BOOKS FOR
SECONDARY SCHOOL
LIBRARIES

BOOKS FOR SECONDARY SCHOOL LIBRARIES

Compiled by a Committee of Librarians
from member schools
of the National Association of
Independent Schools

Fifth Edition

R. R. BOWKER COMPANY
A Xerox Education Company
New York & London, 1976

Published by R. R. Bowker Co. (A Xerox Education Company)
1180 Avenue of the Americas, New York, N.Y. 10036
Copyright © 1976 by Xerox Corporation
All rights reserved
Printed and bound in the United States of America

Library of Congress Cataloging in Publication Data

National Association of Independent Schools
  Books for secondary school libraries.

  Issued by the Library Committee of the Independent Schools Education Board in 1955 under title: 1,000 books for independent school libraries, and in 1961 under title: 3,000 books for secondary school libraries. Issued by the Library Committee of the National Association of Independent Schools in 1968 under title: 4,000 books for secondary school libraries, and in 1971 under title: Books for secondary school libraries.
    1. Bibliography—Best books. 2. School libraries (High school) I. National Association of Independent Schools. Library Committee. Books for secondary school libraries.
II. Title Z1035.N2 1976   028.52   75-37836
ISBN 0-8352-0836-2

CONTENTS

Preface	VII
Professional Tools	1
Reference Works	4
000/General Works	24
100/Philosophy and Psychology	27
200/Religion and Mythology	36
300/Social Sciences	46
400/Language	96
500/Science	98
600/Technology	125
700/Fine Arts and Recreation	144
800/Literature	171
900/Geography, Travel, and History	218
Directory of Publishers	301
Sources for Foreign Books	313
Index	315

PREFACE

This newly expanded edition of *Books for Secondary School Libraries* was compiled by an Ad Hoc Library Committee of the National Association of Independent Schools. The Committee, recognizing that the rapid changes in today's world can cause instant obsolescence in various sections of a book collection, attempted to select books representing high standards of scholarship in the traditional areas. Objectivity of presentation and literary quality were among the guidelines for the selection of books which reflect the immediate and swiftly changing issues, concerns, and problems of the mid-1970s. Because the selection of fiction for a library is highly individualized and so heavily dependent upon the taste and needs of a library's users, the Committee chose to eliminate the fiction section in this edition.

Just as a portion of the books were chosen to speak to today's concerns, others were chosen to reflect special events such as the Bicentennial. Selected series recommendations appear at the end of appropriate sections. Because series tend to be uneven in quality, the Committee emphasizes the need for librarians to choose only those books which will meet the needs and standards of the individual library collections.

The books are arranged by Dewey Decimal Classification numbers and carry Library of Congress subject headings. An entry number is assigned to each book and series to allow for easy access from the Index to the authors, titles, and subjects within the text entries. Prices are from the 1974 edition of *Books in Print*. Some prices and publishers were not always available for foreign books. For those foreign books whose publishers are not included in the Directory of Publishers, a separate section following the Directory called "Sources for Foreign Books" has been included for assistance in locating these books.

Books for Secondary School Libraries has been computerized for the first time, and this has made possible better standardization of subject headings than in previous editions and wider coverage of subjects within the Index. Because of computerization, expansion and revision of subsequent editions will be made easier and the time span between editions will be decreased.

The diversity of challenges which confront today's secondary school library book collections makes it impossible for any one book selection tool to fulfill all the needs. We offer this list with the hope that it will be a useful bibliographic guide for librarians and teachers as they build book collections to meet the needs of college-bound students and to complement the total academic program within the individual school.

Since this list is totally book-oriented, we have deliberately used the words "librarian" and "library"—even as those terms become as obsolete as some of the books in this list are doomed to become obsolete.

Coordinating Editors
  Pauline Anderson, Choate Rosemary Hall, Wallingford, Conn.
  Ronald W. Warden, Fountain Valley School, Colorado Springs, Colo.

Committee
  Rita Adams, Loomis-Chaffee School, Windsor, Conn.
  Jean Edwards, Lincoln School, Providence, R.I.
  John A. Williams, Oregon Episcopal Schools, Portland, Oreg.

PROFESSIONAL TOOLS

011 General Bibliographies

1. Wynar, Christine L. Guide to Reference Books for School Media Centers. Libs Unl. 1973. $17.50.   011.02
1. Instructional Media Centers. 2. Reference Books — Bibliography.

2. Wynkoop, Sally. Subject Guide to Government Reference Books. US Govt Ptg Off. 1972. $11.50.   011.02
1. U. S. — Government Publications — Bibliography.

015-016 Special Bibliographies

3. Books in Print. 4 vols. Bowker. $75.00.   015.73
1. U. S. — Bibliography. 2. U. S. — Imprints.

4. Paperbound Books in Print. An author, title, & subject index with twice-a-year supplements. Bowker. 1-yr. subscription $54.50.   015.73
1. Bibliography — Paperbound Editions.

5. Subject Guide to Books in Print. 2 vols. Bowker. $55.00.   015.73
1. U. S. — Bibliography. 2. U. S. — Imprints.

6. U. S. Superintendent of Documents. Selected U. S. Government Publications. US Govt Ptg Off. free.   015.73
1. Government Publications. 2. U. S. — Government Publications — Bibliography.

7. Encyclopedia Buying Guide, 1975-1976: A Consumer Guide to General Encyclopedias in Print. Kister, Kenneth F., ed.. Bowker. 1976. $15.50.   016
1. Reference Books — Bibliography.

8. Galin, Saul and Spielberg, Peter, eds. Reference Books: How to Select and Use Them. Random. 1969. $7.95; pap. $1.95.   016
1. Reference Books — Bibliography.

9. Pirie, James W., ed. Books for Junior College Libraries. ALA. 1970. $35.00.   016.028
1. Bibliography.

10. Katz, William A. and Gargal, Berry. Magazines for Libraries. 2nd ed. Bowker. 1972. $24.50.   016.05
1. Periodicals — Bibliography.

11. Ulrich's International Periodicals Directory. 2 vols. 16th ed. Bowker. 1975. $50.00.   016.05
1. Periodicals — Bibliography.

12. Scott, Marian H. Periodicals for School Libraries. rev. ed. ALA. 1973. pap. $4.95.   016.051
1. Periodicals — Bibliography.

13. Bradley, Van Allen. The Book Collector's Handbook of Values. Putnam. 1975. $22.50.   016.09
1. Bibliography — Rare Books. 2. Books — Prices.

14. The Reader's Adviser. Vol. 1. Prakken, Sally, ed.. 12th ed. Bowker. 1974. $23.50.   016.42

PROFESSIONAL TOOLS

1. Bibliography — Editions. 2. Books — Reviews. 3. Literature — Bibliography.

15. French Book Corp. of America. French Books: Books, Recordings, Periodicals, Audiovisuals. French Bk. $5.00.   016.44
1. Catalogs, Commercial — Foreign Language Books.

16. Spanish Book Corp. of America. Spanish Books. Spanish Bk. $5.00.   016.46
1. Catalogs, Commercial — Foreign Language Books.

17. Salk, Erwin A. Layman's Guide to Negro History. McGraw. 1967. pap. $6.95.   016.917
1. Negroes — Bibliography. 2. Negroes — History.

18. Irwin, Leonard B. Black Studies. McKinley Pub. 1973. $8.50.   016.9173
1. Negroes — Bibliography.

021 The Library and Society

19. ALA Office for Intellectual Freedom, compiled by. ALA Intellectual Freedom Manual. ALA. $12.75.   021.8
1. Freedom of Information.

022 Library Buildings

20. Ellsworth, Ralph E. Academic Library Buildings. Colo Assoc. 1973. $10.00.   022
1. Library Architecture.

21. Metcalf, Keyes. Planning Academic and Research Library Buildings. McGraw. 1965. $16.00.   022
1. Library Architecture.

22. Taylor, Robert S. The Making of a Library: The Academic Library in Transition. Wiley. 1972. $12.95.   022
1. Libraries, University and College.

025-027 Library Administration

23. NEA, Division of Audiovisual Instruction and NEA, Division of Audiovisual Instruction. Media Programs: District and School. ALA. 1975. pap. $2.95.   025.1
1. Instructional Materials Centers. 2. School Libraries.

24. Miller, Shirley. The Vertical File and Its Satellites. Libs Unl. 1971. $9.00.   025.17
1. Vertical Files (Libraries).

25. Schellenberg, T. R. Modern Archives: Principles and Techniques. U of Chicago Pr. 1956. $8.75.   025.171
1. Archives — Handbooks, Manuals, etc.

26. Harrison, Helen. Film Library Techniques: Principles of Administration. Hastings. $16.50.   025.177
1. Moving-Picture Film Collections.

27. Diaz, A. J. Guide to Microforms in Print. Microcard Edns. pap. $7.50.   025.179
1. Microfilms.

28. Carter, Mary D., ed. Building Library Collections. 4th ed. Scarecrow. 1974. $9.00.   025.2
1. Book Selection.

29. Piercy, Esther J. Commonsense Cataloging: A Manual for the Organization of Books and Other Materials. 2nd ed. Wilson. 1974. $8.00.   025.3
1. Cataloging.

30. Spalding, C. Sumner, ed. Anglo-American Cataloging Rules. ALA. 1967. $10.00; pap. $5.00.   025.3
1. Cataloging.

31. Williams, James G. Classified Library of Congress Subject Headings. Dekker. 1972. Vol. 1: Classified List. $31.25; Vol. 2: Alphabetic List. $43.75.   025.3
1. Cataloging and Classification.

32. Dewey, Melvil. Decimal Classification and Relative Index. 3 vols. 18th ed. Wilson. 1971. $45.00; 10th ed. abr. Forest, 1971 $12.00.   025.43
1. Classification, Decimal.

33. Cunha, George. Conservation of Library Materials: A Manual and Bibliography on the Care, Repair, and Restoration of Library Materials. 2 vols. 2nd ed. Scarecrow. $20.00.   025.8
1. Books — Conservation and Restoration. 2. Manuscripts — Conservation and Restoration. 3. Maps — Conservation and Restoration.

34. Davies, Ruth A. The School Library Media Center. 2nd ed. Bowker. 1973. $12.50.   027.8
1. School Libraries.

35. Gillespie, John T. and Spirt, Diana L. Creating a School Media Program. Bowker. 1973. $11.50.   027.8
1. Instructional Materials Centers — Administration.

028-029 Reading Aids: Documentation

36. American Book Publishing Record. Monthly cumulation of all books listed in Publishers' Weekly Weekly Record during previous month. Bowker. $19.00.   028.1
1. U. S. — Imprints.

37. Book Review Digest. Published monthly, annual cumulations. Wilson. Service basis.   028.1
1. Books — Reviews.

38. Booklist and Subscription Books Bulletin: A Guide to Current Books. 23 issues a yr. ALA. $20.00.   028.1
1. Books — Reviews.

39. Choice: Monthly with Combined July-August Issue. ALA. $35.00.   028.1
1. Books — Reviews.

40. Media and Methods. Monthly, Sept.-May. North Am Pub Co. $9.00.   028.1
1. Audiovisual Materials — Reviews.

41. Previews: Non-Print Software and Hardware News and Reviews. Monthly, Sept.-May. Bowker. $5.00.   028.1
1. Audiovisual Materials — Reviews.

42. School Library Journal. Monthly, Sept.-May. Bowker. $10.50.   028.1
1. Books — Reviews.

43. Science Books and Films. AAAS. $10.00.   028.1
1. Science — Bibliography.

44. Wilson Library Bulletin. Published monthly except July & August. Wilson. $11.00.   028.1
1. Books — Reviews.

45. A.E.C.T. Standards for Cataloging Nonprint Materials. NEA. 1971. pap. $3.50.
    028.7
1. Cataloging of Audio-Visual Materials.

46. Riddle, Jean, et al. Non-Book Materials: The Organization of Integrated Collections. ALA. 1973. $6.50.   028.7
1. Cataloging of Audio-Visual Materials.

47. Artandi, Susan. Introduction to Computers in Information Science. 2nd ed. Scarecrow. 1972. $6.00.   029.8
1. Information Storage and Retrieval Systems. 2. Libraries — Automation.

371 The School

48. National Study of Secondary School Evaluation. Evaluative Criteria. 4th ed. ACE. 1969. $7.50; pap. $6.00.   371.2
1. Educational Surveys.

49. New England Association of Schools & Colleges. Manual for School Evaluation. NEASC. 1972. pap. $5.00.   371.2
1. Educational Surveys.

50. Educators' Guide to Free Films. Diffor, John C. and Horkheimer, Mary F., eds.. rev. 35th ed. Ed Prog. 1975. pap. $12.75.   371.335
1. Moving-Pictures — Catalogs. 2. Moving-Pictures in Education.

778 Photography

51. Andersen, Yvonne. Teaching Film Animation to Children. Van Nos Reinhold. 1971. $8.95.   778.534
1. Moving-Picture Cartoons.

791 Motion Pictures

52. Limbacher, James L., ed. Feature Films on 8mm and 16mm. 3rd ed. Bowker. 1971. $14.50.   791.43
1. Moving-Pictures — Catalogs.

53. Parlato, Salvatore J., Jr., ed. Films Too Good for Words: A Directory of Non-Narrated 16mm Films. Bowker. 1973. $12.50.
    791.43
1. Moving-Pictures — Catalogs.

REFERENCE WORKS

001.5 Information and Communication

54. Cirlot, Juan E. A Dictionary of Symbols. 2nd ed. Philos Lib. 1972. $15.00.   001.5
1. Symbolism — Dictionaries.

016 Subject Bibliographies

55. College and Adult Reading List of Books in Literature and the Fine Arts. Lueders, Edward, ed.. WSP. pap. $0.90.   016
1. Books and Reading.

56. Carter, Ciel M. Guide to Reference Sources in the Computer Sciences. Macmillan. 1974. $25.00.   016.0016
1. Computer Science Literature.

57. Miller, Albert J. Confrontation, Conflict and Dissent. Scarecrow. 1972. $15.00.   016.3
1. Dissenters — U. S. — Bibliography.
2. U. S. — Social Conditions — 1960 — Bibliography.

58. Wasserman, Paul and Paskar, Joanne, eds. Statistics Sources. 4th ed. Gale. 1974. $45.00.   016.31
1. Statistical Services. 2. Statistics — Bibliography.

59. McGraw-Hill Encyclopedia of Science & Technology Editors. Basic Bibliography of Science and Technology. McGraw. 1966. $19.50.   016.5
1. Science — Bibliography.

60. Bullock, Alan and Taylor, A. J., eds. Select List of Books on European History, 1815-1914. 2nd ed. Oxford U Pr. 1954. $1.70.   016.74
1. History, Modern — Europe — Bibliography.

61. Ellis, Jesse C. Index to Illustrations. Faxon. 1966. $13.00.   016.75
1. Illustrations — Bibliography.

62. Thompson, Kenneth. Dictionary of Twentieth Century Composers. St Martin. 1972. $30.00.   016.78
1. Music — Bibliography.

63. Whitburn, Joel. Top Pop Records, 1955-1970. Gale. 1972. $15.00.   016.78
1. Music, Popular (Songs, etc.) — Discography.

64. Baker, Blanche M. Theatre and Allied Arts. Blom. Repr. 1953. $17.50.   016.79
1. Drama — Bibliography. 2. Theater — Bibliography.

65. Weaver, John T. Twenty Years of Silents, 1908-1928. Scarecrow. 1971. $35.00.   016.79
1. Moving-Picture Actors and Actresses. 2. Moving-Pictures, Silent — U. S.

66. Gohdes, Clarence L. Bibliographical Guide to the Study of the Literature of the U. S. A. 3rd ed. Duke. 1970. $5.00.   016.8
1. American Literature — Bibliography.
2. U. S. — Bibliography.

REFERENCE WORKS

67. Breed, Paul F. and Sniderman, Florence M. Dramatic Criticism Index: Bibliography of Commentaries on Playwrights from Ibsen to the Avant-Garde. Gale. 1972. $20.00. 016.809
1. Drama — Twentieth Century — History and Criticism — Indexes.

68. Havlice, Patricia P. Index to Literary Biography. Scarecrow. 1974. $9.00. 016.809
1. Authors — Indexes. 2. Literature — Bio-Bibliography — Bibliography.

69. Gohdes, Clarence L. Literature and Theatre of the States and Regions of the U. S. A.: An Historical Bibliography. Duke. 1967. $10.00. 016.81
1. American Literature — Bibliography.

70. Cambridge Bibliography of English Literature. 5 vols. Cambridge U Pr. $85.00.
016.82
1. English Literature — Bibliography.

71. Temple, Ruth Z. and Tucker, Martin A. Twentieth Century British Literature: A Reference Guide and Bibliography. Ungar. 1967. $6.00. 016.82
1. English Literature — Bibliography.

72. American Universities Field Service. Select Bibliography: Asia, Africa, Eastern Europe, Latin America. Am U Field. 1972. $12.50. 016.9
1. Africa — Bibliography. 2. Asia — Bibliography. 3. Europe, Eastern — Bibliography. 4. Latin America — Bibliography.

73. Wagar, W. Warren. Books in World History: A Guide for Teachers and Students. Ind U Pr. 1973. $4.95. 016.909
1. History — Bibliography.

74. Posner, Arlene, ed. China: A Resource and Curriculum Guide. U of Chicago Pr. 1973. $6.50; pap. $2.95. 016.951
1. China — Books.

75. Stensland, Anna L. Literature by and about the American Indian. NCTE. 1974. $3.95. 016.97
1. Indians of North America — Bibliography.

76. Bemis, Samuel F. and Griffin, G. G. Guide to the Diplomatic History of the United States (1775-1921) Peter Smith. $13.50.
016.973
1. U. S. — Foreign Relations — Bibliography.

77. De Santis, Vincent P. The Gilded Age, 1877-1896. AHM Pub. 1973. pap. $2.95.
016.973
1. U. S. — History — 1865-1898 — Bibliography.

78. Freidel, Frank and Showman, Richard K., eds. Harvard Guide to American History. 2 vols. rev. ed. Harvard U Pr. 1974. $45.00.
016.973
1. U. S. — History — Bibliography. 2. U. S. — History — Study and Teaching.

79. Nevins, Allan, et al, eds. Civil War Books: A Critical Bibliography. 2 vols. La State U Pr. 1967. $11.50 ea.; $20.00 set.
016.973
1. U. S. — History — Civil War — Bibliography.

80. U. S. Library of Congress. A Guide to the Study of the United States of America: Representative Books Reflecting the Development of American Life and Thought by Mugridge, Donald H. and Crum, Blanch P. Lib of Congress. 1960. $7.00. 016.973
1. U. S. — Bibliography. 2. U. S. — Civilization — Bibliography. 3. U. S. — History — Bibliography.

020 Special Libraries

81. Ash, Lee, compiled by. Subject Collections: A Guide to Special Book Collections. Bowker. 1974. $38.50. 026.002
1. Library Resources — Canada — Directories. 2. Library Resources — U. S. — Directories.

028 Reading Aids

82. Todd, Alden. Finding Facts Fast: How to Find Out What You Want to Know Immediately. Morrow. 1972. $5.95; pap. $2.45.
028.7
1. Libraries — Handbooks, Manuals, etc. 2. Reference Books. 3. Research.

030 General Encyclopedic Works

83. Larousse Editors. Grand Larousse Encyclopedique. 10 vols. & suppl. (Fr.). French & Eur. $484.00. 030.4
1. French Language — Encyclopedias and Dictionaries.

5

REFERENCE WORKS

84. Barsa Enciclopedia. 16 vols. (Sp.). Ency Brit Inc. 1970. $148.50. 030.6
1. Spanish Language — Encyclopedias and Dictionaries.

85. Encyclopedia Americana. 30 vols. Grolier Inc. 1975. price on request. 031
1. Encyclopedias and Dictionaries.

86. The New Columbia Encyclopedia. Columbia U Pr. 1975. $79.50. 031
1. Encyclopedias and Dictionaries.

87. The New Encyclopedia Britannica. 30 vols. 15th ed. Ency Brit Inc. 1974. price on request. 031
1. Encyclopedias and Dictionaries.

050-080 Periodicals, Newspapers, and General Collection Indexes

88. Humanities Index. Quarterly. Wilson. By subscription. 050
1. Periodicals — Indexes.

89. Nineteenth-Century Readers' Guide to Periodical Literature: 1890-1899. 2 vols. Wilson. $28.00. 050
1. Periodicals — Indexes.

90. Readers' Guide to Periodical Literature. Semi-monthly, Sept.-June; Monthly, July & Aug. Wilson. 22 issues. yearly $32.00. 050
1. Periodicals — Indexes.

91. Social Sciences Index. Quarterly. Wilson. By subscription. 050
1. Periodicals — Indexes.

92. Center for Curriculum Research. Somewhere Else. Swallow. 1972. $6.00; pap. $3.95. 060.25
1. Associations, Institutions, etc. 2. Directories.

93. The New York Times Index. NY Times. Subscription rates: 24 semi-monthly issues $87.50; cumulative Annual Index $87.50; semi-monthly issues with Annual Index $150.00. 070
1. Newspapers — Indexes.

94. Essay and General Literature Index. Semi-annual. Bound annual & permanent five-year cumulations. Wilson. $20.00. 080
1. Humanities — Indexes. 2. Literature — Bibliography. 3. Literature — Indexes.

100 Philosophy and Psychology

95. Edwards, Paul, ed. Encyclopedia of Philosophy. 4 vols. Free Pr. 1973. $99.50. 103
1. Philosophy — Dictionaries.

96. Encyclopedia of Occult Sciences. Gale. Repr. 1939. $12.50. 133
1. Occult Sciences — Encyclopedias and Dictionaries.

97. Eysenck, H. J., et al, eds. Encyclopedia of Psychology. 3 vols. Seabury. 1972. $75.00. 150.3
1. Psychology — Dictionaries.

98. Wolman, Benjamin B. Dictionary of Behavioral Science. Van Nos Reinhold. 1973. $19.95. 150.3
1. Psychology — Dictionaries.

200 Religion and Mythology

99. Cross, F. L. and Livingstone, Elizabeth A. The Oxford Dictionary of the Christian Church. Oxford U Pr. 1974. $35.00. 203
1. Theology — Dictionaries.

100. Hastings, James, ed. Encyclopedia of Religion and Ethics. 13 vols. Scribner. 1908-1927. $270.00. 203
1. Ethics — Dictionaries. 2. Religion — Dictionaries. 3. Theology — Dictionaries.

101. Stevenson, Burton E. Home Book of Bible Quotations. Har-Row. 1949. $13.50. 220.2
1. Bible. 2. Quotations.

102. Young, Robert. Young's Analytical Concordance to the Bible. rev. ed. Eerdmans. 1955. $13.75. 220.2
1. Bible — Concordances.

103. Miller, Madeline and Lane, J. Harper Bible Dictionary. Har-Row. 1973. $12.50. 220.3
1. Bible — Dictionaries.

104. Interpreter's Bible. 12 vols. Buttrick, G. A., ed.. Abingdon. $8.75 ea.; $89.50 set. 220.7
1. Bible — Commentaries.

105. Interpreter's Dictionary of the Bible. 4 vols. Buttrick, G. A., ed.. Abingdon. 1962. $45.00 set. 220.7
1. Bible — Dictionaries.

REFERENCE WORKS

106. Interpreter's One Volume Commentary on the Bible. Laymon, Charles M., ed.. Abingdon. 1971. $17.50.   220.7
1. Bible — Commentaries.

107. Cambridge History of the Bible. 3 vols. Ackroyd, P. R., & Evans, C. F., eds.. Vol. 1. From Jerome to the Renaissance; Vol. 2. The West from the Fathers to the Reformation; Vol. 3. The West from the Reformation to the Present Day. Cambridge U Pr. $22.50 ea.; $60.00 set.   220.9
1. Bible — History.

108. May, Herbert G. Oxford Bible Atlas. 2nd ed. Oxford U Pr. 1974. $9.95; pap. $3.95.   220.9
1. Bible — Geography. 2. Bible — Maps.

109. Wright, George E. and Filson, Floyd V. Westminster Historical Atlas to the Bible. rev. ed. Westminster. 1956. $9.95.   220.9
1. Bible — Whole — Atlases.

110. Holweck, Frederick G. A Biographical Dictionary of the Saints. Gale. Repr. 1924. $34.00.   235.2
1. Saints — Dictionaries.

111. MacQuarrie, John, ed. Dictionary of Christian Ethics. Westminster. 1967. $7.50.   241
1. Christian Ethics — Dictionaries. 2. Ethics — Dictionaries.

112. Child, Heather and Colles, Dorothy. Christian Symbols Ancient and Modern: A Handbook for Students. Scribner. 1973. $17.50.   246.5
1. Christian Art and Symbolism.

113. Brusher, Joseph S. Popes Through the Ages. Borden. 1960. $12.50.   262.13
1. Papacy. 2. Popes — Biography.

114. Weiser, Francis X. Handbook of Feasts and Customs. HarBraceJ. 1958. $7.50.   264
1. Church Year. 2. Fasts and Feasts.

115. Attwater, Donald, ed. Catholic Dictionary. Macmillan. 1961. pap. $2.45.   280
1. Catholic Church — Dictionaries.

116. Parrinder, Geoffrey. A Dictionary of Non-Christian Religions. Westminster. 1973. $10.95.   290.3
1. Religions — Dictionaries.

117. Brandon, Samuel G. A Dictionary of Comparative Religion. Scribner. 1970. $17.50.   291
1. Religions — Encyclopedias and Dictionaries.

118. Gaskell, G. A. Dictionary of All Scriptures and Myths. Julian. 1960. $15.00.   291
1. Mythology — Dictionaries.

119. MacCulloch, John A., et al, eds. Mythology of All Races. 13 vols. Cooper Sq. Repr. 1932. $175.00.   291
1. Mythology.

120. New Larousse Encyclopedia of Mythology. Guirand, Felix, ed.. rev. ed. Putnam. 1969. $17.95.   291
1. Folk-Lore. 2. Mythology — Dictionaries.

121. Tripp, Edward. Crowell's Handbook of Classical Mythology. T Y Crowell. 1970. $10.00.   291
1. Mythology — Dictionaries.

122. Bridger, David and Wolk, Samuel J., eds. The New Jewish Encyclopedia. Behrman. 1962. $15.00.   296.03
1. Jews — Dictionaries. 2. Judaism — Dictionaries.

123. Encyclopedia Judaica. 16 vols. Keter. 1972. $500.00.   296.03
1. Jews — Dictionaries and Encyclopedias. 2. Judaism — Dictionaries and Encyclopedias.

300 Social Sciences

124. Gallup, George H. The Gallup Poll: 1935-1971. 3 vols. Random. 1973. $108.00.   301.15
1. Public Opinion — U. S.

125. McGraw-Hill Encyclopedia of Environmental Science. McGraw. 1974. $39.95.   301.31
1. Ecology — Dictionaries. 2. Environmental Protection — Dictionaries. 3. Man — Influence on Nature — Dictionaries.

126. Encyclopedia Britannica. Makers of America: A Survey of Ethnic Diversity in the United States. 10 vols. Ency Brit Inc. 1971. price on request.   301.45
1. Minorities — U. S. 2. U. S. — Foreign Population.

REFERENCE WORKS

127. The Negro in American History. 3 vols. Adler, M. J., et. al, eds.. Ency Brit Inc. 1969. price on request. 301.451
1. Negroes — History.

128. The International Encyclopedia of the Social Sciences. 17 vols. Sills, David L., ed.. Macmillan. 1968. $495.00. 303
1. Social Sciences — Dictionaries.

129. Statesman's Yearbook. Paxton, John, ed.. St Martin. 1975. $16.95. 305
1. Statistics — Yearbooks.

130. Preston, Samuel H., et al. Causes of Death: Life Tables for National Populations. Acad Pr. 1972. $22.50. 312.2
1. Mortality.

131. World Almanac and Book of Facts. Long, L., ed.. Doubleday. $4.95; pap. $2.25. 317
1. Almanacs. 2. Statistics — Yearbooks.

132. U. S. Bureau of the Census. Statistical Abstract of the United States. US Govt Ptg Off. $4.00. 317.91
1. U. S. — Census. 2. U. S. — Statistics.

133. Plano, J. C. and Greenberg, M. American Political Dictionary. 3rd rev. ed. HR&W. 1972. pap. $5.95. 320.973
1. U. S. — History — Dictionaries.

134. Hyams, Edward. A Dictionary of Modern Revolution. Taplinger. 1973. $9.95; pap. $4.95. 322.42
1. Revolutionists — Dictionaries. 2. Revolutions — Dictionaries.

135. U. S. Congress. Biographical Directory of the American Congress, 1774-1961. US Govt Ptg Off. 1961. price on request. 328.73
1. U. S. — Biography — Dictionaries. 2. U. S. Congress — Biography. 3. U. S. Continental Congress — Biography.

136. Bain, Richard C. Convention Decisions and Voting Records. 2nd rev. ed. Brookings. 1973. $14.95. 329.02
1. Political Conventions.

137. Schlesinger, Arthur M., Jr. and Israel, F. L. History of American Presidential Elections. 4 vols. McGraw. 1971. $150.00. 329.02
1. Presidents — U. S. — Election — History. 2. U. S. — Politics and Government.

138. Greenwald, Douglas. The McGraw-Hill Dictionary of Modern Economics: A Handbook of Terms and Organizations. 2nd ed. McGraw. 1973. $19.95. 330.03
1. Economics — Dictionaries.

139. Munn, Glenn G. Encyclopedia of Banking and Finance. 7th ed. Garcia, Ferdinand L., ed. Bankers. 1973. $49.75. 332.1
1. Banks and Banking — Dictionaries. 2. Economics — Dictionaries.

140. Staar, Richard F., ed. Yearbook on International Communist Affairs. Hoover Inst Pr. 1974. $25.00. 335.4305
1. Communism — Yearbooks — 1974. 2. Communist Parties — Yearbooks.

141. Hurst, Michael, ed. Key Treaties for the Great Powers, 1814-1914. 2 vols. St Martin. 1972. $35.00. 341.02
1. Treaties — Collections.

142. McGovney, D. O. and McGovney, Howard. Cases on Constitutional Law. 3rd ed. Bobbs. 1955. $13.50. 342.733
1. U. S. — Constitutional Law — Cases.

143. Nader, Ralph. Working on the System: A Comprehensive Manual for Citizen Access to Federal Agencies. Basic. 1974. $15.00. 350.829
1. Consumer Protection.

144. Dupuy, R. Ernest and Dupuy, Trevor N. The Encyclopedia of Military History: From 3500 B.C. to the Present. Har-Row. 1970. $22.50. 355.009
1. Military History.

145. Nash, Jay R. Bloodletters and Badmen: A Narrative Encyclopedia of American Criminals from the Pilgrims to the Present. M Evans. 1973. $16.95. 364.092
1. Crime and Criminals — U. S. — Biography.

146. Fine, Benjamin. Barron's Profiles of American Colleges. Barron. Vol. 1. $18.00; pap. $6.95; Vol. 2. $12.00; pap. $4.95. 378.73
1. Universities and Colleges — U. S. — Directories.

147. Furniss, W. Todd, ed. American Universities and Colleges. 11th ed. ACE. 1973. $38.00. 378.73
1. Colleges — U. S. 2. Universities and Colleges — U. S. — Directories.

REFERENCE WORKS

148. Gleazer, Edmund J., Jr., ed. American Junior Colleges. 8th ed. ACE. 1971. $18.00. 378.73
1. Junior Colleges — U. S. — Directories.

149. Singletary, Otis A., ed. American Universities and Colleges. 11th ed. ACE. 1973. $22.00. 378.73
1. Colleges — U. S. 2. Universities and Colleges — U. S. — Directories.

150. Wilcox, Ruth T. The Dictionary of Costume. Scribner. 1969. $15.00. 391
1. Costume — Dictionaries.

151. Ickis, Marguerite. Book of Festivals and Holidays the World Over. Dodd. 1970. $5.00. 394.2
1. Festivals. 2. Holidays.

152. Myers, Robert J. and Hallmark Cards Editors. Celebrations: The Complete Book of American Holidays. Doubleday. 1972. $8.95. 394.2
1. Festivals — U. S. 2. Holidays — U. S.

153. Ireland, Norma. Index to Fairy Tales, 1949-1972. Including folklore, legends & myths in collections. Faxon. 1973. $18.00. 398.2
1. Fairy Tales — Indexes. 2. Mythology — Indexes.

154. Leach, Maria, ed. Standard Dictionary of Folklore, Mythology and Legend. Funk & W. 1972. $17.95. 398.3
1. Folk-Lore — Dictionaries and Encyclopedias. 2. Mythology — Dictionaries and Encyclopedias.

155. Smith, William G. and Wilson, F. B., eds. The Oxford Dictionary of English Proverbs. Oxford U Pr. 1970. $17.00. 398.9
1. Proverbs, English.

400 Language

156. Guinagh, Kevin, ed. Dictionary of Foreign Phrases and Abbreviations. 2nd ed. Wilson. 1972. $10.00. 418
1. Abbreviations. 2. Polyglot Glossaries, Phrase Books, etc.

157. Holt, Alfred H. Phrase and Word Origins: A Study of Familiar Expressions. 2nd ed. Dover. 1961. pap. $2.50. 422
1. English Language — Etymology — Dictionaries.

158. The Oxford Dictionary of English Etymology. Onions, C. T., et al, eds.. Oxford U Pr. 1966. $20.00. 422
1. English Language — Etymology — Dictionaries.

159. Skeat, Walter W., ed. Etymological Dictionary of the English Language. rev. & enl. ed. Oxford U Pr. 1910. $20.50. 422
1. English Language — Etymology — Dictionaries.

160. Carroll, David. The Dictionary of Foreign Terms in the English Language. Hawthorn. 1973. $9.95. 422.4
1. English Language — Foreign Words and Phrases — Dictionaries.

161. American Heritage Dictionary of the English Language. HM. $7.95; thumb indexed $9.95; deluxe ed. $15.00. 423
1. English Language — Dictionaries.

162. Barnhart, Clarence L., et al, eds. The Barnhart Dictionary of New English Since 1963. Har-Row. 1973. $12.95. 423
1. English Language — Dictionaries. 2. Words, New — English Language — Dictionaries.

163. Burchfield, R. W., ed. Supplement to the Oxford English Dictionary. Vol. 1. Oxford U Pr. 1972. $50.00. 423
1. English Language — Dictionaries.

164. Johnson, Samuel. Johnson's Dictionary: A Modern Selection. McAdam, E. L., Jr. and Milne, George, eds. Pantheon. 1963. $8.95. 423
1. English Language — Dictionaries.

165. Murray, J. A., et al, eds. Oxford English Dictionary. 13 vols. Oxford U Pr. $350.00. 423
1. English Language — Dictionaries.

166. Random House Editors. Random House Dictionary of the English Language. Random. 1966. $30.00; the College edition, 1968 $6.95; thumb indexed $7.95. 423
1. English Language — Dictionaries.

167. Webster's New World Dictionary of the English Language. 2nd college ed. Collins-World. 1974. $9.95. 423
1. English Language — Dictionaries.

168. Webster's Third New International Dictionary: The Great Library of the English Language. Merriam. 1971. $59.95. 423
1. English Language — Dictionaries.

REFERENCE WORKS

169. De Sola, Ralph. Abbreviations Dictionary. 4th ed. Am Elsevier. 1974. $24.50. 423.1
1. Abbreviations, English. 2. Acronyms. 3. Signs and Symbols.

170. Webster's New Dictionary of Synonyms. Merriam. 1968. $7.95. 423.1
1. English Language — Synonyms and Antonyms.

171. Whitford, Harold C. and Dixson, Robert J. Handbook of American Idioms and Idiomatic Usage. rev. ed. Regents Pub. 1973. pap. $2.95. 423.1
1. English Language — Idioms — Dictionaries.

172. Roget, Peter M. Roget's Thesaurus in Dictionary Form. new ed. Putnam. 1965. $4.50. 424
1. English Language — Synonyms and Antonyms.

173. Johnson, Burges, ed. New Rhyming Dictionary and Poets' Handbook. rev. ed. Har-Row. 1957. $6.95. 426
1. English Language — Rime — Dictionaries. 2. Poetics. 3. Versification.

174. Stratmann, Francis H. Middle-English Dictionary: Containing Words Used by English Writers from the Twelfth to the Fifteenth Century. Bradley, Henry, ed. Oxford U Pr. 1891. $15.25. 427.02
1. English Language — Dictionaries.

175. Partridge, Eric. Dictionary of Slang and Unconventional English. 7th ed. Macmillan. 1970. $18.50. 427.09
1. English Language — Slang — Dictionaries.

176. Fowler, Henry M. A Dictionary of Modern English Usage. 2nd ed. Gowers, E., rev. by. Oxford U Pr. 1965. $7.50. 428.3
1. English Language. 2. English Language — Idioms, Corrections, Errors.

177. Shipley, Joseph T. Dictionary of Early English. Littlefield. 1968. pap. $3.45. 429
1. English Language — Dictionaries.

178. Cassell's New German Dictionary. (Ger-Eng & Eng-Ger.). Funk & W. 1965. $8.95; thumb indexed $9.95. 433
1. German Language — Dictionaries.

179. Larousse. Nouveau Petit Larousse. Larousse. 1974. $14.95. 443
1. French Language — Dictionaries.

180. Larousse. Nouveau Dictionnaire Etymologique. Dauzat, A., et al, eds. Larousse. 1964. $14.75. 443
1. French Language — Dictionaries.

181. Ledesert, Rene and Ledesert, D. M. Harrap's New Standard French and English Dictionary. 2 vols. Scribner. 1973. $39.50. 443
1. English Language — Dictionaries — French. 2. French Language — Dictionaries — English.

182. Cassell's Italian Dictionary. (It-Eng & Eng-It.). Funk & W. 1967. $9.95; thumb indexed $10.95. 453
1. Italian Language — Dictionaries.

183. Academia Española. Diccionario de la Lengua Española. 19th ed. S F Bk. 1971. $32.50. 463
1. Spanish Language — Dictionaries.

184. Velazquez-de-la-Cadena, Mariano, et al, eds. New Pronouncing Dictionary of the Spanish and English Languages. rev. ed. P-H. 1973 (Appleton-Century-Crofts). $8.95; thumb indexed $9.95. 463
1. Spanish Language — Dictionaries.

185. Cassell's New Latin Dictionary. (Lat-Eng & Eng-Lat.). Funk & W. 1960. $9.95; thumb indexed $10.95. 473
1. Latin Language — Dictionaries.

186. Lewis, Charlton T. and Short, Charles. Latin Dictionary: Founded on Andrew's Edition of Freund's Latin Dictionary. Oxford U Pr. 1879. $22.00. 473
1. Latin Language — Dictionaries.

187. Liddell, Henry G. and Scott, Robert, eds. Greek-English Lexicon. 9th ed. Oxford U Pr. $51.00; abr. ed. $5.00; Greek-English Lexicon: A Supplement. ed. by Barber, E. A., et al. 1968 $15.25. 483.1
1. Greek Language — Dictionaries.

188. Müller, Vladimir K. English-Russian Dictionary. rev. ed. Dutton. 1973. $12.95. 491.7
1. Russian Language — Dictionaries.

189. Smirnitsky, A. I. Russian-English Dictionary. 7th rev. ed. Dutton. 1973. $11.50. 491.7
1. Russian Language — Dictionaries.

REFERENCE WORKS

190. Goldberg, Nathan. New Functional Hebrew-English, English-Hebrew Dictionary. Ktav. 1958. $5.00. 492.4
1. Hebrew Language — Dictionaries.

191. Wehr, Hans. Dictionary of Modern Written Arabic. 3rd ed. Cowan, J. Milton, ed. Cornell U Pr. 1973. $50.00. 492.7
1. Arabic Language — Dictionaries.

192. Wortabet, J. and Porter, H., eds. English-Arabic, Arabic-English Dictionary. Ungar. $14.00. 492.7
1. Arabic Language — Dictionaries.

193. Fenn, Courtenay H., ed. Five Thousand Dictionary: A Chinese-English Pocket Dictionary and Index to the Character Cards of the College of Chinese Studies. rev. ed. Harvard U Pr. 1942. $8.50. 495.1
1. Chinese Language — Dictionaries.

194. Yale Institute of Far Eastern Languages. Dictionary of Spoken Chinese. (Yale Linguistic Ser). Yale U Pr. 1966. $50.00. 495.1
1. Chinese Language — Dictionaries.

500 Sciences

195. Asimov, Isaac. Asimov's Guide to Science. rev. ed. Basic. 1972. $15.50. 500
1. Science.

196. Suroweicki, John. The Pulse of the Planet: A State of the Earth Report from the Smithsonian Institution Center for Short-Lived Phenomena. Harmony. 1973. $6.95; pap. $2.95. 500.9
1. Meteorites. 2. Natural Disasters. 3. Natural History. 4. Oil Pollution of Rivers, Harbors, etc. 5. Short-Lived Phenomena.

197. Clement, Roland. Nature Atlas of America. rev. ed. Hammond Inc. 1973. $17.95. 500.97
1. Natural History — North America.

198. Asimov, Isaac. More Words of Science. HM. 1972. $6.95. 501.4
1. English Language — Words — History. 2. Science — Terminology.

199. ———. Words of Science and the History Behind Them. HM. 1959. $5.95; pap. $1.25 (NAL). 501.4
1. English Language — Words — History. 2. Science — Terminology.

200. Gray, Peter. Encyclopedia of Microscopy and Micro-Technique. Van Nos Reinhold. 1973. $32.50. 502.8
1. Microscope and Microscopy — Technique — Dictionaries. 2. Microscopy — Encyclopedias.

201. McGraw-Hill Editors. Dictionary of Scientific and Technical Terms. McGraw. 1975. $39.50. 503
1. Science — Dictionaries. 2. Technology — Dictionaries.

202. ———. McGraw-Hill Encyclopedia of Science and Technology. 15 vols. McGraw. 1971. $350.00. 503
1. Science — Dictionaries. 2. Technology — Dictionaries.

203. Van Nostrand. Van Nostrand's Scientific Encyclopedia. 4th ed. Van Nos Reinhold. 1968. $42.75. 503
1. Science — Dictionaries.

204. McGraw-Hill Yearbook of Science and Technology, 1975. McGraw. 1975. $28.00. 505.8
1. Science — Yearbooks. 2. Technology — Yearbooks.

205. Saterstrom, Mary H. and Renner, John W. Educators Guide to Free Science Materials. rev. 16th ed. Ed Prog. 1975. pap. $10.25. 507
1. Science — Study and Teaching — Free Material.

206. Williams, Trevor I. Biographical Dictionary of Scientists. 2nd ed. Halsted Pr. 1975. $17.95. 509.2
1. Scientists — Biography.

207. Asimov, Isaac. Asimov's Biographical Encyclopedia of Science and Technology: The Lives and Achievements of 1195 Great Scientists from Ancient Times to the Present Chronologically Arranged. rev. ed. Doubleday. 1972. $12.95. 509.22
1. Scientists — Biography.

208. Handbook of Tables for Mathematics. CRC Pr. price & edition on request. 510.3
1. Mathematics — Tables, etc.

209. James, Glenn and James, Robert C., eds. Mathematics Dictionary. 3rd ed. Van Nos Reinhold. 1968. $15.95. 510.3
1. Mathematics — Dictionaries.

11

REFERENCE WORKS

210. Newman, James R. World of Mathematics. 4 vols. S&S. 1962. $30.00 set; pap. $14.95 set.   510.3
1. Mathematics.

211. Moore, Patrick. Atlas of the Universe. Rand. 1970. $35.00.   523
1. Astronomy — Atlases.

212. ———. Yearbook of Astronomy, 1975. Norton. 1975. $8.95.   523.058
1. Astronomy — Yearbooks.

213. Besancon, Robert M., ed. Encyclopedia of Physics. 2nd ed. Van Nos Reinhold. 1974. $37.50.   530.3
1. Physics — Dictionaries.

214. Condon, Edward W. and Odishaw, H. Handbook of Physics. 2nd ed. McGraw. 1967. $37.45.   530.3
1. Physics — Dictionaries.

215. Dean, John A. Lange's Handbook of Chemistry. 11th rev. ed. McGraw. 1973. $19.50.   540.2
1. Chemistry, Technical — Tables, etc. 2. Mathematics — Tables, etc.

216. Hampel, Clifford A. and Hawley, Gessner C., eds. Encyclopedia of Chemistry. 3rd ed. Van Nos Reinhold. 1973. $39.50.   540.3
1. Chemistry — Dictionaries.

217. Handbook of Chemistry and Physics. CRC Pr. price & edition on request.   541.9
1. Chemistry — Tables, etc. 2. Physics — Tables, etc.

218. Gordon, Arnold J. and Ford, Richard A. The Chemist's Companion: A Handbook of Practical Data, Techniques, and References. Wiley. 1972. $16.95.   542
1. Chemistry — Handbooks, Manuals, etc.

219. Roberts, Willard Lincoln, et al. Encyclopedia of Minerals. Van Nos Reinhold. 1974. $69.50.   549.03
1. Mineralogy — Dictionaries.

220. American Geological Institute. Dictionary of Geological Terms. abr. ed. Doubleday. 1962. pap. $2.95.   550.3
1. Geology — Dictionaries.

221. Challinor, John. A Dictionary of Geology. Oxford U Pr. 1974. $13.00.   550.3
1. Geology — Dictionaries.

222. Durrenberger, Robert W. Dictionary of the Environmental Sciences. Mayfield Pub. 1973. $7.95; pap. $4.95.   550.3
1. Earth Sciences — Dictionaries. 2. Natural History — Dictionaries. 3. Natural Resources — Dictionaries.

223. Larousse. Encyclopedia of the Earth. Crown. 1972. pap. $6.95.   550.3
1. Earth. 2. Geology — Dictionaries. 3. Mines and Mineral Resources. 4. Physical Geography.

224. U. S. Dept. of Commerce. Earthquake History of the United States: (Thru 1970) (Pub. 41-1). rev. ed. US Govt Ptg Off. 1973. pap. $2.80.   551.22
1. Earthquakes — Statistics.

225. Fairbridge, R., ed. The Encyclopedia of Oceanography. Halsted Pr. 1966. $27.50.   551.46
1. Oceanography — Dictionaries.

226. Todd, David K., ed. The Water Encyclopedia. Water Info. 1970. $27.50.   551.48
1. Hydrology — Tables, Calculations, etc. 2. Water-Supply — Tables, Calculations, etc.

227. Deeson, A. F. The Collector's Encyclopedia of Rocks and Minerals. Potter. 1973. $12.50.   552.003
1. Mineralogy — Dictionaries. 2. Rocks — Dictionaries. 3. Petrology — Dictionaries.

228. Glut, Donald F. The Dinosaur Dictionary. Citadel Pr. 1972. $12.50.   568.1903
1. Dinosaurs.

229. Gray, Peter. The Encyclopedia of the Biological Sciences. 2nd ed. Van Nos Reinhold. 1970. $26.95.   574.03
1. Biology — Dictionaries.

230. Henderson, Isabella F. and Henderson, W. D. Dictionary of Biological Terms. 8th ed. Kenneth, John H., ed. Van Nos Reinhold. 1963. $16.75.   574.03
1. Biology — Dictionaries.

231. Deedy, John and Nobile, Philip, eds. The Complete Ecology Fact Book. Doubleday. 1972. $10.00; pap. $3.95.   574.5
1. Ecology. 2. Ecology — Statistics.

232. Bailey, Liberty H. Manual of Cultivated Plants. rev. ed. Macmillan. 1949. $19.95.   581
1. Botany. 2. Plants, Cultivated.

REFERENCE WORKS

233. Edlin, Herbert L. and Huxley, Anthony. Atlas of Plant Life. John Day. 1973. $10.00. 581
1. Botany. 2. Plants, Cultivated — Geographical Distribution. 3. Vegetation and Climate.

234. Gray, Asa. Manual of Botany. 8th ed. Van Nos Reinhold. 1950. $24.95. 581
1. Botany.

235. Porter, Cedric L. Taxonomy of Flowering Plants. 2nd ed. W H Freeman. 1967. $9.95. 582.1301
1. Angiosperms. 2. Botany — Classification.

236. Johnson, Hugh. The International Book of Trees. S&S. 1973. $29.95. 582.16
1. Ornamental Trees. 2. Trees.

237. Buchanan, Robert E. and Gibbons, Norman E. Bergey's Manual of Determinative Bacteriology. 8th ed. Williams & Wilkins. 1974. $45.00. 589.95
1. Bacteriology — Classification. 2. Schizomycetes.

238. Grzimek, Bernhard. Grzimek's Animal Life Encyclopedia. 13 vols. Van Nos Reinhold. $29.95 ea. 591
1. Zoology — Encyclopedias.

239. Jarman, Cathy. Atlas of Animal Migration. John Day. 1972. $10.00. 591.52
1. Animal Migration.

240. Beazley, Mitchel. Atlas of World Wildlife. Rand. 1973. $25.00. 591.9
1. Animals. 2. Zoogeography.

241. Nayman, Jacqueline. Atlas of Wildlife. John Day. 1972. $10.00. 591.9
1. Animals. 2. Zoogeography.

242. Abbott, R. Tucker. American Seashells. 2nd ed. Van Nos Reinhold. 1974. $49.50.
594.047
1. Shells.

243. Linsenmaier, Walter. Insects of the World. McGraw. 1972. $25.00. 595.7
1. Insects.

244. Tweedie, Michael. Atlas of Insects. John Day. 1974. $10.00. 595.7
1. Insects. 2. Insects — Geographical Distribution.

245. Barruel, Paul. Birds of the World. 2nd ed. Oxford U Pr. 1973. $24.95. 598.25
1. Birds — Behavior.

246. Campbell, Bruce and Holmes, Richard T., eds. The Dictionary of Birds in Color. Viking Pr. 1974. $22.50. 598.29
1. Birds — Dictionaries.

247. Walker, Ernest P., et al. Mammals of the World. 2 vols. 3rd ed. Johns Hopkins. 1975. $37.50. 599
1. Mammals.

600 Technology

248. Dorland, William A. Dorland's Illustrated Medical Dictionary. 25th ed. Saunders. 1974. $21.50. 610.3
1. Medicine — Dictionaries.

249. Merck Manual of Diagnosis and Therapy. 12th ed. Merck. 1972. $8.00. 610.3
1. Diagnosis. 2. Medicine — Dictionaries.

250. Gray, Henry. Gray's Anatomy of the Human Body. 35th ed. Saunders. 1973. $38.50. 611
1. Anatomy, Human.

251. The Trans-Vision Book of Health. Ency Brit Inc. 1974. $39.50. 612
1. Human Physiology. 2. Hygiene.

252. Clark, Randolph L. and Cumley, Russell W. The Book of Health. 3rd ed. Van Nos Reinhold. 1973. $29.95. 616
1. Medicine — Dictionaries.

253. Lingeman, Richard R. Drugs from A to Z: A Dictionary. 2nd rev. ed. McGraw. 1974. $6.95; pap. $3.50. 616.86
1. Drugs — Dictionaries.

254. Baumeister, T. and Marks, Lionel. Standard Handbook for Mechanical Engineers. 7th ed. McGraw. 1967. $33.75. 621.02
1. Mechanical Engineering — Handbooks, Manuals, etc.

255. Institute of Electrical & Electronics Engineers. IEEE Standard Dictionary of Electrical and Electronics Terms. Wiley. 1972. $19.95. 621.303
1. Electric Engineering — Dictionaries. 2. Electronics — Dictionaries.

256. Funk & Wagnalls Editors. Dictionary of Electronics. Funk & W. 1969. $8.95.
621.3803
1. Electronics — Dictionaries.

REFERENCE WORKS

257. Markus, John. Electronics and Nucleonics Dictionary. 3rd ed. McGraw. 1967. $19.25.   621.381
1. Electronics — Dictionaries. 2. Nuclear Engineering — Dictionaries.

258. Sarnoff, Paul. The New York Times Encyclopedic Dictionary of the Environment. Quadrangle. 1972. $10.00; pap. $3.95 (Avon).   628.503
1. Environment — Dictionaries. 2. Pollution — Dictionaries.

259. Turnill, Reginald. The Language of Space: A Dictionary of Astronautics. John Day. 1971. $6.95.   629.403
1. Astronautics — Dictionaries.

260. Hay, Roy and Synge, Patrick M. The Color Dictionary of Flowers and Plants for Home and Garden. Crown. 1969. $15.00.   635.9
1. Flowers — Dictionaries. 2. Plants, Ornamental — Dictionaries.

261. Hope, C. E. and Jackson, G. N. The Encyclopedia of the Horse. Viking Pr. 1973. $22.50.   636.1
1. Horses — Dictionaries.

262. Hervey, George F. and Hems, Jack. Illustrated Encyclopedia of Freshwater Fish. Doubleday. 1973. $14.95.   639.34
1. Aquariums. 2. Fishes, Freshwater — Dictionaries.

263. Hoedeman, J. J. Naturalists' Guide to Freshwater Aquarium Fish. Sterling. 1974. $30.00.   639.34
1. Aquariums. 2. Fishes, Freshwater — Dictionaries.

264. Neal, Jack A., ed. Literary Market Place: The Business Directory of American Book Publishing, 1975-76. Bowker. 1975. pap. $19.95.   655.473
1. Publishers and Publishing.

700 Fine Arts and Recreation

265. Lemke, Antje and Fleiss, Ruth. Museum Companion: A Dictionary of Art Terms and Subjects. Hippocrene Bks. 1974. $6.95.   703
1. Art — Dictionaries.

266. Mayer, Ralph. Dictionary of Art: Terms and Technique. T Y Crowell. 1969. $8.95.   703
1. Art — Dictionaries.

267. The Oxford Companion to Art. Osborne, Harold, ed.. Oxford U Pr. 1970. $25.00.   703
1. Art — Dictionaries.

268. Phaidon Dictionary of Twentieth-Century Art. Praeger. 1973. $15.00.   703
1. Art, Modern — 20th Century — Dictionaries.

269. Janson, Horst W. History of Art. rev. ed. Abrams. 1969. $18.50.   709
1. Art — History.

270. McGraw Encyclopedia of World Art. 15 vols. McGraw. 1959-68. $597.00 set; $50.00 ea.   709
1. Art — History.

271. Praeger Encyclopedia of Art. 5 vols. Ency Brit Inc. price on request.   709
1. Art — History.

272. Larousse Encyclopedia of Prehistoric and Ancient Art. Putnam. 1962. $17.95.   709.01
1. Art, Ancient.

273. Larousse Encyclopedia of Byzantine and Medieval Art. Putnam. 1963. $17.95.   709.02
1. Art, Byzantine. 2. Art, Medieval.

274. McGraw-Hill Dictionary of Art. 5 vols. McGraw. 1974. $89.50.   709.03
1. Art — Dictionaries.

275. Murray, Peter and Murray, Linda. Dictionary of Art and Artists. 3rd ed. Gannon. $5.50; pap. $2.65 1972 (Penguin).   709.03
1. Art — Dictionaries. 2. Art — History. 3. Artists — Dictionaries.

276. Larousse Encyclopedia of Modern Art. Putnam. 1965. $20.00.   709.04
1. Art, Modern.

277. Cummings, Paul. Dictionary of Contemporary American Artists. rev. ed. St Martin. 1971. $25.00.   709.22
1. Artists, American — Dictionaries.

278. Britannica Encyclopedia of American Art. S&S. 1973. $29.95.   709.73
1. Art, American — Dictionaries. 2. Artists — U. S.

REFERENCE WORKS

279. Who's Who in American Art. 11th ed. Bowker. 1973. $34.75.   709.73
1. Artists — U. S.

280. Fleming, J., et al. Penguin Dictionary of Architecture. Gannon. $5.00; pap. $2.10 rev. Penguin 1973.   720
1. Architecture — Dictionaries.

281. Hatje, Gerd, ed. Encyclopedia of Modern Architecture. Abrams. 1964. $17.50; pap. $7.95.   724.9
1. Architecture, Modern — 20th Century — Dictionaries.

282. Aronson, Joseph. The New Encyclopedia of Furniture. rev. ed. Crown. 1965. $7.95.   729.9
1. Furniture — Dictionaries.

283. Krause, Chester L. and Mishler, Clifford, eds. Standard Catalog of World Coins. Krause Pubns. 1974. pap. $12.50.   737.4
1. Coins.

284. Andrews, Charles J. Fell's International Coin Book. 5th ed. Fell. 1973. $4.95; pap. $2.95.   737.409
1. Coins.

285. Angus, Ian. Fell's Guide to Coins and Money Tokens of the World. Fell. 1974. $8.95.   737.409
1. Coins.

286. Reed, Mort. Encyclopedia of U. S. Coins. rev. ed. Regnery. 1972. $10.00.   737.49
1. Coins, American. 2. Coinage — U. S.

287. Conrad, John W. Ceramic Formulas: A Guide to Clay, Glaze, Enamel, Glass and Their Colours. Macmillan. 1973. $10.95.   738.12
1. Ceramic Materials — Tables, Calculations, etc. 2. Pottery — Formulae, Tables, etc.

288. American Crafts Council. Contemporary Crafts Market Place, 1975-1976. Bowker. 1975. $13.95.   745
1. Art Industries and Trade.

289. Savage, George. Dictionary of Antiques. Praeger. 1970. $17.50.   745.103
1. Art Objects — Dictionaries.

290. Hornung, Clarence P. Treasury of American Design: A Pictorial Survey of Popular Folk Arts. 2 vols. Abrams. 1972. $50.00.   745.409
1. Art Industries and Trade, American. 2. Design, Decorative — U. S.

291. Friedberg, Robert. Paper Money of the United States. 7th ed. Coin & Curr. 1972. $14.00.   769.55
1. Paper Money — U. S.

292. Mackay, James A. The Dictionary of Stamps in Color. Macmillan. 1973. $19.95.   769.56
1. Postage-Stamps — Dictionaries.

293. Scott's Specialized Catalog of United States Stamps, 1923- S&S. $7.75.   769.73
1. Postage-Stamps — U. S.

294. Scott's Standard Postage Stamps of the World. 3 vols. S&S. 1972. $8.50 ea.   769.73
1. Postage-Stamps — Catalogs.

295. Focal Press, Ltd. Focal Encyclopedia of Photography. 2 vols. P-H. 1974. $24.50 ea.   770
1. Photography.

296. Apel, Willi. Harvard Dictionary of Music. 2nd rev. & enl. ed. Harvard U Pr. 1969. $20.00.   780.3
1. Music — Dictionaries. 2. Musicians — Dictionaries.

297. Barlow, Harold and Morgenstern, Sam, eds. A Dictionary of Musical Themes. Crown. 1949. $6.95.   780.3
1. Music — Dictionaries.

298. Cross, Milton J. and Ewen, David. Milton Cross' New Encyclopedia of the Great Composers and Their Music. 2 vols. Doubleday. boxed $14.95.   780.3
1. Composers — Dictionaries. 2. Music — Dictionaries.

299. Ewen, David, ed. Composers Since 1900. Wilson. 1969. $17.00.   780.3
1. Composers — Dictionaries.

300. ————. Great Composers: 1300-1900. Wilson. 1966. $12.00.   780.3
1. Composers — Dictionaries.

301. Grove, George. Dictionary of Music and Musicians. 10 vols. with suppl. 5th ed. Blom, E., ed. St Martin. 1954. $15.00 ea.; $149.50 set; pap. $69.50.   780.3
1. Music — Dictionaries. 2. Musicians — Dictionaries.

REFERENCE WORKS

302. Oxford Companion to Music. Scholes, P. A., ed.. 10th ed. Oxford U Pr. 1970. $25.00. 780.3
1. Music — Bibliography. 2. Music — Dictionaries.

303. Siegmeister, Elie, ed. The New Music Lover's Handbook. Harvey. 1973. $29.95.
780.8
1. Composers. 2. Folk Music — History and Criticism. 3. Music.

304. Ewen, David. The Complete Book of Classical Music. P-H. 1965. $14.95. 780.9
1. Music — History and Criticism.

305. New Oxford History of Music. Westrup, J. A., et al, eds.. Vol. 1. Ancient & Oriental Music. $15.00; Vol. 2. Early Medieval Music up to 1300. $15.00; Vol. 3. Ars Nova & the Renaissance, c. 1300-1540. $15.00; Vol. 4. The Age of Humanism, 1540-1630. 1968. $22.50; Vol. 7. The Age of Enlightenment, 1745-1790. 1974. $27.50; Vol. 10. Modern Music, 1890-1960. 1974. $29.00. Oxford U Pr.
780.9
1. Music — History and Criticism.

306. Schonberg, Harold C. The Great Conductors. S&S. 1967. $7.50; pap. $3.95.
780.92
1. Conductors (Music).

307. Stambler, Irwin and London, Grelun. Encyclopedia of Folk, Country and Western Music. St Martin. 1969. $12.95. 781.773
1. Folk Music — U. S. 2. Musicians, American. 3. Music, Popular (Songs, etc.) — Dictionaries.

308. Barlow, Harold and Morgenstern, Sam, eds. Dictionary of Opera and Song Themes. Crown. 1966. $6.95. 782
1. Opera — Dictionaries.

309. Ewen, David. New Encyclopedia of the Opera. Hill & Wang. 1971. $15.00. 782.1
1. Opera — Dictionaries. 2. Operas — Stories, Plots, etc.

310. Roxon, Lillian. Rock Encyclopedia. G&D. 1974. pap. $1.95. 784
1. Music, Popular (Songs, etc.) — Dictionaries. 2. Music — Bio-Bibliography.

311. Shestack, Melvin. Country Music Encyclopedia. T Y Crowell. 1974. $13.95.
784.092
1. Music, Popular (Songs, etc.) — Dictionaries.

312. Amberg, George. The New York Times Film Reviews: A One-Volume Selection 1913-1970. Quadrangle. 1972. $12.50. 791.43
1. Moving-Pictures — Reviews.

313. Halliwell, Leslie. The Filmgoer's Companion: From Nickelodeon to New Wave. 4th ed. Hill & Wang. 1974. $25.00; pap. $15.00. 791.43
1. Moving-Pictures — Biography. 2. Moving-Pictures — Dictionaries.

314. Michael, Paul and Parish, James R., eds. American Movies Reference Book: The Sound Era. P-H. 1969. $29.95. 791.43
1. Moving Picture Actors and Actresses. 2. Moving-Pictures — U. S.

315. Bowman, Walter P. and Ball, Robert H. Theatre Language, a Dictionary. Theatre Arts. 1961. $9.95; pap. $3.95. 792
1. Drama — Dictionaries. 2. Theater — Dictionaries.

316. Melchinger, Siegfried. The Concise Encyclopedia of Modern Drama. Horizon. 1964. $15.00. 792.03
1. Drama — Encyclopedias. 2. Drama — 20th Century — History and Criticism. 3. Theater — Dictionaries.

317. Oxford Companion to the Theatre. Hartnoll, P., ed.. 3rd ed. Oxford U Pr. 1967. $17.50. 792.03
1. Theater — Dictionaries.

318. Guinness Sports Record Book. Sterling. 1972. $3.50; pap. $1.25 1973 (Bantam). 796
1. Sports — Dictionaries.

319. Oxford Companion to World Sports and Games. Arlott, John, ed.. Oxford U Pr. 1975. $29.95. 796
1. Sports — Encyclopedias. 2. Sports — History.

320. Rules of the Game: The Complete Illustrated Encyclopedia of All the Sports in the World. Two Continents. $14.95. 796
1. Sports — Dictionaries.

321. Menke, Frank G. The Encyclopedia of Sports. 5th ed. A S Barnes. 1974. $25.00.
796.03
1. Sports — Encyclopedias.

REFERENCE WORKS

800 Literature

322. Benet, William Rose. The Reader's Encyclopedia. T Y Crowell. 1965. $10.00.   803
1. Literature — Dictionaries.

323. Brewer, Ebenezer C. Dictionary of Phrase and Fable. Centenary ed. by Evans, Ivor H.. Har-Row. 1972. $10.00.   803
1. Allusions. 2. Literature — Dictionaries.

324. ———. Reader's Handbook of Famous Names in Fiction, Allusions. 2 vols. Gale. Repr. 1966. $29.50.   803
1. Allusions. 2. Literature — Dictionaries.

325. Buchanan-Brown, John, ed. Cassell's Encyclopedia of World Literature. new rev. ed. Morrow. Repr. of 1954 ed. 1973. $47.95.   803
1. Authors. 2. Literature — Dictionaries.

326. Shaw, Harry. Dictionary of Literary Terms. McGraw. 1972. $12.50.   803
1. Literature — Terminology.

327. Shipley, Joseph T., ed. Dictionary of World Literary Terms. Writer. $12.95.   803
1. Literature — Dictionaries.

328. Smith, Horatio, ed. Columbia Dictionary of Modern European Literature. Columbia U Pr. 1947. $20.00.   803
1. Literature — Dictionaries.

329. Turabian, Kate L. Manual for Writers of Term Papers, Theses, and Dissertations. 4th ed. U of Chicago Pr. 1973. $5.00; pap. $1.95.   808.02
1. Authorship — Handbooks, Manuals, etc.

330. Fiction Catalog. 8th ed. Wilson. 1971. with 4 annual suppl. vols. $25.00.   808.3
1. Fiction — Bibliography.

331. Abrams, Meyer H. A Glossary of Literary Terms. 3rd ed. HR&W. 1971. pap. $2.00.   808.5
1. Literature — Terminology.

332. Granger, Edith. Granger's Index to Poetry. Smith, W. J., ed. Columbia U Pr. 1973. $80.00.   808.81
1. Poetry — Indexes.

333. Connor, John M. and Connor, Billie M., eds. Ottemiller's Index to Plays in Collections. 5th ed. Scarecrow. 1971. $11.00.   808.82
1. Drama — Indexes.

334. Gassner, John and Quinn, Edward, eds. Reader's Encyclopedia of World Drama. T Y Crowell. 1969. $15.00.   808.82
1. Drama. 2. Drama — History and Criticism.

335. Play Index. 4 vols., 1949-1952, 1953-1960, 1961-1967, 1968-1972. Wilson. 1972. $20.00 ea.   808.82
1. Drama — Indexes.

336. Cook, Dorothy E., et al, eds. Short Story Index, Plus 4 Supplements. Wilson. $69.00.   808.83
1. Short Stories — Indexes.

337. Sutton, Roberta B. Speech Index. 4th ed. Scarecrow. 1966. $20.00.   808.85
1. Speeches — Indexes.

338. Sutton, Roberta B. and Mitchell, Charity. Speech Index: Supplement 1966-1970. Scarecrow. 1972. $7.50.   808.85
1. Speeches — Indexes.

339. Bartlett, John. Bartlett's Familiar Quotations. 14th ed. Beck, Emily M., ed. Little. 1968. $15.00; pap. $1.95.   808.88
1. Poetry — Indexes.

340. Stevenson, Burton E., ed. Home Book of Quotations. rev. ed. Dodd. 1967. $40.00.   808.88
1. Quotations.

341. Curley, Dorothy N. and Curley, Arthur, eds. Modern Romance Literatures. Ungar. 1967. $15.00.   809
1. French Literature — History and Criticism. 2. Romance Literature — History and Criticism. 3. Spanish Literature — History and Criticism.

342. Magill, Frank N., ed. Cyclopedia of Literary Characters. Har-Row. 1964. $15.00.   809
1. Characters and Characteristics in Literature.

343. Seymour-Smith, Martin. The Funk and Wagnalls Guide to Modern World Literature. Funk & W. 1973. $13.95.   809.034
1. Literature, Modern — 19th Century — History and Criticism. 2. Literature, Modern — 20th Century — History and Criticism.

344. Contemporary Literary Criticism: Excerpts from the Works of Today's Novelists, Poets, Playwrights and Other Creative Writers. Riley, Carolyn, ed.. Gale. 1973-74. $30.00 ea.   809.04

REFERENCE WORKS

1. Literature, Modern — 20th Century — History and Criticism.

345. Zell, Hans and Silver, Helene. Reader's Guide to African Literature. Holmes & Meier. 1972. $12.50; pap. $4.95.   809.04
1. English Literature — African Authors — Bio-Bibliography. 2. English Literature — African Authors — History and Criticism. 3. French Literature — African Authors — History and Criticism. 4. French Literature — African Authors — History and Criticism.

346. McGraw-Hill Encyclopedia of World Drama. 4 vols. McGraw. 1972. $129.00 set.   809.2
1. Drama — Bibliography. 2. Drama — Dictionaries.

347. Taylor, John R. Penguin Dictionary of the Theatre. B&N. 1967. $8.00; pap. $1.45 (Penguin).   809.2
1. Drama — Dictionaries.

348. Crowell's Handbook of Contemporary Drama. Anderson, Michael, et al. T Y Crowell. 1971. $10.00.   809.204
1. Drama — 20th Century — Dictionaries.

349. Penguin Companion to European Literature. Thorlby, Anthony, ed.. new ed. Penguin. 1973. $4.95.   809.8
1. European Literature — Dictionaries.

350. Preminger, Alex, et al, eds. Princeton Encyclopedia of Poetry and Poetics. rev. ed. Princeton U Pr. 1974. $27.50; pap. $9.75.   809.81
1. Poetics — Dictionaries. 2. Poetry — Dictionaries. 3. Poetry — History and Criticism.

351. Dudley, D. R. and Lang, D. M., eds. Penguin Companion to Literature, Vol. 4: Classical and Byzantine, Oriental and African. Penguin. 1973. pap. $3.95.   809.891
1. African Literature — Dictionaries.
2. Byzantine Literature — Dictionaries.
3. Classical Literature — Dictionaries.
4. Oriental Literature — Dictionaries.

352. Herdeck, Donald E. African Authors: A Companion to Black African Writing. Vol. I: 1300-1973. Inscape Corp. 1973 (BO). $27.50.   809.896
1. African Literature — Bio-Bibliography.

353. Oxford Companion to American Literature. Hart, J. D., ed.. 4th ed. Oxford U Pr. 1965. $20.00.   810.3
1. American Literature — Dictionaries.

354. Jones, Howard M. and Ludwig, Richard M. Guide to American Literature and Its Backgrounds Since 1890. 4th ed. Harvard U Pr. 1972. $10.00; pap. $2.75.   810.9
1. American Literature — Bio-Bibliography. 2. American Literature — History and Criticism.

355. Penguin Companion to American Literature. Bradbury, Malcolm; Mottram, Eric, & Franco, Jean, eds.. McGraw. 1971. $9.95.   810.9
1. American Literature — Bio-Bibliography. 2. American Literature — History and Criticism.

356. Shockley, Ann A. and Chandler, Sue, eds. Living Black American Authors: A Biographical Directory. Bowker. 1973. $12.95.   810.9
1. American Literature — Negro Authors — Bio-Bibliography. 2. American Literature — 20th Century — Bio-Bibliography.

357. Spiller, Robert E., et al. Literary History of the United States. 4th rev. ed. Macmillan. 1974. $25.00; bibliography $25.00.   810.9
1. American Literature — Bibliography. 2. American Literature — History and Criticism.

358. Malkoff, Karl. Crowell's Handbook of Contemporary American Poetry. T Y Crowell. 1973. $8.95.   811.5
1. American Poetry — 20th Century — History and Criticism.

359. New Century Handbook of English Literature. Barnhart, C. L., & Halsey, W. D., eds.. rev. ed. P-H. 1956. $16.50.   820.3
1. English Literature — Dictionaries.

360. Oxford Companion to English Literature. Harvey, P., & Eagle, D., eds.. 4th ed. Oxford U Pr. 1967. $17.50.   820.3
1. American Literature — Dictionaries. 2. English Literature — Dictionaries.

361. Cambridge History of English Literature. 15 vols. Cambridge U Pr. $13.75 ea; $185.00 set.   820.9
1. English Literature — History and Criticism.

362. Moulton, Charles W. Moulton's Library of Literary Criticism of English and American Authors. abr. ed. Tucker, Martin, ed. Ungar. 1966. $45.00.   820.9
1. American Literature — History and Criticism. 2. Criticism. 3. English Literature — History and Criticism.

REFERENCE WORKS

363. Penguin Companion to English Literature. Daiches, David, ed.. McGraw. 1971. $10.95.   820.9
1. Commonwealth of Nations — Literature — Bio-Bibliography. 2. English Literature — History and Criticism.

364. Sampson, George. The Concise Cambridge History of English Literature. 3rd ed. Cambridge U Pr. 1970. $13.75; pap. $5.00.   820.9
1. English Literature — History and Criticism.

365. Cline, Gloria S. and Baker, Jeffrey A. An Index to Criticism of British and American Poetry. Scarecrow. 1973. $9.00.   821.009
1. American Poetry — History and Criticism — Indexes. 2. American Poetry — Indexes. 3. English Poetry — History and Criticism — Indexes. 4. English Poetry — Indexes.

366. Stevenson, Burton E., ed. The Home Book of Verse, American and English. 2 vols. HR&W. 1953. $30.00.   821.08
1. American Poetry — Collections. 2. English Poetry — Collections.

367. Bartlett, John, ed. Complete Concordance to Shakespeare. St Martin. 1973. $37.50.   822.33
1. Shakespeare, William, 1564-1616 — Concordances.

368. Campbell, Oscar J. and Quinn, Edward G., eds. Reader's Encyclopedia of Shakespeare. T Y Crowell. 1966. $15.00.   822.33
1. Shakespeare, William — Dictionaries, Indexes, etc.

369. Quennell, Peter. Who's Who in Shakespeare. Morrow. 1973. $14.95.   822.33
1. Shakespeare, William, 1564-1616 — Characters. 2. Shakespeare, William, 1564-1616 — Dictionaries, Indexes, etc.

370. Spevack, Marvin. The Harvard Concordance to Shakespeare. Harvard U Pr. 1974. $45.00.   822.33
1. Shakespeare, William, 1564-1616 — Concordances.

371. Stokes, F. G. Dictionary of the Characters and Proper Names in the Works of Shakespeare. Peter Smith. $6.75.   822.33
1. Shakespeare, William, 1564-1616 — Dictionaries.

372. Vinson, James. Contemporary Dramatists. St Martin. 1973. $30.00.   822.9
1. American Drama — 20th Century — Bio-Bibliography. 2. English Drama — 20th Century — Bio-Bibliography.

373. Domandi, Agnes K., ed. Modern Germanic Literature. 2 vols. Ungar. 1972. $30.00.   830
1. German Literature.

374. Oxford Companion to French Literature. Harvey, P., & Heseltine, J. E., eds.. Oxford U Pr. 1959. $15.00.   840.3
1. French Literature — Dictionaries.

375. Newmark, Maxim. Dictionary of Spanish Literature. Littlefield. 1956. pap. $2.25.   860.3
1. Spanish Literature — Dictionaries. 2. Spanish-American Literature — Dictionaries.

376. Prusek, ed. Dictionary of Oriental Literatures. 3 vols. Basic. 1974. boxed set $35.00.   895
1. Oriental Literature.

900 Geography, Travel, and History

377. Wiener, Philip P., ed. Dictionary of the History of Ideas. 4 vols. Scribner. 1973. $140.00 set; $35.00 ea.   901.9
1. Civilization — Collected Works.

378. ———. Index to the Dictionary of the History of Ideas. Scribner. 1974. $35.00.   901.9

379. Langer, William L., ed. Encyclopedia of World History. 5th ed. HM. 1972. $17.50.   902
1. Chronology, Historical. 2. History.

380. Morris, Richard E. and Irwin, Graham, eds. Harper Encyclopedia of the Modern World: A Concise Reference History from 1760 to the Present. Har-Row. 1970. $17.50; pap. $15.79.   909
1. History — Dictionaries. 2. World History — Dictionaries.

381. Storey, Robin L. Chronology of the Medieval World: 800-1491. McKay. 1973. $15.95.   909.07
1. Middle Ages — History — Chronology.

382. Holt, P. M., et al, eds. Cambridge History of Islam. 2 vols. Cambridge U Pr. $55.00.   910.031
1. Civilization, Islamic. 2. Islamic Countries — History.

REFERENCE WORKS

383. Seltzer, L. E., ed. Columbia Lippincott Gazetteer of the World. Columbia U Pr. 1962. with 1961 suppl. $100.00. 910.3
1. Geography — Dictionaries.

384. Webster's New Geographical Dictionary. rev. ed. Merriam. 1972. $14.95. 910.3
1. Geography — Dictionaries.

385. Banks, Arthur. A World Atlas of Military History. 2 vols. Hippocrene Bks. 1973-74. $12.95 ea. 911
1. Military History — Atlases.

386. Shepherd, William R. Shepherd's Historical Atlas. 9th ed. B&N. 1964. $17.50. 911
1. Atlases, Historical. 2. Geography, Historical — Maps.

387. Fox, Edward W. Atlas of European History. Oxford U Pr. 1957. pap. $3.95. 911.4
1. Europe — Historical Geography — Maps.

388. Chew, Allen F. An Atlas of Russian History: Eleven Centuries of Changing Borders. rev. ed. Yale U Pr. 1970. $10.00. 911.47
1. Russia — Historical Geography — Maps.

389. Gilbert, Martin. Atlas of the Arab-Israeli Conflict. Macmillan. 1975. $6.95. 911.56
1. Arabs — Historical Geography — Maps. 2. Jewish-Arab Relations — History. 3. Jews — Historical Geography — Maps. 4. Near East — Historical Geography — Maps.

390. Chi-Bonnardel, Regine V., ed. The Atlas of Africa. Free Pr. 1974. $80.00. 911.60
1. Africa — Historical Geography — Maps.

391. Adams, James T., ed. Atlas of American History. Scribner. $20.00. 911.73
1. U. S. — Historical Geography — Maps.

392. American Heritage Editors. American Heritage Pictorial Atlas of United States History. McGraw. 1967. $16.50. 911.73
1. U. S. — Historical Geography — Maps.

393. Lord, Clifford L. and Lord, Elizabeth S. Historical Atlas of the United States. rev. ed. Johnson Repr. 1969. $21.00. 911.73
1. U. S. — Historical Geography — Maps.

394. Wilgus, A. Curtis. Historical Atlas of Latin America. rev. ed. Cooper Sq. 1967. $6.95. 911.8
1. Latin America — Historical Geography — Maps.

395. Bartholomew, John, ed. Time Atlas of the World: Comprehensive 1 vol. ed. rev. ed. HM. 1971. $65.00. 912
1. Atlases.

396. Cohen, Saul B., ed. Oxford World Atlas. Oxford U Pr. 1973. $19.95; pap. $6.95. 912
1. Atlases.

397. Fitzgerald, Ken, compiled by. The Space-Age Photographic Atlas. Crown. 1970. $7.95. 912
1. Earth — Photographs from Space.

398. Loftus, Tony, ed. The Earth and Man: A Rand McNally World Atlas. Rand. 1972. $35.00. 912
1. Atlases. 2. Man — Influence of Environment.

399. Rand McNally Atlas of the American Revolution. Rand. 1975. $35.00. 912.1
1. U. S. — History — Revolution — Campaigns and Battles. 2. U. S. — History — Revolution — Historical Geography — Maps.

400. Al Faruqi, Isma'il R. Historical Atlas of the Religions of the World. Macmillan. 1974. $12.50. 912.12
1. Religions — Maps.

401. Hawkes, Jacquetta H. Atlas of Ancient Archaeology. McGraw. 1974. $19.50. 912.19
1. Archaeology — Maps. 2. Man, Prehistoric — Maps.

402. Gilbert, Martin. First World War History Atlas. Macmillan. 1971. $4.95. 912.4
1. European War, 1914-1918 — Maps.

403. Young, Peter, ed. Atlas of the Second World War. Putnam. 1974. $17.95. 912.4
1. World War, 1939-1945 — Maps.

404. Hsieh, Chiao-Min and Salter, Christopher L. Atlas of China. McGraw. 1973. $14.95. 912.51
1. China — Economic Conditions — Maps. 2. China — Historical Geography — Maps. 3. China — Maps.

405. Ryuziro, Isido, ed. Atlas of Japan: Physical, Economic and Social. InterCulture. 1974. $30.00. 912.52
1. Japan — Maps.

REFERENCE WORKS

406. Avery, Catherine B., ed. The New Century Handbook of Classical Geography. P-H. 1972. $7.95.   913.003
1. Classical Geography — Dictionaries. 2. Geography, Ancient — Dictionaries.

407. Larousse Encyclopedia of Archaeology. Putnam. 1972. $25.00.   913.03
1. Archaeology — Dictionaries.

408. Feder, Lillian. Crowell's Handbook of Classical Literature. T Y Crowell. 1964. $7.95.   913.38
1. Classical Literature — Dictionaries.

409. The Oxford Classical Dictionary. Hammond, N. G., & Scullard, H. H., eds.. 2nd ed. Oxford U Pr. 1970. $35.00.   913.38
1. Classical Dictionaries.

410. The Oxford Companion to Classical Literature. Harvey, P., ed.. 3rd ed. Oxford U Pr. 1946. $8.50.   913.38
1. Classical Dictionaries. 2. Greek Literature — Dictionaries. 3. Latin Literature — Dictionaries.

411. Avery, Catherine B. New Century Handbook of Leaders of the Classical World. P-H. 1972. $7.95.   920.009
1. Biography — Dictionaries. 2. Classical Biography — Dictionaries.

412. Who Was Who. 5 vols. Vol. 1. 1897-1915; Vol. 2. 1916-1928; Vol. 3. 1929-1940; Vol. 4. 1941-1950; Vol. 5. 1951-1960. St Martin. $17.00 ea.   920.01
1. Great Britain — Biography.

413. Who's Who. 121st ed. St Martin. 1969. $32.50.   920.01
1. Great Britain — Biography.

414. Current Biography. Monthly. Wilson. $10.00; Yearbook $10.00.   920.02
1. Biography — Dictionaries.

415. Current Biography. Cumulated Index, 1940-1970. Wilson. 1973. $6.00.   920.02

416. McGraw-Hill Editors. The McGraw-Hill Encyclopedia of World Biography. 12 vols. McGraw. 1973. $275.00.   920.02
1. Biography — Dictionaries.

417. The New Century Cyclopedia of Names. 3 vols. Barnhart, C., & Halsey, W. D., eds.. P-H. 1954 (Appleton-Century-Crofts). $55.00.   920.02
1. Biography — Dictionaries. 2. Geography — Dictionaries. 3. Names — Dictionaries.

418. Thorne, J. O., ed. Chambers Biographical Dictionary. rev. ed. St Martin. 1969. $17.50.   920.02
1. Biography — Dictionaries.

419. Webster's Biographical Dictionary. rev. ed. Merriam. 1972. $12.95.   920.02
1. Biography — Dictionaries.

420. Dictionary of National Biography. Stephen, Leslie, et al, eds.. Oxford U Pr. 1882-1953. 22 vols. (inc. 1st suppl.) $395.00; suppl. 2 $22.75; suppls. 3 & 4 $18.75 ea.; suppl. 5 $22.50; suppl. 6 $27.25; Concise Dictionary. 2 pts: pt. 1 to 1900 $12.00; pt. 2 1901-1950 $15.25.   920.042
1. Great Britain — Biography — Dictionaries.

421. Dictionary of American Biography, 1927-1972. 16 vols. Scribner. $360.00.   920.073
1. U. S. — Biography — Dictionaries.

422. Who Was Who in America. 6 vols. Marquis. $230.80, set.   920.073
1. U. S. — Biography.

423. Who's Who in America: Vol. 38. 2 vols. Marquis. 1974. $69.50.   920.073
1. U. S. — Biography.

424. Who's Who of American Women. 8th ed. Marquis. 1973. $44.50.   920.073
1. Women in the U. S. — Biography.

425. Contemporary Authors: A Bio-Bibliographical Guide to Current Authors and Their Works. 2 vols. 1 yr. Gale. $30.00, per yr.   928
1. Authors. 2. Biography — Dictionaries.

426. Kunitz, Stanley J. and Colby, Vineta, eds. European Authors, 1000-1900. Wilson. 1967. $24.00.   928
1. Authors, European. 2. Biography — Dictionaries.

427. Kunitz, Stanley J. and Haycraft, Howard, eds. American Authors: 1600-1900. Wilson. 1938. $12.00.   928
1. Authors, American. 2. Biography — Dictionaries.

428. ———. British Authors Before 1800. Wilson. 1952. $10.00.   928
1. Authors, English. 2. Biography — Dictionaries.

REFERENCE WORKS

429. ———. British Authors of the Nineteenth Century. Wilson. 1936. $12.00. 928
1. Authors, English. 2. Biography — Dictionaries.

430. ———. Twentieth Century Authors. Wilson. 1942. $22.00; 1st suppl., 1955 $18.00. 928
1. Authors. 2. Biography — Dictionaries.

431. Sharp, Harold S. Handbook of Pseudonyms and Personal Nicknames. 2 vols. Scarecrow. 1972. $27.50. 929.4
1. Anonyms and Pseudonyms. 2. Nicknames.

432. Smith, Elsdon C. New Dictionary of American Family Names. Har-Row. 1973. $12.95. 929.4
1. Names, Personal — U. S.

433. Franklyn, Julian. An Encyclopediic Dictionary of Heraldry. Pergamon. 1970. $32.00. 929.6
1. Heraldry.

434. Bickerman, Elias J. Chronology of the Ancient World. Cornell U Pr. 1968. $9.75. 930
1. History, Ancient — Chronology.

435. Cambridge Ancient History. 12 vols. Cambridge U Pr. $27.50 ea.; 5 vols. of plates $15.50 ea., (Consult publisher's catalog). 930
1. History, Ancient.

436. Cambridge Medieval History. 8 vols. Cambridge U Pr. Consult publisher's catalog. 940.1
1. Middle Ages — History.

437. Cambridge Modern History. 13 vols. Cambridge U Pr. 1970. $295.00; $27.50 ea. 940.2
1. History, Modern.

438. Vernadsky, George and Fisher, Ralph T., eds. Dictionary of Russian Historical Terms from the Eleventh Century to 1917. Yale U Pr. 1970. $15.00. 947.003
1. Russia — History — Dictionaries. 2. Russian Language — Dictionaries — English.

439. Wu, Yuan-Li, ed. China: A Handbook. Praeger. 1973. $35.00. 951.103
1. China (People's Republic of China, 1949-).

440. Bhattacharya, Sachchidananda. A Dictionary of Indian History. Braziller. 1968. $12.50. 954.003
1. India — History — Dictionaries.

441. Bacharach, Jere L. A Near East Studies Handbook, 570-1974. U of Wash Pr. 1974. $12.50; pap. $4.95. 956.002
1. Islamic Empire — History — Handbooks, Manuals, etc. 2. Near East — History — Handbooks, Manuals, etc.

442. Adams, Michael, ed. The Middle East: A Handbook. Praeger. 1971. $25.00. 956.03
1. Near East — History.

443. Kajubi, Senteza, et al, eds. African Encyclopedia. Oxford U Pr. 1974. $13.00. 960
1. Africa — Dictionaries and Encyclopedias.

444. Rosenthal, Eric, ed. Encyclopedia of Southern Africa. rev. ed. Warne. 1973. $15.00. 968
1. Africa, Southern — Dictionaries and Encyclopedias.

445. Washburn, Wilcomb E., compiled by. The American Indian and the United States: A Documentary History. 4 vols. Random. 1973. $125.00. 970.1
1. Indians of North America — Government Relations. 2. Indians of North America — History.

446. Kappler, Charles J., ed. Indian Treaties, 1778-1883. Interland Pub. Repr. 1904. $67.50. 970.5
1. Indians of North America — Government Relations. 2. Indians of North America — Legal Status, Laws, etc.

447. Oxford Companion to Canadian History and Literature. Story, Norah, ed.. Oxford U Pr. 1967. $18.50. 971
1. Canada — History — Dictionaries. 2. Canadian Literature — Bio-Bibliography. 3. Canadian Literature — Dictionaries.

448. Adams, James T., ed. Album of American History. 6 vols. By subscription only. Scribner. $120.00. 973
1. U. S. — History — Pictorial Works. 2. U. S. — Social Life and Customs.

449. Carruth, Gorton, et al, eds. The Encyclopedia of American Facts and Dates. 6th ed. T Y Crowell. 1972. $9.95. 973.02
1. U. S. — History — Chronology.

450. Adams, James T., ed. Dictionary of American History. 6 vols. & index. By subscription only. Scribner. $120.00. 973.03
1. U. S. — History — Dictionaries.

REFERENCE WORKS

451. Morris, Richard B. and Commager, Henry S., eds. Encyclopedia of American History. rev. ed. Har-Row. 1970. $12.50.
973.03
1. U. S. — History — Chronology. 2. U. S. — History — Dictionaries.

452. Oxford Companion to American History. Hart, James D., ed.. 4th ed. Oxford U Pr. 1965. $20.00. 973.03
1. U. S. — History — Dictionaries.

453. Boatner, Mark M., 3rd. Encyclopedia of the American Revolution. rev. ed. McKay. 1974. $17.50. 973.3
1. U. S. — History — Revolution — Dictionaries.

454. ———. Civil War Dictionary: A Concise Encyclopedia. 3rd ed. McKay. $17.50.
973.7
1. U. S. — History — Civil War — Dictionaries.

455. Delpar, Helen, ed. Encyclopedia of Latin America. McGraw. 1974. $28.50. 980
1. Latin America — Dictionaries and Encyclopedias.

456. Learmonth, Andrew T. and Learmonth, Nancy. Encyclopedia of Australia. new ed. Warne. 1974. $15.00. 994
1. Australia — Dictionaries and Encyclopedias.

000 GENERAL WORKS

001 Knowledge

457. Barzun, Jacques. The House of Intellect. Har-Row. 1959. pap. $1.75.   001
1. Learning and Scholarship. 2. U. S. — Intellectual Life.

458. Snow, Charles P. Two Cultures and a Second Look. Cambridge U Pr. 1969. $3.95; pap. $1.75.   001
1. Science and the Humanities.

459. Pells, Richard H. Radical Visions and American Dreams: Culture and Thought in the Depression Years. Har-Row. 1973. $12.50; pap. $3.95.   001.2
1. U. S. — Intellectual Life.

460. White, Virginia P. Grants: How to Find Out About Them and What to Do Next. Plenum Pub. 1975. $19.50.   001.44
1. Fundraising. 2. Research Grants — U. S.

001.5 Information and Communication

461. Parsegian, V. L. This Cybernetic World of Men, Machines and Earth Systems. Doubleday. 1972. $6.95.   001.5
1. Cybernetics.

462. Rose, M. The Cybernetics Revolution. B&N. 1974. $13.00.   001.5
1. Cybernetics.

463. Schramm, Wilbur. Men, Messages and Media: A Look at Human Communication. Har-Row. 1973. pap. $4.95.   001.5
1. Communication. 2. Mass Media.

464. Van Amerogen, C. The Way Things Work Book of Computers: An Illustrated Encyclopedia of Information Science, Cybernetics and Data Processing. S&S. 1974. $8.95.   001.53
1. Computers. 2. Cybernetics. 3. Information Theory.

465. Kurlansky, Mervin and Naar, Jon. The Faith of Graffiti. Praeger. 1974. $14.95; pap. $7.95.   001.55
1. Graffiti — U. S.

001.6 Data Processing

466. Albrecht, Robert L., et al. Basic. Wiley. 1973. $3.95.   001.64
1. Basic (Computer Program Language).

467. Anger, Arthur L., et al. Computer Science: The PL-1 Language. Wiley. 1972. pap. $6.50.   001.64
1. PL 1 (Computer Program Language).

468. Bezner, Hart C. The Elements of Fortran Four. Goodyear. 1973. pap. $6.95.   001.64
1. Fortran (Computer Program Language).

469. Hawkes, Nigel. The Computer Revolution. Dutton. 1972. $7.95.   001.64
1. Electronic Data Processing. 2. Electronic Digital Processing.

000 GENERAL WORKS

470. Kemeny, John G. Man and the Computer. Scribner. 1972. $6.95; pap. $2.45.   001.64
1. Computers and Civilization. 2. Electronic Data Processing.

471. Spencer, Donald. Computers in Action: How Computers Work. Hayden. 1974. $7.50; pap. $4.95.   001.64
1. Electronic Digital Computers.

001.9 Controversial and Spurious Knowledge

472. Klass, Philip J. UFO's Explained. Random. 1975. $8.95.   001.9
1. Flying Saucers.

473. Von Daniken, Erich. Gods from Outer Space: Return to the Stars, or Evidence for the Impossible. Putnam. 1971. $5.95.   001.9
1. Interplanetary Voyages. 2. Life on Other Planets.

474. ———. In Search of Ancient Gods: My Pictorial Evidence for the Impossible. Putnam. 1974. $8.95.   001.9
1. History, Ancient. 2. Interplanetary Voyages. 3. Man, Prehistoric.

020 Library and Information Sciences

475. Busha, Charles H. Freedom vs. Suppression and Censorship. Libs Unl. 1973. $10.00.   020.8
1. Censorship — Bibliography. 2. Libraries — Censorship.

476. Goodrum, Charles A. The Library of Congress. Praeger. 1974. $9.50.   027.53
1. U. S. Library of Congress.

030 General Encyclopedic Works

477. McWhirter, Norris and McWhirter, Ross, eds. Guinness Book of World Records. rev. ed. Sterling. 1975. $6.95.   030
1. Statistics. 2. World Records.

050 Periodicals

478. Peterson, Theodore. Magazines in the Twentieth Century. 2nd ed. U of Ill Pr. 1964. $10.00.   051
1. American Periodicals — History.

479. Wood, James P. Magazines in the United States. Ronald. 1971. $9.95.   051
1. American Periodicals.

060 Museums

480. Cooper, Barbara and Matheson, Maureen. The World Museum Guide. McGraw. 1974. $9.95.   069.02
1. Museums — Directories.

481. Mills, John F. Treasure Keepers. Doubleday. 1973. $7.95.   069.53
1. Art Objects — Conservation and Restoration. 2. Museum Techniques.

070-080 Journalism, Publishing, and Newspapers

482. Seldes, George. Never Tire of Protesting. Brand, Eileen, ed. Lyle Stuart. 1968. $6.95.   070.1
1. Liberty of the Press — U. S. 2. Press — U. S. 3. U. S. — Politics and Government — 1945- 4. World Politics — 1945-

483. Epstein, Edward J. News from Nowhere: Television and the News. Random. 1973. $7.95; pap. $1.95.   070.43
1. Television Broadcasting and News — U. S.

484. Robinson, Sol. Guidelines for News Reporters. Tab Bks. 1971. $9.95.   070.43
1. English Language — Synonyms and Antonyms. 2. Reporters and Reporting.

485. Gelfand, Louis and Heath, Harry E. Modern Sportswriting. 2nd ed. Iowa St U Pr. 1969. $10.50.   070.44
1. Journalism. 2. Sports Journalism.

486. MacDougall, Curtis D. Principles of Editorial Writing. new ed. Wm C Brown. 1973.   070.44
1. Editorials.

487. Singer, Samuel L. The Student Journalist and Reviewing the Performing Arts. Rosen Pr. 1974. $6.95.   070.44
1. Journalism.

488. Stapler, Harry. The Student Journalist and Sportswriting. Rosen Pr. 1975. $6.96.   070.44
1. Sports Journalism.

489. Hicks, Wilson. Words and Pictures. Arno. 1973. $12.00.   070.49

000 GENERAL WORKS

1. Journalism, Pictorial. 2. Photography, Journalistic.

490. Dessauer, John P. Book Publishing: What It Is, What It Does. Bowker. 1974. $11.95.   070.5
1. Publishers and Publishing.

491. Swanberg, W. A. Luce and His Empire: A Biography. Scribner. 1972. $12.50; pap. $1.95 (Dell).   070.5(B)
1. Luce, Henry Robinson, 1898-1967.

492. Brucker, Herbert. Communication Is Power: Unchanging Values in Changing Journalism. Oxford U Pr. 1973. $9.50.   070.9
1. Journalism — U. S.

493. Merrill, John C. The Elite Press: Great Newspapers of the World. Pitman. 1968. $7.95.   070.9
1. Newspapers.

494. Swanberg, W. A. Citizen Hearst. Scribner. 1961. $12.95; pap. $1.95 (Bantam).   070.9(B)
1. Hearst, William Randolph, 1863-1951. 2. Newspapers. 3. Press — U. S.

495. Lee, Alfred M. The Daily Newspaper in America: The Evolution of a Social Instrument. Octagon. 1973. $25.00.   071
1. American Newspapers — History. 2. Journalism — U. S. 3. Press — U. S.

496. Chalmers, David M. The Muckrake Years. Van Nos Reinhold. 1974. pap. $2.95.   071.3
1. Journalism — U. S. — History. 2. U. S. — Economic Conditions — 1865-1918. 3. U. S. — Social Conditions — 1865-1918.

497. Emery, Edwin. The Press and America: An Interpretation of Mass Media. 3rd ed. P-H. 1972. $12.50.   071.3
1. American Newspapers. 2. Press — U. S.

498. Hynds, Ernest C. American Newspapers in the 1970's. HM. 1975. $12.95.   071.3
1. American Newspapers — History. 2. Journalism — U. S.

499. Leamer, Laurence. The Paper Revolutionaries: The Rise of the Underground Press. S&S. 1972. $8.95; pap. $2.95.   071.3
1. Underground Press — U. S.

500. Reston, James B. The Artillery of the Press: Its Influence on American Foreign Policy. Har-Row. 1967. $5.00.   071.3
1. Government and the Press — U. S. 2. U. S. — Foreign Relations.

501. Rutland, Robert A. The Newsmongers: Journalism in the Life of the Nation, 1690-1972. Dial. 1973. $12.50.   071.3
1. Journalism — U. S. — History.

502. Steffens, Lincoln. Autobiography. HarBraceJ. 1968. $12.00; Vol. 1. pap. $2.55; Vol. 2. pap. $2.95.   071.3(B)
1. Journalists — Correspondence, Reminiscences, etc. 2. Social Problems. 3. Steffens, Lincoln, 1866-1936.

503. Talese, Gay. The Kingdom and the Power. Bantam. 1970. pap. $1.50.   071.4
1. New York Times.

504. Wolfe, Tom. The New Journalism. Har-Row. 1973. $10.95.   081
1. Journalism — U. S.

090 Book Rarities

505. Weber, Carl J. Fore-Edge Painting: Historical Survey of a Curious Art in Book Decoration. Harvey. 1966. $20.00.   096.1
1. Fore-Edge Painting.

506. Haight, Anne L. Banned Books. 3rd ed. Bowker. 1970. $9.75.   098.1
1. Censorship. 2. Prohibited Books.

100 PHILOSOPHY AND PSYCHOLOGY

100-109 Philosophy (Theory and History)

507. Hofstadter, Albert. Agony and Epitaph: Man, His Art and His Painting. Braziller. 1970. $7.50. 100
1. Aesthetics. 2. Art — Philosophy. 3. Man.

508. Hoyle, Fred. Man in the Universe. Columbia U Pr. 1966. $6.00. 100
1. Education. 2. Philosophy, Modern. 3. Universe.

509. Hocking, William E. and Hocking, Richard, eds. Types of Philosophy. 3rd rev. ed. Scribner. 1959. pap. $5.95. 102
1. Philosophy.

510. Allen, Reginald E., ed. Greek Philosophy: Thales to Aristotle. Free Pr. 1966. pap. $3.95. 108
1. Philosophy — Collections.

511. Bronstein, David J., et al. Basic Problems of Philosophy. 4th ed. P-H. 1972. $10.95. 108
1. Philosophy — Collections.

512. Weber, Eugen, ed. Paths to the Present: Aspects of European Thought from Romanticism to Existentialism. Dodd. 1960. pap. $6.75. 108
1. Philosophy — Collections.

513. Clark, Gordon H. Thales to Dewey. HM. 1957. $10.95. 109
1. Philosophy — History.

514. Durant, Will. The Story of Philosophy. rev. ed. S&S. 1961. $7.95; pap. $2.95. 109
1. Philosophers. 2. Philosophy — History.

515. Hartnack, Justus. History of Philosophy. Humanities. 1973. pap. $7.50. 109
1. Philosophy — History.

516. Jaspers, Karl. The Great Philosophers. 2 vols. HarBraceJ. 1962-66. $22.50. 109
1. Philosophers. 2. Philosophers — History.

517. Passmore, John. A Hundred Years of Philosophy. 3rd ed. Basic. 1966. $12.95. 109
1. Philosophy — History.

518. Russell, Bertrand. A History of Western Philosophy. S&S. 1945. $8.95. 109
1. Philosophy — History.

113-115 Metaphysics

519. Bergson, Henri L. Creative Evolution. R West. 1911. $20.00. 113
1. Evolution. 2. Life. 3. Metaphysics.

520. Braybrooke, Neville. Teilhard de Chardin: Pilgrim of the Future. Humanities. 1968. pap. $1.75. 113(B)
1. Teilhard de Chardin, Pierre, 1881-1955.

521. Teilhard de Chardin, Pierre. The Phenomenon of Man. Har-Row. 1959. pap. $1.95. 113
1. Cosmology. 2. Evolution.

522. Fraser, Julius T., ed. Voices of Time. Braziller. 1965. $12.50. 115
1. Time.

100 PHILOSOPHY AND PSYCHOLOGY

120-128 Knowledge, Cause, Purpose, Man

523. Pruyser, Paul W. Between Belief and Unbelief. Har-Row. 1974. $10.00. 121
1. Belief and Doubt.

524. Popkin, Richard H. The History of Scepticism from Erasmus to Descartes. rev. ed. Humanities. 1964. $16.50; pap. $2.95 (Har-Row). 121.5
1. Skepticism — History.

525. Salk, Jonas E. The Survival of the Wisest. Har-Row. 1973. $6.95. 128
1. Human Evolution. 2. Man. 3. Philosophy of Nature. 4. Self (Philosophy). 5. Wisdom.

526. Aries, Philippe. Western Attitudes Toward Death: From the Middle Ages to the Present. Johns Hopkins. 1974. $6.50. 128.5
1. Death — Collected Works.

130-136 Pseudopsychology, Parapsychology, Occultism

527. Freud, Sigmund. The Basic Writings. Modern Lib. $4.95. 131.3
1. Psychoanalysis.

528. Jung, Carl G. Basic Writings of C. G. Jung. Modern Lib. 1959. $2.95. 131.3
1. Psychoanalysis.

529. Heywood, Rosalind. Beyond the Reach of Sense: An Inquiry into Extra-Sensory Perception. Dutton. 1974. pap. $3.45. 133
1. Extrasensory Perception. 2. Psychical Research.

530. Leek, Sybil. ESP: the Magic Within You. Abelard. 1972. $6.95. 133
1. Extrasensory Perception. 2. Psychical Research.

531. Cohen, Daniel. Masters of the Occult. Dodd. 1971. $5.95. 133.09(B)
1. Occult Sciences — Biography.

532. Freedland, Nat. The Occult Explosion. Putnam. 1972. $6.95. 133.09
1. Occult Sciences — U. S. 2. Psychical Research — U. S.

533. Douglas, Alfred. The Tarot: The Origin, Meaning and Uses of the Cards. Taplinger. 1972. $7.95. 133.3
1. Tarot.

534. Cavendish, Richard. The Black Arts. Putnam. 1967. $6.95. 133.4
1. Occult Sciences.

535. Ebon, Martin. The Devil's Bride: Exorcism, Past and Present. Har-Row. 1974. $6.95. 133.4
1. Demonology. 2. Exorcism.

536. Hart, Roger. Witchcraft. Putnam. 1972. $5.95. 133.4
1. Witchcraft.

537. Seligmann, Kurt. Magic, Supernaturalism and Religion. Pantheon. 1973. $10.00; pap. $3.95. 133.4
1. Magic — History. 2. Occult Sciences — History.

538. Carter, Charles E. The Principles of Astrology. Theos Pub Hse. 1963. $2.45. 133.5
1. Astrology.

539. Rudhyar, Dane. The Astrological Houses: The Spectrum of Individual Experience. Doubleday. 1972. $6.95; pap. $2.95. 133.5
1. Astrology.

540. Zolar. The History of Astrology. Zolar. 1972. $7.95. 133.5
1. Astrology — History.

541. Heaps, Willard A. Psychic Phenomena. Nelson. 1974. $5.95. 133.8
1. Psychical Research.

542. Spraggett, Allen. The Case for Immortality. Norton. 1974. $6.95. 133.9
1. Future Life.

543. Fromm, Erich. The Forgotten Language. HR&W. 1951. $7.95; pap. $2.45 (Grove). 135
1. Dreams. 2. Fairy Tales. 3. Mythology.

544. Riesman, David, et al. The Lonely Crowd. abr. ed. Yale U Pr. 1969. $12.50; pap. $3.75. 136.4
1. National Characteristics, American. 2. Race Psychology. 3. U. S. — Social Life and Customs.

545. Gesell, Arnold, et al. Youth: The Years from Ten to Sixteen. Har-Row. 1956. $8.95. 136.7
1. Adolescence. 2. Child Study.

140-149 Specific Philosophies

546. Boller, Paul F. American Transcendentalism, 1830-1860: An Intellectual Inquiry. Putnam. 1974. $6.95; pap. $2.95.   141
1. Philosophy, American — 19th Century. 2. Transcendentalism (New England).

547. Miller, Perry, ed. The Transcendentalists: An Anthology. Harvard U Pr. 1950. $15.00; pap. $2.95.   141
1. Transcendentalism (New England).

548. Forem, Jack. Transcendental Meditation: Maharishi Mahesh Yogi and the Science of Creative Intelligence. Dutton. 1973. $7.95; pap. $2.95.   141.3
1. Transcendental Meditation.

549. Barrett, William. Irrational Man. Doubleday. 1958. pap. $2.50.   142.7
1. Existentialism.

550. ———. What Is Existentialism? Heidegger: The Silent Power of the Possible. Grove. 1964. pap. $2.95.   142.7
1. Existentialism. 2. Heidegger, Martin. 1889-

551. Hubben, William. Dostoevsky, Kierkegaard, Nietzsche and Kafka. Macmillan. 1966. pap. $1.25.   142.7
1. Dostoevsky, Fedor Mikhailovich, 1821-1881. 2. Existentialism. 3. Kafka, Franz, 1883-1924. 4. Kierkegaard, Soren Aabye, 1813-1855. 5. Nietzsche, Friedrich Wilhelm, 1844-1900.

552. Kaufmann, Walter A., ed. Existentialism from Dostoevsky to Sartre. Peter Smith. 1958. $6.00.   142.7
1. Existentialism.

553. MacQuarrie, John. Existentialism. Westminster. 1971. $9.95; pap. $1.95 (Penguin).   142.7
1. Existentialism.

554. Sartre, Jean-Paul. Being and Nothingness. Citadel Pr. 1965. pap. $4.95.   142.7
1. Existentialism.

555. Conkin, Paul K. Puritans and Pragmatists: Eight Eminent American Thinkers. Dodd. 1968. pap. $6.95.   144.3
1. Pragmatism — History. 2. Puritans — U. S.

556. Somerville, John. The Philosophy of Marxism: An Exposition. Random. 1967. pap. $2.95.   146.3
1. Dialectical Materialism. 2. Marx, Karl, 1818-1883.

557. Otto, Rudolf. Mysticism East and West: A Comparative Analysis of the Nature of Mysticism. Macmillan. 1970. pap. $2.45.   149.3
1. Mysticism.

558. Underhill, Evelyn. Mysticism: A Study in the Nature and Development of Man's Spiritual Consciousness. Dutton. 1930. $4.95; pap. $2.95 (NAL).   149.3
1. Mysticism.

150-151 Psychology

559. Adcock, C. J. Fundamentals of Psychology. Penguin. 1964. pap. $1.45.   150
1. Psychology.

560. Murphy, Gardner. Historical Introduction to Modern Psychology. 3rd ed. HarBraceJ. 1972. $12.95.   150
1. Psychology — History.

561. Miller, Jonathan, ed. Freud: The Man, His World, His Influence. Little. 1972. $14.95.
150.19(B)
1. Freud, Sigmund, 1856-1939.

562. Skinner, Burrhus F. Beyond Freedom and Dignity. Knopf. 1971. $6.95; pap. $1.95 (Bantam).   150.19
1. Conditioned Response. 2. Personality and Culture.

563. Storr, Anthony. C. G. Jung. Viking Pr. 1973. $5.95; pap. $1.95.   150.19(B)
1. Jung, Carl Gustav, 1875-1961. 2. Psychoanalysis.

564. Brett, George. Psychology, Ancient and Modern. Cooper Sq. Repr. 1930. $3.75.   150.7
1. Psychology — History.

565. Garrett, Henry E. Great Experiments in Psychology. 3rd ed. Irvington. 1951. $14.95.
150.7
1. Psychology — History. 2. Psychology, Physiological — History.

566. Herrnstein, Richard J. and Boring, Edwin G., eds. Source Book in the History of Psychology. Harvard U Pr. 1969. $15.00; pap. $5.95.   150.8
1. Psychology — Sources.

100 PHILOSOPHY AND PSYCHOLOGY

567. Watson, Robert I. The Great Psychologists: From Aristotle to Freud. 2nd ed. Lippincott. 1968. pap. $7.50.   150.9
1. Psychology — History.

152 Physiological and Experimental Psychology

568. Evans, Ralph M. The Perception of Color. Wiley. 1974. $14.95.   152.1
1. Color — Psychology. 2. Color — Sense. 3. Perception.

569. Madow, Leo. Anger. Scribner. 1972. pap. $2.45.   152.4
1. Anger.

570. May, Rollo. Love and Will. Norton. 1969. $7.95; pap. $1.75 (Dell).   152.4
1. Love. 2. Psychology. 3. Sex (Psychology). 4. Will.

571. Ashley Montagu, compiled by. Man and Aggression. Oxford U Pr. 1973. pap. $2.95.   152.5
1. Aggressiveness.

572. Fromm, Erich. The Anatomy of Human Destructiveness. new ed. HR&W. 1973. $10.95.   152.5
1. Aggressiveness (Psychology). 2. Violence.

153-154 Intelligence and Processes

573. Harrison, Randall P. Beyond Words: An Introduction to Nonverbal Communication. P-H. 1974. $7.95.   153
1. Nonverbal Communication.

574. Ornstein, Robert E. The Psychology of Consciousness. Viking Pr. 1973. $8.95.   153
1. Consciousness.

575. Storr, Anthony. The Dynamics of Creation. Atheneum. 1972. $7.95.   153.3
1. Creative Ability.

576. Woods, Ralph L. and Greenhouse, Herbert B. The New World of Dreams. Macmillan. 1974. $9.95.   153.6
1. Dreams — Collected Works.

577. Cohen, Daniel. Intelligence - What Is It? M Evans. 1974. $4.95.   153.9
1. Intellect. 2. Mental Tests. 3. Psychology, Comparative.

578. Shneour, Elie. The Mal-Nourished Mind. Doubleday. 1974. $6.95; pap. $2.95.   153.9
1. Developmental Psychobiology. 2. Intellect — Nutritional Aspects. 3. Malnutrition.

579. Laird, Donald A. Techniques for Efficient Remembering. McGraw. 1960. $5.75; pap. $2.45.   154.1
1. Mnemonics.

155-156 Genetic and Comparative Psychology

580. Erikson, Erik H. Identity: Youth and Crisis. Norton. 1968. $8.95; pap. $2.95.   155.2
1. Personality. 2. Youth.

581. Evans, Richard I. Jean Piaget: The Man and His Ideas. Dutton. 1973. $8.95; pap. $2.95.   155.4(B)
1. Cognition (Child Psychology). 2. Piaget, Jean, 1896-   3. Psychology.

582. Kagan, Jerome. Personality Development. HarBraceJ. 1971. $3.95.   155.4
1. Child Study. 2. Personality.

583. Becker, Ernest. The Denial of Death. Free Pr. 1974. $7.95.   155.9
1. Death — Psychology.

584. Kubler-Ross, Elisabeth. On Death and Dying. Macmillan. 1974. $4.95.   155.9
1. Death — Psychology.

585. Lifton, Robert J. and Olson, Eric. Living and Dying. Praeger. 1974. $6.50.   155.9
1. Death. 2. Death — Psychology.

586. Wertham, Frederic. Seduction of the Innocent. Kennikat. Repr. 1954. $12.50.   155.92
1. Comic Books and Children. 2. Comic Books, Strips, etc. — History and Criticism.

587. Milne, Lorus and Milne, Margery. The Animal in Man. McGraw. 1973. $7.95.   156
1. Psychology, Comparative.

588. Morris, Desmond. The Human Zoo. McGraw. 1969. $6.95; pap. $2.25 (Dell).   156
1. Human Behavior. 2. Psychology, Comparative.

589. Scientific American Editors. Psychobiology: The Biological Bases of Behavior: Readings from Scientific American. W H Freeman. 1967. $10.00; pap. $5.95.   156.208
1. Psychobiology.

100 PHILOSOPHY AND PSYCHOLOGY

157 Abnormal Psychology

590. Laing, R. D. Self and Others. 2nd rev. ed. Pantheon. 1970. $5.95; pap. $1.25 (Penguin). 157
1. Personality, Disorders of. 2. Schizophrenia. 3. Self.

591. Pietsch, William V. Human Be-Ing: How to Have a Creative Relationship Instead of a Power Struggle. L Hill. $7.95; pap. $1.75 (NAL). 158.2
1. Interpersonal Relationships.

160-164 Logic

592. Carney, James D. and Scheer, Richard. Fundamentals of Logic. Macmillan. 1974. $8.95. 160
1. Logic.

593. Copi, Irving M. Introduction to Logic. 4th ed. Macmillan. 1972. $8.95. 160
1. Logic.

594. Kneale, William and Kneale, Martha. Development of Logic. Oxford U Pr. 1962. $15.00. 160
1. Logic.

595. Salmon, Wesley C. Logic. 2nd ed. P-H. 1973. pap. $2.95. 160
1. Logic.

596. Lieber, Hugh G. and Lieber, Lillian R. Mits, Wits and Logic. 3rd ed. Norton. 1960. $5.95. 164
1. Logic, Symbolic and Mathematical. 2. Science — Philosophy.

170 Ethics

597. Camus, Albert. The Rebel: An Essay on Man in Revolt. Knopf. 1954. $5.95; pap. $1.95 (Random). 170
1. Good and Evil.

598. Dunham, Barrows. Ethics - Dead and Alive. Knopf. 1971. $6.95. 170
1. Ethics.

599. Frankena, William K. Ethics. 2nd ed. P-H. 1973. pap. $2.95. 170
1. Ethics.

600. MacIntyre, Alasdair C. A Short History of Ethics. Macmillan. $4.95; pap. $2.45. 170
1. Ethics — History.

601. Wheelwright, Philip, ed. Critical Introduction to Ethics. 3rd ed. Odyssey Pr. 1959. $5.25. 170
1. Ethics.

602. Simon, Sidney B., et al. Values Clarification: A Handbook of Practical Strategies for Teachers and Students. Hart. 1972. pap. $3.95. 170.2
1. Worth. 2. Youth — Conduct of Life.

603. Hancock, Roger N. Twentieth Century Ethics. Columbia U Pr. 1974. $10.00. 170.9
1. Ethics — History — Great Britain. 2. Ethics — History — U. S.

172-179 Applied Ethics

604. Frank, Jerome D. Sanity and Survival: Psychological Aspects of War and Peace. Random. 1967. pap. $1.95. 172.4
1. Peace. 2. War.

605. Fromm, Erich. The Art of Loving: An Inquiry into the Nature of Love. Har-Row. 1956. $4.95; pap. $0.95. 177.6
1. Love.

606. Timberlake, James H. Prohibition and the Progressive Movement, 1900-1920. Atheneum. 1970. pap. $2.95. 178.5
1. Progressivism (U. S. Politics). 2. Prohibition — U. S.

607. Tillich, Paul. The Courage to Be. Yale U Pr. 1952. $10.00; pap. $2.95. 179
1. Anxiety. 2. Courage. 3. Ontology.

180-181 Ancient, Medieval, and Oriental Philosophy

608. Cornford, Francis M. Before and After Socrates. Cambridge U Pr. 1932. $5.95; pap. $1.65. 180
1. Aristoteles, 384-322 B.C. 2. Philosophy, Ancient. 3. Plato, 427?-347 B.C. 4. Socrates, 470?-399 B.C.

609. Kaplan, Abraham. New World of Philosophy. Random. 1961. $8.95. 180
1. Philosophy.

100 PHILOSOPHY AND PSYCHOLOGY

610. Gilson, Etienne. The Christian Philosophy of Saint Augustine. Random. 1960. $10.00. 180.2
1. Augustinus, Aurelius, Saint, Bp. of Hippo — Philosophy.

611. Kaufmann, Walter A. Philosophic Classics. 2 vols. 2nd ed. P-H. 1968. $10.95 ea. 180.82
1. Philosophy, Ancient. 2. Philosophy, Medieval.

612. Koller, John M. Oriental Philosophies. Scribner. 1970. pap. $4.95. 181
1. Philosophy, Oriental.

613. Fakhry, Majid. A History of Islamic Philosophy. Columbia U Pr. 1970. $15.00. 181.07
1. Philosophy, Islamic — History.

614. Watt, W. Montgomery. Islamic Philosophy and Theology. Aldine. 1962. pap. $5.00. 181.07
1. Islam. 2. Philosophy, Arabic.

615. Chan, Wing-Tsit. A Source Book in Chinese Philosophy. Princeton U Pr. 1963. $17.50; pap. $3.95. 181.1
1. Philosophy, Chinese — Collections. 2. Philosophy — History — China — Sources.

616. Confucius. The Wisdom of Confucius. Modern Lib. 1943. $2.95. 181.1
1. Ethics, Chinese. 2. Philosophy, Chinese.

617. Creel, Herrlee G. Chinese Thought from Confucius to Mao Tse-tung. U of Chicago Pr. 1971. $7.50; pap. $2.95 (NAL). 181.1
1. Philosophy, Chinese.

618. Buber, Martin. Pointing the Way. Bks for Libs. Repr. 1957. $9.75. 181.3
1. Dialectic. 2. Philosophy — Collected Works.

619. Diamond, Malcolm L. Martin Buber: Jewish Existentialist. Gannon. 1970. $8.50. 181.3(B)
1. Buber, Martin, 1878-1965. 2. Existentialism.

620. Iyer, Raghaven. The Moral and Political Thought of Mahatma Gandhi. Oxford U Pr. 1973. $12.50. 181.4
1. Gandhi, Mohandas Karamchand, 1869-1948. 2. Nonviolence. 3. Political Ethics.

621. Krishna, Gopi. The Secret of Yoga. Har-Row. 1972. $6.95. 181.4
1. Yoga.

622. Krishnamurti, Jiddu. The Only Revolution. Luytens, ed. Har-Row. 1970. $4.95. 181.4
1. Philosophy, Hindu.

623. Zimmer, Heinrich. Philosophies of India. Campbell, Joseph, ed. Princeton U Pr. 1969. $14.50; pap. $3.95. 181.4
1. Philosophy, Hindu.

182-189 Ancient and Medieval Western Philosophy

624. Boas, George. Rationalism in Greek Philosophy. Johns Hopkins. 1961. $14.00. 182
1. Philosophy, Greek. 2. Rationalism.

625. Aristoteles. The Basic Works. McKeon, Richard P., ed. Random. 1941. $10.00. 184
1. Philosophy, Ancient.

626. Oates, Whitney J. Stoic and Epicurean Philosophers. Modern Lib. $4.95. 187
1. Epicurus. 2. Philosophy, Ancient. 3. Stoics.

627. De Santillana, Giorgio, ed. The Age of Adventure: The Renaissance Philosophers. Bks for Libs. Repr. 1956. $11.25. 189
1. Philosophy, Renaissance.

628. Fremantle, Anne, ed. The Age of Belief: The Medieval Philosophers. Bks for Libs. 1954. $10.50. 189
1. Philosophy, Medieval.

629. Hyman, Arthur and Walsh, James J., eds. Philosophy in the Middle Ages: The Christian, Islamic and Jewish Traditions. new ed. Hackett Pub. 1973. $15.00; pap. $5.95. 189
1. Philosophy, Medieval. 2. Religious Thought — Middle Ages.

630. Cassirer, Ernst, ed. The Renaissance Philosophy of Man. U of Chicago Pr. 1948. $12.50; pap. $2.95. 189.4
1. Philosophy, Medieval.

631. Maurer, Armand A. Medieval Philosophy. Random. 1962. $10.00. 189.4
1. Philosophy, Medieval.

632. Weinberg, Julius R. A Short History of Medieval Philosophy. Princeton U Pr. 1964. $7.50; pap. $2.95. 189.4
1. Philosophy, Medieval.

100 PHILOSOPHY AND PSYCHOLOGY

633. Weisheipl, James A. Friar Thomas D'Aquino: His Life, Thought and Work. Doubleday. 1974. $8.95.   189.4(B)
1. Thomas Aquinas, Saint, 1225?-1274.

190 Modern Western Philosophy

634. Aiken, Henry D., ed. The Age of Ideology: The 19th Century Philosophers. Bks for Libs. 1956. $11.00.   190
1. Ideology. 2. Philosophy, Modern.

635. Beardsley, Monroe C., ed. European Philosophers from Descartes to Nietzsche. Modern Lib. $4.95.   190
1. Philosophers, Modern. 2. Philosophy, Modern.

636. Flew, Anthony G. An Introduction to Western Philosophy: Ideas and Argument from Plato to Sartre. Bobbs. 1971. $10.00; pap. $2.50.   190
1. Philosophy — Introductions.

637. Gay, Peter, compiled by. The Enlightenment: A Comprehensive Anthology. S&S. 1973. $14.95.   190
1. Enlightenment. 2. Philosophy, Modern — 18th Century.

638. Hampson, Norman. A Cultural History of the Enlightenment. Pantheon. 1969. $6.95.   190
1. Enlightenment — History.

639. White, Morton, ed. The Age of Analysis: Twentieth Century Philosophers. NAL. 1955. $0.95.   190
1. Philosophy, Modern.

640. Bronowski, Jacob and Mazlish, B. Western Intellectual Tradition: From Leonardo to Hegel. Bks for Libs. 1960. $17.50; pap. $3.25 (Har-Row).   190.8
1. Philosophy, Modern.

641. Randall, John H., Jr. The Career of Philosophy: From the Enlightenment to the 19th Century. 2 vols. Columbia U Pr. 1970. $35.00; pap. $7.70.   190.8
1. Philosophy, Medieval. 2. Philosophy, Modern.

191 U. S.

642. Allen, Gay W. William James: A Biography. Viking Pr. 1967. pap. $3.45.   191(B)
1. James, Henry, 1843-1916. 2. James, William, 1842-1910.

643. Fisch, Max H., ed. Classic American Philosophers. P-H. 1961. $7.50.   191
1. Philosophers, American. 2. Philosophy, American.

644. Fuller, R. Buckminster. Synergetics: Explorations in the Geometry of Thinking. Macmillan. 1975. $25.00.   191
1. Mathematics — Philosophy. 2. System Theory. 3. Thought and Thinking.

645. James, William. William James: The Essential Writings. Har-Row. 1972. $4.25.   191
1. Philosophy — Collected Works.

646. Munson, Thomas N. The Essential Wisdom of George Santayana. Columbia U Pr. 1962. $10.00.   191
1. Santayana, George, 1863-1952.

647. Reck, Andrew J. The New American Philosophers: An Exploration of Thought Since World War II. La State U Pr. 1968. $8.95; pap. $2.65.   191
1. Philosophers, American. 2. Philosophy, American — 20th Century.

648. Schlesinger, Arthur M., Jr. and White, Morton M. Paths of American Thought. HM. 1970. pap. $3.75.   191
1. Philosophy, American — History.

649. Schneider, Herbert W. History of American Philosophy. 2nd ed. Columbia U Pr. 1963. $15.00; pap. $7.00.   191
1. Philosophy, American. 2. Philosophy — History — U. S.

650. White, Morton. Science and Sentiment in America: Philosophical Thought from Jonathan Edwards to John Dewey. Oxford U Pr. 1972. $10.00; pap. $2.95.   191
1. Philosophy, American — History.

192 Great Britain

651. Aaron, Richard. John Locke. 3rd ed. Oxford U Pr. 1971. $11.25.   192(B)
1. Locke, John, 1632-1704.

652. Hume, David. Moral and Political Philosophy. Aiken, Henry D., ed. Hafner. 1948. pap. $3.95.   192
1. Ethics.

100 PHILOSOPHY AND PSYCHOLOGY

653. Lawrence, Nathaniel M. Alfred North Whitehead. Twayne. 1973. $6.95. 192(B)
1. Whitehead, Alfred North, 1861-1947.

654. Locke, John. An Essay Concerning Human Understanding. Pringle-Pattison, A. S., ed. Oxford U Pr. 1924. $4.95. 192
1. Knowledge, Theory of.

655. Russell, Bertrand. Basic Writings, 1903-1959. Denonn, Lester E. and Egner, Robert E., eds. S&S. 1961. $10.00; pap. $3.75. 192
1. Philosophy, English.

656. Whitehead, Alfred N. Alfred North Whitehead: An Anthology. Northrop, F. C. and Gross, W., eds. Macmillan. 1961. $6.95; pap. $2.95. 192
1. Philosophy, English.

657. Willey, Basil. The Eighteenth Century Background. Columbia U Pr. 1941. $11.00; pap. $3.45 1961 (Beacon Pr). 192
1. Eighteenth Century. 2. English Literature — History and Criticism. 3. Ethics. 4. Natural Theology. 5. Realism in Literature.

658. ———. More Nineteenth Century Studies: A Group of Honest Doubters. Columbia U Pr. 1956. $11.00. 192
1. English Literature — 19th Century — History and Criticism. 2. Nineteenth Century. 3. Philosophy, Modern. 4. Religious Thought — 19th Century.

659. ———. Nineteenth Century Studies. Columbia U Pr. 1949. $11.00; pap. $1.95 (Har-Row). 192
1. English Literature — History and Criticism. 2. Nineteenth Century. 3. Philosophy, Modern.

660. ———. The Seventeenth Century Background. Columbia U Pr. 1942. $11.00. 192
1. English Poetry — History and Criticism. 2. Philosophy, Modern. 3. Religious Thought — 17th Century. 4. Seventeenth Century.

661. Brabazon, James. Albert Schweitzer. Putnam. 1975. $12.95. 193(B)
1. Schweitzer, Albert, 1875-1965.

662. Jaspers, Karl. Nietzsche: An Introduction to the Understanding of His Philosophical Activity. U of Ariz Pr. 1965. $12.00; pap. $3.95 (Regnery). 193
1. Nietzsche, Friedrich Wilhelm, 1844-1900.

663. Schweitzer, Albert. Albert Schweitzer: An Anthology. Joy, Charles R., ed. Beacon Pr. 1955. pap. $2.45. 193
1. Philosophy, German.

664. Buber, Martin. I and Thou. 2nd ed. Scribner. 1970. $5.95; pap. $1.95. 193.5
1. Philosophy, German. 2. Religion — Philosophy.

665. Hegel, George W. Philosophy. Friedrich, Carl J., ed. Modern Lib. 1953. $2.95. 193.5
1. Philosophy, German.

666. Kant, Immanuel. The Philosophy of Kant. Modern Lib. $2.95. 193.5
1. Philosophy, German.

667. Nietzsche, Friedrich W. Thus Spoke Zarathustra. Modern Lib. $2.95. 193.7
1. Philosophy, German.

668. Schopenhauer, Arthur. Philosophy. Modern Lib. $2.95. 193.7
1. Philosophy, German.

194 France

669. Murdoch, Iris. Sartre: Romantic Rationalist. Yale U Pr. 1953. pap. $1.95. 194
1. Existentialism. 2. Sartre, Jean Paul, 1905-

670. Blum, Carol. Diderot: The Virtue of a Philosopher. Viking Pr. 1974. $8.95. 194.1(B)
1. Diderot, Denis, 1713-1784.

671. Descartes, René. Philosophical Writings. Modern Lib. $2.95. 194.1
1. Philosophy, French.

672. Hazelton, Roger. Blaise Pascal: The Genius of His Thought. Westminster. 1974. $7.50. 194.1(B)
1. Pascal, Blaise, 1623-1662.

673. La Farge, René. Jean-Paul Sartre: His Philosophy. U of Notre Dame Pr. 1970. $6.50. 194.1
1. Sartre, Jean Paul, 1905-

674. Vrooman, Jack R. René Descartes: A Biography. Putnam. 1970. $7.95. 194.1(B)
1. Descartes, René, 1596-1650.

197-199 Russia, Scandinavia and Other Countries

675. Blakeley, Thomas J. Soviet Philosophy: A General Introduction to Contemporary Soviet Thought. Reidel Pub. 1964. $6.00. 197
1. Philosophy, Russian.

676. Zenkovsky, Vasilii V. History of Russian Philosophy. 2 vols. Kline, G. L., tr. Columbia U Pr. 1953. $22.50. 197
1. Philosophy, Russian.

677. Grimsley, Ronald. Kierkegaard: A Biographical Introduction. Scribner. 1974. $5.95. 198.9(B)
1. Kierkegaard, Soren Aabye, 1813-1855.

678. Kierkegaard, Soren. A Kierkegaard Anthology. Modern Lib. 1959. $2.45. 198.9
1. Philosophy, Danish.

679. Spinoza, Benedict. Chief Works. 2 vols. Dover. $8.75 ea. 199
1. Ethics. 2. Philosophy.

680. Davis, Harold E. Latin American Thought: A Historical Introduction. La State U Pr. 1972. $10.00; pap. $3.95 (Free Pr). 199.8
1. Philosophy, Latin American.

200 RELIGION AND MYTHOLOGY

200 Philosophy of Religion

681. Cone, James H. A Black Theology of Liberation. Lippincott. 1970. $5.95; pap. $2.95.   200
1. Freedom (Theology). 2. Negroes — Religion. 3. Theology, Doctrinal.

682. Barbour, Ian G. Myths, Models, and Paradigms: A Comparative Study in Science and Religion. Har-Row. 1974. $6 95.   200.1
1. Religion and Science.

683. Charlesworth, Maxwell J. Philosophy of Religion: The Historic Approaches. Seabury. 1972. $8.95.   200.1
1. Religion — Philosophy.

684. Hick, John. Philosophy of Religion. 2nd ed. P-H. 1973. pap. $2.95.   200.1
1. Religion — Philosophy.

685. Saher, P. J. Eastern Wisdom and Western Thought: A Comparative Study in the Modern Philosophy of Religion. B&N. 1970. $12.75.   200.1
1. Philosophy, Comparative. 2. Religion — Philosophy.

686. Comstock, W. Richard. Religion and Man: Study of Religion and Primitive Religion. Har-Row. 1971. $10.95; pap. $3.50.   200.7
1. Religion. 2. Religions, Primitive.

687. Stroup, Herbert H. Founders of Living Religions. Westminster. 1974. pap. $4.25.   200.9(B)
1. Religions. 2. Religions — Biography.

688. Ellwood, Robert S., Jr. Religious and Spiritual Groups in Modern America. P-H. 1972. $7.95; pap. $3.95.   200.973
1. Cults — U. S. 2. Religions.

689. Gaustad, Edwin S. Dissent in American Religion. U of Chicago Pr. 1973. $6.95.   200.973
1. Religious Thought — U. S. 2. U. S. — Religion.

690. Hudson, Winthrop S. Religion in America: An Historical Account of the Development of American Religious Life. 2nd ed. Scribner. 1973. $12.50; pap. $5.95.   200.973
1. U. S. — Religion.

691. Zaretsky, Irving and Leone, Mark P., eds. Religious Movements in Contemporary America. Princeton U Pr. 1974. $25.00.   200.973
1. U. S. — Religion — 1965- 2. U. S. — Religious Life and Customs.

201-209 Religious Philosophies and Theories

692. Huxley, Aldous L. The Perennial Philosophy. Bks for Libs. Repr. 1945. $12.75.   201
1. Philosophy and Religion. 2. Religion — Philosophy.

693. James, William. Varieties of Religious Experience. Modern Lib. $2.95; pap. $1.50 (Macmillan). 201
1. Religion — Philosophy.

694. Kaufmann, Walter A., ed. Religion from Tolstoy to Camus: Basic Writings on Religions, Truth, and Morals. Har-Row. 1961. pap. $3.25. 201
1. Philosophy and Religion. 2. Religion.

695. Tillich, Paul. Dynamics of Faith. Har-Row. 1958. pap. $1.75. 201
1. Religion — Philosophy.

696. Cox, Harvey. The Seduction of the Spirit: The Use and Misuse of People's Religion. S&S. 1973. $8.95; pap. $2.95. 201.1
1. Religion.

697. Teilhard de Chardin, Pierre. Christianity and Evolution. Hague, René, tr. HarBraceJ. 1971. $5.95; pap. $2.95. 201.1
1. Theology.

698. Burkill, T. Alec. The Evolution of Christian Thought. Cornell U Pr. 1971. $13.50. 201.109
1. Theology, Doctrinal — History.

699. Thomas Aquinas, St. Basic Writings. 2 vols. Random. 1945. $25.00. 208.1
1. Theology — Collected Works — Middle Ages.

210-219 Natural Religion

700. Schilling, Sylvester P. God Incognito. Abingdon. 1974. $5.95. 211
1. Experience (Religion). 2. God.

701. Koestler, Arthur. The Sleepwalkers: A History of Man's Changing Vision of the Universe. G&D. pap. $3.45. 215
1. Religion and Science.

702. Lewis, Clive S. The Problem of Pain. Macmillan. 1943. $4.95; pap. $1.25. 216
1. Good and Evil. 2. Pain. 3. Providence and Government of God.

220 Bible

703. Bible. Holy Bible. Confraternity Edition. Kenedy. see catalog for prices. 220.5
1. Bible.

704. ———. Holy Bible. King James Version. Oxford U Pr. prices vary. 220.5
1. Bible.

705. ———. Holy Bible: Revised Standard Version. Nelson. prices vary. 220.5
1. Bible.

706. ———. New English Bible, with the Apocrypha. Oxford U Pr. 1970. prices vary. 220.5
1. Bible.

707. ———. The Living Bible. Doubleday. 1971. $10.95. 220.52
1. Bible.

708. Bible. The Jerusalem Bible. Jones, Alexander, ed. Doubleday. 1970. $19.95. 220.52
1. Bible.

709. Bible. The New Oxford Annotated Bible. Revised standard version. May, Herbert and Metzger, Bruce M., eds. Oxford U Pr. 1973. $12.50. 220.52
1. Bible.

710. Chase, Mary Ellen. The Bible and the Common Reader. rev. ed. Macmillan. 1962. pap. $1.45. 220.8
1. Bible As Literature. 2. Bible — Study.

711. Baly, Denis A. A Geography of the Bible. rev. ed. Har-Row. 1974. $10.95. 220.9
1. Bible — Geography.

712. Keller, Werner. The Bible As History in Pictures. Morrow. 1964. $10.95. 220.9
1. Bible — History of Biblical Events — Pictorial Works.

713. Keller, Werner. The Bible As History: A Confirmation of the Book of Books. Neil, William, tr. Morrow. 1964. $9.95; pap. $3.50 rev. ed. 1969 (Apollo Eds). 220.9
1. Bible — Antiquities. 2. Bible — History of Biblical Events.

714. National Geographic Society, ed. Everyday Life in Bible Times. Natl Geog. 1968. $9.95. 220.91
1. Bible — Antiquities. 2. Civilization, Ancient.

715. Ahlstrom, Sydney E. A Religious History of the American People. Yale U Pr. 1972. $22.50. 220.973
1. U. S. — Religion.

221-224 Old Testament

716. Bible. The Holy Scriptures. According to the Masoretic Text. Jewish Pubn. 1917. $5.00.   221
1. Bible — Old Testament.

717. Eissfeldt, Otto. The Old Testament: An Introduction. Har-Row. 1965. $11.00.   221
1. Bible — Old Testament — Introductions.

718. Brownlee, William H. The Meaning of the Qumran Scrolls for the Bible. Oxford U Pr. 1964. $10.00.   221.4
1. Bible — Old Testament Isaiah — Criticism, Textual. 2. Dead Sea Scrolls.

719. Burrows, Millar. More Light on the Dead Sea Scrolls: New Scrolls and New Interpretations. Viking Pr. 1958. $6.95.   221.4
1. Dead Sea Scrolls.

720. La Sor, William S. Dead Sea Scrolls and the New Testament. Eerdmans. 1972. pap. $3.95.   221.4
1. Dead Sea Scrolls — Relation to the New Testament.

721. Wilson, Edmund. The Dead Sea Scrolls, 1947-1969. Oxford U Pr. 1969. $7.50.   221.4
1. Dead Sea Scrolls.

722. Anderson, Bernhard W. Understanding the Old Testament. 2nd ed. P-H. 1975. $11.95.   221.9
1. Bible — Old Testament.

723. Baring-Gould, Sabine. Legends of the Patriarch and Prophets and Other Old Testament Characters. Folcroft. Repr. 1872. $30.00.   221.9(B)
1. Bible — Old Testament — Biography.

724. Bewer, Julius A. The Literature of the Old Testament. 3rd ed. Columbia U Pr. 1962. $15.00.   221.9
1. Bible As Literature. 2. Bible — Old Testament.

725. Chase, Mary Ellen. Life and Language in the Old Testament. Norton. 1955. pap. $2.25.   221.9
1. Bible — Old Testament — Criticism, Interpretation, etc.

726. Heaton, Eric W. Everyday Life in Old Testament Times. Scribner. 1956. $8.95.   221.9
1. Bible — Old Testament — Antiquities. 2. Bible — Old Testament — History of Contemporary Events.

727. Wiseman, D. J., ed. Peoples of Old Testament Times. Oxford U Pr. 1973. $17.75.   221.95
1. Near East — Civilization. 2. Near East — History — to 622.

728. Newman, John Henry. Apologia pro Vita Sua: An Annotated Text with Critical Essays. De Laura, David, ed. Norton. 1968. pap. $1.95.   222
1. Catholic Church — Doctrinal and Controversial Works.

729. The Torah: The Five Books of Moses. Jewish Pubn. 1963. $6.00.   222.1
1. Bible — Old Testament Pentateuch.

730. Chase, Mary Ellen. Prophets for the Common Reader. Norton. 1963. $4.50.   224.06
1. Bible — Old Testament — Prophets — Commentaries.

731. Bible. Holy Bible. Four Prophets: Amos, Hosea, First Isaiah, Micah. Phillips, J. B., tr. Macmillan. 1963. $3.95; pap. $1.45.   224.52
1. Amos. 2. Bible — Old Testament — Prophets. 3. Hosea. 4. Isaiah. 5. Micah.

225-226 New Testament

732. Scott, Ernest F. The Literature of the New Testament. Columbia U Pr. 1932. $10.00.   225.5
1. Bible — New Testament.

733. Bouquet, Alan C. Everyday Life in New Testament Times. Scribner. 1953. $8.95.   225.9
1. Bible — New Testament — History of Contemporary Events. 2. Palestine — Social Life and Customs.

734. Brownrigg, Ronald. The Twelve Apostles. Macmillan. 1974. $12.95.   225.9
1. Apostles.

735. Kee, Howard C., et al. Understanding the New Testament. 3rd ed. P-H. 1973. $10.50.   225.9
1. Bible — New Testament — Criticism, Interpretation, etc.

200 RELIGION AND MYTHOLOGY

736. Bonhoeffer, Dietrich. Cost of Discipleship. 2nd ed. Macmillan. 1967. $4.95; pap. $1.95. 226.2
1. Sermon on the Mount.

230 Christian Theology

737. Aulen, Gustaf. The Faith of the Christian Church. rev. ed. Fortress. 1961. pap. $4.25. 230
1. Theology, Doctrinal.

738. Lewis, Clive S. Mere Christianity. Macmillan. 1964. $5.95; pap. $1.45. 230
1. Christianity. 2. U. S. — Religion.

739. MacQuarrie, John. Studies in Christian Existentialism. Westminster. 1966. $6.00. 230
1. Existentialism. 2. Theology.

740. Merton, Thomas. The Asian Journal of Thomas Merton. New Directions. 1973. $12.50. 230.2(B)
1. Meditation. 2. Spiritual Life — Catholic Authors.

741. Mueller, David. Karl Barth. Word Bks. 1972. $4.95. 230.4(B)
1. Barth, Karl, 1886-1968.

742. Reist, Benjamin A. The Promise of Bonhoeffer. Lippincott. 1969. $3.50; pap. $1.95. 230.4
1. Bonhoeffer, Dietrich, 1906-1945.

231 God

743. Altizer, Thomas, ed. Toward a New Christianity: Readings in the Death of God Theology. HarBraceJ. 1967. $6.95. 231
1. God. 2. Theology.

744. Cox, Harvey. The Secular City. rev. ed. Macmillan. 1966. pap. $1.45. 231
1. Church and Social Problems. 2. God.

745. Edwards, David L., ed. Honest to God Debate. Westminster. 1963. pap. $2.25. 231
1. God. 2. Theology.

746. Jones, William R. Is God a White Racist? A Preamble to Black Theology. Doubleday. 1973. $7.95; pap. $2.95. 231
1. Negroes — Religion. 2. Race (Theology).

747. Robinson, John A. Honest to God. Westminster. 1963. pap. $1.65. 231
1. God. 2. Theology.

232 Jesus Christ

748. Baillie, Donald M. God Was in Christ. Scribner. 1948. pap. $1.65. 232
1. Jesus Christ.

749. Bornkamm, Gunther. Jesus of Nazareth. McLuskey, I. and McLuskey, F., trs. Har-Row. 1961. $6.00. 232
1. Jesus Christ.

750. Schweitzer, Albert. Quest of the Historical Jesus. Macmillan. 1968. pap. $3.95. 232
1. Jesus Christ.

751. Johnson, Paul. Pope John XXIII. Little. 1974. $6.95. 236.13(B)
1. Joannes XXIII, Pope, 1881-1963.

238 Creeds

752. Barth, Karl. Dogmatics in Outline. Har-Row. 1959. pap. $2.25. 238.1
1. Apostles' Creed. 2. Theology, Doctrinal.

241 Moral Theology

753. Fletcher, Joseph. Moral Responsibility: Situation Ethics at Work. Westminster. 1967. pap. $1.95. 241
1. Christian Ethics.

754. ———. Situation Ethics: The New Morality. Westminster. 1966. pap. $1.95. 241
1. Christian Ethics.

755. Lewis, Clive S. The Four Loves. HarBraceJ. 1960. $6.25. 241
1. Love. 2. Love (Theology).

756. Robinson, Norman H. The Groundwork of Christian Ethics. Eerdmans. 1972. $7.95. 241
1. Christian Ethics.

757. Barclay, William. Ethics in a Permissive Society. Har-Row. 1972. $5.50. 241.04
1. Christian Ethics.

758. Mensching, Gustav. Tolerance and Truth in Religion. Klimkeit, H. J., tr. U of Ala Pr. 1971. $8.00. 241.4
1. Toleration.

200 RELIGION AND MYTHOLOGY

242-244 Devotional Literature

759. Augustine, St. Confessions of Saint Augustine. Pusey, Edward, tr. Dutton. 1949. $3.95.   242
1. Meditations.

760. Thomas a Kempis. Of the Imitation of Christ. Bruce Pub Co. $2.25.   242.1
1. Thomas a Kempis, 1380-1471.

761. Lewis, Clive S. The Screwtape Letters, and Screwtape Proposes a Toast. Macmillan. $5.95; pap. $1.25.   244
1. Christian Life. 2. Satire.

246 Art in Christianity

762. Brandon, Samuel G. Man and God in Art and Ritual. Scribner. 1975. $20.00.   246
1. Art and Religion. 2. Ritual.

248 Personal Religion

763. Harkness, Georgia. Mysticism: Its Meaning and Message. Abingdon. 1973. $5.50.   248.22
1. Mysticism.

261-269 Social Theology

764. Niebuhr, H. Richard. Christ and Culture. Peter Smith. $4.00.   261
1. Church.

765. Tawney, Richard H. Religion and the Rise of Capitalism. Peter Smith. $4.75; pap. $0.95 (NAL).   261
1. Capitalism. 2. Christianity and Economics. 3. Great Britain — Social Conditions. 4. Religious Thought — History.

766. Brown, William C. Church and State in Contemporary America. Octagon. Repr. 1963. $14.00.   261.7
1. Church and State in the U. S.

767. Bock, Paul. In Search of a Responsible World Society: The Social Teachings of the World Council of Churches. Westminster. 1974. $10.00.   261.8
1. Church and Social Problems. 2. World Council of Churches.

768. Brown, Robert M. Religion and Violence: A Primer for White Americans. Westminster. 1973. pap. $3.95.   261.8
1. Violence — Moral and Religious Aspects.

769. Marrin, Albert, ed. War and the Christian Conscience: From Augustine to Martin Luther King, Jr. Regnery. 1971. $12.50; pap. $3.95.   261.8
1. War and Religion.

770. Merton, Thomas. Faith and Violence: Christian Teaching and Christian Practice. U of Notre Dame Pr. 1968. pap. $2.45.   261.8
1. Violence — Moral and Religious Aspects.

771. Brown, Robert M. Frontiers for the Church Today. Oxford U Pr. 1973. $5.95.   262
1. Christianity — 20th Century Church.

772. Cavert, Samuel M. The American Churches in the Ecumenical Movement, 1900-1968. Assn Pr. 1968. $9.95.   262
1. Christian Union — U. S. 2. Ecumenical Movement — History.

773. Marshall, George and Poling, David. Schweitzer: A Biography. Doubleday. 1971. $7.95.   266.02(B)
1. Schweitzer, Albert, 1875-1965.

774. Schweitzer, Albert. Out of My Life and Thought. HR&W. 1972. $2.95; pap. $1.25 (NAL).   266.02(B)
1. Schweitzer, Albert, 1875-1965.

775. Ellwood, Robert S., Jr. One Way: The Jesus Movement and Its Meaning. P-H. 1973. $6.95; pap. $3.95.   269.2
1. Evangelicalism — U. S. 2. Jesus People.

776. Enroth, Ronald M., et al. The Jesus People: Old Time Religion in the Age of Aquarius. Eerdmans. 1972. pap. $2.95.   269.2
1. Jesus People.

270-274 Christian Church History

777. Bettenson, Henry, ed. Documents of the Christian Church. 2nd ed. Oxford U Pr. 1970. pap. $2.95.   270
1. Church History — Sources.

778. Goodall, Norman. Ecumenical Progress: A Decade of Change in the Ecumenical Movement, 1961-1971. Oxford U Pr. 1972. $10.95.   270
1. Church History — Modern Period. 2. Ecumenical Movement.

779. Manschreck, Clyde L. A History of Christianity in the World: From Persecution to Uncertainty. P-H. 1974. $7.95.   270
1. Church History.

200 RELIGION AND MYTHOLOGY

780. Rouse, Ruth and Neill, Stephen C., eds. History of the Ecumenical Movement, 1517-1948. 2nd ed. Westminster. 1967. $12.50. 270
1. Church History — Modern Period. 2. Ecumenical Movement.

781. Walker, Williston. History of the Christian Church. 3rd ed. Richardson, C. C., et al, eds. Scribner. 1970. $9.50. 270
1. Church History.

782. Bainton, Roland H. Here I Stand. Abingdon. 1951. $6.95; pap. $2.25. 270.6(B)
1. Luther, Martin, 1483-1546. 2. Reformation.

783. ———. Women of the Reformation in France and England. Augsburg. 1973. $8.95. 270.6(B)
1. Reformation — Biography. 2. Women — Biography.

784. ———. Women of the Reformation in Germany and Italy. Augsburg. 1971. $7.95. 270.6(B)
1. Reformation — Biography. 2. Women — Biography.

785. Dickens, Arthur G. The Counter-Reformation. HarBraceJ. 1969. $6.95; pap. $4.50. 270.6
1. Counter-Reformation.

786. Hillerbrand, Hans J. The World of the Reformation. Scribner. 1973. $10.00. 270.6
1. Reformation.

787. Huizinga, Johan. Erasmus and the Age of Reformation. Har-Row. pap. $1.95. 270.6(B)
1. Erasmus, Desiderius, 1466?-1535. 2. Reformation.

788. Luther, Martin. Martin Luther: Selections from His Writings. Dillenberger, John, ed. Doubleday. pap. $2.95. 270.6
1. Lutheran Church. 2. Theology — 16th Century.

789. Mosse, George L. The Reformation. 3rd ed. Peter Smith. 1963. $4.25. 270.6
1. Reformation.

790. Nigg, Walter. Warriors of God: The Great Religious Orders and Their Founders. Knopf. 1959. $8.95. 271
1. Monasticism and Religious Orders.

791. Bishop, Morris. St. Francis of Assisi. Little. 1974. $6.95. 271.3(B)
1. Francesco d'Assisi, Saint, 1182-1226.

792. Foxe, John. Foxe's Book of Martyrs. Revell. $1.25. 272(B)
1. Christian Biography. 2. Martyrs.

793. Norwood, Frederick A. Strangers and Exiles: A History of Religious Refugees. 2 vols. Abingdon. 1969. $25.00. 272.09
1. Dissenters, Religious. 2. Persecution — History. 3. Refugees, Religious.

794. O'Brien, John A. The Inquisition: A Tragic Mistake. Macmillan. 1973. $6.95. 272.2
1. Inquisition.

795. Loades, David M. The Oxford Martyrs. Stein & Day. 1970. $7.95. 272.6(B)
1. Martyrs — England.

796. Ridley, Jasper. Thomas Cranmer. Oxford U Pr. 1956. $11.25; pap. $3.95. 274.2(B)
1. Cranmer, Thomas, Abp. of Canterbury, 1489-1556.

797. Conquest, Robert, ed. Religion in the USSR. Praeger. 1968. $5.50. 274.7
1. Church and State in Russia. 2. Russia — Religion.

798. Curtiss, John S. Church and State in Russia. Octagon. 1965. $14.50. 274.7
1. Church and State in Russia. 2. Russia — Religion.

799. Hayward, Max and Fletcher, William C., eds. Religion and the Soviet State: A Dilemma of Power. Praeger. 1969. $6.50. 274.7
1. Russia — Religion — 1917-

280-289 Denominations and Sects

800. Herberg, Will. Protestant - Catholic - Jew: An Essay in American Religious Society. rev. ed. Peter Smith. $4.25. 280
1. U. S. — Religion.

801. Hudson, Winthrop S. American Protestantism. U of Chicago Pr. 1961. $7.00; pap. $2.75. 280
1. Protestantism — U. S.

802. Mead, Frank S. Handbook of Denominations in the United States. 5th ed, Abingdon. 1970. $3.95. 280
1. U. S. — Religions.

803. Rosten, Leo, ed. Religions in America. rev. ed. S&S. 1963. $7.95. 280
1. Sects — U. S. 2. U. S. — Religion.

RELIGION AND MYTHOLOGY

804. Schneider, Herbert W. Religion in 20th Century America. Atheneum. 1964. pap. $2.95.   280
1. U. S. — Religion.

805. Grant, Robert M. Augustus to Constantine: The Thrust of the Christian Movement in the Roman World. Har-Row. 1970. $10.00.   281.1
1. Church History — Primitive and Early Church.

806. Augustine, St. Basic Writing of Saint Augustine. 2 vols. Oates, W. J., ed. Random. 1948. $11.00 ea.; boxed $20.00.
281.4
1. Theology — Early Church — Collected Writings.

807. Fletcher, William C. The Russian Orthodox Church Underground, 1917-1971. Oxford U Pr. 1971. $12.75.
281.9
1. Church and State in Russia — 1917- 2. Orthodox Eastern Church, Russian. 3. Persecution — Russia.

808. Ellis, John T. American Catholicism. 2nd ed. U of Chicago Pr. 1969. $9.50; pap. $3.25.   282
1. Catholic Church in the U. S.

809. McKenzie, John L. The Roman Catholic Church. HR&W. 1969. $6.95; pap. $4.75.   282
1. Catholic Church. 2. Catholic Church — History.

810. Bethge, Eberhard. Dietrich Bonhoeffer: Man of Vision, Man of Courage. Mosbacher, Eric, et al, trs. Har-Row. 1970. $17.95.
284.1(B)
1. Bonhoeffer, Dietrich, 1906-1945.

811. Bonhoeffer, Dietrich. Letters and Papers from Prison. enl. ed. Macmillan. 1972. $7.95.   284.1
1. Bonhoeffer, Dietrich, 1906-1945.

812. Walker, Williston. John Calvin: The Organizer of Reformed Protestantism, 1509-1564. Schocken. 1969. $8.50; pap. $2.95.
284.2(B)
1. Calvin, John, 1509-1564.

813. Reid, W. Stanford. Trumpeter of God: A Biography of John Knox. Scribner. 1974. $12.50.   285.2(B)
1. Knox, John, 1505-1572.

814. Brodie, Fawn M. No Man Knows My History: The Life of Joseph Smith. Knopf. 1971. $10.00.   289.3(B)
1. Smith, Joseph, 1805-1844.

815. Hinshaw, David. Rufus Jones, Master Quaker. Bks for Libs. Repr. 1951. $12.50.
289.6(B)
1. Jones, Rufus Matthew, 1863-1948.

816. Wildes, Harry E. Voice of the Lord: A Biography of George Fox. U of Pa Pr. 1964. $11.50.   289.6(B)
1. Fox, George, 1624-1691. 2. Friends, Society of.

290 Other Religions and Comparative Religions

817. Bach, Marcus. Major Religions of the World. Abingdon. 1959. $1.25.   290
1. Religions.

818. Ballou, Robert O., et al, eds. The Bible of the World. Viking Pr. 1939. $12.00.   290
1. Religions. 2. Sacred Books.

819. Bouquet, Alan C. Comparative Religions. Penguin. 1961. pap. $1.95.   290
1. Religions.

820. Gaer, Joseph. How the Great Religions Began. rev. ed. Dodd. 1956. $6.00; pap. $0.95 (NAL).   290
1. Religions.

821. ———. What the Great Religions Believe. Dodd. 1963. $6.00; pap. $1.25 (NAL).
290
1. Religions. 2. Sacred Books.

822. Life Magazine Editors. World's Great Religions. Western Pub. 1958. $6.95; pap. $3.95.   290
1. Religions.

823. Noss, John B. Man's Religions. 5th ed. Macmillan. 1974. $8.95.   290
1. Religions.

291 Mythology and Comparative Religions

824. Bulfinch, Thomas. Mythology. T Y Crowell. 1970. $6.95.   291
1. Folk-Lore, European. 2. Folklore — Europe. 3. Mythology.

825. Frazer, James G. The Golden Bough. abr. ed. Macmillan. $7.95; pap. $3.95.   291
1. Folk-Lore. 2. Religions.

RELIGION AND MYTHOLOGY

826. Gayley, Charles M. Classic Myths in English Literature and in Art. rev. ed. Xerox College. 1939. $9.25. 291
1. Mythology, Classical. 2. Mythology, Norse.

827. Graves, Robert. Greek Myths. Braziller. 1959. $7.50. 291
1. Mythology, Classical.

828. Hamilton, Edith. Mythology. Little. 1942. $7.95. 291
1. Mythology.

829. Lowie, Robert H. Primitive Religion. Liveright. 1970. $7.95; pap. $2.95. 291
1. Religion, Primitive.

830. Smith, Huston, et al, eds. Great Religions of the World. Natl Geog. 1971. $11.95. 291
1. Religions.

831. Eliade, Mircea. From Primitives to Zen: A Thematic Sourcebook of the History of Religions. Har-Row. 1967. $10.50. 291.09
1. Religions — History — Sources.

292-294 Classical and Indic Religions

832. Cornford, Francis M. Greek Religious Thought from Homer to the Age of Alexander. AMS Pr. 1923. $7.00. 292.08
1. Greece — Religion. 2. Philosophy, Ancient. 3. Religious Thought. 4. Religious Thought — Ancient Period.

833. Rose, Herbert J. Religion in Greece and Rome. Har-Row. 1959. pap. $1.95. 292.08
1. Greece — Religion. 2. Rome — Religion.

834. Bancroft, Anne. Religions of the East. St Martin. 1974. $12.95. 294
1. Religions.

835. Keith, Arthur B. The Religion and Philosophy of the Veda and Upanishads. 2 vols. Verry. 1971. $22.50. 294.1
1. India — Religion. 2. Philosophy, Hindu. 3. Upanishads. 4. Vedas.

836. De Bary, William T. The Buddhist Tradition in India, China and Japan. Modern Lib. 1969. $2.95; pap. $2.45 (Random). 294.3
1. Buddha and Buddhism — Collections.

837. Dumoulin, Heinrich. A History of Zen Buddhism. Peachey, Paul, tr. Beacon Pr. 1969. pap. $3.45. 294.3
1. Zen (Sect) — History.

838. Oldenberg, Hermann. Buddha: His Life, His Doctrine, His Order. Intl Pubns Serv. Repr. 1882. $12.50. 294.3(B)
1. Buddha and Buddhism.

839. Smith, Howard D. Chinese Religions from 1000 B. C. to the Present Day. HR&W. 1971. pap. $2.45. 294.3
1. Buddha and Buddhism. 2. Confucius and Confucianism.

840. Steinilber-Oberlin, Emile. The Buddhist Sects of Japan: Their History, Philosophical Doctrines and Sanctuaries. Greenwood. Repr. 1938. $14.00. 294.3
1. Buddhist Sects — Japan.

841. Van De Wetering, Janwillem. The Empty Mirror: Experiences in a Japanese Zen Monastery. HM. 1974. $5.95. 294.3
1. Monastic and Religious Life (Zen Buddhism) — Japan.

842. Watts, Alan W. The Way of Zen. Pantheon. 1957. $6.95; pap. $1.95 (Random). 294.3
1. Zen Buddhism.

843. Wright, Arthur F. Buddhism in Chinese History. Stanford U Pr. 1959. $4.75; pap. $1.95 (Atheneum). 294.3
1. Buddha and Buddhism. 2. China — History.

844. Chinmoy, Sri. Commentary on the Bhagavad Gita. Multimedia. 1974. pap. $1.95. 294.5
1. Mahabharata Bhagavadgita.

845. Deutsch, Eliot, ed. Bhagavad Gita. HR&W. 1968. $4.95; pap. $4.00. 294.5
1. Mahabharata Bhagavadgita.

846. Embree, Ainslie T., ed. The Hindu Tradition. Modern Lib. 1966. $2.95. 294.5
1. Hinduism.

847. Hopkins, Edward W. The Religions of India. Verry. 1970. $16.50. 294.5
1. India — Religion.

848. Klostermaier, Klaus. In the Paradise of Krishna: Hindu and Christian Seekers. Westminster. 1971. pap. $1.95. 294.5

200 RELIGION AND MYTHOLOGY

1. Christianity and Other Religions — Hinduism. 2. Hinduism — Relations — Christianity.

849. Menen, Aubrey. The Mystics. Dial. 1974. $15.00.   294.5
1. Mysticism — Hinduism.

850. Gupta, Hari R. History of the Sikh Gurus. South Asia Bks. 1973. $8.50.   294.6(B)
1. Sikh Gurus — Biography. 2. Sikhism — History.

296 Judaism

851. Buber, Martin. On Judaism. Schocken. 1972. pap. $2.95.   296
1. Judaism.

852. Glazer, Nathan. American Judaism. rev. ed. U of Chicago Pr. 1972. $5.95; pap. $1.95.   296
1. Jews in the U. S. 2. Jews — Religion. 3. Judaism.

853. Neusner, Jacob. American Judaism: Adventure in Modernity. P-H. 1972. $8.95; pap. $3.75.   296
1. Judaism — U. S.

854. Ginzberg, Louis. The Legends of the Jews. rev. ed. S&S. 1961. $6.00; pap. $2.45.   296.1
1. Legends, Jewish.

855. Cohen, Abraham. Everyman's Talmud. rev. ed. Dutton. 1949. $6.95.   296.12
1. Talmud.

856. Glatzer, Nahum N., ed. Hammer on the Rock: A Midrash Reader. Schocken. 1962. $4.00; pap. $2.25.   296.14
1. Midrash.

857. Agus, Jacob B. Evolution of Jewish Thought: From Biblical Times to the Openings of the 19th Century. Arno. 1959. $22.00.   296.3
1. Jews — Civilization. 2. Judaism — History.

858. ———. The Vision and the Way: An Interpretation of Jewish Ethics. Ungar. 1966. $8.50; pap. $2.95.   296.3
1. Ethics, Jewish.

859. Schweid, Eliezer. Israel at the Crossroads. Jewish Pubn. 1973. $5.95.   296.3
1. Judaism — Israel.

860. Silver, Daniel J. A History of Judaism. 2 vols. Basic. 1974. $35.00.   296.3
1. Judaism — History.

861. Rapahael, Chaim. A Feast of History: Passover Through the Ages As a Key to the Jewish Experience. S&S. 1972. $12.50.   296.4
1. Jews — Liturgy and Ritual. Haggadah.

297-299 Islamic and Other Religions

862. Farzan, Massaud, compiled by. The Tale of the Reed Pipes: Teachings of the Sufis. Dutton. 1974. pap. $1.95.   297.4
1. Sufism.

863. Glubb, John. The Life and Times of Muhammad. Stein & Day. 1970. pap. $2.95.   297.6(B)
1. Islam. 2. Muhammad, 570-632.

864. Guillaume, Alfred. Islam. Penguin. $1.35.   297.6
1. Islam.

865. Muhammed. Koran. Sale, George, tr. Warne. 1909. $4.95.   297.6
1. Islam.

866. Piggott, Stuart. The Druids. Praeger. 1968. $8.50.   299
1. Druids and Druidism.

867. Breasted, James H. Development of Religion and Thought in Ancient Egypt. U of Pa Pr. 1972. pap. $4.95.   299.31
1. Egypt — Religion.

868. Budge, Ernest A. The Egyptian Book of the Dead. Dover. 1967. pap. $3.95.   299.31
1. Funeral Rites and Ceremonies — Egypt.

869. Liu, Wu-Chi. Confucius, His Life and Time. Greenwood. Repr. 1955. $11.50.   299.5(B)
1. Confucius, ab. 551-479 B.C.

870. Baynes, Cary F., tr. The I Ching; or, Book of Changes. Princeton U Pr. 1967. $8.50.   299.514
1. I Ching.

871. Barrett, Leonard E. Soul-Force: African Heritage in Afro-American Religion. Doubleday. 1974. $7.95; pap. $3.50.   299.6
1. Negroes — Religion.

RELIGION AND MYTHOLOGY

872. King, Noel Q. Religions of Africa: A Pilgrimage into Traditional Religions. Har-Row. 1970. $4.50.   299.6
1. Africa, Sub-Saharan — Religion.

873. Mbiti, John. African Religions and Philosophy. Praeger. 1969. $10.00.   299.6
1. Africa — Religion.

874. Castaneda, Carlos. Tales of Power. S&S. 1974. $7.95.   299.7
1. Hallucinogenic Drugs and Religious Experience. 2. Juan, Don, 1891- 3. Yaqui Indians — Religion and Mythology.

875. ———. The Teachings of Don Juan: A Separate Reality; Journey into Ixian. 3 vols. S&S. 1974. $22.85; pap. $8.85.   299.7
1. Hallucinogenic Drugs and Religious Experience. 2. Juan, Don, 1891- 3. Yaqui Indians — Religion and Mythology.

876. Steiger, Brad. Medicine Power: The American Indian's Revival of His Spiritual Heritage and Its Relevancy for Modern Man. Doubleday. 1974. $6.95; pap. $2.95.   299.7
1. Indians of North America — Religion and Mythology.

877. Eliade, Mircea. Australian Religions: An Introduction. Turner, Victor, ed. Cornell U Pr. 1973. $12.95.   299.9
1. Australia — Religion. 2. Mythology, Australian (Aboriginal).

Recommended Series

878. History of Religion. HR&W.

300 SOCIAL SCIENCES

300 The Social Sciences

879. Hetzler, Stanley A. Technological Growth and Social Change: Achieving Modernization. Praeger. 1969. $7.50.   300
1. Economic Development. 2. Technology and Civilization.

301 Sociology

880. Arendt, Hannah. On Violence. HarBraceJ. 1970. pap. $1.65.   301
1. Violence.

881. Graham, Hugh D., et al, eds. Violence: The Crisis of American Confidence. Johns Hopkins. 1972. $8.50; pap. $2.25.   301
1. Violence — U. S. — History.

882. Graham, Hugh D. and Gurr, Ted R. The History of Violence in America: Historical and Comparative Perspectives. Praeger. 1969. $13.50.   301
1. Violence — U. S. — History.

883. Hartogs, Renatus and Artzt, Eric. Violence: Causes and Solutions. Dell. 1970. pap. $1.25.   301
1. Violence — U. S.

884. Hofstadter, Richard. Social Darwinism in American Thought. rev. ed. Braziller. 1959. $6.00.   301
1. Philosophy, American. 2. Social Evolution.

885. Merton, Robert K. and Nisbet, Robert. Contemporary Social Problems. 3rd ed. HarBraceJ. 1971. $12.50.   301
1. Social Problems.

886. Sarvis, Betty and Rodman, Hyman. The Abortion Controversy. 2nd ed. Columbia U Pr. 1974. $10.00; pap. $3.95.   301
1. Abortion — U. S.

887. Gardner, Howard. The Quest for Mind: Piaget, Levi-Strauss and the Structural Movement. Knopf. 1973. pap. $2.45.   301.045
1. Piaget, Jean, 1896- 2. Levi-Strauss, Claude. 3. Structuralism.

888. Rose, Peter I. Seeing Ourselves: Introductory Readings in Sociology. Knopf. 1972. pap. $4.25.   301.08
1. Sociology.

889. ————. Study of Society: An Integrated Anthology. rev. ed. Knopf. 1972. pap. $6.95.   301.08
1. Sociology.

890. Robertson, John. Modern Humanists Reconsidered. Folcroft. Repr. 1927. $9.75.   301.092
1. Sociology.

301.1 Social Psychology

891. McNeil, Elton B. Being Human, the Psychological Experience. Har-Row. 1973. $8.95.   301.1
1. Social History. 2. Social Psychology.

300 SOCIAL SCIENCES

892. Halacy, D. S., Jr. Social Man. Macrae. 1972. $5.95. 301.11
1. Interpersonal Relations. 2. Social Organization. 3. Sociology.

893. Downton, James V. Rebel Leadership: Commitment and Charisma in the Revolutionary Process. Free Pr. 1973. $10.95. 301.15
1. Leadership. 2. Revolutionists.

894. Golob, Eugene O. The Isms: A History and Evaluation. Bks for Libs. 1954. $15.00. 301.15
1. Economic Policy. 2. Economics — History. 3. Socialism.

895. Harkabi, Yehoshafat. Arab Attitudes to Israel. 2nd ed. Louvish, Misha, tr. Halsted Pr. 1974. $12.50. 301.15
1. Israel — Foreign Opinion. 2. Jewish-Arab Relations.

896. Hoffer, Eric. The True Believer. Har-Row. 1951. $4.50; pap. $0.95. 301.15
1. Fanaticism. 2. Social Psychology.

897. Huxley, Aldous L. Brave New World Revisited. Har-Row. 1932. $6.95; pap. $0.95. 301.15
1. Liberty. 2. Propaganda. 3. Totalitarianism.

898. Bondurant, Joan and Fisher, Margaret W., eds. Conquest of Violence: The Ghandhian Philosophy of Conflict. Lieber-Atherton. 1971. $7.95; pap. $3.95. 301.153
1. Gandhi, Mohandas Karamchand, 1869-1948. 2. Passive Resistance to Government.

899. Schramm, Wilbur and Rivers, William. Responsibility in Mass Communication. rev. ed. Har-Row. 1969. $9.95. 301.153
1. Communication.

900. Mueller, John E. War, Presidents, and Public Opinion. Wiley. 1973. $8.75. 301.154
1. Korean War, 1950-1953 — Public Opinion. 2. Presidents — U. S. — Public Opinion. 3. Public Opinion — U. S. 4. Vietnamese Conflict, 1961-1973 — Public Opinion.

901. Haselden, Kyle. Morality and the Mass Media. Broadman. 1968. $2.50. 301.16
1. Christian Ethics. 2. Mass Media — Moral and Religious Aspects. 3. Mass Media — U. S.

902. Larsen, Otto N., ed. Violence and the Mass Media. Har-Row. 1968. pap. $5.50. 301.16
1. Mass Media — Social Aspects. 2. Mass Media — U. S. 3. Violence in Mass Media.

903. Heaps, Willard A. Riots, U. S. A. 1765-1965. rev. ed. Seabury. 1970. $4.95. 301.18
1. Riots. 2. U. S. — History.

301.2 Culture and Cultural Processes

904. Bock, Philip K., compiled by. Culture Shock: A Reader in Modern Cultural Anthropology. Knopf. 1970. pap. $4.95. 301.2
1. Ethnology — Collections.

905. Fogelson, Robert M. Violence As Protest: A Study of Riots and Ghettos. Doubleday. 1971. $6.95. 301.2
1. Riots — U. S. 2. U. S. — Social Conditions — 1960- 3. Violence — U. S.

906. Gurr, Ted R. Why Men Rebel. Princeton U Pr. 1970. $14.00; pap. $3.45. 301.2
1. Revolutions. 2. Violence.

907. Harris, Marvin. Culture, Man and Nature: An Introduction to General Anthropology. T Y Crowell. 1971. $10.95. 301.2
1. Anthropology.

908. Journal of Urban Law Editors. Riot in the Cities: An Analytical Symposium on the Causes and Effects. Fairleigh Dickinson. 1970. $15.00. 301.2
1. Law Enforcement — U. S. 2. Riots — U. S.

909. Keniston, Kenneth. Uncommitted: Alienated Youth in American Society. HarBraceJ. 1965. $9.50; pap. $2.45 (Delta). 301.2
1. Alienation (Social Psychology).

910. Mead, Margaret. Culture and Commitment. Doubleday. 1970. $5.00; pap. $1.95. 301.2
1. Conflict of Generations. 2. Culture. 3. Social Change.

911. Miller, William R. Nonviolence: A Christian Interpretation. Schocken. 1966. pap. $2.95. 301.2
1. Passive Resistance to Government.

300 SOCIAL SCIENCES

912. Roszak, Theodore. The Making of a Counter Culture: Reflections in the Technocratic Society and Its Youthful Opposition. Doubleday. 1969. $7.95; pap. $1.95. 301.2
1. Civilization, Modern — 1950- 2. Social History — 1945-

913. Toffler, Alvin. Future Shock. Random. 1970. $10.00; pap. $1.95 1971 (Bantam). 301.2
1. Civilization, Modern — 1950- 2. Social Change. 3. Social History — 1945-

914. Newman, Edwin. Strictly Speaking: Will America Be the Death of English? Bobbs. 1974. $7.95. 301.21
1. English Language in the U. S. 2. U. S. — Social Life and Customs.

915. Partridge, William L. The Hippie Ghetto: The Natural History of a Subculture. HR&W. 1973. $2.75. 301.22
1. Hippies — U. S. — Case Studies. 2. U. S. — Social Conditions — 1960-

916. Mead, Margaret. Continuities in Cultural Evolution. Yale U Pr. 1964. $17.50; pap. $3.95. 301.23
1. Social Change.

917. Boulding, Kenneth E. The Meaning of the Twentieth Century: The Great Transition. Har-Row. 1964. pap. $1.95. 301.24
1. Civilization, Modern — 1950-

918. Ferkiss, Victor C. Technological Man: The Myth and the Reality. NAL. 1970. pap. $1.25. 301.24
1. Mass Society. 2. Technology and Civilization.

919. Hall, Edward T. The Silent Language. Doubleday. 1959. $6.95; pap. $1.95. 301.24
1. Intercultural Communication.

920. Loy, John W., Jr. and Kenyon, Gerald S., eds. Sport, Culture and Society: A Reader for the Sociology of Sport. Macmillan. 1969. $10.95. 301.24
1. Sports — Social Aspects.

921. Nikolaieff, George A. Computers and Society. Wilson. 1970. $4.50. 301.24
1. Electronic Digital Computers. 2. Technology and Civilization.

922. Gardner, John W. Self-Renewal: The Individual and the Innovative Society. Har-Row. 1971. pap. $1.25. 301.245
1. Progress.

923. Fanon, Frantz. Wretched of the Earth. Farrington, Constance, tr. Grove. 1965. pap. $1.25. 301.25
1. Algeria — History — 1945- 2. France — Colonies — Africa.

924. Alexander, Yonah and Kittrie, Nicholas N. F., eds. Crescent and Star: Arab and Israeli Perspectives on the Middle East Conflict. AMS Pr. 1973. $25.00. 301.29
1. Jewish-Arab Relations.

925. Ayisi, Eric O. An Introduction to the Study of African Culture. Humanities. 1972. pap. $3.25. 301.29
1. Ethnology — Africa, Sub-Saharan.

926. Briggs, Jean L. Never in Anger: Portrait of an Eskimo Family. Harvard U Pr. 1970. $15.25. 301.29
1. Eskimos — Psychology.

927. Cochran, Thomas. Social Change in America: The Twentieth Century. Har-Row. 1972. $9.00; pap. $2.75. 301.29
1. U. S. — Social Conditions.

928. Hacker, Andrew. The End of the American Era. Atheneum. 1971. $6.50; pap. $2.95. 301.29
1. U. S. — Civilization — 1970- 2. U. S. — Social Conditions — 1960-

929. Iriye, Akira. Across the Pacific: An Inner History of American-East Asian Relations. HarBraceJ. 1967. $9.75. 301.29
1. China — Relations (General) with U. S. 2. East (Far East) — Relations (General) with the U. S. 3. Japan — Relations (General) with U. S. 4. U. S. — Relations (General) with China. 5. U. S. — Relations (General) with Japan.

930. Nystrom, John W. and Haverstock, Nathan A. The Alliance for Progress, Key to Latin America's Development. Van Nos Reinhold. 1962. pap. $2.50. 301.29
1. Alliance for Progress. 2. Latin America — Relations (General) with the U. S. 3. U. S. — Relations (General) with Latin America.

931. Olson, Lawrence A. Japan in Postwar Asia. Praeger. 1970. $10.00. 301.29
1. East (Far East) — Relations (General) with Japan. 2. Japan — Relations (General) with the East (Far East).

932. Turnbull, Colin M. The Mountain People. S&S. 1972. $7.95. 301.29
1. Ik (African People).

301.3 Human Ecology

933. Caldwell, Lynton. Environment: A Challenge for Modern Society. Natural Hist. 1970. $7.95.   301.3
1. Environmental Policy — U. S.

934. Hauser, Philip M. The Population Dilemma. 2nd ed. P-H. 1970. pap. $2.45.   301.3
1. Population.

935. McHale, John. The Ecological Context. new ed. Braziller. 1970. $7.95.   301.3
1. Human Ecology. 2. Twenty-First Century — Forecasts.

936. Mitchell, John G. and Stallings, Constance L., eds. Ectotatics: The Sierra Club Handbook for Environmental Activists. S&S. 1970. pap. $0.95.   301.3
1. Environmental Policy — U. S.

937. Netzer, Dick. Economics and Urban Problems: Diagnoses and Prescriptions. 2nd ed. Basic. 1974. $8.50.   301.3
1. Sociology, Urban.

938. Saltonstall, Richard. Your Environment and What You Can Do About It. Ace Bks. 1972. pap. $1.25.   301.3
1. Environmental Policy — U. S. 2. Pollution — U. S.

939. Adler, Cy A. Ecological Fantasies: Death from Falling Watermelons. Green Eagle Pr. 1974. $9.95.   301.31
1. Ecology. 2. Pollution.

940. Brubaker, Sterling. To Live on Earth: Man and His Environment in Perspective. Johns Hopkins. 1972. $6.95.   301.31
1. Conservation of Natural Resources. 2. Ecology. 3. Human Ecology.

941. Commoner, Barry. The Closing Circle: Nature, Man and Technology. Knopf. 1971. $6.95.   301.31
1. Ecology. 2. Technology and Civilization.

942. Ehrlich, Paul R. and Harriman, Richard L. How to Be a Survivor. Ballantine. 1971. $1.25.   301.31
1. Environmental Policy.

943. Freeman, A. Myrick. The Economics of Environmental Policy. Wiley. 1973. pap. $4.25.   301.31
1. Environmental Policy — U. S.

944. Grayson, Melvin J. and Shepard, Thomas R. The Disaster Lobby: Prophets of Ecological Doom and Other Absurdities. Follett. 1973. $7.95.   301.31
1. Environmental Policy — U. S. 2. Environmental Protection — U. S. — Citizen Participation.

945. Sax, Joseph L. Defending the Environment: A Strategy for Citizen Action. Knopf. 1971. $6.95.   301.31
1. Environmental Law — U. S. 2. Environmental Policy — U. S.

946. Segerberg, Osborn. Where Have All the Flowers, Fishes, Birds, Trees, Water, and Air Gone? What Ecology Is All About. McKay. 1971. $6.95.   301.31
1. Ecology. 2. Human Ecology.

947. Smith, Grahame J., et al. Our Ecological Crisis. Macmillan. 1974. $5.95.   301.31
1. Environmental Policy — U. S. 2. Human Ecology. 3. Pollution — Economic Aspects — U. S.

948. Bird, Caroline. The Crowding Syndrome: Learning to Live with Too Much and Too Many. McKay. 1972. $7.95.   301.32
1. Population. 2. U. S. — Population.

949. Callahan, Daniel J., compiled by. The American Population Debate. Doubleday. 1971. $8.95.   301.32
1. Birth Control — U. S. 2. U. S. — Population.

950. Chamberlain, Neil W. Beyond Malthus: Population and Power. Basic. 1970. $6.95.   301.32
1. Population.

951. Ehrlich, Paul R. The Population Bomb. new rev. ed. Ballantine. 1971. pap. $0.95.   301.32
1. Population.

952. Ehrlich, Paul R. and Ehrlich, Anne H. Population, Resources, Environment: Issues in Human Ecology. 2nd ed. W H Freeman. 1972. $9.95.   301.32
1. Human Ecology. 2. Population.

953. McCormack, Arthur. The Population Problem. T Y Crowell. 1970. $8.95.   301.32
1. Food Supply. 2. Population.

300 SOCIAL SCIENCES

954. Nelson, J. Population and Survival: Can We Win the Race? P-H. 1972. $4.95; pap. $1.84. 301.32
1. Population.

955. Rienow, Robert. Moment in the Sun: A Report on the Deteriorating Quality of the American Environment. Dial. 1967. $7.95; pap. $0.95 (Ballantine). 301.32
1. Human Ecology. 2. Natural Resources — U. S. 3. U. S. — Social Conditions — 1945.

956. Tydings, Joseph D. Born to Starve. Morrow. 1970. pap. $1.95. 301.32
1. Food Supply. 2. Population.

957. U. S. Commission on Population Growth & the American Future. Population and the American Future: The Report. US Govt Ptg Off. 1972. $1.75. 301.32
1. U. S. — Population.

958. Loebl, Suzanne. Conception, Contraception: A New Look. McGraw. 1974. $6.95. 301.321
1. Birth Control.

959. Population Institute. The Population Activist's Handbook. Macmillan. 1974. $8.95; pap. $4.95. 301.329
1. Politics, Practical — Handbooks, Manuals, etc. 2. U. S. — Population — Handbooks, Manuals, etc.

960. Carter, Harold. The Study of Urban Geography. Crane-Russak Co. 1972. $14.50. 301.34
1. Cities and Towns.

961. Downs, Anthony. Opening up the Suburbs: An Urban Strategy for America. Yale U Pr. 1973. $7.95. 301.34
1. Cities and Towns — U. S.

962. Osofsky, Gilbert. Harlem: The Making of a Ghetto; Negro New York, 1890-1930. Har-Row. 1966. $8.95; pap. $2.95. 301.34
1. Harlem, New York (City). 2. Negroes — New York (City).

963. Brinkman, George, ed. The Development of Rural America. U Pr of Kansas. 1974. $8.50. 301.35
1. Community Development — U. S. 2. U. S. — Rural Conditions.

964. Arango, Jorge. The Urbanization of the Earth. Beacon Pr. 1970. $6.95. 301.36
1. Cities and Towns — Planning. 2. Urbanization.

965. Cahill, Susan and Cooper, Michele. The Urban Reader. P-H. 1971. $8.95; pap. $5.75. 301.36
1. Cities and Towns — U. S. — Lectures. 2. Sociology, Urban.

966. Hippler, Arthur E. Hunter's Point: A Black Ghetto. Basic. 1974. $11.95. 301.36
1. Hunters Point, San Francisco. 2. Negroes — San Francisco.

967. McKelvey, Blake. The Emergence of Metropolitan America, 1915-1966. Rutgers U Pr. 1968. $10.00. 301.36
1. Urbanization — U. S.

968. ———. Urbanization of America, 1860-1915. Rutgers U Pr. 1963. $10.00. 301.36
1. Urbanization — U. S. 2. U. S. — Economic Conditions.

969. Riis, Jacob A. How the Other Half Lives. Peter Smith. 1959. $4.00; pap. $4.50 1971 (Dover). 301.36
1. New York (City) — Poor. 2. Tenement Houses — New York (City).

970. Schwartz, Alvin. Central City-Spread City: The Metropolitan Regions Where More and More of Us Spend Our Lives. Macmillan. 1973. $4.95. 301.36
1. Metropolitan Areas. 2. Regional Planning.

971. Tamiment Institute. The Future Metropolis. Rodwin, Lloyd, ed. Braziller. 1968. $6.00; pap. $2.95. 301.36
1. Futurism.

301.4 Social Groups

972. Hemming, James and Maxwell, Zena. Sex and Love. Praeger. 1974. $5.95. 301.41
1. Love. 2. Sex.

973. Kirkendall, Lester A. and Whitehurst, Robert N., eds. The New Sexual Revolution. Prometheus Bks. 1974. $6.95; pap. $3.45. 301.41
1. Sex Customs — U. S.

974. St. George, George. Our Soviet Sister. Luce. 1973. $7.95. 301.41
1. Woman — History and Condition of Women. 2. Women in Russia.

975. Amundsen, Kirsten. The Silenced Majority: Women and American Democracy. P-H. 1971. pap. $2.45. 301.412
1. Women's Rights. 2. Women in the U. S.

976. Bullough, Vernl and Bullough, Bonnie. The Subordinate Sex: A History of Attitudes Toward Women. Penguin. 1974. pap. $2.95. 301.412
1. Woman — History and Condition of Women.

977. Greer, Germaine. The Female Eunich. McGraw. 1971. $6.95. 301.412
1. Woman.

978. ————. Once Upon a Pedestal. T Y Crowell. 1974. $6.95. 301.412
1. Woman — Legal Status, etc. — U. S. 2. Woman — Suffrage — U. S.

979. Gurko, Miriam. The Ladies of Seneca Falls: The Birth of the Woman's Rights Movement. Macmillan. 1974. $7.95. 301.412
1. Women's Rights. 2. Woman — Suffrage — U. S. 3. Women in the U. S. — Biography.

980. Kahn, Kathy. Hillbilly Women. Doubleday. 1973. $7.95. 301.412
1. Coal-Miners — Appalachian Region. 2. Women in the Appalachian Region.

981. Koedt, Anne, et al. Radical Feminism. Quadrangle. 1973. $10.00; pap. $3.95. 301.412
1. Woman — History and Condition of Women. 2. Woman — Psychology. 3. Women in the U. S.

982. Morgan, Robin, ed. Sisterhood Is Powerful: An Anthology of Writings from the Women's Liberation Movement. Random. 1970. $8.95; pap. $2.45. 301.412
1. Women's Rights. 2. Woman — Social and Moral Questions. 3. Women in the U. S. 4. Women's Liberation Movement.

983. Sochen, June. Movers and Shakers: American Women Thinkers and Activities, 1900-1970. Quadrangle. 1974. pap. $3.95. 301.412
1. Woman — History and Condition of Women. 2. Women in the U. S. 3. Women's Liberation Movement — U. S.

984. Hoffman, Martin. The Gay World: Male Homosexuality and the Social Creation of Evil. Basic. 1968. $7.55; pap. $1.95 (Bantam). 301.415
1. Homosexuality.

985. Murphy, John. Homosexual Liberation: A Personal View. Praeger. 1971. $5.95. 301.415
1. Homosexuality — U. S.

986. Pierson, Elaine C. Sex Is Never an Emergency: A Candid Guide for Young Adults. 3rd ed. Lippincott. 1973. $3.95; pap. $1.25. 301.4195
1. Conception — Prevention. 2. Contraception. 3. Sex Instruction for Youth.

987. Demos, John. A Little Commonwealth: Family Life in Plymouth Colony. Oxford U Pr. 1970. $6.95. 301.42
1. Family — Plymouth, Mass. 2. Plymouth, Mass. — Social Life and Customs.

988. Yorburg, Betty. The Changing Family. Columbia U Pr. 1973. $9.00; pap. $2.95. 301.42
1. Family.

989. Barron, Milton L. The Blending American: Patterns of Intermarriage. Quadrangle. 1972. $12.50. 301.422
1. Marriage, Mixed.

990. Lukas, J. Anthony. Don't Shoot - We Are Your Children! Random. 1971. $8.95. 301.427
1. Young Adults — U. S.

991. Epstein, Joseph. Divorced in America. Dutton. 1974. $8.95. 301.428
1. Divorce. 2. Divorce — U. S.

992. Sheresky, Norman and Mannes, M. Uncoupling: The Art of Coming Apart. Viking Pr. 1972. $6.95. 301.428
1. Divorce — U. S.

993. Keniston, Kenneth. Young Radicals: Notes on Committed Youth. HarBraceJ. 1968. $6.95; pap. $2.45. 301.431
1. Radicals and Radicalism. 2. Youth — U. S. — Political Activity.

994. Farson, Richard E. Birthrights. Macmillan. 1974. $6.95. 301.4314
1. Children in the U. S. 2. Children's Rights. 3. Parent and Child.

995. Bensman, Joseph and Vidich, Arthur J. The New American Society: The Revolution of the Middle Class. Quadrangle. 1971. $10.00. 301.441
1. Middle Classes — U. S. 2. Social Classes — U. S.

996. Coles, Robert. Uprooted Children: The Early Life of Migrant Farm Workers. U of Pittsburgh Pr. 1970. $5.95; pap. $0.95 1971 (Har-Row). 301.441

300 SOCIAL SCIENCES

1. Children of Migrant Laborers. 2. Migrant Labor — U. S.

997. Coles, Robert and Clayton, Al. Still Hungry in America. Norton. 1969. $7.95; pap. $2.95 1973 (NAL). 301.441
1. Nutrition. 2. Poverty. 3. U. S. — Social Conditions.

998. Coles, Robert and Erikson, Jon. The Middle Americans: Proud and Uncertain. Little. 1971. $12.50; pap. $3.95. 301.441
1. Middle Classes — U. S. 2. Middle Classes — U. S. — Pictorial Works.

999. Harrington, Michael. The Other America: Poverty in the U. S. rev. ed. Macmillan. 1970. $7.95. 301.441
1. Poor — U. S.

1000. Helmer, John. Bringing the War Home: The American Soldier in Vietnam and After. Free Pr. 1974. $12.95. 301.444
1. Sociology, Military. 2. Veterans — U. S. 3. Vietnamese Conflict, 1961-1973 — Psychological Aspects.

1001. Lansberger, Henry A., ed. Latin American Peasant Movements. Cornell U Pr. 1969. $15.00. 301.4444
1. Latin America — Social Conditions. 2. Peasantry.

1002. Yetman, Norman R., ed. Voices from Slavery: Personal Accounts from the Slave Narrative Collection. HR&W. 1970. $7.95. 301.449
1. Slave Narratives. 2. Slavery in the U. S. — Condition of Slaves.

1003. Davis, David B. The Problem of Slavery in an Age of Revolution, 1770-1823. Cornell U Pr. 1975. $17.50. 301.4493
1. Slavery.

1004. McManus, Edgar J. Black Bondage in the North. Syracuse U Pr. 1973. $9.95. 301.4493
1. Slavery in the U. S. — Middle Atlantic States. 2. Slavery in the U. S. — New England.

301.45 Ethnic Groups

1005. Glock, Charles I. and Siegelman, Ellen. Prejudice, U. S. Praeger. 1969. $6.95; pap. $2.95. 301.45
1. Discrimination — U. S. 2. Minorities — U. S. 3. Prejudice and Antipathies.

1006. Novak, Michael. The Rise of the Unmeltable Ethics: Politics and Culture in the Seventies. Macmillan. 1972. $7.95; pap. $1.95. 301.45
1. Ethnic Attitudes. 2. Minorities — U. S.

1007. Weiss, Karel. Under the Mask: An Anthology About Prejudice in America. Dell. 1973. pap. $1.25. 301.45
1. Minorities — U. S. 2. Prejudices and Antipathies. 3. U. S. — Race Question.

1008. Adoff, Arnold, ed. Black on Black: Commentaries by Negro Americans. Macmillan. 1968. $5.95. 301.451
1. Negroes — History. 2. Negroes — Moral and Social Conditions.

1009. Baldwin, James. The Fire Next Time. Dial. 1963. $3.95; pap. $0.75 (Dell). 301.451
1. Negroes. 2. U. S. — Race Relations.

1010. ———. No Name in the Street. Dial. 1972. $5.95. 301.451
1. Negroes. 2. U. S. — Race Question.

1011. ———. Nobody Knows My Name. Dial. 1961. $4.50; pap. $1.65 (Dell). 301.451
1. Negroes. 2. U. S. — Race Question.

1012. Barbour, Floyd B., ed. The Black Seventies. Sargent. 1970. $5.95; pap. $2.95. 301.451
1. Negroes.

1013. Bloch, Herman D. The Circle of Discrimination: An Economic and Social Study of the Black Man in New York. NYU Pr. 1969. $7.95. 301.451
1. Discrimination. 2. Negroes — Civil Rights.

1014. Breitman, George, ed. Malcolm X Speaks: Selected Speeches and Statements. Grove. 1967. pap. $0.95. 301.451
1. Little, Malcolm, 1925-1965.

1015. Brink, William and Harris, Louis. Black and White: A Study of U. S. Racial Attitudes Today. rev. ed. S&S. 1969. pap. $1.95. 301.451
1. Negroes — Civil Rights. 2. Race Discrimination — U. S.

1016. Clarke, John H., et al. Malcolm X: The Man and His Times. Macmillan. 1969. $7.95; pap. $1.95. 301.451
1. Little, Malcolm, 1925-1965.

300 SOCIAL SCIENCES

1017. Cleaver, Eldridge. Soul on Ice. McGraw. 1968. $6.50; pap. $1.95 (Dell).
301.451
1. Negroes.

1018. Cleaver, Eldridge. Post Prison Writings and Speeches. Scheer, Robert, ed. Random. 1969. pap. $1.95. 301.451
1. Negroes.

1019. Coles, Robert. Children of Crisis: A Study of Courage and Fear. Little. 1967. $8.50. 301.451
1. Black Children. 2. Blacks — Segregation. 3. Fear.

1020. DuBois, William E. W. E. B. DuBois: A Reader. Weinberg, M. and Weinberg, Clark, eds. Har-Row. 1970. $10.00. 301.451
1. Negroes.

1021. Fanon, Frantz. Black Skin, White Masks. Markmann, Charles L., tr. Grove. 1967. $5.00; pap. $1.65. 301.451
1. Negro Race.

1022. Glazer, Nathan and Moynihan, Daniel P. Beyond the Melting Pot: The Negroes, Puerto Ricans, Jews, Italians and Irish of New York City. 2nd ed. MIT Pr. 1970. $10.00; pap. $1.95. 301.451
1. Minorities — New York (City). 2. New York (City) — Foreign Population.

1023. Handlin, Oscar. Race and Nationality in American Life. Little. 1957. $6.95; pap. $1.95 (Doubleday). 301.451
1. Minorities — U. S. 2. U. S. — Race Question.

1024. Hiro, Dilip. Black British, White British. rev. ed. Monthly Rev. 1973. $8.95.
301.451
1. England — Foreign Population. 2. England — Race Question. 3. Race Discrimination — England.

1025. Katz, William L., compiled by. Eyewitness: The Negro in American History. Pitman. 1974. $12.50. 301.451
1. Negroes — History — Sources.

1026. Kellogg, Charles F. NAACP: A History of the National Association for the Advancement of Colored People, 1909-1920. Johns Hopkins. 1967. $11.00; pap. $2.95.
301.451
1. National Association for the Advancement of Colored People.

1027. King, Martin Luther, Jr. Stride Toward Freedom: The Montgomery Story. Har-Row. 1958. $4.95. 301.451
1. Montgomery, Alabama — Race Question. 2. Negroes — Montgomery, Alabama. 3. Segregation in Transportation — Montgomery, Alabama.

1028. ———. Where Do We Go from Here: Chaos or Community. Har-Row. 1967. $6.95; pap. $1.95 (Beacon Pr). 301.451
1. Negroes — Civil Rights. 2. Negroes — History — 1964-

1029. ———. Why We Can't Wait. Har-Row. 1964. $6.95; pap. $0.95 (NAL). 301.451
1. Negroes — Civil Rights.

1030. Lomax, Louis. The Negro Revolt. Har-Row. 1962. $7.95; pap. $1.25 (NAL).
301.451
1. Negroes — Moral and Social Conditions. 2. Negroes — Segregation. 3. U. S. — Race Question.

1031. Malcolm X and Haley, Alex. The Autobiography of Malcolm X. Grove. 1965. pap. $1.95. 301.451
1. Little, Malcolm, 1925-1965. 2. Negroes.

1032. Meier, August. Negro Thought in America, 1880-1915: Radical Ideologies in the Age of Booker T. Washington. U of Mich Pr. 1963. $8.95; pap. $2.25. 301.451
1. Negroes — History. 2. Washington, Booker Taliaferro, 1859-1915.

1033. Mitchell, George. I'm Somebody Important: Young Black Voices from Rural Georgia. U of Ill Pr. 1973. $7.95. 301.451
1. Negro Youth — Georgia.

1034. Proctor, Samuel. Young Negro in America, 1960-1980. Assn Pr. 1966. $3.95.
301.451
1. Negroes — Civil Rights. 2. Negroes — History.

1035. Quarles, Benjamin. The Negro in the Making of America. Macmillan. 1964. pap. $1.25. 301.451
1. Negroes — History.

1036. Schulz, David A. Coming up Black: Patterns of Ghetto Socialization. P-H. 1969. pap. $2.45. 301.451
1. Negroes — Moral and Social Conditions. 2. Negroes — Segregation.

300 SOCIAL SCIENCES

1037. Spear, Allan H. Black Chicago: The Making of a Negro Ghetto, 1890-1920. U of Chicago Pr. 1967. $8.75; pap. $3.45.   301.451
1. Negroes — Chicago — History.

1038. Yette, Samuel F. The Choice. Putnam. 1971. $6.95.   301.451
1. Negroes — Civil Rights. 2. Negroes — Social Conditions — 1964-

1039. Zilversmit, Arthur. The First Emancipation: The Abolition of Slavery in the North. U of Chicago Pr. 1967. $9.50; pap. $2.75.   301.451
1. Slavery in the U. S. — Anti-Slavery Movements.

1040. Castro, Tony. Chicano Power: The Emergence of Mexican America. Sat Rev Pr. 1974. $9.95; pap. $3.95.   301.4516
1. Mexican Americans.

1041. Galarza, Ernesto. Barrio Boy. U of Notre Dame Pr. 1971. $7.95; pap. $3.95.   301.4516
1. Mexican Americans — Social Life and Customs.

1042. Lewis, Oscar. La Vida: A Puerto Rican Family in the Culture of Poverty - San Juan and New York. Random. 1966. $12.50; pap. $2.95.   301.4516
1. New York (City) — Poor. 2. Puerto Ricans in New York (City). 3. San Juan, Puerto Rico — Poor.

1043. Lopez, Alfredo. The Puerto Rican Papers: Notes on the Re-Emergence of a Nation. Bobbs. 1973. $8.95.   301.4516
1. New York (City) — Social Conditions. 2. Puerto Ricans in New York (City). 3. Puerto Rico — History.

1044. Meier, Matthew S. and Rivera, Feliciano. The Chicanos: A History of Mexican Americans. Hill & Wang. 1972. $8.95; pap. $2.65.   301.4516
1. Mexican Americans — History.

1045. Servin, Manuel P., compiled by. An Awakened Minority: The Mexican-Americans. 2nd ed. Glencoe. 1974. $3.95.   301.4516
1. Mexican Americans.

1046. Steiner, Stanley. La Raza: The Mexican Americans. Har-Row. 1970. $10.00.   301.4516
1. Mexican Americans.

1047. Cheng-Tsu Wu, ed. Chink: A Documentary History of Anti-Chinese Prejudice in America. NAL. 1972. pap. $3.95.   301.4519
1. Chinese Americans — Social Life and Customs.

1048. Conroy, Hilary and Miyakawa, T. S., eds. East Across the Pacific: Historical and Sociological Studies of Japanese Immigration and Assimilation. ABC-Clio. 1972. $15.00; pap. $5.75.   301.4519
1. Japan — Emigration and Immigration. 2. Japanese in the U. S.

1049. Frye, William R. In Whitest Africa: The Dynamics of Apartheid. P-H. 1968. $6.95.   301.4519
1. Africa, South — Race Question.

1050. Kaplan, Benjamin. The Jew and His Family. La State U Pr. 1967. $5.95.   301.4519
1. Jewish Families.

1051. Purcell, Victor. The Chinese in Southeast Asia. 2nd ed. Oxford U Pr. 1965. $14.25.   301.4519
1. Chinese in Southeastern Asia.

1052. Selznick, Gertrude J. and Steinberg, Stephen. The Tenacity of Prejudice: Anti-Semitism in Contemporary America. Har-Row. 1969. $10.00; pap. $1.95.   301.4519
1. Antisemitism — U. S. 2. Jews — Political and Social Conditions. 3. Prejudices and Antipathies.

Recommended Series

1053. Patterns of American Prejudice. Har-Row.

301.452 Socioeconomic and Religious Groups

1054. Kahler, Erich. Jews Among the Nations: Three Essays. Ungar. 1967. $4.75.   301.452
1. Jews — History.

1055. Bontemps, Arna, ed. Great Slave Narratives. Beacon Pr. 1969. $7.50; pap. $2.95.   301.4522
1. Slavery in the U. S.

1056. Stampp, Kenneth M. The Peculiar Institution: Slavery in the Ante-Bellum South. Knopf. 1956. $7.95; pap. $1.95 (Random).   301.4522
1. Slavery in the U. S. — Economic Aspects — Southern States.

300 SOCIAL SCIENCES

1057. Still, William. The Underground Railroad. Johnson Chi. 1970. $10.50. 301.4522
1. Slavery in the U. S. — Anti-Slavery Movement. 2. Slavery in the U. S. — Fugitive Slaves. 3. Underground Railroad.

1058. Birmingham, Stephen. Our Crowd: The Great Jewish Families of New York. Har-Row. 1967. $10.00; pap. $1.25 (Dell). 301.4529
1. Banks and Banking — Jews. 2. Jews in New York (City) — Social Life and Customs.

1059. Gilbert, Arthur. A Jew in Christian America. Sheed. 1966. $4.95. 301.4529
1. Antisemitism — U. S. 2. Christianity and Other Religions — Judaism. 3. Jews in the U. S. 4. Judaism — Relations — Christianity.

1060. Husain, S. Abid. Destiny of Indian Muslims. Asia. 1966. $6.95. 301.4529
1. Muslims in India.

1061. Lincoln, C. Eric. The Black Muslims in America. rev. ed. Beacon Pr. 1973. $12.50; pap. $3.95. 301.4529
1. Black Muslims.

301.453 National Origins Group

1062. Conrat, Maisie and Conrat, Richard. Executive Order 9066. MIT Pr. 1971. pap. $3.95. 301.453
1. Concentration Camps — U. S. — Pictorial Works. 2. Japanese in the U. S. — Pictorial Works. 3. World War, 1939-1945 — Evacuation of Civilians.

1063. Girdner, Audrie and Loftis, Anne. The Great Betrayal: The Evacuation of the Japanese-Americans During World War II. Macmillan. 1969. $12.95. 301.453
1. Concentration Camps. 2. Japanese in the U. S. 3. World War, 1939-1945 — Evacuation of Civilians.

1064. Kitagawa, Daisuke. Isei and Nisei: The Internment Years. Seabury. 1967. $5.95. 301.453
1. Concentration Camps. 2. Japanese in the U. S. 3. World War, 1939-1945 — Evacuation of Civilians.

1065. Kitano, Harry L. Japanese Americans: The Evolution of a Subculture. P-H. 1969. $6.40; pap. $2.95. 301.453
1. Japanese in the U. S. — History.

301.5 Institutions

1066. Ackley, Charles Walton. The Modern Military in American Society: A Study in the Nature of Military Power. Westminster. 1972. $10.95. 301.5
1. Sociology, Military. 2. U. S. — Armed Forces.

1067. Ambrose, Stephen E. and Barber, James A., Jr., eds. The Military and American Society. Free Pr. 1972. $10.00; pap. $2.95. 301.5
1. Sociology, Military. 2. U. S. — Armed Forces.

1068. Armstrong, John A. The European Administrative Elite. Princeton U Pr. 1973. $20.00; pap. $9.75. 301.5
1. Economic Development. 2. Leadership. 3. Public Administration.

1069. Binstock, Robert H. and Ely, Katherine. The Politics of the Powerless. Winthrop. 1971. $7.95; pap. $4.95. 301.5
1. Power (Social Sciences). 2. U. S. — Social Conditions.

1070. Fellman, Gordon. The Deceived Majority. Transaction Bks. 1973. $9.95. 301.5
1. Dissent. 2. Middle Classes — Political Activity. 3. Social Classes — U. S.

301.6 Social Conflict

1071. Davis, David B., ed. The Fear of Conspiracy: Images of un-American Subversion from the Revolution to the Present. Cornell U Pr. 1971. $12.50; pap. $3.45. 301.63
1. Subversive Activities — U. S. 2. U. S. — Social Conditions.

1072. Conant, Ralph W. Prospects for Revolution: A Study of Riots, Civil Disobedience, and Insurrection in Contemporary America. Harper Mag Pr. 1971. $8.95. 301.633
1. Government, Resistance to. 2. Riots. 3. Violence — U. S.

1073. Feagin, Joe R. and Hahn, H. Ghetto Revolts. Macmillan. 1973. pap. $3.95. 301.633
1. Riots — U. S. 2. Violence — U. S.

1074. Froman, Robert. Racism. Delacorte. 1972. $5.95; pap. $0.95. 301.636

300 SOCIAL SCIENCES

1. Prejudices and Antipathies. 2. Race Problems. 3. U. S. — Race Question. 4. U. S. — Race Relations.

308 Collections on the Social Sciences

1075. Burke, Edmund. Selected Writings and Speeches on America. Mahoney, T. H., ed. Bobbs. 1964. $6.00; pap. $1.75.   308
1. Political Science — Addresses and Essays.

1076. Jefferson, Thomas. Life and Selected Writings. Modern Lib. 1944. $2.95.   308
1. Jefferson, Thomas, President U. S., 1743-1826. 2. Political Science.

1077. Lincoln, Abraham. Political Thought. Current, R., ed. Bobbs. 1966. $7.50; pap. $3.25.   308
1. Political Science.

1078. Rousseau, Jean-Jacques. Political Writings. Watkins, Frederick M., tr. Nelson. 1953. $3.00.   308
1. Political Science.

Recommended Series

1079. Public Papers of the Presidents. US Govt Ptg Off.

309 Social Situation and Conditions

1080. Braudel, Fernand. Capitalism and Material Life, 1400-1800. Kochan, Miriam, tr. from Fr. Har-Row. 1974. $13.00.   309.1
1. Economic History. 2. Social History.

1081. Kaplan, Lawrence and Kaplan, Carol, eds. Revolutions: A Comparative Study. Random. 1973. $10.00; pap. $3.45.   309.1
1. Revolutions — History.

1082. Spock, Benjamin M. Decent and Indecent. Fawcett World. 1971. pap. $0.95.   309.1
1. Family — U. S. 2. U. S. — Social Conditions — 1960-

1083. Drucker, Peter. The Age of Discontinuity: Guidelines to Our Changing Society. Har-Row. 1969. $10.00.   309.104
1. Economic Development. 2. Economic History — 1945- 3. International Economic Relations. 4. Social Change.

309.14-309.19 Historical and Geographical Treatment

1084. Gilbert, Felix. The End of the European Era, 1890 to the Present. Norton. 1970. $7.50; pap. $3.50.   309.14
1. Europe — Politics — 20th Century. 2. World Politics — 20th Century.

1085. Lloyd, T. O. Empire to Welfare State: English History 1906-1967. Oxford U Pr. 1970. $10.00.   309.142
1. Great Britain — Economic Conditions — 20th Century. 2. Great Britain — History — 20th Century. 3. Great Britain — Politics and Government — 20th Century.

1086. Roebuck, Janet. Making of Modern English Society from 1850. Scribner. 1973. $8.95.   309.142
1. Great Britain — Social Conditions.

1087. Sampson, Anthony. The New Anatomy of Britain. Stein & Day. 1972. $12.50; pap. $4.95.   309.142
1. Great Britain — Civilization — 1945- 2. Great Britain — Politics and Government — 1964-

1088. Dahrendorf, Ralf. Society and Democracy in Germany. Doubleday. 1969. pap. $1.95.   309.143
1. Germany — Politics and Government — 1871- 2. Germany — Social Conditions. 3. National Characteristics, German.

1089. Ardagh, John. The New French Revolution: Social and Economic Study of France, 1945-1968. Har-Row. 1969. $8.95; pap. $2.95.   309.144
1. France — Economic Conditions. 2. France — Social Conditions.

1090. Hollander, Paul. Soviet and American Society: A Comparison. Oxford U Pr. 1973. $12.50.   309.147
1. Russia — Social Conditions. 2. U. S. — Social Conditions — 1960-

1091. Inkeles, Alex. Social Change in Soviet Russia. Harvard U Pr. 1968. $14.00.   309.147
1. Russia — Social Conditions.

1092. Kassof, Allen, ed. Prospects for Soviet Society. Praeger. 1968. $10.00; pap. $4.50.   309.147
1. Russia — Politics and Government — 1953- 2. Russia — Social Conditions — 1945-

300 SOCIAL SCIENCES

1093. Lyons, Eugene. Workers' Paradise Lost: 50 Years of Soviet Communism, a Balance Sheet. Funk & W. 1967. $6.95.
309.147
1. Russia — Economic Conditions. 2. Russia — Politics and Government. 3. Russia — Social Conditions.

1094. Myrdal, Jean. Report from a Chinese Village. Pantheon. 1965. $8.95; pap. $2.45 1972 (Random). 309.15
1. China (People's Republic of China, 1949-). 2. China — Social Life and Customs.

1095. Taylor, Alice, ed. Focus on Southeast Asia. Praeger. 1972. $8.50; pap. $3.95. 309.159
1. Asia, Southeastern — Economic Conditions. 2. Asia, Southeastern — Social Conditions.

1096. Lloyd, Peter C. Africa in Social Change: Changing Traditional Societies in the Modern World. Peter Smith. 1968. $3.75; pap. $1.95 (Penguin). 309.166
1. Africa, West — Politics. 2. Africa, West — Social Conditions.

1097. Morrison, Donald G. Black Africa: A Comparative Handbook. Free Pr. 1972. $29.95. 309.167
1. Africa, Sub-Saharan.

1098. Denoon, Donald. Southern Africa Since Eighteen Hundred. Praeger. 1973. $8.00; pap. $3.50. 309.168
1. Africa, Southern — Economic Conditions. 2. Africa, Southern — Politics.

1099. Kuper, Leo. An African Bourgeoisie: Race, Class, and Politics in South Africa. Yale U Pr. 1965. pap. $2.95. 309.168
1. Africa, South — Social Conditions. 2. Middle Classes — Africa, South. 3. Negroes in South Africa — Segregation.

1100. Lewis, Oscar. Five Families: Mexican Case Studies in the Culture of Poverty. Basic. 1959. $10.00; pap. $0.95 (NAL). 309.172
1. Mexico — Social Conditions.

1101. ———. Life in a Mexican Village: Tepoztlan Restudied. U of Ill Pr. 1963. pap. $3.95. 309.172
1. Mexico — Social Conditions.

1102. Szulc, Tad, ed. The United States and the Carribean. rev. ed. P-H. 1971. pap. $2.45.
309.172
1. West Indies — Politics.

1103. Bell, Daniel. The Coming of Post-Industrial Society: A Venture in Social Forecasting. Basic. 1973. $12.50. 309.173
1. Forecasting. 2. Social History — 20th Century. 3. U. S. — Social Conditions — 1945-

1104. Bernstein, Saul. Alternatives to Violence. Assn Pr. 1970. pap. $2.95. 309.173
1. Poor — U. S. 2. Riots — U. S. 3. U. S. — Race Question. 4. Youth — U. S.

1105. Berthoff, Rowland T. An Unsettled People: Social Order and Disorder in American History. Har-Row. 1971. $12.50.
309.173
1. U. S. — Social Conditions.

1106. Ellis, Edward R. A Nation in Torment: The Great American Depression, 1929-1939. Putnam. $10.00; pap. $3.95.
309.173
1. U. S. — Economic Conditions — 1918-1945. 2. U. S. — Politics and Government — 1933-1945. 3. U. S. — Social Conditions — 1918-1932.

1107. Endleman, Shalom, ed. Violence in the Streets. Quadrangle. 1968. pap. $2.95. 309.173
1. U. S. — Social Conditions — 1945-
2. Violence.

1108. Gardner, John W. The Recovery of Confidence. Norton. 1970. $5.00. 309.173
1. U. S. — Social Policy.

1109. Gardner, John W. No Easy Victories. Rowan, Helen, ed. Har-Row. 1968. pap. $1.45.
309.173
1. Education — U. S. 2. U. S. — Social Conditions — 1945-

1110. Gerzon, Mark. The Whole World Is Watching: A Young Man Looks at Youth's Dissent. Stein & Day. 1972. $6.95; pap. $1.50 1974 (Popular Lib). 309.173
1. U. S. — Social Conditions — 1960-
2. Youth — U. S.

1111. Glad, Paul, ed. The Dissonance of Change, 1919 to the Present. Phila Bk Co. 1970. pap. text ed. $3.95. 309.173
1. U. S. — Politics and Government — 20th Century.

1112. Goodwin, Richard N. The American Condition. Doubleday. 1974. $10.00. 309.173
1. Liberty. 2. U. S. — Social Conditions — 20th Century.

300 SOCIAL SCIENCES

1113. Harrington, Michael. Toward a Democratic Left: A Radical Program for a New Majority. Penguin. 1969. $5.95; pap. $1.25. 309.173
1. U. S. — Economic Conditions — 1945-
2. U. S. — Social Conditions — 1945-

1114. Hofstadter, Richard. America at 1750: A Social Portrait. Knopf. 1971. $6.95. 309.173
1. U. S. — Social Conditions — to 1865.

1115. Newfield, Jack and Greenfield, J. A Populist Manifesto: The Making of a New Majority. Praeger. 1972. $5.95; pap. $1.95. 309.173
1. U. S. — Economic Policy — 1971-
2. U. S. — Politics and Government — 1969-
3. U. S. — Social Policy.

1116. Perrett, Geoffrey. Days of Sadness, Years of Triumph. Coward. 1973. $10.00. 309.173
1. U. S. — History — 1933-1945. 2. World War, 1939-1945 — U. S.

1117. Rockefeller, John D. The Second American Revolution: Some Personal Observations. Har-Row. 1973. $6.50; pap. $1.50. 309.173
1. Social Change. 2. U. S. — Social Conditions — 1960-

1118. Terkel, Studs. Hard Times: An Oral History of the Great Depression in America. Pantheon. 1970. $8.95. 309.173
1. U. S. — Economic Conditions — 1919-1945. 2. U. S. — Social Conditions — 1933-1945.

1119. Udall, Stewart L. Nineteen Seventy-Six: Agenda for Tomorrow. HarBraceJ. 1972. pap. $1.95. 309.173
1. Human Ecology. 2. U. S. — Social Policy.

1120. Brown, Claude. Manchild in the Promised Land. Macmillan. 1965. $7.95; pap. $1.50 (NAL). 309.174
1. Harlem, New York (City) — Social Conditions.

1121. Davis, Allison, et al. Deep South: A Social Anthropological Study of Caste and Class. U of Chicago Pr. 1965. pap. $2.95. 309.175
1. Negroes — Southern States. 2. Southern States — Economic Conditions. 3. Southern States — Social Conditions.

1122. Caudill, Harry M. Night Comes to the Cumberlands: A Biography of a Depressed Area. Little. 1963. $8.50; pap. $2.95. 309.176
1. Appalachian Plateau — Economic Conditions. 2. Appalachian Plateau — Social Conditions.

1123. Bullock, Paul, ed. Watts: The Aftermath by the People of Watts. Grove. 1970. pap. $1.50. 309.179
1. Los Angeles — Riots, 1965. 2. Negroes — Moral and Social Conditions. 3. Watts, California — Social Conditions.

1124. Wiser, William and Wiser, Charlotte. Behind Mud Walls, 1930-1962. U of Cal Pr. 1963. $8.50; pap. $2.85. 309.195
1. India.

309.2 Planning and Assistance

1125. Carey, Robert G. The Peace Corps. Praeger. 1970. $8.95. 309.2
1. U. S. Peace Corps.

1126. Hough, John T., Jr. Peck of Salt: A Year in the Ghetto. Little. 1970. $5.95; pap. $2.95. 309.23
1. U. S. Volunteers in Service to America.

320 Politcal Science

1127. De Grazia, Alfred. Politics for Better or Worse. Scott F. 1973. pap. $6.50. 320
1. Political Science.

1128. Ebenstein, William. Great Political Thinkers: Plato to the Present. 4th ed. HR&W. 1969. text ed. $12.95. 320
1. Political Science — History.

1129. Mill, John Stuart. Utilitarianism, Liberty and Representative Government. Dutton. 1950. $3.95. 320
1. Political Science.

1130. Minow, Newton N., et al. Presidential Television: A Twentieth Century Fund Report. Basic. 1973. $8.95. 320
1. Presidents — U. S. 2. Television in Politics — U. S.

1131. Sabine, George H. History of Political Theory. 4th ed. HR&W. 1973. $13.95. 320
1. Political Science.

300 SOCIAL SCIENCES

1132. Nieburg, Harold L. Political Violence: The Behavioral Process. St Martin. 1969. $5.95; pap. $2.95. 320.01
1. Political Sociology. 2. Violence.

1133. Raphael, David D. Problems of Political Philosophy. Praeger. 1970. $6.00; pap. $2.95. 320.01
1. Political Science. 2. State, The.

1134. Manuel, Frank Edward, ed. Utopias and Utopian Thought. HM. 1966. $6.50. 320.07
1. Utopias.

1135. Burch, Betty B. and Cole, Alan B. Asian Political Systems: Readings on China, Japan, India and Pakistan. Van Nos Reinhold. 1968. pap. $5.95. 320.095
1. Asia — Politics.

1136. Barnett, A. Doak, ed. Chinese Communist Politics in Action. U of Wash Pr. 1969. $12.50; pap. $4.95. 320.0957
1. China (People's Republic of China, 1949-) — Politics and Government. 2. Communist Parties.

1137. Myers, Gustavus. The History of Tammany Hall. new ed. Peter Smith. $6.50. 320.097
1. New York (City) — Politics and Government. 2. Tammany Hall.

1138. Arendt, Hannah. Crises of the Republic: Lying in Politics, Civil Disobedience on Violence, Thoughts on Politics, and Revolution. HarBraceJ. 1972. $6.95. 320.1
1. Government, Resistance to. 2. Revolutions. 3. Vietnamese Conflict, 1961-1973 — U. S. 4. Violence.

1139. Dunn, Mary M. William Penn: Politics and Conscience. Princeton U Pr. 1967. $10.00. 320.1(B)
1. Penn, William, 1644-1718. 2. Pennsylvania — Politics and Government.

1140. Machiavelli, Niccolo. The Prince: Discourses. Ricci, Luigi, tr. Oxford U Pr. 1906. $2.00. 320.1
1. Political Science.

1141. Prezzolini, Giuseppe. Machiavelli. Savine, Giocanda, tr. FS&G. 1967. $8.50. 320.1(B)
1. Machiavelli, Niccolo, 1469-1527.

1142. Blondel, Jean. An Introduction to Comparative Government. Praeger. 1970. $12.00. 320.3
1. Comparative Government.

1143. Macridis, Roy C. and Ward, Robert E., eds. Modern Political Systems: Asia. 3rd ed. P-H. 1972. $12.50. 320.3
1. Comparative Government.

1144. ———. Modern Political Systems: Europe. 2nd ed. P-H. 1968. $10.95. 320.3
1. Comparative Government.

1145. Hendel, Samuel. The Soviet Crucible: Soviet Government in Theory and Practice. 3rd ed. Duxbury Pr. 1973. pap. $6.95. 320.447
1. Russia — Economic Conditions — 1918-
2. Russia — Politics and Government — 1917-

1146. Bell, Leland V. In Hitler's Shadow: The Anatomy of American Nazism. Kennikat. 1973. $7.95. 320.5
1. Fascism — U. S. 2. U. S. — Politics and Government — 1933-1945.

1147. Dawn, C. Ernest. From Ottomanism to Arabism: Essays on the Origins of Arab Nationalism. U of Ill Pr. 1973. $8.95. 320.5
1. Nationalism. 2. Near East — Politics.

1148. Hayes, Paul M. Fascism. Free Pr. 1973. $7.95. 320.5
1. Fascism — History.

1149. Volkomer, Walter E., ed. The Liberal Tradition in American Thought. Putnam. 1969. pap. $2.45. 320.51
1. Liberalism — U. S. 2. Political Science — History — U. S.

1150. Sigler, Jay A., ed. The Conservative Tradition in American Thought: An Anthology. Putnam. 1969. $6.95; pap. $2.45. 320.52
1. Conservatism — U. S. 2. Political Science — History — U. S.

1151. Nolte, Ernest. Three Faces of Fascism: Action Francaise, Italian Fascism, National Socialism. HR&W. 1966. $7.95; pap. $1.95 (NAL). 320.533
1. Fascism — History. 2. National Socialism.

1152. Goldman, Peter L. The Death and Life of Malcolm X. Har-Row. 1973. $8.95; pap. $1.95. 320.54
1. Little, Malcolm, 1925-1965.

320.9 Political Situations and Conditions

1153. An, Tai-Sung. Mao Tse-Tung's Cultural Revolution. Pegasus. 1972. $6.95; pap. $1.95. 320.9
1. China (People's Republic of China, 1949-) — Politics and Government.

1154. Armstrong, Hamilton F., ed. Fifty Years of Foreign Affairs. Praeger. 1972. $12.50. 320.9
1. Economic Conditions. 2. International Relations. 3. World Politics — 20th Century.

1155. Bromke, Adam and Rakowska-Harmstone, Teresa, eds. The Communist States in Disarray, 1965-1971. U of Minn Pr. 1972. $13.50; pap. $4.95. 320.9
1. Communist Countries — Politics.

1156. Congressional Quarterly Service. Congress and the Nation. 3 vols. 1965, 1969, 1973. Congr Quarterly. $105.50. 320.9
1. Legislation — U. S. 2. U. S. Congress. 3. U. S. — Politics and Government — 1945-

1157. Khadduri, Majid. Arab Contemporaries: The Role of Personalities in Politics. Johns Hopkins. 1973. $8.95.
320.917(B)
1. Arab Countries — Biography. 2. Arab Countries — Politics.

1158. ———. Political Trends in the Arab World: The Role of Ideas and Ideals in Politics. Johns Hopkins. 1970. $11.00; pap. $3.00. 320.917
1. Arab Countries — Intellectual Life. 2. Arab Countries — Politics. 3. Political Science — History — Arab Countries.

1159. Skilling, H. Gordon. The Governments of Communist East Europe. T Y Crowell. 1966. $5.95; pap. $3.95. 320.94
1. Communism — Europe, Eastern. 2. Communist State. 3. Europe, Eastern — Politics.

1160. Starr, Richard F. The Communist Regimes in Eastern Europe: An Introduction. rev. ed. Hoover Inst Pr. 1971. pap. $3.95.
320.94
1. Communism — Europe, Eastern. 2. Europe, Eastern — Politics.

1161. Chubb, Basil. The Government and Politics of Ireland. Stanford U Pr. 1970. $10.00. 320.941
1. Ireland — Politics and Government — 1922-1949. 2. Ireland — Politics and Government — 1949-

1162. Bromke, Adam. Poland's Politics: Idealism vs. Realism. Harvard U Pr. 1967. $9.95. 320.943
1. Communism — Poland. 2. Poland — Politics and Government.

1163. Hangen, Welles. The Muted Revolution: East Germany's Challenge to Russia and the West. Knopf. 1966. $6.95.
320.943
1. Germany (Democratic Republic, 1949-) — Politics and Government.

1164. Ritter, Gerhard. The Sword and the Scepter: The Problem of Militarism in Germany. Norden, Heinz, tr. U of Miami Pr. 1969. $15.00. 320.943
1. Germany — History, Military. 2. Germany — Politics and Government. 3. Militarism — Germany. 4. Politics and War.

1165. Vali, Ferenc. The Quest for a United Germany. Johns Hopkins. 1967. $10.00.
320.943
1. German Reunification Question.

1166. Remond, Rene. The Right Wing in France: From 1815 to de Gaulle. 2nd ed. Laux, James M., tr. U of Pa Pr. 1969. $10.00.
320.944
1. France — Politics and Government.

1167. Adams, John C. and Barile, Paolo. The Government of Republican Italy. 3rd ed. HM. 1972. pap. $4.50. 320.945
1. Italy — Politics and Government — 1945-

1168. Hughes, Serge. The Fall and Rise of Modern Italy. Macmillan. 1967. $6.95; pap. $2.95 (Funk & W). 320.945
1. Italy — Politics and Government — 20th Century.

1169. Armstrong, John A. Ideology, Politics and Government in the Soviet Union. 3rd ed. Praeger. 1974. $8.00; pap. $3.50. 320.947
1. Communist Party (Russia). 2. Russia — Politics and Government.

1170. Barghoorn, Frederick C. Politics in the USSR. 2nd ed. Little. 1972. $4.95. 320.947
1. Russia — Politics and Government — 1917-

300 SOCIAL SCIENCES

1171. Tatu, Michel. Power in the Kremlin: From Krushchev to Kosygin. Katel, Helen, tr. Viking Pr. 1969. $10.00; pap. $3.45.   320.947
1. Russia — Politics and Government — 1953-

1172. Kousoulas, D. George. Modern Greece: Profile of a Nation. Scribner. 1974. $10.00; pap. $3.95.   320.949
1. Greece, Modern — Politics and Government — 1821-

1173. Weil, Gordon L. The Benelux Nations: The Politics of Small-Country Democracies. HR&W. 1970. pap. $3.25.   320.949
1. Benelux Countries — Politics.

1174. Henderson, Gregory. Korea, the Politics of the Vortex. Harvard U Pr. 1968. $13.50.   320.95
1. Korea — Politics and Government.

1175. Barnett, A. Doak. China After Mao, with Selected Documents. Princeton U Pr. 1967. $8.50; pap. $3.95.   320.951
1. China (People's Republic of China, 1949-) — Politics and Government. 2. Communist Party. 3. Mao, Tŝe-tung, 1893-

1176. Domes, Juergen. The Internal Politics of China, 1949-1972. Praeger. 1973. $10.00.   320.951
1. China (People's Republic of China, 1949-).

1177. Harrison, James P. The Long March to Power: A History of the Chinese Communist Party, 1921-1972. Praeger. 1972. $18.50; pap. $6.95.   320.951
1. China — Politics and Government — 1912-1949. 2. China (People's Republic of China, 1949-) — Politics and Government. 3. Communism — China.

1178. Lowenthal, Richard, ed. Issues in the Future of Asia: Communist and Non-Communist Alternatives. Praeger. 1969. $6.00.   320.951
1. Asia — Economic Policy. 2. Asia — Politics.

1179. Mao Tŝe-Tung. Selected Readings. China Bks. 1971. $2.25; pap. $1.75.   320.951
1. China (People's Republic of China, 1949-) — Politics and Government. 2. Communism — China (People's Republic of China, 1949-).

1180. Brown, Judith M. Gandhi's Rise to Power: Indian Politics, 1915-1922. Cambridge U Pr. 1972. $19.50; pap. $5.95.   320.954
1. Gandhi, Mohandas Karamchand, 1869-1948. 2. India — Politics and Government — 1919-1947.

1181. Abboushi, W. F. Political Systems of the Middle East in the 20th Century. Dodd. 1970. $8.95.   320.956
1. Near East — Politics.

1182. Allen, Richard. Imperialism and Nationalism in the Fertile Crescent: Sources and Prospects of the Arab-Israeli Conflict. Oxford U Pr. 1974. $8.95; pap. $3.50.   320.956
1. Jewish-Arab Relations — History. 2. Near East — Politics.

1183. Dobson, Christopher. Black September: Its Short Violent History. Macmillan. 1974. $8.95.   320.956
1. Fedayeen. 2. Jewish-Arab Relations — 1967-1973. 3. Munazzamat Aylul al-Aswad.

1184. Quandt, William B. The Politics of Palestinian Nationalism. U of Cal Pr. 1973. $6.95; pap. $2.95.   320.956
1. Fedayeen. 2. Near East — Politics.

1185. Fitzgerald, Frances. Fire in the Lake: The Vietnamese and the Americans in Vietnam. Little. 1972. $12.50.   320.959
1. Vietnam — Politics and Government. 2. Vietnamese Conflict, 1961-1973 — U. S.

1186. Girling, J. L. People's War: Conditions and Consequences in China and Southeast Asia. Praeger. 1969. $7.50.   320.959
1. Asia, Southeastern — Politics. 2. Communism — China.

1187. McAlister, John T., Jr. and Mus, Paul. The Vietnamese and Their Revolution. Har-Row. 1970. pap. $1.95.   320.959
1. Communism — Vietnam. 2. Vietnam — Politics and Government.

1188. Africa Independent: Keesling's Research Report. Scribner. 1971. $10.00; pap. $3.95.   320.96
1. Africa — Politics — 1960-

1189. Boorstin, Daniel J. The Genius of American Politics. U of Chicago Pr. 1953. $6.50; pap. $1.50.   320.97
1. U. S. — Politics and Government.

1190. Mallory, James R. The Structure of Canadian Government. St Martin. 1971. $13.95.   320.971
1. Canada — Constitutional History. 2. Canada — Politics and Government.

300 SOCIAL SCIENCES

1191. Apple, R. W., Jr. The Watergate Hearings: Break-in and Cover-up. Bantam. 1973. pap. $2.50. 320.973
1. U. S. — Politics and Government — 1969-

1192. Bell, Daniel, ed. The Radical Right. Doubleday. 1963. pap. $2.50. 320.973
1. Conservatism. 2. U. S. — Politics and Government — 1953-1961. 3. U. S. — Politics and Government — 1961-

1193. Chisholm, Shirley. The Good Fight. Har-Row. 1973. $6.95. 320.973(B)
1. Chisholm, Shirley, 1924- 2. Presidents — U. S. — Election — 1972. 3. U. S. — Politics and Government — 1969-

1194. Dargo, George. Roots of the Republic. Praeger. 1974. $7.50; pap. $2.95. 320.973
1. U. S. — Constitutional History. 2. U. S. — Politics — Colonial Period.

1195. Dobson, John M. Politics in the Gilded Age: A New Perspective on Reform. Praeger. 1972. $7.50; pap. $2.95. 320.973
1. Civil Service Reform. 2. Political Parties — U. S. 3. U. S. — Politics and Government — 1865-1900.

1196. Levin, Murray B. Political Hysteria in America: The Democratic Capacity for Repression. Basic. 1972. $8.95. 320.973
1. Anti-Communist Movements — U. S. 2. Hysteria (Social Psychology). 3. U. S. — Politics and Government — 20th Century.

1197. McCloskey, Paul N. Truth and Untruth. S&S. 1972. $7.95. 320.973
1. Political Ethics. 2. U. S. — Politics and Government — 1969-

1198. Merriam, Charles E. A History of American Political Theories. Johnson Repr. 1920. $9.00. 320.973
1. Political Science — History — U. S. 2. U. S. — Politics and Government.

1199. Mintz, Morton and Cohen, Jerry S. America, Inc. Who Owns and Operates the United States. Dial. 1971. $10.00. 320.973
1. Big Business — U. S. 2. Business and Politics — U. S. 3. Commercial Crimes — U. S. 4. Industry and State — U. S.

1200. Rather, Dan and Gates, Gary. The Palace Guard. Har-Row. 1974. $8.95. 320.973
1. Cabinet Officers — U. S. 2. Presidents — U. S. — Staff. 3. U. S. — Politics and Government — 1961-

1201. Saffell, David C., ed. Watergate: Its Effects on the American Political System. Winthrop. 1974. pap. $5.95. 320.973
1. U. S. — Politics and Government — 1969- 2. Watergate Affair, 1972-

1202. Steinberg, Alfred. The Bosses. Macmillan. 1972. $8.95. 320.973(B)
1. Corruption (in Politics) — U. S. — Biography. 2. U. S. — Politics and Government — 1901-1953.

1203. Wolff, Robert P., ed. Nineteen Eighty-Four Revisited: Prospects for American Politics. Knopf. 1973. $6.95; pap. $3.25. 320.973
1. Radicalism — U. S. 2. U. S. — Politics and Government — 1945- 3. U. S. — Social Conditions — 1945-

1204. Glassman, Ronald. Political History of Latin America. Funk & W. 1969. $7.95. 320.98
1. Latin America — Politics. 2. Latin America — Social Conditions.

1205. Lambert, Jacques. Latin America: Social Structure and Political Institutions. Katel, Helen, tr. U of Cal Pr. 1968. $12.50; pap. $3.45. 320.98
1. Latin America — Politics. 2. Latin America — Social Conditions.

1206. Tomasek, Robert D., ed. Latin American Politics: Studies of the Contemporary Scenes. 2nd rev. ed. Doubleday. 1970. pap. $2.45. 320.98
1. Latin America — Politics — 1948-

321 Forms of State

1207. Ebenstein, William. Today's Isms: Communism, Fascism, Socialism, Capitalism. 7th ed. P-H. 1973. $7.95; pap. $4.95. 321
1. Capitalism. 2. Communism. 3. Fascism. 4. Socialism.

1208. Eurich, Nell. Science in Utopia: A Mighty Design. Harvard U Pr. 1967. $9.00. 321
1. Utopias.

1209. Fogarty, Robert S., ed. American Utopianism. Peacock Pubs. 1972. pap. $2.95. 321
1. Collective Settlements — U. S. 2. Utopias.

1210. Rossiter, Clinton. Conservatism in America. 2nd ed. Knopf. 1962. $7.95. 321
1. Right and Left (Political Science).

300 SOCIAL SCIENCES

1211. Koebner, Richard and Schmidt, H. D. Imperialism: The Story and Significance of a Political Word, 1840-1960. Cambridge U Pr. 1964. $19.50. 321.03
1. Imperialism.

1212. Arendt, Hannah. On Revolution. Viking Pr. 1965. pap. $2.25. 321.09
1. Revolutions.

1213. Postgate, Raymond W. Revolution from 1789 to 1906: Documents. Peter Smith. 1962. $6.00. 321.09
1. Europe — History — 1789-1900. 2. Revolutions.

1214. Mao Tŝe-Tung. The Political Thought of Mao Tŝe-Tung. rev. & enl. ed. Schram, Stuart, ed. Praeger. 1969. pap. text ed. $4.95. 321.642
1. Communism — China.

1215. Pickles, Dorothy M. Democracy. Basic. 1971. $5.95. 321.8
1. Democracy.

1216. Arendt, Hannah. Origins of Totalitarianism. HarBraceJ. 1973. pap. $4.95. 321.9
1. Antisemitism. 2. Imperialism. 3. Totalitarianism.

1217. Buchheim, Hans. Totalitarian Rule: Its Nature and Characteristics. Hein, Ruth, tr. Wesleyan U Pr. 1968. $7.00; pap. $2.95. 321.9
1. Totalitarianism — Psychology.

1218. Mussolini, Benito. Fascism: Doctrine and Institutions. Fertig. 1935. $11.50. 321.94
1. Fascism.

322 The State and Organized Groups

1219. Cohen, Carl. Civil Disobedience: Conscience, Tactics, and the Law. Columbia U Pr. 1971. $10.00; pap. $2.95. 322
1. Civil Rights — U. S. 2. Government, Resistance to.

1220. Barker, Rodney, ed. Studies in Opposition. St Martin. 1972. $11.95. 322.4
1. Government, Resistance to. 2. Passive Resistance to Government.

1221. Bedau, Hugo A., compiled by. Civil Disobedience: Theory and Practice. Pegasus. 1969. $7.50; pap. $2.25. 322.4
1. Government, Resistance to.

1222. Djilas, Milovan. Memoir of a Revolutionary. HarBraceJ. 1973. $12.00. 322.4(B)
1. Communism — Yugoslavia. 2. Djilas, Milovan, 1911-

1223. Esler, Anthony. Bombs, Beards and Barricades: One Hundred Fifty Years of Youth in Revolt. Stein & Day. 1971. $7.95. 322.4
1. College Students — Political Activity — History. 2. Radicalism — History. 3. Young Adults — Political Activity — History.

1224. Mabee, Carleton. Black Freedom: The Nonviolent Abolitionists from 1830 Through the Civil War. Macmillan. 1969. $9.95. 322.4
1. Abolitionists. 2. Slavery in the U. S. — Anti-Slavery Movements.

1225. Richards, Leonard L. Gentlemen of Property and Standing: Anti-Abolitionist Mobs in Jacksonian America. Oxford U Pr. 1970. $6.95; pap. $1.95. 322.4
1. Mobs. 2. Slavery in the U. S. — Anti-Slavery Movements.

1226. U. S. President's Commission on Campus Unrest. The Report of the President's Commission on Campus Unrest. US Govt Ptg Off. 1970. $2.50. 322.4
1. Student Movements — U. S.

1227. Polner, Murray, ed. When Can I Come Home? A Debate on Amnesty for Exiles, Antiwar Prisoners and Others. Doubleday. 1972. pap. $1.95. 322.409
1. Amnesty — U. S. 2. Conscientious Objectors — U. S.

1228. Bentley, Eric, ed. Thirty Years of Treason: Excerpts from Hearings Before the House Un-American Activities Committee 1938-1968. Viking Pr. 1971. $20.00; pap. $5.50. 322.42
1. Communism — U. S. — 1917. 2. Subversive Activities — U. S.

1229. Geismar, Peter. Fanon. Dial. 1971. $6.95. 322.42(B)
1. Fanon, Frantz, 1925-1961.

1230. Newton, Huey P. To Die for the People. Random. 1972. $7.95; pap. $1.95. 322.42
1. Black Panther Party.

300 SOCIAL SCIENCES

1231. Newton, Huey P. and Blake, Herman. Revolutionary Suicide. HarBraceJ. 1973. $8.95. 322.42(B)
1. Newton, Huey Percy, 1942-

1232. Parker, J. A. Angela Davis: The Making of a Revolutionary. Arlington Hse. 1973. $9.95. 322.42
1. Davis, Angela Yvonne, 1944-

1233. Sale, Kirkpatrick. SDS: Ten Years Toward a Revolution. Random. 1973. $15.00; pap. $3.45. 322.42
1. Radicalism. 2. Students for a Democratic Society — History.

1234. Bermann, Ernest G. Forerunners of Black Power: The Rhetoric of Abolition. P-H. 1971. $9.15; pap. $4.85. 322.44
1. Slavery in the U. S. — Anti-Slavery Movements.

1235. Kobler, John. Ardent Spirits: The Rise and Fall of Prohibition. Putnam. 1973. $8.95. 322.44
1. Prohibition — U. S. — History. 2. Prohibition Party. 3. Temperance — History.

1236. Meier, August and Rudwick, Elliott. CORE: A Story in the Civil Rights Movement, 1942-1968. Oxford U Pr. 1973. $15.00. 322.44
1. Negroes — Civil Rights. 2. Congress of Racial Equality.

1237. Rendon, Armando B. Chicano Manifesto. Macmillan. 1971. $7.95. 322.44
1. Mexican Americans. 2. Social Conflict.

1238. Sorin, Gerald. Abolitionism: A New Perspective. Praeger. 1972. $7.50. 322.44
1. Abolitionists. 2. Slavery in the U. S. — Anti-Slavery Movements.

323 State and Individual

1239. Ballinger, Margaret. From Union to Apartheid: A Trek to Isolation. Praeger. 1970. $12.50. 323.119
1. Africa, West — History — Sources. 2. Slave-Trade — Africa, West.

1240. Bond, Julian. A Time to Speak, a Time to Act. S&S. 1972. pap. $1.95. 323.119
1. Negroes — Politics and Suffrage. 2. Negroes — Civil Rights. 3. U. S. — Race Question.

1241. Draper, Theodore. The Rediscovery of Black Nationalism. Viking Pr. 1970. $5.95; pap. $2.45. 323.119
1. Negroes — Politics and Suffrage. 2. U. S. — Race Question.

1242. Schroeter, Leonard. The Last Exodus. Universe. 1974. $10.95. 323.119
1. Jews in Russia — Persecutions. 2. Jews in Russia — Political and Social Conditions — 1917-

1243. Wilson, Theodore B. Black Codes of the South. U of Ala Pr. 1966. $7.50. 323.119
1. Negroes — Legal Status, Laws, etc. 2. Negroes — Southern States.

1244. Kahn, Ely J. The Separated People: A Look at Contemporary South Africa. Norton. 1968. $6.95. 323.168
1. Africa, South — Race Question.

1245. Erikson, Erik H. Gandhi's Truth: On the Origins of Militant Nonviolence. Norton. 1969. $10.00; pap. $3.95. 323.2
1. Gandhi, Mohandas Karamchand, 1869-1948. 2. Passive Resistance.

1246. Guevara, Che. Episodes of the Revolutionary War. Intl Pub Co. 1968 (NW). pap. $1.65. 323.2
1. Guerrillas — Bolivia. 2. Subversive Activities — Bolivia.

1247. Harris, Richard. Death of a Revolutionary: The Last Days of Ché Guevara. Norton. 1970. $6.95. 323.2
1. Guerrillas — Bolivia. 2. Guevara, Ernesto (Ché), 1928-1967. 3. Subversive Activities — Bolivia.

1248. Headley, Joel Tyler. The Great Riots of New York, 1712-1873. Peter Smith. 1970. $5.00. 323.2
1. New York (City) — History. 2. Riots.

1249. Lasch, Christopher. The Agony of the American Left. Knopf. 1969. $5.95; pap. $1.95 (Random). 323.2
1. Right and Left (Political Science). 2. U. S. — Intellectual Life. 3. U. S. — Politics and Government.

1250. Lockwood, Lee. Conversations with Eldridge Cleaver. Dell. 1970. pap. $1.95. 323.2
1. Cleaver, Eldridge, 1935-

1251. Thoreau, Henry David. The Variorum Civil Disobedience. Harding, Walter, ed. Twayne. 1968. $4.50. 323.2
1. Government, Resistance to.

1252. Lynd, Staughton, ed. Nonviolence in America: A Documentary History. Bobbs. 1966. $7.50; pap. $3.45.   323.209
1. Passive Resistance to Government.

1253. Jacobs, Jane. Death and Life of Great American Cities. Modern Lib. 1969. $2.95; pap. $1.95 (Random).   323.35
1. Sociology, Urban.

323.4 Civil Rights

1254. Chafee, Zecharian, Jr., ed. Documents on Fundamental Human Rights: The Anglo-American Traditions. 2 vols. abr. ed. Atheneum. 1963. pap. $1.95 ea.   323.4
1. Civil Rights — Sources. 2. Civil Rights — U. S. — Sources.

1255. Fager, Charles E. Selma 1965. Scribner. 1974. $7.95.   323.4
1. Civil Rights — Selma, Ala. 2. Selma, Ala. — Race Question.

1256. Grant, Joanne, ed. Black Protest: History, Documents, and Analyses: 1619 to the Present. Fawcett World. 1972. pap. $1.50.   323.4
1. Negroes — Civil Rights — History — Sources.

1257. King, Coretta Scott. My Life with Martin Luther King, Jr. HR&W. 1969. $6.95; pap. $1.50 1970 (Avon).   323.4
1. King, Martin Luther, 1929-1968.

1258. Logan, Rayford W. The Betrayal of the Negro: From Rutherford B. Hayes to Woodrow Wilson. Macmillan. 1965. pap. $1.50.   323.4
1. Negroes — Civil Rights. 2. Negroes — History.

1259. Ianniello, Lynne, ed. Milestones Along the March: 12 Historic Civil Rights Documents from World War II to Selma. Praeger. 1965. $3.95.   323.408
1. Negroes — Civil Rights — Sources.

1260. Abraham, Henry J. Freedom and the Court: Civil Rights and Liberties in the United States. 2nd ed. Oxford U Pr. 1972. $12.50; pap. $3.95.   323.409
1. Civil Rights. 2. U. S. Supreme Court.

1261. Carmichael, Stokely and Hamilton, Charles V. Black Power: The Politics of Liberation in America. Random. 1967. $5.95; pap. $1.95.   323.409
1. Negroes — Civil Rights. 2. Negroes — Politics and Suffrage.

1262. Pallister, Anne. Magna Carta: The Heritage of Liberty. Oxford U Pr. 1971. $7.25.   323.44
1. Magna Carta.

1263. Small, William J. Political Power and the Press. Norton. 1972. $8.95.   323.445
1. Government and the Press — U. S.

1264. Miller, Arthur R. The Assault on Privacy: Computers, Data Banks, and Dossiers. NAL. 1971. pap. $1.50.   323.49
1. Information Storage and Retrieval Systems. 2. Privacy, Right of — U. S.

324 Suffrage

1265. Peirce, Neal R. The People's President: The Electoral College in American History and the Direct-Vote Alternative. S&S. 1968. pap. $2.95.   324.21
1. Presidents — U. S. — Election.

1266. Wilmerding, Lucius, Jr. Electoral College. Rutgers U Pr. 1958. $7.50.   324.21
1. Presidents — U. S. — Election.

1267. Catt, Carrie C. and Shuler, Nettie R. Woman Suffrage and Politics: The Inner Story of the Suffrage Movement. U of Wash Pr. 1970. $10.50; pap. $3.95.   324.3
1. Woman — Suffrage — U. S.

1268. Flexner, Eleanor. Century of Struggle: The Woman's Rights Movement in the United States. rev. ed. Harvard U Pr. 1975. $15.00.   324.3
1. Woman — Suffrage — U. S.

1269. Scammon, Richard M. and Wattenburg, Ben J. The Real Majority: How the Silent Center of the American Electorate Chooses Its President. Coward. 1970. $7.95; pap. $2.95.   324.73
1. Elections — U. S. 2. Public Opinion — U.S.

300 SOCIAL SCIENCES

325 Emigration

1270. Aptheker, Herbert, ed. A Documentary History of the Negro People in the United States. 3 vols. Citadel Pr. Vol. 1. 1962. $15.00; pap. $4.95; Vol. 2. 1964. $17.50; pap. $4.95; Vol. 3. 1974. $17.50. 325.26
1. Negroes — History.

1271. Franklin, John H. From Slavery to Freedom: A History of American Negroes. 4th ed. Knopf. 1974. $13.95; pap. $6.95. 325.26
1. Negroes — History. 2. Slavery in the U. S. — History.

1272. Myrdal, Gunnar. An American Dilemma. rev. ed. Har-Row. 1962. $20.00; pap. $4.95 ea. 1975. 2 vols (Pantheon). 325.26
1. Negroes.

1273. Redding, J. Saunders. The Lonesome Road: The Story of the Negro's Part in America. Doubleday. 1958. $6.95. 325.26
1. Negroes. 2. Negroes — Biography. 3. U. S. — Race Question.

1274. Weaver, Robert C. Negro Ghetto. Russell. Repr. 1948. $16.00. 325.26
1. Negroes — Housing. 2. Negroes — Segregation.

1275. Woodward, C. Vann. The Strange Career of Jim Crow. 3rd rev. ed. Oxford U Pr. 1974. $8.95; pap. $2.50. 325.26
1. Negroes — Segregation.

1276. Kavenagh, W. Keith. Foundations of Colonial America: A Documentary History. 3 vols. HR&W. 1972. $95.00. 325.34
1. U. S. — Politics and Government — Colonial Period — Sources.

1277. Handlin, Oscar. Children of the Uprooted. Braziller. 1966. $8.50; pap. $3.45 (G&D). 325.73
1. U. S. — Foreign Population.

1278. ———. Immigration As a Factor in American History. Peter Smith. 1959. $4.95; pap. $1.95 (P-H). 325.73
1. U. S. — Emigration and Immigration.

1279. ———. The Uprooted. 2nd enl. ed. Little. 1973. $8.95; pap. $3.95. 325.73
1. Acculturation. 2. U. S. — Foreign Population.

1280. Riis, Jacob August. The Making of an American. Macmillan. 1970. $6.95. 325.73(B)
1. Riis, Jacob August, 1849-1914. 2. U. S. — Emigration and Immigration.

326 Slavery and Emancipation

1281. Barnes, Gilbert H. Anti-Slavery Impulse, 1830-1844. Peter Smith. 1957. $5.00; pap. $2.65 (HarBraceJ). 326.0973
1. Slavery in the U. S. — Anti-Slavery Movements.

1282. Dumond, Dwight L. Antislavery: The Crusade for Freedom in America. U of Mich Pr. 1961. $20.00; pap. $2.25 (Norton). 326.0973
1. Slavery in the U. S. — Anti-Slavery Movements.

1283. Elkins, Stanley M. Slavery: A Problem in American Institutional and Intellectual Life. 2nd ed. U of Chicago Pr. 1968. $7.50; pap. $2.45. 326.0973
1. Negroes — Moral and Social Conditions. 2. Slavery in the U. S.

1284. Filler, Louis. Crusade Against Slavery, 1830-1860. Har-Row. 1960. $8.95; pap. $2.45. 326.0973
1. Slavery in the U. S. — Anti-Slavery Movements.

1285. Helper, Hinton R. Impending Crisis of the South: And How to Meet It. Frederickson, George, ed. Harvard U Pr. Repr. of 1857 ed. 1968. $15.00. 326.0973
1. Slavery in the U. S. 2. Slavery in the U. S. — Controversial Literature — 1857.

1286. McKitrick, Eric L., ed. Slavery Defended: The Views of the Old South. Peter Smith. $4.95; pap. $1.95 (P-H). 326.0973
1. Slavery in the U. S. — Controversial Literature. 2. Slavery in the U. S. — Southern States.

1287. Phillips, Ulrich B. American Negro Slavery: A Survey of the Supply, Employment, and Control of Negro Labor As Determined by the Plantation Regime. Peter Smith. 1966. $6.00; pap. $2.95 (La State U Pr). 326.0973
1. Negroes — History. 2. Slavery in the U. S.

1288. Weinstein, Allen and Gatell, Otto, eds. American Negro Slavery: A Modern Reader. 2nd ed. Oxford U Pr. 1973. $9.50; pap. $2.95. 326.0973
1. Slavery in the U. S. — History.

1289. Hume, John. The Abolitionists, Together with Personal Memories of the Struggle for Human Rights, 1830-1964. Negro U Pr. Repr. of 1897 ed. 1975. $9.50. 326.099

300 SOCIAL SCIENCES

1. Abolitionists. 2. Slavery in the U. S. — Anti-Slavery Movements.

1290. Douglass, Frederick. Narrative of the Life of Frederick Douglass, an American Slave, Written by Himself. Quarles, Benjamin, ed. Harvard U Pr. 1960. $5.00; pap. $1.95.
326.92
1. Douglass, Frederick, 1817-1895. 2. Slavery in the U. S.

1291. Quarles, Benjamin. Black Abolitionists. Oxford U Pr. $9.50; pap. $1.95. 326.92
1. Abolitionists. 2. Negroes — History.

1292. Washington, Booker T. Up from Slavery. Doubleday. 1933. $5.50. 326.92
1. Negroes — Biography. 2. Washington, Booker Taliaferro, 1859-1915.

327 International Relations

1293. Brodie, Bernard. War and Politics. Macmillan. 1973. $8.95. 327
1. International Relations. 2. U. S. — Military Policy. 3. War.

1294. Reischauer, Edwin O. Toward the Twenty-First Century: Education for a Changing World. Knopf. 1973. $5.95. 327
1. International Relations.

1295. Marchetti, Victor and Marks, John D. The CIA and the Cult of Intelligence. Knopf. 1974. $8.95. 327.12
1. U. S. Central Intelligence Agency.

1296. Ransom, Harry H. The Intelligence Establishment. rev. & enl. ed. Harvard U Pr. 1970. $10.95. 327.12
1. Intelligence Service — U. S. 2. U. S. Central Intelligence Agency. 3. U. S. — Military Policy.

1297. Sorenson, Thomas C. The World War: The Story of American Propaganda. Har-Row. 1968. $8.95. 327.14
1. Propaganda, American. 2. U. S. — Relations (General) with Foreign Countries.

1298. U. S. Arms Control and Disarmament Agency. Arms Control and Disarmament Agreements, 1959-1972. US Govt Ptg Off. 1972. pap. $0.60. 327.17
1. Disarmament. 2. U. S. — Foreign Relations — Treaties.

1299. Chatfield, Charles. For Peace and Justice: Pacificism in America. U of Tenn Pr. 1971. $11.95. 327.172
1. Pacifism — History.

1300. Newhouse, John. Cold Dawn: The Story of SALT. HR&W. 1973. $7.95. 327.174
1. Atomic Weapons and Disarmament. 2. Strategic Arms Limitation Talks.

1301. Galbraith, John Kenneth. Ambassador's Journal: A Personal Account of the Kennedy Years. HM. 1969. $10.00.
327.209
1. India — Relations (General) with the U. S. 2. U. S. — Relations (General) with India.

327.4 Foreign Relations - European Countries

1302. Bourne, Kenneth. The Foreign Policy of Victorian England, 1830-1902. Oxford U Pr. 1970. $14.50; pap. $7.25. 327.42
1. Great Britain — Foreign Relations — 1837-1901. 2. Great Britain — History — Victoria, 1837-1901 — Sources.

1303. Williamson, Samuel R. The Politics of Grand Strategy: Britain and France Prepare for War, 1904-1914. Harvard U Pr. 1969. $15.00. 327.42
1. European War, 1914-1918 — Causes. 2. France — Foreign Relations — Great Britain. 3. Great Britain — Foreign Relations — France.

1304. Compton, James V. The Swastika and the Eagle: Hitler, the United States and the Origins of World War II. HM. 1967. $6.95.
327.43
1. Germany — Foreign Relations — U. S. 2. Hitler, Adolf, 1889-1945. 3. Japan — Foreign Relations — 1912-1945. 4. U. S. — Foreign Relations — Germany. 5. World War, 1939-1945 — Causes.

1305. Weinberg, Gerhard L. The Foreign Policy of Hitler's Germany: 1933-1936. U of Chicago Pr. 1971. $12.75. 327.43
1. Germany — Foreign Relations — 1933-1945.

1306. Beloff, Max. Foreign Policy of Soviet Russia, 1929-1941. 2 vols. Oxford U Pr. 1947-1949. $9.75 ea. 327.47
1. Russia — Foreign Relations — 1917-1945.

1307. Clubb, Oliver E. China and Russia: The "Great Game". Columbia U Pr. 1971. $15.00; pap. $3.95. 327.47

300 SOCIAL SCIENCES

1. China — Foreign Relations — Russia. 2. Russia — Foreign Relations — China.

1308. Fischer, Louis. Russia's Road from Peace to War: Soviet Foreign Relations, 1917-1941. Har-Row. 1969. $12.50. 327.47
1. Russia — Foreign Relations — 1917-1945.

1309. Kennan, George F. Russia and the West Under Lenin and Stalin. Little. 1961. $8.50; pap. $1.50 (NAL). 327.47
1. Russia — Foreign Relations — 1917-1945.

1310. LaFeber, Walter. America, Russia, and the Cold War, 1945-1971. 2nd ed. Wiley. 1972. pap. $4.00. 327.47
1. Psychological Warfare. 2. Russia — Foreign Relations — U. S. 3. U. S. — Foreign Relations — Russia.

1311. Rapoport, Anatol. The Big Two: Soviet-American Perceptions of Foreign Policy. Pegasus. 1971. $6.95; pap. $2.95. 327.47
1. Russia — Foreign Relations — U. S. 2. U. S. — Foreign Relations — Russia.

1312. Ulam, Adam B. Expansion and Coexistence: History of Soviet Foreign Policy, 1917-1967. Praeger. 1968. $15.00; pap. $4.95. 327.47
1. Russia — Foreign Relations — 1917-1945. 2. Russia — Foreign Relations — 1945-

1313. Welch, William. American Images of Soviet Foreign Policy: An Inquiry into Recent Appraisals from the Academic Community. Yale U Pr. 1970. $12.50. 327.47
1. Russia — Foreign Opinion, American. 2. Russia — Foreign Relations — U. S. 3. U. S. — Foreign Relations — Russia.

327.5 Foreign Relations - Asia and Middle East

1314. Alexander, Garth. The Invisible China: The Overseas Chinese and the Politics of Southeast Asia. Macmillan. 1974. $7.95. 327.51
1. Asia, Southeastern — Foreign Relations — China (People's Republic of China, 1949-).
2. China (People's Republic of China, 1949-) Foreign Relations — Asia, Southeastern.
3. Chinese in Southeastern Asia.

1315. Fairbank, John K. The United States and China. 3rd ed. Harvard U Pr. 1971. $9.95; pap. $3.50. 327.51

1. China — Foreign Relations — U. S. 2. China — History. 3. U. S. — Foreign Relations — China.

1316. Gittings, John, ed. Survey of the Sino-Soviet Dispute: A Commentary and Extracts from the Recent Polemics, 1963-1967. Oxford U Pr. 1969. $14.25. 327.51
1. China (People's Republic of China, 1949-) — Foreign Relations — Russia. 2. Russia — Foreign Relations — China (People's Republic of China).

1317. Hibbert, Christopher. The Dragon Wakes: China and the West, 1793-1911. Har-Row. 1971. $10.00. 327.51
1. China — Foreign Relations.

1318. Lall, Arthur. How Communist China Negotiates. Columbia U Pr. 1968. $12.00; pap. $2.95. 327.51
1. China (People's Republic of China, 1949-) — Foreign Relations.

1319. Ojha, Ishwer C. Chinese Foreign Policy in an Age of Transition: The Diplomacy of Cultural Despair. Beacon Pr. 1969. $5.95; pap. $3.95. 327.51
1. China (People's Republic of China, 1949-) — Foreign Relations.

1320. Sulzberger, C. L. The Coldest War. HarBraceJ. 1974. $5.95. 327.51
1. China (People's Republic of China, 1949-) — Foreign Relations — Russia. 2. China (People's Republic of China, 1949-) — Politics and Government. 3. Russia — Foreign Relations — China (People's Republic of China, 1949-).

1321. Teng, Ssu-Yu. China's Response to the West: A Documentary Survey, 1839-1923. Harvard U Pr. 1954. $8.50; pap. $4.00. 327.51
1. China — Foreign Relations.

1322. Kimche, Jon. There Could Have Been Peace: The Untold Story of Why We Failed with Palestine and Again with Israel. Dial. 1973. $10.00. 327.56
1. Jewish-Arab Relations — History. 2. Near East — History.

1323. Laqueur, Walter, ed. The Israel-Arab Reader: A Documentary History of the Middle East Conquest. Bantam. 1970. pap. $1.65. 327.56
1. Israel — Foreign Relations. 2. Jewish-Arab Relations.

327.73 Foreign Relations - U. S.

1324. Acheson, Dean. Present at the Creation: My Years in the State Department. Norton. 1969. $12.50. 327.73
1. U. S. — Foreign Relations — 1933-1945. 2. U. S. — Foreign Relations — 1945-1953.

1325. Adler, Selig. The Uncertain Giant: 1921-1941: American Foreign Policy Between the Wars. Macmillan. 1966. $6.95; pap. $2.95. 327.73
1. U. S. — Foreign Relations — 20th Century.

1326. Allison, Graham T. Essence of Decision: Explaining the Cuban Missile Crisis. Little. 1971. pap. $4.95. 327.73
1. Cuba — History — 1959- 2. Military Bases, Russian — Cuba. 3. Russia — Foreign Relations — U. S. 4. U. S. — Foreign Relations — Russia.

1327. Aron, Raymond. The Imperial Republic: The United States and the World, 1945-1973. P-H. 1974. $10.00. 327.73
1. U. S. — Foreign Economic Relations. 2. U. S. — Foreign Relations — 1945-

1328. Bailey, Thomas A. Diplomatic History of the American People. 9th ed. P-H. 1974. $11.95. 327.73
1. U. S. — Foreign Relations.

1329. Bartlett, Ruhl J., ed. Record of American Diplomacy. 4th ed. Knopf. 1964. $9.95. 327.73
1. U. S. — Foreign Relations.

1330. Bemis, Samuel F., ed. The American Secretaries of State and Their Diplomacy, 1776-1925. 10 vols. in 5. Cooper Sq. Repr. 1928. $50.00. 327.73
1. Cabinet Office — U. S. 2. Statesmen, American. 3. U. S. — Foreign Relations.

1331. Bohlen, Charles E. Transformation of American Foreign Policy. Norton. 1969. $3.95; pap. $11.50. 327.73
1. U. S. — Foreign Relations.

1332. Craig, Gerald M. The United States and Canada. Harvard U Pr. 1968. $10.95. 327.73
1. Canada — Foreign Relations — U. S. 2. U. S. — Foreign Relations — Canada.

1333. Divine, Robert. The Cuban Missile Crisis. Watts. 1971. $8.95; pap. $2.65. 327.73
1. Military Bases, Russian — Cuba. 2. Russia — Foreign Relations — Cuba. 3. U. S. — Foreign Relations — Russia.

1334. Dulles, Foster R. American Policy Toward Communist China: The Historical Record, 1944-1969. AHM Pub. 1972. $7.95; pap. $5.75. 327.73
1. China (People's Republic of China, 1949-) — Foreign Relations — U. S. 2. U. S. — Foreign Relations — China (People's Republic of China, 1949-).

1335. ———. America's Rise to World Power: 1898-1954. Har-Row. 1955. $8.95; pap. $2.25. 327.73
1. U. S. — Foreign Relations.

1336. Freeland, Richard M. The Truman Doctrine and the Origins of McCarthyism: Foreign Policy, Domestic Politics, and Internal Security, 1946-1948. Knopf. 1972. $10.00. 327.73
1. Communism — U. S. — 1917- 2. Internal Security — U. S. 3. U. S. — Foreign Relations — 1945-1953. 4. U. S. — Politics and Government — 1945-1953.

1337. Fulbright, James W. The Arrogance of Power. Random. 1967. $5.95; pap. $1.95. 327.73
1. U. S. — Foreign Relations — 1945- 2. Vietnam — Politics and Government. 3. World Politics — 1945-

1338. ———. The Crippled Giant: American Foreign Policy and Its Domestic Consequences. Random. 1972. $6.95. 327.73
1. U. S. — Foreign Relations — 1945-

1339. Gaddis, John L. The United States and the Origins of the Cold War, 1941-1947. Columbia U Pr. 1972. $15.00; pap. $4.45. 327.73
1. U. S. — Foreign Realtions — 1933-1945. 2. U. S. — Foreign Relations — 1945-1953.

1340. Gellman, Irwin F. Roosevelt and Batista: Good Neighbor Diplomacy in Cuba, 1933-1945. U of NM Pr. 1973. $12.00. 327.73
1. Batista y Zaldivar, Fulgencio, Pres. Cuba, 1901-1973. 2. Cuba — Foreign Relations — U. S. 3. Cuba — Politics and Government — 1933-1959. 4. Roosevelt, Franklin Delano, President U. S., 1882-1945. 5. U. S. — Foreign Relations — Cuba.

300 SOCIAL SCIENCES

1341. Hilsman, Roger. To Move a Nation: The Politics of Foreign Policy in the Administration of John F. Kennedy. Dell. 1968. pap. $2.95. 327.73
1. Kennedy, John Fitzgerald, President U. S., 1917-1963. 2. U. S. — Foreign Relations — 1961-1963.

1342. Hughes, H. Stuart. United States and Italy. rev. ed. Harvard U Pr. 1965. $8.50; pap. $2.45 (Norton). 327.73
1. Italy — Foreign Relations — U. S. 2. U. S. — Foreign Relations — Italy.

1343. Kennan, George F. Memoirs, 1925-1963. Little. 1972. $12.50. 327.73
1. Diplomats — Correspondence, Reminiscences, etc. 2. Kennan, George, 1904- 3. U. S. — Foreign Relations — Sources.

1344. ———. Realities of American Foreign Policy. Norton. 1966. pap. $1.25. 327.73
1. U. S. — Foreign Relations.

1345. Kissinger, Henry A. American Foreign Policy: Three Essays. Norton. 1969. $3.95; pap. $1.25. 327.73
1. U. S. — Foreign Relations.

1346. Langer, William L. and Gleason, S. E. Challenge to Isolation. 2 vols. Peter Smith. 1952. $11.00. 327.73
1. U. S. — Foreign Relations — 1933-1945. 2. World War, 1939-1945 — Diplomatic History. 3. World War, 1939-1945 — U. S.

1347. Langley, Lester D. The Cuban Policy of the United States: A Brief History. Wiley. 1968. $9.25; pap. $4.95. 327.73
1. Cuba — Foreign Relations — U. S. 2. U. S. — Foreign Relations — Cuba.

1348. Liss, Sheldon B. Canal: Aspects of United States - Panamanian Relations. U of Notre Dame Pr. 1967. pap. $2.25. 327.73
1. Panama — Foreign Relations — U. S. 2. U. S. — Foreign Relations — Panama.

1349. Lycan, Gilbert L. Alexander Hamilton and American Foreign Policy: A Design for Greatness. U of Okla Pr. 1970. $9.95. 327.73
1. Hamilton, Alexander, 1757-1804. 2. U. S. — Foreign Relations — Constitutional Period, 1789-1809.

1350. McColley, Robert. Federalists, Republicans, and Foreign Entanglements, 1789-1815. Irvington. 1969. $5.95. 327.73
1. U. S. — Politics and Government — Constitutional Period, 1789-1809.

1351. Perkins, Dexter. American Approach to Foreign Policy. rev. ed. Harvard U Pr. 1962. $7.00; pap. $2.95 (Atheneum). 327.73
1. U. S. — Foreign Relations.

1352. ———. History of the Monroe Doctrine. rev. ed. Little. 1955. $6.95; pap. $2.95. 327.73
1. Monroe Doctrine.

1353. Reischauer, Edwin O. The United States and Japan. 3rd ed. Harvard U Pr. 1965. $12.50. 327.73
1. Japan — Foreign Relations — U. S. 2. U. S. — Foreign Relations — Japan.

1354. Schlesinger, Arthur M, Jr. The Bitter Heritage: Vietnam and American Democracy, 1941-1966. rev. ed. Fawcett World. 1972. pap. $0.95. 327.73
1. U. S. — Foreign Relations — Vietnam. 2. U. S. — Politics and Government — 1963- 3. Vietnam — History.

1355. Young, Kenneth T. Negotiating with the Chinese Communists: The United States Experience, 1953-1967. McGraw. 1968. $10.95; pap. $3.95. 327.73
1. China (People's Republic of China, 1949-) — Foreign Relations — U. S. 2. U. S. — Foreign Relations — China (People's Republic of China, 1949-).

328 Legislation

1356. Robert, Henry M. Robert's Rules of Order. rev. ed. Scott F. 1970. $7.50. 328.1
1. Parliamentary Practice.

1357. Sturgis, Alice F. Learning Parliamentary Procedure. McGraw. 1953. $7.95. 328.1
1. Parliamentary Practice.

1358. ———. Sturgis' Standard Code of Parliamentary Procedure. 2nd ed. McGraw. 1966. $4.95. 328.1
1. Parliamentary Practice.

1359. Jennings, Ivor. Parliament. Cambridge U Pr. 1969. $17.50; pap. $6.95. 328.42
1. Great Britain — Parliament. 2. Great Britain — Politics and Government.

328.7 Legislative Branch of Government

1360. Chisholm, Shirley. Unbought and Unbossed. HM. 1970. $5.95. 328.73
1. U. S. — Politics and Government — 1969-

300 SOCIAL SCIENCES

1361. Galloway, George B. History of the House of Representatives. T Y Crowell. 1962. $8.95. 328.73
1. U. S. Congress — House.

1362. Goodman, Walter. The Committee: The Extraordinary Career of the House Committee on Un-American Activities. FS&G. 1968. $15.00. 328.73
1. U. S. Congress — House Committee on Un-American Activities.

1363. Grayson, Cary R. and Lukowski, Susan, eds. The Impeachment Congress: The 93rd Congress. Potomac. 1974. $18.50; pap. $2.50. 328.73
1. U. S. Congress — Decisions. 2. U. S. Congress — Registers.

1364. Griffith, Ernest S. Congress: Its Contemporary Role. 5th ed. NYU Pr. 1975. $10.00; pap. $5.95. 328.73
1. U. S. Congress.

1365. Kennedy, John F. Profiles in Courage. Har-Row. 1961. PLB $3.79; pap. $0.95. 328.73(B)
1. Courage. 2. U. S. Congress — Senate — Biography.

1366. Morrow, William L. Congressional Committees. Scribner. 1969. pap. $3.50. 328.73
1. U. S. Congress — Committees.

1367. Polsby, Nelson W., ed. Congressional Behavior. Random. 1970. pap. $4.25. 328.73
1. U. S. Congress.

1368. Ripley, Randall. Majority Party Leadership in Congress. Little. 1969. $6.95. 328.73
1. Executive Power — U. S. 2. U. S. Congress.

1369. Smith, Duane A. Horace Tabor: His Life and the Legend. Colo Assoc. 1973. $12.50. 328.73(B)
1. Tabor, Horace Austin Warner, 1830-1899.

Recommended Series

1370. Praeger Library of U. S. Government Departments and Agencies. Praeger.

329 Political Parties

1371. Brogan, Denis W. Politics in America. Har-Row. pap. $3.95. 329
1. Politics, Practical. 2. U. S. — Politics and Government — 20th Century.

1372. Zink, Harold. City Bosses in the United States. AMS Pr. 1930. $12.50. 329
1. Corruption (in Politics). 2. Municipal Government — U. S. 3. Politics, Practical.

1373. Horn, Stanley F. Invisible Empire: Story of the Ku Klux Klan, 1866-1871. Assoc Bk. 1969. $9.95. 329.006
1. Ku Klux Klan.

1374. Jackson, Kenneth T. The Ku Klux Klan in the City, 1915-1930. Oxford U Pr. 1967. $8.95. 329.006
1. Ku Klux Klan (1915-).

1375. Banner, James M., Jr. To the Hartford Convention: The Federalists and the Origins of Party Politics in Massachusetts, 1789-1815. Knopf. 1970. $8.95. 329.009
1. Hartford Convention, 1814. 2. Massachusetts — Politics and Government.

1376. Reedy, George E. The Presidency in Flux. Columbia U Pr. 1973. $5.95. 329.009
1. Presidents — U. S.

1377. Schlesinger, Arthur M., Jr. History of U. S. Political Parties. 4 vols. Bowker. 1973. $135.00. 329.02
1. Political Parties — U. S. — History.

1378. Mushkat, Jerome. Tammany: The Evolution of a Political Machine, 1789-1865. Syracuse U Pr. 1971. $15.00. 329.021
1. New York (City) — Politics and Government — to 1898. 2. Tammany Hall.

1379. Matthews, Donald R., ed. Perspectives on Presidential Selection. Brookings. 1973. $6.95. 329.022
1. Presidents — U. S. — Election.

1380. Dougherty, Richard. Goodbye Mr. Christian: A Personal Account of McGovern's Rise and Fall. Doubleday. 1973. $7.95. 329.023
1. McGovern, George Stanley, 1922- 2. Presidents — U. S. — Election — 1972.

1381. Polakoff, Keith I. The Politics of Inertia: The Election of 1876 and the End of Reconstruction. La State U Pr. 1973. $10.95. 329.023
1. Presidents — U. S. — Election — 1876. 2. Reconstruction.

300 SOCIAL SCIENCES

1382. Roseboom, Eugene H. A History of Presidential Elections. 3rd ed. Macmillan. 1970. $10.00. 329.023
1. Presidents — U. S. — Election. 2. U. S. — Politics and Government.

1383. Tugwell, Rexford G. Brains Trust. Viking Pr. 1968. pap. $3.25. 329.023
1. Presidents — U. S. — Election — 1932. 2. Roosevelt, Franklin Delano, President U. S., 1882-1945.

1384. Warren, Sidney. Battle for the Presidency. Lippincott. 1968. $7.95. 329.023
1. Presidents — U. S. — Election — History. 2. U. S. — Politics and Government.

1385. White, Theodore H. The Making of the President, 1972. Atheneum. 1973. $10.00. 329.023
1. Presidents — U. S. — Election — 1972.

1386. Thayer, George. Who Shakes the Money Tree? American Campaign Financing Practices from 1789 to the Present. S&S. 1974. pap. $2.95. 329.025
1. Elections — U. S. — Campaign Funds. 2. Elections — U. S. — Campaign Funds — History.

1387. Binkley, Wilfred E. American Political Parties. 4th rev. ed. Knopf. 1963. $10.00. 329.1
1. Political Parties. 2. U. S. — Politics and Government.

1388. Morgan, H. Wayne. From Hayes to McKinley: National Party Politics, 1877-1896. Syracuse U Pr. 1969. $12.95. 329.1
1. Political Parties. 2. U. S. — Politics and Government — 1865-1898.

1389. Cunningham, Noble E., Jr. The Jeffersonian Republicans: The Formation of Party Organization, 1789-1801. U of NC Pr. 1957. $7.50; pap. $2.95. 329.3
1. Democratic Party — History. 2. Political Parties — U. S. — History. 3. U. S. — Politics and Government — Constitutional Period, 1789-1809.

1390. Davis, Lanny J. The Emerging Democratic Majority: Lessons and Legacies from the New Politics. Stein & Day. 1974. $8.95. 329.3
1. Democratic Party. 2. U. S. — Politics and Government — 1963-1969. 3. U. S. — Politics and Government — 1969-

1391. Kent, Frank R. Democratic Party: A History. Johnson Repr. 1968. $23.00. 329.3
1. Democratic Party — History.

1392. Hess, Stephen and Broder, David. The Republican Establishment: The Present and Future of the G.O.P. Har-Row. 1967. $7.95. 329.6
1. Republican Party.

1393. Shannon, David A. Socialist Party of America: A History. Quadrangle. 1967. pap. $2.95. 329.81
1. Political Parties — U. S. 2. Socialist Party.

1394. Hicks, John D. The Populist Revolt: A History of the Farmer's Alliance and the People's Party. U of Nebr Pr. 1961. pap. $2.75. 329.88
1. Agriculture — U. S. — Economic Aspects. 2. Farmer's Alliance. 3. Populist Party.

1395. Bracher, Karl D. The German Dictatorship: The Origins, Structure and Effects of National Socialism. Praeger. 1970. $13.95; pap. $5.95. 329.943
1. Anti-Nazi Movement. 2. Germany — Politics and Government — 1933-1945. 3. National Socialism — History.

1396. Schapiro, Leonard. The Communist Party of the Soviet Union. rev. ed. Random. 1971. $15.00; pap. $3.45. 329.947
1. Communist Party (Russia).

1397. Kousoulas, D. George. Revolution and Defeat: The Story of the Greek Communist Party. Oxford U Pr. 1965. $8.50. 329.9495
1. Communist Party (Greece). 2. Greece, Modern — History — 1944-1949.

1398. Lewis, John W., ed. Party Leadership and Revolutionary Power in China. Cambridge U Pr. 1970. $15.00; pap. $3.95. 329.951
1. China (People's Republic of China, 1949-) — Politics and Government — Congresses. 2. Communist Party (China) — Congresses.

1399. Walton, Hanes, Jr. Black Political Parties: An Historical and Political Analysis. Free Pr. 1972. $7.95. 329.973
1. Negroes — Politics and Suffrage. 2. U. S. — Politics and Government.

330 Economics

1400. Moore, Basil J. An Introduction to

Modern Economic Theory. Free Pr. 1973. $10.95. 330
1. Economics.

1401. Robinson, Joan and Eatwell, John. An Introduction to Modern Economics. McGraw. 1974. $11.50; pap. $7.95. 330
1. Comparative Economics. 2. Economic Policy. 3. Economics.

1402. Samuelson, Paul A., ed. Readings in Economics. 7th ed. McGraw. 1973. $7.95; pap. $5.95. 330
1. Economics — Collections.

1403. Smith, Adam. Wealth of Nations. Modern Lib. $4.95. 330
1. Economics.

1404. Veblen, Thorstein. Theory of the Leisure Class. HM. 1973. $6.95; pap. $1.25 (NAL). 330
1. Economics.

1405. Heilbroner, Robert. Worldly Philosophers. rev. ed. S&S. 1972. $7.95; pap. $2.45. 330.09
1. Economics — History.

1406. Napoleoni, Claudio. Economic Thought of the Twentieth Century. Wiley. 1973. $5.95. 330.09
1. Economics — History — 20th Century.

1407. Bell, Daniel and Kristol, Irving, eds. Capitalism Today. Basic. 1971. $6.95. 330.12
1. Capitalism. 2. Economic History — 1945-

1408. Sweezy, Paul. Modern Capitalism and Other Essays. Monthly Rev. 1972. $5.95; pap. $1.95. 330.12
1. Capitalism. 2. Marxian Economics.

1409. Galbraith, John Kenneth. The New Industrial State. 2nd rev. ed. HM. 1971. $8.95; pap. $3.25. 330.9
1. Industry and State — U. S. 2. U. S. — Industries.

1410. Beard, Charles A. The Industrial Revolution. Greenwood. 1927. $9.25. 330.942
1. Great Britain — Economic Conditions — 1760-1860.

1411. Marshall, Dorothy. Industrial England, 1776-1851. Scribner. 1973. $8.95. 330.942

1. Great Britain — Economic Conditions — 1760-1860. 2. Great Britain — Social Conditions. 3. Social Classes — Great Britain.

1412. George, Pierre. France: A Geographical Study. B&N. 1973. $12.75. 330.944
1. France — Economic Conditions — 1945-

1413. Cole, David C., et al. Korean Development: The Interplay of Politics and Economics. Harvard U Pr. 1971. $12.00. 330.951
1. Korea — Economic Conditions — 1945- 2. Korea — Politics and Government — 1960-

1414. Myrdal, Gunnar. Asian Drama: An Inquiry into the Poverty of Nations. 3 vols. Pantheon. 1968. Set. $30.00; Set. pap. $10.00. 330.954
1. Asia, Southeastern — Economic Conditions. 2. South Asia — Economic Conditions.

1415. Uppal, J. S. and Salkever, Louis K., eds. Africa: Problems in Economic Development. Free Pr. 1972. $11.95. 330.96
1. Africa — Economic Conditions. 2. Africa — Economic Policy.

330.97 U. S. - Economic Conditions

1416. Faulkner, Harold U. American Economic History. 8th ed. Har-Row. 1960. $13.95. 330.973
1. U. S. — Economic Conditions.

1417. Galbraith, John Kenneth. The Affluent Society. 2nd ed. HM. 1969. $6.95; pap. $1.25 (NAL). 330.973
1. Economics. 2. Economics — History — U. S.

1418. Hacker, Louis M. The Course of American Economic Growth and Development. Wiley. 1970. pap. $6.50. 330.973
1. U. S. — Economic Conditions.

1419. ———. Major Documents in American Economic History. 2 vols. Van Nos Reinhold. 1961. pap. $2.95 ea. 330.973
1. U. S. — Economic Conditions.

1420. Haddad, William F. and Pugh, G. Douglas, eds. Black Economic Development. P-H. 1969. pap. $1.95. 330.973
1. Negroes — Economic Conditions. 2. Negroes — Employment.

300 SOCIAL SCIENCES

1421. Hays, Samuel P. Response to Industrialism: 1885-1914. U of Chicago Pr. 1957. $7.00; pap. $2.45. 330.973
1. U. S. — Economic Conditions.

1422. Heilbroner, Robert L. The Limits of American Capitalism. Har-Row. 1966. $5.95; pap. $1.25. 330.973
1. Capitalism. 2. U. S. — Economic Conditions.

1423. Lapp, Ralph E. The Logarithmic Century. P-H. 1973. $7.95. 330.973
1. Consumption (Economics) — U. S. 2. Economic Development. 3. Technology — Social Aspects. 4. U. S. — Economic Conditions — 1971-

1424. Phillips, Ulrich B. Slave Economy of the Old South. Genovese, Eugene D., ed. La State U Pr. 1968. pap. $2.95. 330.975
1. Plantation Life — Southern States. 2. Slavery in the U. S. 3. Southern States — Economic Conditions. 4. Southern States — Social Conditions.

1425. Russel, Robert R. Economic Aspects of Southern Sectionalism, 1840-1861. Arno. 1923. $16.00. 330.975
1. Southern States — Economic Conditions.

1426. Schwab, John C. The Confederate States of America: A Financial and Industrial History of the South During the Civil War. B Franklin. 1901. $8.95. 330.975
1. Confederate States of America. 2. Finance — Confederate States of America. 3. Southern States — Industries.

Recommended Series

1427. Studies in Economics. Novack, David E., gen. ed.. Heath.

331 Labor Economics

1428. Cahn, William. A Pictorial History of American Labor. Crown. 1972. $12.50. 331.1
1. Labor and Laboring Classes — U. S. — History.

1429. Dubofsky, Melvyn, ed. American Labor Since the New Deal. Watts. 1971. pap. $2.95. 331.1
1. Labor and Laboring Classes — U. S. — 1933- 2. Trade Unions — U. S.

1430. Dunnette, Marvin D. Work and Nonwork in the Year 2001. Brooks-Cole. 1973. pap. $5.95. 331.1
1. Employment Forecasting — U. S. 2. Manpower Policy — U. S. 3. Personnel Management — U. S.

1431. Fogel, Robert W. and Engerman, Stanley L. Time on the Cross: The Economics of American Negro Slavery. 2 vols. Little. 1974. Vol. 1. $8.95; pap $4.95; Vol. 2. $12.50; pap. $6.95. 331.1
1. Slavery in the U. S. — Economic Aspects.

1432. Mosse, Claude. The Ancient World at Work. Lloyd, Janet, tr. Norton. 1970. $5.00; pap. $2.45. 331.19
1. Labor and Laboring Classes — Greece. 2. Labor and Laboring Classes — Rome.

1433. Sheppard, Harold L. and Herrick, N. Q. Where Have All the Robots Gone? Worker Dissatisfaction in the Seventies. Free Pr. 1972. $7.95; pap. $3.95. 331.2
1. Industrial Relations. 2. Labor and Laboring Classes.

1434. Terkel, Studs. Working: People Talk About What They Do All Day and How They Feel About What They Do. Pantheon. 1974. $10.00. 331.2
1. Labor and Laboring Classes — U. S. — 1970- — Interviews.

1435. Vecsey, George. One Sunset a Week: The Story of a Coalminer. Sat Rev Pr. 1974. $7.95. 331.762
1. Coal-Miners — West Virginia.

1436. Bimba, Anthony. History of the American Working Class. 3rd ed. Greenwood. 1936. $17.50. 331.819
1. Labor and Laboring Classes — U. S. — History.

1437. ———. The Molly Maguires. Intl Pub Co. 1970. $4.95; pap. $1.65. 331.88
1. Coal Miners — Pennsylvania. 2. Molly Maguires.

1438. Dubofsky, Melvyn. We Shall Be All: A History of the Industrial Workers of the World. Quadrangle. 1969. $12.50. 331.88
1. Industrial Workers of the World.

1439. Dulles, Foster R. Labor in America: A History. 3rd ed. T Y Crowell. 1966. $6.95; pap. $5.95. 331.88
1. Labor and Laboring Classes — U. S. — History. 2. Trade Unions — U. S. — History.

300 SOCIAL SCIENCES

1440. Finely, Joseph E. The Corrupt Kingdom: The Rise and Fall of the United Mine Workers. S&S. 1972. $8.95.   331.88
1. United Mine Workers of America — History.

1441. Hutchinson, John. The Imperfect Union: A History in Corruption in American Trade Unions. Dutton. 1972. $12.50; pap. $3.95.   331.88
1. Extortion — U. S. — History. 2. Racketeering — U. S. — History. 3. Trade-Unions — U. S. — History.

1442. Larrowe, Charles P. Harry Bridges: The Rise and Fall of Radical Labor in the U. S. Hill & Wang. 1972. $8.95.   331.88
1. Bridges, Harry Renton, 1900- 2. Labor and Laboring Classes — U. S. — 1914- 3. Trade-Unions — Longshoremen — U. S.

1443. Lens, Sidney. The Labor Wars: From the Molly Maguires to the Sitdowns. Doubleday. 1973. $9.95; pap. $2.95.   331.88
1. Labor and Laboring Classes — U. S. 2. Labor Unions — History.

1444. London, Joan and Anderson, Henry. So Shall Ye Reap: The Grape Strike. Apollo Eds. 1971. pap. $2.45.   331.88
1. Chavez, Cesar Estrada, 1927- 2. Trade-Unions — Agricultural Laborers — California — History.

1445. Renshaw, Patrick. The Wobblies: The Story of Syndicalism in the United States. Doubleday. 1967. $5.95; pap. $1.45.   331.88
1. Industrial Workers of the World.

1446. Sherican, Walter. The Fall and Rise of Jimmy Hoffa. Sat Rev Pr. 1972. $10.95.   331.88
1. Hoffa, James Riddle, 1913- 2. International Brotherhood of Teamsters, Chauffeurs, Warehousemen and Helpers of America.

1447. Taft, Philip. The A. F. of L. in the Time of Gompers. Octagon. 1957. $17.00.   331.88
1. American Federation of Labor.

1448. Matthiessen, Peter. Sal Si Puedes: Cesar Chavez and the New American Revolution. Random. 1969. $7.95; pap. $1.50 (Dell).   331.89
1. Chavez, Cesar Estrada, 1927- 2. Strikes and Lockouts. 3. United Farm Workers Organization Committee.

332 Financial Institutions

1449. Allen, Frederick L. Lords of Creation. Quadrangle. 1966. pap. $2.95.   332.09
1. Capitalists and Financiers — U. S. 2. Corporations — U. S. 3. Finance — U. S. — History. 4. Wall Street.

1450. Cowles, Virginia. The Rothschilds: Family of Fortune. Knopf. 1973. $17.50.   332.092
1. Rothschild Family.

1451. Fischer, Gerald C. American Banking Structure. Columbia U Pr. 1968. $15.00.   332.1
1. Banks and Banking — U. S.

1452. Hammond, Bray. Banks and Politics in America: From the Revolution to the Civil War. Princeton U Pr. 1957. $17.50; pap. $4.95.   332.1
1. Banks and Banking — U. S.

1453. Redlich, Fritz. Molding of American Banking: Men and Ideas. Johnson Repr. 1951. $49.00.   332.1
1. Banks and Banking — U. S.

1454. Prochnow, Herbert V. Federal Reserve System. Har-Row. 1960. $5.75.   332.4
1. Banks and Banking — U. S.

1455. Friedman, Irving S. Inflation: A World-Wide Disaster. HM. 1973. $8.95; pap. $2.50 (Doubleday).   332.41
1. Inflation (Finance).

1456. Becker, Thomas. The Coin Makers. Doubleday. 1969. $6.95.   332.46
1. Coinage — History.

1457. Krow, Harvey. Stock Market Behavior: The Technical Approach to Understanding Wall Street. Random. 1969. $10.00.   332.6
1. Stock Exchange. 2. Wall Street.

1458. Shannon, David A., ed. The Great Depression. Peter Smith. 1960. $4.95; pap. $1.95 (P-H).   332.6
1. Depressions — U. S. — 1929.

333.7-333.9 Conservation

1459. Fisher, James, et al. Wildlife in Danger. Viking Pr. 1969. $12.95.   333.7
1. Wildlife Conservation. 2. Zoology.

300 SOCIAL SCIENCES

1460. Fisher, John. Energy Crises in Perspective. Wiley. 1974. $9.95.   333.7
1. Power Resources.

1461. Freeman, S. David. Energy: The New Era. Walker & Co. 1974. $14.50; pap. $2.45 (Random).   333.7
1. Energy Conservation. 2. Energy Policy.

1462. Jones, Holway R. John Muir and the Sierra Club: The Battle for Yosemite. Sierra. 1964. $10.00.   333.7
1. Muir, John, 1838-1914. 2. Sierra Club, San Francisco. 3. Yosemite National Park.

1463. Marine, Gene. America the Raped: The Engineering Mentality and the Devastation of a Continent. Avon. 1969. pap. $1.25.   333.7
1. Conservation of Natural Resources.

1464. Nash, Roderick, compiled by. American Environment: Readings in the History of Conservation. A-W. 1968. $3.95.   333.7
1. Conservation of Natural Resources — U. S.

1465. Richardson, Elmo. Dams, Parks and Politics: Resource Development and Preservation in the Truman - Eisenhower Era. U Pr of Ky. 1973. $11.25.   333.7
1. Environmental Policy — U. S. 2. Natural Resources — U. S.

1466. Dorst, Jean. Before Nature Dies. HM. 1970. $8.95.   333.72
1. Conservation of Natural Resources. 2. Man — Influence on Nature.

1467. Mossman, Archie. Conservation. Intext. 1974. $8.50; pap. $4.50.   333.72
1. Conservation of Natural Resources.

1468. Onyx Group, Inc. Environment U. S. A. A Guide to Agencies, People and Resources. Bowker. 1974. $15.95.   333.72
1. Conservation of Natural Resources — U. S. — Directories. 2. Environmental Protection — U. S. — Directories.

1469. Smith, Frank E. The Politics of Conservation. Pantheon. 1966. $7.95.   333.72
1. Natural Resources — U. S. — History.

1470. Udall, Stewart L. Quiet Crisis. HR&W. 1963. $6.95; pap. $1.25 (Avon).   333.72
1. Natural Resources — U. S. — History.

1471. Frome, Michael. Battle for the Wilderness. Praeger. 1974. $8.95.   333.78
1. Nature Conservation — U. S. 2. Wilderness Areas — U. S.

1472. Matthews, William H. A Guide to the National Parks: Their Landscape and Geology. 2 vols. Natural Hist. 1968. $10.95 ea.; pap. $5.95 ea.   333.78
1. Geology — U. S. 2. National Parks and Reserves — U. S.

1473. Congressional Quarterly Service. Energy Crisis in America. Congr Quarterly. 1973. $4.00.   333.8
1. Power Resources — U. S.

1474. Hellman, Harold. Energy in the World of the Future. Lippincott. 1973. $5.95.   333.8
1. Energy Conservation. 2. Power Resources.

1475. Manning, Harvey. Cry Crisis: Rehearsal in Alaska. Friends Earth. 1974. $7.50; pap. $4.95.   333.8
1. Energy Policy — U. S. 2. Petroleum Industry and Trade — Alaska. 3. Power Resources — U. S.

1476. Ridgeway, James. The Last Play: The Struggle to Monopolize the World's Energy Resources. Dutton. 1973. $10.00.   333.8
1. Energy Policy.

1477. Rocks, Lawrence and Runyon, Richard P. The Energy Crisis. Crown. 1972. $5.95.   333.821
1. Power Resources — U. S.

1478. Bardach, John E. Harvest of the Sea. Har-Row. 1968. $7.95; pap. $1.95.   333.9
1. Marine Resources. 2. Oceanography.

1479. Marx, Wesley. The Frail Ocean. Ballantine. 1969. pap. $0.95.   333.9
1. Marine Resources Conservation.

1480. Dary, David. The Buffalo Book: The Full Saga of the American Animal. Swallow. 1973. $15.00.   333.95
1. Bison, American. 2. West — History.

1481. Netboy, Anthony. The Salmon: Their Fight for Survival. HM. 1974. $15.00.   333.95
1. Salmon. 2. Salmon Fisheries. 3. Salmon Fishing.

335 Collectivist Systems

1482. Fried, Albert and Sanders, Ronald, eds. Socialist Thought: A Documentary

History. Doubleday. 1964. pap. $2.95.   335
1. Communism. 2. Socialism.

1483. Gorz, Andre. Socialism and Revolution. Doubleday. 1973. pap. $1.95.   335
1. Socialism.

1484. Kilroy-Silk, Robert. Socialism Since Marx. Taplinger. 1972. $9.95.   335
1. Communism — History. 2. Socialism — History.

1485. Fried, Albert, ed. Socialism in America: From the Shakers to the Third International; A Documentary History. Doubleday. 1970. pap. $3.95.   335.009
1. Socialism in the U. S.

1486. Seidler, Murray B. Norman Thomas: Respectable Rebel. 2nd ed. Syracuse U Pr. 1967. $7.00.   335.009(B)
1. Socialism in the U. S. 2. Socialist Party (U. S.). 3. Thomas, Norman Mattoon, 1884-1968.

1487. Blackmer, Donald L. Unity in Diversity: Italian Communism and the Communist World. MIT Pr. 1968. $15.00.
335.4
1. Communism — Italy. 2. Communism — 1945-

1488. Haimson, Leopold. The Russian Marxists and the Origins of Bolshevism. Harvard U Pr. 1955. $7.50; pap. $2.45 (Beacon Pr).   335.4
1. Revolutionists, Russian. 2. Socialism in Russia.

1489. Mendel, Arthur P., ed. Essential Works of Marxism. Bantam. 1961. pap. $1.25.
335.4
1. Communism. 2. Socialism.

1490. Treadgold, Donald W. Soviet and Chinese Communism: Similarities and Differences. U of Wash Pr. 1967. $10.00; pap. $3.95.   335.4
1. Communism — China (People's Republic of China, 1949-). 2. Communism — Russia.

1491. Berlin, Isaiah. Karl Marx: His Life and Environment. 3rd ed. Oxford U Pr. 1963. pap. $1.95.   335.42(B)
1. Communism. 2. Marx, Karl, 1818-1883. 3. Socialism.

1492. Bottomore, Tom, ed. Karl Marx. P-H. 1973. pap. $2.45.   335.42(B)

1. Dialectical Materialism. 2. Marx, Karl, 1818-1883.

1493. Marx, Karl and Engels, Friedrich. Communist Manifesto: With Principles of Communism, and the Communist Manifesto After One Hundred Years. Sweezy, Paul M. and Huberman, Leo, eds. Monthly Rev. 1968. $4.00; pap. $1.45.   335.42
1. Communism.

1494. Althusser, Louis. Lenin and Philosophy, and Other Essays. Monthly Rev. 1972. $9.50; pap. $3.25.   335.423
1. Lenin, Vladimir Ilyich, 1870-1924. 2. Marx, Karl, 1818-1883. Das Kapital.

1495. Berdyaev, Nicolas. Origin of Russian Communism. U of Mich Pr. 1960. pap. $2.25.
335.43
1. Communism and Religion. 2. Communism — Russia. 3. Religion — Philosophy. 4. Russia — Religion.

1496. Djilas, Milovan. The New Class: An Analysis of the Communist System. Praeger. 1957. $5.95; pap. $1.95.   335.43
1. Communism.

1497. Hyde, Douglas A. Communism Today. U of Notre Dame Pr. 1973. $7.95; pap. $2.95.   335.43
1. Communism. 2. Communism — 1945-

1498. Wilson, Edmund. To the Finland Station. Doubleday. 1953. pap. $2.95.   335.43
1. Communism — Russia. 2. Russia — History — Revolution, 1917-1921.

1499. Chai, Winberg. Essential Works of Chinese Communism. rev. ed. Bantam. 1969. pap. $1.45.   335.434
1. Communism — China. 2. Communism — China (People's Republic of China, 1949-).

1500. Schurmann, Franz. Ideology and Organization in Communist China. 2nd ed. U of Cal Pr. 1968. $12.50; pap. $5.50.   335.434
1. China (People's Republic of China, 1949-) — Politics and Government.

1501. Trotsky, Leon. The Struggle Against Fascism in Germany. Path Pr Inc NY. 1971. $12.50; pap. $3.95.   335.438
1. Communism — Germany. 2. Germany — Politics and Government — 1918-1933.

1502. Fairfield, Richard. Communes USA: A Personal Tour. Penguin. 1972. pap. $3.50.
335.973
1. Collective Settlements — U. S.

300 SOCIAL SCIENCES

1503. Hedgepeth, William and Stock, Dennis. The Alternative: Communal Life in New America. Macmillan. 1970. pap. $3.95. 335.973
1. Collective Settlements — U. S. 2. Hippies — U. S.

1504. Holloway, Mark. Heavens on Earth: Utopian Communities in America, 1680-1880. 2nd ed. Peter Smith. 1966. $4.75. 335.973
1. Collective Settlements — U. S.

1505. Horwitz, Elinor L. Communes in America: The Place Just Right. Lippincott. 1972. $4.95. 335.973
1. Collective Settlements — U. S. — History. 2. U. S. — Social Conditions — 1960-

1506. Melville, Keith. Communes in the Counter Culture: Origins, Theories, Styles of Life. Morrow. 1972. $6.95; pap. $2.45. 335.973
1. Collective Settlements — U. S. — History. 2. Radicalism — U. S. 3. Social Values. 4. U. S. — Social Conditions — 1960-

1507. Curtis, Edith R. A Season in Utopia: The Story of Brook Farm. Russell. 1971. $15.00. 335.974
1. Collective Settlements — U. S.

1508. Robertson, Constance N. Oneida Community: The Breakup, 1876-1881. Syracuse U Pr. 1972. $9.95. 335.974
1. Oneida Community.

1509. Lockwood, George B. The New Harmony Movement. Dover. 1971. pap. $3.50. 335.977
1. Harmony Society. 2. New Harmony, Indiana — History.

338 Production

1510. Tregear, Thomas R. An Economic Geography of China. Am Elsevier. 1970. $12.75. 338.095
1. China (People's Republic of China, 1949-) — Economic Conditions. 2. China (People's Republic of China, 1949-) — Industries.

1511. McGovern, George S., ed. Agricultural Thought in the 20th Century. Bobbs. 1968. $7.50; pap. $3.75. 338.1
1. Agricultural Administration. 2. Agriculture and State. 3. Agriculture — Economic Aspects. 4. Agriculture — U. S.

1512. Paddock, William and Paddock, Paul. Famine 1975: America's Decision, Who Will Survive. Little. 1968. $10.00; pap. $2.65. 338.109
1. Agriculture and State — U. S. 2. Food Supply. 3. Surplus Agricultural Commodities.

1513. Woodham-Smith, Cecil B. The Great Hunger: Ireland 1845-1849. Har-Row. 1963. $10.00. 338.15
1. Ireland — Emigration and Immigration. 2. Ireland — Famines.

1514. Aykroyd, W. R. The Conquest of Famine. Readers Digest Pr. 1975. $7.95. 338.19
1. Food Supply. 2. Population.

1515. Brown, Lester R. By Bread Alone. Praeger. 1974. $8.95. 338.19
1. Food Supply. 2. Population.

1516. Cochrane, Willard W. World Food Problem: A Guardedly Optimistic View. T Y Crowell. 1969. $7.95; pap. $3.95. 338.19
1. Food Supply. 2. Population.

1517. Dumont, Rene and Rosier, Bernard. The Hungry Future. Linnell, Rosamund and Sutcliffe, R. B., trs. Praeger. 1969. $6.95. 338.19
1. Food Supply. 2. Population.

1518. Katz, Robert. A Giant in the Earth: The Green Revolution and a Future with 100 Billion People. Stein & Day. 1972. $8.95. 338.19
1. Agricultural Innovations. 2. Food Supply. 3. Underdeveloped Areas — Agriculture.

1519. Edwin, Ed. Feast or Famine: Food, Farming and Farm Politics in America. Charterhouse. 1974. $7.95. 338.197
1. Agriculture — Economic Aspects — U. S. 2. Food Supply — U. S.

1520. Adelman, Morris A. The World Petroleum Market. Johns Hopkins. 1972. $22.50; pap. $5.95. 338.27
1. Petroleum Industry and Trade.

1521. Berry, Mary C. The Alaska Pipeline. Ind U Pr. 1975. $10.95. 338.27
1. Alaska Pipeline. 2. Petroleum — Alaska — Pipelines. 3. Petroleum — Alaska — Transportation. 4. Petroleum Industry and Trade — Alaska.

300 SOCIAL SCIENCES

1522. Tussing, Arlon R. Alaska Pipeline Report. 2nd ed. U Alaska Inst Res. 1973. $5.00. 338.27
1. Alaska Pipeline. 2. Petroleum — Alaska — Pipelines. 3. Petroleum — Alaska — Transportation. 4. Petroleum Industry and Trade — Alaska.

1523. Viker, Ray. The Kingdom of Oil, The Middle East: Its People and Its Power. Scribner. 1974. $7.95. 338.27
1. Near East — Social Conditions. 2. Petroleum Industry and Trade — Near East.

1524. Metzger, H. Peter. The Atomic Establishment. S&S. 1972. $8.95. 338.4
1. Atomic Energy — Social Aspects — U. S. 2. Atomic Energy Industries — U. S. 3. Atomic Power — Law and Legislation — U. S.

1525. Wall, Joseph F. Andrew Carnegie. Oxford U Pr. 1970. $17.50. 338.4(B)
1. Carnegie, Andrew, 1835-1919.

1526. Goldman, Marshall I. Ecology and Economics: Controlling Pollution in the 70's. P-H. 1972. $6.95; pap. $3.45. 338.47
1. Pollution — U. S.

1527. Knowles, Ruth S. America's Oil Famine. Coward. 1975. $8.95. 338.47
1. Petroleum and Petroleum Industry.

1528. Glyn, Andrew and Sutcliffe, Bob. Capitalism in Crisis. Pantheon. 1972. $8.95. 338.516
1. Great Britain — Economic Conditions — 1918-1945. 2. Great Britain — Economic Conditions — 1945- 3. Profit — Great Britain. 4. Wages — Great Britain.

1529. Collman, Charles A. Our Mysterious Panics, 1830-1930. Greenwood. 1931. $14.50. 338.54
1. Depressions — U. S.

1530. Galbraith, John Kenneth. Great Crash, 1929. 3rd ed. HM. 1972. $5.95; pap. $1.95. 338.54
1. Depressions — U. S. — 1929.

1531. Manchester, William. Arms of Krupp, 1587-1968. Little. 1968. $14.95. 338.7
1. Krupp Family.

1532. Berle, Adolf A., Jr. Twentieth Century Capitalist Revolution. HarBraceJ. 1954. $6.50. 338.74
1. Capitalism. 2. Corporations.

1533. Nevins, Allan. John D. Rockefeller. abr. ed. Scribner. 1959. $10.00. 338.8(B)
1. Petroleum Industry and Trade. 2. Rockefeller, John Davidson, 1839-1937.

1534. Golway, Frank H., et al. Underdevelopment and Economic Nationalism in Southeast Asia. Cornell U Pr. 1969. $16.50. 338.9
1. Asia, Southeastern — Economic Conditions.

1535. Asher, Robert E., et al. Development Assistance in the Seventies: Alternatives for the United States. Brookings. 1970. $6.95. 338.91
1. Economic Assistance. 2. Underdeveloped Areas.

1536. Myrdal, Gunnar. Challenge of World Poverty: A World Poverty Program in Outline. Pantheon. 1970. $8.95. 338.91
1. Economic Conditions. 2. Underdeveloped Areas.

1537. Dreier, John E., ed. The Alliance for Progress: Problems and Perspectives. John Hopkins. 1962. $6.00. 338.917
1. Alliance for Progress.

1538. Galbraith, John Kenneth. Economics and the Public Purpose. HM. 1973. $10.00. 338.973
1. Corporations — U. S. 2. Industry and State — U. S. 3. U. S. — Economic Conditions — 1961- 4. U. S. — Economic Policy — 1961-

1539. Heller, Walter W. New Dimensions of Political Economy. Harvard U Pr. 1966. $5.50. 338.973
1. Fiscal Policy — U. S. 2. Inter-Governmental Fiscal Relations — U. S. 3. U. S. — Economic Policy — 1961-

339 Distribution of Goods

1540. Budd, Edward C., ed. Inequality and Poverty: An Introduction to a Current Issue of Public Policy. Norton. 1968. pap. $1.95. 339.2
1. Income — U. S. 2. Poverty.

1541. Donovan, John C. The Politics of Poverty. 2nd ed. Pegasus. 1973. pap. $1.95. 339.46
1. Poverty. 2. U. S. — Economic Conditions. 3. U. S. — Social Conditions.

300 SOCIAL SCIENCES

1542. Ferman, Louis A., et al, eds. Poverty in America: A Book of Readings. rev. ed. U of Mich Pr. 1968. $12.50; pap. $6.95. 339.46
1. Poverty. 2. Public Welfare. 3. U. S. — Economic Conditions. 4. U. S. — Social Conditions.

1543. Committee for Economic Development. High Employment Without Inflation: A Positive Program for Economic Stabilization. Comm Econ Dev. 1972. pap. $1.50. 339.5
1. Economic Stabilization. 2. U. S. — Economic Policy — 1971-

340 Law

1544. McCarry, Charles. Citizen Nader. Sat Rev Pr. 1972. $7.95. 340.09(B)
1. Nader, Ralph, 1934-

1545. Friedman, Lawrence M. A History of American Law. S&S. 1973. $14.95. 340.097
1. Law — U. S. — History and Criticism.

1546. Brierley, John E. and David, Rene. Major Legal Systems in the World Today. Free Pr. 1969. $10.95. 340.5
1. Comparative Law.

341 International Law

1547. Brock, Peter. Twentieth Century Pacificism. Van Nos Reinhold. 1970. pap. $3.50. 341.1
1. Pacifism.

1548. Carr, Edward H. Twenty Years' Crisis, 1919-1939. 2nd ed. St Martin. 1946. $10.95; pap. $2.45 (Har-Row). 341.1
1. International Relations. 2. World Politics.

1549. Mayer, Peter, ed. The Pacifist Conscience. Regnery. 1967. pap. $2.95. 341.1
1. Pacifism.

1550. Wittner, Lawrence S. Rebels Against War: The American Peace Movement Since 1941. Columbia U Pr. 1969. $12.00; pap. $2.95. 341.1
1. Peace.

1551. Dexter, Byron. The Years of Opportunity: The League of Nations, 1920-1926. Viking Pr. 1967. $8.50. 341.22
1. League of Nations.

1552. Henig, Ruth B. The League of Nations. B&N. 1973. $11.50. 341.22
1. League of Nations.

1553. Barros, James, ed. The United Nations: Past, Present and Future. Free Pr. 1972. $8.95. 341.23
1. United Nations.

1554. Eichelberger, Clark M. UN: The First Twenty-Five Years. 4th ed. Har-Row. 1970. $6.95. 341.23
1. United Nations — History.

1555. Davidson, Eugene. The Nuremberg Falacy: Wars and War Crimes Since World War Two. Macmillan. 1973. $9.95. 341.6
1. International Law. 2. War and Society. 3. World Politics.

1556. Friedman, Leon, ed. The Law of War: A Documentary History. 2 vols. Random. 1973. $65.00. 341.6
1. War (International Law) — History.

1557. Borgese, Elisabeth Mann and Krieger, David, eds. The Tides of Change. Mason & Charter. 1975. $15.00. 341.7
1. Marine Resources and State. 2. Maritime Law. 3. Ocean Bottom (Maritime Law).

1558. Wood, John R. and Serres, Jean. Diplomatic Ceremonial and Protocol. Columbia U Pr. 1970. $25.00. 341.7
1. Diplomatic Protocol. 2. Etiquette.

342 Constitutional Law

1559. Goerner, Edward A., ed. Constitutions of Europe. Regnery. 1966. pap. $2.25. 342.4
1. Constitutions — Collections. 2. Europe — Constitutional Law.

1560. Jennings, Ivor. British Constitution. 5th ed. Cambridge U Pr. 1961. $9.50; pap. $4.95. 342.42
1. Great Britain — Constitutional Law. 2. Great Britain — Politics and Government.

1561. Lovell, Colin R. English Constitutional and Legal History. Oxford U Pr. 1962. $9.95. 342.42
1. Great Britain — Constitutional History.

1562. Callard, Keith, et al. Major Governments of Asia. Cornell U Pr. 1963. $17.50. 342.5

1. China (People's Republic of China, 1949-) — Politics and Government. 2. India — Politics and Government. 3. Indonesia — Politics and Government. 4. Japan — Politics and Government. 5. Pakistan — Politics and Government.

342.73 U. S. - Constitutional Law

1563. Anastaplo, George. The Constitutionalist: Notes of the First Amendment. S Meth U Pr. 1971. $20.00.
342.73
1. Free Speech. 2. Freedom of the Press. 3. U. S. — Constitutional History.

1564. Ashmore, Harry S. Fear in the Air: Broadcasting and the First Amendment; The Anatomy of a Constitutional Crisis. Norton. 1973. $6.95. 342.73
1. Liberty of the Press — U. S. 2. Radio — U. S. — Laws and Regulations. 3. Television — Laws and Legislation — U. S.

1565. Barker, Lucius and Twiley, W. B. Civil Liberties and the Constitution: Cases and Commentaries. P-H. 1969. $9.50; pap. $6.25.
342.73
1. Civil Rights — U. S.

1566. Barron, Jerome A. Freedom of the Press for Whom? The Right of Access to Mass Media. Ind U Pr. 1973. $8.95. 342.73
1. Freedom of Information — U. S. 2. Freedom of the Press — U. S.

1567. Bayh, Birch. One Heartbeat Away: Presidential Disability and Succession. Bobbs. 1968. $7.50. 342.73
1. Presidents — U. S. — Succession.

1568. Beard, Charles A. Economic Interpretation of the Constitution of the United States. Macmillan. 1935. $6.95; pap. $2.95 (Free Pr). 342.73
1. U. S. Constitution.

1569. Berger, Raoul. Impeachment: The Constitutional Problems. Harvard U Pr. 1974. $14.95. 342.73
1. Impeachments — Great Britain. 2. Impeachments — U. S.

1570. Beth, Loren P. The Development of the American Constitution, 1877-1917. Har-Row. 1971. $8.95. 342.73
1. U. S. — Constitutional History.

1571. Black, Charles Lund. Impeachment: A Handbook. Yale U Pr. 1974. $5.95; pap. $1.95. 342.73
1. Impeachments — U. S.

1572. Bowen, Catherine D. Miracle at Philadelphia: The Story of the Constitutional Convention, May to September, 1787. Little. 1966. $11.95. 342.73
1. U. S. Constitutional Convention, 1787.

1573. Cortner, R. and Lytle, C. Modern Constitutional Law. Free Pr. 1971. $8.95.
342.73
1. U. S. — Constitutional Law.

1574. Croly, Herbert. Promise of American Life. Harvard U Pr. 1965. $10.00; pap. $2.50 (Bobbs). 342.73
1. U. S. — Politics and Government. 2. U. S. — Social Conditions.

1575. Cushman, Robert E. Leading Constitutional Decisions. 14th ed. P-H. 1971. pap. $6.50. 342.73
1. U. S. — Constitutional History — Cases.

1576. De Tocqueville, Alexis. Democracy in America. Oxford U Pr. 1947. $6.00; pap. $4.95 1969. (Doubleday). 342.73
1. Democracy. 2. U. S. — Politics and Government. 3. U. S. — Social Conditions.

1577. Garraty, John A., ed. Quarrels That Have Shaped the Constitution. Har-Row. 1964. $4.95; pap. $2.95. 342.73
1. U. S. — Constitutional Law — Cases.

1578. Graham, Gene S. One Man, One Vote: Baker vs. Carr and the American Levellers. Little. 1972. $8.95. 342.73
1. Apportionment (Election Law) — U. S.

1579. Hamilton, Alexander, et al. Federalist: A Commentary on the Constitution of the United States from the Original Text of Alexander Hamilton, John Jay and James Madison. Modern Lib. pap. $2.95. 342.73
1. U. S. — Constitutional History.

1580. Javits, Jacob K. and Kellerman, Don. Who Makes War: The President versus Congress. Morrow. 1973. $8.95; pap. $3.95.
342.73
1. Executive Power. 2. U. S. Congress. 3. War.

1581. Konvitz, Milton R., ed. Bill of Rights Reader: Leading Constitutional Cases. 5th rev. ed. Cornell U Pr. 1973. $19.50. 342.73

300 SOCIAL SCIENCES

1. Civil Rights — U. S. — Cases. 2. U. S. Constitution 1st-10th Amendments. 3. U. S. — Constitutional Law — Cases.

1582. Marnell, William H. The Right to Know: Media and the Common Good. Seabury. 1973. $6.95.   342.73
1. Liberty of the Press — U. S. 2. Security Classification (Government Documents) — U. S.

1583. Mason, Alpheus Thomas. The States Rights Debate: Anti-Federalism in America. 2nd ed. Oxford U Pr. 1972. pap. $1.95. 342.73
1. Federal Government — U. S. 2. States Rights. 3. U. S. — Constitutional History.

1584. Morgan, Richard E. The Supreme Court and Religion. Free Pr. 1972. $7.95; pap. $3.95.   342.73
1. Religious Liberty — U. S. 2. U. S. Supreme Court.

1585. Rossiter, Clinton L. Seventeen Eighty Seven: The Grand Convention. Macmillan. 1966. $7.95; pap. $1.50 (NAL).   342.73
1. U. S. Constitutional Convention, 1787. 2. |U. S. — Politics and Government — 1783-1789.

1586. Schwartz, Bernard. Commentary on the Constitution of the United States. 2 vols. Macmillan. 1963. $25.00.   342.73
1. U. S. — Constitutional Law.

1587. Swieker, Carl B. The Growth of Constitutional Power in the United States. 2nd ed. U of Chicago Pr. 1963. pap. $2.45. 342.73
1. U. S. — Constitutional History. 2. U. S. — Constitutional Law.

1588. U. S. Congress. Senate. Committee on the Judiciary. Subcommittee on Constitutional Rights. Layman's Guide to Individual Rights Under the U. S. Constitution. 3rd ed. US Govt Ptg Off. 1972.   342.73
1. Civil Rights — U. S.

1589. Randall, James G. The Constitutional Problems Under Lincoln. rev. ed. U of Ill Pr. 1964. pap. $2.95.   342.739
1. Lincoln, Abraham, President U. S., 1809-1865. 2. U. S. — Constitutional History. 3. U. S. — Constitutional Law. 4. U. S. — Politics and Government — Civil War.

1590. Fitzgerald, Gerald E., ed. Constitutions of Latin America. Regnery. 1968. $6.95; pap. $2.95.   342.8

1. Constitutions — Collections. 2. Latin America — Constitutions.

343-346 Public, Social and Criminal Law

1591. DeCamp, L. Sprague. The Great Monkey Trial. Doubleday. 1968. $6.95.   343.3
1. Evolution. 2. Scopes Evolution Case. 3. Scopes, John Thomas.

1592. Contempt: Transcript of the Contempt Citations, Sentences, and Responses of the Chicago Conspiracy 10. Swallow. 1970. pap. $1.95.   343.4
1. Chicago — Riot, August, 1968. 2. Dellinger, David T. 1915-

1593. Lincoln, James H. The Anatomy of a Riot: A Detroit Judge's Report. McGraw. 1968. $5.95.   343.4
1. Detroit — Riot, 1967. 2. Juvenile Delinquency — Wayne Co., Mich. 3. Juvenile Detention Homes — Wayne Co., Mich.

1594. Carter, Dan T. Scottsboro: A Tragedy of the American South. La State U Pr. 1969. $10.00; pap. $3.95 (Oxford U Pr).   343.53
1. Scottsboro Case.

1595. Hammer, Richard. The Court Martial of Lt. Calley. Coward. 1971. $7.95.   343.73
1. Calley, William Laws, 1943-

1596. Liston, Robert A. The Right to Know: Censorship in America. Watts. 1973. $5.95.   344.73
1. Censorship — U. S. 2. Executive Privilege (Government Information) — U. S. 3. Obscenity (Law) — U. S.

1597. Stepanian, Michael. Pot Shots. Delacorte. 1972. $6.95.   344.73
1. Marihuana. 2. Narcotic Laws — U. S. 3. Searches and Seizures — U. S.

1598. Kempton, Murray. The Briar Patch: The People of the State of New York vs. Lumumba Shakur et al. Dutton. 1973. $7.95.   345.73
1. Black Panthers Trial, New York, 1970-1971.

1599. Meltsner, Michael. Cruel and Unusual: The Supreme Court and Capital Punishment. Morrow. 1974. pap. $3.95.   345.73
1. Capital Punishment. 2. U. S. Supreme Court.

1600. Schultz, John. Motion Will Be Denied: A New Report on the Chicago Conspiracy Trial. Morrow. 1972. pap. $3.95. 345.73
1. Chicago — Riot, August, 1968. 2. Dellinger, David T., 1915-

347 Civil Procedures

1601. Bland, Randall W. Private Pressure on Public Law: The Legal Career of Justice Thurgood Marshall. Kennikat. 1973. $9.95. 347
1. Marshall, Thurgood, 1908-

1602. Dorman, Michael. Under Twenty-One: A Young People's Guide to Legal Rights. Delacorte. 1970. $5.95. 347.1
1. Children — Law — U. S. 2. Youth — Law — U. S.

1603. Forer, Lois G. No One Will Lissen: How Our Legal System Brutalizes the Youthful Poor. John Day. 1970. $8.95; pap. $2.95. 347.1
1. Juvenile Delinquency — U. S.

1604. Norwick, Kenneth P., ed. Your Legal Rights: Making the Law Work for You. John Day. 1972. $7.95. 347.1
1. Children — Law — U. S. 2. Youth — Law — U. S.

1605. Asch, Sidney H. The Supreme Court and Its Great Justices. Arco. 1971. $5.95. 347.73
1. U. S. Supreme Court — Biography.

1606. Brant, Irving. Impeachment: Trials and Errors. Knopf. 1972. $5.95. 347.73
1. Impeachments — U. S.

1607. Ernst, Morris. The Great Reversals: Tales of the Supreme Court. Weybright. 1973. $7.95. 347.73
1. U. S. Supreme Court.

1608. Kohlmeier, Louis M. God Save This Honorable Court. Scribner. 1972. $8.95. 347.73
1. U. S. Supreme Court.

1609. MacKenzie, John P. The Appearance of Justice. Scribner. 1974. $7.95. 347.73
1. Judges — U. S. 2. Judicial Ethics — U. S.

1610. Simon, James F. In His Own Image: The Supreme Court in Richard Nixon's America. McKay. 1973. $7.95; pap. $3.95. 347.73
1. U. S. Supreme Court.

1611. Stone, Irving. Clarence Darrow for the Defense. Doubleday. 1949. $7.95; pap. $1.95 (NAL). 347.9(B)
1. Darrow, Clarence Seward, 1857-1938.

1612. Ashman, Charles R. The Finest Judges Money Can Buy: And Other Forms of Judicial Pollution. Nash Pub. 1973. $7.95. 347.99
1. Corruption (in Politics). 2. Crime and Criminals. 3. Judges.

1613. Berger, Raoul. Congress v. the Supreme Court. Howard U Pr. 1969. $15.00. 347.99
1. Judicial Review — U. S. 2. U. S. Congress. 3. U. S. Supreme Court.

1614. Bickel, Alexander M. The Supreme Court and the Idea of Progress. Har-Row. 1970. $6.50; pap. $1.95. 347.99
1. U. S. Supreme Court.

1615. Chandler, Peleg W. American Criminal Trials. 2 vols. Bks for Libs. 1844. $38.50 set. 347.99
1. Trials — U. S.

1616. Cox, Archibald. The Warren Court: Constitutional Decisions As an Instrument of Reform. Harvard U Pr. 1968. $4.95; pap. $1.95. 347.99
1. U. S. Supreme Court.

1617. Frankfurter, Felix. Mr. Justice Holmes and the Supreme Court. Atheneum. 1965. $3.00; pap. $1.25. 347.99
1. U. S. Supreme Court.

1618. Friedman, Leon and Israel, F. L., eds. The Justices of the U. S. Supreme Court, 1789-1969: Their Lives and Major Opinions. Bowker. 1969. $128.00. 347.99
1. U. S. Supreme Court — Biography.

1619. Swindler, William F. Court and Constitution in the Twentieth Century. 2 vols. Bobbs. 1969. $12.95. 347.99
1. U. S. Supreme Court.

1620. Todd, Alden L. Justice on Trial: The Case for Louis D. Brandeis. U of Chicago Pr. 1968. pap. $2.95. 347.99
1. Brandeis, Louis Dembitz, 1856-1941. 2. U. S. Supreme Court.

1621. Warren, Charles. Supreme Court in U. S. History. 2 vols. Little. 1960. $20.00. 347.99
1. U. S. Supreme Court.

300 SOCIAL SCIENCES

351 Police Organization

1622. Chambers, Whittaker. Witness. Random. 1952. $10.00. 351.74
1. Communism — U. S. — 1917- 2. Hiss, Alger, 1904-

1623. Whitehead, Donald F. F.B.I. Story. Random. 1956. $8.95. 351.74
1. U. S. Federal Bureau of Investigation.

1624. Wise, David and Ross, Thomas B. The Invisible Government. Random. 1964. $8.95. 351.74
1. Secret Service. 2. U. S. Central Intelligence Agency.

1625. Kohlmeier, Louis M. The Regulators: Watchdog Agencies and the Public Interest. Har-Row. 1969. $8.95; pap. $4.50. 351.8
1. Industry and State — U. S. 2. Public Administration.

352 Local Government

1626. Steffens, Joseph L. The Shame of the Cities. Peter Smith. 1959. $4.00; pap. $2.25 (FS&G). 352
1. Cities and Towns — U. S. 2. Corruption (in Politics). 3. Municipal Government.

1627. Adrian, Charles R. and Press, Charles. Governing Urban America. 4th ed. McGraw. 1972. $11.50. 352.008
1. Municipal Government — U. S.

1628. Banfield, Edward C., ed. Urban Government: A Reader in Administration and Politics. 2nd ed. Macmillan. 1969. $10.95. 352.008
1. Municipal Government — U. S.

1629. Mahood, H. R. and Angus, Edward L., eds. Urban Politics and Problems: A Reader. Scribner. 1969. $5.95. 352.008
1. Cities and Towns — U. S. 2. Local Government — U. S.

1630. Ruchelman, Leonard I., ed. Big City Mayors: The Crisis in Urban Politics. Ind U Pr. 1970. $12.50; pap. $4.95. 352.008
1. Mayors — U. S. 2. Municipal Government.

1631. Maas, Peter. Serpico. Viking Pr. 1973. $7.95; pap. $1.75. 352.07
1. New York (City) — Police. 2. Serpico, Frank.

353 U. S. - Politics and Government

1632. Burns, James M. Deadlock of Democracy: Four-Party Politics in America. P-H. 1963. pap. $2.95. 353
1. U. S. — Politics and Government.

1633. MacDonald, H. Malcolm, et al. Readings in American National Government. T Y Crowell. 1964. pap. $5.50. 353
1. U. S. — Politics and Government — Sources.

1634. Davies, J. Clarence. The Politics of Polution. Pegasus. 1970. $6.00; pap. $1.95. 353.008
1. Environmental Policy — U. S.

1635. Hill, Gladwin. Madman in a Lifeboat: Issues of the Environmental Crisis. John Day. 1972. $5.95; pap. $1.95. 353.008
1. Environmental Policy — U. S. 2. Human Ecology.

1636. Hirsch, Richard. The National Aeronautics and Space Administration. Praeger. 1973. $9.50. 353.008
1. U. S. National Aeronautics and Space Administration.

1637. American Heritage Editors. The American Heritage History of the Presidency. McGraw. 1968. $16.50. 353.03
1. Presidents — U. S.

1638. Anderson, Donald F. William Howard Taft: A Conservative's Conception of the Presidency. Cornell U Pr. 1973. $15.00. 353.03
1. Executive Power — U. S. 2. Taft, William Howard, President U. S., 1857-1930. 3. U. S. — Politics and Government — 1909-1913.

1639. Burns, James M. Presidential Government: Crucible in Leadership. HM. 1966. $7.95. 353.03
1. Executive Power — U. S. 2. Presidents — U. S.

1640. Hinschfield, Robert S., ed. The Power of the Presidency: Concepts and Controversy. 2nd ed. Aldine. 1973. $9.75; pap. $3.95. 353.03
1. Executive Power — U. S. 2. Presidents — U. S.

300 SOCIAL SCIENCES

1641. Hughes, Emmet J. The Living Presidency: The Resources and Dilemmas of the American Presidential Office. Coward. 1973. $10.50; pap. $2.95 (Penguin). 353.03
1. Presidents — U. S.

1642. Novak, Michael. Choosing Our King: Powerful Symbols in Presidential Politics. Macmillan. 1974. $7.95. 353.03
1. National Characteristics, American. 2. Presidents — U. S. — Election.

1643. Pusey, Merlo J. The Way We Go to War. HM. 1969. $5.95. 353.03
1. Executive Power — U. S. 2. U. S. Congress — Powers and Duties. 3. War and Emergency Powers — U. S.

1644. Schnapper, M. B., ed. Presidential Impeachment: A Documentary Overview. Pub Aff Pr. 1974. pap. $4.50. 353.03
1. Impeachments — U. S.

1645. U. S. Congress. House. Committee on the Judiciary. Constitutional Grounds for Presidential Impeachment. Pub Aff Pr. 1974. pap. $1.00. 353.03
1. Impeachments — U. S.

1646. Wicker, Tom. JFK and LBJ: The Influence of Personality Upon Prejudice. Penguin. 1969. pap. $2.25. 353.03
1. Johnson, Lyndon Baines, President U. S., 1908-1973. 2. Kennedy, John Fitzgerald, President U. S., 1917-1963.

1647. Salmond, John A. The Civilian Conservation Corps, 1933-1942: A New Deal Case Study. Duke. 1967. $7.50. 353.09
1. U. S. Civilian Conservation Corps — History.

1648. Harris, Richard. Justice: The Crisis of Law, Order, and Freedom in America. Dutton. 1970. $7.95; pap. $1.65 (Avon). 353.5
1. U. S. Department of Justice. 2. U. S. — Politics and Government.

1649. Fesler, James W., et al. The Fifty States and Their Local Governments. Knopf. 1967. $10.95. 353.9
1. Local Government — U. S. 2. State Governments.

Recommended Series

1650. Ralph Nader Study Groups Reports. Grossman.

354 Governments other than U. S.

1651. Barnett, A. Doak. Cadres, Bureaucracy, and Political Power in Communist China. Columbia U Pr. 1967. $12.00. 354.41
1. China (People's Republic of China, 1949-) — Politics and Government.

1652. Jennings, Ivor. Cabinet Government. 3rd ed. Cambridge U Pr. 1969. $17.50; pap. $5.95. 354.42
1. Cabinet System — Great Britain. 2. Great Britain — Politics and Government.

Recommended Series

1653. Studies in History and Politics. Stearn, Gerald Emanuel, gen. ed.. Heath.

355 Military Science

1654. Adcock, Frank E. Greek and Macedonian Art of War. U of Cal Pr. 1957. $1.65. 355
1. Greece — Army. 2. Macedonia — Army. 3. Military Art and Science.

1655. Clausewitz, Karl von. Principles of War. Stackpole. 1942. $3.25. 355
1. Military Art and Science.

1656. Knorr, Klaus E. Military Power and Potential. Heath. 1970. pap. $3.95. 355
1. Armaments. 2. Armed Forces.

1657. Montross, Lynn. War Through the Ages. rev. ed. Har-Row. 1960. $15.00. 355
1. Military Art and Science.

1658. Beeler, John. Warfare in Feudal Europe, 730-1200. Cornell U Pr. 1971. $9.75; pap. $2.45. 355.009
1. Military Art and Science — History. 2. Military History, Medieval.

1659. Donovan, James A. Militarism, U. S. A. Scribner. 1970. $6.95; pap. $2.95. 355.02
1. Militarism — U. S.

1660. Leckie, Robert. Warfare. Har-Row. 1970. $7.95. 355.02
1. Military Art and Science. 2. War.

300 SOCIAL SCIENCES

1661. Schwarz, Urs. Confrontation and Intervention in the Modern World. Oceana. 1970. $7.50. 355.02
1. Military Policy. 2. World Politics — 1965-

1662. Weigley, Russell F. American Military: Readings in the History of the Military in American Society. A-W. 1969. pap. $3.95. 355.02
1. Militarism — U. S. 2. U. S. — History, Military.

1663. ———. History of the United States Army. Macmillan. 1967. $12.95. 355.02
1. U. S. Army — History. 2. U. S. — History, Military.

1664. Yarmolinsky, Adam. The Military Establishment: Its Impact on American Society. Har-Row. 1971. $10.00; pap. $3.95. 355.02
1. U. S. — Defenses.

1665. Blainey, Geoffrey. The Causes of War. Free Pr. 1973. $7.95; pap. $3.95. 355.027
1. Military History. 2. War.

1666. Collins, John M. Grand Strategy: Principles and Practices. Naval Inst Pr. 1973. $15.00. 355.03
1. Strategy. 2. U. S. — Military Policy. 3. U. S. — National Security.

1667. Martin, Laurence W. Arms and Strategy: The World Power Structure Today. McKay. 1973. $15.95. 355.03
1. Armaments. 2. Strategy. 3. War.

1668. Moss, Norman. Men Who Play God: The Story of the H-Bomb and How the World Came to Live with It. Har-Row. 1969. $8.95. 355.03
1. Hydrogen Bomb. 2. U. S. — Military Policy.

1669. Earle, Edward M., ed. Makers of Modern Strategy: Military Thought from Machiavelli to Hitler. Princeton U Pr. 1943. $16.50; pap. $3.95 (Atheneum). 355.082
1. Military Art and Science — History. 2. Military History. 3. Strategy. 4. War.

1670. Hindley, Geoffrey. Medieval Warfare. Putnam. 1972. $5.95. 355.09
1. Military Art and Science — History. 2. Military History, Medieval.

1671. Kannik, Preben. Military Uniforms of the World in Color. Macmillan. 1968. $5.95. 355.1
1. Uniforms, Military.

1672. Starr, Paul. The Discarded Army: Veterans After Vietnam; the Nader Report on Vietnam Veterans and the Veterans Administration. Charterhouse. 1973. $7.95; pap. $3.95. 355.115
1. U. S. Veterans Administration. 2. Veterans — U. S. 3. Vietnamese Conflict, 1961-1973 — U. S.

1673. Gaylin, Willard. In the Service of Their Country: War Resisters in Prisons. Viking Pr. 1970. $6.95. 355.2
1. Conscientious Objectors — U. S.

1674. Reeves, Thomas and Hess, Karl. The End of the Draft. Random. 1970. $6.95; pap. $1.95. 355.2
1. Military Service, Compulsory — U. S.

1675. Schlissel, Lillian, ed. Conscience in America: A Documentary History of Conscientious Objection in America, 1757-1967. Dutton. 1968. $6.50; pap. $2.75. 355.2
1. Conscientious Objectors — U. S.

1676. James, Dorris C. The Years of MacArthur. HM. 1970. $12.50. 355.3
1. MacArthur, Douglas, 1880-1964.

1677. Marx, Karl. Capital and Other Writings. Modern Lib. $2.95. 355.411
1. Capital. 2. Economics. 3. Socialism.

1678. Weigley, Russell F. The American Way of War: A History of the United States Military Strategy and Policy. Macmillan. 1973. $12.95. 355.42
1. U. S. — History, Military. 2. U. S. — Military Policy.

1679. Fitzgerald, Arthur E. The High Priests of Waste. Norton. 1972. $8.95. 355.6
1. U. S. Department of Defense — Finance. 2. U. S. Department of Defense — Management.

1680. Cleator, Philip E. Weapons of War. T Y Crowell. 1968. $6.95. 355.8
1. Arms and Armor. 2. Ordnance.

1681. Ellis, Christopher. Military Transport of the First World War. Macmillan. 1970. $5.95. 355.83
1. European War, 1914-1918 — Transportation. 2. Vehicles, Military.

1682. ———. Military Transport of World War Two. Macmillan. 1971. $5.95. 355.83

300 SOCIAL SCIENCES

358-359 Technical, Land, Air, Naval, and Forces Space

1683. Batchelor, John and Hogg, Ian. Artillery. Scribner. 1972. $9.95. 358.109
1. Artillery — History.

1684. Taylor, John W. and Taylor, Michael J. Missiles of the World. rev. ed. Scribner. 1975. $6.95. 358.17
1. Guided Missiles.

1685. Hersh, Seymour M. Chemical and Biological Warfare: America's Hidden Arsenal. Doubleday. 1969. pap. $1.95. 358.34
1. Biological Warfare. 2. Chemical Warfare.

1686. Center for the Study of Democratic Institutions. Anti-Ballistic Missile: Yes or No? A Special Report. McDonald, Donald, ed. Hill & Wang. 1969. pap. $1.75. 358.41
1. Antimissile Missiles. 2. U. S. — Military Policy.

1687. Klass, Philip J. Secret Sentries in Space. Random. 1971. $7.95. 358.8
1. Astronautics, Military — Russia. 2. Astronautics, Military — U. S. 3. Earth — Photographs from Space.

1688. Mahan, Alfred T. Influence of Sea Power Upon History, 1660-1783. Peter Smith. $5.00. 359
1. Naval History. 2. Sea Power.

1689. Padfield, Peter. The Battleship Era. McKay. 1973. $9.95. 359.325
1. Battleships — History.

1690. Thomson, George M. Sir Francis Drake. Morrow. 1972. $10.00. 359.33(B)
1. Drake, Francis, Sir, 1540?-1596.

361-363 Social Welfare

1691. Trattner, Walter I. From Poor Law to Welfare State: A History of Social Welfare in America. Free Pr. 1974. $9.00; pap. $3.95. 361
1. Public Welfare. 2. Social Work.

1692. Davis, Allen F. American Heroine: The Life and Legend of Jane Addams. Oxford U Pr. 1973. $10.95. 361.92(B)
1. Addams, Jane, 1860-1935.

1693. Meigs, Cornelia L. Jane Addams, Pioneer for Social Justice: A Biography. Little. 1970. $5.95. 361.922(B)
1. Addams, Jane, 1860-1935.

1694. Bremner, Robert H. American Philanthropy. U of Chicago Pr. 1960. $7.50; pap. $2.25. 361.97
1. Charities — U. S. — History. 2. Social Work.

1695. Cahill, Kevin M. The Untapped Resource: Medicine and Diplomacy. Orbis Bks. 1971. $4.95. 362.1
1. Diplomacy. 2. Medical Assistance, American.

1696. Alexander, Clifton and Alexander, Sandy. How to Kick the Habit: The Drug Withdrawal Handbook. Fell. 1972. $5.95.
362.2
1. Drug Abuse. 2. Drug Abuse — Treatment. 3. Drugs.

1697. Nahas, Gabriel G. Marihuana - The Deceptive Weed. rev. ed. Raven. 1975. $12.50.
362.2
1. Cannabis. 2. Marihuana.

1698. U. S. Commission on Marihuana & Drug Abuse. Drug Use in America: Problem in Perspective; Second Report. US Govt Ptg Off. 1973. $2.60. 362.2
1. Drug Abuse — Treatment — U. S. 2. Drug Abuse — U. S. 3. Narcotics, Control of — U. S.

1699. ———. Marihuana: A Signal of Misunderstanding. NAL. $1.25. 362.2
1. Drug Abuse — U. S. 2. Drugs and Youth — U. S. 3. Marihuana.

1700. Johnson, Bruce D. Marihuana Users and Drug Subculture. Wiley. 1973. $14.25.
362.29
1. Drugs and Youth — U. S. 2. Marihuana.

1701. Clark, Kenneth B. and Hopkins, Jeannette. A Relevant War Against Poverty: A Study of Community Action Programs and Observable Social Change. Har-Row. 1969. $6.95. 362.5
1. Community Action Programs. 2. Poverty.

1702. Hampden-Turner, Charles. From Poverty to Dignity: A Strategy for Poor Americans. Doubleday. 1974. $8.95. 362.5
1. Poverty — Psychological Aspects. 2. U. S. — Economic Conditions.

300 SOCIAL SCIENCES

1703. Davis, Allen F. Spearheads for Reform: The Social Settlements and the Progressive Movement, 1890-1914. Oxford U Pr. 1968. pap. $2.95. 362.973
1. Cities and Towns — U. S. 2. Reformers. 3. Social Settlements. 4. U. S. — Politics and Government.

1704. Ahern, James F. Police in Trouble: Our Frightening Crisis in Law Enforcement. Hawthorn. 1971. $6.95. 363.2
1. Law Enforcement. 2. Police — U. S.

1705. Chalmers, David M. Hooded Americanism: The First Century of the Ku Klux Klan, 1865-1965. Doubleday. 1965. $5.95. 363.973
1. Ku Klux Klan. 2. Ku Klux Klan (1915-).

1706. Randel, William P. The Ku Klux Klan: A Century of Infamy. Chilton. 1965. $5.95. 363.973
1. Ku Klux Klan. 2. Ku Klux Klan (1915-).

364-365 Criminology and Penal Institutions

1707. Fraenkel, Jack R. Crime and Criminals: What Should We Do About Them? P-H. 1970. $5.52; pap. $2.08. 364
1. Crime and Criminals — U. S. 2. Law Enforcement — U. S.

1708. Boetie, Dugmore. Familiarity Is the Kingdom of the Lost: An Imaginary Autobiography. Dutton. 1970. $4.95. 364.1(B)
1. Africa, South.

1709. Cressey, Donald R. Theft of the Nation: The Structure and Operation of Organized Crime in America. Har-Row. 1969. $7.95; pap. $2.25. 364.1
1. Mafia. 2. Racketeering — U. S.

1710. Frank, Gerold. An American Death: The True Story of the Assassination of Dr. Martin Luther King, Jr. and the Greatest Manhunt of Our Time. Bantam. 1973. pap. $1.95. 364.1
1. King, Martin Luther — Assassination. 2. Ray, James Earl, 1928-

1711. Gage, Nicholas. The Mafia Is Not an Equal Opportunity Employer. McGraw. 1971. $5.95. 364.1
1. Mafia.

1712. Ianni, Francis A. and Ianni, E. R. A Family Business: Kinship and Social Control in Organized Crime. Russell Sage. 1972. $8.50; pap. $1.50 (NAL). 364.1
1. Mafia. 2. Racketeering — U. S.

1713. Kobler, John. Capone: The Life and World of Al Capone. Putnam. 1971. $8.95. 364.1(B)
1. Capone, Alphonse, 1899-1947.

1714. Hiss, Alger. In the Court of Public Opinion. Har-Row. 1972. pap. $3.95. 364.13
1. Chambers, Whittaker, 1901-1961. 2. Communism — U. S. — 1917-

1715. Stern, Philip M. and Green, Harold P. The Oppenheimer Case: Security on Trial. Har-Row. 1969. $10.00. 364.131
1. Oppenheimer, Julius Robert, 1904-1967. 2. Trials.

1716. Bernstein, Carl and Woodward, Bob. All the President's Men. S&S. 1974. $8.95. 364.132
1. Watergate Affair, 1972-

1717. Dickinson, William B., ed. Watergate: Chronology of a Crisis. Congr Quarterly. 1975. $35.00. 364.132
1. Watergate Affair, 1972-

1718. White, Theodore H. Breach of Faith: The Fall of Richard Nixon. Atheneum. 1975. $10.95. 364.132
1. Nixon, Richard Milhous, President U. S., 1913- — Impeachment. 2. Watergate Affair, 1972-

1719. Arey, James A. The Sky Pirates. Scribner. 1972. $7.95. 364.135
1. Hijacking of Airplanes.

1720. Maas, Peter. Valachi Papers. Putnam. 1968. $6.95. 364.14
1. Crime and Criminals. 2. Mafia. 3. Valachi, Joseph.

1721. Methvin, Eugene H. The Riot Makers: The Technology of Social Demolition. Arlington Hse. 1970. $10.00. 364.14
1. Communism — History. 2. Riots — History. 3. Riots — U. S.

1722. Platt, Anthony, ed. The Politics of Riot Commissions, 1917-1970: A Collection of Official Reports and Critical Essays. Macmillan. 1971. $8.95; pap. $3.95. 364.14
1. Riots. 2. U. S. President's Commission on Campus Unrest.

300 SOCIAL SCIENCES

1723. Grinshaw, Allen D. Racial Violence in the United States. Aldine. 1969. $15.95.
364.143
1. Negroes — History. 2. Riots — U. S. 3. U. S. — Race Question.

1724. Ehrmann, Herbert B. The Untried Case: The Sacco-Vanzetti Case and the Morelli Gang. Vanguard. 1960. $5.95. 364.15
1. Sacco-Vanzetti Case.

1725. Shneidman, Edwin S. Death and the College Student. Behavioral Pubns. 1972. $10.95; pap. $4.95. 364.152
1. Death. 2. Suicide.

1726. Newsday, Staff & Editors of. The Heroin Trail. HR&W. 1975. $8.95; pap. $1.95 (NAL). 364.157
1. Heroin. 2. Narcotics, Control of.

1727. U. S. Commission on Obscenity & Pornography. The Report. US Govt Ptg Off. 1970. $5.50. 364.17
1. Erotica. 2. Obscenity (Law) — U. S.

1728. Newman, Oscar. Defensible Space: Crime Prevention Through Urban Design. Macmillan. 1972. $9.95. 364.44
1. Architecture, Domestic — New York (City). 2. Crime and Criminals — New York (City). 3. Crime Prevention — New York (City).

1729. Goldfarb, Ronald L. After Conviction. S&S. 1973. $15.95. 364.6
1. Corrections — U. S.

1730. Bedau, Hugo A., ed. The Death Penalty in America: An Anthology. 2nd ed. Aldine. 1968. $12.50. 364.66
1. Capital Punishment — U. S.

1731. McLennan, Barbara N., ed. Crime in Urban Society. Dunellen Pub Co. 1970. $8.95; pap. $3.95. 364.9
1. Crime and Criminals — U. S. 2. Urbanization — U. S.

1732. U. S. President's Commission on Law Enforcement & Administration of Justice. The Challenge of Crime in a Free Society: A Report. Da Capo. 1969. $12.50; pap. $2.45 (Avon). 364.9
1. Crime and Criminals — U. S.

1733. Solzhenitsyn, Aleksandr I. The Gulag Archipelago, 1918-1956: An Experiment in Literary Investigation. Whitney, Thomas P., tr. from Rus. Har-Row. 1974. $12.50; pap. $1.95. 365.45
1. Political Prisoners — Russia.

1734. Charriere, Henri. Banco. Morrow. 1973. $7.95. 365.6(B)
1. Charriere, Henri, 1906- 2. Crime and Criminals — Biography.

1735. Coons, William R. Attica Diary. Stein & Day. 1972. $6.95. 365.6
1. New York. State Prison, Attica. 2. Prisoners — New York (State) — Personal Narratives.

1736. Jackson, George. Soledad Brother: The Prison Letters of George Jackson. Coward. 1970. $5.95. 365.6
1. Prisoners — California — Personal Narratives.

1737. Melville, Samuel. Letters from Attica. Morrow. 1972. pap. $1.95. 365.6
1. New York. State Prison, Attica. 2. Prisoners — Personal Narratives.

1738. Russier, Gabrielle. The Affair of Gabrielle Russier. Knopf. 1971. $5.95. 365.6
1. Prisoners — France — Personal Narratives.

1739. Mitford, Jessica. Kind and Usual Punishment: The Prison Business. Knopf. 1973. $7.95. 365.9
1. Corrections — U. S. 2. Prisons — U. S.

1740. Parker, Tony. The Frying-Pan: A Prison and Its Prisoners. Basic. 1970. $6.95; pap. $2.45 (Har-Row). 365.9
1. Prisons — Great Britain. 2. Rehabilitation of Criminals — Great Britain.

1741. Atkins, Burton M. and Glick, H. R., eds. Prisons, Protest, and Politics. P-H. 1972. $5.95. 365.973
1. Prison Riots — U. S. 2. Prisoners — U. S. 3. Prisons — U. S.

1742. Badillo, Herman and Haynes, Milton. A Bill of No Rights: Attica and the American Prison System. Dutton. 1972. $6.95. 365.973
1. New York. State Prison, Attica. 2. Prison Riots — New York (State).

370 Education

1743. Heath, Douglas. Growing Up in College: Liberal Education and Maturity. Jossey-Bass. 1968. $10.75.   370.01
1. Education, Higher — Aims and Objectives. 2. Maturation (Psychology).

1744. Bruner, Jerome S. Toward a Theory of Instruction. Harvard U Pr. 1966. $4.95; pap. $1.95.   370.1
1. Education — Philosophy.

1745. Dewey, John. John Dewey on Education. U of Chicago Pr. 1974. pap. $4.25.   370.1
1. Education — Philosophy.

1746. Harvard Committee. General Education in a Free Society. Harvard U Pr. 1945. $7.50.   370.1
1. Education — Philosophy.

1747. Reimer, Everett W. School Is Dead: Alternatives in Education. Peter Smith. 1972. $4.00; pap. $1.95 (Doubleday).   370.11
1. Education — U. S. — 1965-

1748. Hawley, Robert C. Human Values in the Classroom: Teaching for Personal and Social Growth. ERA Pr. 1973. pap. $3.75.   370.15
1. Educational Psychology. 2. Worth.

1749. Holt, John. How Children Learn. Pitman. 1969. $5.95; pap. $2.25.   370.15
1. Education of Children.

1750. Holden, Anna. The Bus Stops Here: A Study of School Desegregation in Three Cities. Agathon. 1974. $15.00.   370.19
1. School Integration — Charlottesville, Virginia. 2. School Integration — Providence, Rhode Island. 3. School Integration — Sacramento, California.

1751. Illich, Ivan D. Deschooling Society. Har-Row. 1972. pap. $1.25.   370.19
1. Education — U. S. 2. Educational Sociology — U. S.

1752. Kozol, Jonathan. Death at an Early Age: The Destruction of the Hearts and Minds of Negro Children in the Boston Public Schools. HM. 1967. $5.95; pap. $1.25 (Bantam).   370.19
1. Boston — Public Schools. 2. Discrimination in Education. 3. Negroes — Education — Boston.

1753. Orfield, Gary. Reconstruction of Southern Education. Wiley. 1969. $11.25.   370.19
1. Education and State. 2. Federal Aid to Education. 3. Segregation in Education.

1754. Taylor, Harold. The World As Teacher. S Ill U Pr. 1974. pap. $3.95.   370.19
1. Intercultural Education.

1755. Toffler, Alvin, ed. Learning for Tomorrow: The Role of the Future in Education. Random. 1974. $10.00; pap. $2.95.   370.19
1. Education — U. S. — 1965- 2. Forecasting.

1756. Boyd, William. History of Western Education. 10th ed. King, E. J., ed. B&N. 1973. $10.00; pap. $3.95.   370.9
1. Education — History.

1757. Bowen, James. Soviet Education: Anton Makarenko and the Years of Experiment. U of Wis Pr. 1962. pap. $3.75.   370.947
1. Communist Education — Russia. 2. Education — Russia.

1758. Hans, Nicholas. The Russian Tradition in Education. Greenwood. 1963. $9.75.   370.947
1. Education — Russia — History.

1759. Seybolt, Peter J., compiled by. Revolutionary Education in China: Documents and Commentary. Intl Arts & Sci. 1973. $15.00.   370.951
1. Education — China.

1760. Eurich, Alvin C. Reforming American Education: The Innovative Approach to Improving Our Schools and Colleges. Har-Row. 1969. $7.95.   370.973
1. Education — U. S. — 1945-

1761. Good, Harry G. and Teller, James D. A History of American Education. 3rd ed. Macmillan. 1973. $10.95.   370.973
1. Education — U. S. — History.

1762. Holt, John. The Underachieving School. Pitman. 1969. $5.95; pap. $2.25 (Dell).   370.973
1. Education — Philosophy. 2. Education — U. S.

1763. Leonard, George B. Education and Ecstasy. Delacorte. 1968. $7.95; pap. $2.25 (Dell).   370.973
1. Education — U. S. — 1945-

1764. Silberman, Charles E. Crises in the Classroom: The Remaking of American Education. Random. 1970. $10.00; pap. $2.45. 370.973
1. Education — U. S.

1765. Sizer, Theodore R. Places for Learning, Places for Joy: Speculations on American School Reform. Harvard U Pr. 1973. $7.50. 370.973
1. Education — U. S. — 1965- 2. School Management and Organization — U. S.

371-373 The School

1766. Kozol, Jonathan. Free Schools. HM. 1972. $4.95; pap. $1.50 (Bantam). 371.02
1. Free Schools — U. S.

1767. Kraushaar, Otto F. American Nonpublic Schools. Johns Hopkins. 1972. $12.00. 371.02
1. Private Schools — U. S. — History.

1768. McLachlan, James. American Boarding Schools: A Historical Study. Scribner. 1970. pap. $4.95. 371.02
1. Private Schools — U. S. — History.

1769. Brown, George I. Human Teaching for Human Learning: An Introduction to Confluent Education. Viking Pr. 1971. $8.50; pap. $2.45. 371.3
1. Teaching.

1770. Kohl, Herbert T. The Open Classroom. Random. 1970. $4.95; pap. $1.65. 371.3
1. Teaching.

1771. Neill, Alexander S. Summerhill: A Radical Approach to Teaching. Hart. 1970. $7.95; pap. $2.95. 371.3
1. Child Study. 2. Education — Experimental Methods. 3. Summerhill School, Leiston, England.

1772. Saettler, Paul. History of Instructional Technology. McGraw. 1968. $10.95. 371.3
1. Audio-Visual Education. 2. Education — Philosophy. 3. Teaching — Aids and Devices.

1773. Gattegno, Caleb. Towards a Visual Culture: Educating Through Television. Dutton. 1969. $4.95. 371.335
1. Television in Education.

1774. Wagner, Rudolph F. Dyslexia and Your Child: A Guide for Parents and Teachers. Har-Row. 1971. $6.95. 371.91
1. Dyslexia.

1775. Holt, John. How Children Fail. Pitman. 1964. $5.95; pap. $2.25 (Dell). 372
1. Education of Children.

1776. Silberman, Charles E., ed. Open Classroom Reader. Random. 1973. $12.50; pap. $2.95. 372.13
1. Open Plan Schools.

1777. Kohl, Herbert T. Thirty-Six Children. Norton. 1968. $5.95; pap. $0.95 (NAL). 372.9
1. Negro Children's Writings. 2. Negroes — Education — Harlem, New York (City).

1778. Neill, Alexander S. Neill! Neill! Orange Peel! An Autobiography. Hart. 1972. $10.00; pap. $3.95. 372.9(B)
1. Neill, Alexander Sutherland, 1883-1973. 2. Summerhill School, Leiston, England.

1779. Eurich, Alvin C. and Academy for Educational Development Staff, eds. High School, 1980: The Shape of the Future in American Secondary Education. Pitman. 1970. $8.50. 373.73
1. Education, Secondary — U. S. — 1945-

378 Higher Education

1780. Coyne, John and Hebert, Tom. This Way Out: A Guide to Alternatives to Traditional College Education in the United States, Europe and the Third World. Dutton. 1972. $10.00; pap. $4.95. 378
1. Education — Experimental Methods. 2. Foreign Study. 3. Self-Culture.

1781. Splaver, Sarah. Nontraditional College Routes to Careers. Messner. 1975. $6.95. 378
1. Education, Higher — U. S. 2. University Extension — U. S.

1782. Taylor, Harold. Students Without Teachers: The Crisis in the University. Avon. 1970. pap. $1.45. 378.1
1. Education, Higher — 1965- 2. Intellectual Life.

1783. Adelson, Alan. SDS. Scribner. 1972. $10.00; pap. $2.95. 378.198
1. Students — U. S. — Political Activity. 2. Students for a Democratic Society.

300 SOCIAL SCIENCES

1784. Feuer, Lewis S. The Conflict of Generations: The Character and Significance of Student Movements. Basic. 1969. $12.50. 378.198
1. Student Movements — History. 2. Young Adults. 3. Youth — Radicalism.

1785. Kunen, James S. The Strawberry Statement: Notes of a College Revolutionist. Random. 1969. $4.95; pap. $1.25 (Avon). 378.198
1. College Students — U. S.

1786. Cass, James and Birnbaum, Max. Comparative Guide to American Colleges. 6th ed. Har-Row. 1973-74. pap. $5.95. 378.73
1. Colleges — U. S. 2. Colleges and Universities — U. S. — Directories.

1787. ———. Comparative Guide to Junior and Community Two Year Colleges. Har-Row. 1972. $10.00; pap. $3.95. 378.73
1. Junior Colleges — U. S. — Directories. 2. Technical Education — U. S. — Directories.

1788. Lovejoy, Clarence E. Lovejoy's College Guide. S&S. 1973. $7.95; pap. $4.95. 378.73
1. Colleges — U. S. 2. Colleges and Universities — U. S. — Directories.

1789. Yale Daily News, ed. The Insiders' Guide to the Colleges. 5th rev. ed. Berkley Pub. 1974. pap. $2.25. 378.73
1. Universities and Colleges — U. S. — Directories.

1790. Barron's in-Depth Guide to the Ivy League Schools. Barron. 1971. pap. $3.95. 378.74
1. Universities and Colleges — Atlantic States — Directories.

1791. Davies, Peter. The Truth About Kent State: A Challenge to the American Conscience. FS&G. 1973. $10.00; pap. $3.50. 378.771
1. Ohio State University, Kent — Riot, May 4, 1970.

380 Commerce

1792. DuBois, William E. Suppression of the African Slave Trade, 1638-1870. Schocken. 1969. $7.50; pap. $2.45. 380.1
1. Slave-Trade — U. S.

1793. Georgano, George N. Transportation Through the Ages. McGraw. 1972. $16.95. 380.509
1. Transportation — History.

1794. Reichard, Robert. The Figure Finaglers. new ed. McGraw. 1973. $8.95. 381.3
1. Commercial Statistics. 2. Consumer Education. 3. Statistics.

1795. Calleo, David P. and Rowland, Benjamin M. America and the World Political Economy: Atlantic Dreams and National Realities. Ind U Pr. 1973. $12.50; pap. $2.95. 382
1. Europe — Economic Policy. 2. International Economic Relations. 3. U. S. — Economic Policy.

1796. Thayer, George. The War Business: The International Trade in Armaments. S&S. 1969. $6.95; pap. $3.45. 382.45
1. Firearms Industry and Trade. 2. Munitions.

1797. Taussig, Frank W. Tariff History of the United States. 8th ed. Kelley. Repr. 1931. $15.00; pap. $2.45 (Putnam). 382.7
1. Tariff — U. S. — History.

1798. Krause, Lawrence B. European Economic Integration and the U. S. Brookings. 1968. $6.95. 382.9
1. European Economic Community — U. S. 2. European Free Trade Association — U. S.

1799. Scott Publications, Inc. Scott's Standard Postage Stamp Catalogue. 2 vols. in 1. Scott Pubns. $12.00. 383
1. Postage-Stamps.

1800. Cullinan, Gerald. The United States Postal Service. Praeger. 1973. $10.00. 383.49
1. Postal Service — U. S. — History. 2. U. S. Postal Service.

1801. Sampson, Anthony. The Sovereign State of ITT. Stein & Day. 1973. $10.00. 384.06
1. Business and Politics — Case Studies. 2. International Telephone and Telegraph Corporation.

1802. Bruce, Robert V. Bell: Alexander Graham Bell and the Conquest of Solitude. Little. 1973. $12.50. 384.609(B)
1. Bell, Alexander Graham, 1847-1922.

300 SOCIAL SCIENCES

1803. Drago, Harry S. Canal Days in America: The History and Romance of Old Towpaths and Waterways. Crown. 1972. $10.00. 386
1. Canals — U. S. — History.

1804. Farnie, D. A. East and West of Suez: The Suez Canal in History 1854-1956. Oxford U Pr. 1969. $41.00. 386.43
1. Suez Canal — History.

1805. Mostert, Noel. Supership. Knopf. 1974. $8.95. 387.245
1. Ardshiel (Ship). 2. Ocean Travel. 3. Petroleum — Transportation. 4. Tank — Vessels.

1806. Toland, John. The Great Dirigibles: Their Triumphs and Disasters. Dover. 1972. $3.00. 387.732
1. Airships — History.

1807. Robinson, John. Highways and Our Environment. McGraw. 1971. $26.50. 388.1
1. Environmental Policy — U. S. 2. Roads — U. S. 3. Transportation and State — U. S.

1808. Gilbert, Thomas F. and Gilbert, Marilyn B. Thinking Metric. Wiley. 1973. pap. $2.95. 389.1
1. Metric System. 2. Weights and Measures — Canada. 3. Weights and Measures — U. S.

1809. Deming, Richard. Metric Power: Why and How We Are Going Metric. Nelson. 1974. $5.95. 389.152
1. Metric System. 2. Weights and Measures — U. S.

391 Costume

1810. Barsis, Max. The Common Man Through the Centuries: A Book of Costume Drawings. Ungar. 1973. $16.00. 391
1. Costume — History.

1811. Houston, Mary G. Ancient Egyptian, Mesopotamian and Persian Costume and Decoration. 2nd ed. B&N. 1954. $9.00. 391
1. Costume — History — Ancient.

1812. ———. Ancient Greek, Roman and Byzantine Costume and Decoration. 2nd ed. B&N. 1965. $9.00. 391
1. Costume — History — Ancient.

1813. Kelly, Francis M. and Schwabe, Randolph. Short History of Costume and Armour, 1066-1800. 2 vols. in 1. Blom. 1968. $13.75. 391
1. Arms and Armor. 2. Costume — History.

1814. Truman, Nevil. Historic Costuming. 2nd ed. Pitman. 1966. $12.50. 391
1. Costume — History.

1815. Wilcox, R. Turner. Folk and Festival Costume of the World. Scribner. 1965. $12.95. 391
1. Costume.

1816. Lister, Margot. Costumes of Everyday Life: An Illustrated History of Working Clothes. Plays. 1972. $13.95. 391.009
1. Costume — Europe — History.

1817. Wilcox, R. Turner. Five Centuries of American Costume. Scribner. 1963. $12.95. 391.09
1. Costume — U. S. — History.

394 Public and Social Customs

1818. Christian, Roy. Old English Customs. Drake Pubs. 1973. $7.95. 394.09
1. England — Social Life and Customs. 2. Festivals — England.

1819. Auld, William M. Christmas Traditions. Gale. 1931. $6.50. 394.2
1. Christmas.

1820. Meyer, Robert, Jr. Festivals U.S.A. and Canada. rev. ed. Washburn. 1967. $5.95. 394.2
1. Festivals — Canada. 2. Festivals — U. S.

1821. Gaster, Theodor H. Festivals of the Jewish Year. Peter Smith. 1962. $5.00. 394.26
1. Fasts and Feasts — Judaism.

395 Etiquette

1822. Post, Elizabeth. The New Emily Post's Etiquette. Funk & W. 1975. $8.95. 395
1. Etiquette.

1823. Vanderbilt, Amy. Amy Vanderbilt's Etiquette. rev. ed. Doubleday. 1972. $7.95. 395
1. Etiquette.

398 Folklore

1824. Abrahams, Roger D. Positively Black. P-H. 1969. $5.95; pap. $4.25. 398
1. Folk-Lore, Negro.

300 SOCIAL SCIENCES

1825. Arabian Nights' Entertainment. Burton, Richard, tr.. Modern Lib. $2.45. 398
1. Folk-Lore.

1826. Botkin, Benjamin A. Treasury of American Folklore. Crown. 1944. $5.95. 398
1. Folk-Lore, American.

1827. Briggs, Katharine M. and Tongue, Ruth L. Folktales of England. U of Chicago Pr. 1965. $7.50; pap. $2.95. 398
1. Folk-Lore, English.

1828. Coffin, Tristram P. Folklore in America. Doubleday. 1966. $4.95; pap. $1.95. 398
1. Folk-Lore, American.

1829. ———. Our Living Traditions: An Introduction to American Folklore. Basic. 1968. $7.00. 398
1. Folk-Lore, American.

1830. Coffin, Tristram P. and Cohen, Hennig. Folklore from the Working Folk of America. Doubleday. 1973. $8.95; pap. $3.50. 398
1. Folk-Lore, American.

1831. Colum, Padriac, ed. A Treasury of Irish Folklore: The Stories, Traditions, Legends, Humor, Wisdom, Ballads and Songs of the Irish People. rev. ed. Crown. 1969. $5.95. 398
1. Folk-Lore, Irish.

1832. Hodous, Lewis. Folklore in China. AMS Pr. 1929. $12.50. 398
1. Folk-Lore, Chinese.

1833. Hughes, Langston and Bontemps, Arna W., eds. The Book of Negro Folklore. Dodd. 1958. $7.50; pap. $3.45 1969 (Apollo Eds). 398
1. Folk-Lore, Negro.

1834. Krappe, Alexander H. The Science of Folklore. B&N. 1930. $16.75; pap. $3.00 (Norton). 398
1. Folk-Lore.

1835. Marriott, Alice and Rachlin, Carol K. American Indian Mythology. T Y Crowell. 1968. $7.95. 398
1. Folk-Lore, Indian. 2. Indians of North America — Legends.

1836. Radin, Paul and Sweeney, James J., eds. African Folktales and Sculpture. 2nd ed. Princeton U Pr. 1964. $18.50. 398
1. Folk-Lore.

1837. Rugoff, Milton A., ed. A Harvest of World Folk Tales. Viking Pr. 1949. pap. $3.95. 398
1. Folk-Lore.

1838. Sokolov, Yury M. Russian Folklore. 1966 ed. Gale. 1971. $18.00. 398
1. Folk-Lore, Russian.

1839. Toor, Frances. A Treasury of Mexican Folkways. Crown. 1947. $10.00. 398
1. Folk-Lore, Mexican.

1840. Van Buitenen, Johannes A. B. Tales of Ancient India. U of Chicago Pr. 1959. $7.00; pap. $2.45. 398
1. Folk-Lore, Indic.

1841. Dorson, Richard M. America in Legend: Folklore from the Colonial Period to the Present. Pantheon. 1973. pap. $5.95. 398.042
1. Folk-Lore, American. 2. U. S. — Social Life and Customs.

1842. Brewer, John Mason, compiled by. American Negro Folklore. Quadrangle. 1968. pap. $4.95. 398.09
1. Folk-Lore, Negro.

1843. Andersen, Hans Christian. Andersen's Fairy Tales. Macmillan. 1963. $4.95. 398.2
1. Fairy Tales.

1844. Grimm Brothers. Fairy Tales. G&D. 1949. $1.25. 398.2
1. Fairy Tales.

1845. Weston, Jessie. From Ritual to Romance. Peter Smith. 1957. $4.25; pap. $1.95 (Doubleday). 398.2
1. Grail. 2. Symbolism.

1846. ———. The Quest of the Holy Grail. Haskell. 1973. $11.95. 398.2
1. Grail. 2. Symbolism.

1847. DeCamp, L. Sprague. Lost Continents: The Atlantis Theme in History, Science, and Literature. Dover. 1970. $2.75. 398.23
1. Lost Continents.

1848. Aesop. Aesop's Fables. G&D. $5.95. 398.24
1. Fables.

1849. Briggs, Katharine M. The Fairies in English Tradition and Literature. U of Chicago Pr. 1967. $7.95.   398.4
1. Characters and Characteristics in Literature. 2. Fairies.

1850. Borges, Jorge Luis. The Book of Imaginary Beings. DiGiovanni, Norman T., tr. Dutton. 1969. $5.95.   398.469
1. Animals, Mythical.

399 Arms and Armor

1851. Snodgrass, Anthony M. Arms and Armour of the Greeks. Cornell U Pr. 1967. $7.50.   399
1. Arms and Armor, Greek.

Recommended Series

1852. Reference Shelf. Wilson. Subscription basis.

400 LANGUAGE

400 Language

1853. Katzner, Kenneth. The Languages of the World. T Y Crowell. 1974. $11.95. 400
1. Language and Languages.

1854. Laird, Charlton G. The Miracle of Language. Fawcett World. 1973. pap. $1.25. 400
1. Language and Languages.

1855. Sapir, Edward. Language: An Introduction to the Study of Speech. HarBraceJ. 1955. pap. $1.45. 400
1. Language and Languages.

410 Linguistics and Nonverbal Langauge

1856. Jespersen, Otto. Language: Its Nature, Development and Origin. Norton. 1964. pap. $2.95. 410
1. Language and Languages.

1857. Langacker, Ronald W. Language and Its Structure: Some Fundamental Linguistic Concepts. 2nd ed. HarBraceJ. 1973. pap. $5.30. 410
1. Language and Languages. 2. Linguistics.

1858. Gross, Maurice. Mathematical Models in Linguistics. P-H. 1972. $8.95; pap. $4.95. 410.1
1. Mathematical Linguistics.

1859. Wall, Robert. Introduction to Mathematical Linguistics. P-H. 1972. $13.50. 410.1
1. Mathematical Linguistics.

1860. Ober, J. Hambleton. Writing: Man's Great Invention. Astor-Honor. 1965. $10.00. 411.09
1. Writing — History.

1861. Shapiro, Karl J. and Beum, R. A Prosody Handbook. Har-Row. 1965. $6.00. 416
1. Poetics. 2. Versification.

1862. Pei, Mario. Talking Your Way Around the World: Profiles of the World's Chief Languages. 3rd enl. ed. Har-Row. 1971. $6.95. 418
1. Polyglot Glossaries, Phrase Books, etc.

420 English Language

1863. Chisholm, William. The New English. Funk & W. 1969. $6.95. 420
1. English Language — Study and Teaching.

1864. Laird, Charlton G. You and Your Language. P-H. 1973. $6.95; pap. $2.45. 420
1. English Language — Dialects.

1865. Barnett, Lincoln. The Treasure of Our Tongue. Knopf. 1965. $6.95. 420.9
1. English Language — History.

1866. Baugh, Albert C. A History of the English Language. 2nd ed. P-H. 1957. $9.50. 420.9
1. English Language — History.

400 LANGUAGE

1867. Jespersen, Otto. Growth and Structure of the English Language. 9th ed. Free Pr. 1968. pap. $1.95.   420.9
1. English Language — History.

1868. Pei, Mario. Story of the English Language. rev. ed. Lippincott. 1967. $7.95; pap. $2.95.   420.9
1. English Language — History.

1869. Robertson, Stuart and Cassidy, Frederic G. The Development of Modern English. 2nd ed. P-H. 1954. $9.95.   420.9
1. English Language — History.

1870. Strang, Barbara. A History of English. B&N. 1970. $18.75; pap. $7.50.   420.9
1. English Language — History.

422 Etymology

1871. Partridge, Eric. Adventuring Among Words. Bks for Libs. Repr. 1961. $6.00.   422
1. English Language — Words — History.

1872. Pei, Mario. Double-Speak in America. Hawthorn. 1973. $6.95.   422
1. English Language — Semantics. 2. English Language — Terms and Phrases. 3. Words, New — English.

1873. ———. Words in Sheep's Clothing. Hawthorn. 1969. $6.95.   422
1. English Language — Semantics. 2. English Language — Terms and Phrases. 3. English Language — Words — History.

1874. Ullmann, Stephen. Semantics: An Introduction to the Science of Meaning. B&N. 1962. $9.00.   422
1. Semantics.

427 Nonstandard English

1875. Bailey, Richard W. and Robinson, Jay L. Varieties of Present-Day English. Macmillan. 1973. pap. $5.95.   427
1. English Language in Foreign Countries. 2. English Language in the U. S. — Dialects.

1876. Wakelin, Martyn F. English Dialects. Humanities. 1972. $14.75; pap. $7.50.   427
1. English Language — Dialects.

1877. Dillard, Joey L. Black English: Its History and Usage in the U. S. Random.

1972. $10.00.   427.9
1. Negroes — Language.

1878. Francis, W. N. Structure of American English. Ronald. 1958. $8.50.   427.9
1. Americanisms. 2. English Language.

1879. Marckwardt, Albert H. American English. Oxford U Pr. 1958. $6.50; pap. $2.50.   427.9
1. Americanisms. 2. English Language.

1880. Mencken, Henry L. American Language. 3 vols. 4th ed. Knopf. 1963. $15.00 ea; $45.00 set.   427.9
1. Americanisms. 2. English Language. 3. Names — U. S.

428 Standard English Usage

1881. Copperud, Roy H. A Dictionary of Usage and Style. Hawthorn. 1964. $8.95; pap. $3.50.   428
1. English Language. 2. Rhetoric.

1882. Hayakawa, Samuel I. Language in Thought and Action. 3rd ed. HarBraceJ. 1972. $7.95; pap. $4.95.   428
1. English Language — Semantics.

1883. Partridge, Eric. Usage and Abusage: Guide to Good English. 6th ed. British Bk Ctr. 1965. $9.95; pap. $1.60 1963 (Penguin).   428
1. English Language — Grammar. 2. English Language — Idioms.

1884. Morse, Josiah M. The Irrelevant English Teacher. Temple U Pr. 1972. pap. $2.95.   428.007
1. English Philology — Study and Teaching.

1885. Bernstein, Theodore M. The Careful Writer. Atheneum. 1965. $10.00.   428.3
1. English Language — Idioms.

1886. ———. Watch Your Language. Atheneum. 1965. $4.50.   428.3
1. English Language — Idioms.

1887. Fries, Charles C. Linguistics and Reading. HR&W. 1963. $7.95.   428.4
1. Language and Languages. 2. Reading.

1888. Mares, Colin. Rapid and Efficient Reading. Emerson. 1967. $5.95.   428.4
1. Rapid Reading.

500 SCIENCE

500 Science

1889. Byrd, E. How Things Work: Practical Guide for Teaching Scientific and Technical Principles. P-H. 1973. $8.95.   500
1. Science — Methodology. 2. Science — Study and Teaching. 3. Technology — Study and Teaching.

1890. DeRopp, Robert S. The New Prometheans. Delacorte. 1972. $7.95; pap. $2.65 (Delta).   500
1. Science.

1891. Dessel, N. and Dessel, Nehrich. Science and Human Destiny. McGraw. 1973. $6.95.   500
1. Science — History. 2. Science — Social Aspects. 3. Technology — Social Aspects.

1892. Dietz, David. The New Outline of Science. Dodd. 1972. $17.50.   500
1. Atoms. 2. Earth. 3. Life (Biology). 4. Science. 5. Universe.

1893. Goran, Morris. Science and Anti-Science. Ann Arbor Science. 1974. $10.00.   500
1. Science. 2. Scientists.

1894. Stevens, Peter S. Patterns in Nature. Little. 1974. $10.00.   500
1. Morphology. 2. Nature. 3. Philosophy of Nature.

1895. CRM Staff & Contributing Consultants. Physical Science Today. new ed. CRM Bks. 1973. $12.95.   500.2
1. Astronomy. 2. Chemistry, Physical and Theoretical. 3. Physics.

1896. Haymes, Robert C. Introduction to Space Science. Wiley. 1971. $16.50.   500.5
1. Cosmic Physics.

500.9 Natural History

1897. Cornell, James, ed. It Happened Last Year: Earth Events - 1973. Macmillan. 1974. $7.95.   500.9
1. Meteorites. 2. Natural Disasters. 3. Natural History. 4. Oil Pollution of Rivers, Harbors, etc. 5. Short-Lived Phenomena.

1898. Shepard, Daniel and Shepard, Jean. Earth Watch: Notes on a Restless Planet. Doubleday. 1973. $8.95.   500.9
1. Meteorites. 2. Natural Disasters. 3. Natural History. 4. Oil Pollution of Rivers, Harbors, etc. 5. Short-Lived Phenomena.

1899. Ogburn, Charlton, Jr. The Winter Beach. Morrow. 1966. $7.95; pap. $3.95.   500.909
1. Atlantic Coast — Description and Travel. 2. Natural History — Atlantic States. 3. Seashore.

1900. Botting, Douglas. Humboldt and the Cosmos. Har-Row. 1973. $15.00.   500.924(B)
1. Humboldt, Alexander Freiheur von, 1769-1859.

1901. Gibbons, Euell. Stalking the Far Away Places. McKay. 1973. $6.95.   500.973
1. Natural History — North America. 2. Nature.

1902. Dillard, Annie. Pilgrim at Tinker Creek. Harper Mag Pr. 1974. $7.95.   500.9755
1. Nature.

500 SCIENCE

1903. Leopold, Aldo. A Sand County Almanac and Sketches Here and There. Oxford U Pr. 1949. pap. $1.95.   500.9775
1. Natural History — Outdoor Books. 2. Natural History — U. S. 3. Wildlife Protection.

1904. Sutton, Ann. Yellowstone Park: A Century of the Wilderness Idea. Macmillan. 1972. $25.00.   500.978
1. Natural History — Yellowstone National Park. 2. Yellowstone National Park.

1905. Norton, Boyd. The Grand Tetons. Viking Pr. 1974. $17.95.   500.9787
1. Grand Tetons National Park — Pictorial Works. 2. Natural History — Wyoming — Grand Teton National Park — Pictorial Works.

1906. Sutton, Ann and Sutton, Myron. The Wilderness World of the Grand Canyon: Leave It As It Is. Lippincott. 1971. $8.95.   500.979
1. Grand Canyon National Park. 2. Natural History — Arizona — Grand Canyon Region.

1907. Johnston, Verna. Sierra Nevada. HM. 1970. $7.95.   500.9794
1. Natural History — California — Sierra Nevada Mountains. 2. Sierra Nevada Mountains.

1908. Thornton, Ian. Darwin's Islands: A Natural History of the Galapagos. Natural Hist. 1971. $8.95.   500.986
1. Galapagos Islands. 2. Natural History — Galapagos Islands.

501-509 Philosophy, Miscellany, Historical and Geographical Treatment

1909. Achinstein, Peter. Concepts of Science: A Philosophical Analysis. Johns Hopkins. 1969. $10.00; pap. $2.45.   501
1. Science — Methodology.

1910. Joravsky, David. Soviet Marxism and Natural Science, 1917-1932. Columbia U Pr. 1961. $11.00.   501.47
1. Communism — Russia. 2. Science — Philosophy.

1911. Killeffer, David H. How Did You Think of That? An Introduction to the Scientific Method. Am Chemical. 1969. pap. $2.79.   501.8
1. Science — Methodology.

1912. Adler, Irving. The Changing Tools of Science. rev. ed. John Day. 1973. $4.68.   502.8
1. Physical Instruments. 2. Scientific Apparatus and Instruments.

1913. Klein, Aaron E. The Electron Microscope: A Tool of Discovery. McGraw. 1974. $5.72.   502.8
1. Electron Microscope. 2. Microscope and Microscopy. 3. Scientific Apparatus and Instruments.

1914. Whitehead, Alfred N. Essays in Science and Philosophy. Greenwood. Repr. 1947. $16.00.   504
1. Education — Addresses, Essays, Lectures. 2. Philosophy — Addresses, Essays, Lectures. 3. Science — Addresses, Essays, Lectures.

1915. Oehser, Paul H. The Smithsonian Institute. Praeger. 1970. $8.95.   506.173
1. Smithsonian Institution. 2. U. S. — Government Departments and Agencies.

1916. Beveridge, W. I. Art of Scientific Investigation. rev. ed. Norton. 1957. $4.95; pap. $1.45 (Random).   507
1. Research.

1917. Asimov, Isaac. The Left Hand of the Electron. Doubleday. 1972. $6.95.   508.1
1. Science.

1918. ———. Today and Tomorrow and ... Doubleday. 1973. $6.95.   508.1
1. Science.

1919. Linklater, Eric. The Voyage of the Challenger. Doubleday. 1972. $15.00.   508.3
1. Challenger (Corvette). 2. Challenger Expedition, 1872-1876.

1920. Bradbury, Ray, et al. Mars and the Mind of Man. Har-Row. 1973. $8.95.   508.9923
1. Astronautics and Civilization. 2. Mars (Planet) — Exploration. 3. Project Mariner. 4. Space Flight to Mars.

1921. Bronowski, Jacob. The Ascent of Man. Little. 1974. $15.00.   509
1. Man. 2. Science — History. 3. Science — Philosophy.

500 SCIENCE

1922. Dampier, William C. A History of Science and Its Relation with Philosophy and Religion. Cambridge U Pr. 1949-66. $9.50; pap. $2.45.　509
1. Science — History.

1923. Parry, Albert. The Russian Scientist. Macmillan. 1973. $5.95.　509
1. Science — History — Russia. 2. Scientists, Russian.

1924. Ronan, Colin A. Lost Discoveries: The Forgotten Science of the Ancient World. McGraw. 1973. $10.95.　509.3
1. Inventions. 2. Science, Ancient.

1925. Vucinich, Alexander S. Science in Russian Culture: A History to 1860. Stanford U Pr. 1963. $15.00.　509.47
1. Science — History — Russia.

1926. ———. Science in Russian Culture, 1861-1917. Stanford U Pr. 1970. $18.50.　509.47
1. Science — History — Russia.

510 Mathematics

1927. Abbott, Edwin A. Flatland. 5th rev. ed. B&N. 1963. $3.50; pap. $1.25.　510
1. Mathematics.

1928. Berkeley, Edmund C. Guide to Mathematics for the Intelligent Nonmathematician. S&S. 1957. $6.95; pap. $2.45.　510
1. Mathematics.

1929. Courant, Richard and Robbins, Herbert. What Is Mathematics? Oxford U Pr. 1941. $12.50.　510
1. Mathematics.

1930. Cundy, Henry M. and Rollett, A. P. Mathematical Models. 2nd ed. Oxford U Pr. 1961. $7.50.　510
1. Mathematics.

1931. Dantzig, T. Number, the Language of Science. 4th rev. ed. Macmillan. 1954. $7.95; pap. $2.45 (Free Pr).　510
1. Mathematics. 2. Numbers, Theory of.

1932. Fuchs, Walter R. Mathematics for the Modern Mind. Macmillan. 1967. $6.95.　510
1. Mathematics.

1933. Jacobs, Harold R. Mathematics, a Human Endeavor: A Textbook for Those Who Think They Don't Like the Subject. W H Freeman. 1970. $8.50.　510
1. Mathematics.

1934. Kasner, Edward and Newman, James. Mathematics and the Imagination. S&S. 1940. $6.95; pap. $2.95.　510
1. Mathematical Recreations. 2. Mathematics.

1935. Kline, Morris. Mathematics in Western Culture. Oxford U Pr. 1953. $12.50; pap. $3.95.　510
1. Mathematics.

1936. Kramer, Edna. The Nature and Growth of Modern Mathematics. Hawthorn. 1970. $24.95; pap. $1.95 ea. 2 vols. (Fawcett World).　510
1. Mathematics.

1937. Lang, Serge. Basic Mathematics. A-W. 1971. $10.95.　510
1. Mathematics.

1938. Malkevitch, Joseph and Meyer, Walter. Graphs, Models, and Finite Mathematics. P-H. 1974. $10.95.　510
1. Graph Theory. 2. Mathematical Models. 3. Mathematics.

1939. Scientific American Editors. Mathematics in the Modern World: Readings from Scientific American. W H Freeman. 1968. pap. $6.50.　510
1. Mathematics.

1940. Zaslovsky, Claudia. Africa Counts: Number and Pattern in African Culture. Prindle. 1973. $12.50.　510
1. Games — Africa, Sub-Saharan. 2. Mathematics, Primitive — Africa, Sub-Saharan.

1941. Polya, Gyorgy. Mathematical Discovery on Understanding, Learning and Teaching Problem Solving. 2 vols. Wiley. 1962. $8.50 ea.　510.76
1. Mathematics. 2. Problem Solving.

1942. Eves, Howard. An Introduction to the History of Mathematics. 3rd ed. HR&W. 1969. $11.50.　510.9
1. Mathematics — History.

1943. Meschkowski, Herbert. Ways of Thought of Great Mathematicians. Holden-Day. 1964. $8.95; pap. $4.95.　510.9
1. Mathematicians. 2. Mathematics — History.

500 SCIENCE

1944. Struik, Dirk J. A Concise History of Mathematics. 3rd rev. ed. Dover. 1967. pap. $2.00.   510.9
1. Mathematics — History.

1945. Bell, Eric T. Men of Mathematics. S&S. 1937. $8.50; pap. $3.95.   510.922
1. Mathematicians.

1946. Osen, Lynn M. Women in Mathematics. MIT Pr. 1973. $5.95.   510.922
1. Women Mathematicians — Biography.

1947. Mahoney, M. The Mathematical Career of Pierre de Fermat, 1601-1665. Princeton U Pr. 1973. $20.00.   510.924(B)
1. Fermat, Pierre de, 1601-1665.

1948. Whipkey, Kenneth L. and Whipkey, Mary N. The Power of Calculus. 2nd ed. Wiley. 1975. $10.95.   515
1. Calculus.

1949. Holden, Alan. Shapes, Space, and Symmetry. Columbia U Pr. 1971. $11.00; pap. $4.95.   516.23
1. Polyhedra.

1950. Wenninger, M. J. Polyhedron Models. Cambridge U Pr. 1971. $14.50; pap. $4.95.   516.23
1. Polyhedra — Models.

519 Probability

1951. David, Florence N. Games, Gods and Gambling. Hafner. 1962. $7.50.   519.2
1. Probabilities.

1952. Weaver, Warren. Lady Luck: The Theory of Probability. Doubleday. 1963. pap. $2.50.   519.2
1. Probabilities.

1953. Davis, Morton D. Game Theory: A Nontechnical Introduction. Basic. 1970. $6.95; pap. $2.95.   519.3
1. Games. 2. Probabilities.

1954. McKinsey, John C. Introduction to the Theory of Games. McGraw. 1952. $12.00.   519.3
1. Games. 2. Probabilities.

1955. Silverman, Eliot N. and Brody, Linda A. Statistics: A Common Sense Approach. rev. ed. Prindle. 1973. $10.95.   519.5
1. Statistics.

1956. Tanur, Judith, et al, eds. Statistics: A Guide to the Unknown. Holden-Day. 1972. $7.95.   519.5
1. Statistics.

Recommended Series

1957. New Mathematical Library. Random.

1958. Topics in Mathematics. Heath.

520 Astronomy

1959. Alter, Dinsmore, et al. Pictorial Astronomy. rev. ed. T Y Crowell. 1974. $10.00.   520
1. Astronomy.

1960. Bova, Ben. The New Astronomies. St Martin. 1972. $7.95; pap. $1.95 (NAL).   520
1. Astronomy.

1961. Brandt, John C. and Maran, S. P. New Horizons in Astronomy. W H Freeman. 1972. $12.95.   520
1. Astronomy.

1962. Ditfurth, Hoimar Von. Children of the Universe. Atheneum. 1974. $10.95.   520
1. Astronomy.

1963. Hoyle, Fred. Frontiers of Astronomy. Har-Row. 1955. $7.50.   520
1. Astronomy.

1964. Jastrow, Robert and Thompson, Malcolm H. Astronomy: Fundamentals and Frontiers. 2nd ed. Wiley. 1974. $14.95.   520
1. Astronomy.

1965. Muirden, James. The Amateur Astronomer's Handbook. rev. ed. T Y Crowell. 1974. $8.95.   520
1. Astronomy — Observers' Manuals.

1966. Scientific American Editors. Frontiers of Astronomy: Readings from Scientific American. W H Freeman. 1970. $11.00; pap. $5.95.   520
1. Astronomy.

1967. Wyatt, Stanley P. Principles of Astronomy. 2nd ed. Allyn. 1971. $14.95.   520
1. Astronomy.

1968. Calder, Nigel. Violent Universe: An Eyewitness Account of the New Astronomy. Viking Pr. 1970. $10.95; pap. $3.95.   520.9
1. Astronomy.

500 SCIENCE

1969. Moore, Patrick. Watchers of the Stars: The Scientific Revolution. Putnam. 1974. $15.95.   520.9
1. Astronomers. 2. Astronomy — History.

1970. Ronan, Colin A. Discovering the Universe. Basic. 1971. $6.95.   520.9
1. Astronomy — History.

1971. Whitney, Charles A. The Discovery of Our Galaxy. Knopf. 1971. $10.00.   520.9
1. Astronomy — History.

1972. Adamczewski, Jan. Nicolaus Copernicus and His Epoch. Scribner. 1974. $7.95.   520.924(B)
1. Copernicus, Nicolaus, 1473-1543.

1973. Hoyle, Fred. Nicolaus Copernicus: An Essay on His Life and Work. Har-Row. $5.95.   520.924(B)
1. Copernicus, Nicolaus, 1473-1543.

1974. Ronan, Colin A. Galileo. Putnam. 1974. $14.95.   520.924(B)
1. Astronomers. 2. Galilei, Galileo, 1564-1642.

1975. Howard, Neale E. The Telescope Handbook and Star Atlas. rev. 2nd ed. T Y Crowell. 1975. $14.95.   522.2
1. Astronomy. 2. Telescope.

1976. MacVey, John. Whispers from Space. Macmillan. 1973. $8.95.   522.682
1. Interstellar Communication. 2. Radio Astronomy.

1977. Verschuur, Gerrit L. The Invisible Universe. Springer-Verlag. 1974. pap. $5.90.   522.682
1. Interstellar Communication. 2. Radio Astronomy.

523 Descriptive Astronomy

1978. Hawkins, Gerald S. Beyond Stonehenge. Har-Row. 1973. $10.00.   523
1. Astronomy, Prehistoric. 2. Indians — Astronomy.

1979. Kaufmann, William J. Relativity and Cosmology. Har-Row. 1973. pap. $3.25.   523
1. Cosmology. 2. General Relativity (Physics).

1980. Taylor, John G. Black Holes: The End of the Universe? Random. 1974. $5.95.   523
1. Black Holes. 2. Universe.

1981. Peltier, Leslie C. Guideposts to the Stars: Exploring the Skies Through the Year. Macmillan. 1972. $6.95.   523.002
1. Astronomy — Observers' Manuals. 2. Stars.

1982. Hoyle, Fred. Galaxies, Nuclei and Quasars. Har-Row. 1965. $5.95.   523.01
1. Astronomy.

523.1 Physical Universe

1983. Alfven, Hannes. Worlds-Antiworlds: Antimatter in Cosmology. W H Freeman. 1966. $3.95.   523.1
1. Universe.

1984. Gamow, George. The Creation of the Universe. rev. ed. Viking Pr. 1961. $5.75.   523.1
1. Universe.

1985. Jastrow, Robert. Red Giants and White Dwarfs: Man's Descent from the Stars. rev. ed. Har-Row. 1970. $6.95; pap. $1.50 (NAL).   523.1
1. Evolution. 2. Life — Origin. 3. Universe.

1986. Levitt, I. M. Beyond the Known Universe: From Dwarf Stars to Quasars. Viking Pr. 1974. $10.00.   523.11
1. Astronomy. 2. Mechanics, Celestial.

1987. Shapley, Harlow. Galaxies. 3rd ed. Harvard U Pr. 1972. $10.00.   523.112
1. Universe.

1988. Bok, Bart J. and Bok, Priscilla F. The Milky Way. 4th ed. Harvard U Pr. 1974. $15.00.   523.113
1. Milky Way.

1989. Branley, Franklyn M. The Milky Way: Galaxy Number One. T Y Crowell. 1969. $5.50.   523.113
1. Milky Way.

1990. Hinkelbein, Albert. Origins of the Universe. Watts. 1973. $5.90.   523.12
1. Astronomy. 2. Universe.

1991. Hartmann, William K. Moons and Planets. Wadsworth Pub. 1972. $12.95.   523.2
1. Solar System.

1992. Kuhn, Thomas S. The Copernican Revolution: Planetary Astronomy in the Development of Western Thought. Harvard U Pr. 1957. $9.00; pap. $2.75.   523.2

500 SCIENCE

1. Copernicus, Nicolaus, 1473-1543.
2. Cosmology.

1993. Branley, Franklyn M. The Moon: Earth's Natural Satellite. rev. ed. T Y Crowell. 1972. $4.50.   523.3
1. Moon.

1994. Alter, Dinsmore. Pictorial Guide to the Moon. 3rd ed. T Y Crowell. 1973. $8.95.   523.39
1. Moon — Photographs.

1995. Cardin, Martin. Planetfall. Coward. 1974. $7.95.   523.4
1. Planets — Exploration. 2. Space Probes.

1996. Jackson, Joseph H., 3rd. Pictorial Guide to the Planets. rev. enl. ed. T Y Crowell. 1973. $12.50.   523.4
1. Planets.

1997. Nourse, Alan E. Nine Planets. rev. ed. Har-Row. 1970. $9.95.   523.4
1. Planets. 2. Solar System.

1998. Moore, Patrick and Cross, Charles A. Mars. Crown. 1973. $7.95.   523.43
1. Mars (Planet).

1999. Collins, Stewart A. The Mariner 6 and 7 Pictures of Mars. US Govt Ptg Off. 1971. $4.25.   523.439
1. Mars (Planet) — Photographs from Space. 2. Project Mariner.

2000. Asimov, Isaac. Jupiter: The Largest Planet. Lothrop. 1973. $6.50.   523.45
1. Jupiter (Planet).

2001. Davies, Merton and Murray, Bruce C. The View from Space: Photographic Exploration of the Planets. Columbia U Pr. 1971. $15.00; pap. $4.95.   523.49
1. Planets — Photographs from Space.

2002. McCall, G. J. Meteorites and Their Origins. Halsted Pr. 1973. $12.95.   523.51
1. Meteorites.

2003. Brown, Peter L. Comets, Meteorites and Men. Taplinger. 1974. $9.50.   523.6
1. Comets. 2. Meteorites.

523.7-523.8 Sun and Stars

2004. Ellison, M. A. The Sun and Its Influence. Am Elsevier. 1968. $5.95.   523.7
1. Sun.

2005. Hey, Nigel S. The Mysterious Sun. Putnam. 1971. $3.97.   523.7
1. Sun.

2006. Smith, Alexander G. Radio Exploration of the Sun. Van Nos Reinhold. 1967. pap. $2.50.   523.7
1. Sun.

2007. King, Henry C. Pictorial Guide to the Stars. T Y Crowell. 1967. $8.95.   523.8
1. Astronomy. 2. Stars.

2008. Allen, Richard H. Star Names: Their Lore and Their Meaning. new ed. Dover. 1963. pap. $4.00.   523.89
1. Constellations.

2009. Bodechtel, J. and Gierioff-Emden, H. G. The Earth from Space. Arco. 1973. $16.95.   525.022
1. Earth — Photographs from Space.

2010. National Aeronautics & Space Administration. Earth Photographs from Gemini III, IV, and V. US Govt Ptg Off. 1967. $7.00.   525.022
1. Earth — Photographs from Space.

2011. ———. Earth Photographs from Gemini VI Through XII. US Govt Ptg Off. 1968. $8.00.   525.022
1. Earth — Photographs from Space.

2012. Nicks, Oran W., ed. This Island Earth. US Govt Ptg Off. 1970. $6.00.   525.022
1. Earth — Photographs from Space.

526 Cartography

2013. Greenwood, David. Mapping. rev. ed. U of Chicago Pr. 1964. $8.50; pap. $2.95.   526.8
1. Maps.

530 Physics

2014. Bailey, John M. Liberal Arts Physics: Invariance and Change. W H Freeman. 1974. $12.95.   530
1. Physics.

2015. Benumof, Reuben. Concepts in Physics. 2nd ed. P-H. 1973. $13.95.   530
1. Physics.

2016. Born, Max. The Restless Universe. 2nd ed. Dover. 1951. pap. $3.50.   530
1. Physics. 2. Universe.

500 SCIENCE

2017. Faraday, Michael. On the Various Forces of Nature. T Y Crowell. 1961. $2.75. 530
1. Physics.

2018. Fuchs, Walter R. Physics for the Modern Mind. Macmillan. 1967. $6.95. 530
1. Physics.

2019. Hulsizer, Robert and Lazarus, David. The World of Physics. new ed. A-W. 1972. $7.96. 530
1. Physics.

2020. Taylor, Lloyd W. Physics, the Pioneer Science. 2 vols. Dover. 1941. pap. $2.75 ea. 530
1. Physics.

2021. Thiemer, Otto H. A Gentleman's Guide to Modern Physics. Wadsworth Pub. 1973. $10.95. 530
1. Physics.

2022. Wiggins, Arthur W. Physical Science with Environmental Applications. HM. 1974. $10.95. 530
1. Matter. 2. Physics.

2023. Bernstein, Jeremy. Einstein. Viking Pr. 1973. $6.95; pap. $2.75. 530.092(B)
1. Einstein, Albert, 1879-1955.

2024. Clark, Ronald W. Einstein: The Life and Times. T Y Crowell. 1971. $15.00; pap. $1.95 (Avon). 530.092(B)
1. Einstein, Albert, 1879-1955. 2. Physics.

2025. Hoffman, Banesh and Dukas, Helen. Albert Einstein: Creator and Rebel. Viking Pr. 1972. $8.95; pap. $2.95 (NAL). 530.092(B)
1. Einstein, Albert, 1879-1955.

2026. More, Louis T. Isaac Newton, a Biography. Peter Smith. $5.50. 530.092(B)
1. Newton, Isaac, 1642-1727. 2. Scientists.

2027. Reid, Robert. Marie Curie. Sat Rev Pr. 1974. $8.95. 530.092(B)
1. Curie, Marie Sklodowska, 1867-1934.

2028. Bergmann, Peter G. The Riddle of Gravitation. Scribner. 1969. pap. $2.65. 530.1
1. Gravitation. 2. Relativity (Physics).

2029. Feuer, Lewis. Einstein and the Generations of Science. Basic. 1974. $12.95. 530.1

1. Quantum Theory — History. 2. Relativity (Physics). 3. Science.

2030. Einstein, Albert. The Meaning of Relativity. 5th ed. Princeton U Pr. 1956. $7.50; pap. $2.45. 530.11
1. Relativity (Physics).

2031. Lieber, Lillian R. The Einstein Theory of Relativity. HR&W. 1945. $3.95. 530.11
1. Relativity (Physics).

2032. Hoffman, Banesh. The Strange Story of the Quantum. Dover. 1959. pap. $2.00. 530.12
1. Quantum Theory.

2033. Segré, Emilio. Enrico Fermi, Physicist. U of Chicago Pr. 1970. $8.50; pap. $2.95. 530.12(B)
1. Fermi, Enrico, 1901-1954.

2034. Bova, Ben. The Fourth State of Matter: Plasma Dynamics and Tomorrow's Technology. St Martin. 1971. $5.95; pap. $1.95 1974 (NAL). 530.44
1. Plasma Dynamics. 2. Plasma (Ionized Gases).

2035. Magie, William F. A Source Book in Physics. Harvard U Pr. 1963. $15.00. 530.8
1. Physics — Collected Works. 2. Physics — History.

2036. Ford, Kenneth W. The World of Elementary Particles. Xerox College. 1963. pap. $3.95. 531.1
1. Dynamics of a Particle.

2037. Pierce, John R. Almost All About Waves. MIT Pr. 1974. $8.95. 532.0593
1. Waves.

534-535 Sound and Optics

2038. Koch, Winston E. Seeing Sound. Wiley. 1971. $8.25. 534
1. Sound-waves.

2039. Huygens, Christiaan. Treatise on Light. Thompson, Silvanus P., tr. Dover. 1912. pap. $2.00. 535
1. Refraction.

2040. Jenkins, Francis A. Fundamentals of Optics. 4th ed. McGraw. 1975. $16.50. 535
1. Optics.

500 SCIENCE

2041. Newton, Isaac. Opticks. Dover. pap. $4.00. 535
1. Optics.

2042. Klein, H. Arthur. Holography. Lippincott. 1970. $4.95. 535.5
1. Optics.

536 Thermodynamics

2043. Faires, Virgil M. Thermodynamics. rev. 5th ed. Macmillan. 1970. $14.50. 536.7
1. Thermodynamics.

2044. Rolle, Kurt C. Introduction to Thermodynamics. Merrill. 1973. $15.95. 536.7
1. Thermodynamics.

2045. Zemansky, M. W. Heat and Thermodynamics. 5th ed. McGraw. 1968. $15.95. 536.7
1. Heat. 2. Thermodynamics.

537 Electricity

2046. De France, J. J. Electrical Fundamentals. P-H. 1969. $14.50. 537.07
1. Electricity.

2047. Kip, Arthur F. Fundamentals of Electricity and Magnetism. McGraw. 1969. $12.50. 537.07
1. Electricity. 2. Magnetism.

2048. Marcus, Abraham. Basic Electricity. 3rd ed. P-H. 1969. $11.24. 537.07
1. Electricity.

2049. Meyer, Herbert W. A History of Electricity and Magnetism. MIT Pr. 1972. $10.00. 537.09
1. Electricity — History. 2. Magnetism — History.

2050. Moore, A. D. Electrostatics: Exploring, Controlling and Using Static Electricity. Doubleday. 1968. $5.50; pap. $1.45. 537.2
1. Electricity.

2051. Crowhurst, Norman H. Basic Electronics Course. Tab Bks. 1972. $8.95; pap. $5.95. 537.5
1. Electronics.

539 Modern Physics - Molecular, Atomic and Nuclear Physics

2052. Boorse, Henry A. and Motz, Lloyd, eds. The World of the Atom. 2 vols. Basic. 1966. $38.50. 539
1. Atoms.

2053. Lindsay, Robert B. The Nature of Physics: A Physicist's View on the History and Philosophy of His Science. Brown U Pr. 1968. $8.50. 539
1. Physics.

2054. Taylor, Edwin F. and Wheeler, John A. Spacetime Physics. W H Freeman. 1966. $5.50; pap. $3.50. 539
1. Outer Space. 2. Physics.

2055. Taylor, John G. The New Physics. Basic. 1972. $8.25. 539
1. Physics.

2056. Childs, Herbert. An American Genius: The Life of Ernest Orlando Lawrence, Father of the Cyclotron. Dutton. 1968. $12.95. 539.7(B)
1. Cyclotron. 2. Lawrence, Ernest Orlando, 1901-1958.

2057. Davis, Nuel P. Lawrence and Oppenheimer. S&S. 1968. $7.50; pap. $2.95. 539.7(B)
1. Atomic Bomb. 2. Lawrence, Ernest Orlando, 1901-1958. 3. Nuclear Physics. 4. Oppenheimer, Julius Robert, 1904-1967.

2058. Ellis, R. Hobart, Jr. Knowing the Atomic Nucleus. Lothrop. 1973. $4.95. 539.7
1. Atoms. 2. Nuclear Physics.

2059. Glasstone, Samuel. Sourcebook on Atomic Energy. 3rd ed. Van Nos Reinhold. 1967. $13.95. 539.7
1. Atomic Energy. 2. Nuclear Physics.

2060. Michelsohn, David R. Atomic Energy for Human Needs. Messner. 1973. $5.29. 539.7
1. Atomic Energy.

2061. Moore, Ruth. Niels Bohr: The Man, His Science and the World They Changed. Knopf. 1966. $7.95. 539.7(B)
1. Atomic Bomb. 2. Bohr, Niels Henrik David, 1885-1962.

2062. Royal, D. The Story of J. Robert Oppenheimer. St Martin. 1969. $5.95. 539.7(B)
1. Oppenheimer, Julius Robert, 1904-1967.

500 SCIENCE

2063. Gallant, Roy A. Explorers of the Atom. Doubleday. 1974. $4.95. 539.709
1. Atoms. 2. Radioactivity.

2064. Hillas, A. M. Cosmic Rays. Pergamon. 1972. $12.50. 539.722
1. Cosmic Rays.

540 Chemistry

2065. Andrews, Donald and Kokes, R. J. Fundamental Chemistry. 2nd ed. Wiley. 1965. $14.00. 540
1. Chemistry.

2066. Drummond, A. H., Jr. Molecules in the Service of Man. Lippincott. 1972. $5.95. 540
1. Chemistry. 2. Molecules.

2067. Kieffer, William F. The Mole Concept in Chemistry. 2nd ed. Van Nos Reinhold. 1973. pap. $3.25. 540
1. Chemistry.

2068. Medeiros, Robert W. Chemistry: An Interdisciplinary Approach. Van Nos Reinhold. 1971. $10.95. 540
1. Chemistry.

2069. O'Connor, Raymond. Chemical Principles and Their Biological Implications. Wiley. 1974. $9.95. 540
1. Biological Chemistry. 2. Chemistry.

2070. Pauling, Linus and Pauling, Peter. College Chemistry. 4th ed. W H Freeman. 1975. $13.95. 540
1. Chemistry.

2071. Sherwood, Martin. The New Chemistry. Basic. 1973. $9.50. 540
1. Chemistry.

2072. Smith, Richard F. Chemistry for the Million. Scribner. 1972. $7.95; pap. $2.95. 540
1. Chemistry.

2073. Vaczek, Louis C. The Enjoyment of Chemistry. Viking Pr. 1964. $6.00; pap. $1.65. 540
1. Chemistry.

2074. Grossinger, Richard and Hough, Lindy. Alchemy. 3rd enl. ed. Io Pubns. 1973. pap. $4.00. 540.1
1. Alchemy.

541 Physical Chemistry

2075. Grunwald, Ernest and Johnsen, Russell H. Atoms, Molecules, and Chemical Change. 3rd ed. P-H. 1971. $13.95. 541.2
1. Atoms. 2. Molecules.

2076. Pauling, Linus and Hayward, R. The Architecture of Molecules. W H Freeman. 1970. pap. $4.95. 541.2
1. Molecules.

546-547 Inorganic and Organic Chemistry

2077. Lagowski, J. J. Modern Inorganic Chemistry. Dekker. 1973. $13.75. 546
1. Chemistry, Inorganic.

2078. Basolo, Fred and Pearson, R. G. Mechanisms of Inorganic Reactions. 2nd ed. Wiley. 1967. $24.75. 546.3
1. Chemical Reactions. 2. Chemistry, Inorganic.

2079. Sanderson, Robert T. Inorganic Chemistry. Van Nos Reinhold. 1967. $15.95. 546.3
1. Chemistry, Inorganic.

2080. Asimov, Isaac. The Noble Gases. Basic. 1966. $5.95. 546.75
1. Gases, Rare.

2081. Benfey, Otto F. The Names and Structures of Organic Compounds: A Programmed Text. Wiley. 1966. pap. $4.95. 547
1. Chemistry, Organic.

2082. Butler, George B. and Berlin, K. Darrell. Fundamentals of Organic Chemistry: Theory and Application. Ronald. 1972. $17.95. 547
1. Chemistry, Organic.

2083. Depuy, Charles H. and Rinehart, Kenneth L. Introduction to Organic Chemistry. 2nd ed. Wiley. 1975. $12.50. 547
1. Chemistry, Organic.

2084. Kice, J. L. and Marvell, E. N. Modern Principles of Organic Chemistry: An Introduction. 2nd ed. Macmillan. 1974. $11.95. 547
1. Chemistry, Organic.

2085. Clar, Eric. The Aromatic Sextet. Wiley. 1972. pap. $4.95. 547.6
1. Aromatic Compounds.

Recommended Series

2086. Topics in Modern Chemistry. Bailar, John C., Jr., & Kleineberg, Jacob, gen. eds.. Heath.

549 Mineralogy

2087. Campbell, Jan. Minerals: Nature's Fabulous Jewels. Abrams. 1974. $35.00.   549
1. Mineralogy.

2088. Desautels, Paul E. Rocks and Minerals. G&D. 1974. $12.95.   549
1. Mineralogy — Pictorial Works. 2. Rocks — Pictorial Works.

2089. Hurlbut, Cornelius, Jr. Minerals and Man. Random. 1968. $17.95.   549
1. Mineralogy.

550 Earth Sciences

2090. Bauer, Ernst W. Wonders of the Earth. Watts. 1973. $5.90.   550
1. Earth Sciences. 2. Geology.

2091. C R M Books Editorial Staff. Geology Today. rev. ed. CRM Bks. 1974. $15.95.   550
1. Geology.

2092. Dineley, David. Earth's Voyage Through Time. Knopf. 1974. $8.95.   550
1. Geology.

2093. Fraser, Ronald. The Habitable Earth. Basic. 1965. $5.95.   550
1. Earth. 2. Geology.

2094. Gilluly, James, et al. Principles of Geology. 4th ed. W H Freeman. 1975. $12.95.   550
1. Geology.

2095. Leveson, David. A Sense of the Earth. Doubleday. 1971. $6.95; pap. $3.50.   550
1. Geology.

2096. Menard, H. W. Geology, Resources, and Society: An Introduction to Earth Science. W H Freeman. 1974. $12.95.   550
1. Earth Sciences.

2097. Press, Frank and Siever, Raymond. Earth. W H Freeman. 1974. $13.95.   550
1. Physical Geology.

2098. Shelton, John S. Geology Illustrated. W H Freeman. 1966. $12.50.   550
1. Geology.

2099. Strahler, Arthur N. and Strahler, Alan H. Environmental Geoscience: Interaction Between Natural Systems and Man. Wiley. 1973. $12.95.   550
1. Conservation of Natural Resources. 2. Earth Sciences. 3. Natural Disasters.

2100. Zumberg, James H. and Nelson, Clemens A. Elements of Geology. 3rd ed. Wiley. 1972. $13.25.   550
1. Geology.

2101. Harrington, John W. To See a World. Mosby. 1973. pap. $4.75.   550.1
1. Geology — Philosophy. 2. Science — Philosophy.

2102. Press, Frank and Siever, Raymond, eds. Planet Earth. W H Freeman. 1974. $12.00; pap. $6.95.   550.8
1. Earth Sciences. 2. Force and Energy. 3. Pollution.

2103. Tank, Ronald W., ed. Focus on Environmental Geology: A Collection of Case Histories and Readings from Original Sources. Oxford U Pr. 1973. $8.95; pap. $4.95.   550.8
1. Conservation of Natural Resources. 2. Geology. 3. Mines and Mineral Resources. 4. Natural Disasters.

2104. Moore, Ruth. The Earth We Live On. 2nd ed. Knopf. 1971. $8.95.   550.9
1. Geology — History.

551 Physical Geology

2105. Bascom, Willard. A Hole in the Bottom of the Sea: The Story of the Mohole Project. Doubleday. $6.95.   551
1. Geology. 2. Mohole Project. 3. Ocean.

2106. Brown, F. Martin, et al. Earth Science. 2nd ed. Silver. 1973. $8.26.   551
1. Earth Sciences.

2107. Eardley, Armand I. Science of the Earth. Har-Row. 1972. $11.95.   551
1. Earth Sciences.

2108. Everglyn, L. Through the Crust of the Earth. McGraw. 1973. $10.95.   551
1. Geology.

500 SCIENCE

2109. Flint, Richard F. and Skinner, Brian J. Physical Geology. Wiley. 1974. $12.95. 551
1. Physical Geology.

2110. McAlester, Archie L. and Hay, E. A. Physical Geology: Principles and Perspectives. P-H. 1975. $10.50. 551
1. Physical Geology.

2111. Mather, Kirtley F. The Earth Beneath Us. Random. 1964. $17.95. 551
1. Earth. 2. Geology.

2112. Scientific American Editors. The Biosphere: A Scientific American Book. W H Freeman. 1970. pap. $3.50. 551
1. Ecology. 2. Geochemistry. 3. Geophysics.

2113. Takeuchi, H., et al. Debate About the Earth: An Approach to Geophysics Through Analysis of Continental Drift. rev. ed. Freeman C. 1970. $5.95; pap. $2.80. 551.1
1. Continental Drift. 2. Earth. 3. Geophysics.

2114. Cox, Allan, ed. Plate Tectonics and Geomagnetic Reversals. W H Freeman. 1973. $17.00; pap. $9.95. 551.13
1. Earthquakes. 2. Heat Budget (Geophysics). 3. Paleomagnetism. 4. Plate Tectonics.

2115. Gribbin, John R. and Plagemann, Stephen H. The Jupiter Effect: A Scientific Exploration of the Planets As Triggers of Major Earthquakes. Walker & Co. 1974. $7.95. 551.13
1. Earthquake Prediction. 2. Earthquakes — California. 3. Geology, Structural.

2116. Hallam, A. A Revolution in the Earth Sciences: From Continental Drift to Plate Tectonics. new ed. Oxford U Pr. 1973. $9.75. 551.13
1. Continental Drift — History. 2. Plate Tectonics — History.

2117. Sullivan, Walter. Continents in Motion. McGraw. 1974. $17.95. 551.13
1. Continental Drift.

2118. MacDonald, Gordon A. Volcanoes. P-H. 1972. $18.50. 551.21
1. Volcanoes.

2119. Thorarinsson, Sigurdur. Surtsey: The New Island in the North Atlantic. Viking Pr. 1967. $6.00. 551.21
1. Surtsey Island. 2. Volcanoes.

2120. Fried, John J. Life Along the San Andreas Fault. Sat Rev Pr. 1973. $7.95. 551.22
1. Disaster Relief — California. 2. Earthquakes and Building. 3. Earthquakes — California.

2121. Thomas, Gordon and Witts, Max M. San Francisco Earthquake. Stein & Day. 1971. $7.95; pap. $1.50 (Dell). 551.22
1. Earthquakes — San Francisco — 1906. 2. San Francisco — Earthquake and Fire, 1906.

2122. Zaruba, G. and Mencl, U. Landslides and Their Treatment. Am Elsevier. 1969. $16.50. 551.353
1. Landslides.

551.4 Geomorphology

2123. Calder, Nigel. The Restless Earth: A Report on the New Geology. Viking Pr. 1972. $10.00; pap. $3.95. 551.4
1. Geology.

2124. Ruhe, Robert V. Geomorphology. HM. 1975. $13.95. 551.4
1. Geomorphology.

2125. Golden, Frederic. The Moving Continents. Scribner. 1972. $6.95. 551.41
1. Continental Drift.

2126. Marvin, Ursula B. Continental Drift: The Evolution of a Concept. Smithsonian. 1973. $12.50. 551.41
1. Continental Drift. 2. Geophysics.

2127. Scientific American Editors. Continents Adrift: Readings from Scientific American. W H Freeman. 1972. $7.00; pap. $3.75. 551.41
1. Continental Drift.

2128. Tarling, Don and Tarling, Maureen. Continental Drift: A Study of the Earth's Moving Surface. Doubleday. 1971. $5.95; pap. $1.95 rev. ed. 551.41
1. Continental Drift.

2129. Judson, David M. Ghar Parau. Macmillan. 1973. $10.00. 551.44
1. Adventure and Adventurers. 2. Caves.

2130. Waltham, A. C. Caves. Crown. 1974. $12.50. 551.44
1. Caves.

551.46 Oceanography

2131. Barton, Robert. Atlas of the Sea. John Day. 1974. $10.00. 551.46
1. Marine Resources. 2. Oceanography.

2132. Behrman, Daniel. The New World of the Oceans: Men and Oceanography. Little. 1969. $10.00; pap. $2.95. 551.46
1. Oceanography.

2133. Brown, Joseph E. The Golden Sea: Man's Underwater Adventures. Playboy. 1974. $16.95. 551.46
1. Oceanography — Pictorial Works.

2134. Carson, Rachel. The Sea Around Us. rev. ed. Oxford U Pr. 1961. $7.95. 551.46
1. Oceanography.

2135. Cousteau, Jacques-Yves and Diole, Philippe. Life and Death in a Coral Sea. Doubleday. 1971. $9.95. 551.46
1. Coral Reefs. 2. Marine Biology. 3. Oceanography.

2136. Critchlow, Keith. Into the Hidden Environment: The Oceans. Viking Pr. 1973. $10.95. 551.46
1. Oceanography.

2137. Darby, Ray and Darby, Patricia. Conquering the Deep Sea Frontier. McKay. 1971. $5.95. 551.46
1. Oceanographic Research. 2. Underwater Exploration.

2138. Hickling, Charles F. and Brown, Peter L. The Seas and Oceans in Color. Macmillan. 1974. $5.95. 551.46
1. Oceanography.

2139. Idyll, C. P., ed. Exploring the Ocean World: A History of Oceanography. rev. ed. T Y Crowell. 1972. $14.95. 551.46
1. Oceanography — History.

2140. Ingmanson, Dale E. and Wallace, William J. Oceanology: An Introduction. Wadsworth Pub. 1973. $13.95. 551.46
1. Oceanography.

2141. Ross, David A. Introduction to Oceanography. P-H. 1970. $10.50. 551.46
1. Oceanography.

2142. Schlee, Susan. The Edge of an Unfamiliar World: A History of Oceanography. Dutton. 1973. $10.95. 551.46
1. Oceanography — History.

2143. Scientific American Editors. The Ocean: A Scientific American Book. W H Freeman. 1969. pap. $3.50. 551.46
1. Marine Resources. 2. Oceanography.

2144. ———. Oceanography: Readings from Scientific American. W H Freeman. 1971. $11.00; pap. $5.75. 551.46
1. Oceanography.

2145. Soule, Gardner. The Greatest Depths: Probing the Seas Below 20,000 Feet. Macrae. 1970. $5.95. 551.46
1. Diving Vehicles. 2. Oceanography — Research.

2146. Briggs, Peter. Two Hundred Million Years Beneath the Sea. HR&W. 1971. $7.95. 551.4608
1. Deep Sea Drilling Project. 2. Glomar Challenger (Ship). 3. Submarine Geology.

2147. Shepard, Francis P. The Earth Beneath the Sea. 2nd ed. Johns Hopkins. 1967. $8.50; pap. $2.45 (Atheneum). 551.4608
1. Submarine Geology.

2148. Wertenbaker, William. The Floor of the Sea: Maurice Ewing and the Mysteries of the Earth. Little. 1974. $8.95. 551.4608(B)
1. Ewing, William Maurice, 1906-
2. Marine Geophysics.

2149. Piccard, Jacques. The Sun Beneath the Sea. Scribner. 1971. $12.50. 551.461
1. Ben Franklin (Research Submarine). 2. Gulf Stream. 3. Underwater Exploration.

2150. Smith, F. Walton. The Seas in Motion. T Y Crowell. 1973. $7.95. 551.47
1. Ocean Currents. 2. Ocean Waves. 3. Tides.

2151. Leopold, Luna B. Water: A Primer. W H Freeman. 1974. $4.95; pap. $2.95. 551.48
1. Water.

551.5-551.6 Weather

2152. Ross, Frank, Jr. Storms and Man. Lothrop. 1971. $6.50. 551.55
1. Storms.

500 SCIENCE

2153. Brown, Billye and Brown, Walter R. Historical Catastrophes: Hurricanes and Tornadoes. A-W. 1972. $4.75. 551.552
1. Hurricanes. 2. Tornadoes.

2154. Flora, Snowden D. Tornadoes of the United States. U of Okla Pr. 1973. $6.95; pap. $2.95. 551.553
1. Natural Disasters. 2. Tornadoes. 3. Weather.

2155. Scorer, Richard. Clouds of the World: A Complete Color Encyclopedia. David & Charles. 1972. $35.00. 551.576
1. Clouds — Pictorial Works.

2156. Claiborne, Robert. Climate, Man, and History: An Irreverent View of the Human Environment. Norton. 1970. $8.95. 551.59
1. Climate.

2157. Battan, Louis D. Weather. P-H. 1974. $7.95; pap. $3.50. 551.6
1. Weather.

2158. Rubin, Louis D. and Herbert, Hiram J. Forecasting the Weather. Watts. 1970. $4.95. 551.63
1. Clouds. 2. Weather Forecasting.

2159. Helm, Thomas. Hurricanes: Weather at Its Worst. Dodd. 1967. $6.00. 551.6452
1. Hurricanes. 2. Weather.

2160. Bova, Ben. Man Changes the Weather. A-W. 1973. $4.95. 551.68
1. Air Pollution. 2. Climatology. 3. Weather Control.

551.7-559 Historical Geology

2161. Baars, Donald L. Red Rock Country: The Geologic History of the Colorado Plateau. Natural Hist. 1972. $9.95. 551.7
1. Geology — Colorado Plateau.

2162. Dunbar, Carl O. and Waage, Karl M. Geology. 3rd ed. Wiley. 1969. $15.25. 551.7
1. Geology, Historical. 2. Geology, Stratigraphic. 3. Paleontology.

2163. Mutch, Thomas A. Geology of the Moon: A Stratigraphic View. rev. ed. Princeton U Pr. 1973. $25.00. 551.7
1. Lunar Geology. 2. Lunar Stratigraphy.

2164. Seyfert, Carl K. and Sirkin, Leslie K. Earth History and Plate Tectonics: An Introduction to Historical Geology. Har-Row. 1973. $12.95. 551.7
1. Geology, Historical. 2. Plate Tectonics.

2165. Kurten, Bjorn. The Ice Age. Putnam. 1972. $16.95. 551.792
1. Glacial Epoch.

2166. Schultz, Given. Ice Age Lost. Doubleday. 1974. $10.00. 551.792
1. Glacial Epoch. 2. Glaciers.

2167. Fenton, Carroll L. and Fenton, Mildred A. The Rock Book. Doubleday. 1970. $12.95. 552
1. Mineralogy. 2. Rocks.

2168. Mason, Brian and Melson, William G. Lunar Rocks. Wiley. 1970. $11.00. 552
1. Lunar Rocks.

2169. Tennissen, A. Nature of Earth Materials. P-H. 1974. $11.95. 552
1. Mineral Industries. 2. Mineralogy. 3. Petrology.

2170. Landes, Kenneth K. Petroleum Geology of the United States. Wiley. 1970. $33.25. 553.282
1. Petroleum — Geology — U. S.

2171. Peterson, James A. Finding and Preparing Precious and Semiprecious Stones. Assn Pr. 1974. pap. $6.95. 553.8075
1. Precious Stones — Collectors and Collecting.

2172. Breed, William J., ed. Geology of the Grand Canyon. Mus Northern Ariz. 1974. pap. $5.00. 557.9132
1. Geology. 2. Grand Canyon.

2173. MacDonald, Gordon A. and Abbott, Agatin T. Volcanoes in the Sea: The Geology of Hawaii. U Pr of Hawaii. 1970. $15.00. 559.69
1. Geology — Hawaii. 2. Volcanoes — Hawaii.

560 Paleontology

2174. Fenton, Carroll L. and Fenton, Mildred A. The Fossil Book. Doubleday. 1959. $17.95. 560
1. Fossils.

2175. Flint, Richard F. Earth and Its History. Norton. 1973. $9.95. 560
1. Earth. 2. Paleontology.

2176. Rhodes, Frank H., et al. Fossils. Western Pub. 1962. $4.95; pap. $1.50. 560
1. Fossils.

2177. Lanham, Urless N. The Bone Hunters. Columbia U Pr. 1973. $12.95. 560.75
1. Cope, Edward Drinker, 1840-1897. 2. Marsh, Othniel Charles, 1831-1899. 3. Paleontology — Collectors and Collecting — The West.

2178. Colbert, Edwin H. Evolution of the Vertebrates. 2nd ed. Wiley. 1969. $15.95. 566
1. Phylogeny. 2. Vertebrates. 3. Vertebrates, Fossil.

2179. ———. Dinosaurs. Dutton. 1961. $9.95. 568.19
1. Dinosaurs.

2180. ———. Men and Dinosaurs. Dutton. 1968. $8.95. 568.19
1. Dinosaurs. 2. Fossils.

2181. Daly, Eileen. Dinosaurs. Western Pub. 1974. $3.95; pap. $1.25. 568.19
1. Dinosaurs.

2182. Swinton, William E. Dinosaurs. Wiley. 1970. $11.00. 568.19
1. Dinosaurs.

2183. Silverberg, Robert. Mammoths, Mastodons and Man. McGraw. 1970. $5.50. 569.6
1. Mammoth. 2. Mastodon.

2184. Leakey, Louis S. By the Evidence: Memoirs, 1932-1951. HarBraceJ. 1974. $9.95. 569.9(B)
1. Leakey, Louis Seymour Bazett, 1903-1972.

572 Human Races

2185. Baker, John R. Race. Oxford U Pr. 1973. $15.00. 572
1. Race.

2186. Coon, Carleton S. The Story of Man. 2nd rev. ed. Knopf. 1962. $10.00. 572
1. Anthropology.

2187. Coon, Carleton S. and Hunt, Edward E., Jr. The Living Races of Man. Knopf. 1965. $12.50. 572
1. Ethnology. 2. Race.

500 SCIENCE

2188. Goldsby, R. A. Race and Races. Macmillan. 1971. $5.95; pap. $3.25. 572
1. Race.

2189. National Geographic Society Editors. Vanishing Peoples of the Earth. Natl Geog. 1968. $4.25. 572
1. Ethnology. 2. Society, Primitive.

2190. Pinney, Roy. Vanishing Tribes. T Y Crowell. 1968. $8.95. 572
1. Ethnology.

573 Physical Anthropology

2191. Swanson, Carl P. The Natural History of Man. P-H. 1973. $14.00. 573
1. Anthropology. 2. Human Biology. 3. Human Evolution.

2192. Ardrey, Robert. African Genesis. Atheneum. 1968. $9.95; pap. $1.95 (Delta). 573.2
1. Animals, Habits and Behavior of. 2. Evolution. 3. Man — Origin and Antiquity.

2193. ———. The Social Contract: A Personal Inquiry into the Evolutionary Sources of Order and Disorder. Atheneum. 1970. $10.00. 573.2
1. Animals, Habits and Behavior of. 2. Human Behavior. 3. Human Evolution.

2194. Campbell, Bernard. Human Evolution: An Introduction to Man's Adaptations. 2nd ed. Aldine. 1974. $12.50; pap. $7.95. 573.2
1. Adaptation (Biology). 2. Evolution. 3. Man — Origin and Antiquity.

2195. Coon, Carleton S. The Origin of Races. Knopf. 1962. $12.95. 573.2
1. Anthropology. 2. Ethnology.

2196. Kurten, Bjorn. Not from the Apes. Random. 1972. $5.95; pap. $1.95. 573.2
1. Human Evolution. 2. Man — Origin and Antiquity.

2197. Pfeiffer, John E. The Emergence of Man. rev. enl. ed. Har-Row. 1972. $12.95; pap. $6.95. 573.2
1. Human Evolution. 2. Man, Prehistoric. 3. Society, Primitive.

2198. Simak, Clifford D. Prehistoric Man. St Martin. 1971. $6.95. 573.2

500 SCIENCE

1. Man — Origin and Antiquity. 2. Man, Prehistoric.

2199. Wendt, Herbert. From Ape to Adam. Bobbs. 1972. $15.00. 573.2
1. Man — Origin and Antiquity. 2. Man, Prehistoric.

2200. Young, Louise B., ed. Evolution of Man. Oxford U Pr. 1970. $12.95; pap. $6.95.
573.208
1. Evolution. 2. Human Evolution.

2201. Heintze, Carl. Genetic Engineering: Man and Nature in Transition. Nelson. 1974. $5.95. 573.21
1. Genetic Engineering. 2. Genetics.

2202. McKusick, Victor. Human Genetics. 2nd ed. P-H. 1969. $7.95; pap. $4.95. 573.21
1. Human Genetics.

2203. Stern, Curt. Principles of Human Genetics. 3rd ed. W H Freeman. 1973. $14.50.
573.21
1. Human Genetics.

2204. Sutton, Elton H. Introduction to Human Genetics. HR&W. 1975. $12.95.
573.21
1. Human Genetics.

2205. Janus, Christopher G. and Brashler, William. The Search for Peking Man. Macmillan. 1975. $8.95. 573.3
1. Man, Prehistoric. 2. Peking Man.

2206. Shapiro, Harry L. Peking Man: The Discovery, Disappearance and Mystery of a Priceless Scientific Treasure. S&S. 1974. $8.95.
573.3
1. Man, Prehistoric. 2. Peking Man.

574 Biology

2207. Becker, George. Introductory Concepts in Biology. Macmillan. 1972. $8.95.
574
1. Biology.

2208. Behuke, John A., ed. Challenging Biological Problems: Directions Toward Their Solution. Oxford U Pr. 1972. $10.95. 574
1. Biology — Social Aspects.

2209. Brandwein, Paul F., et al. Life: A Biological Science. HarBraceJ. 1975. $6.75.
574
1. Biology.

2210. Brown, Vinson. Knowing the Outdoors in the Dark. Stackpole. 1972. $6.95; pap. $2.95 (Macmillan). 574
1. Natural History — Outdoor Books. 2. Outdoor Life — Safety Measures.

2211. Clark, Mary E. Contemporary Biology. Saunders. 1973. $11.50. 574
1. Biology.

2212. Curtis, Helena. Invitation to Biology. Worth. 1972. $9.95. 574
1. Biology.

2213. Goin, Coleman J. and Goin, Olive B. Man and the Natural World: An Introduction to Life Science. Macmillan. 1970. $10.95. 574
1. Biology.

2214. Handler, Philip, ed. Biology and the Future of Man. Oxford U Pr. 1970. $14.95; pap. $5.95. 574
1. Biology.

2215. Moore, Ruth. The Coil of Life. Knopf. 1961. $6.95. 574
1. Biochemistry. 2. Life (Biology).

2216. Morowitz, Harold J. and Morowitz, Lucille S. Life on the Planet Earth. new ed. Norton. 1974. $8.95. 574
1. Biology.

2217. Nason, Alvin and Dehaan, Robert L. The Biological World. Wiley. 1973. $14.25.
574
1. Biology.

2218. Thomas, Lewis. The Lives of a Cell: Notes of a Biology Watcher. Viking Pr. 1974. $6.95. 574.01
1. Biology — Philosophy.

2219. Knobloch, Irving W., ed. Readings in Biological Science. 3rd ed. Irvington. 1972. pap. $6.95. 574.08
1. Biology.

2220. Scientific American Editors. Thirty-Nine Steps to Biology: Readings from Scientific American. W H Freeman. 1968. $10.00; pap. $5.45. 574.08
1. Biology.

2221. Bibby, Cyril. Scientist Extraordinary: T. H. Huxley. St Martin. 1972. $8.95.
574.092(B)
1. Huxley, Thomas Henry, 1825-1895.

500 SCIENCE

2222. Brooks, Paul. The House of Life: Rachel Carson at Work. HM. 1972. $8.95; pap. $1.75 (Fawcett World). 574.092(B)
1. Carson, Rachel Louise, 1907-1964.

2223. Sanger, Marjory B. Billy Bartram and His Green World. FS&G. 1972. $6.50.
574.092(B)
1. Bartram, William, 1739-1823. 2. Ornithologists, American.

574.1 Physiology

2224. Still, Henry. Of Time, Tides, and Inner Clocks: Taking Advantage of the Natural Rhythms of Life. Stackpole. 1972. $8.50. 574.1
1. Biology — Periodicity.

2225. Kavaler, Lucy. Freezing Point: Cold As a Matter of Life and Death. John Day. 1970. $8.95. 574.1916
1. Cryobiology.

2226. Butler, J. A. The Life Process. Basic. 1972. $6.95. 574.192
1. Biology.

2227. Jevons, Frederick R. The Biochemical Approach to Life. 2nd ed. Basic. 1968. $5.95.
574.192
1. Biological Chemistry.

2228. Metzger, Norman. Men and Molecules. 2nd ed. Crown. 1972. $5.95.
574.192
1. Biological Chemistry. 2. Chemistry.

2229. Smith, C. U. Molecular Biology: A Structural Approach. MIT Pr. 1969. $12.50.
574.192
1. Biological Chemistry.

574.5 Ecology

2230. Crosby, Alfred W. The Columbian Exchange: Biological and Cultural Consequences of 1492. new ed. Greenwood. 1972. $9.50; pap. $2.95. 574.5
1. Geographical Distribution of Animals and Plants. 2. Indians — Agriculture. 3. Indians — Diseases. 4. Medical Geography — History.

2231. Fridriksson, S. Surtsey: Eveolution of Life on a Volcanic Island. Halsted Pr. 1975. $14.95. 574.5
1. Island Ecology — Iceland — Surtsey. 2. Surtsey. 3. Volcanoes — Iceland.

2232. Mariner, James L. Understanding Ecology. Ind Sch Pr. 1975. $3.75. 574.5
1. Ecology.

2233. Milne, Lorus and Milne, Margery. The Arena of Life: The Dynamics of Ecology. Doubleday. 1972. $15.00. 574.5
1. Ecology.

2234. Odum, Eugene P. Fundamentals of Ecology. 3rd ed. Saunders. 1971. $11.75. 574.5
1. Ecology.

2235. Reid, Keith, et al. Man, Nature and Ecology. Doubleday. 1974. $14.95. 574.5
1. Ecology. 2. Man — Influence on Nature.

2236. Benton, Allen H. and Werner, William E. Field Biology and Ecology. new ed. McGraw. 1974. $13.95. 574.5028
1. Biology — Field Work. 2. Ecology.

2237. Smith, Robert L. Ecology and Field Biology. 2nd ed. Har-Row. 1974. $14.95.
574.5028
1. Biology — Field Work. 2. Ecology.

2238. Scientific American Editors. Ecology, Evolution, and Population Biology: Readings from Scientific American. W H Freeman. 1974. $12.00; pap. $5.95. 574.508
1. Biology. 2. Biotic Community. 3. Ecology. 4. Evolution. 5. Population Biology.

2239. Emmel, Thomas C. An Introduction to Ecology and Population Biology. Norton. 1973. $6.95; pap. $2.95. 574.524
1. Ecology. 2. Man — Influence on Nature. 3. Population Biology.

2240. Gill, Don and Bonnett, Penelope. Nature in the Urban Landscape: A Study of City Ecosystems. York Pr. 1973. $12.00.
574.526
1. Cities and Towns — Planning. 2. Ecology. 3. Nature Conservation. 4. Urban Fauna.

2241. Pringle, Laurence. Wild River. Lippincott. 1972. $15.00. 574.5263
1. Stream Ecology — U. S. 2. Wild and Scenic Rivers — U. S.

2242. Shepherd, Elizabeth. Arms of the Sea: Our Vital Estuaries. Lothrop. 1973. $5.50.
574.5263
1. Estuarine Ecology.

2243. Silverberg, Robert. The World Within the Tide Pool. Weybright. 1972. $6.95.
574.5263
1. Tide Pool Ecology.

500 SCIENCE

2244. Teal, John and Teal, Mildred. Life and Death of the Salt Marsh. Little. 1969. $7.95; pap. $1.25 (Ballantine). 574.5263
1. Marsh Ecology. 2. Marshes, Tide.

2245. Meggers, Betty J., et al. Tropical Forest Ecosystems in Africa and South America: A Comparative Review. Smithsonian. 1973. $15.00; pap. $5.95.
574.5264
1. Forest Ecology — Tropics.

2246. Zwinger, Ann H. and Willard, Beatrice E. Land Above the Trees: A Guide to American Alpine Tundra. Har-Row. 1972. $15.00. 574.5264
1. Alpine Flora — U. S. 2. Mountain Ecology — U. S.

2247. Costello, David F. The Desert World. T Y Crowell. 1972. $7.95. 574.5265
1. Desert Biology — Mexico. 2. Desert Biology — U. S.

2248. Kirk, Ruth. Desert: The American Southwest. HM. 1973. $10.00. 574.5265
1. Desert Ecology — Southwestern States. 2. Natural History — Southwestern States.

574.8 Tissue, Cellular, Molecular Biology

2249. Watson, James D. The Double Helix. Atheneum. 1968. $7.95; pap. $0.95 (NAL).
574.8
1. Biochemistry — Research. 2. DNA. 3. Genetics. 4. Heredity.

2250. Ambrose, E. J. and Easty, Dorothy M. Cell Biology. A-W. 1970. $12.50. 574.87
1. Cells. 2. Cytology.

2251. Dowben, Robert M. Cell Biology. Har-Row. 1971. $14.95. 574.87
1. Cells. 2. Cytology.

2252. Lessing, L. and Fortune Editors. DNA: At the Core of Life Itself. Macmillan. 1967. $3.95. 574.87
1. Cells. 2. Genetics. 3. Heredity.

2253. Scientific American Editors. From Cell to Organism: Readings from Scientific American Magazine. W H Freeman. 1967. pap. $4.45. 574.87
1. Cells. 2. Cytology.

2254. ———. The Living Cell: Readings from Scientific American Magazine. W H Freeman. 1965. pap. $5.95. 574.87
1. Cells. 2. Cytology.

2255. Tufty, Barbara. Cells: Units of Life. new ed. Putnam. 1973. $4.49. 574.87
1. Cells. 2. Cytology.

2256. Borek, Ernest. The Sculpture of Life. Columbia U Pr. 1973. $10.00; pap. $2.95.
574.8761
1. Cancer Cells. 2. Cell Differentiation. 3. Cell Proliferation.

2257. Burnet, MacFarlane. Genes, Dreams and Realities. Basic. 1971. $8.95. 574.88
1. Biology. 2. Human Genetics. 3. Immunology.

2258. Chedd, Graham. The New Biology. Basic. 1972. $8.25. 574.88
1. Biology. 2. Molecular Biology.

574.9 Biology - Geographical Treatment of

2259. Durrell, Gerald. Birds, Beasts, and Relatives. Viking Pr. 1969. $5.95; pap. $2.25.
574.9
1. Corfu — Description and Travel. 2. Natural History — Corfu.

2260. Stephenson, T. A. and Stephenson, Anne. Life Between Tidemarks on Rocky Shores. W H Freeman. 1972. $15.00; pap. $6.95. 574.909
1. Intertidal Zonation. 2. Seashore Ecology.

2261. Amos, William H. The Infinite River. Random. 1970. $6.95; pap. $1.25 (Ballantine).
574.92
1. Aquatic Biology. 2. Hydrologic Cycle.

2262. Carson, Rachel. The Edge of the Sea. HM. 1955. $7.95; pap. $0.95 (NAL). 574.92
1. Seashore Biology.

2263. Faulkner, Douglas. The Living Reef. Quadrangle. 1974. $25.00. 574.92
1. Coral Reef Biology. 2. Fishes. 3. Fishes — Tropics. 4. Pelew Islands.

2264. Greenberg, Jerry. The Living Reef. Seahawk Pr. 1972. pap. $5.95. 574.92
1. Coral Reef Biology. 2. Fishes. 3. Fishes — Tropics.

2265. Hannan, Hans, et al. In the Coral Reefs of the Caribbean, Bahamas, Florida, Bermuda. Doubleday. 1974. $12.50.   574.92
1. Coral Reefs and Islands. 2. Marine Biology.

2266. Platt, Rutherford. Water: The Wonder of Life. P-H. 1971. $8.95.   574.92
1. Marine Biology. 2. Water.

2267. Silverberg, Robert. The World Within the Ocean Wave. Weybright. 1972. $6.95.
574.92
1. Marine Ecology. 2. Marine Plankton.

2268. Ward, Ritchie. Into the Ocean World. Knopf. 1974. $10.00.   574.92
1. Marine Biology. 2. Oceanography.

2269. Russell, Franklin. Watchers at the Pond. Knopf. 1961. $5.95.   574.929
1. Fresh-Water Fauna. 2. Pond Ecology.

2270. Klots, Elsie B. New Field Book of Freshwater Life. Putnam. 1966. $5.95.
574.9297
1. Fresh-Water Biology.

2271. Brown, Leslie. Africa: A Natural History. Random. 1965. $20.00.   574.96
1. Natural History — Africa.

2272. Farb, Peter. The Face of North America: The Natural History of a Continent. Har-Row. 1963. $10.00; pap. $2.95.   574.973
1. Natural History — U. S. 2. Physical Geography — U. S. 3. U. S. — Description and Travel.

2273. Grossman, Mary L. and Hamlet, John N. Our Vanishing Wilderness. G&D. 1969. $14.95.   574.973
1. Ecology. 2. Natural History — U. S.

2274. George, Jean C. Everglades Wildguide. US Govt Ptg Off. 1972. price on request.
574.9759
1. Everglades National Park. 2. Natural History — Florida — Everglades.

2275. Sage, Bryan L. Alaska and Its Wildlife. Viking Pr. 1973. $14.00.   574.9798
1. Natural History — Alaska.

2276. Bennett, Isobel. The Great Barrier Reef. Scribner. 1974. $17.50.   574.9943
1. Great Barrier Reef, Australia. 2. Natural History — Australia — Great Barrier Reef.

2277. Engdahl, Sylvia L. The Planet-Girded Suns. Atheneum. 1974. $7.50.   574.999
1. Life on Other Planets.

500 SCIENCE

575 Organic Evolution

2278. Brace, C. Loring. The Stages of Human Evolution: Human and Cultural Origins. P-H. 1967. pap. $2.40.   575
1. Evolution.

2279. Gastonguay, Paul R. Evolution for Everyone. Pegasus. 1974. $6.95; pap. $3.95.
575
1. Evolution.

2280. Hutchinson, Peter. Evolution Explained. David & Charles. 1974. $12.50.   575
1. Evolution.

2281. Huxley, Julian. Evolution in Action. Har-Row. 1953. $4.95.   575
1. Evolution.

2282. Huxley, Thomas H. On a Piece of Chalk. Scribner. 1965. $6.95; pap. $0.65.   575
1. Evolution.

2283. Stebbins, G. Ledyard. Processes of Organic Evolution. 2nd ed. P-H. 1971. $8.00; pap. $4.50.   575
1. Evolution.

2284. Moore, Ruth. Charles Darwin. Knopf. 1955. $3.95.   575.009(B)
1. Darwin, Charles Robert, 1809-1882.

2285. Bates, Marston and Humphrey, Philip S., eds. The Darwin Reader. Scribner. 1956. pap. $3.95.   575.016
1. Biology. 2. Darwin, Charles Robert, 1809-1882. 3. Evolution.

2286. Darwin, Charles. The Origin of Species and The Descent of Man. Modern Lib. $4.95.
575.016
1. Evolution. 2. Natural Selection. 3. Origin of Species.

2287. DeCamp, L. Darwin and His Great Discovery. Macmillan. 1972. $6.95. 575.016(B)
1. Darwin, Charles Robert, 1809-1882. 2. Evolution.

2288. Moorehead, Alan. Darwin and the Beagle. Har-Row. 1969. $17.50; pap. $5.95.
575.016
1. Beagle Expedition, 1831-1836. 2. Darwin, Charles Robert, 1809-1882. 3. Natural History — South America.

500 SCIENCE

2289. Beddall, Barbara G., ed. Wallace and Bates in the Tropics: An Introduction to the Theory of Natural Selection. Macmillan. 1969. $5.95. 575.0162
1. Bates, Henry Walter, 1825-1892. 2. Natural Selection. 3. Wallace, Alfred Russel, 1823-1913.

2290. McKinney, H. Lewis. Wallace and Natural Selection. Yale U Pr. 1972. $12.50.
575.0162
1. Natural Selection. 2. Wallace, Alfred Russel, 1823-1913.

575.1 Genetics

2291. Borek, Ernest. The Code of Life. Columbia U Pr. 1965. $10.00; pap. $2.25.
575.1
1. Genetics.

2292. Fried, John J. The Mystery of Heredity. John Day. 1971. $6.95. 575.1
1. Genetics.

2293. Gardner, Eldon J. Principles of Genetics. 4th ed. Wiley. 1972. $14.50. 575.1
1. Genetics.

2294. Herskowitz, Irwin H. Principles of Genetics. Macmillan. 1973. $13.50. 575.1
1. Genetics.

2295. Hyde, Margaret O. The New Genetics. Watts. 1974. $6.95. 575.1
1. Genetics.

2296. Jacob, Francois. The Logic of Life: A History of Heredity. Pantheon. 1974. $8.95.
575.1
1. Biology — History. 2. Genetics — History. 3. Life (Biology).

2297. Moore, John A. Heredity and Development. 2nd rev. ed. Oxford U Pr. 1972. pap. $3.50. 575.1
1. Genetics.

2298. Papazian, Haig P. Modern Genetics. Norton. 1967. $8.50. 575.1
1. Genetics.

2299. Scientific American Editors. Facets of Genetics: Readings from Scientific American. W H Freeman. 1970. $10.00; pap. $5.45. 575.1
1. Genetics.

2300. Sootin, Harry. Gregor Mendel: Father of the Science of Genetics. Vanguard. 1958. $4.50. 575.1(B)
1. Genetics. 2. Mendel, Gregor, 1822-1884.

2301. Kuspira, John and Walker, G. W. Genetics: Questions and Problems. McGraw. 1973. pap. $8.95. 575.1076
1. Genetics.

576 Microbiology

2302. Frobisher, Martin, et al. Fundamentals of Microbiology. 9th ed. Saunders. 1974. $16.50. 576
1. Microbiology.

2303. Pelczar, Michael J. and Reid, Roger D. Microbiology. 3rd ed. McGraw. 1972. $14.50. 576
1. Microbiology.

2304. Stanier, Roger Y., et al. Microbial World. 3rd ed. P-H. 1970. $17.50. 576
1. Microbiology.

2305. Wyss, Orville and Eklund, C. E. Micro-Organisms and Man. Wiley. 1971. $9.25. 576
1. Microbiology.

577 General Nature of Life

2306. Calder, Nigel. The Life Game: Evolution of the New Biology. Viking Pr. 1974. $12.50. 577
1. Life (Biology).

2307. Luria, S. E. Life: The Unfinished Experiment. Scribner. 1973. $7.95; pap. $2.95.
577
1. Life (Biology). 2. Molecular Biology.

2308. Anguist, Stanley W. Other Worlds, Other Beings. T Y Crowell. 1973. $4.95.
577.099
1. Life on Other Planets.

578-579 Microscopy and Biological Techniques

2309. Carona, Philip B. Microscope and How to Use It. Gulf Pub. 1970. pap. $2.95.
578
1. Microscope and Microscopy.

500 SCIENCE

2310. Knudsen, Jens W. Biological Techniques: Collecting, Preserving and Illustrating Plants and Animals. Har-Row. 1966. $16.95. 579
1. Biological Specimens — Collection and Preservation.

581 Botany

2311. Jensen, William A. and Salisbury, Frank B. Botany: An Ecological Approach. Wadsworth Pub. 1972. $15.95. 581
1. Botany. 2. Botany — Ecology.

2312. Milne, Lorus and Milne, Margery. Living Plants of the World. Random. 1967. $15.00. 581
1. Plants.

2313. Neushul, M. Botany. Wiley. 1974. $13.95. 581
1. Botany.

2314. Scagel, Robert F., et al. An Evolutionary Survey of the Plant Kingdom. Wadsworth Pub. 1965. $16.95. 581
1. Botany.

2315. Tompkins, Peter and Bird, Christopher. Secret Life of Plants. Har-Row. 1973. $8.95. 581
1. Botany. 2. Plants.

2316. Asimov, Isaac. Photosynthesis. Basic. 1969. $6.95. 581.133
1. Photosynthesis.

2317. Devlin, Robert M. Photosynthesis. Van Nos Reinhold. 1971. $8.95. 581.133
1. Photosynthesis.

2318. Brown, Vinson. Reading the Woods: Seeing More in Nature's Familiar Faces. Stackpole. 1969. $5.95; pap. $2.95 (Macmillan). 581.5
1. Forest Ecology.

2319. Olson, Sigurd F. and Blacklock, Les. The Hidden Forest. Viking Pr. 1969. $14.95. 581.5
1. Forest Ecology.

2320. Gibbons, Euell. Stalking the Healthful Herbs. McKay. 1970. $8.95; pap. $2.95. 581.63
1. Herbs. 2. Plant Lore.

2321. ———. Stalking the Good Life. McKay. 1971. $7.95. 581.632

1. Cookery (Wild Foods). 2. Plants, Edible. 3. Pollution. 4. Wilderness Survival.

2322. Hall, Alan. The Wild Food Trailguide. HR&W. 1973. $6.95; pap. $3.50. 581.632
1. Food, Wild — U. S. 2. Plants, Edible — U. S.

2323. Wilson, Charles M. Green Treasures: Adventures in the Discovery of Edible Plants. Macrae. 1974. $5.95. 581.632
1. Agriculturists — Biography. 2. Plant Collectors — Biography. 3. Plant Introduction — History. 4. Plants, Edible — History.

582 Seed-Bearing Plants

2324. Ary, Sheila and Gregory, Mary. Oxford Book of Wild Flowers. Oxford U Pr. 1970. $12.95. 582.13
1. Wild Flowers.

2325. Martin, Alexander C. Weeds. Western Pub. 1973. $4.95; pap. $1.95. 582.13
1. Weeds — North America. 2. Wild Flowers — North America.

2326. Everett, Thomas H. Living Trees of the World. Doubleday. 1969. $7.95. 582.16
1. Trees.

2327. Ketchum, Richard M. The Secret Life of the Forest. McGraw. 1970. $7.95. 582.16
1. Forest Ecology. 2. Forests and Forestry. 3. Trees.

2328. Constantine, Albert. Know Your Woods. rev. ed. Scribner. 1975. $10.00. 582.1609
1. Trees. 2. Trees — Dictionaries. 3. Wood. 4. Wood — Dictionaries.

589 Algae, Fungi and Mushrooms

2329. Alexopoulos, Constantine J. and Bold, Harold C. Algae and Fungi. Macmillan. 1967. pap. $4.25. 589
1. Algae. 2. Fungi.

2330. Christensen, Clyde M. Molds and Man: An Introduction to the Fungi. 3rd ed. U of Minn Pr. 1965. $8.50. 589
1. Molds (Botany).

2331. Smith, Alexander H. The Mushroom Hunter's Field Guide. rev. & enl. ed. U of Mich Pr. 1963. $9.95. 589
1. Mushrooms.

500 SCIENCE

2332. Bigelow, Howard E. Mushroom Pocket Field Guide. Macmillan. 1974. $3.50.   589.222
1. Mushrooms — Identification.

2333. Miller, Orson K., Jr. Mushrooms of North America. Dutton. 1972. $15.00. 589.222
1. Mushrooms — North America — Identification.

2334. Prescott, G. W. The Algae: A Review. HM. 1968. $12.50.   589.3
1. Algae.

2335. Hardin, James W. and Arena, James W. Human Poisoning from Native and Cultivated Plants. rev. exp. ed. Duke. 1973. $6.75.   589.69
1. Antidotes. 2. Poisonous Plants — U. S. 3. Poisons — Physiological Effect.

590 Zoological Sciences

2336. Storer, Tracy I. and Usinger, Robert L. General Zoology. 5th ed. McGraw. 1972. $12.50.   590
1. Zoology.

2337. Weisz, Paul B. The Science of Zoology. 2nd ed. McGraw. 1973. $12.95.   591
1. Zoology.

2338. Curry-Lindahl, Kai. Let Them Live: A Worldwide Survey of Animals Threatened with Extinction. Morrow. 1972. $9.95; pap. $3.95.   591.042
1. Rare Animals. 2. Wildlife Conservation.

2339. Milne, Lorus and Milne, Margery. The Cougar Doesn't Live Here Anymore. P-H. 1971. $10.70.   591.042
1. Rare Animals. 2. Wildlife Conservation.

2340. National Geographic Society, ed. Vanishing Wildlife of North America. Natl Geog. 1974. $4.25.   591.042
1. Rare Animals — North America. 2. Wildlife Conservation — North America. 3. Wildlife Management — North America.

2341. Time-Life Books Editors. Vanishing Species. Time-Life. 1974. $14.95.   591.042
1. Rare Animals — Pictorial Works.

591.1 Physiology of Animals

2342. Schmidt-Nielsen, Knut. Animal Physiology. 3rd ed. P-H. 1970. $7.95; pap. $4.68.   591.1
1. Zoology.

2343. Lewin, Roger. Nervous System. Doubleday. 1974. pap. $1.95.   591.18
1. Nervous System.

2344. Burton, Maurice. The Sixth Sense of Animals. Taplinger. 1973. $7.95.   591.182
1. Animal Orientation. 2. Senses and Sensation.

2345. Freedman, Russell and Morriss, James E. The Brains of Animals and Man. Holiday. 1972. $5.95.   591.188
1. Brain.

2346. Rudloe, Jack. The Erotic Ocean. T Y Crowell. 1972. $15.00.   591.2
1. Marine Biology. 2. Marine Fauna — Collection and Preservation.

2347. Mayr, Ernst. Populations, Species and Evolution: An Abridgment of Animal Species and Evolution. Harvard U Pr. 1970. $10.00; pap. $4.95.   591.38
1. Evolution. 2. Species. 3. Zoology — Variation.

2348. Romer, Alfred S. The Procession of Life. Universe. 1968. $12.50; pap. $2.95 1972 (Doubleday).   591.38
1. Anatomy, Comparative. 2. Evolution.

2349. Stonehouse, Bernard. Young Animals: The Search for Independent Life. Viking Pr. 1974. $10.95.   591.39
1. Animals, Infancy of.

591.5 Ecology of Animals

2350. Alcock, John. Animal Behavior: An Evolutionary Approach. Sinauer Assoc. 1974. $14.00.   591.5
1. Animals, Habits and Behavior of.

2351. Barnett, Samuel A. Instinct and Intelligence: Behavior of Animals and Men. P-H. 1967. $8.55; pap. $2.95.   591.5
1. Animals, Habits and Behavior of. 2. Psychology, Comparative.

2352. Diole, Philippe. The Errant Ark: Man's Relationship with Animals. Putnam. 1974. $8.95.   591.5
1. Animals and Civilization. 2. Wildlife Conservation.

500 SCIENCE

2353. Halle, Louise J. The Sea and the Ice: A Naturalist in Antarctica. HM. 1973. $8.95.   591.5
1. Birds — Antarctic Regions. 2. Natural History — Antarctic Regions. 3. Zoology — Antarctic Regions.

2354. Lorenz, Konrad. King Solomon's Ring. T Y Crowell. 1952. $6.95; pap. $1.95 (Apollo Eds).   591.5
1. Animals, Habits and Behavior of.

2355. Lorenz, Konrad. On Aggression. Wilson, Marjorie K., tr. HarBraceJ. 1966. $7.95; pap. $3.50.   591.5
1. Aggression (Psychological). 2. Animals, Habits and Behavior of.

2356. Mailer, Peter R., et al. The Marvels of Animal Behavior. Natl Geog. 1972. $11.95.   591.5
1. Animals, Habits and Behavior of.

2357. Roots, Clive. Animals of the Dark. Praeger. 1974. $8.95.   591.5
1. Nocturnal Animals.

2358. Roth, Charles E. Walking Catfish and Other Aliens. A-W. 1973. $4.95.   591.5
1. Animal Introduction — U. S.

2359. Silverstein, Alvin and Silverstein, Virginia. Animal Invaders. Atheneum. 1974. $5.95.   591.5
1. Animal Introduction — U. S.

2360. Ardrey, Robert. The Territorial Imperative: A Personal Inquiry into the Animal Origins of Property and Nations. Atheneum. 1966. $10.95; pap. $2.45 (Delta).   591.51
1. Animals, Habits and Behavior of. 2. Behaviorism (Psychology). 3. Instinct.

2361. Orr, Robert T. Animals in Migration. Macmillan. 1970. $12.50.   591.52
1. Animal Migration.

2362. Prince, J. H. Weather and the Animal World. Nelson. 1974. $5.95.   591.542
1. Bioclimatology. 2. Weather. 3. Zoology.

2363. Hancocks, David. Master Builders of the Animal World. Har-Row. 1973. $8.95.   591.56
1. Animals, Habitations of.

2364. Von Frisch, Karl and Von Frisch, Otto. Animal Architecture. HarBraceJ. 1974. $12.95.   591.56
1. Animals, Habitations of.

2365. Fogden, Michael and Fogden, Patricia. Animals and Their Colors: Camouflage, Warning Coloration, Courtship and Territorial Display, Mimicry. Crown. 1974. $9.95.   591.57
1. Animals, Habits and Behavior of. 2. Camouflage (Biology). 3. Color of Animals.

2366. Von Frisch, Otto. Animal Camouflage. Watts. 1973. $5.90.   591.57
1. Animals, Habits and Behavior of. 2. Camouflage (Biology). 3. Color of Animals.

2367. Cosgrove, Margaret. Messages and Voices. Dodd. 1974. $4.95.   591.59
1. Animal Communications.

2368. Caras, Roger. Venomous Animals of the World. P-H. 1974. $25.00.   591.69
1. Animals, Habits and Behavior of. 2. Poisonous Animals.

591.9 Zoological Sciences - Geographical Treatment of

2369. Perry, Richard. The Polar Worlds. Taplinger. 1973. $7.95.   591.9091
1. Ecology — Polar Regions. 2. Natural History — Polar Regions. 3. Zoology — Polar Regions — Ecology.

2370. Campbell, Elizabeth M. and Solomon, David. The Search for Morag. Walker & Co. 1973. $6.95.   591.92
1. Morag. 2. Sea Serpents.

2371. Costello, Peter. In Search of Lake Monsters. Coward. 1974. $8.95.   591.92
1. Sea Serpents.

2372. Heuvelmans, Bernard. In the Wake of the Sea Serpents. Hill & Wang. 1968. $10.00.   591.92
1. Sea Serpents.

2373. Holiday, F. W. Great Orm of Loch Ness. Norton. 1969. $6.95.   591.92
1. Loch Ness Monster. 2. Sea Serpents.

2374. Perry, Richard. The Unknown Ocean. Taplinger. 1972. $7.95.   591.92
1. Marine Ecology. 2. Marine Fauna.

2375. Stonehouse, Bernard. Animals of the Antarctic: The Ecology of the Far South. HR&W. 1972. $10.95.   591.998

500 SCIENCE

1. Ecology — Antarctic Regions. 2. Natural History — Antarctic Regions. 3. Zoology — Antarctic Regions.

2376. ———. Animals of the Arctic: The Ecology of the Far North. Intl Pubns Serv. 1971. $13.00. 591.998
1. Ecology — Arctic Regions. 2. Natural History — Arctic Regions. 3. Zoology — Arctic Regions.

2377. Sagan, Carl. The Cosmic Connection: An Extraterrestrial Perspective. Doubleday. 1973. $7.95. 591.999
1. Life on Other Planets.

592-593 Invertebrates and Protozoa

2378. Buchsbaum, Ralph. Animals Without Backbones: An Introduction to the Invertebrates. rev. ed. U of Chicago Pr. 1948. $8.50; pap. $4.25. 592
1. Invertebrates.

2379. Buchsbaum, Ralph and Milne, Lorus. Lower Animals: Living Invertebrates of the World. Doubleday. 1960. $14.95. 592
1. Invertebrates.

2380. Nichols, David and Cooke, John. Oxford Book of Invertebrates. Oxford U Pr. 1971. $12.95. 592
1. Invertebrates.

2381. Milne, Lorus and Milne, Margery. Invertebrates of North America. Doubleday. 1972. $9.95. 592.097
1. Invertebrates — North America.

2382. Vickerman, Keith and Cox, F. E. The Protozoa. HM. 1967. pap. $4.60. 593
1. Protozoa.

594 Mollusks

2383. Jenkins, Marie M. The Curious Mollusks. Holiday. 1972. $6.95. 594
1. Mollusks.

2384. Solem, Alan. The Shell Makers: Introducing Mollusks. Wiley. 1974. $9.95. 594
1. Mollusks. 2. Mollusks — Evolution.

2385. Abbott, R. Tucker. Kingdom of the Seashell. Crown. 1972. $14.95. 594.047
1. Mollusks. 2. Shells.

2386. Dance, Peter S. Collector's Encyclopedia of Shells. McGraw. 1974. $19.95. 594.047
1. Shells.

2387. Stix, Hugh and Stix, Marguerite. The Shell: Five Hundred Million Years of Inspired Design. Abrams. 1968. $28.50; pap. $4.95 abr. ed. (Ballantine). 594.047
1. Shells.

2388. Cousteau, Jacques-Yves and Diole, Philippe. Octopus and Squid, the Soft Intelligence. Doubleday. 1973. $9.95. 594.56
1. Octopus. 2. Squids.

595 Insects

2389. Klots, Alexander B. and Klots, Elsie B. Living Insects of the World. Doubleday. 1959. $14.95. 595.7
1. Insects.

2390. Callahan, Philip S. Insects and How They Function. Holiday. 1971. $5.95. 595.701
1. Insects.

2391. ———. The Evolution of Insects. Holiday. 1972. $5.95. 595.7038
1. Insects — Evolution. 2. Insects, Fossil.

2392. Wilson, Edward O. The Insect Societies. Harvard U Pr. 1971. $20.00; pap. $7.95. 595.705
1. Insect Societies.

2393. Klots, Alexander B. and Klots, Elsie B. Insects of North America. Doubleday. 1971. $9.95. 595.709
1. Insects — North America.

2394. Swan, Lester A. and Papp, Charles S. The Common Insects of North America. Har-Row. 1972. $15.00. 595.709
1. Insects — North America. 2. Insects — North America — Identification.

2395. Dickens, Michael and Storey, Eric. The World of Butterflies. Macmillan. 1973. $5.95. 595.789
1. Butterflies.

2396. Ordish, George. The Year of the Butterfly. Scribner. 1975. $8.95. 595.789
1. Butterflies.

2397. Chauvin, Remy. The World of Ants. Hill & Wang. 1971. $5.95. 595.796
1. Ants.

500 SCIENCE

2398. Evans, Howard E. and Eberhard, Mary J. The Wasps. U of Mich Pr. 1970. $7.95; pap. $3.45.   595.798
1. Wasps.

2399. Michener, Charles D. The Social Behavior of the Bees. Harvard U Pr. 1974. $25.00.   595.799
1. Bees — Behavior. 2. Social Behavior in Animals.

596 Vertebrates

2400. Romer, Alfred S. The Vertebrate Body. 4th ed. Saunders. 1970. $10.25.   596
1. Vertebrates — Anatomy.

2401. ———. Vertebrate Story. rev. ed. U of Chicago Pr. 1959. $9.50; pap. $3.95.   596
1. Evolution. 2. Fossils. 3. Vertebrates.

2402. Young, John Z. Life of Vertebrates. 2nd ed. Oxford U Pr. 1962. $12.50.   596
1. Vertebrates.

2403. Nixon, Marion. Oxford Book of Vertebrates. Oxford U Pr. 1972. $14.75.
    596.0942
1. Vertebrates.

2404. Blair, W. F., et al. Vertebrates of the United States. 2nd ed. McGraw. 1968. $21.00.
    596.0973
1. Vertebrates.

597 Fishes

2405. Herald, Earl. Living Fishes of the World. Doubleday. 1961. $16.95.   597
1. Fishes.

2406. Schultz, Leonard, et al. Wondrous World of Fishes. Natl Geog. 1969. $9.95.   597
1. Fishes. 2. Fishing.

2407. Herald, Earl. Fishes of North America. Doubleday. 1972. $9.95.   597.092
1. Fishes — North America.

2408. Brown, Theo W. Sharks: The Silent Savages. Little. 1975. $7.95.   597.31
1. Sharks — Behavior. 2. Sound-waves — Physiological Effect.

2409. Cousteau, Jacques-Yves and Cousteau, Philippe. The Shark: Splendid Savage of the Sea. Doubleday. 1970. $9.95.   597.31
1. Sharks.

2410. Cochran, Doris M. Living Amphibians of the World. Doubleday. 1966. $16.95.   597.6
1. Amphibians.

598.1 Reptiles

2411. Cochran, Doris M. and Goin, Coleman J. New Field Book of Reptiles and Amphibians. Putnam. 1970. $5.95.   598.1
1. Amphibians. 2. Reptiles.

2412. Inger, Robert F. and Schmidt, Karl P. Living Reptiles of the World. Doubleday. 1957. $14.95.   598.1
1. Reptiles.

2413. Minton, Sherman A., Jr. and Minton, Madge R. Giant Reptiles. Scribner. 1973. $9.95.   598.1
1. Reptiles. 2. Serpents (in Religion, Folk-lore, etc.).

2414. Pope, Clifford H. The Reptile World. Knopf. 1955. $8.95.   598.1
1. Reptiles.

2415. Leviton, Alan. Reptiles and Amphibians of North America. Doubleday. 1972. $9.95.   598.1097
1. Amphibians — North America. 2. Reptiles — North America.

2416. Harrison, Hal H. The World of the Snake. Lippincott. 1971. $5.95.   598.12
1. Snakes.

2417. Minton, Sherman A., Jr. and Minton, Madge R. Venomous Reptiles. Scribner. 1969. pap. $3.50.   598.12
1. Poisonous Snakes. 2. Reptiles, Poisonous. 3. Venom.

2418. Shaw, Charles E. and Campbell, Sheldon. Snakes of the American West. Knopf. 1974. $12.50.   598.12
1. Reptiles — The West. 2. Snakes — The West.

2419. Stidworthy, John. Snakes of the World. rev. ed. G&D. 1975. $5.95.   598.12
1. Reptiles. 2. Snakes.

2420. Ernst, Carl and Barbour, Roger W. Turtles of the United States. U Pr of Ky. 1972. $22.50.   598.13
1. Turtles.

500 SCIENCE

2421. Graham, Alistair. Eyelids of Morning: The Mingled Destinies of Crocodiles and Men. NYGS. 1973. $22.50; pap. $7.95 1975 (A-W). 598.14
1. Crocodiles. 2. Crocodiles (in Religions, Folk-Lore, etc.). 3. Lake Rudolph. 4. Reptiles — Kenya — Lake Rudolph.

2422. Guggisberg, C. A. Crocodiles: Their Natural History, Folklore and Conservation. Stackpole. 1972. $7.95. 598.14
1. Crocodiles.

2423. Neill, Wilfred T. The Last of the Ruling Reptiles: Alligators, Crocodiles, and Their Kin. Columbia U Pr. 1971. $17.50. 598.14
1. Alligators. 2. Crocodiles.

2424. Ricciuti, Edward R. The American Alligator: Its Life in the Wild. Har-Row. 1972. $5.95. 598.14
1. Alligators.

598.2 Birds

2425. Gilliard, Thomas E. Living Birds of the World. Doubleday. 1958. $14.95. 598.2
1. Birds.

2426. Anderson, John M. The Changing World of Birds. HR&W. 1973. $5.95. 598.25
1. Birds — Behavior. 2. Birds, Protection of.

2427. Dorst, Jean. The Life of Birds. Columbia U Pr. 1974. $35.00. 598.25
1. Birds. 2. Birds — Behavior.

2428. Matthiessen, Peter. The Wind Birds. Viking Pr. 1973. $9.95. 598.2923
1. Shore Birds — Behavior.

2429. Headstrom, Richard. A Complete Field Guide to Nests in the United States. Washburn. 1970. $10.00. 598.2923
1. Animals, Habitations of. 2. Birds — Eggs and Nests.

2430. Kortright, Francis H. The Ducks, Geese, and Swans of North America. Stackpole. 1942. $7.50. 598.2973
1. Birds — North America.

2431. Rand, Austin L. Birds of North America. Doubleday. 1971. $9.95. 598.2973
1. Birds — North America.

2432. Wetmore, Alexander, et al. Song and Garden Birds of North America. Natl Geog. 1964. $11.95. 598.2973
1. Birds — North America.

2433. ———. Water, Prey, and Game Birds of North America. Natl Geog. 1965. $11.95. 598.2973
1. Birds — North America.

2434. Costello, David F. The World of the Gull. Lippincott. 1971. $5.95. 598.33
1. Gulls.

2435. Hay, John. Spirit of Survival: A Natural and Personal History of Terns. Dutton. 1974. $7.95. 598.33
1. Shore Birds. 2. Terns.

2436. Scott, Peter and Wildfowl Trust. The Swans. HM. 1972. $15.00. 598.41
1. Swans.

2437. Wilmore, Sylvia B. Swans of the World. Taplinger. 1974. $9.95. 598.41
1. Swans.

2438. Callahan, Philip S. The Magnificent Birds of Prey. Holiday. 1974. $6.95. 598.91
1. Birds of Prey.

2439. Durden, Kent. Flight to Freedom. S&S. 1974. $5.95. 598.91
1. Golden Eagle — Legends and Stories.

2440. ———. Gifts of an Eagle. G K Hall. 1973. $6.95; pap. $1.25 (Bantam). 598.91
1. Golden Eagle — Legends and Stories.

2441. Cameron, Angus. The Nightwatchers. Schol Bk Serv. 1971. $8.95. 598.97
1. Owls.

2442. Karalus, Karl E. and Eckert, Allan W. The Owls of North America. Doubleday. 1975. $29.95. 598.97
1. Birds — North America. 2. Owls.

2443. Walker, Lewis W. The Book of Owls. Knopf. 1974. $12.50. 598.97
1. Birds — North America. 2. Owls.

599 Mammals

2444. Burton, Maurice. University Dictionary of Mammals of the World. Peter Smith. $5.50; pap. $2.45 1968 (Apollo Eds). 599
1. Mammals — Dictionaries.

500 SCIENCE

2445. Durrell, Gerald. A Bevy of Beasts. S&S. 1973. $7.95. 599
1. Zoo Animals. 2. Zoological Society of London. Gardens. Whipsnade Park.

2446. Jordan, Emil L. Animal Atlas of the World. Hammond Inc. 1969. $16.95. 599
1. Animals, Habits and Behavior of. 2. Mammals.

2447. Sanderson, Ivan T. Living Mammals of the World. Doubleday. 1955. $15.95. 599
1. Mammals.

2448. Leakey, Louis S. Animals of East Africa. Natl Geog. 1969. $4.25. 599.096
1. Mammals — Africa, East.

2449. Myers, Norman. The Long African Day. Macmillan. 1972. $25.00. 599.096
1. Wildlife Conservation — Africa, East. 2. Zoology — Africa, East. 3. Zoology — Africa, East — Ecology.

2450. Kellog, A. Remington, et al. Wild Animals of North America. 5th ed. Natl Geog. 1971. $7.75. 599.097
1. Mammals — North America.

2451. Orr, Robert T. Mammals of North America. Doubleday. 1971. $9.95. 599.097
1. Mammals — North America.

2452. Rue, Leonard L. Pictorial Guide to the Mammals of North America. 3rd ed. T Y Crowell. 1967. $8.75. 599.097
1. Mammals — North America.

2453. Lockley, R. M. The Private Life of the Rabbit: An Account of the Life History and Social Behavior of the Wild Rabbit. Macmillan. 1974. $6.95. 599.322
1. Rabbits.

599.5 Whales, Dolphins, etc.

2454. Cousteau, Jacques-Yves and Diole, Philippe. The Whale: Mighty Monarch of the Sea. Doubleday. 1972. $9.95. 599.5
1. Whales.

2455. Ommanney, F. D. Lost Leviathan: Whales and Whaling. Dodd. 1971. $7.95.
599.5
1. Whales. 2. Whaling.

2456. Stephen, David. Dolphins, Seals, and Other Sea Mammals. new ed. Putnam. 1973. $6.95. 599.5
1. Dolphins. 2. Marine Mammals. 3. Seals.

2457. Fichtelius, Karl-Erik and Sjolander, Sverre. Smarter Than Man? Intelligence in Whales, Dolphins and Humans. Pantheon. 1973. $6.95; pap. $1.50 (Ballantine). 599.504
1. Animal Intelligence. 2. Brain. 3. Dolphins — Behavior. 4. Human Behavior. 5. Whales — Behavior.

2458. McIntyre, Joan. Mind in the Waters: A Book on Behalf of Whales and Dolphins. Scribner. 1974. $12.50. 599.504
1. Animal Intelligence. 2. Dolphins. 3. Whales.

2459. Cousteau, Jacques-Yves and Diole, Philippe. Dolphins and Freedom. Doubleday. 1975. $12.50. 599.53
1. Dolphins.

2460. Norris, Kenneth S. The Porpoise Watcher. Norton. 1974. $7.95. 599.53
1. Porpoises.

2461. Wood, Forrest G. Marine Mammals and Man: The Navy's Porpoises and Sea Lions. Luce. 1973. $7.95. 599.53
1. Dolphins. 2. Porpoises. 3. Sea Lions.

599.7 Hoofed Mammals

2462. Mochi, Ugo and Carter, T. Donald. Hoofed Mammals of the World. Scribner. 1971. $9.95. 599.7
1. Mammals.

2463. Ryden, Hope. Mustangs: A Return to the Wild. Viking Pr. 1972. $9.95. 599.725
1. Mustangs.

2464. McHugh, Tom. The Time of the Buffalo. Knopf. 1972. $10.00. 599.7358
1. Bison, American. 2. Indians of North America — History — Great Plains. 3. Natural History — Great Plains. 4. Prairie Ecology — Great Plains.

599.74 Cats, Dogs, etc.

2465. Boorer, Michael. Wild Cats. G&D. 1970. $3.95. 599.7442
1. Cats.

2466. Guggisberg, C. A. Wild Cats of the World. Taplinger. 1975. $15.95. 599.7442
1. Cats.

500 SCIENCE

2467. Schaller, George B. Golden Shadows, Flying Hooves. Knopf. 1973. $8.95. 599.7442
1. Lions — Behavior. 2. Natural History — Tanzania — Serengeti Steppe. 3. Predation. 4. Serengeti National Park.

2468. ———. Serengeti: A Kingdom of Predators. Knopf. 1972. $12.95. 599.7442
1. Predation. 2. Predatory Animals — Tanzania. 3. Serengeti National Park.

2469. ———. Serengeti Lion: A Study in Predator-Prey Relations. U of Chicago Pr. 1972. $12.50. 599.7442
1. Lions — Behavior. 2. Natural History — Tanzania — Serengeti Steppe. 3. Predation. 4. Serengeti National Park.

2470. Hopf, Alice L. Wild Cousins of the Dog. Putnam. 1973. $3.86. 599.7444
1. Dogs.

2471. Mowat, Farley. Never Cry Wolf. Little. 1963. $5.95; pap. $0.75 (Dell). 599.7444
1. Animals, Habits and Behavior of. 2. Wolves.

2472. Ryden, Hope. God's Dog. Coward. 1975. $12.50. 599.7444
1. Coyotes.

2473. Van Lawick, Hugo. Solo: The Story of an African Wild Dog. HM. 1974. $6.95. 599.7444
1. Animals, Habits and Behavior of. 2. Dogs.

2474. Van Lawick-Goodall, Jane and Van Lawick-Goodall, Hugo. Innocent Killers. HM. 1971. $10.00; pap. $2.00 (Ballantine). 599.7444
1. Spotted Hyena. 2. Zoology — Africa, East.

2475. Scheffer, Victor B. The Year of the Seal. Scribner. 1970. $7.95; pap. $2.45. 599.748
1. Seals (Animals).

599.8 Primates

2476. Hahn, Emily. On the Side of the Apes. T Y Crowell. 1971. $7.95; pap. $1.95 (Pyramid Pubns). 599.8
1. Primates. 2. Primates — Behavior.

2477. Napier, Prue. Monkeys and Apes. G&D. 1972. $3.95; pap. $1.45 (Bantam). 599.8
1. Apes. 2. Monkeys. 3. Primates.

2478. Bourne, Geoffrey H. Primate Odyssey. Putnam. 1974. $9.95. 599.8045
1. Primates — Behavior. 2. Primates — Evolution.

2479. Reynolds, Vernon. Apes: Gorilla, Chimpanzee, Orangutan, and Gibbon: Their History and Their World. Dutton. 1967. $11.95. 599.88
1. Apes.

2480. Gardner, Richard. The Baboon. Macmillan. 1972. $5.95. 599.884
1. Baboons.

2481. Van Lawick-Goodall, Jane. In the Shadow of Man. HM. 1971. $10.00; pap. $2.95 (Delta). 599.884
1. Chimpanzees — Behavior.

2482. ———. My Friends the Wild Chimpanzees. Natl Geog. 1967. $4.25. 599.884
1. Chimpanzees — Behavior.

2483. Morris, Desmond. The Naked Ape: A Zoologist's Study of the Human Animal. McGraw. 1968. $5.95; pap. $1.25 (Dell). 599.9
1. Human Behavior. 2. Man. 3. Primates.

Recommended Series

2484. Life Nature Library. Time-Life.

2485. Life Science Library. Time-Life.

2486. Science Study Series. Doubleday.

600 TECHNOLOGY

600 Technology

2487. Lodewijk, T., et al. The Way Things Work: An Illustrated Encyclopedia of Technology. Special ed. for young people. S&S. 1973. $9.95. 600
1. Science — Methodology. 2. Science — Study and Teaching. 3. Technology — Methodology.

609 Technology - History

2488. Baldwin, Gordon C. Inventors and Inventions of the Ancient World. Schol Bk Serv. 1973. $6.50. 609
1. Inventions. 2. Man, Prehistoric.

2489. DeBono, Edward. Eureka: An Illustrated History of Inventions from the Wheel to the Computer. HR&W. 1974. $25.00. 609
1. Inventions — History.

2490. Hodges, Henry. Technology in the Ancient World. Knopf. 1970. $10.00. 609
1. Technology — History.

2491. Klemm, Friedrich. A History of Western Technology. MIT Pr. 1964. $12.50; pap. $3.95. 609
1. Technology — History.

2492. Kranzberg, Melvin and Pursell, Carroll W., Jr., eds. Technology of Western Civilization. 2 vols. Oxford U Pr. 1967. $9.95 ea. 609

1. Technology — History. 2. Technology and Civilization.

2493. Rowland, K. T. Eighteenth Century Inventions. B&N. 1974. $10.00. 609.033
1. Inventions — History.

2494. Clark, Ronald W. The Scientific Breakthrough: The Impact of Modern Invention. Putnam. 1974. $14.95. 609.04
1. Inventions — History. 2. Technology — History.

2495. National Geographic Society, ed. Those Inventive Americans. Natl Geog. 1971. $4.25. 609.73
1. Inventors, American.

610 Medical Sciences

2496. Fenten, D. X. Ms.-M.D. Westminster. 1973. $4.95. 610.69
1. Medicine As a Profession. 2. Women in Medicine.

2497. Huxley, Elspeth. Florence Nightingale. Putnam. 1975. $15.00. 610.73(B)
1. Nightingale, Florence, 1820-1910. 2. Nurses and Nursing.

2498. Burgess, Alan. Daylight Must Come. Delacorte. 1975. $6.95. 610.92(B)
1. Physicians — Africa. 2. Roseveare, Helen. 3. Women in Medicine.

2499. Flexner, Simon and Flexner, James T. William Henry Welch and the Heroic Age of American Medicine. Dover. 1967. pap. $3.50. 610.92(B)
1. Welch, William Henry, 1850-1934.

600 TECHNOLOGY

2500. Keynes, Geoffrey. Life of William Harvey. Oxford U Pr. 1966. $20.50. 610.92(B)
1. Harvey, William, 1578-1657.

2501. Weiner, Michael. Earth Medicine - Earth Foods: Plant Remedies, Drugs, and Natural Foods of the North American Indians. Macmillan. 1972. $8.95; pap. $3.95. 610.9701
1. Ethnobotany. 2. Indians of North America — Food. 3. Indians of North America — Medicine.

2502. Marks, Geoffrey and Beatty, William K. The Story of Medicine in America. Scribner. 1974. $10.00. 610.973
1. Medicine — U. S. — History.

611-612 Human Anatomy and Physiology

2503. Francis, Carl C. Introduction to Human Anatomy. 6th ed. Mosby. 1973. $10.95. 611
1. Anatomy, Human.

2504. Gardner, Weston D. and Osburn, William A. Structure of the Human Body. 2nd ed. Saunders. 1973. $11.95. 611
1. Anatomy, Human.

2505. Nilsson, Lennart. Behold Man. Little. 1974. $25.00. 611.013
1. Anatomy, Human.

2506. Gardner, Ernest. Fundamentals of Neurology: A Psychophysiological Approach. 6th ed. Saunders. 1968. price not set. 611.8
1. Nervous System.

2507. Best, Charles H. and Taylor, N. B. The Human Body: Its Anatomy and Physiology. 4th ed. HR&W. 1963. $14.00. 612
1. Anatomy, Human. 2. Human Physiology.

2508. Chaffee, Ellen E. and Greisheimer, Esther M. Basic Physiology and Anatomy. 3rd ed. Lippincott. 1974. $13.50. 612
1. Anatomy, Human. 2. Human Physiology.

2509. DeCoursey, Russell M. The Human Organism. 4th rev. ed. McGraw. 1974. $12.95. 612
1. Anatomy, Human. 2. Human Physiology.

2510. Eckstein, Gustav. The Body Has a Head. Har-Row. 1970. $15.00. 612
1. Human Physiology.

2511. Upton, Arthur C. Radiation Injury: Effects, Principles, and Perspectives. U of Chicago Pr. 1969. $7.50. 612
1. Radiation — Physiological Effect.

2512. Locke, David M. Enzymes: Agents of Life. Crown. 1969. $5.95. 612.015
1. Enzymes.

2513. Brown, Barbara B. New Mind, New Body Biofeedback: New Directions for the Mind. Har-Row. 1974. $9.95. 612.022
1. Biofeedback Training.

2514. Luce, Gay. Body Time: Physiological Rhythms and Social Stress. Pantheon. 1971. $6.95; pap. $1.50 (Bantam). 612.022
1. Biology — Periodicity. 2. Diel Cycles. 3. Stress (Physiology).

2515. Hackett, Earl. Blood. Sat Rev Pr. 1973. $9.95. 612.11
1. Blood. 2. Blood — Diseases. 3. Medicine, Popular.

2516. Wellford, Harrison. Sowing the Wind: A Report on the Politics of Food Safety. Grossman. 1972. $7.95. 612.3
1. Meat Inspection — U. S. 2. Pesticides — U. S. 3. Poultry Inspection — U. S. 4. U. S. Department of Agriculture.

2517. Bohannan, Paul. Love, Sex and Being Human: A Book About the Human Condition for Young People. Doubleday. 1969. $4.95; pap. $1.95. 612.6
1. Sex Instruction for Youth. 2. Sexual Ethics.

2518. Johnson, Eric W. Love and Sex in Plain Language. rev. ed. Lippincott. 1974. $4.95; pap. $0.95 (Bantam). 612.6
1. Sex Instruction for Youth.

2519. Lieberman, E. James and Peck, Ellen. Sex and Birth Control: A Guide for the Young. T Y Crowell. 1973. $5.95. 612.6
1. Birth — U. S. 2. Sex Instruction for Youth.

2520. McCary, James L. Human Sexuality. 2nd ed. Van Nos Reinhold. 1973. $10.95. 612.6
1. Sex Instruction for Youth.

2521. Pomeroy, Wardell B. Girls and Sex. Delacorte. 1969. $5.95; pap. $1.50 (Dell). 612.6
1. Sex Instruction for Youth.

600 TECHNOLOGY

2522. Pomeroy, Wardell B. and Tebbel, John. Boys and Sex. Delacorte. 1968. $5.95; pap. $0.95 (Dell). 612.6
1. Sex Instruction.

2523. Noback, Charles R. The Human Nervous System. 2nd ed. McGraw. 1975. $14.95. 612.8
1. Human Nervous System.

2524. Asimov, Isaac. The Human Brain. HM. 1964. $6.95. 612.82
1. Brain.

2525. Ferguson, Marilyn. The Brain Revolution: The Frontiers of Mind Research. Taplinger. 1973. $9.95. 612.82
1. Brain.

2526. Oatley, Keith. Brain Mechanisms and Mind. Dutton. 1972. $7.95; pap. $3.95. 612.82
1. Brain. 2. Psychology.

2527. Weiss, Malcolm E. The World Within the Brain. Messner. 1974. $6.25. 612.82
1. Brain.

2528. Silverstein, Alvin and Silverstein, Virginia. Sleep and Dreams. Lippincott. 1974. $5.50. 612.821
1. Dreams. 2. Sleep.

613 General and Personal Hygiene

2529. Read, Donald A., et al. Health and Modern Man. Macmillan. 1973. $9.50. 613
1. Medicine, Popular. 2. Public Health.

2530. Rodale, Robert. Sane Living in a Mad World. Rodale Pr Inc. 1972. $7.95; pap. $1.25 (NAL). 613.2
1. Diet. 2. Hygiene. 3. Organic Farming. 4. Organiculture.

613.69 Survival

2531. Angier, Bradford. Living off the Country: How to Stay Alive in the Woods. Stackpole. 1956. $5.00. 613.69
1. Outdoor Life. 2. Survival (After Airplane Accidents, Shipwrecks, etc.).

2532. Berglund, Berndt. Wilderness Survival. Scribner. 1972. $7.95. 613.69
1. Wilderness Survival — North America.

2533. Graves, Richard. Bushcraft: A Serious Guide to Survival and Camping. Schocken. 1972. $10.00; pap. $3.95. 613.69
1. Camping. 2. Wilderness Survival.

2534. Greenbank, Anthony. The Book of Survival. Har-Row. 1968. $6.95; pap. $0.95 (NAL). 613.69
1. Accidents. 2. First Aid in Illness and Injury. 3. Survival (After Airplane Accidents, Shipwrecks, etc.).

2535. Merrill, W. K. The Survival Handbook. Winchester Pr. 1972. $5.95; pap. $1.95 (Arc Bks). 613.69
1. Wilderness Survival.

613.71-613.79 Exercise and Yoga

2536. Cooper, Kenneth H. Aerobics. M Evans. 1968. $4.95; pap. $1.25 (Bantam). 613.71
1. Exercise. 2. Physical Fitness.

2537. Myers, Clayton R. The Official YMCA Physical Fitness Handbook. Popular Lib. 1975. pap. $1.50. 613.71
1. Exercise. 2. Physical Fitness.

2538. Royal Canadian Air Force. The Royal Canadian Air Force Exercise Plan for Physical Fitness. PB. 1972. pap. $0.95. 613.71
1. Exercise. 2. Physical Fitness.

2539. Carr, Rachel. The Yoga Way to Release Tension. Coward. 1974. $7.95. 613.79
1. Relaxation. 2. Yoga, Hatha.

2540. Roberts, Nancy. The Yoga Thing. Hawthorn. 1973. $8.95. 613.79
1. Yoga.

613.8 Addictions and Health

2541. Brecker, Edward M. and Consumer Report Editors. Licit and Illicit Drugs: The Consumers Union Report on Narcotics, Stimulants, Depressants, Inhalants, Hallucinogens and Marijuana - Including Caffeine, Nicotine, and Alcohol. Little. 1972. $14.95; pap. $3.95. 613.8
1. Drug Abuse — U. S. 2. Drugs. 3. Drugs — Physiological. 4. Narcotics.

2542. Grinspoon, Lester. Marihuana Reconsidered. Harvard U Pr. 1971. $13.50; pap. $1.50 (Bantam). 613.8
1. Drug Abuse. 2. Marihuana.

600 TECHNOLOGY

2543. Hyde, Margaret O. Mind Drugs. 3rd ed. McGraw. 1974. $4.95.   613.8
1. Drug Abuse. 2. Drugs and Youth. 3. Narcotic Habit.

2544. Louria, Donald B. Overcoming Drugs: A Program for Action. McGraw. 1971. $6.95.   613.8
1. Drugs. 2. Narcotic Habit.

2545. Anonymous. Go Ask Alice. P-H. 1971. $5.30; pap. $0.95 (Avon).   613.83
1. Drug Abuse. 2. Drugs.

2546. Coles, Robert, et al. Drugs and Youth: Medical, Psychiatric, and Legal Facts. Liveright. 1970. $5.95; pap. $2.45.   613.83
1. Drugs and Youth — U. S.

2547. Jones, Kenneth L., et al. Drugs and Alcohol. 2nd ed. Har-Row. 1973. pap. $3.95.   613.83
1. Alcoholism. 2. Narcotic Habit.

2548. Lieberman, Mark. The Dope Book. Praeger. 1971. $5.95.   613.83
1. Drug Abuse. 2. Drugs. 3. Narcotic Habit.

2549. Weil, Andres. The Natural Mind: A New Way of Looking at Drugs and the Higher Consciousness. HM. 1972. $5.95; pap. $2.95.   613.83
1. Drug Abuse. 2. Narcotic Habit.

2550. Diehl, Harold S. Tobacco and Your Health: The Smoking Controversy. McGraw. 1969. $5.50; pap. $2.95.   613.85
1. Cigarettes. 2. Smoking.

613.94 Birth Control

2551. Fleming, Alice. Contraception, Abortion, Pregnancy. Nelson. 1974. $5.95.   613.94
1. Abortion. 2. Conception — Prevention. 3. Human Reproduction.

2552. Rudel, Harry W. Birth Control: Contraception and Abortion. Macmillan. 1973. $14.50; pap. $9.95.   613.94
1. Abortion. 2. Conception — Prevention.

2553. Fried, John J. Vasectomy: The Truth and Consequences of the Newest Form of Birth Control - Male Sterilization. Sat Rev Pr. 1972. $5.95; pap. $1.50 (Pyramid Pubns).   613.942
1. Sterilization (Birth Control). 2. Vasectomy.

2554. Wylie, Evan McLeod. The New Birth Control: The Case for Voluntary Sterilization. G&D. 1972. $6.95.   613.942
1. Birth Control — U. S. 2. Sterilization (Birth Control).

2555. Mintz, Morton. The Pill: An Alarming Report. Beacon Pr. 1970. $7.50.   613.943
1. Oral Contraceptives.

614.3 Food and Drug Control

2556. Fuller, John. Two Hundred Million Guinea Pigs. Putnam. 1972. $7.95.   614.3
1. Consumer Protection — U. S. 2. Cosmetic Industry — U. S. 3. Drugs — Adulteration and Analysis. 4. Food Adulteration and Inspection — U. S. 5. Medicines, Patent, Proprietary, etc.

2557. Marine, Gene and Van Allan, Judith. Food Pollution: The Violation of Our Inner Ecology. HR&W. 1972. $8.95; pap. $2.95.   614.3
1. Food Adulteration and Inspection. 2. Food Contamination.

2558. Winter, Ruth. Beware of the Food You Eat. rev. ed. Crown. 1971. $5.95.   614.31
1. Food Adulteration and Inspection. 2. Food Contamination.

2559. Wain, Harry. A History of Preventive Medicine. C C Thomas. 1970. $14.75.   614.4
1. Medicine, Preventive — History.

560. Ackerknecht, Erwin H. History and Geography of the Most Important Diseases. Hafner. 1965. $9.95.   614.42
1. Medical Geography. 2. Medicine — History.

2561. Cartwright, Frederick F. and Biddis, Michael D. Disease and History. T Y Crowell. 1972. $7.95; pap. $1.75 (NAL).   614.49
1. Epidemics — History. 2. Medicine — History. 3. World History.

614.7 Pollution as a Threat to Health

2562. Carr, Donald E. The Breath of Life. Norton. 1965. $5.95; pap. $0.75 (Berkley Pub).   614.7
1. Air Pollution.

2563. ———. Death of the Sweet Waters. Norton. 1966. $6.95.   614.7
1. Water Pollution.

600 TECHNOLOGY

2564. Harmer, Ruth. Unfit for Human Consumption. P-H. 1971. $6.95.   614.7
1. Pesticides and the Environment. 2. Pesticides — Toxicology.

2565. Herber, Lewis. Crisis in Our Cities: The Shocking Truth About the Urban Epidemic. P-H. 1965. $6.95.   614.7
1. Air Pollution. 2. Public Health. 3. Water Pollution.

2566. Lewis, Howard. With Every Breath You Take. Crown. 1965. $5.00.   614.71
1. Air Pollution. 2. Public Health — U. S.

2567. Kavaler, Lucy. Noise: The New Menace. John Day. 1974. $7.95.   614.78
1. Noise — Physiological Effect. 2. Noise Pollution.

2568. Lipscomb, David M. Noise: The Unwanted Sounds. Nelson-Hall. 1974. $15.00.   614.78
1. Noise — Physiological Effect. 2. Noise Pollution.

614.8 Safety

2569. American National Red Cross Editors. Advanced First Aid and Emergency Care. Doubleday. 1973. $3.95; pap. $2.50.   614.8
1. Accidents. 2. First Aid in Illness and Injury.

2570. ———. Lifesaving: Rescue and Water Safety. Doubleday. 1974. pap. $2.25.   614.81
1. Accident Prevention. 2. Aquatic Sports — Safety Measures. 3. First Aid. 4. Lifesaving. 5. Respiration, Artificial. 6. Swimming.

2571. Kearney, Paul W. How to Drive Better and Avoid Accidents. 3rd ed. T Y Crowell. 1969. $6.95.   614.86
1. Automobile Driving. 2. Traffic Accidents.

2572. Mitchell, Dick. Mountaineering First Aid: A Guide to Accident Response and First Aid Care. Mountaineers. 1972. pap. $1.95.   614.877
1. First Aid in Illness and Injury. 2. Mountaineering — Accidents.

2573. Nourse, Alan E. The Outdoorsman's Medical Guide: Common Sense Advice and Essential Health Care for Campers, Hikers, and Backpackers. Har-Row. 1974. $3.95.   614.877
1. Camping — Safety Measures. 2. First Aid in Illness and Injury.

615.1 Drugs

2574. Barber, Bernard. Drugs and Society. Russell Sage. 1967. $6.50.   615.1
1. Drugs.

2575. Cohen, Sidney. The Drug Dilemma. 2nd ed. McGraw. 1975. pap. price not set.   615.1
1. Drugs. 2. Narcotics. 3. Narcotic Habit.

2576. Proger, Samuel. The Medicated Society. Macmillan. 1968. $6.95.   615.1
1. Drugs.

2577. Cashman, John A. LSD Story. Fawcett World. 1969. pap. $0.60.   615.78
1. Lysergic Acid Diethylamide. 2. Narcotic Habit.

2578. De Bold, Richard C. and Leaf, Russel C., eds. LSD, Man and Society. Wesleyan U Pr. 1968. $5.00; pap. $1.45.   615.78
1. Lysergic Acid Diethylamide. 2. Narcotic Habit.

2579. Grinspoon, Lester and Hedblom, Peter. The·Speed Culture: Amphetamine Use and Abuse in America. Harvard U Pr. 1975. $15.00.   615.785
1. Amphetamines. 2. Drug Abuse. 3. Narcotic Habit.

615.8 Physical and Other Therapies

2580. Kailins, Marvin and Andrews, Lewis M. Biofeedback: Turning on the Power of Your Mind. Lippincott. 1972. $5.95; pap. $1.25 (Paperback Lib).   615.851
1. Biofeedback Training.

2581. Duke, Marc. Acupuncture. Pyramid Pubns. 1972. $6.95; pap. $1.50.   615.89
1. Acupuncture.

2582. Mann, Felix. Acupuncture. rev. ed. Random. 1973. pap. $1.95.   615.89
1. Acupuncture.

615.9 Toxicology

2583. Montague, Katherine and Montague, Peter. Mercury. Sierra. 1972. pap. $2.25.   615.925

600 TECHNOLOGY

1. Mercury — Toxicology. 2. Pesticides and the Environment.

2584. Schroeder, Henry A. The Poisons Around Us: Toxic Metals in Food, Air and Water. Ind U Pr. 1974. $6.95. 615.9253
1. Metals. 2. Metals — Physiological Effect. 3. Poisons. 4. Pollution.

2585. Arnold, Robert E. What to Do About Bites and Stings of Venomous Animals. Macmillan. 1973. $5.95; pap. $1.95. 615.942
1. First Aid in Illness and Injury. 2. Venom — Physiological Effect.

616 Disease and Medicine

2586. Bennett, Hastin. The International Medical Encyclopedia. Stein & Day. 1972. $17.50. 616
1. Medicine — Dictionaries.

2587. Locke, David M. Viruses: The Smallest Enemy. Crown. 1974. $10.95. 616.0194
1. Virus Diseases. 2. Viruses.

2588. Langone, John. Vital Signs: The Way We Die in America. Little. 1974. $8.95. 616.07
1. Attitude to Death. 2. Death. 3. Philosophy, Medical.

2589. O'Malley, C. D. Andreas Vesalius of Brussels, 1514-1564. U of Cal Pr. 1964. $15.00. 616.07(B)
1. Vesalius, Andreas, 1514-1564.

2590. Fox, Renee C. and Swazy, Judith P. The Courage to Fail: A Social View of Organ Transplants and Dialysis. U of Chicago Pr. 1974. $12.95. 616.09
1. Medicine — Practice. 2. Transplantation of Organs, Tissues, etc.

2591. Roueché, Berton. The Orange Man. Little. 1971. $6.95. 616.09
1. Medicine — Cases, Clinical Reports, Statistics.

2592. Diethrich, Edward B. and Fried, John J. Code Arrest: A Heart Stops. Sat Rev Pr. 1974. $6.96. 616.12
1. Heart — Diseases.

616.8 Diseases of the Nervous System

2593. Klein, Aaron E. Trial by Fury: The Polio Vaccine Controversy. Scribner. 1972. $6.96. 616.835
1. Poliomyelitis — Vaccination.

2594. Killilea, Marie. Karen. P-H. 1962. $6.40; pap. $0.95 (Dell). 616.836(B)
1. Cerebral Palsy. 2. Killilea, Karen.

2595. Saghir, Marcel T. and Robins, Eli. Male and Female Homosexuality: A Comprehensive Investigation. Williams & Wilkins. 1973. $12.95. 616.85
1. Homosexuality.

2596. American Alliance for Health, Physical Education & Recreation. Drug Abuse: Escape to Nowhere. rev. ed. AAHPER. 1969. pap. $2.00. 616.86
1. Narcotic Habit.

2597. Berry, James. Heroin Was My Best Friend. Macmillan. 1971. $4.95; pap. $0.95 (Collier). 616.86
1. Drugs. 2. Narcotic Habit.

2598. Harris, John D. The Junkie Priest. PB. 1969. $0.95. 616.86(B)
1. Egan, Father Daniel, S.A. 2. Narcotic Habit — New York (City).

2599. Bloch, Marvin A. Alcoholism: Its Facets and Phases. John Day. 1965. $7.95. 616.861
1. Alcoholism.

2600. Burgess, Louise B. Alcohol and Your Health. Charles Pub. 1973. $12.50. 616.861
1. Alcohol — Physiological Effect. 2. Alcoholism. 3. Alcoholism — Treatment — U. S. 4. Liquor Problem — U. S.

2601. Kessel, Neil and Walton, Henry. Alcoholism. Penguin. pap. $1.25. 616.861
1. Alcoholism.

2602. Langone, John. Goodbye to Bedlam: Understanding Mental Illness and Retardation. Little. 1974. $5.95. 616.89
1. Mental Deficiency. 2. Psychiatry.

2603. Rogers, Carl R. Carl Rogers on Encounter Groups. Har-Row. 1970. $5.95; pap. $1.95. 616.89
1. Psychotherapy.

2604. Harris, Thomas Anthony. I'm OK, You're OK: A Practical Guide to Transactional Analysis. Har-Row. 1969. $6.95; pap. $1.95 (Revell). 616.891

600 TECHNOLOGY

1. Mental Hygiene. 2. Psychotherapy. 3. Transactional Analysis.

2605. James, Muriel. Born to Love: Transactional Analysis in the Church. A-W. 1973. $5.95. 616.8914
1. Psychology, Religious. 2. Transactional Analysis.

2606. James, Muriel and Jongward, Dorothy. Born to Win: Transactional Analysis with Gestalt Experiments. A-W. 1971. $4.95. 616.8914
1. Gestalt Therapy. 2. Transactional Analysis.

616.9 Bacterial Diseases

2607. Burnet, MacFarlane F. and White, D. O. Natural History of Infectious Disease. 4th ed. Cambridge U Pr. 1972. $14.50; pap. $3.95. 616.9
1. Communicable Diseases.

2608. Fuller, John. Fever: The Hunt for a New Killer Virus. Readers Digest Pr. 1974. $8.95; pap. $1.75 (Ballantine). 616.92
1. Medical Geography — Nigeria. 2. Virus Diseases.

2609. Zinsser, Hans. Rats, Lice and History. Little. 1935. $7.95; pap. $1.45 (Bantam). 616.922
1. Contagion and Contagious Diseases. 2. Epidemics — History. 3. Lice. 4. Rats As Carriers of Disease. 5. Typhus Fever.

2610. Marks, Geoffrey. The Medieval Plague: The Black Death of the Middle Ages. Doubleday. 1971. $3.95. 616.923
1. Plague.

2611. Hyde, Margaret O. V.D. The Silent Epidemic. McGraw. 1973. $4.50. 616.951
1. Venereal Diseases.

2612. Johnson, Eric W. V.D. Lippincott. 1973. $4.75; pap. $1.25 (Bantam). 616.951
1. Venereal Diseases.

2613. Lasagna, Louis. The VD Epidemic. Temple U Pr. 1975. $6.95. 616.951
1. Venereal Diseases.

2614. Rosebury, Theodor. Microbes and Morals: The Strange Story of Venereal Disease. Viking Pr. 1971. $10.00; pap. $1.50 (Ballantine). 616.951
1. Venereal Diseases.

2615. Sgroi, Suzanne M. VD: A Doctor's Answers. HarBraceJ. 1974. $6.50. 616.951
1. Venereal Diseases.

2616. Stiller, Richard. The Love Bugs: A Natural History of the V.D.'s. Nelson. 1974. $5.95; pap. $2.95. 616.951
1. Venereal Diseases.

616.994 Cancer

2617. Glemser, Bernard. Man Against Cancer. Funk & W. 1969. $7.95. 616.994
1. Cancer Research.

2618. Gunther, John. Death Be Not Proud. new ed. Har-Row. 1971. $7.95. 616.994(B)
1. Gunther, John, 1929-1947.

2619. Richards, Victor. Cancer: The Wayward Cell: Its Origins, Nature and Treatment. U of Cal Pr. 1972. $10.00. 616.994
1. Cancer. 2. Cancer Cells.

617 Surgery

2620. Minetree, Harry. Cooley: The Career of a Great Heart Surgeon. Harper Mag Pr. 1973. $8.95. 617.092(B)
1. Cooley, Denton A. 2. Heart — Surgery.

2621. Nolen, William A. The Making of a Surgeon. Random. 1970. $6.95; pap. $1.50 (PB). 617.092(B)
1. Surgery.

2622. Wilkerson, James A., ed. Medicine for Mountaineering. Mountaineers. 1967. $7.50. 617.1
1. Mountaineering — Accidents and Injuries. 2. Sports Medicine.

2623. Root, Leon and Kiernan, Thomas. The Doctor's Guide to Tennis Elbow, Trick Knee, and Other Miseries of the Weekend Athlete. McKay. 1974. $8.95. 617.1027
1. Sports — Accidents and Injuries.

2624. Mowbray, A. Q. The Transplant. McKay. 1974. $8.95. 617.461
1. Kidneys — Transplantation. 2. Transplantation of Organs, Tissues, etc.

2625. Valenstein, Elliot S. Brain Control: A Critical Examination of Brain Stimulation and Psychosurgery. Wiley. 1973. $10.95. 617.481
1. Brain Stimulation. 2. Psychosurgery.

600 TECHNOLOGY

618 Other Branches of Medicine

2626. Zimmerman, David R. Rh: The Intimate History of a Disease and Its Conquest. Macmillan. 1973. $8.95.   618.32
1. Erythroblastosis Fetalis. 2. Rh Factor.

2627. Rubin, Theodore I. Jordi, Lisa and David. Ballantine. 1973. pap. $1.25.   618.92
1. Child Psychiatry.

2628. Axline, Virginia M. Debs: In Search of Self. HM. 1965. $5.95; pap. $1.25 (Ballantine).   618.9289
1. Child Psychotherapy — Cases, Clinical Reports, Statistics.

620 Engineering

2629. Graf, Rudolf F. and Whalen, George J. How It Works: Every Day Devices and Mechanisms. Har-Row. 1974. $10.95.   620
1. Household Appliances. 2. Mechanical Movements.

2630. Parsons, William B. Engineers and Engineering in the Renaissance. MIT Pr. 1968. $12.50.   620
1. Engineering — History, Renaissance.

2631. DeCamp, L. Sprague. The Ancient Engineers. MIT Pr. 1970. pap. $2.95.   620.009
1. Engineering — History.

2632. Kenner, Hugh. Bucky: A Guided Tour of Buckminster Fuller. Morrow. 1973. $7.95; pap. $3.95.   620.092(B)
1. Fuller, Richard Buckminster, 1895-

2633. Taylor, L. B., Jr. For All Mankind. Dutton. 1974. $8.95.   620.419
1. Astronautics — U. S. 2. Outer Space — Exploration. 3. Space Flight — U. S. 4. Space Ships.

621 Applied Physics

2634. Hammond, Allen, et al. Energy and the Future. AAAS. 1973. $9.95; pap. $4.95.   621
1. Energy Conservation. 2. Energy Policy. 3. Power Resources.

2635. Calder, Ritchie. The Evolution of the Machine. Hale. 1969. $4.98.   621.09

1. Machinery — History. 2. Technology — History.

2636. Buban, Peter and Schmitt, Marshall L. Understanding Electricity and Electronics. 3rd ed. McGraw. 1975. $10.40.   621.3
1. Electric Engineering. 2. Electronics.

2637. Lloyd, Tom C. Electric Motors and Their Applications. Wiley. 1969. $10.50.   621.3
1. Electric Motors.

2638. Young, Louise B. Power Over People. Oxford U Pr. 1973. $7.50; pap. $2.95.   621.312
1. Electric Power-Plants — Environmental Aspects.

2639. Brown, Ronald. Lasers: Tools of Modern Technology. Doubleday. 1969. $6.95.   621.366
1. Lasers.

2640. Heavens, O. S. Lasers. Scribner. 1973. $9.95.   621.366
1. Lasers.

2641. Hawker, J. P. Radio and Television: Principles and Applications. Hart. 1970. $12.50.   621.38
1. Radio. 2. Television.

2642. Martin, James. Introduction to Teleprocessing. P-H. 1972. $10.50.   621.38
1. Data Transmission Systems.

2643. Gregor, Arthur. Bell Laboratories. Scribner. 1972. $6.95.   621.3807
1. Bell Telephone Laboratories, Inc. 2. Electronic Apparatus and Appliances.

2644. Branson, Lane. Introduction to Electronics. P-H. 1967. $14.50.   621.381
1. Electronics.

2645. Mandl, Matthew. Fundamentals of Electronics. 3rd ed. P-H. 1973. $13.95.   621.381
1. Electronics.

2646. Pearce, W. E. and Klein, Aaron. Transistors and Circuits: Electronics for Young Experimenters. Doubleday. 1971. $4.95.   621.381
1. Electricity — Experiments. 2. Electronics — Experiments.

2647. Goldstine, Herman H. The Computer from Pascal to Von Neumann. Princeton U Pr. 1972. $12.50.   621.3819
1. Computers — History.

621.384-621.389 Radio and Sound Systems

2648. American Radio Relay League. The Radio Amateur's Handbook. Am Radio. $4.50. 621.384
1. Radio — Amateurs' Manuals.

2649. Marcus, Abraham and Marcus, W. Elements of Radio. 6th ed. P-H. 1972. $13.20. 621.384
1. Radio. 2. Radio — Receivers and Reception.

2650. Bennett, Hank. The Complete Shortwave Listener's Handbook. Tab Bks. 1974. $9.95; pap. $6.95. 621.3841
1. Radio, Shortwave — Receivers and Reception.

2651. Buckwalter, Len. ABC's of Citizens Band Radio. 3rd ed. Sams. 1974. $4.50. 621.3845
1. Citizens Radio Service (Class D). 2. Radio.

2652. Wheeler, Gershon. Radar Fundamentals. P-H. 1967. $10.00. 621.3848
1. Radar.

2653. Coleman, Howard W., ed. Color Television: The Business of Colorcasting. Hastings. 1968. $9.95. 621.388
1. Color Television. 2. Television Industry.

2654. Boyce, William F. Hi-Fi Stereo Handbook. 4th ed. Sams. 1972. $5.95. 621.389
1. High-Fidelity Sound Systems. 2. Stereophonic Sound Systems.

2655. Fantel, Hans. ABC's of Hi-Fi and Stereo. 3rd ed. Sams. 1974. pap. $3.95. 621.389
1. High-Fidelity Sound Systems. 2. Stereophonic Sound Systems.

2656. ———. The True Sound of Music: A Practical Guide to Sound Equipment for the Home. Dutton. 1973. $7.95. 621.389
1. High-Fidelity Sound Systems.

2657. Feldman, Leonard. Four Channel Sound. Sams. 1973. pap. $4.50. 621.389
1. Stereophonic Sound Systems.

2658. Zuckerman, Art. Tape Recording for the Hobbyist. 3rd ed. Sams. 1973. $9.95. 621.389
1. Tape Recorders and Recording.

600 TECHNOLOGY

621.4 Engines and Energy

2659. Faith, Nicholas. Wankel: The Story Behind the World's Most Revolutionary Engine. Stein & Day. 1975. $8.95. 621.434
1. Wankel Engine.

2660. Pipe, Ted. Principles of the Wankel Engine. Sams. 1974. $3.95. 621.434
1. Wankel Engine.

2661. Brinkworth, B. D. Solar Energy for Man. Halsted Pr. 1973. $8.95. 621.47
1. Solar Energy.

2662. Halacy, D. S., Jr. The Coming Age of Solar Energy. rev. ed. Har-Row. 1973. $7.95. 621.47
1. Solar Energy.

2663. Barnaby, Frank. Man and the Atom: The Uses of Nuclear Energy. Funk & W. 1972. $6.95; pap. $3.50. 621.48
1. Atomic Energy.

2664. Ebbin, Steven and Kasper, Raphael. Citizen Groups and the Nuclear Power Controversy: Uses of Scientific and Technological Information. MIT Pr. 1974. $13.95; pap. $7.95. 621.481
1. Atomic Power-Plants — Environmental Aspects — U. S. 2. Environmental Protection — U. S. — Citizen Participation.

2665. Novick, Sheldon. The Careless Atom. HM. 1969. $5.95. 621.483
1. Nuclear Reactors — Accidents. 2. Radioactive Substances.

622 Mining Engineering

2666. Sloane, Howard N. and Sloane, Lucille L. A Pictorial History of American Mining. Crown. 1970. $12.50. 622.0973
1. Mines and Mineral Resources — U. S. — History.

2667. Stacks, John F. Stripping: The Surface Mining of America. Sierra. 1972. pap. $2.95. 622.33
1. Coal Mine Waste. 2. Environmental Policy — U. S. 3. Strip Mining.

623 Military Engineering

2668. Groueff, Stephen. Manhattan Project. Little. 1967. $8.95. 623.4
1. Atomic Bomb — History.

600 TECHNOLOGY

2669. Lamont, Lansing. Day of Trinity. Atheneum. 1965. $6.95.   623.4
1. Atomic Bomb — History.

2670. Lapp, Ralph E. The Weapons Culture. Norton. 1968. $4.95; pap. $1.25 (Penguin).   623.4
1. Atomic Weapons. 2. U. S. — Defenses.

2671. Larus, Joel. Nuclear Weapons Safety and the Common Defense. Ohio St U Pr. 1967. $6.50.   623.4
1. Atomic Weapons — Safety Measures.

2672. Peterson, Harold L. Encyclopedia of Firearms. Dutton. 1964. $16.95.   623.44
1. Firearms — Dictionaries.

2673. Smith, Joseph E. Small Arms of the World. rev. ed. Stackpole. 1973. $7.95.   623.44
1. Firearms.

2674. Cooper, Bryan and Batchelor, John. Fighter. Scribner. 1974. $9.95; pap. $5.95 (Ballantine).   623.746
1. Fighter Planes — History.

2675. Munson, Kenneth. Fighters in Service. Macmillan. 1972. $5.95.   623.746
1. Fighter Planes.

2676. Taylor, John, ed. Jane's Pocket Book of Major Combat Aircraft. Macmillan. 1974. $6.95; pap. $3.95.   623.746
1. Airplanes, Military.

2677. Munson, Kenneth. Bombers in Service Since 1960. Macmillan. 1972. $5.95.   623.7463
1. Airplanes, Military. 2. Bombers.

2678. Foss, Christopher F. Armoured Fighting Vehicles of the World. rev. ed. Scribner. 1975. $7.95.   623.7475
1. Armored Vehicles, Military.

2679. Macksey, Kenneth and Batchelor, John H. Tank: A History of the Armoured Fighting Vehicle. Scribner. 1974. $9.95; pap. $4.95 (Ballantine).   623.7475
1. Armored Vehicles, Military — History. 2. Tanks (Military Science) — History.

623.8 Naval Engineering

2680. Casson, Lionel. Illustrated History of Ships and Boats. Doubleday. 1968. $9.95.   623.8
1. Naval Architecture — History. 2. Ships — Pictorial Works.

2681. Chapman, Charles F. Piloting, Seamanship and Small Boat Handling. new ed. Hearst Bks. 1974. $9.95.   623.8
1. Motorboats. 2. Navigation. 3. Pilots and Piloting. 4. Sailing.

2682. Moore, John E., ed. Jane's Pocket Book of Major Warships. Macmillan. 1974. $6.95; pap. $3.95.   623.825
1. Warships — Recognition.

2683. Cohen, Paul. The Realm of the Submarine. Macmillan. 1969. $5.95.   623.8257
1. Submarine Boats.

2684. Horton, Edward. The Illustrated History of the Submarine. Doubleday. 1974. $10.00.   623.8257
1. Submarine Boats — History. 2. Submarine Warfare — History.

2685. Schroeder, Peter B. Contact at Sea: A History of Maritime Radio Communications. Gregg. 1967. $14.00.   623.85
1. Radio — Installation on Ships.

2686. Ashley, Clifford U. The Ashley Book of Knots. Doubleday. 1944. $16.95.   623.8882
1. Knots and Splices.

2687. Snyder, Paul and Snyder, Arthur. Knots and Lines Illustrated. De Graff. 1970. $6.95.   623.8882
1. Knots and Splices.

2688. Bentley, John. The Thresher Disaster: The Most Tragic Dive in Submarine History. Doubleday. 1975. $8.95.   623.8885
1. Submarine Boats. 2. Thresher (Submarine).

624 Civil Engineering

2689. Jacobs, David, et al. Bridges, Canals, Tunnels. Hale. 1968. $4.98.   624
1. Civil Engineering — U. S. — History.

2690. Condit, Carl. American Building: Materials and Techniques from the First Colonial Settlements to the Present. U of Chicago Pr. 1969. $10.00; pap. $3.95.   624.09
1. Building — U. S. — History.

600 TECHNOLOGY

2691. Plowden, David. Bridges: The Spans of North America. Viking Pr. 1974. $27.50. 624.2
1. Bridges — North America.

2692. Shirley-Smith, H. World's Great Bridges. rev. ed. Har-Row. 1965. $7.95. 624.2
1. Bridges.

2693. McCullough, David. The Great Bridge. S&S. 1972. $10.95. 624.55
1. Bridges. 2. New York (City) — Bridges — Brooklyn Bridge.

627.7 Underwater Operations

2694. Kenny, John. Business of Diving. Gulf Pub. 1972. $14.95. 627.72
1. Diving, Submarine.

2695. Terrell, Mark. The Principles of Diving. A S Barnes. 1967. $8.50. 627.72
1. Diving, Submarine.

2696. Briggs, Peter. Rampage: The Story of Disastrous Floods, Broken Dams, and Human Fallibility. McKay. 1973. $6.95. 627.8
1. Dams — U. S. 2. Floods — U. S.

628 Pollution and Sanitation

2697. Stewart, George R. Not So Rich As You Think. HM. 1967. $6.95. 628
1. Pollution — U. S. 2. Refuse and Refuse Disposal — U. S.

2698. Still, Henry. The Dirty Animal. Hawthorn. 1967. $6.95. 628
1. Pollution.

2699. Overman, Michael. Water: Solutions to a Problem of Supply and Demand. Doubleday. 1969. $6.95. 628.1
1. Water.

2700. Behrman, A. S. Water Is Everybody's Business: The Chemistry of Water Purification. Doubleday. 1968. pap. $1.45. 628.16
1. Water — Analysis. 2. Water — Purification.

2701. Marx, Wesley. Oilspill. Sierra. 1972. pap. $2.75. 628.1683
1. Oil Pollution of Rivers, Harbors, etc. 2. Water — Pollution.

2702. Potter, Jeffrey. Disaster by Oil. Macmillan. 1973. $7.95. 628.1683
1. Oil Pollution of Rivers, Harbors, etc. 2. Water Pollution.

2703. Moorcraft, Colin. Must the Seas Die? Gambit. 1973. $6.95. 628.1686
1. Marine Pollution.

2704. Stevens, Leonard A. Clean Water: Nature's Way to Stop Pollution. Dutton. 1974. $10.00. 628.36
1. Sewage Irrigation.

2705. Goldstein, Jerome. Garbage As You Like It. Rodale Pr Inc. 1969. $5.95. 628.445
1. Compost. 2. Refuse and Refuse Disposal.

2706. Andrews, W. A Guide to the Study of Environmental Pollution. P-H. 1972. $5.95; pap. $3.00. 628.5
1. Pollution.

2707. Linton, Ron. Terracide: America's Destruction of Her Living Environment. Little. 1970. $7.95. 628.5
1. Man — Influence on Nature. 2. Pollution.

2708. Lewis, Alfred. Clean the Air: Fighting Smoke, Smog and Smaze. McGraw. 1965. $3.83. 628.509

2709. Bowen, D. H. Michael. Air Pollution. Am Chemical. 1973. $5.95; pap. $3.50. 628.5308
1. Air Pollution. 2. Environmental Science and Technology.

629.045 Orientation

2710. Mooers, Robert L., Jr. Finding Your Way in the Outdoors. Dutton. 1972. $6.95. 629.045
1. Orientation.

629.1 Aeronautics

2711. Gibbs-Smith, Charles H. Flight Through the Ages. T Y Crowell. 1974. $17.95. 629.109
1. Aeronautics — History.

2712. ———. The Invention of the Aeroplane, 1799-1909. Taplinger. 1966. $14.95. 629.13
1. Aeronautics — History. 2. Airplanes.

2713. Greiner, James D. Wager with the Wind: The Don Sheldon Story. Rand. 1974. $8.95. 629.13(B)

600 TECHNOLOGY

1. Aeronautics — Alaska — History. 2. Alaska — History. 3. Sheldon, Donald Edward.

2714. Harris, Sherwood. The First to Fly. S&S. 1970. $7.50. 629.13
1. Aeronautics — History.

2715. Howard, Frank and Gunston, Bill. The Conquest of the Air. Random. 1972. $25.00. 629.13
1. Aeronautics — History. 2. Airplanes — History.

2716. Lindbergh, Charles A. Spirit of St. Louis. Scribner. 1953. $9.95. 629.13
1. Aeronautics — Flights. 2. Spirit of St. Louis (Airplane).

2717. Mayer, Tom. Climb for the Evening Star. HM. 1974. $5.95. 629.13(B)
1. Air Pilots — Correspondence, Reminiscences, etc. 2. Mayer, Tom.

2718. Scott, Sheila. Barefoot in the Sky. Macmillan. 1974. $7.95. 629.13(B)
1. Scott, Sheila. 2. Women Aviators.

2719. Underwood, John W. Stinsons: Air Pioneers and Aircraft. Aviation. 1969. $9.95; pap. $5.95. 629.13
1. Aeronautics — History. 2. Airplanes.

2720. Gann, Ernest K. Ernest K. Gann's Flying Circus. Macmillan. 1974. $12.95. 629.1309
1. Aeronautics — History.

2721. Flying Magazine Editors. America's Flying Book. Scribner. 1972. $12.95. 629.132
1. Airplanes — Piloting. 2. Private Flying.

2722. Kershmer, William K. Flight Instructor's Manual. Iowa St U Pr. 1974. $14.95. 629.132
1. Flight Training.

629.133 Aircraft Types

2723. Carter, William T. Soaring. Macmillan. 1973. $6.95. 629.133
1. Gliders (Aeronautics). 2. Gliding and Soaring.

2724. Munson, Kenneth. Airliners Between the Wars, 1919 to 1939. Macmillan. 1972. $5.95. 629.133
1. Transport Planes.

2725. ————. Airliners Since 1946. rev. ed. Macmillan. 1972. $5.95. 629.133
1. Transport Planes.

2726. ————. Helicopters and Other Rotocraft Since 1907. Macmillan. 1969. $5.95. 629.133
1. Autogiros — History. 2. Helicopters — History.

2727. ————. Pioneer Aircraft 1903-1914. Macmillan. 1969. $5.95. 629.133
1. Airplanes — History.

2728. ————. Pocket Encyclopedia of Seaplanes and Flying Boats. Macmillan. 1971. $5.95. 629.133
1. Seaplanes.

2729. Taylor, John, ed. Jane's Pocket Book of Commercial Transport Aircraft. Macmillan. 1974. $6.95; pap. $3.95. 629.133
1. Transport Planes.

2730. ————. Milestones of the Air: Jane's 100 Significant Aircraft. McGraw. 1971. $10.00. 629.133
1. Airplanes — History.

2731. Taylor, John W. Civil Aircraft of the World. rev. ed. Scribner. 1975. $6.95. 629.133
1. Airplanes, Private. 2. Transport Planes.

2732. Collier, Basil. The Airship: A History. Putnam. 1975. $12.95. 629.1332
1. Airships — History.

2733. Dwiggins, Don. Riders of the Winds: The Story of Ballooning. Hawthorn. 1973. $6.95. 629.1332
1. Airships. 2. Balloons.

2734. Ege, Lennart. Balloons and Airships. Macmillan. 1974. $5.95. 629.1332
1. Airships. 2. Balloons.

2735. Mooney, Michael M. The Hindenburg. Dodd. 1972. $8.95; pap. $1.95 (Bantam). 629.1332
1. Airships. 2. Hindenburg (Airship).

2736. Robinson, Douglas H. Giants in the Sky: A History of the Rigid Airship. U of Wash Pr. 1973. $15.00. 629.1332
1. Airships — History.

2737. Siberry, K. M. Instruments of Flight. Crane-Russak Co. 1974. $7.50. 629.135
1. Aeronautical Instruments.

600 TECHNOLOGY

629.2 Automobiles

2738. May, George S. A Most Unique Machine: A History of the Automobile Industry in Michigan. Eerdmans. 1974. $6.95.
629.2
1. Automobile Industry and Trade — History.

2739. Nader, Ralph. Unsafe at Any Speed: The Designed-in Dangers of the American Automobile. rev. ed. Grossman. 1972. $7.95; pap. $1.95 (Bantam). 629.2
1. Automobile Industry and Trade. 2. Automobiles — Design and Construction.

2740. Automobile Quarterly. Auto Quarterly. $7.95; annual subscription (4 issues) $28.50. 629.205
1. Automobiles, Antique. 2. Automobiles — History. 3. Automobiles, Racing — History. 4. Sports Cars — History.

2741. Butterworth, W. E. Wheels and Pistons: The Story of the Automobile. Schol Bk Serv. 1971. $5.95. 629.222
1. Automobiles — History.

2742. Automobile Quarterly, ed. The American Car Since 1775. Dutton. 1971. $11.95. 629.2222
1. Automobiles, American — History.

2743. Georgano, George N. The Complete Encyclopedia of Motorcars. rev. ed. Dutton. 1973. $30.00. 629.2222
1. Automobiles — History.

2744. Jutty, Sam. How Your Car Works. Har-Row. 1974. $11.95. 629.2222
1. Automobiles.

2745. Time-Life Books Editors. The Time-Life Book of the Family Car. Time-Life. 1974. $14.95. 629.2222
1. Automobiles. 2. Automobiles — Maintenance and Repair.

2746. Coles, Clarence W. and Glenn, Harold T. Glenn's Complete Bicycle Manual: Selection, Maintenance, Repair. Crown. 1973. $7.95; pap. $5.95. 629.2272
1. Bicycles and Tricycles — Maintenance and Repair.

2747. Engel, Lyle K. The Complete Motorcycle Book. Schol Bk Serv. 1974. $6.95.
629.2275
1. Motorcycle Racing. 2. Motorcycles. 3. Motorcycling.

2748. Roth, Bernhard A. The Complete Beginner's Guide to Motorcycling. Doubleday. 1974. $4.95. 629.2275
1. Motorcycles. 2. Motorcycling.

2749. Schilling, Phil. The Motorcycle World. Random. 1974. $17.95. 629.2275
1. Motorcycles. 2. Motorcycling.

2750. Campbell, Colin. The Sports Car: Its Design and Performance. 3rd ed. Bentley. 1969. $9.95. 629.228
1. Sports Cars.

2751. Lurani, Giovanni. History of the Racing Car: Man and Machine. T Y Crowell. 1972. $14.95. 629.228
1. Automobile Racing — History.

2752. Billiet, Walter E. Automotive Engines: Maintenance and Repair. 4th ed. Am Technical. 1973. $9.95. 629.25
1. Automobiles — Motors — Maintenance and Repair.

2753. Crouse, W. H. and Anglin, D. L. Automotive Engines. 5th ed. McGraw. 1976. price not set. 629.25
1. Automobiles — Motors.

2754. Gunston, William T. Hydrofoils and Hovercraft. Doubleday. 1970. $6.95. 629.3
1. Ground Effect Machines. 2. Hydrofoil Boats.

629.4 Astronautics

2755. Gatland, K. Robot Explorers. Macmillan. 1972. $5.95. 629.4
1. Astronautics. 2. Robots.

2756. McCall, Robert. Our World in Space. NYGS. 1973. $22.50. 629.4
1. Astronautics. 2. Outer Space — Exploration.

2757. Moore, Patrick and Hardy, David A. Challenge of the Stars. Rand. 1972. $6.95.
629.4
1. Outer Space — Exploration.

2758. Ordway, Frederick I., 3rd, et al. Dividends from Space. T Y Crowell. 1972. $10.00. 629.4

600 TECHNOLOGY

1. Artificial Satellites — Scientific Applications. 2. Astronautics — U. S. 3. Remote Sensing Systems. 4. Technology Transfer.

2759. Riabchikov, Eugeny. Russians in Space. Intl Pubns Serv. 1972. $12.50.   629.4
1. Astronautics — Russia. 2. Astronauts — Russia.

2760. Ordway, Frederick I., Jr. and Braun, Wernher Von. History of Rocketry and Space Travel. rev. ed. T Y Crowell. 1975. $19.95.
629.409
1. Astronautics — History. 2. Rocketry — History.

2761. Smolders, Peter L. Soviets in Space. Taplinger. 1974. $9.95.   629.409
1. Astronautics — Russia.

2762. Collins, Michael. Carrying the Fire: An Astronaut's Journeys. FS&G. 1974. $10.00.   629.4092
1. Apollo 11 (Spacecraft). 2. Project Apollo. 3. Space Flight to the Moon.

2763. Anderton, David A. Apollo 17 at Taurus Littrow. US Govt Ptg Off. 1973. pap. $1.25.   629.454
1. Moon — Exploration. 2. Project Apollo.

2764. Armstrong, Neil, et al. First on the Moon: The Astronauts' Own Story. Little. 1970. $7.95.   629.454
1. Project Apollo.

2765. Cooper, Henry S., Jr. Thirteen: The Flight That Failed. Dial. 1973. $6.95.   629.454
1. Apollo 13 (Spacecraft). 2. Project Apollo. 3. Space Flight to the Moon.

2766. Froehlich, Walter. Apollo 14: Science at Fra Mauro. US Govt Ptg Off. 1971. pap. $1.25.   629.454
1. Moon — Exploration. 2. Project Apollo.

2767. Lewis, Richard S. The Voyages of Apollo: The Exploration of the Moon. Quadrangle. 1974. $10.00.   629.454
1. Moon — Exploration. 2. Project Apollo. 3. Space Flight to the Moon.

2768. Gatland, K. Manned Spacecraft. Macmillan. 1967. $3.50.   629.47
1. Astronautics. 2. Manned Space Flight.

2769. Lowry, Peter and Griffith, Field. Model Rocketry: Hobby of Tomorrow. Doubleday. 1972. $4.50.   629.47
1. Rockets (Astronautics) — Models.

629.8 Automation

2770. August, Stanley W. Closing the Loop: The Story of Feedback. T Y Crowell. 1973. $4.95.   629.83
1. Feedback Control Systems.

2771. Young, J. F. Robotics. Halsted Pr. 1974. $18.95.   629.892
1. Automation.

630 Agriculture

2772. Hayter, Earl W. The Troubled Farmer: Rural Adjustments to Industrialism, 1850-1900. N Ill U Pr. 1969. pap. $5.00.   630
1. Agriculture — U. S. — History. 2. Farm Life — U. S.

2773. Bickel, Lennard. Facing Starvation: A Biography of Dr. Norman E. Borlang. Readers Digest Pr. 1974. $8.95.   630.92(B)
1. Borlang, Norman E. 2. Starvation.

631.4 Soil and Soil Conservation

2774. Held, R. Burnell and Clawson, Marion. Soil Conservation in Perspective. Johns Hopkins. 1965. $11.00.   631.4
1. Soil Conservation.

2775. Kohn, Bernice. The Organic Living Book. Viking Pr. 1972. $4.50; pap. $1.25.
631.58
1. Cookery. 2. Organiculture.

2776. Slack, A. V. Defense Against Famine. Doubleday. 1970. $5.95.   631.8
1. Fertilizers and Manures.

2777. Swan, Lester. Beneficial Insects. Har-Row. 1964. $8.95.   632.2
1. Insects, Injurious and Beneficial.

632.9 Pest Control

2778. Carson, Rachel. Silent Spring. HM. 1962. $6.95; pap. $2.95.   632.9
1. Insects, Injurious and Beneficial — Biological Control. 2. Pesticides — Toxicology. 3. Wildlife Conservation.

2779. Fletcher, W. W. The Pest War. Halsted Pr. 1974. $11.95.   632.9
1. Pest Control. 2. Pesticides.

600 TECHNOLOGY

2780. Pringle, Laurence. Pests and People: The Search for Sensible Pest Control. Macmillan. 1972. $4.95. 632.9
1. Agricultural Pests. 2. Pesticides.

2781. Graham, Frank, Jr. Since Silent Spring. HM. 1970. $6.95; pap. $1.25 (Fawcett World). 632.95
1. Carson, Rachel Louise. Silent Spring. 2. Ecology. 3. Pesticides.

2782. Whorton, James. Before Silent Spring: Pesticides in pre-DDT America. Princeton U Pr. 1974. $12.50. 632.95
1. Food Adulteration and Inspection — U. S. 2. Food Contamination. 3. Pesticide Residues. 4. Pesticides — Toxicology.

2783. Deback, P. Biological Control by Natural Enemies. Cambridge U Pr. 1974. $14.95; pap. $5.95. 632.96
1. Pest Control — Biological Control.

2784. Hunter, Beatrice T. Gardening Without Poisons. 2nd ed. HM. 1972. $6.95. 632.96
1. Garden Pests. 2. Insect Control — Biological Control.

634.9 Forestry

2785. Frome, Michael. The Forest Service. Praeger. 1971. $8.75. 634.9
1. Forest Conservation — U. S. 2. U. S. Forest Service.

2786. Brown, A. A. and Davis, Kenneth P. Forest Fire: Control and Use. 2nd ed. McGraw. 1973. $16.50. 634.9618
1. Forest Fires.

2787. Wood, Nancy. Clear-Cut: The Deforestation of America. Sierra. 1972. pap. $2.75. 634.982
1. Clear-Cutting — U. S. 2. Forests and Forestry — Clear-Cutting — U. S.

635 Horticulture

2788. Faust, Joan L. The New York Times Book of Vegetable Gardening. Quadrangle. 1975. $9.95. 635
1. Vegetable Gardening.

2789. Harrison, S. G., et al. The Oxford Book of Food Plants. Oxford U Pr. 1969. $13.95. 635
1. Plants, Edible.

2790. Wyman, Donald. Wyman's Gardening Encyclopedia. Macmillan. 1971. $17.50. 635.03
1. Gardening — Dictionaries. 2. Plants, Cultivated — Dictionaries.

2791. Flemer, William. Nature's Guide to Successful Gardening and Landscaping. 3rd ed. T Y Crowell. 1972. $8.95. 635.9
1. Gardening. 2. Landscape Gardening.

2792. Faust, Joan L., ed. The New York Times Garden Book. 2nd rev. ed. Knopf. 1973. $10.00. 635.908
1. Gardening.

2793. Lamb, Edgar and Lamb, Brian. Colorful Cacti of the American Deserts. Macmillan. 1974. $5.95. 635.933
1. Cactus — Pictorial Works. 2. Desert Flora — U. S. — Pictorial Works.

2794. Compton, Joan. House Plants. G&D. 1972. $3.95. 635.965
1. House Plants.

2795. Faust, Joan L. The New York Times Book of House Plants. Quadrangle. 1973. $9.95; pap. $5.95 (A & W Visual Library). 635.965
1. House Plants.

2796. Langer, Richard W. Grow It Indoors. Sat Rev Pr. 1975. $9.95. 635.965
1. House Plants.

2797. Loewer, H. Peter. The Indoor Water Gardener's How-to Handbook. Walker & Co. 1973. $5.95; pap. $1.25 (Popular Lib). 635.965
1. House Plants. 2. Hydroponics.

2798. McDonald, Elvin. The World Book of House Plants. new updated ed. Funk & W. 1975. $8.95. 635.965
1. House Plants.

2799. Evans, Charles and Pliner, Roberta. The Terrarium Book. Random. 1973. $7.95; pap. $3.95. 635.98
1. Terrariums.

2800. Kayatta, Ken and Schmidt, Steven. Successful Terrariums: A Step-by-Step Guide. HM. 1975. $14.95. 635.98
1. Terrariums.

600 TECHNOLOGY

2801. Kramer, Jack. The Complete Book of Terrarium Gardening. Scribner. 1974. $9.95. 635.98
1. Terrariums.

2802. Northen, Henry T. and Northen, Rebecca T. Greenhouse Gardening. 2nd ed. Ronald. 1973. $10.50. 635.982
1. Greenhouse Management. 2. Plants, Ornamental.

636 Animal Husbandry

2803. Carson, Gerald. Men, Beasts, and Gods: A History of Cruelty and Kindness to Animals. Scribner. 1972. pap. $2.95. 636.083
1. Animals, Treatment of — History.

2804. Herriot, James. All Creatures Great and Small. St Martin. 1972. $7.95; pap. $1.75 (Bantam). 636.089(B)
1. Veterinarians — Correspondence, Reminiscences, etc.

2805. ———. All Things Bright and Beautiful. St Martin. 1974. $8.95. 636.089(B)
1. Veterinarians — Correspondence, Reminiscences, etc.

2806. Haines, Francis. Horses in America. T Y Crowell. 1971. $7.95. 636.1
1. Horses — U. S. — History.

2807. Ryden, Hope. America's Last Wild Horses. Dutton. 1970. $8.95; pap. $2.00 (Ballantine). 636.1
1. Horses — U. S.

2808. Taylor, Louis. Harper's Encyclopedia for Horsemen: The Complete Book of the Horse. Har-Row. 1973. $15.00. 636.1
1. Horsemanship — Dictionaries. 2. Horses — Dictionaries.

2809. American Kennel Club. The Complete Dog Book: The Official Publication of the American Kennel Club. new 15th ed. Howell Bk. 1975. $7.95. 636.7
1. Dog Breeds. 2. Dogs.

2810. Fiorone, Frorenzo. Encyclopedia of Dogs. T Y Crowell. 1973. $25.00. 636.7
1. Dog Breeds. 2. Dogs.

2811. National Geographic Society, ed. Man's Best Friend. rev. ed. Natl Geog. 1971. $9.85. 636.7
1. Dogs.

2812. Ing, Catherine and Pond, Grace. Champion Cats of the World. St Martin. 1972. $15.00. 636.8
1. Cat Breeds. 2. Cats.

638.5 Insects - Collection and Preservation

2813. Ewbank, Connie. Insect Zoo. Walker & Co. 1973. $4.50. 638.5
1. Insects — Collection and Preservation.

639 Nondomesticated Animals and Plants

2814. Scheffer, Victor B. A Voice for Wildlife. Scribner. 1974. $8.95. 639
1. Wildlife Conservation. 2. Wildlife Management.

639.2 Commercial Fishing and Whaling

2815. Bradley, Wendell P. They Live by the Wind: The Lore and Romance of the Last Sailing Workboats. Knopf. 1969. $7.95. 639.22
1. Sailing Ships. 2. Seafaring Life.

2816. Haley, Nelson C. Whale Hunt. Washburn. 1967. $5.50. 639.28
1. Charles W. Morgan (Ship). 2. Whaling.

639.3 Culture of Cold-Blooded Vertebrates

2817. Bardach, John E., et al. Aquaculture: The Farming and Husbandry of Freshwater and Marine Organisms. Wiley. 1972. $37.50. 639.3
1. Aquaculture.

2818. Wolfe, Louis. Aquaculture: Farming in Water. Putnam. 1972. $3.69. 639.3
1. Aquaculture.

2819. Innes, William T. Exotic Aquarium Fishes. 19th ed. Dutton. 1964. $6.95. 639.34
1. Aquariums. 2. Fishes.

2820. Schiotz, Arne. A Guide to Aquarium Fishes and Plants. Lippincott. 1972. $6.95. 639.34
1. Aquarium Fishes. 2. Aquarium Plants.

2821. Spotte, Stephen. Marine Aquarium Keeping: The Science, Animals, and Art. Wiley. 1973. $10.95. 639.34
1. Marine Aquariums.

600 TECHNOLOGY

2822. Kauffeld, Carl. Snakes: The Keeper and the Kept. Doubleday. 1969. $6.95. 639.39
1. Snakes As Pets.

639.9 Conservation of Biological Resources

2823. Collett, Rosemary K. My Orphans of the Wild: Rescue and Home Care of Native Wildlife. Lippincott. 1974. $8.95. 639.9
1. Naturalists. 2. Wildlife Rescue.

2824. Ehrenfeld, David. Conserving Life on Earth. Oxford U Pr. 1972. $10.00. 639.9
1. Ecology. 2. Nature Conservation.

2825. Walsh, John and Gannon, Robert. Time Is Short and the Water Rises: Operation Gwamba - the Story of the Rescue of 10,000 Animals from Certain Death in a South American Rain Forest. Dutton. 1967. $8.95. 639.9
1. Surinam — Description and Travel. 2. Wildlife Conservation — Surinam. 3. Zoology — Surinam.

2826. Hickman, Mae and Guy, Maxine. Care of the Wild Feathered and Furred: A Guide to Wildlife Handling and Care. Unity Pr. 1973. $7.95; pap. $3.95. 639.96
1. Wildlife Diseases. 2. Wildlife Rescue.

2827. Olsen, Jack. Slaughter the Animals, Poison the Earth. S&S. 1971. $6.95; pap. $1.75 (Manor Bks). 639.97
1. Pesticides. 2. U. S. Fish and Wildlife Service. 3. Wildlife Conservation.

640 Home Economics

2828. Laurel, Alicia B. Living on the Earth. Random. 1971. $7.95; pap. $3.95. 640
1. Handicraft. 2. Home Economics. 3. Outdoor Life.

641 Food and Cookery

2829. Horizon Cookbook Editors. The Horizon Cookbook and Illustrated History of Eating and Drinking Through the Ages. Doubleday. 1968. $16.50. 641
1. Cookery — History. 2. Dinners and Dining. 3. Menus.

2830. Lamb, Lawrence E. What You Need to Know About Food and Cooking for Health. Viking Pr. 1973. $10.00. 641.1
1. Cookery. 2. Nutrition.

2831. Hunter, Beatrice T. The Natural Foods Primer. S&S. 1972. $4.95; pap. $1.95. 641.3
1. Food. 2. Nutrition.

2832. Margolius, Sidney. Health Foods: Facts and Fakes. Walker & Co. 1973. $6.95. 641.3
1. Food. 2. Food Industry and Trade — U. S. 3. Nutrition.

2833. Tannahill, Reay. Food in History. Stein & Day. 1973. $15.00; pap. $4.95. 641.3009
1. Food — History.

2834. American Heritage Editors. The American Heritage Cookbook. rev. ed. McGraw. 1969. $6.95. 641.5
1. Cookery.

2835. DeKnight, Freda. The Ebony Cookbook: A Date with a Dish. Johnson Chi. 1970. $4.95; pap. $0.95 (Pyramid Pubns). 641.5
1. Cookery. 2. Cookery, Afro-American.

2836. Farmer, Fannie. The Fannie Farmer Cookbook. 11th rev. enl. ed. Little. 1965. $8.95. 641.5
1. Cookery.

2837. Berglund, Berndt and Bolsby, Clare. Wilderness Cooking. Scribner. 1973. $7.95. 641.578
1. Cookery (Wild Foods). 2. Outdoor Cookery.

646 Sewing, Clothing, Personal Grooming

2838. Better Homes & Gardens. Better Homes and Gardens Sewing Book. rev. ed. BH&G. 1970. $8.95. 646.4
1. Dressmaking. 2. Sewing.

2839. Rosenberg, Sharon and Wiener, Joan. The Illustrated Hassle-Free Make Your Own Clothes Book. Bantam. 1972. pap. $1.25. 646.4
1. Dressmaking. 2. Sewing.

2840. Erwin, Mabel D. and Kinchen, Lila A. Clothing for Moderns. 5th ed. Macmillan. 1974. $9.95. 646.43
1. Clothing and Dress. 2. Dressmaking.

2841. Chase, Deborah. The Medically Based No-Nonsense Beauty Book. Knopf. 1974. $8.95. 646.72

600 TECHNOLOGY

1. Beauty, Personal. 2. Cosmetics. 3. Women — Health and Hygiene.

649 Child Rearing

2842. Bronfenbrenner, Urie. Two Worlds of Childhood: U. S. and U. S. S. R. Russell Sage. 1970. $7.95; pap. $2.95 (S&S). 649.1
1. Children in Russia. 2. Children in the U. S. 3. Socialization.

651 Office Services

2843. Doris, Lillian and Miller, Bessemay. Complete Secretary's Handbook. 3rd ed. P-H. 1970. $7.95. 651.02
1. Office Management — Handbooks, Manuals, etc. 2. Secretaries.

2844. Cloke, Marjane and Wallace, Robert. The Modern Business Letter-Writer's Manual. Doubleday. 1969. $5.95; pap. $1.95. 651.7
1. Business Letters.

2845. Emery, Glyn. Electronic Data Processing. Am Elsevier. 1969. $8.75. 651.8
1. Electronic Data Processing.

2846. Langerbach, Robert. Introduction to Automated Data Processing. P-H. 1968. $8.95. 651.8
1. Electronic Data Processing.

655 Printing and Related Activites

2847. Dahl, Svend. History of the Book. 2nd ed. Scarecrow. 1968. $7.00. 655.1
1. Books. 2. Printing — History.

2848. Lehmann-Haupt, Hellmut. The Book in America: A History of the Making and Selling of Books in the United States. 2nd ed. Bowker. 1951. $16.95. 655.1
1. Books. 2. Printing — History.

2849. University of Chicago Press Editors. A Manual of Style. rev. 12th ed. U of Chicago Pr. 1969. $12.50. 655.2
1. Authorship — Handbooks, Manuals, etc. 2. Printing — Style Manuals.

2850. Madison, Charles A. Book Publishing in America. McGraw. 1966. $12.50. 655.4
1. Publishers and Publishing.

2851. Wolseley, Roland E. Understanding Magazines. 2nd ed. Iowa St U Pr. 1969. $8.95. 655.5
1. Periodicals, Publishing of.

658 Management

2852. Peter, Laurence J. and Hill, Raymond. The Peter Principle: Why Things Always Go Wrong. Morrow. 1969. $5.95; pap. $2.45. 658.002
1. Management — Anecdotes, Facetiae, Satire, etc.

2853. Townsend, Robert C. Up the Organization. Knopf. 1970. $5.95; pap. $1.25 rev. ed. 1971 (Fawcett World). 658.4
1. Business. 2. Executive Ability.

2854. Clark, Leta W. How to Make Money with Your Crafts. Morrow. 1974. $6.95. 658.91
1. Business. 2. Handicraft. 3. Small Business.

659.1 Advertising

2855. Cohen, Dorothy. Advertising. Wiley. 1972. $12.50. 659.1
1. Advertising.

2856. Key, Wilson B. Subliminal Seduction: Ad Media's Manipulation of a Not So Innocent America. P-H. 1973. $7.95; pap. $1.95 (NAL). 659.1
1. Advertising — Psychological Aspects. 2. Advertising — U. S.

2857. Mandell, Maurice. Advertising. 2nd ed. P-H. 1974. $12.95. 659.1
1. Advertising.

2858. Packard, Vance O. The Hidden Persuaders. McKay. 1957. $7.50; pap. $0.95 (PB). 659.1
1. Advertising.

2859. Stevens, Paul. I Can Sell You Anything. Wyden. 1972. $5.95; pap. $1.25 (Ballantine). 659.143
1. Television Advertising — U. S.

660 Chemical and Related Technologies

2860. Vanderbilt, B. M. Thomas Edison, Chemist. Am Chemical. 1971. $5.95. 660.092(B)
1. Edison, Thomas Alva, 1847-1931.

600 TECHNOLOGY

2861. Clark, John D. Ignition: An Informal History of Liquid Rocket Propellants. Rutgers U Pr. 1972. $10.00. 662.666
1. Liquid Propellants.

2862. Hunter, Beatrice T. Consumer Beware! S&S. 1971. $8.95; pap. $3.95. 664
1. Food Adulteration and Inspection. 2. Food Industry and Trade.

2863. Lyttle, Richard B. Paints, Inks, and Dyes: The Story of Colors at Work. Holiday. 1974. $6.50. 667
1. Colors.

684.8 Woodworking

2864. Shea, John G. Woodworking for Everybody. 4th rev. ed. Van Nos Reinhold. 1970. $12.95. 684.8
1. Woodwork.

686 Printing (Book Arts)

2865. Harris, Brayton. Johann Gutenberg and the Invention of Printing. Watts. 1972. $4.33. 686.109(B)
1. Gutenburg, Johann, 1397?-1468. 2. Printing — History.

2866. Gates, David. Type. Watson-Guptill. 1973. $10.00. 686.224
1. Printing — Specimens. 2. Type and Typefounding — History.

2867. Morison, Stanley and Day, Kenneth. The Typographic Book, 1450-1935. U of Chicago Pr. 1964. $42.50. 686.224
1. Printing — Specimens. 2. Type and Typefounding.

2868. Updike, Daniel B. Printing Types: Their History, Forms and Use, a Study in Survival. 2 vols. 3rd ed. Harvard U Pr. 1962. $18.00 set. 686.224
1. Printing — Specimens. 2. Type and Typefounding — History.

693.852 Earthquake-Resistant Construction

2869. Yanev, Peter. Peace of Mind in Earthquake Country: How to Save Your Home and Life. Chronicle Bks. 1974. $9.95; pap. $4.95. 693.852
1. Dwellings — The West. 2. Earthquakes and Building.

694 Carpentry

2870. Wagner, Willis H. Modern Carpentry. Goodheart. 1973. $9.28. 694
1. Carpentry.

700 FINE ARTS AND RECREATION

700-701 The Arts - Philosophy and Theory

2871. Davis, Douglas M. Art and the Future: A History-Prophecy of the Collaboration Between Science, Technology and Art. Praeger. 1973. $20.00. 700
1. Art and Science. 2. Art and Technology. 3. Art, Modern — 20th Century.

2872. Linn, Charles F. The Golden Mean: Mathematics and the Fine Arts. Doubleday. 1974. $4.95. 700.151
1. Arts — Mathematics.

2873. Janson, Horst W. and Kerman, Joseph. History of Art and Music. Abrams. 1968. $15.00; pap. $8.95. 700.9
1. Art — History. 2. Music — History and Criticism.

2874. Butcher, Margaret J. Negro in American Culture. 2nd ed. Knopf. 1972. $7.95. 700.973
1. Negro Arts — U. S.

2875. Feldman, Edmund B. Varieties of Visual Experience: Art As Image and Idea. P-H. $17.50; pap. $8.95. 701
1. Art — Philosophy. 2. Composition (Art).

2876. Gombrich, Ernst H. Art and Illusion. 2nd ed. Princeton U Pr. 1961. $17.50. 701
1. Art. 2. Art — Psychology.

2877. Knobler, Nathan. The Visual Dialogue: An Introduction to the Appreciation of Art. Brown Bk. 1974. $11.50. 701
1. Art Criticism.

2878. Matisse, Henri. Matisse on Art. Phaidon. 1973. $12.50. 701
1. Art Criticism.

2879. Richardson, John A. Art: The Way It Is. Abrams. 1974. $15.00; pap. $7.95. 701
1. Art — Philosophy.

2880. Weitz, Morris. Problems in Aesthetics. 2nd ed. Macmillan. 1970. $11.50. 701
1. Aesthetics.

2881. Hauser, Arnold. The Social History of Art. 4 vols. Vol. 1. Prehistoric to Middle Ages; Vol. 2. Renaissance to Baroque; Vol. 3. Rococo to Romanticism; Vol. 4. Naturalism to the Film Age. Random. pap. $1.95 ea. 701.1
1. Art and Society. 2. Art — History.

2882. Arnheim, Rudolf. Art and Visual Perception. New version. U of Cal Pr. 1974. $14.95; pap. $5.95. 701.15
1. Art — Psychology. 2. Visual Perception.

2883. Ehrenzweig, Aaron. The Hidden Order of Art: A Study in the Psychology of Artistic Imagination. U of Cal Pr. 1967. $9.95; pap. $3.95. 701.15
1. Art — Psychology.

2884. Weismann, Donald L. The Visual Arts - As Human Experience. P-H. 1970. $18.50. 701.15
1. Art — Philosophy. 2. Art — Psychology.

700 FINE ARTS AND RECREATION

2885. Thurston, Jacqueline and Carraher, Ronald G. Optical Illusions. Van Nos Reinhold. 1966. $8.95. 701.8
1. Art. 2. Optical Illusions.

704 Art Criticism

2886. Henri, Robert. The Art Spirit. Ryerson, Margery A., compiled by. Lippincott. 1960. $7.95; pap. $2.25. 704
1. Art Criticism.

2887. Toynbee, Jocelyn M. C. Animals in Roman Life and Art. Cornell U Pr. 1973. $17.50. 704.9432
1. Animals in Art. 2. Rome — Antiquities.

2888. Stanford, William B. and Luce, John V. The Quest for Ulysses. Praeger. 1974. $17.50. 704.947
1. Odysseus — Art.

2889. Grube, Ernst J. Classical Style in Islamic Painting. Orientalia. 1968. $4.95. 704.948
1. Art, Islamic.

2890. Kampf, Avram. Contemporary Synagogue Art. UAHC. 1966. $14.50. 704.948
1. Synagogue Architecture — U. S.

2891. Rice, David T. and Rice, Tamara T. Icons and Their History. Viking Pr. 1974. $35.00. 704.948
1. Icons.

2892. Roth, Cecil. Jewish Art: An Illustrated History. NYGS. 1971. $25.00. 704.948
1. Art, Jewish.

2893. Tomkins, Calvin. Merchants and Masterpieces: The Story of the Metropolitan Museum of Art. Dutton. 1970. $10.00; pap. $3.95. 708.974
1. Metropolitan Museum of Art.

709 Art - History

2894. Butterberry, Ariane R. Pantheon Story of Art for Young People. rev. ed. Pantheon. 1975. $2.95. 709
1. Art — History.

2895. Gardner, Helen. Art Through the Ages. 6th ed. HarBraceJ. 1976. $13.95. 709
1. Art — History.

2896. Gombrich, Ernst H. Story of Art. 12th ed. Phaidon. 1972. $15.00; pap. $7.95. 709
1. Art — History.

2897. Boas, Franz. Primitive Art. Peter Smith. 1962. $5.50. 709.01
1. Art, Primitive. 2. Literature, Primitive.

2898. Feder, Norman. American Indian Art. Abrams. 1974. $15.00. 709.01
1. Indians of North America — Art.

2899. Powell, Ann. The Origins of Western Art. HarBraceJ. 1973. $6.95. 709.01
1. Art, Ancient — History.

2900. Wolf, Walther. The Origins of Western Art: Egypt, Mesopotamia, the Aegean. Universe. 1972. $7.95. 709.01
1. Art, Ancient. 2. Art — Near East.

2901. Hollander, Hans. Early Medieval Art. Universe. 1974. $7.95. 709.02
1. Art, Medieval.

2902. Rice, David T. The Appreciation of Byzantine Art. Oxford U Pr. 1972. $14.50. 709.02
1. Art, Byzantine.

2903. Sehug-Wille, Christa. Art of the Byzantine World. Abrams. 1971. $8.95. 709.02
1. Art, Byzantine.

2904. Clark, Kenneth. The Romantic Rebellion: Romantic Versus Classic Art. Har-Row. 1974. $15.00. 709.034
1. Art — History.

2905. Amaya, Mario. Pop Art and After. Viking Pr. 1972. pap. $3.25. 709.04
1. Modernism (Art).

2906. Art without Boundaries. Woods, Gerald, et al, eds. Praeger. 1974. $8.50; pap. $4.95. 709.04
1. Art, Modern — 20th Century.

2907. Ashton, Dore. A Reading of Modern Art. Har-Row. 1971. pap. $4.95. 709.04
1. Art, Modern — 20th Century.

2908. Canaday, John. Mainstreams of Modern Art. HR&W. 1959. $14.00. 709.04
1. Art — History. 2. Modernism (Art).

2909. Faulkner, Ray, et al. Art Today. HR&W. 1969. $13.00. 709.04
1. Aesthetics. 2. Art Industries and Trade.

700 FINE ARTS AND RECREATION

2910. Henri, Adrian. Total Art: Environments, Happenings, and Performance. rev. ed. Praeger. 1974. $10.00; pap. $5.95. 709.04
1. Happening (Art).

2911. Lancaster, John. Introducing Op Art. Watson-Guptill. 1973. $8.95. 709.04
1. Optical Art.

2912. Richardson, Tony and Stangos, Nikos, eds. Concepts of Modern Art. Har-Row. 1974. $12.50; pap. $4.95. 709.04
1. Art, Modern — 20th Century.

2913. Steinberg, Leo. Other Criteria: Confrontations with 20th Century Art. Oxford U Pr. 1972. $7.95. 709.04
1. Art, Modern — 20th Century.

2914. Locke, Alain, ed. The Negro in Art. Hacker. Repr. 1940. $15.00. 709.22
1. Black Americans in Art.

2915. Lange, Kurt and Hirmer, Max. Egypt: Architecture, Sculpture, Painting. 4th ed. Phaidon. 1968. $29.50. 709.32
1. Art, Egyptian. 2. Egypt — Civilization.

709.37 Roman Art

2916. Brilliant, Richard. Arts of the Ancient Greeks. McGraw. 1973. $16.95. 709.37
1. Art, Greek.

2917. ———. Roman Art, from the Republic to Constantine. Praeger. 1974. $15.00; pap. $6.95. 709.37
1. Art, Roman.

2918. Kahler, Heinz. The Art of Rome and Her Empire. Crown. 1965. $6.95. 709.37
1. Art, Roman.

709.38 Greek Art

2919. Pollitt, Jerry J. Art and Experience in Classical Greece. Cambridge U Pr. 1972. $11.95; pap. $4.95. 709.38
1. Art, Greek. 2. Art — Psychology.

2920. Richter, Gisela M. Handbook of Greek Art. 6th ed. Phaidon. 1969. $10.00; pap. $5.95. 709.38
1. Art, Greek.

709.415 Irish Art

2921. Lucas, A. T. Treasures of Ireland: Irish Pagan and Early Christian Art. Viking Pr. 1974. $14.95. 709.415
1. Art, Ancient — Ireland. 2. Art, Early Christian — Ireland. 3. Art, Irish.

709.45 Italian Art

2922. Brandes, Georg. Michelangelo: His Life, His Times, His Era. Ungar. 1967. $12.00. 709.45(B)
1. Michelangelo Buonarotti, 1475-1564.

2923. Chastel, Andre. Italian Art: Architecture, Sculpture and Painting. Humanities. 1965. $22.00; pap. $5.95 (Har-Row). 709.45
1. Architecture, Italian. 2. Sculpture, Italian.

2924. Decker, Heinrich. Renaissance in Italy: Architecture, Frescoes, Sculpture. Viking Pr. 1969. $22.50. 709.45
1. Art, Italian. 2. Art, Renaissance.

2925. Hartt, Frederick. History of Italian Renaissance Art: Painting, Sculpture, Architecture. Abrams. 1969. $28.50. 709.45
1. Art, Italian. 2. Art, Renaissance.

2926. Vasari, Giorgio. Vasari's Lives of the Painters, Sculptors and Architects. 4 vols. Dutton. $3.95 ea; pap. $2.95 (S&S). 709.45(B)
1. Art — Italian — History. 2. Artists, Italian.

709.47 Russian Art

2927. Frankel, Tobia. The Russian Artist. Macmillan. 1972. $5.95. 709.47
1. Art, Russian — History. 2. Russia — Civilization.

2928. Horizon Editors. Horizon Book of the Arts of Russia. McGraw. 1970. $20.00. 709.47
1. Art, Russian.

709.5-709.6 Oriental and African Art

2929. Binyon, Lawrence. Flight of the Dragon (Wisdom of the East) Paragon. $3.50. 709.51
1. Art, Chinese.

700 FINE ARTS AND RECREATION

2930. Horizon Editors. The Horizon Book of the Arts of China. Am Heritage. 1969. $20.00. 709.51
1. Art, Chinese.

2931. Smith, Bradley and Weng, Wan-Go. China: A History in Art. Har-Row. 1973. $25.00. 709.51
1. Art, Chinese. 2. China — Civilization.

2932. Sullivan, Michael. The Arts of China. rev. ed. U of Cal Pr. 1973. $14.50. 709.51
1. Art, Chinese.

2933. Smith, Bradley. Japan: A History in Art. S&S. 1964. $30.00. 709.52
1. Art, Japanese. 2. Japan — History.

2934. Soper, A. and Paine, R. Art and Architecture of Japan. rev. ed. Penguin. 1974. $39.50; pap. $12.50. 709.52
1. Architecture, Japanese. 2. Art, Japanese.

2935. Goetz, Hermann. The Art of India. Crown. 1964. $6.95. 709.54
1. Art, India.

2936. Bodrogi, Tibor. Art of Indonesia. NYGS. 1972. $17.50. 709.598
1. Art, Indonesian.

2937. Bravmann, Rene A. Open Frontiers: The Mobility of Art in Black Africa. U of Wash Pr. 1973. $8.95; pap. $4.95. 709.67
1. Art, African.

709.7 American Art

2938. Dockstader, Frederick J. Indian Art in America: The Arts and Crafts of the North American Indian. 3rd ed. NYGS. 1968. $27.50. 709.7
1. Indians of North America — Art.

2939. Bell, Michael, compiled by. Painters in a New Land: From Annapolis Royal to the Klondike. NYGS. 1973. $25.00. 709.71
1. Art, Canadian. 2. Canada — Discovery and Exploration.

2940. Duval, Paul. Four Decades: The Canadian Group of Painters and Their Contemporaries, 1930-1970. Clark Irwin. 1973. $24.95. 709.71
1. Art, Canadian.

2941. Brenner, Anita. Idols Behind Altars. Biblo. Repr. of 1929 ed. 1967. $15.00; pap. $3.95 1970 (Beacon Pr). 709.72
1. Art — Mexico. 2. Artists — Mexican. 3. Indians of Mexico. 4. Mexico — Antiquities.

2942. Rodman, Selden. The Miracle of Haitian Art. Doubleday. 1974. $4.95. 709.72
1. Art, Haitian.

2943. Alloway, Lawrence. American Pop Art. Macmillan. 1974. pap. $4.95. 709.73
1. Art, Modern — U. S. 2. Pop Art — U. S.

2944. Davidson, Marshall B. The American Heritage History of the Artists' America. Am Heritage. 1973. $19.95. 709.73
1. Art, American — History.

2945. Hunter, Sam and Jacobus, John. American Art of the 20th Century: Painting, Sculpture and Architecture. rev. ed. Abrams. 1974. $20.00. 709.73
1. Art, American.

2946. McLanathan, Richard B. Art in America: A Brief History. HarBraceJ. 1973. pap. $4.50. 709.73
1. Art, American — History.

2947. Rose, Barbara, ed. Readings in American Art Since 1900: A Documentary Survey. Praeger. 1968. $8.50; pap. $3.95. 709.73
1. Art, American — History. 2. Art, Modern — 20th Century — U. S.

2948. Tufts, Eleanor. Our Hidden Heritage: Five Centuries of Women Artists. Two Continents. 1974. $12.95. 709.73
1. Women in the Arts.

2949. Castedo, Leopoldo. A History of Latin American Art and Architecture from Pre-Columbian Times to the Present. Praeger. 1969. $9.95; pap. $4.95. 709.8
1. Architecture, Latin American. 2. Art, Latin American.

711 City Planning

2950. Blake, Peter. God's Own Junkyard: The Planned Deterioration of America's Landscape. HR&W. 1964. $6.95; pap. $2.95. 711
1. Cities and Towns — Civic Improvement. 2. U. S. — Description and Travel.

2951. Mumford, Lewis. The City in History. HarBraceJ. 1961. $15.00; pap. $4.95. 711
1. Cities and Towns — History.

700 FINE ARTS AND RECREATION

2952. Saalman, Howard. Medieval Cities. Collins, G. R., ed. Braziller. 1968. $5.95; pap. $2.95. 711
1. Cities and Towns, Medieval.

2953. Macaulay, David. City: A Story of Roman Planning and Construction. HM. 1974. $7.95. 711.4
1. Building — Rome. 2. Civil Engineering — Rome. 3. Rome — Antiquities.

2954. Moholy-Nagy, Sibyl. Matrix of Man: An Illustrated History of Urban Environment. Praeger. 1968. $15.00. 711.4
1. Cities and Towns — Planning — History.

2955. Ewald, William R., ed. Environment for Man: The Next Fifty Years. Ind U Pr. 1967. $8.50; pap. $2.95. 711.409
1. Cities and Towns — Planning — U. S. 2. Man — Influence of Environment.

2956. Specter, David K. Urban Spaces. NYGS. 1973. $15.00. 711.74
1. Architecture — Psychology. 2. Space (Architecture).

2957. Newton, Norman T. Design on the Land: The Development of Landscape Architecture. Harvard U Pr. 1971. $25.00. 712.09
1. Landscape Architecture — History.

2958. Roper, Laura W. Flo: A Biography of Frederick Law Olmsted. Johns Hopkins. 1974. $15.00. 712.092(B)
1. Landscape Architecture — U. S. 2. Olmsted, Frederick Law, 1822-1903.

720 Architecture

2959. Muschenheim, William. Elements of the Art of Architecture. Viking Pr. 1964. $6.50. 720
1. Architecture, American — History. 2. Architecture, European — History. 3. Architecture — Views.

2960. Hohauser, Sanford. Architectural and Interior Models. Van Nos Reinhold. 1970. $22.50. 720.2
1. Architectural Models.

2961. Blake, Peter. The Master Builders. Knopf. 1961. $12.50. 720.9
1. Jeanneret-Gris, Charles Edouard, 1887-1965. 2. Van der Rohe, Mies. 3. Wright, Frank Lloyd, 1869-1959.

2962. Fletcher, Banister. The History of Architecture. 17th ed. Scribner. 1961. $18.95. 720.9
1. Architecture — History.

2963. Jacobs, David. Architecture. Newsweek. 1974. $6.95. 720.9
1. Architecture — History.

2964. Twombly, Robert C. Frank Lloyd Wright: An Interpretive Biography. Har-Row. 1973. $10.00; pap. $3.95. 720.924(B)
1. Wright, Frank Lloyd, 1869-1959.

2965. Gould, Heywood. Sir Christopher Wren. Watts. 1970. $4.33. 720.94(B)
1. Wren, Sir Christopher, 1632-1723.

2966. Pevsner, Nikolaus. Outline of European Architecture. 7th ed. Penguin. 1974. $9.95. 720.94
1. Architecture — Europe — History.

2967. Betjeman, John. Ghastly Good Taste, a Depressing Story of the Rise and Fall of English Architecture. St Martin. 1971. $10.00. 720.942
1. Architecture — England.

2968. Mumford, Lewis. Sticks and Stones: A Study of American Architecture and Civilization. rev. ed. Dover. 1955. pap. $2.00. 720.97
1. Architecture, American.

2969. Saarinen, Eero. Eero Saarinen on His Work. rev. ed. Saarinen, Aline B., ed. Yale U Pr. 1968. $22.50. 720.97
1. Architecture, American. 2. Saarinen, Eero, 1910-1961.

2970. Kurtz, Stephen A. Wasteland: Building the American Dream. Praeger. 1973. $7.95; pap. $3.95. 720.973
1. Architecture — U. S. 2. Cities and Towns — Planning — U. S.

2971. Boethius, Axel and Ward-Perkins, J. B. Etruscan and Roman Architecture. Penguin. 1970. $29.50. 722.7
1. Architecture, Etruscan. 2. Architecture, Roman.

2972. Lowry, Bates. Renaissance Architecture. Braziller. 1962. $5.95; pap. $2.95. 724.1
1. Architecture, Renaissance.

700 FINE ARTS AND RECREATION

2973. Jencks, Charles. Modern Movements in Architecture. Doubleday. 1973. $10.00; pap. $4.95. 724.9
1. Architecture, Modern.

2974. Scully, Vincent J. Modern Architecture. Braziller. 1974. $8.95; pap. $3.95. 724.9
1. Architecture, Modern — 20th Century.

2975. Hughes, Quentin. Military Architecture. St Martin. 1975. $20.00. 725.18
1. Fortification — History. 2. Military Architecture — History.

2976. Horizon Editors. The Horizon Book of Great Cathedrals. HM. 1968. $20.00. 726.6
1. Cathedrals.

2977. Macaulay, David. Cathedral: The Story of Its Construction. HM. 1973. $6.95. 726.6
1. Architecture, Gothic. 2. Cathedrals.

2978. Boericke, Art and Shapiro, Barry. Handmade Houses: A Guide to the Wood Butcher's Art. Scrimshaw. 1973. $12.95; pap. $5.95 (A & W Visual Library). 728.6
1. Building, Wooden. 2. House Construction.

Recommended Series

2979. History of Architecture. Braziller.

730 Sculpture

2980. Cheney, Sheldon. Sculpture of the World: A History. Viking Pr. 1968. $15.00. 730.9
1. Sculpture — History.

2981. Cellini, Benvenuto. Autobiography. Symonds, John A., tr. Doubleday. pap. $1.25. 730.924(B)
1. Cellini, Benvenuto, 1500-1571. 2. Sculptors — Correspondence, Reminiscences, etc.

2982. Sylvester, David. Henry Moore. Praeger. 1968. $10.00. 730.924(B)
1. Moore, Henry, 1898-

2983. Ashton, Dore. Modern American Sculpture. Abrams. 1968. $28.50. 730.973
1. Sculpture, American.

2984. Craven, Wayne. Sculpture in America. T Y Crowell. 1968. $18.50. 730.973
1. Sculpture, American.

2985. Gladstone, M. J. A Carrot for a Nose: The Form of Folk Sculpture on America's City Streets and Country Roads. Scribner. 1974. $9.95. 730.973
1. Folk Art, American.

2986. Panting, John. Sculpture in Fiberglass. Watson-Guptill. 1972. $8.95. 731.2
1. Plastic Sculpture.

2987. Baldwin, John. Contemporary Sculpture Techniques: Direct Metal and Fiber-Glass. Van Nos Reinhold. 1967. $10.95. 731.4
1. Sculpture — Technique.

2988. Cowley, David. Working with Clay and Plaster. Watson-Guptill. 1973. $8.95. 731.4
1. Clay. 2. Modeling. 3. Plaster Casts.

2989. Zaidenberg, Arthur. Anyone Can Sculpt. rev. ed. Har-Row. 1972. $9.95. 731.4
1. Sculpture — Technique.

2990. Meilach, Dona Z. Contemporary Art with Wood. Crown. 1968. $7.95. 731.46
1. Wood-Carving.

2991. Tangerman, Elmer J. The Modern Book of Whittling and Woodcarving. McGraw. 1973. $8.95. 731.462
1. Wood-Carving.

2992. Mackett-Beeson, E. J. Chessmen. Roy. 1968. $3.98. 731.8
1. Chessmen.

2993. Segy, L. African Sculpture. Peter Smith. $4.50; pap. $2.50 (Dover). 732.2
1. Sculpture, African.

2994. ———. African Sculpture Speaks. rev. ed. Hill & Wang. 1969. $14.95. 732.2
1. Sculpture, African.

2995. Richter, Gisela. Sculpture and Sculptors of the Greeks. 4th ed. Yale U Pr. 1970. $35.00. 733
1. Sculptors, Greek. 2. Sculpture.

2996. Wilenski, Reginald H. The Meaning of Modern Sculpture. Beacon Pr. 1961. pap. $1.95. 735
1. Sculpture, Modern.

2997. Flayderman, E. Norman. Scrimshaw and Scrimshanders, Whales and Whalemen. Flayderman. 1972. $19.95. 736.6
1. Scrimshaws.

700 FINE ARTS AND RECREATION

737 Numismatics

2998. Coffin, Joseph. The Complete Book of Coin Collecting. 4th ed. Coward. 1973. $6.95. 737
1. Coins.

2999. Grant, Michael. Roman History from Coins: Some Uses of the Imperial Coinage to the Historian. Cambridge U Pr. 1968. $5.50; pap. $2.45. 737.4
1. Coins, Roman. 2. Rome — History.

3000. Davis, Norman M. The Complete Book of United States Coin Collecting. Macmillan. 1970. $7.95. 737.49
1. Coins, American.

738 Ceramic Arts

3001. Rothenberg, Polly. The Complete Book of Ceramic Art. Crown. 1972. $8.95. 738
1. Pottery.

739 Art Metalwork

3002. Hood, Graham. American Silver: A History of Style, 1650-1900. Praeger. 1971. $15.00. 739.23
1. Silversmithing — U. S. — History.

3003. Montgomery, Charles F. A History of American Pewter. Praeger. 1973. $17.50. 739.533
1. Pewter.

741 Drawing

3004. Collier, Graham. Form, Space and Vision. 3rd ed. P-H. 1972. $16.60. 741
1. Drawing — Instruction.

3005. Bowman, William J. Graphic Communication. Wiley. 1968. $12.75. 741.4
1. Communication — Audio-Visual. 2. Graphic Arts — Technique.

3006. Robinson, Jerry. The Comics: An Illustrated History of Comic Strip Art. Putnam. 1974. $15.00. 741.5
1. Caricatures and Cartoons.

3007. Bernstein, Burton. Thurber: A Biography. Dodd. 1975. $15.00. 741.59(B)
1. Thurber, James, 1894-1961.

3008. Hogg, Syd. The Art of Cartooning. Stravon. 1973. $7.95. 741.597
1. Cartoons and Cartooning.

3009. Suares, Jean-Claude, ed. Art of the Times. Universe. 1973. $8.95; pap. $3.95 (Avon). 741.65
1. Graphic Arts — Collections.

3010. White, Gwen. Perspective: A Guide for Artists, Architects and Designers. Watson-Guptill. 1968. $8.95. 742
1. Perspective.

3011. Barcsay, Jeno. Anatomy for the Artist. Tudor. Repr. 1958. $14.95. 743
1. Anatomy, Artistic.

745 Design and Crafts

3012. Paz, Octavio. In Praise of Hands: Contemporary Crafts of the World. NYGS. 1974. $19.95. 745
1. Handicraft.

3013. Jones, Barbara and Howell, Bill. Popular Arts of the First World War. McGraw. 1972. $14.95. 745.09
1. European War, 1914-1918 — Art and the War. 2. Kitsch.

3014. Muraoka, Kageo and Okamura, Kichiemon. Folk Arts and Crafts of Japan. Weatherhill. 1973. $10.00. 745.0952
1. Art Industries and Trade, Japanese. 2. Folk Art — Japan.

3015. Sieber, Roy. African Textiles and Decorative Arts. NYGS. 1972. $15.00; pap. $7.95. 745.096
1. Decoration and Ornament, African. 2. Textile Industry and Fabrics, African.

3016. Lipman, Jean and Winchester, Alice. The Flowering of American Folk Art 1776-1876. Viking Pr. 1974. $19.95. 745.097
1. Folk Art — U. S. 2. Primitivism in Art — U. S.

3017. Kelley, Austin P. and Sotheby Parke Bernet Staff. Anatomy of Antiques: A Collector's Guide. Viking Pr. 1974. $12.95. 745.103
1. Antiques — Collecting.

3018. Evans, Helen M. Man the Designer. Macmillan. 1973. $11.95. 745.4
1. Aesthetics. 2. Design.

700 FINE ARTS AND RECREATION

3019. Dayan, Ruth and Feinberg, Wilburt. Crafts of Israel. Macmillan. 1974. $14.95. 745.449
1. Handicraft — Israel.

3020. Harvey, Marian. Crafts of Mexico. Macmillan. 1973. $12.95. 745.5
1. Folk Art, Mexican. 2. Handicraft — Mexico.

3021. Ecke, Tseng Y. Chinese Calligraphy. Godine. 1971. $17.50. 745.6
1. Calligraphy, Chinese.

3022. Gibbs-Smith, Charles H. Bayeux Tapestry. Phaidon. 1973. $7.50. 746.4
1. Bayeux Tapestry. 2. Tapestry.

3023. Boger, Louise A. Complete Guide to Furniture Styles. rev. ed. Scribner. 1969. $19.95. 749
1. Furniture.

3024. Bishop, Robert. How to Know American Antique Furniture. Dutton. 1973. pap. $4.95. 749.273
1. Collectors and Collecting. 2. Furniture — U. S.

759 History of Painting

3025. Bazin, Germain. The Avant-Garde in Painting. S&S. 1969. $29.95. 759
1. Painting, Medieval — History. 2. Painting, Modern — History.

3026. Howat, John K. The Hudson River and Its Painters. Viking Pr. 1972. $25.00. 759
1. Hudson Valley — Description and Travel — Views. 2. Landscape Painting, American.

3027. Jaffe, Hans. Twenty Thousand Years of World Painting. Abrams. 1967. $30.00. 759
1. Painting — History.

3028. Pignatti, Terisio. Painting: Through the Eighteenth Century. Newsweek. 1974. $6.95. 759
1. Painting — History.

3029. Roters, Eberhard. Painters of the Bauhaus. Praeger. 1969. $18.50. 759
1. Art, Modern — 20th Century — History. 2. Bauhaus.

3030. Rewald, John. The History of Impressionism. 4th ed. NYGS. 1973. $27.50. 759.05
1. Impressionism (Art).

3031. Cooper, Douglas. The Cubist Epoch. Phaidon. 1971. $12.50. 759.06
1. Cubism. 2. Post-Impressionism (Art).

3032. Dube, Wolf D. Expressionism. Praeger. 1973. $10.00; pap. $5.95. 759.06
1. Expressionism (Art).

3033. Gaunt, William. The Surrealists. Putnam. 1972. $30.00. 759.06
1. Painting, Modern. 2. Surrealism.

3034. Rubin, William S. Dada, Surrealism, and Their Heritage. NYGS. 1968. $10.95; pap. $5.95. 759.06
1. Dadaism. 2. Surrealism.

3035. Canaday, John. Lives of the Painters. 4 vols. Norton. 1969. $24.95. 759.092(B)
1. Art — History. 2. Painters.

3036. Baigell, Matthew. The American Scene: American Painting of the 1930's. Praeger. 1974. $29.50. 759.13
1. Federal Art Project. 2. Painting, American. 3. Social Realism.

3037. The Brandywine Heritage: Howard Pyle, N. C. Wyeth, Andrew Wyeth, James Wyeth. NYGS. 1971. $14.50. 759.13
1. Pyle, Howard, 1853-1911. 2. Wyeth Family.

3038. Buechner, Thomas S., ed. Norman Rockwell: A Sixty-Year Retrospective. Abrams. 1972. $15.00; pap. $5.95. 759.13
1. Rockwell, Norman, 1894-

3039. Corn, Wanda M., ed. The Art of Andrew Wyeth. NYGS. 1973. $19.95. 759.13
1. Wyeth, Andrew, 1917-

3040. Geldzahler, Henry. American Painting in the Twentieth Century. Metro Mus Art. 1965. pap. $4.95. 759.13
1. Painting, American.

3041. Goodrich, Lloyd. Winslow Homer. NYGS. 1973. $14.95. 759.13
1. Homer, Winslow, 1836-1910.

3042. Goodrich, Lloyd and Bry, Doris. Georgia O'Keefe. Praeger. 1970. $18.50. 759.13
1. O'Keefe, Georgia, 1887-

700 FINE ARTS AND RECREATION

3043. Hendricks, Gordon. The Life and Works of Thomas Eakins. Grossman. 1974. $37.50. 759.13(B)
1. Eakins, Thomas, 1844-1916.

3044. Hoopes, Donelson F. The American Impressionists. Watson-Guptill. 1972. $25.00. 759.13
1. Impressionism (Art) — U. S. 2. Painting, Modern — 19th Century — U. S.

3045. Kallir, Otto. Grandma Moses. Abrams. 1973. $40.00. 759.13
1. Moses, Anna Mary (Robertson), 1860-1961.

3046. Richardson, E. P. A Short History of Painting in America. T Y Crowell. 1963. pap. $5.25. 759.13
1. Painting, American.

3047. Weintraub, Stanley. Whistler, a Biography. Weybright. 1974. $12.50. 759.13(B)
1. Whistler, James, 1834-1903.

3048. Whitley, William T. Gilbert Stuart. Da Capo. 1932. $12.50. 759.13(B)
1. Stuart, Gilbert, 1755-1825.

3049. Gaunt, William. The Restless Century: Painting in Britain, 1800-1900. Phaidon. 1972. $25.00. 759.2
1. Painting, British. 2. Painting, Modern — 19th Century — Great Britain.

3050. Taylor, Basil. Constable: Paintings, Drawings, Watercolors. Praeger. 1973. $25.00. 759.2
1. Constable, John, 1776-1837.

3051. Koschatzy, Walter. Durer Watercolors. St Martin. 1973. $45.00. 759.3
1. Durer, Albrecht, 1471-1528.

3052. Hibbard, Howard. Poussin: The Holy Family on the Steps. Viking Pr. 1974. $8.95. 759.4
1. Painting, French.

3053. Huisman, Philippe and Dortu, M. G. Lautrec by Lautrec. Bellow, Corinne, tr. Viking Pr. 1964. $14.95. 759.4(B)
1. Toulouse-Lautrec Monfa, Henri Marie Raymond de, 1864-1901.

3054. Lindsay, Jack. Cézanne: His Life and Art. NYGS. 1969. $14.95. 759.4(B)
1. Cézanne, Paul, 1839-1906.

3055. Berenson, Bernard. Italian Painters of the Renaissance. 2 vols. Phaidon. 1968. pap. $3.95 ea. 759.5(B)
1. Painting, Italian.

3056. Berti, Luciano. Raphael. Norton. 1962. $5.95. 759.5(B)
1. Raffaele Sanzio, 1483-1520.

3057. Calder, Ritchie. Leonardo. S&S. 1970. $12.95. 759.5(B)
1. Leonardo da Vinci, 1452-1519.

3058. ———. Leonardo and the Age of the Eye. Intl Pubns Serv. 1970. $21.00. 759.5(B)
1. Leonardo da Vinci, 1452-1519.

3059. Pope-Hennessey, John. Fra Angelico. Cornell U Pr. 1974. $42.50. 759.5(B)
1. Fra Angelico (Giovanni da Fiesole), 1387-1455.

3060. Werner, Alfred. Modigliani. Abrams. 1967. $18.50. 759.5(B)
1. Modigliani, Amadeo, 1884-1920.

3061. Arnheim, Rudolf. The Genesis of a Painting: Picasso's Guernica. U of Cal Pr. 1962. $12.50; pap. $5.95. 759.6
1. Picasso, Pablo, 1881-1973.

3062. Guidiol, Jose. El Greco. Viking Pr. 1973. $38.50. 759.6
1. El Greco (Theotocopuli, Dominico), 1541-1614.

3063. Horwitz, Sylvia L. Francisco Goya: Painter of Kings and Demons. Har-Row. 1974. $5.95. 759.6(B)
1. Goya y Lucientes, Francisco, 1746-1828.

3064. Ortega Y Gasset, Jose. Velasquez, Goya and the Dehumanization of Art. Norton. 1972. $17.50. 759.6
1. Painting, Spanish.

3065. Picasso, Pablo. Picasso. Felicie Presse. 1974. $35.00. 759.6
1. Picasso, Pablo, 1881-1973.

3066. Smith, Bradley. Spain: A History in Art. S&S. 1966. $30.00. 759.6
1. Art — History.

3067. Haftman, Werner. Chagall. Abrams. 1974. $22.50. 759.7
1. Chagall, Marc, 1887-

700 FINE ARTS AND RECREATION

3068. Auden, Wystan H., ed. Van Gogh: A Self Portrait. NYGS. 1961. $12.50.
759.9492(B)
1. Van Gogh, Vincent, 1853-1890.

3069. Clark, Kenneth. Rembrandt and the Italian Renaissance. NYU Pr. 1966. $12.50; pap. $2.65 1968 (Norton). 759.9492
1. Rembrandt Hermenszoon van Rijn, 1606-1669.

3070. Lassaigne, Jacques. Van Gogh. Doubleday. 1974. $9.95. 759.9492(B)
1. Van Gogh, Vincent, 1853-1890.

3071. Nash, J. M. The Age of Rembrandt and Vermeer. HR&W. 1972. $25.00. 759.9492
1. Vermeer, Jan, 1632-1675.

3072. Slive, Seymour. Frans Hals. 2 vols. Phaidon. 1971. $30.00. 759.9492
1. Hals, Frans, 1850?-1666.

3073. White, Christopher. Rembrandt and His World. Viking Pr. 1964. $6.95. 759.9492
1. Rembrandt, Hermenszoon van Rijn, 1606-1669.

3074. Bruegel, Pieter The Elder. Bruegel. Abrams. 1970. $22.50. 759.9493
1. Bruegel, Pieter the Elder, 1525?-1569.

3075. White, Christopher. Rubens and His World. Viking Pr. 1968. $6.95. 759.9493
1. Rubens, Sir Peter Paul, 1577-1640.

3076. Arquin, Florence. Diego Rivera: The Shaping of an Artist. U of Okla Pr. 1971. $8.95. 759.972
1. Rivera, Diego, 1886-1957.

Recommended Series

3077. Art Treasures of the World. McGraw. $6.95.

3078. The Arts of Mankind. Braziller. $30.00 ea.

3079. Discovering Art. McGraw.

3080. Great Museums of the World. Newsweek Magazine editors, eds. S&S.

3081. Library of Great Museums. Abrams.

3082. Library of Great Painters. Abrams.

3083. Time-Life Library of Art. Time-Life.

3084. Unesco World Art Series. Unesco.

3085. World of Art. Praeger.

760 Graphic Arts

3086. Daniels, Harvey. Printmaking. Viking Pr. 1972. $16.95. 760
1. Graphic Arts.

3087. Peterdi, Gabor. Printmaking: Methods Old and New. rev. ed. Macmillan. 1971. $17.50. 760
1. Engraving.

3088. Jacobs, G. Walker. Stranger Stop and Cast an Eye: A Guide to Gravestones and Gravestone Rubbing. Greene. 1973. $4.95.
760.28
1. Rubbings. 2. Symbolism in Art — New England. 3. Tombs.

3089. Ebert, John and Ebert, Katherine. Old American Prints for the Collector. Scribner. 1974. $15.00. 760.8
1. Print-Making.

3090. Michener, James A. Modern Japanese Print: (an Appreciation) C E Tuttle. 1968. $10.00. 761
1. Engraving.

3091. Knigin, Michael and Zimiles, Murray. The Technique of Fine Art Lithography. Van Nos Reinhold. 1970. $15.95. 763
1. Lithography — Technique.

3092. Paulson, Ronald. Hogarth: His Life, Art and Times. abr. ed. Yale U Pr. 1974. $20.00; pap. $8.95. 769(B)
1. Hogarth, William, 1697-1764.

3093. Sachs, Paul J. Modern Prints and Drawings. Knopf. 1954. $12.50. 769
1. Engravings.

3094. Ward, Lynd K. Storyteller without Words: The Wood Engravings. Abrams. 1974. $25.00. 769
1. Wood-Engravers, American.

3095. Zigrosser, Carl. Prints and Their Creators. Crown. 1974. $12.50. 769
1. Engravings.

3096. Constantine, Mildred and Fern, Alan. Revolutionary Soviet Film Posters. Johns Hopkins. 1974. $12.95. 769.5
1. Film Posters, Russian.

700 FINE ARTS AND RECREATION

3097. Gallo, Max. The Poster in History. McGraw. 1974. $22.50. 769.5
1. Posters — History.

3098. Currier, Nathaniel and Ives, J. M. World of Currier and Ives. King, Roy and Davis, Burke, eds. Random. 1968. $30.00. 769.922
1. Currier and Ives. 2. Lithographs.

770 Photography

3099. Nurnberg, Walter. Lighting for Photography. 6th ed. Amphoto. 1968. $12.95. 770
1. Photography.

3100. Adams, Ansel. Artificial Light Photography. Morgan. 1968. $5.95. 770.153
1. Photography — Lighting.

3101. ———. Natural Light Photography. Morgan. 1969. $5.95. 770.153
1. Photography — Lighting.

3102. Hattersley, Ralph. Discover Yourself Through Photography. Assn Pr. 1971. $14.95. 770.23
1. Photography, Artistic.

3103. Feininger, Andreas. The Complete Photographer. P-H. 1965. $9.95. 770.28
1. Photography.

3104. ———. Darkroom Techniques. 2 vols. P-H. 1974. $7.95 ea. 770.28
1. Photography — Processing.

3105. Sussman, Aaron. The Amateur Photographer's Handbook. 8th ed. T Y Crowell. 1973. $8.95. 770.28
1. Photography — Handbooks, Manuals, etc.

3106. Adams, Ansel. The Negative. Morgan. 1968. $5.95. 770.283
1. Photography — Negatives.

3107. Berg, W. Exposure. 4th ed. Amphoto. 1971. $15.95. 770.284
1. Photography — Exposure.

3108. Croy, D. R. The Complete Art of Printing and Enlarging. Amphoto. 1970. $13.50. 770.284
1. Photography — Enlarging. 2. Photography — Printing.

3109. Newhall, Beaumont. History of Photography: 1839 to the Present Day. NYGS. 1972. $15.00; pap. $6.95 (Museum Mod Art). 770.9
1. Photography — History.

3110. Adams, Ansel. Camera and Lens: The Creative Approach. rev. ed. Morgan. 1969. $12.00. 771.352
1. Camera. 2. Lenses. 3. Photography.

3111. Lootens, J. Ghislain. Lootens on Photographic Enlarging and Print Quality. 8th ed. Bogen, L. H., ed. Amphoto. 1974. $12.95. 778.13
1. Photography — Enlarging.

3112. Bobker, Lee R. Making Movies from Script to Screen. HarBraceJ. 1973. $10.00; pap. $6.50. 778.53
1. Moving-Pictures — Production and Direction.

3113. Petzold, Paul. All-in-One Movie Book. Amphoto. 1974. $5.95. 778.53
1. Moving-Pictures — Production and Direction.

3114. Young Filmakers Foundation. Young Animators and Their Discoveries. Praeger. 1973. $6.50. 778.53
1. Moving-Picture Cartoons.

3115. Yulsman, Jerry. The Complete Book of 8mm Movie Making. Coward. 1972. $6.95; pap. $2.50 1974 (B&N). 778.53
1. Moving-Pictures — Production and Direction.

3116. Mattingly, Grayson and Smith, Welby. Introducing the Single-Camera VTR System. Scribner. 1973. $8.95. 778.59
1. Video Tape Recorders and Recording.

3117. Videofreex (Organization) The Spaghetti City Video Manual: A Guide to Use, Repair and Maintenance. Praeger. 1973. $7.95. 778.59
1. Video Tape Recorders and Recording.

3118. Feininger, Andreas. The Color Photo Book. P-H. 1969. $12.95. 778.6
1. Color Photography — Handbooks, Manuals, etc.

3119. Warner, James A. The Darker Brother. Dutton. 1974. $18.95. 778.9
1. Black Americans — Pictorial Works.

700 FINE ARTS AND RECREATION

3120. Hoskins, Eric and Gooders, John. Wildlife Photography: A Field Guide. Praeger. 1974. $9.95. 778.932
1. Photography of Animals.

3121. Meltzer, Milton and Cole, Bernard. The Eye of Conscience: Photographers and Social Change. Follett. 1974. $6.95. 778.99
1. Photographers. 2. Social History — Pictorial Works.

3122. Ackley, Clifford, ed. Private Realities: Recent American Photography. NYGS. 1974. $15.00. 779
1. Photography, American.

3123. Arbus, Diane. Diane Arbus. Aperture. 1972. $15.00. 779
1. Photography, Experimental.

3124. Steichen, Edward. The Family of Man. S&S. 1967. $4.95; pap. $2.95 (NAL). 779
1. Photography — Portraits.

3125. ———. A Life in Photography. Doubleday. 1968. $9.95. 779(B)
1. Photographers.

3126. Adams, Ansel. Ansel Adams: Singular Images. Morgan. 1974. pap. $7.95. 779.092
1. Photography, Artistic.

3127. Eisenstaedt, Alfred. People. Viking Pr. 1973. $17.95. 779.2
1. Photography — Portraits.

3128. Russell, Terry and Russell, Renny. On the Loose. Sierra. 1972. $7.95; pap. $3.95 (Ballantine). 779.3
1. Nature Photography.

Recommended Series

3129. Life Library of Photography. Morgan.

780 Music

3130. Lockspeiser, Edward. Music and Painting: A Study in Comparative Ideas from Turner to Schoenberg. Har-Row. 1973. $8.50; pap. $4.95. 780.08
1. Art and Music.

3131. Bernstein, Leonard. The Joy of Music. S&S. 1959. $6.50; pap. $2.45. 780.15
1. Music — Analysis, Appreciation.

3132. Stringham, Edwin John. Listening to Music Creatively. 2nd ed. P-H. 1959. $10.95. 780.15
1. Music — Analysis, Appreciation.

3133. Winold, Allen. Elements of Musical Understanding. P-H. 1966. $9.95. 780.15
1. Music — Analysis, Appreciation.

780.9 Music - History and Criticism

3134. Bauer, Marion and Peyser, Ethel. Music Through the Ages. rev. ed. Putnam. 1967. $8.95. 780.9
1. Music — History and Criticism.

3135. Boyden, David D. An Introduction to Music. 2nd ed. Knopf. 1970. $10.95. 780.9
1. Music — Analysis, Appreciation.

3136. Grout, Donald J. A History of Western Music. rev. ed. Norton. 1973. $9.95. 780.9
1. Music — History and Criticism.

3137. Grunfeld, Frederic V. Music. Newsweek. 1974. $6.95. 780.9
1. Music — History and Criticism.

3138. Haggin, B. H. A Decade of Music. Horizon. 1973. $10.00. 780.9
1. Music — History and Criticism — 20th Century.

3139. Raynor, Henry. A Social History of Music from the Middle Ages to Beethoven. Schocken. 1972. $12.00. 780.9
1. Music and Society.

3140. Shippen, Katherine B. and Seidlova, Anca. The Heritage of Music. Viking Pr. 1963. $6.00. 780.9
1. Composers. 2. Music — History and Criticism.

3141. Ulrich, Homer and Pisk, Paul A. History of Music and Musical Style. HarBraceJ. 1963. $10.95. 780.9
1. Music — History and Criticism.

3142. Walter, Don C. Men and Music in Western Culture. P-H. 1969. $4.75. 780.9
1. Music — History and Criticism.

3143. Sternfeld, Frederick W. Music from the Middle Ages to the Renaissance. Praeger. 1973. $20.00. 780.902
1. Music — History and Criticism.

700 FINE ARTS AND RECREATION

3144. Bukofzer, Manfred F. Music in the Baroque Era: From Monteverdi to Bach. Norton. 1947. $8.95. 780.903
1. Music, Baroque. 2. Music — History and Criticism — 17th Century. 3. Music — History and Criticism — 18th Century.

3145. ———. Studies in Medieval and Renaissance Music. Norton. 1950. pap. $2.25. 780.903
1. Music — History and Criticism — Medieval. 2. Music — History and Criticism — 16th Century.

3146. Davison, Archibald T. and Apel, Willi. Historical Anthology of Music. 2 vols. Vol. 1. Oriental, Medieval & Renaissance Music. rev. ed. 1949; Vol. 2. Baroque, Rococo & Preclassical Music. Harvard U Pr. 1950. $12.00 ea. 780.903
1. Music — Collections. 2. Music — History and Criticism.

3147. Palisca, Claude U. Baroque Music. P-H. 1968. pap. $4.00. 780.903
1. Music, Baroque.

3148. Pauly, Reinhard G. Music in the Classic Period. 2nd ed. P-H. 1973. $7.95; pap. $4.50. 780.903
1. Music — History and Criticism — 18th Century. 2. Music — History and Criticism — 19th Century.

3149. Austin, William. Music in the 20th Century. Norton. 1966. $11.00. 780.904
1. Music — History and Criticism — 20th Century.

3150. Myers, Rolls H., ed. Twentieth Century Music: Its Forms, Trends and Interpretations Throughout the World. Grossman. 1968. $7.50. 780.904
1. Music — History and Criticism — 20th Century.

3151. Sternfeld, Frederick W. Music in the Modern Age: A History of Western Music. Praeger. 1973. $20.00. 780.904
1. Music — History and Criticism.

780.92 Musicians

3152. Barzun, Jacques. Berlioz and His Century: An Introduction to the Age of Romanticism. Peter Smith. $5.00. 780.92(B)
1. Berlioz, Hector, 1803-1869.

3153. Blunt, Wilfred. On Wings of Song: A Biography of Felix Mendelssohn. Scribner. 1974. $17.50. 780.92(B)
1. Mendelssohn-Bartholdy, Felix, 1809-1847.

3154. Ewen, David. Composers of Tomorrow's Music. Dodd. 1971. $5.00; pap. $1.95. 780.92(B)
1. Music — History and Criticism — 20th Century. 2. Composers.

3155. ———. Instrumental and Chamber Music: Its Story Told Through the Lives and Works of Its Foremost Composers. Watts. 1974. $9.95. 780.92(B)
1. Composers.

3156. ———. The World of Twentieth-Century Music. P-H. 1968. $14.95. 780.92(B)
1. Composers. 2. Music — History and Criticism — 20th Century.

3157. Freedland, Michael. Irving Berlin. Stein & Day. 1974. $8.95. 780.92(B)
1. Berlin, Irving, 1888-

3158. Geiringer, Karl and Geiringer, Irene. Johann Sebastian Bach: The Culmination of an Era. Oxford U Pr. 1966. $12.50. 780.92(B)
1. Bach, Johann Sebastian, 1685-1750.

3159. Lesznai, Lajos. Bartok. Octagon. 1973. $8.50. 780.92(B)
1. Bartok, Bela, 1881-1945.

3160. Perenyi, Eleanor. Liszt: The Artist As Romantic Hero. Little. 1974. $15.00. 780.92(B)
1. Liszt, Franz, 1811-1886.

3161. Perlis, Vivian. Charles Ives Remembered. Yale U Pr. 1974. $12.50. 780.92(B)
1. Ives, Charles, 1874-1954.

3162. Warrack, John H. Tchaikovsky. Scribner. 1973. $14.95. 780.92(B)
1. Tchaikovsky, Peter Ilyich, 1840-1893.

3163. Wechsberg, Joseph. Verdi. Putnam. 1974. $15.00. 780.92(B)
1. Verdi, Giuseppe, 1813-1901.

3164. Chiapusso, Jan. Bach's World. Ind U Pr. 1969. $12.50. 780.924(B)
1. Bach, Johann Sebastian, 1685-1750.

3165. Davies, Laurence. Cesar Franck and His Circle. HM. 1970. $10.00. 780.924
1. Franck, Cesar, 1822-1890. 2. Musicians.

700 FINE ARTS AND RECREATION

3166. Fischer, Hans S. and Besch, Lutz. The Life of Mozart. St Martin. 1969. $10.00. 780.924(B)
1. Mozart, Wolfgang Amadeus, 1756-1791.

3167. Geiringer, Karl. Haydn: A Creative Life in Music. rev. ed. U of Cal Pr. 1968. $13.75; pap. $4.50. 780.924(B)
1. Haydn, Joseph, 1732-1809.

3168. Geiringer, Karl. Brahms, His Life and Work. 2nd rev. ed. Weiner, H. D. and Nirall, Bernard, trs. Oxford U Pr. 1947. $14.00. 780.924(B)
1. Brahms, Johannes, 1833-1897.

3169. Goldberg, Isaac. George Gershwin: A Study in American Music. Ungar. 1958. $8.50; pap. $1.95. 780.924(B)
1. Gershwin, George, 1898-1937.

3170. Gutman, Robert W. Richard Wagner: The Man, His Mind, and His Music. HarBraceJ. 1968. $12.50; pap. $4.50. 780.924(B)
1. Wagner, Richard, 1813-1883.

3171. Hedley, Arthur. Chopin. Octagon. 1949. $8.50. 780.924(B)
1. Chopin, Frederick François, 1810-1849.

3172. Hughes, Gervase. Dvorak: His Life and Music. Dodd. 1968. $5.00. 780.924(B)
1. Dvorak, Antonin, 1841-1904.

3173. Krause, Ernst. Richard Strauss: The Man and His Work. Crescendo. 1970. $11.00. 780.924(B)
1. Strauss, Richard, 1864-1949.

3174. Lang, Paul H. George Frederic Handel. Norton. 1966. $15.00. 780.924(B)
1. Handel, Georg Friedrich, 1685-1759.

3175. Lockspeiser, Edward. Debussy. 4th ed. McGraw. 1972. pap. $2.95. 780.924(B)
1. Debussy, Claude, 1862-1918.

3176. Mahler, Alma. Gustav Mahler: Memories and Letters. enl. & rev. ed. U of Wash Pr. 1971. $6.95; pap. $3.95. 780.924(B)
1. Mahler, Gustav, 1860-1911.

3177. Marek, George R. Beethoven: Biography of a Genius. Funk & W. 1969. $12.50; pap. $4.95 (Apollo Eds). 780.924(B)
1. Beethoven, Ludwig Van, 1770-1827.

3178. Nestyev, Israel V. Prokofiev. Jonas, Florence, tr. Stanford U Pr. 1960. $17.50. 780.924(B)
1. Prokofiev, Sergei Sergeevich, 1891-1953.

3179. Pincherle, Marc. Vivaldi: Genius of the Baroque. Norton. 1962. pap. $2.95. 780.924(B)
1. Vivaldi, Antonio, 1680?-1743.

3180. Stravinsky, Igor. Autobiography. Norton. 1962. pap. $1.95. 780.924(B)
1. Stravinskii, Igor Fedorovich, 1882-1971.

3181. Schwarz, Boris. Music and Musical Life in Soviet Russia 1917-1970. Norton. 1972. $13.50. 780.947
1. Music, Russian — 1917-

3182. Howard, John T. Our American Music: A Comprehensive History from 1620 to the Present. 4th ed. T Y Crowell. 1965. $12.95. 780.973
1. Music, American — History and Criticism.

3183. Nanry, Charles, ed. American Music: From Storyville to Woodstock. Transaction Bks. 1972. $9.95; pap. $3.95. 780.973
1. Music, American — History and Criticism.

3184. Sablosky, Irving L. American Music. U of Chicago Pr. 1969. $8.50; pap. $2.25. 780.973
1. Music, American — History and Criticism.

3185. Thomson, Virgil. American Music Since 1910. HR&W. 1971. $8.95; pap. $2.95. 780.973
1. Music, American — History and Criticism.

781 Music - Theory and Technique

3186. Seegar, Pete. Henscratches and Flyspecks: How to Read Melodies from Songbooks in Twelve Confusing Lessons. Putnam. 1973. $7.95. 781.24
1. Musical Notation.

3187. Dexter, Dave. The Jazz Story from the '90's to the '60's. P-H. 1964. pap. $2.45. 781.57
1. Jazz Music. 2. Music — History and Criticism — 20th Century.

3188. Feather, Leonard. Book of Jazz: From Then till Now. rev. ed. Horizon. 1965. $6.95. 781.57
1. Music — History and Criticism — 20th Century.

700 FINE ARTS AND RECREATION

3189. Gitler, Ira. Jazz Masters of the '40's. Macmillan. 1966. $5.95; pap. $2.95.   781.57
1. Jazz Music.

3190. Hadlock, Richard. Jazz Masters of the '20's. Macmillan. 1965. $5.95; pap. $2.95.   781.57
1. Jazz Music.

3191. Schuller, Gunther. Early Jazz: Its Roots and Musical Development. Oxford U Pr. 1968. $12.50.   781.57
1. Jazz Music.

3192. Ulanov, Barry. A History of Jazz in America. Da Capo. Repr. 1955. $12.50.   781.57
1. Jazz Music.

3193. Schafer, William J., et al. The Art of Ragtime: Form and Meaning of an Original Black American Art. La State U Pr. 1973. $10.00.   781.572
1. Black Music — History and Criticism. 2. Ragtime Music — History and Criticism.

3194. Cook, Bruce. Listen to the Blues. Scribner. 1973. $8.95; pap. $2.95.   781.573
1. Blues (Songs, Etc.) — History and Criticism.

3195. Sackheim, Eric, compiled by. The Blues Line: A Collection of Blues Lyrics. Grossman. 1969. $20.00.   781.573
1. Songs.

3196. Jones, Leroi. Black Music. Morrow. 1967. $7.95; pap. $1.95.   781.7
1. Musicians, American. 2. Jazz Music. 3. Negro Musicians. 4. Negroes.

3197. Roach, Hildred. Black American Music: Past and Present. Crescendo. 1973. $9.50; pap. $5.00.   781.773
1. Black Music — History and Criticism.

3198. Walton, Ortiz. Music: Black, White and Blue: A Sociological Survey of the Use and Misuse of Afro-American Music. Morrow. 1972. $6.95; pap. $2.45.   781.773
1. Black Music — History and Criticism.

781.91 Musical Instruments

3199. Buchner, Alexander. Musical Instruments: An Illustrated History. rev. ed. Crown. 1973. $12.50.   781.91
1. Musical Instruments — History.

3200. Donington, Robert. Instruments of Music. 3rd ed. B&N. 1970. $12.50; pap. $6.00.   781.91
1. Musical Instruments.

3201. Sachs, Curt. The History of Musical Instruments. Norton. 1940. $10.00.   781.91
1. Musical Instruments.

3202. Dylan, Bob. Writings and Drawings. Knopf. 1973. $6.95.   781.96
1. Music, Popular (Songs, etc.).

782.1 Opera

3203. Grout, Donald J. A Short History of Opera. 2nd ed. Columbia U Pr. 1965. $13.50.   782.1
1. Opera.

3204. Harewood and Kobbè. Kobbè's Complete Opera Book. 3rd ed. Harewood, Lord, ed. Putnam. 1972. $12.95.   782.1
1. Opera — Stories, Plots, etc.

3205. Jackson, Stanley. Caruso. Stein & Day. 1972. $7.95.   782.1
1. Caruso, Enrico, 1873-1921.

3206. Knapp, J. Merrill. The Magic of Opera. Har-Row. 1972. $10.95; pap. $6.95.   782.1
1. Opera — History and Criticism.

3207. Kolodin, Irving. The Metropolitan Opera, 1883-1966: A Candid History. rev. ed. Knopf. 1966. $17.50.   782.1
1. Opera, American.

3208. Orrey, Leslie. A Concise History of Opera. Scribner. 1973. $7.95; pap. $4.95.   782.1
1. Opera — History and Criticism.

782.8 Theater Music

3209. Laufe, Abe. Broadway's Greatest Musicals. Funk & W. 1970. $10.00.   782.8
1. Musical Revue, Comedy, etc.

3210. Baily, Leslie. Gilbert and Sullivan: Their Lives and Times. Viking Pr. 1974. $7.95.   782.81(B)
1. Gilbert, (Sir) William Schwenele, 1836-1911.2. Sullivan, (Sir) Arthur Seymour, 1842-1900.

700 FINE ARTS AND RECREATION

3211. Ewen, David. New Complete Book of the American Musical Theater. HR&W. 1970. $15.00. 782.81
1. Musical Revue, Comedy, etc.

3212. Green, Stanley. World of Musical Comedy. 2nd ed. A S Barnes. 1973. $15.00. 782.81
1. Composer, American. 2. Librettists, American. 3. Musical Revue, Comedy, etc. — U. S.

3213. Jablonski, Edward and Stewart, Lawrence D. The Gershwin Years. rev. ed. Doubleday. 1973. $12.95. 782.81(B)
1. Gershwin, George, 1898-1937. 2. Gershwin, Ira, 1896-

3214. Lewine, Richard and Alfred, Simon. Songs of the American Theater, 1900-1971. Dodd. 1973. $15.00. 782.81
1. Musical Revues, Comedies, etc.

3215. Nassour, Ellis and Broderick, Richard. Rock Opera: The Creation of Jesus Christ Superstar. Hawthorn. 1973. $8.95; pap. $3.95. 782.81
1. Jesus Christ Superstar.

3216. New York Times Great Songs of Broadway. Quadrangle. 1973. $17.50. 782.81
1. Musical Revues, Comedies, etc. 2. Songs — Collections.

3217. Rodgers, Richard and Hammerstein, Oscar, 3rd. Rodgers and Hammerstein Song Book. S&S. 1968. $15.00. 782.81
1. Musical Revues, Comedies, etc.

783 Sacred Music

3218. Routley, Erik. Words, Music and the Church. Abingdon. 1968. $4.95. 783
1. Church Music.

3219. Cook, Harold E. Shaker Music: A Manifestation of American Folk Culture. Bucknell U Pr. 1972. $18.00. 783.026
1. Shakers — Music — History and Criticism.

3220. Oxford Book of Carols. Dearmer, P., et al, eds. Oxford U Pr. Repr. 1928. $6.00; words & melody $1.75. 783.65
1. Carols.

784 Vocal Music

3221. Boeckman, Charles. And the Beat Goes on: A History of Pop Music in America. Luce. 1972. $5.95. 784
1. Music, Popular (Songs, etc.).

3222. Jahn, Mike. Rock: A Social History of the Music from 1945-1972. Quadrangle. 1973. $9.95. 784
1. Rock Music — England — History and Criticism. 2. Rock Music — U. S. — History and Criticism.

3223. Pleasants, Henry. The Great American Popular Singers. S&S. 1974. $9.95. 784(B)
1. Music, Popular (Songs, etc.). 2. Singers.

3224. Price, Steven D. Take Me Home: Country and Western Music. Praeger. 1974. $6.95. 784
1. Music, American. 2. Music, Popular (Songs, etc.).

3225. Schiotz, Askel. The Singer and His Art. Har-Row. 1970. $6.95. 784
1. Singing.

3226. Wolman, Baron, et al. Festival: The Book of American Music Celebrations. Macmillan. 1970. $6.95. 784
1. Music Festivals. 2. Music, Popular (Songs, etc.) — U. S. — History and Criticism.

3227. Malone, Bill C. Country Music U.S.A. A Fifty-Year History. U of Tex Pr. 1974. $10.00; pap. $4.75. 784.09
1. Music, American — History and Criticism.

3228. Albertson, Chris. Bessie. Stein & Day. 1972. $7.95; pap. $2.95. 784.092(B)
1. Smith, Bessie, 1898-1937.

3229. Friedman, Myra. Buried Alive: The Biography of Janis Joplin. Morrow. 1973. $7.95; pap. $1.95. 784.092(B)
1. Joplin, Janis, 1943-1970.

3230. Gray, Michael. Song and Dance Man: The Art of Bob Dylan. Dutton. 1973. $7.95. 784.092(B)
1. Dylan, Bob, 1941-

3231. Hopkins, Jerry. Elvis: A Biography. S&S. 1971. $7.95; pap. $1.50 (PB). 784.092(B)
1. Presley, Elvis Aron, 1935-

3232. Mellers, Wilfred. Twilight of the Gods: The Beatles in Retrospect. Viking Pr. 1974. $7.95. 784.092(B)
1. Beatles, The.

700 FINE ARTS AND RECREATION

3233. Greenberg, Noah, et al, eds. Anthology of Elizabethan Lute Songs, Madrigals and Rounds. Norton. 1970. $2.65.   784.1
1. Songs, English.

3234. ———. Anthology of English Medieval and Renaissance Vocal Music. Norton. 1968. pap. $2.45.   784.1
1. Songs, English.

3235. Keil, Charles. Urban Blues. U of Chicago Pr. 1966. $7.50; pap. $2.45.   784.4
1. Folk-Songs, American.

3236. Landeck, Beatrice. Echoes of Africa in Folk Songs of the Americas. 2nd ed. McKay. 1969. $7.95.   784.4
1. Folk-Songs, African. 2. Folk-Songs, American.

3237. Lomax, John A. and Lomax, Alan. American Ballads and Folk Songs. Macmillan. 1934. $10.00.   784.4
1. American Ballads and Songs. 2. Folk-Songs, American.

3238. Seegar, Pete. The Incompleat Folksinger. S&S. 1972. $12.50.   784.4
1. Folk-Songs — Collections.

3239. Cone, James H. The Spirituals and the Blues. Seabury. 1972. $4.95; pap. $2.95.   784.756
1. Black Music.

785 Instrumental Ensemble

3240. Lang, Paul H., ed. Symphony, 1800-1900. Norton. 1969. $6.95.   785
1. Symphony.

3241. Ulrich, Homer. Symphonic Music. Columbia U Pr. 1952. $12.50.   785
1. Symphony.

3242. Fernett, Gene. Swing Out: Great Negro Dance Bands. Pendell Pub. 1970. $10.00.   785.066
1. Dance Orchestra — U. S. 2. Negro Musicians.

3243. Simon, George T. The Big Bands. rev. ed. Macmillan. 1971. $10.00; pap. $3.95.   785.066
1. Dance Orchestras — U. S. 2. Jazz Musicians.

3244. Ewen, David. Orchestra Music: Its Story Told Through the Lives and Works of Its Foremost Composers. Watts. 1973. $9.95.   785.09(B)
1. Composers. 2. Orchestra Music — History and Criticism.

3245. Antek, Samuel. This Was Toscanini. Vanguard. 1963. $17.50.   785.092(B)
1. Toscanini, Arturo, 1867-1957.

3246. Kirk, H. L. Pablo Casals: A Biography. HR&W. 1974. $15.00.   785.092(B)
1. Casals, Pablo, 1876-1973.

3247. Buerkle, Jack V. and Barker, Danny. Bourbon Street Black: The New Orleans Black Jazzmen. Oxford U Pr. 1973. $7.95; pap. $2.95.   785.42(B)
1. Black Musicians. 2. Jazz Musicians. 3. Music — Louisiana — New Orleans.

3248. Ellington, Duke. Music Is My Mistress. Doubleday. 1973. $14.95.   785.42(B)
1. Ellington, Edward K., 1899-1974.

3249. Guralnick, Peter. Feel Like Going Home: Portraits in Blues and Rock'n Roll. Dutton. 1971. $6.95; pap. $2.95.   785.42(B)
1. Jazz Musicians.

3250. Ulrich, Homer. Chamber Music. 2nd ed. Columbia U Pr. 1966. $12.50; pap. $7.50.   785.7
1. Chamber Music. 2. Instrumental Ensembles.

3251. Silverman, Jerry. How to Play the Guitar. Doubleday. 1968. pap. $3.95.   787.61
1. Guitar — Methods — Self-Instruction.

3252. Camp, John. Bellringing. A S Barnes. 1974. $7.95.   789
1. Handbell Ringing.

3253. Hatch, Eric. The Little Book of Bells. Hawthorn. 1964. $3.50.   789
1. Bells.

3254. Schwartz, Elliott S. Electronic Music: A Listener's Guide. Praeger. 1973. $12.50.   789.9
1. Electronic Music.

3255. History of Music in Sound. Oxford U Pr.

Recommended Series

3256. History of Music. P-H.

700 FINE ARTS AND RECREATION

3257. History of Music Series. Goldron, Romain, ed.. Doubleday.

790-791 Performing Arts and Public Performances

3258. Willeford, William. The Fool and His Scepter: A Study in Clowns and Jesters and Their Audience. Northwestern U Pr. 1969. $9.50. 790.2
1. Clowns.

3259. Toll, Robert C. Blacking up: The Minstrel Show in Nineteenth-Century America. Oxford U Pr. 1974. $10.95. 791.12
1. Musical Revue, Comedy, etc. — U. S. 2. Negro Minstrels.

3260. Fox, Charles P. and Parkinson, Tom. The Circus in America. Country Beautiful. 1969. $25.00. 791.3
1. Circus — U. S.

3261. Blum, Daniel. A Pictorial History of the Silent Screen. Putnam. 1953. $7.95; pap. $4.95. 791.4084
1. Moving-Pictures, Silent — History.

3262. Pratt, George C. Spellbound in Darkness: A History of the Silent Film. rev. ed. NYGS. 1973. $22.50; pap. $8.95. 791.4084
1. Moving-Pictures, Silent — History.

3263. Agee, James. Agee on Film. 2 vols. G&D. 1969. pap. $2.95 ea. 791.43
1. Moving-Picture Plays.

3264. Bergman, Andrew. We're in the Money: Depression America and Its Films. NYU Pr. 1971. $8.95; pap. $3.95. 791.43
1. Moving-Pictures — History.

3265. Blum, Daniel. A New Pictorial History of the Talkies. rev. ed. Putnam. 1973. $10.00; pap. $5.95. 791.43
1. Moving-Pictures — Pictorial Works. 2. Moving-Pictures, Talking — History.

3266. Bobker, G. R. Elements of Film. 2nd ed. HarBraceJ. 1974. pap. $5.95. 791.43
1. Moving-Pictures — Criticism.

3267. Bogle, Donald. Toms, Coons, Mulattoes, Mammies, and Bucks: An Interpretive History of Blacks in American Films. Viking Pr. 1973. $12.50; pap. $2.25 (Bantam). 791.43
1. Moving-Pictures — U. S. — History. 2. Negroes in Moving-Pictures.

3268. Brosnan, John. Movie Magic: Special Effects Men and Their Crafts. St Martin. 1974. $10.95. 791.43
1. Moving-Pictures — Setting and Scenery.

3269. Crowther, Bosley. Great Films: Fifty Golden Years of Motion Pictures. Putnam. 1967. $10.00; pap. $4.95. 791.43
1. Moving-Pictures.

3270. Curtis, David. Experimental Cinema: A Fifty-Year Evolution. Universe. 1971. $7.95. 791.43
1. Experimental Films.

3271. Fenin, George N. and Everson, William K. The Western: From Silents to the Seventies. rev. ed. Grossman. 1973. $15.00. 791.43
1. Western Films — History and Criticism.

3272. Fielding, Raymond. The American Newsreel, 1911-1967. U of Okla Pr. 1972. $9.95. 791.43
1. Moving-Pictures, Documentary.

3273. Fulton, Albert R. Motion Pictures: The Development of an Art from Silent Films to the Age of Television. U of Okla Pr. Repr. 1960. $6.95. 791.43
1. Moving-Pictures — History.

3274. Higham, Charles. The Art of the American Film, 1900-1971. Doubleday. 1973. $12.50; pap. $4.95. 791.43
1. Moving-Pictures — History and Criticism.

3275. Jacobs, Lewis, compiled by. The Documentary Tradition: From Nanook to Woodstock. Hopkinson. 1971. $10.00; pap. $5.50. 791.43
1. Moving-Pictures, Documentary.

3276. ———. The Emergence of Film Art: The Evolution and Development of the Motion Picture As an Art, from Nineteen Hundred to the Present. Hopkinson. 1969. $10.00; pap. $5.50. 791.43
1. Moving-Pictures.

3277. Kauffman, Stanley. Living Images: Film Criticism and Comment. Har-Row. 1975. $10.00; pap. $4.95. 791.43
1. Moving-Pictures — Reviews.

3278. Kinder, Marsha and Houston, Beverle. Close-up: A Critical Perspective on Film. HarBraceJ. 1972. pap. $5.95. 791.43
1. Moving-Pictures — Criticism.

700 FINE ARTS AND RECREATION

3279. McCaffrey, Donald W. The Golden Age of Sound Comedy: Comic Films and Comedians of the Thirties. A S Barnes. 1973. $15.00. 791.43
1. Comedy Films.

3280. Rosen, Marjorie. Popcorn Venus: Women, Movies and the American Dream. Coward. 1973. $9.95. 791.43
1. Actresses. 2. Moving-Picture Industry — U. S. 3. Moving-Picture Plays — History and Criticism.

3281. Sarris, Andrew. The American Cinema: Director and Directions, 1929-1968. Dutton. 1969. pap. $2.95. 791.43
1. Moving-Pictures — Biography. 2. Moving-Pictures — Production and Direction.

3282. Schickel, Richard. Movies: The History of an Art and an Institution. Basic. 1964. $6.45. 791.43
1. Moving-Pictures — History.

3283. Vogel, Amos. Film As a Subversive Art. Random. 1974. $15.00. 791.43
1. Experimental Films.

3284. Edmondson, Madeleine and Rounds, David. The Soaps: Daytime Serials of Radio and TV. Stein & Day. 1973. $8.95. 791.44
1. Soap Operas.

3285. Anderson, Chuck. The Electric Journalist: An Introduction to Video. Praeger. 1973. $6.50. 791.45
1. Television — Production and Direction.

3286. Fettig, Hansjurgen. Hand and Rod Puppets: A Handbook of Technique. Plays. 1974. $9.95. 791.53
1. Puppets and Puppet-Plays.

3287. Strong, Roy. Splendor at Court: Renaissance Spectacle and the Theater of Power. HM. 1973. $15.00. 791.609
1. Festivals. 2. Pageants. 3. Theater — Europe — History.

3288. Collins, Larry and LaPierre, Dominique. Or I'll Dress You in Mourning. S&S. 1968. $8.95; pap. $1.25. 791.8
1. Benitez Pérez, Manuel. 2. Bull-Fights.

3289. Hall, Douglas K. Let 'er Buck! Sat Rev Pr. 1973. $7.95. 791.8
1. Rodeos.

3290. Hemingway, Ernest. Death in the Afternoon. Scribner. 1932. $10.00; pap. $2.95. 791.8
1. Bull-Fights.

792 Theater

3291. Bentley, Eric. The Theatre of Commitment and Other Essays on Drama in Our Society. Atheneum. 1967. $5.00. 792
1. Drama — History and Criticism. 2. Theater.

3292. Brecht, Bertolt. Brecht on Theatre. Willett, John, ed. Hill & Wang. 1964. $6.50; pap. $3.45. 792
1. Theater.

3293. Grotowski, Jerzy, ed. Towards a Poor Theatre. S&S. 1969. $6.50; pap. $2.45. 792
1. Acting. 2. Theater.

3294. Joseph, Stephen. Theatre in the Round. Taplinger. 1968. $6.50. 792
1. Arena Theatre.

3295. Spolin, Viola. Improvization for the Theatre: A Handbook of Teaching and Directing Techniques. Northwestern U Pr. 1963. $10.00. 792
1. Improvization.

3296. Stanislavski, Constantin. An Actor Prepares. Theatre Arts. $4.95. 792
1. Acting.

3297. Weisman, John. Guerilla Theatre: Scenarios for Revolution. Doubleday. 1973. pap. $3.50. 792
1. Experimental Theater.

3298. Allensworth, Carl, et al. The Complete Play Production Handbook. T Y Crowell. 1973. $8.95. 792.02
1. Theater — Production and Direction.

3299. Cole, Toby and Chinoy, Helen K., eds. Directors on Directing. rev. ed. Bobbs. 1963. $5.00; pap. $3.50. 792.02
1. Theater — Production and Direction.

3300. Engel, Lehman. Getting Started in the Theater. Macmillan. 1973. $6.95; pap. $2.95. 792.023
1. Theater As a Profession.

3301. Selden, Samuel, Jr. and Rezzuto, Tom. Essentials of Stage Scenery. P-H. 1972. $11.50. 792.025
1. Theaters — Stage-Setting and Scenery.

700 FINE ARTS AND RECREATION

3302. Sellman, Hunton D. Essentials of Stage Lighting. P-H. 1972. $11.50.   792.025
1. Stage Lighting.

3303. Barton, Lucy. Historic Costume for the Stage. rev. ed. Baker's Plays. 1961. $10.95.   792.026
1. Costume.

3304. Russell, Douglas A. Stage Costume Design: Theory, Technique and Style. P-H. 1973. $15.00.   792.026
1. Costume, Theatrical.

3305. Corson, Richard. Stage Makeup. 5th ed. P-H. 1974. $13.50.   792.027
1. Makeup, Theatrical.

3306. Skinner, Cornelia O. Madame Sarah. Dell. 1968. pap. $0.95.   792.028(B)
1. Bernhardt, Sarah, 1844-1923.

792.09 Theater History

3307. Blum, Daniel. Pictorial History of the American Theatre: 1860-1970. 3rd ed. Crown. 1970. $12.50.   792.09
1. Theater — U. S. — Pictorial Works.

3308. Brockett, Oscar G. History of the Theatre. 2nd ed. Allyn. 1974. $13.95.   792.09
1. Drama — History and Criticism. 2. Theater — History.

3309. Brockett, Oscar G. and Findley, R. Century of Innovation: A History of European and American Theater and Drama, 1870-1970. P-H. 1973. $14.50.   792.09
1. Theater — History.

3310. Cheney, Sheldon. The Theatre: Three Thousand Years of Drama, Acting, and Stage Craft. new ed. McKay. 1972. $14.95.   792.09
1. Acting. 2. Drama — History and Criticism. 3. Theater — History.

3311. Croyden, Margaret. Lunatics, Lovers and Poets: The Contemporary Experimental Theater. McGraw. 1974. $9.95; pap. $3.25 (Dell).   792.09
1. Drama — 20th Century — History and Criticism. 2. Experimental Theater.

3312. Driver, Tom F. Romantic Quest and Modern Query: A History of the Modern Theatre. Delacorte. 1970. $7.50; pap. $2.95.   792.09
1. Drama — History and Criticism. 2. Theater — History.

3313. Freedley, George and Reeves, John A. History of the Theatre. rev. ed. Crown. 1968. $10.00.   792.09
1. Drama — History and Criticism. 2. Theater — History.

3314. Kernodle, George Riley. Invitation to the Theatre. HarBraceJ. 1967. $10.50.   792.09
1. Drama — History and Criticism. 2. Theater — History.

3315. Nadel, Norman. A Pictorial History of the Theatre Guild: Special Material by Langer, Lawrence and Marshall, Armina. Crown. 1969. $10.00.   792.09
1. Theater — U. S. 2. Theater — U. S.

3316. Nagler, A. M. Source Book in Theatrical History. Peter Smith. 1952. $6.00; pap. $4.00 1952 (Dover).   792.09
1. Theater — History — Sources.

3317. Sainer, Arthur. The Radical Theatre Notebook. Avon. 1975. $2.65.   792.09
1. Drama — 20th Century — History and Criticism. 2. Experimental Theater.

3318. Adams, John C. The Globe Playhouse: Its Design and Equipment. 2nd ed. A S Barnes. 1961. $12.50.   792.094
1. Theater — History.

3319. Nicoll, Allardyce. The World of Harlequin: A Critical Study of the Commedia dell'Arte. Cambridge U Pr. 1963. $24.50.   792.0945
1. Commedia dell'Arte. 2. Theater, Italian.

3320. Atkinson, J. Brooks and Hirschfeld, Albert. The Lively Years, 1920-1973. Assn Pr. 1973. $12.50.   792.097
1. Drama — 20th Century — History and Criticism. 2. Theater — New York (City) — History.

3321. Williams, Jay. Stage Left. Scribner. 1974. $8.95.   792.097
1. Theater — U. S. — History.

3322. Alberts, David. Pantomime: Elements and Exercise. U Pr of Kansas. 1971. $5.50.   792.3
1. Pantomime.

3323. Kimmell, Stanley. The Mad Booths of Maryland. 2nd rev. ed. Dover. 1970. pap. $3.75.   792.42(B)
1. Actors and Acting. 2. Booth Family.

700 FINE ARTS AND RECREATION

792.8 Ballet

3324. Balanchine, George. Balanchine's New Complete Stories of the Great Ballets. Mason, Francis, ed. Doubleday. 1968. $10.00. 792.8
1. Ballets — Stories, Plots, etc.

3325. Kerensky, Oleg. Anna Pavlova. Dutton. 1973. $6.95. 792.8(B)
1. Ballet. 2. Pavlova, Anna, 1885-1931.

3326. Kraus, Richard. History of the Dance: In Art and Education. P-H. 1969. $10.50. 792.8
1. Dancing — History.

3327. Mazo, Joseph H. Dance Is a Contact Sport. Sat Rev Pr. 1974. $9.95. 792.8
1. Ballet. 2. New York City Ballet.

3328. Clarke, Mary and Crisp, Clement. Ballet: An Illustrated History. Universe. 1973. $15.00. 792.809
1. Ballet — History.

793 Indoor Games and Amusements

3329. McDonagh, Don. Martha Graham: A Biography. Praeger. 1973. $10.95. 793.092(B)
1. Dance. 2. Graham, Martha, 1894(?)-

3330. Schurman, Nona and Clark, Sharon. Modern Dance Fundamentals. Macmillan. 1972. pap. $8.50. 793.3
1. Modern Dance.

3331. Lawson, Joan. European Folk Dance: Its National and Musical Characteristics. Pitman. 1953. $18.95. 793.31
1. Dancing — Folk and National Dances. 2. Folk Music.

3332. Gardner, Martin. Martin Gardner's Sixth Book of Mathematical Games from Scientific American. W H Freeman. 1971. $9.95. 793.74
1. Mathematical Recreations.

3333. Kordemsky, Boris. The Moscow Puzzles: Three Hundred and Fifty-Nine Mathematical Recreations. Scribner. 1972. $10.00. 793.74
1. Mathematical Recreations.

3334. Christopher, Milbourne. The Illustrated History of Magic. T Y Crowell. 1973. $12.95. 793.8
1. Conjuring — History. 2. Magic.

3335. Hay, Henry. Amateur Magician's Handbook. rev. ed. T Y Crowell. 1972. $7.95; pap. $1.95 (NAL). 793.8
1. Conjuring.

3336. Horowitz, I. A. The World Chess Championship: A History. Macmillan. 1973. $6.95. 794.1
1. Chess. 2. Chess — Tournaments.

3337. Murray, Harold J. Short History of Chess. Oxford U Pr. 1963. $3.75. 794.1
1. Chess — History.

3338. Reinfeld, Fred. How to Be a Winner at Chess. Doubleday. $4.95; pap. $0.95 (Fawcett World). 794.1
1. Chess.

3339. Korschelt, O. The Theory and Practice of Go. C E Tuttle. 1965. $5.95. 794.2
1. Go (Game).

3340. Berger, Gene. Bowling for Everyone. St Martin. 1974. $5.50. 794.6
1. Bowling.

3341. Foster, Robert F. Foster's Complete Hoyle. rev. ed. Lippincott. 1963. $6.95. 795
1. Bridge (Game). 2. Canasta (Game). 3. Cards.

3342. Scarne, John. Scarne's Encyclopedia of Games. Har-Row. 1973. $13.95. 795.03
1. Games.

3343. Goren, Charles H. Goren's Modern Backgammon Complete. Doubleday. 1974. $7.95; pap. $1.95 (Cornerstone). 795.1
1. Backgammon.

3344. Berndt, Fredrick. The Domino Book: Games, Solitaire, Puzzles. Nelson. 1974. $5.95. 795.3
1. Dominoes.

3345. Hervey, George F. The Complete Illustrated Book of Card Games. Doubleday. 1973. $14.95. 795.4
1. Cards. 2. Games.

3346. Reese, Terence and Dormer, Albert. The Complete Book of Bridge. Sat Rev Pr. 1974. $9.95. 795.415
1. Bridge Whist.

700 FINE ARTS AND RECREATION

3347. Stanyon, Ellis. Card Tricks for Everyone. rev. ed. Emerson. 1968. $4.95. 795.438
1. Card Tricks.

796 Athletics and Outdoor Sports and Games

3348. Vecsey, George, ed. The Way It Was. McGraw. 1974. $14.95. 796
1. Sports — History.

3349. Severn, William. A Carnival of Sports: Spectacles, Stunts, Crazes and Unusual Sports Events. McKay. 1974. $6.95. 796.08
1. Sports.

3350. Brasch, Rudolph. How Did Sports Begin? A Look at the Origins of Man at Play. McKay. 1969. $9.95. 796.09
1. Sports — History.

3351. Edwards, Harry. The Revolt of the Black Athlete. Free Pr. 1969. $5.95; pap. $2.95. 796.09
1. Negro Athletes.

3352. Newman, Lee S. and Newman, Jay H. Kite Craft: The History and Processes of Kitemaking Throughout the World. Crown. 1974. $8.95; pap. $4.95. 796.15
1. Kites.

796.3 Ball Games

3353. Cousy, Robert and Power, Frank G., Jr. Basketball: Concepts and Techniques. Allyn. 1970. $12.95. 796.32
1. Basketball.

3354. Hollander, Zander, ed. Modern Encyclopedia of Basketball. rev. ed. Schol Bk Serv. 1972. $14.95. 796.32
1. Basketball.

3355. Holzman, William and Lewin, Leonard. Holzman's Basketball: Winning Strategy and Tactics. Macmillan. 1973. $6.95. 796.32
1. Basketball.

3356. Monroe, Earl and Unseld, Wes. The Basketball Skill Book. Atheneum. 1973. $5.95. 796.32
1. Basketball.

3357. Shondell, Donald S. and McManama, Jerry. Volleyball. P-H. 1971. $4.95; pap. $1.60. 796.327
1. Volleyball.

3358. Bradley, Gordon and Toye, Clive. Playing Soccer the Professional Way. Har-Row. 1973. $8.95. 796.33
1. Soccer.

3359. National Football League. Official Encyclopedia History of Professional Football. Macmillan. 1973. $14.95. 796.33
1. Football — History.

3360. Smith, Burt. Offensive and Defensive Football. A S Barnes. 1969. $7.95. 796.33
1. Football.

3361. Blount, Roy. About Three Bricks Shy of a Load. Little. 1974. $7.95. 796.332
1. Football, Professional.

796.34 Tennis and Lacrosse

3362. King, Billie J. and Hyams, Joseph. Billie Jean King's Secrets of Winning Tennis. new ed. HR&W. 1974. $6.95. 796.34
1. Tennis.

3363. Laver, Rod and Pollard, Jack. How to Play Championship Tennis. Macmillan. 1970. $7.95. 796.34
1. Tennis.

3364. Lichtenstein, Grace. A Long Way, Baby: Behind the Scenes in Women's Pro Tennis. Morrow. 1974. $6.95. 796.34
1. Tennis.

3365. Hawkey, Richard B. Beginner's Guide to Squash. Transatlantic. 1973. $7.50. 796.343
1. Squash Rackets.

3366. Evans, G. Heberton and Anderson, R. E. Lacrosse Fundamentals. A S Barnes. 1966. $7.95. 796.347
1. Lacrosse.

796.35 Ball Games (Club, Mallet, Bat, etc.)

3367. Coyne, John, ed. Better Golf. Follett. 1972. $9.95. 796.352
1. Golf.

3368. Golf Magazine. Golf Magazine's Encyclopedia of Golf. rev. ed. Har-Row. 1973. $13.95; pap. $5.95. 796.352
1. Golf.

700 FINE ARTS AND RECREATION

3369. McAdams, Cliff, ed. How to Break Ninety-Eight-Par. Winchester Pr. 1973. $6.95. 796.352
1. Golf.

3370. Scott, Tom and Cousins, Geoffrey. The Golf Immortals. new ed. Hart. 1974. pap. $2.95. 796.352(B)
1. Golf — Biography.

3371. Allen, Ethan. Baseball Play and Strategy. 2nd ed. Ronald. 1969. $9.50. 796.357
1. Baseball.

3372. Alston, Walter and Weiskopf, Donald. The Complete Baseball Handbook: Strategies and Techniques for Winning. Allyn. 1972. $14.95. 796.357
1. Baseball.

3373. Jenkins, Ferguson. Inside Pitching. Regnery. 1972. $5.95; pap. $3.95. 796.357
1. Pitching (Baseball).

3374. Litwhiler, Daniel. Baseball. 4th ed. P-H. 1967. $10.95. 796.357
1. Baseball.

3375. McCrory, G. Jacobs. Softball Rules in Pictures. G&D. 1974. pap. $1.95. 796.357
1. Softball.

3376. Smith, Robert M. Illustrated History of Baseball. G&D. 1973. $12.95. 796.357
1. Baseball — History.

3377. Tanner, Chuck and Enright, Jim, eds. The Official Major League Baseball Playbook. P-H. 1974. $9.95. 796.357
1. Baseball.

3378. Turkin, Hy. The Official Encyclopedia of Baseball. 7th ed. A S Barnes. 1974. $13.95. 796.357
1. Baseball.

796.4 Athletic Exercises and Gymnastics

3379. Beecham, Justin. Olga: Her Life and Her Gymnastics. Two Continents. 1974. $2.95. 796.4
1. Gymnastics. 2. Women Athletes.

3380. Holm, Nora S. Runner's Bible. HM. $3.95. 796.4
1. Running.

3381. Vincent, William. Gymnastic Routines for Men. Saunders. 1972. pap. $2.25. 796.4
1. Gymnastics.

3382. Loken, Newton C. Tumbling and Trampolining. Sterling. 1969. $3.95. 796.47
1. Tumbling.

3383. Durant, John. Highlights of the Olympics from Ancient Times to the Present. 4th ed. Hastings. 1974. $6.95. 796.48
1. Olympic Games.

3384. Johnson, William O., Jr. All That Glitters Is Not Gold: The Olympic Games. Putnam. 1972. $7.95. 796.48
1. Olympic Games — Revival, 1896-

3385. Kieran, John and Daley, Arthur. Story of the Olympic Games: 776 B.C. to 1972. rev. ed. Lippincott. 1973. $10.95. 796.48
1. Olympic Games.

796.5 Outdoor Life

3386. Kelsey, Robert J. Walking in the Wild: Complete Guide to Hiking and Backpacking. Funk & W. 1973. $6.95. 796.5
1. Backpacking. 2. Hiking.

3387. Fletcher, Colin. The New Complete Walker. Knopf. 1974. $8.95. 796.51
1. Hiking. 2. Walking.

3388. Casewit, Curtis W. and Pownall, Richard. Mountaineering Handbook: An Invitation to Climbing. Lippincott. 1968. $6.50. 796.52
1. Mountaineering.

3389. Kjellstrom, Bjorn. Be Expert with Map and Compass: The Orienteering Handbook. Scribner. 1972. pap. $3.50. 796.52
1. Maps. 2. Compass.

3390. Petzoldt, Paul. The Wilderness Handbook. Norton. 1974. $7.95. 796.52
1. Wilderness.

3391. Herzog, Maurice. Annapurna: First Conquest of an 8,000 Meter Peak. Dutton. 1953. $7.95; pap. $0.75 1969 (Popular Lib). 796.522
1. India. 2. Mountaineering.

3392. Hunt, John. The Conquest of Everest. Dutton. 1954. $8.95. 796.522
1. Everest, Mount. 2. Mount Everest Expedition, 1953. 3. Mountaineering.

700 FINE ARTS AND RECREATION

3393. Rebuffat, Gaston. On Ice and Snow and Rock. Oxford U Pr. 1971. $15.00. 796.522
1. Rock Climbing.

3394. Robbins, Royal. Basic Rockcraft. La Siesta. 1970. pap. $1.95. 796.522
1. Mountaineering. 2. Rock Climbing.

3395. Ullman, James R. Age of Mountaineering. rev. ed. Lippincott. 1964. $8.95. 796.522
1. Mountaineering.

3396. McClurg, David R. The Amateur's Guide to Caves and Caving: Skill-Building Ways to Finding and Exploring the Underground Wilderness. Stackpole. 1973. $5.95; pap. $2.95. 796.525
1. Caves.

3397. Colby, C. B. and Angier, B. The Art and Science of Taking to the Woods. Macmillan. 1971. pap. $4.95. 796.54
1. Camping. 2. Wilderness.

3398. Riviere, William A. Backcountry Camping. Doubleday. 1971. $6.95; pap. $3.95. 796.54
1. Backpacking. 2. Camping.

3399. Rutstrum, Calvin. Paradise Below Zero. Macmillan. 1972. pap. $2.45. 796.54
1. Camping. 2. Winter.

3400. Bridge, Raymond. Freewheeling: The Bicycle Camping Book. Stackpole. 1974. $5.95. 796.6
1. Bicycles. 2. Camping.

3401. Sloane, Eugene A. The New Complete Book of Bicycling. S&S. 1974. $12.50. 796.6
1. Cycling.

796.7 Driving Motor Vehicles

3402. Bledsoe, Jerry. The World's Number One, Flat-Out, All-Time, Great, Stock Car Racing Book. Doubleday. 1975. $8.95. 796.7
1. Automobile Racing.

3403. Ball, Adrian, ed. My Greatest Race, by Twenty of the Finest Motor Racing Drivers of All Time. Dutton. 1974. $8.95. 796.72(B)
1. Automobile Racing — Biography.

3404. Cutter, Bob and Fendell, Bob. The Encyclopedia of Auto Racing Greats. P-H. 1973. $17.50. 796.72(B)
1. Automobile Racing — Biography.

3405. Engel, Lyle K. The Indianapolis 500: The World's Most Exciting Auto Race. rev. ed. Schol Bk Serv. 1972. $7.95. 796.72
1. Automobile Racing. 2. Indianapolis Speedway Race.

3406. Hayward, Elizabeth. Grand Prix: The Complete Book of Formula 1 Racing. Dodd. 1971. $5.95. 796.72
1. Grand Prix Racing.

3407. Sox, Ronnie, et al. Sox and Martin Book of Drag Racing. Regnery. 1974. $15.00. 796.72
1. Automobile Racing. 2. Drag Racing.

3408. Spence, James and Brown, Gar. Motorcycle Racing in America: A Definitive Look at the Sport. O'Hara. $8.95. 796.75
1. Motorcycle Racing.

796.8 Combat Sports

3409. Keen, Clifford P., et al. Championship Wrestling. rev. ed. Arco. 1973. pap. $3.95. 796.8
1. Wrestling.

3410. Masters, Robert V., compiled by. Complete Book of Karate and Self-Defense. Sterling. 1974. $7.95. 796.8
1. Self-Defense.

796.9 Winter Sports

3411. Bass, Howard. International Encyclopedia of Winter Sports. Great Albion. 1972. $7.95. 796.9
1. Winter Sports.

3412. Beddoes, Richard. Hockey! The Story of the World's Fastest Sport. 3rd ed. Macmillan. 1973. $9.95. 796.9
1. Hockey.

3413. Gilbert, Rod and Park, Brad. Playing Hockey the Professional Way. Har-Row. 1972. $7.95. 796.9
1. Hockey.

3414. Hollander, Zander and Bock, Hal, eds. The Complete Encyclopedia of Ice Hockey. rev. ed. P-H. 1974. $14.95. 796.9
1. Hockey.

700 FINE ARTS AND RECREATION

3415. Ogilvie, Robert S. Basic Ice Skating Skills. Lippincott. 1968. $6.95; pap. $3.95.
796.9
1. Skating.

3416. Noyes, Tina and Alexander, Freda. I Can Teach You to Figure Skate. Hawthorn. 1973. $6.95; pap. $2.95. 796.91
1. Skating.

3417. Steck, Allen and Tejada-Flores, Lito. Wilderness Skiing. Sierra. 1972. $6.95. 796.93
1. Skiis and Skiing.

3418. Taylor, Clif. GLM: The New Way to Ski. G&D. 1973. pap. $2.95. 796.93
1. Skiis and Skiing.

3419. Tokle, Art and Luray, Martin. Complete Guide to Cross-Country Skiing and Touring. HR&W. 1973. $6.95; pap. $2.95 (Random). 796.93
1. Skiis and Skiing.

3420. Witherell, Warren. How the Racers Ski. Norton. 1972. $6.95. 796.93
1. Skiis and Skiing.

797 Aquatic and Air Sports

3421. Gabrielsen, Milton A., et al. Aquatics Handbook. 2nd ed. P-H. 1968. $10.50. 797
1. Aquatic Sports.

3422. Andrews, Howard and Russel, Alexander. Basic Boating: Piloting and Seamanship. P-H. 1964. $9.95. 797.1
1. Boats and Boating.

3423. Urban, John T., ed. White Water Handbook for Canoe and Kayak. Appalach Mtn. 1965. $1.50. 797.1
1. Canoes and Canoeing.

3424. Wilson, Paul C. Modern Rowing. Stackpole. 1969. $6.50. 797.1
1. Rowing.

3425. Zadig, Ernest A. The Complete Book of Boating: An Owner's Book. P-H. 1972. $12.95. 797.1
1. Boats and Boating.

3426. Malo, John W. Malo's Complete Guide to Canoeing and Canoe-Camping. rev. ed. Quadrangle. 1974. $7.95. 797.122
1. Canoes and Canoeing.

3427. Bavier, Robert N. Sailing to Win. rev. ed. Dodd. 1973. $8.95. 797.14
1. Yacht Racing.

3428. Hammond, Geoffrey F. Showdown at Newport: The Race for the America's Cup. Walden Bk Co. 1974. $12.95. 797.14
1. Yachts and Yachting.

3429. Ogilvy, C. Stanley. Thoughts on Small Boat Racing. 2nd ed. Little. 1974. pap. $2.95.
797.14
1. Sailboat Racing.

3430. Walker, Stuart H., ed. Techniques of Small Boat Racing. Norton. 1960. $8.50.
797.14
1. Sailboat Racing.

3431. Nelson, William D. Surfing: A Handbook. rev. ed. Mason & Charter. 1973. $9.95. 797.17
1. Surf Riding.

3432. Sports Illustrated Editors. Sports Illustrated Swimming and Diving. rev. ed. Lippincott. 1973. $4.50; pap. $1.75. 797.2
1. Diving. 2. Swimming.

3433. Schollander, Don and Cohne, Joel H. Inside Swimming. Regnery. 1974. $5.95; pap. $3.95. 797.21
1. Swimming.

3434. Allen, Barry. Sports Illustrated Skin Diving and Snorkeling. Lippincott. 1973. $4.50; pap. $1.75. 797.23
1. Skin Diving.

3435. Borstein, Larry and Berkowitz, Henry. Scuba, Spear and Snorkel. Regnery. 1971. $4.95. 797.23
1. Aqualung. 2. Skin Diving.

3436. Council for National Co-Operation in Aquatics. New Science of Skin and Scuba Diving. new rev. ed. Assn Pr. 1974. $6.95; pap. $4.95. 797.23
1. Aqualung. 2. Skin Diving.

3437. Cousteau, Jacques-Yves and Dugan, J. Captain Cousteau's Underwater Treasury. Har-Row. 1959. $10.00. 797.23
1. Skin and Scuba Diving.

3438. May, Judy G. Scuba Diver's Guide to Underwater Ventures. Stackpole. 1973. $5.95; pap. $2.95. 797.23
1. Aqualung. 2. Skin Diving.

700 FINE ARTS AND RECREATION

3439. Emrich, Linn. The Complete Book of Sky Sports. Macmillan. 1970. pap. $2.95. 797.5
1. Aeronautical Sports.

3440. Carrier, Rick. Fly: The Complete Book of Sky Sailing. McGraw. 1974. $7.95. 797.55
1. Gliding and Soaring.

3441. Dedera, Don. Hang Gliding: The Flyingest Flying. Northland. 1975. $14.50; pap. $8.50. 797.55
1. Gliding and Soaring.

3442. Poynter, Dan. Hang Gliding, the Basic Handbook of Skysurfing. rev. ed. Parachuting Pubns. 1974. $9.95; pap. $5.95. 797.55
1. Gliding and Soaring.

3443. ———. Manned Kiting: The Basic Handbook of Tow Launched Hang Gliding. Parachuting Pubns. 1974. pap. $3.95. 797.55
1. Gliding and Soaring.

3444. Ryan, Charles W. Sport Parachuting. Regnery. 1975. $10.00; pap. $4.95. 797.56
1. Skydiving.

3445. Sellick, Bud. Parachutes and Parachuting: A Modern Guide to the Sport. P-H. 1971. $7.95. 797.56
1. Parachuting.

798.2 Horsemanship

3446. Young, John R. The Schooling of the Western Horse. rev. ed. U of Okla Pr. $6.95. 798.22
1. Horse-Training.

3447. Back, Joe. Horses, Hitches and Rocky Trails. Swallow. 1959. $5.00. 798.23
1. Harness Making and Trade. 2. Horsemanship.

3448. Hedges, David and Meyer, Fred. Horses and Courses: A Pictorial History of Racing. Viking Pr. 1972. $22.50. 798.4
1. Horse-Racing.

3449. Pettingill, O. E. Born to Run: The Making of a Racehorse. Arco. 1973. $12.50. 798.4
1. Horse-Racing. 2. Race Horses.

799 Fishing, Hunting, Target Shooting

3450. Mason, Jerry, ed. The American Sportsman Treasury. Knopf. 1971. $14.95. 799.08
1. Fishing. 2. Hunting.

3451. Bates, Joseph D. Fishing: An Encyclopedic Guide to Tackle and Tactics for Fresh and Salt Water. Dutton. 1974. $14.95. 799.1
1. Fishing.

3452. Brooks, Joseph W. Complete Guide to Fishing Across North America. Har-Row. 1966. $9.75. 799.1
1. Fishing — North America.

3453. Kreh, Bernard L. Fly Fishing in Salt Water. Crown. 1974. $8.95. 799.1
1. Fishing.

3454. Scharff, Robert. Standard Handbook of Saltwater Fishing. rev. ed. T Y Crowell. 1966. $8.95. 799.1
1. Salt-Water Fishing.

3455. Netherby, Steve, ed. The Experts' Book of Freshwater Fishing. S&S. 1974. $9.95. 799.11
1. Fishing.

3456. Ovington, Roy. Basic Fly Fishing and Fly Tying. Stackpole. 1973. $5.95; pap. $2.95. 799.12
1. Fly Fishing. 2. Fly Tying.

3457. Knap, Jerome J. The Hunter's Handbook: A Guide to Hunting in North America. Scribner. 1973. $7.95. 799.2
1. Game and Gamebirds — North America. 2. Hunting — North America.

3458. O'Connor, Jack, et al. Complete Book of Shooting: Rifles, Shotguns, Handguns. Times Mirror Mag. 1965. $7.95. 799.2
1. Hunting. 2. Shooting.

3459. Ormond, Clyde. Complete Book of Hunting. rev. ed. Har-Row. 1972. $7.95. 799.2
1. Hunting.

3460. Riviere, William A. The Gunner's Bible: The Complete Guide to Sporting Firearms. rev. ed. Doubleday. 1973. pap. $2.50. 799.2
1. Firearms — Handbooks, Manuals, etc. 2. Shooting.

700 FINE ARTS AND RECREATION

3461. Bear, Fred. The Archer's Bible.
Doubleday. 1968. pap. $2.50.   799.215
1. Archery. 2. Hunting.

800 LITERATURE

801 Literature - Philosophy and Theory

3462. Abrams, Meyer H. The Mirror and the Lamp. Oxford U Pr. 1953. $10.95; pap. $2.75 1968 (Norton). 801
1. Criticism. 2. Romanticism.

3463. Lipking, Lawrence I. and Litz, Walton A., eds. Modern Literary Criticism, 1900-1970. Atheneum. 1972. $12.95. 801
1. Criticism.

3464. Steiner, George. Language and Silence: Essays on Language, Literature, and the Inhuman. Atheneum. 1970. $8.00; pap. $3.95. 801
1. Literature — History and Criticism. 2. Literature — Philosophy.

3465. Hall, Vernon, Jr. A Short History of Literary Criticism. NYU Pr. 1963. $8.00; pap. $2.45. 801.95
1. Criticism.

3466. Wellek, Rene. Concepts of Criticism. Nichols, Stephen G., Jr., ed. Yale U Pr. 1963. $20.00; pap. $3.95. 801.95
1. Criticism. 2. Literature — History and Criticism.

808 Rhetoric

3467. Burack, A. A., ed. The Writer's Handbook. new ed. Writer. 1974. $12.50. 808
1. English Language — Style. 2. Style, Literary.

3468. Engle, Paul, ed. On Creative Writing. Dutton. 1964. $6.50. 808
1. Authorship. 2. Style, Literary.

3469. Perrin, Porter G. and Ebbitt, Wilma R. Writer's Guide and Index to English. 5th ed. Scott F. 1972. $8.75; pap. $6.95. 808
1. English Language — Rhetoric.

3470. Strunk, William S., Jr. and White, E. B. The Elements of Style. Macmillan. $2.95; pap. $0.95. 808
1. English Language — Style. 2. Style, Literary.

808.1 Poetry - Style

3471. Bowra, Cecil M. Heroic Poetry. St Martin. 1952. $14.00; pap. $6.95. 808.1
1. Epic Poetry — History and Criticism.

3472. Brooks, Cleanth and Warren, Robert P. Understanding Poetry. 3rd ed. HarBraceJ. 1960. $10.95. 808.1
1. Poetry — History and Criticism.

3473. Cotter, Janet. Invitation to Poetry. Winthrop. 1971. pap. $4.25. 808.1
1. Poetry.

3474. Deutsch, Babette. Poetry Handbook: A Dictionary of Terms. Funk & W. 1974. $5.95; pap. $1.50 (G&D). 808.1
1. Poetics.

3475. Drew, Elizabeth. Poetry: A Modern Guide to Its Understanding and Enjoyment. Norton. 1959. $5.95; pap. $0.60 (Dell). 808.1
1. Poetry.

800 LITERATURE

3476. Eliot, Thomas S. On Poetry and Poets. FS&G. 1957. $4.50; pap. $2.95. 808.1
1. Poetry.

3477. MacLeish, Archibald. Poetry and Experience. HM. 1961. $6.95. 808.1
1. Poetry. 2. Poetry — History and Criticism.

3478. Nemerov, Howard. Reflections on Poetry and Poets. Rutgers U Pr. 1972. $10.00. 808.1
1. Poetry.

3479. Untermeyer, Louis. The Pursuit of Poetry: A Guide to Its Understanding and Appreciation with an Explanation of Its Forms and a Dictionary of Poetic Terms. S&S. 1969. $6.95. 808.1
1. Poetry — History and Criticism.

808.2 Drama - Style

3480. Busfield, Roger M. Playwright's Art: Stage, Radio, Television, Motion Pictures. Greenwood. 1971. $13.00. 808.2
1. Drama — Technique. 2. Playwriting.

3481. Clark, Barrett H. European Theories of the Drama. rev. ed. Popkin, Henry, ed. Crown. 1965. $7.50. 808.2
1. Drama — History and Criticism.

3482. Lucas, Frank L. Tragedy: Serious Drama in Relation to Aristotle's Poetics. Macmillan. 1966. pap. $1.25. 808.2
1. Drama — History and Criticism.
2. Literature — History and Criticism.
3. Tragedy — History and Criticism.

3483. Olson, Elder. Theory of Comedy. Ind U Pr. 1968. $6.50; pap. $1.95. 808.2
1. Comedy.

3484. Sewall, Richard B. The Vision of Tragedy. Yale U Pr. 1959. $8.50; pap. $2.45. 808.2
1. Drama — History and Criticism.
2. Literature — History and Criticism.
3. Tragedy.

3485. Vale, Eugene. Technique of Screenplay Writing. G&D. 1973. pap. $2.95. 808.23
1. Moving-Picture Plays.

808.3 Fiction - Style

3486. Allott, Miriam, ed. Novelists on the Novel. Columbia U Pr. 1959. $12.00; pap. $2.45. 808.3
1. Fiction — History and Criticism. 2. Fiction — Technique.

3487. Forster, Edward M. Aspects of the Novel. HarBraceJ. 1947. $6.95; pap. $1.45. 808.3
1. Fiction — History and Criticism.

3488. James, Henry. Theory of Fiction. Miller, James E., Jr., ed. U of Nebr Pr. 1972. $12.00; pap. $3.95. 808.3
1. Fiction — History and Criticism.

3489. Lubbock, Percy. The Craft of Fiction. Viking Pr. 1957. pap. $2.25. 808.3
1. Fiction — History and Criticism.

3490. West, Ray Benedict and Stallman, Robert W. The Art of Modern Fiction. HR&W. 1956. pap. $6.00. 808.3
1. Fiction — History and Criticism.

808.5 Speech

3491. Ott, John. How to Write and Deliver a Speech. Trident. 1970. $6.50. 808.5
1. Oral Communication. 2. Public Speaking. 3. Speech.

3492. Smith, Craig R. and Hunsaker, David M. The Bases of Argument: Ideas in Conflict. Bobbs. 1972. pap. $1.45. 808.53
1. Debates and Debating.

808.8 Literature - Collections

3493. Ellmann, Richard and Fiedelson, Charles, Jr., eds. Modern Tradition: Backgrounds to Modern Literature. Oxford U Pr. 1965. $17.50. 808.8
1. Literature — Collections.

3494. Friedlander, Albert H., ed. Out of the Whirlwind: A Reader of Holocaust Literature. Doubleday. 1968. $8.65. 808.803
1. Holocaust, Jewish (1939-1945).

808.81 Poetry - Collections

3495. Allen, Samuel W. Poems from Africa. T Y Crowell. 1973. $4.50. 808.81
1. African Poetry.

3496. Barnes, Richard G. Episodes in Fine Poetic Traditions. Chandler Pub. 1972. pap. $6.75. 808.81
1. Poetry — Collections.

3497. Eberhart, Richard and Rodman, S., eds. War and the Poet, 1800 B.C.-1945 A.D. Anthology. Devin. 1945. $12.50. 808.81
1. War — Poetry.

3498. Lomax, Alan and Abdul, Raoul, eds. Three Thousand Years of Black Poetry. Dodd. 1970. $6.95; pap. $1.25. 808.81
1. Negro Poetry — Collections.

3499. The Oxford Book of Canadian Verse in English and French. Smith, A. J., ed.. Oxford U Pr. 1962. $8.00; pap. $3.25. 808.81
1. Canadian Poetry — Collections. 2. French Canadian Poetry — Collections.

3500. Pound, Ezra and Spann, Marcella, eds. Confucius to Cummings: An Anthology of Poetry. New Directions. 1964. pap. $3.25. 808.81
1. Poetry — Collections.

3501. Van Doren, Mark. Anthology of World Poetry. HarBraceJ. $16.50. 808.81
1. Poetry — Collections.

3502. Williams, Oscar. Little Treasury of Great Poetry. rev. ed. Scribner. 1955. $7.50. 808.81
1. Poetry — Collections.

3503. ———. Little Treasury of Modern Poetry. rev. ed. Scribner. 1955. $8.95. 808.81
1. Poetry — Collections.

3504. Lucie-Smith, Edward. Primer of Experimental Poetry. Bobbs. $6.50. 808.8104
1. Poetry, Modern — 20th Century.

3505. Hutson, Arthur E. and McCoy, Patricia, trs. Epics of the Western World. Bks for Libs. 1954. $16.50. 808.813
1. Epic Poetry.

808.82 Drama - Collections

3506. Kernan, Alvin B., ed. Classics of the Modern Theater: Realism and After. HarBraceJ. 1965. pap. $6.50. 808.82
1. Drama — Collections.

3507. MacDonald, J. W. and Saxton, J. C., eds. Four Stages: The Development of World Drama. St Martin. 1966. $4.50. 808.82

1. Drama — Collections. 2. Drama — History and Criticism.

3508. Plays for a New Theater. (Playbook 2). New Directions. $7.50; pap. $2.95. 808.82
1. Drama — Collections.

3509. Richards, Stanley, ed. Best Mystery and Suspense Plays of the Modern Theatre. Dodd. 1971. $10.00. 808.82
1. Drama — Collections. 2. Mystery and Detective Plays.

3510. ———. Best Plays of the Sixties: A Dramatic Prologue to the Seventies. Doubleday. 1970. $10.00. 808.82
1. Drama — Collections.

3511. Raines, Robert A., ed. Modern Drama and Social Change. P-H. 1972. pap. $5.25. 808.8204
1. Drama — 20th Century. 2. Social Change.

3512. Dukore, Bernard F. Drama and Revolution. HR&W. 1971. pap. $7.00. 808.829
1. Revolution — Drama.

3513. Wellrath, George E. Theatre of Protest and Paradox: Developments in Avante-Garde Drama. 2nd ed. NYU Pr. 1970. $10.00; pap. $3.95. 808.829
1. Drama — 20th Century.

808.83 Fiction - Collections

3514. Barnet, Sylvan, et al. Nine Modern Classics: An Anthology of Short Novels. Little. 1973. pap. $5.95. 808.831
1. Short Stories, English — Translations from Foreign Literature.

3515. Stegner, Wallace E. The Writer's Art: A Collection of Short Stories. Greenwood. Repr. of 1950 ed. $16.25. 808.831
1. Short Stories.

808.84 Essays - Collections

3516. Mead, Douglas S., ed. Great English and American Essays. rev. ed. HR&W. 1957. pap. $3.95. 808.84
1. American Essays. 2. English Essays. 3. Essays.

3517. Reaske, Christopher. Seven Essayists: Varieties of Excellence in English Prose. Scott F. 1969. pap. $6.00. 808.84
1. Essays.

800 LITERATURE

808.85 Speeches - Collections

3518. Baird, A. C. American Public Addresses. McGraw. 1956. $8.95; pap. $5.50. 808.85
1. Orations.

3519. Peterson, Houston, ed. Treasury of the World's Greatest Speeches. rev. ed. S&S. 1965. $9.95; pap. $3.95. 808.85
1. Orations.

808.87 Satire and Humor - Collections

3520. Untermeyer, Louis, ed. Treasury of Great Humor. McGraw. 1972. $9.95. 808.87
1. Wit and Humor.

809 Literature - History and Criticism

3521. Berthoff, Warner. Fictions and Events: Essays in Criticism and Literary History. Dutton. 1971. $10.00. 809
1. American Literature. 2. Literature.

3522. Downs, Robert B. Books That Changed America. Macmillan. 1970. $7.95; pap. $1.25 (NAL). 809
1. American Literature — History and Criticism. 2. Books and Reading. 3. U. S. — Civilization.

3523. Rahv, Philip. Literature and the Sixth Sense. HM. 1969. $10.00; pap. $2.95. 809
1. Literature.

3524. Ivask, Ivar and Von Wilpert, Gero. World Literature Since 1945: Critical Surveys of the Contemporary Literature of Europe and the Americas. Ungar. 1973. $25.00. 809.03
1. Literature, Modern — 20th Century — History and Criticism.

3525. Graves, Robert. The White Goddess, a Historical Grammar of Poetic Myth. rev. & enl. ed. FS&G. 1966. pap. $3.45. 809.1
1. Mythology. 2. Poetry — History and Criticism.

3526. Esslin, Martin. The Theatre of the Absurd. Doubleday. 1969. pap. $2.50. 809.2
1. Drama — 20th Century — History and Criticism.

3527. Lumley, Frederick. New Trends in 20th Century Drama: A Survey Since Ibsen and Shaw. 4th ed. Oxford U Pr. 1972. $8.50. 809.2
1. Drama — 20th Century — History and Criticism.

3528. Williams, Raymond. Drama from Ibsen to Brecht. rev. & enl. ed. Oxford U Pr. 1969. $6.50. 809.2
1. Drama — History and Criticism.

3529. Corrigan, Robert W. Tragedy: A Critical Anthology. HM. 1971. pap. $6.50. 809.251
1. Drama — Collections. 2. Tragedy.

3530. Sorrell, Walter. Facets of Comedy. G&D. 1973. pap. $2.95. 809.252
1. Comedy.

3531. McNally, Raymond T. and Florescu, Radu. In Search of Dracula: A True History of Dracula and Vampire Legends. NYGS. 1972. $8.95. 809.933
1. Vlad II, Dracul, Prince of Wallachia. 2. Vampires.

810.8 American Literature

3532. Chapman, Abraham, ed. Black Voices: An Anthology of Afro-American Literature. NAL. 1968. pap. $1.75. 810.8
1. American Literature — Negro Authors. 2. American Literature — 20th Century.

3533. ———. New Black Voices. NAL. pap. $1.50. 810.8
1. American Literature — Negro Authors. 2. American Literature — 20th Century.

3534. Solzman, Jack, ed. Years of Protest: A Collection of American Writings of the 1930's. Pegasus. 1967. $7.50; pap. $2.95. 810.8
1. American Literature — Collections.

3535. Chevez, Albert C., ed. Yearnings: Mexican-American Literature. Pendulum Pr. 1972. pap. $1.45. 810.808
1. American Literature — Mexican-American Authors. 2. American Literature — 20th Century.

3536. Gross, Theodore L. Literature of the American Jews. Free Pr. 1973. $12.95. 810.808
1. American Literature — Jewish-American Authors. 2. Jews in Literature.

3537. Edwards, Mary Jane. The Evolution of Canadian Literature in English. HR&W Canada. 1973. price on request. 810.809
1. Canadian Literature.

800 LITERATURE

3538. Miller, Perry and Johnson, Thomas H., eds. The Puritans: A Sourcebook of Their Writings. 2 vols. Har-Row. 1963. pap. $5.70. 810.82
1. American Literature — New England. 2. Puritans.

810.9 American Literature - History and Criticism

3539. Curley, Dorothy Nyren, et al, eds. Modern American Literature. 3 vols. 4th enl. ed. Ungar. 1969. $45.00. 810.9
1. American Literature — History and Criticism.

3540. Hoffman, Frederick J. The Twenties: American Writing in the Postwar Decade. Viking Pr. 1955. $8.00; pap. $3.95 (Free Pr). 810.9
1. American Literature — History and Criticism. 2. U. S. — History — 20th Century.

3541. Hoffman, Michael J. The Subversive Vision: American Romanticism in Literature. new ed. Kennikat. 1973. $8.95. 810.9
1. American Literature — 19th Century — History and Criticism. 2. Romanticism.

3542. Morgan, H. Wayne. American Writers in Rebellion, from Mark Twain to Dreiser. Hill & Wang. 1965. pap. $1.75. 810.9
1. American Literature — History and Criticism.

3543. Spiller, Robert E., ed. The American Literary Revolution, 1783-1837. NYU Pr. 1967. $10.00. 810.9
1. American Literature — History and Criticism.

811 American Poetry

3544. Sprague, Rosemary. Imaginary Poets: A Study of Five American Poets. Chilton. 1969. $5.95. 811.008
1. Poets, American. 2. Poets, Women.

3545. Stepanchev, Stephen. American Poetry Since 1945: A Critical Survey. Har-Row. pap. $1.95. 811.009
1. American Poetry — History and Criticism.

3546. Waggoner, Hyatt H. American Poets. Dell. 1970. pap. $2.95. 811.009
1. American Poetry — History and Criticism.

811.08 American Poetry - Collections

3547. Berg, Stephen, ed. Naked Poetry: Recent American Poetry in Open Forms. Bobbs. 1969. $8.50; pap. $2.95. 811.08
1. American Poetry — Collections.

3548. Dunning, Stephen and Lueders, Edward, eds. Some Haystacks Don't Even Have Any Needle, and Other Complete Modern Poems. Lothrop. 1969. $5.95. 811.08
1. American Poetry — Collections.

3549. Gelpi, Albert J., compiled by. The Poet in America, 1650 to Present. Heath. 1973. $10.95. 811.08
1. American Poetry — Collections.

3550. Lowenfels, Walter, ed. The Writing on the Wall: 108 American Poems of Protest. Doubleday. 1969. $4.95; pap. $1.95. 811.08
1. American Poetry — Collections.

3551. Untermeyer, Louis, ed. Modern American Poetry. rev. ed. HarBraceJ. 1962. $8.95. 811.08
1. American Poetry — Collections.

3552. Williams, Oscar. Little Treasury of American Poetry. rev. ed. Scribner. 1955. $10.00. 811.08
1. American Poetry — Collections.

3553. ———. New Pocket Anthology of American Verse. rev. ed. WSP. 1972. pap. $1.25. 811.08
1. American Poetry — Collections.

811.09 American Poetry - History and Criticism

3554. Cambon, Glauco. The Inclusive Flame: Studies in American Poetry. Peter Smith. 1963. $5.00; pap. $2.45 (Ind U Pr). 811.09
1. American Poetry — History and Criticism.

811.3 Middle 19th Century

3555. Bryant, William Cullen. Poetical Works. AMS Pr. 1969. $15.00. 811.3

3556. Duberman, Martin B. James Russell Lowell. HM. 1966. $8.00. 811.3(B)
1. Lowell, James Russell, 1819-1891.

800 LITERATURE

3557. Longfellow, Henry Wadsworth. Poems. Fuller, Edmund, ed. T Y Crowell. 1967. $3.95. 811.3

3558. Lowell, James Russell. Complete Poetical Works. HM. $7.00. 811.3

3559. Poe, Edgar Allan. Poems of Edgar Allan Poe. Stovall, Floyd, ed. U Pr of Va. 1965. $10.00. 811.3

3560. Smeaton, Oliphant. Longfellow and His Poetry. Folcroft. 1913. $7.25. 811.3(B)
1. Longfellow, Henry Wadsworth, 1807-1882.

3561. Van Doren, Mark, ed. Portable Emerson. Viking Pr. 1946. $5.95; pap. $3.35. 811.3
1. Emerson, Ralph Waldo, 1803-1882.

3562. Waskow, Howard J. Whitman: Explorations in Form. U of Chicago Pr. 1966. $10.75. 811.3
1. Whitman, Walt — Criticism.

3563. Whitman, Walt. Complete Poetry, Selected Prose and Letters. Random. 1961. $15.00. 811.3

3564. ———. Leaves of Grass. Modern Lib. $4.95. 811.3

811.4 Later 19th Century

3565. Crane, Stephen. Poems of Stephen Crane. McDonald, Gerald D., ed. T Y Crowell. 1964. $3.95. 811.4
1. Crane, Stephen, 1871-1900.

3566. Cunningham, Virginia. Paul Lawrence Dunbar and His Song. Biblo. Repr. of 1947 ed. $10.00. 811.4(B)
1. Dunbar, Paul Lawrence, 1872-1906.

3567. Dickinson, Emily. Complete Poems of Emily Dickinson. Little. 1960. $15.00. 811.4

3568. Johnson, Thomas Herbert. Emily Dickinson: An Interpretive Biography. Harvard U Pr. 1955. $7.50; pap. $3.45 1967 (Atheneum). 811.4(B)
1. Dickinson, Emily Elizabeth, 1830-1886.

3569. Lanier, Sidney. Poems of Sidney Lanier. U of Ga Pr. 1944. $5.00. 811.4

3570. Mazzaro, Jerome, ed. Modern American Poetry: Essays in Criticism. McKay. 1970. $7.95; pap. $4.95. 811.4
1. American Poetry — History and Criticism.

811.5 20th Century

3571. Eliot, Thomas S. Complete Poems and Plays, 1909-1950. HarBraceJ. 1952. $8.50. 811.5

3572. Hall, Donald. Marianne Moore: The Cage and the Animal. Pegasus. 1970. $6.95. 811.5(B)
1. Moore, Marianne Craig — Criticism and Interpretation.

3573. Humphries, Rolfe. Coat on a Stick: Late Poems. Ind U Pr. 1969. $5.95. 811.5

3574. ———. Collected Poems of Rolfe Humphries. Ind U Pr. 1965. $7.50. 811.5

3575. Jeffers, Robinson. Beginning and the End, and Other Poems. Random. 1963. $5.95. 811.5

3576. Lowenfels, Walter. From the Belly of the Shark: Poems by Chicanos, Eskimos, Hawaiians, Indians, Puerto Ricans in the United States with Related Poems by Others. Random. 1973. pap. $1.95. 811.5
1. American Poetry — 20th Century.

3577. McGinley, Phyllis. Times Three: Selected Verse from Three Decades. Viking Pr. 1960. $5.50; pap. $1.65 1968. 811.5

3578. Matthiessen, Francis O. The Achievement of T. S. Eliot: An Essay on the Nature of Poetry. 3rd ed. Oxford U Pr. 1958. $7.50; pap. $2.75. 811.5
1. Eliot, Thomas Stearns — Criticism and Interpretation. 2. Poetry.

3579. Moore, Marianne. Complete Poems of Marianne Moore. Viking Pr. 1967. $10.00. 811.5

3580. Nash, Ogden. Verses from Nineteen Twenty-Nine on. Modern Lib. $2.45. 811.5

3581. Patchen, Kenneth. Collected Poems. New Directions. 1969. pap. $4.25. 811.5

3582. Pound, Ezra. Cantos of Ezra Pound: No. 1-117. New Directions. 1970. $12.50. 811.5

3583. ———. Selected Poems. New Directions. 1957. pap. $1.50. 811.5

3584. Rexroth, Kenneth. Collected Shorter Poems. New Directions. 1967. $8.75; pap. $2.95. 811.5

3585. Roethke, Theodore. Collected Poems. Doubleday. 1975. pap. $3.95. 811.5

3586. Smith, Chard. Where the Light Falls: A Portrait of Edwin Arlington Robinson. Macmillan. 1965. $7.50. 811.5(B)
1. Robinson, Edwin Arlington, 1869-1935.

3587. Stevens, Wallace. Collected Poems of Wallace Stevens. Knopf. 1954. $10.00. 811.5

3588. Stock, Noel. Life of Ezra Pound. Pantheon. 1970. $10.00. 811.5(B)
1. Pound, Ezra Loomis, 1885-1972.

3589. Tate, Allen. Poems. Swallow. 1960. $2.50. 811.5

3590. Warren, Robert Penn. Brother to Dragons. Random. 1953. $7.95. 811.5

3591. ———. Selected Poems: New and Old, 1923-1966. Random. 1966. $7.95. 811.5

3592. Williams, William C. Collected Later Poems: 1949-1950. rev. ed. New Directions. 1962. $6.50. 811.5

3593. ———. Selected Poems. rev. & enl. ed. New Directions. 1969. pap. $1.75. 811.5

811.52 Early 20th Century

3594. Aiken, Conrad. Selected Poems. Oxford U Pr. 1961. pap. $2.50. 811.52

3595. Benet, Stephen Vincent. John Brown's Body. Capps, J. L. and Kemble, C. R., eds. HR&W. 1969. $4.12. 811.52
1. Benet, Stephen Vincent, 1898-1943.

3596. Callahan, North. Carl Sandburg: A Biography. NYU Pr. 1969. $8.00. 811.52(B)
1. Sandburg, Carl, 1878-1967.

3597. Cox, Sidney. Swinger of Birches: A Portrait of Robert Frost. Macmillan. 1961. pap. $0.95. 811.52(B)
1. Frost, Robert, 1875-1963.

3598. Crane, Hart. Complete Poems and Selected Letters and Prose. Weber, B., ed. Doubleday. 1966. pap. $2.50. 811.52

3599. Cullen, Countee. On These I Stand. Har-Row. 1947. $6.95. 811.52

3600. Cummings, E. E. Complete Poems. HarBraceJ. 1962. $12.50. 811.52

3601. Friedman, Norman. E. E. Cummings: The Growth of a Writer. S Ill U Pr. 1964. $4.95. 811.52(B)
1. Cummings, Edward Estlin, 1894-1962.

3602. Frost, Robert. Poetry. HR&W. 1969. $12.95. 811.52

3603. Johnson, James W. Gods Trombones. Viking Pr. 1927. $3.95. 811.52

3604. Lindsay, Vachel. Selected Poems. Macmillan. 1963. $5.95; pap. $1.95 1967. 811.52

3605. Lowell, Amy. Complete Poetical Works. HM. 1955. $10.00. 811.52

3606. MacLeish, Archibald. The Wild Old Wicked Man and Other Poems. HM. 1968. $4.00. 811.52

3607. Massa, Ann. Vachel Lindsay: Fieldworker for the American Dream. Ind U Pr. 1970. $12.50. 811.52(B)
1. Lindsay, Vachel, 1879-1931.

3608. Masters, Edgar L. New Spoon River Anthology. Macmillan. 1968. $5.95; pap. $1.25. 811.52

3609. Mazzaro, Jerome. William Carlos Williams, the Later Poems. Cornell U Pr. 1973. $8.75. 811.52
1. Williams, William Carlos, 1883-1963.

3610. Millay, Edna S. Collected Poems. Har-Row. 1956. $10.95. 811.52

3611. Morrison, Kathleen. Robert Frost: A Pictorial Chronicle. new ed. HR&W. 1974. $10.95. 811.52
1. Frost, Robert, 1875-1963.

3612. Parker, Dorothy. Collected Poetry. Modern Lib. $2.45. 811.52

3613. Ransom, John C. Selected Poems. 3rd ed. Knopf. 1969. $5.00. 811.52

3614. Robinson, Edwin A. Collected Poems. Macmillan. 1937. $12.50. 811.52

800 LITERATURE

3615. ———. Selected Poems. Macmillan. 1965. $5.00. 811.52

3616. Sandburg, Carl. The Complete Poems of Carl Sandburg. rev. ed. HarBraceJ. 1970. $14.00. 811.52

3617. Sarton, May. Collected Poems: 1930-1973. Norton. 1974. $10.00. 811.52

3618. Sheean, Vincent. The Indigo Bunting: A Memoir of Edna St. Vincent Millay. Schocken. 1973. $2.95. 811.52(B)
1. Millay, Edna St. Vincent, 1892-1950.

3619. Thompson, Lawrence. Robert Frost: The Years of Triumph, 1915-1938. HR&W. 1970. $15.00. 811.52(B)
1. Frost, Robert, 1875-1963.

3620. Thompson, Lawrence R. Fire and Ice: The Art and Thought of Robert Frost. Russell. Repr. 1942. $10.00. 811.52
1. Frost, Robert, 1875-1963 — Criticism and Interpretation.

3621. Unterecker, John. Voyager: A Life of Hart Crane. FS&G. 1969. $15.00. 811.52(B)
1. Crane, Hart, 1899-1932.

811.54 Later 20th Century

3622. Antonius, Bro. Hazards of Holiness: Poems, 1957-1960. Serendipity. 1962. $3.50. 811.54

3623. Berry, Wendell. Openings. HarBraceJ. 1969. $4.50. 811.54

3624. Berryman, John. His Toy, His Dream, His Rest. FS&G. 1968. $6.50. 811.54

3625. ———. Seventy-Seven Dream Songs. FS&G. 1964. $4.95; pap. $1.95. 811.54

3626. Bishop, Elizabeth. Complete Poems. FS&G. 1969. $7.50; pap. $2.95. 811.54

3627. Bogan, Louise. The Blue Estuaries: Poems, Nineteen Twenty Three-Nineteen Sixty Eight. FS&G. 1968. pap. $1.95. 811.54

3628. Brooks, Gwendolyn. Selected Poems. Har-Row. 1963. $6.95; pap. $2.25. 811.54

3629. ———. The World of Gwendolyn Brooks. Har-Row. 1971. $10.00. 811.54

3630. Ciardi, John. Thirty-Nine Poems. Rutgers U Pr. 1959. $3.00. 811.54

3631. Cohen, Leonard. Selected Poems, 1956-1968. Viking Pr. 1968. $5.00; pap. $1.95. 811.54

3632. Cowley, Malcolm. Blue Juniata: Collected Poems. Viking Pr. 1968. $5.95. 811.54

3633. Davison, Peter. Walking the Boundaries. Atheneum. 1974. $6.95. 811.54

3634. Deutsch, Babette. Coming of Age: New and Selected Poems. Ind U Pr. 1963. pap. $1.75. 811.54

3635. Dickey, James. Poems Nineteen Fifty Seven-Nineteen Sixty Seven. Wesleyan U Pr. 1967. $9.95; pap. $1.95 1968 (Macmillan). 811.54

3636. Dugan, Alan. Collected Poems. Yale U Pr. 1969. pap. $2.75. 811.54

3637. Eberhart, Richard. Collected Poems, 1909-1960. Oxford U Pr. 1960. $7.50. 811.54

3638. Ferlinghetti, Lawrence. A Coney Island of the Mind. New Directions. 1968. gift ed. $5.50; pap. $1.00. 811.54

3639. ———. Starting from San Francisco. enl. & rev. ed. New Directions. 1967. pap. $1.00. 811.54

3640. Ginsberg, Allen. Howl, and Other Poems. City Lights. 1956. pap. $1.00. 811.54

3641. ———. Reality Sandwiches, 1953-1960. City Lights. 1963. pap. $1.50. 811.54

3642. Giovanni, Nikki. My House. Morrow. 1972. $5.95; pap. $1.95. 811.54

3643. Hughes, Langston. I Wonder As I Wander: An Autobiographical Journey. Hill & Wang. 1964. pap. $3.95. 811.54(B)
1. Hughes, Langston, 1902-1967.

3644. ———. Langston Hughes Reader. Braziller. 1958. $5.95. 811.54

3645. Jarrell, Randall. Complete Poems. FS&G. 1969. $12.95; pap. $4.95. 811.54

3646. Kramer, Jane. Allen Ginsberg in America. Random. 1969. pap. $1.95. 811.54(B)
1. Ginsberg, Allen, 1926-

800 LITERATURE

3647. Lee, Don L. Directionscore: Selected and New Poems. Broadside. 1971. $6.00; pap. $3.75. 811.54

3648. Levertov, Denise. The Sorrow Dance. New Directions. 1967. pap. $1.60. 811.54

3649. ———. With Eyes in the Back of Our Heads. New Directions. 1960. pap. $1.50. 811.54

3650. Lowell, Robert. Life Studies: For the Union Dead. FS&G. 1967. pap. $2.25. 811.54

3651. ———. Lord Weary's Castle: Mills of the Kavanaughs. HarBraceJ. 1968. pap. $1.45. 811.54

3652. McKuen, Rod. In Someone's Shadow. Random. 1969. $3.95. 811.54

3653. ———. Listen to the Warm. Random. 1967. $3.75. 811.54

3654. Merrill, James. Braving the Elements. Atheneum. 1972. $5.95; pap. $3.95. 811.54

3655. Nemerov, Howard. Blue Swallows. U of Chicago Pr. 1967. pap. $5.75; pap. $1.95 1969. 811.54

3656. ———. New and Selected Poems. U of Chicago Pr. 1960. $5.95; pap. $2.95. 811.54

3657. Plath, Sylvia. Winter Trees. Har-Row. 1972. $6.95. 811.54

3658. Rukeyser, Muriel. Breaking Open. Random. 1973. $6.00; pap. $1.95. 811.54

3659. ———. Speed of Darkness. Random. 1968. $6.95. 811.54

3660. Schwartz, Delmore. Selected Poems: Summer Knowledge (Orig. Title: Summer Knowledge) New Directions. 1967. pap. $1.75. 811.54

3661. Sexton, Anne. The Book of Folly. HM. 1972. $5.95; pap. $2.95. 811.54

3662. ———. Live or Die. HM. 1966. $4.00; pap. $2.95. 811.54

3663. Shapiro, Karl. Selected Poems. Random. 1973. pap. $2.45. 811.54

3664. Simpson, Louis. Selected Poems. HarBraceJ. 1965. $4.95; pap. $1.45. 811.54

3665. Swenson, May. To Mix with Time: New and Selected Poems. Scribner. 1963. pap. $1.45. 811.54

3666. Wild, Peter. Cochise. Doubleday. 1973. $5.95. 811.54

3667. Wood, Nancy. Many Winters. Doubleday. 1974. $6.95. 811.54

3668. Adoff, Arnold, ed. The Poetry of Black America: Anthology of the 20th Century. Har-Row. 1973. $12.50. 811.5408
1. American Poetry — Negro Authors.

3669. Van Den Heuvel, Cor, ed. The Haiku Anthology: English Language Haiku by Contemporary American and Canadian Poets. Doubleday. 1974. pap. $2.95. 811.5408
1. Haiku, American. 2. Haiku, Canadian.

812.08 American Drama - Collections

3670. Couch, William, Jr., ed. New Black Playwrights, an Anthology. La State U Pr. 1970. $6.95. 812.08
1. American Drama — Collections. 2. Negro Literature. 3. One-Act Plays.

3671. Orzel, Nick, ed. Eight Plays from off-off Broadway. Bobbs. 1966. $4.95; pap. $1.95. 812.08
1. Drama — Collections.

3672. Parone, Edward, ed. Collision Course. Random. 1968. $5.95; pap. $1.95. 812.08
1. Drama — Collections. 2. Drama — History and Criticism.

Recommended Series

3673. Best American Plays Series. Gassner, John, & Barnes, Clive, eds.. Crown.

812.5 American Drama - 20th Century

3674. Eliot, Thomas S. Complete Plays of T. S. Eliot. HarBraceJ. $8.50. 812.5

3675. Rodgers, Richard and Hammerstein, Oscar, 2nd. Six Plays: (South Pacific; The King and I; Me and Juliet; Oklahoma; Allegro; Carousel) Modern Lib. 1959. $2.95. 812.5

179

800 LITERATURE

3676. Patterson, Lindsay, ed. Black Theater: A Twentieth-Century Collection of the Works of Its Best Playwrights. Dodd. 1971. $12.95; pap. $3.95 (NAL). 812.508
1. American Drama — Negro Authors. 2. American Drama — 20th Century.

812.52 Early 20th Century

3677. Gelb, Barbara and Gelb, Arthur. O'Neill. rev. ed. Har-Row. 1974. $17.50; pap. $6.95. 812.52(B)
1. O'Neill, Eugene, 1888-1953. 2. Theater.

3678. Hellman, Lillian. The Collected Plays. Little. 1972. $15.00. 812.52

3679. ———. An Unfinished Woman. Little. 1969. $7.50. 812.52(B)
1. Hellman, Lillian, 1905-

3680. McCullers, Carson. Member of the Wedding. HM. 1969. $4.95; pap. $0.75 (Bantam). 812.52

3681. Miller, Arthur. Collected Plays. Viking Pr. 1957. $6.95. 812.52

3682. Nelson, Benjamin. Arthur Miller: Portrait of a Playwright. McKay. 1970. $5.95. 812.52(B)
1. Miller, Arthur, 1915-

3683. Odets, Clifford. Six Plays: (Waiting for Lefty; Awake and Sing; till the Day I Die; Paradise Lost; Golden Boy; Rocket to the Moon) Modern Lib. 1959. $2.95. 812.52

3684. O'Neill, Eugene. Nine Plays. Modern Lib. $4.95. 812.52

3685. ———. Plays. 3 vols. Random. $25.00 set. 812.52

3686. Rice, Elmer. Three Plays: (Street Scene; Adding Machine; Dream Girl) Hill & Wang. 1965. $4.95; pap. $2.25. 812.52

812.54 Later 20th Century

3687. Albee, Edward. American Dream: Zoo Story. NAL. pap. $0.75. 812.54

3688. ———. Sandbox; Sad Death of Bessie Smith. NAL. 1964. pap. $0.60. 812.54

3689. ———. Tiny Alice. Atheneum. 1965. $4.50; pap. $1.25 (PB). 812.54

3690. ———. Who's Afraid of Virginia Woolf. Atheneum. 1962. pap. $3.95; pap. $1.25 (PB). 812.54

3691. Anderson, Robert. You Know I Can't Hear You When the Water's Running. Random. 1967. $5.50. 812.54

3692. Gelber, Jack. The Connection. Grove. 1960. $2.45. 812.54

3693. Gilroy, Frank. The Subject Was Roses, and About Those Roses. Random. 1965. $5.50. 812.54

3694. Hansberry, Lorraine. A Raisin in the Sun. Random. 1959. $5.50. 812.54

3695. ———. The Sign in Sidney Brustein's Window. Random. 1965. $5.50. 812.54

3696. Inge, William. Four Plays: (Come Back Little Sheba; Picnic; Bus Stop; The Dark at the Top of the Stairs) Random. 1958. $7.50. 812.54

3697. Jones, LeRoi. Four Black Revolutionary Plays. Bobbs. 1969. $5.00; pap. $2.95. 812.54

3698. ———. Two Plays: (the Dutchman; The Slave) Morrow. 1964. $3.95; pap. $1.50. 812.54

3699. Kopit, Arthur. Indians. Bantam. 1971. pap. $1.65. 812.54

3700. ———. Oh Dad Poor Dad, Mama's Hung You in the Closet and I'm Feelin' So Sad. Hill & Wang. 1960. pap. $1.95. 812.54

3701. Nemiroff, Robert, ed. To Be Young, Gifted and Black: Lorraine Hansberry in Her Own Words. P-H. 1969. $8.95. 812.54
1. Hansberry, Lorraine, 1930-1965.

3702. Rutenberg, Michael E. Edward Albee: Playwright in Protest. Hill & Wang. 1969 (Drama). $6.95. 812.54
1. Albee, Edward — Criticism and Interpretation.

3703. Sackler, Howard. The Great White Hope. Bantam. 1968. $4.95; pap. $0.95. 812.54
1. Johnson, John Arthur.

3704. Simon, Neil. Comedy of Neil Simon. Random. 1971. $12.95. 812.54

3705. ———. The Sunshine Boys. Random. 1973. $4.95. 812.54

3706. Van Itallie, Jean-Claude. The Serpent: A Play. Atheneum. 1969. $4.95; pap. $3.95. 812.54

3707. Vonnegut, Kurt, Jr. Happy Birthday, Wanda June. Delacorte. 1971. $7.95. 812.54

3708. Williams, Tennessee. Cat on a Hot Tin Roof. NAL. 1955. pap. $0.95. 812.54

3709. ———. Glass Menagerie. New Directions. 1945. $1.50. 812.54

3710. ———. Night of the Iguana. NAL. 1964. pap. $0.95. 812.54

3711. ———. Streetcar Named Desire. New Directions. 1947. $5.25; pap. $0.95 1952 (NAL). 812.54

813 American Fiction

3712. Lutwack, Leonard. Heroic Fiction: The Epic Tradition and American Novels of the Twentieth Century. S Ill U Pr. 1971. $5.95. 813.03
1. American Fiction — 20th Century — History and Criticism.

813.09 American Fiction - History and Criticism

3713. Stegner, Wallace, ed. The American Novel: From James Fenimore Cooper to William Faulkner. Basic. 1965. text ed. $6.50. 813.09
1. American Fiction — History and Criticism.

3714. Fiedler, Leslie A. Love and Death in the American Novel. rev. ed. Stein & Day. 1966. $12.50. 813.093
1. American Fiction — History and Criticism.2. Death in Literature. 3. Love in Literature. 4. National Characteristics, American.

3715. Baumbach, Jonathan. The Landscape of Nightmare: Studies in the Contemporary American Novel. NYU Pr. 1965. $6.95; pap. $1.95. 813.095
1. American Fiction — History and Criticism.

3716. Field, Leslie A., compiled by. Thomas Wolfe: Three Decades of Criticism. NYU Pr. 1968. $8.95; pap. $2.45. 813.095

1. Wolfe, Thomas — Criticism and Interpretation.

3717. Harper, Howard M., Jr. Desperate Faith: A Study of Bellow, Salinger, Mailer, Baldwin and Updike. U of NC Pr. 1967. pap. $1.95. 813.095
1. American Fiction — History and Criticism.

813.3 Middle 19th Century

3718. Hoeltje, Hubert H. Inward Sky: The Mind and Heart of Nathaniel Hawthorne. Duke. 1962. $12.00. 813.3(B)
1. Hawthorne, Nathaniel, 1804-1864.

3719. Arvin, Newton. Herman Melville. Greenwood. Repr. 1950. $13.50. 813.36(B)
1. Melville, Herman, 1819-1891.

3720. Freeman, John. Herman Melville. Haskell. 1974. $11.95. 813.36(B)
1. Melville, Herman, 1819-1891.

813.4 Later 19th Century

3721. O'Connor, Richard. Ambrose Bierce: A Biography. Little. 1967. $8.95. 813.4(B)
1. Bierce, Ambrose, 1842-1914.

3722. Quinn, Arthur H. Edgar Allan Poe: A Critical Biography. Cooper Sq. Repr. 1941. $17.50. 813.4(B)
1. Poe, Edgar Allan, 1809-1849.

813.5 20th Century

3723. Lewis, Richard W. Edith Wharton: A Biography. Har-Row. 1975. $15.00. 813.5(B)
1. Wharton, Edith Newbold Jones, 1862-1937.

3724. Westbrook, Max, ed. The Modern American Novel: Essays in Criticism. Peter Smith. $5.00. 813.509
1. American Fiction — 20th Century — History and Criticism.

813.52 Early 20th Century

3725. Baker, Carlos. Ernest Hemingway: A Life Story. Scribner. 1969. $12.50; pap. $1.95 (Bantam). 813.52(B)
1. Hemingway, Ernest, 1899-1961.

800 LITERATURE

3726. ———. Hemingway and His Critics: An International Anthology. Hill & Wang. 1961. pap. $2.25.   813.52
1. Hemingway, Ernest — Criticism and Interpretation.

3727. Carr, Virginia S. The Lonely Hunter: A Biography of Carson McCullers. Doubleday. 1975. $12.50.   813.52(B)
1. McCullers, Carson Smith, 1917-1967.

3728. Farr, Finis. Margaret Mitchell of Atlanta. Avon. 1974. $1.75.   813.52(B)
1. Mitchell, Margaret, 1900-1949.

3729. Howe, Irving. Sherwood Anderson. Stanford U Pr. 1951. $8.50; pap. $2.95.   813.52(B)
1. Anderson, Sherwood, 1876-1941.

3730. Kazin, Alfred. Bright Book of Life: American Novelists and Storytellers from Hemingway to Mailer. Little. 1973. $8.95; pap. $1.95 (Dell).   813.52
1. American Fiction — 20th Century — History and Criticism.

3731. Lundquist, James. Sinclair Lewis. Ungar. 1972. $6.00.   813.52
1. Lewis, Sinclair — Criticism and Interpretation.

3732. Martin, Jay. Nathaniel West: The Art of His Life. FS&G. 1970. $10.00.   813.52(B)
1. West, Nathaniel, 1904-1940.

3733. Milford, Nancy. Zelda: A Biography. Har-Row. 1970. $10.95.   813.52(B)
1. Fitzgerald, Zelda (Sayre), 1900-1948.

3734. Millgate, Michael. The Achievement of William Faulkner. Random. 1966. $8.95; pap. $1.95.   813.52
1. Faulkner, William — Criticism and Interpretation.

3735. Mizener, Arthur. The Far Side of Paradise: Biography of F. Scott Fitzgerald. HM. 1965. pap. $2.85.   813.52(B)
1. Fitzgerald, Francis Scott, 1896-1940.

3736. Stone, Irving. Jack London, Sailor on Horseback. Doubleday. 1947. $6.95; pap. $1.25 (NAL).   813.52(B)
1. London, Jack, 1876-1916.

3737. Swanberg, W. A. Dreiser. Scribner. 1965. $12.50.   813.52(B)
1. Dreiser, Theodore, 1871-1945.

3738. Tedlock, Ernest and Wicker, Cecil. Steinbeck and His Critics: A Record of 25 Years. U of NM Pr. 1969. pap. $3.45.   813.52
1. Steinbeck, John — Criticism and Interpretation.

3739. Turnbull, Andrew. Thomas Wolfe. S&S. 1970. pap. $2.95.   813.52(B)
1. Wolfe, Thomas, 1900-1938.

3740. Watkins, Floyd C. Thomas Wolfe's Characters: Portraits from Life. U of Okla Pr. 1957. $5.95.   813.52
1. Wolfe, Thomas — Criticism and Interpretation.

3741. Webb, Constance. Richard Wright: A Biography. Putnam. 1968. $9.95.   813.52(B)
1. Wright, Richard, 1908-1960.

813.54 Later 20th Century

3742. Clarke, John H., ed. William Styron's Nat Turner: Ten Black Writers Respond. Beacon Pr. 1968. $4.95; pap. $1.95.   813.54
1. Confessions of Nat Turner. 2. Styron, William — The Confessions of Nat Turner. 3. Turner, Nat, 1800?-1831.

3743. Eckman, Fern M. The Furious Passage of James Baldwin. Popular Lib. 1967. pap. $0.75.   813.54(B)
1. Baldwin, James, 1924-

3744. Panshin, Alexi. Heinlein in Dimension, a Critical Analysis. Advent. 1969. $7.00; pap. $2.75.   813.54
1. Heinlein, Robert Anson, 1907-

3745. Bewley, Marius. Eccentric Design: Form in the Classic American Novel. Columbia U Pr. 1959. pap. $1.95.   813.9
1. American Fiction.

814 American Essays

3746. Mersand, Joseph, ed. Great Narrative Essays. WSP. 1968. pap. $0.95.   814.008
1. Essays — Collections.

3747. British and American Essays: 1905-1956. Anderson, C. L. and Williams, G. W., eds.. HR&W. 1959. pap. $5.00.   814.08
1. American Essays. 2. English Essays.

3748. Shaw, Charles B., ed. American Essays. NAL. 1955 (Ment). pap. $0.95.   814.08
1. American Essays.

800 LITERATURE

3749. Bode, Carl. Ralph Waldo Emerson: A Profile. Hill & Wang. 1968. pap. $1.95. 814.3(B)
1. Emerson, Ralph Waldo, 1803-1882.

3750. Anderson, Charles R., ed. Thoreau's Vision: The Major Essays. P-H. 1973. pap. $2.45. 814.4

817 American Satire and Humor

3751. Kaplan, Martin, compiled by. The Harvard Lampoon Centennial Celebration, 1876-1973. Little. 1973. $29.95. 817.008
1. American Wit and Humor.

3752. Twain, Mark. Autobiography of Mark Twain. Neider, C., ed. Har-Row. 1959. $10.00. 817.3(B)
1. Clemens, Samuel Langhorne, 1835-1910.

3753. Wagenknecht, Edward C. Mark Twain: The Man and His Work. 3rd ed. U of Okla Pr. 1967. $6.95. 817.3
1. Clemens, Samuel Langhorne — Criticism.

3754. Bierce, Ambrose. Devil's Dictionary. Hill & Wang. 1957. pap. $1.95. 817.4

818 Miscellaneous Writings

3755. Franklin, Benjamin. Poor Richard's Almanac. McKay. $2.25. 818.1
1. Almanacs, American.

3756. Clemens, Samuel L. Mark Twain's Notebook. Paine, Albert B., ed. Cooper Sq. 1972. $23.50. 818.4

3757. Cummings, E. E. Six Non Lectures. Harvard U Pr. 1953. $4.50; pap. $2.50. 818.5

3758. Kaplan, Justin. Lincoln Steffens. S&S. 1974. $10.00. 818.5(B)
1. Steffens, Joseph Lincoln, 1866-1936.

3759. Mailer, Norman. The Armies of the Night: History As a Novel, the Novel As History. NAL. 1971. pap. $1.50. 818.5
1. Vietnamese Conflict, 1961-1973 — Protests, Demonstrations, etc. against.

3760. Toklas, Alice B. Staying on Alone: Letters of Alice B. Toklas. Burns, Edward, ed. Liveright. 1973. $11.95. 818.5(B)
1. Stein, Gertrude, 1874-1946. 2. Toklas, Alice B.

3761. Baker, Carlos. Hemingway, the Writer As Artist. 4th ed. Princeton U Pr. 1973. $12.50; pap. $2.95. 818.52
1. Hemingway, Ernest — Criticism and Interpretation.

3762. Brinnin, John M. The Third Rose: Gertrude Stein and Her World. Peter Smith. 1959. $7.50. 818.52(B)
1. Stein, Gertrude, 1874-1946.

3763. Nabokov, Vladimir. Speak, Memory: An Autobiography Revisited. Putnam. 1966. $6.75. 818.52(B)
1. Nabokov, Vladimir, 1899-

3764. Ohlin, Peter. Agee. Astor-Honor. 1968. $6.95; pap. $2.45. 818.52
1. Agee, James — Criticism and Interpretation.

3765. Mellow, James R. Charmed Circle: Gertrude Stein and Co. new ed. Praeger. 1974. $12.95. 818.5209(B)
1. Stein, Gertrude, 1874-1946.

3766. Parker, Dorothy. The Portable Dorothy Parker. rev. ed. Viking Pr. 1973. $5.95; pap. $2.95. 818.5209
1. Parker, Dorothy, 1893-1967.

3767. Capote, Truman. Selected Writings. Random. 1963. $7.95. 818.54

Recommended Series

3768. University of Minnesota Pamphlets on American Writers. Ungar, Leonard, & Wright, George T., eds.. U of Minn Pr. 818.999

3769. Twayne's United States Authors Series. Twayne.

820.9 English Literature - History and Criticism

3770. Bergonzi, Bernard. The Turn of the Century: Essays on Victorian and Modern English Literature. B&N. 1973. $13.75. 820.9
1. English Literature — History and Criticism.

3771. Penguin Companion to Literature. Vol. 2. Daiches, Davis, ed.. Penguin. 1973. pap. $4.95. 820.9(B)
1. English Literature — History and Criticism.

3772. Quennell, Peter. A History of English Literature. Merriam. 1973. $15.00. 820.9
1. English Literature — History and Criticism.

800 LITERATURE

3773. Wedgwood, Cicely V. Seventeenth Century Literature. Oxford U Pr. 1970. pap. $2.50. 820.904
1. English Literature — History and Criticism.

821.08 English Poetry - Collections

3774. Auden, W. H. and Pearson, Norman H., eds. Poets of the English Language. 5 vols. Vol. 1. Langland to Spenser; Vol. 2. Marlowe to Marvell; Vol. 3. Milton to Goldsmith; Vol. 4. Blake to Poe; Vol. 5. Tennyson to Yeats. Viking Pr. 1950. $5.95 ea. 821.08
1. English Poetry — Collections.

3775. Coffin, Charles M. and Roelofs, Gerrit, eds. Major Poets: English and American. 2nd ed. HarBraceJ. 1969. pap. $4.95. 821.08
1. American Poetry — Collections. 2. English Poetry — Collections.

3776. Cole, William, ed. A Book of Love Poems. Viking Pr. 1965. $3.95. 821.08
1. Love Poetry. 2. Poetry — Collections.

3777. Corson, Hiram. A Primer of English Verse. Folcroft. 1973. $10.00. 821.08
1. English Poetry — Collections.

3778. Garrity, Durin, ed. New Irish Poets, Anthology. Devin. $6.50. 821.08
1. Irish Poetry — Collections.

3779. New Yorker (Periodical) The New Yorker Book of Poems. Viking Pr. 1969. $12.50. 821.08
1. American Poetry — Collections. 2. English Poetry — Collections.

3780. Oxford Anthology of English Poetry. Lowry, H. F., & Thorp, W., eds. 2nd ed. Oxford U Pr. $9.95. 821.08
1. English Poetry — Collections.

3781. Oxford Book of Ballads. Kingsley, James, ed.. Oxford U Pr. 1969. $12.00. 821.08
1. Ballads, English. 2. Ballads, Scottish.

3782. Oxford Book of Light Verse. Auden, W. H., ed.. Oxford U Pr. 1938. $10.00; pap. $4.95. 821.08
1. American Poetry — Collections. 2. English Poetry — Collections.

3783. Sitwell, Edith, ed. The Atlantic Book of British and American Poetry. Little. 1958. $16.50. 821.08
1. American Poetry — Collections. 2. English Poetry — Collections.

3784. Stevenson, Burton E., ed. The Home Book of Modern Verse. 2nd ed. HR&W. 1953. $10.95. 821.08
1. American Poetry — Collections. 2. English Poetry — Collections.

3785. Untermeyer, Louis, ed. The Book of Living Verse. HarBraceJ. $4.95. 821.08
1. American Poetry — Collections. 2. English Poetry — Collections.

3786. ————. Modern British Poetry. rev. ed. HarBraceJ. 1962. $7.50. 821.08
1. English Poetry — Collections.

3787. Williams, Oscar. Little Treasury of British Poetry. rev. ed. Scribner. 1955. $7.00. 821.08

3788. ————. Little Treasury of Modern Poetry: English and American. rev. ed. Scribner. $3.95. 821.08
1. American Poetry — Collections. 2. English Poetry — Collections.

3789. Abrams, Meyer H., ed. English Romantic Poets: Modern Essays in Criticism. Oxford U Pr. 1960. pap. $2.50. 821.09
1. English Poetry — History and Criticism.

821.1-821.6 Early English - Later 18th Century

3790. Chaucer, Geoffrey. Complete Works. Skeat, Walter, ed. Oxford U Pr. 1933. $9.50. 821.1

3791. French, Robert D. A Chaucer Handbook. 2nd ed. P-H. 1947. $8.50. 821.1
1. Chaucer, Geoffrey — Handbooks, Manuals, etc.

3792. Rowland, Beryl, ed. Companion to Chaucer Studies. Oxford U Pr. 1968. pap. $2.95. 821.1
1. Chaucer, Geoffrey — Handbooks, Manuals, etc.

3793. Herbert, George. Poems of George Herbert. 2nd ed. Oxford U Pr. 1961. $3.00. 821.3

800 LITERATURE

3794. Spenser, Edmund. Complete Poetical Works. Dodge, R. Neil, ed. HM. 1908. $10.00.
821.3

3795. Bald, R. C. John Donne: A Life. Oxford U Pr. 1970. $15.00. 821.4(B)
1. Donne, John, 1573-1631.

3796. Donne, John. The Complete Poetry and Selected Prose. Modern Lib. $2.95. 821.4

3797. Dryden, John. Complete Poetical Works. Noyes, George R., ed. HM. $10.95.
821.4

3798. Handford, James H. A Milton Handbook. 5th ed. P-H. 1970. $9.50. 821.4
1. Milton, John, 1608-1674.

3799. Herrick, Robert. Poems. Martin, L. C., ed. Oxford U Pr. 1965. $8.00. 821.4

3800. Marvell, Andrew. The Complete Poems. Donno, Elizabeth S., ed. Penguin. 1973. pap. $3.95. 821.4

3801. Milton, John. Complete Poetry and Selected English Prose. Visiak, E. H., ed. Random. 1942. $12.50. 821.4

3802. Tillyard, Eustace M. Milton. Macmillan. 1967. pap. $2.45. 821.4(B)
1. Milton, John, 1608-1674.

3803. Gray, Thomas. Complete Poems of Thomas Gray: English, Latin and Greek. Oxford U Pr. 1966. $15.25. 821.5

3804. Pope, Alexander. Poetical Works. Davis, Herbert, ed. Oxford U Pr. 1966. $8.00.
821.5

3805. Burns, Robert. Complete Poetical Works. HM. $7.00. 821.6

3806. Cowper, William. Poems. Dutton. $3.95. 821.6

821.7 Early 19th Century

3807. Bate, Walter Jackson. Coleridge. Macmillan. 1968. $5.95. 821.7(B)
1. Coleridge, Samuel Taylor, 1772-1834.

3808. Blake, William. Complete Writings of William Blake, with Variant Readings. Keynes, G., ed. Oxford U Pr. 1966. $10.00; pap. $4.75. 821.7

3809. Bronowski, Jacob. William Blake and the Age of Revolution: A Biography. Har-Row. 1969. pap. $1.95. 821.7(B)
1. Blake, William, 1757-1827.

3810. Byron, George G. Poetical and Dramatic Works. 3 vols. Dutton. $3.50 ea.
821.7

3811. Coleridge, Samuel T. Poems. Coleridge, E. H., ed. Oxford U Pr. 1912. $9.00; pap. $4.25. 821.7

3812. Keats, John. Complete Poetical Works. Scudder, Horace E., ed. HM. $7.00.
821.7

3813. Marchand, Leslie A. Byron: A Portrait. Knopf. 1970. $13.95. 821.7(B)
1. Byron, George Gordon Noel Byron, 6th Baron, 1788-1824.

3814. Maurois, Andre. Ariel: The Life of Shelley. Ungar. 1957. $7.50; pap. $2.75.
821.7(B)
1. Shelley, Percy Bysshe, 1792-1882.

3815. Read, Herbert E. Wordsworth. Humanities. 1949. pap. $2.00. 821.7(B)
1. Wordsworth, William, 1770-1850.

3816. Scott, Walter. Poetical Works. Robertson, J. L., ed. Oxford U Pr. 1904. $4.50. 821.7

3817. Shelley, Percy B. Poems. T Y Crowell. 1968. $3.50. 821.7

3818. Shelley, Percy B. Complete Poetical Works. Hutchinson, T., ed. Oxford U Pr. 1934. $5.00. 821.7

3819. Ward, Aileen. John Keats: The Making of a Poet. Viking Pr. 1963. $8.95; pap. $1.85. 821.7(B)
1. Keats, John, 1795-1821.

3820. Wordsworth, William. Complete Poetical Works. George, A. J., ed. HM. 1932. $8.50. 821.7

821.8 Victorian Period

3821. Arnold, Matthew. Poetry and Criticism of Matthew Arnold. HM. 1961. pap. $3.50. 821.8

3822. Browning, Elizabeth B. Poetical Works. HM. 1974. $10.00. 821.8

3823. Browning, Robert. Poetical Works. HM. 1974. $12.50. 821.8

800 LITERATURE

3824. Buckley, Jerome. Tennyson: The Growth of a Poet. Harvard U Pr. 1960. $8.50; pap. $4.95 (HM). 821.8(B)
1. Tennyson, Alfred Tennyson, Baron, 1809-1892.

3825. Hardy, Thomas. Collected Poems. Macmillan. 1926. $10.95. 821.8

3826. Hopkins, Gerard M. Poems. Gardner, W. H. and MacKenzie, N. H., eds. Oxford U Pr. 1967. $9.75; pap. $3.95. 821.8

3827. Kipling, Rudyard. Verse. Doubleday. 1940. $10.00. 821.8

3828. Lear, Edward. Complete Nonsense Book. 9th ed. Strachey, Lady, ed. Dodd. 1942. $5.95. 821.8

3829. Rossetti, Dante G. Poems and Translations: Hand and Soul. Oxford U Pr. 1913. $6.00. 821.8

3830. Ruggles, Eleanor. Gerard Manley Hopkins: A Life. Kennikat. Repr. 1944. $9.00. 821.8(B)
1. Hopkins, Gerard Manley, 1844-1889.

3831. Swinburne, Algernon C. Selected Poetry and Prose. Rosenberg, John D., ed. Modern Lib. $2.95. 821.8

3832. Tennyson, Alfred. Poetical Works. HM. 1974. $12.50. 821.8

3833. Thompson, Francis. Poems. Oxford U Pr. 1937. $6.50. 821.8

3834. Woolf, Virginia. Flush: A Biography. HarBraceJ. 1933. $6.95; pap. $0.45. 821.8(B)
1. Browning, Elizabeth Barrett, 1806-1861.

821.9-821.91 20th Century

3835. Brooke, Rupert. Collected Poems. Dodd. 1930. $3.95. 821.9

3836. Brophy, James D. Edith Sitwell: The Symbolist Order. S Ill U Pr. 1968. $4.95. 821.9
1. Sitwell, Edith — Criticism and Interpretation.

3837. Housman, Alfred E. Collected Poems of A. E. Housman. rev. ed. HarBraceJ. 1971. pap. $2.45. 821.9

3838. Lawrence, David H. Selected Poems. Viking Pr. 1959. pap. $1.65. 821.9

3839. Masefield, John. Poems. Collected ed. in 1 vol. rev. ed. Macmillan. 1953. $10.50. 821.9

3840. Sitwell, Edith. Collected Poems of Edith Sitwell. Vanguard. 1954. $10.00. 821.9

3841. Sparrow, John. Robert Bridges. British Bk Ctr. 1962. $2.95; pap. $1.20. 821.9(B)
1. Bridges, Robert Seymour, 1844-1930.

3842. Auden, Wystan H. Collected Longer Poems. Random. 1966. $7.50. 821.91

3843. ————. Collected Shorter Poems: 1927-1957. Random. 1966. $8.95. 821.91

3844. Betjeman, John. Collected Poems. 2nd ed. HM. 1971. $7.50. 821.91

3845. Clarke, Austin. Poetry in Modern Ireland. Folcroft. 1972. $7.50. 821.91

3846. Dickey, James. Babel to Byzantium: Poets and Poetry Now. Octagon. Repr. 1968. $11.50; pap. $2.95 1971 (G&D). 821.91
1. American Poetry — 20th Century. 2. English Poetry — 20th Century.

3847. Durrell, Lawrence. Poetry. Dutton. pap. $1.45. 821.91

3848. Ellmann, Richard. Yeats: The Man and the Masks. Dutton. 1948. $2.45. 821.91(B)
1. Yeats, William Butler, 1865-1939.

3849. Fitzgibbon, Constantine. Life of Dylan Thomas. Little. 1965. pap. $2.65. 821.91(B)
1. Thomas, Dylan, 1914-1953.

3850. MacNeice, Louis. Collected Poems, 1925-1963. Oxford U Pr. 1967. $11.50. 821.91

3851. Spender, Stephen. Collected Poems. Random. 1955. $6.50. 821.91

3852. Thomas, Dylan. Collected Poems. New Directions. 1971. $2.75. 821.91

3853. Yeats, William B. Collected Poems. 2nd ed. Macmillan. 1956. $8.95. 821.91

822 English Drama

3854. Hogan, Robert G. After the Irish Renaissance: A Critical History of Irish Drama Since The Plough and The Stars. U of Minn Pr. 1967. $8.50. 822
1. English Drama — Irish Authors — History and Criticism. 2. Irish Drama (English) — History and Criticism.

3855. ———. Seven Irish Plays, 1946-1964. U of Minn Pr. 1967. $10.00. 822
1. English Drama — Irish Authors. 2. Irish Drama (English).

822.09 English Drama - History and Criticism

3856. Symonds, John A. Shakespeare's Predecessors in the English Drama. Cooper Sq. 1967. $9.95. 822.09
1. English Drama — History and Criticism.

822.3 Elizabethan Period

3857. Beaumont, Francis and Fletcher, John. King and No King. Turner, Robert K., ed. U of Nebr Pr. 1963. $4.75; pap. $1.85. 822.3

3858. ———. Knight of the Burning Pestle. Griffith, Benjamin, Jr., ed. Barron. 1963. pap. $1.25. 822.3

3859. ———. Maid's Tragedy. Norland, Howard B., ed. U of Nebr Pr. 1969. $4.75. 822.3

3860. Jonson, Ben. Five Plays. Oxford U Pr. 1953. $3.75. 822.3

3861. Marlowe, Christopher. Works. Brooke, C. F., ed. Oxford U Pr. 1910. $6.00. 822.3

3862. Webster, John and Tourneur, Cyril. Four Plays: White Devil; Duchess of Malfi; Atheist's Tragedy; Revenger's Tragedy. Hill & Wang. 1956. pap. $2.65. 822.3

822.33 Shakespeare

3863. Bradley, Andrew C. Shakespearean Tragedy. 2nd ed. St Martin. 1905. $12.95; pap. $2.75 1956. 822.33
1. Shakespeare, William, 1564-1616 — Tragedy.

3864. Charlton, Henry B. Shakespearean Comedy. B&N. 1961. pap. $4.50. 822.33
1. Shakespeare, William, 1564-1616 — Characters.

3865. Chute, Marchette. Shakespeare of London. Dutton. 1949. $8.95; pap. $2.25. 822.33(B)
1. Shakespeare, William, 1564-1616.

3866. Coe, Charles N. Shakespeare's Villains. AMS Pr. 1957. $6.50. 822.33
1. Shakespeare, William, 1564-1616 — Characters.

3867. Palmer, John. Political and Comic Characters of Shakespeare. St Martin. 1967. pap. $6.95. 822.33
1. Shakespeare, William, 1564-1616 — Characters.

3868. Partridge, Eric. Shakespeare's Bawdy: A Literary and Psychological Essay and a Comprehensive Glossary. rev. ed. Dutton. 1947. pap. $1.95. 822.33
1. Shakespeare, William, 1564-1616 — Dictionaries, Indexes, etc.

3869. Rowse, Alfred L. Shakespeare the Man. Har-Row. 1973. $10.00. 822.33(B)
1. Shakespeare, William, 1564-1616.

3870. Smith, Irwin. Shakespeare's Globe Playhouse. Scribner. 1956. $12.50. 822.33
1. Globe Theatre. 2. Shakespeare, William, 1564-1616 — Stage History.

822.4-822.8 Post-Elizabethan - Victorian Period

3871. Congreve, William. Complete Plays. Davis, Herbert, ed. U of Chicago Pr. 1967. $15.00. 822.4

3872. Dryden, John. All for Love or The World Well Lost. Barron. 1960. $4.25; pap. $1.25. 822.4

3873. Wycherley, William. Complete Plays. Weales, Gerald, ed. Norton. 1971. pap. $3.45. 822.4

3874. Gay, John. The Beggar's Opera. Lewis, Peter, ed. B&N. 1973. $7.50; pap. $3.25. 822.5

3875. Goldsmith, Oliver. She Stoops to Conquer. Friedman, Arthur, ed. Oxford U Pr. 1968. pap. $1.50. 822.6

3876. Sheridan, Richard B. Six Plays: (The Rivals; St. Patrick's Day; The Duenna; A Trip to Scarborough; The School for Scandal; The Critic) Kronenberger, Louis, ed. Hill & Wang. 1957. pap. $2.25. 822.6

800 LITERATURE

3877. Agate, James. Oscar Wilde and the Theatre. Folcroft. Repr. 1947. $6.50. 822.8
1. Wilde, Oscar — Criticism and Interpretation. 2. Wilde, Oscar — Stage History.

3878. Gilbert, William S. Savoy Operas. 2 vols. Oxford U Pr. $2.50 ea. 822.8
1. Sullivan, (Sir) Arthur Seymour, 1842-1900.

3879. Synge, John M. The Complete Works. Random. 1935. $7.95. 822.8

3880. Wilde, Oscar. Portable Oscar Wilde. Aldington, Richard, ed. Viking Pr. 1946. $6.50; pap. $3.25. 822.8

822.9-822.91 20th Century

3881. Barrie, James M. Plays. Scribner. 1928. $8.95. 822.9

3882. Crompton, Louis. Shaw the Dramatist. U of Nebr Pr. 1969. $7.95. 822.9
1. Shaw, George Bernard — Criticism and Interpretation.

3883. Gregory, Isabella A. Seven Short Plays. Scholarly. Repr. 1909. $14.50. 822.9

3884. Pearson, Hesketh. George Bernard Shaw: His Life and Personality. Atheneum. 1963. pap. $1.95. 822.9(B)
1. Shaw, George Bernard, 1856-1950.

3885. Shaw, George B. Four Plays: (Candida; Devil's Disciple; Caesar and Cleopatra; Captain Brasshound's Conversion) Dell. 1957. pap. $0.95. 822.9

3886. ———. Pygmalion. WSP. 1973. pap. $0.75. 822.9

3887. Shaw, George B. Plays: (Major Barbara; Heartbreak House; Saint Joan; Too Good to Be True) Smith, Warren, ed. Norton. $8.00; pap. $2.65. 822.9

3888. Taylor, John R. Second Wave: British Drama for the Seventies. Hill & Wang. 1971. $6.95. 822.9
1. English Drama — 20th Century — History and Criticism.

3889. Yeats, William B. Collected Plays. rev. ed. Macmillan. 1953. $8.95. 822.9

3890. Carroll, Paul Vincent. Irish Stories and Plays: (the Conspirators; Beauty Is Fled; Interlude; the Devil Came from Dublin) Devin. 1958. $5.95. 822.91

3891. O'Casey, Sean. Selected Plays of Sean O'Casey: (The Shadow of a Gunman; Juno and the Paycock; The Plough and the Stars; The Silver Tassle; Within the Gates; Purple Dust; Red Roses for Me; Bed Time Story and Time to Go) Braziller. 1956. $7.50. 822.91

3892. Rattigan, Terance. Collected Plays. 3 vols. Intl Pubns Serv. $8.00 ea. 822.91

3893. Van Druten, John. I Am a Camera: A Play in Three Acts. Greenwood. Repr. 1952. $11.50. 822.91

822.912 Early 20th Century

3894. Adams, Hazard. Lady Gregory. Bucknell U Pr. 1973. $4.50; pap. $1.95. 822.912
1. Gregory, Isabella Augusta, Lady, 1852-1932.

3895. Galsworthy, John. Plays. Scribner. 1928. $12.50. 822.912

3896. Jones, David. The Plays of T. S. Eliot. U of Toronto Pr. 1960. pap. $2.75. 822.912
1. Eliot, Thomas Stearns, 1888-1965.

3897. Martin, Graham. Eliot in Perspective. Humanities. 1970. $12.00. 822.912
1. Eliot, Thomas Stearns, 1888-1965.

822.914 Later 20th Century

3898. Behan, Brendan. The Quare Fellow; The Hostage. Grove. 1965. pap. $1.95. 822.914

3899. Bolt, Robert. A Man for All Seasons. Random. 1962. $6.50; pap. $1.65. 822.914

3900. Delaney, Shelagh. A Taste of Honey. Grove. pap. $1.95. 822.914

3901. Esslin, Martin. The Peopled World of Harold Pinter. Doubleday. 1970. pap. $1.45. 822.914
1. Pinter, Harold, 1930-

3902. Fry, Christopher. Lady's Not for Burning. Oxford U Pr. 1950. $3.95. 822.914

800 LITERATURE

3903. ———. Three Plays: (First Born; Thor with Angel; Sleep of Prisoners) Oxford U Pr. pap. $2.25. 822.914

3904. Nichols, Peter. Joe Egg. Grove. 1968. $1.95. 822.914

3905. Osborne, John. Inadmissible Evidence. Grove. 1965. pap. $2.45. 822.914

3906. ———. Look Back in Anger. S G Phillips. 1957. $4.95; pap. $0.95 (Bantam). 822.914

3907. ———. Luther. NAL. pap. $0.95. 822.914

3908. Pinter, Harold. The Birthday Party: Room. Grove. 1961. pap. $1.95. 822.914

3909. ———. The Caretaker and the Dumb Waiter. Grove. 1961. pap. $1.75. 822.914

3910. ———. Early Plays: (Night Out; Night School; Review Sketches) Grove. 1968. pap. $1.95. 822.914

3911. ———. Five Screenplays. Grove. 1973. $10.00; pap. $3.95. 822.914

3912. ———. Homecoming. Grove. 1967. $1.95. 822.914

3913. Shaffer, Peter. Black Comedy and White Lies. Stein & Day. 1967. pap. $1.95. 822.914

3914. ———. Equus and Shrivings. Atheneum. 1974. $7.95. 822.914

3915. Stoppard, Tom. Rosencrantz and Guildenstern Are Dead. Grove. 1967. pap. $1.95. 822.914

3916. Thomas, Dylan. Under Milk Wood: A Play for Voices. New Directions. 1959. pap. $1.50. 822.914

3917. Wesker, Arnold. The Wesker Trilogy: (Chicken Soup with Barley; Roots; I'm Talking About Jerusalem) Penguin. 1964. pap. $1.25. 822.914

823 English Fiction

3918. Adburgham, Alison. Women in Print: Writing Women and Women's Magazines from the Restoration to the Accession of Victoria. Humanities. 1973. $18.25. 823
1. Women Authors.

3919. Calkins, Elizabeth. Teaching Tomorrow: A Handbook of Science Fiction for Teachers. Pflaum-Standard. 1972. $2.20. 823.0876
1. English Language — Study and Teaching.
2. Science Fiction — Study and Teaching.

3920. Hillegas, Mark R. The Future As Nightmare; H. G. Wells and the Anti-Utopians. Ill U Pr. 1974. $7.00; pap. $2.45. 823.09
1. Science Fiction — History and Criticism. 2. Wells, Herbert George, 1866-1946.

823.5-823.8 Queen Anne Period - Victorian Period

3921. Moore, John R. Daniel Defoe: Citizen of the Modern World. U of Chicago Pr. 1958. $10.50. 823.5(B)
1. Defoe, Daniel, 1661-1731.

3922. Hodge, Jane A. Only a Novel: The Double Life of Jane Austen. Coward. 1972. $6.95. 823.7(B)
1. Austen, Jane, 1775-1817.

3923. Jenkins, Elizabeth. Jane Austen. Funk & W. 1969. pap. $2.95. 823.7(B)
1. Austen, Jane, 1775-1817.

3924. Laski, Marghanita. Jane Austen and Her World. Viking Pr. 1969. $8.95. 823.7
1. Austen, Jane — Criticism and Interpretation.

3925. Gerin, Winifred. Charlotte Brontë: The Evolution of a Genius. Oxford U Pr. 1967. $15.00; pap. $2.95. 823.8(B)
1. Brontë, Charlotte, 1816-1855.

3926. Hanson, Lawrence and Hanson, Elizabeth. The Four Brontës: The Lives and Works of Charlotte, Branwell, Emily and Anne Brontë. 4th ed. Shoe String. 1967. $12.00. 823.8(B)
1. Brontë Family.

3927. Hewish, John. Emily Brontë. St Martin. 1969. $8.95. 823.8(B)
1. Brontë, Emily Jane, 1818-1848.

3928. Johnson, Edgar. Charles Dickens: His Tragedy and Triumph. 2 vols. Little. 1965. $20.00. 823.8(B)
1. Dickens, Charles, 1812-1870.

800 LITERATURE

3929. Redinger, Ruby V. George Eliot: The Emergent Self. Knopf. 1975. $15.00. 823.8(B)
1. Eliot, George, pseud., 1819-1880.

823.9 20th Century

3930. Karl, Frederick R. Reader's Guide to the Contemporary English Novel. Octagon. 1972. $13.00; pap. $2.95 1963 (FS&G). 823.9
1. English Fiction — History and Criticism.

3931. Marcus, Steven. Dickens: From Pickwick to Dombey. Basic. 1965. $8.95; pap. $2.45 (S&S). 823.9
1. Dickens, Charles — Criticism and Interpretation.

3932. Stallybrass, Oliver, ed. Aspects of E. M. Forster: Essays and Recollections Written for His Ninetieth Birthday, January 1, 1969. HarBraceJ. 1969. $5.95. 823.9
1. Forster, Edward Morgan — Criticism and Interpretation.

3933. West, Paul. Modern Novel. Vol. 1. England & France. 2nd ed. 1967; Vol. 2. The United States & Other Countries. 1970. Humanities. pap. $2.00 ea. 823.9
1. American Fiction — History and Criticism. 2. English Fiction — History and Criticism. 3. French Fiction — History and Criticism.

3934. Karl, Frederick R. An Age of Fiction: The Nineteenth Century British Novel. FS&G. 1964. pap. $2.25. 823.908
1. English Fiction — History and Criticism.

823.912 Early 20th Century

3935. Anderson, Chester G. James Joyce and His World. Viking Pr. 1968. $6.95. 823.912(B)
1. Joyce, James, 1882-1941.

3936. Atkins, John. George Orwell: A Literary and Biographical Study. Ungar. 1955. $7.50. 823.912(B)
1. Orwell, George, 1903-1950.

3937. Barker, Dudley. The Man of Principle: A Biography of John Galsworthy. Stein & Day. 1970. pap. $2.45. 823.912(B)
1. Galsworthy, John, 1867-1933.

3938. Dickson, Lovat. H. G. Wells, His Turbulent Life and Times. Atheneum. 1969. $10.00; pap. $3.45. 823.912(B)
1. Wells, Herbert George, 1866-1946.

3939. Ellmann, Richard. James Joyce. Oxford U Pr. 1959. $17.50; pap. $2.50. 823.912(B)
1. Joyce, James, 1882-1941.

3940. Foster, Malcolm. Joyce Cary, a Biography. HM. 1968. $10.00. 823.912(B)
1. Cary, Joyce, 1888-1957.

3941. Gurko, Leo. Two Lives of Joseph Conrad. T Y Crowell. 1965. $3.95. 823.912(B)
1. Conrad, Joseph, 1857-1924.

3942. Isaacs, Neil D. and Zimbardo, Rose A., eds. Tolkien and the Critics: Essays on J. R. R. Tolkien's The Lord of the Rings. U of Notre Dame Pr. 1969. $9.95; pap. $3.45. 823.912
1. Tolkien, John Ronald Reuel — Criticism and Interpretation.

3943. Lucas, Robert. Frieda Lawrence: The Story of Frieda von Richtofen and D. H. Lawrence. Skelton, Geoffrey, tr. from Ger. Viking Pr. 1973. $8.95. 823.912(B)
1. Lawrence, David Herbert, 1885-1930.

3944. Moore, Harry T. and Roberts, Warren. D. H. Lawrence and His World. Viking Pr. 1966. $6.95. 823.912(B)
1. Lawrence, David Herbert, 1885-1930.

3945. Pippett, Aileen. Moth and the Star: A Biography of Virginia Woolf. Kraus Repr. 1955. $15.00. 823.912(B)
1. Woolf, Virginia, 1882-1941.

3946. Pryce-Jones, David. Evelyn Waugh and His World. Little. 1973. $12.95. 823.912(B)
1. Waugh, Evelyn, 1903-1966.

3947. Ready, William. The Tolkien Relation: A Personal Inquiry. Regnery. 1968. $3.95. 823.912
1. Tolkien, John Ronald Reuel — Criticism and Interpretation.

3948. Stone, Wilfred. The Cave and the Mountain: Study of E. M. Forster. Stanford U Pr. 1966. $10.00; pap. $3.85. 823.912(B)
1. Forster, Edward Morgan, 1879-1970.

3949. Weber, Carl J. Hardy of Wessex: His Life and Literary Career. 2nd ed. Columbia U Pr. 1965. $12.50. 823.912(B)
1. Hardy, Thomas, 1835-1902.

800 LITERATURE

3950. Woodcock, George. The Crystal Spirit: A Study of George Orwell. Little. 1966. $7.95; pap. $2.45 (Funk & W). 823.912
1. Orwell, George, 1903-1950.

3951. ———. Dawn and the Darkest Hour: A Study of Aldous Huxley. Viking Pr. 1972. $7.95. 823.912
1. Huxley, Aldous, 1894-1963.

3952. Kinkead-Weekes, Mark and Gregoe, Ian. William Golding: A Critical Study. HarBraceJ. 1967. $6.95. 823.914
1. Golding, William — Criticism and Interpretation.

824 English Essays

3953. Jones, Edmund D., ed. English Critical Essays: Nineteenth Century. Oxford U Pr. 1971. pap. $2.75. 824.008

3954. ———. English Critical Essays: Sixteenth to Eighteenth Centuries. Oxford U Pr. pap. $1.95. 824.008

3955. Jones, Phyllis M., ed. English Critical Essays: Twentieth Century. Oxford U Pr. $2.25. 824.008
1. Essays.

3956. Carlyle, Thomas. Selected Writings. Shelston, Alan, ed. Penguin. 1971. pap. $2.45. 824.8

3957. Feldberg, Katherine, ed. Of Men and Morals: The Englishman and His World. U of Miami Pr. 1970. $10.00. 824.9

827 English Satire and Humor

3958. Orel, Harold, ed. World of Victorian Humor. Irvington. pap. $4.95. 827
1. English Wit and Humor — History and Criticism.

3959. Parkinson, C. Northcote. Parkinson's Law. HM. 1957. $3.50; pap. $1.75. 827
1. English Wit and Humor.

3960. Punch Magazine. Century of Punch Cartoons. Williams, R. E., ed. S&S. 1955. $4.95. 827
1. English Wit and Humor — History and Criticism.

3961. Jerrold, Walter C. A Book of Famous Wits. Gryphon Hse. 1971. $14.00. 827.009

1. English Wit and Humor — History and Criticism.

3962. MacDonald, Dwight, ed. Parodies: An Anthology from Chaucer to Beerbohm - and After. Random. 1960. $10.00. 827.082

828 English Miscellany

3963. Boswell, James. Life of Samuel Johnson. Modern Lib. pap. $1.95. 828.6(B)
1. Johnson, Samuel, 1709-1784.

3964. Johnson, Edgar. Sir Walter Scott, the Great Unknown. 2 vols. Macmillan. 1970. $25.00. 828.709(B)
1. Scott, Sir Walter, 1771-1832.

3965. Stewart, J. I. Rudyard Kipling. Dodd. 1966. $5.00. 828.809(B)
1. Kipling, Rudyard, 1865-1936.

3966. Dunbar, Janet. J. M. Barrie: The Man Behind the Image. HM. 1970. $8.95. 828.91(B)
1. Barrie, Sir James Matthew, Bart., 1890-1937.

3967. Russell, Bertrand. The Autobiography of Bertrand Russell. Little. 1967. $7.95. 828.912(B)
1. Russell, Bertrand Russell, 3rd Earl, 1872-1970.

3968. Baker, James. William Golding: A Critical Study. St Martin. 1965. $3.95. 828.914
1. Golding, William, 1911-

3969. Beowulf. Alexander, Michael, tr.. Penguin. 1973. pap. $1.05. 829.3

Recommended Series

3970. Twayne's English Authors Series. Twayne.

3971. Twentieth Century Interpretation Series. Mack, Maynard, ed.. P-H.

3972. Twentieth Century Views Series. Mack, Maynard, ed.. P-H.

830 German Literature

3973. Droste-Huelshoff, Annette Von. Werke. (Ger.). Bergland, Walter I., ed. S F Bk. $4.60. 830
1. German Literature.

800 LITERATURE

3974. Goethe, Johann Wolfgang Von. Werke in Sechs Banden. (Ger.). Insel-Verlag. $14.00. 830
1. German Literature.

3975. Heine, Heinrich. Werke. 4 banden. (Ger.). Insel-Verlag. 1968. $11.80. 830
1. German Literature.

3976. Hofmannsthal, Hugo Von. Selected Writings. 3 vols. Hamburger, M., ed. Princeton U Pr. 1952-63. $15.00. 830
1. German Literature.

3977. Kleist, Heinrich Von. Works. 2 vols. (Ger.). S F Bk. $5.00. 830
1. German Literature.

3978. Schiller, Friedrich Von. Werke. 4 vols. (Ger.). Insel-Verlag. 1966. $7.95. 830
1. German Literature.

3979. Storm, Theodor. Werke in Zwei Banden. (Ger.). Aufbau-Verlag. 1966. $3.00. 830
1. German Literature.

3980. Tucholsky, Kurt. Deutschland, Deutschland, Uber Alles. Halley, Anne, tr. U of Mass Pr. 1972. $12.50. 830

3981. Tucholsky, Kurt. Eine Auswahl. Schwarz, Egon, tr. Norton. 1963. pap. $1.25. 830

3982. Fleissner, Otto S. and Deutsches, E. M. Literaturlesebuch. (Ger.). 4th ed. P-H. 1968 (Appleton-Century-Crofts). $3.75. 830.8
1. German Literature — Collections. 2. German Language — Readers.

3983. Bloecker, J. Die Neuen Wirklichkeiten: Linien und Profile der Modernen Literatur. (Ger.). 3rd ed. Berlin. 1961. $3.60. 830.9
1. German Literature — History and Criticism.

3984. Demetz, Peter. Postwar German Literature: A Critical Introduction. Pegasus. 1970. $6.95. 830.9
1. German Literature — 20th Century — History and Criticism.

3985. Gray, Ronald D. German Tradition in Literature, 1871-1945. Cambridge U Pr. 1966. $11.50. 830.9
1. German Literature — 20th Century — History and Criticism. 2. Politics and Literature.

3986. Hatfield, Henry C. Modern German Literature: The Major Figures in Context. Ind U Pr. 1968. pap. $1.85. 830.9
1. German Literature — History and Criticism.

3987. Heller, Erich. Disinherited Mind. Collins-World (Mer). pap. $3.45. 830.9
1. Germany — Intellectual Life. 2. German Literature — History and Criticism.

3988. Huebener, Theodore. The Literature of East Germany. Ungar. 1970. $6.00. 830.9
1. German Literature (East).

3989. Martini, Fritz. Deutsche Literaturgeschichte von den Anfangen bis zur Gegenwart. 4 aufl. (Ger.). Kroner. 1952. 830.9
1. German Literature — History and Criticism.

3990. Robertson, J. G. History of German Literature. rev. 6th ed. British Bk Ctr. 1971. $11.50. 830.9
1. German Literature — History and Criticism.

3991. Rose, Ernst. History of German Literature. NYU Pr. 1960. $7.50; pap. $2.75. 830.9
1. German Literature — History and Criticism.

3992. Sokel, Walter H. The Writer in Extremis: Expressionism in Twentieth Century German Literature. Stanford U Pr. 1959. $7.50. 830.9
1. German Literature — 20th Century — History and Criticism.

3993. Wilpert, Gero Von. Deutsche Literatur in Bildern. (Ger.). Kroner. 1957. 830.9
1. German Literature — History and Criticism.

831 German Poetry

3994. Benn, Gottfried. Gottfried Benn Dargestellt von Walter Lennig. (Ger.). Rowohlt. $1.25. 831

3995. Goethe, Johann Wolfgang Von. Poems. Gray, R., ed. Cambridge U Pr. 1966. $4.95; pap. $2.45. 831

3996. Heine, Heinrich. Lyric Poems and Ballads. (Eng. & Ger.). Feise, Ernst, tr. U of Pittsburgh Pr. 1969. pap. $2.25. 831

3997. Langgasser, Elisabeth. Mithras. Lyrik und Prosa. (Ger.). Fischer Bucherei. $1.25. 831

3998. Peters, H. Frederick. Rainer Maria Rilke: Masks and the Man. U of Wash Pr. 1960. $6.50. 831
1. Rilke, Rainer Maria, 1875-1926. 2. Rilke, Rainer Maria — Criticism.

3999. Rilke, Rainer Maria. Selected Poems. Bilingual. (Ger.). 2nd ed. MacIntyre, C. F., tr. U of Cal Pr. 1941. pap. $1.50. 831

4000. Sachs, Nelly. O the Chimneys. (Ger. & Eng.). Hamburger, M., et al, trs. FS&G. 1967. $7.50. 831
1. German Poetry.

4001. Vogelweide, Walther Von Der. Gedichte. Mittelhochdeutscher Text und Ubertragung. (Ger.). Fischer Bucherei. $1.50. 831

4002. Echtemeyer, T. H., ed. Deutsche Gedichte. (Ger.). school ed. August Bagel Verlag. 1966. $3.30. 831.08
1. German Poetry — Collections.

4003. Flores, Angel, ed. Anthology of German Poetry from Holderlin to Rilke. Peter Smith. $5.50. 831.08
1. German Poetry — Collections.

4004. Forster, Leonard Wilson, ed. The Penguin Book of German Verse. Ger. with prose tr. (Ger.). Penguin. 1964. $1.45. 831.08
1. German Poetry — Collections.

4005. Middleton, Christopher and Hamburger, Michael, eds. Modern German Poetry: 1910-1960. (Ger-Eng.). Grove. 1962. pap. $2.95. 831.08
1. German Poetry — Collections.

4006. Brod, Max. Heinrich Heine: The Artist in Revolt. Macmillan. 1962. pap. $1.50. 831.09
1. German Poetry — History and Criticism.

4007. Gray, Ronald D. Introduction to German Poetry. Cambridge U Pr. 1965. $3.75; pap. $1.95. 831.09
1. German Poetry — History and Criticism.

4008. Wiese, Benno Von. Die Deutsche Lyrik: Form und Geschichte. 2 vols. (Ger.). Adler. 1964. $19.50. 831.09
1. German Poetry — History and Criticism.

800 LITERATURE

4009. Hofrichter, Laura. Heinrich Heine. Fairley, Barker, tr. Oxford U Pr. 1963. $6.10. 831.7
1. Heine, Heinrich, 1797-1856. 2. Heine, Heinrich — Criticism and Interpretation.

832 German Drama

4010. Benn, Gottfried. Die Stimme Hinter dem Vorhang. (Ger.). Deutscher Taschenbuch Verlag. $1.25. 832

4011. Brecht, Bertolt. Die Mutter. (Ger.). Rowohlt. $1.00. 832

4012. Brecht, Bertolt. Seven Plays. Bentley, Eric, ed. Grove. 1961. $8.50. 832

4013. Buchner, Georg. Complete Plays and Prose. Hill & Wang. 1963. $3.95; pap. $1.75. 832

4014. Durrenmatt, Friedrich. The Visit. Bowles, Patrick, tr. Grove. 1962. pap. $1.75. 832

4015. Durrenmatt, Friedrich. Die Physiker. (Ger.). Helbing, R. E., ed. Oxford U Pr. 1965. pap. $2.50. 832

4016. Goethe, Johann Wolfgang Von. Faust: A Tragedy in Two Parts. Taylor, Bayard, tr. Oxford U Pr. $3.50. 832

4017. Grillparzer, Franz. Werke. 2 vols. (Ger.). Stapf, P., ed. Tempel. $11.80. 832

4018. Hauptmann, Gerhart. Das Friedensfest-Einsame Menschen. (Ger.). Fischer Bucherei. $1.25. 832

4019. Hochhuth, Rolf. The Deputy. Grove. 1964. $5.95; pap. $1.25. 832

4020. ———. Soldiers. Grove. 1968. $5.95; pap. $1.50. 832
1. German Drama.

4021. Horspiele: Von Ilse Aichinger-Ingeborg Bachmann-Heinrich Böll-Günter Eich-Wolfgang Hildescheimer-Jan Rhys. (Ger.). Fischer Bücherei. $1.25. 832

4022. Lessing, Gotthold E. Dramen. (Ger.). Fischer Bücherei. 1962. pap. $1.25. 832

800 LITERATURE

4023. Wedekind, Frank. The Lulu Plays: Earth Spirit, Pandora's Box, Death and the Devil. Newly translated & with an intro. by Mueller, Carl Richard. Fawcett World. 1967. pap. $0.75. 832
1. German Drama.

4024. Zuckmayer, Carl. Meister Dramen. (Ger.). G B Fischer. 1966. $4.95. 832

4025. Bentley, Eric, ed. Classic Theatre, Five German Plays. Vol. 2. Doubleday. pap. $1.95. 832.08
1. German Drama — Collections.

4026. ———. Five German Plays. Doubleday. 1959. $1.95. 832.08
1. German Drama — Collections.

4027. Corrigan, Robert W., ed. Masterpieces of the Modern German Theatre. Macmillan. 1967. pap. $1.50. 832.08
1. German Drama — Collections.

4028. Garten, H. F. Modern German Drama. Grove. 1962. pap. $2.45. 832.09
1. German Drama — History and Criticism.

4029. Shaw, Leroy, ed. German Theater Today. U of Tex Pr. 1963. $4.50. 832.09
1. German Drama — History and Criticism.

4030. Wiese, Benno Von. Die Deutsche Tragodie von Lessing bis Hebbel. (Ger.). Hamburg. 1958. $8.40. 832.09
1. German Drama — History and Criticism.

4031. Willett, John. The Theatre of Bertolt Brecht. New Directions. 1968. $3.50. 832.09
1. Brecht, Bertolt, 1898-1956. 2. German Drama — History and Criticism.

4032. Esslin, Martin. Brecht: The Man and His Worlds. Norton. 1974. pap. $3.95. 832.91
1. Brecht, Bertolt, 1898-1956.

4033. Fuegi, John. The Essential Brecht. Hennessey. 1972. $12.95. 832.91
1. Brecht, Bertolt, 1898-1956. 2. German Drama, Modern.

4034. Weiss, Peter. The Persecution and Assassination of Jean-Paul Marat As Performed by the Inmates of the Asylum of Charenton Under the Direction of the Marquis de Sade. Atheneum. 1966. $4.50; pap. $2.95. 832.914

833 German Fiction

4035. Boll, Heinrich. Billiards at Half-Past Nine. McGraw. 1973. pap. $2.95. 833

4036. ———. Eighteen Stories. McGraw. $5.95; pap. $2.95. 833

4037. ———. Group Portrait with Lady. Avon. 1974. pap. $1.75. 833

4038. ———. Nicht Nur Zur Weignschtzeit: Der Mann mit Den Messern. (Ger.). Van Nos Reinhold. 1954. pap. $1.95. 833

4039. Boll, Heinrich. Abenteuer Eines Blotbentles un Andere Geschichten. (Ger.). Plant, Richard, ed. Norton. 1957. pap. $1.25. 833

4040. Boll, Heinrich. And Where Were You, Adam? Vennewitz, Leila, tr. McGraw. 1974. pap. $2.95. 833

4041. Brecht, Bertolt. Kalendergeschichten. (Ger.). Gebrüder Weiss. 1966. $4.75. 833

4042. Durrenmatt, Friedrich. Richter und Sein Henken. (Ger.). Gillis, William and Neumaler, J. J., eds. HM. 1964. pap. $3.80. 833

4043. ———. Der Verdacht. (Ger.). Gillis, William, ed. HM. 1964. $3.80. 833

4044. Fallada, Hans. Kleiner Mann - Was Nun? (Ger.). Rowohlt. 1960. pap. $1.00. 833

4045. Fontane, Theodor. Effi Briest. (Ger.). Cooper, W. A., tr. Ungar. $6.50; pap. $2.45. 833

4046. Fontane, Theodor. Irrungen, Wirrungen. (Ger.). Field, G. W., tr. St Martin. 1967. $3.95. 833

4047. Fontane, Theodor. Frau Jenny Treibel. (Ger.). Garland, H. B., ed. St Martin. 1968. $3.95. 833

4048. Frisch, Max. I'm Not Stiller. Random. 1958. pap. $1.95. 833

4049. Frisch, Max. Homo Faber. Ackerman, Paul K., ed. HM. 1973. pap. $4.40. 833

4050. Frisch, Max. Andorra. Bullock, Michael, tr. Hill & Wang. 1964. $3.50; pap. $1.95. 833

4051. Grass, Gunther. Cat and Mouse. Manheim, Ralph, tr. HarBraceJ. 1963. $5.95; pap. $0.95 1964 (NAL). 833

4052. ———. Local Anesthetic. Manheim, Ralph, tr. HarBraceJ. 1970. $6.95; pap. $1.50 1974 (Fawcett World). 833

4053. ———. Tin Drum. Manheim, Ralph, tr. Pantheon. 1963. $8.95; pap. $2.45 1971 (Random). 833

4054. Handke, Peter. Goalie's Anxiety at the Penalty Kick. Roloff, Michael, tr. FS&G. 1972. $6.95. 833

4055. Hesse, Hermann. Der Steppenwolf. (Ger.). Deutscher Taschenbuch Verlag. pap. $1.25. 833

4056. Hesse, Hermann. Beneath the Wheel. Roloff, Michael, tr. from Ger. FS&G. 1968. pap. $1.95. 833

4057. Hesse, Hermann. Gertrude. Rosner, Hilda, tr. FS&G. 1969. $4.95. 833

4058. Hesse, Hermann. Glass Bead Game. Winston, Richard and Winston, Clara, trs. HR&W. 1969. $7.95. 833

4059. Kafka, Franz. Die Romane. Contents: America, The Trial, The Castle. (Ger.). S. Fischer. 1965. $5.20. 833

4060. ———. Das Urteil und Andere Erzählungen: (The Judgment and Other Stories) (Ger.). Fischer Bücherei. pap. $1.50. 833

4061. Langgasser, Elizabeth. Das Unauslöschliche Siegel. (Ger.). Rowohlt. pap. $1.50. 833

4062. Lenz, Siegfried. The German Lesson. Hill & Wang. 1972. $8.95; pap. $1.95 1973 (Avon). 833

4063. ———. The Lightship. Hill & Wang. 1962. $3.50. 833

4064. Mann, Thomas. Bekenntnisse des Hochstaplers, Felix Krull: (Confessions of Felix Krull, the Confidence Man) (Ger.). Fischer. 1962. $4.30. 833

4065. ———. Buddenbrooks. (Ger.). Fischer Bücherei. 1960. pap. $2.00. 833

4066. ———. Magic Mountain. (Ger.). S F Bk. $6.00. 833

4067. ———. Der Tod in Venedig und Andere Erzählungen: (Death in Venice and Other Stories) (Ger.). Fischer Bücherei. 1960. pap. $1.25. 833

4068. Remarque, Erich M. Im Westen Nichts Neues. (Ger.). Verlag Ullstein GMBH. pap. $1.15. 833

4069. Storm, Theodor. Immensee. (Ger.). Zeydel, E. H., ed. Irvington. $6.95; pap. $3.95. 833

4070. Zweig, Arnold. Junge Frau von 1914. (Ger.). Verlag Ullstein GMBH. pap. $1.15. 833

4071. Hofmannstal, Hugo Von. Deutsche Erzahler, Ausgewahlt und Eingeleitet von Hugo von Hofmannsthal. 2 vols. (Ger.). Insel-Verlag. 1946. 833.08
1. German Fiction — Collections.

4072. Wiese, Benno Von, ed. Deutschland Erzählt, Von Büchner bis Hauptmann. (Ger.). Fischer Bücherei. pap. $1.50. 833.08
1. German Short Stories.

4073. ———. Deutschland Erzählt, Von Göethe bis Tieck. (Ger.). Fischer Bücherei. pap. $1.50. 833.08
1. German Short Stories.

4074. ———. Deutschland Erzählt, Von Schnitzler bis Johnson. (Ger.). Fischer Bücherei. 1966. pap. $1.50. 833.08
1. German Short Stories.

4075. Hatfield, Henry C. Thomas Mann. rev. ed. New Directions. 1952. pap. $1.45. 833.09
1. German Fiction — History and Criticism.

4076. Reiss, H. S. Franz Kafka: Eine Betrachtung Seines Werkes. (Ger.). Heidelberg. 1951. $3.30. 833.09
1. German Literature — History and Criticism.

4077. Wiese, Benno Von. Die Deutsche Novelle von Goethe bis Kafka: Interpretationen. (Ger.). 4th ed. Dusseldorf. 1962. $4.90. 833.09
1. German Fiction — History and Criticism.

800 LITERATURE

4078. Berendsohn, Walter A. Thomas Mann: Artist and Partisan in Troubled Times. U of Ala Pr. 1973. $10.00. 833.91
1. Mann, Thomas, 1875-1955.

4079. Wilkinson, Elizabeth M. and Willoughby, Leonard. Goethe: Poet and Thinker. B&N. 1962. $5.50. 838.6(B)
1. Goethe, Johann Wolfgang von, 1749-1832.

4080. Brod, Max. Franz Kafka: A Biography. 2nd ed. Schocken. 1960. $4.50; pap. $1.95. 838.912(B)
1. Kafka, Franz, 1883-1924.

4081. Tank, Kurt L. Günter Grass. Conway, John, tr. Ungar. 1968. $4.50. 838.914
1. Grass, Günter — Criticism and Interpretation.

839 Scandinavian Literature

4082. Bredsdorff, Elias, et al. Introduction to Scandinavian Literature. Greenwood. Repr. 1951. $11.50. 839
1. Scandinavian Literature — History and Criticism.

4083. Godden, Rumer. Hans Christian Andersen. R West. 1955. $10.00. 839
1. Andersen, Hans Christian, 1805-1875.

4084. Topsoe-Jensen, H. G. Scandinavian Literature from Brandes to Our Day. Kraus Repr. 1929. $15.00. 839
1. Scandinavian Literature — History and Criticism.

4085. Weigand, Hermann J. Modern Ibsen. Bks for Libs. Repr. 1953. $14.50; pap. $2.25 (Dutton). 839
1. Ibsen, Henrik, 1828-1906.

4086. Gustafson, Alrik. Six Scandinavian Novelists: Lie, Jacobsen, Heidenstam, Selma Lagerlof, Hamsun, Sigrid Undset. Biblo. 1968. $7.50. 839.5
1. Novelists, Scandinavian. 2. Scandinavian Fiction — History and Criticism.

4087. Hallmundson, Hallberg, ed. An Anthology of Scandinavian Literature, from the Viking Period to the Twentieth Century. Macmillan. 1966. pap. $3.45. 839.5
1. English Literature — Translations from Scandinavian. 2. Scandinavian Literature — Translations from English.

4088. Bergman, Ingmar. Four Screen Plays. S&S. 1969. pap. $2.95. 839.72
1. Moving Picture Plays.

4089. Strindberg, August. Eight Famous Plays. Bjorkman, E. and Erichsen, N., trs. Hillary. 1953. $8.25. 839.72
1. Swedish Drama.

4090. Strindberg, August. Plays. Sprigge, Elizabeth, tr. Doubleday. 1960. pap. $1.95. 839.72

4091. Berendsohn, Walter A. Selma Lagerlof, Her Life and Work. Kennikat. 1931. $6.00. 839.73(B)
1. Lagerlof, Selma, 1858-1940.

4092. Hammarskjold, Dag. Markings. Knopf. 1964. $5.95. 839.78

4093. Migel, Parmenia. Titania: The Biography of Isak Dinesen. Random. 1967. $10.00. 839.81(B)
1. Blixen, Karen, 1885-1962. 2. Dinesen, Isak, 1885-1962.

4094. Ibsen, Henrik. Eleven Plays. Modern Lib. $4.95. 839.82

4095. Downs, Brian. Modern Norwegian Literature, 1860-1918. Cambridge U Pr. 1966. $12.50. 839.83
1. Norwegian Literature — History and Criticism.

840 French Literature

4096. Bree, Germaine. Women Writers in France: Variations on a Theme. Rutgers U Pr. 1973. $5.00. 840
1. Women As Authors.

4097. Hall, Marie-Louise Michaud and Michaud, C. Regis. Lectures Classiques et Modernes. (Fr.). Odyssey Pr. 1956. $3.45. 840
1. French Literature.

840.8 French Literature - Collections

4098. Brée, Germaine. Twentieth Century French Literature: An Anthology of Prose and Poetry. Macmillan. 1962. $8.95. 840.8
1. French Literature — Collections.

4099. Cattanes, Helene and Robert, Osmond T. Promenades Littéraires et Historiques. (Fr.). rev. ed. Har-Row. 1948. $7.95. 840.8
1. French Literature — Collections.

800 LITERATURE

4100. Fellows, Otis E. and Torrey, N. L. The Age of Enlightenment. (Fr.). P-H. 1971 (Appleton-Century-Crofts). $9.50. 840.8
1. French Literature — Collections.

4101. Haac, Oscar A., et al. Points de Vue. (Fr.). Appleton. 1959. $4.50. 840.8
1. French Literature — Collections.

4102. Peyre, Henri. Contemporary French Literature: A Critical Anthology. Har-Row. 1964. $7.75. 840.8
1. French Literature — Collections.

840.9 French Literature - History and Criticism

4103. Abry, Emile, et al. Histoire Illustrée de la Littérature Française. (Fr.). Didier. 1942. pap. $3.10. 840.9
1. French Literature — History and Criticism.

4104. Benac, H. Guide de Ideés Littéraires. (Fr.). Hachette. 1961. $3.95. 840.9
1. French Literature — History and Criticism.

4105. Castex, Pierre-Georges and Surer, Paul. Manuel des Études Littéraires Françaises. (Fr.). Vol. 1. Moyen Age. $2.95; Vol. 2. XVI Siecle. $2.95; Vol. 3. XVII Siecle. $4.50; Vol. 4. XVIII Siecle. $4.50; Vol. 5. XIX Siecle. $4.95; Vol. 6. XX Siecle. $4.95. French & Eur. 840.9
1. French Literature — History and Criticism.

4106. Cazamian, Louis. History of French Literature. Oxford U Pr. 1955. $13.00; pap. $4.95. 840.9
1. French Literature — History and Criticism.

4107. Des Granges, C. M. Histoire de la Littérature Française. (Fr.). French & Eur. $6.50. 840.9
1. French Literature — History and Criticism.

4108. Fowlie, Wallace. A Guide to Contemporary French Literature. Peter Smith. $6.00. 840.9
1. French Literature — History and Criticism.

4109. Lagarde, André and Michard, Laurent. Les Grands Auteurs Français Du Programme. 6 vols. (Fr.). Bordas. $21.10 set. 840.9
1. French Literature — History and Criticism.

4110. Lalou, René. Histoire de las Littérature Française Contemporaine. 2 vols. (Fr.). French & Eur. $7.75. 840.9
1. French Literature — History and Criticism.

4111. Lanson, Gustave and Tuffrau, Paul. Manuel Illustré d'Histoire de la Littérature Française. (Fr.). French & Eur. $7.50. 840.9
1. French Literature — History and Criticism.

4112. Mason, Germaine. A Survey of French Literature. Littlefield. 1964. pap. $1.95. 840.9
1. French Literature.

4113. Nitze, William and D'Argan, E. History of French Literature. 3rd ed. HR&W. 1938. $9.85. 840.9
1. French Literature — History and Criticism.

4114. Peyre, Henri, ed. Lanson, Gustave. Essais de Méthode de Critique et d'Histoire Littéraire. (Fr.). Hachette. 1965. $2.80. 840.9
1. French Literature — History and Criticism.

4115. Pollman, Leo. Sartre and Camus; Literature in Existence. Ungar. 1970. $8.50. 840.9
1. Camus, Albert — Criticism and Interpretation. 2. Sartre, Jean Paul — Criticism and Interpretation.

4116. Shroder, Maurice Z. Icarus. Harvard U Pr. 1961. $5.75. 840.9
1. France — Intellectual Life. 2. French Literature — History and Criticism. 3. Romanticism — France.

4117. Steinhauer, Harry and Walter, Felix, eds. Omnibus of French Literature. 2 vols. Macmillan. 1941. $8.95 ea. 840.9
1. French Literature — History and Criticism.

841 French Poetry

4118. Baudelaire, Charles P. Les Fleurs du Mal. (Fr.). French & Eur. pap. $1.25. 841

4119. Beaumont, Pierre de. La Chanson de Roland. (Fr.). Didier. 1964. pap. $0.63. 841
1. Legends, French. 2. Roland.

4120. ———. Le Cheval Fou. (Fr.). Didier. 1963. $0.63. 841

4121. Gasztold, Carmen B., ed. Prayers from the Ark. (Fr.). French & Eur. $6.95. 841

800 LITERATURE

4122. Giese, Frank S. and Wilder, W. F., eds. French Lyric Poetry. (Fr.). Odyssey Pr. 1965. pap. $2.25. 841

4123. Hugo, Victor. La Légende des Siecles. (Fr.). French & Eur. $8.95; pap. $5.95. 841

4124. Lamartine, Alphonse de. Jocelyn. (Fr.). French & Eur. $9.95; pap. $1.25. 841

4125. ———. Meditations, Poétiques. (Fr.). Larousse. pap. $1.25. 841

4126. Mallarme, Stephanie. Selected Poems. (Fr.). MacIntyre, C. F., tr. U of Cal Pr. 1957. $4.50; pap. $2.45. 841

4127. Prévert, Jacques. Paroles. (Fr.). French & Eur. pap. $4.50. 841

4128. Rimbaud, Arthur. Selected Verse. Bernard, Oliver, tr. Peter Smith. $3.75. 841

4129. Ronsard, Pierre de. Póesies. 2 vols. (Fr.). Larousse. $0.95 ea. 841

4130. Tristan. The Romance of Tristan and Iseult. Penguin. 1970. pap. $1.45. 841

4131. Verlaine, Paul-Marie. Selected Poems. Bilingual, Eng. & Fr.. MacIntyre, C. F., tr. U of Cal Pr. 1948. pap. $2.25. 841

4132. Vigny, Alfred de. Destinées. (Fr.). Larousse. pap. $1.25. 841

4133. Villon, François. Oeuvres Poétiques. (Fr.). Odyssey Pr. 1964. pap. $0.95. 841

4134. Villon, François. Complete Works of François Villon. Bonner, Anthony, tr. McKay. 1960. $3.95. 841

4135. Boase, Alan M. The Poetry of France. 4 vols. Vol. 1. 1400-1600. 1964. $8.50; Vol. 2. 1600-1800. 1973. $17.50; Vol. 3. 1800-1900. 2nd ed. 1967. $8.50; Vol. 4. 1900-1965. 1969. $8.50. B&N. 841.008

4136. Brereton, Geoffrey. Introduction to the French Poets: Villon to the Present Day. B&N. 1957. pap. $6.75. 841.08
1. French Poetry — Collections.

4137. Flores, Angel, ed. Anthology of French Poetry from Nerval to Valéry. English tr. Peter Smith. $4.25. 841.08
1. French Poetry — Collections.

4138. Gide, Andre, ed. Anthologie de la Póesie Francaise. (Fr.). Pantheon. 1949. $7.95. 841.08
1. French Poetry — Collections.

4139. Oxford Book of French Verse, Thirteenth to Twentieth Century. Lucas, St. John, & Jones, P. M., eds.. (Fr.). 2nd ed. Oxford U Pr. $8.00. 841.08
1. French Poetry — Collections.

4140. The Penguin Book of French Verse. Woledge, B., ed.. (Fr.). Penguin. $4.25. 841.08
1. French Poetry — Collections.

4141. Sonnenfeld, Albert, ed. Thirty-Six French Poems. (Fr.). HM. 1961. $2.25. 841.08
1. French Poetry — Collections.

842 French Drama

4142. Anouilh, Jean. L' Alouette. (Fr.). French & Eur. pap. $3.50. 842

4143. ———. Antigone. (Fr.). Larousse. 1966. pap. $1.50. 842

4144. ———. Becket. (Fr.). French & Eur. pap. $4.50. 842

4145. ———. L' Hurluberlu, ou Le Réactionnaire Amoureu. (Fr.). French & Eur. pap. $2.50. 842

4146. ———. Le Voyageur sans Bagages, and Le Bal des Voleurs. (Fr.). French & Eur. pap. $1.25. 842

4147. Beaumarchais, Pierre-Auguste Caron de. The Barber of Seville, and The Marriage of Figaro. Luciani, Vincent, tr. Barron. 1964. pap. $1.75. 842

4148. ———. Le Barbier de Séville, Le Mariage de Figaro. 2 vols. (Fr.). Larousse. pap. $1.25. 842

4149. Beckett, Samuel. Waiting for Godot: Tragi-Comedy in Two Acts. Grove. 1966. pap. $1.95. 842

4150. Camus, Albert. Caligula and Three Other Plays. Knopf. 1958. $5.95; pap. $1.95 (Random). 842

4151. Claudel, Paul. L' Annonce Faite a Marie. (Fr.). French & Eur. pap. $7.50. 842

800 LITERATURE

4152. Cocteau, Jean. Five Plays. Hill & Wang. 1961. pap. $1.95. 842

4153. ———. La Machine Infernale. (Fr.). French & Eur. pap. $3.50. 842

4154. ———. Théâtre. 2 vols. (Fr.). French & Eur. 1948. Vol. 1. pap. $5.50; Vol. 2. pap. $7.50; pap. $8.95 set. 842

4155. Corneille, Pierre. Chief Plays of Corneille. rev. ed. Lockert, L., tr. Princeton U Pr. 1957. $9.50. 842

4156. Fowlie, Wallace. Jean Cocteau: The History of a Poet's Age. Ind U Pr. 1966. $6.95. 842(B)
1. Cocteau, Jean, 1889-1963. 2. Cocteau, Jean — Criticism.

4157. Genet, Jean. The Maids; Deathwatch. Frechtman, Bernard, tr. Grove. 1956. pap. $2.95. 842

4158. Giraudoux, Jean. Amphitryon. (Fr.). French & Eur. pap. $3.50. 842

4159. ———. La Folle de Chaillot. (Fr.). French & Eur. 1960. pap. $4.50. 842

4160. ———. La Guerre de Troi n'aura Pas Lieu. (Fr.). French & Eur. pap. $3.50. 842

4161. ———. Intermezzo. (Fr.). French & Eur. pap. $3.50. 842

4162. Giraudoux, Jean. Four Plays. Valency, Maurice, ed. Hill & Wang. pap. $2.25. 842

4163. Gossman, Lionel. Men and Masks: A Study of Moliere. Johns Hopkins. 1963. $10.00; pap. $2.95. 842
1. Molière, Jean Baptiste, 1622-1673. 2. Molière, Jean Baptiste — Criticism and Interpretation.

4164. Hugo, Victor. Hernani, Librairie. (Fr.). French & Eur. pap. $2.50. 842

4165. ———. Ruy Blas. (Fr.). French & Eur. pap. $1.00. 842

4166. Ionesco, Eugene. Rhinoceros and Other Plays. Prouse, Derek, tr. Peter Smith. $4.00. 842

4167. Labichne, Eugene and Martin, E. Voyage de Monsieur Perrichon. (Fr.). French & Eur. pap. $3.50. 842

4168. Le Sage, Laurent. Jean Giraudoux: His Life and Works. Pa St U Pr. 1959. $8.50. 842(B)
1. Giraudoux, Jean, 1882-1944.

4169. Marivaux, Pierre C. de. Les Fausses Confidences. (Fr.). French & Eur. pap. $1.75. 842

4170. ———. Le Jeu de l'Amour et du Hasard. (Fr.). French & Eur. 1964. pap. $0.95. 842

4171. ———. Le Paysan Parvenu. (Fr.). French & Eur. 1966. pap. $1.75. 842

4172. Molière, Jean B. Complete Works. (Fr.). S F Bk. 1963. $8.50. 842

4173. Musset, Alfred de. Oeuvres Complétes. (Fr.). Larousse. 1963. $9.95. 842

4174. Pagnol, Marcel. Fanny. (Fr.). French & Eur. $7.95. 842

4175. ———. Marius. (Fr.). French & Eur. pap. $3.50. 842

4176. ———. Topaze. (Fr.). French & Eur. pap. $3.50. 842

4177. Prévert, Jacques. Spectacle. (Fr.). French & Eur. $5.95. 842

4178. Racine, Jean B. Complete Works. (Fr.). S F Bk. $8.50. 842

4179. Racine, Jean B. Best Plays. Lockert, Lacy, tr. Princeton U Pr. 1936. pap. $3.95. 842

4180. Romains, Jules. Knock. (Fr.). French & Eur. $6.95; pap. $1.25 (Barron). 842

4181. Rostand, Edmond. Cyrano de Bergerac. (Fr.). Meras, L. R., ed. Har-Row. pap. $3.95. 842

4182. Sartre, Jean-Paul. No Exit, and Flies. Knopf. 1947. $4.95. 842

4183. ———. Théâtre. (Fr.). French & Eur. 1947. $7.95. 842

4184. Bentley, Eric, ed. Classic Theatre, Six French Plays. Vol. 4. Doubleday. pap. $2.95. 842.08
1. French Drama — Collections.

800 LITERATURE

4185. Peyre, Henri and Seronde, Joseph, eds. Nine Classic French Plays. rev. ed. Heath. 1974. pap. $8.95. 842.08
1. French Drama — Collections.

4186. Pucciani, Oreste F., ed. The French Theatre Since 1930. Xerox College. 1954. $9.75. 842.08
1. French Drama — Collections.

4187. Grossvogel, D. E. Twentieth Century French Drama. Gordian. 1966. $7.50; pap. $2.25 1958 (Columbia U Pr). 842.09
1. French Drama — History and Criticism.

4188. Pronko, Leonard C. Avant-Garde: The Experimental Theater in France. U of Cal Pr. 1962. $6.50. 842.09
1. French Drama — History and Criticism.

4189. Freeman, E. The Theatre of Albert Camus: A Critical Study. B&N. 1971. $9.00. 842.9

4190. Corrigan, Robert W. Masterpieces of Modern French Theater. Macmillan. 1967. pap. $1.50. 842.91
1. French Drama, Modern.

843 French Fiction

4191. Aymé, Marcel. Le Passe-Muraille. (Fr.). French & Eur. pap. $7.95. 843

4192. Balzac, Honoré de. César Birotteau. (Fr.). French & Eur. $12.95; pap. $5.95. 843

4193. ———. La Cousine Bette. (Fr.). French & Eur. $6.95; pap. $1.50. 843

4194. ———. Le Curé de Tours. (Fr.). French & Eur. $8.95; pap. $3.95. 843

4195. ———. Eugénie Grandet. (Fr.). French & Eur. pap. $1.75. 843

4196. ———. Le Lys dans la Vallée. (Fr.). French & Eur. $12.95; pap. $1.75. 843

4197. ———. Le Pére Goriot. (Fr.). French & Eur. $5.95; pap. $1.75. 843

4198. Camus, Albert. La Chute. (Fr.). French & Eur. $6.95. 843

4199. ———. L' Etranger. (Fr.). French & Eur. $7.50. 843

4200. ———. L' Exile et le Royaume. (Fr.). French & Eur. $7.50. 843

4201. ———. L' Homme Revolté. (Fr.). French & Eur. 1951. $8.95; pap. $2.50. 843

4202. Chateaubriand, François René de. Atala. (Fr.). P-H. pap. $3.50. 843

4203. ———. René. (Fr.). Larousse. $1.25. 843

4204. Daninos, Pierre. Les Carnets du Major Thompson. (Fr.). French & Eur. $3.50; pap. $1.25. 843

4205. Daudet, Alphonse. Lettres de Mon Moulin. (Fr.). French & Eur. $1.75. 843

4206. ———. Le Petit Chose. (Fr.). French & Eur. $4.95; pap. $0.95. 843

4207. Daudet, Alphonse. Tartarin de Tarascon. (Fr.). Siepmann, Otto, ed. St Martin. pap. $2.50. 843

4208. Dumas, Alexandre. Les Trois Mousquetaires. (Fr.). French & Eur. $11.90; pap. $3.95. 843

4209. Flaubert, Gustave. Madame Bovary. (Fr.). French & Eur. pap. $1.75. 843

4210. ———. Salammbô. (Fr.). French & Eur. $5.95; pap. $1.75. 843

4211. ———. Trois Contes. (Fr.). French & Eur. $9.95; pap. $1.25. 843

4212. France, Anatole. Le Crime de Sylvestre Bonnard. (Fr.). Braun, S. and Bree, G., eds. French & Eur. 1958. $4.50. 843

4213. Gary, Romain. L' Education Européenne. (Fr.). French & Eur. pap. $2.95. 843

4214. Gide, André. L' Immoraliste. (Fr.). French & Eur. $7.50. 843

4215. ———. La Porte Étroite. (Fr.). French & Eur. $7.50. 843

4216. ———. Si le Grain Ne Meurt. (Fr.). French & Eur. $7.95; pap. $0.95. 843

4217. ———. La Symphonie Pastorale. (Fr.). French & Eur. $6.95. 843

800 LITERATURE

4218. Guerard, Albert J. André Gide. rev. ed. Harvard U Pr. 1969. $6.95. 843(B)
1. Gide, André, 1869-1951.

4219. Hugo, Victor. Les Miserables. (Fr.). Dodd. 1925. $5.50; pap. $3.75 1970 (Amsco Sch). 843

4220. ———. Notre Dame de Paris. (Fr.). French & Eur. $9.95; pap. $1.75. 843

4221. ———. Quatre-Vingt Treize. (Fr.). French & Eur. $9.95; pap. $1.75. 843

4222. LaFayette, Marie M. de. La Princesse de Clèves. (Fr.). French & Eur. pap. $1.95. 843

4223. La Fontaine, Jean de. Fables. (Fr.). P-H. 1967. pap. $2.50. 843

4224. La Fontaine, Jean de. Selected Fables. Clark, Eunice, tr. Dover. 1968. pap. $1.50. 843

4225. Lamartine, Alphonse de. Graziella and Raphael. (Fr.). French & Eur. $8.95; pap. $8.95. 843

4226. Le Sage, Alain-René. Gil Blas. 2 vols. (Fr.). French & Eur. pap. $7.50. 843

4227. ———. Turcaret. (Fr.). French & Eur. pap. $0.95. 843

4228. Loti, Pierre. Pêcheur d'islande. (Fr.). French & Eur. $6.50. 843

4229. Malraux, André. La Condition Humaine. (Fr.). French & Eur. $9.95; pap. $0.95 (Larousse). 843

4230. Maupassant, Guy de. Contes Choisis. (Fr.). Larousse. pap. $1.25. 843

4231. ———. Pierre et Jean. (Fr.). French & Eur. pap. $1.25. 843

4232. Mauriac, François. Désert de l'Amour. (Fr.). French & Eur. 1961. $7.50. 843

4233. ———. Le Noeud de Vipères. (Fr.). French & Eur. $8.95. 843

4234. ———. Thérèse Desqueyroux. (Fr.). French & Eur. $7.50. 843

4235. Maurois, André. Prometheus: The Life of Balzac. Denny, Norman, tr. Har-Row. 1966. $10.00. 843(B)
1. Balzac, Honoré de, 1799-1850.

4236. Merimée, Prosper. Colomba. (Fr.). French & Eur. pap. $1.25. 843

4237. Montherlant, Henri de. Célibataires. (Fr.). French & Eur. $3.50. 843

4238. Musset, Alfred de. La Confession d'un Enfant du Siècle. (Fr.). French & Eur. pap. $3.95. 843

4239. Prévost, Abbé. Manon Lescaut. (Fr.). French & Eur. pap. $1.25. 843

4240. Proust, Marcel. Combray. (Fr.). P-H (Appleton-Century-Crofts). pap. $2.70. 843

4241. Rabelais, François. Gargantua. (Fr.). French & Eur. pap. $1.75. 843

4242. ———. Pantagruel. (Fr.). French & Eur. $2.50; pap. $1.75. 843

4243. Renard, Jules. Poil de Carotte. (Fr.). St Martin. 1968. $3.95. 843

4244. Rolland, Romain. Jean-Christophe. 3 vols. (Fr.). French & Eur. pap. $4.50. 843

4245. Rousseau, Jean-Jacques. Emile. (Fr.). French & Eur. $9.95; $5.95. 843

4246. ———. Julie, ou La Nouvelle Héloise. (Fr.). French & Eur. $12.95; pap. $5.95. 843

4247. Sagan, François. Bonjour Tristesse. (Fr.). French & Eur. $7.50; pap. $0.95 (Popular Lib). 843

4248. Saint Exupéry, Antoine de. Petit Prince. (Fr.). French & Eur. $5.95; pap. $4.50. 843

4249. ———. Terre des Hommes. (Fr.). French & Eur. $7.50. 843

4250. Sand, George. La Mare au Diable. (Fr.). French & Eur. $9.95; pap. $5.95. 843

4251. Starkie, Enid. Flaubert. Atheneum. 1967. $10.00. 843(B)
1. Flaubert, Gustave, 1821-1880.

4252. Stendhal. La Chartreuse de Parme. (Fr.). French & Eur. $5.95. 843

4253. ———. Le Rouge et le Noir. (Fr.). French & Eur. pap. $5.95. 843

4254. Vercors. Le Silence de la Mer. (Fr.). French & Eur. pap. $3.50. 843

800 LITERATURE

4255. Verne, Jules. Le Tour de Monde en 80 Jours. (Fr.). St Martin. pap. $1.75. 843

4256. ———. Vingt Mille Lieues Sous les Mers. (Fr.). St Martin. pap. $2.50. 843

4257. ———. Voyage au Centre de la Terre. (Fr.). St Martin. 1962. pap. $1.75. 843

4258. Voltaire, Francois M. de. Candide. (Fr.). HR&W. 1969. $3.75. 843

4259. Zola, Émile. L' Assommoir. (Fr.). French & Eur. pap. $3.50. 843

4260. ———. Germinal. (Fr.). NAL. 1970. $1.75. 843

4261. ———. Nana. (Fr.). Macmillan. 1962 (Collier). pap. $0.65. 843

4262. Fowlie, Wallace, ed. French Stories. (Fr.). Bantam. pap. $1.25. 843.08
1. Short Stories, French.

4263. Yale University, Dept. of French. Contes et Nouvelles D'aujourd 'hui. (Fr.). Har-Row. 1966. $5.95. 843.08
1. Short Stories — French.

4264. Levin, Harry. Gates of Horn. Oxford U Pr. 1963. $10.50; pap. $3.95. 843.09
1. French Fiction — History and Criticism. 2. Realism in Literature.

4265. Peyre, Henri. French Novelists of Today. Oxford U Pr. 1967. pap. $3.50. 843.09
1. French Fiction — History and Criticism.

4266. Turnell, Martin. The Art of French Fiction. New Directions. 1968. pap. $2.95. 843.09
1. French Fiction — History and Criticism.

4267. Brée, Germaine and Guiton, Margaret. The Age of Fiction. Rutgers U Pr. 1957. $7.50. 843.91
1. French Fiction — 20th Century.

844 French Essays

4268. Camus, Albert. The Myth of Sisyphus, and Other Essays. Knopf. 1955. $5.95; pap. $1.65 (Random). 844
1. French Essays.

4269. ———. Resistance, Rebellion and Death. Modern Lib. 1963. $2.95. 844
1. French Essays.

4270. Frame, Donald. Montaigne: A Biography. HarBraceJ. 1965. $10.00. 844(B)
1. Montaigne, Michel Eyguem de, 1533-1592.

4271. Montaigne, Michel E. de. Essais. 2 vols. (Fr.). French & Eur. pap. $11.95. 844
1. French Essays.

4272. ———. Selected Essays. Modern Lib. $2.45. 844
1. French Essays.

4273. Montesquieu, Charles de. Oeuvres Complètes. 2 vols. (Fr.). French & Eur. $37.50. 844

848 French Miscellany

4274. Griffiths, Richard, ed. Claudel: A Reappraisal. Dufour. 1970. $13.95. 848
1. Claudel, Paul, 1868-1955. 2. Claudel, Paul — Criticism and Interpretation.

4275. La Bruyère, Jean de. Les Caractéres. (Fr.). French & Eur. $9.95; pap. $1.50. 848

4276. Lanson, Gustave. Voltaire. Wagoner, Robert A., tr. Wiley. 1966. $9.95; pap. $5.50. 848(B)
1. Voltaire, François, 1694-1778.

4277. La Rochefoucald, François Duc De. Maximes. (Fr.). French & Eur. pap. $1.75. 848

4278. Malraux, André. Anti-Memoirs. French & Eur. 1967. $12.50. 848
1. Gaulle, Charles De, President of France, 1890-1970. 2. Malraux, André, 1901- 3. Mao Tŝe-tung, 1893- | 4. Nehru, Jawaharlal, 1889-1964.

4279. Maurois, André. Victor Hugo. French & Eur. $7.50. 848(B)
1. Hugo, Victor Marie, Comte, 1802-1885.

4280. Pascal, Blaise. Pensées. (Fr.). French & Eur. $8.95; pap. $1.75. 848

4281. Rabelais, François. Portable Rabelais. Putnam, S., ed. & tr. Viking Pr. 1946. $4.95; pap. $2.95. 848

4282. Voltaire, François M. de. Portable Voltaire. Redman, Ben R., ed. Viking Pr. 1949. $6.50; pap. $2.95. 848

4283. Josephson, Matthew. Stendhal; or the Pursuit of Happiness. Russell. 1969. $14.50. 848.7(B)
1. Beyle, Marie Henri, 1783-1842.

800 LITERATURE

4284. Cohn, Ruby. Back to Beckett. Princeton U Pr. 1974. $12.50. 848.9
1. Beckett, Samuel, 1906-

4285. Colette, Sidonie. Earthly Paradise: Colette's Autobiography Drawn from the Writings of Her Lifetime. Phelps, Robert, ed. Briffault, H., et al, trs. FS&G. 1966. $6.95; pap. $2.65. 848.9(B)
1. Colette, Sidonie, 1873-1954.

4286. Kenner, Hugh. A Reader's Guide to Samuel Beckett. FS&G. 1973. $7.95. 848.9
1. Beckett, Samuel, 1906-

850 Italian Literature

4287. Wilkins, Ernest H. History of Italian Literature. Harvard U Pr. 1954. $13.50. 850.9
1. Italian Literature — History and Criticism.

4288. Dante Alighieri. The Divine Comedy. Carlyle, John A., et al, trs. Modern Lib. pap. $1.95. 851

4289. Dante Alighieri. Dante's Lyric Poetry. 2 vols. Foster, Kenelm and Boyde, Patrick, trs. Oxford U Pr. 1967. $34.00. 851

4290. Quasimodo, Salvatore. Selected Writings of Salvatore Quasimodo. Mandelbaum, Allen, tr. Funk & W. 1969. pap. $2.95. 851

4291. De Luca, A. Michael and Giulianos, William. Selections from Italian Poetry. Harvey. 1966. $4.89. 851.08
1. Italian Poetry — Collections.

4292. Betti, Ugo. Crime on Goat Island. Reed, Henry, tr. Chandler Pub. 1961. pap. $0.95. 852

4293. Goldoni, Carlo. Three Comedies: (Mine Hostess; The Boors; The Fan) Oxford U Pr. 1961. $2.90. 852
1. Italian Drama.

4294. Pirandello, Luigi. Naked Masks: Five Plays. Dutton. 1952. $3.25. 852
1. Italian Drama.

4295. Bentley, Eric, ed. Classic Theatre, Six Italian Plays. Vol. 1. Doubleday. pap. $1.45. 852.08
1. Italian Drama — Collections.

4296. ———. Genius of the Italian Theatre. NAL. pap. $0.95. 852.08
1. Italian Drama — Collections.

4297. Corrigan, Robert W., ed. Masterpieces of the Modern Italian Theatre. Macmillan. 1965. pap. $1.50. 852.08
1. Italian Drama — Collections.

4298. Pacifici, Sergio J. The Modern Italian Novel from Manzoni to Svevo. S Ill U Pr. 1967. $4.95. 853.9
1. Italian Fiction — History and Criticism.

4299. Leopardi, Giacomo. Poems and Prose. Flores, Angel, ed. Ind U Pr. 1966. pap. $2.95. 858
1. Italian Essays. 2. Italian Poetry.

4300. Michelangelo. Complete Poems and Selected Letters. Modern Lib. $2.45. 858
1. Italian Letters. 2. Italian Poetry.

860 Spanish Literature

4301. Castro, Americo. Iberoamérica. (Sp.). 4th ed. HR&W. 1971. pap. $5.25. 860
1. Spanish America — Civilization.

4302. Hays, H. R., ed. Twelve Spanish-American Poets: An Anthology. Beacon Pr. 1972. $12.50; pap. $3.95. 860
1. Spanish-American Poetry.

4303. Anderson-Imbert, Enrique and Florit, E. Literatura Hispanoamericana, Antologia e Introducción Historica. 2 vols. (Sp.). rev. ed. HR&W. 1970. pap. $7.75 ea. 860.08
1. Spanish-American Literature (Selections: Extracts, etc.).

4304. Chandler, Richard E. and Schwartz, Kessel, eds. New Anthology of Spanish Literature. 2 vols. La State U Pr. 1967. Vol. 1. $7.50; Vol. 2. $8.50. 860.08
1. Spanish Literature — Collections.

4305. Del Río, Amelia and Del Río, Angel. Antología General de la Literatura Española. 2 vols. (Sp.). rev ed. HR&W. 1960. $13.95. 860.08
1. Spanish Literature — Collections.

4306. Onís, Harriet de, ed. The Golden Land: An Anthology of Latin American Folklore. Knopf. 1961. $6.95. 860.08
1. Folk-Lore, Brazilian. 2. Folk-Lore, Spanish American.

800 LITERATURE

4307. Resnick, Seymour and Pasmantier, Jeanne, eds. Anthology of Spanish Literature in English Translation. 2 vols. Ungar. 1958. $15.00. 860.08
1. Spanish Literature — Collections.

4308. Alborg, Juan Luis. Hora Actual Dela Novela Espanola. Taurus. 860.9
1. Spanish Literature — History and Criticism.

4309. Brenan, Gerald. The Literature of the Spanish People. 2nd ed. Cambridge U Pr. 1953. $16.50. 860.9
1. Spanish Literature — History and Criticism.

4310. Chandler, Richard E. and Schwartz, Kessel. New History of Spanish Literature. La State U Pr. 1961. $12.00. 860.9
1. Spanish Literature — History and Criticism.

4311. Corre, Gustavo. El Simbolismo Religioso en las Novelas de Perez Galdos. Editoria Gredos. 860.9
1. Spanish Literature — History and Criticism.

4312. Del Río, Angel. Historia de la Literatura Española. 2 vols. (Sp.). rev. ed. HR&W. 1963. $8.30. 860.9
1. Spanish Literature — History and Criticism.

4313. Deriquer, Martin. Aproximaciónal Quixote. Editoria Teide. 860.9
1. Spanish Literature — History and Criticism.

4314. Franco, Jean. An Introduction to Spanish-American Literature. Cambridge U Pr. 1969. $13.95. 860.9
1. Spanish-American Literature — History and Criticism.

4315. Northup, George T. An Introduction to Spanish Literature. 3rd ed. U of Chicago Pr. 1960. $10.00; pap. $3.95. 860.9
1. Spanish Literature — History and Criticism.

4316. Torrente, Ballesteros. Panorama de la Literatura Espanola. Ediciones Guadarrama. 860.9
1. Spanish Literature — History and Criticism.

4317. Torres-Rioseco, Arturo. Epic of Latin American Literature. U of Cal Pr. 1942. pap. $2.25. 860.9
1. Brazilian Literature — History and Criticism. 2. Spanish-American Literature — History and Criticism.

861 Spanish Poetry

4318. Berceo, Gonzalo de. Milagros de Nuestra Señora. (Sp.). French & Eur. pap. $2.95. 861

4319. Darío, Ruben. Azul and Otras Versos. S F Bk. $3.00. 861

4320. Darío, Ruben. Selected Poems of Ruben Darío. Kemp, Lysander, tr. U of Tex Pr. 1965. $5.75. 861

4321. García Lorca, Federico and Jimenez, Juan Ramon. Selected Poems. Bly, Robert, ed. Beacon Pr. 1973. $7.95; pap. $2.95. 861

4322. Godoy Alcayaga, Lucilla. Selected Poems of Gabriela Mistral. Dana, Doris, ed. & tr. Johns Hopkins. 1971. $10.00. 861
1. Spanish Poetry.

4323. Gongora, Luis de. Obras Completas. Schoenhof. $14.50. 861

4324. Guillén, Jorge. Cantico. (Sp.). Di Giovanni, N. T., ed. Little. 1965. pap. $2.95. 861

4325. Hernandez, Jose. Gaucho Martin Fierro. Carrino, Frank G. and Carlos, Albert J., eds. Ward, Catherine E., tr. State U NY Pr. 1967. $10.00. 861

4326. Machado, Antonio. Poesías Completas. (Sp.). French & Eur. $9.95; pap. $1.25. 861

4327. Machado, Antonio. Juan de Mairena: Epigrams, Maxims, Memoranda, and Memoirs of an Apocryphal Professor. Belitt, Ben, tr. U of Cal Pr. 1963. $4.95; pap. $1.50. 861

4328. Martí, José. Páginas Escogidas. Collection. (Sp.). French & Eur. pap. $1.25. 861

4329. Mistral, Gabriela. Selected Poems. Hughes, L., tr. Ind U Pr. 1957. $3.50; pap. $1.75. 861

800 LITERATURE

4330. Neruda, Pablo. Selected Poems. Belitt, Ben, ed. Grove. 1961. pap. $2.95. 861

4331. Salinas, Pedro. Sea of San Juan. Brandon. $2.95. 861

4332. Simpson, Lesley B., tr. The Poem of the Cid. U of Cal Pr. 1957. pap. $1.95. 861

4333. Smith, Colin, ed. Poema de Mio Cid. (Sp.). Oxford U Pr. 1972. $12.75. 861

4334. Valle-Inclán, Ramón Del. Sonata de Primavera. (Sp.). HR&W. 1941. $4.20. 861

4335. Flores, Angel. Anthology of Spanish Poetry from Garcilaso to García Lorca: In English Translation with Spanish Originals. Doubleday. pap. $1.45. 861.08
1. Spanish Poetry — Collections.

4336. Hernandez, Miguel. El Rayo Que No Cesa. (Sp.). Austral. 861.08
1. Spanish Poetry — Collections.

4337. The Oxford Book of Spanish Verse: 13th Century to 20th Century. Fitzmaurice-Kelly, James & Trend, J. B., ed.. (Sp.). 2nd ed. Oxford U Pr. 1940. $8.00. 861.08

4338. Resnick, Seymour. Selections from Spanish Poetry. Harvey. 1962. $3.50. 861.08
1. Spanish Poetry — Collections.

4339. ———. Spanish-American Poetry: A Bilingual Selection. Harvey. 1964. $4.29. 861.08
1. Spanish-American Poetry — Collections.

4340. Turnbull, Eleanor L., ed. Ten Centuries of Spanish Poetry: An Anthology in English Verse. Johns Hopkins. 1969. $12.00; pap. $3.95. 861.08
1. Spanish Poetry — Collections.

4341. Barea, Arturo. Lorca, the Poet and His People. Cooper Sq. 1973. $6.00. 861.09
1. Garcia Lorca, Federico, 1899-1936.

4342. Young, Howard T. The Victorious Expression: A Study of Four Contemporary Spanish Poets, Unamuno, Machado, Jiménez and Lorca. U of Wis Pr. 1964. $8.50; pap. $3.50. 861.09
1. Spanish Poetry — History and Criticism.

4343. Jiménez, Juan Ramon. Three Hundred Poems, 1903-1953. Roach, Eloise, tr. U of Tex Pr. 1962. $10.00. 861.64

862 Spanish Drama

4344. Benevente, Jacinto. Bonds of Interest. Alpeen, Hymen, ed. Underhill, J. G., tr. Ungar. 1967. $4.50; pap. $1.75. 862

4345. Benevente, Jacinto. Malquerida. Manchester, Paul T., ed. Irvington. $3.50. 862

4346. Buero Vallejo, Antonio. La Doble Historia del Doctor Valmy. French & Eur. 862

4347. ———. Hoy Es Fiesta. (Sp.). Heath. 1967. $3.50. 862

4348. ———. Las Meninas. Scribner. 1963. $2.95. 862

4349. Buero Vallejo, Antonio. Historia de una Escalera. (Sp.). Sanchez, Jose, ed. Scribner. 1955. pap. $2.95. 862

4350. Buero Vallejo, Antonio. En la Ardiente Obscuridad. (Sp.). Wofsy, Samuel A., ed. Scribner. 1954. pap. $2.95. 862

4351. Calderón de la Barca, Pedro. Four Plays. Honig, Edwin, tr. Hill & Wang. 1961. pap. $2.95. 862

4352. Casona, Alejandro. La Barca Sin Pescador. (Sp.). Balseiro, J. A., ed. Owre, J. R., tr. Oxford U Pr. 1955. $2.95. 862

4353. Casona, Alejandro. La Dama del Alba. (Sp.). Rodriguez Castellano, Juan, ed. Scribner. 1947. $3.50. 862

4354. De Rojas, Fernando. Celestina. (Sp.). Hispanic Soc. 1970. $7.50. 862

4355. García Lorca, Federico. Three Tragedies: Blood Wedding; Yerma; House of Bernarda Alba. New Directions. 1956. pap. $1.75. 862

4356. Lope de Vega, Felix de. Five Plays. Hill & Wang. 1961. $4.50; pap. $2.45. 862

4357. Usigli, Rodolfo. El Gesticulador: Pieza para Demogogos en Tres Actos. (Sp.). Ballinger, Rex E., ed. P-H. 1963 (Appleton-Century-Crofts). pap. $3.25. 862

4358. Colecchia, Francesca Maria. Selected Latin American One-Act Plays. U of Pittsburgh Pr. 1974. pap. $3.95. 862.04
1. Spanish-American Drama.

800 LITERATURE

4359. Benedikt, Michael and Wellwarth, George. Modern Spanish Theatre: An Anthology of Plays. Dutton. 1968. pap. $2.95. 862.08
1. Spanish Drama — Collections.

4360. Bentley, Eric, ed. Classic Theatre, Six Spanish Plays. Vol. 3. Doubleday. pap. $2.50. 862.08
1. Spanish Drama — Collections.

4361. Corrigan, Robert W., ed. Masterpieces of the Modern Spanish Theatre. Macmillan. 1967. pap. $1.50. 862.08
1. Spanish Drama — Collections.

4362. Flynn, Gerard C. Manuel Tamayo y Baus. Twayne. 1973. $6.95. 862.5

4363. Sastre, Alfonso. Teatro Selecto. Aquilar. 862.9
1. Spanish Drama — History and Criticism.

4364. Shergold, N. D. History of the Spanish Stage from Medieval Times Until the End of the Seventeenth Century. Oxford U Pr. 1967. $20.50. 862.9
1. Spanish Drama — History and Criticism.

863 Spanish Fiction

4365. Ayala, Francisco. El Rapto. Boring, Phyllis Zatlim, ed. H-B. 1971. $2.95. 863

4366. Azorin. Dona Ines. (Sp.). Irvington. pap. $4.95. 863

4367. Azuela, Mariano. Los de Abajo. (Sp.). Englekirk, J. E. and Kiddle, L. B., eds. P-H. 1971. pap. $2.25. 863

4368. Baroja, Pio. Las Cuidades. Alianza Editorial. 863

4369. ———. Zalacain, e Aventurero. (Sp.). HM. 1926. pap. $1.95. 863

4370. Casalduero, Joaquin. Vida y Obra de Galdos. Editorial Gredos. 863

4371. Cela, Camilo José. La Familia de Pascual Duarte. (Sp.). P-H. 1961. pap. $3.25. 863

4372. Cervantes, Miguel de. Don Quijote. (Sp.). S F Bk. $4.00. 863

4373. ———. Novelas Ejemplares. (Sp.). S F Bk. $3.00. 863

4374. Delibes, Miguel. El Camino. (Sp.). HR&W. $3.45. 863

4375. ———. Cinco Horas con Mario. French & Eur. 863

4376. Gallegos, Romulo. Doña Bárbara. (Sp.). Dunham, Lowell, ed. P-H. 1961 (Appleton-Century-Crofts). pap. $4.50. 863

4377. Gironella, José María. Los Cipreses Creen en Dios. (Sp.). HR&W. 1969. $3.75. 863

4378. Guiraldes, Ricardo. Don Segundo Sombra. (Sp.). Dellepiane, Angelo B., tr. P-H. 1971. pap. $5.25. 863

4379. Howes, Barbara, ed. The Eye of the Heart: Short Stories from Latin America. Bobbs. 1973. pap. $5.95. 863
1. Spanish Fiction. 2. Spanish-American Fiction.

4380. Jiménez, Juan Ramón. Platero and I. Roach, Gloise, tr. U of Tex Pr. $4.75. 863

4381. Pérez Galdós, Benito. Gloria. (Sp.). French & Eur. $3.95 set. 863

4382. ———. Misericordia. (Sp.). HR&W. $4.45. 863

4383. Pérez Galdós, Benito. Doña Perfecta. DeOnis, Harriet, tr. Barron. pap. $1.50. 863

4384. Sabato, Ernest R. Tunel. (Sp.). Pérez, L. C., ed. Macmillan. 1965. pap. $2.50. 863

4385. Sarmiento, Domingo F. Facundo. (Sp.). Mayer, James, tr. O'Hara. 1974. $10.00. 863

4386. Sender, Ramón J. Mosén Millán. Heath. 1964. pap. $2.50. 863

4387. Sender, Ramón J. Cronica del Alba. (Sp.). Sender, Florence H., ed. Irvington. pap. $3.95. 863

4388. Unamuno, Miguel de. Galdós' Novelista Moderno. Kerrigan, Anthony, tr. Regnery. pap. $1.95. 863

4389. Unamuno, Miguel de. Niebla. Valdés, Mario J., ed. P-H. 1969. $4.25. 863

800 LITERATURE

4390. Nelson, Lowry, Jr., ed. Cervantes: A Collection of Critical Essays. P-H. 1969. $6.50; pap. $1.95.   863.08
1. Cervantes Saavedra, Miguel de, 1547-1616. 2. Spanish Fiction — History and Criticism.

4391. Eoff, Sherman. Modern Spanish Novel. NYU Pr. 1961. $8.50; pap. $1.95.
863.09
1. Literature, Comparative. 2. Spanish Fiction — History and Criticism.

4392. Ledesma, Francisco N. Cervantes: The Man and the Genius. Charterhouse. 1972. $9.95.   863.3(B)
1. Cervantes Saavedra, Miguel de, 1547-1616.

4393. Tunamuno. Vida de Don Quixote y Sancho. Espasa-Calpe.   868
1. Spanish Literature.

870 Latin Literature

4394. Davenport, Basil, ed. Portable Roman Reader. Viking Pr. 1951. $6.50; pap. $2.95.
870.8
1. Latin Literature — Collections.

4395. Guinagh, Kevin and Dorjahn, Alfred P., eds. Latin Literature in Translation. 2nd ed. McKay. 1952. $7.95.   870.8
1. Latin Literature — Collections.

4396. Duff, John W. Literary History of Rome. 2 vols. Duff, M. A., ed. Vol. 1. From the Origins to the Close of the Golden Age. 3rd ed. 1964. $8.75; pap. $2.95; Vol. 2. Silver Age: from Tiberius to Hadrian. 2nd ed. 1960. $10.00; pap. $4.25 3rd ed. 1964. B&N. 870.9
1. Latin Literature — History and Criticism.

4397. Frank, Tenney. Life and Literature in the Roman Republic. U of Cal Pr. 1930. pap. $2.65.   870.9
1. Latin Literature — History and Criticism. 2. Rome — Civilization.

4398. Hadas, Moses. A History of Latin Literature. Columbia U Pr. 1952. $14.00; pap. $2.95.   870.9
1. Latin Literature — History and Criticism.

4399. Hamilton, Edith. Roman Way. Norton. 1932. $6.95; pap. $1.25.   870.9
1. Latin Literature — History and Criticism. 2. Rome — Civilization.

4400. Rose, Herbert J. Handbook of Latin Literature. Dutton. $7.95; pap. $2.45.   870.9
1. Latin Literature — History and Criticism.

871 Latin Poetry

4401. Britain, Frederick, ed. Penguin Book of Latin Verse. Bilingual. (Lat. & Eng.). Peter Smith. 1962. pap. $4.00.   871.08
1. Latin Poetry — Collections.

4402. The Oxford Book of Latin Verse from the Earliest Fragments to the End of the 5th Century. (Lat.). Oxford U Pr. 1912. $11.25.
871.08
1. Latin Poetry — Collections.

4403. Waddell, Helen. The Wandering Scholars. 7th ed. B&N. 1968. $6.50.   871.08
1. Goliards. 2. Latin Poetry, Medieval and Modern.

4404. Mendell, Clarence. Latin Poetry: The Age of Rhetoric and Satire. Shoe String. 1967. $6.00.   871.09
1. Latin Poetry — History and Criticism.

4405. Sellar, William Y. Roman Poets of the Republic. 3rd ed. Biblo. 1889. $12.50.   871.09
1. Latin Poetry — History and Criticism.

4406. Lucretius Carus, Titus. De Rerum Natura. (Lat.). Leonard, William E. and Smith, Stanley B., eds. U of Wis Pr. 1942. $12.50.   871.1
1. Latin Poetry.

4407. Otis, Brooks. Ovid As an Epic Poet. 2nd ed. Cambridge U Pr. 1971. $19.50. 871.2
1. Latin Poetry — History and Criticism. 2. Ovidius Naso, Publius — Criticism, Interpretation, etc.

4408. Ovidius Naso, Publius. Metamorphoses. 2 vols. (Lat.). Harvard U Pr. $5.50 ea.   871.2
1. Latin Poetry.

872 Latin Drama

4409. Duckworth, George E., ed. Complete Roman Drama. 2 vols. Random. 1942. $20.00.
872.08
1. Latin Drama — Collections.

4410. Dorey, T. A. and Dudley, D. R., eds. Roman Drama. Basic. 1965. $5.95.   872.09
1. Latin Drama — History and Criticism.

800 LITERATURE

4411. Duckworth, George E. The Nature of Roman Comedy. Princeton U Pr. 1971. $17.50; pap. $3.95.   872.09
1. Latin Drama (Comedy) — History and Criticism.

873-874 Latin Epic Poetry, Fiction and Lyric Poetry

4412. Otis, Brooks. Virgil: A Study in Civilized Poetry. Oxford U Pr. 1964. $11.00.   873.1
1. Latin Poetry — History and Criticism. 2. Vergilius Maro, Publius — Criticism and Interpretation, etc.

4413. Vergilius Maro, Publius. Eclogues, Georgics, Aeneid, Minor Poems. 2 vols. (Lat.). Harvard U Pr. $5.50 ea.   873.1
1. Latin Poetry.

4414. Vergilius Maro, Publius. The Aeneid: A Verse Translation. Humphries, Rolfe, tr. Scribner. 1951. $7.95; pap. $2.95.   873.1
1. Latin Poetry.

4415. Catallus, Gaius Valerius. Works. (Lat.). Merrill, Elmer T., ed. Harvard U Pr. 1893. $6.00.   874.1
1. Latin Poetry. 2. Pervigilium Veneris. 3. Tibullus.

4416. Catullus, Gaius Valerius. Complete Poetry. Copley, Frank O., tr. U of Mich Pr. 1957. pap. $1.95.   874.1
1. Latin Poetry.

4417. Horatius Flaccus, Quintus. Odes and Epodes. (Lat.). Harvard U Pr. $5.50.   874.5
1. Latin Poetry.

4418. ———. Satires, Epistles, and Ars Poetica. (Lat.). Harvard U Pr. $4.00.   874.5
1. Latin Poetry.

4419. Martialis, Marcus Valerius. The Epigrams. 2 vols. (Lat.). Harvard U Pr. $5.50 ea.   874.5
1. Latin Poetry.

875 Latin Orations

4420. Cicero, Marcus Tullius. Speeches. 2 vols. (Lat.). Harvard U Pr. 1958. $4.00 ea.   875.2

4421. ———. Tusculan Disputations. (Lat.). Harvard U Pr. 1927. $5.50.   875.2
1. Latin Orations.

877 Latin Satire and Humor

4422. Highet, Gilbert. Juvenal the Satirist. Oxford U Pr. 1954. $7.20; pap. $2.95.   877.7
1. Juvenalis, Decimus Junius. 2. Latin Literature. 3. Satire, Latin.

4423. Juvenalis, Decimus Junius. Satires. Mazzaro, Jerome, tr. U of Mich Pr. 1965. $5.00.   877.7
1. Latin Literature. 2. Satire, Latin.

878 Latin Miscellany

4424. Caesar, Gaius Julius. Gallic War. (Lat.). Harvard U Pr. $5.50.   878.1
1. Latin Literature.

4425. Sallustius Crispus, Gaius. War with Catiline, War with Jugurtha, etc. (Lat.). Harvard U Pr. $5.50.   878.2
1. Latin Literature.

4426. Livius, Titus. Roman History with an English Translation. Bks. 1 & 5. (Lat.). Foster, B. O., tr. Harvard U Pr. $5.50.   878.4
1. Latin Literature.

4427. Tacitus, Cornelius. Dialogus, Agricola, Germania. (Lat.). Harvard U Pr. $5.50.   878.6
1. Latin Literature.

4428. Plinius Caecilius Secundus, Gaius. Letters. 2 vols. (Lat.). Harvard U Pr. $5.50 ea.   878.9
1. Latin Literature.

879 Latin Literature, Medieval and Modern

4429. Bestiary: The Book of Beasts. White, T. H., tr. Putnam. 1960. pap. $2.95.   879
1. Latin Literature, Medieval and Modern — History and Criticism.

4430. Curtius, Ernst R. European Literature and the Latin Middle Ages. Trask, Willard R., tr. Princeton U Pr. 1973. $20.00; pap. $3.95 (Har-Row).   879
1. Civilization, Medieval. 2. Latin Literature, Medieval and Modern — History and Criticism.

4431. Haskins, Charles. The Renaissance of the Twelfth Century. Harvard U Pr. 1971. $12.00; pap. $2.75.   879

800 LITERATURE

1. Civilization, Medieval. 2. Latin Literature, Medieval and Modern — History and Criticism. 3. Twelfth Century.

4432. Erasmus, Desiderius. In Praise of Folly. Radice, Betty, tr. Penguin. pap. $1.95. 879.7
1. Folly.

880 Greek Literature

4433. Lattimore, Richmond. Themes in Greek and Latin Epitaphs. U of Ill Pr. 1962. pap. $1.95. 880.09
1. Epitaphs. 2. Greek Literature — Epitaphs. 3. Roman Literature — Epitaphs.

4434. Stuart, Duane Reed. Epochs of Greek and Roman Biography. Biblo. 1928. $7.50. 880.09
1. Biography (As a Literary Form). 2. Greek Literature — History and Criticism. 3. Latin Literature — History and Criticism.

4435. Auden, Wystan H., ed. Portable Greek Reader. Viking Pr. 1948. $6.95; pap. $3.50. 880.8
1. Greek Literature — Collections.

4436. Oates, Whitney J. and Murphy, C. T., eds. Greek Literature in Translation. McKay. 1944. $7.95. 880.8
1. Greek Literature — Collections.

4437. Baldry, H. C. Ancient Greek Literature in Its Living Context. McGraw. 1968. $5.50; pap. $2.95. 880.9
1. Greek Literature — History and Criticism.

4438. Hadas, Moses. A History of Greek Literature. Columbia U Pr. 1950. $12.50. 880.9
1. Greek Literature — History and Criticism.

4439. Hamilton, Edith. Echo of Greece. Norton. 1957. $6.95; pap. $2.45. 880.9
1. Civilization, Greek. 2. Greek Literature — History and Criticism.

4440. ———. The Greek Way. Norton. 1930. $6.95; pap. $1.25. 880.9
1. Civilization, Greek. 2. Greek Literature — History and Criticism.

4441. Rose, Herbert J. Handbook of Greek Literature. rev. ed. Dutton. pap. $2.45. 880.9
1. Greek Literature — History and Criticism.

881 Greek Poetry

4442. Oxford Book of Greek Verse. Murray, Gilbert, et al, eds. (Gr.). Oxford U Pr. 1930. $8.00. 881.08
1. Greek Poetry — Collections.

4443. Bowra, Cecil M. Early Greek Elegists. Cooper Sq. 1969. $6.00. 881.09
1. Greek Poetry — History and Criticism.

4444. MacKail, John W. Lectures on Greek Poetry. Biblo. $7.50. 881.09
1. Greek Poetry — History and Criticism.

882 Greek Drama

4445. Casson, Lionel, ed. Masters of Ancient Comedy. Funk & W. 1967. pap. $2.95. 882.08
1. Greek Drama (Comedy). 2. Latin Drama (Comedy).

4446. Cooper, Lane, ed. Fifteen Greek Plays. Murray, Gilbert, et al, trs. Oxford U Pr. 1943. $9.95. 882.08
1. Greek Drama — Collections.

4447. Fitts, Dudley, ed. Greek Plays in Modern Translation. Dial. 1947. $7.50. 882.08
1. English Drama. 2. Greek Drama (Tragedy).

4448. Grene, David and Lattimore, Richmond. Complete Greek Tragedies. 3 vols. U of Chicago Pr. Vol. 1. pap. $1.75; Vol. 2. pap. $1.50; Vol. 3. pap. $1.95. 882.08
1. Greek Drama — Collections.

4449. Oates, Whitney J. and O'Neill, Eugene, Jr., eds. Complete Greek Dramas. 2 vols. Random. 1938. $20.00. 882.08
1. Greek Drama — Collections.

4450. Bieber, Margarete. The History of the Greek and Roman Theater. rev. ed. Princeton U Pr. 1961. $25.00. 882.09
1. Art, Greek. 2. Art, Rome. 3. Theater — Greece. 4. Theater — Rome.

4451. Bowra, Cecil M. Sophoclean Tragedy. Oxford U Pr. 1944. pap. $3.95. 882.09
1. Greek Drama — History and Criticism.

4452. Harsh, Philip W. Handbook of Classical Drama. Stanford U Pr. 1944. $12.50; pap. $3.85. 882.09

800 LITERATURE

1. Classical Literature — History and Criticism. 2. Drama — History and Criticism. 3. Greek Literature — History and Criticism. 4. Latin Literature — History and Criticism.

4453. Jones, John F. On Aristotle and Greek Tragedy. Oxford U Pr. 1968. pap. $2.95. 882.09
1. Greek Drama — History and Criticism.

4454. Kitto, Humphrey D. Form and Meaning in Drama: A Study of Six Greek Plays and of Hamlet. B&N. 1957. $9.00. 882.09
1. Greek Drama (Tragedy) — History and Criticism. 2. Hamlet.

4455. ———. Greek Tragedy: A Literary Study. 3rd ed. B&N. 1961. $10.00; pap. $5.00. 882.09
1. Greek Drama — History and Criticism.

4456. Aeschylus. Plays. Cookson, G. M., tr. Dutton. 1956. $3.95. 882.1
1. Greek Drama.

4457. Whitman, Cedric H. Sophocles: A Study of Heroic Humanism. Harvard U Pr. 1951. $8.00. 882.2(B)
1. Sophocles, 496?-406 B.C.

4458. Euripides. Plays. 2 vols. Dutton. $3.95 ea. 882.3
1. Greek Drama.

4459. Aristophanes. Eleven Comedies. Liveright. $7.95. 882.4
1. Greek Drama.

883 Greek Epic Poetry

4460. Finley, Moses I., ed. The World of Odysseus. Viking Pr. 1965. pap. $1.95. 883.01
1. Civilization, Homeric. 2. Greece — Civilization.

4461. Bowra, Cecil M. Tradition and Design in the Iliad. Oxford U Pr. 1930. $8.95. 883.1
1. Homer — Criticism and Interpretation. 2. Iliad.

4462. Bradford, Ernle D. Ulysses Found. HarBraceJ. 1966. pap. $1.65. 883.1
1. Classical Geography. 2. Homer. 3. Odyssey.

4463. Homer. The Iliad: With an English Translation by Murray, A. T. 2 vols. (Gr.). Harvard U Pr. $5.50 ea. 883.1
1. Epic Poetry, Greek.

4464. ———. The Odyssey: With an English Tr. by Murray, A. T. 2 vols. (Gr.). Harvard U Pr. 1919. $5.50 ea. 883.1
1. Epic Poetry, Greek.

4465. Homer. Odyssey. Fitzgerald, Robert and Fitzgerald, Robert, eds. Doubleday. 1961. pap. $1.95. 883.1
1. Epic Poetry, Greek.

4466. Homer. Iliad. 2nd ed. Lattimore, Richmond, tr. U of Chicago Pr. 1962. $6.95. 883.1
1. Epic Poetry, Greek.

4467. Stanford, William B. The Ulysses Theme. U of Mich Pr. 1968. pap. $2.65. 883.1
1. Odyssey.

4468. Steiner, George and Fagles, Robert, eds. Homer: A Collection of Critical Essays. P-H. 1963. $5.95. 883.1
1. Homer — Criticism and Interpretation.

4469. Whitman, Cedric H. Homer and the Heroic Tradition. Harvard U Pr. 1958. $10.00; pap. $2.75 (Norton). 883.1
1. Homer. 2. Iliad — Criticism and Interpretation. 3. Odyssey — Criticism and Interpretation.

884 Greek Lyric Poetry

4470. Pindarus. Odes, and Fragments. (Gr.). Sandys, Sir John, tr. Harvard U Pr. $5.50. 884.5

4471. Plato. The Portable Plato. Buchanan, Scott, ed. Viking Pr. 1948. $6.95; pap. $3.35. 888.4
1. Philosophy, Ancient.

4472. Plato. The Collected Dialogues of Plato. Hamilton, Edith and Huntington, Cairns, eds. Princeton U Pr. 1961. $10.00. 888.4
1. Philosophy, Ancient.

4473. Plutarch. Lives. Dryden, John, tr. Modern Lib. $4.95. 888.8(B)
1. Greece — Biography. 2. Rome — Biography.

4474. Brown, Demetra V. and Phoutrides, Aristides, trs. Modern Greek Stories. AMS Pr. 1920. $8.50. 889.3

Recommended Series

4475. Loeb Classical Library. Warnington, E. H., ed.. Harvard U Pr.

890-891.6 Literature of Other Languages

4476. Feinburg, Leonard, compiled by. Asian Laughter: An Anthology of Oriental Satire and Humor. Weatherhill. 1971. $15.00. 890
1. Oriental Literature.

4477. Yohannan, John D. A Treasury of Asian Literature. NAL. 1959. pap. $1.50. 890.8
1. Oriental Literature.

4478. Alphonso-Karkala, John B., compiled by. An Anthology of Indian Literature. Penguin. 1971. pap. $2.95. 891.1
1. Indian Literature.

4479. Singh, Khushwant. Train to Pakostan: Mano Majra. Grove. 1956. pap. $1.95. 891.3

4480. Banerji, Bibhutibhushan. Pather Panchali: Song of the Road. Clart, T. W. and Mukherji, Tarapada, trs. Ind U Pr. 1969. $7.50. 891.4

4481. Kalidasa. Shakuntala and Other Writings. Dutton. 1959. pap. $1.35. 891.4
1. Indian Drama.

4482. Markandaya, Kamala. A Handful of Rice. John Day. 1966. $7.95; pap. $0.75 1971 (Fawcett World). 891.4

4483. ———. Nectar in a Sieve. John Day. 1955. $4.95; pap. $1.25 (NAL). 891.4

4484. Narayan, R. K. The Financial Expert. Mich St U Pr. 1953. $4.00; pap. $2.50 1959 (FS&G). 891.4

4485. ———. Swami and Friends and The Bachelor of Arts: Two Novels of Malgudi. Mich St U Pr. 1954. $3.95. 891.4

4486. Narasimhan, C. U., tr. The Mahabharata. Columbia U Pr. 1964. $11.00; pap. $3.95. 891.41
1. Indian Literature.

4487. Tagore, Rabindranath. Sheaves: Poems and Songs. 2nd ed. Cupta, Nagendranath, tr. Greenwood. Repr. of 1950 ed. $9.00. 891.44

4488. Tagore, Rabindranath. The Broken Nest. Lago, Mary M. and Sen, Supriga, trs. U of Mo Pr. 1971. pap. $2.50. 891.44

4489. Baroja, Pío. Restlessness of Shanti Andía and Other Writings. Kerrigan, Anthony, tr. U of Mich Pr. 1959. $7.50. 891.5
1. Persian Literature.

4490. Omar Khayyam. Rubáiyát. Fitzgerald, Edward, tr. T Y Crowell. 1964. $5.00. 891.5
1. Persian Literature.

4491. Jackson, Kenneth H., ed. A Celtic Miscellany: Translations from the Celtic Literatures. Penguin. 1971. pap. $2.65. 891.6
1. Celtic Literature — Translations into English. 2. English Literature — Translations from Celtic.

4492. Greene, David H. An Anthology of Irish Literature. 2 vols. NYU Pr. 1971. $12.95; pap. $5.95. 891.62
1. English Literature — Translations from Irish. 2. Irish Literature — Translations into English.

891.7 Russian Literature

4493. Brown, Edward J. Russian Literature Since the Revolution. 2nd ed. Macmillan. 1969. pap. $2.95. 891.7
1. Russian Literature — History and Criticism.

4494. Guerney, Bernard G., ed. Anthology of Russian Literature in the Soviet Period from Gorki to Pasternak. Random (Vin). pap. $1.95. 891.7
1. Russian Literature — Collections.

4495. ———. The Portable Russian Reader. Viking Pr. 1947. $5.50. 891.7
1. Russian Literature — Collections.

4496. ———. Treasury of Russian Literature. Vanguard. 1943. $10.00. 891.7
1. Russian Literature — Collections.

4497. Mirsky, D. S. A History of Russian Literature. Knopf. 1949. $7.95. 891.7
1. Russian Literature — History and Criticism.

4498. Segel, Harold B., tr. The Literature of Eighteenth Century Russia. 2 vols. Dutton. 1967. pap. $2.95 ea. 891.7
1. Russian Literature — Collections.

800 LITERATURE

4499. Struve, Gleb. Russian Literature Under Lenin and Stalin, 1917-1953. U of Okla Pr. 1971. $9.95; pap. $4.95. 891.7
1. Russian Literature — History and Criticism.

4500. Turkevich, Ludmilla B., ed. Masterpieces of Russian Literature: From the Beginnings to 1863. Van Nos Reinhold. 1964. $8.95. 891.7
1. Russian Literature — Collections.

4501. Wiener, Leo, ed. Anthology of Russian Literature. 2 vols. Blom. 1965. $25.00. 891.7
1. Russian Literature — Collections.

4502. Yarmolinsky, Avrahm. Aspects of Russian Imagination. Funk & W. 1969. $8.95. 891.7
1. Russian Literature — Collections.

4503. ———. Russians: Then and Now. Macmillan. 1963. $8.50. 891.7
1. Russian Literature — Collections.

4504. Zavalishin, Viacheslav. Early Soviet Writers. Bks for Libs. 1970. $15.50. 891.7
1. Russian Literature — 20th Century — History and Criticism.

891.71 Russian Poetry

4505. Akhmatova, Anna. Works. (Rus.). Interlanguage Literary Associates. 1965. $4.50. 891.71

4506. Brodsky, Joseph. Selected Poems. Kline, tr. Har-Row. 1973. $5.95. 891.71
1. Broskii, Iosif.

4507. Brown, Edward J. Mayakovsky: A Poet in the Revolution. Princeton U Pr. 1973. $16.00. 891.71
1. Russian Poetry — History and Criticism.

4508. Lermontov, Mikhail Y. Demon. Bradda Bks. $1.25; pap. $0.80. 891.71

4509. Mayakovski, Vladimir. Stikhovoreniia Poemy. (Rus.). Four Continent Bk Corp. $1.75. 891.71

4510. Nabokov, Vladimir, tr. Song of Igor's Campaign: An Epic of the 12th Century. Random. $1.95. 891.71

4511. Nekrasov, Nikolai. Izbrannye Proizv. 2 vols. (Rus.). Four Continent Bk Corp. $3.25. 891.71

4512. Pasternak, Boris L. In the Interlude: Poems, 1945-1960. Katkov, George, ed. Kamen, Henry, tr. Oxford U Pr. 1962. $8.00; pap. $1.75. 891.71

4513. Pushkin, Aleksandr. Poems of Pushkin. Bilingual. Jones, Henry, tr. Citadel Pr. 1964. pap. $1.25. 891.71

4514. Troyat, Henri. Pushkin. Amphoux, Nancy, tr. from Fr. Doubleday. 1970. $10.00. 891.71(B)
1. Pushkin, Aleksandr Sergeyevich, 1799-1837.

4515. Voznesenskii, Andrei. Antimiry. (Rus.). Molodaya Gvardiya. 1964. $1.75. 891.71

4516. Voznesenskii, Andrei. Antiworlds. (Rus.). Blake, Patricia and Hayward, Max, eds. Schocken. 1973. pap. $3.95. 891.71

4517. Yevtushenko, Yevgeny. Stolen Apples: Poetry by Yevgeny Yevtushenko. Doubleday. 1971. $8.95. 891.71
1. Russian Poetry — Translations into English. 2. Yevtushenko, Yevgeny, 1933-

4518. Yevtushenko, Yevgeny. Precocious Autobiography. MacAndrew, Andrew, tr. Dutton. 1963. pap. $1.25. 891.71(B)
1. Yevtushenko, Yevgeny, 1933-

4519. Yevtushenko, Yevgeny. Selected Poetry. Milner-Gulland, R., ed. Pergamon. 1963. $4.00; pap. $3.00. 891.71

4520. Carlisle, Olga. Poets on Street Corners: Portraits of Fifteen Russian Poets. Bilingual. Random. 1970. $7.98; pap. $2.95. 891.718
1. Russian Poetry — Collections. 2. Russian Poetry — History and Criticism.

4521. Deutsch, Babette and Yarmolinsky, Avrahm. Modern Russian Poetry: An Anthology. Kraus Repr. 1968. $8.50. 891.718
1. Russian Poetry — Collections.

4522. Markov, Vladimir and Sparks, Merrill, eds. Modern Russian Poetry. Bilingual. (Rus.). Bobbs. 1969. $12.50; pap. $5.95. 891.718
1. Russian Poetry — Collections.

4523. Milner-Gulland, Robin, ed. Soviet Russian Verse: An Anthology. (Rus.). Pergamon. 1964. $5.50; pap. $4.50. 891.718

4524. Obolensky, Dimitri, ed. The Penguin Book of Russian Verse. (Rus.). Penguin. 1962. $1.95. 891.718

4525. Markov, Vladimir. Russian Futurism: A History. U of Cal Pr. 1968. $14.50. 891.719
1. Russian Poetry — History and Criticism.

891.72 Russian Drama

4526. Chekhov, Anton P. Chaika. (Rus.). Bradda Bks. $2.00. 891.72

4527. ———. Diadia Vania. (Rus.). Bradda Bks. $2.50. 891.72

4528. ———. P'esy. (Rus.). Bradda Bks. $3.15. 891.72

4529. Chekhov, Anton P. Best Plays. Young, Stark, tr. Modern Lib. $2.45. 891.72

4530. Fonvizin, Denis I. Nedorosl' (Rus.). Bradda Bks. 1965. $1.75. 891.72

4531. Gogol, Nikolai V. Revizor. (Rus.). Bradda Bks. 1964. $1.75. 891.72

4532. Gorky, Maxim. Lower Depths and Other Plays. Bakshy, Alexander, tr. Yale U Pr. 1959. pap. $2.75. 891.72

4533. Griboyedov, Aleksandr. Gore ot Uma. (Rus.). Four Continent Bk Corp. $0.75. 891.72

4534. Hare, Richard. Maxim Gorky, Romantic Realist and Conservative Revolutionary. Oxford U Pr. 1962. $5.00. 891.72(B)
1. Gorky, Maxim, 1868-1936.

4535. Pushkin, Aleksandr S. Boris Godunov. (Rus.). Bradda Bks. 1965. $1.75. 891.72

4536. Simmons, Ernest J. Chekhov. U of Chicago Pr. 1970. $10.00; pap. $3.95. 891.72(B)
1. Chekhov, Anton, 1860-1904.

4537. Tolstoy, Aleksei. Piesy. (Rus.). Four Continent Bk Corp. $1.75. 891.72

4538. Corrigan, Robert W., ed. Masterpieces of the Modern Russian Theatre. Macmillan. 1967. pap. $1.50. 891.728
1. Russian Drama — Collections.

4539. Noyes, George R., ed. Masterpieces of the Russian Drama. 2 vols. Dover. 1933. pap. $3.00 ea. 891.728
1. Russian Drama — Collections.

4540. Patrick, Ludmilla A. Six Soviet One-Act Plays. (Rus.). Pitman. 1963. $5.00. 891.728

4541. Reeve, Franklin D., ed. Nineteenth Century Russian Plays: 1790-1890. Norton. 1973. pap. $3.95. 891.728
1. Russian Drama — Collections.

4542. ———. Twentieth Century Russian Plays. Norton. 1973. pap. $3.95. 891.728
1. Russian Drama — Collections.

891.73 Russian Fiction

4543. Chekhov, Anton P. Shest' Rasskazov. (Rus.). Bradda Bks. 1963. $1.25. 891.73

4544. Dostoevsky, Feodor M. Brat'ya Karamazovy. 2 vols. (Rus.). Goslitizdat. 1963. $3.95. 891.73

4545. ———. Prestuplenie: Nakozanie. (Rus.). Bradda Bks. $3.85. 891.73

4546. ———. Zapiski: Iz Podpol'ia. (Rus.). Bradda Bks. $2.25. 891.73

4547. Friedberg, Maurice, ed. Russian Short Stories. 2 vols. Bilingual. (Rus.). Random. 1964. Vol. 1. pap. $1.95; Vol. 2. Ed. By Friedberg, M., & Maguire, R. A. $6.95. 891.73
1. Russian Short Stories — Collections.

4548. Gibian, George and Samilov, M., eds. Modern Russian Short Stories. (Rus.). Har-Row. 1965. $7.95. 891.73
1. Russian Short Stories — Collections.

4549. Gogol, Nikolai V. Mertvye Dushi. (Rus.). Four Continent Bk Corp. $1.50. 891.73

4550. ———. Shinel' (Rus.). Bradda Bks. 1963. $1.35. 891.73

4551. Goncharov, Ivan. Oblomov. (Rus.). Four Continent Bk Corp. $1.50. 891.73

4552. Harper, Kenneth, et al, eds. New Voices: Contemporary Soviet Short Stories. (Rus.). HarBraceJ. 1966. pap. $4.70. 891.73
1. Russian Short Stories — Collections.

800 LITERATURE

4553. Kaun, Alexander S. Leonid Andreyev: A Critical Study. AMS Pr. 1970. $9.50.
891.73(B)
1. Andreev, Leonid Nikolaevich, 1871-1919.

4554. Leonov, Leonid. Vor. (Rus.). Four Continent Bk Corp. $2.00. 891.73

4555. Lermontov, Mikhail Y. Geroi Nashego Vremeni. (Rus.). Bradda Bks. 1965. $2.00.
891.73

4556. Milne, Alan A. Vinni - Pukh I Vse-Vse-Vse. (Rus.). Zakhoder, Boris, tr. Dutton. 1967. $4.95. 891.73

4557. Payne, Robert. The Three Worlds of Boris Pasternak. Ind U Pr. 1963. pap. $1.95.
891.73(B)
1. Pasternak, Boris Leonidovich, 1890-1960.

4558. Pushkin, Aleksandr S. Kapitanskaia Dochka. (Rus.). Four Continent Bk Corp. $0.85. 891.73

4559. ———. Pikovaya Dara. (Rus.). Bradda Bks. 1963. $1.40. 891.73

4560. Pushkin, Aleksandr S. Eugene Onegin. Arndt, Walter, tr. Dutton. pap. $1.75. 891.73

4561. Solzhenitsyn, Aleksandr I. Izbrannoe. Eng. tr. (Rus.). Kamin Bk Store. 1965. $2.50.
891.73

4562. Solzhenitsyn, Aleksandr I. Stories and Prose Poems. Glenny, Michael, tr. FS&G. 1971. $7.95. 891.73

4563. Tolstoi, Leo N. Anna Karenina. 2 vols. (Rus.). Four Continent Bk Corp. $3.00.
891.73

4564. ———. Voina I Mir. 2 vols. (Rus.). Detskaya Lit. 1966. $4.50. 891.73

4565. Tolstoi, Leo N. Selections. Duddington, N. and Gorodetzky, N., eds. Oxford U Pr. 1959. $3.50. 891.73

4566. Tolstoi, Leo N. Kavkazskii Plennik. Fitzjohn, Bernard S., ed. Bradda Bks. 1962. $1.15. 891.73

4567. Turgenev, Ivan S. Ottsy i Deti. (Rus.). Bradda Bks. 1965. $2.50. 891.73

4568. ———. Zapiski Okhotnika. (Rus.). Bradda Bks. 1965. $2.50. 891.73

4569. Whitney, Thomas P., ed. & tr. The New Writing in Russia. U of Mich Pr. 1964. $6.95; pap. $4.95. 891.73

4570. Yarmolinsky, Avrahm, ed. Treasury of Great Russian Short Stories. (Rus.). Macmillan. 1944. $9.75. 891.73
1. Russian Short Stories — Collections.

4571. ———. Turgenev: The Man, His Art and His Age. Macmillan (Collier). pap. $1.50.
891.73(B)
1. Turgenev, Ivan Sergeyevich, 1818-1883.

4572. Davie, Donald, ed. Russian Literature and Modern English Fiction. U of Chicago Pr. 1965. $6.95; pap. $1.95. 891.739
1. Literature, Comparative — English and Russian. 2. Literature, Comparative — Russian and English. 3. Russian Literature.

891.78 Russian Literary Miscellany

4573. Chekhov, Anton P. Letters on the Short Story, the Drama and Other Literary Topics. Friedland, ed. Peter Smith. $4.50.
891.78
1. Russian Literature.

4574. Chekhov, Anton P. Portable Chekhov. Yarmolinsky, Avrahm, ed. Viking Pr. 1955. $6.95; pap. $3.25. 891.78

4575. Dostoevsky, Feodor M. Occasional Writings. Magarshack, David, ed. & tr. Random. 1963. $5.95. 891.78

4576. Gogol, Nikolai V. The Collected Tales and Plays. Kent, Leonard J., ed. Modern Lib. $4.95. 891.78

4577. Gorky, Maxim. Moi Universitety. (Rus.). Bradda Bks. 1966. $1.00. 891.78

4578. Lermontov, Mikhail Y. Lermontov Reader. Daniels, G., ed. Macmillan. 1964. $5.00. 891.78

4579. Moody, Christopher. Solzhenitsyn. B&N. 1973. $5.75. 891.78
1. Solzhenitsyn, Aleksandr Isaevich, 1918-

800 LITERATURE

4580. Pasternak, Boris L. Sochinenia: (Works in Russian) 4 vols. (Rus.). Struve, Gleb and Filipoff, Boris, eds. Vol. 1. Early Poetry, 1912-1932. $10.00; Vol. 2. Short Prose, 1915-1958. $8.50; Vol. 3. Later Poetry & Miscellaneous Writings, 1961. $9.00; Vol. 4. Doktor Zhivago, 1959. $7.50. U of Mich Pr. 891.78

4581. Pushkin, Aleksandr S. Poems, Prose, and Plays. Yarmolinsky, Avrahm, ed. Modern Lib. $4.95. 891.78

4582. Simmons, Ernest J. Pushkin. Peter Smith. $7.50. 891.78(B)
1. Pushkin, Aleksandr Sergeyevich, 1799-1837.

4583. Turgenev, Ivan S. Vintage Turgenev. 2 vols. Random. 1960. pap. $1.95 ea. 891.78

4584. Zenkovsky, Serge A. Medieval Russia's Epics, Chronicles and Tales. Dutton. 1963. pap. $2.95. 891.78

891.79 Russian Literature - History and Criticism

4585. Hayward, Max and Crowley, E. L., eds. Soviet Literature in the Sixties. Praeger. 1964. $6.00. 891.79
1. Russian Literature — 20th Century — History and Criticism.

891.8 Yugoslav Literature - History and Criticism

4586. Mikasinovich, Branko, et al, eds. Introduction to Yugoslav Literature. Twayne. 1973. $9.95. 891.8
1. Yugoslav Literature — History and Criticism.

892-896 Literature of Other Languages

4587. Agnon, Shmuel Y. Guest for the Night. Schocken. 1968. $6.95. 892.4
1. Hebrew Literature — History and Criticism.

4588. ———. Two Tales. Schocken. 1966. $4.95. 892.4
1. Hebrew Literature — History and Criticism.

4589. Mezey, Robert, compiled by. Poems from the Hebrew. T Y Crowell. 1973. $4.50. 892.4
1. Hebrew Poetry.

4590. Aleichem, Sholem. Collected Stories of Sholem Aleichem. 2 vols. Crown. 1965. $10.00. 892.49
1. Hebrew Literature — History and Criticism.

4591. Asch, Shalom. Children of Abraham. Samuel, Maurice, tr. Bks for Libs. Repr. 1942. $14.50. 892.49
1. Asch, Shalom, 1880-1957. 2. Hebrew Literature — History and Criticism.

4592. Klausner, Joseph. A History of Modern Hebrew Literature. Danby, Herbert, tr. Greenwood. Repr. 1932. $10.50. 892.49
1. Hebrew Literature, Modern — History and Criticism.

4593. Madison, Charles A. Yiddish Literature: Its Scope and Major Writers. Schocken. 1968. pap. $4.50. 892.49
1. Yiddish Literature — History and Criticism.

4594. Rapoport, Solomon. The Dybbuk: A Play in Four Acts. Liveright. Repr. 1926. pap. $2.95. 892.492
1. Hebrew Drama.

4595. Gibran, Kahlil. The Prophet. Knopf. 1923. $4.50. 892.7

4596. Gibran, Kahlil. A Treasury of Kahlil Gibran. Ferris, Anthony R., tr. Citadel Pr. 1951. $4.95. 892.7

4597. Kritzeck, James, ed. Modern Islamic Literature. NAL. 1972. pap. $1.95. 892.7
1. Arabic Literature — Collections. 2. Persian Literature — Collections.

4598. Nicholson, Reynold A. A Literary History of the Arabs. 2nd ed. Cambridge U Pr. 1969. $17.50; pap. $5.75. 892.7
1. Arabic Literature — History and Criticism.

4599. Brandon, James R., ed. Traditional Asian Plays. Hill & Wang. 1972. $7.50; pap. $2.95. 895
1. Chinese Drama. 2. Indian Drama. 3. Japanese Drama.

4600. Payne, Robert, ed. The White Pony. NAL. $1.25. 895
1. Poetry, Chinese.

800 LITERATURE

4601. Wells, Henry W., tr. Ancient Poetry from China, Japan and India. U of SC Pr. 1968. $14.95. 895
1. Poetry, Chinese. 2. Poetry, Indian. 3. Poetry, Japanese.

4602. Chai, Chu and Chai, Winberg, eds. A Treasury of Chinese Literature. Hawthorn. 1965. $8.95; pap. $4.25 (Apollo Eds). 895.1
1. Chinese Drama. 2. Chinese Fiction.

4603. Hsueh-Chin, Tsao. Dream of the Red Chamber. Wang, Chi-Eng, tr. Doubleday. pap. $2.50. 895.1

4604. Kai-Yu, Hsu, ed. Twentieth Century Chinese Poetry Anthology. Cornell U Pr. 1970. pap. $3.45. 895.11

4605. Meserve, Walter J. and Meserve, Ruth, eds. Modern Drama from Communist China. NYU Pr. 1970. $10.00; pap. $3.95. 895.12

4606. Bachmann, Robert. The Hand of a Thousand Rings and Other Chinese Stories. Bks for Libs. Repr. 1924. $9.25. 895.13

4607. Wu Ch'Eng-En. Monkey. Waley, Arthur, tr. Grove. 1958. pap. $2.95. 895.14

4608. Bhattacharya, Bhabani, ed. Contemporary Indian Short Stories. 2 vols. InterCulture. 1967. $2.35. 895.4

4609. Kawabata, Yasunari. Snow Country. Bd. with Thousand Cranes. Knopf. 1969. $6.95. 895.6

4610. Keene, Donald, ed. Anthology of Japanese Literature: Earliest Era to Mid-Nineteenth Century. Grove. 1956. pap. $3.95. 895.6
1. Japanese Literature — Collections.

4611. ———. Modern Japanese Literature from 1868 to Present Day. Grove. 1960. pap. $3.95. 895.6
1. Japanese Literature.

4612. Shiffert, Edith and Sawa, Yuki, trs. Anthology of Modern Japanese Poetry. C E Tuttle. 1972. $6.25. 895.6
1. English Poetry — Translations from Japanese. 2. Japanese Poetry — Translations into English.

4613. Buchanan, Daniel C., tr. One Hundred Famous Haiku. Japan Pubns. 1973. pap. $3.25. 895.61
1. English Poetry — Translations from Japanese. 2. Haiku. 3. Haiku — Translations into English.

4614. Cohen, William H. To Walk in Seasons: An Introduction to Haiku. C E Tuttle. 1972. pap. $2.50. 895.61
1. English Poetry — Translations from Japanese. 2. Haiku. 3. Haiku — Translations into English.

4615. Keene, Donald, tr. from Jap. Twenty Plays of the No Theater. Columbia U Pr. 1970. $4.95. 895.62

4616. ———. Modern Japanese Novels and the West. U Pr of Va. 1961. $3.75. 895.63
1. Japanese Fiction — History and Criticism.

4617. Miyoshi, Masao. Accomplices of Silence: The Modern Japanese Novel. U of Cal Pr. 1974. $7.95. 895.63

4618. Scott-Stokes, Henry. The Life and Death of Yukio Mishima. FS&G. 1974. $10.00. 895.63(B)
1. Mishima, Yukio, Pseudonym.

4619. Mishima, Yukio. Sound of Waves. Knopf. 1956. $4.95; pap. $1.25 1971 (Berkley Pub). 895.65

4620. ———. Temple of the Golden Pavillion. Knopf. 1959. $6.95; pap. $1.74 1971 (Berkley Pub). 895.65

4621. Mishima, Yukio. Confessions of a Mask. Weatherby, Meredith, tr. New Directions. 1968. pap. $2.25. 895.65

4622. Morris, Ivan I., ed. Modern Japanese Stories: An Anthology. C E Tuttle. 1961. $7.75. 895.7

4623. Nguyen, Du and Nguyen, Huynh-Sang. The Tale of Kieu: The Classic Vietnamese Verse Novel. Random. 1973. pap. $1.95. 895.9

4624. Beier, Ulli. Introduction to African Literature. Northeastern U Pr. 1967. $9.00. 896
1. African Literature.

4625. Cartey, Wilfred, ed. Palaver: Modern African Writings. Nelson. 1970. $5.95. 896
1. African Literature — Translations into English. 2. English Literature — Translations from African Languages.

800 LITERATURE

4626. Djoleto, S. A. and Kwami, T. S., eds. West African Prose. Humanities. 1973. $1.75.   896

4627. Olney, James. Tell Me Africa: An Approach to African Literature. Princeton U Pr. 1974. $15.00; pap. $3.45.   896

4628. Scheob, Harold, ed. African Images. McGraw. 1972. $3.44.   896

4629. Rutherfoord, Peggy, ed. African Voices: An Anthology of African Writings. Vanguard. 1959. $6.95.   896.08
1. African Literature — Collections.

4630. Beier, Ulli, ed. African Poetry. Cambridge U Pr. 1966. $4.95; pap. $2.95.   896.1
1. African Poetry — Collections.

4631. ———. Three Nigerian Plays. Humanities. 1967. pap. $2.00.   896.2
1. African Drama — Collections.

4632. Gleason, Judith I. This Africa: Novels by West Africans in English and French. Northwestern U Pr. 1965. $6.50.   896.3
1. Africa, West — Fiction.

4633. Killam, G. D. The Novels of Chinua Achebe. Holmes & Meier. 1970 (Africana). $5.50; pap. $2.50.   896.3
1. Achebe, Chinua — Criticism and Interpretation.

4634. Litto, Frederic M. Plays from Black Africa. Hill & Wang. 1969. pap. $1.95.   896.82
1. African Drama. 2. Drama — Collections.

897 American Indian Literature

4635. Allen, Paula C., et al. Four Indian Poets. U of S Dakota Pr. 1974. pap. $1.95.   897

4636. Astrov, Margot, ed. American Indian Prose and Poetry: An Anthology. John Day. 1972. $7.95; pap. $2.45 1962 (Putnam).   897
1. English Literature — Translations from Indian Languages. 2. Indian Literature — Translations into English.

4637. Bierhorst, John, ed. Four Masterpieces of American Indian Literature. FS&G. 1974. $10.00.   897
1. American Literature — Translations from Indian Languages. 2. Indian Literature — Translations into English.

4638. ———. In the Trail of the Wind: American Indian Poems and Ritual Orations. FS&G. 1971. $4.95; pap. $2.45 1972.   897

4639. Rothenberg, Jerome, ed. Shaking the Pumpkin: Traditional Poetry of the Indian of North Americas. Doubleday. 1972. $8.95; pap. $4.95.   897

4640. Steiner, Stan and Witt, Shirley. The Way: An Anthology of American Indian Literature. Knopf. 1972. $7.95; pap. $1.95 1972 (Random).   897

Recommended Series

4641. Contemporary Writers in Christian Perspective Series. Jellema, Roderick, ed.. Eerdmans. $0.85 ea; or $0.95 ea.

4642. Modern Masters. Kermode, Frank, ed.. Viking Pr.

4643. Twayne's World Authors Series. Twayne.

900 GEOGRAPHY, TRAVEL, AND HISTORY

901 History - Philosophy and Theory

4644. Brinton, Crane, et al. Civilization in the West. 3rd ed. P-H. 1973. $12.50; pap. $7.50. 901
1. Civilization — History. 2. Civilization, Occidental.

4645. Carr, Edward H. What Is History? Knopf. 1962. $4.95; pap. $1.95 (Random). 901
1. History — Philosophy.

4646. Muller, Herbert J. The Uses of the Past: Profiles of Former Societies. Oxford U Pr. 1952. $8.95; pap. $2.25. 901
1. Civilization — History.

4647. Ortega Y Gasset, José. Revolt of the Masses. Norton. 1957. $5.95; pap. $1.50. 901
1. Civilization. 2. Europe — Civilization. 3. Proletariat.

4648. Toynbee, Arnold J. A Study of History. Abridgement of vols. 1-10, in 2 vols. Somervell, D. C., ed. Oxford U Pr. Vols. 1-6. 1947. $8.50. Vols. 7-10. 1957. $7.50. 901
1. Civilization. 2. History — Philosophy.

4649. Zinn, Howard. The Politics of History. Beacon Pr. 1970. $7.50; pap. $3.45. 901
1. History — Philosophy.

4650. Fischer, David H. Historian's Fallacies: Toward a Logic of Historical Thought. Har-Row. 1970. $10.00; pap. $2.45. 901.8
1. History — Methodology.

4651. Clark, Kenneth. Civilisation: A Personal View. Har-Row. 1970. $17.95; pap. $6.95. 901.9
1. Art — History. 2. Civilization — History.

4652. Mumford, Lewis. The Pentagon of Power: The Myth of the Machine. Vol. 2. HarBraceJ. 1970. $12.95; pap. $4.95. 901.9
1. Civilization — History. 2. Technology and Civilization.

4653. ———. Technics and Human Development: The Myth of the Machine. Vol. 1. HarBraceJ. 1967. $12.00; pap. $3.45. 901.9
1. Civilization — History. 2. Technology and Civilization.

4654. Alves, Rubem A. Tomorrow's Child: Imagination, Creativity and the Rebirth of Culture. Har-Row. 1972. $6.95. 901.94
1. Civilization, Modern — 1950-
2. Forecasting. 3. Imagination.

4655. Barrett, William. Time of Need: Forms of Imagination in the Twentieth Century. Har-Row. 1972. $10.00; pap. $2.95. 901.94
1. Arts and Society. 2. Civilization, Modern — 1950- 3. Civilization — Philosophy.

4656. Fabun, Don. The Dynamics of Change. P-H. 1967. pap. $6.50. 901.94
1. Civilization, Modern — 1950-

4657. Heilbroner, Robert L. An Inquiry into the Human Prospect. Norton. 1974. $5.95; pap. $1.95. 901.94

900 GEOGRAPHY, TRAVEL, AND HISTORY

1. Civilization, Modern — 1950- 2. Regression (Civilization).

4658. Muller, Herbert J. The Uses of the Future. Ind U Pr. 1974. $10.00. 901.94
1. Civilization, Modern — 1950- 2. Twenty-First Century — Forecasts. 3. U. S. — Civilization — 1970-

4659. Nelson, Jack L. and Carlson, K., eds. Radical Ideas and the Schools. HR&W. 1972. $5.00. 901.94
1. Civilization, Modern — 1950- 2. Educational Sociology. 3. Radicalism. 4. U. S. — Civilization — 1945-

4660. Berry, Adrian. The Next Ten Thousand Years: A Vision of Man's Future in the Universe. Sat Rev Pr. 1974. $8.95. 901.95
1. Civilization, Modern — 1950- 2. Forecasting.

4661. Farmer, Richard N. The Real World of 1984: A Look at the Foreseeable Future. McKay. 1973. $6.95. 901.95
1. U. S. — History — Prophecies.

907.2 Historiography

4662. Bloch, Marc. Historian's Craft. Knopf. 1953. $4.95; pap. $1.95 (Random). 907.2
1. Historiography. 2. History — Methodology.

4663. Block, Jack. Understanding Historical Research: A Search for Truth. Research Pubns. 1971. $5.00. 907.2
1. Historical Research.

4664. Elton, Geoffrey R. The Practice of History. Apollo Eds. 1970. pap. $2.25. 907.2
1. History — Methodology.

4665. Gottschalk, Louis. Understanding History: A Primer of Historical Method. Knopf. 1969. pap. $3.95. 907.2
1. Historiography. 2. History — Methodology.

4666. Winks, Robin W., ed. The Historian As Detective: Essays on Evidence. Har-Row. 1969. $10.95; pap. $2.95. 907.2
1. Historiography. 2. History — Methodology.

909 World History

4667. Beals, Carleton. The Nature of Revolution. T Y Crowell. 1970. $8.95. 909

1. History, Modern. 2. Revolutions.

4668. Coblentz, Stanton A. The Militant Dissenters. A S Barnes. 1970. $10.00. 909
1. Dissenters. 2. Revolutions — History.

4669. Creasy, Edward S. and Mitchell, J. P. Twenty Decisive Battles of the World. Macmillan. 1964. $7.95. 909
1. Battles.

4670. Eggenberger, David. Dictionary of Battles. T Y Crowell. 1967. $14.95. 909
1. Battles — Dictionaries.

4671. Fuller, John F. A Military History of the Western World. 3 vols. Funk & W. 1954-56. $22.50; pap. $10.85. 909
1. Battles. 2. Military History.

4672. Palmer, Robert R. and Colton, Joel. A History of the Modern World. 4th ed. Knopf. 1971. $16.95. 909
1. History, Modern.

4673. Snyder, Louis L. Great Turning Points in History. Van Nos Reinhold. 1971. $5.95. 909
1. World History.

4674. Spengler, Oswald. The Decline of the West. 2 vols. Knopf. 1945. $22.50. 909
1. Civilization — History.

4675. Falls, Cyril. Hundred Years of War: 1815-1950. 2nd ed. Macmillan. 1962. pap. $1.50. 909.8
1. War. 2. World Politics — 19th Century. 3. World Politics — 20th Century.

4676. Brzezinski, Zbigniew. The Soviet Bloc: Unity and Conflict. rev. & enl. ed. Harvard U Pr. 1967. $15.00; pap. $4.95. 909.82
1. Communist Countries.

4677. Langsam, Walter C. The World Since 1919. 8th ed. Macmillan. 1971. $11.95. 909.82
1. European War, 1914-1918 — Influence and Result. 2. History, Modern — 20th Century. 3. World Politics — 20th Century. 4. World War, 1939-1945.

4678. Mydans, Carl and Mydans, Shelley. Violent Peace: A Report on Wars in the Postwar World. Atheneum. 1968. $12.50. 909.826
1. History, Modern — 1945- 2. Military History, Modern — 20th Century.

900 GEOGRAPHY, TRAVEL, AND HISTORY

910 General Geography and Travel

4679. Darden, Lloyd. The Earth in the Looking Glass. Doubleday. 1974. $7.95. 910
1. Geography. 2. Remote Sensing Systems.

4680. Trewartha, G. T., et al. Elements of Geography. 5th ed. McGraw. 1967. $13.95. 910
1. Geography.

4681. Fitzgerald, Brian P. Developments in Geographical Methods. Oxford U Pr. 1974. pap. $1.80. 910.01
1. Geography — Methodology.

4682. Bercovici, Konrad. The Story of the Gypsies. Gale. Repr. 1928. $14.00. 910.03
1. Gipsies.

4683. Bradford, Ernle D. Mediterranean: Portrait of a Sea. HarBraceJ. 1971. $10.00. 910.03
1. Mediterranean Region.

4684. Christopher, John B. The Islamic Tradition. Har-Row. 1972. pap. $3.50. 910.03
1. Civilization, Islamic. 2. Islam.

4685. Maenchen-Helfen, Otto J. The World of the Huns: Studies in Their History and Culture. U of Cal Pr. 1973. $20.00. 910.03
1. Attila, d. 453. 2. Huns.

4686. Berlitz, Charles F. and Valentine, J. Manson. The Bermuda Triangle. Doubleday. 1974. $7.95. 910.09
1. Bermuda Triangle. 2. Shipwrecks — Bermuda Triangle.

4687. Heyerdahl, Thor. The RA Expeditions. Doubleday. 1971. $10.00; pap. $1.95 (NAL). 910.09
1. Ra (Boat). 2. Voyages and Travels — 1951-

4688. Matthews, Constance M. Place Names of the English Speaking World. Scribner. 1972. $8.95. 910.09
1. Names, Geographical — English.

4689. Braudel, Fernand. The Mediterranean and the Mediterranean World in the Age of Philip II. 2 vols. Har-Row. 1972-74. $17.50 ea. 910.091
1. Mediterranean Region — History. 2. Physical Geography — Mediterranean Region.

4690. Barnaby, Kenneth C. Some Ship Disasters and Their Causes. A S Barnes. 1970. $10.00. 910.4
1. Shipwrecks.

4691. Chichester, Francis. Gipsy Moth Circles the World. Coward. 1968. $6.95; pap. $0.95 (PB). 910.4
1. Gipsy Moth (Sailing Yacht). 2. Voyages Around the World — 1951-

4692. Dana, Richard H. Two Years Before the Mast. Dutton. $3.95; pap. $2.25. 910.4
1. Voyages and Travels.

4693. Exquemelin, Alexandre O. The Buccaneers and Marooners of America. Gale. Repr. 1971. $17.50. 910.4
1. Buccaneers. 2. Pirates. 3. Spanish Main. 4. West Indies — History.

4694. Freuchen, Peter and Loth, David. Book of the Seven Seas. S&S. 1957. $9.95; pap. $3.95. 910.4
1. Ocean.

4695. Hakluyt, Richard. Portable Hakluyt's Voyages. Viking Pr. 1965. $4.95. 910.4
1. Discoveries (in Geography). 2. Voyages and Travels.

4696. Hampden, John, compiled by. Francis Drake, Privateer: Contemporary Narratives and Documents. U of Ala Pr. 1972. $12.75. 910.4
1. Drake, Francis, Sir, 1540?-1596.

4697. Heyerdahl, Thor. Kon-Tiki. Rand. 1950. $8.95; pap. $2.95 (Ballantine). 910.4
1. Ethnology — Polynesia. 2. Pacific Ocean. 3. Voyages and Travels.

4698. Marcus, Geoffrey. The Maiden Voyage. Viking Pr. 1969. $8.95. 910.4
1. Titanic (Steamship).

4699. Parry, John H. The Discovery of the Sea. Dial. 1974. $20.00. 910.45
1. Discoveries (in Geography) — History. 2. Ocean Travel — History.

4700. Bettex, Albert. The Discovery of the World. S&S. 1960. $22.50. 910.9
1. Discoveries (in Geography).

4701. Beaglehole, John C. The Life of Captain John Cook. Stanford U Pr. 1974. $18.50. 910.92(B)
1. Cook, James, 1728-1779.

4702. Roditi, Edouard. Magellan of the Pacific. McGraw. 1973. $6.95. 910.92(B)
1. Magalhaes, Fernao de, d. 1521.

900 GEOGRAPHY, TRAVEL, AND HISTORY

4703. Parry, John H. The Age of Reconnaissance: Discovery, Exploration, and Settlement, 1450-1650. Praeger. 1970. $10.00; pap. $1.50 (NAL). 910.94
1. Colonization — History. 2. Discoveries (in Geography).

4704. ———. The European Reconnaissance: Selected Documents. Walker & Co. 1968. $12.50. 910.94
1. Discoveries (in Geography).

4705. Pounds, Norman J. Political Geography. 2nd ed. McGraw. 1972. $13.50. 911
1. Geography, Political.

4706. Smith, C. T. An Historical Geography of Western Europe Before 1800. Praeger. 1967. $15.00. 911.4
1. Europe — Historical Geography.

913 Ancient World

4707. Ceram, C. W. March of Archaeology. Knopf. 1970. $17.95; pap. $4.95. 913
1. Archaeology — History.

4708. Schreiber, Hermann and Schreiber, Georg. Vanished Cities. Knopf. 1957. $7.95. 913
1. Archaeology. 2. Cities and Towns, Ruined, Extinct, etc.

4709. Avebury, John L. Pre-Historic Times As Illustrated by Ancient Remains and the Manners and Customs of Modern Savages. 7th ed. Humanities. Repr. 1969. $24.75. 913.03
1. Man, Prehistoric. 2. Man, Primitive.

4710. Ceram, C. W. Gods, Graves and Scholars. rev. ed. Knopf. 1967. $8.95. 913.03
1. Archaeology — History.

4711. ———. Hands on the Past: Pioneer Archaeologists Tell Their Own Story. Knopf. 1966. $10.00; pap. $3.95. 913.03
1. Archaeologists. 2. Archaeology. 3. Excavations (Archaeology).

4712. Clark, Grahame. Stone Age Hunters. McGraw. 1967. $5.50; pap. $2.95. 913.03
1. Man, Prehistoric. 2. Stone Age.

4713. Goodyear, Frank. Archaeological Site Science. Am Elsevier. 1971. $10.00. 913.03
1. Archaeology — Methodology.

4714. Piggott, Stuart, ed. The Dawn of Civilization: The First World Survey of Human Cultures in Early Times. McGraw. 1961. $32.75. 913.03
1. Archaeology. 2. Civilization, Ancient.

4715. Roe, Derek. Prehistory: An Introduction. U of Cal Pr. 1970. $7.95; pap. $3.25. 913.03
1. Archaeology. 2. Man, Prehistoric.

4716. Bass, George F. Archaeology Under Water. Praeger. 1966. $8.50; pap. $1.95 (Penguin). 913.031
1. Underwater Archaeology.

4717. Throckmorton, Peter. Shipwrecks and Archaeology: The Unharvested Sea. Little. 1970. $7.95. 913.031
1. Shipwrecks. 2. Underwater Archaeology.

4718. Treistman, Judith M. The Prehistory of China: An Archaeological Exploration. Natural Hist. 1972. $5.95; pap. $1.95. 913.31
1. China — History — Early to 1766 B.C.
2. China — History — 1766 B.C.-220 A.D.

4719. Kenyon, Kathleen M. Archaeology in the Holy Land. 3rd ed. Praeger. 1970. $9.00; pap. $4.50. 913.33
1. Palestine — Antiquities.

4720. Chiera, Edward. They Wrote on Clay: The Babylonian Tablets Speak Today. U of Chicago Pr. 1938. $7.50; pap. $1.95. 913.35
1. Cuneiform Inscriptions. 2. Excavations (Archaeology) — Mesopotamia. 3. Mesopotamia — Antiquities.

4721. Cottrell, Leonard. The Quest for Sumer. Putnam. 1965. $5.95. 913.35
1. Sumerians.

4722. Mellaart, James. Earliest Civilizations of the Near East. McGraw. 1966. $5.95; pap. $3.95. 913.35
1. Civilization, Ancient. 2. Near East — Antiquities. 3. Stone Age.

4723. Piggott, Stuart. Ancient Europe: From the Beginnings of Agriculture to Classical Antiquity. Aldine. 1966. $12.50; pap. $3.95. 913.36
1. Europe — Antiquities. 2. Europe — History — to 476.

4724. Renfrew, Colin. Before Civilization: The Radiocarbon Revolution and Prehistoric Europe. Knopf. 1973. $8.95. 913.36
1. Man, Prehistoric. 2. Radiocarbon Dating.

900 GEOGRAPHY, TRAVEL, AND HISTORY

4725. Bord, Janet and Bord, Colin. Mysterious Britain. Doubleday. 1973. $14.95.   913.362
1. Great Britain — Antiquities. 2. Great Britain — History. 3. Man, Prehistoric — Great Britain.

4726. MacKendrick, Paul. Roman France. St Martin. 1972. $10.95.   913.364
1. France — Antiquities, Roman.

4727. ———. The Mute Stones Speak: Story of Archaeology in Italy. St Martin. 1960. $7.50; pap. $1.50 (NAL).   913.37
1. Italy — Antiquities. 2. Rome — Antiquities.

4728. Pearson, John. Arena: The Story of the Colosseum. McGraw. 1973. $10.00.   913.37
1. Rome (City) — Colosseum — History.

4729. Keller, Werner. The Etruscans. Knopf. 1974. $12.50.   913.375
1. Etruria — History.

4730. Grant, Michael. Cities of Vesuvius: Pompeii and Herculaneum. Macmillan. 1972. $10.00.   913.377
1. Herculaneum. 2. Pompeii.

4731. Furguson, John. Heritage of Hellenism: The Greek World from 323-31 B.C. HarBraceJ. 1973. pap. $4.95.   913.38
1. Civilization, Greek. 2. Hellenism.

4732. MacKendrick, Paul. The Greek Stones Speak: Story of Archaeology in Greek Lands. rev. ed. St Martin. 1962. $8.50; pap. $1.75 (NAL).   913.38
1. Greece — Antiquities.

4733. Bibby, Geoffrey. Looking for Dilmun. Knopf. 1969. $10.00; pap. $2.25 (NAL).   913.39
1. Arabia — Antiquities. 2. Dilmun. 3. Excavations (Archaeology) — Arabia.

4734. Hood, Sinclair. The Minoans. Praeger. 1971. $10.00.   913.39
1. Civilization, Minoan. 2. Crete.

4735. Savory, Hubert N. Spain and Portugal: The Prehistory of the Iberian Peninsula. Praeger. 1968. $10.00.   913.39
1. Man, Prehistoric — Portugal. 2. Man, Prehistoric — Spain. 3. Portugal — Antiquities. 4. Spain — Antiquities.

4736. Ceram, C. W. The First American: A Story of North American Archaeology. HarBraceJ. 1971. $9.95.   913.7
1. America — Antiquities. 2. Indians of North America — Antiquities.

4737. Leonard, Jonathan N. Ancient America. Silver. 1967. $8.80.   913.7
1. America — Antiquities. 2. Indians of Mexico — Antiquities. 3. Indians of South America — Antiquities.

4738. Giddings, James L. Ancient Men of the Arctic. Knopf. 1967. $12.50.   913.98
1. Alaska — Antiquities. 2. Arctic Regions — Antiquities. 3. Eskimos. 4. Man, Prehistoric.

914-919 Geography of and Travel in Specific Locations

4739. Anderson, William. Castles of Europe from Charlemagne to the Renaissance. Random. 1970. $35.00.   914.03
1. Castles — Europe.

4740. Davidson, Marshall B. The Horizon Book of Great Historic Places of Europe. McGraw. 1974. $25.00.   914.03
1. Europe — Description and Travel. 2. Historic Sites — Europe.

4741. Crouzet, Maurice. The European Renaissance Since 1945. HarBraceJ. 1971. $6.95; pap. $3.95.   914.035
1. Europe — Civilization — 1945-

4742. Oakes, George and Chapman, Alexandria. Turn Right at the Fountain: Walking Tours. HR&W. 1971. $5.95.   914.045
1. Europe — Description and Travel — Guidebooks.

4743. Cowie, Donald. Scotland: The Land and the People. A S Barnes. 1973. $10.00.   914.1
1. Scotland — Description and Travel.

4744. Linklater, Eric and Smith, Edwin. Scotland. Viking Pr. 1968. $12.50.   914.1
1. Scotland — Description and Travel.

4745. Boll, Heinrich. Irish Journal. McGraw. 1967. $1.95.   914.15
1. Ireland — Description and Travel.

4746. Alcock, Leslie. Arthur's Britain: History and Archaeology A.D. 367-634. St Martin. 1972. $12.95.   914.2

900 GEOGRAPHY, TRAVEL, AND HISTORY

1. Arthur, King. 2. Great Britain — Antiquities. 3. Great Britain — History — Roman Period, 55 B.C.-449 A.D. 4. Great Britain — History — Anglo Saxon Period, 449-1066.

4747. Gloucester, Richard. The Face of London. Phaidon. 1973. $7.95. 914.2
1. London — Description.

4748. Kitson-Clark, George S. The Making of Victorian England. Atheneum. 1967. pap. $3.25. 914.2
1. Great Britain — Civilization.

4749. Richardson, Albert E. Georgian England: A Survey of Social Life, Trades, Industries and Art from 1700-1820. Bks for Libs. Repr. 1931. $18.50. 914.2
1. Art — English — History. 2. England — Social Life and Customs — 18th Century. 3. Industrial Arts — History.

4750. Wilson, John D. Life in Shakespeare's England: A Book of Elizabethan Prose. Folcroft. 1920. $5.95. 914.2
1. England — Social Life and Customs — 16th Century. 2. English Prose Literature — Early Modern (to 1700). 3. Shakespeare, William, 1564-1616 — Contemporary England.

4751. Oakes, George. Turn Left at the Pub: Walking Tours of the English Countryside. new ed. McKay. 1974. $6.95. 914.204
1. Great Britain — Description and Travel — Guidebooks.

4752. Marsden, Walter. The Rhineland. Hastings. 1973. $8.95. 914.3
1. Rhine Valley — Description and Travel. 2. Rhineland — Palatinate — Description and Travel.

4753. Adams, Marion. The German Tradition. Wiley. 1971. $7.95. 914.303
1. Arts, German. 2. Austria — Intellectual Life — History. 3. Germany — Intellectual Life — History. 4. Switzerland — Intellectual Life — History.

4754. Friedrich, Otto. Before the Deluge: A Portrait of Berlin in the 1920's. Har-Row. 1972. $10.00; pap. $1.95 (Avon). 914.315
1. Berlin — History — 1918-1945. 2. Berlin — Intellectual Life.

4755. Hurlimann, Martin. France. new ed. Viking Pr. 1968. $12.95. 914.4
1. France — Description and Travel.

4756. Zeldin, Theodore. France, 1848-1945: Ambition, Love and Politics. Oxford U Pr. 1973. $19.50. 914.403
1. France — History — 19th Century. 2. France — History — 20th Century.

4757. Dunlop, Ian. Versailles. Taplinger. 1970. $12.00. 914.43
1. France — Court and Courtiers. 2. Versailles — History.

4758. Hamblin, Dora J. The Appian Way: A Journey. Random. 1974. $10.00. 914.5
1. Appian Way.

4759. Pereira, Anthony. Rome. Hastings. 1975. $12.50. 914.56
1. Rome (City) — Description.

4760. Chejne, Anwar G. Muslim Spain: Its History and Culture. U of Minn Pr. 1974. $24.75. 914.603
1. Muslims in Spain. 2. Spain — Civilization — 711-1492.

4761. Gallop, Rodney. A Book of the Basques. U of Nev Pr. Repr. 1930. $7.00. 914.66
1. Basques.

4762. Reich, Hanns, ed. Portugal. Hill & Wang. 1968. $8.50. 914.69
1. Portugal — Description and Travel.

4763. Cartier-Bresson, Henri. About Russia. Viking Pr. 1973. $18.95. 914.7
1. Russia — Description and Travel.

4764. Gerstenmaier, Cornelia. The Voices of the Silent. Hart. 1973. $10.00; pap. $3.95. 914.703
1. Russia — Intellectual Life — 1917- 2. Underground Literature — Russia.

4765. Kennett, Audrey and Kennett, Vincent. The Palaces of Leningrad. Putnam. 1973. $25.00. 914.745
1. Leningrad — Palaces.

4766. Fullerton, Brian and Williams, Alan. Scandinavia. Praeger. 1972. $9.00. 914.8
1. Scandinavia — Description and Travel.

4767. Clark, Ronald. The Alps. Knopf. 1973. $15.95. 914.94
1. Alps — Description and Travel. 2. Mountaineering — History.

900 GEOGRAPHY, TRAVEL, AND HISTORY

4768. Rebuffat, Gaston. Men and the Matterhorn. Oxford U Pr. 1973. $17.50. 914.94
1. Matterhorn. 2. Mountaineering.

4769. Simpson, Colin. Greece: The Unclouded Eye. Fielding. 1969. $10.95. 914.95
1. Greece, Modern — Description and Travel — 1950-

4770. Edwards, Lovett F. Yugoslavia: People and Places. Intl Pubns Serv. 1974. $8.50. 914.97
1. Yugoslavia — Description and Travel.

4771. East, William G., et al, eds. The Changing Map of Asia: A Political Geography. 5th ed. B&N. 1971. $23.50; pap. $12.00. 915
1. Asia — Historical Geography. 2. Asia — Politics.

4772. Welty, Paul T. The Asians: Their Heritage and Their Destiny. 4th ed. Lippincott. 1973. pap. $3.25. 915.03
1. Asia — Civilization. 2. Asia — History.

4773. Gary, Dorothy H. and Payne, Robert. Splendors of Asia. Viking Pr. 1965. $12.50. 915.04
1. Asia — Description and Travel.

4774. Polo, Marco. Travels. Liveright. $6.95. 915.04
1. Asia — Description and Travel. 2. Voyages and Travel.

4775. Capa, Cornell, ed. Behind the Great Wall of China: Photographs from 1870 to the Present. Metro Mus Art. 1972. $12.50. 915.103
1. China — Description and Travel — Views.

4776. Rand, Christopher. Hongkong: The Island Between. AMS Pr. Repr. 1952. $12.00. 915.125
1. Hongkong — Description and Travel.

4777. Osgood, Cornelius B. The Koreans and Their Culture. Ronald. 1951. $9.95. 915.19
1. Korea — Civilization.

4778. Hurlimann, Martin and King, Francis. Japan. Viking Pr. 1970. $14.95. 915.2
1. Japan — Description and Travel.

4779. Maraini, Fosco. Japan: Patterns of Continuity. Kodansha. 1971. $17.50. 915.2
1. Japan — Civilization.

4780. Seward, Jack. The Japanese. Morrow. 1972. $6.95. 915.2
1. National Characteristics, Japanese.

4781. Freeth, Zahra and Winestone, H. V. Kuwait: Prosperity and Reality. Crane-Russak Co. 1973. $20.50. 915.3
1. Kuwait (State) — History. 2. Petroleum Industry and Trade — Kuwait (State).

4782. Bernstein, Jeremy. Nepal: A Profile. S&S. 1970. $7.95. 915.49
1. Nepal — Description and Travel.

4783. Fantin, Mario. Sherpa, Himalaya, Nepal. Intl Pubns Serv. 1974. $28.00. 915.49
1. Himalaya Mountains — Description and Travel. 2. Nepal — Description and Travel. 3. Sherpas.

4784. Hawkes, Jacquetta H. First Great Civilization. Knopf. 1970. $12.50. 915.6
1. India — Civilization. 2. Near East — Civilization.

4785. Payne, Robert. Splendor of Israel. Har-Row. 1963. $9.95. 915.694
1. Israel — Description and Travel.

4786. Pearlman, Moshe. Historical Sites of Israel. S&S. 1969. $14.95. 915.694
1. Israel — Antiquities. 2. Israel — Description and Travel. 3. Palestine — Antiquities. 4. Palestine — Description and Travel.

4787. Belenitsky, Aleksandr. Central Asia. Hippocrene Bks. 1968. $19.50. 915.8
1. Asia, Central — Antiquities.

4788. Siegner, Otto. Egypt. Scribner. 1970. $9.95. 915.8
1. Egypt — Description and Travel.

4789. Dobby, Ernest H. G. Southeast Asia. 11th ed. Verry. 1974. $12.50. 915.9
1. Asia, Southeastern — Description and Travel.

4790. Bohannan, Paul and Curtin, Philip. Africa and Africans. rev ed. Doubleday. 1971. $7.95; pap. $2.95 (Natural Hist). 916.03
1. Africa — Civilization.

4791. Davidson, Basil. The Lost Cities of Africa. rev. ed. Little. 1970. $10.00; pap. $2.75. 916.03
1. Africa, Sub-Saharan — Civilization — History.

900 GEOGRAPHY, TRAVEL, AND HISTORY

4792. Jackson, John G. Introduction to African Civilization. Univ Bks. 1970. $10.00; pap. $3.95 (Citadel Pr). 916.03
1. Africa — Civilization. 2. Africa — History.

4793. Matthiessen, Peter and Porter, Eliot. The Tree Where Man Was Born. Dutton. 1972. $12.95. 916.7
1. Africa, East — Description and Travel.

4794. Hall, Richard S. Stanley: An Adventurer Explored. HM. 1975. $12.50. 916.704(B)
1. Stanley, Henry Morton, Sir, 1844-1904.

4795. Jeal, Tim. Livingstone. Putnam. 1973. $10.00; pap. $2.25. 916.704(B)
1. Livingstone, David, 1813-1873.

4796. Van Der Post, Laurens. The Heart of the Hunter. Morrow. 1971. pap. $2.50. 916.8
1. Bushmen. 2. Kalahari Desert — Description and Travel.

4797. ———. The Lost World of the Kalahari. Pyramid Pubns. 1972. $0.95. 916.81
1. Bushmen. 2. Kalahari Desert — Description and Travel.

4798. Platt, Rutherford. Great American Forest. P-H. 1965. pap. $2.95. 917.095
1. Forests and Forestry — U. S. 2. Natural History — U. S.

4799. Toppings, Earl, ed. Canada. McGraw. 1973. $19.95. 917.1
1. Canada — Description and Travel.

4800. Bernal, Ignacio. Mexico, Three Thousand Years of Art and Life: As Seen in the National Museum of Anthropology, Mexico City. Abrams. 1969. $8.50. 917.2
1. Mexico — Antiquities. 2. Mexico — Civilization.

4801. Hannan, Hans W. Islands of the Caribbean. Hastings. 1974. $5.95. 917.2
1. Caribbean Area — Description and Travel.

4802. Peissel, Michel. The Lost World of Quintana Roo: Alone on Foot in the Jungles of Yucatan. Dutton. 1963. $6.50. 917.2
1. Mayas — Antiquities. 2. Mexico — Description and Travel. 3. Quintana Roo.

4803. Hunter, C. Bruce. A Guide to Ancient Maya Ruins. U of Okla Pr. 1974. $9.95; pap. $4.95. 917.203
1. Central America — Antiquities. 2. Mayas — Antiquities. 3. Mexico — Antiquities.

4804. Espy, Hilda C. and Creamer, Lex. Another World: Central America. Viking Pr. 1970. $10.00. 917.28
1. Central America — Description and Travel.

4805. Slater, Mary. The Caribbean Islands. Viking Pr. 1968. $6.95. 917.29
1. West Indies — Description and Travel.

4806. Caute, David. Cuba, Yes? McGraw. 1974. $7.95. 917.291
1. Cuba — Politics and Government — 1959-
2. Cuba — Social Conditions.

4807. Wagenheim, Kal. Puerto Rico: A Profile. Praeger. 1971. $8.50; pap. $2.95. 917.295
1. Puerto Rico.

4808. American Heritage Editors and Jenson, Oliver. American Album. McGraw. 1968. $17.50. 917.3
1. U. S. — Social Life and Customs.

4809. Andrist, Ralph K. American Century: One Hundred Years of Changing Life Styles in America. McGraw. 1972. $16.95. 917.3
1. U. S. — Civilization — 1865-1918. 2. U. S. — Civilization — 1918-1945. 3. U. S. — Civilization — 1945-

4810. Bennett, Ross, ed. The New America's Wonderlands: Our National Parks. Natl Geog. 1975. $8.15. 917.3
1. National Parks and Reserves — U. S.
2. U. S. — Description and Travel — 1960-

4811. Cooke, Alistair. Alistair Cooke's America. Knopf. 1973. $15.00. 917.3
1. U. S. — Civilization.

4812. Nash, Roderick. Wilderness and the American Mind. Yale U Pr. 1973. $12.50; pap. $3.25. 917.3
1. Frontier and Pioneer Life — U. S. 2. Nature Conservation — U. S. 3. U. S. — Civilization.

4813. National Geographic Society, ed. Wilderness U. S. A. Natl Geog. 1973. $9.95. 917.3
1. Camping — U. S. 2. Wilderness Areas — U. S.

4814. Noel Hume, Ivor. A Guide to Artifacts of Colonial America. Knopf. 1970. $10.00. 917.3
1. U. S. — Antiquities.

900 GEOGRAPHY, TRAVEL, AND HISTORY

4815. Pirsig, Robert. Zen and the Art of Motorcycle Maintenance: An Inquiry into Values. Morrow. 1974. $7.95.   917.3(B)
1. Pirsig, Robert M.

4816. Shimer, John A. Field Guide to Landforms in the U. S. Macmillan. 1972. $10.95.   917.3
1. Landforms — U. S.

4817. Steinbeck, John. America and Americans. Viking Pr. 1966. $14.95; pap. $1.25 (Bantam).   917.3
1. National Characteristics, American. 2. U. S. — Civilization. 3. U. S. — Description and Travel. 4. U. S. — Social Life and Customs.

4818. ———. Travels with Charley: In Search of America. Viking Pr. 1962. $4.95; pap. $1.65.   917.3
1. U. S. — Description and Travel.

4819. Time-Life Books Editors. This Fabulous Century. 8 vols. Silver. 1969-70. $10.60 ea.   917.3
1. U. S. — Civilization — 20th Century. 2. U. S. — Social Life and Customs — Pictorial Works.

4820. Wiebe, Robert H. The Segmented Society: An Introduction to the Meaning of America. Oxford U Pr. 1975. $7.95.   917.3
1. U. S. — Civilization.

4821. Birmingham, Stephen. Real Lace: America's Irish Rich. Har-Row. 1973. $10.00; pap. $1.75 (Popular Lib).   917.306(B)
1. Irish in the U. S. — Biography. 2. U. S. — Social Life and Customs.

4822. Cooper, Paulette, ed. Growing up Puerto Rican. Arbor Hse. 1972. $6.95; pap. $1.25 (NAL).   917.306
1. Puerto Ricans in the U. S.

4823. Gambino, Richard. Blood of My Blood: The Dilemma of the Italian-Americans. Doubleday. 1974. $7.95.   917.306
1. Italians in the U. S.

4824. Moquin, Wayne and Van Doren, Charles, eds. A Documentary History of the Italian-Americans. Praeger. 1974. pap. $4.95.   917.306
1. Italian Americans.

4825. Samora, Julian, ed. La Raza: Forgotten Americans. U of Notre Dame Pr. 1966. $7.95.   917.306
1. Mexican Americans.

4826. Weber, David J., compiled by. Foreigners in Their Native Land: Historical Roots of the Mexican Americans. U of NM Pr. 1973. $12.00; pap. $4.95.   917.306
1. Mexican Americans — History — Sources.

4827. Cruse, Harold. The Crisis of the Negro Intellectual. Morrow. 1967. $10.00; pap. $3.50.   917.309
1. Negroes — Intellectual Life.

4828. Miller, Perry. Life of the Mind in America: From the Revolution to the Civil War. HarBraceJ. 1970. pap. $2.50.   917.313
1. U. S. — Civilization — 1783-1865. 2. U. S. — Intellectual Life.

4829. ———. The New England Mind: From Colony to Province. Harvard U Pr. 1953. $12.50; pap. $4.95 (Beacon Pr).   917.313
1. American Literature — Colonial Period — History and Criticism. 2. American Literature — New England. 3. Puritans. 4. Religious Literature in America.

4830. Teller, Walter M. Cape Cod and the Offshore Islands. P-H. 1970. $8.95.   917.44
1. Cape Cod — Description and Travel. 2. Martha's Vineyard, Massachusetts — Description and Travel. 3. Nantucket, Massachusetts — Description and Travel.

4831. Boyle, Robert H. The Hudson River: A Natural and Unnatural History. Norton. 1969. $7.95.   917.473
1. Hudson River.

4832. Wigginton, Brooks E., ed. The Foxfire Book. Doubleday. 1972. $8.95; pap. $3.95.   917.58
1. Country Life — Georgia. 2. Handicraft. 3. Rabun Gap.

4833. ———. Foxfire 2. Doubleday. 1973. $10.00; pap. $4.95.   917.58
1. Country Life — Georgia — Rabun Gap. 2. Handicraft. 3. Rabun Gap.

4834. ———. Foxfire 3. Doubleday. 1975. $10.00; pap. $4.95.   917.58
1. Country Life — Georgia — Rabun Gap. 2. Handicraft. 3. Rabun Gap.

4835. Peirce, Neal R. The Deep South States of America: People, Politics and Power in the Seven Deep South Stats. Norton. 1974. $12.95.   917.6
1. Southern States — Civilization. 2. Southern States — Politics and Government — 1951- 3. Southern States — Race Question.

900 GEOGRAPHY, TRAVEL, AND HISTORY

4836. O'Connor, Richard. The German-Americans: An Informal History. Little. 1968. $10.00. 917.603
1. Germans in the U.S.

4837. Branch, Douglas. The Cowboy and His Interpreters. Cooper Sq. 1961. $5.50. 917.8
1. Cowboys.

4838. Crouch, Steve. Steinbeck Country. Am West. 1973. $18.50. 917.94
1. Monterey County, California — Description and Travel. 2. Salinas Valley, California.

4839. Morris, John J., ed. Alaska. Graphic Arts Ctr. 1972. $25.00. 917.98
1. Alaska — Description and Travel.

4840. National Geographic Society, ed. Alaska. Natl Geog. 1969. $4.25. 917.98
1. Alaska — Description and Travel.

4841. Matthiessen, Peter. The Cloud Forest: A Chronicle of the South American Wilderness. Viking Pr. 1961. $6.50; pap. $1.65 (Ballantine). 918
1. South America — Description and Travel.

4842. Schreider, Helen and Schreider, Frank. Exploring the Amazon. Natl Geog. 1970. $4.25. 918.11
1. Amazon River. 2. Amazon Valley.

4843. Robinson, K. W. Australia, New Zealand and the Southwest Pacific. 2nd ed. British Bk Ctr. 1968. $7.00. 919.4
1. Australia — Description and Travel.
2. New Zealand — Description and Travel.
3. Pacific Islands — Description and Travel.

4844. Simpson, Colin. The New Australia. Dutton. 1972. $12.50. 919.4
1. Australia — Description and Travel. 2. Mines and Mineral Resources — Australia.

4845. Heyerdahl, Thor. Aku-Aku: The Secret of Easter Island. Rand. 1958. $8.95. 919.6
1. Easter Island.

4846. Chickering, William H. Within the Sound of These Waves. Greenwood. Repr. 1941. $16.75. 919.69
1. Cook, James, 1728-1779. 2. Hawaii — Kings and Rulers. 3. Vancouver, George, 1757-1808.

4847. Siers, James. Hawaii. Har-Row. 1973. $9.95. 919.69
1. Hawaii — Description and Travel.

4848. Birket-Smith, Kaj. Eskimos. Crown. 1971. $17.95. 919.8
1. Eskimos.

4849. Bruemmer, Fred. The Arctic. Quadrangle. 1974. $25.00. 919.8
1. Arctic Regions.

4850. Henson, Matthew A. A Black Explorer at the North Pole: An Autobiographical Report. Walker & Co. 1969. $4.50. 919.8(B)
1. Arctic Regions. 2. North Pole. 3. Peary, Robert Edwin, 1856-1920.

4851. King, H. G. R. Antarctic. Arco. 1969. $9.95. 919.8
1. Antarctic Regions.

4852. Mountfield, David. A History of Polar Exploration. Dial. 1974. $17.50. 919.8
1. Polar Regions — Discovery and Explorations.

4853. Brent, Peter. Captain Scott and the Antarctic Tragedy. Sat Rev Pr. 1974. $12.50. 919.9(B)
1. Scott, Robert Falcon, 1868-1913.

Recommended Series

4854. The Centers of Civilization. U of Okla Pr. $2.95 ea.

4855. Fodor's Modern Travel Guides. McKay.

4856. Life World Library. Time-Life. $4.95 ea.

4857. Sierra Club. Sierra.

920-928 Collected Biography

4858. Hitti, Philip K. Makers of Arab History. St Martin. 1968. $6.95; pap. $3.25 (Har-Row). 920.009(B)
1. Islamic Empire — Biography.

4859. Horizon Editors. The Horizon Book of Makers of Modern Thought. McGraw. 1972. $15.00. 920.009(B)
1. Philosophers, Modern — Biography.

900 GEOGRAPHY, TRAVEL, AND HISTORY

4860. Rogers, J. A. World's Great Men of Color. 2 vols. Macmillan. 1972. $9.95 ea. 920.009(B)
1. Negroes — Biography. 2. Negroes — History.

4861. Churchill, Winston L. Great Contemporaries. Bks for Libs. Repr. 1937. $13.50. 920.02(B)
1. Biography — 20th Century. 2. Great Britain — Biography.

4862. Thomas, Norman M. Great Dissenters. Norton. 1970. pap. $1.95. 920.02(B)
1. Dissenters.

4863. Untermeyer, Louis. Makers of the Modern World. S&S. 1955. $12.50. 920.02(B)
1. Artists. 2. Authors. 3. Composers. 4. Inventors. 5. Philosophers. 6. Scientists. 7. Statesmen.

4864. Birmingham, Stephen. The Grandees: America's Sephardic Elite. Har-Row. 1971. $10.00; pap. $1.50 (Dell). 920.073(B)
1. Jews in the U. S. — Biography. 2. Sephardim — U. S. — Biography.

4865. Wecter, Dixon. The Hero in America: A Chronicle of Hero-Worship. Scribner. 1972. $12.50. 920.073(B)
1. Heroes. 2. U. S. — Biography.

4866. Davis, Harold E. Revolutionaries, Traditionalists, and Dictators in Latin America. Cooper Sq. 1972. $7.50. 920.08(B)
1. Latin America — Biography.

4867. Brawley, Benjamin G. Negro Genius. Apollo Eds. 1970. pap. $2.45. 920.097(B)
1. American Literature — Negro Authors — History and Criticism. 2. Negro Art. 3. Negro Artists. 4. Negro Authors. 5. Negro Musicians.

4868. Lippmann, Walter. Men of Destiny. U of Wash Pr. 1970. $7.50; pap. $2.95. 920.7(B)
1. U. S. — Biography. 2. U. S. — Politics and Government — 20th Century.

4869. Jones, Rufus. Spiritual Reformers of the 16th and 17th Centuries. Peter Smith. 1959. $6.00. 922.86(B)
1. Reformers.

4870. Madison, Charles A. Critics and Crusaders: A Century of American Protest. 2nd ed. Ungar. 1959. $9.75. 923.673(B)
1. Abolitionists. 2. Reformers.

4871. Untermeyer, Louis. Lives of the Poets. S&S. 1959. $9.95; pap. $3.95. 928.02(B)
1. Poets, American. 2. Poets, English.

929 Genealogy, Heraldry, Names

4872. Greenwood, Val D. Researcher's Guide to American Genealogy. Scribner. 1974. $14.95. 929.1
1. Archives — U. S. 2. Canada — Genealogy. 3. U. S. — Genealogy.

4873. Brook-Little, J. P. Heraldic Alphabet. Arco. 1973. $8.95. 929.6
1. Heraldry.

4874. Franklyn, Julian. Shield and Crest: An Account of the Art and Science of Heraldry. rev. 3rd ed. Genealog Pub. Repr. 1967. $17.50. 929.6
1. Heraldry.

4875. Patterson, Jerry E. Autographs: A Collector's Guide. Crown. 1973. $6.95. 929.8
1. Autographs — Collectors and Collecting.

930 Ancient History

4876. Casson, Lionel. The Ancient Mariners: Seafarers and Sea Fighters of the Mediterranean in Ancient Times. Macmillan. 1959. $6.95; pap. $2.75 (Funk & W). 930
1. History, Ancient. 2. Naval History, Ancient.

4877. Herodotus. Histories. 2 vols. Blakeney, E. H., ed. Rawlinson, George, tr. Dutton. 1964. $3.95 ea. 930
1. History, Ancient.

4878. Maspero, Gaston C. The Dawn of Civilization: Egypt and Chaldea. 2 vols. Ungar. Repr. 1969. $20.00. 930
1. Babylonia — Antiquities. 2. Egypt — Antiquities. 3. History, Ancient.

4879. Robinson, Charles A. Ancient History. 2nd ed. Boegehold, A. L., ed. Macmillan. 1967. $10.95. 930
1. History, Ancient.

4880. Roebuck, Carl. The World of Ancient Times. Scribner. 1966. $15.00; pap. $5.95. 930
1. Civilization, Ancient. 2. History, Ancient.

4881. Starr, Chester G. A History of the Ancient World. 2nd ed. Oxford U Pr. 1974. $15.00. 930
1. History, Ancient.

900 GEOGRAPHY, TRAVEL, AND HISTORY

932 Egypt

4882. Aldred, Cyril. Egypt to the End of the Old Kingdom. McGraw. 1965. $5.95; pap. $2.95. 932
1. Egypt — Antiquities. 2. Egypt — Civilization. 3. Egypt — History — Ancient to 640 A.D.

4883. Breasted, James H. History of Egypt. Scribner. 1909. $15.00. 932
1. Egypt — History — Ancient to 640 A.D.

4884. Cottrell, Leonard. Lady of the Two Lands: Five Queens of Ancient Egypt. Bobbs. 1967. $7.50. 932
1. Egypt — Social Life and Customs.

4885. Fakhry, Ahmed. Pyramids. 2nd ed. U of Chicago Pr. 1969. $10.50; pap. $3.25. 932
1. Egypt — Civilization. 2. Pyramids.

4886. Gardiner, Alan. Egypt of the Pharaohs: An Introduction. Oxford U Pr. 1966. pap. $3.50. 932
1. Egypt — History — Ancient to 640 A.D.

4887. Grant, Michael. Cleopatra. S&S. 1973. $10.00. 932(B)
1. Cleopatra, Queen of Egypt, d. B. C. 30.

4888. Harris, John R., ed. The Legacy of Egypt. 2nd ed. Oxford U Pr. 1971. $10.00. 932
1. Egypt — Civilization.

4889. Kaster, Joseph, ed. Wings of the Falcon: Life and Thought of Ancient Egypt. HR&W. 1968. $8.95. 932
1. Egypt — Civilization. 2. English Literature — Translations from Egyptian.

4890. Mendelssohn, Kurt. The Riddle of the Pyramids. Praeger. 1974. $12.95. 932
1. Pyramids — Construction.

4891. Montet, Pierre. Eternal Egypt. NAL. 1968. pap. $1.25. 932
1. Egypt — Civilization.

4892. ———. Everyday Life in Egypt in the Days of Ramesses the Great. Greenwood. 1958. $17.75. 932
1. Egypt — Social Life and Customs.

4893. Murray, Margaret A. The Splendour That Was Egypt: A General Survey of Egyptian Culture and Civilization. rev. ed. Praeger. 1969. $9.50. 932
1. Egypt — Antiquities. 2. Egypt — Civilization.

4894. Steindorff, George and Seele, Keith C. When Egypt Ruled the East. rev. ed. U of Chicago Pr. 1957. $8.50; pap. $2.50. 932
1. Egypt — Civilization. 2. Egypt — History — Ancient to 640 A.D.

4895. Tompkins, Peter. Secrets of the Great Pyramid. Har-Row. 1971. $15.00. 932
1. Pyramids.

4896. Vatikiotis, Panagiotis J. The Modern History of Egypt. Praeger. 1969. $9.50. 932
1. Egypt — History — 1798-

4897. Weigall, Arthur E. The Glory of the Pharaohs. Kennikat. Repr. 1923. $12.50. 932
1. Egypt — Antiquities.

4898. ———. The Life and Times of Akhnaton, Pharaoh of Egypt. Kennikat. Repr. 1922. $12.50. 932(B)
1. Amenhotep IV, King of Egypt, 1388-1358 B.C. 2. Egypt — History — to 332 B.C. 3. Egypt — Religion.

933 Palestine to 70 A.D.

4899. Bright, John. A History of Israel. 2nd ed. Westminster. 1972. $9.95. 933
1. Jews — History — to 70 A.D.

4900. Brodsky, Alyn. The Kings Depart: A Saga of the Empire Judah Maccabee Created and His Heirs Destroyed. Har-Row. 1974. $8.95. 933
1. Maccabees.

4901. Dawidowicz, Lucy S. Golden Tradition: Jewish Life and Thought in Eastern Europe, 1772-1939. HR&W. 1967. $8.95; pap. $3.45 (Beacon Pr). 933
1. Jews — Civilization. 2. Jews — History. 3. Jews in Eastern Europe.

4902. Join-Lambert, Michel. Jerusalem. Holdane, C., tr. Ungar. 1967. $9.00. 933
1. Jerusalem — Antiquities.

4903. Jones, Arnold H. Herods of Judaea. Oxford U Pr. 1938. $6.50. 933
1. Herod, House of. 2. Palestine — History.

900 GEOGRAPHY, TRAVEL, AND HISTORY

4904. Josephus, Flavius. Complete Works. 4 vols. Baker Bk. $29.95.   933
1. Jews — Antiquities. 2. Jews — History to 70 A.D.

4905. Orlinsky, Harry M. Ancient Israel. 2nd ed. Cornell U Pr. 1954. $7.50; pap. $1.95.   933
1. Jews — History.

4906. Sachar, Abram. A History of the Jews. rev. ed. Knopf. 1965. $10.00; pap. $6.50.   933
1. Jews — History.

4907. Schweitzer, Frederick M. A History of the Jews Since the First Century A.D. Macmillan. 1971. $7.95; pap. $1.95.   933
1. Jews — History.

935 Mesopotamia and Iranian Plateau

4908. Contenau, Georges. Everyday Life in Babylon and Assyria. St Martin. 1954. $13.95; pap. $2.25 (Norton).   935
1. Assyria — Social Life and Customs. 2. Babylonia — Social Life and Customs.

4909. Huart, Clément I. Ancient Persia and Iranian Civilization. B&N. 1927. $11.25.   935
1. Civilization, Iranian. 2. Iran — History — Ancient to 640 A.D.

4910. Mallowan, Max E. Early Mesopotamia and Iran. McGraw. 1965. pap. $3.95.   935
1. Iran — Antiquities. 2. Iran — Civilization. 3. Mesopotamia — Antiquities. 4. Mesopotamia — Civilization. 5. Sumerians.

4911. Oppenheim, A. Leo. Ancient Mesopotamia: Portrait of a Dead Civilization. U of Chicago Pr. 1964. $8.50; pap. $3.95.   935
1. Civilization, Assyro-Babylonian. 2. Mesopotamia — Civilization.

4912. Roux, Georges. Ancient Iraq. Humanities. 1964. $12.75; pap. $2.45 (Penguin).   935
1. Iraq — History. 2. Mesopotamia — Civilization.

4913. Kramer, Samuel Noah. The Sumerians: Their History, Culture and Character. U of Chicago Pr. 1963. $10.00; pap. $2.95.   935.01
1. Sumerians.

4914. Woolley, Charles. The Sumerians. AMS Pr. 1929. $8.50.   935.01
1. Sumerians.

4915. Saggs, H. W. The Greatness That Was Babylon: A Survey of the Ancient Civilization of the Tigris-Euphrates Valley. Praeger. 1969. $13.00.   935.02
1. Civilization, Assyro-Babylonian.

4916. Olmstead, Albert T. History of Assyria. U of Chicago Pr. Repr. 1923. $19.50.   935.03
1. Assyria — History.

4917. Culican, William. The Medes and Persians. Praeger. 1965. $8.50.   935.05
1. Iran — History — Ancient to 640 A.D.

4918. Olmstead, Arthur T. History of the Persian Empire: Achaemenid Period. U of Chicago Pr. 1948. pap. $5.95.   935.05
1. Iran — History — Ancient to 640 A.D.

937 Rome

4919. Abbott, Frank F. History and Description of Roman Political Institutions. 3rd ed. Biblo. 1910. $7.50.   937
1. Rome — Politics and Government.

4920. Gelzer, Mathias. The Roman Nobility. Seager, Robin, tr. B&N. 1970. $7.00.   937
1. Nobility. 2. Rome — Politics and Government. 3. Rome — Social Conditions.

4921. Grant, Michael. Gladiators. Delacorte. 1968. $4.50.   937
1. Gladiators. 2. Rome — History.

4922. Johnston, Harold W. The Private Life of the Romans. Cooper Sq. Repr. 1903. $15.00.   937
1. Rome — Social Life and Customs.

4923. Johnston, Mary. Roman Life. Lothrop. 1957. $15.75.   937
1. Rome — Civilization. 2. Rome — Social Life and Customs.

4924. Scullard, Howard H. History of the Roman World, 753 to 146 B.C. 3rd ed. B&N. 1969. $13.50; pap. $6.75.   937
1. Rome — History — Kings 753-510 B.C. 2. Rome — History — Republic, 510-265 B.C.

4925. Showerman, Grant. Rome and the Romans. Cooper Sq. Repr. 1931. $15.00.   937
1. Rome — Social Life and Customs.

4926. Banti, Luisa. Etruscan Cities and Their Culture. U of Cal Pr. 1974. $14.50.   937.01
1. Etruria.

900 GEOGRAPHY, TRAVEL, AND HISTORY

4927. Bloch, Raymond. Etruscans. Praeger. 1958. $8.50. 937.01
1. Etrurians.

4928. Dyer, Thomas H. The History of the Kings of Rome. Kennikat. Repr. 1868. $17.50. 937.01
1. Rome — History — Kings, 753-510 B.C.

4929. Richardson, Emeline. The Etruscans: Their Art and Civilization. U of Chicago Pr. 1964. $9.50. 937.01
1. Art, Etruscan. 2. Civilization, Etruscan.

4930. Marsh, Frank B. History of the Roman World, 146 to 30 B.C. 3rd ed. B&N. 1969. $13.50; pap. $6.50. 937.02
1. Rome — History — Republic, 265-30 B.C.

4931. Liddell Hart, Basil H. A Greater Than Napoleon: Scipio Africanus. Biblo. Repr. 1927. $12.50. 937.04(B)
1. Scipio the Elder (Scipio Africanus Major, Publius Cornelius).

4932. Proctor, Dennis. Hannibal's March in History. Oxford U Pr. 1971. $13.75. 937.04
1. Hannibal — Crossing of the Alps, 218 B.C.

4933. Boissier, Gaston. Cicero and His Friends: A Study of Roman Society in the Times of Caesar. Cooper Sq. Repr. 1970. $11.00. 937.05
1. Cicero, Marcus Tullius — Contemporary Rome. 2. Rome — History — Republic, 265-30 B.C.

4934. Cowell, Frank R. Cicero and the Roman Republic. rev ed. Penguin. 1973. $4.25; pap. $1.95. 937.05
1. Cicero, Marcus Tullius, 106-43 B.C. 2. Rome — Civilization. 3. Rome — History — Republic, 510-30 B.C.

4935. Fowler, William W. Social Life at Rome in the Age of Cicero. R West. 1916. $25.00. 937.05
1. Rome — Social Conditions.

4936. Geeler, Matthias. Caesar: Politician and Statesman. 6th ed. Harvard U Pr. 1968. $12.50. 937.05(B)
1. Caesar, Gaius Julius, 100-44 B.C.

4937. Grant, Michael. Army of the Caesars. Scribner. 1974. $10.00. 937.05
1. Caesar, Gaius Julius, 100-44 B.C. 2. Military Art and Science — History. 3. Rome — Army.

4938. Scullard, Howard H. From the Gracchi to Nero: A History of Rome from 133 B.C. to A.D. 68. 3rd ed. B&N. 1970. pap. $4.50. 937.05
1. Rome — History — Republic, 265-30 B.C. 2. Rome — History — The Five Julii, 30 B.C.-68 A.D.

4939. Syme, Ronald. Roman Revolution. Oxford U Pr. 1939. pap. $5.75. 937.05
1. Augustus, Emperor of Rome, 63 B.C.-14 A.D. 2. Rome — History — Empire, 30 B.C.-476 A.D. 3. Rome — History — Republic 510-30 B.C. 4. Rome — Politics and Government.

4940. Taylor, Lily R. Party Politics in the Age of Caesar. Peter Smith. 1962. $4.75. 937.05
1. Political Parties — Rome. 2. Rome — Politics and Government.

4941. Africa, Thomas W. Rome of the Caesars. Wiley. 1965. pap. $4.25. 937.06
1. Rome — Civilization. 2. Rome — History — Empire, 30 B.C.-284 A.D.

4942. Grant, Michael. The World of Rome. NAL. pap. $1.50. 937.06
1. Rome — Civilization.

4943. Hadas, Moses. Imperial Rome. Silver. 1965. $6.95. 937.06
1. Rome — Civilization. 2. Rome — History — Empire 30 B.C.-476 A.D.

4944. Marsh, Henry. The Caesars: Rulers of the Roman Empire. St Martin. 1972. $5.95. 937.06(B)
1. Rome — History — Empire, 30 B.C.-476 A.D. 2. Roman Emperors.

4945. Rostovtzeff, Mikhail. Social and Economic History of the Roman Empire. 2 vols. Frazer, P. M., ed. Oxford U Pr. 1957. $59.50. 937.06
1. Rome — Economic Conditions. 2. Rome — History — Empire, 30 B.C.-476 A.D. 3. Rome — Social Conditions.

4946. Sedgwick, Henry D. Marcus Aurelius: A Biography. AMS Pr. 1921. $8.00. 937.06(B)
1. Aurelius Antoninus, Marcus, Emperor of Rome, 121-180. 2. Roman Emperors. 3. Rome — History — Empire, 30 B.C.-284 A.D.

4947. Starr, Chester G. Civilization and the Caesars: The Intellectual Revolution in the Roman Empire. Norton. 1965. pap. $3.25. 937.06
1. Rome — Civilization.

900 GEOGRAPHY, TRAVEL, AND HISTORY

4948. Warrington, Brian H. Nero: Reality and Legend. Norton. 1970. pap. $1.65.
937.06(B)
1. Nero, Emperor of Rome, 37-68.

4949. Seager, Robin. Tiberius. U of Cal Pr. 1972. $12.95. 937.07(B)
1. Tiberius, Emperor of Rome, 42 B.C.-37 A.D.

4950. MacMullen, Ramsay. Constantine. Dial. 1970. $7.95; pap. $2.95 (Har-Row).
937.08(B)
1. Constantine I, the Great, Emperor of Rome, 280?-337. 2. Roman Emperors. 3. Rome — History — Empire, 30 B.C.-476 A.D.

4951. Jones, Arnold H. The Later Roman Empire, 284 to 602. 2 vols. U of Okla Pr. 1966. $24.95. 937.09
1. Byzantine Empire — History. 2. Rome — History — Empire, 284-476.

938 Greece

4952. Bowra, Cecil M. The Greek Experience. Collins-World. 1970. $10.00; pap. $1.25 (NAL). 938
1. Civilization, Greek.

4953. Bury, John B. History of Greece. 3rd ed. St Martin. 1951. $10.95. 938
1. Greece — History.

4954. Dickinson, G. Lowes. The Greek View of Life. U of Mich Pr. 1958. pap. $1.85. 938
1. Civilization, Greek. 2. Greece — Civilization.

4955. Finley, Moses I. The Ancient Greeks: An Introduction to Their Life and Thought. Viking Pr. 1963. pap. $1.45. 938
1. Civilization, Greek. 2. Greece — Antiquities.

4956. Forrest, William G. Emergence of Greek Democracy. McGraw. 1967. $4.95; pap. $2.45. 938
1. Greece — History.

4957. Gardiner, Edward N. Athletics of the Ancient World. Oxford U Pr. 1930. $20.50.
938
1. Athletics — History. 2. Greece — Social Life and Customs. 3. Sports — Greece.

4958. Green, Peter. Ancient Greece: An Illustrated History. Viking Pr. 1973. $13.95.
938
1. Civilization, Greek. 2. Greece — Antiquities.

4959. Kitto, Humphrey D. The Greeks. Peter Smith. 1951. $3.75. 938
1. Civilization, Greek. 2. Greece — History.

4960. Livingstone, Richard W., ed. Legacy of Greece. Oxford U Pr. 1921. pap. $2.50. 938
1. Civilization, Greek.

4961. Lloyd, Alan. Marathon: The Story of Civilizations on a Collision Course. Random. 1973. $6.95. 938
1. Civilization, Greek. 2. Iran — History — Ancient to 640 A.D. 3. Marathon, Battle of, 490 B.C.

4962. Starr, Chester G. The Ancient Greeks. Oxford U Pr. 1971. $10.00; pap. $3.95. 938
1. Civilization, Greek. 2. Greece — History.

4963. Burn, Andrew R. Minoans, Philistines, and Greeks: B.C. 1400-900. Greenwood. Repr. 1930. $18.50. 938.01
1. Civilization, Homeric. 2. Crete — Antiquities. 3. Etruscans. 4. Philistines.

4964. ———. The World of Hesiod: A Study of the Greek Middle Ages, 900-700 B.C. Blom. 1936. $12.50. 938.01
1. Civilization, Greek. 2. Hesiod.

4965. Ehrenberg, Victor. From Solon to Socrates: Greek History and Civilization During the 4th and 5th Centuries B.C. 2nd ed. B&N. 1973. $12.75; pap. $0.75. 938.02
1. Civilization, Greek. 2. Greece — History.

4966. Bowra, Maurice. Classical Greece. Silver. 1965. $8.80. 938.03
1. Art, Greek. 2. Civilization, Greek — Pictorial Works.

4967. De Selincourt, Aubrey. The World of Herodotus. Little. 1963. pap. $2.45. 938.03
1. Civilization, Greek. 2. Greece — History.

4968. Herodotus. The Persian Wars. Rawlinson, George, tr. Modern Lib. 1947. pap. $1.95. 938.03
1. Greece — History — Persian Wars, 500-499 B.C.

4969. Usher, Stephen. The Historians of Greece and Rome. Taplinger. 1970. $6.50.
938.03
1. Greek Historians. 2. Latin Historians.

900 GEOGRAPHY, TRAVEL, AND HISTORY

4970. Xenophon. Anabasis: The March up Country. Rouse, William H., tr. U of Mich Pr. 1958. pap. $2.45. 938.03
1. Greece — History — Persian Wars, 500-499 B.C. 2. Iran — History — Ancient to 640 A.D.

4971. Burn, Andrew R. Pericles and Athens. Verry. 1948. $4.00; pap. $1.25 (Macmillan).
938.04
1. Athens — History. 2. Pericles, 449-429 B.C.

4972. Henderson, Bernard W. The Great War Between Athens and Sparta. Arno. Repr. 1927. $28.00. 938.05
1. Greece — History — Peloponnesian War, 431-404 B.C.

4973. Thucydides. History of the Peloponnesian War. Livingstone, Richard W., ed. Oxford U Pr. 1943. $4.00; pap. $2.50.
938.05
1. Greece — History — Peloponnesian War, 431-404 B.C.

4974. Arrianus, Flavius. The Campaigns of Alexander. Penguin. 1972. $2.45. 938.07
1. Alexander the Great, 356-323 B.C. — Campaigns.

4975. Lane-Fox, Robin. Alexander the Great. Dial. 1974. $10.00. 938.07(B)
1. Alexander the Great, 356-323 B.C.
2 Greece — History.

4976. Bury, John B., et al. Hellenistic Age: Aspects of Hellenistic Civilization. Kraus Repr. 1923. $8.00; pap. $1.85 (Norton). 938.08
1. Civilization, Greek. 2. Hellenism.

4977. Rostovtzeff, Mikhail. Social and Economic History of the Hellenistic World. 2 vols. Oxford U Pr. 1957. $59.50. 938.08
1. Greece — Economic Conditions. 2. Greece — History. 3. Greece — Social Conditions.

4978. Michell, Humphrey. Sparta. Cambridge U Pr. 1964. $13.95. 938.9
1. Sparta — History.

939 Other Parts of the Ancient World

4979. Cottrell, Leonard. The Bull of Minos. HR&W. 1958. $5.00. 939.1
1. Civilization, Mycenaean. 2. Crete — Antiquities.

4980. Mylonas, George E. Mycenae and the Mycenaean Age. Princeton U Pr. 1966. $27.50. 939.1
1. Civilization, Mycenaean. 2. Mycenae.

4981. Taylour, William. The Mycenaeans. Praeger. 1964. $8.50. 939.1
1. Civilization, Mycenaean. 2. Crete — Antiquities.

4982. Schliemann, Heinrich. Ilios: The City and the Country of the Trojans. Blom. Repr. 1971. $18.50. 939.21
1. Troy.

4983. Rawlinson, George. Phoenicia. Bks for Libs. Repr. 1889. $16.50. 939.4
1. Phoenicians.

4984. Ceram, C. W. The Secret of the Hittites. Knopf. 1956. $8.95. 939.45
1. Hittites.

4985. Graham, Alexander. Roman Africa. Bks for Libs. Repr. 1902. $18.75. 939.7
1. Africa, North — History — to 647.
2. Rome — Provinces — Africa.

4986. Picard, Gilbert C. and Picard, Colette. The Life and Death of Carthage: A Survey of Punic History and Culture from Its Birth to the Final Tragedy. Taplinger. 1969. $13.95.
939.7
1. Carthage — History. 2. Punic Wars. 3. Rome — History — Republic, 260-30 B.C.

Recommended Series

4987. Ancient Peoples and Places. Praeger.

940 European History

4988. Ferguson, Wallace K. and Bruun, Geoffrey. A Survey of European Civilization. 3 vols. 4th ed. HM. 1969. $10.75; pap. $6.95.
940
1. Civilization, European. 2. Europe — History.

4989. Hayes, Carlton J., et al. History of Western Civilization Since 1500. 2nd ed. Macmillan. 1967. $10.95. 940
1. Civilization, European. 2. Europe — History.

4990. Mendenhall, Thomas C., et al. Ideas and Institutions in European History, 800-1715. HR&W. 1948. pap. $7.95. 940
1. Europe — History — Sources.

900 GEOGRAPHY, TRAVEL, AND HISTORY

4991. Roucek, Joseph S., ed. Central-Eastern Europe: Crucible of World Wars. Greenwood. 1970. $25.25. 940
1. Central Europe — History.

4992. McNeil, William H. The Shape of European History. Oxford U Pr. 1974. $7.50. 940.07
1. Europe — Historiography. 2. Europe — History.

940.1 Middle Ages

4993. Adams, Jeremy DuQuesnay. Patterns of Medieval Society. P-H. 1969. $6.95; pap. $3.15. 940.1
1. Civilization, Medieval. 2. Middle Ages.

4994. Artz, Frederick B. The Mind of the Middle Ages, A.D. 200-1500. 3rd ed. Knopf. 1958. $8.50. 940.1
1. Civilization, Medieval. 2. Middle Ages — Intellectual Life.

4995. Bishop, Morris. The Horizon Book of the Middle Ages. HM. 1968. $22.50. 940.1
1. Civilization, Medieval.

4996. Coulton, George G. Medieval Village: Manor and Monastery. Peter Smith. 1960. $6.00. 940.1
1. Civilization, Medieval. 2. Middle Ages — History.

4997. Davis, William. Life on a Medieval Barony: A Picture of a Typical Feudal Community in the 13th Century. Har-Row. 1928. $5.49. 940.1
1. Civilization, Medieval.

4998. Froissart, Jean. Chronicles of England, France, Spain. Dutton. 1961. pap. $2.75. 940.1
1. Europe — History — 476-1492. 2. Middle Ages — History.

4999. Gies, Joseph and Gies, Francis. Life in a Medieval Castle. T Y Crowell. 1974. $6.95. 940.1
1. Castles. 2. Civilization, Medieval. 3. Middle Ages.

5000. Huizinga, Johan. The Waning of the Middle Ages: Study of the Forms of Life, Thought and Art in France and the Netherlands in the 14th and 15th Centuries. St Martin. 1924. $10.95. 940.1
1. Civilization, Medieval. 2. France — Social Life and Customs. 3. Middle Ages — Intellectual Life. 4. Netherlands — Social Life and Customs.

5001. Lot, Ferdinand. The End of the Ancient World and the Beginnings of the Middle Ages. Leon, Philip and Leon, Mariette, trs. Har-Row. pap. $2.95. 940.1
1. Civilization, Medieval. 2. Europe — History — 392-814.

5002. Oman, Charles. Art of War in the Middle Ages: A.D. 378-1575. rev. ed. Cornell U Pr. 1960. pap. $2.95. 940.1
1. Middle Ages — History. 2. War.

5003. Pirenne, Henri. Economic and Social History of Medieval Europe. Clegg, I. E., tr. HarBraceJ. 1956. pap. $1.65. 940.1
1. Europe — Economic Conditions. 2. Europe — Social Conditions. 3. Middle Ages — History.

5004. Power, Eileen E. Medieval People. 10th rev. ed. B&N. 1963. $6.00; pap. $2.95. 940.1
1. Civilization, Medieval. 2. Greece — Civilization.

5005. Previte-Orton, Charles. The Shorter Cambridge Medieval History. 2 vols. Grierson, P., ed. Cambridge U Pr. 1952. $28.50. 940.1
1. Cambridge Medieval History. 2. Middle Ages — History.

5006. Price, Mary R. and Howell, Margaret. From Barbarism to Chivalry: A Portrait of Europe. Oxford U Pr. 1973. $10.50; pap. $5.50. 940.1
1. Europe — History — 476-1492.

5007. Rand, Edward K. Founders of the Middle Ages. Dover. 1928. pap. $2.50. 940.1
1. Civilization, Medieval. 2. Literature, Medieval — History and Criticism. 3. Middle Ages — History.

5008. Taylor, Henry O. The Medieval Mind: A History of the Development of Thought and Emotion in the Middle Ages. 2 vols. 4th ed. Harvard U Pr. 1959. $18.50 set. 940.1
1. Civilization, Medieval. 2. Middle Ages — Intellectual Life. 3. Philosophy, Medieval.

5009. Thatcher, Oliver J. and McNeal, E. H. The Source Book for Medieval History: Selected Documents. AMS Pr. 1905. $18.50. 940.1

900 GEOGRAPHY, TRAVEL, AND HISTORY

5010. Thorndike, Lynn. History of Medieval Europe. 3rd ed. HM. 1949. $10.95. 940.1
1. Europe — History. 2. Middle Ages — History.

5011. Tierney, Brian. Western Europe in the Middle Ages, 300-1475. Knopf. 1974. $16.95. 940.1
1. Middle Ages — History.

5012. Gordon, Colin D. The Age of Attila: 5th Century Byzantium and the Barbarians. U of Mich Pr. 1960. pap. $2.45. 940.11
1. Attila, d. 453. 2. Byzantine Empire — History.

5013. Bloch, Marc. Feudal Society. Manyon, L. A., tr. U of Chicago Pr. 1968. $6.95. 940.14
1. Europe — History — 476-1492. 2. Feudalism.

5014. Cox, Eugene L. The Eagles of Savoy: The House of Savoy in 13th Century Europe. Princeton U Pr. 1974. $22.50. 940.17
1. Savoy, House of.

5015. Evans, Joan. The Flowering of the Middle Ages. McGraw. 1966. $34.50. 940.17
1. Civilization, Medieval. 2. Middle Ages — History.

5016. Perroy, Edouard. The Hundred Years' War. Putnam. 1965. pap. $2.95. 940.17
1. Europe — History — 476-1492. 2. Hundred Years' War, 1339-1453.

5017. Cheyney, Edward P. The Dawn of a New Era: 1250-1453. Har-Row. 1936. $10.00; pap. $2.45. 940.18
1. Europe — History — 476-1492.

5018. Runciman, Steven. A History of the Crusades. 3 vols. Cambridge U Pr. 1962-66. $16.50 ea. 940.18
1. Crusades. 2. Middle Ages — History.

5019. Treece, Henry. The Crusades. Random. 1963. $7.95. 940.18
1. Crusades.

940.2 Modern History, 1453-1914

5020. Brinton, Crane, ed. Portable Age of Reason Reader. Viking Pr. 1956. $4.95; pap. $3.35. 940.2
1. Enlightenment. 2. Literature — Collections.

5021. Larkin, Maurice. Gathering Pace: Continental Europe, 1870-1945. Humanities. 1970. $8.25; pap. $5.50. 940.2
1. Europe — History — 1871-1918. 2. Europe — History — 1918-1945.

5022. Mendenhall, Thomas C., et al. Quest for a Principle of Authority in Europe, 1715 to the Present. HR&W. 1948. $7.25. 940.2
1. Europe — History — Sources.

5023. Ogg, David. Europe in the Seventeenth Century. 8th ed. Macmillan. 1962. pap. $1.95. 940.2
1. Europe — History — 17th Century.

5024. Ranum, Orest A. The Century of Louis XIV. Walker & Co. 1972. $12.50; pap. $3.95 (Har-Row). 940.2
1. Europe — History — 1648-1715 — Sources. 2. France — History — Louis XIV, 1643-1715 — Sources.

5025. Roberts, Martin. Machines and Liberty: A Portrait of Europe, 1789-1914. Oxford U Pr. 1973. $10.50. 940.2
1. Europe — History — 1789-1900.

5026. Schapiro, Jacob S. Modern and Contemporary European History. HM. 1953. $12.95. 940.2
1. Europe — Civilization. 2. Europe — History — 1789-1900. 3. Europe — History — 20th Century.

5027. Wolf, John B. The Emergence of the Great Powers: 1685-1715. Har-Row. 1951. pap. $2.45. 940.2
1. Europe — Intellectual Life. 2. Europe — Politics — 1648-1715.

5028. Gilmore, Myron P. The World of Humanism: 1453-1517. Har-Row. 1952. pap. $2.25. 940.21
1. Europe — History — 476-1492. 2. Europe — History — 1492-1648. 3. Humanism. 4. Renaissance.

5029. Plumb, J. H., ed. The Horizon Book of the Renaissance. Doubleday. 1961. $17.50. 940.21
1. Renaissance.

5030. Ross, James B. and McLaughlin, Mary M., eds. The Portable Medieval Reader. Viking Pr. 1946. $6.50; pap. $3.75. 940.21
1. Literature, Medieval. 2. Renaissance.

900 GEOGRAPHY, TRAVEL, AND HISTORY

5031. Setton, Kenneth M. The Renaissance: Maker of Modern Man. Natl Geog. 1970. $11.95. 940.21
1. Renaissance.

5032. Dorn, Walter L. Competition for Empire, 1740-1763. Har-Row. 1940. $8.95. 940.22
1. Europe — History — 1648-1789.

5033. Gershoy, Leo. From Despotism to Revolution: 1763-1789. Har-Row. 1944. $8.95; pap. $2.75. 940.22
1. Europe — History — 1648-1789.

5034. Krieger, Leonard. Kings and Philosophers, 1689-1789. Norton. 1970. $7.00; pap. $2.95. 940.22
1. Enlightenment. 2. Europe — Politics — 1648-1789. 3. Philosophy, Modern — 18th Century.

5035. Roberts, Penfield. Quest for Security; 1715-1740. Har-Row. 1947. pap. $2.95. 940.22
1. Europe — History — 18th Century.

5036. Williams, E. Neville. The Ancien Régime in Europe: Government and Society in the Major States, 1648-1789. Har-Row. 1970. $10.00. 940.22
1. Europe — Economic Conditions. 2. Europe — Politics — 1648-1789.

5037. Elliott, J. H. Europe Divided: 1559-1598. Har-Row. 1969. $7.95; pap. $2.75. 940.23
1. Europe — History — 1517-1648.

5038. Elton, Geoffrey R. Reformation Europe: 1517-1559. Har-Row. 1966. $7.95. 940.23
1. Europe — History — 1517-1648. 2. Reformation.

5039. Wedgwood, Cicely V. The Thirty Years' War. Peter Smith. $6.00. 940.24
1. Europe — History — 1517-1648. 2. Habsburg, House of. 3. Thirty Years' War — 1618-1648.

5040. Durant, Will. Rousseau and Revolution. S&S. 1967. $15.00. 940.25
1. Civilization — History. 2. Europe — History — 1648-1789. 3. Rousseau, Jean Jacques, 1712-1778.

5041. Friedrich, Carl J. Age of the Baroque: 1610-1660. Har-Row. 1952. $7.95; pap. $2.95. 940.25
1. Europe — History — 17th Century.

5042. Nussbaum, Frederick L. Triumph of Science and Reason, 1660-1685. Har-Row. 1953. $8.95. 940.25
1. Europe — History — 1492-1789. 2. Seventeenth Century.

5043. Ogg, David. Europe of the Ancient Régime: 1715-1783. Har-Row. 1966. pap. $2.75. 940.25
1. Europe — History — 18th Century.

5044. Palmer, Robert R. The Age of the Democratic Revolution. A Political History of Europe and America, 1760-1800. 2 vols. Vol. 1. Challenge. 1959; Vol. 2. Struggle. 1964. Princeton U Pr. $15.00 ea.; pap. $3.45 ea. 940.25
1. Constitutional History. 2. Europe — Politics — 18th Century.

5045. Bruun, Geoffrey. Europe and the French Imperium: 1799-1814. Har-Row. 1938. $8.95. 940.27
1. Europe — History — 1789-1815. 2. France — History — Consulate and Empire, 1799-1815. 3. Napoleon I, Emperor of the French, 1769-1821.

5046. Chandler, David G. The Campaigns of Napoleon. Macmillan. 1973. $17.50. 940.27
1. Europe — History — 1789-1815. 2. France — History, Military — 1789-1815. 3. Napoleon I, Emperor of the French, 1769-1821.

5047. Holtman, Robert B. The Napoleonic Revolution. Lippincott. 1967. $4.50; pap. $2.45. 940.27
1. Europe — Politics — 1789-1900. 2. Napoleon I, Emperor of the French, 1769-1821.

5048. Nicolson, Harold G. The Congress of Vienna: A Study in Allied Unity, 1812-1822. Peter Smith. $5.00. 940.27
1. Europe — Politics — 1789-1815. 2. Vienna Congress, 1814-1815.

5049. Palmer, Robert R. The World of the French Revolution. Har-Row. 1971. $8.50; pap. $2.95. 940.27
1. Europe — History — 1789-1815. 2. France — History — Revolution, 1789-1793 — Influence.

5050. Albrecht-Carrié, René, ed. The Concert of Europe. Har-Row. 1968. pap. $3.95. 940.28
1. Europe — History — 20th Century.

900 GEOGRAPHY, TRAVEL, AND HISTORY

5051. ———. A Diplomatic History of Europe Since the Congress of Vienna. rev ed. Har-Row. 1973. pap. $7.50.   940.28
1. Europe — History — 1789-1900. 2. Europe — History — 20th Century.

5052. Artz, Frederick B. Reaction and Revolution: 1814-1832. Har-Row. 1935. $7.95; pap. $2.25.   940.28
1. Europe — History — 1815-1848.

5053. Binkley, Robert C. Realism and Nationalism: 1852-1871. Har-Row. 1935. $8.95; pap. $2.45.   940.28
1. Europe — History — 1848-1871.

5054. Droz, Jacques. Europe Between Revolutions: 1815-1848. Baldick, Robert, tr. Har-Row. 1968. $6.95; pap. $2.25.   940.28
1. Europe — Economic Conditions. 2. Europe — History — 1815-1848. 3. Europe — Social Conditions.

5055. Hayes, Carlton J. Generation of Materialism: 1871-1900. Har-Row. 1941. $8.95; pap. $3.25.   940.28
1. Europe — History — 1789-1900.

5056. Hobshawm, Eric J. The Age of Revolution, Europe: 1789-1848. NAL. pap. $1.75.   940.28
1. Europe — History — 1789-1900. 2. Industry — History.

5057. Langer, William L. The Diplomacy of Imperialism, 1890-1902. Knopf. 1935. $15.00.   940.28
1. History, Modern — 19th Century. 2. Imperialism. 3. World Politics.

5058. ———. Political and Social Upheaval, 1832-1852. Har-Row. 1970. $10.00.   940.28
1. Europe — Intellectual Life. 2. Europe — Politics — 1789-1900.

5059. Lichtheim, George. Europe in the Twentieth Century. Praeger. 1974. pap. $5.95.   940.28
1. Europe — History — 20th Century.

5060. Robertson, Priscilla. Revolutions of 1848, a Social History. Princeton U Pr. 1952. $12.50; pap. $3.95.   940.28
1. Europe — History — 1848-1849. 2. Revolutions — Europe.

5061. Schenk, Hans G. The Aftermath of the Napoleonic Wars: The Concert of Europe - an Experiment. Fertig. 1967. $10.50.   940.28
1. Europe — History — 19th Century.

5062. Stearns, Peter N. Eighteen Forty-Eight: The Revolutionary Tide in Europe. Norton. 1974. $8.95; pap. $2.75.   940.28
1. Europe — History — 1848-1849.

5063. Taylor, Alan J. P. Struggle for Mastery in Europe: 1848-1918. Oxford U Pr. 1954. $14.50; pap. $4.95.   940.28
1. Europe — History — 1848-1871. 2. Europe — History — 1871-1918.

5064. Thomson, David. Europe Since Napoleon. 2nd ed. Knopf. 1962. $13.95.   940.28
1. Europe — History — 1789-1900. 2. Europe — History — 20th Century.

5065. Walker, Mack, ed. Metternich's Europe. Har-Row. 1968. $3.75.   940.28
1. Europe — History — 1815-1848 — Sources.

5066. Woodward, Llewellyn. Prelude to Modern Europe, 1815-1914. B&N. 1972. $9.00; pap. $3.50.   940.28
1. Europe — Politics — 1815-1871. 2. Europe — Politics — 1871-1918.

940.3-940.4 World War I, 1914-1918

5067. American Heritage Editors. American Heritage History of World War I. McGraw. 1964. $16.50.   940.3
1. European War, 1914-1918 — Pictorial Works.

5068. Cruttwell, Charles R. A History of the Great War, 1914-1918. 2nd ed. Oxford U Pr. 1936. $12.00.   940.3
1. European War, 1914-1918.

5069. Falls, Cyril. The Great War: 1914-1918. Putnam. 1961. pap. $3.45.   940.3
1. European War, 1914-1918.

5070. Ferro, Marc. The Great War, 1914-1918. Routledge & Kegan. 1973. $11.75.   940.3
1. European War, 1914-1918.

5071. Bloch, Camille. The Causes of the World War: An Historical Survey. Soames, Jane, tr. Fertig. 1968. $11.00.   940.31
1. European War, 1914-1918 — Causes.

5072. Czernin, Ferdinand. Versailles, Nineteen Nineteen: The Forces, Events and Personalities That Shaped the Treaty. Putnam. 1964. $6.95; pap. $2.45.   940.31

900 GEOGRAPHY, TRAVEL, AND HISTORY

5073. Fischer, Fritz. Germany's Aims in the First World War. Norton. 1967. $15.00; pap. $4.50. 940.31
1. Versailles, Treaty of, June 28, 1919 (Germany).
1. European War, 1914-1918 — Causes. 2. European War, 1914-1918 — Germany. 3. Germany — Foreign Relations — 1888-1918.

5074. Geiss, Immanuel, compiled by. July, Nineteen Fourteen: The Outbreak of the First World War, Selected Documents. Norton. 1967. pap. $3.95. 940.31
1. European War, 1914-1918 — Causes. 2. European War, 1914-1918 — Sources.

5075. Kellogg, Walter G. The Conscientious Objector. Da Capo. Repr. 1919. $8.95. 940.31
1. European War, 1914-1918 — Conscientious Objectors — U. S.

5076. Lafore, Laurence. The Long Fuse: An Interpretation of the Origins of World War I. Lippincott. 1965. $4.50; pap. $2.45. 940.31
1. European War, 1914-1918 — Causes.

5077. Tuchman, Barbara W. The Zimmerman Telegram. Macmillan. 1966. $6.95. 940.31
1. European War, 1914-1918 — Causes. 2. Zimmerman, Arthur, 1864-1940.

5078. Bailey, Thomas A. Woodrow Wilson and the Lost Peace. Peter Smith. 1944. $5.00; pap. $2.95 (Watts). 940.314
1. European War, 1914-1918 — U.S. 2. Paris Peace Conference, 1919. 3. Versailles, Treafy of, June 28, 1919. 4. Wilson, Woodrow, President U. S., 1856-1924.

5079. May, Ernest. The World War and American Isolation, 1914-1917. Harvard U Pr. 1959. $7.50; pap. $2.95 (Quadrangle). 940.32
1. European War, 1914-1918 — Diplomatic History. 2. U. S. — Foreign Relations — 1913-1921.

5080. Seymour, Charles. American Diplomacy During the World War. Shoe String. 1942. $12.00. 940.32
1. European War, 1914-1918 — U. S. 2. U. S. — Foreign Relations — 1913-1921. 3. Wilson, Woodrow, President U. S., 1856-1924.

5081. Gatzke, Hans W. Germany's Drive to the West: A Study of Germany's Western War Aims During the First World War. Johns Hopkins. 1950. $12.00; pap. $2.95. 940.343
1. European War, 1914-1918 — Germany. 2. Germany — Politics and Government — 1888-1918.

5082. Millis, Walter. Road to War: America, 1914-1917. Fertig. 1935. $15.50. 940.37
1. European War, 1914-1918 — U. S. 2. U. S. — Foreign Relations — 1913-1921.

5083. Tansill, Charles Callan. America Goes to War. Peter Smith. 1963. $11.00. 940.37
1. European War, 1914-1918 — U. S. 2. U. S. — Foreign Relations — 1913-1921. 3. U. S. — Neutrality.

5084. Lasswell, Harold D. Propaganda Technique in World War I. MIT Pr. 1971. $10.00; pap. $2.95. 940.4
1. European War, 1914-1918 — Propaganda.

5085. Liddell Hart, Basil H. The Real War, 1914-1918. Little. 1964. pap. $2.65. 940.4
1. European War, 1914-1918.

5086. Barbeau, Arthur E. The Unknown Soldiers: Black American Troops in World War I. Temple U Pr. 1974. $10.00. 940.403
1. European War, 1914-1918 — Negroes. 2. U. S. Army — Negro Troops.

5087. Coffman, Edward M. The War to End All Wars: The American Military Experience in World War I. Oxford U Pr. 1968. $12.50. 940.41
1. European War, 1914-1918 — U. S.

5088. Tuchman, Barbara W. The Guns of August. Macmillan. 1962. $10.00; pap. $1.75 (Dell). 940.421
1. European War, 1914-1918 — Causes.

5089. Rudin, Harry R. Armistice, 1918. Shoe String. 1967. $12.50. 940.439
1. European War, 1914-1918 — Armistices. 2. Germany — History — 1918-1933.

5090. Simpson, Colin. The Lusitania. Little. 1973. $8.95; pap. $1.75 (Ballantine). 940.45
1. Lusitania (Steamship).

940.5 20th Century, 1918-

5091. Black, Cyril E. and Helmreich, E. C. Twentieth Century Europe. 4th rev. ed. Knopf. 1972. $15.95. 940.5
1. Europe — History — 20th Century.

900 GEOGRAPHY, TRAVEL, AND HISTORY

5092. Hughes, H. Stuart. Contemporary Europe: A History. 3rd ed. P-H. 1971. $11.95. 940.5
1. Europe — History — 20th Century.

5093. Rothschild, Joseph. East Central Europe Between the Two World Wars. U of Wash Pr. 1974. $14.95. 940.5
1. Europe, Eastern — History.

5094. Wiskemann, Elizabeth. Europe of the Dictators, 1919-1945. Har-Row. 1966. $6.95; pap. $2.25. 940.5
1. Europe — History — 1918-1945.

5095. Craig, Gordon A. and Gilbert, Felix, eds. Diplomats: 1919-1939. 2 vols. Atheneum. 1963. Vol. 1. pap. $3.45; Vol. 2. pap. $2.95. 940.51
1. World Politics.

5096. Berghahn, Volker R. Germany and the Approach of War in 1914. St Martin. 1973. $9.95; pap. $3.95. 940.53
1. European War, 1914-1918 — Germany. 2. Germany — Politics and Government — 1888-1915.

5097. Bethell, Nicholas. The War Hitler Won: The Fall of Poland, September, 1939. HR&W. 1973. $10.00. 940.53
1. World War, 1939-1945 — Poland.

5098. Churchill, Winston L. The Gathering Storm; Their Finest Hour; The Grand Alliance; The Hinge of Fate; Closing the Ring; Triumph and Tragedy. HM. 1948-53. $50.00 set; $8.50 ea; pap. $2.25 ea. (Bantam). 940.53
1. World War, 1939-1945. 2. World War, 1939-1945 — Great Britain.

5099. Dank, Milton. The French Against the French: Collaboration and Resistance. Lippincott. 1974. $12.50. 940.53
1. France — History — German Occupation, 1900-1945. 2. World War, 1939-1945 — Collaborationists — France. 3. World War, 1939-1945 — Underground Movements.

5100. Fourcade, Marie M. Noah's Ark. Dutton. 1974. $10.00. 940.53
1. World War, 1939-1945 — Underground Movements — France.

5101. Liddell Hart, Basil H. History of the Second World War. 2 vols. Putnam. 1971. $12.50. 940.53
1. World War, 1939-1945.

5102. Parkinson, Roger. A Day's March Nearer Home: The War History from Alamein to VE Day Based on the War Cabinet Papers of 1942-1945. McKay. 1974. $9.95. 940.53
1. Great Britain — Foreign Relations — 1936-1945. 2. World War, 1939-1945 — Diplomatic History. 3. World War, 1939-1945 — Great Britain.

5103. Wright, Gordon. The Ordeal of Total War, 1939-1945. Har-Row. 1969. $8.95; pap. $2.75. 940.53
1. Europe — History — 1914-1945. 2. World War, 1939-1945.

5104. Feingold, Henry L. The Politics of Rescue: The Roosevelt Administration and the Holocaust, 1938-1945. Rutgers U Pr. 1970. $12.50. 940.531
1. U. S. — Foreign Relations — 1933-1945. 2. World War, 1939-1945 — Jews — Rescue.

5105. Levin, Nora. The Holocaust: The Destruction of European Jewry, 1933-1945. T Y Crowell. 1968. $12.50; pap. $6.95 (Schocken). 940.531
1. Jews — Political and Social Conditions. 2. World War, 1939-1945 — Jews.

5106. Taylor, Alan J. P. The Origins of the Second World War. Atheneum. 1962. $6.95. 940.531
1. World War, 1939-1945 — Causes.

5107. Dawidowicz, Lucy S. The War Against the Jews, 1933-1945. HR&W. 1975. $15.00. 940.5315
1. Holocaust, Jewish (1939-1945) — History.

5108. Ciano, Galeazzo. The Ciano Diaries, 1939-1943. Fertig. Repr. $16.50. 940.532(B)
1. Italy — Foreign Relations — 1922-1945. 2. World War, 1939-1945 — Italy.

5109. Deane, John R. The Strange Alliance: The Story of Our Efforts at Wartime Cooperation with Russia. Ind U Pr. 1973. pap. $3.50. 940.532
1. Russia — Foreign Relations — U. S. 2. U. S. — Foreign Relations — Russia. 3. World War, 1939-1945 — Russia.

5110. Feis, Herbert. Between War and Peace: The Potsdam Conferences. Princeton U Pr. 1960. $12.50; pap. $3.95. 940.532
1. Berlin, Conference, 1945. 2. World War, 1939-1945 — Diplomatic History.

900 GEOGRAPHY, TRAVEL, AND HISTORY

5111. ———. Churchill-Roosevelt-Stalin: The War They Waged and the Peace They Sought. 2nd ed. Princeton U Pr. 1967. $15.00; pap. $3.95. 940.532
1. World War, 1939-1945 — Diplomatic History.

5112. Feis, Herbert. The Road to Pearl Harbor: The Coming of the War Between the United States and Japan. Princeton U Pr. 1950. $12.50; pap. $2.95. 940.532
1. Japan — Foreign Relations — U. S. 2. U. S. — Foreign Relations — Japan. 3. World War, 1939-1945 — Japan. 4. World War, 1939-1945 — U. S.

5113. Bialer, Seweryn, ed. Stalin and His Generals: Soviet Military Memoirs of World War II. Pegasus. 1969. $10.00. 940.534
1. Stalin, Joseph Vissarionvich, 1879-1953. 2. World War, 1939-1945 — Personal Narratives. 3. World War, 1939-1945 — Russia.

5114. Frank, Anne. Diary of a Young Girl. Modern Lib. $2.95. 940.534(B)
1. Frank, Anne, 1929-1945. 2. Netherlands — History — German Occupation, 1939-1945. 3. World War, 1939-1945 — Jews.

5115. Korbonski, Stefan. Fighting Warsaw: The Story of the Polish Underground State 1939-1945. Funk & W. 1969. $6.00; pap. $2.95. 940.534
1. Poland — History — Occupation, 1939-1945. 2. World War, 1939-1945 — Underground Movements — Poland.

5116. Warmbrunn, Werner. The Dutch Under German Occupation, 1940-1945. Stanford U Pr. 1963. $10.00. 940.534
1. Netherlands — History — German Occupation, 1939-1945. 2. World War, 1939-1945 — Underground Movements — Netherlands.

5117. Bergamini, David. Japan's Imperial Conspiracy. Morrow. 1971. $14.95; pap. $2.25 (PB). 940.535
1. Hirohito, Emperor of Japan, 1901- 2. Japan — Politics and Government — 1912-1945. 3. World War, 1939-1945 — Japan.

5118. Butow, Robert J. Japan's Decision to Surrender. Stanford U Pr. 1967. $8.50; pap. $2.95. 940.535
1. World War, 1939-1945 — Japan. 2. World War, 1939-1945 — Peace.

5119. Toland, John. The Rising Sun: The Decline and Fall of the Japanese Empire, 1936-1945. Random. 1970. $12.95. 940.535
1. World War, 1939-1945 — Japan.

5120. Buchanan, A. Russell. U. S. and World War II. 2 vols. Har-Row. 1964. $8.95 ea; pap. $4.95 ea. 940.539
1. World War, 1939-1945 — U. S.

940.54 World War II, 1939-1945

5121. Humble, Richard. Hitler's Generals. Doubleday. 1974. $5.95. 940.54(B)
1. Hitler, Adolf, 1889-1945. 2. World War, 1939-1945 — Germany.

5122. Sulzberger, C. L. The American Heritage Picture History of World War II. McGraw. 1970. $6.95; pap. $2.95. 940.54
1. World War, 1939-1945 — Pictorial Works.

5123. Whaley, Barton. Codeword Barbarossa. MIT Pr. 1973. $10.00; pap. $4.95. 940.541
1. World War, 1939-1945 — Germany. 2. World War, 1939-1945 — Russia. 3. World War, 1939-1945 — Secret Service.

5124. Baldwin, Hanson. Battles Lost and Won: Great Campaigns of World War II. Har-Row. 1966. $10.00; pap. $1.25 (Avon). 940.542
1. World War, 1939-1945 — Campaigns.

5125. Belote, James H. and Belote, William M. Corregidor: The Saga of a Fortress. Har-Row. 1967. $8.95. 940.542
1. Corregidor Island. 2. World War, 1939-1945 — Campaigns — Philippine Islands.

5126. Clark, Alan. Barbarossa: The Russian-German Conflict, 1941-1945. Morrow. 1965. $10.95. 940.542
1. World War, 1939-1945 — Campaigns — Eastern. 2. World War, 1939-1945 — Germany. 3. World War, 1939-1945 — Russia.

5127. Farago, Ladislas. Patton: Ordeal and Triumph. Astor-Honor. 1964. $15.00; pap. $1.25 (Dell). 940.542(B)
1. Patton, George Smith, 1885-1945. 2. World War, 1939-1945 — Campaigns and Battles.

5128. Lord, Walter. Day of Infamy. HR&W. 1957. $5.95; pap. $1.25 (Bantam). 940.542
1. Pearl Harbor, Attack on, 1941.

900 GEOGRAPHY, TRAVEL, AND HISTORY

5129. Moorehead, Alan. The March to Tunis: The North African War, 1940-1943. Har-Row. 1969. $8.50.   940.542
1. World War, 1939-1945 — Africa, North. 2. World War, 1939-1945 — Mediterranean Sea. 3. World War, 1939-1945 — Personal Narratives, England.

5130. Petrow, Richard. The Bitter Years: The Invasion and Occupation of Denmark and Norway, April, 1940-May, 1945. Morrow. 1974. $10.95.   940.542
1. Denmark — History — German Occupation, 1940-1945. 2. Norway — History — German Occupation, 1940-1945. 3. World War, 1939-1945 — Campaigns — Denmark. 4. World War, 1939-1945 — Campaigns — Norway.

5131. Ryan, Cornelius. A Bridge Too Far. S&S. 1974. $12.50.   940.542
1. Arnheim, Battle of, 1944.

5132. ———. The Last Battle. S&S. 1966. $7.50; pap. $1.25 (PB).   940.542
1. Berlin, Battle of, 1945. 2. World War, 1939-1945 — Germany — Berlin.

5133. ———. The Longest Day: June 6, 1944. S&S. 1959. $7.95; pap. $1.50 (Popular Lib).   940.542
1. Normandy, Attack on, 1944. 2. World War, 1939-1945 — Campaigns.

5134. Salisbury, Harrison E. The Nine Hundred Days: The Siege of Leningrad. Har-Row. 1969. $10.95.   940.542
1. Leningrad — Siege, 1941-1944. 2. World War, 1939-1945 — Campaigns and Battles.

5135. Schmidt, Paul K. Hitler Moves East, 1941-1943. Little. 1965. $12.50; pap. $1.65 (Ballantine).   940.542
1. World War, 1939-1945 — Campaigns, Eastern.

5136. ———. Scorched Earth. Little. 1970. $12.50; pap. $1.65.   940.542
1. World War, 1939-1945 — Campaigns, Eastern.

5137. Toland, John. The Last Hundred Days. Random. 1966. $10.00; pap. $1.65 (Bantam).   940.542
1. World War, 1939-1945 — Europe.

5138. Young, Desmond. Rommel, the Desert Fox. Har-Row. 1951. $7.95; pap. $1.25 (Berkley Pub).   940.542(B)

1. Rommel, Erwin, 1891-1944. 2. World War, 1939-1945 — Campaigns — Africa.

5139. Bekker, Cajus. The Lutwaffe War Diaries. Ziegler, Frank, tr. Ballantine. 1972. pap. $1.65.   940.544
1. World War, 1939-1945 — Aerial Operations — Germany.

5140. Hersey, John R. Hiroshima. Modern Lib. 1946. $2.95.   940.544
1. Atomic Bomb. 2. Hiroshima — Bombardment, 1945. 3. World War, 1939-1945 — Japan — Hiroshima.

5141. Lifton, Robert J. Death in Life: Survivors of Hiroshima. Random. 1969. pap. $2.95.   940.544
1. Atomic Warfare — Psychological Aspects. 2. Hiroshima — Bombardment, 1945. 3. World War, 1939-1945 — Japan — Hiroshima.

5142. Yass, Marion. Hiroshima. Putnam. 1972. $5.95.   940.544
1. Atomic Bomb — History. 2. Hiroshima — Bombardment, 1945. 3. Nagasaki — Bombardment, 1945.

5143. Morison, Samuel E. History of the United States Naval Operations in World War II. 15 vols. Little. 1947-60. $150.00; $10.00 ea.   940.545
1. World War, 1939-1945 — Naval Operations, American.

5144. ———. The Two-Ocean War: Short History of United States Navy in the Second World War. Little. 1963. $15.00.   940.545
1. World War, 1939-1945 — Naval Operations.

5145. Roscoe, Theodore. United States Submarine Operations in World War II. Naval Inst Pr. 1949. $22.50.   940.545
1. World War, 1939-1945 — Naval Operations — Submarine.

5146. Ruge, Friedrich. Der Seekrieg: The German Navy's Story, 1939-1945. Naval Inst Pr. 1957. $9.50.   940.545
1. World War, 1939-1945 — Germany — Naval Operations.

5147. Bosworth, Allan. America's Concentration Camps. Norton. 1967. $7.95.   940.547
1. Concentration Camps — U. S. 2. World War, 1939-1945 — Prisoners and Prisons, American.

900 GEOGRAPHY, TRAVEL, AND HISTORY

5148. Gordon, Ernest. Through the Valley of the Kwai. Har-Row. 1962. $4.95. 940.547
1. Burma-Siam Railroad. 2. World War, 1939-1945 — Prisoners and Prisons, Japanese.

5149. Farago, Ladislas. The Broken Seal: The Story of Operation Magic and the Pearl Harbor Disaster. Random. 1967. $10.00. 940.548
1. Cryptography. 2. Japan — Foreign Relations — U. S. 3. U. S. — Foreign Relations — Japan. 4. World War, 1939-1945 — U. S.

5150. Winterbotham, Frederick. The Ultra Secret. Har-Row. 1974. $8.95. 940.5486
1. World War, 1939-1945 — Crytography. 2. World War, 1939-1945 — Secret Service — Great Britain.

941 Scotland, Ireland

5151. Donaldson, Gordon. Scotland: James V to James VII. B&N. 1974. $13.50. 941
1. Scotland — History — 16th Century. 2. Scotland — History — 17th Century.

5152. Mitchison, Rosalind. A History of Scotland. B&N. 1970. $12.00; pap. $6.00. 941
1. Scotland — History.

5153. Pine, Leslie G. The Highland Clans. C E Tuttle. 1972. $7.50. 941
1. Scotland — History.

5154. Prebble, John. The Lion in the North: A Personal View of Scotland's History. Coward. 1971. $17.95. 941
1. Scotland — History.

5155. Chadwick, Hector M. Early Scotland: The Picts, the Scots and the Welsh of Southern Scotland. Octagon. 1972. $10.50. 941.01
1. Scotland — History — to 1057.

5156. Nicholson, Ranald. Scotland: The Later Middle Ages. B&N. 1974. $25.00. 941.02
1. Scotland — History — 1057-1603.

5157. Fraser, Antonia. Mary, Queen of Scots. Delacorte. 1969. $10.00. 941.05(B)
1. Mary Stuart, Queen of the Scots, 1542-1587.

5158. Daiches, David. The Last Stuart: The Life and Times of Bonnie Prince Charlie. Putnam. 1973. $10.00. 941.07(B)
1. Charles Edward, the Young Pretender, 1720-1788. 2. Jacobite Rebellion, 1745-1746.

5159. Kellas, James C. Modern Scotland: The Nation Since 1870. Praeger. 1968. $8.00. 941.08
1. Scotland — History.

5160. Beckett, James G. The Making of Modern Ireland, 1603-1923. Knopf. 1966. $10.00. 941.5
1. Ireland — History — 1691- 2. Ireland — History — 17th Century.

5161. Connery, Donald S. The Irish. S&S. 1968. $7.95; pap. $2.95. 941.5
1. Ireland — Civilization.

5162. O'Brien, Connor C. and O'Brien, Maire. The Story of Ireland. Viking Pr. 1972. $12.95. 941.5
1. Ireland — History.

5163. Bell, J. Bowyer. The Secret Army: A History of the IRA. MIT Pr. 1974. pap. $3.95. 941.59
1. Ireland — History — 20th Century. 2. Irish Republican Army — History. 3. Northern Ireland — History.

5164. Coogan, Timothy P. Ireland Since the Rising. Praeger. 1970. $8.95. 941.59
1. Ireland — History — 1920-

5165. Fitzgibbon, Constantine and Morrison, George. The Life and Times of Eamon de Valera. Macmillan. 1974. $8.95. 941.59(B)
1. De Valera, Eamon, 1882-1975. 2. Ireland — Politics and Government — 20th Century.

5166. Kee, Robert. The Green Flag: The Turbulent History of the Irish National Movement. Delacorte. 1972. $15.00. 941.59
1. Ireland — Politics and Government — 19th Century. 2. Ireland — Politics and Government — 20th Century. 3. Irish Question.

5167. Hastings, Max. Barricades in Belfast: The Fight for the Civil Rights in Northern Ireland. Taplinger. 1970. $5.95. 941.609
1. Northern Ireland — History. 2. Northern Ireland — Social Conditions.

5168. Mansbach, Richard W., ed. Northern Ireland: Half a Century of Partition. Facts on File. 1974. $7.95. 941.609
1. Northern Ireland — History.

900 GEOGRAPHY, TRAVEL, AND HISTORY

5169. Budge, Ian and O'Leary, Cornelius. Belfast: Approach to Crisis. St Martin. 1973. $10.95. 941.61
1. Belfast — Politics and Government.

942 England

5170. Ashley, Maurice P. Great Britain to 1688. U of Mich Pr. 1961. $7.50. 942
1. Great Britain — History.

5171. Churchill, Winston L. A History of the English-Speaking Peoples. 4 vols. Vol. 1. Birth of Britain (to 1485) 1956; Vol. 2. New World (1485-1688) 1956; Vol. 3. Age of Revolution (1688-1815) 1957; Vol. 4. Great Democracies (1815-1901) 1958. Dodd. $6.95 ea.; boxed set $25.00. 942
1. Great Britain — History.

5172. ———. Island Race. Dodd. 1968. $27.50; smaller format $9.95. 942
1. Great Britain — History.

5173. Fulford, Roger. Hanover to Windsor: British Monarchs from 1830-1936. Watts (Fontana Pap). pap. $1.75. 942(B)
1. Edward VII, King of Great Britain, 1841-1910. 2. George V, King of Great Britain, 1865-1936. 3. Victoria, Queen of Great Britain, 1819-1901. 4. William IV, King of Great Britain, 1765-1837.

5174. Morris, Jean. The Monarchs of England. McKay. 1975. $14.95. 942
1. Great Britain — Kings and Rulers.

5175. Smellie, K. B. Great Britain Since 1688. U of Mich Pr. 1962. $7.50. 942
1. Great Britain — History. 2. Great Britain — History — Modern Period, 1485-

5176. Trevelyan, George M. History of England. 3 vols. Doubleday. pap. $6.45 set. 942
1. Great Britain — History.

5177. ———. Illustrated English Social History. 4 vols. McKay. 1949-1952. $11.95 ea. 942
1. Great Britain — History. 2. Great Britain — Social Conditions.

942.01 Early History, 410-1066

5178. Ashe, Geoffrey. The Quest for Arthur's Britain. Praeger. 1968. $13.50. 942.01

1. Arthur, King. 2. Excavations (Archaeology). 3. Great Britain — Antiquities. 4. Great Britain — History — to 1066.

5179. Blair, Peter H. An Introduction to Anglo-Saxon England. Cambridge U Pr. 1954. $14.50; pap. $4.95. 942.01
1. Great Britain — History — Anglo-Saxon Period, 449-1066.

5180. ———. Roman Britain and Early England, 55 B.C. to A.D. 871. Norton. 1966. $2.45. 942.01
1. Great Britain — History — Anglo-Saxon Period, 449-1066. 2. Great Britain — History — Roman Period, 55 B.C.-449 A.D.

5181. Brown, Reginald A. Origins of English Feudalism. B&N. 1973. $8.50. 942.01
1. Great Britain — History — to 1066.

5182. Garmonsway, G. N., ed. The Anglo-Saxon Chronicle. Dutton. 1934. $3.95. 942.01
1. Anglo-Saxons. 2. Great Britain — History — Anglo-Saxon Period, 449-1066 — Sources.

5183. Grohskopf, Bernice, ed. The Treasure of Sutton Hoo: Ship-Burial for an Anglo-Saxon King. Atheneum. 1973. pap. $2.95. 942.01
1. Ship Burial. 2. Suffolk, England — Antiquities.

5184. Hawkins, Gerald S. Stonehenge Decoded. Doubleday. 1965. $6.95; pap. $2.25 (Dell). 942.01
1. Astronomy, Ancient. 2. Great Britain — History — to 1066.

5185. Helm, Peter J. Alfred the Great. T Y Crowell. 1965. $4.95. 942.01(B)
1. Alfred the Great, King of England, 849-901. 2. Great Britain — History — Anglo-Saxon Period, 449-1066.

5186. Jusserand, Jean A. English Wayfaring Life in the Middle Ages. Smith, Lucy T., tr. Corner Hse. Repr. $12.50. 942.01
1. England — Social Life and Customs. 2. Pilgrims and Pilgrimages. 3. Travel, Medieval. 4. Wayfaring Life — Great Britain.

5187. Lloyd, Alan. The Making of the King, 1066. HR&W. 1966. $6.00. 942.01
1. Great Britain — History — to 1066. 2. Harold II, King of England, 1022-1066. 3. Harold III, King of Norway. 1015-1066. 4. William I, the Conqueror, King of England, 1027-1087.

900 GEOGRAPHY, TRAVEL, AND HISTORY

5188. Morris, John. The Age of Arthur: A History of the British Isles from 350 to 650. Scribner. 1973. $17.50. 942.01
1. Great Britain — History — Anglo-Saxon Period, 449-1066. 2. Great Britain — History — Roman Period, 55 B.C-449 A.D.

5189. Richmond, Ian A. Roman Britain. rev. ed. Gannon. $5.00. 942.01
1. Great Britain — History — Roman Period, 55 B.C.-449 A.D.

5190. Stanton, Frank M. Anglo-Saxon England. 3rd ed. Oxford U Pr. 1971. $12.75. 942.01
1. Anglo-Saxons. 2. Great Britain — History — Anglo-Saxon Period, 449-1066.

942.02 Norman Period, 1066-1154

5191. Baker, Timothy. The Normans: The Men Who Made the English-Speaking World. Macmillan. 1969. pap. $2.45. 942.02
1. Great Britain — History — Edward, the Confessor, 1042-1066. 2. Great Britain — History — William I, 1066-1087. 3. Normans in England.

5192. Barlow, Frank. Edward the Confessor. U of Cal Pr. 1970. $13.75. 942.02(B)
1. Edward, the Confessor, King of England, Saint, d. 1066.

5193. Barrow, G. W. Feudal Britain: The Completion of the Medieval Kingdoms, 1066-1314. St Martin. 1956. $9.95. 942.02
1. Feudalism — Great Britain. 2. Great Britain — Politics and Government — 1066-1485.

5194. Beeler, John. Warfare in England, 1066-1189. Cornell U Pr. 1966. $19.50. 942.02
1. Great Britain — History, Military — Medieval Period.

5195. Brown, Reginald A. The Normans and the Norman Conquest. T Y Crowell. 1970. $7.50. 942.02
1. Great Britain — History — Norman Period, 1066-1154. 2. Normandy — History.

5196. Coulton, George G. Medieval Panorama: The English Scene from Conquest to Reformation. Norton. 1974. pap. $4.95. 942.02
1. England — Civilization — Medieval Period, 1066-1485.

5197. Douglas, David C. The Norman Achievement: 1050-1100. U of Cal Pr. 1969. $10.75. 942.02
1. Great Britain — History — Norman Period, 1066-1154. 2. Normans.

5198. ———. William the Conqueror: The Norman Impact Upon England. U of Cal Pr. 1964. $12.50; pap. $3.85. 942.02(B)
1. Great Britain — History — Norman Period, 1066-1154. 2. Normans. 3. William I, the Conqueror, King of England, 1027-1087.

942.03 House of Plantagenet, 1154-1339

5199. Barnie, John. War in Medieval English Society: Social Values in the Hundred Years War, 1337-1399. Cornell U Pr. 1974. $10.00. 942.03
1. England — Civilization — Medieval Period, 1066-1485. 2. Hundred Years' War, 1339-1453.

5200. Bennett, Henry S. Life on the English Manor: A Study of Peasant Conditions 1150-1400. Cambridge U Pr. 1960. $11.50; pap. $3.95. 942.03
1. England — Social Life and Customs.
2. Great Britain — History — 1066-1687.
3. Peasantry.

5201. Costain, Thomas B. Conquering Family. Popular Lib. 1971. pap. $1.25. 942.03
1. Great Britain — History — Plantagenets, 1154-1399. 2. John, King of England, 1167-1216.

5202. ———. Last Plantagenets. Popular Lib. 1971. pap. $1.25. 942.03
1. Great Britain — History — Plantagenets, 1154-1399. 2. Great Britain — History — Lancaster and York, 1399-1485. 3. Richard II, King of England, 1367-1400.

5203. ———. Magnificent Century. Popular Lib. 1971. pap. $1.25. 942.03
1. Great Britain — History — Plantagenets, 1154-1399. 2. Henry III, King of England, 1207-1272. 3. Magna Carta.

5204. ———. Three Edwards. Popular Lib. 1971. pap. $1.25. 942.03
1. Edward I, King of England, 1239-1307. 2. Edward II, King of England, 1284-1327. 3. Edward III, King of England, 1312-1377. 4. Great Britain — History.

5205. Hart, Roger. English Life in Chaucer's Day. Putnam. 1973. $6.95. 942.03

900 GEOGRAPHY, TRAVEL, AND HISTORY

1. Chaucer, Geoffrey, d. 1400 — Contemporary England. 2. Civilization, Medieval — Pictorial Works.

5206. Kelly, Amy. Eleanor of Aquitane and the Four Kings. Harvard U Pr. 1950. $15.00; pap. $2.75. 942.03(B)
1. Eleanor of Aquitane, Consort of Henry II, King of England, 1122?-1204.

5207. Warren, Wilfred L. Henry II. U of Cal Pr. 1973. $20.00. 942.03(B)
1. Great Britain — Politics and Government — 1154-1189. 2. Henry II, King of England, 1133-1189.

5208. Winston, Richard. Thomas Becket. Knopf. 1967. $10.00. 942.03(B)
1. Thomas á Becket, Saint, Archbishop of Canterbury, 1118?-1170.

942.04 House of Lancaster and York, 1399- 1485

5209. Clive, Mary. This Sun of York: A Biography of Edward IV. Knopf. 1974. $10.00. 942.04(B)
1. Edward IV, King of England, 1442-1483. 2. Great Britain — History — Edward IV, 1461-1483.

5210. Kendall, Paul M. Richard III. Norton. 1965. $8.95; pap. $1.95. 942.04(B)
1. Great Britain — History — War of the Roses. 2. Richard III, King of England, 1452-1485.

5211. ———. The Yorkist Age: Daily Life During the Wars of Roses. Norton. 1961. pap. $4.25. 942.04
1. Great Britain — History — Wars of the Roses, 1455-1485. 2. Great Britain — Social Life and Customs.

942.05 Tudor Period, 1485-1603

5212. Bowen, Catherine D. Francis Bacon: The Temper of a Man. Little. 1963. $7.50; pap. $1.95. 942.05(B)
1. Bacon, Francis, Viscount St. Albans, 1561-1626.

5213. Bruce, Marie L. Anne Boleyn. Coward. 1972. $10.00; pap. $1.75 (Paperback Lib). 942.05(B)
1. Anne Boleyn, Consort of Henry VIII, King of England, 1507-1536.

5214. Cavendish, George. Thomas Wolsey, Late Cardinal. Rowman. Repr. 1962. $7.50. 942.05(B)
1. Wolsey, Thomas, Cardinal, 1475?-1530.

5215. Chapman, Hester W. The Last Tudor King. Macmillan. 1959. $4.95. 942.05(B)
1. Edward VI, King of England, 1537-1553.

5216. Chrimes, Stanley B. Henry VII. U of Cal Pr. 1973. $16.00. 942.05(B)
1. Great Britain — Politics and Government — 1485-1509. 2. Henry VII, King of England, 1457-1509.

5217. Elton, Geoffrey R. England Under the Tudors. 2nd ed. B&N. 1974. $10.00. 942.05
1. Great Britain — History — Tudors, 1485-1603.

5218. Ferguson, Charles Wright. Naked to Mine Enemies, the Life of Cardinal Wolsey. Little. 1958. $8.95; pap. $2.45. 942.05(B)
1. Great Britain — History — Tudors, 1485-1603. 2. Henry VII, King of England, 1457-1509. 3. Henry VIII, King of England, 1491-1547. 4. Wolsey, Thomas, Cardinal, 1475?-1530.

5219. Graham, Winston. The Spanish Armadas. Doubleday. 1972. $14.95. 942.05
1. Armada, 1588. 2. Great Britain — History, Naval — Tudors, 1485-1603. 3. Spain — History, Naval.

5220. Lacey, Robert. Robert, Earl of Essex. Atheneum. 1971. $8.95. 942.05(B)
1. Essex, Robert Devereux, Earl of, 1566-1601.

5221. ———. Sir Walter Raleigh. Atheneum. 1974. $10.95. 942.05(B)
1. Raleigh, Walter, 1552?-1618.

5222. Martienssen, Anthony K. Queen Catherine Parr. McGraw. 1974. $7.95. 942.05(B)
1. Catherine Parr, Consort of Henry VIII, King of England, 1512-1548.

5223. Mathew, David. Lady Jane Grey: The Setting of the Reign. B&N. 1972. $14.00. 942.05(B)
1. Dudley, Lady Jane, 1537-1554. 2. Great Britain — Politics and Government — 1485-1603.

5224. Mattingly, Garrett. The Armada. HM. 1959. $7.50; pap. $2.65. 942.05
1. Armada, 1588.

900 GEOGRAPHY, TRAVEL, AND HISTORY

5225. ———. Catherine of Aragon. Peter Smith. $4.50; pap. $1.95 (Random). 942.05(B)
1. Catherine of Aragon, Consort of Henry VIII, King of England, 1512-1548.

5226. Maynard, Theodore. The Humanist As Hero: The Life of Sir Thomas More. Hafner. Repr. 1947. $11.95. 942.05(B)
1. More, Sir Thomas, Saint, 1478-1535.

5227. Neale, John. Queen Elizabeth I. St Martin. 1959. $10.95. 942.05(B)
1. Elizabeth I, Queen of England, 1533-1603. 2. Great Britain — History — 1492-1648.

5228. Richardson, Walter C. Mary Tudor, the White Queen. U of Wash Pr. 1969. $10.00. 942.05(B)
1. Mary, Consort of Louis XII, King of France, 1496-1533.

5229. Rowse, Alfred L. The Elizabethan Renaissance: The Life of the Society. Scribner. 1972. $12.50. 942.05
1. England — Civilization — 16th Century. 2. Great Britain — Social Conditions.

5230. Scarisbrick, J. J. Henry VIII. U of Cal Pr. 1968. $12.50. 942.05(B)
1. Henry VIII, King of England, 1491-1547.

5231. Smith, Lacey B., ed. The Elizabethan World. HM. 1971. $6.50; pap. $2.25. 942.05
1. Europe — History — 1492-1648. 2. Great Britain — Civilization. 3. Great Britain — History — Tudors, 1485-1603.

5232. Waldman, Milton. The Lady Mary. Scribner. 1972. $7.95. 942.05(B)
1. Mary I, Queen of England, 1516-1558.

5233. Wernham, R. B. Before the Armada: The Emergence of the English Nation, 1485-1588. Norton. 1972. pap. $3.25. 942.05
1. Great Britain — Foreign Relations — 16th Century. 2. Great Britain — History — Tudors, 1485-1603.

942.06 Stuart Period, 1603-1714

5234. Ashley, Maurice. England in the Seventeenth Century: 1603-1714. Penguin. 1961. $1.75. 942.06
1. Great Britain — History — Stuarts, 1603-1714.

5235. Barnett, Correlli. The First Churchill: Marlborough, Soldier and Statesman. Putnam. 1974. $14.95. 942.06(B)
1. Marlborough, John Churchill, 1st Duke of, 1650-1722.

5236. Bowen, Catherine D. The Lion and the Throne: The Life and Times of Sir Edward Coke. Little. 1957. $10.00; pap. $3.45. 942.06(B)
1. Coke, Sir Edward, 1552-1634. 2. Great Britain — History.

5237. Bridenbaugh, Carl. Vexed and Troubled Englishmen, 1590-1642. Oxford U Pr. 1968. $12.50. 942.06
1. Great Britain — Emigration and Immigration. 2. Great Britain — History — Early Stuarts — 1603-1649.

5238. Fraser, Antonia. Cromwell, the Lord Protector. Knopf. 1973. $12.50. 942.06(B)
1. Cromwell, Oliver, 1599-1658.

5239. Hill, John E. The World Turned Upside Down: Radical Ideas During the English Revolution. Viking Pr. 1972. $10.95; pap. $2.95. 942.06
1. Great Britain — History — Puritan Revolution, 1642-1660. 2. Great Britain — Intellectual Life — 17th Century. 3. Great Britain — Religion — 17th Century.

5240. Mathew, David. James First. U of Ala Pr. 1968. $10.00. 942.06(B)
1. James I, King of Great Britain, 1566-1625.

5241. Notestein, Wallace. English People on the Eve of Colonization: 1603-1630. Har-Row. 1954. $10.00; pap. $2.95. 942.06
1. Early Stuarts, 1603-1649. 2. Great Britain — History. 3. Great Britain — Social Conditions.

5242. Pepys, Samuel. Diary. 2 vols. Random. 1946. $20.00. 942.06(B)
1. Great Britain — History — Stuarts, 1603-1714. 2. Great Britain — Social Life and Customs.

5243. Prall, Stuart E., compiled by. The Puritan Revolution: A Documentary History. Peter Smith. $5.75. 942.06
1. Great Britain — History — Puritan Revolution — 1642-1660.

5244. Trease, Geoffrey. Samuel Pepys and His World. Putnam. 1972. $6.95. 942.06(B)
1. England — Social Life and Customs — 17th Century. 2. Pepys, Samuel, 1633-1703.

900 GEOGRAPHY, TRAVEL, AND HISTORY

5245. Trevelyan, George M. England Under the Stuarts. 21st ed. B&N. 1961. $12.00; pap. $6.00. 942.06
1. Great Britain — History — Stuarts, 1603-1714.

5246. ———. The English Revolution, 1688-1689. Peter Smith. 1939. $3.75. 942.06
1. Great Britain — History — Revolution of 1688.

5247. Van Der Zee, Henri and Van der Zee, Barbara. William and Mary. Knopf. 1973. $12.50. 942.06(B)
1. Great Britain — History — William and Mary, 1689-1702. 2. Mary II, Queen of England, 1662-1694. 3. William III, King of Great Britain, 1650-1702.

5248. Wilson, David H. King James VI and I. Oxford U Pr. 1967. pap. $3.95. 942.06(B)
1. James I, King of Great Britain, 1566-1625.

942.07 House of Hanover, 1714-1837

5249. Green, Vivian H. The Hanoverians, 1714-1815. St Martin. 1948. $6.95. 942.07
1. Great Britain — History- 1714-1837. 2. Great Britain — History — 18th Century.

5250. Lloyd, Alan. The King Who Lost America: A Portrait of the Life and Times of George III. Doubleday. 1971. $7.95. 942.07(B)
1. George III, King of Great Britain, 1738-1820.

5251. Longford, Elizabeth. Wellington: Pillar of State. Har-Row. 1973. $12.50. 942.07(B)
1. Wellington, Arthur Wellesley, 1st Duke of, 1769-1852.

5252. ———. Wellington: The Years of the Sword. Har-Row. 1969. $12.50. 942.07(B)
1. Wellington, Arthur Wellesley, 1st Duke of, 1769-1852.

5253. Namier, Lewis. England in the Age of the American Revolution. 2nd ed. St Martin. 1961. $13.50; pap. $7.95. 942.07
1. Great Britain — History — Revolution — 18th Century. 2. Great Britain — History — George III, 1760-1820. 3. U. S. — History — Revolution.

5254. Southey, Robert. Life of Nelson. AMS Pr. Repr. 1922. $18.50. 942.07(B)
1. Nelson, Horatio, 1758-1805.

5255. Ziegler, Philip. King William the Fourth. Har-Row. 1973. $12.50. 942.07(B)
1. Great Britain — History — William IV, 1830-1837. 2. William IV, King of Great Britain, 1765-1837.

942.08 Victoria and House of Windsor, 1837

5256. Cecil, David. Melbourne. Greenwood. Repr. 1954. $19.25. 942.08(B)
1. Melbourne, William Lamb, 1779-1848. 2. Victoria, Queen of Great Britain, 1819-1901.

5257. Evans, R. J. The Victorian Age, 1815-1914. 2nd ed. St Martin. 1968. $7.95. 942.08
1. Great Britain — History — Victoria, 1837-1901.

5258. Longford, Elizabeth. Queen Victoria: Born to Succeed. Har-Row. 1965. $12.50; pap. $1.95. 942.08(B)
1. Great Britain — History — 19th Century. 2. Victoria, Queen of Great Britain, 1819-1901.

5259. MacDonald, Donald F. The Age of Transition: Britain in the 19th and 20th Centuries. St Martin. 1967. $8.95. 942.08
1. Great Britain — History — 19th Century. 2. Great Britain — History — 20th Century.

5260. Magnus, Philip. Kitchener: Portrait of an Imperialist. Dutton. 1968. $7.50; pap. $2.95. 942.08(B)
1. Kitchener, Horatio Herbert, 1st Earl, 1850-1916. 2. Great Britain — History — 19th Century. 3. Great Britain — History — 20th Century.

5261. Morris, James. Heaven's Command: An Imperial Progress. HarBraceJ. 1973. $11.50. 942.08
1. Great Britain — Colonies — History. 2. Great Britain — History — Victoria, 1837-1901.

5262. Reader, W. J. Victorian England. Putnam. 1974. $10.00. 942.08

5263. Ridley, Jasper G. Lord Palmerston. Dutton. 1971. $12.50. 942.08(B)
1. Palmerston, Henry John Temple, 3rd Viscount, 1784-1865.

5264. Tingsten, Herbert L. Victoria and the Victorians. Delacorte. 1972. $15.00. 942.08
1. Victoria, Queen of Great Britain, 1819-1901.

900 GEOGRAPHY, TRAVEL, AND HISTORY

5265. Woodham-Smith, Cecil B. The Reason Why. McGraw. 1971. $7.95; pap. $2.25 (Dutton). 942.08
1. Crimean War, 1853-1856. 2. Great Britain — History — 19th Century. 3. Light Brigade.

5266. Young, George M. Victorian England: Portrait of an Age. 2nd ed. Oxford U Pr. 1964. pap. $1.95. 942.08
1. Great Britain — History — Victoria, 1837-1901.

5267. Briggs, Asa. Victorian People: A Reassessment of Persons and Themes, 1851-67. U of Chicago Pr. 1970. $7.50. 942.081
1. Great Britain — History — Victoria, 1837-1901.

5268. Barnett, Correlli. The Collapse of British Power. Morrow. 1972. $15.00. 942.082
1. Commonwealth of Nations — History. 2. Great Britain — Foreign Relations — 20th Century. 3. Great Britain — Politics and Government — 20th Century.

5269. Battiscombe, Georgina. Queen Alexandra, 1844-1925. HM. 1970. $7.50. 942.082(B)
1. Alexandra, Queen Consort of Edward VII, King of England, 1844-1925. 2. Great Britain — History — 20th Century.

5270. Cross, Colin. The Fall of the British Empire, 1918-1968. Coward. 1969. $8.95. 942.082
1. Commonwealth of Nations. 2. Great Britain — Colonies. 3. Great Britain — History — 20th Century.

5271. Medlicott, William N. Contemporary England: 1914-1964. McKay. 1967. $10.95. 942.082
1. Great Britain — History — 20th Century.

5272. Graves, Robert and Hodge, Alan. The Long Week-End: A Social History of Great Britain, 1918-1939. Norton. 1963. pap. $2.95. 942.083
1. Great Britain — History — 20th Century. 2. Great Britain — Social Life and Customs.

5273. Mowat, Charles L. Britain Between the Wars; 1918-1940. U of Chicago Pr. 1955. $13.50; pap. $4.95 (Beacon Pr). 942.083
1. Great Britain — History — 20th Century.

5274. Calder, Angus. The People's War: Britain, 1939-1945. Pantheon. 1969. $8.95; pap. $2.50 1972 (Ace Bks). 942.084
1. Great Britain — History — 20th Century. 2. World War, 1939-1945 — Great Britain.

5275. Hibbert, Christopher. Edward the Uncrowned King. St Martin. 1973. $10.95. 942.084
1. Edward VIII, King of Great Britain, 1894-1972.

5276. Taylor, Alan J. P. English History, 1914-1945. Oxford U Pr. 1965. $12.50; pap. $4.50. 942.085
1. Great Britain — History — 20th Century.

5277. Costigan, Giovanni. Makers of Modern England: The Force of Individual Genius in History. Macmillan. 1967. $6.95. 942.09(B)
1. Great Britain — Biography.

942.9 Wales

5278. Habgood, Noel. Heritage of Wales. Porter. 1971. $5.00. 942.9
1. Wales — History.

5279. Roderick, Arthur J., ed. Wales Through the Ages. 2 vols. Dufour. $12.50. 942.9
1. Wales — History.

Recommended Series

5280. English Monarchs Series. U of Cal Pr.

5281. The Oxford History of England. Clark, George, ed.. Oxford U Pr. for complete list see Oxford University Press catalogue.

943 Germany

5282. Barraclough, Geoffrey. The Origins of Modern Germany. Putnam. 1963. pap. $2.95. 943
1. Germany — History.

5283. Butler, Rohan D. The Roots of National Socialism, 1783-1933. Fertig. 1968. $13.00. 943
1. Germany — Civilization. 2. Germany — Politics and Government. 3. National Socialism.

5284. Carsten, Franz L. Origins of Prussia. Oxford U Pr. 1954. $7.25; pap. $4.25. 943
1. Prussia — History.

900 GEOGRAPHY, TRAVEL, AND HISTORY

5285. Halecki, Oscar. Borderlands of Western Civilization: A History of East Central Europe. Ronald. 1952. $9.50. 943
1. Central Europe — History. 2. Slavs — History.

5286. Holborn, Hajo. A History of Modern Germany. 3 vols. Knopf. 1956-69. Vol. 1. $10.00; Vol. 2. $10.75; Vol. 3. $13.95. 943
1. Germany — History.

5287. Palmer, Alan W. The Lands Between: A History of East-Central Europe Since the Congress of Vienna. Macmillan. 1970. $9.95. 943
1. Central Europe — History. 2. Europe, Eastern — History.

5288. Reinhardt, Kurt F. Germany: Two Thousand Years. 2 vols. rev. ed. Ungar. $14.00; pap. $7.40. 943
1. Germany — History.

943.02-943.07 Early Holy Roman Empire - Unification

5289. Barraclough, Geoffrey, tr. Medieval Germany, 911-1250. 2 vols. B&N. 1961. $12.50. 943.02
1. Church and State in Germany. 2. Germany — Constitutional History. 3. Germany — History — to 1517.

5290. Ritter, Gerhard. Frederick the Great: A Historical Profile. Paret, Peter, tr. U of Cal Pr. 1968. $8.75; pap. $2.85. 943.053(B)
1. Frederick the Great, King of Prussia, 1712-1786.

5291. Padover, Saul K. Revolutionary Emperor: Joseph the Second of Austria. rev. ed. Shoe String. 1967. $9.00. 943.057(B)
1. Austria — History. 2. Joseph II, Emperor of Germany, 1741-1790.

5292. Böhme, Helmut, compiled by. The Foundation of the German Empire: Select Documents. Oxford U Pr. 1971. $12.00. 943.07
1. Germany — History — 1848-1870 — Sources.

943.08 Empire, Third Reich, Republic, 1866-

5293. Howard, Michael. The Franco-Prussian War: The German Invasion of France, 1870-1871. Macmillan. 1962. pap. $3.95. 943.08
1. Franco-German War, 1870-1871.

5294. Kohn, Hans. The Mind of Germany: The Education of a Nation. Har-Row. 1960. pap. $2.75. 943.08
1. Germany — History — 1866- 2. Germany — Intellectual Life. 3. Nationalism.

5295. Meyer, Henry C. The Long Generation: Germany from Empire to Ruin, 1913-1945. Walker & Co. 1973. $12.50; pap. $5.50 (Har-Row). 943.08
1. Germany — History — William II, 1888-1918 — Sources. 2. Germany — History — 1918-1933 — Sources. 3. Germany — History — 1933-1945 — Sources.

5296. Pinson, Koppel S. Modern Germany. 2nd ed. Macmillan. 1966. $11.50. 943.08
1. Germany — History — 1789-1900. 2. Germany — History — 20th Century.

5297. Rosenberg, Arthur. Imperial Germany: The Birth of the German Republic, 1871-1918. Morrow, Ian F., tr. Oxford U Pr. pap. $2.95. 943.08
1. Germany — History — 1871-1918. 2. Germany — History — Revolution, 1918.

5298. Ryder, A. J. Twentieth Century Germany. Columbia U Pr. 1972. $12.05. 943.08
1. Germany — History — William II, 1888-1918. 2. Germany — History — 20th Century.

5299. Taylor, Alan J. P. Bismarck. Knopf. 1955. $5.95. 943.083(B)
1. Bismarck, Otto von, 1815-1898. 2. Germany — History — 1789-1900.

5300. Balfour, Michael. The Kaiser and His Times. Norton. 1972. pap. $3.95. 943.084(B)
1. Germany — History — 1871-1918. 2. Wilhelm II, German Emperor, 1859-1941.

5301. Carsten, Franz L. The Reichswehr and Politics: 1918-1933. Oxford U Pr. 1974. pap. $4.25. 943.085
1. Germany — Politics and Government — 1918-1933. 2. Germany, Reichswehr.

5302. Gay, Peter. Weimar Culture: The Outsider As Insider. Har-Row. 1968. $5.95; pap. $1.95. 943.085
1. Germany — History — 1918-1933.

5303. Laqueur, Walter. Weimar: A Cultural History, 1918-1933. Putnam. 1974. $8.95. 943.085

900 GEOGRAPHY, TRAVEL, AND HISTORY

1. Germany — Intellectual Life — 1918-1933.
2. Germany — Politics and Government — 1918-1933.

5304. Nicholls, A. J. Weimar and the Rise of Hitler. Thorne, Christopher, ed. St Martin. 1969. $6.95; pap. $3.50.   943.085
1. Germany — History — 1918-1933. 2. Germany — Politics and Government — 1918-1933. 3. Hitler, Adolf, 1889-1945.

5305. Vogt, Hannah. Burden of Guilt: A Short History of Germany, 1914-1945. Oxford U Pr. 1964. $7.50; pap. $2.95.   943.085
1. Germany — History — 1918-1933. 2. Germany — History — 1933-1945.

5306. Watt, Richard M. Kings Depart: The Tragedy of Germany: Versailles and the German Revolution. S&S. 1969. $10.00; pap. $3.45.   943.085
1. Germany — History — Revolution, 1918. 2. Germany — Politics and Government, 1918-1933. 3. Versailles, Treaty of, June 28, 1919 (Germany).

5307. Wheeler-Bennett, John W. Nemesis of Power: The German Army in Politics, 1918-1945. 2nd ed. St Martin. 1964. $15.00; pap. $5.95.   943.085
1. Germany — Army — History — 1918-1933. 2. Germany — History — 1933-1945. 3. Germany — Politics and Government — 1918-1933. 4. Germany — Politics and Government — 1933-1945. 5. World War, 1939-1945 — Germany.

5308. Bullock, Alan. Hitler, a Study in Tyranny. rev ed. Har-Row. 1964. pap. $4.75.   943.086(B)
1. Germany — History — 1933-1945. 2. Germany — Politics and Government — 20th Century. 3. Hitler, Adolf, 1889-1945.

5309. Davidson, Eugene. Trial of the Germans. Macmillan. 1966. $12.50; pap. $3.95.   943.086
1. Nuremberg Trial of Major German War Criminals, 1945-1946.

5310. Deutsch, Harold C. The Conspiracy Against Hitler in the Twilight War. U of Minn Pr. 1968. $10.00.   943.086
1. Anti-Nazi Movement. 2. Hitler, Adolf, 1889-1945. 3. Pius XII, Pope, 1876-1958.

5311. Fest, Joachim C. Hitler. HarBraceJ. 1974. $15.00.   943.086(B)
1. Hitler, Adolf, 1889-1945.

5312. Fest, Joachim C. The Face of the Third Reich: Portraits of the Nazi Leadership. Bullock, Michael, tr. Pantheon. 1970. $12.50.   943.086
1. Germany — Biography. 2. National Socialism.

5313. Grunberger, Richard. The Twelve Year Reich: A Social History of Nazi Germany, 1933-1945. HR&W. 1971. $10.00.   943.086
1. Germany — Intellectual Life. 2. Germany — Politics and Government — 1933-1945. 3. Germany — Social Conditions.

5314. Heiber, Helmut. Goebbels. Hawthorn. 1972. $9.95.   943.086(B)
1. Goebbels, Joseph, 1897-1945.

5315. Heiden, Konrad. Der Fuehrer: Hitler's Rise to Power. Fertig. 1968. $16.75; pap. $3.95 (Beacon Pr).   943.086
1. Germany — History — 1933-1945. 2. Hitler, Adolf, 1889-1945.

5316. Hitler, Adolf. Mein Kampf. Manheim, Ralph, tr. HM. 1943. $10.00; pap. $3.95.   943.086
1. Germany — History — 1933-1945. 2. Germany — Politics and Government. 3. National Socialism.

5317. Hohne, Heinz. The Order of the Death's Head: The Story of Hitler's S.S. Barry, Richard, tr. Coward. 1970. $12.50.   943.086
1. Germany — History — 1933-1945. 2. National Socialist Party (Germany). 3. World War, 1939-1945 — Germany.

5318. Hutton, J. Bernard. Hess: The Man and His Mission. Macmillan. 1971. $6.95.   943.086(B)
1. Germany — History — 1933-1945. 2. Hess, Rudolf, 1894-

5319. Mayer, Milton S. They Thought They Were Free: The Germans, 1933-1945. 2nd ed. U of Chicago Pr. 1966. $10.00; pap. $2.45.   943.086
1. Germany — History — 1933-1945. 2. Germany — Social Conditions — Case Studies. 3. Jews in Germany. 4. National Socialism.

5320. Mosse, George L. The Crisis of German Ideology: Intellectual Origins of the Third Reich. G&D. 1964. $5.95; pap. $2.95.   943.086

900 GEOGRAPHY, TRAVEL, AND HISTORY

1. Germany — Intellectual Life. 2. National Socialism.

5321. Neumann, Franz. Behemoth: The Structure and Practice of National Socialism, 1933-1944. 2nd ed. Octagon. 1963. $18.50; pap. $4.25 (Har-Row). 943.086
1. Germany — History — 1933-1945. 2. National Socialism.

5322. O'Neill, Robert J. The German Army and the Nazi Party, 1933-1939. Heineman. 1967. $8.50. 943.086
1. Germany — Army. 2. Germany — Politics and Government — 1933-1945. 3. National Socialist Party.

5323. Remak, Joachim, ed. The Nazi Years: A Documentary History. P-H. 1969. $4.95; pap. $2.45. 943.086
1. Germany — History — 1918-1933. 2. Germany — History — 1933-1945. 3. National Socialism.

5324. Shirer, William L. The Rise and Fall of the Third Reich: A History of Nazi Germany. S&S. 1960. $12.50; pap. $5.95 2 vols. 943.086
1. Germany — History — 1918-1933. 2. Germany — History — 1933-1945. 3. Hitler, Adolf, 1889-1945.

5325. Smith, Bradley F. Heinrich Himmler: A Nazi in the Making, 1900-1926. Hoover Inst Pr. 1971. $6.95. 943.086
1. Himmler, Heinrich, 1900-1945.

5326. Speer, Albert. Inside the Third Reich. Winston, Richard and Winston, Clara, trs. from Ger. Macmillan. 1970. $12.50; pap. $1.95 (Avon). 943.086
1. Germany — History — 1918-1933. 2. Germany — History — 1933-1945.

5327. Stein, George H. The Waffen S.S. Hitler's Elite Guard at War, 1939-1945. Cornell U Pr. 1966. $12.50. 943.086
1. Germany — History — 1933-1945. 2. World War, 1939-1945 — Germany.

5328. Wiesel, Elie. Legends of Our Time. Donadio, Stephen, tr. HR&W. 1968. $5.95; pap. $1.25 (Avon). 943.086
1. Jews — Persecutions.

5329. Armstrong, Anne. Berliners: Both Sides of the Wall. Rutgers U Pr. 1973. $12.50. 943.087
1. Berlin — Politics and Government — 1945- 2. Berlin — Social Life and Customs.

5330. Bailey, George. Germany: The Biography of an Obsession. T Y Crowell. 1972. $10.00. 943.087
1. Germans. 2. Germany — History — Allied Occupation, 1945-

5331. Balfour, Michael. West Germany. Praeger. 1968. $7.50. 943.087
1. Germany (Federal Republic, 1949-). 2. Germany — Politics and Government.

5332. Childs, David. East Germany. Praeger. 1969. $8.50. 943.087
1. Germany (Democratic Republic, 1949-

5333. Gimbel, John. American Occupation of Germany: Politics and the Military, 1945-1949. Stanford U Pr. 1968. $10.00. 943.087
1. Germany — History — Allied Occupation, 1945-

5334. Harris, Whitney R. Tyranny on Trial: The Evidence at Nuremberg. S Meth U Pr. 1954. $10.00. 943.087
1. War Crimes — Trials — Nuremberg, 1945-

5335. Prittie, Terence C. Willy Brandt: Portrait of a Statesman. Schocken. 1974. $10.50. 943.087(B)
1. Brandt, Willy, 1913-

5336. Walton, Henry. Germany. Walker & Co. 1969. $8.50. 943.087
1. Germany (Federal Republic, 1949-) — History.

943.1 Northeastern Germany

5337. Morris, Eric. Blockade: Berlin and the Cold War. Stein & Day. 1973. $10.00. 943.1
1. Berlin — Blockade, 1948-1949. 2. Berlin Question (1945-).

5338. Nelson, Walter H. The Soldier Kings: The House of Hohenzollern. Putnam. 1970. $8.95. 943.1
1. Hohenzollern, House of. 2. Prussia — History.

943.6 Austria

5339. Crankshaw, Edward. The Habsburgs: Portrait of a Dynasty. Viking Pr. 1971. $16.95. 943.6
1. Austria — Politics and Government. 2. Habsburg, House of — History.

900 GEOGRAPHY, TRAVEL, AND HISTORY

5340. Lingelbach, William E. Austria-Hungary: Based on the Work of Paul Louis Leger. Arno. Repr. 1967. $22.00. 943.6
1. Austria — Hungary.

5341. May, Arthur J. Age of Metternich, 1814-1848. rev. ed. Peter Smith. $5.00; pap. $3.00 (HR&W). 943.6
1. Europe — Politics — 1815-1848.

5342. Bright, James F. Maria Theresa. Bks for Libs. Repr. 1897. $9.75. 943.603(B)
1. Austria — History — Maria Theresa, 1740-1780. 2. Maria Theresa, Empress of Austria, 1717-1780.

5343. Tapié, Victor L. The Rise and Fall of the Habsburg Monarchy. Praeger. 1971. $15.00. 943.603
1. Austria — Politics and Government. 2. Bohemia — Politics and Government. 3. Habsburg, House of. 4. Hungary — Politics and Government.

5344. Valliana, Leo. The End of Austria-Hungary. Knopf. 1973. $15.00. 943.604
1. Austria — Politics and Government — 1868-1917. 2. Karl I, Emperor of Austria — 1887-1922. 3. Nationalism — Austria.

5345. Baden, William B. Austria Between East and West, 1945-1955. Stanford U Pr. 1966. $8.50. 943.605
1. Austria — History — Allied Occupation, 1945-1955.

5346. Barker, Elisabeth. Austria, 1918-1972. U of Miami Pr. 1973. $12.50. 943.605
1. Austria — Politics and Government — 1918-1938. 2. Austria — Politics and Government — 1938-1945. 3. Austria — Politics and Government — 1945-

5347. Stadler, Karl R. Austria. Praeger. 1971. $9.50. 943.605
1. Austria — History — 20th Century.

5348. Wagner, Dieter and Tomkowitz, Gerhard. Anschluss: The Week Hitler Seized Vienna. St Martin. 1971. $8.95. 943.605
1. Anschluss Movement — 1918-1938. 2. Austria — History — 1918-1938.

943.7 Czechoslovakia

5349. Mamatey, Victor S. and Luza, Radomir. A History of the Czechoslovak Republic, 1918-1948. Princeton U Pr. 1973. $22.50; pap. $9.75. 943.7
1. Czechoslovak Republic — History.

5350. Seton-Watson, Robert W. A History of the Czechs and Slovaks. Shoe String. 1965. $10.00. 943.7
1. Bohemia — History. 2. Czechoslovak Republic — History. 3. Slovakia — History.

5351. Wellek, Rene, ed. The Meaning of Czech History by Thomas Masaryk. U of NC Pr. 1974. $9.95. 943.7
1. Czechoslovak Republic — History.

5352. Masaryk, Thomas G. Making of a State. Fertig. 1927. $15.00. 943.703
1. Czechoslovak Republic — History.

5353. Dubcek, Alexander. Czechoslovakia's Blueprint for Freedom. Ello, Paul, ed. Acropolis. 1968. pap. $2.95. 943.704
1. Czechoslovak Republic — History — Intervention, 1968. 2. Czechoslovak Republic — Politics and Government — 1968.

5354. Remington, Robin A., ed. Winter in Prague: Documents on Czechoslovak Communism in Crisis. MIT Pr. 1969. $12.50; pap. $2.95. 943.704
1. Czechoslovak Republic — Politics and Government — 1968- 2. Czechoslovak Republic — History — Intervention — 1968- — Sources.

5355. Schwartz, Harry. Prague's 200 Days: The Struggle for Democracy in Czechoslovakia. Praeger. 1969. $7.50. 943.704
1. Czechoslovak Republic — History. 2. Czechoslovak Republic — Politics and Government — 1968-

5356. Shawcross, William. Dubcek. S&S. 1971. $7.95. 943.704(B)
1. Czechoslovak Republic — Politics and Government — 1968-

5357. Szulc, Tad. Czechoslovakia Since World War II. Viking Pr. 1973. $14.00.
943.704
1. Czechoslovak Republic — History — 1945-

5358. Taborsky, Edward. Communism in Czechoslovakia, 1948-1960. Princeton U Pr. 1961. $17.50. 943.704
1. Communism — Czechoslovak Republic. 2. Czechoslovak Republic — Politics and Government.

900 GEOGRAPHY, TRAVEL, AND HISTORY

5359. Windsor, Philip and Roberts, Adam. Czechoslovakia 1968: Reform, Repression and Resistance. Columbia U Pr. 1969. $10.00; pap. $2.50. 943.704
1. Czechoslovak Republic — History — Intervention, 1968- 2. Czechoslovak Republic — Politics and Government.

943.8 Poland

5360. Bethell, Nicholas. Gomulka: His Poland, His Communism. Penguin. 1973. $2.65. 943.8(B)
1. Gomulka, Wladyslaw, 1906- 2. Poland — Politics and Government — 1945.

5361. Hiscocks, Richard. Poland: Bridge for the Abyss. Oxford U Pr. 1963. $8.50. 943.8
1. Communism — Poland. 2. Poland — History.

5362. Kaplan, Chaim A. Scroll of Agony: The Warsaw Diary of Chaim A. Kaplan. Katsh, Abraham I., ed. & tr. Macmillan. 1965. $6.95. 943.8
1. Jews in Warsaw — History — Sources. 2. World War, 1939-1945 — Atrocities.

5363. Reddaway, William W., et al, eds. Cambridge History of Poland. 2 vols. Octagon. Repr. 1941. $60.00. 943.8
1. Poland — History.

5364. Kosary, Domokos G. A History of Hungary. Arno. Repr. 1941. $21.00. 943.9
1. Hungary — History.

5365. Nagy-Talavera, Nicholas M. The Green Shirts and the Others: A History of Fascism in Hungary and Rumania. Hoover Inst Pr. 1970. $9.95. 943.905
1. Hungary — Politics and Government — 1918-1945. 2. Rumania — Politics and Government.

943.91 Hungary

5366. Barber, Noel. Seven Days of Freedom: The Hungarian Uprising. Stein & Day. 1974. $8.95. 943.9105
1. Hungary — History — Revolution, 1956.

5367. Kecskemeti, Paul. Unexpected Revolution. Stanford U Pr. 1961. $7.50. 943.9105
1. Hungary — History — Revolution, 1956.

5368. Sartre, Jean-Paul. The Ghost of Stalin. Fletcher, Martha, tr. Braziller. 1968. $4.50. 943.9105
1. Communism — Russia. 2. Hungary — History — Revolution, 1956. 3. Hungary — Politics and Government — 1945-

944 France

5369. Cobban, Alfred. A History of Modern France. Braziller. 1965. $10.00. 944
1. France — History.

5370. De Gramont, Sanche. The French: Portrait of a People. Putnam. 1969. $7.95. 944
1. France — Civilization. 2. National Characteristics, French.

5371. Guerard, Albert L. France: A Modern History. U of Mich Pr. 1969. $10.00. 944
1. France — History.

5372. Knapton, Ernest J. France: An Interpretative History. Scribner. 1971. $15.00. 944
1. France — History.

944.01-944.03 Early History - House of Bourbon, 1589-1789

5373. Bullough, Donald. The Age of Charlemagne. Putnam. 1966. $15.00. 944.01
1. Charlemagne, 742-814. 2. France — History — Carlovingian and Early Period to 987.

5374. Cabaniss, Allen. Charlemagne. Twayne. 1971. $6.95. 944.01(B)
1. Charlemagne, 742-814.

5375. Guerard, Albert L. French Civilization from Its Origins to the Close of the Middle Ages. Cooper Sq. Repr. 1921. $8.50. 944.02
1. France — Civilization.

5376. Kendall, Paul M. Louis XI: "...the Universal Spider". Norton. 1970. $10.00. 944.02(B)
1. France — History — House of Valois, 1328-1589. 2. Louis XI, King of France, 1423-1483.

5377. Michelet, Jules. Joan of Arc. Guerard, Albert, tr. U of Mich Pr. 1957. pap. $1.95. 944.02(B)
1. France — History. 2. Joan of Arc, Saint, 1412-1431.

900 GEOGRAPHY, TRAVEL, AND HISTORY

5378. Vale, M. G. A. Charles VII. U of Cal Pr. 1974. $18.00.   944.02(B)
1. Charles VII, King of France, 1403-1461.

5379. Auchincloss, Louis. Richelieu. Viking Pr. 1972. $16.95.   944.03(B)
1. Richelieu, Armand Jean du Plessis, Cardinal, duc de, 1585-1642.

5380. Castelot, Andre. Queen of France. Har-Row. 1957. $10.00.   944.03(B)
1. Marie Antoinette, Consort of Louis XIV, King of France, 1755-1793.

5381. Guerard, Albert L. French Civilization in the 19th Century: A Historical Introduction. Cooper Sq. Repr. 1918. $8.50.   944.03
1. France — Civilization — 1830-1900.

5382. Lewis, Warren H. The Splendid Century: Life in the France of Louis XIV. Morrow. 1971. pap. $2.50.   944.03
1. France — Social Conditions. 2. Louis XIV, King of France, 1638-1715. 3. Seventeenth Century.

5383. Mitford, Nancy. Madame de Pompadour. Har-Row. 1968. $17.50. 944.03(B)
1. Pompadour, Jeanne Antoinete, Marquise de, 1721-1764.

5384. ———. The Sun King: Louis Fourteenth at Versailles. Har-Row. 1966. $15.00.   944.03(B)
1. France — History — Bourbons, 1589-1789. 2. Louis XIV, King of France, 1638-1715.

5385. Rule, John C. Louis XIV and the Craft of Kingship. Ohio St U Pr. 1970. $12.00.   944.03
1. Louis XIV, King of France, 1638-1715.

5386. Saint-Simon, Louis. Louis XIV at Versailles. Flower, Desmond, ed. & tr. Dufour. 1954. $3.95.   944.03
1. France — Court and Courtiers. 2. France — History — Louis XIV, 1643-1715.

5387. Treasure, Geoffrey. Seventeenth Century France. B&N. 1966. $10.00.   944.03
1. France — History — Louis XIII, 1610-1643. 2. France — History — Louis XIV, 1643-1715.

5388. Voltaire, Francois M. de. Age of Louis XIV. Pollack, Martin P., tr. Dutton. 1926. $3.95; pap. $1.95.   944.03
1. France — History — Louis XIV, 1643-1715.

944.04 Revolution, 1789-1804

5389. Beraud, Henri. Twelve Portraits of the French Revolution. Boyd, M., tr. Bks for Libs. 1928. $11.50.   944.04(B)
1. France — History — Revolution, 1789-1793 — Biography.

5390. Bernard, Jack F. Talleyrand: A Biography. Putnam. 1973. $12.95; pap. $4.95.   944.04(B)
1. Talleyrand-Perigord, Charles Maurice de, Prince de Benevent, 1754-1838.

5391. Bizardel, Yvon. The First Expatriates: Americans in Paris During the French Revolution. HR&W. 1975. $10.00.   944.04
1. Americans in France. 2. France — History — Revolution, 1789-1793.

5392. De Tocqueville, Alexis. The Old Regime and the French Revolution. Gilbert, Stuart, tr. Peter Smith. 1955. $4.00; pap. $2.50 (Doubleday).   944.04
1. France — History — Revolution, 1789-1793 — Causes.

5393. Gershoy, Leo. The Era of the French Revolution, 1789 to 1793: Ten Years That Shook the World. Peter Smith. 1957. $3.00.   944.04
1. France — History — Revolution — 1789-1793.

5394. ———. The French Revolution and Napoleon. P-H. 1964. $10.50.   944.04
1. France — History — Consulate and Empire, 1799-1815. 2. France — History — Revolution, 1789-1793. 3. Napoleon I, Emperor of the French, 1769-1821.

5395. Kafker, Frank A. and Laux, James M., eds. The French Revolution: Conflicting Interpretations. Random. 1968. pap. $4.95.   944.04
1. France — History — Revolution — 1789-1793.

5396. Lefebvre, Georges. The Coming of the French Revolution. Palmer, Robert R., tr. Princeton U Pr. 1957. $8.50; pap. $2.95 (Random).   944.04
1. France — History — Revolution, 1789-1793 — Causes.

900 GEOGRAPHY, TRAVEL, AND HISTORY

5397. Lefebvre, Georges, et al, eds. French Revolution from 1793-1799. 2 vols. Stewart, J. H. and Friguglietti, J., trs. Columbia U Pr. 1961-1962. $15.00 ea.; pap. $3.45 ea.   944.04
1. France — History — Revolution, 1789-1793.

5398. Palmer, Robert R. Twelve Who Ruled: The Year of the Terror in the French Revolution. Princeton U Pr. 1941. $10.00; pap. $2.95.   944.04(B)
1. France — History — Revolution, 1789-1793. 2. France — History — Revolution, 1789-1793 — Biography.

5399. Stewart, John H. A Documentary Survey of the French Revolution. Macmillan. 1951. $10.95.   944.04
1. France — History — Revolution, 1789-1793 — Sources.

5400. Sydenham, M. J. The First French Republic, 1792-1804. U of Cal Pr. 1973. $13.00.   944.04
1. France — History — Revolution, 1789-1793. 2. France — History — Consulate and Empire, 1799-1815.

5401. Thompson, James M. Leaders of the French Revolution. B&N. 1929. $4.50; pap. $1.95 (Har-Row).   944.04(B)
1. France — History — Revolution, 1789-1793 — Biography.

5402. ———. Robespierre and the French Revolution. Verry. 1952. $5.50.   944.04
1. France — History — Revolution, 1789-1793. 2. Robespierre, Maximilien Marie Isidore de, 1758-1794.

5403. Herold, Christopher J. and Horizon Editors. The Horizon Book of the Age of Napoleon. Har-Row. 1963. $18.95.   944.046
1. France — History — Consulate and Empire, 1799-1815. 2. Napoleon I, Emperor of the French, 1769-1821.

5404. Thompson, James M. Napoleon Bonaparte: His Rise and Fall. Oxford U Pr. 1952. $9.50.   944.046
1. France — History — Consulate and Empire, 1799-1815. 2. Napoleon I, Emperor of the French, 1769-1821.

5405. Young, Peter. Napoleon's Marshals. Hippocrene Bks. 1973. $12.50.   944.046
1. France — History — Consulate and Empire, 1799-1815. 2. Marshals, France.

944.05-944.07 First Empire, Second Republic, Second Empire, 1804-1870

5406. Knapton, Ernest J. Empress Josephine. Harvard U Pr. 1963. $10.00.   944.05(B)
1. Josephine, Consort of Napoleon I, 1763-1814.

5407. Amann, Peter. Revolution and Mass Democracy: The Paris Club Movement in 1848. Princeton U Pr. 1974. $14.50.   944.06
1. France — History — February Revolution, 1848. 2. Political Clubs.

5408. Artz, Frederick B. France Under the Bourbon Restoration, 1814-1830. Russell. 1931. $11.00.   944.06
1. France — History — Restoration, 1814-1830.

5409. Brogan, Denis W. The French Nation: From Napoleon to Petain, 1814-1940. Gannon. 1970. $6.50.   944.06
1. France — History — 1799-1914. 2. France — History — 1914-1940.

5410. De Bertier De Sauvigny, Guillaume. Bourbon Restoration. Case, Lynn M., tr. U of Pa Pr. 1967. $12.50.   944.06
1. France — History — Restoration, 1814-1830.

5411. Smith, William H. Napoleon III. St Martin. 1973. $14.95.   944.07
1. Napoleon III, Emperor of the French, 1808-1873.

5412. Thompson, James M. Louis Napoleon and the Second Empire. Norton. 1967. pap. $2.95.   944.07
1. France — History — Second Empire, 1852-1870. 2. Napoleon III, Emperor of the French, 1808-1873.

944.08 Third, Fourth, Fifth Republic, 1870

5413. Brogan, Denis W. France Under the Republic: The Development of Modern France, 1870-1939. 2 vols. rev. ed. Peter Smith. $11.00.   944.08
1. France — History — Third Republic, 1870-1940. 2. France — Politics and Government — 1870-1940.

5414. Snyder, Louis L. Dreyfus Case: A Documentary History. Rutgers U Pr. 1973. $17.50.   944.08(B)
1. Dreyfus, Alfred, 1859-1935.

900 GEOGRAPHY, TRAVEL, AND HISTORY

5415. Thomson, David. Democracy in France Since 1870. 5th ed. Oxford U Pr. 1969. pap. $2.95. 944.08
1. France — Politics and Government — 1870-1940.

5416. ———. France: Empire and Republic, 1850-1940: Historical Documents. Har-Row. 1968. pap. $3.95. 944.08
1. France — Constitutional History. 2. France — History — Second Empire, 1852-1870 — Sources. 3. France — History — Third Republic, 1870-1940 — Sources.

5417. Aron, Robert. The Vichy Regime: 1940-1944. Hare, Humphrey, tr. Beacon Pr. 1969. $3.95. 944.081
1. France — History — German Occupation, 1940-1945. 2. France — Politics and Government — 1940-1945.

5418. Sedgwick, Alexander. Third French Republic, 1870-1924. T Y Crowell. 1969. pap. $2.95. 944.081
1. France — History — 1870-1940.

5419. Shirer, William L. The Collapse of the Third Republic. PB. 1971. $1.95. 944.081
1. France — History — 1870-1940.

5420. Werth, Alexander. The Twilight of France, 1933-1940. Fertig. 1966. $15.00. 944.081
1. France — Foreign Relations — 1914-1940. 2. France — Politics and Government — 1914-1940. 3. World War, 1939-1945 — France.

5421. Crozier, Brian. DeGaulle. Scribner. 1974. $12.50. 944.083(B)
1. Gaulle, Charles de, President France, 1890-1970.

5422. Williams, Philip M. and Harrison, Martin. Politics and Society in De Gaulle's Republic. Doubleday. 1973. $2.95. 944.083
1. France — Politics and Government — 1958-

5423. Willianis, Philip M. French Politicians and Elections, 1951-1969. Cambridge U Pr. 1970. $11.50; pap. $3.25. 944.083
1. France — Politics and Government — 1958.

5424. Werth, Alexander. De Gaulle: A Political Biography. S&S. 1966. $7.50. 944.084(B)
1. Gaulle, Charles De, President of France, 1890-1970.

Recommended Series

5425. French Monarchs Series. U of Cal Pr.

945 Italy

5426. Barzini, Luigi. The Italians. Atheneum. 1964. $6.95. 945
1. Italy — Social Life and Customs. 2. National Characteristics, Italian.

5427. Hearder, H. and Waley, Daniel P. Short History of Italy. Cambridge U Pr. 1963. $7.50; pap. $3.95. 945
1. Italy — History.

5428. Mallett, Michael. The Borgias: The Rise and Fall of a Renaissance Dynasty. B&N. 1969. $11.50. 945
1. Borgia Family.

5429. Trevelyan, Janet P. A Short History of the Italian People. 4th ed. Pitman. 1956. $10.95. 945
1. Italy — History.

945.05 Renaissance Period, 1300-1494

5430. Ady, Julia M. Beatrice d'Este, Duchess of Milan, 1475-1497: A Study of the Renaissance. AMS Pr. Repr. 1905. $17.50. 945.05(B)
1. Beatrice d'Este, Consort of Ladovico Sforza, Duke of Milan, 1475-1497. 2. Italy — History — 1268-1492.

5431. Burckhardt, Jacob. The Civilization of the Renaissance in Italy. 2 vols. Peter Smith. $9.00. 945.05
1. Italy — Civilization. 2. Renaissance — Italy.

5432. Guicciardini, Francesco. The History of Italy. Alexander, Sydney, tr. Macmillan. 1970. $12.50. 945.05
1. Italy — Civilization. 2. Renaissance — Italy.

5433. Machiavelli, Niccolo. History of Florence and of the Affairs of Italy: From the Earliest Times to the Death of Lorenzo the Magnificent. Peter Smith. $6.00. 945.05
1. Florence — History. 2. Italy — History — to 1599. 3. Medici, House of.

900 GEOGRAPHY, TRAVEL, AND HISTORY

5434. Schevill, Ferdinand. The Medici. Peter Smith. 1960. $4.00; pap. $1.95 (Har-Row). 945.05
1. Italy — History — to 1559. 2. Medici, House of.

5435. Corvo, Frederick B. Chronicles of the House of Borgia. Peter Smith. $5.00. 945.06
1. Borgia Family. 2. Francisco de Borja, Saint, 1510-1572. 3. Italy — History — 1492-1559.

5436. Hale, John R. Machiavelli and Renaissance Italy. Verry. 1961. $5.50. 945.06
1. Machiavelli, Niccolo, 1469-1527. 2. Renaissance — Italy.

945.08 Growth of Nationalism, 1796-1870

5437. Delzell, Charles F., ed. Unification of Italy, 1859-1861: Cavour, Mazzini, or Garibaldi? Peter Smith. $5.00. 945.08
1. Italy — History — 1815-1870.

5438. Hibbert, Christopher. Garibaldi and His Enemies: The Clash of Arms and Personalities in the Making of Italy. NAL. 1970. pap. $3.95. 945.08
1. Garibaldi, Giuseppe, 1807-1882. 2. Italy — History — 19th Century.

5439. Larg, David G. Giuseppe Garibaldi: A Biography. Kennikat. Repr. 1934. $12.00.
945.08(B)
1. Garibaldi, Giuseppe, 1807-1882.

5440. Salvemini, Gaetano. Mazzini. Stanford U Pr. 1957. $6.00. 945.08(B)
1. Mazzini, Giuseppe, 1805-1872.

5441. Thayer, William R. The Life and Times of Cavour. 2 vols. Fertig. Repr. 1911. $28.50. 945.08(B)
1. Cavour, Camillo Benso, Conte di, 1810-1861. 2. Italy — History — 1849-1870.

5442. Trevelyan, George M. Garibaldi and the Making of Italy. Humanities. 1948. $7.25.
945.08
1. Garibaldi, Giuseppe, 1807-1882. 2. Italy — History — 19th Century. 3. Italy — History — War of 1860-1861.

945.09 Unified Kingdom, Fascist Regime, Republic, 1870

5443. Albrecht-Carrie, René. Italy from Napoleon to Mussolini. Peter Smith. 1950. $5.50; pap. $1.95 (Columbia U Pr). 945.09
1. Italy — History — 1870-1915. 2. Italy — History — 1914-1945.

5444. Katz, Robert. The Fall of the House of Savoy. Macmillan. 1971. $12.50. 945.09
1. Savoy, House of.

5445. Keene, Frances, ed. Neither Liberty nor Bread: The Meaning and Tragedy of Fascism. Kennikat. 1940. $12.50. 945.09
1. Fascism — Italy. 2. Italy — History — Fascist Movement.

5446. Mack-Smith, Denis. Italy: A Modern History. U of Mich Pr. 1969. $9.50. 945.09
1. Italy — History.

5447. Mammarella, Giuseppe. Italy After Fascism: A Political History, 1943-1965. Velen, E. and Velen, V., trs. U of Notre Dame Pr. 1966. $9.95. 945.09
1. Italy — History — 1922-1945. 2. Italy — History — 1945-

5448. Chabod, Federico. A History of Italian Fascism. Fertig. Repr. 1963. $10.00.
945.091
1. Fascism — Italy. 2. Italy — History — 1914-1945.

5449. Deakin, Frederick W. The Brutal Friendship. Har-Row. 1963. $15.00. 945.091
1. Germany — Foreign Relations — Italy. 2. Hitler, Adolf, 1889-1945. 3. Italy — Foreign Relations — Germany. 4. Mussolini, Benito, 1883-1945. 5. World War, 1939-1945.

5450. Gallo, Max. Mussolini's Italy: 20 Years of the Fascist Era. Macmillan. 1973. $10.95. 945.091
1. Fascism — Italy. 2. Italy — History — 1922-1945. 3. Mussolini, Benito, 1883-1945.

5451. Leeds, Christopher A. Italy Under Mussolini. Putnam. 1973. $5.95. 945.091
1. Italy — History — 1922-1945. 2. Mussolini, Benito, 1883-1945.

5452. Wiskemann, Elizabeth. Fascism in Italy: Its Development and Influence. St Martin. 1969. pap. $3.50. 945.091
1. Fascism — Italy. 2. Italy — History — 1941-1945.

5453. Partner, Peter. The Lands of St. Peter: The Papal State in the Middle Ages and the Early Renaissance. U of Cal Pr. 1972. $18.75.
945.6
1. Papal States — History.

900 GEOGRAPHY, TRAVEL, AND HISTORY

5454. Croce, Benedetto. History of the Kingdom of Naples. U of Chicago Pr. 1970. $11.00; pap. $2.95. 945.73
1. Naples (Kingdom) — History.

946 Spain

5455. Altamira y Crevea, Rafael. History of Spanish Civilization. Volkov, P., tr. Biblo. Repr. 1930. $10.00. 946
1. Spain — Civilization.

5456. Arribas, Antonio. The Iberians. Praeger. 1964. $8.50. 946
1. Iberians. 2. Spain — Antiquities.

5457. Brenan, Gerald. The Spanish Labyrinth: An Account of the Social and Political Background of the Civil War. 2nd ed. Cambridge U Pr. 1960. $14.50; pap. $3.95. 946
1. Spain — History. 2. Spain — Politics and Government.

5458. De Madariaga, Salvador. Spain. Praeger. 1958. $12.50. 946
1. Spain. 2. Spain — History.

5459. Michener, James A. Iberia: Spanish Travels and Reflections. Random. 1968. $12.50. 946
1. Spain — Civilization. 2. Spain — Description and Travel — 1951-

5460. Salmon, Edward D. Imperial Spain: The Rise of the Empire and the Dawn of Modern Sea Power. Greenwood. Repr. 1931. $9.50. 946

5461. Smith, Rhea M. Spain: A Modern History. U of Mich Pr. 1965. $8.75. 946
1. Spain — History.

946.04-946.07 Early Habsburg Rulers-Bourbon Restoration, 1516-1868

5462. Bergamini, John D. The Spanish Bourbons: The History of a Tenacious Dynasty. Putnam. 1974. $12.95. 946.04
1. Bourbon, House of. 2. Spain — History — Bourbons.

5463. Davies, R. Trevor. The Golden Century of Spain, 1501-1621. rev. ed. Har-Row. pap. $2.75. 946.04
1. Spain — History — 16th Century.

5464. Grierson, Edward. King of Two Worlds: Philip II of Spain. Putnam. 1974. $12.95. 946.04(B)
1. Felipe II, King of Spain, 1527-1598.

5465. Carr, Raymond. Spain 1808-1939. Oxford U Pr. 1966. $14.50. 946.06
1. Spain — Politics and Government — 19th Century. 2. Spain — Politics and Government — 20th Century. 3. Spain — Social Conditions.

946.08 Later 19th and 20th Centuries, 1868-

5466. Benson, Frederick R. Writers in Arms: The Literary Impact of the Spanish Civil War. NYU Pr. 1967. $9.75; pap. $2.95. 946.08
1. Literature, Modern — 20th Century — History and Criticism. 2. Spain — History — Civil War, 1936-1939 — Literature and the War.

5467. Broué, Pierre and Témime, Emile. The Revolution and the Civil War in Spain. MIT Pr. 1972. $12.50. 946.08
1. Spain — History — Civil War, 1936-1939.

5468. Payne, Stanley G. Politics and the Military in Modern Spain. Stanford U Pr. 1967. $15.00. 946.08
1. Spain — Politics and Government.

5469. Thomas, Hugh. The Spanish Civil War. Har-Row. 1961. $15.00; pap. $3.45. 946.08
1. Spain — History — Civil War, 1936-1939.

5470. Jackson, Gabriel. Spanish Republic and the Civil War, 1931-1939. Princeton U Pr. 1965. $16.00; pap. $3.45. 946.081
1. Spain — History — Civil War, 1936-1939.

5471. Koestler, Arthur. Dialogue with Death: The Journal of a Condemned Prisoner of the Fascists in the Spanish Civil War. Macmillan. 1967. $5.95; pap. $1.25. 946.081
1. Spain — History — Civil War, 1936-1939 — Personal Narrative. 2. Spain — History — Civil War, 1936-1939 — Prisoners and Prisons.

5472. Payne, Stanley G. Falange: A History of Spanish Fascism. Stanford U Pr. 1961. $8.50; pap. $2.95. 946.081
1. Fascism — Spain. 2. Spain — Politics and Government.

900 GEOGRAPHY, TRAVEL, AND HISTORY

5473. Rosenstone, Robert A. Crusade of the Left: The Lincoln Battalion in the Spanish Civil War. Pegasus. 1969. $8.95.   946.081
1. Spain — History — Civil War, 1936-1939 — Foreign Participation — American.

5474. Gallo, Max. Spain Under France: A History. Dutton. 1974. $12.50.   946.082
1. Spain — Politics and Government — 1939.

5475. Trythall, J. W. El Caudillo: A Political Biography of Franco. Intl Pubns Serv. 1970. $10.50.   946.082(B)
1. Franco Bahamonde, Francisco, 1892- 2. Spain — History — 20th Century.

946.9 Portugal

5476. Bradford, Sarah. Portugal. Walker & Co. 1973. $8.50.   946.9
1. Portugal.

5477. Livermore, Harold B. New History of Portugal. Cambridge U Pr. 1966. $14.50; pap. $4.95.   946.9
1. Portugal — History.

5478. Marques, Antonio H. R. de. History of Portugal. 2 vols. Columbia U Pr. 1972. $15.00 ea.   946.9
1. Portugal — History.

5479. Nowell, Charles. Portugal. P-H. 1973. $6.95.   946.9
1. Portugal — History.

947 Russia

5480. Avrich, Paul. Russian Rebels, 1600-1800. Schocken. 1972. $10.00.   947(B)
1. Revolutions — Russia.

5481. Billington, James H. The Icon and the Axe. Random. 1970. pap. $3.95.   947
1. Russia — Intellectual Life.

5482. Florinsky, Michael T. Russia: A History and Interpretation. 2 vols. Macmillan. 1954. $9.95 ea.   947
1. Russia — History.

5483. Grey, Ian. The Horizon History of Russia. McGraw. 1970. $22.00.   947
1. Russia — History.

5484. Harcave, Sidney. Russia: A History. 6th ed. Lippincott. 1968. $10.95.   947
1. Russia — History.

5485. Hindus, Maurice G. Cossacks: The Story of a Warrior People. Greenwood. Repr. 1945. $15.75.   947
1. Cossacks.

5486. Kerner, Robert J. The Urge to the Sea: The Course of Russian History. Russell. Repr. 1942. $14.00.   947
1. Russia — History.

5487. Kohn, Hans, ed. Mind of Modern Russia: Historical and Political Thought of Russia's Great Age. Har-Row. 1962. pap. $2.25.   947
1. Russia — Intellectual Life.

5488. Longworth, Philip. Cossacks. HR&W. 1970. $8.95.   947
1. Cossacks.

5489. Masaryk, Thomas G. The Spirit of Russia. 3 vols. rev. ed. B&N. 1961. $45.00.   947
1. Dostoevsky, Fedor Mikhailovich, 1821-1881. 2. Philosophy, Russian. 3. Russia — History. 4. Russian Literature — History and Criticism.

5490. Pares, Bernard. A History of Russia. Knopf. 1953. $12.50; pap. $2.95 (Random).   947
1. Russia — History.

5491. Riasanovsky, Nicholas V. A History of Russia. 2nd ed. Oxford U Pr. 1969. $15.00.   947
1. Russia — History.

5492. Riha, Thomas, ed. Readings in Russian Civilization. 3 vols. rev. ed. U of Chicago Pr. 1969. Vols. 1-2. $8.75 ea.; Vol. 3. $9.50; Vols. 1-2. pap. $3.95 ea.; Vol. 3. pap. $4.35.   947
1. Civilization, Russian. 2. Russia — History.

5493. Seton-Watson, Hugh. Eastern Europe Between the Wars, 1918-1941. 3rd ed. Har-Row. 1967. pap. $3.75.   947
1. Europe, Eastern — History.

5494. Vernadsky, George. History of Russia. rev. ed. Yale U Pr. 1961. $17.50; pap. $3.45.   947
1. Russia — History.

5495. ———. A Source Book for Russian History from Early Times to 1917. 3 vols. Yale U Pr. 1972. $40.00.   947
1. Russia — History — Sources.

900 GEOGRAPHY, TRAVEL, AND HISTORY

5496. Yarmolinsky, Avrahm. Road to Revolution: A Century of Russian Radicalism. Macmillan. 1962. pap. $1.50.   947
1. Russia — Politics and Government.

5497. Platanov, Sergei. Boris Godunov: Tsar of Russia. Academic Intl. 1973. $11.00.
    947.04(B)
1. Boris Godunov, Czar of Russia, 1551-1605. 2. Russia — History — 1598-1605.

947.05-947.07 Peter the Great - Early 19th Century, 1689-1855

5498. Klyuchevsky, V. Peter the Great. St Martin. $10.50; pap. $1.95 (Random).
    947.05(B)
1. Peter I, The Great, Emperor of Russia, 1672-1725.

5499. Curtiss, Mina S. A Forgotten Empress: Anna Ivanovna and Her Era, 1730-1740. Ungar. 1974. $12.50.   947.06(B)
1. Anne, Empress of Russia, 1693-1740. 2. Russia — History — Anne, 1730-1740.

5500. Oldenbourg, Zoe. Catherine the Great. Carter, A., tr. Pantheon. 1965. $8.95.
    947.06(B)
1. Catherine II (Catherine the Great), Empress of Russia, 1729-1796. 2. Russia — History.

5501. Herzen, Alexander I. My Past and Thoughts: The Memoirs of Alexander Herzen. Garnett, Constance, tr. Random. 1974. pap. $4.95.   947.07(B)
1. Herzen, Aleksandr Ivanovich, 1812-1870.

5502. Thaden, Edward C. Russia Since 1801: The Making of a New Society. Wiley. 1971. $11.95.   947.07
1. Russia — History — 19th Century. 2. Russia — History — 20th Century.

947.08 Later 19th and 20th Centuries, 1855-

5503. Charques, Richard. Twilight of Imperial Russia. Oxford U Pr. 1965. pap. $3.50.   947.08
1. Russia — History — 19th Century. 2. Russia — History — 1904-1914.

5504. Kropotkin, Petr. Memoirs of a Revolutionist. Rogers, James H., ed. Peter Smith. 1967. $4.50.   947.08(B)
1. Anarchism and Anarchists. 2. Russia — Politics and Government.

5505. Lyons, Marvin. Nicholas II: The Last Tsar. St Martin. 1975. $16.95.   947.08(B)
1. Nicholas II, Emperor of Russia, 1868-1918. 2. Russia — Politics and Government — 1894-1917.

5506. Massie, Robert. Nicholas and Alexandra. Atheneum. 1967. $12.95; pap. $1.75 (Dell).   947.08(B)
1. Alexandra, Consort of Nicholas II, Emperor of Russia, 1872-1918. 2. Nicholas II, Emperor of Russia, 1868-1918. 3. Russia — Politics and Government — 1894-1917.

5507. Maynard, John. Russia in Flux: Before October. Macmillan. 1962. pap. $2.45.   947.08
1. Peasantry — Russia. 2. Russia — History.

5508. Pipes, Richard. Formation of the Soviet Union: Communism and Nationalism, 1917-1923. rev. ed. Harvard U Pr. 1964. $9.50; pap. $3.45 1968 (Atheneum).   947.08
1. Russia — History — 1917.

5509. Wolfe, Bertram D. Three Who Made a Revolution. Dell. pap. $2.95.   947.08(B)
1. Lenin, Vladimir Ilyich, 1870-1924. 2. Russia — History — Revolution, 1917-1921. 3. Stalin, Joseph Vissarionvich, 1879-1953. 4. Trotsky, Leon, 1879-1940.

5510. Carr, Edward H. Bolshevik Revolution, 1917-1923. 3 vols. Macmillan. 1951-53. $7.50 ea.   947.084
1. Russia — History — Revolution, 1917-1921.

5511. Cohen, Stephen F. Bukharin and the Bolshevik Revolution: A Political Biography. Knopf. 1973. $15.00; pap. $3.95 (Random).
    947.084(B)
1. Bukharin, Nikolai Ivanovich, 1888-1938. 2. Russia — Economic Policy — 1917-1928. 3. Russia — Politics and Government — 1917-1936.

5512. Conquest, Robert. The Great Terror: Stalin's Purge of the Thirties. rev ed. Macmillan. 1973. $8.95; pap. $4.95.   947.084
1. Russia — Politics and Government. 2. Terrorism — Russia.

5513. Curtiss, John S. The Russian Revolutions of 1917. Van Nos Reinhold. 1957. pap. $2.95.   947.084
1. Russia — History — Revolution, 1917-1921.

900 GEOGRAPHY, TRAVEL, AND HISTORY

5514. Deutscher, Isaac. Prophet Armed: Trotsky, 1879-1921. Oxford U Pr. 1954. $12.50; pap. $2.45 (Random). 947.084(B)
1. Russia — History — Revolution, 1917-1921. 2. Trotsky, Leon, 1879-1940.

5515. ———. Prophet Outcast: Trotsky, 1929-1940. Oxford U Pr. 1963. $12.50; pap. $2.45 (Random). 947.084(B)
1. Trotsky, Leon, 1879-1940.

5516. ———. Prophet Unarmed: Trotsky, 1921-1929. Oxford U Pr. 1959. $12.50; pap. $2.45 (Random). 947.084(B)
1. Trotsky, Leon, 1879-1940.

5517. ———. Stalin: A Political Biography. 2nd ed. Oxford U Pr. 1967. $15.00; pap. $3.95. 947.084(B)
1. Russia — History — 20th Century. 2. Stalin, Joseph Vissarionvich, 1879-1953.

5518. ———. The Unfinished Revolution: Russia 1917-1967. Oxford U Pr. 1969. $3.95; pap. $1.95. 947.084
1. Revolutions. 2. Russia — History — Revolution, 1917-1921 — Influence. 3. Russia — Social Conditions — 1917-

5519. Ferro, Marc. The Russian Revolution of February, 1917. P-H. 1972. $9.95. 947.084
1. Russia — History — February Revolution, 1917.

5520. Haupt, Georges and Marie, Jean-J. Makers of the Russian Revolution: Biography of Bolshevik Leaders. Cornell U Pr. 1974. $15.00. 947.084(B)
1. Communists — Russia.

5521. Kerensky, Alexander. The Catastrophe: Kerensky's Own Story of the Russian Revolution. Kraus Repr. 1927. $12.00. 947.084
1. Russia — History — Revolution, 1917-1921.

5522. Pipes, Richard E., ed. Revolutionary Russia. Harvard U Pr. 1968. $9.50. 947.084
1. Russia — History — Revolution, 1917-1921.

5523. Reed, John. Ten Days That Shook the World. Intl Pub Co. 1967 (NW). $7.50; pap. $1.95. 947.084
1. Russia — History — Revolution, 1917-1921.

5524. Rosenberg, Arthur. A History of Bolshevism, from Marx to the First Five Years' Plan. Morrow, Ian F., tr. Russell. 1934. $8.50. 947.084
1. Communism — History. 2. Communism — Russia.

5525. Shukman, Harold. Lenin and the Russian Revolution. Putnam. 1968. pap. $2.45. 947.084
1. Lenin, Vladimir Ilyich, 1870-1924. 2. Revolutionists, Russian. 3. Russia — History — Revolution, 1917-1921.

5526. Tucker, Robert C. Stalin As Revolutionary, 1879-1929: A Study in History and Personality. Norton. 1973. $12.95; pap. $3.95. 947.084
1. Stalin, Joseph Vissarionvich, 1879-1953.

5527. Ulam, Adam B. Stalin: The Man and His Era. Viking Pr. 1973. $12.95; pap. $4.95. 947.084(B)
1. Stalin, Joseph Vissarionvich, 1879-1953.

5528. Werth, Alexander. Russia: The Postwar Years. Taplinger. 1972. $12.00. 947.084
1. Russia — History — 1925-1953.

5529. Dornberg, John. Brezhnev: The Masks of Power. Basic. 1974. $10.00. 947.085(B)
1. Brezhev, Leonid Ilyich, 1906-

5530. Khrushchev, Nikita S. Khruschev Remembers. Little. 1971. $12.95. 947.085
1. Russia — Politics and Government — 1936-1953. 2. Russia — Politics and Government — 1953-

5531. Salisbury, Harrison E., ed. The Soviet Union: The Fifty Years. HarBraceJ. 1967. $10.00. 947.085
1. Russia — History — 1917-

5532. Hrushevy, Michael. A History of Ukraine. Shoe String. Repr. 1941. $15.00. 947.71
1. Ukraine — History.

948 Northern Europe/Scandinavia

5533. Butler, Ewan. The Horizon Concise History of Scandinavia. McGraw. 1974. $8.95. 948
1. Finland — History. 2. Scandinavia — History.

900 GEOGRAPHY, TRAVEL, AND HISTORY

5534. Connery, Donald. The Scandinavians. S&S. 1966. $9.95. 948
1. Scandinavia.

5535. Fleisher, Frederic K. The New Sweden. McKay. 1967. $6.95. 948
1. Sweden — Economic Conditions. 2. Sweden — Social Conditions.

5536. Jones, Gwyn. A History of the Vikings. Oxford U Pr. 1968. $12.50. 948.01
1. Northmen — History.

5537. Sawyer, P. H. The Age of the Vikings. 2nd ed. St Martin. 1972. $11.95. 948.01
1. Vikings.

5538. Wilson, David M. The Vikings and Their Origins: Scandinavia in the First Millenium. McGraw. 1970. pap. $2.95. 948.01
1. Civilization, Scandinavian. 2. Northmen.

5539. Derry, Thomas K. A Short History of Norway. Humanities. 1960. $7.25. 948.1
1. Norway — History.

5540. Oakley, Stewart. A Short History of Sweden. Praeger. 1966. $8.50. 948.5
1. Sweden — History.

5541. Scobbie, Irene. Sweden. Praeger. 1972. $10.00. 948.5
1. Sweden.

5542. Oakley, Stewart. A Short History of Denmark. Praeger. 1972. $10.00. 948.9
1. Denmark — History.

5543. Bailey, Anthony. Horizon Concise History of the Low Countries. McGraw. 1974. $8.95. 949.2
1. Benelux Countries — History.

5544. Wedgwood, Cicely V. William the Silent: William of Nassau, Prince of Orange, 1533-1584. Humanities. 1960. $6.50; pap. $2.45 (Norton). 949.2(B)
1. William I, Prince of Orange, 1533-1584.

5545. De Meeus, Adrien. History of the Belgians. Praeger. 1962. $7.50. 949.3
1. Belgium — History.

5546. Howarth, David. Waterloo: Day of Battle. Atheneum. 1968. $7.95. 949.3
1. Waterloo, Battle of, 1815.

949.5 Greece

5547. Barker, John W. Justinian and the Later Roman Empire. U of Wis Pr. 1966. $12.50. 949.5
1. Byzantine Empire — History. 2. Justinianus I, Emperor of the East, 483-565.

5548. Byron, Robert. The Byzantine Achievements. Russell. 1964. $11.00. 949.5
1. Byzantine Empire — Civilization.

5549. Campbell, John and Sherrard, Philip. Modern Greece. Praeger. 1968. $10.00. 949.5
1. Byzantine Empire — History. 2. Greece, Modern — History.

5550. Franzius, Enno. History of the Byzantine Empire: Mother of Nations. Funk & W. 1967. $10.00. 949.5
1. Byzantine Empire — Civilization.

5551. Vasiliev, Alexander A. A History of the Byzantine Empire, 324-1453. 2 vols. Peter Smith. $11.00; pap. $4.75 ea (U of Wis Pr). 949.5
1. Byzantine Empire — History.

5552. Vryonis, Speros. Byzantium and Europe. HarBraceJ. 1967. pap. $4.75. 949.5
1. Byzantine Empire — Civilization. 2. Byzantine Empire — History.

5553. Phillips, Walter A. The War of Greek Independence. Fertig. $14.00. 949.506
1. Greece, Modern — History — War of Independence, 1821-1829.

5554. Holden, David. Greece Without Columns: The Making of the Modern Greeks. Lippincott. 1972. $7.50. 949.507
1. Greece, Modern — History. 2. National Characteristics, Greek (Modern).

949.6 Balkan Peninsula

5555. Barber, Noel. The Sultans. S&S. 1973. $9.95. 949.6
1. Turkey — History.

5556. Forbes, Nevil, et al. The Balkans: A History of Bulgaria, Serbia, Greece, Rumania, Turkey. AMS Pr. 1915. $10.50. 949.6
1. Balkan Peninsula — History.

5557. Wolff, Robert. The Balkans in Our Time. Harvard U Pr. 1956. $12.50; pap. $3.45. 949.6
1. Balkan Peninsula — History. 2. Communism — Balkan Peninsula.

900 GEOGRAPHY, TRAVEL, AND HISTORY

5558. Balfour, Patrick. Atatürk: A Biography of Mustafa Kemâl, Father of Modern Turkey. Morrow. 1966. $10.00. 949.61(B)
1. Atatürk, Kemâl, President of Turkey, d. 1938. 2. Turkey — History — 1909-

949.7-949.8 Yugoslavia, Bulgaria, Romania

5559. Clissold, Stephen, et al. A Short History of Yugoslavia from Early Times to 1966. Cambridge U Pr. 1968. $10.75; pap. $3.75. 949.7
1. Yugoslavia — History.

5560. Tomasevic, N. Yugoslavia: Past and Present. Vanous. 1970. $20.00. 949.7
1. Yugoslavia — History.

5561. Vucinich, Wayne S., ed. Contemporary Yugoslavia: 20 Years of Socialist Experiment. U of Cal Pr. 1969. $12.75. 949.7
1. Yugoslavia — History — 20th Century.

5562. Auty, Phyllis. Tito: A Biography. Ballantine. 1972. pap. $1.00. 949.702(B)
1. Tito, Josip Broz, President Yugoslavia, 1892-

5563. Campbell, John C. Tito's Separate Road: America and Yugoslavia in World Politics. Har-Row. 1967. $3.95. 949.702
1. Yugoslavia — Foreign Relations — 1945-
2. Yugoslavia — Politics and Government — 1945-

5564. Fischer-Galati, Stephen. The New Rumania: From People's Democracy to Socialist Republic. MIT Pr. 1967. $8.95. 949.8
1. Rumania — History — 1944- 2. Rumania — Politics and Government — 1945-

5565. Willetts, Ronald F. Ancient Crete: A Social History from Early Times Until the Roman Occupation. U of Toronto Pr. 1965. $10.00. 949.98
1. Crete — History.

Recommended Series

5566. History of the Western World Series. Merriam.

5567. Problems of European Civilization. Greenlaw, Ralph W. & Lee, Dwight E., gen. eds.. Heath.

5568. The Rise of Modern Europe. Langer, William L., ed.. Har-Row.

950 Asian History

5569. Fairbank, John K., et al. East Asia: Tradition and Transformation. HM. 1973. $20.00. 950
1. East (Far East) — History.

5570. Latourette, Kenneth S. A Short History of the Far East. 4th ed. Macmillan. 1964. $11.95. 950
1. East (Far East) — History.

5571. Reischauer, Edwin O., et al. History of East Asian Civilization. 2 vols. HM. $13.95 ea. 950
1. Asia — History.

951 China and Adjacent Areas

5572. Bloodworth, Dennis. Chinese Looking Glass. FS&G. 1967. $7.95; pap. $1.25 (Dell). 951
1. China — Civilization.

5573. Bodde, Derk. China's Cultural Tradition - What and Whither? HR&W. 1957. pap. $2.50. 951
1. China — Civilization.

5574. Chang, Chun-shu. Making of China: Main Themes in Pre-Modern Chinese History. P-H. 1975. $14.95. 951
1. China — History — Ch'ing Dynasty, 1644-1912. 2. China — History — Early to 1643.

5575. De Bary, William T., et al, eds. Source of Chinese Tradition. Columbia U Pr. 1960. $17.50. 951
1. China — Civilization. 2. China — History — Sources.

5576. Fairbank, John K. China: The People's Middle Kingdom and the U. S. A. Harvard U Pr. 1967. $5.00. 951
1. U. S. — Foreign Relations — China. 2. China — Foreign Relations — U. S. 3. China — History.

5577. Fitzgerald, Charles P. and Horizon Editors. History of China. McGraw. 1969. $22.00. 951
1. China — History.

900 GEOGRAPHY, TRAVEL, AND HISTORY

5578. Goodrich, L. Carrington. A Short History of the Chinese People. 3rd rev. ed. Har-Row. 1959. pap. $1.75. 951
1. China — History.

5579. Heren, Louis, et al. China's Three Thousand Years: The Story of a Great Civilization. Macmillan. 1974. $8.95; pap. $3.95. 951
1. China — Civilization — History. 2. China — History. 3. China (People's Republic of China, 1949-).

5580. Latourette, Kenneth S. The Chinese: Their History and Culture. 2 vols. in 1. 4th rev. ed. Macmillan. 1964. $12.50. 951
1. China — History. 2. China — Civilization.

5581. Schurmann, Franz and Schell, Orville, eds. China Reader. 3 vols. Random. 1967. pap. $7.30. 951
1. China — History.

951.03 Ch'ing Dynasty, 1644-1912

5582. Franke, Wolfgang. A Century of Chinese Revolution, 1851-1949. U of SC Pr. 1970. $5.95; pap. $1.95 (Har-Row). 951.03
1. China — History — 19th Century. 2. China — History — 1900- 3. Revolutions — China.

5583. Hsü, Immanuel C. Y. The Rise of Modern China. Oxford U Pr. 1970. $15.00. 951.03
1. China — History — Ch'ing Dynasty, 1644-1912. 2. China — History — 1900.

5584. O'Connor, Richard. The Spirit Soldiers: A Historical Narrative of the Boxer Rebellion. Putnam. 1973. $8.95. 951.03
1. Boxers.

5585. Spence, Jonathan D. Emperor of China: Self Portrait of K'ang Hsi, 1661-1772. Knopf. 1974. $8.95. 951.03(B)
1. Ch'ing Sheng-Tsu, Emperor of China, 1654-1722.

5586. Tan, Chester G. Boxer Catastrophe. Octagon. Repr. 1967. $10.50; pap. $2.25 (Norton). 951.03
1. Boxers. 2. China — History — 1900.

5587. Wright, Mary C., ed. China in Revolution: The First Phase, 1900-1913. Yale U Pr. 1968. $17.50; pap. $5.95. 951.03
1. China — History — Ching Dynasty — 1644-1912. 2. China — History — Revolution — 1911-1912.

5588. Yu Wen, Jen. The Taiping Revolutionary Movement. Yale U Pr. 1973. $19.50. 951.03
1. Taiping Rebellion, 1850-1864.

951.04 Early 20th Century, 1912-1949

5589. Clubb, Oliver E. Twentieth Century China. rev. ed. Columbia U Pr. 1972. $15.00; pap. $3.95. 951.04
1. China — History — 1900-

5590. Martin, Bernard. Strange Vigor: A Biography of Sun Yat-Sen. Kennikat. Repr. 1944. $2.95. 951.04(B)
1. China — History — Revolution, 1911-1912. 2. China — History — Republic, 1912-1949. 3. Sun Yat-Sen, 1866-1925.

5591. Milton, David, et al, eds. The China Reader: The Cultural Revolution and After, 1966-1972. Random. 1974. $15.00. 951.04
1. China — History — 1900-

5592. Snow, Edgar. Red Star Over China. Grove. 1968. $10.00. 951.04
1. China — History — Republic, 1912-1949. 2. Communism — China.

5593. Barnett, A. Doak. China on the Eve of the Communist Take Over. Praeger. 1963. pap. $3.50. 951.042
1. China — Economic Conditions. 2. China — History.

5594. Berkov, Robert. Strong Man of China. Bks for Libs. Repr. 1938. $11.00. 951.042(B)
1. Chiang, Kai-Shek, 1886-1975.

5595. Melby, John F. The Mandate of Heaven: Record of a Civil War, China 1945-1949. U of Toronto Pr. 1968. $15.00; pap. $1.95 1971 (Doubleday). 951.042
1. China — History — Civil War, 1945-1949.

5596. Rice, Edward. Mao's Way. U of Cal Pr. 1972. $12.95; pap. $0.95. 951.042
1. Communism — China. 2. Mao, Tse-tung, 1893-

5597. Wilson, Richard G. The Long March, 1935: The Epic of Chinese Communism's Survival. Viking Pr. 1972. $8.95. 951.042
1. Long March, 1934-1935.

900 GEOGRAPHY, TRAVEL, AND HISTORY

951.05 Period of People's Republic, 1949-

5598. Cheng, Peter P. Chronology of the People's Republic of China from October 1, 1969. Littlefield. 1972. pap. $3.95. 951.05
1. China (People's Republic of China, 1949-) — History — Chronology.

5599. MacFarquhar, Roderick. The Origins of the Cultural Revolution. Columbia U Pr. 1974. $14.95. 951.05
1. China — Politics and Government — 1945-

5600. Mao, Tse-tung. Mao. Papers: Anthology and Bibliography. Oxford U Pr. 1970. $10.00. 951.05
1. China — Politics and Government — 1949-

5601. Moravia, Alberto. Red Book and the Great Wall: An Impression of Mao's China. Strom, Ronald, tr. FS&G. 1968. pap. $1.95. 951.05
1. China (People's Republic of China, 1949-).

5602. Salisbury, Harrison E. Orbit of China. Har-Row. 1967. $6.95. 951.05
1. China (People's Republic of China, 1949-).

5603. Snow, Edgar. Red China Today: The Other Side of the River. rev. ed. Random. 1971. $20.00; pap. $3.45. 951.05
1. China (People's Republic of China, 1949-) — History.

5604. Chiu, Hungdah. China and the Question of Taiwan: Documents and Analysis. Praeger. 1973. $18.50. 951.2
1. Taiwan — History — Sources.

951.9 Korea

5605. Choy, Bong-Youn. Korea: A History. C E Tuttle. 1971. $13.75. 951.9
1. Korea — History.

5606. Hatada, Takashi. A History of Korea. ABC-Clio. 1969. $8.75; pap. $3.95. 951.9
1. Korea — History.

5607. McCune, Shannon. Korea's Heritage: A Regional and Social Geography. C E Tuttle. 1964. $6.95. 951.9
1. Korea — Geography. 2. Korea — Social Life and Customs.

5608. Choi, Woonsang. Fall of the Hermit Kingdom. Oceana. 1967. $7.50. 951.901
1. Japan — Foreign Relations — Korea. 2. Korea — Foreign Relations. 3. Korea — History — 1868-1910.

5609. Clark, Mark W. From the Danube to the Yalu. Greenwood. Repr. 1954. $16.75. 951.904
1. Korean War, 1950-1953.

5610. Collins, Joseph L. War in Peacetime: The History and Lessons of Korea. HM. 1969. $8.95. 951.904
1. Korean War, 1950-1953.

5611. McGovern, James. To the Yalu: From the Chinese Invasion of Korea to MacArthur's Dismissal. Morrow. 1972. $6.95. 951.904
1. Korean War, 1950-1953. 2. MacArthur, Douglas, 1880-1964.

5612. Ridgway, Matthew B. The Korean War: How We Met the Challenge, How All-Out Asian War Was Averted, Why MacArthur Was Dismissed, Why Today's War Objectives Must Be Limited. Doubleday. 1967. $7.95. 951.904
1. Korean War, 1950-1953.

5613. Stone, Isidor F. Hidden History of the Korean War. rev. ed. Monthly Rev. 1969. pap. $3.95. 951.904
1. Korean War, 1950-1953. 2. U. S. — Foreign Relations — 1945-1953.

952 Japan

5614. De Bary, William T., et al, eds. Sources of Japanese Tradition. 2 vols. Columbia U Pr. 1958. pap. $7.00. 952
1. Japan — Civilization. 2. Japan — History — Sources.

5615. Hall, John W., et al, eds. Studies in the Institutional History of Early Modern Japan. Princeton U Pr. 1970. $12.50; pap. $3.95. 952
1. Japan — History.

5616. Hane, Mikiso. Japan: A Historical Survey. Scribner. 1972. $15.00; pap. $6.95. 952
1. Japan — History.

5617. Reischauer, Edwin O. Japan: The Story of a Nation. rev. ed. Knopf. 1974. $7.95. 952
1. Japan — History.

5618. Sansom, George B. Japan: A Short Cultural History. rev. ed. P-H. 1962. $9.50. 952
1. Japan — Civilization. 2. Japan — History.

900 GEOGRAPHY, TRAVEL, AND HISTORY

952.03 Re-establishment of Imperial Power, 1868-1945

5619. Beasley, William G. The Modern History of Japan. 2nd ed. Praeger. 1974. $10.00; pap. $4.95.   952.03
1. Japan — History — 1868-

5620. Borton, Hugh. Japan's Modern Century: From Perry to 1970. 2nd ed. Ronald. 1970. $10.50.   952.03
1. Japan — History.

5621. Livingston, Jon. Imperial Japan, 1800-1945. Pantheon. 1973. $15.00.   952.03
1. Japan — History — 1787-1868 — Sources. 2. Japan — History — Meiji Period, 1868-1912 — Sources. 3. Japan — History — 1912-1945 — Sources.

5622. Walder, David. The Short Victorious War: The Russo-Japanese Conflict, 1904-1905. Har-Row. 1974. $10.00.   952.03
1. Russo-Japanese War, 1904-1905.

5623. Livingston, Jon. Postwar Japan, 1945 to the Present. Pantheon. 1973. $15.00.   952.04
1. Japan — History — 1945- — Sources.

953 Arabian Peninsula

5624. Doughty, Charles M. Travels in Arabia Deserts. Garnett, Edward, ed. Peter Smith. $4.50.   953
1. Arabia — Description and Travel. 2. Arabia — Social Life and Customs.

5625. Hitti, Philip K. History of the Arabs. 10th ed. St Martin. 1970. $16.95; pap. $8.95.   953
1. Arabia — History. 2. Arab States.

954 India

5626. Basham, Arthur L. The Wonder That Was India: A Survey of the History and Culture of the Indian Sub-Continent Before the Coming of the Muslims. 3rd ed. Taplinger. 1968. $13.50.   954
1. India — Civilization. 2. India — History — Early to 324 B.C. 3. India — History — 324 B.C.-1000 A.D.

5627. De Bary, William T., et al, eds. Sources of Indian Tradition. Columbia U Pr. 1958. $17.50.   954
1. India — Civilization. 2. India — History — Sources.

5628. Ikram, Sheikh M. Muslim Civilization in India. Embree, A. T., ed. Columbia U Pr. 1964. $12.00.   954
1. Civilization, Mohammedan.

5629. Kublin, Hyman. India: Selected Readings. rev. ed. HM. 1973. pap. $2.96.   954
1. India.

5630. Spear, Percival. India, a Modern History. U of Mich Pr. 1972. $10.00.   954
1. India — History.

954.03 British Rule, 1774-1947

5631. Bhatia, Krishan. Indira: A Biography of Prime Minister Gandhi. Praeger. 1974. $10.00.   954.03(B)
1. Gandhi, Indira Nehru, 1917- 2. India — Politics and Government — 1947-

5632. Gandhi, Mohandas. Autobiography. Beacon Pr. 1957. pap. $3.95.   954.03(B)
1. Gandhi, Mohandas Karamchand, 1869-1948.

5633. Keer, Bhananjay. Mahatma Gandhi: Political Saint and Unarmed Prophet. South Asia Bks. 1973. $17.00.   954.03(B)
1. Gandhi, Mohandas Karamchaud, 1869-1948.

5634. Shiva Rao, B. India's Freedom Movement: Some Notable Figures. Intl Pubns Serv. 1974. $13.50.   954.03(B)
1. India — Biography. 2. India — Politics and Government. 3. Nationalism — India.

5635. Gandhi, Indira. Indira Gandhi Speaks on Democracy, Socialism, and Third World Nonalignment. Taplinger. 1975. $8.95.   954.04
1. India — History — 1947- 2. India — Social Conditions — 1947-

5636. Seton, Marie. Panditji: A Portrait of Jawaharlal Nehru. Taplinger. 1967. $13.95.   954.04(B)
1. Nehru, Jawaharlal, 1889-1964.

954.9 Pakistan

5637. Jackson, Robert V. South Asian Crisis: India, Pakistan and Bangla Desh: a Political and Historical Analysis of the 1971 War. Praeger. 1974. $11.00.   954.9

900 GEOGRAPHY, TRAVEL, AND HISTORY

1. Asia, Southeastern — Politics. 2. India-Pakistan Conflict, 1971-

5638. Payne, Robert. Massacre. Macmillan. 1973. $5.95. 954.9
1. Bangladesh — Politics and Government — 1971- 2. Political Atrocities — Bangladesh.

5639. Zeylanicus. Ceylon: Between Orient and Occident. Humanities. 1970. $7.25. 954.93
1. Ceylon — History.

955 Iran

5640. Avery, Peter. Modern Iran. Praeger. 1965. $11.00. 955
1. Iran — History — 19th Century. 2. Iran — History — 1909-

5641. Banani, Amin. The Modernization of Iran, 1921-1941. Stanford U Pr. 1961. $6.00. 955
1. Iran — History — 1909-

956 Near East

5642. Holt, Peter M. Egypt and the Fertile Crescent: A Political History. Cornell U Pr. 1956. $8.50; pap. $2.45. 956
1. Asia, Western — Relations (General) with Egypt. 2. Egypt — History — 640-1882. 3. Egypt — History — 1882-1952. 4. Egypt — Relations (General) with Western Asia. 5. Near East — History. 6. Turkey — History.

5643. Collins, Larry and LaPierre, Dominique. O Jerusalem! S&S. 1972. $10.00. 956.044
1. Israel-Arab War, 1948-1949 — Jerusalem. 2. Jerusalem — Siege, 1948.

5644. Laffin, John. Fedayeen: The Arab-Israeli Dilemma. Free Pr. 1973. $5.95. 956.044
1. Fedayeen. 2. Israel-Arab Border Conflicts, 1949- 3. Jewish-Arab Relations.

5645. Lorch, Netaniel. Israel's War of Independence, 1947-1949. 2nd ed. Hartmore. 1969. $12.50. 956.044
1. Israel-Arab War, 1948-1949 — Campaigns and Battles.

5646. Love, Kenneth. Suez: The Twice-Fought War; a History. McGraw. 1970. $10.00. 956.044
1. Egypt — History — Intervention, 1956. 2. Jewish-Arab Relations.

956.046-956.08 Israel-Arab Wars

5647. Abu-Lughod, Ibrahim, ed. The Arab-Israeli Confrontation of June, 1967: An Arab Perspective. Northwestern U Pr. 1970. $7.00. 956.046
1. Israel-Arab War, 1967-

5648. Draper, Theodore. Israel and World Politics: Roots of the Third Arab-Israeli War. Viking Pr. 1968. $5.75; pap. $2.25. 956.046
1. Israel-Arab War, 1967- 2. World Politics — 1945-

5649. Laqueur, Walter. The Road to Jerusalem: The Origins of the Arab-Israel Conflict. Macmillan. 1968. $6.95. 956.046
1. Israel-Arab War, 1967-

5650. O'Ballance, Edgar. The Third Arab-Israeli War. Shoe String. 1972. $10.00. 956.046
1. Israel-Arab War, 1967-

5651. Laqueur, Walter. Confrontation: The Middle East and World Politics. Quadrangle. 1974. $8.95; pap. $1.95 (Bantam). 956.048
1. Israel-Arab War, 1973-

5652. Sunday Times, London. The Yom Kippur War. Doubleday. 1974. $10.00. 956.048
1. Israel-Arab War, 1973-

956.1 Turkey and Cyprus

5653. Hotham, David. The Turks. Intl Pubns Serv. 1972. $15.00. 956.1
1. Turkey — History. 2. Turkey — Social Life and Customs.

5654. Lewis, Geoffrey L. Modern Turkey. Praeger. 1974. $10.00. 956.1
1. Turkey — History.

5655. Miller, William. The Ottoman Empire and Its Successors, 1801-1927. Octagon. Repr. 1966. $16.00. 956.1
1. Eastern Question (Balkans). 2. Turkey — History.

5656. Foley, Charles and Scobie, W. I. The Struggle for Cyprus. Hoover Inst Pr. 1974. $7.95. 956.45
1. Cyprus — History.

5657. Purcell, H. D. Cyprus. Praeger. 1969. $9.00. 956.45
1. Cyprus — History.

900 GEOGRAPHY, TRAVEL, AND HISTORY

5658. Der Nersessian, Strarpie. The Armenians. Praeger. 1970. $8.50. 956.6
1. Armenia — Civilization. 2. Armenia — History.

5659. O'Ballance, Edgar. The Kurdish Revolt, 1961-1970. Shoe String. 1973. $7.50. 956.7
1. Iraq — Politics and Government. 2. Kurds in Iraq.

956.94 Palestine/Israel

5660. Bauer, Yehuda. From Diplomacy to Resistance: A History of Jewish Palestine, 1939-1945. Winters, Alton M., tr. Atheneum. 1970. pap. $4.65. 956.94
1. Palestine — History — 1929-1948.

5661. Ben-Gurion, David, ed. The Jews in Their Land. new rev. ed. Doubleday. 1974. $17.50. 956.94
1. Israel — History. 2. Jews in Palestine — History.

5662. Dodd, Charles H., compiled by. Israel and the Arab World. Routledge & Kegan. 1970. $7.00. 956.94
1. Jewish-Arab Relations — History — Sources.

5663. Eban, Abba A. My Country: The Story of Modern Israel. Random. 1972. $15.00. 956.94
1. Israel — History.

5664. Halpern, Ben. The Idea of the Jewish State. rev. ed. Harvard U Pr. 1969. $15.00. 956.94
1. Palestine — History — 1917-1948. 2. Zionism — History.

5665. Lucas, Noah. The Modern History of Israel. Praeger. 1975. $17.50. 956.94
1. Israel — History. 2. Palestine — History — 1917-1948.

5666. Meir, Golda. A Land of Our Own: An Oral Biography. Putnam. 1973. $6.95. 956.94(B)
1. Meir, Golda Mabovitz, 1898-

5667. Naamani, Israel T. Israel: A Profile. Praeger. 1972. $8.50. 956.94
1. Israel.

5668. Parkes, James W. Whose Land? A History of the Peoples of Palestine. Taplinger. 1971. $10.00; pap. $1.95 (Penguin). 956.94
1. Palestine — History.

5669. Teveth, Shabati. Moshe Dayan: The Soldier, the Man, the Legend. HM. 1973. $8.95; pap. $1.95 (Dell). 956.94(B)
1. Dayan, Moshe, 1915-

959 Southeast Asia

5670. Bastin, John and Benda, Harry J. A History of Modern Southeast Asia: Colonialism, Nationalism and Decolonization. P-H. 1968. $6.95; pap. $2.45. 959
1. Asia, Southeastern — History.

5671. Benda, Harry J. and Larkin, J. A., eds. The World of Southeast Asia: Selected Historical Readings. Taplinger. 1967. $5.95. 959
1. Asia, Southeastern.

5672. Buchanan, Keith. The Southeast Asian World: An Introductory Essay. rev. ed. Doubleday. 1970. pap. $2.95. 959
1. Asia, Southeastern.

5673. Shaplen, Robert. Time Out of Hand: Revolution and Reaction in Southeast Asia. Har-Row. 1969. $8.95. 959
1. Asia, Southeastern — History. 2. Asia, Southeastern — Politics.

5674. Von Der Mebhen, Fred R. Southeast Asia, 1930-1970: The Legacy of Colonialism and Nationalism. Norton. 1974. $7.95; pap. $3.45. 959
1. Asia, Southeastern — History. 2. Asia, Southeastern — Politics.

5675. Hall, Daniel G. Burma. AMS Pr. 1974. $9.50. 959.1
1. Burma — History.

5676. Gullick, J. M. Malaysia and Its Neighbors. B&N. 1967. $4.50. 959.505
1. Malaysia — History — Sources.

959.7 Vietnam

5677. Fall, Bernard B. The Two Vietnams: A Political and Military History. 2nd rev. ed. Praeger. 1967. $7.95. 959.7
1. Vietnam — History.

900 GEOGRAPHY, TRAVEL, AND HISTORY

5678. Halberstam, David. The Making of a Quagmire. Random. 1965. $7.95. 959.7
1. U. S. — Foreign Relations — Vietnam. 2. Vietnam — Politics and Government.

5679. McAlister, John T. Vietnam: The Origins of Revolution. Knopf. 1969. $7.95; pap. $2.95 (Doubleday). 959.7
1. Vietnam — Politics and Government.

5680. Smith, Ralph B. Vietnam and the West. Cornell U Pr. 1971. $6.50; pap. $1.95. 959.7
1. Vietnam — History.

5681. Caldwell, Malcolm and Tan, Lek. Cambodia in the Southeast Asian War. Monthly Rev. 1973. $15.00; pap. $4.95. 959.704
1. Laos — Politics and Government. 2. Vietnamese Conflict, 1961-1973 — Laos. 3. Vietnamese Conflict, 1961-1973 — U. S.

5682. Halberstam, David. Ho. Random. 1971. $4.95; pap. $1.65. 959.704(B)
1. Ho-Chi-Minh, President, Democratic Republic of Vietnam, 1894?-1969.

5683. Hersh, Seymour M. My Lai 4: A Report on the Massacre and the Aftermath. Random. 1970. $5.95. 959.704
1. Vietnamese Conflict, 1961-1973 — Atrocities. 2. Vietnamese Conflict, 1961-1973 — Campaigns — My Lai (4), Vietnam.

5684. Huyen, N. Kha. Vision Accomplished: The Enigma of Ho Chi Minh. Macmillan. 1971. $8.95; pap. $2.95. 959.704
1. Ho-Chi-Minh, President, Democratic Republic of Vietnam, 1894?-1969.

5685. Kendrick, Alexander. The Wound Within: America in the Vietnam Years, 1945-1974. Little. 1974. $12.95. 959.704
1. U. S. — History — 1945- 2. Vietnamese Conflict, 1961-1973 — U. S.

5686. Polner, Murray. No Victory Parades: The Return of the Vietnam Veteran. HR&W. 1971. $5.95; pap. $2.95. 959.704
1. Veterans — U. S. 2. Vietnamese Conflict, 1961-1973.

5687. Sheehan, Neil, et al. The Pentagon Papers. Quadrangle. 1971. $15.00. 959.704
1. U. S. — Foreign Relations — Vietnam. 2. Vietnamese Conflict, 1961-1973.

5688. Zagoria, Donald S. Vietnam Triangle: Moscow, Peking, Hanoi. Pegasus. 1967. $6.95; pap. $2.30. 959.704
1. Vietnam (Democratic Republic, 1946-) — Foreign Relations. 2. Vietnamese Conflict, 1961-1973.

959.8 Indonesia

5689. Neill, Wilfred. Twentieth Century Indonesia. Columbia U Pr. 1973. $15.00; pap. $4.95. 959.8
1. Indonesia — Civilization. 2. Indonesia — History. 3. Natural History — Indonesia.

5690. Wehl, David. The Birth of Indonesia. AMS Pr. 1948. $11.00. 959.8
1. Indonesia — History — Revolution, 1945-1949.

5691. Quezon, Manuel L. The Good Fight. AMS Pr. Repr. 1946. $18.00. 959.9
1. Philippine Islands — History — 1898-1946. 2. Quezon, Manuel Luis, President Philippines, 1879-1944. 3. World War, 1939-1945 — Philippine Islands.

Recommended Series

5692. The Great Ages of Man. Time-L

5693. Problems in Asian Civilization: Prepared by the University Committee on Oriental Studies, Columbia University, William T. de Bary, Chmn. Heath.

960 African History

5694. Aynor, H. S. Notes from Africa. Praeger. 1969. $5.95. 960
1. Africa — Civilization. 2. Africa — Economic Conditions.

5695. Davidson, Basil. Africa: A History of a Continent. Macmillan. 1972. $12.95. 960
1. Africa — History.

5696. ———. African Kingdoms. Silver. 1966 (Pub. by Time-Life). $8.80. 960
1. Africa — History.

5697. ———. The African Past: Chronicles from Antiquity to Modern Times. G&D. 1964. pap. $2.95. 960
1. Africa — History.

900 GEOGRAPHY, TRAVEL, AND HISTORY

5698. Grove, Alfred T. Africa South of the Sahara. Oxford U Pr. 1970. $10.95.   960
1. Africa.

5699. Herskovits, Melville J. The Human Factor in Changing Africa. Knopf. 1962. $8.95; pap. $2.45 (Random).   960
1. Africa.

5700. ———. The Myth of the Negro Past. Beacon Pr. 1958. pap. $2.95.   960
1. Africa — Civilization. 2. Africa — History. 3. Negroes.

5701. Hodgson, Robert D. and Stoneman, Elryn. A Changing Map of Africa. Van Nos Reinhold. 1968. pap. $2.95.   960
1. Africa — History.

5702. Josephy, Alvin M., et al, eds. The Horizon History of Africa. 2 vols. McGraw. 1971. $25.00.   960
1. Africa — History.

5703. McEwan, P. J., ed. Africa from Early Times to 1800. Oxford U Pr. 1968. $10.25.   960
1. Africa — History.

5704. ———. Nineteenth-Century Africa. Oxford U Pr. $10.25.   960
1. Africa — History.

5705. ———. Twentieth-Century Africa. Oxford U Pr. $10.25; pap. $5.50.   960
1. Africa — History.

5706. Murphy, E. Jefferson. History of African Civilization. T Y Crowell. 1972. $12.50; pap. $3.45 (Dell).   960
1. Africa — History.

5707. Oliver, Roland A. and Atmore, Anthony. Africa Since 1800. Cambridge U Pr. 1972. $11.95; pap. $3.75.   960
1. Africa — History.

5708. Ranger, Terence O. Emerging Themes of African History. Northwestern U Pr. 1968. $6.00.   960
1. Africa — History.

960.2 Early History, 640-1900

5709. Gailey, Harry A. History of Africa: From Earliest Times to 1800. HR&W. 1970. pap. $6.00.   960.2
1. Africa — History — to 1884.

5710. ———. History of Africa: From 1800 to the Present. HR&W. 1972. pap. $7.00.   960.2
1. Africa — History — 1884-1960. 2. Africa — History — 1960-

5711. Hallett, Robin. Africa Since 1875: A Modern History. U of Mich Pr. 1974. $15.00.   960.2
1. Africa — History — 1884-

5712. ———. Africa to 1875: A Modern History. U of Mich Pr. 1970. $8.95.   960.2
1. Africa — History — to 1884.

962 Countries of the Nile

5713. Moorehead, Alan. The Blue Nile. Har-Row. 1974. pap. $1.25.   962
1. Africa — History. 2. Nile River.

5714. ———. The White Nile. Har-Row. 1971. $17.50.   962
1. Africa — History. 2. Nile River.

5715. Dekmejian, R. Hrair. Egypt Under Nasser: A Study in Political Dynamics. State U NY Pr. 1971. $10.00.   962.05
1. Egypt — Politics and Government — 1952- 2. Nasser, Gamal Abdel, President United Arab Republic, 1918-1970.

5716. Haykal, Muhammad H. The Cairo Documents: The Inside Story of Nasser and His Relationship with World Leaders, Rebels, and Statesmen. Doubleday. 1973. $10.00.   962.05
1. Egypt — Foreign Relations. 2. Nasser, Gamal Abdel, President United Arab Republic, 1918-1970.

5717. McLeave, Hugh. The Last Pharaoh: Farouk of Egypt. Tower. 1971. pap. $1.25.   962.05(B)
1. Egypt — History — 1919- 2. Farouk I, King of Egypt, 1920-1965.

5718. Thomas, Hugh. Suez. Har-Row. 1967. $5.95; pap. $2.45.   962.15
1. Egypt — History — Intervention, 1956. 2. Suez Canal.

963 Ethiopia

5719. Hess, Robert L. Ethiopia: The Modernization of Autocracy. Cornell U Pr. 1970. $8.95; pap. $2.95.   963
1. Ethiopia — History.

900 GEOGRAPHY, TRAVEL, AND HISTORY

5720. Baer, George W. The Coming of the Italian-Ethiopian War. Harvard U Pr. 1967. $12.00. 963.056
1. Italo-Ethiopian War, 1935-1936 — Causes.

5721. Hardie, Frank. The Abyssian Crisis. Shoe String. 1974. $15.00. 963.056
1. Great Britain — Foreign Relations — 1910-1936. 2. Italo-Ethiopian War, 1935-1936 — Diplomatic History. 3. League of Nations.

966 West Africa

5722. Davidson, Basil. A History of West Africa to the 19th Century. rev. ed. Doubleday. 1966. pap. $1.95. 966
1. Africa, West.

5723. July, Robert W. The Origins of Modern African Thought: Its Development in West Africa During the 19th and 20th Centuries. Praeger. 1968. $10.00. 966
1. Africa, West.

5724. Webster, J. B. History of West Africa: The Revolutionary Years - 1815 to Independence. Praeger. 1970. $9.00. 966
1. Africa, French West — History.

5725. Davidson, Basil. Black Star: A View of the Life and Times of Kwame Nkrumah. Praeger. 1974. $7.95. 966.7(B)
1. Nkrumah, Kwame, President Ghana, 1909-1972.

5726. Kimble, David. A Political History of Ghana: The Rise of Gold Coast Nationalism, 1850-1928. Oxford U Pr. 1963. $20.50. 966.7
1. Ghana.

5727. Omari, T. Peter. Kwame Nkrumah: The Anatomy of an African Dictatorship. Holmes & Meier. 1970. $12.50. 966.7
1. Ghana — Politics and Government — 1957- 2. Nkrumah, Kwame, President Ghana, 1909-1972.

5728. De St. Jorre, John. The Brothers' War: Biafra and Nigeria. HM. 1972. $10.00. 966.9
1. Nigeria — History — Civil War, 1967-1970.

5729. Schwarz, Walter. Nigeria. Praeger. 1968. $9.00. 966.9
1. Nigeria — History.

5730. Davidson, Basil. Black Mother: The Years of the African Slave Trade. Little. 1961. $10.00. 967
1. Africa — History. 2. Slave Trade.

5731. Ranger, Terence O., ed. Aspects of Central African History. Northwestern U Pr. 1968. $10.00. 967
1. Africa, Central — History.

5732. Scott, Ian. Tumbled House: The Congo at Independence. Oxford U Pr. 1969. $5.75. 967.24
1. Congo (Democratic Republic) — History — Early Period to 1908.

5733. Miller, Charles. The Lunatic Express: An Entertainment in Imperialism. Macmillan. 1971. $10.95. 967.6
1. Africa, East — History. 2. Great Britain — Colonies — Africa. 3. Railroads — Africa, East.

968 South Africa

5734. Cope, John. South Africa. rev. ed. Praeger. 1967. $8.50. 968
1. Africa, South — History. 2. Africa, South — Race Question.

5735. Hale, Hugh M. Passing of the Black Kings. Negro U Pr. Repr. 1932. $14.95. 968
1. Africa, South — History.

5736. Macmillan, William M. Bantu, Boer and Briton: The Making of the South African Native Problems. rev. ed. Oxford U Pr. 1963. $12.00. 968
1. Africa, South.

5737. Morris, Donald. The Washing of the Spears: The Rise and Fall of the Zulu Nation. S&S. 1965. $12.00; pap. $3.45. 968
1. Africa — History. 2. Cettiwayo, King of Zulu-Land. 3. Chaka, Zulu Chief. 4. Zulu War, 1879.

5738. Were, Gideon S. A History of South Africa. Holmes & Meier. 1974. $8.95; pap. $4.95. 968
1. Africa, South — History.

5739. Flint, John E. Cecil Rhodes. Little. 1974. $6.95. 968.04(B)
1. Rhodes, Cecil John, 1853-1902.

5740. Crafford, F. S. Jan Smuts: A Biography. Greenwood. Repr. 1943. $17.50. 968.05(B)
1. Smuts, Jan Christian, 1870-1950.

900 GEOGRAPHY, TRAVEL, AND HISTORY

5741. Mahan, Alfred T. Story of the War in South Africa. Greenwood. Repr. 1900. $12.00. 968.2
1. South African War, 1899-1902.

5742. Wills, Alfred J. An Introduction to the History of Central Africa. 3rd ed. Oxford U Pr. 1973. $13.00; pap. $6.95. 968.9
1. Malawi — History. 2. Rhodesia — History.

970.1 Indians of North America

5743. Armstrong, Virginia I., ed. I Have Spoken: American History Through the Voices of the Indians. Swallow. 1971. $6.00; pap. $2.95. 970.1
1. Indians of North America — History — Sources. 2. Indians of North America — Oratory.

5744. Brandon, William. The Last Americans: The Indians in American Culture. McGraw. 1974. $12.95. 970.1
1. Indians of North America — Civilization.

5745. Debo, Angie. History of the Indians of the United States. U of Okla Pr. 1970. $8.95. 970.1
1. Indians of North America.

5746. Deloria, Vine, Jr. Custer Died for Your Sins: An Indian Manifesto. Macmillan. 1969. $6.95. 970.1
1. Custer, George Armstrong, 1839-1876. 2. Indians of North America.

5747. Driver, Harold E. Indians of North America. 2nd ed. U of Chicago Pr. 1969. $15.00; pap. $6.85. 970.1
1. Indians of Central America. 2. Indians of Mexico. 3. Indians of North America.

5748. Embree, Edwin R. Indians of the Americas. HM. 1939. $5.95. 970.1
1. Indians of North America. 2. Indians of South America.

5749. Farb, Peter. Man's Rise to Civilization As Shown by the Indians of North America, from Primeval Times to the Coming of the Industrial State. Dutton. 1968. $11.95; pap. $1.65 (Avon). 970.1
1. Anthropology. 2. Indians of North America. 3. Social Change.

5750. Gridley, Marion E. American Indian Women. Hawthorn. 1974. $5.95. 970.1(B)
1. Indians of North America — Biography. 2. Indians of North America — Women.

5751. Hyde, George E. Indians of the High Plains: From the Prehistoric Period to the Coming of the Europeans. U of Okla Pr. 1959. $6.50. 970.1
1. Indians of North America.

5752. ———. Indians of the Woodlands, from Prehistoric Times to 1725. U of Okla Pr. 1970. $8.95; pap. $3.95. 970.1
1. Indians of North America.

5753. Josephy, Alvin M. The Indian Heritage of America. Knopf. 1968. $10.00. 970.1
1. Indians of Central America — History. 2. Indians of Mexico — History. 3. Indians of North America — History. 4. Indians of South America — History.

5754. Manuel, George and Posluns, Michael. The Fourth World: An Indian Reality. Free Pr. 1974. $7.95. 970.1
1. Indians of North America — Canada. 2. Indians of North America — Civilization.

5755. Oswalt, Wendell H. This Land Was Theirs: A Study of the North American Indians. 2nd ed. Wiley. 1973. $13.95. 970.1
1. Indians of North America.

5756. Vogel, Virgil J. This Country Was Ours: A Documentary History of the American Indian. Har-Row. 1972. $12.95; pap. $1.95. 970.1
1. Indians — History — Sources. 2. Indians of North America — History — Sources.

970.3 Specific Indian Tribes

5757. Caso, Alfonso. Aztecs, People of the Sun. Dunham, Lowell, tr. U of Okla Pr. 1958. $9.95. 970.3
1. Aztecs. 2. Indians of Mexico — History. 3. Indians of Mexico — Religion and Mythology.

5758. Coe, Michael D. The Maya. Praeger. 1966. $8.50. 970.3
1. Mayas — Antiquities.

5759. Debo, Angie. The Road to Disappearance: A History of the Creek Indians. U of Okla Pr. 1941. $8.95. 970.3
1. Creek Indians. 2. Indians, Treatment of — U. S.

900 GEOGRAPHY, TRAVEL, AND HISTORY

5760. Ewers, John C. The Blackfeet: Raiders on the Northwestern Plains. U of Okla Pr. 1958. $7.95. 970.3
1. Kainah Indians. 2. Piegan Indians. 3. Siksiba Indians.

5761. Geronimo. Geronimo: His Own Story. Dutton. 1970. $7.95; pap. $1.25 1974 (Ballantine). 970.3(B)
1. Apache Indians. 2. Geronimo, Apache Chief, 1829-1909.

5762. Hassrick, Royal B., et al. The Sioux: Life and Customs of a Warrior Society. U of Okla Pr. 1964. $8.95. 970.3
1. Dakota Indians.

5763. Okane, Walter C. Hopis: Portrait of a Desert People. U of Okla Pr. 1953. $8.95. 970.3
1. Hopi Indians. 2. Indians of North America.

5764. Red Fox, William. The Memoirs of Chief Red Fox. McGraw. 1970. $6.95. 970.3(B)
1. Dakota Indians. 2. Indians of North America — the West.

970.5 Government Relations with Indians

5765. Brown, Dee A. Bury My Heart at Wounded Knee: An Indian History of the American West. HR&W. 1971. $10.95; pap. $1.95 1972 (Bantam). 970.5
1. Indians of North America — the West. 2. Indians of North America — Wars. 3. West — History.

5766. Commission on the Rights and Liberties and Responsibilities of the American Indians. The Indian: America's Unfinished Business. Brophy, William A., et al, eds. U of Okla Pr. 1966. $6.95. 970.5
1. Indians of North America — Economic Conditions. 2. Indians of North America — Government Relations. 3. Indians of North America — Social Conditions. 4. Indians, Treatment of — U. S.

5767. Debo, Angie. And Still the Waters Run. Gordian. 1940. $9.00; pap. $2.95 (Princeton U Pr). 970.5
1. Indians of North America — Government Relations. 2. Indians, Treatment of — U. S.

5768. Deloria, Vine, Jr. Behind the Trail of Broken Treaties. Delacorte. 1974. $8.95; pap. $2.95 (Dell). 970.5

1. Indians of North America — Government Relations. 2. Indians of North America — Legal Status, Laws, etc.

5769. Foreman, Grant. Advancing the Frontier, 1830-1960. U of Okla Pr. 1933. $8.95. 970.5
1. Indians of North America — Government Relations. 2. Indians of North America — Oklahoma. 3. Indians of North America — Wars. 4. Indians, Treatment of — U. S.

5770. ———. Indian Removal: The Emigration of the Five Civilized Tribes of Indians. U of Okla Pr. 1932. $8.95. 970.5
1. Indians of North America — Government Relations. 2. Indians, Treatment of — U. S. 3. Indians of North America — Oklahoma.

5771. ———. The Last Trek of the Indians. Russell. Repr. 1946. $20.00. 970.5
1. Indians of North America — Government Relations. 2. Indians of North America — Indian Territory. 3. Indians of North America — Land Transfers. 4. Indians of North America — Ohio Valley.

5772. Jacobs, Wilbur R. Dispossessing the American Indian: Indians and Whites on the Colonial Frontier. Scribner. 1972. $7.95; pap. $3.95. 970.5
1. Indians of North America — Government Relations — to 1789.

5773. McNickle, D'Arcy. Native American Tribalism: Indian Survival and Renewals. new ed. Oxford U Pr. 1973. $6.95; pap. $1.95. 970.5
1. Indians of North America — Government Relations. 2. Indians of North America — History.

5774. Marshall, Samuel L. Crimsoned Prairie: The Wars Between the United States and the Plains Indians During the Winning of the West. Scribner. 1972. $8.95. 970.5
1. Indians of North America — Great Plains — West.

5775. Turner, Katharine C. Red Men Calling on the Great White Father. U of Okla Pr. 1951. $7.95. 970.5
1. Indians of North America — Government Relations. 2. Indians, Treatment of — U. S.

5776. Mead, Margaret. Changing Culture of an Indian Tribe. AMS Pr. 1932. $14.50. 970.6

900 GEOGRAPHY, TRAVEL, AND HISTORY

1. Indians of North America — Culture. 2. Indians of North America — Social Life and Customs. 3. Indians of North America — Women.

5777. Vogel, Virgil J. American Indian Medicine. U of Okla Pr. 1970. $12.50; pap. $1.95 (Ballantine).   970.6
1. Indians of North America — Medicine.

Recommended Series

5778. The Civilization of the American Indian. U of Okla Pr.

971 Canada

5779. Careless, James M. and Brown, R. C. Canadians, 1867-1967. St Martin. 1968. $5.95.   971
1. Canada — History.

5780. Creighton, Donald. Canada's First Century. St Martin. 1970. $12.75.   971
1. Canada — History.

5781. Hill, Brian H., compiled by. Canada, 1875-1973: A Chronology and Fact Book. Oceana. 1973. $7.50.   971
1. Canada — History — Chronology. 2. Canada — History — Sources.

5782. Masters, Donald C., ed. Canada: A Modern History. U of Mich Pr. 1970. $10.00.   971
1. Canada — History.

5783. Park, Julian, ed. Culture of Contemporary Canada. Cornell U Pr. 1957. $16.50.   971
1. Canada — Civilization. 2. Canada — Intellectual Life.

5784. Wade, Mason. French Canadians. 2 vols. rev. ed. St Martin. 1968. $21.50 set.   971
1. Canada — History. 2. French Canadians.

5785. Ward, Norman. Public Purse: A Study in Canadian Democracy. U of Toronto Pr. 1962. $22.50.   971
1. Canada — History.

5786. Burpee, Lawrence J. The Discovery of Canada. Bks for Libs. Repr. 1944. $15.50.   971.01
1. America — Discovery and Exploration. 2. Canada — Exploring Expeditions. 3. Canada — History. 4. New France — Discovery and Exploration.

5787. Thwaites, Reuben G. France in America, 1497-1763. Greenwood. Repr. 1905. $12.00.   971.01
1. Canada — History — to 1763 (New France). 2. French in North America.

5788. Zoitvany, Yves F., ed. French Tradition in America. U of SC Pr. 1969. $7.95; pap. $2.95 (Har-Row).   971.01
1. Canada — History — to 1763 (New France) — Sources. 2. Canada — History — 1763-1867 — Sources.

971.02 Early British Rule, 1763-1791

5789. Bradley, Arthur G. The United Empire Loyalists: Founders of British Canada. AMS Pr. Repr. 1932. $24.50.   971.02
1. American Loyalists. 2. American Loyalists — Canada. 3. Canada — History — 1763-1867. 4. U. S. — History — Revolution. 5. U. S. — History — War of 1812.

5790. Lanctot, Gustave. Canada and the American Revolution, 1774-1783. Harvard U Pr. 1967. $8.50.   971.02
1. Canada — History — 1775-1783. 2. U. S. — History — Revolution.

5791. Smith, Justin H. Our Struggle for the 14th Colony: Canada and the American Revolution. 2 vols. Da Capo. Repr. 1907. $65.00.   971.02
1. Canada — History — 1775-1783. 2. Canadian Invasion — 1775-1783.

5792. Trotter, Reginald G. Canadian Federation: Its Origins and Achievement, a Study in Nation Building. Russell. Repr. 1924. $18.00.   971.02
1. Canada — History — 1763-1867.

971.03-971.05 Separate Colonies - Dominion of Canada, 1791-1911

5793. Morison, Samuel E. Samuel De Champlain: Father of New France. Little. 1972. $10.00.   971.03(B)
1. America — Discovery and Exploration — French. 2. Champlain, Samuel de, 1567-1635. 3. Indians of North America — Canada. 4. New France — Discovery and Exploration.

900 GEOGRAPHY, TRAVEL, AND HISTORY

5794. Talman, James J. Basic Documents in Canadian History. Peter Smith. $3.25. 971.03
1. Canada — History — Sources.

5795. Boyd, James. Sir George Etienne Cartier: His Life and Times, a Political History of Canada from 1814 Until 1873. Bks for Libs. Repr. 1914. $27.50. 971.04(B)
1. Canada — Politics and Government — 19th Century. 2. Cartier, Sir George Etienne, bart., 1814-1873.

5796. Winks, Robin W. The Blacks in Canada: A History. Yale U Pr. 1971. $15.00. 971.04
1. Negroes — Canada — History.

5797. Pope, Joseph. Memoirs of the Right Honorable Alexander Macdonald. 2 vols. AMS Pr. Repr. 1894. $19.00. 971.05(B)
1. Canada — Politics and Government — 19th Century. 2. Macdonald, Sir John Alexander, 1815-1891.

971.06 20th Century, 1911-

5798. Pearson, Lester N. Words and Occasions: An Anthology of Speeches and Articles from His Papers. Harvard U Pr. 1970. $10.00. 971.06
1. Canada — Politics and Government — 1945-

5799. Stacy, C. P., ed. Historical Documents of Canada, 1914-1945. St Martin. 1972. $20.00. 971.06
1. Canada — History — Sources.

5800. Westell, Anthony. Paradox: Trudeau As Prime Minister. P-H. 1972. $7.50. 971.06
1. Canada — Politics and Government — 1945- 2. Trudeau, Pierre Elliot, 1919-

5801. Cline, Gloria G. Peter Skene Ogden and the Hudson's Bay Company. U of Okla Pr. 1974. $8.95. 971.2(B)
1. Hudson's Bay Company. 2. Ogden, Peter Skene, 1790-1854.

972 Mexico

5802. Cheetham, Nicolas. Mexico: A Short History. T Y Crowell. 1971. $7.50. 972
1. Mexico — History.

5803. Cumberland, Charles C. Mexico: The Struggle for Modernity. Oxford U Pr. 1968. $8.95; pap. $2.95. 972
1. Mexico — History.

5804. Diaz del Castillo, Bernal. Discovery and Conquest of Mexico. FS&G. 1956. pap. $4.95. 972
1. Cortes, Hernando, 1485-1547. 2. Mexico — History — Conquest, 1519-1540.

5805. Flandrau, Charles M. Viva Mexico. Peter Smith. $4.00; pap. $1.95 (U of Ill Pr). 972
1. Mexico.

5806. Lansing, Marion F. Liberators and Heroes of Mexico and Central America. Bks for Libs. Repr. 1941. $14.50. 972(B)
1. Central America — Biography. 2. Mexico — Biography.

5807. Parkes, Henry B. History of Mexico. rev. ed. HM. 1960. $6.75; pap. $3.45. 972
1. Mexico — History.

5808. Soustelle, Jacques. Daily Life Among the Aztecs. Macmillan. 1962. $5.95. 972
1. Aztecs. 2. Indians of Mexico.

5809. Thompson, John E. Rise and Fall of the Maya Civilization. U of Okla Pr. 1954. $6.95. 972.015
1. Mayas.

5810. Burland, Cottie A. Montezuma: Lord of the Aztecs. Putnam. 1973. $15.00. 972.02(B)
1. Mexico — History — Conquest, 1519-1540. 2. Montezuma II, Emperor of Mexico, 1480?-1521.

5811. Davies, Nigel. The Aztecs: A History. Putnam. 1974. $10.00. 972.02
1. Aztecs. 2. Mexico — History — to 1519.

5812. Flores Caballero, Romeo. Counterrevolution: The Role of the Spaniards in the Independence of Mexico, 1804-1838. U of Nebr Pr. 1974. $10.95. 972.03
1. Mexico — History — Spanish Colony — 1540-1810. 2. Spaniards in Mexico.

5813. Gutierrez de Lara, Lazaro. The Mexican People: Their Struggle for Freedom. Arno. Repr. 1914. $15.00. 972.03
1. Mexico — History — 1810-

5814. Smart, Charles A. Viva Juarez: The Founder of Modern Mexico. Lippincott. 1963. $7.95. 972.05(B)

900 GEOGRAPHY, TRAVEL, AND HISTORY

1. Juarez, Benito Pablo, President Mexico, 1806-1872. 2. Mexico — History — 1867-1910.

5815. Hanna, Alfred J. and Hanna, Kathryn A. Napoleon Third and Mexico: American Triumph Over Monarchy. U of NC Pr. 1971. $11.25.   972.07
1. Mexico — History — European Intervention, 1861-1867. 2. U. S. — Foreign Relations — 1861-1865.

5816. Smith, Gene. Maximilian and Carlota: A Tale of Romance and Tragedy. Morrow. 1973. $8.95.   972.07(B)
1. Charlotte, Consort of Maximilian, Emperor of Mexico, 1840-1927. 2. Maximilian, Emperor of Mexico, 1832-1867.

972.08 Republic 1867-

5817. Brenner, Anita. The Wind That Swept Mexico: The History of the Mexican Revolution, 1910-1942. U of Tex Pr. 1971. $10.00.   972.08
1. Mexico — History — 1910-1946.

5818. Cumberland, Charles C. Mexican Revolution: The Constitutionalist Years. U of Tex Pr. 1972. $10.00; pap. $4.35.   972.08
1. Mexico — History — 1910-1946.

5819. Hofstadter, Dan. Mexico, 1946-1973. Facts on File. 1974. $6.95.   972.08
1. Mexico — History — 1946- 2. Mexico — Politics and Government — 1946-

5820. Pinchon, Edgums. Viva Villa! Arno. Repr. 1933. $15.00.   972.08
1. Mexico — History — 1910-1946. 2. Villa, Francisco, 1878-1923.

5821. Tannenbaum, Frank. Mexico: The Struggle for Peace and Bread. Knopf. 1950. $6.95.   972.08
1. Mexico — Economic Conditions. 2. Mexico — Foreign Relations. 3. Mexico — Politics and Government — 1910- 4. Mexico — Social Conditions.

5822. Womack, John. Zapata and the Mexican Revolution. Knopf. 1969. $10.00; pap. $2.95 (Random).   972.08
1. Mexico — History — 1910-1946. 2. Zapata, Emiliano, 1877?-1919.

5823. Brandenburg, Frank R. The Making of Modern Mexico. P-H. 1964. $10.95.   972.082

1. Mexico — History — 1910-1946. 2. Mexico — History — 1946-

972.9 West Indies

5824. Fagg, John E. Cuba, Haiti and the Dominican Republic. P-H. 1965. pap. $1.95.   972.9
1. Cuba — History. 2. Dominican Republic — History. 3. Haiti — History.

5825. Sherlock, Philip M. West Indian Nations: A New History. St Martin. 1974. $14.95.   972.9
1. West Indies — History.

972.91 Cuba

5826. Aguilar, Luis E. Cuba Nineteen Thirty-Three: Prologue to Revolution. Norton. 1972. pap. $2.95.   972.91
1. Cuba — History — 1895- 2. Cuba — History — Revolution, 1933.

5827. Bonachea, Ramon L. The Cuban Insurrection, 1952-1959. Transaction Bks. 1974. $12.95.   972.91
1. Cuba — History — 1933-1959.

5828. Castro, Fidel. History Will Absolve Me. Grossman. 1969. $3.50; pap. $1.95. 972.91
1. Cuba — Politics and Government.

5829. ———. Revolutionary Struggle, 1947-1958. MIT Pr. 1972. $12.50.   972.91(B)
1. Communism — Cuba. 2. Cuba — History — 1933-1959. 3. Cuba — History — 1959-

5830. Draper, Theodore. Castroism: Theory and Practice. Praeger. 1969. $7.50; pap. $2.75.   972.91
1. Castro, Fidel, 1927- 2. Communism — Cuba, 1927- 3. Cuba — History — 1933-1959. 4. Cuba — History — 1959-

5831. Fagen, Richard R., et al. Cubans in Exile: Disaffection and the Revolution. Stanford U Pr. 1968. $5.95.   972.91
1. Cuba — History — 1959- 2. Cubans in Miami, Florida. 3. Refugees, Cuban.

5832. Guevara, Ché. Reminiscences of the Cuban Revolutionary War. Grove. 1968. $6.95.   972.91
1. Cuba — History — 1959-

900 GEOGRAPHY, TRAVEL, AND HISTORY

5833. Johnson, Haynes. Bay of Pigs: The Leaders' Story of Brigade 2506. Norton. 1964. $8.95.   972.91
1. Cuba — History — Invasion, 1961.

5834. Lizaso, Felix. Marti, Martyr of Cuban Independence. Greenwood. Repr. 1953. $12.00.   972.91(B)
1. Marti, Jose, 1853-1895.

5835. Lockwood, Lee. Castro's Cuba: Cuba's Fidel. Macmillan. 1967. $9.95; pap. $2.95 (Random).   972.91
1. Castro, Fidel, 1927- 2. Cuba.

5836. Ruiz, Roman E. Cuba: The Making of a Revolution. U of Mass Pr. 1968. $9.50; pap. $1.85 (Norton).   972.91
1. Cuba — History. 2. Cuba — Politics and Government — 1959- 3. Cuba — Social Conditions.

5837. Suarez, Andres. Cuba: Castroism and Communism, 1959-1966. Carmichael, Joel and Halperin, Ernst, trs. MIT Pr. 1969. $10.00; pap. $2.45.   972.91
1. Castro, Fidel, 1927- 2. Cuba — History — 1959- 3. Cuba — Social Conditions.

5838. Suchlicki, Jaime. Cuba: From Columbus to Castro. Scribner. 1974. $8.95; pap. $3.95.   972.91
1. Cuba — History.

5839. Thomas, Hugh. Cuba: The Pursuit of Freedom, 1762-1969. Har-Row. 1971. $25.00.   972.91
1. Cuba — History.

972.93 Dominican Republic

5840. Clausner, Marlin D. Rural Santo Domingo: Settled, Unsettled and Resettled. Temple U Pr. 1973. $11.50.   972.93
1. Dominican Republic — History. 2. Land Tenure — Dominican Republic.

5841. Galindez, Jesus de. The Era of Trujillo: Dominican Dictator. U of Ariz Pr. 1973. pap. $4.50.   972.93(B)
1. Trujillo, Molina Rafael Leonidas, President Dominican Republic, 1891-1961.

5842. Knight, Melvin M. The American in Santo Domingo. Arno. Repr. 1928. $8.00.   972.93
1. Dominican Republic — History — American Occupation. 2. Dominican Republic — Politics and Government — 1844-1930.

5843. Mansbach, Richard W. Dominican Crisis, 1965. Facts on File. 1971. pap. $2.45.   972.93
1. Dominican Republic — Politics and Government — 1961-

5844. Rodman, Selden. Quisqueya: A History of the Dominican Republic. U of Wash Pr. 1964. $6.95.   972.93
1. Dominican Republic — History.

5845. Wiarda, Howard J. The Dominican Republic: Nation in Transition. Praeger. 1969. $7.00.   972.93
1. Dominican Republic — History. 2. Dominican Republic — Politics and Government. 3. Dominican Republic — Social Conditions.

972.94 Haiti

5846. Bird, Mark B. The Black Man: Or, Haytian Independence. Bks for Libs. Repr. 1869. $18.50.   972.94
1. Haiti — History — 1804-1844. 2. Haiti — History — 1844-1915.

5847. Korngold, Ralph. Citizen Touissant. Hill & Wang. 1965. pap. $2.95.   972.94(B)
1. Haiti — History — Revolution, 1791-1804. 2. Touissant Louverture, Francois Dominique, 1743-1803.

5848. Leyburn, James G. The Haitian People. Yale U Pr. 1966. $15.00.   972.94
1. Haiti — Social Conditions.

5849. Ott, Thomas. The Haitian Revolution, 1789-1804. U of Tenn Pr. 1973. $8.95.   972.94
1. Haiti — History — Revolution, 1791-1804. 2. Haiti — History — to 1791.

5850. Logan, Rayford W. Haiti and the Dominican Republic. Oxford U Pr. 1968. $6.75.   972.95
1. Dominican Republic — History. 2. Haiti — History.

5851. Maldonado, Manuel. Puerto Rico: An Historic Social Interpretation. Random. 1972. $8.95; pap. $2.45.   972.95
1. Nationalism — Puerto Rico. 2. Puerto Rico — History.

5852. Wagenheim, Kal, compiled by. The Puerto Ricans: A Documentary History. Praeger. 1973. $12.50.   972.95
1. Puerto Ricans in the U. S. 2. Puerto Rico — History — Sources.

900 GEOGRAPHY, TRAVEL, AND HISTORY

973 United States History

5853. Barzman, Sol. Madmen and Geniuses: The Vice-Presidents of the United States. Follett. 1974. $8.95.   973(B)
1. Vice-Presidents — U. S. — Biography.

5854. Brogan, Denis W. American Character. Peter Smith. 1956. $4.00.   973
1. U. S. — Civilization. 2. National Characteristics, American.

5855. Butterfield, Roger, ed. The American Past. 2nd rev. ed. S&S. 1966. $9.95.   973
1. U. S. — History.

5856. Carman, Harry J., et al. History of the American People. 2 vols. Knopf. pap. $6.95 ea.   973
1. U. S. — History.

5857. Commager, Henry S. The American Mind. Yale U Pr. 1950. $17.50; pap. $3.95.   973
1. National Characteristics, American. 2. U. S. — Civilization. 3. U. S. — Intellectual Life.

5858. Curti, Merle E. Growth of American Thought. 3rd ed. Har-Row. 1964. $14.95.   973
1. U. S. — Intellectual Life. 2. U. S. — Civilization.

5859. Degler, Carl N. Out of Our Past: The Forces That Shaped Modern America. Har-Row. 1969. $10.00; pap. $2.95.   973
1. U. S. — Civilization. 2. U. S. — History.

5860. Gabriel, Ralph H. The Course of American Democratic Thought. 2nd ed. Ronald. 1956. $8.25.   973
1. Democracy. 2. Philosophy, American. 3. U. S. — Intellectual Life.

5861. Hofstadter, Richard. American Political Tradition. new ed. Knopf. 1973. $7.95; pap. $1.95 (Random).   973
1. U. S. — Biography. 2. U. S. — Politics and Government.

5862. Hofstadter, Richard and Wallace, Michael, eds. American Violence: A Documentary History. Knopf. 1970. $10.00; pap. $2.95 (Random).   973
1. U. S. — History. 2. Violence — U. S.

5863. Krout, John A. and Fox, Dixon R. The Completion of Independence, 1790-1830. Watts. 1971. pap. $3.45.   973
1. U. S. — Civilization — History. 2. U. S. — History — 1783-1865.

5864. Lerner, Max. America As a Civilization. S&S. 1957. $12.00; pap. $2.45 ea. 2 vols.   973
1. National Characteristics, American. 2. U. S. — Civilization.

5865. Meier, August. From Plantation to Ghetto: An Interpretive History of American Negroes. rev. ed. Hill & Wang. 1970. $6.95; pap. $2.45.   973
1. Negroes — History.

5866. Morison, Samuel E. The Oxford History of the American People. Oxford U Pr. 1965. $16.95; pap. $1.95 ea. 3 vols (NAL).   973
1. U. S. — History.

5867. Morison, Samuel E., et al. The Growth of the American Republic. 2 vols. 6th ed. Leuchtenburg, William, ed. Oxford U Pr. 1969. $35.00 set.   973
1. U. S. — History.

5868. Paxson, Frederic L. History of the American Frontier, 1763-1893. Berg. 1967. $20.00.   973
1. Mississippi Valley — History. 2. U. S. — History. 3. West — History.

5869. Schlesinger, Arthur, Jr. The Imperial Presidency. HM. 1973. $10.00.   973
1. Executive Power — U. S. — History. 2. Presidents — U. S. — History.

5870. Schlesinger, Arthur M., Jr. Paths to the Present. HM. 1963. pap. $1.95.   973
1. National Characteristics, American. 2. U. S. — Civilization — History. 3. U. S. — History. 4. U. S. — Politics and Government.

5871. Slater, Philip E. The Pursuit of Loneliness: American Culture at the Breaking Point. Beacon Pr. 1971. $7.50; pap. $2.45.   973
1. National Characteristics, American. 2. U. S. — Civilization — 1945-

5872. Turner, Frederick J. The Frontier in American History. HR&W. $5.95; pap. $5.50.   973
1. U. S. — History. 2. West — History.

5873. Wish, Harvey. Society and Thought in America. 2 vols. McKay. 1950-1962. $10.00.   973
1. U. S. — Civilization. 2. U. S. — Intellectual Life.

900 GEOGRAPHY, TRAVEL, AND HISTORY

5874. Young, Desmond. American Roulette: The History and Dilemma of the Vice Presidency. HR&W. 1972. $7.95; pap. $3.95 (Viking Pr). 973
1. Vice-Presidents — U.S.

5875. Moquin, Wayne and Van Doren, Charles, eds. Documentary History of the Mexican Americans. Praeger. 1972. $13.50; pap. $4.95. 973.046
1. Mexican Americans — History.

973.08 Sources

5876. Bailey, Thomas A. American Spirit: U. S. History As Seen by Contemporaries. 2 vols. 3rd ed. Heath. 1973. $5.95 ea. 973.08
1. U. S. — History — Sources.

5877. Boorstin, Daniel J., ed. An American Primer. 2 vols. U of Chicago Pr. 1969. $12.50. 973.08
1. U. S. — History — Sources.

5878. Commager, Henry S., ed. Documents of American History. 9th ed. P-H. 1974. $17.50. 973.08
1. U. S. — History — Sources.

5879. ———. Living Ideas in America. rev. ed. Har-Row. 1964. $8.50; pap. $3.95. 973.08
1. American Literature — Collections. 2. U. S. — Civilization — Sources. 3. U. S. — History — Sources.

5880. Commager, Henry S. and Nevins, A., eds. Heritage of America: Readings in American History. 2nd rev. ed. Little. 1949. $15.00. 973.08
1. American Literature — Collections. 2. U. S. — History — Sources.

5881. Hofstadter, Richard, ed. Progressive Movement, 1900-1915. Peter Smith. 1967. $4.95; pap. $1.95 (P-H). 973.08
1. Progressivism (U. S. Politics) — Sources. 2. U. S. — Politics and Government — 20th Century — Sources. 3. U. S. — Social Conditions — Sources.

5882. Fishel, Leslie H. and Quarles, Benjamin. The Black American: A Documentary History. rev. ed. Scott F. 1970. pap. $7.75. 973.09
1. Negroes — History — Sources.

5883. Jordan, Winthrop D. White Over Black: American Attitudes Toward the Negro, 1550-1812. U of NC Pr. 1968. $12.50; pap. $2.95 (Penguin). 973.09
1. Negroes — History.

973.1 Discovery and Exploration to 1607

5884. Blegen, Theodore C. The Kensington Rune Stone: New Light on an Old Riddle. Minn Hist. 1968. $4.50. 973.1
1. America — Discovery and Exploration — Norse. 2. Kensington Rune Stone.

5885. Cumming, William P., et al. The Discovery of North America. McGraw. 1972. $25.00. 973.1
1. America — Discovery and Exploration.

5886. DeVoto, Bernard A. The Course of Empire. HM. 1952. $8.50. 973.1
1. North America — Discovery and Exploration. 2. U. S. — Territorial Expansion. 3. Indians of North America — History.

5887. Enterline, James R. Viking America: The Norse Crossing and Their Legacy. Doubleday. 1972. $6.95. 973.1
1. America — Discovery and Exploration — Norse.

5888. Hermannsson, Halldor. The Vinland Sagas. Kraus Repr. 1944. pap. $6.50. 973.1
1. America — Discovery and Exploration — Norse. 2. Sagas.

5889. Morison, Samuel E. Admiral of the Ocean Sea. Little. 1942. $15.00. 973.1(B)
1. Columbus, Christopher, 1446?-1506.

5890. ———. The European Discovery of America: The Northern Voyages. Oxford U Pr. 1971. $15.00. 973.1
1. America — Discovery and Exploration. 2. Voyages and Travels.

5891. ———. The European Discovery of America: The Southern Voyages. Oxford U Pr. 1974. $17.50. 973.1
1. America — Discovery and Exploration. 2. Voyages and Travels.

5892. Priestley, Herbert I. The Coming of the White Man, 1492-1848. Watts. 1971. pap. $3.45. 973.1

900 GEOGRAPHY, TRAVEL, AND HISTORY

1. Canada — History — to 1763 (New France). 2. North America — History. 3. Spain — Colonies — North America. 4. U. S. — History — Colonial Period.

973.2 Colonial Period, 1607-1775

5893. Andrews, Charles. Colonial Background of the American Revolution. rev. ed. Yale U Pr. 1961. $10.00; pap. $2.95. 973.2
1. U. S. — History — Colonial Period.
2. U. S. — History — Revolution.

5894. Boorstin, Daniel J. The Americans. 2 vols. Random. 1965. $12.50 ea. 973.2
1. National Characteristics, American. 2. U. S. — Civilization — History.

5895. Bradford, William. Bradford's History of Plymouth Plantation, 1606-1646. Davis, W. T., ed. B&N. 1908. $6.50. 973.2
1. U. S. — History — Colonial Period.

5896. Bridenbaugh, Carl. Cities in Revolt: Urban Life in America, 1743-1776. Knopf. 1955. $10.95; pap. $4.50 (Oxford U Pr) 973.2
1. Cities and Towns — U. S. 2. U. S. — History — Colonial Period. 3. U. S. — Social Life and Customs — Colonial Period.

5897. ———. Cities in the Wilderness: The First Century of Urban Life in America, 1625-1742. Knopf. 1955. $10.95; pap. $4.50 (Oxford U Pr). 973.2
1. Cities and Towns — U. S. 2. U. S. — History — Colonial Period. 3. U. S. — Social Life and Customs — Colonial Period.

5898. Burr, George L., ed. Narratives of the Witchcraft Cases, 1648 to 1706. B&N. 1914. $6.50. 973.2
1. U. S. — History — Colonial Period. 2. Witchcraft — New England.

5899. Gipson, Lawrence H. Coming of the Revolution: 1763-1775. Har-Row. 1954. $8.95; pap. $3.25. 973.2
1. U. S. — History — Colonial Period.

5900. Greene, Evarts B. The Revolutionary Generation, 1763-1790. Watts. 1971. pap. $3.45. 973.2
1. U. S. — Civilization — History. 2. U. S. — History — Colonial Period. 3. U. S. — History — Revolution.

5901. Hawke, David. The Colonial Experience. Bobbs. 1966. $8.50. 973.2

1. U. S. — History — Colonial Period.
2. U. S. — History — Revolution.

5902. Leach, Douglas E. Arms for Empire: A Military History of the British Colonies in North America, 1607-1763. Macmillan. 1973. $14.95. 973.2
1. Canada — History, Military. 2. North America — History — Colonial Period. 3. U. S. — History, Military.

5903. Morgan, Edmund S. The Puritan Dilemma: The Story of John Winthrop. Little. 1958. $5.00; pap. $2.95. 973.2(B)
1. U. S. — History — Colonial Period. 2. Winthrop, John, 1606-1676.

5904. Nash, Gary B. Red, White and Black: The Peoples of Early America. P-H. 1974. $9.95; pap. $5.95. 973.2
1. America — Discovery and Exploration. 2. U. S. — History — Colonial Period.

5905. Nettels, Curtis P. Roots of American Civilization. 2nd ed. Irvington. 1963. $14.95. 973.2
1. U. S. — Civilization — to 1783. 2. U. S. — History — Colonial Period.

5906. Parkman, Francis. Half-Century of Conflict. Peter Smith. $4.00. 973.2
1. U. S. — History — Colonial Period.

5907. Peckham, Howard H. Colonial Wars, 1689-1762. U of Chicago Pr. 1964. $7.50; pap. $2.25. 973.2
1. U. S. — History — Colonial Period.
2. U. S. — History — Military — to 1900.

5908. Schlesinger, Arthur M., Jr. The Birth of the Nation: A Portrait of the American People on the Eve of Independence. Knopf. 1698. $7.95. 973.2
1. U. S. — History — Colonial Period.
2. U. S. — Social Life and Customs — Colonial Period.

5909. Vaughan, Alden T. American Genesis: Captain John Smith and the Founding of Virginia. Little. 1975. $8.95. 973.2
1. Virginia — History — Colonial Period. 2. Smith, John, 1580-1631.

5910. Wright, Louis B. Cultural Life of the American Colonies: 1607-1763. Har-Row. 1957. $10.00. 973.2
1. U. S. — Civilization. 2. U. S. — Intellectual Life.

900 GEOGRAPHY, TRAVEL, AND HISTORY

5911. Bird, Harrison. Battle for a Continent. Oxford U Pr. 1965. $7.95.   973.26
1. U. S. — History — French and Indian War, 1755-1763.

973.3 Revolution and Confederation, 1775-1789

5912. Alden, John R. History of the American Revolution. Knopf. 1969. $10.00.   973.3
1. U. S. — History — Revolution.

5913. Bailyn, Bernard. The Ideological Origins of the American Revolution. Harvard U Pr. $9.50; pap. $2.95.   973.3
1. U. S. — History — Revolution — Causes.

5914. Bailyn, Bernard and Garrett, J. N., eds. Pamphlets on the American Revolution, 1750-1776. Harvard U Pr. 1965. $15.00.   973.3
1. U. S. — History — Revolution — Pamphlets.

5915. Becker, Carl L. Declaration of Independence: A Study in the History of Political Ideas. Knopf. 1942. $5.95; pap. $1.95.   973.3
1. Jefferson, Thomas, President U. S., 1743-1826. 2. U. S. — Declaration of Independence.3. U. S. — Politics and Government — Revolution.

5916. Flexner, John T. The Traitor and the Spy. Little. 1975. $15.00.   973.3
1. André, John, 1751-1780. 2. Arnold, Benedict, 1741-1801.

5917. Jameson, J. Franklin. The American Revolution Considered As a Social Movement. Princeton U Pr. 1940. $4.50; pap. $1.95.   973.3
1. U. S. — History — Revolution. 2. U. S. — Social Conditions.

5918. Lancaster, Bruce. The American Heritage Book of the Revolution. McGraw. 1971. $19.95.   973.3
1. U. S. — History — Revolution — Pictures, Illustrations, etc.

5919. Main, Jackson T. The Sovereign States 1775-1783. new ed. Watts. 1973. $10.00; pap. $4.95.   973.3
1. U. S. — History — Revolution.

5920. Miller, John C. Origins of the American Revolution. Stanford U Pr. 1959. $12.50; pap. $4.95.   973.3

1. U. S. — History — Colonial Period.
2. U. S. — History — Revolution.

5921. ———. The Triumph of Freedom, 1775-1783. Little. 1948. pap. $3.95.   973.3
1. U. S. — History — Revolution.

5922. Mitchell, Broadus. The Price of Independence: A Realistic View of the American Revolution. Oxford U Pr. 1974. $9.50.   973.3
1. U. S. — History — Revolution.

5923. Morgan, Edmund S. The Birth of the Republic, 1763-1789. U of Chicago Pr. 1956. $5.50; pap. $1.75.   973.3
1. U. S. — History — Confederation, 1783-1789. 2. U. S. — History — Revolution.

5924. Morison, Samuel E., ed. Sources and Documents Illustrating the American Revolution, 1764-1788, and the Formation of the Federal Constitution. 2nd ed. Oxford U Pr. 1965. $2.95.   973.3
1. U. S. — Constitutional History — Sources.2. U. S. — History — Revolution — Sources. 3. U. S. — History — Confederation, 1783-1789 — Sources.

5925. Morris, Richard B. The Peacemakers: Great Powers and American Independence. Har-Row. 1965. $10.00; pap. $3.75.   973.3
1. Europe — Politics — 18th Century. 2. Paris, Treaty of, 1783. 3. U. S. — Foreign Relations — Revolution.

5926. Nye, Russel B. The Cultural Life of the New Nation: 1776-1830. Har-Row. 1960. $8.95; pap. $2.75.   973.3
1. U. S. — Civilization. 2. U. S. — Intellectual Life.

5927. Robson, Eric. The American Revolution in Its Political and Military Aspects, 1763-1783. Norton. 1966. pap. $1.95.   973.3
1. U. S. — History — Revolution.

5928. Trevelyan, George O. The American Revolution. Morris, Richard B., ed. McKay. 1964. $12.50.   973.3
1. U. S. — History — Revolution.

5929. Tyler, Moses C. Literary History of the American Revolution. 2 vols. Ungar. 1957. $20.00.   973.3
1. U. S. — History — Revolution — Literature.

900 GEOGRAPHY, TRAVEL, AND HISTORY

5930. Van Tyne, Claude H. Causes of the War of Independence. Peter Smith. $6.75. 973.3
1. U. S. — History — Revolution — Causes.

5931. Commager, Henry S. and Morris, Richard B., eds. The Spirit of '76: The Story of the American Revolution As Told by Participants. Har-Row. 1967. $20.00. 973.308
1. U. S. — History — Revolution — Personal Narratives. 2. U. S. — History — Revolution — Sources.

5932. Bowen, Catherine D. John Adams and the American Revolution. Little. 1950. $5.95; pap. $3.45 (G&D). 973.3092(B)
1. Adams, John, President U. S., 1735-1826. 2. U. S. — History — Revolution.

5933. Boylan, Brian R. Benedict Arnold: The Dark Eagle. Norton. 1973. $6.95. 973.3092(B)
1. André, John, 1751-1780. 2. Arnold, Benedict, 1741-1801. 3. U. S. — History — Revolution.

5934. Gottschalk, Louis. Lafayette and the Close of the American Revolution. U of Chicago Pr. 1974. $17.50. 973.3092(B)
1. Lafayette, Marie Joseph Paul ..., Marquis De, 1757-1834. 2. U. S. — History — Revolution.

5935. Kaplan, Sidney. The Black Presence in the Era of Revolution, 1770-1800. NYGS. 1973. $17.50. 973.3092(B)
1. Negroes — Biography. 2. U. S. — History — Revolution — Negroes.

5936. Lewis, Paul. The Grand Incendiary: A Biography of Samuel Adams. Dial. 1973. $8.95. 973.3092(B)
1. Adams, Samuel, 1772-1803. 2. U. S. — History — Revolution — Causes.

5937. Morris, Richard B. Seven Who Shaped Our Destiny: The Founding Fathers As Revolutionaries. Har-Row. 1973. $8.95. 973.3092(B)
1. U. S. — History — Revolution — Biography. 2. U. S. — History — Revolution — Causes.

5938. Quarles, Benjamin. Negroes in the American Revolution. U of NC Pr. 1967. $6.95; pap. $1.95 (Norton). 973.3092
1. U. S. — History — Revolution — Negroes.

5939. Rankin, Hugh F. Francis Marion: The Swamp Fox. T Y Crowell. 1973. $10.00. 973.3092(B)
1. Marion, Francis, 1732-1792. 2. U. S. — History — Revolution.

5940. Tyler, Moses C. Patrick Henry. AMS Pr. Repr. 1898. $12.50. 973.3092(B)
1. Henry, Patrick, 1736-1799.

5941. Davidson, Philip G. Propaganda and the American Revolution. U of NC Pr. 1941. $7.50; pap. $3.45 (Norton). 973.311
1. Propaganda, American. 2. U. S. — History — Revolution — Causes.

5942. Martin, James K. Men in Rebellion: Governmental Leaders and the Coming of the American Revolution. Rutgers U Pr. 1973. $12.50. 973.311
1. U. S. — Politics and Government — Colonial Period.

5943. Stout, Neil R. The Royal Navy in America, 1760-1775: A Study of Enforcement of British Colonial Policy in the Era of the American Revolution. Naval Inst Pr. 1973. $12.50. 973.311
1. Great Britain — History, Naval — 18th Century. 2. Great Britain — Navy. 3. U. S. — History — Revolution — Causes.

5944. Berkin, Carol. Jonathan Sewall: Odyssey of an American Loyalist. Columbia U Pr. 1974. $10.95. 973.314(B)
1. Sewall, Jonathan, 1728-1796.

5945. Calhoon, Robert M. The Loyalists in Revolutionary America, 1760-1781. HarBraceJ. 1973. $17.50. 973.314
1. American Loyalists. 2. U. S. — History — Revolution — Causes. 3. U. S. — Politics and Government — Colonial Period.

5946. Crary, Catherine S. Price of Loyalty: Tory Writings from the Revolutionary Era. McGraw. 1973. $12.50. 973.314
1. American Loyalists. 2. U. S. — History — Revolution — Sources.

5947. Einstein, Lewis. Divided Loyalties: Americans in England During the War of Independence. Russell. Repr. 1933. $13.50. 973.314(B)
1. American Loyalists in England. 2. Secret Service — Great Britain. 3. U. S. — History — Revolution — Biography.

900 GEOGRAPHY, TRAVEL, AND HISTORY

5948. Evans, Elizabeth. Weathering the Storm: Women of the American Revolution. Scribner. 1974. $10.00. 973.315(B)
1. U. S. — History — Revolution. 2. U. S. — History — Revolution — Women.

5949. Bowen, Catherine D. The Most Dangerous Man in America: Scenes from the Life of Benjamin Franklin. Little. 1974. $8.95. 973.32(B)
1. Franklin, Benjamin, 1706-1790.

5950. Fleming, Thomas, ed. Benjamin Franklin: A Biography in His Own Words. Har-Row. 1972. $15.00. 973.32
1. Franklin, Benjamin, 1706-1790.

5951. Billias, George A., ed. George Washington's Opponents: British Generals and Admirals in the American Revolution. Apollo Eds. pap. $2.95. 973.341
1. Great Britain — History, Military — Biography. 2. U. S. — History — Revolution — Biography.

5952. Ketchum, Richard M. The Winter Soldiers. Doubleday. 1973. $10.00. 973.344
1. U. S. Army — Continental Army. 2. U. S. — History — Revolution — Campaigns and Battles.

5953. Tucker, Glenn. Mad Anthony Wayne and the New Nation. Stackpole. 1973. $10.00. 973.344
1. Wayne, Anthony, 1745-1796.

5954. Miller, Nathan. Sea of Glory: The Continental Navy Fights for Independence, 1775-1783. McKay. 1974. $12.95. 973.35
1. U. S. — History — Revolution — Naval Operations.

5955. Morison, Samuel E. John Paul Jones: A Sailor's Biography. Little. 1959. $10.00; pap. $2.95. 973.35(B)
1. Jones, John Paul, 1747-1792. 2. U. S. — History — Revolution — Naval Operations.

5956. Dorson, Richard M. America Rebels: Narratives of the Patriots. Greenwood. Repr. 1953. $14.75. 973.381
1. U. S. — History — Revolution — Personal Narratives.

5957. Van Doren, Carl C. Secret History of the American Revolution. Kelley. Repr. 1941. $17.50; pap. $1.50 (Popular Lib). 973.381
1. Arnold, Benedict, 1741-1801. 2. Secret Service — Great Britain. 3. Treason — U. S. 4. U. S. — History — Revolution.

Recommended Series

5958. American and French Accounts of the American Revolution. Gregg.

5959. Era of the American Revolution Series. Da Capo.

5960. Eyewitness Accounts of the American Revolution. Arno.

5961. Leaders of the American Revolution Series. T Y Crowell.

973.4 Constitutional Period, 1789-1809

5962. Bowers, Claude G. Jefferson and Hamilton. HM. $8.50; pap. $2.65. 973.4
1. Hamilton, Alexander, 1757-1804. 2. Jefferson, Thomas, President U. S., 1743-1826. 3. U. S. — History — Constitutional Period, 1789-1809.

5963. Cunliffe, Marcus. The Nation Takes Shape, 1789-1837. U of Chicago Pr. 1959. $6.50; pap. $1.95. 973.4
1. U. S. — History — 1783-1865.

5964. Fiske, John. Critical Period of American History, 1783-1789. Norwood Edns. Repr. 1901. $12.50. 973.4
1. U. S. — History — Confederation, 1783-1789.

5965. Jensen, Merrill. The New Nation. Knopf. 1950. $7.95; pap. $2.65 (Random). 973.4
1. U. S. — History — Confederation, 1783-1789.

5966. Ketcham, Ralph L. From Colony to Country: The Revolution in American Thought, 1750-1820. Macmillan. 1974. $9.95. 973.4
1. U. S. — Intellectual Life.

5967. Miller, John C. The Federalist Era, 1789-1801. Har-Row. 1960. $8.95; pap. $2.25. 973.4
1. U. S. — History — Constitutional Period, 1789-1809.

5968. Rossiter, Clinton. The American Quest, 1790-1860: An Emerging Nation in Search of Identity, Unity and Modernity. HarBraceJ. 1971. $9.50. 973.4
1. U. S. — History — 1783-1865.

900 GEOGRAPHY, TRAVEL, AND HISTORY

5969. Schachner, Nathan. Alexander Hamilton. A S Barnes. 1961. pap. $2.95. 973.409(B)
1. Hamilton, Alexander, 1757-1804.

5970. Flexner, James T. George Washington. 4 vols. Little. 1965-72. $15.00 ea. 973.410(B)
1. Washington, George, President U. S., 1732-1779.

5971. Richards, Laura E. Abigail Adams and Her Time. Gale. Repr. 1917. $12.50. 973.44(B)
1. Adams, Abigail (Smith), 1744-1818.

5972. Alexander, Holmes. Aaron Burr, the Proud Pretender. Greenwood. Repr. 1937. $16.00. 973.46
1. Burr, Aaron, 1756-1836.

5973. Houck, Louis. Boundaries of the Louisiana Purchase: A Historical Study. Arno. Repr. 1901. $6.00. 973.46
1. Louisiana Purchase.

5974. Petersen, Merrill D. Thomas Jefferson and the New Nation: A Biography. Oxford U Pr. 1970. $17.50. 973.46
1. Jefferson, Thomas, President U. S., 1743-1826.

973.5 Early 19th Century, 1809-1845

5975. Abels, Jules. Man on Fire: John Brown and the Cause of Liberty. Macmillan. 1971. $12.50. 973.5
1. Brown, John, 1800-1859. 2. Harper's Ferry, West Virginia — John Brown's Raid, 1859.

5976. Coit, Margaret L. John C. Calhoun. HM. 1950. $8.50; pap. $4.95. 973.5(B)
1. Calhoun, John Caldwell, 1782-1850.

5977. McCaughey, Robert A. Josiah Quincy, 1772-1864: The Last Federalist. Harvard U Pr. 1974. $12.00. 973.5(B)
1. Quincy, Josiah, 1772-1864.

5978. Turner, Frederick J. Rise of the New West 1819-1829. Peter Smith. 1959. $6.00; pap. $1.25 (Macmillan). 973.5
1. Mississippi Valley — History. 2. U. S. — Politics and Government — 1815-1861. 3. West — History.

5979. Tyler, Alice F. Freedom's Ferment: Phases of American Social History from the Colonial Period to the Outbreak of the Civil War. Bks for Libs. 1944. $22.75; pap. $3.50 (Har-Row). 973.5
1. U. S. — History — 1815-1861. 2. U. S. — Social Life and Customs.

5980. Webster, Daniel. Speak for Yourself, Daniel: A Life of Webster in His Own Words. Lewis, Walker, ed. HM. 1969. $8.95. 973.5(B)
1. Webster, Daniel, 1782-1852.

5981. Ammon, Henry. James Monroe: The Quest for National Identity. McGraw. 1971. $12.95. 973.51
1. Monroe, James, President U. S., 1758-1831. 2. U. S. — Politics and Government — 1817-1825.

5982. Arnett, Ethel S. Mrs. James Madison: The Incomparable Dolley. Straughan. 1972. $10.95. 973.51(B)
1. Madison, Dolley (Payne) Todd, 1768-1849.

5983. Hunt, Gaillard. Life of James Madison. Russell. Repr. 1902. $10.00. 973.51(B)
1. Madison, James, President U. S., 1751-1836.

5984. Myers, Marvin, ed. The Mind of the Founder: Sources of the Political Thought of James Madison. Bobbs. 1973. $10.00; pap. $4.95. 973.51
1. U. S. — History — 1783-1865 — Sources.

5985. Forester, Cecil S. The Age of Fighting Sail. Doubleday. 1956. $7.95. 973.52
1. U. S. — History — War of 1812. 2. U. S. — History, Naval.

5986. Hitsman, J. Mackay. Incredible War of 1812: A Military History. U of Toronto Pr. 1965. $10.00; pap. $3.25. 973.52
1. Canada — History, Military. 2. U. S. — History — War of 1812 — Campaigns and Battles.

5987. Perkins, Bradford. Prologue to War: England and the United States, 1805-1812. U of Cal Pr. 1961. $9.00; pap. $4.65. 973.521
1. Great Britain — Foreign Relations — U. S. 2. U. S. — Foreign Relations — Great Britain. 3. U. S. — History — War of 1812 — Causes.

5988. Dangerfield, George. The Era of Good Feelings. Peter Smith. 1952. $7.50; pap. $3.75 (HarBraceJ). 973.54
1. Ghent, Treaty of, 1814. 2. Monroe Doctrine. 3. U. S. — History — 1815-1861.

5989. Morgan, George. Life of James Monroe. AMS Pr. Repr. 1921. $12.75. 973.54(B)
1. Monroe, James, President U. S., 1758-1831.

900 GEOGRAPHY, TRAVEL, AND HISTORY

5990. Bemis, Samuel F. John Quincy Adams. 2 vols. Knopf. 1949-56. $25.00. 973.55
1. Adams, John Quincy, President U. S., 1767-1848. 2. U. S. — Politics and Government — 1817-1825.

5991. Hecht, Marie B. John Quincy Adams: A Personal History of an Independent Man. Macmillan. 1972. $14.95. 973.55(B)
1. Adams, John Quincy, President U. S., 1767-1848.

5992. Aptheker, Herbert. Nat Turner's Slave Rebellion. Grove. 1968. pap. $0.95. 973.56
1. Southampton, Insurrection, 1831. 2. Turner, Nat, 1800?-1831.

5993. Eby, Cecil D. That Disgraceful Affair: The Black Hawk War. Norton. 1973. $9.95. 973.56
1. Black Hawk War, 1832.

5994. Freehling, William H., ed. Nullification Era: A Documentary Record. Har-Row. 1966. pap. $2.75. 973.56
1. Nullification. 2. South Carolina — History — Sources.

5995. Rogin, Michael P. Fathers and Children: Andrew Jackson and the Subjugation of the American Indian. Knopf. 1975. $13.95. 973.56
1. Indians of North America — Government Relations, 1789-1869. 2. Indians of North America — Land Transfers. 3. Jackson, Andrew, President U. S., 1767-1845.

5996. Schlesinger, Arthur M., Jr. The Age of Jackson. Little. 1945. $10.00; pap. $3.95. 973.56
1. Jackson, Andrew, President U. S., 1767-1845. 2. U. S. — History — 1815-1861.

5997. Van Deusen, Glyndon G. Jacksonian Era: 1828-1848. Har-Row. 1959. $8.95; pap. $2.45. 973.56
1. Jackson, Andrew, President U.S., 1767-1845. 2. U. S. — History — 1815-1861.

5998. Ward, John. Andrew Jackson: Symbol for an Age. Oxford U Pr. 1962. pap. $1.95. 973.56(B)
1. Jackson, Andrew, President U. S., 1767-1845.

5999. Curtis, James C. The Fox at Bay: Martin Van Buren and the Presidency, 1837-1841. U Pr of Ky. 1970. $8.50. 973.57(B)
1. U. S. — Politics and Government — 1837-1841. 2. Van Buren, Martin, President U. S., 1782-1862.

6000. Goebel, Dorothy B. William Henry Harrison: A Political Biography. Porcupine Pr. Repr. 1926. $17.50. 973.58(B)
1. Harrison, William Henry, President U. S., 1773-1841.

6001. Morgan, Robert J. A Whig Embattled: The Presidency Under John Tyler. Shoe String. Repr. 1954 (Archon). $10.00. 973.58
1. Tyler, John, President U. S., 1780-1862. 2. U. S. — Politics and Government — 1841-1845.

973.6 Middle 19th Century, 1845-1861

6002. Bode, Carl, compiled by. Midcentury America: Life in the 1850's. S Ill U Pr. 1972. $15.00. 973.6
1. U. S. — Civilization — 1783-1865. 2. U. S. — History — 1815-1861 — Sources.

6003. Clendenen, Clarence. Blood on the Border: The United States Army and the Mexican Irregulars. Macmillan. 1969. $12.50. 973.6
1. U. S. — Foreign Relations — Mexico. 2. U. S. — History, Military.

6004. Cole, Arthur C. The Irrepressible Conflict, 1850-1865. Watts. 1934. pap. $3.45. 973.6
1. U. S. — History — 1849-1877. 2. U. S. — History — Civil War.

6005. Commager, Henry S. Era of Reform, 1830-1860. Van Nos Reinhold. 1960. pap. $2.95. 973.6
1. Reformers. 2. U. S. — Social Conditions.

6006. Craven, Avery O. The Coming of the Civil War. 2nd ed. U of Chicago Pr. 1957. $13.50; pap. $2.95. 973.6
1. U. S. — History — 1815-1861. 2. U. S. — History — Civil War — Causes.

6007. ———. Edmund Ruffin, Southerner: A Study in Secession. La State U Pr. 1966. pap. $2.75. 973.6
1. Ruffin, Edmund, 1794-1865. 2. Secession.

6008. Fish, Carl R. The Rise of the Common Man, 1830-1850. Watts. 1971. pap. $3.45. 973.6
1. U. S. — Civilization — History. 2. U. S. — Economic Conditions.

900 GEOGRAPHY, TRAVEL, AND HISTORY

6009. Nevins, Allan. Ordeal of the Union. 8 vols. Scribner. 1947-1971. $15.00 ea.   973.6
1. U. S. — History — 1815-1861.

6010. Nichols, Roy F. Stakes of Power: 1845-1877. Hill & Wang. 1961. $4.50; pap. $1.95.   973.6
1. U. S. — History — 1849-1877. 2. U. S. — Politics and Government — 1849-1877.

6011. Nye, Russel B. Society and Culture in America, 1830-1860. Har-Row. 1974. $16.00.   973.6
1. U. S. — Civilization — 1783-1865. 2. National Characteristics, American. 3. Reformers.

6012. Oates, Stephen B. To Purge This Land with Blood: A Biography of John Brown. Har-Row. 1970. $10.95; pap. $3.95.   973.6(B)
1. Brown, John, 1800-1859.

6013. Quarles, Benjamin. Lincoln and the Negro. Oxford U Pr. 1962. $8.95.   973.6
1. Lincoln, Abraham, President U.S., 1809-1865. 2. Negroes. 3. Slavery in the U. S.

6014. Van Deusen, Glyndon G. William Henry Seward. Oxford U Pr. 1967. $15.00.   973.6(B)
1. Seward, William Henry, 1801-1872.

6015. Vestal, Stanley. Sitting Bull, Champion of the Sioux: A Biography. rev ed. U of Okla Pr. Repr. 1957. $7.95.   973.6(B)
1. Sitting Bull, 1834-1890.

6016. Pletcher, David M. The Diplomacy of Annexation: Texas, Oregon and the Mexican War. U of Mo Pr. 1973. $20.00.   973.61
1. Oregon. 2. U. S. — Foreign Relations — 1815-1861. 3. U. S. — History — War with Mexico, 1845-1848. 4. U. S. — Territorial Expansion.

6017. Bill, Alfred H. Rehearsal for Conflict: The War with Mexico, 1846-1848. Cooper Sq. 1945. $8.95.   973.62
1. U. S. — History — War with Mexico, 1845-1848.

6018. Brooks, Nathan C. Complete History of the Mexican War. Rio Grande. 1965. $17.50.   973.62
1. U. S. — History — War with Mexico, 1845-1848.

6019. Fuller, John D. The Movement for the Acquisition of All Mexico, 1846-1848. Johns Hopkins. Repr. 1936. $11.00.   973.62

1. U. S. — History — War with Mexico, 1845-1848. 2. U. S. — Territorial Expansion.

6020. Singletary, Otis A. The Mexican War. U of Chicago Pr. 1960. $6.75; pap. $2.95.   973.62
1. U. S. — History — War with Mexico, 1845-1848.

6021. Eaton, Clement. Henry Clay and the Art of American Politics. Little. 1957. $5.00; pap. $2.95.   973.63
1. Clay, Henry, 1777-1852.

6022. Rayback, Robert J. Millard Fillmore: Biography of a President. Stewart. 1972. $15.00.   973.64
1. Fillmore, Millard, President U. S., 1800-1874.

6023. Johannsen, Robert W. Stephen A. Douglas. Oxford U Pr. 1973. $19.95.   973.68(B)
1. Douglas, Stephen Arnold, 1813-1861.

6024. Quarles, Benjamin, ed. Blacks on John Brown. U of Ill Pr. 1972. $6.95.   973.68
1. Brown, John, 1800-1859.

973.7 Civil War, 1861-1865

6025. Catton, Bruce. The American Heritage Picture History of the Civil War. Doubleday. 1960. $24.95.   973.7
1. U. S. — History — Civil War — Pictures, Illustrations, etc.

6026. ———. This Hallowed Ground. Doubleday. 1956. $6.50.   973.7
1. U. S. — History — Civil War.

6027. Commager, Henry S. The Blue and the Gray: The Story of the Civil War As Told by Participants. Bobbs. 1950. $11.95; pap. $2.25 ea. 2 vols. (NAL).   973.7
1. U. S. — History — Civil War — Personal Narratives.

6028. Cruden, Robert. The War That Never Ended: The American Civil War. P-H. 1973. $8.95.   973.7
1. U. S. — History — Civil War — Influence.

6029. Donald, David. Charles Sumner and the Coming of the Civil War. Knopf. 1960. $8.95.   973.7
1. Sumner, Charles, 1811-1874. 2. U. S. — History — Civil War.

900 GEOGRAPHY, TRAVEL, AND HISTORY

6030. Dupuy, R. Ernest and Dupuy, Trevor N. Compact History of the Civil War. Macmillan. 1962. pap. $1.50. 973.7
1. U. S. — History — Civil War.

6031. Nichols, Roy F., ed. Battles and Leaders of the Civil War. 4 vols. A S Barnes. 1957. $50.00 set. 973.7
1. U. S. — History — Civil War — Biography. 2. U. S. — History — Civil War — Campaigns and Battles.

6032. O'Connor, Thomas H. The Disunited States: The Era of Civil War and Reconstruction. Dodd. 1972. pap. $4.50. 973.7
1. Reconstruction. 2. U. S. — History — 1849-1877. 3. U. S. — History — Civil War.

6033. Quarles, Benjamin. Negro in the Civil War. Russell. 1953. $15.00; pap. $2.65 (Little). 973.7
1. U. S. — History — Civil War — Negroes.

6034. Niven, John. Gideon Welles: Lincoln's Secretary of the Navy. Oxford U Pr. 1973. $17.50. 973.7092(B)
1. Welles, Gideon, 1802-1870.

6035. Sandburg, Carl. Abraham Lincoln: The Prairie Years and the War Years. 6 vols. HarBraceJ. $120.00; 1-vol. ed $10.95; pap. $2.95 set 3 vols (Dell). 973.7092(B)
1. Lincoln, Abraham, President U. S., 1809-1865. 2. U. S. — History — Civil War.

6036. Thomas, Benjamin P. Abraham Lincoln: A Biography. Modern Lib. 1965. $4.95. 973.7092(B)
1. Lincoln, Abraham, President U. S., 1809-1865.

6037. Thomas, Benjamin P. and Hyman, Harold M. Stanton: The Life and Times of Lincoln's Secretary of War. Knopf. 1962. $10.00. 973.7092(B)
1. Stanton, Edwin McMasters, 1814-1869. 2. U. S. — History — Civil War.

6038. Turner, Justin G. and Turner, Linda L., eds. Mary Todd Lincoln: Her Life and Letters. Knopf. 1972. $15.00. 973.7092(B)
1. Lincoln, Mary (Todd), 1818-1882.

6039. Bartlett, Irving H. Wendell Phillips. Greenwood. Repr. 1961. $16.25. 973.71(B)
1. Phillips, Wendell, 1811-1884.

6040. Stampp, Kenneth M., ed. The Causes of the Civil War. rev. ed. Peter Smith. 1965. $4.95; pap. $2.45 (P-H). 973.71
1. U. S. — History — Civil War — Causes.

6041. Stern, Philip V. Prologue to Sumter: The Beginnings of the Civil War. Greenwood. 1961. $19.75. 973.71
1. Fort Sumter. 2. U. S. — History — Civil War — Causes. 3. U. S. — Politics and Government — 1857-1861.

6042. Van Deusen, Glyndon G. Horace Greeley: Nineteenth Century Crusader. U of Pa Pr. 1953. $10.00; pap. $2.45 (Hill & Wang). 973.71
1. Greeley, Horace, 1811-1872.

6043. Channing, Steven A. Crisis of Fear: Secession in South Carolina. S&S. 1970. $7.95; pap. $2.95 (Norton). 973.713
1. Secession. 2. South Carolina — History — Civil War. 3. South Carolina — Politics and Government — 1775-1865.

6044. Dumond, Dwight L., ed. Southern Editorials on Secession. Peter Smith. 1974. $8.00. 973.713
1. Secession. 2. U. S. — Politics and Government — 1857-1861.

6045. Perkins, H. C. Northern Editorials on Secession. 2 vols. Peter Smith. $16.00. 973.713
1. Secession. 2. U. S. — Politics and Government — 1857-1861.

6046. Ross, Ishbel. First Lady of the South: The Life of Mrs. Jefferson Davis. Greenwood. Repr. 1958. $17.50. 973.713(B)
1. Davis, Varina (Howell), 1826-1906.

6047. Tate, Allen. Jefferson Davis: His Rise and Fall: a Biographical Narrative. Kraus Repr. 1929. $12.00. 973.713(B)
1. Confederate States of America. 2. Davis, Jefferson, 1808-1889. 3. Southern States — History.

6048. Freeman, Douglas. Lee's Lieutenants. 3 vols. Scribner. 1942-1944. $17.50 ea. 973.73(B)
1. U. S. — History — Civil War — Biography.

6049. ———. Robert E. Lee. 4 vols. Scribner. 1935. $17.50 ea. 973.73(B)
1. Lee, Robert Edward, 1807-1870. 2. U. S. — History — Civil War — Campaigns and Battles.

6050. Thomason, John W. Jeb Stuart. Scribner. 1970. $9.95. 973.73(B)

900 GEOGRAPHY, TRAVEL, AND HISTORY

6050. Stuart, James Ewell Brown, 1833-1864. 2. U. S. — History — Civil War — Campaigns and Battles.

6051. Vandiver, Frank E. Mighty Stonewall. Greenwood. Repr. 1957. $22.50.   973.73(B)
1. Jackson, Thomas Jonathan, 1824-1863.

6052. Warner, Ezra. Generals in Gray: Lives of the Confederate Commanders. La State U Pr. 1959. $12.95.   973.73(B)
1. Generals — U. S. 2. U. S. — History — Civil War — Biography.

6053. Bruce, Robert V. Lincoln and the Tools of War. Greenwood. 1956. $15.00.   973.741
1. Lincoln, Abraham, President U. S., 1809-1865. 2. U. S. — History — Civil War — Supplies. 3. U. S. — Armed Forces — Ordnance and Ordnance Stores.

6054. Hassler, Warren W. General George B. McClellan, Shield of the Union. Greenwood. 1957. $17.00.   973.741(B)
1. McClellan, George Brinton, 1826-1885.

6055. Merrill, James M. William Tecumseh Sherman. Rand. 1971. $10.00.   973.741(B)
1. Sherman, William Tecumseh, 1820-1891.

6056. Cochran, Hamilton. Blockade Runners of the Confederacy. Greenwodd. 1958. $14.25.   973.757
1. U. S. — History — Civil War — Blockade.

6057. Davis, Jefferson. The Rise and Fall of the Confederate Government. 2 vols. A S Barnes. $25.00.   973.782
1. Confederate States of America — History. 2. U. S. — History — Civil War.

6058. Jones, Katharine M. Heroines of Dixie: Confederate Women Tell the Story of the War. Greenwood. Repr. 1958. $18.50.   973.782
1. Confederate States of America — History. 2. U. S. — History — Civil War — Personal Narratives — Confederate Side. 3. Women in the Confederate States of America.

6059. Kean, Robert G. Inside the Confederate Government. Greenwood. Repr. 1957. $12.00.   973.782
1. Confederate States of America — History — Sources. 2. Kean, Robert Garlick Hill, 1828-1898. 3. U. S. — History — Civil War — Personal Narratives — Confederate Side.

6060. Simkins, Francis B. The Women of the Confederacy. Scholarly. Repr. 1936. $16.00.   973.782
1. U. S. — History — Civil War. 2. Women in the Confederate States of America.

973.8 Later 19th Century, 1865-1901

6061. Bontemps, Arna. Free at Last: The Life of Frederick Douglass. Dodd. 1971. $7.95.   973.8(B)
1. Douglass, Frederick, 1817-1895.

6062. Carter, Hodding. The Angry Scar: The Story of Reconstruction, 1865-1890. Greenwood. 1959. $17.25.   973.8
1. Reconstruction. 2. U. S. — History — 1865-1898.

6063. Cox, Lawanda and Cox, John H. Politics, Principle and Prejudice, 1865-1866: Dilemma of Reconstruction America. Atheneum. 1969. pap. $3.75.   973.8
1. Reconstruction. 2. U. S. — History — 1865-1898.

6064. Daniels, Jonathan. Prince of Carpetbaggers. Greenwood. Repr. 1958. $14.00.   973.8(B)
1. Littlefield, Milton Smith, 1830-1895.

6065. Faulkner, Harold U. Politics, Reform and Expansion: 1890-1900. Har-Row. 1959. $8.95; pap. $2.25.   973.8
1. U. S. — Economic Conditions. 2. U. S. — Politics and Government — 1865-1898.

6066. Fleming, Walter L. Documentary History of Reconstruction: Political, Military, Social, Religious, Educational, and Industrial. 2 vols. in 1. Peter Smith. 1960. $12.50.   973.8
1. Reconstruction — Sources.

6067. Franklin, John H. Reconstruction After the Civil War. U of Chicago Pr. 1961. $6.50; pap. $1.95.   973.8
1. Reconstruction. 2. U. S. — History — 1863-1877.

6068. Goldman, Eric F. Rendezvous with Destiny: A History of Modern American Reform. Knopf. 1952. $7.95; pap. $1.95 (Random).   973.8
1. Reformers. 2. U. S. — Politics and Government. 3. U. S. — Social Problems.

6069. Grant, Ulysses S. Personal Memoirs. AMS Pr. 1894. $30.00.   973.8(B)

900 GEOGRAPHY, TRAVEL, AND HISTORY

1. Grant, Ulysses Simpson, President U. S., 1822-1885. 2. U. S. — History — Civil War.

6070. Josephson, Matthew. The Politicos. HarBraceJ. 1963. pap. $4.95.   973.8
1. U. S. — History — 1865-1898.

6071. ———. Robber Barons: The Great American Capitalists, 1861-1901. HarBraceJ. 1934. pap. $2.85.   973.8
1. Capitalists and Financiers. 2. U. S. — Industries.

6072. Morgan, H. Wayne. Gilded Age: A Reappraisal. rev. ed. Syracuse U Pr. $11.95; pap. $3.95.   973.8
1. U. S. — Civilization — 1865-1918.

6073. Rister, Carl C. Border Command: General Phil Sheridan in the West. Greenwood. Repr. 1944. $13.00.   973.8(B)
1. Indians of North America — Wars — 1866-1895. 2. Sheridan, Philip Henry, 1831-1888. 3. West — History — 1848-1950.

6074. Schlesinger, Arthur M. The Rise of the City, 1878-1898. Watts. 1971. pap. $3.45.   973.8
1. Cities and Towns — U. S. 2. U. S. — Civilization — History.

6075. Stampp, Kenneth M. Era of Reconstruction: 1865-1877. Knopf. 1965. $5.95; pap. $1.95 (Random).   973.8
1. Reconstruction. 2. U. S. — Politics and Government — 1865-1898.

6076. Stampp, Kenneth M. and Litwack, Leon F., eds. Reconstruction: An Anthology of Revisionist Writings. La State U Pr. 1969. $12.00; pap. $4.95.   973.8
1. Reconstruction. 2. U. S. — History — 1865-1898.

6077. Trelease, Allen W. White Terror: The Ku Klux Klan Conspiracy and Southern Reconstruction. Har-Row. 1971. $15.00; pap. $4.95.   973.8
1. Ku Klux Klan. 2. Reconstruction.

6078. Utley, Robert M. Frontier Regulars: The United States Army and the Indian, 1866-1891. Macmillan. 1973. $12.95.   973.8
1. Indians of North America — Wars, 1866-1895. 2. U. S. Army — History. 3. West — History.

6079. Woodward, C. Vann. Reunion and Reaction: The Compromise of 1877 and the End of Reconstruction. Little. 1966. $7.95; pap. $2.45.   973.8
1. Reconstruction. 2. U. S. — Politics and Government — 1877-1881.

6080. Beale, Howard K. The Critical Year: A Study of Andrew Johnson and the Reconstruction. Ungar. 1958. $11.50.   973.81
1. Johnson, Andrew, President U. S., 1808-1875. 2. Reconstruction.

6081. Benedict, Michael. The Impeachment and Trial of Andrew Johnson. Norton. 1973. $6.95; pap. $2.45.   973.81
1. Johnson, Andrew, President U. S., 1808-1875 — Impeachment.

6082. Bowers, Claude G. Tragic Era: The Revolution After Lincoln. HM. 1962. pap. $2.85.   973.81
1. Johnson, Andrew, President U. S., 1808-1875. 2. Reconstruction. 3. U. S. — History — 1865-1898. 4. U. S. — Politics and Government — 1865-1898.

6083. DeWitt, David. The Impeachment and Trial of Andrew Johnson. State Hist Soc Wis. 1967. $8.50.   973.81
1. Johnson, Andrew, President U. S., 1808-1875 — Impeachment.

6084. McKitrick, Eric L. Andrew Johnson and Reconstruction. U of Chicago Pr. 1960. $15.00; pap. $3.25.   973.81
1. Johnson, Andrew, President U. S., 1808-1875. 2. Reconstruction.

6085. Perman, Michael. Reunion Without Compromise: The South and Reconstruction, 1865-1868. Cambridge U Pr. 1973. $17.50.   973.81
1. Reconstruction. 2. Southern States — Politics and Government — 1865-1950.

6086. Rosenberg, Bruce A. Custer and the Epic of Defeat. Pa St U Pr. 1974. $12.95.   973.81(B)
1. Custer, George Armstrong, 1839-1876.

6087. Simon, John Y., ed. The Personal Memoirs of Julia Dent Grant. Putnam. 1975. $12.50.   973.82(B)
1. Grant, Julia Dent, 1826-1902.

6088. Barnard, Harry. Rutherford B. Hayes and His America. Russell. 1954. $17.50.   973.83

900 GEOGRAPHY, TRAVEL, AND HISTORY

1. Hayes, Rutherford Birchard, President U. S., 1822-1893. 2. U. S. — History — 1865-1898.

6089. Davison, Kenneth B. The Presidency of Rutherford B. Hayes. Greenwood. Repr. 1972. $12.00. 973.83(B)
1. Hayes, Rutherford Birchard, President U. S., 1882-1893.

6090. Bates, Richard O. The Gentleman from Ohio: A Biography of James A. Garfield. Moore Pub Co. $7.95. 973.84(B)
1. Garfield, James Abram, President U. S., 1831-1881.

6091. Reeves, Thomas C. Gentleman Boss: The Life of Chester Alan Arthur. Knopf. 1975. $15.00. 973.84(B)
1. Arthur, Chester Alan, President U. S., 1830-1886.

6092. Nevins, Allan. Grover Cleveland: A Study in Courage. Dodd. 1932. $12.00. 973.85(B)
1. Cleveland, Grover, President U. S., 1837-1908. 2. U. S. — History — 1865-1898.

6093. Glad, Paul W. McKinley, Bryan and the People. Lippincott. 1964. pap. $2.45. 973.88
1. Bryan, William Jennings, 1860-1925. 2. McKinley, William, President U. S., 1843-1901. 3. Presidents — U. S. — Election — 1896. 4. U. S. — Politics and Government — 1865-1898.

6094. Pratt, Julius W. Expansionists of 1898: The Acquisition of Hawaii and the Spanish Islands. Quadrangle. 1964. pap. $2.95. 973.88
1. Hawaii — History. 2. U. S. — Foreign Relations. 3. U. S. — Territorial Expansion.

6095. Cosmas, Graham A. An Army for Empire: The United States Army in the Spanish-American War. U of Mo Pr. 1971. $11.50. 973.89
1. U. S. Army — History — War of 1898.

6096. Foner, Philip S. The Spanish-Cuban-American War and the Birth of American Imperialism, 1895-1902. 2 vols. Monthly Rev. 1973. $22.50; pap. $8.50. 973.89
1. Cuba — Foreign Relations — U. S. 2. Cuba — History — Revolution, 1895-1898. 3. U. S. — Foreign Relations — Cuba. 4. U. S. — History — War of 1898.

6097. Freidel, Frank. Splendid Little War. Little. 1958. $12.50. 973.89
1. U. S. — History — War of 1898.

6098. Jones, Virgil C. Roosevelt's Rough Riders. Doubleday. 1971. $10.00. 973.89
1. U. S. Army. 1st Calvalry (Volunteer). 2. U. S. — History — War of 1898.

973.9 20th Century, 1901-

6099. Abernethy, Robert G. Introduction to Tomorrow: The United States and the Wider World, 1945-1965. HarBraceJ. 1966. $6.95. 973.9
1. History, Modern — 1945- 2. U. S. — Foreign Relations — 1945-

6100. American Heritage Editors. The American Heritage History of the 20's and 30's. McGraw. 1970. $19.95. 973.9
1. U. S. — History.

6101. Barck, Oscar T., ed. America in the World: 20th Century History in Documents. Peter Smith. $4.25. 973.9
1. U. S. — History — 20th Century — Sources.

6102. Hacker, Louis M. and Kendrick, Benjamin B. The United States Since 1865. 4th ed. Irvington. 1949. $14.95. 973.9
1. U. S. — History — 1865-1898. 2. U. S. — History — 1898-

6103. Josephson, Matthew. President Makers, 1896-1919. Ungar. 1964. $12.00. 973.9
1. Statesmen, American. 2. U. S. — Politics and Government — 1865-1933.

6104. Leighton, Isabel, ed. Aspirin Age, 1919-41. S&S. 1968. pap. $2.95. 973.9
1. U. S. — Civilization. 2. U. S. — Politics and Government — 20th Century.

6105. Shannon, David A. Twentieth Century America: The U. S. Since the 1890's. 3 vols. 3rd ed. Rand. 1973. pap. $4.75 ea. 973.9
1. U. S. — History — 20th Century.

6106. Wish, Harvey. Contemporary America: The National Scene Since 1900. 4th ed. Har-Row. 1966. $12.95. 973.9
1. U. S. — Foreign Relations — 20th Century. 2. U. S. — History — 20th Century.

900 GEOGRAPHY, TRAVEL, AND HISTORY

973.91 Early 20th Century, 1901-1953

6107. Allen, Frederick L. Only Yesterday: An Informal History of the 1920's. Har-Row. 1957. $7.95; pap. $0.95. 973.91
1. U. S. — Economic Conditions. 2. U. S. — History — 1919-1933. 3. U. S. — Social Conditions — 1919-1933.

6108. Barck, Oscar T. Since Nineteen Hundred: A History of the United States in Our Times. 5th ed. Macmillan. 1974. $12.95. 973.91
1. U. S. — History — 20th Century.

6109. Braeman, John. Albert J. Beveridge: An American Nationalist. U of Chicago Pr. 1971. $13.50. 973.910(B)
1. Beveridge, Albert Jeremiah, 1862-1927.

6110. Hofstadter, Richard. The Age of Reform: From Bryan to F.D.R. Knopf. 1955. $6.95. 973.91
1. Progressivism (U. S. Politics). 2. Reformers. 3. U. S. — Politics and Government — 1898.

6111. Leuchtenburg, William E. The Periods of Prosperity, 1914-1932. U of Chicago Pr. 1958. $7.50; pap. $2.45. 973.91
1. European War, 1914-1918 — Economic Aspects — U. S. 2. U. S. — Economic Conditions — 1918-1945. 3. U. S. — History — 1919-1933.

6112. Link, Arthur S., et al. American Epoch: A History of the United States Since the 1890's. 3rd ed. Knopf. 1967. $11.95; pap. $2.95. 973.91
1. U. S. — History — 20th Century.

6113. Lippmann, Walter. Early Writings. new ed. Liveright. 1971. $7.50; pap. $2.95. 973.91
1. U. S. — Politics and Government — 1898-1919. 2. U. S. — Politics and Government — 1919-1933.

6114. Merz, Charles. Dry Decade. U of Wash Pr. 1970. $9.50; pap. $3.45. 973.91
1. Prohibition — U. S. 2. U. S. — History — 20th Century.

6115. Mowry, George E. Era of Theodore Roosevelt: 1900-1912. Har-Row. 1958. $8.95; pap. $2.75. 973.911
1. Roosevelt, Theodore, President U. S., 1858-1919. 2. U. S. — Politics and Government — 1901-1909. 3. U. S. — Politics and Government — 1909-1913.

6116. Pringle, Henry F. Theodore Roosevelt: A Biography. HarBraceJ. 1956. pap. $2.65. 973.911(B)
1. Roosevelt, Theodore, President U. S., 1858-1919.

6117. Daniels, Josephus. The Wilson Era: Years of Peace, 1910-1917. Greenwood. Repr. 1944. $27.00. 973.913
1. U. S. — Politics and Government — 1913-1921. 2. Wilson, Woodrow, President U. S., 1856-1924.

6118. Link, Arthur S. Woodrow Wilson: A Profile. Hill & Wang. 1968. $5.95; pap. $2.25. 973.913(B)
1. Wilson, Woodrow, President U. S., 1856-1924.

6119. ———. Woodrow Wilson and the Progressive Era: 1910-1917. Har-Row. 1954. $8.95; pap. $2.75. 973.913
1. U. S. — History — 1898-1919. 2. Wilson, Woodrow, President U. S., 1856-1924.

6120. Murray, Robert K. Red Scare: A Study in National Hysteria, 1919-1920. McGraw. 1964. pap. $2.95. 973.913
1. Communism — U. S. — 1917- 2. Hysteria (Social Psychology) — Case Studies. 3. Subversive Activities — U. S. 4. U. S. — History — 20th Century.

6121. Smith, Gene. When the Cheering Stopped: The Last Years of Woodrow Wilson. Morrow. 1971. $6.95; pap. $2.95. 973.913(B)
1. Wilson, Woodrow, President U. S., 1856-1924.

6122. Wilson, Woodrow. Case for the League of Nations. Foley, H., ed. Kennikat. 1923. $8.50. 973.913
1. European War, 1914-1918 — Peace. 2. League of Nations. 3. U. S. — History — 20th Century.

6123. McKenna, Marian C. Borah. U of Mich Pr. 1961. $7.50. 973.914
1. Borah, William Edgar, 1865-1940.

6124. Murray, Robert K. The Harding Era: Warren G. Harding and His Administration. U of Minn Pr. 1969. $13.50. 973.914
1. Harding, Warren Gamaliel, President U. S., 1865-1923. 2. U. S. — History — 1919-1933. 3. U. S. — History — 20th Century.

900 GEOGRAPHY, TRAVEL, AND HISTORY

6125. ———. The Politics of Normalcy: Governmental Theory and Practice in the Harding-Coolidge Era. Norton. 1973. $6.95; pap. $2.45. 973.914
1. Coolidge, Calvin, President U. S., 1872-1933. 2. Harding, Warren Gamaliel, President U. S., 1865-1923. 3. U. S. — Politics and Government — 1921-1923.

6126. Josephson, Matthew. Al Smith: Hero of the Cities: a Political Portrait. HM. 1969. $7.95. 973.915(B)
1. Smith, Alfred Emanuel, 1873-1944.

6127. McCoy, Donald. Calvin Coolidge: The Quiet President. Macmillan. 1967. $8.95. 973.915(B)
1. Coolidge, Calvin, President U.S., 1872-1933. 2. U. S. — History — 1919-1933. 3. U. S. — Politics and Government — 1919-1933.

6128. Elder, Glen H. Children of the Great Depression: Social Change in Life Experience. U of Chicago Pr. 1974. $15.00. 973.916
1. U. S. — History — 20th Century.

6129. Warren, Harris A. Herbert Hoover and the Great Depression. Norton. 1967. pap. $3.15. 973.916
1. Depressions — 1929 — U. S. 2. Hoover, Herbert Clark, President U. S., 1874-1964. 3. U. S. — Politics and Government — 1929-1933.

6130. Aaron, Daniel and Bendiner, Robert, eds. The Strenuous Decade: A Social and Intellectual Record of the 1930's. Doubleday. 1970. pap. $2.95. 973.917
1. U. S. — Civilization — 1918-1945. 2. U. S. — Politics and Government — 1933-1945.

6131. The Age of the Great Depression,1929-1941. Wecter, Dixon. Watts. 1971. pap. $3.45. 973.917
1. U. S. — Civilization. 2. U. S. — Economic Conditions — 1918-1945. 3. U. S. — History — 1933-1945. 4. U. S. — Politics and Government — 1933-1945. 5. U. S. — Social Conditions.

6132. Bowles, Chester. Promises to Keep: My Years in Public Life, 1941-1969. Har-Row. 1971. $12.95; pap. $3.95. 973.917
1. Connecticut — Politics and Government — 1951- 2. India — Foreign Relations — U. S. 3. U. S. — Foreign Relations — India. 4. U. S. — Politics and Government — 1933-1945.

6133. Burns, James M. Roosevelt: The Lion and the Fox. HarBraceJ. 1956. $12.50; pap. $3.45. 973.917(B)
1. Roosevelt, Franklin Delano, President U. S., 1882-1945.

6134. ———. Roosevelt: The Soldier of Freedom. HarBraceJ. 1970. $12.50; pap. $4.45. 973.917
1. Roosevelt, Franklin Delano, President U. S., 1882-1945. 2. World War, 1939-1945 — U. S.

6135. Kimball, Warren F. The Most Unsordid Act: Lend-Lease, 1939-1941. Johns Hopkins. 1969. $12.00. 973.917
1. U. S. — Politics and Government — 1933-1945. 2. World War, 1939-1945 — Economic Aspects.

6136. Lash, Joseph P. Eleanor and Franklin. Norton. 1971. $17.50; pap. $1.95 (NAL). 973.917(B)
1. Roosevelt, Eleanor (Roosevelt), 1884-1962. 2. Roosevelt, Franklin Delano, President U.S., 1882-1945.

6137. ———. Eleanor: The Years Alone. Norton. 1972. $9.95. 973.917(B)
1. Roosevelt, Eleanor (Roosevelt), 1884-1962.

6138. Leuchtenburg, William E. Franklin D. Roosevelt and the New Deal: 1932-1940. Har-Row. 1963. pap. $2.45. 973.917
1. Roosevelt, Franklin Delano, President U. S., 1882-1945. 2. U. S. — Economic Conditions — 1933-1945. 3. U. S. — History — 1933-1945.

6139. Lindley, Ernest K. Roosevelt Revolution. Da Capo. Repr. 1974. $13.50. 973.917
1. Roosevelt, Franklin Delano, President U. S., 1882-1945. 2. U. S. — Politics and Government — 1933-1945.

6140. Manchester, William. The Glory and the Dream: A Narrative History of America, 1932-1972. 2 vols. Little. 1974. $20.00. 973.917
1. U. S. — History — 1933-1945. 2. U. S. — History — 1945-

6141. Markowitz, Norman D. The Rise and Fall of the People's Century: Henry A. Wallace and American Liberalism, 1941-1948. Free Pr. 1973. $8.95. 973.917(B)
1. U. S. — Politics and Government — 1933-1945. 2. U. S. — Politics and Government — 1945- 3. Wallace, Henry Agard, 1888-1965.

900 GEOGRAPHY, TRAVEL, AND HISTORY

6142. Perkins, Dexter. The New Age of Franklin Roosevelt: 1932-1945. U of Chicago Pr. 1957. $6.95; pap. $1.95. 973.917
1. Roosevelt, Franklin D., President U. S., 1882-1945. 2. U. S. — History — 1933-1945.

6143. Phillips, Cabell. From the Crash to the Blitz, 1929-1939: A New York Times Chronicle of American Life. Macmillan. 1969. $12.50. 973.917
1. Roosevelt, Franklin Delano, President U. S., 1882-1945. 2. U. S. — Economic Conditions — 1933-1945. 3. U. S. — History — 1933-1945.

6144. Schlesinger, Arthur M., Jr. The Age of Roosevelt. 3 vols. HM. 1957-59. $30.00 set; pap. $11.85. 973.917
1. Roosevelt, Franklin Delano, President U. S., 1882-1945. 2. U. S. — History — 1919-1933. 3. U. S. — History — 1933-1945.

6145. Shannon, David A. Between the Wars: America, 1919-1941. HM. 1965. pap. $4.95. 973.917
1. U. S. — History — 1901-1953.

6146. Tugwell, Rexford G. In Search of Roosevelt. Harvard U Pr. 1972. $12.95. 973.917
1. Roosevelt, Franklin Delano, President U. S., 1882-1945.

6147. Bernstein, Barton J., ed. The Politics and Policies of the Truman Administration. Watts. 1970. $10.00; pap. $4.95. 973.918
1. Truman, Harry S., President U. S., 1884-1972. 2. U. S. — Foreign Relations — 1945-1953. 3. U. S. — Politics and Government — 1945-1953.

6148. Bernstein, Barton J. and Matusow, A. J., eds. The Truman Administration: A Documentary History. Har-Row. 1968. pap. $3.95. 973.918
1. Truman, Harry S., President U. S., 1884-1972. 2. U. S. — Foreign Relations — 1945-1953 — Sources. 3. U. S. — Politics and Government — 1933-1953 — Sources.

6149. Cochran, Bert. Harry Truman and the Crisis Presidency. Funk & W. 1973. $10.00. 973.918
1. Truman, Harry S., President U. S., 1884-1972. 2. U. S. — Politics and Government — 1945-1953.

6150. Goldman, Eric F. The Crucial Decade and After: America, 1945-1960. Knopf. 1956. $6.95; pap. $1.95. 973.918
1. U. S. — History — 1945-

6151. Hamby, Alonzo L. Beyond the New Deal: Harry S. Truman and American Liberalism. Columbia U Pr. 1973. $12.95. 973.918
1. Liberalism — U. S. 2. Truman, Harry S., President U. S., 1884-1972. 3. U. S. — Politics and Government — 1945-1953.

6152. Leuchtenburg, William E. A Troubled Feast: American Society Since 1945. Little. 1973. pap. $3.95. 973.918
1. U. S. — Civilization — 1945-

6153. Miller, Merle. Plain Speaking: An Oral Biography of Harry S. Truman. Putnam. 1974. $8.95. 973.918(B)
1. Truman, Harry S., President U. S., 1884-1972. 2. U. S. — Politics and Government — 1945-1953.

6154. Truman, Harry S. Memoirs. 2 vols. Doubleday. 1958. $8.95. 973.918(B)
1. U. S. — Politics and Government — 1945-1952 — Sources.

6155. Truman, Margaret. Harry S. Truman. Morrow. 1973. $10.95. 973.918(B)
1. Truman, Harry S., President U. S., 1884-1972. 2. U. S. — Politics and Government — 1945-1953.

973.92 Later 20th Century, 1953-

6156. Druks, Herbert. From Truman Through Johnson: A Documentary History. 2 vols. Speller. 1971. $12.50 ea. 973.92
1. U. S. — Politics and Government — 1945- — Sources.

6157. Link, Arthur S. and Catton, William B. The Era of the Cold War, 1946-1973. 4th ed. Knopf. 1974. pap. $4.95. 973.92
1. U. S. — History — 1945-

6158. Nixon, Richard M. Six Crises. Doubleday. 1962. $8.95. 973.92
1. U. S. — History — 1945-

6159. Wittner, Lawrence S. Cold-War America. Praeger. 1974. $12.50. 973.92
1. U. S. — History — 1945-

6160. Griffith, Robert. A Politics of Fear: Joseph R. McCarthy and the Senate. Hayden. 1971. $4.30. 973.921
1. McCarthy, Joseph Raymond, 1908-1957.

293

900 GEOGRAPHY, TRAVEL, AND HISTORY

6161. Johnson, Walter and Evans, Carol, eds. The Papers of Adlai E. Stevenson. 3 vols. Little. 1972-73. $45.00. 973.921(B)
1. Stevenson, Adlai Ewing, 1900-1965.

6162. Lyon, Peter. Eisenhower: Portrait of the Hero. Little. 1974. $15.00. 973.921(B)
1. Eisenhower, Dwight David, President U. S., 1890-1969.

6163. Abel, Elie. The Missile Crisis. Lippincott. 1966. $6.50. 973.922
1. Cuba — History — 1959. 2. Military Bases.3. Russia — Foreign Relations — U. S. 4. U. S. — Foreign Relations — Russia.

6164. Gould-Adams, Richard J. John Foster Dulles: A Reappraisal. Greenwood. Repr. 1962. $13.75. 973.922(B)
1. Dulles, John Foster, 1888-1959. 2. U. S. — Foreign Relations — 1953-1961.

6165. Halberstam, David. The Best and the Brightest. Random. 1972. $10.00; pap. $1.95 (Fawcett World). 973.922
1. U. S. — Foreign Relations — Vietnam. 2. U. S. — Politics and Government — 1961-1963. 3. U. S. — Politics and Government — 1963-1969. 4. Vietnam.

6166. Kennedy, Robert F. Thirteen Days: A Memoir of the Cuban Missile Crisis. Norton. 1969. $5.50; pap. $0.95 (NAL). 973.922
1. Cuba — History — 1959- 2. Russia — Foreign Relations. 3. U. S. — Foreign Relations — Russia. 4. U. S. — Politics and Government — 1961-

6167. Kennedy, Rose F. Times to Remember. Doubleday. 1974. $12.50. 973.922(B)
1. Kennedy, Rose Fitzgerald, 1890-

6168. Koskoff, David E. Joseph P. Kennedy: A Life and Times. P-H. 1974. $10.00. 973.922(B)
1. Kennedy, Joseph Patrick, 1888-1969.

6169. Sorensen, Theodore. Kennedy. Har-Row. 1965. $12.50; pap. $1.95 (Bantam). 973.922(B)
1. Kennedy, John Fitzgerald, President U. S., 1917-1963.

6170. Goldman, Eric F. The Tragedy of Lyndon Johnson. Knopf. 1969. $8.95; pap. $1.50 (Dell). 973.923
1. Johnson, Lyndon Baines, President U. S., 1908-1973. 2. U. S. — Politics and Government — 1961-

6171. Johnson, Lady Bird. A White House Diary. HR&W. 1970. $10.95. 973.923(B)
1. Johnson, Lyndon Baines, President U. S., 1908-1973.

6172. Joseph, Peter. Good Times: An Oral History of America in the 1960's. Charterhouse. 1973. $10.95; pap. $3.95 (Morrow). 973.923
1. U. S. — Civilization — 1945- — Sources.

6173. Cohen, Richard M. A Heartbeat Away: The Investigation and Resignation of Vice-President Spiro T. Agnew. Viking Pr. 1973. $10.00. 973.924(B)
1. Agnew, Spiro Theodore, 1918-

6174. Congressional Quarterly Service. President Ford: The Man and His Record. Congr Quarterly. 1974. $4.50. 973.924
1. Ford, Gerald Rudolph, President U. S., 1913-

6175. Kalb, Marvin L. Kissinger. Little. 1974. $12.50. 973.924(B)
1. Kissinger, Henry Alfred, 1923- 2. U. S. — Foreign Relations — 1969-

6176. Michener, James A. Kent State: What Happened and Why. Random. 1971. $10.00. 973.924
1. Ohio State University, Kent — Riot, May 4, 1970.

6177. New York Times. The End of a Presidency. Bantam. 1974. $2.25. 973.924(B)
1. Nixon, Richard Milhous, President U. S., 1913- 2. Watergate Affair, 1972-

6178. ———. The White House Transcripts: The Full Text. Viking Pr. 1974. $15.00. 973.924(B)
1. Nixon, Richard Milhous, President U. S., 1913- 2. Watergate Affair, 1972-

6179. Washington Post. The Fall of a President. Delacorte. 1974. $8.95. 973.924(B)
1. Nixon, Richard Milhous, President U. S., 1913- 2. Watergate Affair, 1972-

6180. Ter Horst, Jerald F. Gerald Ford and the Future of the Presidency. Third Pr. 1974. $9.95. 973.925(B)
1. Ford, Gerald Rudolph, President U. S., 1913-

6181. ———. Gerald Ford: Past, Present, Future. Third Pr. 1974. $10.00. 973.925
1. Ford, Gerald Rudolph, President U. S., 1913-

900 GEOGRAPHY, TRAVEL, AND HISTORY

Recommended Series

6182. American Epochs Series. Freidel, Frank, ed. Braziller. $8.50 ea.

6183. Chicago History of American Civilization. Boorstin, Daniel J., ed.. U of Chicago Pr.

6184. Chronicles of America (Yale Chronicles) US Pubs.

6185. A History of American Life Series. Schlesinger, A. M. & Fox, D. R., eds.. Macmillan.

6186. The New American Nation Series. Har-Row.

6187. Problems in American Civilization. Rozwenc, Edwin C., gen. ed.. Heath.

974 Northeastern States

6188. Adams, James T. History of New England. 3 vols. Scholarly. 1923. $39.50 set. 974
1. New England — History.

6189. Leach, Douglas E. The Northern Colonial Frontier, 1607-1763. U of NM Pr. 1973. $7.95. 974
1. Frontier and Pioneer Life — Northeastern States. 2. Northeastern States — History — Colonial Period.

6190. Miller, Perry. New England Mind: The Seventeenth Century. Harvard U Pr. 1954. $12.50; pap. $3.95 (Beacon Pr). 974
1. American Literature — New England. 2. New England — History — Colonial Period. 3. Puritans.

6191. Vaughan, Alden T. New England Frontier: Indians and Puritans, 1620-1675. Little. 1965. $7.50; pap. $2.95. 974
1. Indians of North America — New England. 2. New England — History — Colonial Period.

6192. ————. Puritan Tradition in America, 1620-1730. Har-Row. 1971. pap. $3.25. 974
1. New England — History — Colonial Period — Sources. 2. Puritans — New England.

6193. Haffenden, Philip S. New England in the English Nation, 1689-1713. Oxford U Pr. 1974. $18.50. 974.02
1. Great Britain — Colonies — American. 2. New England — History — Colonial Period.

6194. Langdon, George D., Jr. Pilgrim Colony: A History of New Plymouth, 1620-1691. Yale U Pr. 1966. $10.00. 974.4
1. Massachusetts — History — Colonial Period (New Plymouth).

6195. Garrett, John. Roger Williams: Witness Beyond Christendom. Macmillan. 1970. $7.50. 974.5(B)
1. Rhode Island — History — Colonial Period. 2. Williams, Roger, 1604?-1683.

6196. Callow, Alexander B., Jr. The Tweed Ring. Oxford U Pr. 1969. pap. $2.95. 974.7
1. Corruption (in Politics) — New York (City). 2. Tweed Ring.

6197. Mann, Arthur. La Guardia: A Fighter Against His Time, 1882-1933. U of Chicago Pr. 1969. pap. $2.95. 974.7(B)
1. La Guardia, Fiorello Henry, 1882-1947. 2. New York (City).

6198. ————. La Guardia Comes to Power, 1933. U of Chicago Pr. 1969. pap. $1.95. 974.8(B)
1. La Guardia, Fiorello Henry, 1882-1947. 2. New York (City).

6199. Wildes, Harry E. William Penn. Macmillan. 1974. $14.95. 974.8
1. Penn, William, 1644-1718.

975 Southeastern States

6200. Blassingame, John W. The Slave Community: Plantation Life in the Antebellum South. Oxford U Pr. 1972. $8.95. 975
1. Plantation Life — Southern States. 2. Slavery in the U. S. — Southern States.

6201. Cash, Wilbur J. The Mind of the South. Knopf. 1960. $7.95; pap. $1.95 (Random). 975
1. Southern States — Civilization. 2. Southern States — Social Conditions.

6202. Eaton, Clement. Growth of Southern Civilization: 1790-1860. Har-Row. 1961. $8.95; pap. $3.00. 975
1. Southern States — Civilization. 2. Southern States — Social Conditions.

6203. ————. The Mind of the Old South. rev. ed. La State U Pr. 1967. $6.95; pap. $2.95. 975

900 GEOGRAPHY, TRAVEL, AND HISTORY

1. National Characteristics, American. 2. Southern States — Biography. 3. Southern States — Civilization.

6204. ———. The Waning of the Old South Civilization, 1860-1880. U of Ga Pr. 1968. $6.00; pap. $1.95 (Pegasus). 975
1. Southern States — Civilization.

6205. Eaton, Clement. Civilization of the Old South: Writings of Clement Eaton. Kirwan, Albert, ed. U Pr of Ky. 1968. $7.50. 975
1. Southern States — Civilization. 2. Southern States — History.

6206. Franklin, John H. The Militant South, 1800-1861. Harvard U Pr. 1956. $7.50. 975
1. Militarism. 2. Southern States — History — 1775-1865.

6207. Gaston, Paul M. The New South Creed: A Study in Southern Myth Making. Knopf. 1970. $7.95; pap. $2.45 (Random). 975
1. Southern States — Civilization. 2. Southern States — Race Question.

6208. Genovese, Eugene D. Roll, Jordan, Roll: The World the Slaves Made. Pantheon. 1974. $17.50. 975
1. Slavery in the U. S. — Condition of Slaves.

6209. Hesseltine, William B. and Smiley, D. The South in American History. 2nd ed. P-H. 1960. $12.50. 975
1. Southern States — History.

6210. McGill, Ralph. The South and the Southerner. Little. 1963. $7.50; pap. $1.95. 975
1. Southern States — Civilization. 2. Southern States — History.

6211. Olmstead, Frederick L. Cotton Kingdom. Schlesinger, Arthur M., ed. Knopf. 1953. $10.00. 975
1. Cotton Growing — Southern States. 2. Slavery in the U. S. 3. Southern States — Description and Travel. 4. Southern States — Economic Conditions.

6212. Phillips, Ulrich B. The Course of the South to Secession. Peter Smith. 1960. $4.00. 975
1. Southern States — History. 2. Southern States — Politics and Government.

6213. ———. Life and Labor in the Old South. Little. 1929. $8.50; pap. $2.45. 975

1. Slavery in the U. S. 2. Southern States. 3. Southern States — Economic Conditions. 4. Southern States — Social Conditions.

6214. ———. Plantation and Frontier Documents, 1649-1863. 2 vols. B Franklin. 1909. $32.50. 975
1. Southern States — History — Sources. 2. U. S. — History — Sources.

6215. Potter, David M. The South and the Sectional Conflict. La State U Pr. 1968. $7.50; pap. $2.95. 975
1. Southern States — History. 2. U. S. — History — Civil War.

6216. Taylor, William R. Cavalier and Yankee: The Old South and American National Character. Braziller. 1961. $6.00; pap. $2.95 (Har-Row). 975
1. National Characteristics, American. 2. Southern States — History — 1775-1865 — Philosophy.

6217. Vandiver, Frank E., ed. The Idea of the South. U of Chicago Pr. 1964. $4.75. 975
1. Southern States — Civilization — Addresses, Essays, etc.

6218. Woodward, C. Vann. The Burden of Southern History. rev. ed. La State U Pr. 1968. $5.95; pap. $2.45. 975
1. Southern States — Civilization.

Recommended Series

6219. A History of the South. Stepenson, Wendell Holmes & Coulter, E. Merton, eds.. La State U Pr.

976-977 Southwestern and Middlewestern States

6220. Faulk, Odie B. Destiny Road: The Gila Trail and the Opening of the Southwest. Oxford U Pr. 1973. $7.50. 976
1. Southwest, New — History.

6221. Horgan, Paul. The Heroic Triad: Backgrounds of Our Three Southwestern Cultures. HR&W. 1970. $7.95. 976
1. Indians of North America — Southwest, New. 2. Southwest, New — Social Life and Customs. 3. Spaniards in the New Southwest.

6222. Williams, T. Harry. Huey Long. Knopf. 1969. $12.50; pap. $1.95 (Bantam). 976.3(B)

900 GEOGRAPHY, TRAVEL, AND HISTORY

1. Long, Huey Pierce, 1893-1935. 2. U. S. — Politics and Government — 1919-1935.

6223. Haskins, James. Pinckney Benton Stewart Pinchback. Macmillan. 1973. $8.95. 976.306
1. Negroes — Biography. 2. Pinchback, Pinckney Benton Stewart, 1837-1921.

6224. Barker, Eugene C. The Life of Stephen F. Austin, Founder of Texas, 1793-1836. Tex St Hist Assn. 1949. $10.00; pap. $3.25 (U of Tex Pr). 976.4(B)
1. Austin, Stephen Fuller, 1793-1836. 2. Texas — History — to 1846.

6225. James, Marquis. The Raven. Berg. 1968. $14.95. 976.4(B)
1. Houston, Samuel, 1793-1863. 2. U. S. — History — 1815-1861.

6226. Walker, Daniel. Rights in Conflict: Convention Week in Chicago, August 25-29, 1968. Dutton. 1969. $6.95. 977.3
1. Chicago — Police. 2. Chicago — Riot, August, 1968. 3. Democratic Party, National Convention, Chicago, 1968.

978 Western States

6227. Billington, Ray A. America's Frontier Heritage. U of NM Pr. 1973. pap. $4.95. 978
1. Frontier and Pioneer Life — U. S. 2. National Characteristics, American.

6228. ———. Far Western Frontier: 1830-1860. Har-Row. 1956. $8.95. 978
1. West — History.

6229. ———. Westward Expansion: History of the American Frontier. 4th ed. Macmillan. 1974. $12.95. 978
1. U. S. — Territorial Expansion. 2. West — History.

6230. DeVoto, Bernard A. Across the Wide Missouri. HM. 1947. $12.50; pap. $3.95. 978
1. Fur Trade. 2. Indians of North America. 3. West — History.

6231. ———. Year of Decision, 1846. HM. 1950. $7.50; pap. $3.95. 978
1. U. S. — History — 1851-1861. 2. U. S. — History — War with Mexico. 3. West — History.

6232. Drago, Harry S. The Great Range Wars: Violence on the Grasslands. Dodd. 1970. $7.50. 978

1. Crime and Criminals — The West. 2. West — History — 1848-1950.

6233. Eide, Ingvard H., compiled by. American Odyssey: The Journey of Lewis and Clark. Rand. 1969. $14.95. 978
1. Lewis and Clark Expeditions. 2. West — Description and Travel — Views.

6234. Hewitt, James, compiled by. Eye-Witness to Wagon Trains West. Scribner. 1974. $7.95. 978
1. Overland Journeys to the Pacific. 2. West — History — to 1848 — Sources.

6235. Katz, William L. The Black West. rev. ed. Doubleday. 1973. pap. $5.95. 978
1. Frontier and Pioneer Life — U. S. 2. Negroes — The West.

6236. Lavendar, David. American Heritage History of the Great West. McGraw. 1965. $16.50. 978
1. West — History.

6237. Nash, Gerald D. The American West in the 20th Century: A Short History of an Urban Oasis. P-H. 1973. $9.95; pap. $4.95. 978
1. West — History — 1848-1950. 2. West — History — 1951-

6238. Parkman, Francis. The Oregon Trail. U of Wis Pr. 1969. $20.00. 978
1. Frontier and Pioneer Life. 2. West — History.

6239. Stone, Irving. Men to Match My Mountains: The Story of the Opening of the Far West, 1840-1900. Doubleday. 1956. $9.95. 978
1. West — Biography. 2. West — History.

6240. Vandiver, Clarence H. Fur-Trade and Early Western Exploration. Cooper Sq. Repr. 1929. $8.95. 978
1. Fur Trade — Northwest, Canadian. 2. Fur Trade — The West. 3. Northwest, Canadian — Discovery and Exploration. 4. West — Discovery and Exploration.

6241. Webb, Walter P. Great Plains. G&D. 1957. pap. $2.95. 978
1. West — History.

979 Far Western States

6242. Lavendar, David. Land of the Giants. Doubleday. 1958. $8.95. 979
1. Northwest Pacific — History.

900 GEOGRAPHY, TRAVEL, AND HISTORY

6243. Wellman, Paul I. Glory, God and Gold. Doubleday. 1956. $7.95.　　979
1. Southwest, New — History.

6244. Jackson, Joseph H. Anybody's Gold: The Story of California's Mining Towns. Chronicle Bks. Repr. 1941. $7.95.　　979.4
1. California — Gold Discoveries. 2. Frontier and Pioneer Life — California.

6245. Sears, David O. and McConahy, John B. The Politics of Violence: The New Urban Blacks and the Watts Riot. HM. 1973. pap. $5.50.　　979.4
1. Los Angeles — Riots, 1965. 2. Negroes — Los Angeles.

6246. Cook, Warren L. Flood Tide of Empire: Spain and the Pacific Northwest, 1543-1819. Yale U Pr. 1973. $17.50.　　979.5
1. Northwest Coast of North America — Discovery and Exploration. 2. Northwest Pacific — History. 3. Spain — Exploring Expeditions.

6247. Chevigny, Hector. Russian America: The Great Alaskan Venture. Viking Pr. 1965. $5.95.　　979.8
1. Alaska — History — to 1867. 2. Russians in Alaska.

6248. Hinckley, Ted C. The Americanization of Alaska, 1867-1897. Pacific Bks. 1972. $8.95.　　979.8
1. Alaska — Annexation. 2. Alaska — History — 1867-1959. 3. Frontier and Pioneer Life — Alaska.

6249. Hulley, Clarence C. Alaska: Past and Present. 3rd rev. & enl. ed. Binford. 1970. $10.00.　　979.8
1. Alaska — History.

6250. Morgan, Lael. And the Land Provides: Alaskan Natives in the Year of Transition. Doubleday. 1974. $10.00.　　979.8
1. Aleuts. 2. Eskimos — Alaska. 3. Indians of North America — Alaska.

6251. Wharton, David B. The Alaska Gold Rush. Ind U Pr. 1972. $10.00.　　979.8
1. Klondike Gold Fields.

980 South American History

6252. Alba, Victor. The Latin Americans. Praeger. 1969. $10.00; pap. $4.95.　　980
1. Latin America.

6253. Arciniegas, German. Latin America: A Cultural History. Knopf. 1967. $10.00.　　980
1. Latin America — Civilization. 2. Latin America — History.

6254. Bailey, Helen M., et al. Latin America: The Development of Its Civilization. 3rd ed. P-H. 1973. $12.50.　　980
1. Latin America — History. 2. South America — History.

6255. Collier, Simon D. From Cortés to Castro: An Introduction to the History of Latin America, 1492-1973. Macmillan. 1974. $12.95.　　980
1. Latin America — History.

6256. Haring, Clarence H. The Spanish Empire in America. HarBraceJ. 1963. pap. $3.25.　　980
1. Latin America — History. 2. South America — History.

6257. Herring, Hubert. History of Latin America. 3rd ed. Knopf. 1968. $14.95.　　980
1. Latin America — History. 2. South America — History.

6258. Nicholson, Irene. The Liberators: A Study of Independence Movements in Spanish America. Praeger. 1969. $8.95.　　980
1. Latin America — Biography. 2. Latin America — History.

6259. Prescott, William H. The Conquest of Mexico, and The Conquest of Peru. Modern Lib. $4.95.　　980
1. Cortes, Hernando, 1485-1547. 2. Mexico — History — Conquest, 1519-1540. 3. Peru — History — to 1548. 4. Pizarro, Francisco, 1470?-1541.

6260. Kirkpatrick, Frederick A. Spanish Conquistadors. 2nd ed. B&N. 1946. $10.00.　　980.01
1. America — Discovery and Exploration — Spanish. 2. Latin America — History — to 1600.

6261. Lynch, John. The Spanish American Revolutions, 1808-1826. Norton. 1973. $15.00; pap. $4.65.　　980.02
1. Latin America — History — Wars of Independence, 1806-1830.

6262. Masur, Gerhard. Simon Bolivar. rev. ed. U of NM Pr. 1969. $15.00.　　980.02(B)
1. Bolivar, Simon, 1783-1830.

900 GEOGRAPHY, TRAVEL, AND HISTORY

6263. O'Leary, Daniel F. Bolivar and the War of Independence. U of Tex Pr. 1970. $9.50. 980.02
1. Bolivar, Simon, 1783-1830. 2. Latin America — History — Wars of Independence, 1806-1830. 3. Venezuela — History — War of Independence, 1810-1823.

6264. Sauvage, Leo. Ché Guevera: The Failure of a Revolutionary. P-H. 1973. $6.95. 980.03(B)
1. Guevara, Ernesto (Ché), 1928-1967.

6265. Hardoy, Jorge E. Pre-Columbian Cities. Walker & Co. 1973. $19.95. 980.1
1. Cities and Towns, Ruined, Extinct, etc. — Latin America. 2. Indians — Antiquities. 3. Latin America — Antiquities.

6266. Brundage, Burr C. Empire of the Inca. U of Okla Pr. 1963. $8.95. 980.3
1. Incas. 2. Peru — History.

6267. Hemming, John. The Conquest of the Incas. HarBraceJ. 1970. $14.00; pap. $4.95. 980.3
1. Incas.

6268. Martin, Luis. The Kingdom of the Sun: A Short Histoy of Peru. Scribner. 1974. $12.50. 980.3
1. Peru — History.

6269. Metraux, Alfred. History of the Incas. Pantheon. 1969. $5.95. 980.3
1. Incas.

981 Brazil

6270. Burns, E. Bradford. A History of Brazil. Columbia U Pr. 1971. $15.00; pap. $3.95. 981
1. Brazil — History.

6271. Poppins, Rollie E. Brazil: The Land and People. Oxford U Pr. 1973. $9.50; pap. $2.95. 981
1. Brazil — History.

6272. Rodrigues, José H. Brazilians: Their Character and Aspirations. Dimmick, Ralph, tr. U of Tex Pr. 1967. $7.95. 981
1. Brazil — Social Conditions.

6273. Alexander, Robert J. An Introduction to Argentina. Praeger. 1969. $6.50. 982
1. Argentine Republic.

6274. Read, Piers P. Alive: The Story of the Andes Survivors. Lippincott. 1974. $10.00. 982.6
1. Aeronautics — Accidents — 1972. 2. Cannibalism. 3. Survival (After Airplane Accidents, Shipwrecks, etc.).

6275. Guevara, Ché. Complete Bolivian Diaries of Che Guevara, and Other Captured Documents. James, Daniel, ed. Stein & Day. 1969. $6.95; pap. $2.95. 984.05
1. Bolivia — History. 2. Guevara, Ernesto (Ché), 1928-1967. 3. Guerrilla Warfare.

6276. Dezarate, Augustin. The Discovery and Conquest of Peru. Folcroft. Repr. 1581. $25.00. 985.02
1. Peru — History — Conquest, 1522-1548.

6277. Hemming, John. The Conquest of the Incas. HarBraceJ. 1970. $14.00. 985.02
1. Incas. 2. Peru — History — Conquest, 1522-1548.

6278. Niemeier, Jean. The Panama Story. Binford. 1968. $5.59; pap. $4.50. 986.2
1. Panama — History.

6279. Alisky, Marvin. Uruguay, a Contemporary Survey. Praeger. 1969. $8.00. 989
1. Uruguay.

Recommended Series

6280. Problems in Latin American Civilization. Lienwen, Edwin, gen. ed.. Heath.

990 Oceania and Australia

6281. Grattan, C. Hartley. The Southwest Pacific. 2 vols. Vol. 1. To 1900. $17.50; Vol. 2. Since 1900. $10.00. U of Mich Pr. 1963. $17.50 set. 990
1. Australia — History. 2. Oceanica — History.

6282. Fischer, Louis. The Story of Indonesia: Old Land, New Nation. Greenwood. 1959. $14.50. 991
1. Indonesia — History.

6283. Kahin, George McT. Nationalism and Revolution in Indonesia. Cornell U Pr. 1952. $12.50; pap. $3.95. 991
1. Indonesia.

900 GEOGRAPHY, TRAVEL, AND HISTORY

6284. Malcolm, George A. The Commonwealth of the Philippines. Bks for Libs. Repr. 1936. $32.50.　991.4
1. Philippine Islands.

6285. Cameron, William J. New Zealand. P-H. 1965. $5.95.　993
1. New Zealand — History.

6286. Alexander, Frederick. Australia Since Federation: A Narrative and Critical Analysis. 2nd ed. Verry. 1973. pap. $7.50.　994
1. Australia — History.

6287. Clark, Charles M. History of Australia. 2 vols. Intl Schol Bk Serv. 1968 (Pub. by Melbourne U Pr). $15.85 ea.　994
1. Australia — History.

6288. Pike, D. Australia: The Quiet Continent. Cambridge U Pr. 1970. $12.50.　994
1. Australia — History.

6289. Daws, Gavan. Shoal of Time: A History of the Hawaiian Islands. U Pr of Hawaii. 1974. pap. $4.95.　996
1. Hawaii — History.

6290. Joesting, Edward. Hawaii: An Uncommon History. Norton. 1972. $10.95.　996
1. Hawaii — History.

998 Arctic Islands and Antarctica

6291. Payne, Donald G. Antarctica: The Last Continent. Little. 1974. $15.00.　998
1. Antarctic Regions.

DIRECTORY OF PUBLISHERS

A & W Visual Library. A & W Visual Library, 95 Madison Ave., New York, NY 10016

A S Barnes. Barnes, A. S., & Co., Inc., P.O. Box 421, Cranbury, NJ 08512 Tel 609-655-0190

A-W. Addison-Wesley Publishing Co., Inc., Jacob Way, Reading, MA 01867 Tel 617-944-3700

AAAS. American Assn. for the Advancement of Science, 1776 Massachusetts Ave., N.W., Washington, DC 20036 Tel 202-467-4400

AAHPER. American Alliance for Health, Physical Education & Recreation, Affiliate of National Education Assn., 1201 16th St., N. W., Washington, DC 20036 Tel 202-833-5555

ABC-Clio. American Bibliographical Center-Clio Press, 2040 Alameda Padre Serra, Box 4397, Santa Barbara, CA 93101 Tel 805-963-4221

Abelard. Abelard-Schuman Ltd., 666 Fifth Ave., New York, NY 10019

Abingdon. Abingdon Press, 201 Eighth Ave., S., Nashville, TN 37202 Tel 615-749-6000

Abrams. Abrams, Harry N., Inc, Subs. of Times Mirror Co., 110 E. 59th St., New York, NY 10022 Tel 212-758-8600

Acad Pr. Academic Press, Inc., 11 Fifth Ave., New York, NY 10003

Academic Intl. Academic International, P.O. Box 555, Gulf Breeze, FL 32561

ACE. American Council on Education, 1 Dupont Circle, Washington, DC 20036 Tel 202-833-4700

Ace Bks. Ace Books, Div. of Charter Communications Inc., 1120 Ave. of the Americas, New York, NY 10036 Tel 212-867-5050

Acropolis. Acropolis Books, 2400 17th St., N. W., Washington, DC 20009 Tel 202-387-6800

Adler. Adler's Foreign Books, Inc., 162 Fifth Ave., New York, NY 10010

Advent. Advent Pubs., Inc., P.O. Box A3228, Chicago, IL 60690

Agathon. Agathon Press Inc., 150 Fifth Ave., New York, NY 10011 Tel 212-924-5440

AHM Pub. AHM Publishing Corp., 899 Skokie Blvd., Northbrook, IL 60062 Tel 312-498-5660

ALA. American Library Assn., 50 E. Huron St., Chicago, IL 60611 Tel 312-944-6780

Aldine. Aldine Publishing Co., 529 S. Wabash Ave., Chicago, IL 60605 Tel 312-939-5190

Allyn. Allyn & Bacon, Inc., 470 Atlantic Ave., Boston, MA 02210 Tel 617-482-9220

Am Chemical. American Chemical Society, 1155 16th St., N.W., Washington, DC 20036 Tel 202-872-4600

Am Elsevier. American Elsevier Publishing Co., Inc., Orders to: 52 Vanderbilt Ave., New York, NY 10017 Tel 212-686-5277

Am Heritage. American Heritage Publishing Co., 1221 Ave. of the Americas, New York, NY 10036

Am Radio. American Radio Relay League, Inc., 225 Main St., Newington, CT 06111 Tel 203-666-1541

DIRECTORY OF PUBLISHERS

Am Technical. American Technical Society, 5608 Stony Island Ave., Chicago, IL 60637

Am U Field. American Universities Field Staff, Inc., 3 Lebanon St., Hanover, NH 03755   Tel 603-643-2110

Am West. American West Publishing Co., 599 College Ave., Palo Alto, CA 94306   Tel 415-327-4660

Amphoto. American Photographic Book Publishing Co., Inc., 750 Zeckendorf Blvd., Garden City, NY 11530   Tel 516-248-2233

AMS Pr. AMS Press, Inc., 56 E. 13th St., New York, NY 10003 Tel 212-777- 4700

Ann Arbor Science. Ann Arbor Science Pubs., P. O. Box 1425, Ann Arbor, MI 48106   Tel 313-761-5010

Aperture. Aperture, Inc., Elm St., Millerton, NY 12546   Tel 914-789-4491

Apollo Eds. Apollo Editions, 666 5th Ave., New York, NY 10019

Appalach Mtn. Appalachian Mountain Club, 5 Joy St., Boston, MA 02108

Appleton. See **P-H**

Arbor Hse. Arbor House Publishing Co., 641 Lexington Ave., New York, NY 10022   Tel 212-832-3810

Arc Bks. Arc Books, 219 Park Ave., S., New York, NY 10003

Arco. Arco Publishing Co., Inc., 219 Park Ave., S., New York, NY 10003   Tel 212-673-6600

Arlington Hse. Arlington House Pubs., 165 Huguenot St., New Rochelle, NY 10801   Tel 914-639-3850

Arno. Arno Press, 330 Madison Ave., New York, NY 10017   Tel 212-697-0044

Assn Pr. Association Press, 291 Broadway, New York, NY 10007   Tel 212-374-2130

Assoc Bk. Associated Booksellers, 147 McKinley Ave., Bridgeport, CT 06606   Tel 203-366-5294

Astor-Honor. Astor-Honor, Inc., 48 E. 43rd St., New York, NY 10017

Atheneum. Atheneum Pubs., 122 E. 42nd St., New York, NY 10017   Tel 212-661-4500

Augsburg. Augsburg Publishing House, 426 S. Fifth St., Minneapolis, MN 55415   Tel 612-332-4561

Auto Quarterly.   Automobile Quarterly, Inc., 245 Main St., Kutztown, PA 19530.

Aviation. Aviation Book Co., 555 W. Glenoaks Blvd., Box 4187, Glendale, CA 91202   Tel 213-240-1771

Avon. Avon Books, 959 Eighth Ave., New York, NY 10019   Tel 212-262-5700

B Franklin. Franklin, Burt, Pub., Dist. by: Lenox Hill Publishing & Distributing Corp., 235 E. 44th St., New York, NY 10017

Baker Bk. Baker Book House, 1019 Wealthy St., S.E., Grand Rapids, MI 49506   Tel 616-676-9186

Baker's Plays. Baker, Walter H., Co., 100 Chauncy St., Boston, MA 02111   Tel 617-482-1280

Ballantine. Ballantine Books, Inc, Div. of Random House, Inc., 201 E. 50th St., New York, NY 10022   Tel 212-751-2600

B&N. Barnes & Noble, Inc, Div of Harper & Row Pubs., Inc., 10 E. 53rd St., New York, NY 10022   Tel 212-593-7000

Bankers. Bankers Publishing Co., 210 South St., Boston, MA 02111   Tel 617-426-4495

Bantam. Bantam Books, Inc., 666 Fifth Ave., New York, NY 10019   Tel 212-765-6500

Barron. Barron's Educational Series, Inc., 113 Crossways Park Dr., Woodbury, NY 11797   Tel 516-921-8750

Basic. Basic Books, Inc., 10 E. 53rd St., New York, NY 10022   Tel 212-593-7057

Beacon Pr. Beacon Press, Inc., 25 Beacon St., Boston, MA 02108   Tel 617-942-2110

Behavioral Pubns. Behavioral Pubns., Inc., 72 Fifth Ave., New York, NY 10011   Tel 212-243-6000

Behrman. Behrman House, Inc., 1261 Broadway, New York, NY 10001   Tel 212-684-2742

Bentley. Bentley, Robert, Inc., 872 Massachusetts Ave., Cambridge, MA 02139   Tel 617-547-4170

Berg. Berg, Norman S., Pub., "Sellanraa", 2690 Mount Vernon Hwy., Box 88384, Dunwoody, GA 30338   Tel 404-457-4120

Berkley Pub. Berkley Publishing Corp, Affiliate of G. P. Putnam's Sons, 200 Madison Ave., New York, NY 10016   Tel 212-883-5500

BH&G. Better Homes & Gardens Books, Div. of Meredith Corp., 1716 Locust St., Des Moines, IA 50336   Tel 515-284-9011

Biblo. Biblo & Tannen Booksellers & Pubs., Inc., 63 Fourth Ave., New York, NY 10003   Tel 212-475-1257

Binford. Binford & Mort Pubs, 2536 S. E. 11th Ave., Portland, OR 97202   Tel 503-235-8641

DIRECTORY OF PUBLISHERS

Bks for Libs. Books for Libraries, Inc., 1 Dupont St., Plainview, NY 11803

Bobbs. Bobbs-Merrill Co., Inc, Subs. of Howard W. Sams & Co., 4 W. 58th St., New York, NY 10019 Tel 212-688-6350

Borden. Borden Publishing Co., 1855 W. Main St., Alhambra, CA 91801 Tel 213-283-5031

Bowker. Bowker, R. R., Co, a Xerox Education Co., 1180 Ave. of the Americas, New York, NY 10036 Tel 212-764-5100

Brandon. Brandon Books, Div. of American Art Enterprises, Inc., 21322 Lassen St., Chatsworth, CA 91311 Tel 213-882-5900

Braziller. Braziller, George, Inc., 1 Park Ave., New York, NY 10016 Tel 212-889-5900

British Bk Ctr. British Book Center, 153 E. 78th St., New York, NY 10021 Tel 212-879-6577

Broadman. Broadman Press, 127 Ninth Ave., N., Nashville, TN 37203 Tel 615-254-5461

Broadside. Broadside Press Pubns., 12651 Old Mill Place, Detroit, MI 48238 Tel 313-491-8960

Brookings. Brookings Institution, 1775 Massachusetts Ave., N.W., Washington, DC 20036 Tel 202-797-6000

Brooks-Cole. Brooks/Cole Publishing Co, Subs. of Wadsworth Publishing Co., 540 Abrego St., Monterey, CA 93940 Tel 408-373-0728

Brown Bk. Brown Book Co., 519 Acorn St., Deer Park, NY 11729 Tel 516-586-5500

Brown U Pr. Brown Univ. Press, 71 George St., Box 1881, Providence, RI 02912 Tel 401-863-2455

Bruce Pub Co. Bruce Books, 866 Third Ave., New York, NY 10022

Bucknell U Pr. Bucknell Univ. Press, Lewisburg, PA 17837 Tel 717-524-3674

C C Thomas. Thomas, Charles C., Pubs., 301-327 E. Lawrence Ave., Springfield, IL 62703 Tel 217-789-8980

C E Tuttle. Tuttle, Charles E., Co., Inc., 28 S. Main St., Rutland, VT 05701 Tel 802-773-8930

Cambridge U Pr. Cambridge Univ. Press, 32 E. 57th St., New York, NY 10022 Tel 212-688-8885

Chandler Pub. Chandler Publishing Co, Div. of Intext Educational Pubs., 257 Park Ave., S., New York, NY 10010

Charles Pub. Charles Publishing Co., 12125 Riverside Dr., Suite 201, North Hollywood, CA 91607

Charterhouse. Charterhouse Books, Inc, Affiliate of David McKay Co., Inc., 750 Third Ave., New York, NY 10017

Chilton. Chilton Book Co., Orders to: Sales Service Dept., 201 King of Prussia Rd., Radnor, PA 19089 Tel 215-687-8200

China Bks. China Books & Periodicals, 2929 24th St., San Francisco, CA 94110

Chronicle Bks. Chronicle Books, Div. of Chronicle Publishing Co., 54 Mint St., San Francisco, CA 94103

Citadel Pr. Citadel Press, Subs. of Lyle Stuart, Inc., 120 Enterprise Ave., Secaucus, NJ 07094 Tel 201-866-0490

City Lights. City Lights Books, 1562 Grant Ave., San Francisco, CA 94133 Tel 415-362-3112

Clark Irwin. Clark, Irwin & Co., Ltd., Dist. by: Universe Books, Inc., 381 Park Ave., S., New York, NY 10016

Coin & Curr. Coin & Currency Institute, Inc., 393 Seventh Ave., New York, NY 10001 Tel 212-947-0370

Collins-World. Collins, William, & World Publishing Co., Inc., 2080 W. 117th St., Cleveland, OH 44111

Colo Assoc. Colorado Associated Univ. Press, Univ. of Colorado, 1424 15th St., Boulder, CO 80302 Tel 303-443-2211

Columbia U Pr. Columbia Univ. Press, 562 W. 113th St., New York, NY 10025 Tel 212-678-6777

Comm Econ Dev. Committee for Economic Development, 477 Madison Ave., New York, NY 10022 Tel 212-688-2063

Congr Quarterly. Congressional Quarterly, Inc., 1414 22nd St., N.W., Washington, DC 20037 Tel 202-296-6800

Cooper Sq. Cooper Square Pubs., Inc., 59 Fourth Ave., New York, NY 10003 Tel 212-674-5296

Cornell U Pr. Cornell Univ. Press, 124 Roberts Place, Ithaca, NY 14850 Tel 607-273-5155

Corner Hse. Corner House Pubs., Green River Rd., Williamstown, MA 01267 Tel 413-458-8561

Cornerstone. Cornerstone Library, Inc, Div. of Simon & Schuster, Inc., 630 Fifth Ave., New York, NY 10020 Tel 212-245-6400

Country Beautiful. Country Beautiful Corp., 24198 W. Bluemound Rd., Waukesha, WI 53186 Tel 414-542-9361

Coward. Coward, McCann & Geoghegan, Inc., 200 Madison Ave., New York, NY 10016 Tel 212-883-5500

DIRECTORY OF PUBLISHERS

Crane-Russak Co. Crane, Russak & Co., Inc., 347 Madison Ave., New York, NY 10017 Tel 212-889-1403

CRC Pr. CRC Press, 18901 Cranwood Pkwy., Cleveland, OH 44128

Crescendo. Crescendo Publishing Co., 48-50 Melrose St., Boston, MA 02116 Tel 617-482-2420

CRM Bks. Communications Research Machines, Inc., 201 E. 50th St., New York, NY 10022 Tel 212-751-2600

Crown. Crown Pubs., Inc., 419 Park Ave., S., New York, NY 10016 Tel 212-685-8550

Da Capo. Da Capo Press, Inc., 227 W. 17th St., New York, NY 10011 Tel 212-255-0713

David & Charles. David & Charles, Inc., P. O. Box 57, North Pomfret, VT 05053 Tel 802-457-1911

De Graff. De Graff, John, Inc., 34 Oak Ave., Clinton Corners, NY 12514

Dekker. Dekker, Marcel, Inc., 270 Madison Ave., New York, NY 10016 Tel 212-679-7000

Delacorte. Delacorte Press, Dist. by: Dial Press, 1 Dag Hammarskjold Plaza, 245 E. 47th St., New York, NY 10017

Dell. Dell Publishing Co., Inc., 1 Dag Hammarskjold Plaza, 245 E. 47th St., New York, NY 10017 Tel 212-986-6300

Denison. Denison, T. S., & Co., Inc., 5100 W. 82nd St., Minneapolis, MN 55437 Tel 612-831-1221

Devin. Devin-Adair Co., Inc., 143 Sound Beach Ave., Old Greenwich, CT 06870 Tel 203-637-4531

Dial. Dial Press, 1 Dag Hammarskjold Plaza, 245 E. 47th St., New York, NY 10017 Tel 212-832-7300

Dodd. Dodd, Mead & Co., 79 Madison Ave., New York, NY 10016 Tel 212-685-6464

Doubleday. Doubleday & Co., Inc., 245 Park Ave., New York, NY 10017 Tel 212-953-4561

Dover. Dover Pubns., Inc., 180 Varick St., New York, NY 10014 Tel 212-255-3755

Drake Pubs. Drake Pubs., Inc., 381 Park Ave.,S., New York, NY 10016 Tel 212-679-4500

Dufour. Dufour Editions, Inc., Chester Springs, PA 19425 Tel 215-458-5005

Duke. Duke Univ. Press, 6697 College Sta., Durham, NC 27708 Tel 919-648-2173

Dunellen Pub Co. Dunellen Publishing Co., Inc., Dist. by: Kennikat Press, 90 S. Bayles Ave., Port Washington, NY 10050

Dutton. Dutton, E. P., & Co., Inc., 201 Park Ave., S., New York, NY 10003 Tel 212-674-5900

Duxbury Pr. Duxbury Press, Div. of Wadsworth Pub. Co., 6 Bound Brook Ct., N. Scituate, MA 02060

Ed Prog. Educators Progress Services, Inc., Dept. A4A, Randolph, WI 53956

Eerdmans. Eerdmans, Wm. B., Publishing Co., 255 Jefferson Ave., S. E., Grand Rapids, MI 49502 Tel 616-459-4591

Emerson. Emerson Books, Inc., Reynolds Lane, Buchanan, NY 10511 Tel 914-739-3506

Ency Brit Inc. Encyclopaedia Britannica, Inc., 425 N. Michigan Ave., Chicago, IL 60611.

ERA Pr. ERA Press, P.O. Box 767, Amherst, MA 01002

Facts on File. Facts on File, Inc., 119 W. 57th St., New York, NY 10019 Tel 212-265-2011

Fairleigh Dickinson. Fairleigh Dickinson Univ. Press, P.O. Box 421, Cranbury, NJ 08512 Tel 609-655-0190

Fawcett World. Fawcett World Library, 1515 Broadway, New York, NY 10036 Tel 212-869-3000

Faxon. Faxon, F. W., Co., Inc., 15 Southwest Park, Westwood, MA 02090 Tel 617-329-3350

Fertig. Fertig, Howard, Inc., 80 E. 11th St., New York, NY 10003 Tel 212-982-7922

Fielding. Fielding Pubns., 105 Madison Ave., New York, NY 10016 Tel 212-889-3050

Flayderman. Flayderman, N., & Co., Inc., Kent Rd., New Milford, CT 06776

Folcroft. Folcroft Library Editions, P.O. Box 182, Folcroft, PA 19032

Follett. Follett Publishing Co, Div. of Follett Corp., 1010 W. Washington Blvd., Chicago, IL 60607 Tel 312-666-5858

Fortress. Fortress Press, 2900 Queen Lane, Philadelphia, PA 19129 Tel 215-848-6800

Free Pr. Free Press, 866 Third Ave., New York, NY 10022

Freeman C. Freeman, Cooper & Co., 1736 Stockton St., San Francisco, CA 94133 Tel 415-362-6171

DIRECTORY OF PUBLISHERS

French & Eur. French & European Pubns., Inc., Rockefeller Center Promenade, 610 Fifth Ave., New York, NY 10020

French Bk. French Book Corp. of America, 636 11th Ave., New York, NY 10036.

Friends Earth. Friends of the Earth, Inc., 529 Commercial St., San Francisco, CA 94111 Tel 415-391-4270

FS&G. Farrar, Straus & Giroux, Inc., 19 Union Square, W., New York, NY 10003 Tel 212-741-6900

Funk & W. Funk & Wagnalls Co., Dist. by: Thomas Y. Crowell Co., 666 Fifth Ave., New York, NY 10019

G K Hall. Hall, G. K., & Co., 70 Lincoln St., Boston, MA 02111 Tel 617-423-3990

Gale. Gale Research Co., Book Tower, Detroit, MI 48226 Tel 313-961-2242

Gambit. Gambit, Inc., 306 Dartmouth, Boston, MA 02116 Tel 617-536-0077

G&D. Grosset & Dunlap, Inc., 51 Madison Ave., New York, NY 10010 Tel 212-689-9200

Gannon. Gannon, William, P.O. Box 2610, Santa Fe, NM 87501 Tel 505-983-1579

Genealog Pub. Genealogical Publishing Co., Inc., 521-523 St. Paul Place, Baltimore, MD 21202

Glencoe. Glencoe Press, Dist. by: Macmillan Co., Riverside, NJ 08075

Godine. Godine, David R., Pub., 306 Dartmouth St., Boston, MA 02116

Goodheart. Goodheart-Willcox Co., Inc., 123 W. Taft Dr., South Holland, IL 60473 Tel 312-333-7200

Goodyear. Goodyear Publishing Co., 15115 Sunset Blvd., Pacific Palisades, CA 90272 Tel 213-459-2733

Gordian. Gordian Press, Inc., 85 Tompkins St., Staten Island, NY 10304 Tel 212-273-4700

Graphic Arts Ctr. Graphic Arts Center, 2000 N. W. Wilson, Portland, OR 97209 Tel 503-224-7777

Great Albion. Great Albion Books, Dist. by: A. S. Barnes & Co., Inc., Cranbury, NJ 08512

Green Eagle Pr. Green Eagle Press, 99 Nassau St., New York, NY 10038 Tel 212-267-2532

Greene. Greene, Stephen, Press, P. O. Box 1000, Fessenden Rd., Indian Flat, Battleboro, VT 05301 Tel 802-257-7757

Greenwood. Greenwood Press, Inc., 51 Riverside Ave., Westport, CT 06880 Tel 203-226-3571

Gregg. Gregg Press, Inc., 70 Lincoln St., Boston, MA 02111 Tel 617-423-3990

Grolier Inc. Grolier, Inc., 575 Lexington Ave., New York, NY 10022 Tel 212-751-3600

Grossman. Grossman Pubs., Inc., Dist. by: Viking Press, 625 Madison Ave., New York, NY 10022

Grove. Grove Press, Inc., 196 W. Houston St., New York, NY 10014 Tel 212-242-4900

Gryphon Hse. Gryphon House, Div. of Maya Enterprises, Inc., 1333 Connecticut Ave., N.W., Washington, DC 20036 Tel 202-223-1738

Gulf Pub. Gulf Publishing Co., P.O. Box 2608, Houston, TX 77001 Tel 713-529-4301

Hacker. Hacker Art Books, 54 W. 57th St., New York, NY 10019 Tel 212-757-1450

Hackett Pub. Hackett Publishing Co., P. O. Box 55573, 4047 N. Pennsylvania St., Indianapolis, IN 46208 Tel 317-283-8187

Hafner. Hafner Press, 866 Third Ave., New York, NY 10022 Tel 212-935-2000

Hale. Hale, E. M., & Company, 1201 S. Hastings Way, Eau Claire, WI 54701 Tel 715-832-8303

Halsted Pr. Halsted Press, Div. of John Wiley & Sons, Inc., 605 Third Ave., New York, NY 10016 Tel 212-867-9800

Hammond Inc. Hammond, Inc., Maplewood, NJ 07040 Tel 201-763-6000

Har-Row. Harper & Row Pubs., Inc., 10 E. 53rd St., New York, NY 10022 Tel 212-593-7000

HarBraceJ. Harcourt Brace Jovanovich, Inc., 757 Third Ave., New York, NY 10017 Tel 212-754-3100

Harmony. Harmony, Dist. by: Crown Pubs., Inc., 419 Park Ave., S., New York, NY 10016

Harper Mag Pr. Harper Magazine Press, 10 E. 53rd St., New York, NY 10022 Tel 212-593-7198

Hart. Hart Publishing Co., 15 W. 4th St., New York, NY 10012 Tel 212-260-2430

Hartmore. Hartmore House, Dist. by: Associated Booksellers, 147 McKinley Ave., Bridgeport, CT 06606

Harvard U Pr. Harvard Univ. Press, 79 Garden St., Cambridge, MA 02138 Tel 617-495-2600

Harvey. Harvey House, Inc., Pubs., c/o E.M. Hale & Co., 1201 South Hastings Way, Eau Claire, WI 54701

DIRECTORY OF PUBLISHERS

Haskell. Haskell House Pubs., Inc., 280 Lafayette St., New York, NY 10012 Tel 212-226-6064

Hastings. Hastings House Pubs., Inc., 10 E. 40th St., New York, NY 10016 Tel 212-689-5400

Hawthorn. Hawthorn Books, Inc., 260 Madison Ave., New York, NY 10016 Tel 212-725-7740

Hayden. Hayden Book Co., Inc., 50 Essex St., Rochelle Park, NJ 07662 Tel 201-843-0550

Hearst Bks. Hearst Books, Div. of Hearst Magazines, 250 W. 55th St., New York, NY 10019 Tel 212-757-5020

Heath. Heath, D.C., & Co., College Dept., 125 Spring St., Lexington, MA 02173 Tel 617-862-6650

Heineman. Heineman, James H., Inc., Pub., 475 Park Ave., New York, NY 10022 Tel 212-688-2028

Hennessey. Hennessey & Ingalls, Inc., 8321 Campion Dr., Los Angeles, CA 90045

Hill & Wang. Hill & Wang, Inc, Div. of Farrar, Straus & Giroux, Inc, 19 Union Square, New York, NY 10003 Tel 212-741-6900

Hillary. Hillary House Pubs., Ltd, Div. of Humanities Press, Inc., Atlantic Highlands, NJ 07716

Hippocrene Bks. Hippocrene Books, Inc., 171 Madison Ave., New York, NY 10016 Tel 212-685-4371

Hispanic Soc. Hispanic Society of America, 613 W. 155th St., New York, NY 10032 Tel 212-926-2234

HM. Houghton Mifflin Co., 2 Park St., Boston, MA 02107 Tel 617-725-5000; 551 Fifth Ave., New York, NY 10017

Holden-Day. Holden-Day, Inc., 500 Sansome St., San Francisco, CA 94111 Tel 415-433-0220

Holiday. Holiday House, Inc., 18 E. 53rd St., New York, NY 10022 Tel 212-688-0085

Holmes & Meier. Holmes & Meier Pubs., Inc., 101 Fifth Ave., New York, NY 10003 Tel 212-691-5252

Hoover Inst Pr. Hoover Institution Press, Stanford University, Stanford, CA 94305 Tel 415-321-2300

Hopkinson. Hopkinson & Blake, Pubs., 329 Fifth Ave., New York, NY 10016 Tel 212-689-5369

Horizon. Horizon Press Pubs., 156 Fifth Ave., New York, NY 10010 Tel 212-924-9225

Howard U Pr. Howard Univ. Press, 2935 Upton St. N. W., Washington, DC 20001 Tel 202-636-6100

Howell Bk. Howell Book House, Inc., 730 Fifth Ave., New York, NY 10019

HR&W. Holt, Rinehart & Winston, Inc., 383 Madison Ave., New York, NY 10017 Tel 212-688-9100

Humanities. Humanities Press, Inc., Atlantic Highlands, NJ 07716

Ind Sch Pr. Independent School Press, 51 River St., Wellesley Hills, MA 02181 Tel 617-237-2591

Ind U Pr. Indiana Univ. Press, Tenth & Morton Sts., Bloomington, IN 47401 Tel 812-337-4203

Inscape Corp. Inscape Corp., 1629 K St., N. W., Suite 5107, Washington, DC 20006

InterCulture. InterCulture Associates, Quaddick Rd., P.O. Box 277, Thompson, CT 06277 Tel 203-923-9494

Interland Pub. Interland Publishing, Inc., 799 Broadway, New York, NY 10003 Tel 212-673-8280

Intext. Intext Educational Pubs., 257 Park Ave., S., New York, NY 10010 Tel 212-533-9000

Intl Arts & Sci. International Arts & Sciences Press, Inc., 901 N. Broadway, White Plains, NY 10603 Tel 914-428-8700

Intl Pub Co. International Pubs. Co., Inc., 381 Park Ave., S., Suite 1301, New York, NY 10016 Tel 212-685-2864

Intl Pubns Serv. International Pubns. Service, 114 E. 32nd St., New York, NY 10016 Tel 212-685-9351

Intl Schol Bk Serv. International Scholarly Book Services, Inc., P.O. Box 555, Forest Grove, OR 97116

Io Pubns. Io Pubns., Dist. by: Book People, 2940 Seventh St., Berkeley, CA 94710

Iowa St U Pr. Iowa State Univ. Press, South State Ave., 112 C Press Office, Ames, IA 50010 Tel 515-294-5280

Irvington. Irvington Pubs., 551 Fifth Ave., New York, NY 10017 Tel 212-697-8100

Japan Pubns. Japan Pubns Trading Center (U.S.A.), Inc., 200 Clearbrook Rd., Elmsford, NY 10523 Tel 914-592-2077

Jewish Pubn. Jewish Publication Society of America, 1528 Walnut St., Suite 800, Philadelphia, PA 19102 Tel 215-567-4218

John Day. John Day Co., Inc., 666 Fifth Ave., New York, NY 10019 Tel 212-533-9000

Johns Hopkins. Johns Hopkins Press, Baltimore, MD 21218 Tel 301-366-9600

DIRECTORY OF PUBLISHERS

Johnson Chi. Johnson Publishing Co., Inc., 820 S. Michigan Ave., Chicago, IL 60605 Tel 312-786-7600
Johnson Repr. Johnson Reprint Corp, Subs. of Harcourt, Brace & Jovanovich, Inc., 111 Fifth Ave., New York, NY 10003 Tel 212-741-6873
Jossey-Bass. Jossey-Bass Inc., Pubs., 615 Montgomery St., San Francisco, CA 94111 Tel 415-433-1740
Julian. Julian Press Inc., Pubs., 150 Fifth Ave., New York, NY 10011 Tel 212-691-9625
Kelley. Kelley, Augustus M., Pubs., 305 Allwood Rd., Clifton, NJ 07012 Tel 201-778-3365
Kenedy. Kenedy, P. J., & Sons, Subs. of Macmillan Publishing Co., 866 Third Ave., New York, NY 10022 Tel 212-935-2000
Kennikat. Kennikat Press, Corp, Subs. of Taylor Publishing Co., 90 S. Bayles Ave., Port Washington, NY 11050 Tel 516-883-0570
Knopf. Knopf, Alfred A., Inc, Subs. of Random House, Inc., 201 E. 50th St., New York, NY 10022 Tel 212-757-2600
Kodansha. Kodansha International, Ltd., 10 E. 53rd St., New York, NY 10022
Kraus Repr. Kraus Reprint Co, Div. of Kraus-Thompson Organization, Ltd., Millwood, NY 10546
Krause Pubns. Krause Pubns., Inc., 700 E. State St., Iola, WI 54945 Tel 715-445-2219
Ktav. Ktav Publishing House, Inc., 120 E. Broadway, New York, NY 10022
L Hill. See Lawrence Hill
La Siesta. La Siesta Press, P. O. Box 406, Glendale, CA 91209 Tel 213-244-9305
La State U Pr. Louisiana State Univ. Press, Baton Rouge, LA 70803 Tel 504-388-2071
Larousse. Larousse & Co., Inc., 572 Fifth Ave., New York, NY 10036 Tel 212-575-9515
Lawrence Hill. Hill, Lawrence, & Co., Inc., 150 Fifth Ave., New York, NY 10011 Tel 212-741-3789
Lib of Congress. Library of Congress, Washington, DC 20540.
Libs Unl. Libraries Unlimited, Inc., c/o Colorado Bibliographic Institute, P.O. Box 263, Littleton, CO 80120
Lieber-Atherton. Lieber-Atherton, Inc., 1841 Broadway, New York, NY 10023 Tel 212-586-2118

Lippincott. Lippincott, J. B., Co., East Washington Sq., Philadelphia, PA 19105 Tel 215-574-4296
Little. Little, Brown & Co., 34 Beacon St., Boston, MA 02106 Tel 617-227-0730
Littlefield. Littlefield, Adams, & Co., 81 Adams Dr., Totowa, NJ 07512 Tel 201-256-8600
Liveright. Liveright Publishing Corp, Subs. of W. W. Norton Co., Inc., 500 Fifth Ave., New York, NY 10036
Lothrop. Lothrop, Lee & Shepard Co, Div. of William Morrow & Co., Inc., 105 Madison Ave., New York, NY 10016 Tel 212-889-3050
Luce. Luce, Robert B., Inc., 2000 "N" St., N. W., Washington, DC 20036 Tel 202-296-2690
Lyle Stuart. Stuart, Lyle, Inc., 120 Enterprise Ave., Secaucus, NJ 07094 Tel 201-866-4188
M Evans. Evans, M., & Co., Inc., 216 E. 49th St., New York, NY 10017 Tel 212-688-2810
McGraw. McGraw-Hill Book Co., 1221 Ave. of the Americas, New York, NY 10036 Tel 212-997-1221
McKay. McKay, David, Co., Inc., 750 Third Ave., New York, NY 10017 Tel 212-661-1700
McKinley Pub. McKinley Publishing Co., P.O. Box 77, Ocean City, NJ 08226
Macmillan. Macmillan Publishing Co., Inc., 866 Third Ave., New York, NY 10022 Tel 212-935-2000
Macrae. Macrae Smith Co., 225 S. 15th St., Philadelphia, PA 19102 Tel 215-545-4270
Manor Bks. Manor Books, Inc., 432 Park Ave., New York, NY 10016 Tel 212-686-9100
Marquis. Marquis-Who's Who Books, 200 E. Ohio St., Chicago, IL 60611 Tel 312-787-2008
Mason Charter. Mason/Charter, 641 Lexington Ave., New York, NY 10022 Tel 212-695-1555
Mayfield Pub. Mayfield Publishing Co., 285 Hamilton Ave., Palo Alto, CA 94301
Melbourne U Pr. See Intl Schol Bk Serv.
Mer. See Collins-World
Merck. Merck & Co., Inc., Rahway, NJ 07065
Merriam. Merriam, G. & C., Co, Subs. of Encyclopaedia Britannica, Inc., 47 Federal St., Springfield, MA 01101 Tel 413-734-3148
Merrill. Merrill, Charles E., Publishing Co, Div. of Bell & Howell Co., 1300 Alum Creek Dr., Columbus, OH 43216 Tel 614-258-8441

DIRECTORY OF PUBLISHERS

Messner. Messner, Julian, Inc., Dist. by: Simon & Schuster, Inc., 1 W. 39th St., New York, NY 10018

Metro Mus Art. Metropolitan Museum of Art, New York, NY 10028

Mich St U Pr. Michigan State Univ. Press, 1405 S. Harrison Rd., 25 Manly Miles Bldg., East Lansing, MI 48823 Tel 517-355-1855

Microcard Edns. Microcard Editions Books, Div. of Information Handling Services, 5500 S. Valentia Way, Englewood, CO 80110

Minn Hist. Minnesota Historical Society, 690 Cedar St., St. Paul, MN 55101 Tel 612-335-4667

MIT Pr. M. I. T. Press, 28 Carleton St., Cambridge, MA 02142 Tel 617-253-5646

Modern Lib. Modern Library, Inc., 201 E. 50th St., New York, NY 10022 Tel 212-751-2600

Monthly Rev. Monthly Review Press, 62 W. 14th St., New York, NY 10011 Tel 212-691-2555

Moore Pub Co. Moore Publishing Co., P.O. Box 3143, W. Durham Sta., Durham, NC 27705 Tel 919-286-2550

Morgan. Morgan & Morgan, Inc., 145 Palisades St., Dobbs Ferry, NY 10522 Tel 914-693-9303

Morrow. Morrow, William, & Co., Inc., 105 Madison Ave., New York, NY 10016 Tel 212-889-3050

Mosby. Mosby, C. V., Co., 11830 Westline Industrial Dr., St. Louis, MO 63141

Mountaineers. Mountaineers, P.O. Box 122, Seattle, WN 98111

Multimedia. Multimedia Publishing Corp., 100 S. Western Hwy., Blauvelt, NY 10913 Tel 914-359-5537

Mus Northern Ariz. Museum of Northern Arizona, Rte. 4, Box 720, Flagstaff, AZ 86001 Tel 602-774-2443

Museum Mod Art. Museum of Modern Art, 11 W. 53rd St., New York, NY 10019

N Ill U Pr. Northern Illinois Univ. Press, 515 Garden Rd., DeKalb, IL 60115 Tel 815-753-1826

NAL. New American Library, 1301 Ave. of the Americas, New York, NY 10019 Tel 212-956-3800

Nash Pub. Nash Publishing Corp., 1 Dupont St., Plainview, NY 11803 Tel 516-938-8100

Natl Geog. National Geographic Society, 17th & "M" Sts., N.W., Washington, DC 20036 Tel 202-296-7500

Natural Hist. Natural History Press, Dist. by: Doubleday & Co., Inc., 501 Franklin Ave., Garden City, NY 11530

Naval Inst Pr. Naval Institute Press, Annapolis, MD 21402 Tel 301-208-6110

NCTE. National Council of Teachers of English, 1111 Kenyon Rd., Urbana, IL 61801 Tel 217-328-3870

NEA. National Education Assn., 1201 16th St., N.W., Washington, DC 20036

NEASC. New England Assn., of Schools & Colleges, 13 Middlesex, Burlington, MA 01803.

Negro U Pr. Negro Universities Press, Affiliate of Greenwood Press, Inc., 51 Riverside Ave., Westport, CT 06880 Tel 203-226-3571

Nelson. Nelson, Thomas, Inc., 30 E. 42nd St., New York, NY 10017 Tel 212-697-5573

Nelson-Hall. Nelson-Hall Co., 325 W. Jackson Blvd., Chicago, IL 60606 Tel 312-922-0856

New Directions. New Directions Publishing Corp., 333 Ave. of the Americas, New York, NY 10014 Tel 212-255-0230

Newsweek. Newsweek, 444 Madison Ave., New York, NY 10022 Tel 212-350-2528

North Am Pub Co. North American Publishing Co., 401 N. Broad St., Philadelphia, PA 19108

Northland. Northland Press, P.O. Box N, Flagstaff, AZ 86001 Tel 602-774-5251

Northwestern U Pr. Northwestern Univ. Press, 1735 Benson Ave., Evanston, IL 60201 Tel 312-492-5313

Norton. Norton, W. W., & Co., Inc., 500 Fifth Ave., New York, NY 10036

Norwood Edns. Norwood Editions, P.O. Box 38, Norwood, PA 19074 Tel 215-583-4550

NW. See **Intl Pub Co.**

NY Times. New York Times Co., Book Div., 330 Madison Ave., New York, NY 10017.

NYGS. New York Graphic Society, Ltd., 11 Beacon St., Suite 503, Boston, MA 02108

NYU Pr. New York Univ. Press, Washington Square, New York, NY 10003 Tel 212-598-2882

Oceana. Oceana Pubns., Dobbs Ferry, NY 10522 Tel 914-693-1320

Octagon. Octagon Books, 19 Union Square W., New York, NY 10003 Tel 212-741-6961

Odyssey Pr. Odyssey Press, Dist. by: Bobbs-Merrill Co., Inc., 4300 W. 62nd St., Indianapolis, IN 46268

DIRECTORY OF PUBLISHERS

O'Hara. O'Hara, J. Philip, Inc., Pubs., 20 E. Huron, Chicago, IL 60611 Tel 312-787-9637

Ohio St U Pr. Ohio State Univ. Press, Hitchcock Hall, Rm. 316, 2070 Neil Ave., Columbus, OH 43210 Tel 614-422-6930

Orbis Bks. Orbis Books, Maryknoll, NY 10545 Tel 914-941-7590

Orientalia. Orientalia, Inc., 61 Fourth Ave., New York, NY 10003 Tel 212-473-6730

Oxford U Pr. Oxford Univ. Press, Inc., 200 Madison Ave., New York, NY 10016 Tel 212-679-7300

P-H. Prentice-Hall, Inc., Englewood Cliffs, NJ 07632 Tel 201-592-2000

Pa St U Pr. Pennsylvania State Univ. Press, 215 Wagner Bldg., University Park, PA 16802 Tel 814-865-1327

Pacific Bks. Pacific Books, Pubs., P.O. Box 558, Palo Alto, CA 94302 Tel 415-323-5529

Pantheon. Pantheon Books, Div. of Random House, Inc., 201 E. 50 St., New York, NY 10022 Tel 212-751-2600

Paperback Lib. Warner Paperback Library, 75 Rockefeller Plaza, New York, NY 10019 Tel 212-484-8000

Parachuting Pubns. Parachuting Pubns., P.O. Box 4232-R, Santa Barbara, CA 93103

Paragon. Paragon Book Reprint Corp., 14 E. 38th St., New York, NY 10016

Path Pr Inc NY. Pathfinder Press, Inc. (N.Y.) 410 West St., New York, NY 10003

Parker. See **P-H**

PB. Pocket Books, Inc, Div. of Simon & Schuster, Inc., 630 Fifth Ave., New York, NY 10020

Peacock Pubs. Peacock, F. T., Pubs., Inc., 401 W. Irving Park Rd., Itasca, IL 60143 Tel 312-773-1155

Pegasus. Pegasus, Affiliated with Bobbs-Merrill Co., Inc., 4300 W. 62nd St., Indianapolis, IN 46268 Tel 317-291-3100

Pendell Pub. Pendell Publishing Co., P.O. Box 1666 PT, Midland, MI 48640

Pendulum Pr. Pendulum Press, Inc., Academic Bldg., Saw Mill Rd., West Haven, CT 06516

Penguin. Penguin Books, Inc., 72 Fifth Ave., New York, NY 10011 Tel 212-924-8801

Pergamon. Pergamon Press, Inc., Maxwell House, Fairview Park, Elmsford, NY 10523 Tel 914-592-7700

Peter Smith. Smith, Peter, Publisher Inc., 6 Lexington Ave., Gloucester, MA 01930 Tel 617-525-3562

Pflaum-Standard. Pflaum/Standard, 2285 Arbor Blvd., Dayton, OH 45439

Phaidon. Phaidon Art Books, Dist. by: Praeger, 111 Fourth Ave., New York, NY 10003

Phila Bk Co. Philadelphia Book Co., Inc., Philadelphia, PA 19127 Tel 215-482-6100

Philos Lib. Philosophical Library, Inc., 15 E. 40th St., New York, NY 10016 Tel 212-683-2945

Pitman. Pitman Publishing Corp., 6 Davis Dr., Belmont, CA 94002 Tel 415-592-7810

Playboy. Playboy Press, Div. of Playboy Enterprises, Inc., 919 N. Michigan Ave., Chicago, IL 60611 Tel 312-751-8000

Plays. Plays, Inc., 8 Arlington St., Boston, MA 02116 Tel 617-536-7420

Plenum Pub. Plenum Publishing Corp., 227 W. 17th St., New York, NY 10011 Tel 212-255-0713

Popular Lib. Popular Library, Inc, Unit of CBS Pubns., 600 Third Ave., New York, NY 10011 Tel 212-661-4200

Porcupine Pr. Porcupine Press, Inc., 1317 Filbert St., Philadelphia, PA 19107 Tel 215-563-2288

Porter. Porter, Bern, 106 High St., Belfast, ME 04915

Potomac. Potomac Books, Inc., Pubs., P. O. Box 40604, Palisades Sta., Washington, DC 20016 Tel 202-338-5774

Potter. Potter, Clarkson N., Inc., Dist. by: Crown Pubs., 419 Park Ave., S., New York, NY 10016

Praeger. Praeger Pubs., 111 Fourth Ave., New York, NY 10003 Tel 212-254-4100

Princeton U Pr. Princeton Univ. Press, 41 William St., Princeton, NJ 08540 Tel 609-452-4900

Prindle. Prindle, Weber & Schmidt, Inc., 20 Newbury St., Boston, MA 02116

Prometheus Bks. Prometheus Books, 923 Kensington Ave., Buffalo, NY 14215 Tel 716-837-0306

Pub Aff Pr. Public Affairs Press, 419 New Jersey Ave., Washington, DC 20003 Tel 202-544-3024

Putnam. Putnam's, G. P., Sons, 200 Madison Ave., New York, NY 10016 Tel 212-883-5500

Pyramid Pubns. Pyramid Pubns., Inc., 9 Garden St, Moonachie, NJ 07074 Tel 201-641-3311

Quadrangle. Quadrangle/The New York Times Co., 10 E. 53rd St., New York, NY 10022 Tel 212-593-7800

DIRECTORY OF PUBLISHERS

R West. West, Richard, Box 6404, Philadelphia, PA 19145
Rand. Rand McNally & Co., P.O. Box 7600, Chicago, IL 60680 Tel 312-673-9100
Random. Random House, Inc., 201 E. 50th St., New York, NY 10022 Tel 212-751-2600
Raven. Raven Press, 1140 Ave. of the Americas, New York, NY 10036 Tel 212-575-0335
Readers Digest Pr. Reader's Digest Press, Dist. by: E. P. Dutton & Co., Inc., 201 Park Ave., S., New York, NY 10003
Regents Pub. Regents Publishing Co., Inc., 2 Park Ave., New York, NY 10016 Tel 212-889-2780
Regnery. Regnery, Henry, Co., 180 N. Michigan Ave., Chicago, IL 60601 Tel 312-782-9181
Reidel Pub. Reidel, D., Publishing Co., 160 Old Derby St., Hingham, MA 02043
Research Pubns. Research Pubns., P. O. Box 801, Glen Rock, NJ 07452
Revell. Revell, Fleming H., Co., Old Tappan, NJ 07675 Tel 201-768-8060
Rio Grande. Rio Grande Press, Inc., Glorieta, NM 87535 Tel 505-757-6275
Rodale Pr Inc. Rodale Press, Inc., 33 E. Minor St., Emmaus, PA 18049 Tel 215-965-9881
Ronald. Ronald Press Co., 79 Madison Ave., New York, NY 10016 Tel 212-683-9070
Rosen Pr. Rosen, Richards, Press, Inc., 29 E. 21st St., New York, NY 10010 Tel 212-777-3017
Routledge & Kegan. Routledge & Kegan Paul, Ltd., 9 Park St., Boston, MA 02108 Tel 617-742-5863
Rowman. Rowman & Littlefield, Inc, Div. of Littlefield, Adams, & Co., 81 Adams Dr., Totowa, NJ 07512 Tel 201-256-8600
Roy. Roy Pubs., Inc., 30 E. 74th St., New York, NY 10021 Tel 212-879-5935
Russell. Russell & Russell, Div. of Atheneum Pubs., 122 E. 42nd St., New York, NY 10017 Tel 212-661-4500
Russell Sage. Russell Sage Foundation, 230 Park Ave., New York, NY 10017 Tel 212-689-6622
Rutgers U Pr. Rutgers Univ. Press, 30 College Ave., New Brunswick, NJ 08903 Tel 201-247-1766
S F Bk. S. F. Book Imports, P.O. Box 526, San Francisco, CA 94101
S G Phillips. Phillips, S. G., Inc., 305 W. 86th St., New York, NY 10024

S Ill U Pr. Southern Illinois Univ. Press, P.O. Box 3697, Carbondale, IL 62901 Tel 618-453-2281
S Meth U Pr. Southern Methodist Univ. Press, Dallas, TX 75275 Tel 214-692-2263
Sams. Sams, Howard W., & Co., Inc, Subs. of ITT, 4300 W. 62nd St., Box 558, Indianapolis, IN 46206 Tel 317-291-3100
S&S. Simon & Schuster, Inc., 630 Fifth Ave., New York, NY 10020 Tel 212-245-6400
Sargent. Sargent, Porter, Inc., 11 Beacon St., Boston, MA 02108 Tel 617-523-1670
Sat Rev Pr. Saturday Review Press, 201 Park Ave., S., New York, NY 10017
Saunders. Saunders, W. B., Co, Subs. of Columbia Broadcasting System, W. Washington Square, Philadelphia, PA 19105 Tel 215-574-4700
Scarecrow. Scarecrow Press, Inc, Subs. of Grolier Educational Corp., 52 Liberty St., Box 656, Metuchen, NJ 08840 Tel 201-548-8600
Schocken. Schocken Books, Inc., 200 Madison Ave., New York, NY 10016 Tel 212-685-6500
Schoenhof. Schoenhof's Foreign Books, Inc., 1280 Massachusetts Ave., Cambridge, MA 02138
Schol Bk Serv. Scholastic Book Services, Div. of Scholastic Magazines, 50 W. 44th St., New York, NY 10036 Tel 212-867-7700
Scholarly. Scholarly Press, 22929 Industrial Dr., E., Saint Clair Shores, MI 48080 Tel 313-773-4250
Scott F. Scott, Foresman & Co., 1900 E. Lake Ave., Glenview, IL 60025 Tel 312-729-3000
Scribner. Scribner's, Charles, Sons, 597 Fifth Ave., New York, NY 10017 Tel 212-486-2700
Scrimshaw. Scrimshaw Press, P.O. Box 728, Cape Cod, MA 02632
Seabury. Seabury Press, Inc., 815 Second Ave., New York, NY 10017 Tel 212-557-0500
Seahawk Pr. Seahawk Press, 6840 S.W. 92nd St., Miami, FL 33156 Tel 305-667-4051
Serendipity. Serendipity Books, 1790 Shattuck Ave., Berkeley, CA 94709 Tel 415-841-7455
Sheed. Sheed & Ward, Inc., 6700 Squibb Rd., Mission, KS 66202 Tel 913-362-1523
Shoe String. Shoe String Press, Inc., 995 Sherman Ave., Hamden, CT 06514 Tel 203-248-6307

DIRECTORY OF PUBLISHERS

Sierra. Sierra Club Books, 1050 Mills Tower, San Francisco, CA 94104

Silver. Silver Burdett Co, Div. of General Learning Co., 250 James St., Morristown, NJ 07960 Tel 201-536-0400

Sinauer Assoc. Sinauer Associates, Inc., Sunderland, MA 01375

Smithsonian. Smithsonian Institution Press, Washington, DC 20560 Tel 202-381-5143

South Asia Bks. South Asia Books, P. O. Box 502, Columbia, MO 65201 Tel 314-657-2239

Spanish Bk. Spanish Book Corp. of America, 636 11th Ave., New York, NY 10036.

Speller. Speller, Robert, & Sons, Pub., Inc., 10 E. 23rd St., New York, NY 10010 Tel 212-477-9953

Springer-Verlag. Springer-Verlag New York, Inc., 175 Fifth Ave., New York, NY 10010 Tel 212-673-2660

St Martin. St. Martin's Press, Inc., 175 Fifth Ave., New York, NY 10010 Tel 212-674-5151

Stackpole. Stackpole Books, Cameron & Keller Sts., Harrisburg, PA 17105 Tel 717-234-5091

Stanford U Pr. Stanford Univ. Press, Stanford, CA 94305 Tel 415-323-9471

State Hist Soc Wis. State Historical Society of Wisconsin, 816 State St., Madison, WI 53706 Tel 608-262-9603

State U NY Pr. State Univ. of New York Press, 99 Washington Ave., Albany, NY 12210 Tel 518-474-6050

Stein & Day. Stein & Day, 7 E. 48th St., New York, NY 10017 Tel 212-753-7285

Sterling. Sterling Publishing Co., Inc., 419 Park Ave., S., New York, NY 10016 Tel 212-532-7160

Stewart. Stewart, Henry, Inc., 249 Bowen Rd., East Aurora, NY 14052

Straughan. Straughan's Book Shop, Inc., 220 N. Elm St., Greensboro, NC 27401

Stravon. Stravon Educational Press, 595 Madison Ave., New York, NY 10022 Tel 212-371-2880

Swallow. Swallow Press, 1139 S. Wabash Ave., Chicago, IL 60605 Tel 312-922-8377

Syracuse U Pr. Syracuse Univ. Press, 1011 E. Water St., Syracuse, NY 13210 Tel 315-423-2596

T Y Crowell. Crowell, Thomas Y., Co., 666 Fifth Ave., New York, NY 10003 Tel 212-489-2200

Tab Bks. TAB Books, Blue Ridge Summit, PA 17214 Tel 717-794-2191

Taplinger. Taplinger Publishing Co., Inc., 200 Park Ave., S., New York, NY 10003 Tel 212-533-6110

Temple U Pr. Temple Univ. Press, Philadelphia, PA 19122 Tel 215-787-8787

Tex St Hist Assn. Texas State Historical Assn., Richardson Hall, 2/306 Univ. Sta., Austin, TX 78712 Tel 512-471-1525

Theatre Arts. Theatre Arts Books, 333 Ave. of the Americas, New York, NY 10014 Tel 212-675-1815

Theos Pub Hse. Theosophical Publishing House, P.O. Box 270, Wheaton, IL 60187 Tel 312-665-0123

Third Pr. Third Press-Joseph Okpaku Publishing Co., Inc., 444 Central Park, W., New York, NY 10025 Tel 212-866-9140

Time-Life. Time-Life Books, Div. of Time, Inc., Time & Life Bldg., Rockefeller Center, New York, NY 10020 Tel 212-586-1212

Times Mirror Mag. Times Mirror Magazine, 380 Madison Ave., New York, NY 10017 Tel 212-697-4070

Tower. Tower Pubns., Inc., Orders to: Belmont-Tower Books, Inc., 185 Madison Ave., New York, NY 10016 Tel 212-679-7707

Transaction Bks. Transaction Books, Rutgers State Univ., New Brunswick, NJ 08903 Tel 201-932-2280

Transatlantic. Transatlantic Arts, Inc., N. Village Green, Levittown, NY 11756 Tel 516-735-4777

Trident. Trident Press, Div. of Simon & Schuster, Inc., 630 Fifth Ave., New York, NY 10020 Tel 212-245-6400

Tudor. Tudor Publishing Co., 31 W. 46th St., New York, NY 10036

Twayne. Twayne Pubs., Dist. by: G. K. Hall & Co., 70 Lincoln St., Boston, MA 02111

Two Continents. Two Continents Publishing Group, Inc., 30 E. 42nd St., New York, NY 10017 Tel 212-661-7520

U Alaska Inst Res. Univ. of Alaska, Institute of Social, Economic, & Government Research, College, AK 99701 Tel 907-479-7436

U of Ala Pr. Univ. of Alabama Press, Drawer 2877, University, AL 35486 Tel 205-348-5180

U of Ariz Pr. Univ. of Arizona Press, P.O. Box 3398, Tucson, AZ 85722

U of Cal Pr. Univ. of California Press, 2223 Fulton St., Berkeley, CA 94720 Tel 415-642-4247

DIRECTORY OF PUBLISHERS

U of Chicago Pr. Univ. of Chicago Press, 5801 Ellis Ave., Chicago, IL 60637 Tel 312-753-1234

U of Ga Pr. Univ. of Georgia Press, Waddell Hall, Athens, GA 30602 Tel 404-542-2830

U of Ill Pr. Univ. of Illinois Press, Urbana, IL 61801 Tel 217-333-0950

U of Mass Pr. Univ. of Massachusetts Press, P.O. Box 429, Amherst, MA 01002 Tel 413-545-2217

U of Miami Pr. Univ. of Miami Press, Drawer 9088, Coral Gables, FL 33124 Tel 305-284-5885

U of Mich Pr. Univ. of Michigan Press, 615 E. University, Ann Arbor, MI 48106 Tel 313-764-1817

U of Minn Pr. Univ. of Minnesota Press, 2037 University Ave., S.E., Minneapolis, MN 55455 Tel 612-313-3266

U of Mo Pr. Univ. of Missouri Press, 107 Swallow Hall, Columbia, MO 65201 Tel 314-882-7641

U of NC Pr. Univ. of North Carolina Press, P.O Box 2288, Chapel Hill, NC 27514 Tel 919-933-2105

U of Nebr Pr. Univ. of Nebraska Press, 901 N. 17th St., Lincoln, NB 68588 Tel 402-472-3581

U of Nev Pr. Univ. of Nevada Press, Reno, NE 89507 Tel 702-784-6573

U of NM Pr. Univ. of New Mexico Press, Albuquerque, NM 87131 Tel 505-277-2346

U of Notre Dame Pr. Univ. of Notre Dame Press, Notre Dame, IN 46556 Tel 219-283-6346

U of Okla Pr. Univ. of Oklahoma Press, 1005 Asp Ave., Norman, OK 73069 Tel 405-325-5111

U of Pa Pr. Univ. of Pennsylvania Press, 3933 Walnut St., Philadelphia, PA 19174 Tel 215-594-6261

U of Pittsburgh Pr. Univ. of Pittsburgh Press, 127 N. Bellefield Ave., Pittsburgh, PA 15260 Tel 412-621-3500

U of S Dakota Pr. Univ. of South Dakota Press, Vermillion, SD 57069 Tel 605-677-8531

U of SC Pr. Univ. of South Carolina Press, Columbia, SC 29208 Tel 803-777-5243

U of Tenn Pr. Univ. of Tennessee Press, 293 Communications Bldg., Knoxville, TN 37916 Tel 615-974-3321

U of Tex Pr. Univ. of Texas Press, P.O. Box 7819, University Sta., Austin, TX 78712 Tel 512-471-7233

U of Toronto Pr. Univ. or Toronto Press, Orders to: 33 E. Tupper St., Buffalo, NY 14208

U of Wash Pr. Univ. of Washington Press, Seattle, WN 98105 Tel 206-543-4050

U of Wis Pr. Univ. of Wisconsin Press, P.O. Box 1379, Madison, WI 53701 Tel 608-262-1116

U Pr of Hawaii. Univ. Press of Hawaii, 2840 Kolowalu St., Honolulu, HI 96822 Tel 808-536-6051

U Pr of Kansas. Univ. Press of Kansas, 366 Watson Library, Lawrence, KS 66045 Tel 918-864-4154

U Pr of Ky. Univ. Press of Kentucky, Lexington, KY 40506 Tel 606-258-2951

U Pr of Va. Univ. Press of Virginia, P.O. Box 3608, University Sta., Charlottesville, VA 22903

UAHC. Union of American Hebrew Congregations, 838 Fifth Ave., New York, NY 10021 Tel 212-249-0100

UNESCO. See **Unipub**

Ungar. Ungar, Frederick, Publishing Co., Inc., 250 Park Ave., S., New York, NY 10003 Tel 212-473-7885

Unipub. Unipub, Inc, a Xerox Education Co., P.O. Box 433, Murray Hill Sta., New York, NY 10016 Tel 212-686-4707

Unity Pr. Unity Press, P.O. Box 1037, Santa Cruz, CA 95061 Tel 408-476-5711

Univ Bks. University Books, Inc, Div. of Lyle Stuart, Inc., 120 Enterprise Ave., Secaucus, NJ 07094 Tel 212-736-1141

Universe. Universe Books, Inc., 381 Park Ave., S., New York, NY 10016 Tel 212-689-0276

US Govt Ptg Off. United States Govt. Printing Office, Div. of Public Documents, Washington, DC 20402.

US Pubs. U. S. Pubs. Assn., Inc., 46 Lafayette Ave., New Rochelle, NY 10801

Van Nos Reinhold. Van Nostrand Reinhold Co, Div. of Litton Educational Publishing, Inc., 450 W. 33rd St., New York, NY 10001 Tel 212-594-8660

Vanguard. Vanguard Press, Inc., 424 Madison Ave., New York, NY 10017 Tel 212-753-3906

Vanous. Vanous, Arthur, Co., 616 Kinderkamack Rd., Riveredge, NJ 07661 Tel 201-265-7555

Verry. Verry, Lawrence, Inc., 16 Holmes St., Mystic, CT 06355 Tel 203-536-1212

Viking Pr. Viking Press, Inc., 625 Madison Ave., New York, NY 10022 Tel 212-755-4330

DIRECTORY OF PUBLISHERS

Vinebrook Prods. Vinebrook Productions, Inc., P.O. Box U, Bedford, MA 01730 Tel 617-275-2280

W H Freeman. Freeman, W. H., & Co., 660 Market St., San Francisco, CA 94104 Tel 415-391-5870

Wadsworth Pub. Wadsworth Publishing Co., Inc., 10 Davis Dr., Belmont, CA 94002 Tel 415-592-1300

Walden Bk Co. Walden Book Co., Dist. by: Dial-Delacorte, 1 Dag Hammarskjold Plaza, 245 E. 47th St., New York, NY 10017

Walker & Co. Walker & Co., 720 Fifth Ave., New York, NY 10019 Tel 212-265-3632

Warne. Warne, Frederick, & Co., Inc., 101 Fifth Ave., New York, NY 10003 Tel 212-675-1151

Washburn. Washburn, Ives, Inc, Subs. of David McKay Co., Inc., 750 Third Ave., New York, NY 10017 Tel 212-661-1700

Water Info. Water Information Center, Inc., 14 Vanderventer Ave., Rm 200, Port Washington, NY 11050 Tel 516-883-6780

Watson-Guptill. Watson-Guptill Pubns., Inc., 1 Astor Plaza, New York, NY 10036 Tel 212-764-1300

Watts. Watts, Franklin, Inc, Subs. of Grolier Inc., 845 Third Ave., New York, NY 10022 Tel 212-751-3600

Weatherhill. Weatherhill, John, Inc., 149 Madison Ave., New York, NY 10016 Tel 212-889-6970

Wesleyan U Pr. Wesleyan Univ. Press, 365 Washington St., Middletown, CT 06457 Tel 203-347-6965

Western Pub. Western Publishing Co., Inc., 850 Third Ave., New York, NY 10022 Tel 212-753-8500

Westminster. Westminster Press, Room 905, Witherspoon Bldg., Philadelphia, PA 19107 Tel 215-735-6722

Weybright. Weybright & Talley, Inc, Div. of David McKay, Inc., 750 Third Ave., New York, NY 10017 Tel 212-490-1155

Wiley. Wiley, John, & Sons, Inc., 605 Third Ave., New York, NY 10016 Tel 212-867-9800

Williams & Wilkins. Williams & Wilkins Co., 428 E. Preston St., Baltimore, MD 21202 Tel 301-528-4000

Wilson. Wilson, H. W., 950 University Ave., Bronx, NY 10452 Tel 212-588-8400

Winchester Pr. Winchester Press, 205 E. 42nd St., New York, NY 10017 Tel 212-679-6301

Winthrop. Winthrop Publishing Co, Subs. of Prentice-Hall, Inc., 17 Dunster St., Cambridge, MA 02138 Tel 617-868-1750

Wm C Brown. Brown, William C., Co., Pubs., 2460 Kerper Blvd., Dubuque, IA 52001 Tel 319-588-1451

Word Bks. Word, Inc., P.O. Box 1790, Waco, TX 76703 Tel 817-772-7650

Worth. Worth Pubs., Inc., 444 Park Ave., S., New York, NY 10016

Writer. Writer, Inc., 8 Arlington St., Boston, MA 02116 Tel 617-536-7420

WSP. Washington Square Press, Inc, Div. of Simon & Schuster, Inc., 630 Fifth Ave., New York, NY 10020

Wyden. Wyden, Peter H., Inc., Dist. by: David McKay Co., Inc., 750 Third Ave., New York, NY 10017

Xerox College. Xerox College Publishing, a Xerox Education Co., 191 Spring St., Lexington, MA 02173 Tel 617-861-1670

Yale U Pr. Yale Univ. Press, 92A Yale Sta., New Haven, CT 06520 Tel 203-432-4969

York Pr. York Press, Inc., 101 E. 32nd St., Baltimore, MD 21218 Tel 301-235-5505

Zolar. Zolar Publishing Co., 335 W. 52nd St., New York, NY 10019

Sources for Foreign Books

French (f); German (G); Russian (R); Spanish (S). Prices quoted in the entries are not stable and may vary from store to store.

Adler's Foreign Books, Inc. 162 Fifth Ave., New York, NY 10010 (F, G)

European Book Center. P.O. B. 4 1700 Fribourg 2 Bourg Switzerland

Four Continent Book Store. 156 Fifth Ave., New York, NY 10011 (R)

French Book Corporation of America. 636 11th Ave., New York, NY 10036 (F)

Gerald J. Fuchs. 2061 Broadway New York, NY 10025 (G)

Larousse & Co., Inc. 572 Fifth Ave., New York, NY 10036 (F)

Spanish Book Corporation of America. 610 Fifth Ave., New York, NY 10003 (S)

INDEX

Computerization of this edition has necessitated several modifications in style in order to adapt to the particular program used to generate the data for this index. Therefore, the user should note the following adjustments in the order and style before looking up author, subject or title information:

1. *Filing.* Wherever possible identical data has been filed in the familiar sequence of author, subject, title. In all other cases the information will file in strict alphabetical order:
   Agee. Ohlin, Peter, 3764
   Agee, James. Agee on Film, 3263
   AGEE, JAMES, 3764
   Agee on Film. Agee, James, 3263
2. *Subjects.* Capitalized entries refer to subject classifications. Subjects with chronological significance have their dates in parentheses to avoid confusion with entry numbers. See U.S. entry and subdivisions.
3. *Entry Numbers.* Listings in the index refer to entry numbers found in the main text, not page numbers.

A. F. of L. in the Time of Gompers. Taft, Philip, 1447
A L A Intellectual Freedom Manual. ALA Office for Intellectual Freedom, compiled by. 19
Aaron Burr, the Proud Pretender. Alexander, Holmes, 5972
Aaron, Daniel and Bendiner, Robert, eds. The Strenuous Decade, 6130
Aaron, Richard. John Locke, 651
Abbott, Agatin T. *see* MacDonald, Gordon A.
Abbott, Edwin A. Flatland, 1927
Abbott, Frank F. History and Description of Roman Political Institutions, 4919
Abbott, R. Tucker. American Seashells, 242
———. Kingdom of the Seashell, 2385
Abboushi, W. F. Political Systems of the Middle East in the 20th Century, 1181
ABBREVIATIONS, 156, 169
Abbreviations Dictionary. De Sola, Ralph, 169
ABC's of Citizens Band Radio. Buckwalter, Len, 2651
ABC's of Hi-Fi and Stereo. Fantel, Hans, 2655
Abdul, Raoul, *see* Lomax, Alan
Abel, Elie. The Missile Crisis, 6163
Abels, Jules. Man on Fire, 5975
Abenteuer Eines Blotbentles un Andere Geschichten. Boll, Heinrich, 4039
Abernethy, Robert G. Introduction to Tomorrow, 6099
Abigail Adams and Her Time. Richards, Laura E, 5971
Abolitionism. Sorin, Gerald, 1238

ABOLITIONISTS, 1224, 1238, 1289, 1291
Abolitionists, Together with Personal Memories of the Struggle for Human Rights, 1830-1964. Hume, John, 1289
ABORTION, 886, 2551-2552
Abortion Controversy. Sarvis, Betty and Rodman, Hyman. 886
About Russia. Cartier-Bresson, Henri, 4763
About Three Bricks Shy of a Load. Blount, Roy, 3361
Abraham, Henry J. Freedom and the Court, 1260
Abraham Lincoln. Sandburg, Carl, 6035
Abraham Lincoln. Thomas, Benjamin P, 6036
Abrahams, Roger D. Positively Black, 1824
Abrams, Meyer H., ed. English Romantic Poets, 3789
———. A Glossary of Literary Terms, 331
———. The Mirror and the Lamp, 3462
Abry, Emile, et al. Histoire Illustrée de la Littérature Française, 4103
Abu-Lughod, Ibrahim, ed. The Arab-Israeli Confrontation of June, 1967, 5647
Abyssian Crisis. Hardie, Frank, 5721
Academia Española. Diccionario de la Lengua Española, 183
Academic Library Buildings. Ellsworth, Ralph E, 20
Academy for Educational Development Staff, *see* Eurich, Alvin C.
ACCIDENT PREVENTION, 2570
Accomplices of Silence. Miyoshi, Masao, 4617
ACCULTURATION, 1279
ACHEBE, CHINUA, 4633
Acheson, Dean. Present at the Creation, 1324

INDEX

Achievement of T. S. Eliot. Matthiessen, Francis O, 3578
Achievement of William Faulkner. Millgate, Michael, 3734
Achinstein, Peter. Concepts of Science, 1909
Ackerknecht, Erwin H. History and Geography of the Most ImportantDiseases, 2560
Ackley, Charles Walton. The Modern Military in American Society, 1066
Ackley, Clifford, ed. Private Realities, 3122
ACRONYMS, 169
Across the Pacific. Iriye, Akira, 929
Across the Wide Missouri. DeVoto, Bernard A, 6230
ACTING, 3280, 3293, 3296, 3310, 3323
An Actor Prepares. Stanislavski, Constantin, 3296
ACUPUNCTURE, 2581-2582
Acupuncture. Duke, Marc, 2581
Acupuncture. Mann, Felix, 2582
Adamczewski, Jan. Nicolaus Copernicus and His Epoch, 1972
ADAMS, ABIGAIL (SMITH), 5971
Adams, Ansel. Ansel Adams, 3126
———. Artificial Light Photography, 3100
———. Camera and Lens, 3110
———. Natural Light Photography, 3101
———. The Negative, 3106
Adams, Hazard. Lady Gregory, 3894
Adams, James T., ed. Album of American History, 448
———. Atlas of American History, 391
———. Dictionary of American History, 450
———. History of New England, 6188
Adams, Jeremy DuQuesnay. Patterns of Medieval Society, 4993
ADAMS, JOHN, 5932
Adams, John C. The Globe Playhouse, 3318
Adams, John C. and Barile, Paolo. The Government of Republican Italy, 1167
ADAMS, JOHN QUINCY, 5990-5991
Adams, Marion. The German Tradition, 4753
Adams, Michael, ed. The Middle East, 442
ADAMS, SAMUEL, 5936
ADAPTATION (BIOLOGY), 2194
Adburgham, Alison. Women in Print, 3918
Adcock, C. J. Fundamentals of Psychology, 559
Adcock, Frank E. Greek and Macedonian Art of War, 1654
ADDAMS, JANE, 1692-1693
Adelman, Morris A. The World Petroleum Market, 1520
Adelson, Alan. SDS, 1783
Adler, Cy A. Ecological Fantasies, 939
Adler, Irving. The Changing Tools of Science, 1912
Adler, Selig. The Uncertain Giant, 1325
Admiral of the Ocean Sea. Morison, Samuel E, 5889
Adoff, Arnold, ed. Black on Black, 1008
———. The Poetry of Black America, 3668
ADOLESCENCE, 545
Adrian, Charles R. and Press, Charles. Governing Urban America, 1627
Advanced First Aid and Emergency Care. American National Red Cross Editors, 2569
Advancing the Frontier, 1830-1960. Foreman, Grant, 5769
ADVENTURE AND ADVENTURERS, 2129
Adventuring Among Words. Partridge, Eric, 1871
ADVERTISING, 2855-2859
Advertising. Cohen, Dorothy, 2855
Advertising. Mandell, Maurice, 2857
Ady, Julia M. Beatrice d'Este, Duchess of Milan, 1475-1497, 5430
A.E.C.T. Standards for Cataloging Nonprint Materials. 45
Aeneid. Vergilius Maro, Publius, 4414
Aerobics. Cooper, Kenneth H, 2536
AERONAUTICS, 2713, 2716, 6274
  HISTORY, 2711-2712, 2714-2715, 2717, 2719-2720
Aeschylus. Plays, 4456
Aesop. Aesop's Fables, 1848
Aesop's Fables. Aesop, 1848
AESTHETICS, 507, 2880, 2909, 3018
Affair of Gabrielle Russier. Russier, Gabrielle, 1738
Affluent Society. Galbraith, John Kenneth, 1417
AFRICA, 1097, 4793, 5698-5699, 5722-5723
  BIBLIOGRAPHY, 72
  CIVILIZATION, 4790, 4792, 5694, 5700
  DICTIONARIES AND ENCYCLOPEDIAS, 443
  ECONOMIC CONDITIONS, 1098, 1415, 5694
  HISTORICAL GEOGRAPHY — MAPS, 390
  HISTORY, 1239, 4791-4792, 4985, 5695-5697, 5700-5714, 5724, 5730-5735, 5737-5738
  POLITICS, 1096, 1098, 1188
  RELIGION, 872-873
Africa. Brown, Leslie, 2271
Africa. Davidson, Basil, 5695
Africa. Uppal, J. S. and Salkever, Louis K., eds. 1415

Africa and Africans. Bohannan, Paul and Curtin, Philip. 4790
Africa Counts. Zaslovsky, Claudia, 1940
Africa from Early Times to 1800. McEwan, P. J., ed, 5703
Africa in Social Change. Lloyd, Peter C, 1096
Africa Independent. 1188
Africa Since 1800. Oliver, Roland A. and Atmore, Anthony. 5707
Africa Since 1875. Hallett, Robin, 5711
AFRICA, SOUTH, 1708, 5736
    RACE QUESTION, 1049, 1244, 5734
    SOCIAL CONDITIONS, 1099
Africa South of the Sahara. Grove, Alfred T, 5698
Africa, Thomas W. Rome of the Caesars, 4941
Africa to 1875. Hallett, Robin, 5712
African Authors. Herdeck, Donald E, 352
An African Bourgeoisie. Kuper, Leo, 1099
AFRICAN DRAMA, 4631, 4634
African Encyclopedia. Kajubi, Senteza, et al, eds. 443
African Folktales and Sculpture. Radin, Paul and Sweeney, James J., eds. 1836
African Genesis. Ardrey, Robert, 2192
African Images. Scheob, Harold, ed, 4628
African Kingdoms. Davidson, Basil, 5696
AFRICAN LITERATURE, 351-352, 4624-4625, 4629
African Past. Davidson, Basil, 5697
AFRICAN POETRY, 3495, 4630
African Poetry. Beier, Ulli, ed, 4630
African Religions and Philosophy. Mbiti, John, 873
African Sculpture. Segy, L, 2993
African Sculpture Speaks. Segy, L, 2994
African Textiles and Decorative Arts. Sieber, Roy, 3015
African Voices. Rutherfoord, Peggy, ed, 4629
After Conviction. Goldfarb, Ronald L, 1729
After the Irish Renaissance. Hogan, Robert G, 3854
Aftermath of the Napoleonic Wars. Schenk, Hans G, 5061
Agate, James. Oscar Wilde and the Theatre, 3877
Age of Adventure. De Santillana, Giorgio, ed, 627
Age of Analysis. White, Morton, ed, 639
Age of Arthur. Morris, John, 5188
Age of Attila. Gordon, Colin D, 5012
Age of Belief. Fremantle, Anne, ed, 628
Age of Charlemagne. Bullough, Donald, 5373
Age of Discontinuity. Drucker, Peter, 1083

Age of Enlightenment. Fellows, Otis E. and Torrey, N. L. 4100
Age of Fiction. Brée, Germaine and Guiton, Margaret. 4267
An Age of Fiction. Karl, Frederick R, 3934
Age of Fighting Sail. Forester, Cecil S, 5985
Age of Ideology. Aiken, Henry D., ed, 634
Age of Jackson. Schlesinger, Arthur M., Jr, 5996
Age of Louis XIV. Voltaire, Francois M. de, 5388
Age of Metternich, 1814-1848. May, Arthur J, 5341
Age of Mountaineering. Ullman, James R, 3395
Age of Reconnaissance. Parry, John H, 4703
Age of Reform. Hofstadter, Richard, 6110
Age of Rembrandt and Vermeer. Nash, J. M, 3071
Age of Revolution, Europe. Hobshawm, Eric J, 5056
Age of Roosevelt. Schlesinger, Arthur M., Jr, 6144
Age of the Baroque. Friedrich, Carl J, 5041
Age of the Democratic Revolution. A Political History of Europe and America, 1760-1800. Palmer, Robert R, 5044
Age of the Great Depression, 1929-1941. Wecter, Dixon, 6131
Age of the Vikings. Sawyer, P. H, 5537
Age of Transition. MacDonald, Donald F, 5259
Agee. Ohlin, Peter, 3764
Agee, James. Agee on Film, 3263
AGEE, JAMES, 3764
Agee on Film. Agee, James, 3263
AGGRESSION (PSYCHOLOGICAL), 2355
AGNEW, SPIRO THEODORE, 6173
Agnon, Shmuel Y. Guest for the Night, 4587
————. Two Tales, 4588
Agony and Epitaph. Hofstadter, Albert, 507
Agony of the American Left. Lasch, Christopher, 1249
AGRESSIVENESS, 571-572
AGRICULTURAL PESTS, 2780
Agricultural Thought in the 20th Century. McGovern, George S., ed, 1511
AGRICULTURE
    ECONOMIC ASPECTS, 1394, 1511-1512, 1519
    HISTORY, 2772

INDEX

Aguilar, Luis E. Cuba Nineteen Thirty-Three, 5826
Agus, Jacob B. Evolution of Jewish Thought, 857
———. The Vision and the Way, 858
Ahern, James F. Police in Trouble, 1704
Ahlstrom, Sydney E. A Religious History of the American People, 715
Aiken, Conrad. Selected Poems, 3594
Aiken, Henry D., ed. The Age of Ideology, 634
AIR POLLUTION, 2160, 2562, 2565-2566, 2709
Air Pollution. Bowen, D. H. Michael, 2709
Airliners Between the Wars, 1919 to 1939. Munson, Kenneth, 2724
Airliners Since 1946. Munson, Kenneth, 2725
AIRPLANES, 2676-2677, 2712, 2715, 2719, 2721, 2724-2725, 2728-2731
Airship. Collier, Basil, 2732
AIRSHIPS, 1806, 2732-2736
Akhmatova, Anna. Works, 4505
Aku-Aku. Heyerdahl, Thor, 4845
Al Smith. Josephson, Matthew, 6126
ALASKA, 2713, 4738, 4839-4840, 6247-6249
Alaska. Hulley, Clarence C, 6249
Alaska. Morris, John J., ed, 4839
Alaska. National Geographic Society, ed, 4840
Alaska and Its Wildlife. Sage, Bryan L, 2275
Alaska Gold Rush. Wharton, David B, 6251
Alaska Pipeline. Berry, Mary C, 1521
Alaska Pipeline Report. Tussing, Arlon R, 1522
Alba, Victor. The Latin Americans, 6252
Albee, Edward. American Dream, 3687
———. Sandbox; Sad Death of Bessie Smith, 3688
———. Tiny Alice, 3689
———. Who's Afraid of Virginia Woolf, 3690
ALBEE, EDWARD, 3702
Albert Einstein. Hoffman, Banesh and Dukas, Helen. 2025
Albert J. Beveridge. Braeman, John, 6109
Albert Schweitzer. Brabazon, James, 661
Albert Schweitzer. Schweitzer, Albert, 663
Alberts, David. Pantomime, 3322
Albertson, Chris. Bessie, 3228

Alborg, Juan Luis. Hora Actual Dela Novela Espanola, 4308
Albrecht, Robert L., et al. Basic, 466
Albrecht-Carrié, René, ed. The Concert of Europe, 5050
———. A Diplomatic History of Europe Since the Congress of Vienna, 5051
———. Italy from Napoleon to Mussolini, 5443
Album of American History. Adams, James T., ed, 448
ALCHEMY, 2074
Alchemy. Grossinger, Richard and Hough, Lindy. 2074
Alcock, John. Animal Behavior, 2350
Alcock, Leslie. Arthur's Britain, 4746
Alcohol and Your Health. Burgess, Louise B, 2600
ALCOHOLISM, 2547, 2599, 2600-2601
Alcoholism. Bloch, Marvin A, 2599
Alcoholism. Kessel, Neil and Walton, Henry. 2601
Alden, John R. History of the American Revolution, 5912
Aldred, Cyril. Egypt to the End of the Old Kingdom, 4882
Aleichem, Sholem. Collected Stories of Sholem Aleichem, 4590
Alexander, Clifton and Alexander, Sandy. How to Kick the Habit, 1696
Alexander, Freda. see Noyes, Tina
Alexander, Frederick. Australia Since Federation, 6286
Alexander, Garth. The Invisible China, 1314
Alexander Hamilton. Schachner, Nathan, 5969
Alexander Hamilton and American Foreign Policy. Lycan, Gilbert L, 1349
Alexander, Holmes. Aaron Burr, the Proud Pretender, 5972
Alexander, Robert J. An Introduction to Argentina, 6273
Alexander, Sandy. see Alexander, Clifton
ALEXANDER THE GREAT, 4974-4975
Alexander the Great. Lane-Fox, Robin, 4975
Alexander, Yonah and Kittrie, Nicholas N. F., eds. Crescent and Star, 924
ALEXANDRA, CONSORT OF NICHOLAS II, 5506
ALEXANDRA, QUEEN CONSORT OF EDWARD VII, KING OF ENGLAND, 5269
Alexopoulos, Constantine J. and Bold, Harold C. Algae and Fungi, 2329
Al Faruqi, Isma'il R. Historical Atlas of the Religions of the World, 400
Alfred North Whitehead. Lawrence, Nathaniel M, 653

INDEX

Alfred North Whitehead. Whitehead, Alfred N, 656
Alfred, Simon. *see* Lewine, Richard
ALFRED THE GREAT, 5185
Alfred the Great. Helm, Peter J, 5185
Alfven, Hannes. Worlds-Antiworlds, 1983
ALGAE, 2329, 2334
Algae. Prescott, G. W, 2334
Algae and Fungi. Alexopoulos, Constantine J. and Bold, Harold C. 2329
ALGERIA — HISTORY, 923
ALIENATION (SOCIAL PSYCHOLOGY), 909
Alisky, Marvin. Uruguay, a Contemporary Survey, 6279
Alistair Cooke's America. Cooke, Alistair, 4811
Alive. Read, Piers P, 6274
All Creatures Great and Small. Herriot, James, 2804
All for Love or The World Well Lost. Dryden, John, 3872
All-in-One Movie Book. Petzold, Paul, 3113
All That Glitters Is Not Gold. Johnson, William O., Jr, 3384
All the President's Men. Bernstein, Carl and Woodward, Bob. 1716
All Things Bright and Beautiful. Herriot, James, 2805
Allen, Barry. Sports Illustrated Skin Diving and Snorkeling, 3434
Allen, Ethan. Baseball Play and Strategy, 3371
Allen, Frederick L. Lords of Creation, 1449
———. Only Yesterday, 6107
Allen, Gay W. William James, 642
Allen Ginsberg in America. Kramer, Jane, 3646
Allen, Paula C., et al. Four Indian Poets, 4635
Allen, Reginald E., ed. Greek Philosophy, 510
Allen, Richard. Imperialism and Nationalism in the Fertile Crescent, 1182
Allen, Richard H. Star Names, 2008
Allen, Samuel W. Poems from Africa, 3495
Allensworth, Carl, et al. The Complete Play Production Handbook, 3298
ALLIANCE FOR PROGRESS, 930, 1537
Alliance for Progress. Dreier, John E., ed, 1537
Alliance for Progress, Key to Latin America's Development. Nystrom, John W. and Haverstock, Nathan A. 930

ALLIGATORS, 2423-2424
Allison, Graham T. Essence of Decision, 1326
Allott, Miriam, ed. Novelists on the Novel, 3486
Alloway, Lawrence. American Pop Art, 2943
ALMANACS, 131, 3755
Almost All About Waves. Pierce, John R, 2037
L' Alouette. Anouilh, Jean, 4142
Alphonso-Karkala, John B., compiled by. An Anthology of Indian Literature, 4478
ALPINE FLORA — U. S., 2246
Alps. Clark, Ronald, 4767
Alston, Walter and Weiskopf, Donald. The Complete Baseball Handbook, 3372
Altamira y Crevea, Rafael. History of Spanish Civilization, 5455
Alter, Dinsmore, et al. Pictorial Astronomy, 1959
———. Pictorial Guide to the Moon, 1994
Alternative. Hedgepeth, William and Stock, Dennis. 1503
Alternatives to Violence. Bernstein, Saul, 1104
Althusser, Louis. Lenin and Philosophy, and Other Essays, 1494
Altizer, Thomas, ed. Toward a New Christianity, 743
Alves, Rubem A. Tomorrow's Child, 4654
Amann, Peter. Revolution and Mass Democracy, 5407
Amateur Astronomer's Handbook. Muirden, James, 1965
Amateur Magician's Handbook. Hay, Henry, 3335
Amateur Photographer's Handbook. Sussman, Aaron, 3105
Amateur's Guide to Caves and Caving. McClurg, David R, 3396
Amaya, Mario. Pop Art and After, 2905
AMAZON RIVER, 4842
Ambassador's Journal. Galbraith, John Kenneth, 1301
Amberg, George. The New York Times Film Reviews, 312
Ambrose Bierce. O'Connor, Richard, 3721
Ambrose, E. J. and Easty, Dorothy M. Cell Biology, 2250
Ambrose, Stephen E. and Barber, James A., Jr., eds. The Military and American Society, 1067
AMENHOTEP IV, 4898
AMERICA
   ANTIQUITIES, 4736-4737
   DISCOVERY AND EXPLORATION, 5786, 5793, 5884-5888, 5890-5891, 5904, 6260

319

INDEX

America and Americans. Steinbeck, John, 4817
America and the World Political Economy. Calleo, David P. and Rowland, Benjamin M. 1795
America As a Civilization. Lerner, Max, 5864
America at 1750. Hofstadter, Richard, 1114
America Goes to War. Tansill, Charles Callan, 5083
America in Legend. Dorson, Richard M, 1841
America in the World. Barck, Oscar T., ed, 6101
America, Inc. Who Owns and Operates the United States. Mintz, Morton and Cohen, Jerry S. 1199
America Rebels. Dorson, Richard M, 5956
America, Russia, and the Cold War, 1945-1971. LaFeber, Walter, 1310
America the Raped. Marine, Gene, 1463
American Album. American Heritage Editors and Jenson, Oliver. 4808
American Alliance for Health, Physical Education & Recreation. Drug Abuse, 2596
American Alligator. Ricciuti, Edward R, 2424
American and French Accounts of the American Revolution. 5958
American Approach to Foreign Policy. Perkins, Dexter, 1351
American Art of the 20th Century. Hunter, Sam and Jacobus, John. 2945
American Authors. Kunitz, Stanley J. and Haycraft, Howard, eds. 427
American Ballads and Folk Songs. Lomax, John A. and Lomax, Alan. 3237
American Banking Structure. Fischer, Gerald C, 1451
American Boarding Schools. McLachlan, James, 1768
American Book Publishing Record. 36
American Building. Condit, Carl, 2690
American Car Since 1775. Automobile Quarterly, ed, 2742
American Catholicism. Ellis, John T, 808
American Century. Andrist, Ralph K, 4809
American Character. Brogan, Denis W, 5854
American Churches in the Ecumenical Movement, 1900-1968. Cavert, Samuel M, 772
American Cinema. Sarris, Andrew, 3281
American Condition. Goodwin, Richard N, 1112
American Crafts Council. Contemporary Crafts Market Place, 1975-1976, 288

American Criminal Trials. Chandler, Peleg W, 1615
An American Death. Frank, Gerold, 1710
An American Dilemma. Myrdal, Gunnar, 1272
American Diplomacy During the World War. Seymour, Charles, 5080
AMERICAN DRAMA, 373, 3670, 3676
American Dream. Albee, Edward, 3687
American Economic History. Faulkner, Harold U, 1416
American English. Marckwardt, Albert H, 1879
American Environment. Nash, Roderick, compiled by. 1464
American Epoch. Link, Arthur S., et al. 6112
American Epochs Series. 6182
American Essays. Shaw, Charles B., ed, 3748
AMERICAN FICTION, 3712-3715, 3717, 3724, 3730, 3745, 3933
American Foreign Policy. Kissinger, Henry A, 1345
American Genesis. Vaughan, Alden T, 5909
An American Genius. Childs, Herbert, 2056
American Geological Institute. Dictionary of Geological Terms, 220
American Heritage Book of the Revolution. Lancaster, Bruce, 5918
American Heritage Cookbook. American Heritage Editors, 2834
American Heritage Dictionary of the English Language. 161
American Heritage Editors. The American Heritage Cookbook, 2834
———. The American Heritage History of the Presidency, 1637
———. The American Heritage History of the 20's and 30's, 6100
———. American Heritage History of World War I, 5067
———. American Heritage Pictorial Atlas of United States History, 392
American Heritage Editors and Jenson, Oliver. American Album, 4808
American Heritage History of the Artists' America. Davidson, Marshall B, 2944
American Heritage History of the Great West. Lavendar, David, 6236
American Heritage History of the Presidency. American Heritage Editors, 1637
American Heritage History of the 20's and 30's. American Heritage Editors, 6100
American Heritage History of World War I. American Heritage Editors, 5067

American Heritage Pictorial Atlas of United States History. American Heritage Editors, 392
American Heritage Picture History of the Civil War. Catton, Bruce, 6025
American Heritage Picture History of World War II. Sulzberger, C. L, 5122
American Heroine. Davis, Allen F, 1692
American Images of Soviet Foreign Policy. Welch, William, 1313
American Impressionists. Hoopes, Donelson F, 3044
American in Santo Domingo. Knight, Melvin M, 5842
American Indian and the United States. Washburn, Wilcomb E., compiled by. 445
American Indian Art. Feder, Norman, 2898
American Indian Medicine. Vogel, Virgil J, 5777
American Indian Mythology. Marriott, Alice and Rachlin, Carol K. 1835
American Indian Prose and Poetry. Astrov, Margot, ed, 4636
American Indian Women. Gridley, Marion E, 5750
American Judaism. Glazer, Nathan, 852
American Judaism. Neusner, Jacob, 853
American Junior Colleges. Gleazer, Edmund J., Jr., ed, 148
American Kennel Club. The Complete Dog Book, 2809
American Labor Since the New Deal. Dubofsky, Melvyn, ed, 1429
American Language. Mencken, Henry L, 1880
American Literary Revolution, 1783-1837. Spiller, Robert E., ed, 3543
AMERICAN LITERATURE, 356, 3521, 3532-3533, 3535, 3541
    BIBLIOGRAPHY, 66, 69, 354-355, 357
    COLLECTIONS, 3534, 5879-5880
    DICTIONARIES, 353, 360
    HISTORY AND CRITICISM, 354-355, 357, 362, 3522, 3539, 3540-3543
    JEWISH-AMERICAN AUTHORS, 3536
    MEXICAN-AMERICAN AUTHORS, 3535
    NEGRO AUTHORS, 356, 3532-3533, 4867
AMERICAN LOYALISTS, 5789, 5945-5947
American Military. Weigley, Russell F, 1662
American Mind. Commager, Henry S, 5857
American Movies Reference Book. Michael, Paul and Parish, James R., eds. 314
American Music. Nanry, Charles, ed, 3183
American Music. Sablosky, Irving L, 3184
American Music Since 1910. Thomson, Virgil, 3185
American National Red Cross Editors. Advanced First Aid and Emergency Care, 2569
———. Lifesaving, 2570
American Negro Folklore. Brewer, John Mason, compiled by. 1842
American Negro Slavery. Phillips, Ulrich B, 1287
American Negro Slavery. Weinstein, Allen and Gatell, Otto, eds. 1288
AMERICAN NEWSPAPERS, 495, 497-498
American Newspapers in the 1970's. Hynds, Ernest C, 498
American Newsreel, 1911-1967. Fielding, Raymond, 3272
American Nonpublic Schools. Kraushaar, Otto F, 1767
American Novel. Stegner, Wallace, ed, 3713
American Occupation of Germany. Gimbel, John, 5333
American Odyssey. Eide, Ingvard H., compiled by. 6233
American Painting in the Twentieth Century. Geldzahler, Henry, 3040
American Past. Butterfield, Roger, ed, 5855
AMERICAN PERIODICALS, 478-479
American Philanthropy. Bremner, Robert H, 1694
AMERICAN POETRY, 3576, 3846
    COLLECTIONS, 366, 3547-3553, 3775, 3779, 3782-3785, 3788
    HISTORY AND CRITICISM, 358, 3545-3546, 3554, 3570
    INDEXES, 365
American Poetry Since 1945. Stepanchev, Stephen, 3545
American Poets. Waggoner, Hyatt H, 3546
American Policy Toward Communist China. Dulles, Foster R, 1334
American Political Dictionary. Plano, J. C. and Greenberg, M. 133
American Political Parties. Binkley, Wilfred E, 1387
American Political Tradition. Hofstadter, Richard, 5861
American Pop Art. Alloway, Lawrence, 2943
American Population Debate. Callahan, Daniel J., compiled by. 949

INDEX

An American Primer. Boorstin, Daniel J., ed, 5877
American Protestantism. Hudson, Winthrop S, 801
American Public Addresses. Baird, A. C, 3518
American Quest, 1790-1860. Rossiter, Clinton, 5968
American Radio Relay League. The Radio Amateur's Handbook, 2648
American Revolution. Trevelyan, George O, 5928
American Revolution Considered As a Social Movement. Jameson, J. Franklin, 5917
American Revolution in Its Political and Military Aspects, 1763-1783. Robson, Eric, 5927
American Roulette. Young, Desmond, 5874
American Scene. Baigell, Matthew, 3036
American Seashells. Abbott, R. Tucker, 242
American Secretaries of State and Their Diplomacy, 1776-1925. Bemis, Samuel F., ed, 1330
American Silver. Hood, Graham, 3002
American Spirit. Bailey, Thomas A, 5876
American Sportsman Treasury. Mason, Jerry, ed, 3450
American Transcendentalism, 1830-1860. Boller, Paul F, 546
American Universities and Colleges. Furniss, W. Todd, ed, 147
American Universities and Colleges. Singletary, Otis A., ed, 149
American Universities Field Service. Select Bibliography, 72
American Utopianism. Fogarty, Robert S., ed, 1209
American Violence. Hofstadter, Richard and Wallace, Michael, eds. 5862
American Way of War. Weigley, Russell F, 1678
American West in the 20th Century. Nash, Gerald D, 6237
AMERICAN WIT AND HUMOR, 3751
American Writers in Rebellion, from Mark Twain to Dreiser. Morgan, H. Wayne, 3542
AMERICANISMS, 1878-1880
Americanization of Alaska, 1867-1897. Hinckley, Ted C, 6248
Americans. Boorstin, Daniel J, 5894
America's Concentration Camps. Bosworth, Allan, 5147
America's Flying Book. Flying Magazine Editors, 2721
America's Frontier Heritage. Billington, Ray A, 6227
America's Last Wild Horses. Ryden, Hope, 2807
America's Oil Famine. Knowles, Ruth S, 1527
America's Rise to World Power. Dulles, Foster R, 1335
Ammon, Henry. James Monroe, 5981
AMNESTY — U. S., 1227
Amos, William H. The Infinite River, 2261
AMPHIBIANS, 2410-2411, 2415
Amphitryon. Giraudoux, Jean, 4158
Amundsen, Kirsten. The Silenced Majority, 975
Amy Vanderbilt's Etiquette. Vanderbilt, Amy, 1823
An, Tai-Sung. Mao Tse-Tung's Cultural Revolution, 1153
Anabasis. Xenophon, 4970
ANARCHISM AND ANARCHISTS, 5504
Anastaplo, George. The Constitutionalist, 1563
ANATOMY, ARTISTIC, 3011
ANATOMY, COMPARATIVE, 2348
Anatomy for the Artist. Barcsay, Jeno, 3011
ANATOMY, HUMAN, 250, 2503-2505, 2507-2509
Anatomy of a Riot. Lincoln, James H, 1593
Anatomy of Antiques. Kelley, Austin P. and Sotheby Parke Bernet Staff. 3017
Anatomy of Human Destructiveness. Fromm, Erich, 572
Ancien Régime in Europe. Williams, E. Neville, 5036
Ancient America. Leonard, Jonathan N, 4737
Ancient Crete. Willetts, Ronald F, 5565
Ancient Egyptian, Mesopotamian and Persian Costume and Decoration. Houston, Mary G, 1811
Ancient Engineers. DeCamp, L. Sprague, 2631
Ancient Europe. Piggott, Stuart, 4723
Ancient Greece. Green, Peter, 4958
Ancient Greek Literature in Its Living Context. Baldry, H. C, 4437
Ancient Greek, Roman and Byzantine Costume and Decoration. Houston, Mary G, 1812
Ancient Greeks. Finley, Moses I, 4955
Ancient Greeks. Starr, Chester G, 4962
Ancient History. Robinson, Charles A, 4879
Ancient Iraq. Roux, Georges, 4912
Ancient Israel. Orlinsky, Harry M, 4905
Ancient Mariners. Casson, Lionel, 4876
Ancient Men of the Arctic. Giddings, James L, 4738

Ancient Mesopotamia. Oppenheim, A. Leo, 4911
Ancient Peoples and Places. 4987
Ancient Persia and Iranian Civilization. Huart, Clément I, 4909
Ancient Poetry from China, Japan and India. Wells, Henry W., tr, 4601
Ancient World at Work. Mosse, Claude, 1432
And Still the Waters Run. Debo, Angie, 5767
And the Beat Goes on. Boeckman, Charles, 3221
And the Land Provides. Morgan, Lael, 6250
And Where Were You, Adam? Boll, Heinrich, 4040
Andersen, Hans Christian. Andersen's Fairy Tales, 1843
ANDERSEN, HANS CHRISTIAN, 4083
Andersen, Yvonne. Teaching Film Animation to Children, 51
Andersen's Fairy Tales. Andersen, Hans Christian, 1843
Anderson, Bernhard W. Understanding the Old Testament, 722
Anderson, Charles R., ed. Thoreau's Vision, 3750
Anderson, Chester G. James Joyce and His World, 3935
Anderson, Chuck. The Electric Journalist, 3285
Anderson, Donald F. William Howard Taft, 1638
Anderson, Henry. see London, Joan
Anderson, John M. The Changing World of Birds, 2426
Anderson, R. E. see Evans, G. Heberton
Anderson, Robert. You Know I Can't Hear You When the Water's Running, 3691
ANDERSON, SHERWOOD, 3729
Anderson, William. Castles of Europe from Charlemagne to the Renaissance, 4739
Anderson-Imbert, Enrique and Florit, E. Literatura Hispanoamericana, Antologia e Introducción Historica, 4303
Anderton, David A. Apollo 17 at Taurus Littrow, 2764
Andorra. Frisch, Max, 4050
André Gide. Guerard, Albert J, 4218
ANDRÉ, JOHN, 5916, 5933
Andreas Vesalius of Brussels, 1514-1564. O'Malley, C. D, 2589
ANDREEV, LEONID NIKOLAEVICH, 4553
Andrew Carnegie. Wall, Joseph F, 1525
Andrew Jackson. Ward, John, 5998
Andrew Johnson and Reconstruction. McKitrick, Eric L, 6084

Andrews, Charles. Colonial Background of the American Revolution, 5893
Andrews, Charles J. Fell's International Coin Book, 284
Andrews, Donald and Kokes, R. J. Fundamental Chemistry, 2065
Andrews, Howard and Russel, Alexander. Basic Boating, 3422
Andrews, Lewis M. see Kailins, Marvin
Andrews, W. A Guide to the Study of Environmental Pollution, 2706
Andrist, Ralph K. American Century, 4809
Angela Davis. Parker, J. A, 1232
ANGER, 569
Anger. Madow, Leo, 569
Anger, Arthur L., et al. Computer Science, 467
Angier, B. see Colby, C. B.
Angier, B. Living off the Country, 2531
Anglin, D. L. see Crouse, W. H.
Anglo-American Cataloging Rules. Spalding, C. Sumner, ed, 30
Anglo-Saxon Chronicle. Garmonsway, G. N., ed, 5182
Anglo-Saxon England. Stanton, Frank M, 5190
ANGLO-SAXONS, 5182, 5190
Angry Scar. Carter, Hodding, 6062
Anguist, Stanley W. Other Worlds, Other Beings, 2308
Angus, Edward L., see Mahood, H. R.
Angus, Ian. Fell's Guide to Coins and Money Tokens of the World, 285
Animal Architecture. Von Frisch, Karl and Von Frisch, Otto. 2364
Animal Atlas of the World. Jordan, Emil L, 2446
Animal Behavior. Alcock, John, 2350
Animal Camouflage. Von Frisch, Otto, 2366
ANIMAL COMMUNICATIONS, 2367
Animal in Man. Milne, Lorus and Milne, Margery. 587
ANIMAL INTELLIGENCE, 2457-2458
ANIMAL INTRODUCTION — U. S., 2358-2359
Animal Invaders. Silverstein, Alvin and Silverstein, Virginia. 2359
ANIMAL MIGRATION, 239, 2361
Animal Physiology. Schmidt-Nielsen, Knut, 2342
ANIMALS, 240-241, 2352
   HABITATIONS OF, 2363-2364, 2429
   HABITS AND BEHAVIOR OF, 2192-2193, 2350-2351, 2354-2356, 2360, 2365-2366, 2368, 2446, 2471, 2473
   INFANCY OF, 2349
   MYTHICAL, 1850
   TREATMENT OF — HISTORY, 2803

INDEX

Animals and Their Colors. Fogden, Michael and Fogden, Patricia. 2365
Animals in Migration. Orr, Robert T, 2361
Animals in Roman Life and Art. Toynbee, Jocelyn M. C, 2887
Animals of East Africa. Leakey, Louis S, 2448
Animals of the Antarctic. Stonehouse, Bernard, 2375
Animals of the Arctic. Stonehouse, Bernard, 2376
Animals of the Dark. Roots, Clive, 2357
Animals Without Backbones. Buchsbaum, Ralph, 2378
Anna Karenina. Tolstoi, Leo N, 4563
Anna Pavlova. Kerensky, Oleg, 3325
Annapurna. Herzog, Maurice, 3391
Anne Boleyn. Bruce, Marie L, 5213
ANNE, EMPRESS OF RUSSIA, 5499
L' Annonce Faite à Marie. Claudel, Paul, 4151
Anonymous. Go Ask Alice, 2545
ANONYMS AND PSEUDONYMS, 431
Another World. Espy, Hilda C. and Creamer, Lex. 4804
Anouilh, Jean. L' Alouette, 4142
———. Antigone, 4143
———. Becket, 4144
———. L' Hurluberlu, ou Le Réactionnaire Amoureu, 4145
———. Le Voyageur sans Bagages, and Le Bal des Voleurs, 4146
Anschluss. Wagner, Dieter and Tomkowitz, Gerhard. 5348
Ansel Adams. Adams, Ansel, 3126
Antarctic. King, H. G. R, 4851
ANTARCTIC REGIONS, 4851, 6291
Antarctica. Payne, Donald G, 6291
Antek, Samuel. This Was Toscanini, 3245
Anthologie de la Póesie Française. Gide, André, ed, 4138
Anthology of Elizabethan Lute Songs, Madrigals and Rounds. Greenberg, Noah, et al, eds. 3233
Anthology of English Medieval and Renaissance Vocal Music. Greenberg, Noah, et al, eds. 3234
Anthology of French Poetry from Nerval to Valéry. Flores, Angel, ed, 4137
Anthology of German Poetry from Holderlin to Rilke. Flores, Angel, ed, 4003
An Anthology of Indian Literature. Alphonso-Karkala, John B., compiled by. 4478
An Anthology of Irish Literature. Greene, David H, 4492
Anthology of Japanese Literature. Keene, Donald, ed, 4610
Anthology of Modern Japanese Poetry. Shiffert, Edith and Sawa, Yuki, trs. 4612
Anthology of Russian Literature. Wiener, Leo, ed, 4501
Anthology of Russian Literature in the Soviet Period from Gorki to Pasternak. Guerney, Bernard G., ed, 4494
An Anthology of Scandinavian Literature, from the Viking Period to the Twentieth Century. Hallmundson, Hallberg, ed, 4087
Anthology of Spanish Literature in English Translation. Resnick, Seymour and Pasmantier, Jeanne, eds. 4307
Anthology of Spanish Poetry from Garcilaso to García Lorca. Flores, Angel, 4335
Anthology of World Poetry. Van Doren, Mark, 3501
ANTHROPOLOGY, 907, 2186, 2191, 2195, 5749
Anti-Ballistic Missile. Center for the Study of Democratic Institutions, 1686
ANTI-COMMUNIST MOVEMENTS — U. S., 1196
Antigone. Anouilh, Jean, 4143
Anti-Memoirs. Malraux, Andre, 4278
Antimiry. Voznesenskii, Andrei, 4515
ANTI-NAZI MOVEMENT, 1395, 5310
ANTIQUES — COLLECTING, 3017
ANTISEMITISM, 1052, 1059, 1216
Antislavery. Dumond, Dwight L, 1282
Anti-Slavery Impulse, 1830-1844. Barnes, Gilbert H. 1281
Antiworlds. Voznesenskii, Andrei. 4516
Antología General de la Literatura Española. Del Río, Amelia and Del Río, Angel. 4305
Antonius, Bro. Hazards of Holiness, 3622
ANTS, 2397
Anybody's Gold. Jackson, Joseph H, 6244
Anyone Can Sculpt. Zaidenberg, Arthur, 2989
Apel, Willi. Harvard Dictionary of Music, 296
Apel, Willi. see Davison, Archibald T.
APES, 2477, 2479
Apes. Reynolds, Vernon, 2479
Apollo 14. Froehlich, Walter, 2763
Apollo 17 at Taurus Littrow. Anderton, David A, 2764
Apologia pro Vita Sua. Newman, John Henry, 728
Appearance of Justice. MacKenzie, John P, 1609
Appian Way. Hamblin, Dora J, 4758
Apple, R. W., Jr. The Watergate Hearings, 1191
Appreciation of Byzantine Art. Rice, David T, 2902

INDEX

Aproximacional Quixote. Deriquer, Martin, 4313
Aptheker, Herbert, ed. A Documentary History of the Negro People in the United States, 1270
———. Nat Turner's Slave Rebellion, 5992
AQUACULTURE, 2817-2818
Aquaculture. Bardach, John E., et al. 2817
Aquaculture. Wolfe, Louis, 2818
AQUARIUMS, 262-263, 2819-2821
Aquatics Handbook. Gabrielsen, Milton A., et al. 3421
Arab Attitudes to Israel. Harkabi, Yehoshafat, 895
Arab Contemporaries. Khadduri, Majid, 1157
ARAB COUNTRIES — POLITICS, 1157-1158
Arab-Israeli Confrontation of June, 1967. Abu-Lughod, Ibrahim, ed, 5647
ARABIA
  ANTIQUITIES, 4733
  HISTORY, 389, 5625
  SOCIAL LIFE AND CUSTOMS, 5624
Arabian Nights' Entertainment. 1825
ARABIC LANGUAGE —
  DICTIONARIES, 191-192
ARABIC LITERATURE
  COLLECTIONS, 4597
  HISTORY AND CRITICISM, 4598
Arango, Jorge. The Urbanization of the Earth, 964
Arbus, Diane. Diane Arbus, 3123
Archaeological Site Science. Goodyear, Frank, 4713
ARCHAEOLOGY, 401, 407, 4707-4708, 4710-4711, 4713-4715, 5178
Archaeology in the Holy Land. Kenyon, Kathleen M, 4719
Archaeology Under Water. Bass, George F, 4716
Archer's Bible. Bear, Fred, 3461
ARCHERY, 3461
Architectural and Interior Models. Hohauser, Sanford, 2960
ARCHITECTURAL MODELS, 2960
ARCHITECTURE, 1728, 2890, 2923, 2934, 2949, 2956, 2967-2974, 2977
  DICTIONARIES, 280-281
  HISTORY, 2959, 2962-2963, 2966
Architecture. Jacobs, David, 2963
Architecture of Molecules. Pauling, Linus and Hayward, R. 2076
ARCHIVES — HANDBOOKS, MANUALS, ETC., 250
ARCHIVES — U. S., 4872
Arciniegas, German. Latin America, 6253
Arctic. Bruemmer, Fred, 4849

ARCTIC REGIONS, 4738, 4849-4850
Ardagh, John. The New French Revolution, 1089
Ardent Spirits. Kobler, John, 1235
Ardrey, Robert. African Genesis, 2192
———. The Social Contract, 2193
———. The Territorial Imperative, 2360
Arena. Pearson, John, 4728
Arena, James W. see Hardin, James W.
Arena of Life. Milne, Lorus and Milne, Margery. 2233
Arendt, Hannah. Crises of the Republic, 1138
———. On Revolution, 1212
———. On Violence, 880
———. Origins of Totalitarianism, 1216
Arey, James A. The Sky Pirates, 1719
ARGENTINE REPUBLIC, 6273
Ariel. Maurois, Andre, 3814
Aries, Philippe. Western Attitudes Toward Death, 526
Aristophanes. Eleven Comedies, 4459
Aristoteles. The Basic Works, 625
Armada. Mattingly, Garrett, 5224
ARMAMENTS, 1656, 1667
ARMENIA — HISTORY, 5658
Armenians. Der Nersessian, Strarpie, 5658
Armies of the Night. Mailer, Norman, 3759
Armistice, 1918. Rudin, Harry R, 5089
Armoured Fighting Vehicles of the World. Foss, Christopher F, 2678
ARMS AND ARMOR, 1680, 1813, 1851
Arms and Armour of the Greeks. Snodgrass, Anthony M, 1851
Arms and Strategy. Martin, Laurence W, 1667
Arms Control and Disarmament Agreements, 1959-1972. U. S. Arms Control and Disarmament Agency, 1298
Arms for Empire. Leach, Douglas E, 5902
Arms of Krupp, 1587-1968. Manchester, William, 1531
Arms of the Sea. Shepherd, Elizabeth, 2242
Armstrong, Anne. Berliners, 5329
Armstrong, Hamilton F., ed. Fifty Years of Foreign Affairs, 1154
Armstrong, John A. The European Administrative Elite, 1068
———. Ideology, Politics and Government in the Soviet Union, 1169
Armstrong, Neil, et al. First on the Moon, 2765
Armstrong, Virginia I., ed. I Have Spoken, 5743
An Army for Empire. Cosmas, Graham A, 6095

325

INDEX

Army of the Caesars. Grant, Michael, 4937
Arnett, Ethel S. Mrs. James Madison, 5982
Arnheim, Rudolf. Art and Visual Perception, 2882
———. The Genesis of a Painting, 3061
ARNOLD, BENEDICT, 5916, 5933, 5957
Arnold, Matthew. Poetry and Criticism of Matthew Arnold, 3821
Arnold, Robert E. What to Do About Bites and Stings of Venomous Animals, 2585
Aromatic Sextet. Clar, Eric, 2085
Aron, Raymond. The Imperial Republic, 1327
Aron, Robert. The Vichy Regime, 5417
Aronson, Joseph. The New Encyclopedia of Furniture, 282
Arquin, Florence. Diego Rivera, 3076
Arrianus, Flavius. The Campaigns of Alexander, 4974
Arribas, Antonio. The Iberians, 5456
Arrogance of Power. Fulbright, James W, 1337
ART, 272-273, 2876, 2885, 2889, 2892, 2897, 2900-2903, 2915-2919, 2921, 2924-2925, 2928-2937, 2939-2942, 2945, 2949, 4450, 4753, 4929, 4966
    CRITICISM, 2877-2878, 2886
    DICTIONARIES, 265-268, 274-275, 278, 289
    HISTORY, 269-271, 275, 2873, 2881, 2894-2896, 2896, 2899, 2904, 2908, 2927, 2944, 2946-2947, 3029, 3035, 3066, 4651, 4749
    INDUSTRIES AND TRADE, 288, 290, 2909, 3014
    MODERN, 276, 2871, 2906-2907, 2912-2913, 2943
    PHILOSOPHY, 507, 875, 879, 884
    PSYCHOLOGY, 2876, 2882-2884, 2919
Art. Richardson, John A, 2879
Art and Architecture of Japan. Soper, A. and Paine, R. 2934
Art and Experience in Classical Greece. Pollitt, Jerry J, 2919
Art and Illusion. Gombrich, Ernst H, 2876
Art and Science of Taking to the Woods. Colby, C. B. and Angier, B. 3397
Art and the Future. Davis, Douglas M, 2871
Art and Visual Perception. Arnheim, Rudolf, 2882
Art in America. McLanathan, Richard B, 2946
ART OBJECTS — CONSERVATION AND RESTORATION, 481
Art of Andrew Wyeth. Corn, Wanda M., ed, 3039
Art of Cartooning. Hogg, Syd, 3008
Art of French Fiction. Turnell, Martin, 4266
Art of India. Goetz, Hermann, 2935
Art of Indonesia. Bodrogi, Tibor, 2936
Art of Loving. Fromm, Erich, 605
Art of Modern Fiction. West, Ray Benedict and Stallman, Robert W. 3490
Art of Ragtime. Schafer, William J., et al. 3193
Art of Rome and Her Empire. Kahler, Heinz, 2918
Art of Scientific Investigation. Beveridge, W. I, 1916
Art of the American Film, 1900-1971. Higham, Charles, 3274
Art of the Byzantine World. Schug-Wille, Christa, 2903
Art of the Times. Suares, Jean-Claude, ed, 3009
Art of War in the Middle Ages. Oman, Charles, 5002
Art Spirit. Henri, Robert, 2886
Art Through the Ages. Gardner, Helen, 2895
Art Today. Faulkner, Ray, et al. 2909
Art Treasures of the World. 3077
Art without Boundaries. Woods, Gerald, et al, eds. 2906
Artandi, Susan. Introduction to Computers in Information Science, 47
ARTHUR, CHESTER ALAN, 6091
Arthur Miller. Nelson, Benjamin, 3682
Arthur's Britain. Alcock, Leslie, 4746
Artificial Light Photography. Adams, Ansel, 3100
Artillery. Batchelor, John and Hogg, Ian. 1683
ARTILLERY — HISTORY, 1683
Artillery of the Press. Reston, James B, 500
ARTISTS, 275, 277-279, 2926, 2941, 4863, 4867
Arts of China. Sullivan, Michael, 2932
Arts of Mankind. 3078
Arts of the Ancient Greeks. Brilliant, Richard, 2916
Artz, Frederick B. France Under the Bourbon Restoration, 1814-1830, 5408
———. The Mind of the Middle Ages, A.D. 200-1500, 4994
———. Reaction and Revolution, 5052
Artzt, Eric. see Hartogs, Renatus
Arvin, Newton. Herman Melville, 3719
Ary, Sheila and Gregory, Mary. Oxford Book of Wild Flowers, 2324
Ascent of Man. Bronowski, Jacob, 1921
Asch, Shalom. Children of Abraham, 4591
ASCH, SHALOM, 4591
Asch, Sidney H. The Supreme Court and Its Great Justices, 1605

Ash, Lee, compiled by. Subject Collections, 81
Ashe, Geoffrey. The Quest for Arthur's Britain, 5178
Asher, Robert E., et al. Development Assistance in the Seventies, 1535
Ashley Book of Knots. Ashley, Clifford U, 2686
Ashley, Clifford U. The Ashley Book of Knots, 2686
Ashley, Maurice. England in the Seventeenth Century, 5234
———. Great Britain to 1688, 5170
Ashley Montagu, compiled by. Man and Aggression, 571
Ashman, Charles R. The Finest Judges Money Can Buy, 1612
Ashmore, Harry S. Fear in the Air, 1564
Ashton, Dore. Modern American Sculpture, 2983
———. A Reading of Modern Art, 2907
ASIA, 4773-4774
    BIBLIOGRAPHY, 72
    HISTORY, 4772, 5571
    POLITICS, 1135, 1178, 4771
ASIA, CENTRAL — ANTIQUITIES, 4787
ASIA, SOUTHEASTERN, 4789, 5671-5672
    ECONOMIC CONDITIONS, 1095, 1414, 1534
    HISTORY, 5670, 5673-5674
    POLITICS, 1186, 1314, 5637, 5673-5674
Asian Drama. Myrdal, Gunnar, 1414
Asian Journal of Thomas Merton. Merton, Thomas, 740
Asian Laughter. Feinburg, Leonard, compiled by. 4476
Asian Political Systems. Burch, Betty B. and Cole, Alan B. 1135
Asians. Welty, Paul T, 4772
Asimov, Isaac. Asimov's Biographical Encyclopedia of Science and Technology, 207
———. Asimov's Guide to Science, 195
———. The Human Brain, 2524
———. Jupiter, 2000
———. The Left Hand of the Electron, 1917
———. More Words of Science, 198
———. The Noble Gases, 2080
———. Photosynthesis, 2316
———. Today and Tomorrow and .., 1918
———. Words of Science and the History Behind Them, 199
Asimov's Biographical Encyclopedia of Science and Technology. Asimov, Isaac, 207
Asimov's Guide to Science. Asimov, Isaac, 195

Aspects of Central African History. Ranger, Terence O., ed, 5731
Aspects of E. M. Forster. Stallybrass, Oliver, ed, 3930
Aspects of Russian Imagination. Yarmolinsky, Avrahm, 4502
Aspects of the Novel. Forster, Edward M, 3487
Aspirin Age, 1919-41. Leighton, Isabel, ed, 6104
Assault on Privacy. Miller, Arthur R, 1264
L' Assommoir. Zola, Émile, 4259
ASSYRIA — HISTORY, 4908, 4916
Astrological Houses. Rudhyar, Dane, 539
ASTROLOGY, 538-540
ASTRONAUTICS, 259, 1687, 1920, 2633, 2755-2756, 2758-2761, 2768
ASTRONOMY, 211-212, 1895, 1959-1971, 1974-1975, 1978, 1981-1982, 1986, 1990, 2007, 5184
Astronomy. Jastrow, Robert and Thompson, Malcolm H. 1964
Astrov, Margot, ed. American Indian Prose and Poetry, 4636
Atala. Chateaubriand, François René de, 4202
Atatürk. Balfour, Patrick, 5558
ATATÜRK, KEMÂL, 5558
Athletics of the Ancient World. Gardiner, Edward N, 4957
Atkins, Burton M. and Glick, H. R., eds. Prisons, Protest, and Politics, 1741
Atkins, John. George Orwell, 3936
Atkinson, J. Brooks and Hirschfeld, Albert. The Lively Years, 1920-1973, 3320
Atlantic Book of British and American Poetry. Sitwell, Edith, ed, 3783
Atlas of Africa. Chi-Bonnardel, Regine V., ed, 390
Atlas of American History. Adams, James T., ed, 391
Atlas of Ancient Archaeology. Hawkes, Jacquetta H, 401
Atlas of Animal Migration. Jarman, Cathy, 239
Atlas of China. Hsieh, Chiao-Min and Salter, Christopher L. 404
Atlas of European History. Fox, Edward W, 387
Atlas of Insects. Tweedie, Michael, 244
Atlas of Japan. Ryuziro, Isido, ed, 405
Atlas of Plant Life. Edlin, Herbert L. and Huxley, Anthony. 233
An Atlas of Russian History. Chew, Allen F, 388
Atlas of the Arab-Israeli Conflict. Gilbert, Martin, 389
Atlas of the Sea. Barton, Robert, 2131

INDEX

Atlas of the Second World War. Young, Peter, ed, 403
Atlas of the Universe. Moore, Patrick, 211
Atlas of Wildlife. Nayman, Jacqueline, 241
Atlas of World Wildlife. Beazley, Mitchel, 240
ATLASES, 386, 395-396, 398
Atmore, Anthony. see Oliver, Roland A.
ATOMIC BOMB, 2057, 2061, 2668-2669, 5140, 5142
ATOMIC ENERGY, 1524, 2059-2060, 2663
Atomic Energy for Human Needs. Michelsohn, David R, 2060
Atomic Establishment. Metzger, H. Peter, 1524
ATOMIC WEAPONS, 1300, 2670-2671
ATOMS, 1892, 2052, 2058, 2063, 2075
Atoms, Molecules, and Chemical Change. Grunwald, Ernest and Johnsen, Russell H. 2075
Attica Diary. Coons, William R, 1735
ATTILA, 4685, 5012
Attwater, Donald, ed. Catholic Dictionary, 115
Auchincloss, Louis. Richelieu, 5379
Auden, W. H. Collected Longer Poems, 3842
———. Collected Shorter Poems, 3843
———. Portable Greek Reader, 4435
———. Van Gogh, 3068
Auden, W. H. and Pearson, Norman H., eds. Poets of the English Language, 3774
AUDIO-VISUAL EDUCATION, 1772
AUDIOVISUAL MATERIALS —
  REVIEWS, 40-41
August, Stanley W. Closing the Loop, 2770
Augustine, St. Basic Writing of Saint Augustine, 806
———. Confessions of Saint Augustine, 759
AUGUSTINUS, AURELIUS, SAINT, 610
AUGUSTUS, 4339
Augustus to Constantine. Grant, Robert M, 805
Auld, William M. Christmas Traditions, 1819
Aulén, Gustaf. The Faith of the Christian Church, 737
AURELIUS ANTONINUS, MARCUS, 4946
AUSTEN, JANE, 3922-3924
AUSTIN, STEPHEN FULLER, 6224
Austin, William. Music in the 20th Century, 3149
AUSTRALIA, 2276
  DESCRIPTION AND TRAVEL, 4843-4844
  DICTIONARIES AND ENCYCLOPEDIAS, 456
  HISTORY, 6281, 6286-6288
  RELIGION, 877
Australia. Pike, D, 6288
Australia, New Zealand and the Southwest Pacific. Robinson, K. W, 4843
Australia Since Federation. Alexander, Frederick, 6286
Australian Religions. Eliade, Mircea, 877
AUSTRIA
  HISTORY, 4753, 5291, 5340, 5342, 5345, 5347-5348
  POLITICS AND GOVERNMENT, 5343-5344, 5339, 5346
Austria. Stadler, Karl R, 5347
Austria Between East and West, 1945-1955. Baden, William B, 5345
Austria-Hungary. Lingelbach, William E, 5340
Austria, 1918-1972. Barker, Elisabeth, 5346
Eine Auswahl. Tucholsky, Kurt, 3981
AUTHORS, 325, 425-430, 4863, 4867
  INDEXES, 68
AUTHORSHIP, 329, 2849, 3468
Autobiography. Cellini, Benvenuto, 2981
Autobiography. Gandhi, Mohandas, 5632
Autobiography. Steffens, Lincoln, 502
Autobiography. Stravinsky, Igor, 3180
Autobiography of Bertrand Russell. Russell, Bertrand, 3967
Autobiography of Malcolm X. Malcolm X and Haley, Alex. 1031
Autobiography of Mark Twain. Twain, Mark, 3752
Autographs. Patterson, Jerry E, 4875
AUTOGRAPHS — COLLECTORS AND COLLECTING, 4875
AUTOMATION, 2771
AUTOMOBILE DRIVING, 2571
AUTOMOBILE INDUSTRY AND TRADE, 2738-2739
Automobile Quarterly, ed. The American Car Since 1775, 2742
Automobile Quarterly. 2740
AUTOMOBILE RACING, 2751, 3402-3405, 3407
AUTOMOBILES, 2744-2745, 2750
  HISTORY, 2740-2743
  MOTORS, 2752-2753
Automotive Engines. Billiet, Walter E, 2752
Automotive Engines. Crouse, W. H. and Anglin, D. L. 2753
Auty, Phyllis. Tito, 5562
Avant-Garde. Pronko, Leonard C, 4188
Avant-Garde in Painting. Bazin, Germain, 3025

328

INDEX

Avebury, John L. Pre-Historic Times As Illustrated by Ancient Remains and the Manners and Customs of Modern Savages, 4709
Avery, Catherine B., ed. The New Century Handbook of Classical Geography, 406
———. New Century Handbook of Leaders of the Classical World, 411
Avery, Peter. Modern Iran, 5640
Avrich, Paul. Russian Rebels, 1600-1800, 5480
An Awakened Minority. Servin, Manuel P., compiled by. 1045
Axline, Virginia M. Debs, 2628
Ayala, Francisco. El Rapto, 4365
Ayisi, Eric O. An Introduction to the Study of African Culture, 925
Aykroyd, W. R. The Conquest of Famine, 1514
Aymé, Marcel. Le Passe-Muraille, 4191
Aynor, H. S. Notes from Africa, 5694
Azorin. Dona Ines, 4366
AZTECS, 5757, 5808, 5811
Aztecs. Davies, Nigel, 5811
Aztecs, People of the Sun. Caso, Alfonso, 5757
Azuela, Mariano. Los de Abajo, 4367
Azul and Otras Versos. Darío, Ruben, 4319

Baars, Donald L. Red Rock Country, 2161
Babel to Byzantium. Dickey, James, 3846
Baboon. Gardner, Richard, 2480
BABOONS, 2480
BABYLONIA — ANTIQUITIES, 4878, 4908
BACH, JOHANN SEBASTIAN, 3158, 3164
Bach, Marcus. Major Religions of the World, 817
Bacharach, Jere L. A Near East Studies Handbook, 570-1974, 441
Bachmann, Robert. The Hand of a Thousand Rings and Other Chinese Stories, 4606
Bach's World. Chiapusso, Jan, 3164
Back, Joe. Horses, Hitches and Rocky Trails, 3447
Back to Beckett. Cohn, Ruby, 4284
Backcountry Camping. Riviere, William A, 3398
BACKGAMMON, 3343
BACKPACKING, 3386, 3398
BACON, FRANCIS, 5212
BACTERIOLOGY — CLASSIFICATION, 237
Baden, William B. Austria Between East and West, 1945-1955, 5345
Badillo, Herman and Haynes, Milton. A Bill of No Rights, 1742

Baer, George W. The Coming of the Italian-Ethiopian War, 5720
Baigell, Matthew. The American Scene, 3036
Bailey, Anthony. Horizon Concise History of the Low Countries, 5543
Bailey, George. Germany, 5330
Bailey, Helen M., et al. Latin America, 6254
Bailey, John M. Liberal Arts Physics, 2014
Bailey, Liberty H. Manual of Cultivated Plants, 232
Bailey, Richard W. and Robinson, Jay L. Varieties of Present-Day English, 1875
Bailey, Thomas A. American Spirit, 5876
———. Diplomatic History of the American People, 1328
———. Woodrow Wilson and the Lost Peace, 5078
Baillie, Donald M. God Was in Christ, 748
Baily, Leslie. Gilbert and Sullivan, 3210
Bailyn, Bernard. The Ideological Origins of the American Revolution, 5913
Bailyn, Bernard and Garrett, J. N., eds. Pamphlets on the American Revolution, 1750-1776, 5914
Bain, Richard C. Convention Decisions and Voting Records, 136
Bainton, Roland H. Here I Stand, 782
———. Women of the Reformation in France and England, 783
———. Women of the Reformation in Germany and Italy, 784
Baird, A. C. American Public Addresses, 3518
Baker, Blanche M. Theatre and Allied Arts, 64
Baker, Carlos. Ernest Hemingway, 3725
———. Hemingway and His Critics, 3726
———. Hemingway, the Writer As Artist, 3761
Baker, James. William Golding, 3968
Baker, Jeffrey A. see Cline, Gloria S.
Baker, John R. Race, 2185
Baker, Timothy. The Normans, 5191
Balanchine, George. Balanchine's New Complete Stories of the Great Ballets, 3324
Balanchine's New Complete Stories of the Great Ballets. Balanchine, George, 3324
Bald, R. C. John Donne, 3795
Baldry, H. C. Ancient Greek Literature in Its Living Context, 4437
Baldwin, Gordon C. Inventors and Inventions of the Ancient World, 2488
Baldwin, Hanson. Battles Lost and Won, 5124
Baldwin, James. The Fire Next Time, 1009
———. No Name in the Street, 1010
———. Nobody Knows My Name, 1011

INDEX

BALDWIN, JAMES, 3237
Baldwin, John. Contemporary Sculpture Techniques, 2987
Balfour, Michael. The Kaiser and His Times, 5300
———. West Germany, 5331
Balfour, Patrick. Atatürk, 5558
Balkans. Forbes, Nevil, et al. 5556
Balkans in Our Time. Wolff, Robert, 5557
Ball, Adrian, ed. My Greatest Race, by Twenty of the Finest Motor Racing Drivers of All Time, 3403
Ball, Robert H. see Bowman, Walter P.
BALLADS, 3237, 3781
BALLET, 3324-3325, 3327-3328
Ballet. Clarke, Mary and Crisp, Clement. 3328
Ballinger, Margaret. From Union to Apartheid, 1239
Balloons and Airships. Ege, Lennart, 2734
Ballou, Robert O., et al, eds. The Bible of the World, 818
Baly, Denis A. A Geography of the Bible, 711
Balzac, Honoré de. César Birotteau, 4192
———. La Cousine Bette, 4193
———. Le Curé de Tours, 4194
———. Eugénie Grandet, 4195
———. Le Lys dans la Vallée, 4196
———. Le Père Goriot, 4197
BALZAC, HONORÉ DE, 4235
Banani, Amin. The Modernization of Iran, 1921-1941, 5641
Banco. Charriere, Henri, 1734
Bancroft, Anne. Religions of the East, 834
Banerji, Bibhutibhushan. Pather Panchali, 4480
Banfield, Edward C., ed. Urban Government, 1628
BANGLADESH — POLITICS AND GOVERNMENT, 5638
BANKS AND BANKING
DICTIONARIES, 139
U. S., 1451-1454
Banks and Politics in America. Hammond, Bray, 1452
Banks, Arthur. A World Atlas of Military History, 385
Banned Books. Haight, Anne L, 506
Banner, James M., Jr. To the Hartford Convention, 1375
Banti, Luisa. Etruscan Cities and Their Culture, 4926
Bantu, Boer and Briton. Macmillan, William M, 5736
Barbarossa. Clark, Alan, 5126
Barbeau, Arthur E. The Unknown Soldiers, 5086
Barber, Bernard. Drugs and Society, 2574

Barber, James A., Jr., see Ambrose, Stephen E.
Barber, Noel. Seven Days of Freedom, 5365
———. The Sultans, 5555
Barber of Seville, and The Marriage of Figaro. Beaumarchais, Pierre-Augustine Caron de, 4147
Le Barbier de Séville, Le Mariage de Figaro. Beaumarchais, Pierre-Augustine Caron de, 4148
Barbour, Floyd B., ed. The Black Seventies, 1012
Barbour, Ian G. Myths, Models, and Paradigms, 682
Barbour, Roger W. see Ernst, Carl
La Barca Sin Pescador. Casona, Alejandro, 4352
Barck, Oscar T., ed. America in the World, 6101
———. Since Nineteen Hundred, 6108
Barclay, William. Ethics in a Permissive Society, 757
Barcsay, Jeno. Anatomy for the Artist, 3011
Bardach, John E., et al. Aquaculture, 2817
———. Harvest of the Sea. , 1478
Barea, Arturo. Lorca, the Poet and His People, 4341
Barefoot in the Sky. Scott, Sheila, 2718
Barghoorn, Frederick C. Politics in the USSR, 1170
Barile, Paolo. see Adams, John C.
Baring-Gould, Sabine. Legends of the Patriarch and Prophets and Other Old Testament Characters, 723
Barker, Danny. see Buerkle, Jack V.
Barker, Dudley. The Man of Principle, 3937
Barker, Elisabeth. Austria, 1918-1972, 5346
Barker, Eugene C. The Life of Stephen F. Austin, Founder of Texas, 1793-1836, 6224
Barker, John W. Justinian and the Later Roman Empire, 5547
Barker, Lucius and Twiley, W. B. Civil Liberties and the Constitution, 1565
Barker, Rodney, ed. Studies in Opposition, 1220
Barlow, Frank. Edward the Confessor, 5192
Barlow, Harold and Morgenstern, Sam, eds. A Dictionary of Musical Themes, 297
———. Dictionary of Opera and Song Themes, 308
Barnaby, Frank. Man and the Atom, 2663
Barnaby, Kenneth C. Some Ship Disasters and Their Causes, 4690
Barnard, Harry. Rutherford B. Hayes and His America, 6088

Barnes, Gilbert H. Anti-Slavery Impulse, 1830-1844, 1281
Barnes, Richard G. Episodes in Fine Poetic Traditions, 3496
Barnet, Sylvan, et al. Nine Modern Classics, 3514
Barnett, A. Doak. Cadres, Bureaucracy, and Political Power in Communist China, 1651
———. China After Mao, with Selected Documents, 1175
———. China on the Eve of the Communist Take Over, 5593
———. Chinese Communist Politics in Action, 1136
Barnett, Correlli. The Collapse of British Power, 5268
———. The First Churchill, 5235
Barnett, Lincoln. The Treasure of Our Tongue, 1865
Barnett, Samuel A. Instinct and Intelligence, 2351
Barnhart, Clarence L., et al, eds. The Barnhart Dictionary of New English Since 1963, 162
Barnhart Dictionary of New English Since 1963. Barnhart, Clarence L., et al, eds. 162
Barnie, John. War in Medieval English Society, 5199
Baroja, Pío. Las Cuidades, 4368
———. Restlessness of Shanti Andía and Other Writings, 4489
———. Zalacain, e Aventurero, 4369
Baroque Music. Palisca, Claude U, 3147
Barraclough, Geoffrey, tr. Medieval Germany, 911-1250, 5289
———. The Origins of Modern Germany, 5282
Barrett, Leonard E. Soul-Force, 871
Barrett, William. Irrational Man, 549
———. Time of Need, 4655
———. What Is Existentialism? Heidegger, 550
Barricades in Belfast. Hastings, Max, 5167
Barrie, James M. Plays, 3881
BARRIE, SIR JAMES MATTHEW, 3966
Barrio Boy. Galarza, Ernesto, 1041
Barron, Jerome A. Freedom of the Press for Whom? The Right of Access to Mass Media, 1566
Barron, Milton L. The Blending American, 989
Barron's in-Depth Guide to the Ivy League Schools. 1790
Barron's Profiles of American Colleges. Fine, Benjamin, 146
Barros, James, ed. The United Nations, 1553
Barrow, G. W. Feudal Britain, 5193

Barruel, Paul. Birds of the World, 245
Barsa Enciclopedia. 84
Barsis, Max. The Common Man Through the Centuries, 1810
Barth, Karl. Dogmatics in Outline, 752
BARTH, KARL, 741
Bartholomew, John, ed. Time Atlas of the World, 395
Bartlett, Irving H. Wendell Phillips, 6039
Bartlett, John. Bartlett's Familiar Quotations, 339
———. Complete Concordance to Shakespeare, 367
Bartlett, Ruhl J., ed. Record of American Diplomacy, 1329
Bartlett's Familiar Quotations. Bartlett, John, 339
Bartok. Lesznai, Lajos, 3159
BARTOK, BELA, 3159
Barton, Lucy. Historic Costume for the Stage, 3303
Barton, Robert. Atlas of the Sea, 2131
BARTRAM, WILLIAM, 2223
Barzini, Luigi. The Italians, 5426
Barzman, Sol. Madmen and Geniuses, 5853
Barzun, Jacques. Berlioz and His Century, 3152
———. The House of Intellect, 457
Bascom, Willard. A Hole in the Bottom of the Sea, 2105
BASEBALL, 3371-3374, 3376-3378
Baseball. Litwhiler, Daniel, 3374
Baseball Play and Strategy. Allen, Ethan, 3371
Bases of Argument. Smith, Craig R. and Hunsaker, David M. 3492
Basham, Arthur L. The Wonder That Was India, 5626
Basic. Albrecht, Robert L., et al. 466
Basic Bibliography of Science and Technology. McGraw-Hill Encyclopedia of Science & Technology Editors, 59
Basic Boating. Andrews, Howard and Russel, Alexander. 3422
BASIC (COMPUTER PROGRAM LANGUAGE), 466
Basic Documents in Canadian History. Talman, James J, 5794
Basic Electricity. Marcus, Abraham, 2048
Basic Electronics Course. Crowhurst, Norman H, 2051
Basic Fly Fishing and Fly Tying. Ovington, Roy, 3456
Basic Ice Skating Skills. Ogilvie, Robert S, 3415
Basic Mathematics. Lang, Serge, 1937
Basic Physiology and Anatomy. Chaffee, Ellen E. and Greisheimer, Esther M. 2508

INDEX

Basic Problems of Philosophy. Bronstein, David J., et al. 511
Basic Rockcraft. Robbins, Royal, 3394
Basic Works. Aristoteles, 625
Basic Writing of Saint Augustine. Augustine, St. 806
Basic Writings. Freud, Sigmund, 527
Basic Writings. Thomas Aquinas, St. 699
Basic Writings of C. G. Jung. Jung, Carl G, 528
Basic Writings, 1903-1959. Russell, Bertrand, 655
BASKETBALL, 3353-3356
Basketball. Cousy, Robert and Power, Frank G., Jr. 3353
Basketball Skill Book. Monroe, Earl and Unseld, Wes. 3356
Basolo, Fred and Pearson, R. G. Mechanisms of Inorganic Reactions, 2078
BASQUES, 4761
Bass, George F. Archaeology Under Water, 4716
Bass, Howard. International Encyclopedia of Winter Sports, 3411
Bastin, John and Benda, Harry J. A History of Modern Southeast Asia, 5670
Batchelor, John and Hogg, Ian. Artillery, 1683
Batchelor, John. see Cooper, Bryan
Batchelor, John H. see Macksey, Kenneth
Bate, Walter Jackson. Coleridge, 3807
BATES, HENRY WALTER, 2289
Bates, Joseph D. Fishing, 3451
Bates, Marston and Humphrey, Philip S., eds. The Darwin Reader, 2285
Bates, Richard O. The Gentleman from Ohio, 6090
BATISTA Y ZALDIVAR, FULGENCIO, 1340
Battan, Louis D. Weather, 2157
Battiscombe, Georgina. Queen Alexandra, 1844-1925, 5269
Battle for a Continent. Bird, Harrison, 5911
Battle for the Presidency. Warren, Sidney, 1384
Battle for the Wilderness. Frome, Michael, 1471
BATTLES, 4669-4671
Battles and Leaders of the Civil War. Nichols, Roy F., ed, 6031
Battles Lost and Won. Baldwin, Hanson, 5124
Battleship Era. Padfield, Peter, 1689
BATTLESHIPS — HISTORY, 1689
Baudelaire, Charles P. Les Fleurs du Mal, 4118
Bauer, Ernst W. Wonders of the Earth, 2090

Bauer, Marion and Peyser, Ethel. Music Through the Ages, 3134
Bauer, Yehuda. From Diplomacy to Resistance, 5660
Baugh, Albert C. A History of the English Language, 1866
Baumbach, Jonathan. The Landscape of Nightmare, 3715
Baumeister, T. and Marks, Lionel. Standard Handbook for Mechanical Engineers, 254
Bavier, Robert N. Sailing to Win, 3427
Bay of Pigs. Johnson, Haynes, 5833
Bayeux Tapestry. Gibbs-Smith, Charles H, 3022
Bayh, Birch. One Heartbeat Away, 1567
Baynes, Cary F., tr. The I Ching; or, Book of Changes, 870
Bazin, Germain. The Avant-Garde in Painting, 3025
Be Expert with Map and Compass. Kjellstrom, Bjorn, 3389
Beaglehole, John C. The Life of Captain John Cook, 4701
Beale, Howard K. The Critical Year, 6080
Beals, Carleton. The Nature of Revolution, 4667
Bear, Fred. The Archer's Bible, 3461
Beard, Charles A. Economic Interpretation of the Constitution of the United States, 1568
———. The Industrial Revolution, 1410
Beardsley, Monroe C., ed. European Philosophers from Descartes to Nietzsche, 635
Beasley, William G. The Modern History of Japan, 5619
BEATLES, THE, 3232
BEATRICE D'ESTE, 5430
Beatrice d'Este, Duchess of Milan, 1475-1497. Ady, Julia M, 5430
Beatty, William K. see Marks, Geoffrey
Beaumarchais, Pierre-Augustine Caron de. The Barber of Seville, and The Marriage of Figaro, 4147
———. Le Barbier de Séville, Le Mariage de Figaro, 4148
Beaumont, Francis and Fletcher, John. King and No King, 3857
———. Knight of the Burning Pestle, 3858
———. Maid's Tragedy, 3859
Beaumont, Pierre de. La Chanson de Roland, 4119
———. Le Cheval Fou, 4120
Beazley, Mitchel. Atlas of World Wildlife, 240
Becker, Carl L. Declaration of Independence, 5915
Becker, Ernest. The Denial of Death, 583

Becker, George. Introductory Concepts in Biology, 2207
Becker, Thomas. The Coin Makers, 1456
Becket. Anouilh, Jean, 4144
Beckett, James G. The Making of Modern Ireland, 1603-1923, 5160
Beckett, Samuel. Waiting for Godot, 4149
BECKETT, SAMUEL, 4284, 4286
Bedau, Hugo A., compiled by. Civil Disobedience, 1221
———. The Death Penalty in America, 1730
Beddall, Barbara G., ed. Wallace and Bates in the Tropics, 2289
Beddoes, Richard. Hockey! The Story of the World's Fastest Sport, 3412
Beecham, Justin. Olga, 3379
Beeler, John. Warfare in England, 1066-1189, 5194
———. Warfare in Feudal Europe, 730-1200, 1658
BEES — BEHAVIOR, 2399
Beethoven. Marek, George R, 3177
BEETHOVEN, LUDWIG VAN, 3177
Before and After Socrates. Cornford, Francis M, 608
Before Civilization. Renfrew, Colin, 4724
Before Nature Dies. Dorst, Jean, 1466
Before Silent Spring. Whorton, James, 2782
Before the Armada. Wernham, R. B, 5233
Before the Deluge. Friedrich, Otto, 4754
Beggar's Opera. Gay, John, 3874
Beginner's Guide to Squash. Hawkey, Richard B, 3365
Beginning and the End, and Other Poems. Jeffers, Robinson, 3575
Behan, Brendan. The Quare Fellow; The Hostage, 3898
BEHAVIORISM (PSYCHOLOGY), 2360
Behemoth. Neumann, Franz, 5321
Behind Mud Walls, 1930-1962. Wiser, William and Wiser, Charlotte. 1124
Behind the Great Wall of China. Capa, Cornell, ed, 4775
Behind the Trail of Broken Treaties. Deloria, Vine, Jr, 5768
Behold Man. Nilsson, Lennart, 2505
Behrman, A. S. Water Is Everybody's Business, 2700
Behrman, Daniel. The New World of the Oceans, 2132
Behuke, John A., ed. Challenging Biological Problems, 2208
Beier, Ulli, ed. African Poetry, 4630
———. Introduction to African Literature, 4624
———. Three Nigerian Plays, 4631
Being and Nothingness. Sartre, Jean-Paul, 554

Being Human, the Psychological Experience. McNeil, Elton B, 891
Bekenntnisse des Hochstaplers, Felix Krull. Mann, Thomas, 4064
Bekker, Cajus. The Lutwaffe War Diaries, 5139
Belenitsky, Aleksandr. Central Asia, 4787
Belfast. Budge, Ian and O'Leary, Cornelius. 5169
BELGIUM — HISTORY, 5545
Bell. Bruce, Robert V, 1802
BELL, ALEXANDER GRAHAM, 1802
Bell, Daniel, ed. The Radical Right, 1192
———. The Coming of Post-Industrial Society, 1103
Bell, Daniel and Kristol, Irving, eds. Capitalism Today, 1407
Bell, Eric T. Men of Mathematics, 1945
Bell, J. Bowyer. The Secret Army, 5163
Bell Laboratories. Gregor, Arthur, 2643
Bell, Leland V. In Hitler's Shadow, 1146
Bell, Michael, compiled by. Painters in a New Land, 2939
Bellringing. Camp, John, 3252
BELLS, 3253
Beloff, Max. Foreign Policy of Soviet Russia, 1929-1941, 1306
Belote, James H. and Belote, William M. Corregidor, 5125
Belote, William M. see Belote, James H.
Bemis, Samuel F., ed. The American Secretaries of State and Their Diplomacy, 1776-1925, 1330
———. John Quincy Adams, 5990
Bemis, Samuel F. and Griffin, G. G. Guide to the Diplomatic History of the United States (1775-1921), 76
Benac, H. Guide de Ideés Littéraires, 4104
Benda, Harry J. and Larkin, J. A., eds. The World of Southeast Asia, 5671
Benda, Harry J. see Bastin, John
Bendiner, Robert, see Aaron, Daniel
Beneath the Wheel. Hesse, Hermann, 4056
Benedict Arnold. Boylan, Brian R, 5933
Benedict, Michael. The Impeachment and Trial of Andrew Johnson, 6081
Benedikt, Michael and Wellwarth, George. Modern Spanish Theatre, 4359
Beneficial Insects. Swan, Lester, 2777
BENELUX COUNTRIES — HISTORY, 1173, 5543
Benelux Nations. Weil, Gordon L, 1173
Benét, Stephen Vincent. John Brown's Body, 3595
BENÉT, STEPHEN VINCENT, 3595
Benet, William Rose. The Reader's Encyclopedia, 322
Benevente, Jacinto. Bonds of Interest, 4344
———. Malquerida, 4345

INDEX

Benfey, Otto F. The Names and Structures of Organic Compounds, 2081
Ben-Gurion, David, ed. The Jews in Their Land, 5661
BENITEZ PÉREZ, MANUEL, 3288
Benjamin Franklin. Fleming, Thomas, ed, 5950
Benn, Gottfried. Gottfried Benn Dargestellt von Walter Lennig, 3994
———. Die Stimme Hinter dem Vorhang, 4010
Bennett, Hank. The Complete Shortwave Listener's Handbook, 2650
Bennett, Hastin. The International Medical Encyclopedia, 2586
Bennett, Henry S. Life on the English Manor, 5200
Bennett, Isobel. The Great Barrier Reef, 2276
Bennett, Ross, ed. The New America's Wonderlands, 4810
Bensman, Joseph and Vidich, Arthur J. The New American Society, 995
Benson, Frederick R. Writers in Arms, 5466
Bentley, Eric, ed. Classic Theatre, Five German Plays, 4025
———. Classic Theatre, Six French Plays, 4184
———. Classic Theatre, Six Italian Plays, 4295
———. Classic Theatre, Six Spanish Plays, 4360
———. Five German Plays, 4026
———. Genius of the Italian Theatre, 4296
———. The Theatre of Commitment and Other Essays on Drama in Our Society, 3291
———. Thirty Years of Treason, 1228
Bentley, John. The Thresher Disaster, 2688
Benton, Allen H. and Werner, William E. Field Biology and Ecology, 2236
Benumof, Reuben. Concepts in Physics, 2015
Beowulf. 3969
Beraud, Henri. Twelve Portraits of the French Revolution, 5389
Berceo, Gonzalo de. Milagros de Nuestra Señora, 4318
Bercovici, Konrad. The Story of the Gypsies, 4682
Berdyaev, Nicolas. Origin of Russian Communism, 1495
Berendsohn, Walter A. Selma Lagerlof, Her Life and Work, 4091
———. Thomas Mann, 4078
Berenson, Bernard. Italian Painters of the Renaissance, 3055
Berg, Stephen, ed. Naked Poetry, 3547
Berg, W. Exposure, 3107

Bergamini, David. Japan's Imperial Conspiracy, 5117
Bergamini, John D. Spanish Bourbons, 5462
Berger, Gene. Bowling for Everyone, 3340
Berger, Raoul. Congress v. the Supreme Court, 1613
———. Impeachment, 1569
Bergey's Manual of Determinative Bacteriology. Buchanan, Robert E. and Gibbons, Norman E. 237
Berghahn, Volker R. Germany and the Approach of War in 1914, 5096
Berglund, Berndt. Wilderness Survival, 2532
Berglund, Berndt and Bolsby, Clare. Wilderness Cooking, 2837
Bergman, Andrew. We're in the Money, 3264
Bergman, Ingmar. Four Screen Plays, 4088
Bergmann, Peter G. The Riddle of Gravitation, 2028
Bergonzi, Bernard. The Turn of the Century, 3770
Bergson, Henri L. Creative Evolution, 519
Berkeley, Edmund C. Guide to Mathematics for the Intelligent Nonmathematician, 1928
Berkin, Carol. Jonathan Sewall, 5944
Berkov, Robert. Strong Man of China, 5594
Berkowitz, Henry. see Borstein, Larry
Berle, Adolf A., Jr. Twentieth Century Capitalist Revolution, 1532
BERLIN
  BLOCKADE, 5337
  HISTORY, 4754, 5110, 5132, 5337
BERLIN, IRVING, 3157
Berlin, Isaiah. Karl Marx, 1491
Berlin, K. Darrell. see Butler, George B.
Berliners. Armstrong, Anne, 5329
Berlioz and His Century. Barzun, Jacques, 3152
BERLIOZ, HECTOR, 3152
Berlitz, Charles F. and Valentine, J. Manson. The Bermuda Triangle, 4686
Bermann, Ernest G. Forerunners of Black Power, 1234
Bermuda Triangle. Berlitz, Charles F. and Valentine, J. Manson. 4686
Bernal, Ignacio. Mexico, Three Thousand Years of Art and Life, 4800
Bernard, Jack F. Talleyrand, 5390
Berndt, Fredrick. The Domino Book, 3344
BERNHARDT, SARAH, 3306
Bernstein, Barton J., ed. The Politics and Policies of the Truman Administration, 6147
Bernstein, Barton J. and Matusow, A. J., eds. The Truman Administration, 6148
Bernstein, Burton. Thurber, 3007

Bernstein, Carl and Woodward, Bob. All the President's Men, 1716
Bernstein, Jeremy. Einstein, 2023
———. Nepal, 4782
Bernstein, Leonard. The Joy of Music, 3131
Bernstein, Saul. Alternatives to Violence, 1104
Bernstein, Theodore M. The Careful Writer, 1885
———. Watch Your Language, 1886
Berry, Adrian. The Next Ten Thousand Years, 4660
Berry, James. Heroin Was My Best Friend, 2597
Berry, Mary C. The Alaska Pipeline, 1521
Berry, Wendell. Openings, 3623
Berryman, John. His Toy, His Dream, His Rest, 3624
———. Seventy-Seven Dream Songs, 3625
Berthoff, Rowland T. An Unsettled People, 1105
Berthoff, Warner. Fictions and Events, 3521
Berti, Luciano. Raphael, 3056
Besancon, Robert M., ed. Encyclopedia of Physics, 213
Besch, Lutz. see Fischer, Hans S.
Bessie. Albertson, Chris, 3228
Best American Plays Series. 3673
Best and the Brightest. Halberstam, David, 6165
Best, Charles H. and Taylor, N. B. The Human Body, 2507
Best Mystery and Suspense Plays of the Modern Theatre. Richards, Stanley, ed, 3509
Best Plays. Chekhov, Anton P, 4529
Best Plays. Racine, Jean B, 4179
Best Plays of the Sixties. Richards, Stanley, ed, 3510
Bestiary. 4429
Beth, Loren P. The Development of the American Constitution, 1877-1917, 1570
Bethell, Nicholas. Gomulka, 5360
———. The War Hitler Won, 5097
Bethge, Eberhard. Dietrich Bonhoeffer, 810
Betjeman, John. Collected Poems, 3844
———. Ghastly Good Taste, a Depressing Story of the Rise and Fall of English Architecture, 2967
Betrayal of the Negro. Logan, Rayford W, 1258
Bettenson, Henry, ed. Documents of the Christian Church, 777
Better Golf. Coyne, John, ed, 3367
Better Homes & Gardens. Better Homes and Gardens Sewing Book, 2838

Better Homes and Gardens Sewing Book. Better Homes & Gardens, 2838
Bettex, Albert. The Discovery of the World, 4700
Betti, Ugo. Crime on Goat Island, 4292
Between Belief and Unbelief. Pruyser, Paul W, 523
Between the Wars. Shannon, David A, 6145
Between War and Peace. Feis, Herbert, 5110
Beum, R. see Shapiro, Karl J.
BEVERIDGE, ALBERT JEREMIAH, 6109
Beveridge, W. I. Art of Scientific Investigation, 1916
A Bevy of Beasts. Durrell, Gerald, 2445
Beware of the Food You Eat. Winter, Ruth, 2558
Bewer, Julius A. The Literature of the Old Testament, 724
Bewley, Marius. Eccentric Design, 3745
BEYLE, MARIE HENRI, 4283
Beyond Freedom and Dignity. Skinner, Burrhus F, 562
Beyond Malthus. Chamberlain, Neil W, 950
Beyond Stonehenge. Hawkins, Gerald S, 1978
Beyond the Known Universe. Levitt, I. M, 1986
Beyond the Melting Pot. Glazer, Nathan and Moyihan, Daniel P. 1022
Beyond the New Deal. Hamby, Alonzo L, 6151
Beyond the Reach of Sense. Heywood, Rosalind, 529
Beyond Words. Harrison, Randall P, 573
Bezner, Hart C. The Elements of Fortran Four, 468
Bhagavad Gita. Deutsch, Eliot, ed, 845
Bhatia, Krishan. Indira, 5631
Bhattacharya, Bhabani, ed. Contemporary Indian Short Stories, 4608
Bhattacharya, Sachchidananda. A Dictionary of Indian History, 440
Bialer, Seweryn, ed. Stalin and His Generals, 5113
Bibby, Cyril. Scientist Extraordinary, 2221
Bibby, Geoffrey. Looking for Dilmun. , 4733
BIBLE, 101, 703-709
   ANTIQUITIES, 713-714
   COMMENTARIES, 104, 106
   DICTIONARIES, 103, 105
   GEOGRAPHY, 108, 711
   HISTORY OF BIBLICAL EVENTS, 712-713
   MAPS, 108-109
   NEW TESTAMENT, 732-733, 735
   OLD TESTAMENT, 716-717, 722-

INDEX

  726, 730-731
  ISAIAH — CRITICISM, TEXTUAL, 718
  PENTATEUCH, 729
Bible. Holy Bible, 705
———. Holy Bible. Confraternity Edition, 703
———. Holy Bible. Four Prophets, 731
———. Holy Bible. King James Version, 704
———. The Holy Scriptures. According to the Masoretic Text, 716
———. The Jerusalem Bible, 708
———. The Living Bible, 707
———. New English Bible, with the Apocrypha, 706
———. The New Oxford Annotated Bible, 709
Bible and the Common Reader. Chase, Mary Ellen, 710
Bible As History. Keller, Werner, 713
Bible As History in Pictures. Keller, Werner, 712
BIBLE AS LITERATURE, 710, 724
Bible of the World. Ballou, Robert O., et al, eds. 818
Bibliographical Guide to the Study of the Literature of the U. S. A. Gohdes, Clarence L, 66
BIBLIOGRAPHY — PAPERBOUND EDITIONS, 4
Bickel, Alexander M. The Supreme Court and the Idea of Progress, 1614
Bickel, Lennard. Facing Starvation, 2773
Bickerman, Elias J. Chronology of the Ancient World, 434
BICYCLES, 2746, 3400
Biddis, Michael D. *see* Cartwright, Frederick F.
Bieber, Margarete. The History of the Greek and Roman Theater, 4450
Bierce, Ambrose. Devil's Dictionary, 3754
BIERCE, AMBROSE, 3721
Bierhorst, John, ed. Four Masterpieces of American Indian Literature, 4637
———. In the Trail of the Wind, 4638
Big Bands. Simon, George T, 3243
Big City Mayors. Ruchelman, Leonard I., ed, 1630
Big Two. Rapoport, Anatol, 1311
Bigelow, Howard E. Mushroom Pocket Field Guide, 2332
Bill, Alfred H. Rehearsal for Conflict, 6017
A Bill of No Rights. Badillo, Herman and Haynes, Milton. 1742
Bill of Rights Reader. Konvitz, Milton R., ed, 1581
Billiards at Half-Past Nine. Boll, Heinrich, 4035

Billias, George A., ed. George Washington's Opponents, 5951
Billie Jean King's Secrets of Winning Tennis. King, Billie J. and Hyams, Joseph. 3362
Billiet, Walter E. Automotive Engines, 2752
Billington, James H. The Icon and the Axe, 5481
Billington, Ray A. America's Frontier Heritage, 6227
———. Far Western Frontier, 6228
———. Westward Expansion, 6229
Billy Bartram and His Green World. Sanger, Marjory B, 2223
Bimba, Anthony. History of the American Working Class, 1436
———. The Molly Maguires, 1437
Binkley, Robert C. Realism and Nationalism, 5053
Binkley, Wilfred E. American Political Parties, 1387
Binstock, Robert H. and Ely, Katherine. The Politics of the Powerless, 1069
Binyon, Lawrence. Flight of the Dragon (Wisdom of the East), 2929
Biochemical Approach to Life. Jevons, Frederick R, 2227
BIOCHEMISTRY, 2215, 2249
Biofeedback. Kailins, Marvin and Andrews, Lewis M. 2580
BIOFEEDBACK TRAINING, 2513, 2580
Biographical Dictionary of Scientists. Williams, Trevor I, 206
A Biographical Dictionary of the Saints. Holweck, Frederick G, 110
Biographical Directory of the American Congress, 1774-1961. U. S. Congress, 135
BIOGRAPHY, 411, 414, 416-419, 425-430, 4434, 4861
BIOLOGICAL CHEMISTRY, 2069, 2227-2229
Biological Control by Natural Enemies. Deback, P, 2783
BIOLOGICAL SPECIMENS — COLLECTION AND PRESERVATION, 2310
Biological Techniques. Knudsen, Jens W, 2310
BIOLOGICAL WARFARE, 1685
Biological World. Nason, Alvin and Dehaan, Robert L. 2217
BIOLOGY, 229-230, 2207-2209, 2211-2220, 2224, 2226, 2236-2238, 2257-2258, 2285, 2296, 2514
Biology and the Future of Man. Handler, Philip, ed, 2214
Biosphere. Scientific American Editors, 2112

Bird, Caroline. The Crowding Syndrome, 948
Bird, Christopher. *see* Tompkins, Peter
Bird, Harrison. Battle for a Continent, 5911
Bird, Mark B. The Black Man, 5846
BIRDS, 245-246, 2353, 2425-2433, 2435-2438, 2442-2443
Birds, Beasts, and Relatives. Durrell, Gerald, 2259
Birds of North America. Rand, Austin L, 2431
Birds of the World. Barruel, Paul, 245
Birket-Smith, Kaj. Eskimos, 4848
Birmingham, Stephen. The Grandees, 4864
———. Our Crowd, 1058
———. Real Lace, 4821
Birnbaum, Max. *see* Cass, James
BIRTH CONTROL, 949, 958, 2553-2555
Birth Control. Rudel, Harry W, 2552
Birth of Indonesia. Wehl, David, 5690
Birth of the Nation. Schlesinger, Arthur M., Jr, 5908
Birth of the Republic, 1763-1789. Morgan, Edmund S, 5923
Birthday Party. Pinter, Harold, 3908
Birthrights. Farson, Richard E, 994
Bishop, Elizabeth. Complete Poems, 3626
Bishop, Morris. The Horizon Book of the Middle Ages, 4995
———. St. Francis of Assisi, 791
Bishop, Robert. How to Know American Antique Furniture, 3024
Bismarck. Taylor, Alan J. P, 5299
BISMARCK, OTTO VON, 5299
BISON, AMERICAN, 1480, 2464
Bitter Heritage. Schlesinger, Arthur M, Jr, 1354
Bitter Years. Petrow, Richard, 5130
Bizardel, Yvon. The First Expatriates, 5391
Black Abolitionists. Quarles, Benjamin, 1291
Black Africa. Morrison, Donald G, 1097
Black American. Fishel, Leslie H. and Quarles, Benjamin. 5882
Black American Music. Roach, Hildred, 3197
Black and White. Brink, William and Harris, Louis. 1015
Black Arts. Cavendish, Richard, 534
Black Bondage in the North. McManus, Edgar J, 1004
Black British, White British. Hiro, Dilip, 1024
Black, Charles Lund. Impeachment, 1571
Black Chicago. Spear, Allan H, 1037
Black Codes of the South. Wilson, Theodore B, 1243
Black Comedy and White Lies. Shaffer, Peter, 3913

Black, Cyril E. and Helmreich, E. C. Twentieth Century Europe, 5091
Black Economic Development. Haddad, William F. and Pugh, G. Douglas, eds. 1420
Black English. Dillard, Joey L, 1877
A Black Explorer at the North Pole. Henson, Matthew A, 4850
Black Freedom. Mabee, Carleton, 1224
BLACK HAWK WAR, 5993
Black Holes. Taylor, John G, 1980
Black Man. Bird, Mark B, 5846
Black Mother. Davidson, Basil, 5730
Black Music. Jones, Leroi, 3196
BLACK MUSLIMS, 1061
Black Muslims in America. Lincoln, C. Eric, 1061
Black on Black. Adoff, Arnold, ed, 1008
BLACK PANTHER PARTY, 1230, 1598
Black Political Parties. Walton, Hanes, Jr, 1399
Black Power. Carmichael, Stokely and Hamilton, Charles V. 1261
Black Presence in the Era of Revolution, 1770-1800. Kaplan, Sidney, 5935
Black Protest. Grant, Joanne, ed, 1256
Black September. Dobson, Christopher, 1183
Black Seventies. Barbour, Floyd B., ed, 1012
Black Skin, White Masks. Fanon, Frantz, 1021
Black Star. Davidson, Basil, 5725
Black Studies. Irwin, Leonard B, 18
Black Theater. Patterson, Lindsay, ed, 3676
A Black Theology of Liberation. Cone, James H, 681
Black Voices. Chapman, Abraham, ed, 3532
Black West. Katz, William L, 6235
Blackfeet. Ewers, John C, 5760
Blacking up. Toll, Robert C, 3259
Blacklock, Les. *see* Olson, Sigurd F.
Blackmer, Donald L. Unity in Diversity, 1487
Blacks in Canada. Winks, Robin W, 5796
Blacks on John Brown. Quarles, Benjamin, ed, 6024
Blainey, Geoffrey. The Causes of War, 1665
Blair, Peter H. An Introduction to Anglo-Saxon England, 5179
———. Roman Britain and Early England, 55 B.C. to A.D. 871, 5180
Blair, W. F., et al. Vertebrates of the United States, 2404
Blaise Pascal. Hazelton, Roger, 672
Blake, Herman. *see* Newton, Huey P.
Blake, Peter. God's Own Junkyard, 2950

INDEX

———. The Master Builders, 2961
Blake, William. Complete Writings of William Blake, with Variant Readings, 3808
BLAKE, WILLIAM, 3809
Blakeley, Thomas J. Soviet Philosophy, 675
Bland, Randall W. Private Pressure on Public Law, 1601
Blassingame, John W. The Slave Community, 6200
Bledsoe, Jerry. The World's Number One, Flat-Out, All-Time, Great, Stock Car Racing Book, 3402
Blegen, Theodore C. The Kensington Rune Stone, 5884
Blending American. Barron, Milton L, 989
BLIXEN, KAREN, 4093
Bloch, Camille. The Causes of the World War, 5071
Bloch, Herman D. The Circle of Discrimination, 1013
Bloch, Marc. Feudal Society, 5013
———. Historian's Craft, 4662
Bloch, Marvin A. Alcoholism, 2599
Bloch, Raymond. Etruscans, 4927
Block, Jack. Understanding Historical Research, 4663
Blockade. Morris, Eric, 5337
Blockade Runners of the Confederacy. Cochran, Hamilton, 6056
Bloecker, J. Die Neuen Wirklichkeiten, 3983
Blondel, Jean. An Introduction to Comparative Government, 1142
Blood. Hackett, Earl, 2515
Blood of My Blood. Gambino, Richard, 4823
Blood on the Border. Clendenen, Clarence, 6003
Bloodletters and Badmen. Nash, Jay R, 145
Bloodworth, Dennis. Chinese Looking Glass, 5572
Blount, Roy. About Three Bricks Shy of a Load, 3361
Blue and the Gray. Commager, Henry S, 6027
Blue Estuaries. Bogan, Louise, 3627
Blue Juniata. Cowley, Malcolm, 3632
Blue Nile. Moorehead, Alan, 5713
Blue Swallows. Nemerov, Howard, 3655
Blues Line. Sackheim, Eric, compiled by. 3195
Blum, Carol. Diderot, 670
Blum, Daniel. A New Pictorial History of the Talkies, 3265
———. Pictorial History of the American Theatre, 3307
———. A Pictorial History of the Silent Screen, 3261

Blunt, Wilfred. On Wings of Song, 3153
Boas, Franz. Primitive Art, 2897
Boas, George. Rationalism in Greek Philosophy, 624
Boase, Alan M. The Poetry of France, 4135
Boatner, Mark M., 3rd. Civil War Dictionary, 454
———. Encyclopedia of the American Revolution, 453
BOATS AND BOATING, 2681, 3422, 3425, 3427-3430
Bobker, G. R. Elements of Film, 3266
Bobker, Lee R. Making Movies from Script to Screen, 3112
Bock, Hal, see Hollander, Zander
Bock, Paul. In Search of a Responsible World Society, 767
Bock, Philip K., compiled by. Culture Shock, 904
Bodde, Derk. China's Cultural Tradition - What and Whither?, 5573
Bode, Carl, compiled by. Midcentury America, 6002
———. Ralph Waldo Emerson, 3749
Bodechtel, J. and Gierioff-Emden, H. G. The Earth from Space, 2009
Bodrogi, Tibor. Art of Indonesia, 2936
Body Has a Head. Eckstein, Gustav, 2510
Body Time. Luce, Gay, 2514
Boeckman, Charles. And the Beat Goes on, 3221
Boericke, Art and Shapiro, Barry. Handmade Houses, 2978
Boethius, Axel and Ward-Perkins, J. B. Etruscan and Roman Architecture, 2971
Boetie, Dugmore. Familiarity Is the Kingdom of the Lost, 1708
Bogan, Louise. The Blue Estuaries, 3627
Boger, Louise A. Complete Guide to Furniture Styles, 3023
Bogle, Donald. Toms, Coons, Mulattoes, Mammies, and Bucks, 3267
Bohannan, Paul. Love, Sex and Being Human, 2517
Bohannan, Paul and Curtin, Philip. Africa and Africans, 4790
BOHEMIA — HISTORY, 5343, 5350
Bohlen, Charles E. Transformation of American Foreign Policy, 1331
Bohme, Helmut, compiled by. The Foundation of the German Empire, 5292
BOHR, NIELS HENRIK DAVID, 2061
Boissier, Gaston. Cicero and His Friends, 4933
Bok, Bart J. and Bok, Priscilla F. The Milky Way, 1988

Bold, Harold C. *see* Alexopoulos, Constantine J.
Bolivar and the War of Independence. O'Leary, Daniel F, 6263
BOLIVAR, SIMON, 6262-6263
BOLIVIA — HISTORY, 6275
Boll, Heinrich. Abenteuer Eines Blotbentles un Andere Geschichten, 4039
———. And Where Were You, Adam?, 4040
———. Billiards at Half-Past Nine, 4035
———. Eighteen Stories, 4036
———. Group Portrait with Lady, 4037
———. Irish Journal, 4745
———. Nicht Nur Zur Weignschtzeit, 4038
Boller, Paul F. American Transcendentalism, 1830-1860, 546
Bolsby, Clare. *see* Berglund, Berndt
Bolshevik Revolution, 1917-1923. Carr, Edward H, 5510
Bolt, Robert. A Man for All Seasons, 3899
BOMBERS, 2677
Bombers in Service Since 1960. Munson, Kenneth, 2677
Bombs, Beards and Barricades. Esler, Anthony, 1223
Bonachea, Ramon L. The Cuban Insurrection, 1952-1959, 5827
Bond, Julian. A Time to Speak, a Time to Act, 1240
Bonds of Interest. Benevente, Jacinto, 4344
Bondurant, Joan and Fisher, Margaret W., eds. Conquest of Violence, 898
Bone Hunters. Lanham, Urless N, 2177
Bonhoeffer, Dietrich. Cost of Discipleship, 736
———. Letters and Papers from Prison, 811
BONHOEFFER, DIETRICH, 742, 810-811
Bonjour Tristesse. Sagan, Francois, 4247
Bonnett, Penelope. *see* Gill, Don
Bontemps, Arna. Free at Last, 6061
———. Great Slave Narratives, 1055
Bontemps, Arna W., *see* Hughes, Langston
Book Collector's Handbook of Values. Bradley, Van Allen, 13
Book in America. Lehmann-Haupt, Hellmut, 2848
A Book of Famous Wits. Jerrold, Walter C, 3961
Book of Festivals and Holidays the World Over. Ickis, Marguerite, 151
Book of Folly. Sexton, Anne, 3661
Book of Health. Clark, Randolph L. and Cumley, Russell W. 252
Book of Imaginary Beings. Borges, Jorge Luis, 1850
Book of Jazz. Feather, Leonard, 3188

Book of Living Verse. Untermeyer, Louis, ed, 3785
A Book of Love Poems. Cole, William, ed, 3776
Book of Negro Folklore. Hughes, Langston and Bontemps, Arna W., eds. 1833
Book of Owls. Walker, Lewis W, 2443
Book of Survival. Greenbank, Anthony, 2534
A Book of the Basques. Gallop, Rodney, 4761
Book of the Seven Seas. Freuchen, Peter and Loth, David. 4694
Book Publishing. Dessauer, John P, 490
Book Publishing in America. Madison, Charles A, 2850
Book Review Digest. 37
BOOK SELECTION, 28
Booklist and Subscription Books Bulletin. 38
BOOKS, 55, 2847-2848, 3522,
   CONSERVATION AND RESTORATION, 33
   PRICES, 13
   REVIEWS, 14, 37-39, 42, 44
Books for Junior College Libraries. Pirie, James W., ed, 9
Books in Print. 3
Books in World History. Wagar, W. Warren, 73
Books That Changed America. Downs, Robert B, 3522
Boorer, Michael. Wild Cats, 2465
Boorse, Henry A. and Motz, Lloyd, eds. The World of the Atom, 2052
Boorstin, Daniel J., ed. An American Primer, 5877
———. The Americans, 5894
———. The Genius of American Politics, 1189
BOOTH FAMILY, 3323
Borah. McKenna, Marian C, 6123
BORAH, WILLIAM EDGAR, 6123
Bord, Colin. *see* Bord, Janet
Bord, Janet and Bord, Colin. Mysterious Britain, 4725
Border Command. Rister, Carl C, 6073
Borderlands of Western Civilization. Halecki, Oscar, 5285
Borek, Ernest. The Code of Life, 2291
———. The Sculpture of Life, 2256
Borges, Jorge Luis. The Book of Imaginary Beings, 1850
Borgese, Elisabeth Mann and Krieger, David, eds. The Tides of Change, 1557
BORGIA FAMILY, 5428, 5435
Borgias. Mallett, Michael, 5428
Boring, Edwin G., *see* Herrnstein, Richard J.

INDEX

BORIS GODUNOV, 5497
Boris Godunov. Platanov, Sergei, 5497
Boris Godunov. Pushkin, Aleksandr S, 4535
BORLANG, NORMAN E., 2773
Born, Max. The Restless Universe, 2016
Born to Love. James, Muriel, 2605
Born to Run. Pettingill, O. E, 3449
Born to Starve. Tydings, Joseph D, 956
Born to Win. James, Muriel and Jongward, Dorothy. 2606
Bornkamm, Gunther. Jesus of Nazareth, 749
Borstein, Larry and Berkowitz, Henry. Scuba, Spear and Snorkel, 3435
Borton, Hugh. Japan's Modern Century, 5620
Bosses. Steinberg, Alfred, 1202
BOSTON — PUBLIC SCHOOLS, 1752
Boswell, James. Life of Samuel Johnson, 3963
Bosworth, Allan. America's Concentration Camps, 5147
BOTANY, 232-235, 2311, 2313-2315
Botany. Jensen, William A. and Salisbury, Frank B. 2311
Botany. Neushul, M, 2313
Botkin, Benjamin A. Treasury of American Folklore, 1826
Botting, Douglas. Humboldt and the Cosmos, 1900
Bottomore, Tom, ed. Karl Marx, 1492
Boulding, Kenneth E. The Meaning of the Twentieth Century, 917
Boundaries of the Louisiana Purchase. Houck, Louis, 5973
Bouquet, Alan C. Comparative Religions, 819
———. Everyday Life in New Testament Times, 733
BOURBON, HOUSE OF, 5462
Bourbon Restoration. De Bertier De Sauvigny, Guillaume, 5410
Bourbon Street Black. Buerkle, Jack V. and Barker, Danny. 3247
Bourne, Geoffrey H. Primate Odyssey, 2478
Bourne, Kenneth. The Foreign Policy of Victorian England, 1830-1902, 1302
Bova, Ben. The Fourth State of Matter, 2034
———. Man Changes the Weather, 2160
———. The New Astronomies, 1960
Bowen, Catherine D. Francis Bacon, 5212
———. John Adams and the American Revolution, 5932
———. The Lion and the Throne, 5236
———. Miracle at Philadelphia, 1572
———. The Most Dangerous Man in America, 5949

Bowen, D. H. Michael. Air Pollution, 2709
Bowen, James. Soviet Education, 1757
Bowers, Claude G. Jefferson and Hamilton, 5962
———. Tragic Era, 6082
Bowles, Chester. Promises to Keep, 6132
BOWLING, 3340
Bowling for Everyone. Berger, Gene, 3340
Bowman, Walter P. and Ball, Robert H. Theatre Language, a Dictionary, 315
Bowman, William J. Graphic Communication, 3005
Bowra, Cecil M. Early Greek Elegists, 4443
———. The Greek Experience, 4952
———. Heroic Poetry, 3471
———. Sophoclean Tragedy, 4451
———. Tradition and Design in the Iliad, 4461
Bowra, Maurice. Classical Greece, 4966
Boxer Catastrophe. Tan, Chester G, 5586
BOXERS, 5584, 5586
Boyce, William F. Hi-Fi Stereo Handbook, 2654
Boyd, James. Sir George Etienne Cartier, 5795
Boyd, William. History of Western Education, 1756
Boyden, David D. An Introduction to Music, 3135
Boylan, Brian R. Benedict Arnold, 5933
Boyle, Robert H. The Hudson River, 4831
Boys and Sex. Pomeroy, Wardell B. and Tebbel, John. 2522
Brabazon, James. Albert Schweitzer, 661
Brace, C. Loring. The Stages of Human Evolution, 2278
Bracher, Karl D. The German Dictatorship, 1395
Bradbury, Ray, et al. Mars and the Mind of Man, 1920
Bradford, Ernle D. Mediterranean, 4683
———. Ulysses Found, 4462
Bradford, Sarah. Portugal, 5476
Bradford, William. Bradford's History of Plymouth Plantation, 1606-1646, 5895
Bradford's History of Plymouth Plantation, 1606-1646. Bradford, William, 5895
Bradley, Andrew C. Shakespearean Tragedy, 3863
Bradley, Arthur G. The United Empire Loyalists, 5789
Bradley, Gordon and Toye, Clive. Playing Soccer the Professional Way, 3358
Bradley, Van Allen. The Book Collector's Handbook of Values, 13
Bradley, Wendell P. They Live by the Wind, 2815
Braeman, John. Albert J. Beveridge, 6109

Brahms, His Life and Work. Geiringer, Karl, 3168
BRAHMS, JOHANNES, 3168
BRAIN, 2345, 2457, 2524-2527, 2625
Brain Control. Valenstein, Elliot S, 2625
Brain Mechanisms and Mind. Oatley, Keith, 2526
Brain Revolution. Ferguson, Marilyn, 2525
Brains of Animals and Man. Freedman, Russell and Morriss, James E. 2345
Brains Trust. Tugwell, Rexford G, 1383
Branch, Douglas. The Cowboy and His Interpreters, 4837
BRANDEIS, LOUIS DEMBITZ, 1620
Brandenburg, Frank R. The Making of Modern Mexico, 5823
Brandes, Georg. Michelangelo, 2922
Brandon, James R., ed. Traditional Asian Plays, 4599
Brandon, Samuel G. A Dictionary of Comparative Religion, 117
———. Man and God in Art and Ritual, 762
Brandon, William. The Last Americans, 5744
Brandt, John C. and Maran, S. P. New Horizons in Astronomy, 1961
BRANDT, WILLY, 5335
Brandwein, Paul F., et al. Life, 2209
Brandywine Heritage. 3037
Branley, Franklyn M. The Milky Way, 1989
———. The Moon, 1993
Branson, Lane. Introduction to Electronics, 2644
Brant, Irving. Impeachment, 1606
Brasch, Rudolph. How Did Sports Begin? A Look at the Origins of Man at Play, 3350
Brashler, William. see Janus, Christopher G.
Brat'ya Karamazovy. Dostoevsky, Feodor M, 4544
Braudel, Fernand. Capitalism and Material Life, 1400-1800, 1080
———. The Mediterranean and the Mediterranean World in the Age of Philip II, 4689
Braun, Wernher Von. see Ordway, Frederick I., Jr.
Brave New World Revisited. Huxley, Aldous L, 897
Braving the Elements. Merrill, James, 3654
Bravmann, Rene A. Open Frontiers, 2937
Brawley, Benjamin G. Negro Genius, 4867
Braybrooke, Neville. Teilhard de Chardin, 520
Brazil. Poppins, Rollie E, 6271

BRAZIL — HISTORY, 6270-6272
Brazilians. Rodrigues, José H, 6272
Breach of Faith. White, Theodore H, 1718
Breaking Open. Rukeyser, Muriel, 3658
Breasted, James H. Development of Religion and Thought in Ancient Egypt, 867
———. History of Egypt, 4883
Breath of Life. Carr, Donald E, 2562
Brecht. Esslin, Martin, 4032
Brecht, Bertolt. Brecht on Theatre, 3292
———. Kalendergeschichten, 4041
———. Die Mutter, 4011
———. Seven Plays, 4012
BRECHT, BERTOLT, 4031-4033
Brecht on Theatre. Brecht, Bertolt, 3292
Brecker, Edward M. and Consumer Report Editors. Licit and Illicit Drugs, 2541
Bredsdorff, Elias, et al. Introduction to Scandinavian Literature, 4082
Brée, Germaine. Twentieth Century French Literature, 4098
———. Women Writers in France, 4096
Brée, Germaine and Guiton, Margaret. The Age of Fiction, 4267
Breed, Paul F. and Sniderman, Florence M. Dramatic Criticism Index, 67
Breed, William J., ed. Geology of the Grand Canyon, 2172
Breitman, George, ed. Malcolm X Speaks, 1014
Bremner, Robert H. American Philanthropy, 1694
Brenan, Gerald. The Literature of the Spanish People, 4309
———. The Spanish Labyrinth, 5457
Brenner, Anita. Idols Behind Altars. , 2941
———. The Wind That Swept Mexico, 5817
Brent, Peter. Captain Scott and the Antarctic Tragedy, 4853
Brereton, Geoffrey. Introduction to the French Poets, 4136
Brett, George. Psychology, Ancient and Modern, 564
Brewer, Ebenezer C. Dictionary of Phrase and Fable. , 323
———. Reader's Handbook of Famous Names in Fiction, Allusions, 324
Brewer, John Mason, compiled by. American Negro Folklore, 1842
Brezhnev. Dornberg, John, 5529
BREZHNEV, LEONID ILYICH, 5529
Briar Patch. Kempton, Murray, 1598
Bridenbaugh, Carl. Cities in Revolt, 5896
———. Cities in the Wilderness, 5897
———. Vexed and Troubled Englishmen, 1590-1642, 5237
Bridge, Raymond. Freewheeling, 3400
A Bridge Too Far. Ryan, Cornelius, 5131

INDEX

Bridger, David and Wolk, Samuel J., eds. The New Jewish Encyclopedia, 122
BRIDGES, 2691-2693
Bridges. Plowden, David, 2691
Bridges, Canals, Tunnels. Jacobs, David, et al. 2689
BRIDGES, HARRY RENTON, 1442
BRIDGES, ROBERT SEYMOUR, 3841
Brierley, John E. and David, Rene. Major Legal Systems in the World Today, 1546
Briggs, Asa. Victorian People, 5267
Briggs, Jean L. Never in Anger, 926
Briggs, Katharine M. The Fairies in English Tradition and Literature, 1849
Briggs, Katharine M. and Tongue, Ruth L. Folktales of England, 1827
Briggs, Peter. Rampage, 2696
———. Two Hundred Million Years Beneath the Sea, 2146
Bright Book of Life. Kazin, Alfred, 3730
Bright, James F. Maria Theresa, 5342
Bright, John. A History of Israel, 4899
Brilliant, Richard. Arts of the Ancient Greeks, 2916
———. Roman Art, from the Republic to Constantine, 2917
Bringing the War Home. Helmer, John, 1000
Brink, William and Harris, Louis. Black and White, 1015
Brinkman, George, ed. The Development of Rural America, 963
Brinkworth, B. D. Solar Energy for Man, 2661
Brinnin, John M. The Third Rose, 3762
Brinton, Crane, et al. Civilization in the West, 4644
———. Portable Age of Reason Reader, 5020
Britain Between the Wars; 1918-1940. Mowat, Charles L, 5273
Britain, Frederick, ed. Penguin Book of Latin Verse, 4401
Britannica Encyclopedia of American Art. 278
British and American Essays. 3747
British Authors Before 1800. Kunitz, Stanley J. and Haycraft, Howard, eds. 428
British Authors of the Nineteenth Century. Kunitz, Stanley J. and Haycraft, Howard, eds. 429
British Constitution. Jennings, Ivor, 1560
Broadway's Greatest Musicals. Laufe, Abe, 3209
Brock, Peter. Twentieth Century Pacificism, 1547
Brockett, Oscar G. History of the Theatre, 3308
Brockett, Oscar G. and Findley, R. Century of Innovation, 3309

Brod, Max. Franz Kafka, 4080
———. Heinrich Heine, 4006
Broder, David. see Hess, Stephen
Broderick, Richard. see Nassour, Ellis
Brodie, Bernard. War and Politics, 1293
Brodie, Fawn M. No Man Knows My History, 814
Brodsky, Alyn. The Kings Depart, 4900
Brodsky, Joseph. Selected Poems, 4506
Brody, Linda A. see Silverman, Eliot N.
Brogan, Denis W. American Character, 5854
———. France Under the Republic, 5413
———. The French Nation, 5409
———. Politics in America, 1371
Broken Nest. Tagore, Rabindranath, 4488
Broken Seal. Farago, Ladislas, 5149
Bromke, Adam. Poland's Politics, 1162
Bromke, Adam and Rakowska-Harmstone, Teresa, eds. The Communist States in Disarray, 1965-1971. 1155
Bronfenbrenner, Urie. Two Worlds of Childhood, 2842
Bronowski, Jacob. The Ascent of Man, 1921
———. William Blake and the Age of Revolution, 3809
Bronowski, Jacob and Mazlish, B. Western Intellectual Tradition, 640
Bronstein, David J., et al. Basic Problems of Philosophy, 511
BRONTE, CHARLOTTE, 3925
BRONTË, EMILY JANE, 3927
BRONTË FAMILY, 3926
Brooke, Rupert. Collected Poems, 3835
Brook-Little, J. P. Heraldic Alphabet, 4873
Brooks, Cleanth and Warren, Robert P. Understanding Poetry, 3472
Brooks, Gwendolyn. Selected Poems, 3628
———. The World of Gwendolyn Brooks, 3629
Brooks, Joseph W. Complete Guide to Fishing Across North America, 3452
Brooks, Nathan C. Complete History of the Mexican War, 6018
Brooks, Paul. The House of Life, 2222
Brophy, James D. Edith Sitwell, 3836
BROSKII, IOSIF, 4506
Brosnan, John. Movie Magic, 3268
Brother to Dragons. Warren, Robert Penn, 3590
Brothers' War. De St. Jorre, John, 5728
Broué, Pierre and Témime, Emile. The Revolution and the Civil War in Spain, 5467
Brown, A. A. and Davis, Kenneth P. Forest Fire, 2786
Brown, Barbara B. New Mind, New Body Biofeedback, 2513
Brown, Billye and Brown, Walter R. Historical Catastrophes, 2153

342

INDEX

Brown, Claude. Manchild in the Promised Land, 1120
Brown, Dee A. Bury My Heart at Wounded Knee, 5765
Brown, Demetra V. and Phoutrides, Aristides, trs. Modern Greek Stories, 4474
Brown, Edward J. Mayakovsky, 4507
———. Russian Literature Since the Revolution, 4493
Brown, F. Martin, et al. Earth Science, 2106
Brown, Gar. see Spence, James
Brown, George I. Human Teaching for Human Learning, 1769
BROWN, JOHN, 5975, 6012, 6024
Brown, Joseph E. The Golden Sea, 2133
Brown, Judith M. Gandhi's Rise to Power, 1180
Brown, Leslie. Africa, 2271
Brown, Lester R. By Bread Alone, 1515
Brown, Peter L. Comets, Meteorites and Men, 2003
Brown, Peter L. see Hickling, Charles F.
Brown, R. C. see Careless, James M.
Brown, Reginald A. The Normans and the Norman Conquest, 5195
———. Origins of English Feudalism, 5181
Brown, Robert M. Frontiers for the Church Today, 771
———. Religion and Violence, 768
Brown, Ronald. Lasers, 2639
Brown, Theo W. Sharks, 2408
Brown, Vinson. Knowing the Outdoors in the Dark, 2210
———. Reading the Woods, 2318
Brown, Walter R. see Brown, Billye
Brown, William C. Church and State in Contemporary America, 766
Browning, Elizabeth B. Poetical Works, 3822
BROWNING, ELIZABETH BARRETT, 3834
Browning, Robert. Poetical Works, 3823
Brownlee, William H. The Meaning of the Qumran Scrolls for the Bible, 718
Brownrigg, Ronald. The Twelve Apostles, 734
Brubaker, Sterling. To Live on Earth, 940
Bruce, Marie L. Anne Boleyn, 5213
Bruce, Robert V. Bell, 1802
———. Lincoln and the Tools of War, 6053
Brucker, Herbert. Communication Is Power, 492
Bruegel. Bruegel, Pieter The Elder, 3074
BRUEGEL, PIETER THE ELDER, 3074
Bruemmer, Fred. The Arctic, 4849

Brundage, Burr C. Empire of the Inca, 6266
Bruner, Jerome S. Toward a Theory of Instruction, 1744
Brusher, Joseph S. Popes Through the Ages, 113
Brutal Friendship. Deakin, Frederick W, 5449
Bruun, Geoffrey. Europe and the French Imperium, 5045
Bruun, Geoffrey. see Ferguson, Wallace K.
Bry, Doris. see Goodrich, Lloyd
BRYAN, WILLIAM JENNINGS, 6093
Bryant, William Cullen. Poetical Works, 3555
Brzezinski, Zbigniew. The Soviet Bloc, 4676
Buban, Peter and Schmitt, Marshall L. Understanding Electricity and Electronics, 2636
Buber, Martin. I and Thou, 664
———. On Judaism, 851
———. Pointing the Way, 618
BUBER, MARTIN, 619
Buccaneers and Marooners of America. Exquemelin, Alexandre O, 4693
Buchanan, A. Russell. U. S. and World War II, 5120
Buchanan, Daniel C., tr. One Hundred Famous Haiku, 4613
Buchanan, Keith. The Southeast Asian World, 5672
Buchanan, Robert E. and Gibbons, Norman E. Bergey's Manual of Determinative Bacteriology, 237
Buchanan-Brown, John, ed. Cassell's Encyclopedia of World Literature, 325
Buchheim, Hans. Totalitarian Rule, 1217
Buchner, Alexander. Musical Instruments, 3199
Buchner, Georg. Complete Plays and Prose, 4013
Buchsbaum, Ralph. Animals Without Backbones, 2378
Buchsbaum, Ralph and Milne, Lorus. Lower Animals, 2379
Buckley, Jerome. Tennyson, 3824
Buckwalter, Len. ABC's of Citizens Band Radio, 2651
Bucky. Kenner, Hugh, 2632
Budd, Edward C., ed. Inequality and Poverty, 1540
Buddenbrooks. Mann, Thomas, 4065
Buddha. Oldenberg, Hermann, 838
BUDDHA AND BUDDHISM, 836, 838-839, 843
Buddhism in Chinese History. Wright, Arthur F, 843
BUDDHIST SECTS — JAPAN, 840
Buddhist Sects of Japan. Steinilber-Oberlin, Emile, 840

INDEX

Buddhist Tradition in India, China and Japan. De Bary, William T, 836
Budge, Ernest A. The Egyptian Book of the Dead, 868
Budge, Ian and O'Leary, Cornelius. Belfast, 5169
Buechner, Thomas S., ed. Norman Rockwell, 3038
Buerkle, Jack V. and Barker, Danny. Bourbon Street Black, 3247
Buero Vallejo, Antonio. La Doble Historia del Doctor Valmy, 4346
———. En la Ardiente Obscuridad, 4350
———. Historia de una Escalera, 4349
———. Hoy Es Fiesta, 4347
———. Las Meninas, 4348
Buffalo Book. Dary, David, 1480
Building Library Collections. Carter, Mary D., ed, 28
Bukharin and the Bolshevik Revolution. Cohen, Stephen F, 5511
BUKHARIN, NIKOLAI IVANOVICH, 5511
Bukofzer, Manfred F. Music in the Baroque Era, 3144
———. Studies in Medieval and Renaissance Music, 3145
Bulfinch, Thomas. Mythology, 824
BULL-FIGHTS, 3288, 3290
Bull of Minos. Cottrell, Leonard, 4979
Bullock, Alan. Hitler, a Study in Tyranny, 5308
Bullock, Alan and Taylor, A. J., eds. Select List of Books on European History, 1815-1914, 60
Bullock, Paul, ed. Watts, 1123
Bullough, Bonnie. *see* Bullough, Vern1
Bullough, Donald. The Age of Charlemagne, 5373
Bullough, Vern1 and Bullough, Bonnie. The Subordinate Sex, 976
Burack, A. A., ed. Writer's Handbook, 3467
Burch, Betty B. and Cole, Alan B. Asian Political Systems, 1135
Burchfield, R. W., ed. Supplement to the Oxford English Dictionary, 163
Burckhardt, Jacob. The Civilization of the Renaissance in Italy, 5431
Burden of Guilt. Vogt, Hannah, 5305
Burden of Southern History. Woodward, C. Vann, 6218
Burgess, Alan. Daylight Must Come, 2498
Burgess, Louise B. Alcohol and Your Health, 2600
Buried Alive. Friedman, Myra, 3229
Burke, Edmund. Selected Writings and Speeches on America, 1075
Burkill, T. Alec. The Evolution of Christian Thought, 698
Burland, Cottie A. Montezuma, 5810

Burma. Hall, Daniel G, 5675
BURMA — HISTORY, 5675
Burn, Andrew R. Minoans, Philistines, and Greeks, 4963
———. Pericles and Athens, 4971
———. The World of Hesiod, 4964
Burnet, MacFarlane. Genes, Dreams and Realities, 2257
Burnet, MacFarlane and White, D. O. Natural History of Infectious Disease, 2607
Burns, E. Bradford. A History of Brazil, 6270
Burns, James M. Deadlock of Democracy, 1632
———. Presidential Government, 1639
———. Roosevelt, 6133
———. Roosevelt, 6134
Burns, Robert. Complete Poetical Works, 3805
Burpee, Lawrence J. The Discovery of Canada, 5786
BURR, AARON, 5972
Burr, George L., ed. Narratives of the Witchcraft Cases, 1648 to 1706, 5898
Burrows, Millar. More Light on the Dead Sea Scrolls, 719
Burton, Maurice. The Sixth Sense of Animals, 2344
———. University Dictionary of Mammals of the World, 2444
Bury, John B., et al. Hellenistic Age, 4976
———. History of Greece, 4953
Bury My Heart at Wounded Knee. Brown, Dee A, 5765
Bus Stops Here. Holden, Anna, 1750
Busfield, Roger M. Playwright's Art, 3480
Busha, Charles H. Freedom vs. Suppression and Censorship, 475
Bushcraft. Graves, Richard, 2533
BUSINESS, 2853-2854
BUSINESS AND POLITICS CASE STUDIES, 1801
U. S., 1199
Business of Diving. Kenny, John, 2694
Butcher, Margaret J. Negro in American Culture, 2874
Butler, Ewan. The Horizon Concise History of Scandinavia, 5533
Butler, George B. and Berlin, K. Darrell. Fundamentals of Organic Chemistry, 2082
Butler, J. A. The Life Process, 2226
Butler, Rohan D. The Roots of National Socialism, 1783-1933, 5283
Butow, Robert J. Japan's Decision to Surrender, 5118
Butterberry, Ariane R. Pantheon Story of Art for Young People, 2894

INDEX

Butterfield, Roger, ed. American Past, 5855
BUTTERFLIES, 2395-2396
Butterworth, W. E. Wheels and Pistons, 2741
By Bread Alone. Brown, Lester R, 1515
By the Evidence. Leakey, Louis S, 2184
Byrd, E. How Things Work, 1889
Byron. Marchand, Leslie A, 3813
Byron, George G. Poetical and Dramatic Works, 3810
BYRON, GEORGE GORDON, 3813
Byron, Robert. The Byzantine Achievements, 5548
Byzantine Achievements. Byron, R. , 5548
BYZANTINE EMPIRE — HISTORY, 4951, 5012, 5547-5552
BYZANTINE LITERATURE — DICTIONARIES, 351
Byzantium and Europe. Vryonis, Speros, 5552

C. G. Jung. Storr, Anthony, 563
C R M Books Editorial Staff. Geology Today, 2091
C R M Staff & Contributing Consultants. Physical Science Today, 1895
Cabaniss, Allen. Charlemagne, 5374
Cabinet Government. Jennings, Ivor, 1652
CABINET OFFICERS, 1200, 1330
CACTUS — PICTORIAL WORKS, 2793
Cadres, Bureaucracy, and Political Power in Communist China. Barnett, A. Doak, 1651
Caesar. Geeler, Matthias, 4936
Caesar, Gaius Julius. Gallic War, 4424
CAESAR, GAIUS JULIUS, 4936-4937
Caesars. Marsh, Henry, 4944
Cahill, Kevin M. Untapped Resource, 1695
Cahill, Susan and Cooper, Michele. The Urban Reader, 965
Cahn, William. A Pictorial History of American Labor, 1428
Cairo Documents. Haykal, Muhammad H, 5716
CALCULUS, 1948
Calder, Angus. The People's War, 5274
Calder, Nigel. The Life Game, 2306
———. The Restless Earth, 2123
———. Violent Universe, 1968
Calder, Ritchie. The Evolution of the Machine, 2635
———. Leonardo, 3057
———. Leonardo and the Age of the Eye, 3058
Calderón de la Barca, Pedro. Four Plays, 4351
Caldwell, Lynton. Environment, 933
Caldwell, Malcolm and Tan, Lek. Cambodia in the Southeast Asian War, 5681

Calhoon, Robert M. The Loyalists in Revolutionary America, 1760-1781, 5945
CALHOUN, JOHN CALDWELL, 5976
CALIFORNIA — GOLD DISCOVERIES, 6244
Caligula and Three Other Plays. Camus, Albert, 4150
Calkins, Elizabeth. Teaching Tomorrow, 3919
Callahan, Daniel J., compiled by. The American Population Debate, 949
Callahan, North. Carl Sandburg, 3596
Callahan, Philip S. The Evolution of Insects, 2391
———. Insects and How They Function, 2390
———. The Magnificent Birds of Prey, 2438
Callard, Keith, et al. Major Governments of Asia, 1562
Calleo, David P. and Rowland, Benjamin M. America and the World Political Economy, 1795
CALLEY, WILLIAM LAWS, 1595
CALLIGRAPHY, CHINESE, 3021
Callow, Alexander B., Jr. The Tweed Ring, 6196
Calvin Coolidge. McCoy, Donald, 6127
CALVIN, JOHN, 812
Cambodia in the Southeast Asian War. Caldwell, Malcolm and Tan, Lek. 5681
Cambon, Glauco. The Inclusive Flame, 3554
Cambridge Ancient History. 435
Cambridge Bibliography of English Literature. 70
Cambridge History of English Literature. 361
Cambridge History of Islam. Holt, P. M., et al, eds. 382
Cambridge History of Poland. Reddaway, William W., et al, eds. 5363
Cambridge History of the Bible. 107
Cambridge Medieval History. 436
Cambridge Modern History. 437
Camera and Lens. Adams, Ansel, 3110
Cameron, Angus. The Nightwatchers, 2441
Cameron, William J. New Zealand, 6285
El Camino. Delibes, Miguel, 4374
CAMOUFLAGE (BIOLOGY), 2365-2366
Camp, John. Bellringing, 3252
Campaigns of Alexander. Arrianus, Flavius, 4974
Campaigns of Napoleon. Chandler, David G, 5046
Campbell, Bernard. Human Evolution, 2194

INDEX

Campbell, Bruce and Holmes, Richard T., eds. The Dictionary of Birds in Color, 246
Campbell, Colin. The Sports Car, 2750
Campbell, Elizabeth M. and Solomon, David. The Search for Morag, 2370
Campbell, Jan. Minerals, 2087
Campbell, John and Sherrard, Philip. Modern Greece, 5549
Campbell, John C. Tito's Separate Road, 5563
Campbell, Oscar J. and Quinn, Edward G., eds. Reader's Encyclopedia of Shakespeare, 368
Campbell, Sheldon. *see* Shaw, Charles E.
CAMPING, 2533, 2537, 3397-3400, 4813
Camus, Albert. Caligula and Three Other Plays, 4150
———. La Chute, 4198
———. L' Etranger, 4199
———. L' Exile et le Royaume, 4200
———. L' Homme Revolté, 4201
———. The Myth of Sisyphus, and Other Essays, 4268
———. The Rebel, 597
———. Resistance, Rebellion and Death, 4269
CAMUS, ALBERT, 4115
CANADA
   DESCRIPTION AND TRAVEL, 4799
   DISCOVERY AND EXPLORATION, 2939
   FOREIGN RELATIONS — U. S., 1332
   GENEALOGY, 4872
   HISTORY, 447, 5779-5792, 5794, 5799, 5892, 5902, 5986
Canada. Masters, Donald C., ed. 5782
Canada. Toppings, Earl, ed, 4799
Canada and the American Revolution, 1774-1783. Lanctot, Gustave, 5790
Canada, 1875-1973. Hill, Brian H., compiled by. 5779
Canada's First Century. Creighton, Donald, 5781
Canaday, John. Lives of the Painters, 3035
———. Mainstreams of Modern Art, 2908
Canadian Federation. Trotter, Reginald G, 5792
CANADIAN LITERATURE, 447, 3499, 3537
Canadians, 1867-1967. Careless, James M. and Brown, R. C. 5780
Canal. Liss, Sheldon B, 1348
Canal Days in America. Drago, Harry S, 1803
CANALS — U. S. — HISTORY, 1803
CANCER, 2256, 2617, 2619
Cancer. Richards, Victor, 2619
Candide. Voltaire, François M. de, 4258

CANOES AND CANOEING, 3423, 3426
Cantico. Guillén, Jorge, 4324
Cantos of Ezra Pound. Pound, Ezra, 3582
Capa, Cornell, ed. Behind the Great Wall of China, 4775
CAPE COD — DESCRIPTION AND TRAVEL, 4830
Cape Cod and the Offshore Islands. Teller, Walter M, 4830
Capital and Other Writings. Marx, Karl, 1677
CAPITAL PUNISHMENT, 1599, 1730
CAPITALISM, 765, 1207, 1407-1408, 1422, 1532
Capitalism and Material Life, 1400-1800. Braudel, Fernand, 1080
Capitalism in Crisis. Glyn, Andrew and Sutcliffe, Bob. 1528
Capitalism Today. Bell, Daniel and Kristol, Irving, eds. 1407
CAPITALISTS AND FINANCIERS, 1449, 6071
Capone. Kobler, John, 1713
CAPONE, ALPHONSE, 1713
Capote, Truman. Selected Writings, 3767
Captain Cousteau's Underwater Treasury. Cousteau, Jacques-Yves and Dugan, J. 3437
Captain Scott and the Antarctic Tragedy. Brent, Peter, 4853
Les Caractères. La Bruyere, Jean de, 4275
Caras, Roger. Venomous Animals of the World, 2368
CARD TRICKS, 3347
Card Tricks for Everyone. Stanyon, Ellis, 3347
Cardin, Martin. Planetfall, 1995
CARDS, 3341, 3345-3346
Care of the Wild Feathered and Furred. Hickman, Mae and Guy, Maxine. 2826
Career of Philosophy. Randall, John H., Jr, 641
Careful Writer. Bernstein, Theodore M, 1885
Careless Atom. Novick, Sheldon, 2665
Careless, James M. and Brown, R. C. Canadians, 1867-1967, 5780
Caretaker and the Dumb Waiter. Pinter, Harold, 3909
Carey, Robert G. The Peace Corps, 1125
CARIBBEAN AREA — DESCRIPTION AND TRAVEL, 4801
Caribbean Islands. Slater, Mary, 4805
CARICATURES AND CARTOONS, 3006
Carl Rogers on Encounter Groups. Rogers, Carl R, 2603
Carl Sandburg. Callahan, North, 3596
Carlisle, Olga. Poets on Street Corners, 4520

INDEX

Carlson, K., *see* Nelson, Jack L.
Carlyle, Thomas. Selected Writings, 3956
Carman, Harry J., et al. History of the American People, 5856
Carmichael, Stokely and Hamilton, Charles V. Black Power, 1261
CARNEGIE, ANDREW, 1525
Les Carnets du Major Thompson. Daninos, Pierre, 4204
Carney, James D. and Scheer, Richard. Fundamentals of Logic, 592
A Carnival of Sports. Severn, William, 3349
Carona, Philip B. Microscope and How to Use It, 2309
CARPENTRY, 2870
Carr, Donald E. The Breath of Life, 2562
———. Death of the Sweet Waters, 2563
Carr, Edward H. Bolshevik Revolution, 1917-1923, 5510
———. Twenty Years' Crisis, 1919-1939, 1548
———. What Is History?, 4645
Carr, Rachel. The Yoga Way to Release Tension, 2539
Carr, Raymond. Spain 1808-1939, 5465
Carr, Virginia S. The Lonely Hunter, 3727
Carraher, Ronald G. *see* Thurston, Jacqueline
Carrier, Rick. Fly, 3440
Carroll, David. The Dictionary of Foreign Terms in the English Language, 160
Carroll, Paul Vincent. Irish Stories and Plays, 3890
A Carrot for a Nose. Gladstone, M. J, 2985
Carruth, Gorton, et al, eds. The Encyclopedia of American Facts and Dates, 449
Carrying the Fire. Collins, Michael, 2762
Carson, Gerald. Men, Beasts, and Gods, 2803
Carson, Rachel. The Edge of the Sea. 2262
———. The Sea Around Us, 2134
———. Silent Spring, 2778
CARSON, RACHEL LOUISE, 2222, 2781
Carsten, Franz L. Origins of Prussia, 5284
———. The Reichswehr and Politics, 5301
Carter, Charles E. The Principles of Astrology, 538
Carter, Ciel M. Guide to Reference Sources in the Computer Sciences, 56
Carter, Dan T. Scottsboro, 1594
Carter, Harold. The Study of Urban Geography, 960
Carter, Hodding. The Angry Scar, 6062
Carter, Mary D., ed. Building Library Collections, 28
Carter, T. Donald. *see* Mochi, Ugo

Carter, William T. Soaring, 2723
Cartey, Wilfred, ed. Palaver, 4625
CARTHAGE — HISTORY, 4986
CARTIER, SIR GEORGE ETIENNE, 5795
Cartier-Bresson, Henri. About Russia, 4763
CARTOONS AND CARTOONING, 3008
Cartwright, Frederick F. and Biddis, Michael D. Disease and History, 2561
Caruso. Jackson, Stanley, 3205
CARUSO, ENRICO, 3205
CARY, JOYCE, 3940
Casalduero, Joaquin. Vida y Obra de Galdos, 4370
CASALS, PABLO, 3246
Case for Immortality. Spraggett, Allen, 542
Case for the League of Nations. Wilson, Woodrow, 6122
Cases on Constitutional Law. McGovney, D. O. and McGovney, Howard. 142
Casewit, Curtis W. and Pownall, Richard. Mountaineering Handbook, 3388
Cash, Wilbur J. The Mind of the South, 6201
Cashman, John A. LSD Story, 2577
Caso, Alfonso. Aztecs, People of the Sun, 5757
Casona, Alejandro. La Barca Sin Pescador, 4352
———. La Dama del Alba, 4353
Cass, James and Birnbaum, Max. Comparative Guide to American Colleges, 1786
———. Comparative Guide to Junior and Community Two Year Colleges, 1787
Cassell's Encyclopedia of World Literature. Buchanan-Brown, John, ed, 325
Cassell's Italian Dictionary. 182
Cassell's New German Dictionary. 178
Cassell's New Latin Dictionary. 185
Cassidy, Frederic G. *see* Robertson, Stuart
Cassirer, Ernst, ed. The Renaissance Philosophy of Man, 630
Casson, Lionel. The Ancient Mariners, 4876
———. Illustrated History of Ships and Boats, 2680
———. Masters of Ancient Comedy, 4445
Castaneda, Carlos. Tales of Power, 874
———. The Teachings of Don Juan, 875
Castedo, Leopoldo. A History of Latin American Art and Architecture from Pre-Columbian Times to the Present, 2949
Castelot, Andre. Queen of France, 5380
Castex, Pierre-Georges and Surer, Paul. Manuel des Études Littéraires Françaises, 4105

INDEX

CASTLES, 4739, 4999
Castles of Europe from Charlemagne to the Renaissance. Anderson, William, 4739
Castro, Americo. Iberoamérica, 4301
Castro, Fidel. History Will Absolve Me, 5828
———. Revolutionary Struggle, 1947-1958, 5829
CASTRO, FIDEL, 5830, 5835, 5837
Castro, Tony. Chicano Power, 1040
Castroism. Draper, Theodore, 5830
Castro's Cuba. Lockwood, Lee, 5835
Cat and Mouse. Grass, Günther, 4051
Cat on a Hot Tin Roof. Williams, Tennessee, 3708
CATALOGING, 29-30
CATALOGING AND CLASSIFICATION, 31
CATALOGING OF AUDIO-VISUAL MATERIALS, 45-46
CATALOGS, COMMERCIAL, 15-16
Catastrophe. Kerensky, Alexander, 5521
Cathedral. Macaulay, David, 2977
CATHEDRALS, 2976-2977
CATHERINE II, 5500
CATHERINE OF ARAGON, 5225
Catherine of Aragon. Mattingly, Garrett, 5225
CATHERINE PARR, 5222
Catherine the Great. Oldenbourg, Zoe, 5500
CATHOLIC CHURCH, 115, 728, 808-809
Catholic Dictionary. Attwater, Donald, ed, 115
CATS, 2465-2466, 2812
Catt, Carrie C. and Shuler, Nettie R. Woman Suffrage and Politics, 1267
Cattanes, Helene and Robert, Osmond T. Promenades Littéraires et Historiques, 4099
Catton, Bruce. The American Heritage Picture History of the Civil War, 6025
———. This Hallowed Ground, 6026
Catton, William B. see Link, Arthur S.
Catullus, Gaius Valerius. Complete Poetry, 4416
———. Works, 4415
Caudill, Harry M. Night Comes to the Cumberlands, 1122
El Caudillo. Trythall, J. W, 5475
Causes of Death. Preston, Samuel H., et al. 130
Causes of the Civil War. Stampp, Kenneth M., ed, 6040
Causes of the War of Independence. Van Tyne, Claude H, 5930
Causes of the World War. Bloch, Camille, 5071
Causes of War. Blainey, Geoffrey, 1665
Caute, David. Cuba, Yes?, 4806

Cavalier and Yankee. Taylor, William R, 6216
Cave and the Mountain. Stone, Wilfred, 3948
Cavendish, George. Thomas Wolsey, Late Cardinal, 5214
Cavendish, Richard. The Black Arts, 534
Cavert, Samuel M. The American Churches in the Ecumenical Movement, 1900-1968, 772
CAVES, 2129-2130, 3396
Caves. Waltham, A. C, 2130
Cazamian, Louis. History of French Literature, 4106
Cecil, David. Melbourne, 5256
Cecil Rhodes. Flint, John E, 5739
Cela, Camilo José. La Familia de Pascual Duarte, 4371
Celebrations. Myers, Robert J. and Hallmark Cards Editors. 152
Celestina. De Rojas, Fernando, 4354
Celibataires. Montherlant, Henri de, 4237
Cell Biology. Ambrose, E. J. and Easty, Dorothy M. 2250
Cell Biology. Dowben, Robert M, 2251
Cellini, Benvenuto. Autobiography, 2981
CELLINI, BENVENUTO, 2981
CELLS, 2250-2256
Cells. Tufty, Barbara, 2255
CELTIC LITERATURE — TRANSLATIONS INTO ENGLISH, 4491
A Celtic Miscellany. Jackson, Kenneth H., ed, 4491
CENSORSHIP, 475, 506, 1596
Center for Curriculum Research. Somewhere Else, 92
Center for the Study of Democratic Institutions. Anti-Ballistic Missile, 1686
Centers of Civilization. 4854
Central Asia. Belenitsky, Aleksandr, 4787
Central City-Spread City. Schwartz, Alvin, 970
Central-Eastern Europe. Roucek, Joseph S., ed, 4991
CENTRAL EUROPE — HISTORY, 4991, 5285, 5287
A Century of Chinese Revolution, 1851-1949. Franke, Wolfgang, 5582
Century of Innovation. Brockett, Oscar G. and Findley, R. 3309
Century of Louis XIV. Ranum, Orest A, 5024
Century of Punch Cartoons. Punch Magazine, 3960
Century of Struggle. Flexner, Eleanor, 1268
Ceram, C. W. The First American, 4736
———. Gods, Graves and Scholars, 4710

——. Hands on the Past, 4711
——. March of Archaeology. , 4707
——. The Secret of the Hittites, 4984
Ceramic Formulas. Conrad, John W, 287
CEREBRAL PALSY, 2594
Cervantes. Ledesma, Francisco N, 4392
Cervantes. Nelson, Lowry, Jr., ed, 4390
Cervantes, Miguel de. Don Quijote, 4372
——. Novelas Ejemplares, 4373
CERVANTES SAAVEDRA, MIGUEL DE, 4390, 4392
César Birotteau. Balzac, Honoré de, 4192
Cesar Franck and His Circle. Davies, Laurence, 3165
Ceylon. Zeylanicus, 5639
CEYLON — HISTORY, 5639
Cézanne. Lindsay, Jack, 3054
CÉZANNE, PAUL, 3054
Chabod, Federico. A History of Italian Fascism, 5448
Chadwick, Hector M. Early Scotland, 5155
Chafee, Zecharian, Jr., ed. Documents on Fundamental Human Rights, 1254
Chaffee, Ellen E. and Greisheimer, Esther M. Basic Physiology and Anatomy, 2508
Chagall. Haftman, Werner, 3067
CHAGALL, MARC, 3067
Chai, Chu and Chai, Winberg, eds. A Treasury of Chinese Literature, 4602
Chai, Winberg. Essential Works of Chinese Communism, 1499
Chai, Winberg, see Chai, Chu
Chaika. Chekhov, Anton P, 4526
Challenge of Crime in a Free Society. U. S. President's Commission on Law Enforcement & Administration of Justice, 1732
Challenge of the Stars. Moore, Patrick and Hardy, David A. 2757
Challenge of World Poverty. Myrdal, Gunnar, 1536
Challenge to Isolation. Langer, William L. and Gleason, S. E. 1346
Challenging Biological Problems. Behuke, John A., ed, 2208
Challinor, John. A Dictionary of Geology, 221
Chalmers, David M. Hooded Americanism, 1705
——. The Muckrake Years, 496
Chamber Music. Ulrich, Homer, 3250
Chamberlain, Neil W. Beyond Malthus, 950
Chambers Biographical Dictionary. Thorne, J. O., ed, 418
Chambers, Whittaker. Witness, 1622
CHAMBERS, WHITTAKER, 1714
Champion Cats of the World. Ing, Catherine and Pond, Grace. 2812

Championship Wrestling. Keen, Clifford P., et al. 3409
CHAMPLAIN, SAMUEL DE, 5793
Chan, Wing-Tsit. A Source Book in Chinese Philosophy, 615
Chandler, David G. The Campaigns of Napoleon, 5046
Chandler, Peleg W. American Criminal Trials, 1615
Chandler, Richard E. and Schwartz, Kessel, eds. New Anthology of Spanish Literature, 4304
——. New History of Spanish Literature, 4310
Chandler, Sue, see Shockley, Ann A.
Chang, Chun-shu. Making of China, 5574
Changing Culture of an Indian Tribe. Mead, Margaret, 5776
Changing Family. Yorburg, Betty, 988
A Changing Map of Africa. Hodgson, Robert D. and Stoneman, Elryn. 5701
Changing Map of Asia. East, William G., et al, eds. 4771
Changing Tools of Science. Adler, Irving, 1912
Changing World of Birds. Anderson, John M, 2426
Channing, Steven A. Crisis of Fear, 6043
La Chanson de Roland. Beaumont, Pierre de, 4119
Chapman, Abraham, ed. Black Voices, 3532
——. New Black Voices, 3533
Chapman, Alexandria. see Oakes, George
Chapman, Charles F. Piloting, Seamanship and Small Boat Handling, 2681
Chapman, Hester W. The Last Tudor King, 5215
CHARITIES — U. S. — HISTORY, 1694
CHARLEMAGNE, 5373-5374
Charlemagne. Cabaniss, Allen, 5374
Charles VII. Vale, M. G. A, 5378
CHARLES VII, KING OF FRANCE, 5378
Charles Darwin. Moore, Ruth, 2284
Charles Dickens. Johnson, Edgar, 3928
Charles Ives Remembered. Perlis, Vivian, 3161
Charles Sumner and the Coming of the Civil War. Donald, David, 6029
Charlesworth, Maxwell J. Philosophy of Religion, 683
Charlotte Brontë. Gerin, Winifred, 3925
CHARLOTTE, CONSORT OF MAXIMILIAN, 5816
Charlton, Henry B. Shakespearean Comedy, 3864
Charmed Circle. Mellow, James R, 3765
Charques, Richard. Twilight of Imperial Russia, 5503
Charriere, Henri. Banco, 1734

INDEX

CHARRIERE, HENRI, 1734
La Chartreuse de Parme. Stendhal, 4252
Chase, Deborah. The Medically Based Non-Nonsense Beauty Book, 2841
Chase, Mary Ellen. The Bible and the Common Reader, 710
———. Life and Language in the Old Testament, 725
———. Prophets for the Common Reader, 730
Chastel, Andre. Italian Art, 2923
Chateaubriand, François René de. Atala, 4202
———. Réné, 4203
Chatfield, Charles. For Peace and Justice, 1299
Chaucer, Geoffrey. Complete Works, 3790
CHAUCER, GEOFFREY, 3791-3792, 5205
A Chaucer Handbook. French, Robert D, 3791
Chauvin, Remy. The World of Ants, 2397
CHAVEZ, CESAR, 1444, 1448
Ché Guevara. Sauvage, Leo, 6264
Chedd, Graham. The New Biology, 2258
Cheetham, Nicolas. Mexico, 5802
Chejne, Anwar G. Muslim Spain, 4760
Chekhov. Simmons, Ernest J, 4536
Chekhov, Anton P. Best Plays, 4529
———. Chaika, 4526
———. Diadia Vania, 4527
———. Letters on the Short Story, the Drama and Other Literary Topics, 4573
———. P'esy, 4528
———. Portable Chekhov, 4574
———. Shest' Rasskazov, 4543
CHEKHOV, ANTON P., 4536
Chemical and Biological Warfare. Hersh, Seymour M, 1685
Chemical Principles and Their Biological Implications. O'Connor, Raymond, 2069
CHEMISTRY, 2065-2073, 2228
  DICTIONARIES, 216
  HANDBOOKS, MANUALS, ETC., 218
  TABLES, ETC., 215, 217
Chemistry. Medeiros, Robert W, 2068
Chemistry for the Million. Smith, Richard F, 2072
CHEMISTRY, INORGANIC, 2077-2079
CHEMISTRY, ORGANIC, 2081-2084
Chemist's Companion. Gordon, Arnold J. and Ford, Richard A. 218
Cheney, Sheldon. Sculpture of the World, 2980
———. The Theatre, 3310
Cheng, Peter P. Chronology of the People's Republic of China from October 1, 1969, 5598
Cheng-Tsu Wu, ed. Chink, 1047

CHESS, 2992, 3336-3338
Chessmen. Mackett-Beeson, E. J, 2992
Le Cheval Fou. Beaumont, Pierre de, 4120
Chevez, Albert C., ed. Yearnings, 3535
Chevigny, Hector. Russian America, 6247
Chew, Allen F. An Atlas of Russian History, 388
Cheyney, Edward P. The Dawn of a New Era, 5017
CHIANG, KAI-SHEK, 5594
Chiapusso, Jan. Bach's World, 3164
Chi-Bonnardel, Regine V., ed. The Atlas of Africa, 390
CHICAGO — RIOT, AUGUST, (1968), 1592, 1600, 6226
Chicago History of American Civilization. 6183
Chicano Manifesto. Rendon, Armando B, 1237
Chicano Power. Castro, Tony, 1040
Chicanos. Meier, Matthew S. and Rivera, Feliciano. 1044
Chichester, Francis. Gipsy Moth Circles the World, 4691
Chickering, William H. Within the Sound of These Waves, 4846
Chief Plays of Corneille. Corneille, Pierre, 4155
Chief Works. Spinoza, Benedict, 679
Chiera, Edward. They Wrote on Clay, 4720
Child, Heather and Colles, Dorothy. Christian Symbols Ancient and Modern, 112
CHILD STUDY, 545, 582, 1771
CHILDREN, 994, 996, 1602, 1604, 2842
Children of Abraham. Asch, Shalom, 4591
Children of Crisis. Coles, Robert, 1019
Children of the Great Depression. Elder, Glen H, 6128
Children of the Universe. Ditfurth, Hoimar Von, 1962
Children of the Uprooted. Handlin, Oscar, 1277
Childs, David. East Germany, 5332
Childs, Herbert. An American Genius, 2056
CHIMPANZEES — BEHAVIOR, 2481-2482
CHINA
  CIVILIZATION, 2931, 5572-5575, 5580
  FOREIGN RELATIONS, 1307, 1317, 1321
  HISTORY, 843, 1315, 4718, 5574-5583, 5586-5587, 5589-5593, 5595
  POLITICS AND GOVERNMENT, 1193, 1177, 5599, 5600
China. Fairbank, John K, 5576
China. Posner, Arlene, ed, 74

INDEX

China. Smith, Bradley and Weng, Wan-Go. 2931
China. Wu, Yuan-Li, ed, 439
China After Mao, with Selected Documents. Barnett, A. Doak, 1175
China and Russia. Clubb, Oliver E, 1307
China and the Question of Taiwan. Chiu, Hungdah, 5604
China in Revolution. Wright, Mary C., ed, 5587
China on the Eve of the Communist Take Over. Barnett, A. Doak, 5593
China Reader. Milton, David, et al, eds. 5591
China Reader. Schurmann, Franz and Schell, Orville, eds. 5581
CHINA(PEOPLE'S REPUBLIC OF CHINA), 94, 439, 1136, 1153, 1175-1177, 1179, 1314, 1316, 1318-1320, 1334, 1355, 1398, 1500, 1510, 1562, 1651, 5579, 5598, 5601-5603
China's Cultural Tradition - What and Whither? Bodde, Derk, 5573
China's Response to the West. Teng, Ssu-Yu, 1321
China's Three Thousand Years. Heren, Louis, et al. 5579
Chinese. Latourette, Kenneth S, 5580
Chinese Calligraphy. Ecke, Tseng Y, 3021
Chinese Communist Politics in Action. Barnett, A. Doak, ed, 1136
CHINESE DRAMA, 4599, 4602
CHINESE FICTION, 4602
Chinese Foreign Policy in an Age of Transition. Ojha, Ishwer C, 1319
Chinese in Southeast Asia. Purcell, Victor, 1051
CHINESE LANGUAGE — DICTIONARIES, 193-194
Chinese Looking Glass. Bloodworth, Dennis, 5572
CHINESE POETRY, 4600-4601
Chinese Religions from 1000 B. C. to the Present Day. Smith, Howard D, 839
Chinese Thought from Confucius to Mao Tse-tung. Creel, Herrlee G, 617
CH'ING SHENG-TSU, 5585
Chink. Cheng-Tsu Wu, ed, 1047
Chinmoy, Sri. Commentary on the Bhagavad Gita, 844
Chinoy, Helen K., see Cole, Toby
Chisholm, Shirley. The Good Fight, 1193
———. Unbought and Unbossed, 1360
CHISHOLM, SHIRLEY, 1193
Chisholm, William. The New English, 1863
Chiu, Hungdah. China and the Question of Taiwan, 5604
Choi, Woonsang. Fall of the Hermit Kingdom, 5608
Choice. 39
Choice. Yette, Samuel F, 1038

Choosing Our King. Novak, Michael, 1642
Chopin. Hedley, Arthur, 3171
CHOPIN, FREDERICK FRANÇOIS, 3171
Choy, Bong-Youn. Korea, 5605
Chrimes, Stanley B. Henry VII, 5216
Christ and Culture. Niebuhr, H. Richard, 764
Christensen, Clyde M. Molds and Man, 2330
CHRISTIAN ART AND SYMBOLISM, 112
CHRISTIAN ETHICS, 111, 753-754, 756-757, 901
Christian Philosophy of Saint Augustine. Gilson, Etienne, 610
Christian, Roy. Old English Customs, 1818
Christian Symbols Ancient and Modern. Child, Heather and Colles, Dorothy. 112
Christianity and Evolution. Teilhard de Chardin, Pierre, 697
CHRISTMAS, 1819
Christmas Traditions. Auld, William M, 1819
Christopher, John B. The Islamic Tradition, 4684
Christopher, Milbourne. The Illustrated History of Magic, 3334
Chronicles of America (Yale Chronicles) 6184
Chronicles of England, France, Spain. Froissart, Jean, 4998
Chronicles of the House of Borgia. Corvo, Frederick B, 5435
Chronology of the Ancient World. Bickerman, Elias J, 434
Chronology of the Medieval World. Storey, Robin L, 381
Chronology of the People's Republic of China from October 1, 1969. Cheng, Peter P, 5598
Chubb, Basil. The Government and Politics of Ireland, 1161
Church and State in Contemporary America. Brown, William C, 766
Church and State in Russia. Curtiss, John S, 798
CHURCH HISTORY, 777-781, 805
Churchill-Roosevelt-Stalin. Feis, Herbert, 5111
Churchill, Winston L. Closing the Ring, 5098
———. The Gathering Storm, 5098
———. The Grand Alliance, 5098
———. Great Contemporaries, 4861
———. The Hinge of Fate, 5098
———. A History of the English-Speaking Peoples, 5171
———. Island Race, 5172
———. Their Finest Hour, 5098
———. Triumph and Tragedy, 5098

INDEX

La Chute. Camus, Albert, 4198
Chute, Marchette. Shakespeare of London, 3865
CIA and the Cult of Intelligence. Marchetti, Victor and Marks, John D. 1295
Ciano Diaries, 1939-1943. Ciano, Galeazzo, 5108
Ciano, Galeazzo. The Ciano Diaries, 1939-1943, 5108
Ciardi, John. Thirty-Nine Poems, 3630
Cicero and His Friends. Boissier, Gaston, 4933
Cicero and the Roman Republic. Cowell, Frank R, 4934
Cicero, Marcus Tullius. Speeches, 4420
———. Tusculan Disputations, 4421
Cinco Horas con Mario. Delibes, Miguel, 4375
Los Cipreses Creen en Dios. Gironella, José María, 4377
Circle of Discrimination. Bloch, Herman D, 1013
CIRCUS — U. S., 3260
Circus in America. Fox, Charles P. and Parkinson, Tom. 3260
Cirlot, Juan E. A Dictionary of Symbols, 54
CITIES AND TOWNS, 960, 964, 2240, 2950-2951, 2954-2955, 2970
U. S., 961, 965, 1626, 1629, 1703, 5896-5897, 6074
Cities in Revolt. Bridenbaugh, Carl, 5896
Cities in the Wilderness. Bridenbaugh, Carl, 5897
Cities of Vesuvius. Grant, Michael, 4730
Citizen Groups and the Nuclear Power Controversy. Ebbin, Steven and Kasper, Raphael. 2664
Citizen Hearst. Swanberg, W. A, 494
Citizen Nader. McCarry, Charles, 1544
Citizen Touissant. Korngold, Ralph, 5847
City. Macaulay, David, 2953
City Bosses in the United States. Zink, Harold, 1372
City in History. Mumford, Lewis, 2951
Civil Aircraft of the World. Taylor, John W, 2731
Civil Disobedience. Bedau, Hugo A., compiled by. 1221
Civil Disobedience. Cohen, Carl, 1219
Civil Liberties and the Constitution. Barker, Lucius and Twiley, W. B. 1565
CIVIL RIGHTS, 1013, 1015, 1027-1029, 1034, 1038, 1219, 1236, 1240, 1254-1256, 1258-1260, 1261, 1565, 1581, 1588, 1750, 1753
CIVIL SERVICE REFORM, 1195
Civil War Books. Nevins, Allan, et al, eds. 79

Civil War Dictionary. Boatner, Mark M., 3rd, 454
Civilian Conservation Corps, 1933-1942. Salmond, John A, 1647
Civilisation. Clark, Kenneth, 4651
CIVILIZATION, 377, 4647-4648
HISTORY, 4644, 4646, 4651-4653, 4674, 5040
CIVILIZATION, ANCIENT, 714, 4714, 4722, 4880
Civilization and the Caesars. Starr, Chester G, 4947
CIVILIZATION, ASSYRO-BABYLONIAN, 4911, 4915
CIVILIZATION, EUROPEAN, 4988-4989
CIVILIZATION, GREEK, 4439-4440, 4731, 4952, 4954-4955, 4958-4962, 4964-4965, 4967, 4976
CIVILIZATION, HOMERIC, 4460, 4963
Civilization in the West. Brinton, Crane, et al. 4644
CIVILIZATION, MEDIEVAL, 4430-4431, 4993-4997, 4999-5001, 5004, 5007-5008, 5015, 5205
CIVILIZATION, MINOAN, 4734
CIVILIZATION, MODERN, 912-913, 917, 4654-4660
CIVILIZATION, MOHAMMEDAN, 5628
CIVILIZATION, MYCENAEAN, 4979-4981
Civilization of the American Indian. 5778
Civilization of the Old South. Eaton, Clement, 6205
Civilization of the Renaissance in Italy. Burckhardt, Jacob, 5431
CIVILIZATION, RUSSIAN, 5492
CIVILIZATION, SCANDINAVIAN, 5538
Claiborne, Robert. Climate, Man, and History, 2156
Clar, Eric. The Aromatic Sextet, 2085
Clarence Darrow for the Defense. Stone, Irving, 1611
Clark, Alan. Barbarossa, 5126
Clark, Barrett H. European Theories of the Drama, 3481
Clark, Charles M. History of Australia, 6287
Clark, Gordon H. Thales to Dewey, 513
Clark, Grahame. Stone Age Hunters, 4712
Clark, John D. Ignition, 2861
Clark, Kenneth. Civilisation, 4651
———. Rembrandt and the Italian Renaissance, 3069
———. The Romantic Rebellion, 2904
Clark, Kenneth B. and Hopkins, Jeannette. A Relevant War Against Poverty, 1701
Clark, Leta W. How to Make Money with Your Crafts, 2854
Clark, Mark W. From the Danube to the Yalu, 5609

INDEX

Clark, Mary E. Contemporary Biology, 2211
Clark, Randolph L. and Cumley, Russell W. The Book of Health, 252
Clark, Ronald. The Alps, 4767
Clark, Ronald W. Einstein, 2024
———. The Scientific Breakthrough, 2494
Clark, Sharon. *see* Schurman, Nona
Clarke, Austin. Poetry in Modern Ireland, 3845
Clarke, John H., et al. Malcolm X, 1016
———. William Styron's Nat Turner, 3742
Clarke, Mary and Crisp, Clement. Ballet, 3328
Classic American Philosophers. Fisch, Max H., ed, 643
Classic Myths in English Literature and in Art. Gayley, Charles M, 826
Classic Theatre, Five German Plays. Bentley, Eric, ed, 4025
Classic Theatre, Six French Plays. Bentley, Eric, ed, 4184
Classic Theatre, Six Italian Plays. Bentley, Eric, ed, 4295
Classic Theatre, Six Spanish Plays. Bentley, Eric, ed, 4360
CLASSICAL DICTIONARIES, 409, 410
CLASSICAL GEOGRAPHY, 406, 4462
Classical Greece. Bowra, Maurice, 4966
CLASSICAL LITERATURE
  DICTIONARIES, 351
  GEOGRAPHY, 408, 4452
Classical Style in Islamic Painting. Grube, Ernst J, 2889
Classics of the Modern Theater. Kernan, Alvin B., ed, 3506
CLASSIFICATION, DECIMAL, 32
Classified Library of Congress Subject Headings. Williams, James G, 31
Claudel. Griffiths, Richard, ed, 4274
Claudel, Paul. L' Annonce Faite à Marie, 4151
CLAUDEL, PAUL, 4274
Clausewitz, Karl von. Principles of War, 1655
Clausner, Marlin D. Rural Santo Domingo, 5840
Clawson, Marion. *see* Held, R. Burnell
CLAY, HENRY, 6021
Clayton, Al. *see* Coles, Robert
Clean the Air. Lewis, Alfred, 2708
Clean Water. Stevens, Leonard A, 2704
Clear-Cut. Wood, Nancy, 2787
Cleator, Philip E. Weapons of War, 1680
Cleaver, Eldridge. Post Prison Writings and Speeches, 1018
———. Soul on Ice, 1017
CLEAVER, ELDRIDGE, 1250
Clemens, Samuel L. Mark Twain's Notebook, 3756

CLEMENS, SAMUEL LANGHORNE, 3752-3753
Clement, Roland. Nature Atlas of America, 197
Clendenen, Clarence. Blood on the Border, 6003
Cleopatra. Grant, Michael, 4887
CLEOPATRA, QUEEN OF EGYPT, 4887
CLEVELAND, GROVER, 6092
CLIMATE, 2156
Climate, Man, and History. Claiborne, Robert, 2156
Climb for the Evening Star. Mayer, Tom, 2717
Cline, Gloria G. Peter Skene Ogden and the Hudson's Bay Company, 5801
Cline, Gloria S. and Baker, Jeffrey A. An Index to Criticism of British and American Poetry, 365
Clissold, Stephen, et al. A Short History of Yugoslavia from Early Times to 1966, 5559
Clive, Mary. This Sun of York, 5209
Cloke, Marjane and Wallace, Robert. The Modern Business Letter-Writer's Manual, 2844
Close-up. Kinder, Marsha and Houston, Beverle. 3278
Closing Circle. Commoner, Barry, 941
Closing the Loop. August, Stanley W, 2770
CLOTHING AND DRESS, 2840
Clothing for Moderns. Erwin, Mabel D. and Kinchen, Lila A. 2840
Cloud Forest. Matthiessen, Peter, 4841
CLOUDS, 2155, 2158
Clouds of the World. Scorer, Richard, 2155
CLOWNS, 3258
Clubb, Oliver E. China and Russia, 1307
———. Twentieth Century China, 5589
COAL-MINERS, 980, 1435, 1437
Coat on a Stick. Humphries, Rolfe, 3573
Cobban, Alfred. A History of Modern France, 5369
Coblentz, Stanton A. The Militant Dissenters, 4668
Cochise. Wild, Peter, 3666
Cochran, Bert. Harry Truman and the Crisis Presidency, 6149
Cochran, Doris M. Living Amphibians of the World, 2410
Cochran, Doris M. and Goin, Coleman J. New Field Book of Reptiles and Amphibians, 2411
Cochran, Hamilton. Blockade Runners of the Confederacy, 6056
Cochran, Thomas. Social Change in America, 927
Cochrane, Willard W. World Food Problem, 1516

353

INDEX

Cocteau, Jean. Five Plays, 4152
———. La Machine Infernale, 4153
———. Théâtre, 4154
COCTEAU, JEAN, 4156
Code Arrest. Diethrich, Edward B. and Fried, John J. 2592
Code of Life. Borek, Ernest, 2291
Codeword Barbarossa. Whaley, Barton, 5123
Coe, Charles N. Shakespeare's Villains, 3866
Coe, Michael D. The Maya, 5758
Coffin, Charles M. and Roelofs, Gerrit, eds. Major Poets, 3775
Coffin, Joseph. The Complete Book of Coin Collecting, 2998
Coffin, Tristram P. Folklore in America, 1828
———. Our Living Traditions, 1829
Coffin, Tristram P. and Cohen, Hennig. Folklore from the Working Folk of America, 1830
Coffman, Edward M. The War to End All Wars, 5087
Cohen, Abraham. Everyman's Talmud, 855
Cohen, Carl. Civil Disobedience, 1219
Cohen, Daniel. Intelligence - What Is It?, 577
———. Masters of the Occult, 531
Cohen, Dorothy. Advertising, 2855
Cohen, Hennig. see Coffin, Tristram P.
Cohen, Jerry S. see Mintz, Morton
Cohen, Leonard. Selected Poems, 1956-1968, 3631
Cohen, Paul. Realm of the Submarine, 2683
Cohen, Richard M. A Heartbeat Away, 6173
Cohen, Saul B., ed. Oxford World Atlas, 396
Cohen, Sidney. The Drug Dilemma, 2575
Cohen, Stephen F. Bukharin and the Bolshevik Revolution, 5511
Cohen, William H. To Walk in Seasons, 4614
Cohn, Ruby. Back to Beckett, 4284
Cohne, Joel H. see Schollander, Don
Coil of Life. Moore, Ruth, 2215
Coin Makers. Becker, Thomas, 1456
COINS, 283-286, 1456, 2999-3000
Coit, Margaret L. John C. Calhoun, 5976
COKE, SIR EDWARD, 5236
Colbert, Edwin H. Dinosaurs, 2179
———. Evolution of the Vertebrates, 2178
———. Men and Dinosaurs, 2180
Colby, C. B. and Angier, B. The Art and Science of Taking to the Woods, 3397
Colby, Vineta, see Kunitz, Stanley J.
Cold Dawn. Newhouse, John, 1300
Cold-War America. Wittner, Lawrence S, 6159

Coldest War. Sulzberger, C. L, 1320
Cole, Alan B. see Burch, Betty B.
Cole, Arthur C. The Irrepressible Conflict, 1850-1865, 6004
Cole, Bernard. see Meltzer, Milton
Cole, David C., et al. Korean Development, 1413
Cole, Toby and Chinoy, Helen K., eds. Directors on Directing, 3299
Cole, William, ed. A Book of Love Poems, 3776
Colecchia, Francesca Maria. Selected Latin American One-Act Plays, 4358
Coleman, Howard W., ed. Color Television, 2653
Coleridge. Bate, Walter Jackson, 3807
Coleridge, Samuel T. Poems, 3811
COLERIDGE, SAMUEL TAYLOR, 3807
Coles, Clarence W. and Glenn, Harold T. Glenn's Complete Bicycle Manual, 2746
Coles, Robert. Children of Crisis, 1019
———. Drugs and Youth, 2546
———. Uprooted Children, 996
Coles, Robert and Clayton, Al. Still Hungry in America, 997
Coles, Robert and Erikson, Jon. The Middle Americans, 998
Colette, Sidonie. Earthly Paradise, 4285
COLETTE, SIDONIE, 4285
Collapse of British Power. Barnett, Correlli, 5268
Collapse of the Third Republic. Shirer, William L, 5419
Collected Dialogues of Plato. Plato, 4472
Collected Later Poems. Williams, William C, 3592
Collected Longer Poems. Auden, Wystan H, 3842
Collected Plays. Hellman, Lillian, 3678
Collected Plays. Miller, Arthur, 3681
Collected Plays. Rattigan, Terance, 3892
Collected Plays. Yeats, William B, 3889
Collected Poems. Betjeman, John, 3844
Collected Poems. Brooke, Rupert, 3835
Collected Poems. Dugan, Alan, 3636
Collected Poems. Hardy, Thomas, 3825
Collected Poems. Millay, Edna S, 3610
Collected Poems. Patchen, Kenneth, 3581
Collected Poems. Robinson, Edwin A. 3614
Collected Poems. Roethke. Theodore, 3585
Collected Poems. Sarton, May, 3617
Collected Poems. Spender, Stephen, 3851
Collected Poems. Thomas, Dylan, 3852
Collected Poems. Yeats, William B, 3853
Collected Poems, 1909-1960. Eberhart, Richard, 3637
Collected Poems, 1925-1963. MacNeice, Louis, 3850
Collected Poems of A. E. Housman. Housman, Alfred E. 3837

Collected Poems of Edith Sitwell. Sitwell, Edith, 3840
Collected Poems of Rolfe Humphries. Humphries, Rolfe, 3574
Collected Poems of Wallace Stevens. Stevens, Wallace. 3587
Collected Poetry. Parker, Dorothy, 3612
Collected Shorter Poems. Auden, Wystan H, 3843
Collected Shorter Poems. Rexroth, Kenneth, 3584
Collected Stories of Sholem Aleichem. Aleichem, Sholem, 4590
Collected Tales and Plays. Gogol, Nikolai V, 4576
COLLECTIVE SETTLEMENTS — U. S., 1209, 2502-1507
Collector's Encyclopedia of Rocks and Minerals. Deeson, A. F, 227
Collector's Encyclopedia of Shells. Dance, Peter S, 2386
College and Adult Reading List of Books in Literature and the Fine Arts. 55
College Chemistry. Pauling, Linus and Pauling, Peter. 2070
COLLEGES — U. S., 147, 149, 1786, 1788
Colles, Dorothy. *see* Child, Heather
Collett, Rosemary K. My Orphans of the Wild, 2823
Collier, Basil. The Airship, 2732
Collier, Graham. Form, Space and Vision, 3004
Collier, Simon D. From Cortés to Castro, 6255
Collins, John M. Grand Strategy, 1666
Collins, Joseph L. War in Peacetime, 5610
Collins, Larry and LaPierre, Dominique. O Jerusalem!, 5643
———. Or I'll Dress You in Mourning, 3288
Collins, Michael. Carrying the Fire, 2762
Collins, Stewart A. The Mariner 6 and 7 Pictures of Mars, 1999
Collision Course. Parone, Edward, ed, 3672
Collman, Charles A. Our Mysterious Panics, 1830-1930, 1529
Colomba. Merimée, Prosper, 4236
Colonial Background of the American Revolution. Andrews, Charles, 5893
Colonial Experience. Hawke, David, 5901
Colonial Wars, 1689-1762. Peckham, Howard H, 5907
COLOR — PSYCHOLOGY, 568
Color Dictionary of Flowers and Plants for Home and Garden. Hay, Roy and Synge, Patrick M. 260
Color Photo Book. Feininger, Andreas, 3118
COLOR PHOTOGRAPHY — HANDBOOKS, MANUALS, ETC., 3118
COLOR TELEVISION, 2653
Color Television. Coleman, Howard W., ed, 2653
Colorful Cacti of the American Deserts. Lamb, Edgar and Lamb, Brian. 2793
COLORS, 2863
Colton, Joel. *see* Palmer, Robert R.
Colum, Padriac, ed. A Treasury of Irish Folklore, 1831
Columbia Dictionary of Modern European Literature. Smith, Horatio, ed, 328
Columbia Lippincott Gazetteer of the World. Seltzer, L. E., ed, 383
Columbian Exchange. Crosby, Alfred W, 2230
COLUMBUS, CHRISTOPHER, 5889
Combray. Proust, Marcel, 4240
COMEDY, 3483, 3530
COMEDY FILMS, 3279
Comedy of Neil Simon. Simon, Neil, 3704
Comets, Meteorites and Men. Brown, Peter L, 2003
COMIC BOOKS, STRIPS, ETC. — HISTORY AND CRITICISM, 586
Comics. Robinson, Jerry, 3006
Coming Age of Solar Energy. Halacy, D. S., Jr, 2662
Coming of Age. Deutsch, Babette, 3634
Coming of Post-Industrial Society. Bell, Daniel, 1103
Coming of the Civil War. Craven, Avery O, 6006
Coming of the French Revolution. Lefebvre, Georges, 5396
Coming of the Italian-Ethiopian War. Baer, George W, 5720
Coming of the Revolution. Gipson, Lawrence H, 5899
Coming of the White Man, 1492-1848. Priestley, Herbert I, 5892
Coming up Black. Schulz, David A, 1036
Commager, Henry S. American Mind, 5857
———. The Blue and the Gray, 6027
———. Documents of American History, 5878
———. Era of Reform, 1830-1860, 6005
———. Living Ideas in America, 5879
Commager, Henry S. and Morris, Richard B., eds. The Spirit of '76, 5931
Commager, Henry S. and Nevins, A., eds. Heritage of America, 5880
Commentary on the Bhagavad Gita. Chinmoy, Sri, 844
Commentary on the Constitution of the United States. Schwartz, Bernard, 1586

INDEX

Commission on the Rights and Liberties and Responsibilities of the American Indians. The Indian, 5766
Committee. Goodman, Walter, 1362
Committee for Economic Development. High Employment Without Inflation, 1543
Common Insects of North America. Swan, Lester A. and Papp, Charles S. 2394
Common Man Through the Centuries. Barsis, Max, 1810
Commoner, Barry. The Closing Circle, 941
Commonsense Cataloging. Piercy, Esther J, 29
COMMONWEALTH OF NATIONS, 363, 5268, 5270
Commonwealth of the Philippines. Malcolm, George A, 6284
Communes in America. Horwitz, Elinor L, 1505
Communes in the Counter Culture. Melville, Keith, 1506
Communes USA. Fairfield, Richard, 1502
COMMUNICABLE DISEASES, 2607
COMMUNICATION, 463, 899, 3005
Communication Is Power. Brucker, Herbert, 492
COMMUNISM, 1207, 1482, 1489, 1491, 1493, 1496-1497
    BALKAN PENINSULA, 5557
    CHINA, 1177, 1186, 1214, 1499, 5592, 5596
    EUROPE, EASTERN, 1159-1160
    HISTORY, 1484, 1721, 5524
    ITALY, 1487
    RUSSIA, 1490, 1495, 1498, 1910, 5368, 5524
    U. S. — (1917), 1228, 1336, 1622, 1714, 6120
    YUGOSLAVIA, 1222
Communism in Czechoslovakia, 1948-1960. Taborsky, Edward, 5358
Communism Today. Hyde, Douglas A, 1497
COMMUNIST COUNTRIES, 1155, 4676
Communist Manifesto. Marx, Karl and Engels, Friedrich. 1493
COMMUNIST PARTIES, 140, 1136
COMMUNIST PARTY, 1169, 1175, 1396
Communist Party of the Soviet Union. Schapiro, Leonard, 1396
Communist Regimes in Eastern Europe. Starr, Richard F, 1160
Communist States in Disarray, 1965-1971. Bromke, Adam and Rakowska-Harmstone, Teresa, eds. 1155
COMMUNISTS — RUSSIA, 5520
Compact History of the Civil War. Dupuy, R. Ernest and Dupuy, Trevor N. 6030

Companion to Chaucer Studies. Rowland, Beryl, ed, 3792
COMPARATIVE GOVERNMENT, 1142-1144
Comparative Guide to American Colleges. Cass, James and Birnbaum, Max. 1786
Comparative Guide to Junior and Community Two Year Colleges. Cass, James and Birnbaum, Max. 1787
COMPARATIVE LAW, 1546
Comparative Religions. Bouquet, Alan C, 819
COMPASS, 3389
Competition for Empire, 1740-1763. Dorn, Walter L, 5032
Complete Art of Printing and Enlarging. Croy, D. R, 3108
Complete Baseball Handbook. Alston, Walter and Weiskopf, Donald. 3372
Complete Beginner's Guide to Motorcycling. Roth, Bernhard A, 2748
Complete Bolivian Diaries of Ché Guevara, and Other Captured Documents. Guevara, Ché, 6275
Complete Book of Boating. Zadig, Ernest A, 3425
Complete Book of Bridge. Reese, Terence and Dormer, Albert. 3346
Complete Book of Ceramic Art. Rothenberg, Polly, 3001
Complete Book of Classical Music. Ewen, David, 304
Complete Book of Coin Collecting. Coffin, Joseph, 2998
Complete Book of Hunting. Ormond, Clyde, 3459
Complete Book of Karate and Self-Defense. Masters, Robert V., compiled by. 3410
Complete Book of Shooting. O'Connor, Jack, et al. 3458
Complete Book of Sky Sports. Emrich, Linn, 3439
Complete Book of Terrarium Gardening. Kramer, Jack, 2801
Complete Book of United States Coin Collecting. Davis, Norman M, 3000
Complete Book of 8mm Movie Making. Yulsman, Jerry, 3115
Complete Concordance to Shakespeare. Bartlett, John, ed, 367
Complete Dog Book. American Kennel Club, 2809
Complete Ecology Fact Book. Deedy, John and Nobile, Philip, eds. 231
Complete Encyclopedia of Ice Hockey. Hollander, Zander and Bock, Hal, eds. 3414

INDEX

Complete Encyclopedia of Motorcars. Georgano, George N, 2743
A Complete Field Guide to Nests in the United States. Headstrom, Richard, 2429
Complete Greek Dramas. Oates, Whitney J. and O'Neill, Eugene, Jr., eds. 4449
Complete Greek Tragedies. Grene, David and Lattimore, Richmond. 4448
Complete Guide to Cross-Country Skiing and Touring. Tokle, Art and Luray, Martin. 3419
Complete Guide to Fishing Across North America. Brooks, Joseph W, 3452
Complete Guide to Furniture Styles. Boger, Louise A, 3023
Complete History of the Mexican War. Brooks, Nathan C, 6018
Complete Illustrated Book of Card Games. Hervey, George F, 3345
Complete Motorcycle Book. Engel, Lyle K, 2747
Complete Nonsense Book. Lear, Edward, 3828
Complete Photographer. Feininger, Andreas, 3103
Complete Play Production Handbook. Allensworth, Carl, et al. 3298
Complete Plays. Congreve, William, 3871
Complete Plays. Wycherley, William, 3873
Complete Plays and Prose. Buchner, Georg, 4013
Complete Plays of T. S. Eliot. Eliot, Thomas S, 3674
Complete Poems. Bishop, Elizabeth, 3626
Complete Poems. Cummings, E. E, 3600
Complete Poems. Jarrell, Randall, 3645
Complete Poems. Marvell, Andrew, 3800
Complete Poems and Plays, 1909-1950. Eliot, Thomas S, 3571
Complete Poems and Selected Letters and Prose. Crane, Hart, 3598
Complete Poems and Selected Letters. Michelangelo, 4300
Complete Poems of Carl Sandburg. Sandburg, Carl, 3616
Complete Poems of Emily Dickinson. Dickinson, Emily, 3567
Complete Poems of Marianne Moore. Moore, Marianne, 3579
Complete Poems of Thomas Gray. Gray, Thomas, 3803
Complete Poetical Works. Burns, Robert, 3805
Complete Poetical Works. Dryden, John, 3797
Complete Poetical Works. Keats, John, 3812
Complete Poetical Works. Lowell, Amy, 3605
Complete Poetical Works. Lowell, James Russell, 3558
Complete Poetical Works. Shelley, Percy B, 3818
Complete Poetical Works. Spenser, Edmund, 3794
Complete Poetical Works. Wordsworth, William, 3820
Complete Poetry. Catullus, Gaius Valerius, 4416
Complete Poetry and Selected English Prose. Milton, John, 3801
Complete Poetry and Selected Prose. Donne, John, 3796
Complete Poetry, Selected Prose and Letters. Whitman, Walt, 3563
Complete Roman Drama. Duckworth, George E., ed, 4409
Complete Secretary's Handbook. Doris, Lillian and Miller, Bessemay. 2843
Complete Shortwave Listener's Handbook. Bennett, Hank, 2650
Complete Works. Chaucer, Geoffrey, 3790
Complete Works. Josephus, Flavius, 4904
Complete Works. Molière, Jean B, 4172
Complete Works. Racine, Jean B, 4178
Complete Works. Synge, John M, 3879
Complete Works of François Villon. Villon, François, 4134
Complete Writings of William Blake, with Variant Readings. Blake, William, 3808
Completion of Independence, 1790-1830. Krout, John A. and Fox, Dixon R. 5863
COMPOSERS, 303, 3140, 3154-3156, 3212, 3244, 4863
   DICTIONARIES, 298-300
Composers of Tomorrow's Music. Ewen, David, 3154
Composers Since 1900. Ewen, David, ed, 299
Compton, James V. The Swastika and the Eagle, 1304
Compton, Joan. House Plants, 2794
Computer from Pascal to Von Neumann. Goldstine, Herman H, 2647
Computer Revolution. Hawkes, Nigel, 469
Computer Science. Anger, Arthur L., et al. 467
COMPUTER SCIENCE LITERATURE, 56
COMPUTERS, 464, 469-470, 2647, 2845-2846
Computers and Society. Nikolaieff, George A, 921
Computers in Action. Spencer, Donald, 471
Comstock, W. Richard. Religion and Man, 686

INDEX

Conant, Ralph W. Prospects for Revolution, 1072
CONCENTRATION CAMPS, 1063-1064, 5147
CONCEPTION — PREVENTION, 986, 2551-2552
Conception, Contraception. Loebl, Suzanne, 958
Concepts in Physics. Benumof, Reuben, 2015
Concepts of Criticism. Wellek, Rene, 3466
Concepts of Modern Art. Richardson, Tony and Stangos, Nikos, eds. 2912
Concepts of Science. Achinstein, Peter, 1909
Concert of Europe. Albrecht-Carrié, René, ed, 5050
Concise Cambridge History of English Literature. Sampson, George, 364
Concise Encyclopedia of Modern Drama. Melchinger, Siegfried, 316
A Concise History of Mathematics. Struik, Dirk J, 1944
A Concise History of Opera. Orrey, Leslie, 3208
Condit, Carl. American Building, 2690
La Condition Humaine. Malraux, André, 4229
Condon, Edward W. and Odishaw, H. Handbook of Physics, 214
CONDUCTORS (MUSIC), 306
Cone, James H. A Black Theology of Liberation, 681
———. The Spirituals and the Blues, 3239
A Coney Island of the Mind. Ferlinghetti, Lawrence, 3638
CONFEDERATE STATES OF AMERICA, 1426, 6047, 6057-6059
Confederate States of America. Schwab, John C, 1426
La Confession d'un Enfant du Siecle. Musset, Alfred de, 4238
Confessions of a Mask. Mishima, Yukio, 4621
Confessions of Saint Augustine. Augustine, St. 759
Conflict of Generations. Feuer, Lewis S, 1784
Confrontation. Laqueur, Walter, 5651
Confrontation and Intervention in the Modern World. Schwarz, Urs, 1661
Confrontation, Conflict and Dissent. Miller, Albert J, 57
Confucius. The Wisdom of Confucius, 616
CONFUCIUS, 869
CONFUCIUS AND CONFUCIANISM, 839
Confucius, His Life and Time. Liu, Wu-Chi, 869

Confucius to Cummings. Pound, Ezra and Spann, Marcella, eds. 3500
Congress. Griffith, Ernest S, 1364
Congress and the Nation. Congressional Quarterly Service, 1156
Congress of Vienna. Nicolson, Harold G, 5048
Congress v. the Supreme Court. Berger, Raoul, 1613
Congressional Behavior. Polsby, Nelson W., ed, 1367
Congressional Committees. Morrow, William L, 1366
Congressional Quarterly Service. Congress and the Nation, 1156
———. Energy Crisis in America, 1473
———. President Ford, 6174
Congreve, William. Complete Plays, 3871
CONJURING, 3334-3335
Conkin, Paul K. Puritans and Pragmatists, 555
Connection. Gelber, Jack, 3692
Connery, Donald. The Irish, 5161
———. The Scandinavians, 5534
Connor, Billie M., see Connor, John M.
Connor, John M. and Connor, Billie M., eds. Ottemiller's Index to Plays in Collections, 333
Conquering Family. Costain, Thomas B, 5201
Conquering the Deep Sea Frontier. Darby, Ray and Darby, Patricia. 2137
Conquest of Everest. Hunt, John, 3392
Conquest of Famine. Aykroyd, W. R, 1514
Conquest of Mexico, and The Conquest of Peru. Prescott, William H, 6259
Conquest of the Air. Howard, Frank and Gunston, Bill. 2715
Conquest of the Incas. Hemming, John, 6267
Conquest of Violence. Bondurant, Joan and Fisher, Margaret W., eds. 898
Conquest, Robert. The Great Terror, 5512
———. Religion in the USSR, 797
Conrad, John W. Ceramic Formulas, 287
CONRAD, JOSEPH, 3941
Conrat, Maisie and Conrat, Richard. Executive Order 9066, 1062
Conrat, Richard. see Conrat, Maisie
Conroy, Hilary and Miyakawa, T. S., eds. East Across the Pacific, 1048
Conscience in America. Schlissel, Lillian, ed, 1675
Conscientious Objector. Kellogg, Walter G, 5075

358

CONSCIENTIOUS OBJECTORS, 1227, 1673, 1675
Conservation. Mossman, Archie, 1467
Conservation of Library Materials. Cunha, George, 33
CONSERVATION OF NATURAL RESOURCES, 940, 2463-1464, 1466-1468, 2099, 2103
CONSERVATISM, 1150, 1192
Conservatism in America. Rossiter, Clinton, 1210
Conservative Tradition in American Thought. Sigler, Jay A., ed, 1150
Conserving Life on Earth. Ehrenfeld, David, 2824
Conspiracy Against Hitler in the Twilight War. Deutsch, Harold C, 5310
Constable. Taylor, Basil, 3050
CONSTABLE, JOHN, 3050
Constantine. MacMullen, Ramsay, 4950
Constantine, Albert. Know Your Woods, 2328
CONSTANTINE I, 4950
Constantine, Mildred and Fern, Alan. Revolutionary Soviet Film Posters, 3096
Constitutional Grounds for Presidential Impeachment. U. S. Congress. House. Committee on the Judiciary, 1645
Constitutional Problems Under Lincoln. Randall, James G, 1589
Constitutionalist. Anastaplo, George, 1563
CONSTITUTIONS — COLLECTIONS, 1559, 1590
Constitutions of Europe. Goerner, Edward A., ed, 1559
Constitutions of Latin America. Fitzgerald, Gerald E., ed, 1590
Consumer Beware! Hunter, Beatrice T, 2862
CONSUMER EDUCATION, 1794
CONSUMER PROTECTION, 143, 2556
Consumer Report Editors. see Brecker, Edward M.
Contact at Sea. Schroeder, Peter B, 2685
Contemporary America. Wish, Harvey, 6106
Contemporary Art with Wood. Meilach, Dona Z, 2990
Contemporary Authors. 425
Contemporary Biology. Clark, Mary E, 2211
Contemporary Crafts Market Place, 1975-1976. American Crafts Council, 288
Contemporary Dramatists. Vinson, James, 372
Contemporary England. Medlicott, William N, 5271
Contemporary Europe. Hughes, H. Stuart, 5092

Contemporary French Literature. Peyre, Henri, 4102
Contemporary Indian Short Stories. Bhattacharya, Bhabani, ed, 4608
Contemporary Literary Criticism. 344
Contemporary Sculpture Techniques. Baldwin, John, 2987
Contemporary Social Problems. Merton, Robert K. and Nisbet, Robert. 885
Contemporary Synagogue Art. Kampf, Avram, 2890
Contemporary Writers in Christian Perspective Series. 4641
Contemporary Yugoslavia. Vucinich, Wayne S., ed, 5561
Contempt. 1592
Contenau, Georges. Everyday Life in Babylon and Assyria, 4908
Contes Choisis. Maupassant, Guy de, 4230
Contes et Nouvelles D'aujourd 'hui. Yale University, Dept. of French, 4263
CONTINENTAL DRIFT, 2113, 2116-2117, 2125-2128
Continental Drift. Marvin, Ursula B, 2126
Continental Drift. Tarling, Don and Tarling, Maureen. 2128
Continents Adrift. Scientific American Editors, 2127
Continents in Motion. Sullivan, Walter, 2117
Continuities in Cultural Evolution. Mead, Margaret, 916
Contraception, Abortion, Pregnancy. Fleming, Alice, 2551
Convention Decisions and Voting Records. Bain, Richard C, 136
Conversations with Eldridge Cleaver. Lockwood, Lee, 1250
Coogan, Timothy P. Ireland Since the Rising, 5164
Cook, Bruce. Listen to the Blues, 3194
Cook, Dorothy E., et al, eds. Short Story Index, Plus 4 Supplements, 336
Cook, Harold E. Shaker Music, 3219
COOK, JAMES, 4701-4846
Cook, Warren L. Flood Tide of Empire, 6246
Cooke, Alistair. Alistair Cooke's America, 4811
Cooke, John. see Nichols, David
COOKERY, 2321, 2775, 2829-2830, 2834-2837
Cooley. Minetree, Harry, 2620
COOLEY, DENTON A, 2620
COOLIDGE, CALVIN, 6125, 6127
Coon, Carleton S. Origin of Races, 2195
————. The Story of Man, 2186
Coon, Carleton S. and Hunt, Edward E., Jr. The Living Races of Man, 2187
Coons, William R. Attica Diary, 1735

INDEX

Cooper, Barbara and Matheson, Maureen. The World Museum Guide, 480
Cooper, Bryan and Batchelor, John. Fighter, 2674
Cooper, Douglas. The Cubist Epoch, 3031
Cooper, Henry S., Jr. Thirteen, 2766
Cooper, Kenneth H. Aerobics, 2536
Cooper, Lane, ed. Fifteen Greek Plays, 4446
Cooper, Michele. see Cahill, Susan
Cooper, Paulette, ed. Growing up Puerto Rican, 4822
COPE, EDWARD DRINKER, 2177
Cope, John. South Africa, 5734
Copernican Revolution. Kuhn, Thomas S, 1992
COPERNICUS, NICOLAUS, 1972-1973, 1992
Copi, Irving M. Introduction to Logic, 593
Copperud, Roy H. A Dictionary of Usage and Style, 1881
CORAL REEFS, 2135, 2263-2265
CORE. Meier, August and Rudwick, Elliott. 1236
Corn, Wanda M., ed. The Art of Andrew Wyeth, 3039
Corneille, Pierre. Chief Plays of Corneille, 4155
Cornell, James, ed. It Happened Last Year, 1897
Cornford, Francis M. Before and After Socrates, 608
———. Greek Religious Thought from Homer to the Age of Alexander, 832
CORPORATIONS, 1449, 1532, 1538
Corre, Gustavo. El Simbolismo Religioso en las Novelas de Perez Galdos, 4311
Corregidor. Belote, James H. and Belote, William M. 5125
Corrigan, Robert W. Masterpieces of Modern French Theater, 4190
———. Masterpieces of the Modern German Theatre, 4027
———. Masterpieces of the Modern Italian Theatre, 4297
———. Masterpieces of the Modern Russian Theatre, 4538
———. Masterpieces of the Modern Spanish Theatre, 4361
———. Tragedy, 3529
Corrupt Kingdom. Finely, Joseph E, 1440
CORRUPTION (IN POLITICS), 1202, 1373, 1612, 1626, 6196
Corson, Hiram. A Primer of English Verse, 3777
Corson, Richard. Stage Makeup, 3305
CORTES, HERNANDO, 5804, 6259
Cortner, R. and Lytle, C. Modern Constitutional Law, 1573

Corvo, Frederick B. Chronicles of the House of Borgia, 5435
Cosgrove, Margaret. Messages and Voices, 2367
Cosmas, Graham A. An Army for Empire, 6095
Cosmic Connection. Sagan, Carl, 2377
COSMIC PHYSICS, 1896
COSMIC RAYS, 2064
Cosmic Rays. Hillas, A. M, 2064
COSMOLOGY, 521, 1979, 1992
COSSACKS, 5485, 5488
Cossacks. Hindus, Maurice G, 5485
Cossacks. Longworth, Philip, 5488
Cost of Discipleship. Bonhoeffer, Dietrich, 736
Costain, Thomas B. Conquering Family, 5201
———. Last Plantagenets, 5202
———. Magnificent Century, 5203
———. Three Edwards, 5204
Costello, David F. The Desert World, 2247
———. The World of the Gull, 2434
Costello, Peter. In Search of Lake Monsters, 2371
Costigan, Giovanni. Makers of Modern England, 5277
COSTUME, 150, 1810-1817, 3303-3304
Costumes of Everyday Life. Lister, Margot, 1816
Cotter, Janet. Invitation to Poetry, 3473
Cotton Kingdom. Olmstead, Frederick L, 6211
Cottrell, Leonard. The Bull of Minos, 4979
———. Lady of the Two Lands, 4884
———. The Quest for Sumer. , 4721
Couch, William, Jr., ed. New Black Playwrights, an Anthology, 3670
Cougar Doesn't Live Here Anymore. Milne, Lorus and Milne, Margery. 2339
Coulton, George G. Medieval Panorama, 5196
———. Medieval Village, 4996
Council for National Co-Operation in Aquatics. New Science of Skin and Scuba Diving, 3436
Counter-Reformation. Dickens, Arthur G, 785
Counterrevolution. Flores Caballero, Romeo, 5812
COUNTRY LIFE — GEORGIA, 4832-4834
Country Music Encyclopedia. Shestack, Melvin, 311
Country Music U.S.A. A Fifty-Year History. Malone, Bill C, 3227
Courage to Be. Tillich, Paul, 607
Courage to Fail. Fox, Renee C. and Swazy, Judith P. 2590

Courant, Richard and Robbins, Herbert. What Is Mathematics?, 1929
Course of American Democratic Thought. Gabriel, Ralph H, 5860
Course of American Economic Growth and Development. Hacker, Louis M, 1418
Course of Empire. DeVoto, Bernard A, 5386
Course of the South to Secession. Phillips, Ulrich B, 6212
Court and Constitution in the Twentieth Century. Swindler, William F, 1619
Court Martial of Lt. Calley. Hammer, Richard, 1595
Cousine Bette. Balzac, Honore de, 4193
Cousins, Geoffrey. *see* Scott, Tom
Cousteau, Jacques-Yves and Cousteau, Philippe. The Shark, 2409
Cousteau, Jacques-Yves and Diole, Philippe. Dolphins and Freedom, 2459
———. Life and Death in a Coral Sea, 2135
———. Octopus and Squid, the Soft Intelligence, 2388
———. The Whale, 2454
Cousteau, Jacques-Yves and Dugan, J. Captain Cousteau's Underwater Treasury, 3437
Cousteau, Philippe. *see* Cousteau, Jacques-Yves
Cousy, Robert and Power, Frank G., Jr. Basketball, 3353
Cowboy and His Interpreters. Branch, Douglas, 4837
Cowell, Frank R. Cicero and the Roman Republic, 4934
Cowie, Donald. Scotland, 4743
Cowles, Virginia. The Rothschilds, 1450
Cowley, David. Working with Clay and Plaster, 2988
Cowley, Malcolm. Blue Juniata, 3632
Cowper, William. Poems, 3806
Cox, Allan, ed. Plate Tectonics and Geomagnetic Reversals, 2114
Cox, Archibald. The Warren Court, 1616
Cox, Eugene L. The Eagles of Savoy, 5014
Cox, F. E. *see* Vickerman, Keith
Cox, Harvey. The Secular City, 744
———. The Seduction of the Spirit, 696
Cox, Lawanda and Cox, John H. Politics, Principle and Prejudice, 1865-1866, 6063
Cox, Sidney. Swinger of Birches, 3597
Coyne, John, ed. Better Golf, 3367
Coyne, John and Hebert, Tom. This Way Out, 1780
COYOTES, 2472
Crafford, F. S. Jan Smuts, 5740
Craft of Fiction. Lubbock, Percy, 3489
Crafts of Israel. Dayan, Ruth and Feinberg, Wilburt, 3019

Crafts of Mexico. Harvey, Marian, 3020
Craig, Gerald M. The United States and Canada, 1332
Craig, Gordon A. and Gilbert, Felix, eds. Diplomats, 5095
Crane, Hart. Complete Poems and Selected Letters and Prose, 3598
CRANE, HART, 3621
Crane, Stephen. Poems of Stephen Crane, 3565
CRANE, STEPHEN, 3565
Crankshaw, Edward. The Habsburgs, 5339
CRANMER, THOMAS, 796
Crary, Catherine S. Price of Loyalty, 5946
Craven, Avery O. The Coming of the Civil War, 6006
———. Edmund Ruffin, Southerner, 6007
Craven, Wayne. Sculpture in America, 2984
Creamer, Lex. *see* Espy, Hilda C.
Creasy, Edward S. and Mitchell, J. P. Twenty Decisive Battles of the World, 4669
Creating a School Media Program. Gillespie, John T. and Spirt, Diana L. 35
Creation of the Universe. Gamow, George, 1984
Creative Evolution. Bergson, Henri L, 519
Creel, Herrlee G. Chinese Thought from Confucius to Mao Tse-tung, 617
Creighton, Donald. Canada's First Century, 5781
Crescent and Star. Alexander, Yonah and Kittrie, Nicholas N. F., eds. 924
Cressey, Donald R. Theft of the Nation, 1709
CRETE, 4734, 4963, 4979, 4981, 5565
CRIME AND CRIMINALS, 145, 1612, 1707, 1720, 1728, 1731-1732, 1734, 6235
Crime and Criminals. Fraenkel, Jack R, 1707
Le Crime de Sylvestre Bonnard. France, Anatole, 4212
Crime in Urban Society. McLennan, Barbara N., ed, 1731
Crime on Goat Island. Betti, Ugo, 4292
CRIMEAN WAR, (1853-1856), 5265
Crimsoned Prairie. Marshall, Samuel L, 5774
Crippled Giant. Fulbright, James W, 1338
Crises in the Classroom. Silberman, Charles E, 1764
Crises of the Republic. Arendt, Hannah, 1138
Crisis in Our Cities. Herber, Lewis, 2565
Crisis of Fear. Channing, Steven A, 6043
Crisis of German Ideology. Mosse, George L, 5320

INDEX

Crisis of the Negro Intellectual. Cruse, Harold, 4827
Crisp, Clement. *see* Clarke, Mary
Critchlow, Keith. Into the Hidden Environment, 2136
Critical Introduction to Ethics. Wheelwright, Philip, ed, 601
Critical Period of American History, 1783-1789. Fiske, John, 5964
Critical Year. Beale, Howard K, 6080
Critics and Crusaders. Madison, Charles A, 4870
Croce, Benedetto. History of the Kingdom of Naples, 5454
CROCODILES, 2421-2423
Crocodiles. Guggisberg, C. A, 2422
Croly, Herbert. Promise of American Life, 1574
Crompton, Louis. Shaw the Dramatist, 3882
CROMWELL, OLIVER, 5238
Cromwell, the Lord Protector. Fraser, Antonia, 5238
Crónica del Alba. Sender, Ramón J, 4387
Crosby, Alfred W. The Columbian Exchange, 2230
Cross, Charles A. *see* Moore, Patrick
Cross, Colin. The Fall of the British Empire, 1918-1968, 5270
Cross, F. L. and Livingstone, Elizabeth A. The Oxford Dictionary of the Christian Church, 99
Cross, Milton J. and Ewen, David. Milton Cross' New Encyclopedia of the Great Composers and Their Music, 298
Crouch, Steve. Steinbeck Country, 4838
Crouse, W. H. and Anglin, D. L. Automotive Engines, 2753
Crouzet, Maurice. The European Renaissance Since 1945, 4741
Crowding Syndrome. Bird, Caroline, 948
Crowell's Handbook of Classical Literature. Feder, Lillian, 408
Crowell's Handbook of Classical Mythology. Tripp, Edward, 121
Crowell's Handbook of Contemporary American Poetry. Malkoff, Karl, 358
Crowell's Handbook of Contemporary Drama. 348
Crowhurst, Norman H. Basic Electronics Course, 2051
Crowley, E. L., *see* Hayward, Max
Crowther, Bosley. Great Films, 3269
Croy, D. R. The Complete Art of Printing and Enlarging, 3108
Croyden, Margaret. Lunatics, Lovers and Poets, 3311
Crozier, Brian. DeGaulle, 5421

Crucial Decade and After. Goldman, Eric F, 6150
Cruden, Robert. The War That Never Ended, 6028
Cruel and Unusual. Meltsner, Michael, 1599
Crusade Against Slavery, 1830-1860. Filler, Louis, 1284
Crusade of the Left. Rosenstone, Robert A, 5473
CRUSADES, 5018-5019
Crusades. Treece, Henry, 5019
Cruse, Harold. The Crisis of the Negro Intellectual, 4827
Cruttwell, Charles R. A History of the Great War, 1914-1918, 5068
Cry Crisis. Manning, Harvey, 1475
CRYOBIOLOGY, 2225
CRYPTOGRAPHY, 5149
Crystal Spirit. Woodcock, George, 3950
CUBA, 5835
   HISTORY, 1326, 5824, 5826-5827, 5829-5833, 5836-5839, 6036, 6163, 6166
   POLITICS AND GOVERNMENT, 1340, 4806, 5828, 5836
Cuba. Ruiz, Roman E, 5836
Cuba. Suarez, Andres, 5837
Cuba. Suchlicki, Jaime, 5838
Cuba. Thomas, Hugh, 5839
Cuba, Haiti and the Dominican Republic. Fagg, John E, 5824
Cuba Nineteen Thirty-Three. Aguilar, Luis E, 5826
Cuba, Yes? Caute, David, 4806
Cuban Insurrection, 1952-1959. Bonachea, Ramon L, 5827
Cuban Missile Crisis. Divine, Robert, 1333
Cuban Policy of the United States. Langley, Lester D, 1347
Cubans in Exile. Fagen, Richard R., et al. 5831
CUBISM, 3031
Cubist Epoch. Cooper, Douglas, 3031
Las Cuidades. Baroja, Pio, 4368
Culican, William. The Medes and Persians. 4917
Cullen, Countee. On These I Stand, 3599
Cullinan, Gerald. The United States Postal Service, 1800
CULTS — U. S., 688
A Cultural History of the Enlightenment. Hampson, Norman, 638
Cultural Life of the American Colonies. Wright, Louis B, 5910
Cultural Life of the New Nation. Nye, Russel B, 5926
Culture and Commitment. Mead, Margaret, 910

Culture, Man and Nature. Harris, Marvin, 907
Culture of Contemporary Canada. Park, Julian, ed, 5783
Culture Shock. Bock, Philip K., compiled by. 904
Cumberland, Charles C. Mexican Revolution, 5818
———. Mexico, 5803
Cumley, Russell W. see Clark, Randolph L.
Cumming, William P., et al. The Discovery of North America, 5885
Cummings, E. E. Complete Poems, 3600
———. Six Non Lectures, 3757
CUMMINGS, EDWARD ESTLIN, 3601
Cummings, Paul. Dictionary of Contemporary American Artists, 277
Cundy, Henry M. and Rollett, A. P. Mathematical Models, 1930
CUNEIFORM INSCRIPTIONS, 4720
Cunha, George. Conservation of Library Materials, 33
Cunliffe, Marcus. The Nation Takes Shape, 1789-1837, 5963
Cunningham, Noble E., Jr. The Jeffersonian Republicans, 1389
Cunningham, Virginia. Paul Lawrence Dunbar and His Song, 3566
Le Curé de Tours. Balzac, Honoré de, 4194
CURIE, MARIE SKLODOWSKA, 2027
Curious Mollusks. Jenkins, Marie M, 2383
Curley, Arthur, see Curley, Dorothy N.
Curley, Dorothy N. and Curley, Arthur, eds. Modern Romance Literatures, 341
Curley, Dorothy N., et al, eds. Modern American Literature, 3539
Current Biography. 414
Current Biography. Cumulated Index, 1940-1970. 415
Currier, Nathaniel and Ives, J. M. World of Currier and Ives, 3098
Curry-Lindahl, Kai. Let Them Live, 2338
Curti, Merle E. Growth of American Thought, 5858
Curtin, Philip. see Bohannan, Paul
Curtis, David. Experimental Cinema, 3270
Curtis, Edith R. A Season in Utopia, 1507
Curtis, Helena. Invitation to Biology, 2212
Curtis, James C. The Fox at Bay, 5999
Curtiss, John S. Church and State in Russia, 798
———. The Russian Revolutions of 1917, 5513
Curtiss, Mina S. A Forgotten Empress, 5499
Curtius, Ernst R. European Literature and the Latin Middle Ages, 4430

Cushman, Robert E. Leading Constitutional Decisions, 1575
Custer and the Epic of Defeat. Rosenberg, Bruce A, 6086
Custer Died for Your Sins. Deloria, Vine, Jr, 5746
CUSTER, GEORGE ARMSTRONG, 5746, 6086
Cutter, Bob and Fendell, Bob. The Encyclopedia of Auto Racing Greats, 3404
CYBERNETICS, 461-462, 464
Cybernetics Revolution. Rose, M, 462
Cyclopedia of Literary Characters. Magill, Frank N., ed, 342
CYCLOTRON, 2056
Cyprus. Purcell, H. D, 5657
CYPRUS — HISTORY, 5656-5657
Cyrano de Bergerac. Rostand, Edmond, 4181
CYTOLOGY, 2250-2251, 2253-2255
CZECHOSLOVAK REPUBLIC
HISTORY, 5349-5355, 5357, 5359
POLITICS AND GOVERNMENT, 5354-5356, 5358-5359
Czechoslovakia 1968. Windsor, Philip and Roberts, Adam. 5359
Czechoslovakia Since World War II. Szulc, Tad, 5357
Czechoslovakia's Blueprint for Freedom. Dubcek, Alexander, 5353
Czernin, Ferdinand. Versailles, Nineteen Nineteen, 5072

D. H. Lawrence and His World. Moore, Harry T. and Roberts, Warren. 3944
Dada, Surrealism, and Their Heritage. Rubin, William S, 3034
DADAISM, 3034
Dahl, Svend. History of the Book, 2847
Dahrendorf, Ralf. Society and Democracy in Germany, 1088
Daiches, David. The Last Stuart, 5158
Daily Life Among the Aztecs. Soustelle, Jacques, 5808
Daily Newspaper in America. Lee, Alfred M, 495
Daley, Arthur. see Kieran, John
Daly, Eileen. Dinosaurs, 2181
La Dama del Alba. Casona, Alejandro, 4353
Dampier, William C. A History of Science and Its Relation with Philosophy and Religion, 1922
DAMS — U. S., 2696
Dams, Parks and Politics. Richardson, Elmo, 1465
Dana, Richard H. Two Years Before the Mast, 4692

INDEX

DANCE, 3242-3243, 3326, 3329, 3331
Dance Is a Contact Sport. Mazo, Joseph H, 3327
Dance, Peter S. Collector's Encyclopedia of Shells, 2386
Dangerfield, George. The Era of Good Feelings, 5988
Daniel Defoe. Moore, John R, 3921
Daniels, Harvey. Printmaking, 3086
Daniels, Jonathan. Prince of Carpetbaggers, 6064
Daniels, Josephus. The Wilson Era, 6117
Daninos, Pierre. Les Carnets du Major Thompson, 4204
Dank, Milton. The French Against the French, 5099
Dante Alighieri. Dante's Lyric Poetry, 4289
———. The Divine Comedy, 4288
Dante's Lyric Poetry. Dante Alighieri, 4289
Dantzig, T. Number, the Language of Science, 1931
Darby, Patricia. see Darby, Ray
Darby, Ray and Darby, Patricia. Conquering the Deep Sea Frontier, 2137
Darden, Lloyd. The Earth in the Looking Glass, 4679
D'Argan, E. see Nitze, William
Dargo, George. Roots of the Republic, 1194
Darío, Ruben. Azul and Otras Versos, 4319
———. Selected Poems of Ruben Darío, 4320
Darker Brother. Warner, James A, 3119
Darkroom Techniques. Feininger, Andreas, 3104
DARROW, CLARENCE SEWARD, 1611
Darwin and His Great Discovery. DeCamp, L, 2287
Darwin and the Beagle. Moorehead, Alan, 2288
Darwin, Charles. The Origin of Species and The Descent of Man, 2286
DARWIN, CHARLES ROBERT, 2284-2285, 2287-2288
Darwin Reader. Bates, Marston and Humphrey, Philip S., eds. 2285
Darwin's Islands. Thornton, Ian, 1908
Dary, David. The Buffalo Book, 1480
DATA TRANSMISSION SYSTEMS, 2642
Daudet, Alphonse. Lettres de Mon Moulin, 4205
———. Le Petit Chose, 4206
———. Tartarin de Tarascon, 4207
Davenport, Basil, ed. Portable Roman Reader, 4394
David, Florence N. Games, Gods and Gambling, 1951

David, Rene. see Brierley, John E.
Davidson, Basil. Africa, 5695
———. African Kingdoms, 5696
———. The African Past, 5697
———. Black Mother, 5730
———. Black Star, 5725
———. A History of West Africa to the 19th Century, 5722
———. The Lost Cities of Africa, 4791
Davidson, Eugene. The Nuremberg Falacy, 1555
———. Trial of the Germans, 5309
Davidson, Marshall B. The American Heritage History of the Artists' America, 2944
———. The Horizon Book of Great Historic Places of Europe, 4740
Davidson, Philip G. Propaganda and the American Revolution, 5941
Davie, Donald, ed. Russian Literature and Modern English Fiction, 4572
Davies, J. Clarence. The Politics of Polution, 1634
Davies, Laurence. Cesar Franck and His Circle, 3165
Davies, Merton and Murray, Bruce C. The View from Space, 2001
Davies, Nigel. The Aztecs, 5811
Davies, Peter. The Truth About Kent State, 1791
Davies, R. Trevor. The Golden Century of Spain, 1501-1621, 5463
Davies, Ruth A. The School Library Media Center, 34
Davis, Allen F. American Heroine, 1692
———. Spearheads for Reform, 1703
Davis, Allison, et al. Deep South, 1121
DAVIS, ANGELA YVONNE, 1232
Davis, David B., ed. The Fear of Conspiracy, 1071
———. The Problem of Slavery in an Age of Revolution, 1770-1823, 1003
Davis, Douglas M. Art and the Future, 2871
Davis, Harold E. Latin American Thought, 680
———. Revolutionaries, Traditionalists, and Dictators in Latin America, 4866
Davis, Jefferson. The Rise and Fall of the Confederate Government, 6057
DAVIS, JEFFERSON, 6047
Davis, Kenneth P. see Brown, A. A.
Davis, Lanny J. The Emerging Democratic Majority, 1390
Davis, Morton D. Game Theory, 1953
Davis, Norman M. The Complete Book of United States Coin Collecting, 3000
Davis, Nuel P. Lawrence and Oppenheimer, 2057

INDEX

DAVIS, VARINA (HOWELL), 6046
Davis, William. Life on a Medieval Barony, 4997
Davison, Archibald T. and Apel, Willi. Historical Anthology of Music, 3146
Davison, Kenneth B. The Presidency of Rutherford B. Hayes, 6089
Davison, Peter. Walking the Boundaries, 3633
Dawidowicz, Lucy S. Golden Tradition, 4901
———. The War Against the Jews, 1933-1945, 5107
Dawn and the Darkest Hour. Woodcock, George, 3951
Dawn, C. Ernest. From Ottomanism to Arabism, 1147
Dawn of a New Era. Cheyney, Edward P, 5017
Dawn of Civilization. Maspero, Gaston C, 4878
Dawn of Civilization. Piggott, Stuart, ed, 4714
Daws, Gavan. Shoal of Time, 6289
Day, Kenneth. *see* Morison, Stanley
Day of Infamy. Lord, Walter, 5128
Day of Trinity. Lamont, Lansing, 2669
DAYAN, MOSHE, 5669
Dayan, Ruth and Feinberg, Wilburt. Crafts of Israel, 3019
Daylight Must Come. Burgess, Alan, 2498
A Day's March Nearer Home. Parkinson, Roger, 5102
Days of Sadness, Years of Triumph. Perrett, Geoffrey, 1116
DEAD SEA SCROLLS, 718-721
Dead Sea Scrolls and the New Testament. La Sor, William S, 720
Dead Sea Scrolls, 1947-1969. Wilson, Edmund, 721
Deadlock of Democracy. Burns, James M, 1632
Deakin, Frederick W. The Brutal Friendship, 5449
Dean, John A. Lange's Handbook of Chemistry, 215
Deane, John R. The Strange Alliance, 5109
DEATH, 526, 583-585, 1725, 2588, 3714
Death and Life of Great American Cities. Jacobs, Jane, 1253
Death and Life of Malcolm X. Goldman, Peter L, 1152
Death and the College Student. Shneidman, Edwin S, 1725
Death at an Early Age. Kozol, Jonathan, 1752
Death Be Not Proud. Gunther, John, 2618
Death in Life. Lifton, Robert J, 5141
Death in the Afternoon. Hemingway, Ernest, 3290
Death of a Revolutionary. Harris, Richard, 1247
Death of the Sweet Waters. Carr, Donald E, 2563
Death Penalty in America. Bedau, Hugo A., ed, 1730
Deback, P. Biological Control by Natural Enemies, 2783
De Bary, William T. The Buddhist Tradition in India, China and Japan, 836
———. Source of Chinese Tradition, 5575
———. Sources of Indian Tradition, 5627
———. Sources of Japanese Tradition, 5614
Debate About the Earth. Takeuchi, H., et al. 2113
DEBATES AND DEBATING, 3492
De Bertier De Sauvigny, Guillaume. Bourbon Restoration, 5410
Debo, Angie. And Still the Waters Run, 5767
———. History of the Indians of the United States, 5745
———. The Road to Disappearance, 5759
De Bold, Richard C. and Leaf, Russel C., eds. LSD, Man and Society, 2578
DeBono, Edward. Eureka, 2489
Debs. Axline, Virginia M, 2628
Debussy. Lockspeiser, Edward, 3175
DEBUSSY, CLAUDE, 3175
A Decade of Music. Haggin, B. H, 3138
DeCamp, L. Darwin and His Great Discovery, 2287
DeCamp, L. Sprague. The Ancient Engineers, 2631
———. The Great Monkey Trial, 1591
———. Lost Continents, 1847
Deceived Majority. Fellman, Gordon, 1070
Decent and Indecent. Spock, Benjamin M, 1082
Decimal Classification and Relative Index. Dewey, Melvil, 32
Decker, Heinrich. Renaissance in Italy, 2924
Declaration of Independence. Becker, Carl L, 5915
Decline of the West. Spengler, Oswald, 4674
DeCoursey, Russell M. The Human Organism, 2509
Dedera, Don. Hang Gliding, 3441
Deedy, John and Nobile, Philip, eds. The Complete Ecology Fact Book, 231
DEEP SEA DRILLING PROJECT, 2146
Deep South. Davis, Allison, et al. 1121
Deep South States of America. Peirce, Neal R, 4835

INDEX

Deeson, A. F. The Collector's Encyclopedia of Rocks and Minerals, 227
Defending the Environment. Sax, Joseph L, 945
Defense Against Famine. Slack, A. V, 2776
Defensible Space. Newman, Oscar, 1728
DEFOE, DANIEL, 3921
De France, J. J. Electrical Fundamentals, 2046
DeGaulle. Crozier, Brian, 5421
De Gaulle. Werth, Alexander, 5424
DE GAULLE, CHARLES, 4278, 5421, 5424
Degler, Carl N. Out of Our Past, 5859
De Gramont, Sanche. The French, 5370
De Grazia, Alfred. Politics for Better or Worse, 1127
Dehaan, Robert L. see Nason, Alvin
Dekmejian, R. Hrair. Egypt Under Nasser, 5715
DeKnight, Freda. Ebony Cookbook, 2835
Del Río, Angel. see Del Río, Amelia
Delaney, Shelagh. A Taste of Honey, 3900
Delibes, Miguel. El Camino, 4374
———. Cinco Horas con Mario, 4375
DELLINGER, DAVID T., 1592, 1600
Deloria, Vine, Jr. Behind the Trail of Broken Treaties, 5768
———. Custer Died for Your Sins, 5746
Delpar, Helen, ed. Encyclopedia of Latin America, 455
Del Río, Amelia and Del Río, Angel. Antología General de la Literatura Española, 4305
Del Río, Angel. Historia de la Literatura Española, 4312
De Luca, A. Michael and Giulianos, William. Selections from Italian Poetry, 4291
Delzell, Charles F., ed. Unification of Italy, 1859-1861, 5437
De Madariaga, Salvador. Spain, 5458
De Meeus, Adrien. History of the Belgians, 5545
Demetz, Peter. Postwar German Literature, 3984
Deming, Richard. Metric Power, 1809
DEMOCRACY, 1215, 1576, 5860
Democracy. Pickles, Dorothy M, 1215
Democracy in America. De Tocqueville, Alexis, 1576
Democracy in France Since 1870. Thomson, David, 5415
DEMOCRATIC PARTY, 1389-1390, 6226
Democratic Party. Kent, Frank R, 1391
Demon. Lermontov, Mikhail Y, 4508
DEMONOLOGY, 535
Demos, John. A Little Commonwealth, 987
Denial of Death. Becker, Ernest, 583

DENMARK — HISTORY, 5130, 5542
Denoon, Donald. Southern Africa Since Eighteen Hundred, 1098
DEPRESSIONS, 1458, 1529-1530, 6129
Deputy. Hochhuth, Rolf, 4019
Depuy, Charles H. and Rinehart, Kenneth L. Introduction to Organic Chemistry, 2083
Deriquer, Martin. Aproximaciónal Quixote, 4313
Der Nersessian, Strarpie. The Armenians, 5658
De Rojas, Fernando. Celestina, 4354
DeRopp, Robert S. The New Prometheans, 1890
Derry, Thomas K. A Short History of Norway, 5539
De St. Jorre, John. The Brothers' War, 5728
De Santillana, Giorgio, ed. The Age of Adventure, 627
De Santis, Vincent P. The Gilded Age, 1877-1896, 77
Desautels, Paul E. Rocks and Minerals, 2088
Descartes, René. Philosophical Writings, 671
DESCARTES, RENÉ, 674
Deschooling Society. Illich, Ivan D, 1751
De Selincourt, Aubrey. The World of Herodotus, 4967
Desert. Kirk, Ruth, 2248
DESERT BIOLOGY — U. S., 2247
Desert de l'Amour. Mauriac, François, 4232
DESERT ECOLOGY — SOUTHWESTERN STATES, 2248
DESERT FLORA — U. S. — PICTORIAL WORKS, 2793
Desert World. Costello, David F, 2247
Des Granges, C. M. Histoire de la Littérature Française, 4107
DESIGN, 290, 2793
Design on the Land. Newton, Norman T, 2957
De Sola, Ralph. Abbreviations Dictionary, 169
Desperate Faith. Harper, Howard M., Jr, 3717
Dessauer, John P. Book Publishing, 490
Dessel, N. and Dessel, Nehrich. Science and Human Destiny, 1891
Dessel, Nehrich. see Dessel, N.
Destinées. Vigny, Alfred de, 4132
Destiny of Indian Muslims. Husain, S. Abid, 1060
Destiny Road. Faulk, Odie B, 6220
De Tocqueville, Alexis. Democracy in America, 1576

INDEX

———. The Old Regime and the French Revolution, 5392
DETROIT — RIOT, (1967), 1593
Deutsch, Babette. Coming of Age, 3634
———. Poetry Handbook, 3474
Deutsch, Babette and Yarmolinsky, Avrahm. Modern Russian Poetry, 4521
Deutsch, Eliot, ed. Bhagavad Gita, 845
Deutsch, Harold C. The Conspiracy Against Hitler in the Twilight War, 5310
Deutsche Erzahler, Ausgewahlt und Eingeleitet von Hugo von Hofmannsthal. Hofmannstal, Hugo Von, 4071
Deutsche Gedichte. Echtemeyer, T. H., ed, 4002
Deutsche Literatur in Bildern. Wilpert, Gero Von, 3993
Deutsche Literaturgeschichte von den Anfangen bis zur Gegenwart. Martini, Fritz, 3989
Deutsche Lyrik. Wiese, Benno Von, 4008
Die Deutsche Novelle von Goethe bis Kafka. Wiese, Benno Von, 4077
Die Deutsche Tragodie von Lessing bis Hebbel. Wiese, Benno Von, 4030
Deutscher, Isaac. Prophet Armed, 5514
———. Prophet Outcast, 5515
———. Prophet Unarmed, 5516
———. Stalin, 5517
———. The Unfinished Revolution, 5518
Deutsches, E. M. *see* Fleissner, Otto S.
Deutschland, Deutschland, Uber Alles. Tucholsky, Kurt, 3980
Deutschland Erzählt, Von Buchner bis Hauptmann. Wiese, Benno Von, ed, 4072
Deutschland Erzählt, Von Goethe bis Tieck. Wiese, Benno Von, ed, 4073
Deutschland Erzählt, Von Schnitzler bis Johnson. Wiese, Benno Von, ed, 4074
DE VALERA, EAMON, 5165
Development Assistance in the Seventies. Asher, Robert E., et al. 1535
Development of Logic. Kneale, William and Kneale, Martha. 594
Development of Modern English. Robertson, Stuart and Cassidy, Frederic G. 1869
Development of Religion and Thought in Ancient Egypt. Breasted, James H, 867
Development of Rural America. Brinkman, George, ed, 963
Development of the American Constitution, 1877-1917. Beth, Loren P, 1570
Developments in Geographical Methods. Fitzgerald, Brian P, 4681
Devil's Bride. Ebon, Martin, 535
Devil's Dictionary. Bierce, Ambrose, 3754
Devlin, Robert M. Photosynthesis, 2317

DeVoto, Bernard A. Across the Wide Missouri, 6230
———. The Course of Empire, 5886
———. Year of Decision, 1846, 6231
Dewey, John. John Dewey on Education, 1745
Dewey, Melvil. Decimal Classification and Relative Index, 32
DeWitt, David. The Impeachment and Trial of Andrew Johnson, 6083
Dexter, Byron. The Years of Opportunity, 1551
Dexter, Dave. The Jazz Story from the '90's to the '60's, 3187
Dezarate, Augustin. The Discovery and Conquest of Peru, 6276
Diadia Vania. Chekhov, Anton P, 4527
Dialogue with Death. Koestler, Arthur, 5471
Dialogus, Agricula, Germania. Tacitus, Cornelius, 4427
Diamond, Malcolm L. Martin Buber, 619
Diane Arbus. Arbus, Diane, 3123
Diary. Pepys, Samuel, 5242
Diary of a Young Girl. Frank, Anne, 5114
Diaz, A. J. Guide to Microforms in Print, 27
Diaz del Castillo, Bernal. Discovery and Conquest of Mexico, 5804
Diccionario de la Lengua Española. Academia Española, 183
Dickens. Marcus, Steven, 3932
Dickens, Arthur G. The Counter-Reformation, 785
DICKENS, CHARLES, 3928, 3932
Dickens, Michael and Storey, Eric. The World of Butterflies, 2395
Dickey, James. Babel to Byzantium, 3846
———. Poems Nineteen Fifty Seven-Nineteen Sixty Seven, 3635
Dickinson, Emily. Complete Poems of Emily Dickinson, 3567
DICKINSON, EMILY ELIZABETH, 3568
Dickinson, G. Lowes. The Greek View of Life, 4954
Dickinson, William B., ed. Watergate, 1717
Dickson, Lovat. H. G. Wells, His Turbulent Life and Times, 3938
Dictionary of All Scriptures and Myths. Gaskell, G. A, 118
Dictionary of American Biography, 1927-1972. 421
Dictionary of American History. Adams, James T., ed, 450
Dictionary of Antiques. Savage, George, 289
Dictionary of Art. Mayer, Ralph, 266
Dictionary of Art and Artists. Murray, Peter and Murray, Linda. 275

INDEX

Dictionary of Battles. Eggenberger, David, 4670
Dictionary of Behavioral Science. Wolman, Benjamin B, 98
Dictionary of Biological Terms. Henderson, Isabella F. and Henderson, W. D. 230
Dictionary of Birds in Color. Campbell, Bruce and Holmes, Richard T., eds. 246
Dictionary of Christian Ethics. MacQuarrie, John, ed, 111
A Dictionary of Comparative Religion. Brandon, Samuel G, 117
Dictionary of Contemporary American Artists. Cummings, Paul, 277
Dictionary of Costume. Wilcox, Ruth T, 150
Dictionary of Early English. Shipley, Joseph T, 177
Dictionary of Electronics. Funk & Wagnalls Editors, 256
Dictionary of Foreign Phrases and Abbreviations. Guinagh, Kevin, ed, 156
Dictionary of Foreign Terms in the English Language. Carroll, David, 160
Dictionary of Geological Terms. American Geological Institute, 220
A Dictionary of Geology. Challinor, John, 221
A Dictionary of Indian History. Bhattacharya, Sachchidananda, 440
Dictionary of Literary Terms. Shaw, Harry, 326
A Dictionary of Modern English Usage. Fowler, Henry M, 176
A Dictionary of Modern Revolution. Hyams, Edward, 134
Dictionary of Modern Written Arabic. Wehr, Hans, 191
Dictionary of Music and Musicians. Grove, George, 301
A Dictionary of Musical Themes. Barlow, Harold and Morgenstern, Sam, eds. 297
Dictionary of National Biography. 420
A Dictionary of Non-Christian Religions. Parrinder, Geoffrey, 116
Dictionary of Opera and Song Themes. Barlow, Harold and Morgenstern, Sam, eds. 308
Dictionary of Oriental Literatures. Prusek, ed, 376
Dictionary of Phrase and Fable. Brewer, Ebenezer C, 323
Dictionary of Russian Historical Terms from the Eleventh Century to 1917. Vernadsky, George and Fisher, Ralph T., eds. 438
Dictionary of Scientific and Technical Terms. McGraw-Hill Editors, 201
Dictionary of Slang and Unconventional English. Partridge, Eric, 175
Dictionary of Spanish Literature. Newmark, Maxim, 375
Dictionary of Spoken Chinese. Yale Institute of Far Eastern Languages, 194
Dictionary of Stamps in Color. Mackay, James A, 292
A Dictionary of Symbols. Cirlot, Juan E, 54
Dictionary of the Characters and Proper Names in the Works of Shakespeare. Stokes, F. G, 371
Dictionary of the Environmental Sciences. Durrenberger, Robert W, 222
Dictionary of the History of Ideas. Wiener, Philip P., ed, 377
Dictionary of Twentieth Century Composers. Thompson, Kenneth, 62
A Dictionary of Usage and Style. Copperud, Roy H, 1881
Dictionary of World Literary Terms. Shipley, Joseph T., ed, 327
Diderot. Blum, Carol, 670
DIDEROT, DENIS, 670
Diego Rivera. Arquin, Florence, 3076
Diehl, Harold S. Tobacco and Your Health, 2550
Diethrich, Edward B. and Fried, John J. Code Arrest, 2592
Dietrich Bonhoeffer. Bethge, Eberhard, 810
Dietz, David. The New Outline of Science, 1892
Dillard, Annie. Pilgrim at Tinker Creek, 1902
Dillard, Joey L. Black English, 1877
Dineley, David. Earth's Voyage Through Time, 2092
DINESEN, ISAK, 4093
Dinosaur Dictionary. Glut, Donald F, 228
DINOSAURS, 228, 2179-2182
Dinosaurs. Colbert, Edwin H, 2179
Dinosaurs. Daly, Eileen, 2181
Dinosaurs. Swinton, William E, 2182
Diole, Philippe. The Errant Ark, 2352
Diole, Philippe. see Cousteau, Jacques-Yves
Diplomacy of Annexation. Pletcher, David M, 6016
Diplomacy of Imperialism, 1890-1902. Langer, William L, 5057
Diplomatic Ceremonial and Protocol. Wood, John R. and Serres, Jean. 1558
A Diplomatic History of Europe Since the Congress of Vienna. Albrecht-Carrié, René, ed, 5051

INDEX

Diplomatic History of the American People. Bailey, Thomas A, 1328
Diplomats. Craig, Gordon A. and Gilbert, Felix, eds. 5095
Directionscore. Lee, Don L, 3647
Directors on Directing. Cole, Toby and Chinoy, Helen K., eds. 3299
Dirty Animal. Still, Henry, 2698
DISARMAMENT, 1298
Disarmament Agency. see U. S. Arms Control
Disaster by Oil. Potter, Jeffrey, 2702
Disaster Lobby. Grayson, Melvin J. and Shepard, Thomas R. 944
Discarded Army. Starr, Paul, 1672
Discover Yourself Through Photography. Hattersley, Ralph, 3102
Discovering Art. 3079
Discovering the Universe. Ronan, Colin A, 1970
Discovery and Conquest of Mexico. Diaz del Castillo, Bernal, 5804
Discovery and Conquest of Peru. Dezarate, Augustin, 6276
Discovery of Canada. Burpee, Lawrence J, 5786
Discovery of North America. Cumming, William P., et al. 5885
Discovery of Our Galaxy. Whitney, Charles A, 1971
Discovery of the Sea. Parry, John H, 4699
Discovery of the World. Bettex, Albert, 4700
DISCRIMINATION, 1005, 1013, 1752
Disease and History. Cartwright, Frederick F. and Biddis, Michael D. 2561
Disinherited Mind. Heller, Erich, 3987
Dispossessing the American Indian. Jacobs, Wilbur R, 5772
DISSENT, 1070
Dissent in American Religion. Gaustad, Edwin S, 689
DISSENTERS, 57, 793, 4668, 4862
Dissonance of Change, 1919 to the Present. Glad, Paul, ed, 1111
Disunited States. O'Connor, Thomas H, 6032
Ditfurth, Hoimar Von. Children of the Universe, 1962
Divided Loyalties. Einstein, Lewis, 5947
Dividends from Space. Ordway, Frederick I., 3rd, et al. 2758
Divine Comedy. Dante Alighieri, 4288
Divine, Robert. The Cuban Missile Crisis, 1333
DIVING, SUBMARINE, 2694-2695
DIVING VEHICLES, 2145
DIVORCE, 991-992
Divorced in America. Epstein, Joseph, 991
Dixson, Robert J. see Whitford, Harold C.

Djilas, Milovan. Memoir of a Revolutionary, 1222
———. The New Class, 1496
DJILAS, MILOVAN, 1222
Djoleto, S. A. and Kwami, T. S., eds. West African Prose, 4626
DNA. Lessing, L. and Fortune Editors. 2252
DNA, 2249
Dobby, Ernest H. G. Southeast Asia, 4789
La Doble Historia del Doctor Valmy. Buero Vallejo, Antonio, 4346
Dobson, Christopher. Black September, 1183
Dobson, John M. Politics in the Gilded Age, 1195
Dockstader, Frederick J. Indian Art in America, 2938
Doctor's Guide to Tennis Elbow, Trick Knee, and Other Miseries of the Weekend Athlete. Root, Leon and Kiernan, Thomas, 2623
Documentary History of Reconstruction. Fleming, Walter L, 6066
A Documentary History of the Italian-Americans. Moquin, Wayne and Van Doren, Charles, eds. 4824
Documentary History of the Mexican Americans. Moquin, Wayne and Van Doren, Charles, eds. 5875
A Documentary History of the Negro People in the United States. Apteker, Herbert, ed, 1270
A Documentary Survey of the French Revolution. Stewart, John H, 5399
Documentary Tradition. Jacobs, Lewis, compiled by. 3275
Documents of American History. Commager, Henry S., ed, 5878
Documents of the Christian Church. Bettenson, Henry, ed, 777
Documents on Fundamental Human Rights. Chafee, Zecharian, Jr., ed, 1254
Dodd, Charles H., compiled by. Israel and the Arab World, 5662
Dogmatics in Outline. Barth, Karl, 752
DOGS, 2470, 2473, 2809, 2811
DOLPHINS, 2456-2459, 2461
Dolphins and Freedom. Cousteau, Jacques-Yves and Diole, Philippe. 2459
Dolphins, Seals, and Other Sea Mammals. Stephen, David, 2456
Domandi, Agnes K., ed. Modern Germanic Literature, 373
Domes, Juergen. The Internal Politics of China, 1949-1972, 1176
Dominican Crisis, 1965. Mansbach, Richard W, 5843
Dominican Republic. Wiarda, Howard J, 5845

INDEX

DOMINICAN REPUBLIC — HISTORY, 5824, 5840, 5842-5845, 5850
Domino Book. Berndt, Fredrick, 3344
Don Quijote. Cervantes, Miguel de, 4372
Don Segundo Sombra. Guiraldes, Ricardo, 4378
Doña Bárbara. Gallegos, Romulo, 4376
Doña Ines. Azorin, 4366
Doña Perfecta. Pérez Galdós, Benito, 4383
Donald, David. Charles Sumner and the Coming of the Civil War, 6029
Donaldson, Gordon. Scotland, 5151
Donington, Robert. Instruments of Music, 3200
Donne, John. The Complete Poetry and Selected Prose, 3796
DONNE, JOHN, 3795
Donovan, James A. Militarism, U. S. A, 1659
Donovan, John C. The Politics of Poverty, 1541
Don't Shoot - We Are Your Children! Lukas, J. Anthony, 990
Dope Book. Lieberman, Mark, 2548
Dorey, T. A. and Dudley, D. R., eds. Roman Drama, 4410
Doris, Lillian and Miller, Bessemay. Complete Secretary's Handbook, 2843
Dorjahn, Alfred P., *see* Guinagh, Kevin
Dorland, William A. Dorland's Illustrated Medical Dictionary, 248
Dorland's Illustrated Medical Dictionary. Dorland, William A, 248
Dorman, Michael. Under Twenty-One, 1602
Dormer, Albert. *see* Reese, Terence
Dorn, Walter L. Competition for Empire, 1740-1763, 5032
Dornberg, John. Brezhnev, 5529
Dorson, Richard M. America in Legend, 1841
———. America Rebels, 5956
Dorst, Jean. Before Nature Dies. , 1466
———. The Life of Birds, 2427
Dortu, M. G. *see* Huisman, Philippe
Dostoevsky, Feodor M. Brat'ya Karamazovy, 4544
———. Occasional Writings, 4575
———. Prestuplenie, 4545
———. Zapiski, 4546
DOSTOEVSKY, FEODOR MIKHAILOVICH, 551, 5489
Dostoevsky, Kierkegaard, Nietzsche and Kafka. Hubben, William, 551
Double Helix. Watson, James D, 2249
Double-Speak in America. Pei, Mario, 1872
Dougherty, Richard. Goodbye Mr. Christian, 1380

Doughty, Charles M. Travels in Arabia Deserts, 5624
Douglas, Alfred. The Tarot, 533
Douglas, David C. The Norman Achievement, 5197
———. William the Conqueror, 5198
DOUGLAS, STEPHEN ARNOLD, 6023
Douglass, Frederick. Narrative of the Life of Frederick Douglass, an American Slave, Written by Himself, 1290
DOUGLASS, FREDERICK, 1290, 6061
Dowben, Robert M. Cell Biology, 2251
Downs, Anthony. Opening up the Suburbs, 961
Downs, Brian. Modern Norwegian Literature, 1860-1918, 4095
Downs, Robert B. Books That Changed America, 3522
Downton, James V. Rebel Leadership, 893
Drago, Harry S. Canal Days in America, 1803
———. The Great Range Wars, 6232
Dragon Wakes. Hibbert, Christopher, 1317
DRAKE, FRANCIS, SIR, 1690, 4696
DRAMA, 334
    BIBLIOGRAPHY, 64, 346
    COLLECTIONS, 3506-3510, 3529, 3671-3672, 4634
    DICTIONARIES, 315, 346-348
    ENCYCLOPEDIAS, 316
    HISTORY AND CRITICISM, 316, 334, 3291, 3308, 3310-3314, 3317, 3320, 3481-3482, 3484, 3507, 3526-3528, 3672, 4452
Drama and Revolution. Dukore, Bernard F, 3512
Drama from Ibsen to Brecht. Williams, Raymond, 3528
Dramatic Criticism Index. Breed, Paul F. and Sniderman, Florence M. 67
Dramen. Lessing, Gotthold E, 4022
Draper, Theodore. Castroism, 5830
———. Israel and World Politics, 5648
———. The Rediscovery of Black Nationalism, 1241
DRAWING — INSTRUCTION, 3004
Dream of the Red Chamber. Hsueh-Chin, Tsao, 4603
DREAMS, 543, 476, 2528
Dreier, John E., ed. The Alliance for Progress, 1537
Dreiser. Swanberg, W. A, 3737
DREISER, THEODORE, 3737
Drew, Elizabeth. Poetry, 3475
DREYFUS, ALFRED, 5414
Dreyfus Case. Snyder, Louis L, 5414
Driver, Harold E. Indians of North America, 5747
Driver, Tom F. Romantic Quest and Modern Query, 3312

Droste-Huelshoff, Annette Von. Werke, 3973
Droz, Jacques. Europe Between Revolutions, 5054
Drucker, Peter. The Age of Discontinuity, 1083
DRUG ABUSE, 1696, 1698-1699, 2541-2543, 2545, 2548-2549, 2579
Drug Abuse. American Alliance for Health, Physical Education & Recreation, 2596
Drug Dilemma. Cohen, Sidney, 2575
Drug Use in America. U. S. Commission on Marihuana & Drug Abuse, 1698
DRUGS, 1696, 2541, 2544-2545, 2548, 2556, 2574-2576, 2597
    DICTIONARIES, 253
Drugs and Alcohol. Jones, Kenneth L., et al. 2547
Drugs and Society. Barber, Bernard, 2574
DRUGS AND YOUTH, 1699-1700, 2543, 2546
Drugs and Youth. Coles, Robert, et al. 2546
Drugs from A to Z. Lingeman, Richard R, 253
Druids. Piggott, Stuart, 866
DRUIDS AND DRUIDISM, 866
Druks, Herbert. From Truman Through Johnson, 6156
Drummond, A. H., Jr. Molecules in the Service of Man, 2066
Dry Decade. Merz, Charles, 6114
Dryden, John. All for Love or The World Well Lost, 3872
———. Complete Poetical Works, 3797
Dubcek. Shawcross, William, 5356
Dubcek, Alexander. Czechoslovakia's Blueprint for Freedom, 5353
Dube, Wolf D. Expressionism, 3032
Duberman, Martin B. James Russell Lowell, 3556
Dubofsky, Melvyn, ed. American Labor Since the New Deal, 1429
———. We Shall Be All, 1438
DuBois, William E. Suppression of the African Slave Trade, 1638-1870, 1792
———. W. E. B. DuBois, 1020
Ducks, Geese, and Swans of North America. Kortright, Francis H, 2430
Duckworth, George E., ed. Complete Roman Drama, 4409
———. The Nature of Roman Comedy, 4411
Dudley, D. R. and Lang, D. M., eds. Penguin Companion to Literature, Vol. 4, 351
Dudley, D. R., see Dorey, T. A.
DUDLEY, LADY JANE, 5223
Duff, John W. Literary History of Rome, 4396

Dugan, Alan. Collected Poems, 3636
Dugan, J. see Cousteau, Jacques-Yves
Dukas, Helen. see Hoffman, Banesh
Duke, Marc. Acupuncture, 2581
Dukore, Bernard F. Drama and Revolution, 3512
Dulles, Foster R. American Policy Toward Communist China, 1334
———. America's Rise to World Power, 1335
———. Labor in America, 1439
DULLES, JOHN FOSTER, 6164
Dumas, Alexandre. Les Trois Mousquetaires, 4208
Dumond, Dwight L. Antislavery, 1282
———. Southern Editorials on Secession, 6044
Dumont, Rene and Rosier, Bernard. The Hungry Future, 1517
Dumoulin, Heinrich. A History of Zen Buddhism, 837
Dunbar, Carl O. and Waage, Karl M. Geology, 2162
Dunbar, Janet. J. M. Barrie, 3966
DUNBAR, PAUL LAWRENCE, 3566
Dunham, Barrows. Ethics - Dead and Alive, 598
Dunlop, Ian. Versailles, 4757
Dunn, Mary M. William Penn, 1139
Dunnette, Marvin D. Work and Nonwork in the Year 2001, 1430
Dunning, Stephen and Lueders, Edward, eds. Some Haystacks Don't Even Have Any Needle, and Other Complete Modern Poems, 3548
Dupuy, R. Ernest and Dupuy, Trevor N. Compact History of the Civil War, 6030
———. The Encyclopedia of Military History, 144
Dupuy, Trevor N. see Dupuy, R. Ernest
Durant, John. Highlights of the Olympics from Ancient Times to the Present, 3383
Durant, Will. Rousseau and Revolution, 5040
———. The Story of Philosophy, 514
Durden, Kent. Flight to Freedom, 2439
———. Gifts of an Eagle, 2440
DÜRER, ALBRECHT, 3051
Dürer Watercolors. Koschatzy, Walter, 3051
Durrell, Gerald. A Bevy of Beasts, 2445
———. Birds, Beasts, and Relatives, 2259
Durrell, Lawrence. Poetry, 3847
Durrenberger, Robert W. Dictionary of the Environmental Sciences, 222
Durrenmatt, Friedrich. Die Physiker, 4015
———. Richter und Sein Henken, 4042
———. Der Verdacht, 4043

INDEX

———. The Visit, 4014
Dutch Under German Occupation, 1940-1945. Warmbrunn, Werner, 5116
Duval, Paul. Four Decades, 2940
Dvorak. Hughes, Gervase, 3172
DVORAK, ANTONIN, 3172
Dwiggins, Don. Riders of the Winds, 2733
Dybbuk. Rapoport, Solomon, 4594
Dyer, Thomas H. The History of the Kings of Rome, 4928
Dylan, Bob. Writings and Drawings, 3202
DYLAN, BOB, 3230
Dynamics of Change. Fabun, Don, 4656
Dynamics of Creation. Storr, Anthony, 575
Dynamics of Faith. Tillich, Paul, 695
Dyslexia and Your Child. Wagner, Rudolph F, 1774

E. E. Cummings. Friedman, Norman, 3601
Eagles of Savoy. Cox, Eugene L, 5014
EAKINS, THOMAS, 3043
Eardley, Armand I. Science of the Earth, 2107
Earle, Edward M., ed. Makers of Modern Strategy, 1669
Earliest Civilizations of the Near East. Mellaart, James, 4722
Early Greek Elegists. Bowra, Cecil M, 4443
Early Jazz. Schuller, Gunther, 3191
Early Medieval Art. Hollander, Hans, 2901
Early Mesopotamia and Iran. Mallowan, Max E, 4910
Early Plays. Pinter, Harold, 3910
Early Scotland. Chadwick, Hector M, 5155
Early Soviet Writers. Zavalishin, Viacheslav, 4504
Early Writings. Lippmann, Walter, 6113
EARTH, 223, 1892, 2093, 2111, 2113, 2175
  PHOTOGRAPHS FROM SPACE, 397, 1687, 2009-2012
Earth. Press, Frank and Siever, Raymond. 2097
Earth and Its History. Flint, Richard F, 2175
Earth and Man. Loftus, Tony, ed, 398
Earth Beneath the Sea. Shepard, Francis P, 2147
Earth Beneath Us. Mather, Kirtley F, 2111
Earth from Space. Bodechtel, J. and Gierioff-Emden, H. G. 2009
Earth History and Plate Tectonics. Seyfert, Carl K. and Sirkin, Leslie K. 2164
Earth in the Looking Glass. Darden, Lloyd, 4679

Earth Medicine - Earth Foods. Weiner, Michael, 2501
Earth Photographs from Gemini III, IV, and V. National Aeronautics & Space Administration, 2010
Earth Photographs from Gemini VI Through XII. National Aeronautics & Space Administration, 2011
Earth Science. Brown, F. Martin, et al. 2106
EARTH SCIENCES, 2090, 2096, 2099, 2102, 2106-2107
  DICTIONARIES, 222
Earth Watch. Shepard, Daniel and Shepard, Jean. 1898
Earth We Live On. Moore, Ruth, 2104
Earthly Paradise. Colette, Sidonie, 4285
Earthquake History of the United States. U. S. Dept. of Commerce, 224
EARTHQUAKES, 224, 2114-2115, 2120-2121
Earth's Voyage Through Time. Dineley, David, 2092
East Across the Pacific. Conroy, Hilary and Miyakawa, T. S., eds. 1048
East and West of Suez. Farnie, D. A, 1804
East Asia. Fairbank, John K., et al. 5569
East Central Europe Between the Two World Wars. Rothschild, Joseph, 5093
EAST (FAR EAST) — HISTORY, 929, 931, 5569-5570
East Germany. Childs, David, 5332
East, William G., et al, eds. The Changing Map of Asia, 4771
EASTER ISLAND, 4845
Eastern Europe Between the Wars, 1918-1941. Seton-Watson, Hugh, 5493
Eastern Wisdom and Western Thought. Saher, P. J, 685
Easty, Dorothy M. see Ambrose, E. J.
Eaton, Clement. Civilization of the Old South, 6205
———. Growth of Southern Civilization, 6202
———. Henry Clay and the Art of American Politics, 6021
———. The Mind of the Old South, 6203
———. The Waning of the Old South Civilization, 1860-1880, 6204
Eatwell, John. see Robinson, Joan
Eban, Abba A. My Country, 5663
Ebbin, Steven and Kasper, Raphael. Citizen Groups and the Nuclear Power Controversy, 2664
Ebbitt, Wilma R. see Perrin, Porter G.
Ebenstein, William. Great Political Thinkers, 1128
———. Today's Isms, 1207
Eberhard, Mary J. see Evans, Howard E.

Eberhart, Richard. Collected Poems, 1909-1960, 3637
Eberhart, Richard and Rodman, S., eds. War and the Poet, 1800 B.C.-1945 A.D. Anthology, 3497
Ebert, John and Ebert, Katherine. Old American Prints for the Collector, 3089
Ebert, Katherine. *see* Ebert, John
Ebon, Martin. The Devil's Bride, 535
Ebony Cookbook. DeKnight, Freda, 2835
Eby, Cecil D. That Disgraceful Affair, 5993
Eccentric Design. Bewley, Marius, 3745
Echo of Greece. Hamilton, Edith, 4439
Echoes of Africa in Folk Songs of the Americas. Landeck, Beatrice, 3236
Echtemeyer, T. H., ed. Deutsche Gedichte, 4002
Ecke, Tseng Y. Chinese Calligraphy, 3021
Eckert, Allan W. *see* Karalus, Karl E.
Eckman, Fern M. The Furious Passage of James Baldwin, 3743
Eckstein, Gustav. Body Has a Head, 2510
Ecological Context. McHale, John, 935
Ecological Fantasies. Adler, Cy A, 939
Ecologues, Georgics, Aeneid, Minor Poems. Vergilius Maro, Publius, 4413
ECOLOGY, 125, 231, 939-941, 946, 2112, 2232-2240, 2273, 2375-2376, 2781, 2824
Ecology and Economics. Goldman, Marshall I, 1526
Ecology and Field Biology. Smith, Robert L, 2237
Ecology, Evolution, and Population Biology. Scientific American Editors, 2238
Economic and Social History of Medieval Europe. Pirenne, Henri, 5003
Economic Aspects of Southern Sectionalism, 1840-1861. Russel, Robert R, 1425
ECONOMIC CONDITIONS, 1154, 1536
ECONOMIC DEVELOPMENT, 879, 1068,1083, 1423
An Economic Geography of China. Tregear, Thomas R, 1510
ECONOMIC HISTORY, 1080, 1083, 1407
Economic Interpretation of the Constitution of the United States. Beard, Charles A, 1568
ECONOMIC STABILIZATION, 1543
Economic Thought of the Twentieth Century. Napoleoni, Claudio, 1406
ECONOMICS, 894, 1400-1406, 1417, 1677
  DICTIONARIES, 138-139
Economics and the Public Purpose. Galbraith, John Kenneth, 1538
Economics and Urban Problems. Netzer, Dick, 937
Economics of Environmental Policy. Freeman, A. Myrick, 943

Ectotatics. Mitchell, John G. and Stallings, Constance L., eds. 936
ECUMENICAL MOVEMENT, 772, 778, 780
Ecumenical Progress. Goodall, Norman, 778
Edgar Allan Poe. Quinn, Arthur H, 3722
Edge of an Unfamiliar World. Schlee, Susan, 2142
Edge of the Sea. Carson, Rachel, 2262
EDISON, THOMAS ALVA, 2860
Edith Sitwell. Brophy, James D, 3836
Edith Wharton. Lewis, Richard W, 3723
EDITORIALS, 486
Edlin, Herbert L. and Huxley, Anthony. Atlas of Plant Life, 233
Edmondson, Madeleine and Rounds, David. The Soaps, 3284
Edmund Ruffin, Southerner. Craven, Avery O, 6007
EDUCATION, 48-49, 508, 1744-1746, 1749, 1756, 1762, 1771-1772, 1775, 1780, 1914
  CHINA, 1759
  RUSSIA, 1757-1758
  U. S., 1109, 1743, 1747, 1751, 1755, 1760-1765, 1779, 1781-1782
Education and Ecstasy. Leonard, George B, 1763
L' Education Européenne. Gary, Romain, 4213
EDUCATIONAL PSYCHOLOGY, 1748
EDUCATIONAL SOCIOLOGY, 1751, 4659
Educators' Guide to Free Films. 50
Educators Guide to Free Science Materials. Saterstrom, Mary H. and Renner, John W. 205
EDWARD I, 5204
EDWARD II, 5204
EDWARD III, 5204
EDWARD IV, 5209
EDWARD VI, 5215
EDWARD VII, 5172
EDWARD VIII, 5274
Edward Albee. Rutenberg, Michael E, 3702
Edward the Confessor. Barlow, Frank, 5192
Edward the Uncrowned King. Hibbert, Christopher, 5275
Edwards, David L., ed. Honest to God Debate, 745
Edwards, Harry. The Revolt of the Black Athlete, 3351
Edwards, Lovett F. Yugoslavia, 4770
Edwards, Mary Jane. The Evolution of Canadian Literature in English, 3537
Edwards, Paul, ed. Encyclopedia of Philosophy, 95

INDEX

Edwin, Ed. Feast or Famine, 1519
Eero Saarinen on His Work. Saarinen, Eero, 2969
Effi Briest. Fontane, Theodor, 4045
Ege, Lennart. Balloons and Airships, 2734
Eggenberger, David. Dictionary of Battles, 4670
EGYPT
    ANTIQUITIES, 4878, 4882, 4893, 4897
    CIVILIZATION, 2915, 4882, 4885, 4888-4889, 4891, 4893-4894
    HISTORY, 4882-4884, 4886, 4892, 4894, 4896, 4898, 5642, 5646, 5715-5718
    RELIGION, 867, 4898
Egypt. Lange, Kurt and Hirmer, Max. 2915
Egypt. Siegner, Otto, 4788
Egypt and the Fertile Crescent. Holt, Peter M, 5642
Egypt of the Pharaohs. Gardiner, Alan, 4886
Egypt to the End of the Old Kingdom. Aldred, Cyril, 4882
Egypt Under Nasser. Dekmejian, R. Hrair, 5715
Egyptian Book of the Dead. Budge, Ernest A, 868
Ehrenberg, Victor. From Solon to Socrates, 4965
Ehrenfeld, David. Conserving Life on Earth, 2824
Ehrenzweig, Aaron. The Hidden Order of Art, 2883
Ehrlich, Anne H. *see* Ehrlich, Paul R.
Ehrlich, Paul R. The Population Bomb, 951
Ehrlich, Paul R. and Ehrlich, Anne H. Population, Resources, Environment, 952
Ehrlich, Paul R. and Harriman, Richard L. How to Be a Survivor, 942
Ehrmann, Herbert B. Untried Case, |1724
Eichelberger, Clark M. UN, 1554
Eide, Ingvard H., compiled by. American Odyssey, 6233
Eight Famous Plays. Strindberg, August, 4089
Eight Plays from off-off Broadway. Orzel, Nick, ed, 3671
Eighteen Forty-Eight. Stearns, Peter N, 5062
Eighteen Stories. Boll, Heinrich, 4036
Eighteenth Century Background. Willey, Basil, 657
Eighteenth Century Inventions. Rowland, K. T, 2493
Einstein. Bernstein, Jeremy, 2023
Einstein. Clark, Ronald W, 2024

Einstein, Albert. The Meaning of Relativity, 2030
EINSTEIN, ALBERT, 2023-2025
Einstein and the Generations of Science. Feuer, Lewis, 2029
Einstein, Lewis. Divided Loyalties, 5947
Einstein Theory of Relativity. Lieber, Lillian R, 2031
Eisenhower. Lyon, Peter, 6162
EISENHOWER, DWIGHT DAVID, 6162
Eisenstaedt, Alfred. People, 3127
Eissfeldt, Otto. The Old Testament, 717
Eklund, C. E. *see* Wyss, Orville
EL GRECO, 3062
El Greco. Guidiol, Jose, 3062
Elder, Glen H. Children of the Great Depression, 6128
Eleanor. Lash, Joseph P, 6137
Eleanor and Franklin. Lash, Joseph P, 6136
ELEANOR OF AQUITANE, 5206
Eleanor of Aquitane and the Four Kings. Kelly, Amy, 5206
ELECTIONS — U. S., 1269, 1386
Electoral College. Wilmerding, Lucius, Jr, 1266
ELECTRIC ENGINEERING, 255, 2636
Electric Journalist. Anderson, Chuck, 3285
ELECTRIC MOTORS, 2637
Electric Motors and Their Applications. Lloyd, Tom C, 2637
ELECTRIC POWER-PLANTS — ENVIRONMENTAL ASPECTS, 2638
Electrical Fundamentals. De France, J. J, 2046
ELECTRICITY, 2046-2050, 2646
Electron Microscope. Klein, Aaron E, 1913
ELECTRONIC APPARATUS AND APPLIANCES, 2643
Electronic Data Processing. Emery, Glyn, 2845
ELECTRONIC MUSIC, 3254
Electronic Music. Schwartz, Elliott S, 3254
ELECTRONICS, 2051, 2636, 2644-2645
    DICTIONARIES, 255-257
Electronics and Nucleonics Dictionary. Markus, John, 257
Electrostatics. Moore, A. D, 2050
Elements of Film. Bobker, G. R, 3266
Elements of Fortran Four. Bezner, Hart C, 468
Elements of Geography. Trewartha, G. T., et al. 4680
Elements of Geology. Zumberg, James H. and Nelson, Clemens A. 2100
Elements of Musical Understanding. Winold, Allen, 3133

INDEX

Elements of Radio. Marcus, Abraham and Marcus, W. 2649
Elements of Style. Strunk, William S., Jr. and White, E. B. 3470
Elements of the Art of Architecture. Muschenheim, William, 2959
Eleven Comedies. Aristophanes, 4459
Eleven Plays. Ibsen, Henrik, 4094
Eliade, Mircea. Australian Religions, 877
———. From Primitives to Zen, 831
ELIOT, GEORGE, 3929
Eliot in Perspective. Martin, Graham, 3897
Eliot, Thomas S. Complete Plays of T. S. Eliot, 3674
———. Complete Poems and Plays, 1909-1950, 3571
———. On Poetry and Poets, 3476
ELIOT, THOMAS STEARNS, 3578, 3896-3897
Elite Press. Merrill, John C, 493
ELIZABETH I, 5227
Elizabethan Renaissance. Rowse, Alfred L, 5229
Elizabethan World. Smith, Lacey B., ed, 5231
Elkins, Stanley M. Slavery, 1283
Ellington, Duke. Music Is My Mistress, 3248
ELLINGTON, EDWARD K, 3248
Elliott, J. H. Europe Divided, 5037
Ellis, Christopher. Military Transport of the First World War, 1681
———. Military Transport of World War Two, 1682
Ellis, Edward R. A Nation in Torment, 1106
Ellis, Jesse C. Index to Illustrations, 61
Ellis, John T. American Catholicism, 808
Ellis, R. Hobart, Jr. Knowing the Atomic Nucleus, 2058
Ellison, M. A. Sun and Its Influence, 2004
Ellmann, Richard. James Joyce, 3939
———. Yeats, 3848
Ellmann, Richard and Fiedelson, Charles, Jr., eds. Modern Tradition, 3493
Ellsworth, Ralph E. Academic Library Buildings, 20
Ellwood, Robert S., Jr. One Way, 775
———. Religious and Spiritual Groups in Modern America, 688
Elton, Geoffrey R. England Under the Tudors, 5217
———. The Practice of History, 4664
———. Reformation Europe, 5038
Elvis. Hopkins, Jerry, 3231
Ely, Katherine. see Binstock, Robert H.
Embree, Ainslie T., ed. The Hindu Tradition, 846
Embree, Edwin R. Indians of the Americas, 5748
Emergence of Film Art. Jacobs, Lewis, compiled by. 3276
Emergence of Greek Democracy. Forrest, William G, 4956
Emergence of Man. Pfeiffer, John E, 2197
Emergence of Metropolitan America, 1915-1966. McKelvey, Blake, 967
Emergence of the Great Powers. Wolf, John B, 5027
Emerging Democratic Majority. Davis, Lanny J, 1390
Emerging Themes of African History. Ranger, Terence O, 5708
EMERSON, RALPH WALDO, 3561, 3749
Emery, Edwin. The Press and America, 497
Emery, Glyn. Electronic Data Processing, 2845
Emile. Rousseau, Jean-Jacques, 4245
Emily Brontë. Hewish, John, 3927
Emily Dickinson. Johnson, Thomas Herbert, 3568
Emmel, Thomas C. An Introduction to Ecology and Population Biology, 2239
Emperor of China. Spence, Jonathan D, 5585
Empire of the Inca. Brundage, Burr C, 6266
Empire to Welfare State. Lloyd, T. O, 1085
Empress Josephine. Knapton, Ernest J, 5406
Empty Mirror. Van De Wetering, Janwillem, 841
Emrich, Linn. The Complete Book of Sky Sports, 3439
En la Ardiente Obscuridad. Buero Vallejo, Antonio, 4350
Encyclopedia Americana. 85
Encyclopedia Britannica. Makers of America, 126
Encyclopedia Buying Guide, 1975-1976. 7
Encyclopedia Judaica. 123
Encyclopedia of American Facts and Dates. Carruth, Gorton, et al, eds. 449
Encyclopedia of American History. Morris, Richard B. and Commager, Henry S., eds. 451
Encyclopedia of Australia. Learmonth, Andrew T. and Learmonth, Nancy. 456
Encyclopedia of Auto Racing Greats. Cutter, Bob and Fendell, Bob. 3404
Encyclopedia of Banking and Finance. Munn, Glenn G, 139
Encyclopedia of Chemistry. Hampel, Clifford A. and Hawley, Gessner C., eds. 216

INDEX

Encyclopedia of Dogs. Fiorone, Frorenzo, 2810
Encyclopedia of Firearms. Peterson, Harold L, 2672
Encyclopedia of Folk, Country and Western Music. Stambler, Irwin and London, Grelun. 307
Encyclopedia of Latin America. Delpar, Helen, ed, 455
Encyclopedia of Microscopy and Micro-Technique. Gray, Peter, 200
Encyclopedia of Military History. Dupuy, R. Ernest and Dupuy, Trevor N. 144
Encyclopedia of Minerals. Roberts, Willard Lincoln, et al. 219
Encyclopedia of Modern Architecture. Hatje, Gerd, ed, 281
Encyclopedia of Occult Sciences. 96
Encyclopedia of Oceanography. Fairbridge, R., ed, 225
Encyclopedia of Philosophy. Edwards, Paul, ed, 95
Encyclopedia of Physics. Besancon, Robert M., ed, 213
Encyclopedia of Psychology. Eysenck, H. J., et al, eds. 97
Encyclopedia of Religion and Ethics. Hastings, James, ed, 100
Encyclopedia of Southern Africa. Rosenthal, Eric, ed, 444
Encyclopedia of Sports. Menke, Frank G, 321
Encyclopedia of the American Revolution. Boatner, Mark M., 3rd, 453
Encyclopedia of the Biological Sciences. Gray, Peter, 229
Encyclopedia of the Earth. Larousse, 223
Encyclopedia of the Horse. Hope, C. E. and Jackson, G. N. 261
Encyclopedia of U. S. Coins. Reed, Mort, 286
Encyclopedia of World History. Langer, William L., ed, 379
ENCYCLOPEDIAS AND DICTIONARIES, 85-87
An Encyclopediic Dictionary of Heraldry. Franklyn, Julian, 433
End of a Presidency. New York Times, 6177
End of Austria-Hungary. Valliana, Leo, 5344
End of the American Era. Hacker, Andrew, 928
End of the Ancient World and the Beginnings of the Middle Ages. Lot, Ferdinand, 5001
End of the Draft. Reeves, Thomas and Hess, Karl. 1674
End of the European Era, 1890 to the Present. Gilbert, Felix, 1084

Endleman, Shalom, ed. Violence in the Streets, 1107
Energy. Freeman, S. David, 1461
Energy and the Future. Hammond, Allen, et al. 2634
ENERGY CONSERVATION, 1461, 1474, 2634
Energy Crises in Perspective. Fisher, John, 1460
Energy Crisis. Rocks, Lawrence and Runyon, Richard P. 1477
Energy Crisis in America. Congressional Quarterly Service, 1473
Energy in the World of the Future. Hellman, Harold, 1474
ENERGY POLICY, 1461, 1475-1476, 2634
Engdahl, Sylvia L. The Planet-Girded Suns, 2277
Engel, Lehman. Getting Started in the Theater, 3300
Engel, Lyle K. The Complete Motorcycle Book, 2747
———. The Indianapolis 500, 3405
Engels, Friedrich. see Marx, Karl
Engerman, Stanley L. see Fogel, Robert W.
ENGINEERING — HISTORY, 2630-2631
Engineers and Engineering in the Renaissance. Parsons, William B, 2630
ENGLAND
 CIVILIZATION, 5196, 5199, 5229
 SOCIAL LIFE AND CUSTOMS, 4749-4750, 5186, 5200, 5244
England in the Age of the American Revolution. Namier, Lewis, 5253
England in the Seventeenth Century. Ashley, Maurice, 5234
England Under the Stuarts. Trevelyan, George M, 5245
England Under the Tudors. Elton, Geoffrey R, 5217
Engle, Paul, ed. On Creative Writing, 3468
English-Arabic, Arabic-English Dictionary. Wortabet, J. and Porter, H., eds. 192
English Constitutional and Legal History. Lovell, Colin R, 1561
English Critical Essays. Jones, Edmund D., ed, 3954
English Critical Essays. Jones, Edmund D., ed, 3953
English Critical Essays. Jones, Phyllis M., ed, 3955
English Dialects. Wakelin, Martyn F, 1876
ENGLISH DRAMA, 372, 3856, 3888, 4447
ENGLISH FICTION, 3931, 3933-3934
English History, 1914-1945. Taylor, Alan J. P, 5276

INDEX

ENGLISH LANGUAGE, 176, 1878-1881, 3467, 3470
   DIALECTS, 1864, 1875-1876
   DICTIONARIES, 161-168, 174-175, 177, 181
   ETYMOLOGY — DICTIONARIES, 157-159
   FOREIGN WORDS AND PHRASES — DICTIONARIES, 160
   HISTORY, 198-199, 1865-1871, 1873
   IDIOMS, 171, 176, 1883, 1885-1886
   RIME — DICTIONARIES, 173
   SEMANTICS, 1872-1873, 1882
   SYNONYMS AND ANTONYMS, 170, 172, 484
English Life in Chaucer's Day. Hart, Roger, 5205
ENGLISH LITERATURE, 4889
   BIBLIOGRAPHY, 70-71,
   DICTIONARIES, 359-360
   HISTORY AND CRITICISM, 361-364, 657-659, 3770-3773
English Monarchs Series. 5280
English People on the Eve of Colonization. Notestein, Wallace, 5241
ENGLISH POETRY
   COLLECTIONS, 366, 3774-3775, 3777, 3779-3780, 3782-3786, 3788
   HISTORY AND CRITICISM, 365, 660, 3789
English Revolution, 1688-1689. Trevelyan, George M, 5246
English Romantic Poets. Abrams, Meyer H., ed, 3789
English-Russian Dictionary. Müller, Vladimir K, 188
English Wayfaring Life in the Middle Ages. Jusserand, Jean A, 5186
ENGLISH WIT AND HUMOR, 3958-3961
ENGRAVING, 3087, 3090
ENGRAVINGS, 3093, 3095
Enjoyment of Chemistry. Vaczek, Louis C, 2073
ENLIGHTENMENT, 637-638, 5020, 5034
Enlightenment. Gay, Peter, compiled by. 637
Enrico Fermi, Physicist. Segré, Emilio, 2033
Enright, Jim, see Tanner, Chuck
Enroth, Ronald M., et al. The Jesus People, 776
Enterline, James R. Viking America, 5887
Environment. Caldwell, Lynton, 933
ENVIRONMENT — DICTIONARIES, 125, 258
Environment for Man. Ewald, William R., ed, 2955
Environment U. S. A. A Guide to Agencies, People and Resources. Onyx Group, Inc, 1468

Environmental Geoscience. Strahler, Arthur N. and Strahler, Alan H. 2099
ENVIRONMENTAL POLICY — U. S., 933, 936, 938, 943-945, 947, 1465, 1468, 1634-1635, 1807, 2664, 2667
ENZYMES, 2512
Enzymes. Locke, David M, 2512
Eoff, Sherman. Modern Spanish Novel, 4391
Epic of Latin American Literature. Torres-Rioseco, Arturo, 4317
EPIC POETRY, 3505
   HISTORY AND CRITICISM, 3471
EPIC POETRY, GREEK, 4463-4466
Epics of the Western World. Hutson, Arthur E. and McCoy, Patricia, trs. 3505
EPIDEMICS — HISTORY, 2561, 2609
Epigrams. Martialis, Marcus Valerius, 4419
Episodes in Fine Poetic Traditions. Barnes, Richard G, 3496
Episodes of the Revolutionary War. Guevara, Che, 1246
EPITAPHS, 4433
Epochs of Greek and Roman Biography. Stuart, Duane Reed, 4434
Epstein, Edward J. News from Nowhere, 483
Epstein, Joseph. Divorced in America, 991
Equus and Shrivings. Shaffer, Peter, 3914
Era of Good Feelings. Dangerfield, George, 5988
Era of Reconstruction. Stampp, Kenneth M, 6075
Era of Reform, 1830-1860. Commager, Henry S, 6005
Era of the American Revolution Series. 5959
Era of the Cold War, 1946-1973. Link, Arthur S. and Catton, William B. 6157
Era of the French Revolution, 1789 to 1793. Gershoy, Leo, 5393
Era of Theodore Roosevelt. Mowry, George E, 6115
Era of Trujillo. Galindez, Jesus de, 5841
Erasmus and the Age of Reformation. Huizinga, Johan, 787
Erasmus, Desiderius. In Praise of Folly, 4432
ERASMUS, DESIDERIUS, 787
Erikson, Erik H. Gandhi's Truth, 1245
———. Identity, 580
Erikson, Jon. see Coles, Robert
Ernest Hemingway. Baker, Carlos, 3725
Ernest K. Gann's Flying Circus. Gann, Ernest K, 2720
Ernst, Carl and Barbour, Roger W. Turtles of the United States, 2420

INDEX

Ernst, Morris. The Great Reversals, 1607
Erotic Ocean. Rudloe, Jack, 2346
Errant Ark. Diole, Philippe, 2352
Erwin, Mabel D. and Kinchen, Lila A. Clothing for Moderns, 2840
ESKIMOS, 926, 4738, 4848, 6250
Eskimos. Birket-Smith, Kaj, 4848
Esler, Anthony. Bombs, Beards and Barricades, 1223
ESP. Leek, Sybil, 530
Espy, Hilda C. and Creamer, Lex. Another World, 4804
Essais. Montaigne, Michel E. de, 4271
Essay and General Literature Index. 94
An Essay Concerning Human Understanding. Locke, John, 654
ESSAYS, 3516-3517, 3746-3748, 4268-4269, 4271-4272, 4299
Essays in Science and Philosophy. Whitehead, Alfred N, 1914
Essence of Decision. Allison, Graham T, 1326
Essential Brecht. Fuegi, John, 4033
Essential Wisdom of George Santayana. Munson, Thomas N, 646
Essential Works of Chinese Communism. Chai, Winberg, 1499
Essential Works of Marxism. Mendel, Arthur P., ed, 1489
Essentials of Stage Lighting. Sellman, Hunton D, 3302
Essentials of Stage Scenery. Selden, Samuel, Jr. and Rezzuto, Tom. 3301
ESSEX, ROBERT DEVEREUX, 5220
Esslin, Martin. Brecht, 4032
———. The Peopled World of Harold Pinter, 3901
———. The Theatre of the Absurd, 3526
Eternal Egypt. Montet, Pierre, 4891
ETHICS, 598-599, 601, 652, 657, 679
   DICTIONARIES, 100, 111
   HISTORY, 600, 603
Ethics. Frankena, William K, 599
Ethics - Dead and Alive. Dunham, Barrows, 598
Ethics in a Permissive Society. Barclay, William, 757
Ethiopia. Hess, Robert L, 5719
ETHIOPIA — HISTORY, 5719
ETHNIC ATTITUDES, 1006
ETHNOLOGY, 904, 925, 4697, 2187, 2189-2190, 2195
ETIQUETTE, 1558, 1822-1823
L' Etranger. Camus, Albert, 4199
ETRURIA, 4729, 4926-4927
Etruscan and Roman Architecture. Boethius, Axel and Ward-Perkins, J. B. 2971
Etruscan Cities and Their Culture. Banti, Luisa, 4926

ETRUSCANS, 4963
Etruscans. Bloch, Raymond, 4927
Etruscans. Keller, Werner, 4729
Etruscans. Richardson, Emeline, 4929
Etymological Dictionary of the English Language. Skeat, Walter W., ed, 159
Eugene Onegin. Pushkin, Aleksandr S, 4560
Eugénie Grandet. Balzac, Honoré de, 4195
Eureka. DeBono, Edward, 2489
Eurich, Alvin C. Reforming American Education, 1760
Eurich, Alvin C. and Academy for Educational Development Staff, eds. High School, 1980, 1779
Eurich, Nell. Science in Utopia, 1208
Euripides. Plays, 4458
EUROPE
   CIVILIZATION, 4647, 4741, 5026
   CONSTITUTIONAL LAW, 1559
   DESCRIPTION AND TRAVEL, 4740, 4742
   ECONOMIC CONDITIONS, 5003, 5036, 5054
   ECONOMIC POLICY, 1795
   HISTORICAL GEOGRAPHY, 387, 4706
   HISTORY, 1213, 4723, 4988-4989, 4992, 4998, 5001, 5006, 5010, 5013, 5016-5017, 5012, 5023, 5025-5026, 5028, 5032-5033, 5035, 5037-5043, 5045-5046, 5049-5056, 5059-5064, 5091-5092, 5094, 5103
      SOURCES, 5009, 5024, 5065
   POLITICS, 1084, 5027, 5034, 5036, 5044, 5047-5048, 5058, 5066, 5341, 5925
   SOCIAL CONDITIONS, 5003, 5054
Europe and the French Imperium. Bruun, Geoffrey, 5045
Europe Between Revolutions. Droz, Jacques, 5054
Europe Divided. Elliott, J. H, 5037
EUROPE, EASTERN
   BIBLIOGRAPHY, 72
   HISTORY, 5093, 5287, 5493
   POLITICS, 1159-1160
Europe in the Seventeenth Century. Ogg, David, 5023
Europe in the Twentieth Century. Lichtheim, George, 5059
Europe of the Ancient Régime. Ogg, David, 5043
Europe of the Dictators, 1919-1945. Wiskemann, Elizabeth, 5094
Europe Since Napoleon. Thomson, David, 5064
European Administrative Elite. Armstrong, John A, 1068

European Authors, 1000-1900. Kunitz, Stanley J. and Colby, Vineta, eds. 426
European Discovery of America. Morison, Samuel E, 5891
European Discovery of America. Morison, Samuel E, 5890
European Economic Integration and the U. S. Krause, Lawrence B, 1798
European Folk Dance. Lawson, Joan, 3331
EUROPEAN LITERATURE — DICTIONARIES, 349
European Literature and the Latin Middle Ages. Curtius, Ernst R, 4430
European Philosophers from Descartes to Nietzsche. Beardsley, Monroe C., ed, 635
European Reconnaissance. Parry, John H., ed, 4704
European Renaissance Since 1945. Crouzet, Maurice, 4741
European Theories of the Drama. Clark, Barrett H, 3481
EUROPEAN WAR, (1914-1918), 402, 1681, 3013, 4677, 5067-5070, 5074, 5079, 5084-5086, 5089, 6122
    CAUSES, 1303, 5071, 5073-5074, 5076-5077, 5088
    GERMANY, 5073, 5081, 5096
    U. S., 5075, 5078, 5080, 5082-5083, 5087, 6111
Evaluative Criteria. National Study of Secondary School Evaluation, 48
Evans, Carol, see Johnson, Walter
Evans, Charles and Pliner, Roberta. The Terrarium Book, 2799
Evans, Elizabeth. Weathering the Storm, 5948
Evans, G. Heberton and Anderson, R. E. Lacrosse Fundamentals, 3366
Evans, Helen M. Man the Designer, 3018
Evans, Howard E. and Eberhard, Mary J. The Wasps, 2398
Evans, Joan. The Flowering of the Middle Ages, 5015
Evans, R. J. The Victorian Age, 1815-1914, 5257
Evans, Ralph M. The Perception of Color, 568
Evans, Richard I. Jean Piaget, 581
Evelyn Waugh and His World. Pryce-Jones, David, 3946
Everett, Thomas H. Living Trees of the World, 2326
Everglades Wildguide. George, Jean C, 2274
Everglyn, L. Through the Crust of the Earth, 2108
Everson, William K. see Fenin, George N.

Everyday Life in Babylon and Assyria. Contenau, Georges, 4908
Everyday Life in Bible Times. National Geographic Society, ed, 714
Everyday Life in Egypt in the Days of Ramesses the Great. Montet, Pierre, 4892
Everyday Life in New Testament Times. Bouquet, Alan C, 733
Everyday Life in Old Testament Times. Heaton, Eric W, 726
Everyman's Talmud. Cohen, Abraham, 855
Eves, Howard. An Introduction to the History of Mathematics, 1942
EVOLUTION, 519, 521, 1591, 1985, 2192, 2194, 2200, 2238, 2278-2283, 2285-2287, 2347-2348, 2401
Evolution Explained. Hutchinson, Peter, 2280
Evolution for Everyone. Gastonguay, Paul R, 2279
Evolution in Action. Huxley, Julian, 2281
Evolution of Canadian Literature in English. Edwards, Mary Jane, 3537
Evolution of Christian Thought. Burkill, T. Alec, 698
Evolution of Insects. Callahan, Philip S, 2391
Evolution of Jewish Thought. Agus, Jacob B, 857
Evolution of Man. Young, Louise B., ed, 2200
Evolution of the Machine. Calder, Ritchie, 2635
Evolution of the Vertebrates. Colbert, Edwin H, 2178
An Evolutionary Survey of the Plant Kingdom. Scagel, Robert F., et al. 2314
Ewald, William R., ed. Environment for Man, 2955
Ewbank, Connie. Insect Zoo, 2813
Ewen, David. The Complete Book of Classical Music, 304
———. Composers of Tomorrow's Music, 3154
———. Composers Since 1900, 299
———. Great Composers, 300
———. Instrumental and Chamber Music, 3155
———. New Complete Book of the American Musical Theater, 3211
———. New Encyclopedia of the Opera, 309
———. Orchestra Music, 3244
———. The World of Twentieth-Century Music, 3156
Ewen, David. see Cross, Milton J.
Ewers, John C. The Blackfeet, 5760

INDEX

EWING, WILLIAM MAURICE, 2148
Executive Order 9066. Conrat, Maisie and Conrat, Richard. 1062
EXECUTIVE POWER — U. S., 1368, 1580, 1638-1640, 1643, 5869
L' Exile et le Royaume. Camus, Albert, 4200
EXISTENTIALISM, 549-554, 619, 669, 739
Existentialism. MacQuarrie, John, 553
Existentialism from Dostoevsky to Sartre. Kaufmann, Walter A., ed, 552
EXORCISM, 535
Exotic Aquarium Fishes. Innes, William T, 2819
Expansion and Coexistence. Ulam, Adam B, 1312
Expansionists of 1898. Pratt, Julius W, 6094
Experimental Cinema. Curtis, David, 3270
EXPERIMENTAL FILMS, 3270, 3283
EXPERIMENTAL THEATER, 3297, 3311, 3317
Experts' Book of Freshwater Fishing. Netherby, Steve, ed, 3455
Explorers of the Atom. Gallant, Roy A, 2063
Exploring the Amazon. Schreider, Helen and Schreider, Frank. 4842
Exploring the Ocean World. Idyll, C. P., ed, 2139
Exposure. Berg, W, 3107
Expressionism. Dube, Wolf D, 3032
EXPRESSIONISM (ART), 3032
Exquemelin, Alexandre O. The Buccaneers and Marooners of America, 4693
EXTRASENSORY PERCEPTION, 529-530
Eye of Conscience. Meltzer, Milton and Cole, Bernard. 3121
Eye of the Heart. Howes, Barbara, ed, 4379
Eye-Witness to Wagon Trains West. Hewitt, James, compiled by. 6234
Eyelids of Morning. Graham, Alistair, 2421
Eyewitness. Katz, William L., compiled by. 1025
Eyewitness Accounts of the American Revolution. 5960
Eysenck, H. J., et al, eds. Encyclopedia of Psychology, 97

FABLES, 1848
Fables. La Fontaine, Jean de, 4223
Fabun, Don. Dynamics of Change, 4656
Face of London. Gloucester, Richard, 4747
Face of North America. Farb, Peter, 2272

Face of the Third Reich. Fest, Joachim C, 5312
Facets of Comedy. Sorrell, Walter, 3530
Facets of Genetics. Scientific American Editors, 2299
Facing Starvation. Bickel, Lennard, 2773
Facundo. Sarmiento, Domingo F, 4385
Fagen, Richard R., et al. Cubans in Exile, 5831
Fager, Charles E. Selma 1965, 1255
Fagg, John E. Cuba, Haiti and the Dominican Republic, 5824
Fagles, Robert, see Steiner, George
Fairbank, John K. China, 5576
———. East Asia, 5569
———. The United States and China, 1315
Fairbridge, R., ed. The Encyclopedia of Oceanography, 225
Faires, Virgil M. Thermodynamics, 2043
Fairfield, Richard. Communes USA, 1502
FAIRIES, 1849
Fairies in English Tradition and Literature. Briggs, Katharine M, 1849
FAIRY TALES, 153, 543, 1843-1844
Fairy Tales. Grimm Brothers, 1844
Faith and Violence. Merton, Thomas, 770
Faith, Nicholas. Wankel, 2659
Faith of Graffiti. Kurlansky, Mervin and Naar, Jon. 465
Faith of the Christian Church. Aulén, Gustaf, 737
Fakhry, Ahmed. Pyramids, 4885
Fakhry, Majid. A History of Islamic Philosophy, 613
Falange. Payne, Stanley G, 5472
Fall and Rise of Jimmy Hoffa. Sherican, Walter, 1446
Fall and Rise of Modern Italy. Hughes, Serge, 1168
Fall, Bernard B. The Two Vietnams, 5677
Fall of a President. Washington Post, 6179
Fall of the British Empire, 1918-1968. Cross, Colin, 5270
Fall of the Hermit Kingdom. Choi, Woonsang, 5608
Fall of the House of Savoy. Katz, Robert, 5444
Fallada, Hans. Kleiner Mann - Was Nun?, 4044
Falls, Cyril. The Great War, 5069
———. Hundred Years of War, 4675
La Familia de Pascual Duarte. Cela, Camilo José, 4371
Familiarity Is the Kingdom of the Lost. Boetie, Dugmore, 1708
A Family Business. Ianni, Francis A. and Ianni, E. R. 1712
Family of Man. Steichen, Edward, 3124
Famine 1975. Paddock, William and Paddock, Paul. 1512

INDEX

Fannie Farmer Cookbook. Farmer, Fannie, 2836
Fanny. Pagnol, Marcel, 4174
Fanon. Geismar, Peter, 1229
Fanon, Frantz. Black Skin, White Masks, 1021
———. Wretched of the Earth, 923
FANON, FRANTZ, 1229
Fantel, Hans. ABC's of Hi-Fi and Stereo, 2655
———. The True Sound of Music, 2656
Fantin, Mario. Sherpa, Himalaya, Nepal, 4783
Far Side of Paradise. Mizener, Arthur, 3735
Far Western Frontier. Billington, Ray A, 6228
Faraday, Michael. On the Various Forces of Nature, 2017
Farago, Ladislas. The Broken Seal, 5149
———. Patton, 5127
Farb, Peter. The Face of North America, 2272
———. Man's Rise to Civilization As Shown by the Indians of North America, from Primeval Times to the Coming of the Industrial State, 5749
Farmer, Fannie. The Fannie Farmer Cookbook, 2836
Farmer, Richard N. The Real World of 1984, 4661
Farnie, D. A. East and West of Suez, 1804
FAROUK I, 5717
Farr, Finis. Margaret Mitchell of Atlanta, 3728
Farson, Richard E. Birthrights, 994
Farzan, Massaud, compiled by. The Tale of the Reed Pipes, 862
FASCISM, 1148, 1151, 1207, 1218
  ITALY, 5445, 5448, 5450, 5452
  SPAIN, 5472
  U. S., 1146
Fascism. Hayes, Paul M, 1148
Fascism. Mussolini, Benito, 1218
Fascism in Italy. Wiskemann, Elizabeth, 5452
Fathers and Children. Rogin, Michael P, 5995
Faulk, Odie B. Destiny Road, 6220
Faulkner, Douglas. The Living Reef, 2263
Faulkner, Harold U. American Economic History, 1416
———. Politics, Reform and Expansion, 6065
Faulkner, Ray, et al. Art Today, 2909
FAULKNER, WILLIAM, 3734
Les Fausses Confidences. Marivaux, Pierre C. de, 4169
Faust. Goethe, Johann Wolfgang Von, 4016

Faust, Joan L. The New York Times Book of House Plants, 2795
———. The New York Times Book of Vegetable Gardening, 2788
———. The New York Times Garden Book, 2792
F.B.I. Story. Whitehead, Donald F, 1623
Feagin, Joe R. and Hahn, H. Ghetto Revolts, 1073
Fear in the Air. Ashmore, Harry S, 1564
Fear of Conspiracy. Davis, David B., ed, 1071
A Feast of History. Rapahael, Chaim, 861
Feast or Famine. Edwin, Ed, 1519
Feather, Leonard. Book of Jazz, 3188
Feature Films on 8mm and 16mm. Limbacher, James L., ed, 52
FEDAYEEN, 1183-1184, 5644
Fedayeen. Laffin, John, 5644
Feder, Lillian. Crowell's Handbook of Classical Literature, 408
Feder, Norman. American Indian Art, 2898
FEDERAL GOVERNMENT — U. S., 1583
Federal Reserve System. Prochnow, Herbert V, 1454
Federalist. Hamilton, Alexander, et al. 1579
Federalist Era, 1789-1801. Miller, John C, 5967
Federalists, Republicans, and Foreign Entanglements, 1789-1815. McColley, Robert, 1350
Feel Like Going Home. Guralnick, Peter, 3249
Feinberg, Wilburt. see Dayan, Ruth
Feinburg, Leonard, compiled by. Asian Laughter, 4476
Feingold, Henry L. The Politics of Rescue, 5104
Feininger, Andreas. The Color Photo Book, 3118
———. The Complete Photographer, 3103
———. Darkroom Techniques, 3104
Feis, Herbert. Between War and Peace, 5110
———. Churchill-Roosevelt-Stalin, 5111
———. The Road to Pearl Harbor, 5112
Feldberg, Katherine, ed. Of Men and Morals, 3957
Feldman, Edmund B. Varieties of Visual Experience, 2875
Feldman, Leonard. Four Channel Sound, 2657
FELIPE II., 5464
Fellman, Gordon. The Deceived Majority, 1070
Fellows, Otis E. and Torrey, N. L. The Age of Enlightenment, 4100

INDEX

Fell's Guide to Coins and Money Tokens of the World. Angus, Ian, 285
Fell's International Coin Book. Andrews, Charles J, 284
Female Eunich. Greer, Germaine, 977
Fendell, Bob. *see* Cutter, Bob
Fenin, George N. and Everson, William K. The Western, 3271
Fenn, Courtenay H., ed. Five Thousand Dictionary, 193
Fenten, D. X. Ms.-M.D, 2496
Fenton, Carroll L. and Fenton, Mildred A. The Fossil Book, 2174
———. The Rock Book, 2167
Fenton, Mildred A. *see* Fenton, Carroll L.
Ferguson, Charles Wright. Naked to Mine Enemies, the Life of Cardinal Wolsey, 5218
Ferguson, Marilyn. The Brain Revolution, 2525
Ferguson, Wallace K. and Bruun, Geoffrey. A Survey of European Civilization, 4988
Ferkiss, Victor C. Technological Man, 918
Ferlinghetti, Lawrence. A Coney Island of the Mind, 3638
———. Starting from San Francisco, 3639
Ferman, Louis A., et al, eds. Poverty in America, 1542
FERMAT, PIERRE DE, 1947
FERMI, ENRICO, 2033
Fern, Alan. *see* Constantine, Mildred
Fernett, Gene. Swing Out, 3242
Ferro, Marc. The Great War, 1914-1918, 5070
———. The Russian Revolution of February, 1917, 5519
Fesler, James W., et al. The Fifty States and Their Local Governments, 1649
Fest, Joachim C. The Face of the Third Reich, 5312
———. Hitler, 5311
Festival. Wolman, Baron, et al. 3226
FESTIVALS, 151, 1818, 1820, 3287
Festivals of the Jewish Year. Gaster, Theodor H, 1821
Festivals U.S.A. and Canada. Meyer, Robert, Jr, 1820
Fettig, Hansjurgen. Hand and Rod Puppets, 3286
Feudal Britain. Barrow, G. W, 5193
Feudal Society. Bloch, Marc, 5013
FEUDALISM, 5013
Feuer, Lewis S. The Conflict of Generations, 1784
———. Einstein and the Generations of Science, 2029
Fever. Fuller, John, 2608

Fichtelius, Karl-Erik and Sjolander, Sverre. Smarter Than Man? Intelligence in Whales, Dolphins and Humans, 2457
FICTION
 BIBLIOGRAPHY, 330
 HISTORY AND CRITICISM, 3486-3490
Fiction Catalog. 330
Fictions and Events. Berthoff, Warner, 3521
Fiedelson, Charles, Jr., *see* Ellmann, Richard
Fiedler, Leslie A. Love and Death in the American Novel, 3714
Field Biology and Ecology. Benton, Allen H. and Werner, William E. 2236
Field Guide to Landforms in the U. S. Shimer, John A, 4816
Field, Leslie A., compiled by. Thomas Wolfe, 3716
Fielding, Raymond. The American Newsreel, 1911-1967, 3272
Fifteen Greek Plays. Cooper, Lane, ed, 4446
Fifty States and Their Local Governments. Fesler, James W., et al. 1649
Fifty Years of Foreign Affairs. Armstrong, Hamilton F., ed, 1154
Fighter. Cooper, Bryan and Batchelor, John. 2674
Fighters in Service. Munson, Kenneth, 2675
Fighting Warsaw. Korbonski, Stefan, 5115
Figure Finaglers. Reichard, Robert, 1794
Filler, Louis. Crusade Against Slavery, 1830-1860, 1284
FILLMORE, MILLARD, 6022
Film As a Subversive Art. Vogel, Amos, 3283
Film Library Techniques. Harrison, Helen, 26
FILM POSTERS, RUSSIAN, 3096
Filmgoer's Companion. Halliwell, Leslie, 313
Films Too Good for Words. Parlato, Salvatore J., Jr., ed, 53
Filson, Floyd V. *see* Wright, George E.
FINANCE — U. S. — HISTORY, 1449
Financial Expert. Narayan, R. K, 4484
Finding and Preparing Precious and Semiprecious Stones. Peterson, James A, 2171
Finding Facts Fast. Todd, Alden, 82
Finding Your Way in the Outdoors. Mooers, Robert L., Jr, 2710
Findley, R. *see* Brockett, Oscar G.
Fine, Benjamin. Barron's Profiles of American Colleges, 146
Finely, Joseph E. The Corrupt Kingdom, 1440

INDEX

Finest Judges Money Can Buy. Ashman, Charles R, 1612
FINLAND — HISTORY, 5533
Finley, Moses I. The Ancient Greeks, 4955
———. The World of Odysseus, 4460
Fiorone, Frorenzo. Encyclopedia of Dogs, 2810
Fire and Ice. Thompson, Lawrence R, 3620
Fire in the Lake. Fitzgerald, Frances, 1185
Fire Next Time. Baldwin, James, 1009
FIREARMS, 1796, 2672-2673, 3460
FIRST AID, 2534, 2569-2570, 2572-2573, 2585
First American. Ceram, C. W, 4736
First Churchill. Barnett, Correlli, 5235
First Emancipation. Zilversmit, Arthur, 1039
First Expatriates. Bizardel, Yvon, 5391
First French Republic, 1792-1804. Sydenham, M. J, 5400
First Great Civilization. Hawkes, Jacquetta H, 4784
First Lady of the South. Ross, Ishbel, 6046
First on the Moon. Armstrong, Neil, et al. 2765
First to Fly. Harris, Sherwood, 2714
First World War History Atlas. Gilbert, Martin, 402
Fisch, Max H., ed. Classic American Philosophers, 643
Fischer, David H. Historian's Fallacies, 4650
Fischer, Fritz. Germany's Aims in the First World War, 5073
Fischer, Gerald C. American Banking Structure, 1451
Fischer, Hans S. and Besch, Lutz. The Life of Mozart, 3166
Fischer, Louis. Russia's Road from Peace to War, 1308
———. The Story of Indonesia, 6282
Fischer-Galati, Stephen. The New Rumania, 5564
Fish, Carl R. The Rise of the Common Man, 1830-1850, 6008
Fishel, Leslie H. and Quarles, Benjamin. The Black American, 5882
Fisher, James, et al. Wildlife in Danger, 1459
Fisher, John. Energy Crises in Perspective, 1460
Fisher, Margaret W., see Bondurant, Joan
Fisher, Ralph T., see Vernadsky, George
FISHES, 2263-2264
FISHES, FRESHWATER — DICTIONARIES, 262-263
Fishes of North America. Herald, Earl, 2407
FISHING, 2406, 3450-3453-3456
Fishing. Bates, Joseph D, 3451
Fiske, John. Critical Period of American History, 1783-1789, 5964
Fitts, Dudley, ed. Greek Plays in Modern Translation, 4447
Fitzgerald, Arthur E. The High Priests of Waste, 1679
Fitzgerald, Brian P. Developments in Geographical Methods, 4681
Fitzgerald, Charles P. and Horizon Editors. History of China, 5577
Fitzgerald, Frances. Fire in the Lake, 1185
FITZGERALD, FRANCIS SCOTT, 3735
Fitzgerald, Gerald E., ed. Constitutions of Latin America, 1590
Fitzgerald, Ken, compiled by. The Space-Age Photographic Atlas, 397
FITZGERALD, ZELDA (SAYRE), 3733
Fitzgibbon, Constantine. Life of Dylan Thomas, 3849
Fitzgibbon, Constantine and Morrison, George. The Life and Times of Eamon de Valera, 5165
Five Centuries of American Costume. Wilcox, R. Turner, 1817
Five Families. Lewis, Oscar, 1100
Five German Plays. Bentley, Eric, ed, 4026
Five Plays. Cocteau, Jean, 4152
Five Plays. Jonson, Ben, 3860
Five Plays. Lope de Vega, Felix de, 4356
Five Screenplays. Pinter, Harold, 3911
Five Thousand Dictionary. Fenn, Courtenay H., ed, 193
Flandrau, Charles M. Viva Mexico, 5805
Flatland. Abbott, Edwin A, 1927
Flaubert. Starkie, Enid, 4251
Flaubert, Gustave. Madame Bovary, 4209
———. Salammbo, 4210
———. Trois Contes, 4211
FLAUBERT, GUSTAVE, 4251
Flayderman, E. Norman. Scrimshaw and Scrimshanders, Whales and Whalemen, 2997
Fleisher, Frederic K. New Sweden, 5535
Fleiss, Ruth. see Lemke, Antje
Fleissner, Otto S. and Deutsches, E. M. Literaturlesebuch, 3982
Flemer, William. Nature's Guide to Successful Gardening and Landscaping, 2791
Fleming, Alice. Contraception, Abortion, Pregnancy, 2551
Fleming, J., et al. Penguin Dictionary of Architecture, 280
Fleming, Thomas, ed. Benjamin Franklin, 5950
Fleming, Walter L. Documentary History of Reconstruction, 6066

INDEX

Fletcher, Banister. The History of Architecture, 2962
Fletcher, Colin. The New Complete Walker, 3387
Fletcher, John. see Beaumont, Francis
Fletcher, Joseph. Moral Responsibility, 753
———. Situation Ethics, 754
Fletcher, W. W. The Pest War, 2779
Fletcher, William C. The Russian Orthodox Church Underground, 1917-1971, 807
Fletcher, William C., see Hayward, Max
Les Fleurs du Mal. Baudelaire, Charles P, 4118
Flew, Anthony G. An Introduction to Western Philosophy, 636
Flexner, Eleanor. Century of Struggle, 1268
Flexner, James T. George Washington. , 5970
Flexner, James T. see Flexner, Simon
Flexner, John T. Traitor and the Spy, 5916
Flexner, Simon and Flexner, James T. William Henry Welch and the Heroic Age of American Medicine, 2499
Flight Instructor's Manual. Kershmer, William K, 2722
Flight of the Dragon (Wisdom of the East) Binyon, Lawrence, 2929
Flight Through the Ages. Gibbs-Smith, Charles H, 2711
Flight to Freedom. Durden, Kent, 2439
Flint, John E. Cecil Rhodes, 5739
Flint, Richard F. Earth and Its History, 2175
Flint, Richard F. and Skinner, Brian J. Physical Geology, 2109
Flo. Roper, Laura W, 2958
Flood Tide of Empire. Cook, Warren L, 6246
FLOODS — U. S., 2696
Floor of the Sea. Wertenbaker, William, 2148
Flora, Snowden D. Tornadoes of the United States, 2154
FLORENCE — HISTORY, 5433
Florence Nightingale. Huxley, Elspeth, 2497
Flores, Angel, ed. Anthology of French Poetry from Nerval to Valéry, 4137
———. Anthology of German Poetry from Holderlin to Rilke, 4003
———. Anthology of Spanish Poetry from Garcilaso to García Lorca, 4335
Flores Caballero, Romeo. Counterrevolution, 5812
Florescu, Radu. see McNally, Raymond T
Florinsky, Michael T. Russia, 5482
Florit, E. see Anderson-Imbert, Enrique
Flowering of American Folk Art 1776-1876. Lipman, Jean and Winchester, Alice. 3016
Flowering of the Middle Ages. Evans, Joan, 5015
FLOWERS — DICTIONARIES, 260
Flush. Woolf, Virginia, 3834
Fly. Carrier, Rick, 3440
Fly Fishing in Salt Water. Kreh, Bernard L, 3453
Flying Magazine Editors. America's Flying Book, 2721
FLYING SAUCERS, 472
Flynn, Gerard C. Manuel Tamayo y Baus, 4362
Focal Encyclopedia of Photography. Focal Press, Ltd, 295
Focal Press, Ltd. Focal Encyclopedia of Photography, 295
Focus on Environmental Geology. Tank, Ronald W., ed, 2103
Focus on Southeast Asia. Taylor, Alice, ed, 1095
Fodor's Modern Travel Guides. 4855
Fogarty, Robert S., ed. American Utopianism, 1209
Fogden, Michael and Fogden, Patricia. Animals and Their Colors, 2365
Fogden, Patricia. see Fogden, Michael
Fogel, Robert W. and Engerman, Stanley L. Time on the Cross, 1431
Fogelson, Robert M. Violence As Protest, 905
Foley, Charles and Scobie, W. I. The Struggle for Cyprus, 5656
Folk and Festival Costume of the World. Wilcox, R. Turner, 1815
FOLK ART, 2985, 3014, 3016, 3020
Folk Arts and Crafts of Japan. Muraoka, Kageo and Okamura, Kichiemon. 3014
FOLK-LORE, 120, 824-825, 1824-1842, 4306
FOLK MUSIC, 303, 307, 3331
FOLK-SONGS, 3235-3238
Folklore from the Working Folk of America. Coffin, Tristram P. and Cohen, Hennig. 1830
Folklore in America. Coffin, Tristram P, 1828
Folklore in China. Hodous, Lewis, 1832
Folktales of England. Briggs, Katharine M. and Tongue, Ruth L. 1827
La Folle de Chaillot. Giraudoux, Jean, 4159
Foner, Philip S. The Spanish-Cuban-American War and the Birth of American Imperialism, 1895-1902, 6096
Fontane, Theodor. Effi Briest, 4045
———. Frau Jenny Treibel, 4047
———. Irrungen, Wirrungen, 4046
Fonvizin, Denis I. Nedorosl', 4530

INDEX

FOOD, 2831-2833
FOOD ADULTERATION AND INSPECTION, 2556-2558, 2862
Food in History. Tannahill, Reay, 2833
Food Pollution. Marine, Gene and Van Allan, Judith. 2557
FOOD SUPPLY, 953, 956, 1512, 1514-1519
Fool and His Scepter. Willeford, William, 3258
FOOTBALL, 3359-3361
For All Mankind. Taylor, L. B., Jr, 2633
For Peace and Justice. Chatfield, Charles, 1299
Forbes, Nevil, et al. The Balkans, 5556
FORD, GERALD RUDOLPH, 6174, 6180-6181
Ford, Kenneth W. The World of Elementary Particles, 2036
Ford, Richard A. see Gordon, Arnold J.
Fore-Edge Painting. Weber, Carl J, 505
Forecasting the Weather. Rubin, Louis D. and Herbert, Hiram J. 2158
Foreign Policy of Hitler's Germany. Weinberg, Gerhard L, 1305
Foreign Policy of Soviet Russia, 1929-1941. Beloff, Max, 1306
Foreign Policy of Victorian England, 1830-1902. Bourne, Kenneth, 1302
Foreigners in Their Native Land. Weber, David J., compiled by. 4826
Forem, Jack. Transcendental Meditation, 548
Foreman, Grant. Advancing the Frontier, 1830-1960, 5769
———. Indian Removal, 5770
———. The Last Trek of the Indians, 5771
Forer, Lois G. No One Will Lissen, 1603
Forerunners of Black Power. Bermann, Ernest G, 1234
FOREST ECOLOGY, 2245, 2318-2319, 2327
Forest Fire. Brown, A. A. and Davis, Kenneth P. 2786
Forest Service. Frome, Michael, 2785
Forester, Cecil S. The Age of Fighting Sail, 5985
FORESTS AND FORESTRY, 2327, 2786-2787, 4798
A Forgotten Empress. Curtiss, Mina S, 5499
Forgotten Language. Fromm, Erich, 543
Form and Meaning in Drama. Kitto, Humphrey D, 4454
Form, Space and Vision. Collier, Graham, 3004
Formation of the Soviet Union. Pipes, Richard, 5508
Forrest, William G. Emergence of Greek Democracy, 4956

Forster, Edward M. Aspects of the Novel, 3487
FORSTER, EDWARD MORGAN, 3930, 3948
Forster, Leonard Wilson, ed. The Penguin Book of German Verse, 4004
FORT SUMTER, 6041
FORTRAN (COMPUTER PROGRAM LANGUAGE), 468
Fortune Editors. see Lessing, L.
Foss, Christopher F. Armoured Fighting Vehicles of the World, 2678
Fossil Book. Fenton, Carroll L. and Fenton, Mildred A. 2174
FOSSILS, 2174, 2176, 2180, 2401
Fossils. Rhodes, Frank H., et al. 2176
Foster, Malcolm. Joyce Cary, a Biography, 3940
Foster, Robert F. Foster's Complete Hoyle, 3341
Foster's Complete Hoyle. Foster, Robert F, 3341
Foundation of the German Empire. Böhme, Helmut, compiled by. 5292
Foundations of Colonial America. Kavenagh, W. Keith, 1276
Founders of Living Religions. Stroup, Herbert H, 687
Founders of the Middle Ages. Rand, Edward K, 5007
Four Black Revolutionary Plays. Jones, LeRoi, 3697
Four Brontës. Hanson, Lawrence and Hanson, Elizabeth. 3926
Four Channel Sound. Feldman, Leonard, 2657
Four Decades. Duval, Paul, 2940
Four Indian Poets. Allen, Paula C., et al. 4635
Four Loves. Lewis, Clive S, 755
Four Masterpieces of American Indian Literature. Bierhorst, John, ed, 4637
Four Plays. Calderón de la Barca, Pedro, 4351
Four Plays. Giraudoux, Jean, 4162
Four Plays. Inge, William, 3696
Four Plays. Shaw, George B, 3885
Four Plays. Webster, John and Tourneur, Cyril. 3862
Four Screen Plays. Bergman, Ingmar, 4088
Four Stages. MacDonald, J. W. and Saxton, J. C., eds. 3507
Fourcade, Marie M. Noah's Ark, 5100
Fourth State of Matter. Bova, Ben, 2034
Fourth World. Manuel, George and Posluns, Michael. 5754
Fowler, Henry M. A Dictionary of Modern English Usage, 176
Fowler, William W. Social Life at Rome in the Age of Cicero, 4935

INDEX

Fowlie, Wallace, ed. French Stories, 4262
——. A Guide to Contemporary French Literature, 4108
——. Jean Cocteau, 4156
Fox at Bay. Curtis, James C, 5999
Fox, Charles P. and Parkinson, Tom. The Circus in America, 3260
Fox, Dixon R. see Krout, John A.
Fox, Edward W. Atlas of European History, 387
FOX, GEORGE, 816
Fox, Renee C. and Swazy, Judith P. The Courage to Fail, 2590
Foxe, John. Foxe's Book of Martyrs, 792
Foxe's Book of Martyrs. Foxe, John, 792
Foxfire Book. Wigginton, Brooks E., ed, 4832
Foxfire 2. Wigginton, Brooks E., ed, 4833
Foxfire 3. Wigginton, Brooks E., ed, 4834
FRA ANGELICO, 3059
Fra Angelico. Pope-Hennessey, John, 3059
Fraenkel, Jack R. Crime and Criminals, 1707
Frail Ocean. Marx, Wesley, 1479
Frame, Donald. Montaigne, 4270
FRANCE, 4726
    CIVILIZATION, 5370, 5375, 5381
    COLONIES — AFRICA, 923
    CONSTITUTIONAL HISTORY, 5416
    ECONOMIC CONDITIONS, 1089, 1412
    FOREIGN RELATIONS, 1303, 5420
    HISTORY, 4756, 5024, 5045-5046, 5099, 5369, 5371-5373, 5376-5377, 5384, 5386-5388, 5394, 5400, 5403-5405, 5407-5410, 5412-5413, 5416-5419
        REVOLUTION, 5049, 5389, 5391-5402
    POLITICS AND GOVERNMENT, 1166, 5413, 5415, 5417, 5422, 5423
France. George, Pierre, 1412
France. Guerard, Albert L, 5371
France. Hurlimann, Martin, 4755
France. Knapton, Ernest J, 5372
France. Thomson, David, 5416
France, Anatole. Le Crime de Sylvestre Bonnard, 4212
FRANCE BAHAMONDE, FRANCISCO, 5475
France in America, 1497-1763. Thwaites, Reuben G, 5787
France Under the Bourbon Restoration, 1814-1830. Artz, Frederick B, 5408
France Under the Republic. Brogan, Denis W, 5413
France, 1848-1945. Zeldin, Theodore, 4756
FRANCESCO D'ASSISI, SAINT, 791
Francis Bacon. Bowen, Catherine D, 5212

Francis, Carl C. Introduction to Human Anatomy, 2503
Francis Drake, Privateer. Hampden, John, compiled by. 4696
Francis Marion. Rankin, Hugh F, 5939
Francis, W. N. Structure of American English, 1878
FRANCISCO DE BORJA, SAINT, 5435
Francisco Goya. Horwitz, Sylvia L, 3063
FRANCO-GERMAN WAR, 5293
Franco, Jean. An Introduction to Spanish-American Literature, 4314
Franco-Prussian War. Howard, Michael, 5293
Frank, Anne. Diary of a Young Girl, 5114
FRANK, ANNE, 5114
Frank, Gerold. An American Death, 1710
Frank, Jerome D. Sanity and Survival, 604
Frank Lloyd Wright. Twombly, Robert C, 2964
Frank, Tenney. Life and Literature in the Roman Republic, 4397
Franke, Wolfgang. A Century of Chinese Revolution, 1851-1949, 5582
Frankel, Tobia. The Russian Artist, 2927
Frankena, William K. Ethics, 599
Frankfurter, Felix. Mr. Justice Holmes and the Supreme Court, 1617
Franklin, Benjamin. Poor Richard's Almanac, 3755
FRANKLIN, BENJAMIN, 5949-5950
Franklin D. Roosevelt and the New Deal. Leuchtenburg, William E, 6138
Franklin, John H. From Slavery to Freedom, 1271
——. The Militant South, 1800-1861, 6206
——. Reconstruction After the Civil War, 6067
Franklyn, Julian. An Encyclopediic Dictionary of Heraldry, 433
——. Shield and Crest, 4874
Frans Hals. Slive, Seymour, 3072
Franz Kafka. Brod, Max, 4080
Franz Kafka. Reiss, H. S, 4076
Franzius, Enno. History of the Byzantine Empire, 5550
Fraser, Antonia. Cromwell, the Lord Protector., 5238
——. Mary, Queen of Scots, 5157
Fraser, Julius T., ed. Voices of Time, 522
Fraser, Ronald. The Habitable Earth, 2093
Frau Jenny Treibel. Fontane, Theodor, 4047
Frazer, James G. The Golden Bough, 825
FREDERICK THE GREAT, 5290
Frederick the Great. Ritter, Gerhard, 5290
Free at Last. Bontemps, Arna, 6061
Free Schools. Kozol, Jonathan, 1766

FREE SCHOOLS — U. S., 1766
Freedland, Michael. Irving Berlin, 3157
Freedland, Nat. The Occult Explosion, 532
Freedley, George and Reeves, John A. History of the Theatre, 3313
Freedman, Russell and Morriss, James E. The Brains of Animals and Man, 2345
Freedom and the Court. Abraham, Henry J, 1260
FREEDOM OF INFORMATION, 19, 1566
FREEDOM OF THE PRESS, 482, 1563-1564, 1566, 1582
Freedom of the Press for Whom? The Right of Access to Mass Media. Barron, Jerome A, 1566
Freedom vs. Suppression and Censorship. Busha, Charles H, 475
Freedom's Ferment. Tyler, Alice F, 5979
Freehling, William H., ed. Nullification Era, 5994
Freeland, Richard M. The Truman Doctrine and the Origins of McCarthyism, 1336
Freeman, A. Myrick. The Economics of Environmental Policy, 943
Freeman, Douglas. Lee's Lieutenants, 6048
———. Robert E. Lee, 6049
Freeman, E. The Theatre of Albert Camus, 4189
Freeman, John. Herman Melville, 3720
Freeman, S. David. Energy, 1461
Freeth, Zahra and Winestone, H. V. Kuwait, 4781
Freewheeling. Bridge, Raymond, 3400
Freezing Point. Kavaler, Lucy, 2225
Freidel, Frank. Splendid Little War, 6097
Freidel, Frank and Showman, Richard K., eds. Harvard Guide to American History, 78
Fremantle, Anne, ed. The Age of Belief, 628
French. De Gramont, Sanche, 5370
French Against the French. Dank, Milton, 5099
French Book Corp. of America. French Books, 15
French Books. French Book Corp. of America, 15
FRENCH CANADIANS, 5784
French Canadians. Wade, Mason, 5784
French Civilization from Its Origins to the Close of the Middle Ages. Guerard, Albert L, 5375
French Civilization in the 19th Century. Guerard, Albert L, 5381
FRENCH DRAMA, 4184-4188, 4190
FRENCH FICTION, 3933, 4264-4267
FRENCH LANGUAGE
DICTIONARIES, 179-181
ENCYCLOPEDIAS AND DICTIONARIES, 83
FRENCH LITERATURE, 345, 4097, 4112
COLLECTIONS, 4098-4102
DICTIONARIES, 374
HISTORY AND CRITICISM, 341, 4103-4111, 4113-4114, 4116-4117
French Lyric Poetry. Giese, Frank S. and Wilder, W. F., eds. 4122
French Monarchs Series. 5425
French Nation. Brogan, Denis W, 5409
French Novelists of Today. Peyre, Henri, 4265
FRENCH POETRY — COLLECTIONS, 4136-4140
French Politicians and Elections, 1951-1969. Willianis, Philip M, 5423
French Revolution. Kafker, Frank A. and Laux, James M., eds. 5395
French Revolution and Napoleon. Gershoy, Leo, 5394
French Revolution from 1793-1799. Lefebvre, Georges, et al, eds. 5397
French, Robert D. A Chaucer Handbook, 3791
French Stories. Fowlie, Wallace, ed, 4262
French Theatre Since 1930. Pucciani, Oreste F., ed, 4186
French Tradition in America. Zoitvany, Yves F., ed, 5788
FRESH-WATER BIOLOGY, 2269-2270
Freuchen, Peter and Loth, David. Book of the Seven Seas, 4694
Freud. Miller, Jonathan, ed, 561
Freud, Sigmund. The Basic Writings, 527
FREUD, SIGMUND, 561
Friar Thomas D'Aquino. Weisheipl, James A, 633
Fridriksson, S. Surtsey, 2231
Fried, Albert, ed. Socialism in America, 1485
Fried, Albert and Sanders, Ronald, eds. Socialist Thought, 1482
Fried, John J. Life Along the San Andreas Fault, 2120
———. The Mystery of Heredity, 2292
———. Vasectomy, 2553
Fried, John J. see Diethrich, Edward B.
Frieda Lawrence. Lucas, Robert, 3943
Friedberg, Maurice, ed. Russian Short Stories, 4547
Friedberg, Robert. Paper Money of the United States, 291
Das Friedensfest-Einsame Menschen. Hauptmann, Gerhart, 4018
Friedlander, Albert H., ed. Out of the Whirlwind, 3494
Friedman, Irving S. Inflation, 1455
Friedman, Lawrence M. A History of American Law, 1545

INDEX

Friedman, Leon, ed. The Law of War, 1556
Friedman, Leon and Israel, F. L., eds. The Justices of the U. S. Supreme Court, 1789-1969, 1618
Friedman, Myra. Buried Alive, 3229
Friedman, Norman. E. E. Cummings, 3601
Friedrich, Carl J. Age of the Baroque, 5041
Friedrich, Otto. Before the Deluge, 4754
FRIENDS, SOCIETY OF, 816
Fries, Charles C. Linguistics and Reading, 1887
Frisch, Max. Andorra, 4050
———. Homo Faber, 4049
———. I'm Not Stiller, 4048
Frobisher, Martin, et al. Fundamentals of Microbiology, 2302
Froehlich, Walter. Apollo 14, 2763
Froissart, Jean. Chronicles of England, France, Spain, 4998
From Ape to Adam. Wendt, Herbert, 2199
From Barbarism to Chivalry. Price, Mary R. and Howell, Margaret. 5006
From Cell to Organism. Scientific American Editors, 2253
From Colony to Country. Ketcham, Ralph L, 5966
From Cortés to Castro. Collier, Simon D, 6255
From Despotism to Revolution. Gershoy, Leo, 5033
From Diplomacy to Resistance. Bauer, Yehuda, 5660
From Hayes to McKinley. Morgan, H. Wayne, 1388
From Ottomanism to Arabism. Dawn, C. Ernest, 1147
From Plantation to Ghetto. Meier, August, 5865
From Poor Law to Welfare State. Trattner, Walter I, 1691
From Poverty to Dignity. Hampden-Turner, Charles, 1702
From Primitives to Zen. Eliade, Mircea, 831
From Ritual to Romance. Weston, Jessie, 1845
From Slavery to Freedom. Franklin, John H, 1271
From Solon to Socrates. Ehrenberg, Victor, 4965
From the Belly of the Shark. Lowenfels, Walter, 3576
From the Crash to the Blitz, 1929-1939. Phillips, Cabell, 6143
From the Danube to the Yalu. Clark, Mark W, 5609
From the Gracchi to Nero. Scullard, Howard H, 4938
From Truman Through Johnson. Druks, Herbert, 6156
From Union to Apartheid. Ballinger, Margaret, 1239
Froman, Robert. Racism, 1074
Frome, Michael. Battle for the Wilderness, 1471
———. The Forest Service, 2785
Fromm, Erich. The Anatomy of Human Destructiveness, 572
———. The Art of Loving, 605
———. The Forgotten Language, 543
FRONTIER AND PIONEER LIFE, 4812, 6189, 6227, 6235, 6238, 6244, 6248
Frontier in American History. Turner, Frederick J, 5872
Frontier Regulars. Utley, Robert M, 6078
Frontiers for the Church Today. Brown, Robert M, 771
Frontiers of Astronomy. Hoyle, Fred, 1963
Frontiers of Astronomy. Scientific American Editors, 1966
Frost, Robert. Poetry, 3602
FROST, ROBERT, 3597, 3611, 3619-3620
Fry, Christopher. Lady's Not for Burning, 3902
———. Three Plays, 3903
Frye, William R. In Whitest Africa, 1049
Frying-Pan. Parker, Tony, 1740
Fuchs, Walter R. Mathematics for the Modern Mind, 1932
———. Physics for the Modern Mind, 2018
Fuegi, John. The Essential Brecht, 4033
Der Fuehrer. Heiden, Konrad, 5315
Fulbright, James W. The Arrogance of Power, 1337
———. The Crippled Giant, 1338
Fulford, Roger. Hanover to Windsor, 5173
Fuller, John. Fever, 2608
———. Two Hundred Million Guinea Pigs, 2556
Fuller, John D. The Movement for the Acquisition of All Mexico, 1846-1848, 6019
Fuller, John F. A Military History of the Western World, 4671
Fuller, R. Buckminster. Synergetics, 644
FULLER, RICHARD BUCKMINSTER, 2632
Fullerton, Brian and Williams, Alan. Scandinavia, 4766
Fulton, Albert R. Motion Pictures, 3273
Fundamental Chemistry. Andrews, Donald and Kokes, R. J. 2065
Fundamentals of Ecology. Odum, Eugene P, 2234
Fundamentals of Electricity and Magnetism. Kip, Arthur F, 2047

Fundamentals of Electronics. Mandl, Matthew, 2645
Fundamentals of Logic. Carney, James D. and Scheer, Richard. 592
Fundamentals of Microbiology. Frobisher, Martin, et al. 2302
Fundamentals of Neurology. Gardner, Ernest, 2506
Fundamentals of Optics. Jenkins, Francis A, 2040
Fundamentals of Organic Chemistry. Butler, George B. and Berlin, K. Darrell. 2082
Fundamentals of Psychology. Adcock, C. J, 559
FUNERAL RITES AND CEREMONIES — EGYPT, 868
FUNGI, 237, 2329
Funk & Wagnalls Editors. Dictionary of Electronics, 256
Funk and Wagnalls Guide to Modern World Literature. Seymour-Smith, Martin, 343
FUR TRADE, 6230, 6240
Fur-Trade and Early Western Exploration. Vandiver, Clarence H, 6240
Furguson, John. Heritage of Hellenism, 4731
Furious Passage of James Baldwin. Eckman, Fern M, 3743
Furniss, W. Todd, ed. American Universities and Colleges, 147
FURNITURE, 282, 3023-3024
Future As Nightmare; H. G. Wells and the Anti-Utopians. Hillegas, Mark R, 3920
Future Metropolis. Tamiment Institute, 971
Future Shock. Toffler, Alvin, 913
FUTURISM, 971

Gabriel, Ralph H. The Course of American Democratic Thought, 5860
Gabrielsen, Milton A., et al. Aquatics Handbook, 3421
Gaddis, John L. The United States and the Origins of the Cold War, 1941-1947, 1339
Gaer, Joseph. How the Great Religions Began, 820
———. What the Great Religions Believe, 821
Gage, Nicholas. The Mafia Is Not an Equal Opportunity Employer, 1711
Gailey, Harry A. History of Africa, 5709
———. History of Africa, 5710
GALAPAGOS ISLANDS, 1908
Galarza, Ernesto. Barrio Boy, 1041
Galaxies. Shapley, Harlow, 1987
Galaxies, Nuclei and Quasars. Hoyle, Fred, 1982
Galbraith, John Kenneth. The Affluent Society, 1417
———. Ambassador's Journal, 1301
———. Economics and the Public Purpose, 1538
———. Great Crash, 1929, 1530
———. The New Industrial State, 1409
Galdós' Novelista Moderno. Unamuno, Miguel de, 4388
GALILEI, GALILEO, 1974
Galileo. Ronan, Colin A, 1974
Galin, Saul and Spielberg, Peter, eds. Reference Books, 8
Galindez, Jesus de. Era of Trujillo, 5841
Gallant, Roy A. Explorers of the Atom. , 2063
Gallegos, Romulo. Doña Bárbara, 4376
Gallic War. Caesar, Gaius Julius, 4424
Gallo, Max. Mussolini's Italy, 5450
———. The Poster in History, 3097
———. Spain Under France, 5474
Gallop, Rodney. A Book of the Basques, 4761
Galloway, George B. History of the House of Representatives, 1361
Gallup, George H. The Gallup Poll, 124
Gallup Poll. Gallup, George H, 124
Galsworthy, John. Plays, 3895
GALSWORTHY, JOHN, 3937
Gambino, Richard. Blood of My Blood, 4823
Game Theory. Davis, Morton D, 1953
GAMES, 1940, 1953-1954, 3342, 3345
Games, Gods and Gambling. David, Florence N, 1951
Gamow, George. The Creation of the Universe, 1984
Gandhi, Indira. Indira Gandhi Speaks on Democracy, Socialism, and Third World Nonalignment, 5635
GANDHI, INDIRA NEHRU, 5631
Gandhi, Mohandas. Autobiography, 5632
GANDHI, MOHANDAS KARAMCHAND, 620, 898, 1180, 1245, 5632-5633
Gandhi's Rise to Power. Brown, Judith M, 1180
Gandhi's Truth. Erikson, Erik H, 1245
Gann, Ernest K. Ernest K. Gann's Flying Circus, 2720
Gannon, Robert. see Walsh, John
Garbage As You Like It. Goldstein, Jerome, 2705
García Lorca, Federico. Three Tragedies, 4355
GARCÍA LORCA, FEDERICO, 4341
García Lorca, Federico and Jimenez, Juan Ramon. Selected Poems, 4321

INDEX

GARDENING, 2788, 2790-2792
Gardening Without Poisons. Hunter, Beatrice T, 2784
Gardiner, Alan. Egypt of the Pharaohs, 4886
Gardiner, Edward N. Athletics of the Ancient World, 4957
Gardner, Eldon J. Principles of Genetics, 2293
Gardner, Ernest. Fundamentals of Neurology, 2506
Gardner, Helen. Art Through the Ages, 2895
Gardner, Howard. The Quest for Mind, 887
Gardner, John W. No Easy Victories, 1109
———. The Recovery of Confidence, 1108
———. Self-Renewal, 922
Gardner, Martin. Martin Gardner's Sixth Book of Mathematical Games from Scientific American, 3332
Gardner, Richard. The Baboon, 2480
Gardner, Weston D. and Osburn, William A. Structure of the Human Body, 2504
GARFIELD, JAMES ABRAM, 6090
Gargal, Berry. see Katz, William A.
Gargantua. Rabelais, François, 4241
GARIBALDI, 5438-5439, 5442
Garibaldi and His Enemies. Hibbert, Christopher, 5438
Garibaldi and the Making of Italy. Trevelyan, George M, 5442
Garmonsway, G. N., ed. The Anglo-Saxon Chronicle, 5182
Garraty, John A., ed. Quarrels That Have Shaped the Constitution, 1577
Garrett, Henry E. Great Experiments in Psychology, 565
Garrett, J. N., see Bailyn, Bernard
Garrett, John. Roger Williams, 6195
Garrity, Durin, ed. New Irish Poets, Anthology, 3778
Garten, H. F. Modern German Drama, 4028
Gary, Dorothy H. and Payne, Robert. Splendors of Asia, 4773
Gary, Romain. L' Education Européenne, 4213
Gaskell, G. A. Dictionary of All Scriptures and Myths, 118
Gassner, John and Quinn, Edward, eds. Reader's Encyclopedia of World Drama, 334
Gaster, Theodor H. Festivals of the Jewish Year, 1821
Gaston, Paul M. The New South Creed, 6207
Gastonguay, Paul R. Evolution for Everyone, 2279

Gasztold, Carmen B., ed. Prayers from the Ark, 4121
Gatell, Otto, see Weinstein, Allen
Gates, David. Type, 2866
Gates, Gary. see Rather, Dan
Gates of Horn. Levin, Harry, 4264
Gathering Pace. Larkin, Maurice, 5021
Gathering Storm; Their Finest Hour; The Grand Alliance; The Hinge of Fate; Closing the Ring; Triumph and Tragedy. Churchill, Winston L, 5098
Gatland, K. Manned Spacecraft 2768
———. Robot Explorers, 2755
Gattegno, Caleb. Towards a Visual Culture, 1773
Gatzke, Hans W. Germany's Drive to the West, 5081
Gaucho Martin Fierro. Hernandez, Jose, 4325
Gaunt, William. Restless Century, 3049
———. The Surrealists, 3033
Gaustad, Edwin S. Dissent in American Religion, 689
Gay, John. The Beggar's Opera, 3874
Gay, Peter, compiled by. The Enlightenment, 637
———. Weimar Culture, 5302
Gay World. Hoffman, Martin, 984
Gayley, Charles M. Classic Myths in English Literature and in Art, 826
Gaylin, Willard. In the Service of Their Country, 1673
Gedichte. Mittelhochdeutscher Text und Ubertragung. Vogelwiede, Walther Von Der, 4001
Geeler, Matthias. Caesar, 4936
Geiringer, Irene. see Geiringer, Karl
Geiringer, Karl. Haydn, 3167
Geiringer, Karl and Geiringer, Irene. Johann Sebastian Bach, 3158
Geiringer, Karl. Brahms, His Life and Work, 3168
Geismar, Peter. Fanon, 1229
Geiss, Immanuel, compiled by. July, Nineteen Fourteen, 5074
Gelb, Arthur. see Gelb, Barbara
Gelb, Barbara and Gelb, Arthur. O'Neill, 3677
Gelber, Jack. The Connection, 3692
Geldzahler, Henry. American Painting in the Twentieth Century, 3040
Gelfand, Louis and Heath, Harry E. Modern Sportswriting, 485
Gellman, Irwin F. Roosevelt and Batista, 1340
Gelpi, Albert J., compiled by. The Poet in America, 1650 to Present, 3549

INDEX

Gelzer, Mathias. The Roman Nobility, 4920
General Education in a Free Society. Harvard Committee, 1746
General George B. McClellan, Shield of the Union. Hassler, Warren W, 6054
General Zoology. Storer, Tracy I. and Usinger, Robert L. 2336
Generals in Gray. Warner, Ezra, 6052
Generation of Materialism. Hayes, Carlton J, 5055
Genes, Dreams and Realities. Burnet, MacFarlane, 2257
Genesis of a Painting. Arnheim, Rudolf, 3061
Genet, Jean. The Maids; Deathwatch, 4157
Genetic Engineering. Heintze, Carl, 2201
GENETICS, 2201, 2249, 2252, 2291-2301
Genetics. Kuspira, John and Walker, G. W. 2301
Genius of American Politics. Boorstin, Daniel J, 1189
Genius of the Italian Theatre. Bentley, Eric, ed, 4296
Genovese, Eugene D. Roll, Jordan, Roll, 6208
Gentleman Boss. Reeves, Thomas C, 6091
Gentleman from Ohio. Bates, Richard O, 6090
A Gentleman's Guide to Modern Physics. Thiemer, Otto H, 2021
Gentlemen of Property and Standing. Richards, Leonard L, 1225
GEOGRAPHY, 4679-4681
    DICTIONARIES, 383-384, 406, 417
    HISTORICAL — MAPS, 386
    POLITICAL, 4705
A Geography of the Bible. Baly, Denis A, 711
GEOLOGY, 1472, 2090-2095, 2098, 2100, 2103, 2105, 2108, 2111, 2115, 2123, 2161-2162, 2164, 2172-2173
    DICTIONARIES, 220-221, 223
Geology. Dunbar, Carl O. and Waage, Karl M. 2162
Geology Illustrated. Shelton, John S, 2098
Geology of the Grand Canyon. Breed, William J., ed, 2172
Geology of the Moon. Mutch, Thomas A, 2163
Geology, Resources, and Society. Menard, H. W, 2096
Geology Today. C R M Books Editorial Staff, 2091
Geomorphology. Ruhe, Robert V, 2124
GEOPHYSICS, 2112-2113, 2126
Georgano, George N. The Complete Encyclopedia of Motorcars, 2743
———. Transportation Through the Ages, 1793

GEORGE III, 5250
GEORGE V, 5173
George Bernard Shaw. Pearson, Hesketh, 3884
George Eliot. Redinger, Ruby V, 3929
George Frederic Handel. Lang, Paul H, 3174
George Gershwin. Goldberg, Isaac, 3169
George, Jean C. Everglades Wildguide, 2274
George Orwell. Atkins, John, 3936
George, Pierre. France, 1412
George Washington. Flexner, James T, 5970
George Washington's Opponents. Billias, George A., ed, 5951
Georgia O'Keefe. Goodrich, Lloyd and Bry, Doris. 3042
Georgian England. Richardson, Albert E, 4749
Geothe, Johann Wolfgang Von. Werke in Sechs Banden, 3974
Gerald Ford. Ter Horst, Jerald F, 6181
Gerald Ford and the Future of the Presidency. Ter Horst, Jerald F, 6180
Gerard Manley Hopkins. Ruggles, Eleanor, 3830
Gerin, Winifred. Charlotte Brontë, 3925
German-Americans. O'Connor Richard, 4836
German Army and the Nazi Party, 1933-1939. O'Neill, Robert J, 5322
German Dictatorship. Bracher, Karl D, 1395
GERMAN DRAMA, 4020, 4023, 4025-4031, 4033
GERMAN FICTION, 4071, 4075, 4077
GERMAN LANGUAGE, 178, 3982
German Lesson. Lenz, Siegfried, 4062
GERMAN LITERATURE, 373, 3973-3979
    COLLECTIONS, 3982
    HISTORY AND CRITICISM, 3983-3987, 3989-3993, 4076
GERMAN LITERATURE (EAST), 3988
GERMAN POETRY, 4000
    COLLECTIONS, 4002-4005
    HISTORY & CRITICISM, 4006-4008
GERMAN SHORT STORIES, 4072-4074
German Theater Today. Shaw, Leroy, ed, 4029
German Tradition. Adams, Marion, 4753
German Tradition in Literature, 1871-1945. Gray, Ronald D, 3985
GERMANY
    ARMY, 5307, 5322
    BIOGRAPHY, 5312
    FOREIGN RELATIONS, 1304-1305, 5073, 5449

INDEX

HISTORY, 1164, 5089, 5282, 5286, 5288, 5294, 5292-5300, 5302, 5304-5308, 5315-5319, 5321, 5323-5324, 5326-5327, 5330, 5333
    SOURCES, 5292, 5295
POLITICS AND GOVERNMENT, 1088, 1164, 1395, 1501, 5081, 5096, 5283, 5301, 5303-5304, 5306-5308, 5313, 5316, 5331
    SOCIAL CONDITIONS, 1088, 5313, 5319
Germany. Bailey, George, 5330
Germany. Reinhardt, Kurt F, 5288
Germany. Walton, Henry, 5336
Germany and the Approach of War in 1914. Berghahn, Volker R, 5096
GERMANY (DEMOCRATIC REPUBLIC, 1949-), 1163, 5332
GERMANY (FEDERAL REPUBLIC, 1949-), 5331, 5336
Germany's Aims in the First World War. Fischer, Fritz, 5073
Germany's Drive to the West. Gatzke, Hans W, 5081
Germinal. Zola, Émile, 4260
Geroi Nashego Vremeni. Lermontov, Mikhail Y, 4555
Geronimo. Geronimo, 5761
GERONIMO, APACHE CHIEF, 5761
Gershoy, Leo. The Era of the French Revolution, 1789 to 1793, 5393
———. The French Revolution and Napoleon, 5394
———. From Despotism to Revolution, 5033
GERSHWIN, GEORGE, 3169, 3213
GERSHWIN, IRA, 3213
Gershwin Years. Jablonski, Edward and Stewart, Lawrence D. 3213
Gerstenmaier, Cornelia. The Voices of the Silent, 4764
Gertrude. Hesse, Hermann, 4057
Gerzon, Mark. The Whole World Is Watching, 1110
Gesell, Arnold, et al. Youth, 545
GESTALT THERAPY, 2606
El Gesticulador. Usigli, Rodolfo, 4357
Getting Started in the Theater. Engel, Lehman, 3300
GHANA, 5726-5727
Ghar Parau. Judson, David M, 2129
Ghastly Good Taste, a Depressing Story of the Rise and Fall of English Architecture. Betjeman, John, 2967
GHENT, TREATY OF, 5988
Ghetto Revolts. Feagin, Joe R. and Hahn, H. 1073
Ghost of Stalin. Sartre, Jean-Paul, 5368
A Giant in the Earth. Katz, Robert, 1518

Giant Reptiles. Minton, Sherman A., Jr. and Minton, Madge R. 2413
Giants in the Sky. Robinson, Douglas H, 2736
Gibbons, Euell. Stalking the Far Away Places, 1901
———. Stalking the Good Life, 2321
———. Stalking the Healthful Herbs, 2320
Gibbons, Norman E. *see* Buchanan, Robert E.
Gibbs-Smith, Charles H. Bayeux Tapestry, 3022
———. Flight Through the Ages, 2711
———. The Invention of the Aeroplane, 1799-1909, 2712
Gibian, George and Samilov, M., eds. Modern Russian Short Stories, 4548
Gibran, Kahlil. The Prophet, 4595
———. A Treasury of Kahlil Gibran, 4596
Giddings, James L. Ancient Men of the Arctic, 4738
Gide, André, ed. Anthologie de la Poesie Francaise, 4138
———. L' Immoraliste, 4214
———. La Porte Étroite, 4215
———. Si le Grain Ne Meurt, 4216
———. La Symphonie Pastorale, 4217
GIDE, ANDRÉ, 4218
Gideon Welles. Niven, John, 6034
Gierioff-Emden, H. G. *see* Bodechtel, J.
Gies, Francis. *see* Gies, Joseph
Gies, Joseph and Gies, Francis. Life in a Medieval Castle, 4999
Giese, Frank S. and Wilder, W. F., eds. French Lyric Poetry, 4122
Gifts of an Eagle. Durden, Kent, 2440
Gil Blas. Le Sage, Alain-René, 4226
Gilbert and Sullivan. Baily, Leslie, 3210
Gilbert, Arthur. A Jew in Christian America, 1059
Gilbert, Felix. The End of the European Era, 1890 to the Present, 1084
Gilbert, Felix, *see* Craig, Gordon A.
Gilbert, Marilyn B. *see* Gilbert, Thomas F.
Gilbert, Martin. Atlas of the Arab-Israeli Conflict, 389
———. First World War History Atlas, 402
Gilbert, Rod and Park, Brad. Playing Hockey the Professional Way, 3413
GILBERT, (SIR) WILLIAM SCHWENELE, 3210
Gilbert Stuart. Whitley, William T, 3048
Gilbert, Thomas F. and Gilbert, Marilyn B. Thinking Metric, 1808
Gilbert, William S. Savoy Operas, 3878
Gilded Age. Morgan, H. Wayne, 6072
Gilded Age, 1877-1896. De Santis, Vincent P, 77

Gill, Don and Bonnett, Penelope. Nature in the Urban Landscape, 2240
Gillespie, John T. and Spirt, Diana L. Creating a School Media Program, 35
Gilliard, Thomas E. Living Birds of the World, 2425
Gilluly, James, et al. Principles of Geology, 2094
Gilmore, Myron P. The World of Humanism, 5028
Gilroy, Frank. The Subject Was Roses, and About Those Roses, 3693
Gilson, Etienne. The Christian Philosophy of Saint Augustine, 610
Gimbel, John. American Occupation of Germany, 5333
Ginsberg, Allen. Howl, and Other Poems, 3640
―――. Reality Sandwiches, 1953-1960, 3641
GINSBERG, ALLEN, 3646
Ginzberg, Louis. The Legends of the Jews, 854
Giovanni, Nikki. My House, 3642
GIPSIES, 4682
Gipson, Lawrence H. Coming of the Revolution, 5899
Gipsy Moth Circles the World. Chichester, Francis, 4691
Giraudoux, Jean. Amphitryon, 4158
―――. La Folle de Chaillot, 4159
―――. Four Plays, 4162
―――. La Guerre de Troi n'aura Pas Lieu, 4160
―――. Intermezzo, 4161
GIRAUDOUX, JEAN, 4168
Girdner, Audrie and Loftis, Anne. The Great Betrayal, 1063
Girling, J. L. People's War, 1186
Girls and Sex. Pomeroy, Wardell B, 2521
Gironella, José María. Los Cipreses Creen en Dios, 4377
Gitler, Ira. Jazz Masters of the '40's, 3189
Gittings, John, ed. Survey of the Sino-Soviet Dispute, 1316
Giulianos, William. see De Luca, A. Michael
Giuseppe Garibaldi. Larg, David G, 5439
GLACIAL EPOCH, 2165-2166
GLACIERS, 2166
Glad, Paul, ed. The Dissonance of Change, 1919 to the Present, 1111
―――. McKinley, Bryan and the People, 6093
GLADIATORS, 4921
Gladiators. Grant, Michael, 4921
Gladstone, M. J. A Carrot for a Nose, 2985
Glass Bead Game. Hesse, Hermann, 4058

Glass Menagerie. Williams, Tennessee, 3709
Glassman, Ronald. Political History of Latin America, 1204
Glasstone, Samuel. Sourcebook on Atomic Energy, 2059
Glatzer, Nahum N., ed. Hammer on the Rock, 856
Glazer, Nathan. American Judaism, 852
Glazer, Nathan and Moyihan, Daniel P. Beyond the Melting Pot, 1022
Gleason, Judith I. This Africa, 4632
Gleason, S. E. see Langer, William L.
Gleazer, Edmund J., Jr., ed. American Junior Colleges, 148
Glemser, Bernard. Man Against Cancer, 2617
Glenn, Harold T. see Coles, Clarence W.
Glenn's Complete Bicycle Manual. Coles, Clarence W. and Glenn, Harold T. 2746
Glick, H. R., see Atkins, Burton M.
GLIDERS (AERONAUTICS), 2723
GLIDING AND SOARING, 2723, 3440-3443
GLM. Taylor, Clif, 3418
Globe Playhouse. Adams, John C, 3318
GLOBE THEATRE, 3870
Glock, Charles I. and Siegelman, Ellen. Prejudice, U. S, 1005
Gloria. Pérez Galdós, Benito, 4381
Glory and the Dream. Manchester, William, 6140
Glory, God and Gold. Wellman, Paul I, 6243
Glory of the Pharaohs. Weigall, Arthur E, 4897
A Glossary of Literary Terms. Abrams, Meyer H, 331
Gloucester, Richard. Face of London, 4747
Glubb, John. The Life and Times of Muhammad, 863
Glut, Donald F. The Dinosaur Dictionary, 228
Glyn, Andrew and Sutcliffe, Bob. Capitalism in Crisis, 1528
Go Ask Alice. Anonymous, 2545
GO (GAME), 3339
Goalie's Anxiety at the Penalty Kick. Handke, Peter, 4054
GOD, 700, 743-745, 747
God Incognito. Schilling, Sylvester P, 700
God Save This Honorable Court. Kohlmeier, Louis M, 1608
God Was in Christ. Baillie, Donald M, 748
Godden, Rumer. Hans Christian Andersen, 4083
Godoy Alcayaga, Lucilla. Selected Poems of Gabriela Mistral, 4322

INDEX

God's Dog. Ryden, Hope, 2472
Gods from Outer Space. Von Daniken, Erich, 473
Gods, Graves and Scholars. Ceram, C. W, 4710
God's Own Junkyard. Blake, Peter, 2950
Gods Trombones. Johnson, James W, 3603
Goebbels. Heiber, Helmut, 5314
GOEBBELS, JOSEPH, 5314
Goebel, Dorothy B. William Henry Harrison, 6000
Goerner, Edward A., ed. Constitutions of Europe, 1559
Goethe. Wilkinson, Elizabeth M. and Willoughby, Leonard. 4079
Goethe, Johann Wolfgang Von. Faust, 4016
———. Poems, 3995
GOETHE, JOHANN WOLFGANG VON, 4079
Goetz, Hermann. The Art of India, 2935
Gogol, Nikolai V. The Collected Tales and Plays, 4576
———. Mertvye Dushi, 4549
———. Revizor, 4531
———. Shinel', 4550
Gohdes, Clarence L. Bibliographical Guide to the Study of the Literature of the U. S. A, 66
———. Literature and Theatre of the States and Regions of the U. S. A., 69
Goin, Coleman J. and Goin, Olive B. Man and the Natural World, 2213
Goin, Coleman J. see Cochran, Doris M.
Goin, Olive B. see Goin, Coleman J.
Goldberg, Isaac. George Gershwin, 3169
Goldberg, Nathan. New Functional Hebrew-English, English-Hebrew Dictionary, 190
Golden Age of Sound Comedy. McCaffrey, Donald W, 3279
Golden Bough. Frazer, James G, 825
Golden Century of Spain, 1501-1621. Davies, R. Trevor, 5463
Golden, Frederic. The Moving Continents, 2125
Golden Land. Onís, Harriet de, ed, 4306
Golden Mean. Linn, Charles F, 2872
Golden Sea. Brown, Joseph E, 2133
Golden Shadows, Flying Hooves. Schaller, George B, 2467
Golden Tradition. Dawidowicz, Lucy S, 4901
Goldfarb, Ronald L. After Conviction, 1729
GOLDING, WILLIAM, 3952, 3968
Goldman, Eric F. The Crucial Decade and After, 6150
———. Rendezvous with Destiny, 6068

———. The Tragedy of Lyndon Johnson, 6170
Goldman, Marshall I. Ecology and Economics, 1526
Goldman, Peter L. The Death and Life of Malcolm X, 1152
Goldoni, Carlo. Three Comedies, 4293
Goldsby, R. A. Race and Races, 2188
Goldsmith, Oliver. She Stoops to Conquer, 3875
Goldstein, Jerome. Garbage As You Like It, 2705
Goldstine, Herman H. The Computer from Pascal to Von Neumann, 2647
GOLF, 3367-3370
Golf Immortals. Scott, Tom and Cousins, Geoffrey. 3370
Golf Magazine. Golf Magazine's Encyclopedia of Golf, 3368
Golf Magazine's Encyclopedia of Golf. Golf Magazine, 3368
GOLIARDS, 4403
Golob, Eugene O. The Isms, 894
Golway, Frank H., et al. Underdevelopment and Economic Nationalism in Southeast Asia, 1534
Gombrich, Ernst H. Art and Illusion, 2876
———. Story of Art, 2896
Gomulka. Bethell, Nicholas, 5360
GOMULKA, WLADYSLAW, 5360
Goncharov, Ivan. Oblomov., 4551
Gongora, Luis de. Obras Completas, 4323
Good Fight. Chisholm, Shirley, 1193
Good Fight. Quezon, Manuel L, 5691
Good, Harry G. and Teller, James D. A History of American Education, 1761
Good Times. Joseph, Peter, 6172
Goodall, Norman. Ecumenical Progress, 778
Goodbye Mr. Christian. Dougherty, Richard, 1380
Goodbye to Bedlam. Langone, John, 2602
Gooders, John. see Hoskins, Eric
Goodman, Walter. The Committee, 1362
Goodrich, L. Carrington. A Short History of the Chinese People, 5578
Goodrich, Lloyd. Winslow Homer, 3041
Goodrich, Lloyd and Bry, Doris. Georgia O'Keefe, 3042
Goodrum, Charles A. The Library of Congress, 476
Goodwin, Richard N. The American Condition, 1112
Goodyear, Frank. Archaeological Site Science, 4713
Goran, Morris. Science and Anti-Science, 1893
Gordon, Arnold J. and Ford, Richard A. The Chemist's Companion, 218
Gordon, Colin D. The Age of Attila, 5012

INDEX

Gordon, Ernest. Through the Valley of the Kwai, 5148
Gore ot Uma. Griboyedov, Aleksandr, 4533
Goren, Charles H. Goren's Modern Backgammon Complete, 3343
Goren's Modern Backgammon Complete. Goren, Charles H, 3343
Gorky, Maxim. Lower Depths and Other Plays, 4532
———. Moi Universitety, 4577
GORKY, MAXIM, 4534
Gorz, Andre. Socialism and Revolution, 1483
Gossman, Lionel. Men and Masks, 4163
Gottfried Benn Dargestellt von Walter Lennig. Benn, Gottfried, 3994
Gottschalk, Louis. Lafayette and the Close of the American Revolution, 5934
———. Understanding History, 4665
Gould, Heywood. Sir Christopher Wren, 2965
Gould-Adams, Richard J. John Foster Dulles, 6164
Governing Urban America. Adrian, Charles R. and Press, Charles. 1627
Government and Politics of Ireland. Chubb, Basil, 1161
Government of Republican Italy. Adams, John C. and Barile, Paolo. 1167
Governments of Communist East Europe. Skilling, H. Gordon, 1159
GOYA Y LUCIENTES, FRANCISCO, 3063
Graf, Rudolf F. and Whalen, George J. How It Works, 2629
GRAFFITI — U. S., 465
Graham, Alexander. Roman Africa, 4985
Graham, Alistair. Eyelids of Morning, 2421
Graham, Frank, Jr. Since Silent Spring, 2781
Graham, Gene S. One Man, One Vote, 1578
Graham, Hugh D., et al, eds. Violence, 881
Graham, Hugh D. and Gurr, Ted R. The History of Violence in America, 882
GRAHAM, MARTHA, 3329
Graham, Winston. The Spanish Armadas. 5219
Grand Incendiary. Lewis, Paul, 5936
Grand Larousse Encyclopedique. Larousse Editors, 83
Grand Prix. Hayward, Elizabeth, 3406
GRAND PRIX RACING, 3406
Grand Strategy. Collins, John M, 1666
Grand Tetons. Norton, Boyd, 1905
Grandees. Birmingham, Stephen, 4864
Grandma Moses. Kallir, Otto, 3045

Les Grands Auteurs Français Du Programme. Lagarde, André and Michard, Laurent. 4109
Granger, Edith. Granger's Index to Poetry, 332
Granger's Index to Poetry. Granger, Edith, 332
Grant, Joanne, ed. Black Protest, 1256
GRANT, JULIA DENT, 6087
Grant, Michael. Army of the Caesars, 4937
———. Cities of Vesuvius, 4730
———. Cleopatra, 4887
———. Gladiators, 4921
———. Roman History from Coins, 2999
———. The World of Rome, 4942
Grant, Robert M. Augustus to Constantine, 805
Grant, Ulysses S. Personal Memoirs, 6069
GRANT, ULYSSES SIMPSON, 6069
Grants. White, Virginia P, 460
GRAPHIC ARTS, 3005, 3009, 3086
Graphic Communication. Bowman, William J, 3005
Graphs, Models, and Finite Mathematics. Malkevitch, Joseph and Meyer, Walter. 1938
GRASS, GÜNTER, 4081
Grass, Günther. Cat and Mouse, 4051
———. Local Anesthetic, 4052
———. Tin Drum, 4053
Grattan, C. Hartley. Southwest Pacific, 6281
Graves, Richard. Bushcraft, 2533
Graves, Robert. Greek Myths, 827
———. The White Goddess, a Historical Grammar of Poetic Myth, 3525
Graves, Robert and Hodge, Alan. The Long Week-End, 5272
GRAVITATION, 2028
Gray, Asa. Manual of Botany, 234
Gray, Henry. Gray's Anatomy of the Human Body, 250
Gray, Michael. Song and Dance Man, 3230
Gray, Peter. Encyclopedia of Microscopy and Micro-Technique, 200
———. The Encyclopedia of the Biological Sciences, 229
Gray, Ronald D. German Tradition in Literature, 1871-1945, 3985
———. Introduction to German Poetry, 4007
Gray, Thomas. Complete Poems of Thomas Gray, 3803
Gray's Anatomy of the Human Body. Gray, Henry, 250
Grayson, Cary R. and Lukowski, Susan, eds. The Impeachment Congress, 1363
Grayson, Melvin J. and Shepard, Thomas R. The Disaster Lobby, 944

INDEX

Graziella and Raphael. Lamartine, Alphonse de, 4225
Great Ages of Man. 5692
Great American Forest. Platt, Rutherford, 4798
Great American Popular Singers. Pleasants, Henry, 3223
Great Barrier Reef. Bennett, Isobel, 2276
Great Betrayal. Girdner, Audrie and Loftis, Anne. 1063
Great Bridge. McCullough, David, 2693
GREAT BRITAIN
    CIVILIZATION, 1087, 4748, 5231
    COLONIES, 5261, 5270, 5733, 6193
    DESCRIPTION AND TRAVEL — GUIDEBOOKS, 4751
    ECONOMIC CONDTIONS, 1085, 1410-1411, 1528
    EMIGRATION AND IMMIGRATION, 5237
    FOREIGN RELATIONS, 1302-1303, 5233, 5102, 5721, 5987
    HISTORY, 5170-5277
    KINGS AND RULERS, 5174
    POLITICS AND GOVERNMENT, 1085, 1087, 1359, 1560, 1652, 5207, 5193, 5216, 5223, 5239, 5268
    SOCIAL CONDITIONS, 765, 1086, 1411, 5177, 5229, 5241
    SOCIAL LIFE AND CUSTOMS, 5211, 5242, 5272
Great Britain Since 1688. Smellie, K. B, 5175
Great Britain to 1688. Ashley, Maurice P, 5170
Great Composers. Ewen, David, ed, 300
Great Conductors. Schonberg, Harold C, 306
Great Contemporaries. Churchill, Winston L, 4861
Great Crash, 1929. Galbraith, John Kenneth, 1530
Great Depression. Shannon, David A., ed, 1458
Great Dirigibles. Toland, John, 1806
Great Dissenters. Thomas, Norman M, 4862
Great English and American Essays. Mead, Douglas S., ed, 3516
Great Experiments in Psychology. Garrett, Henry E, 565
Great Films. Crowther, Bosley, 3269
Great Hunger. Woodham-Smith, Cecil B, 1513
Great Monkey Trial. DeCamp, L. Sprague, 1591
Great Museums of the World. 3080
Great Narrative Essays. Mersand, Joseph, ed, 3746
Great Orm of Loch Ness. Holiday, F. W, 2373
Great Philosophers. Jaspers, Karl, 516
Great Plains. Webb, Walter P, 6241
Great Political Thinkers. Ebenstein, William, 1128
Great Psychologists. Watson, Robert I, 567
Great Range Wars. Drago, Harry S, 6232
Great Religions of the World. Smith, Huston, et al, eds. 830
Great Reversals. Ernst, Morris, 1607
Great Riots of New York, 1712-1873. Headley, Joel Tyler, 1248
Great Slave Narratives. Bontemps, Arna, ed, 1055
Great Terror. Conquest, Robert, 5512
Great Turning Points in History. Snyder, Louis L, 4673
Great War Between Athens and Sparta. Henderson, Bernard W, 4972
Great War. Falls, Cyril, 5069
Great War, 1914-1918. Ferro, Marc, 5070
Great White Hope. Sackler, Howard, 3703
A Greater Than Napoleon. Liddell Hart, Basil H, 4931
Greatest Depths. Soule, Gardner, 2145
Greatness That Was Babylon. Saggs, H. W, 4915
GREECE
    ANTIQUITIES, 4732, 4955, 4958
    ARMY, 1654
    CIVILIZATION, 4460, 4954, 5004
    ECONOMIC CONDITIONS, 4977
    HISTORY, 4953, 4956, 4959, 4962, 4965, 4967-4968, 4970-4973, 4975, 4977-4978, 4982
    RELIGION, 832-833
Greece. Simpson, Colin, 4769
GREECE, MODERN
    HISTORY, 1397, 5549, 5553-5554
    POLITICS AND GOVERNMENT, 1172
Greece Without Columns. Holden, David, 5554
Greek and Macedonian Art of War. Adcock, Frank E, 1654
GREEK DRAMA, 4446, 4448-4449, 4451, 4453, 4455-4456, 4458-4459
GREEK DRAMA (COMEDY), 4445
GREEK DRAMA (TRAGEDY), 4447, 4454
Greek-English Lexicon. Liddell, Henry G. and Scott, Robert, eds. 187
Greek Experience. Bowra, Cecil M, 4952

GREEK HISTORIANS, 4969
GREEK LANGUAGE — DICTIONARIES, 187
GREEK LITERATURE
    COLLECTIONS, 4435-4436
    DICTIONARIES, 410
    HISTORY AND CRITICISM, 4434, 4437-4441, 4452
Greek Literature in Translation. Oates, Whitney J. and Murphy, C. T., eds. 4436
Greek Myths. Graves, Robert, 827
Greek Philosophy. Allen, Reginald E., ed, 510
Greek Plays in Modern Translation. Fitts, Dudley, ed, 4447
GREEK POETRY,
    COLLECTIONS, 4442
    HISTORY AND CRITICISM, 4443-4444
Greek Religious Thought from Homer to the Age of Alexander. Cornford, Francis M, 832
Greek Stones Speak. MacKendrick, Paul, 4732
Greek Tragedy. Kitto, Humphrey D, 4455
Greek View of Life. Dickinson, G. Lowes, 4954
Greek Way. Hamilton, Edith, 4440
Greeks. Kitto, Humphrey D, 4959
GREELEY, HORACE, 6042
Green Flag. Kee, Robert, 5166
Green, Harold P. see Stern, Philip M.
Green, Peter. Ancient Greece, 4958
Green Shirts and the Others. Nagy-Talavera, Nicholas M, 5365
Green, Stanley. World of Musical Comedy, 3212
Green Treasures. Wilson, Charles M, 2323
Green, Vivian H. The Hanoverians, 1714-1815, 5249
Greenbank, Anthony. The Book of Survival, 2534
Greenberg, Jerry. The Living Reef, 2264
Greenberg, M. see Plano, J. C.
Greenberg, Noah, et al, eds. Anthology of Elizabethan Lute Songs, Madrigals and Rounds, 3233
———. Anthology of English Medieval and Renaissance Vocal Music, 3234
Greene, David H. An Anthology of Irish Literature, 4492
Greene, Evarts B. The Revolutionary Generation, 1763-1790, 5900
Greenfield, J. see Newfield, Jack
Greenhouse Gardening. Northen, Henry T. and Northen, Rebecca T. 2802
Greenhouse, Herbert B. see Woods, Ralph L.

Greenwald, Douglas. The McGraw-Hill Dictionary of Modern Economics, 138
Greenwood, David. Mapping, 2013
Greenwood, Val D. Researcher's Guide to American Genealogy, 4872
Greer, Germaine. The Female Eunich, 977
———. Once Upon a Pedestal, 978
Gregoe, Ian. see Kinkead-Weekes, Mark
Gregor, Arthur. Bell Laboratories, 2643
Gregor Mendel. Sootin, Harry, 2300
Gregory, Isabella A. Seven Short Plays, 3883
GREGORY, ISABELLA AUGUSTA, 3894
Gregory, Mary. see Ary, Sheila
Greiner, James D. Wager with the Wind, 2713
Greisheimer, Esther M. see Chaffee, Ellen E.
Grene, David and Lattimore, Richmond. Complete Greek Tragedies, 4448
Grey, Ian. The Horizon History of Russia, 5483
Gribbin, John R. and Plagemann, Stephen H. The Jupiter Effect, 2115
Griboyedov, Aleksandr. Gore ot Uma, 4533
Gridley, Marion E. American Indian Women, 5750
Grierson, Edward. King of Two Worlds, 5464
Griffin, G. G. see Bemis, Samuel F.
Griffith, Ernest S. Congress, 1364
Griffith, Field. see Lowry, Peter
Griffith, Robert. A Politics of Fear, 6160
Griffiths, Richard, ed. Claudel, 4274
Grillparzer, Franz. Werke, 4017
Grimm Brothers. Fairy Tales, 1844
Grimsley, Ronald. Kierkegaard, 677
Grinshaw, Allen D. Racial Violence in the United States, 1723
Grinspoon, Lester. Marihuana Reconsidered, 2542
Grinspoon, Lester and Hedblom, Peter. The Speed Culture, 2579
Grohskopf, Bernice, ed. The Treasure of Sutton Hoo, 5183
Gross, Maurice. Mathematical Models in Linguistics, 1858
Gross, Theodore L. Literature of the American Jews, 3536
Grossinger, Richard and Hough, Lindy. Alchemy, 2074
Grossman, Mary L. and Hamlet, John N. Our Vanishing Wilderness, 2273
Grossvogel, D. E. Twentieth Century French Drama, 4187
Grotowski, Jerzy, ed. Towards a Poor Theatre, 3293
Groueff, Stephen. Manhattan Project, 2668

INDEX

GROUND EFFECT MACHINES, 2754
Groundwork of Christian Ethics. Robinson, Norman H, 756
Group Portrait with Lady. Boll, Heinrich, 4037
Grout, Donald J. A History of Western Music, 3136
———. A Short History of Opera, 3203
Grove, Alfred T. Africa South of the Sahara, 5698
Grove, George. Dictionary of Music and Musicians, 301
Grover Cleveland. Nevins, Allan, 6092
Grow It Indoors. Langer, Richard W, 2796
Growing Up in College. Heath, Douglas, 1743
Growing up Puerto Rican. Cooper, Paulette, ed, 4822
Growth and Structure of the English Language. Jespersen, Otto, 1867
Growth of American Thought. Curti, Merle E, 5858
Growth of Constitutional Power in the United States. Swieker, Carl B, 1587
Growth of Southern Civilization. Eaton, Clement, 6202
Growth of the American Republic. Morison, Samuel E., et al. 5867
Grube, Ernst J. Classical Style in Islamic Painting, 2889
Grunberger, Richard. The Twelve Year Reich, 5313
Grunfeld, Frederic V. Music, 3137
Grunwald, Ernest and Johnsen, Russell H. Atoms, Molecules, and Chemical Change, 2075
Grzimek, Bernhard. Grzimek's Animal Life Encyclopedia, 238
Grzimek's Animal Life Encyclopedia. Grzimek, Bernhard, 238
Guerard, Albert J. Andre Gidé, 4218
Guerard, Albert L. France, 5371
———. French Civilization from Its Origins to the Close of the Middle Ages, 5375
———. French Civilization in the 19th Century, 5381
Guerilla Theatre. Weisman, John, 3297
Guerney, Bernard G., ed. Anthology of Russian Literature in the Soviet Period from Gorki to Pasternak, 4494
———. The Portable Russian Reader, 4495
———. Treasury of Russian Literature, 4496
La Guerre de Troi n'aura Pas Lieu. Giraudoux, Jean, 4160
GUERRILLA WARFARE, 6275
Guest for the Night. Agnon, Shmuel Y, 4587

Guevara, Ché. Complete Bolivian Diaries of Ché Guevara, and Other Captured Documents, 6275
———. Episodes of the Revolutionary War, 1246
———. Reminiscences of the Cuban Revolutionary War, 5832
GUEVARA, ERNESTO (CHÉ), 1247, 6264, 6275
Guggisberg, C. A. Crocodiles, 2422
———. Wild Cats of the World, 2466
Guicciardini, Francesco. The History of Italy, 5432
Guide de Ideés Littéraires. Benac, H, 4104
Guide to American Literature and Its Backgrounds Since 1890. Jones, Howard M. and Ludwig, Richard M. 354
A Guide to Ancient Maya Ruins. Hunter, C. Bruce, 4803
A Guide to Aquarium Fishes and Plants. Schiotz, Arne, 2820
A Guide to Artifacts of Colonial America. Noel Hume, Ivor, 4814
A Guide to Contemporary French Literature. Fowlie, Wallace, 4108
Guide to Mathematics for the Intelligent Nonmathematician. Berkeley, Edmund C, 1928
Guide to Microforms in Print. Diaz, A. J, 27
Guide to Reference Books for School Media Centers. Wynar, Christine L, 1
Guide to Reference Sources in the Computer Sciences. Carter, Ciel M, 56
Guide to the Diplomatic History of the United States (1775-1921) Bemis, Samuel F. and Griffin, G. G. 76
A Guide to the National Parks. Matthews, William H, 1472
A Guide to the Study of Environmental Pollution. Andrews, W, 2706
A Guide to the Study of the United States of America. U. S. Library of Congress, 80
GUIDED MISSILES, 1684, 1686
Guidelines for News Reporters. Robinson, Sol, 484
Guideposts to the Stars. Peltier, Leslie C, 1981
Guidiol, Jose. El Greco, 3062
Guillaume, Alfred. Islam, 864
Guillén, Jorge. Cantico, 4324
Guinagh, Kevin, ed. Dictionary of Foreign Phrases and Abbreviations, 156
Guinagh, Kevin and Dorjahn, Alfred P., eds. Latin Literature in Translation, 4395
Guinness Book of World Records. McWhirter, Norris and McWhirter, Ross, eds. 477

INDEX

Guinness Sports Record Book. 318
Guiraldes, Ricardo. Don Segundo Sombra, 4378
Guiton, Margaret. *see* Brée, Germaine
Gulag Archipelago, 1918-1956. Solzhenitsyn, Aleksandr I, 1733
GULF STREAM, 2149
Gullick, J. M. Malaysia and Its Neighbors, 5676
GULLS, 2434
Gunner's Bible. Riviere, William A, 3460
Guns of August. Tuchman, Barbara W, 5088
Gunston, Bill. *see* Howard, Frank
Gunston, William T. Hydrofoils and Hovercraft, 2754
Günter Grass. Tank, Kurt L, 4081
Gunther, John. Death Be Not Proud, 2618
GUNTHER, JOHN, 2618
Gupta, Hari R. History of the Sikh Gurus, 850
Guralnick, Peter. Feel Like Going Home, 3249
Gurko, Leo. Two Lives of Joseph Conrad, 3941
Gurko, Miriam. Ladies of Seneca Falls, 979
Gurr, Ted R. Why Men Rebel, 906
Gurr, Ted R. *see* Graham, Hugh D.
Gustafson, Alrik. Six Scandinavian Novelists, 4086
Gustav Mahler. Mahler, Alma, 3176
GUTENBURG, JOHANN, 2865
Gutierrez de Lara, Lazaro. The Mexican People, 5813
Gutman, Robert W. Richard Wagner, 3170
Guy, Maxine. *see* Hickman, Mae
Gymnastic Routines for Men. Vincent, William, 3381
GYMNASTICS, 3379, 3381

H. G. Wells, His Turbulent Life and Times. Dickson, Lovat, 3938
Haac, Oscar A., et al. Points de Vue, 4101
Habgood, Noel. Heritage of Wales, 5278
Habitable Earth. Fraser, Ronald, 2093
HABSBURG, HOUSE OF, 5039, 5339, 5343
Habsburgs. Crankshaw, Edward, 5339
Hacker, Andrew. The End of the American Era, 928
Hacker, Louis M. The Course of American Economic Growth and Development, 1418
———. Major Documents in American Economic History, 1419
Hacker, Louis M. and Kendrick, Benjamin B. The United States Since 1865, 6102
Hackett, Earl. Blood, 2515
Hadas, Moses. A History of Greek Literature, 4438
———. A History of Latin Literature, 4398
———. Imperial Rome, 4943
Haddad, William F. and Pugh, G. Douglas, eds. Black Economic Development, 1420
Hadlock, Richard. Jazz Masters of the '20's, 3190
Haffenden, Philip S. New England in the English Nation, 1689-1713, 6193
Haftman, Werner. Chagall, 3067
Haggin, B. H. A Decade of Music, 3138
Hahn, Emily. On the Side of the Apes, 2476
Hahn, H. *see* Feagin, Joe R.
Haight, Anne L. Banned Books, 506
HAIKU, 3669, 4613-4614
Haiku Anthology. Van Den Heuvel, Cor, ed, 3669
Haimson, Leopold. The Russian Marxists and the Origins of Bolshevism, 1488
Haines, Francis. Horses in America, 2806
HAITI — HISTORY, 5824, 5847-5850
Haiti and the Dominican Republic. Logan, Rayford W, 5850
Haitian People. Leyburn, James G, 5848
Haitian Revolution, 1789-1804. Ott, Thomas, 5849
Hakluyt, Richard. Portable Hakluyt's Voyages, 4695
Halacy, D. S., Jr. The Coming Age of Solar Energy, 2662
———. Social Man, 892
Halberstam, David. The Best and the Brightest, 6165
———. Ho, 5682
———. The Making of a Quagmire, 5678
Hale, Hugh M. Passing of the Black Kings, 5735
Hale, John R. Machiavelli and Renaissance Italy, 5436
Halecki, Oscar. Borderlands of Western Civilization, 5285
Haley, Alex. *see* Malcolm X
Haley, Nelson C. Whale Hunt, 2816
Half-Century of Conflict. Parkman, Francis, 5906
Hall, Alan. The Wild Food Trailguide, 2322
Hall, Daniel G. Burma, 5675
Hall, Donald. Marianne Moore, 3572
Hall, Douglas K. Let 'er Buck!, 3289
Hall, Edward T. The Silent Language, 919
Hall, John W., et al, eds. Studies in the Institutional History of Early Modern Japan, 5615
Hall, Marie-Louise Michaud and Michaud, C. Regis. Lectures Classiques et Modernes, 4097
Hall, Richard S. Stanley, 4794

INDEX

Hall, Vernon, Jr. A Short History of Literary Criticism, 3465
Hallam, A. A Revolution in the Earth Sciences, 2116
Halle, Louise J. The Sea and the Ice, 2353
Hallett, Robin. Africa Since 1875, 5711
———. Africa to 1875, 5712
Halliwell, Leslie. The Filmgoer's Companion, 313
Hallmark Cards Editors. see Myers, Robert J.
Hallmundson, Hallberg, ed. An Anthology of Scandinavian Literature, from the Viking Period to the Twentieth Century, 4087
HALLUCINOGENIC DRUGS AND RELIGIOUS EXPERIENCE, 874-875
Halpern, Ben. The Idea of the Jewish State, 5664
HALS, FRANS, 3072
Hamblin, Dora J. The Appian Way, 4758
Hamburger, Michael, see Middleton, Christopher
Hamby, Alonzo L. Beyond the New Deal, 6151
Hamilton, Alexander, et al. Federalist, 1579
HAMILTON, ALEXANDER, 1349, 5962, 5969
Hamilton, Charles V. see Carmichael, Stokely
Hamilton, Edith. Echo of Greece, 4439
———. The Greek Way, 4440
———. Mythology, 828
———. Roman Way, 4399
Hamlet, John N. see Grossman, Mary L.
Hammarskjold, Dag. Markings, 4092
Hammer on the Rock. Glatzer, Nahum N., ed, 856
Hammer, Richard. The Court Martial of Lt. Calley, 1595
Hammerstein, Oscar, 2nd. see Rodgers, Richard
Hammerstein, Oscar, 3rd. see Rodgers, Richard
Hammond, Allen, et al. Energy and the Future, 2634
Hammond, Bray. Banks and Politics in America, 1452
Hammond, Geoffrey F. Showdown at Newport, 3428
Hampden, John, compiled by. Francis Drake, Privateer, 4696
Hampden-Turner, Charles. From Poverty to Dignity, 1702
Hampel, Clifford A. and Hawley, Gessner C., eds. Encyclopedia of Chemistry, 216
Hampson, Norman. A Cultural History of the Enlightenment, 638

Hancock, Roger N. Twentieth Century Ethics, 603
Hancocks, David. Master Builders of the Animal World, 2363
Hand and Rod Puppets. Fettig, Hansjurgen, 3286
Hand of a Thousand Rings and Other Chinese Stories. Bachmann, Robert, 4606
HANDBELL RINGING, 3252
Handbook of American Idioms and Idiomatic Usage. Whitford, Harold C. and Dixson, Robert J. 171
Handbook of Chemistry and Physics. 217
Handbook of Classical Drama. Harsh, Philip W, 4452
Handbook of Denominations in the United States. Mead, Frank S, 802
Handbook of Feasts and Customs. Weiser, Francis X, 114
Handbook of Greek Art. Richter, Gisela M, 2920
Handbook of Greek Literature. Rose, Herbert J, 4441
Handbook of Latin Literature. Rose, Herbert J, 4400
Handbook of Physics. Condon, Edward W. and Odishaw, H. 214
Handbook of Pseudonyms and Personal Nicknames. Sharp, Harold S, 431
Handbook of Tables for Mathematics. 208
HANDEL, GEORGE FREIDRICH, 3174
Handford, James H. A Milton Handbook, 3798
A Handful of Rice. Markandaya, Kamala, 4482
HANDICRAFT, 2828, 2854, 3012, 3019-3020, 4832-4834
Handke, Peter. Goalie's Anxiety at the Penalty Kick, 4054
Handler, Philip, ed. Biology and the Future of Man, 2214
Handlin, Oscar. Children of the Uprooted, 1277
———. Immigration As a Factor in American History, 1278
———. Race and Nationality in American Life, 1023
———. The Uprooted, 1279
Handmade Houses. Boericke, Art and Shapiro, Barry. 2978
Hands on the Past. Ceram, C. W., ed, 4711
Hane, Mikiso. Japan, 5616
Hang Gliding. Dedera, Don, 3441
Hang Gliding, the Basic Handbook of Skysurfing. Poynter, Dan, 3442
Hangen, Welles. The Muted Revolution, 1163

Hanna, Alfred J. and Hanna, Kathryn A. Napoleon Third and Mexico, 5815
Hanna, Kathryn A. *see* Hanna, Alfred J.
Hannan, Hans, et al. In the Coral Reefs of the Caribbean, Bahamas, Florida, Bermuda, 2265
Hannan, Hans W. Islands of the Caribbean, 4801
HANNIBAL — CROSSING OF THE ALPS, 218 B.C., 4932
Hannibal's March in History. Proctor, Dennis, 4932
Hanover to Windsor. Fulford, Roger, 5173
Hanoverians, 1714-1815. Green, Vivian H, 5249
Hans Christian Andersen. Godden, Rumer, 4083
Hans, Nicholas. The Russian Tradition in Education, 1758
Hansberry, Lorraine. A Raisin in the Sun, 3694
———. The Sign in Sidney Brustein's Window, 3695
HANSBERRY, LORRAINE, 3701
Hanson, Elizabeth. *see* Hanson, Lawrence
Hanson, Lawrence and Hanson, Elizabeth. The Four Brontës, 3926
Happy Birthday, Wanda June. Vonnegut, Kurt, Jr, 3707
Harcave, Sidney. Russia, 5484
Hard Times. Terkel, Studs, 1118
Hardie, Frank. The Abyssian Crisis, 5721
Hardin, James W. and Arena, James W. Human Poisoning from Native and Cultivated Plants, 2335
Harding Era. Murray, Robert K, 6124
HARDING, WARREN GAMABIEL, 6124-6125
Hardoy, Jorge E. Pre-Columbian Cities, 6265
Hardy, David A. *see* Moore, Patrick
Hardy of Wessex. Weber, Carl J, 3949
Hardy, Thomas. Collected Poems, 3825
HARDY, THOMAS, 3949
Hare, Richard. Maxim Gorky, Romantic Realist and Conservative Revolutionary, 4534
Harewood and Kobbe. Kobbe's Complete Opera Book, 3204
Haring, Clarence H. The Spanish Empire in America, 6256
Harkabi, Yehoshafat. Arab Attitudes to Israel, 895
Harkness, Georgia. Mysticism, 763
Harlem. Osofsky, Gilbert, 962
HARLEM, NEW YORK (CITY), 962, 1120
Harmer, Ruth. Unfit for Human Consumption, 2564

HAROLD II, KING OF ENGLAND, 5187
Harper Bible Dictionary. Miller, Madeline and Lane, J. 103
Harper Encyclopedia of the Modern World. Morris, Richard E. and Irwin, Graham, eds. 380
Harper, Howard M., Jr. Desperate Faith, 3717
Harper, Kenneth, et al, eds. New Voices, 4552
Harper's Encyclopedia for Horsemen. Taylor, Louis, 2808
HARPER'S FERRY, WEST VIRGINIA — JOHN BROWN'S RAID, 1859, 5975
Harrap's New Standard French and English Dictionary. Ledesert, Rene and Ledesert, D. M. 181
Harriman, Richard L. *see* Ehrlich, Paul R.
Harrington, John W. To See a World, 2101
Harrington, Michael. The Other America, 999
———. Toward a Democratic Left, 1113
Harris, Brayton. Johann Gutenberg and the Invention of Printing, 2865
Harris, John D. The Junkie Priest, 2598
Harris, John R., ed. The Legacy of Egypt, 4888
Harris, Louis. *see* Brink, William
Harris, Marvin. Culture, Man and Nature, 907
Harris, Richard. Death of a Revolutionary, 1247
———. Justice, 1648
Harris, Sherwood. The First to Fly, 2714
Harris, Thomas Anthony. I'm OK, You're OK, 2604
Harris, Whitney R. Tyranny on Trial, 5334
Harrison, Hal H. The World of the Snake, 2416
Harrison, Helen. Film Library Techniques, 26
Harrison, James P. The Long March to Power, 1177
Harrison, Martin. *see* Williams, Philip M.
Harrison, Randall P. Beyond Words, 573
Harrison, S. G., et al. The Oxford Book of Food Plants, 2789
HARRISON, WILLIAM HENRY, 6000
Harry Bridges. Larrowe, Charles P, 1442
Harry S. Truman. Truman, Margaret, 6155
Harry Truman and the Crisis Presidency. Cochran, Bert, 6149
Harsh, Philip W. Handbook of Classical Drama, 4452
Hart, Roger. English Life in Chaucer's Day, 5205
———. Witchcraft, 536

INDEX

HARTFORD CONVENTION, (1814), 1375
Hartmann, William K. Moons and Planets, 1991
Hartnack, Justus. History of Philosophy, 515
Hartogs, Renatus and Artzt, Eric. Violence, 883
Hartt, Frederick. History of Italian Renaissance Art, 2925
Harvard Committee. General Education in a Free Society, 1746
Harvard Concordance to Shakespeare. Spevack, Marvin, 370
Harvard Dictionary of Music. Apel, Willi, 296
Harvard Guide to American History. Freidel, Frank and Showman, Richard K., eds. 78
Harvard Lampoon Centennial Celebration, 1876-1973. Kaplan, Martin, compiled by. 3751
Harvest of the Sea. Bardach, John E, 1478
A Harvest of World Folk Tales. Rugoff, Milton A., ed, 1837
Harvey, Marian. Crafts of Mexico, 3020
Haselden, Kyle. Morality and the Mass Media, 901
Haskins, Charles. The Renaissance of the Twelfth Century, 4431
Haskins, James. Pinckney Benton Stewart Pinchback, 6223
Hassler, Warren W. General George B. McClellan, Shield of the Union, 6054
Hassrick, Royal B., et al. The Sioux, 5762
Hastings, James, ed. Encyclopedia of Religion and Ethics, 100
Hastings, Max. Barricades in Belfast, 5167
Hatada, Takashi. A History of Korea, 5606
Hatch, Eric. The Little Book of Bells, 3253
Hatfield, Henry C. Modern German Literature, 3986
———. Thomas Mann, 4075
Hatje, Gerd, ed. Encyclopedia of Modern Architecture, 281
Hattersley, Ralph. Discover Yourself Through Photography, 3102
Haupt, Georges and Marie, Jean-J. Makers of the Russian Revolution, 5520
Hauptmann, Gerhart. Das Friedensfest-Einsame Menschen, 4018
Hauser, Arnold. The Social History of Art, 2881
Hauser, Philip M. The Population Dilemma, 934
Haverstock, Nathan A. see Nystrom, John W.
Havlice, Patricia P. Index to Literary Biography, 68

HAWAII
 DESCRIPTION AND TRAVEL, 4847
 HISTORY, 4846-4847, 6094, 6289-6290
Hawaii. Joesting, Edward, 6290
Hawaii. Siers, James, 4847
Hawke, David. The Colonial Experience, 5901
Hawker, J. P. Radio and Television, 2641
Hawkes, Jacquetta H. Atlas of Ancient Archaeology, 401
———. First Great Civilization, 4784
Hawkes, Nigel. The Computer Revolution, 469
Hawkey, Richard B. Beginner's Guide to Squash, 3365
Hawkins, Gerald S. Beyond Stonehenge, 1978
———. Stonehenge Decoded, 5184
Hawley, Gessner C., see Hampel, Clifford A.
Hawley, Robert C. Human Values in the Classroom, 1748
HAWTHORNE, NATHANIEL, 3718
Hay, E. A. see McAlester, Archie L.
Hay, Henry. Amateur Magician's Handbook, 3335
Hay, John. Spirit of Survival, 2435
Hay, Roy and Synge, Patrick M. The Color Dictionary of Flowers and Plants for Home and Garden, 260
Hayakawa, Samuel I. Language in Thought and Action, 1882
Haycraft, Howard, see Kunitz, Stanley J.
Haydn. Geiringer, Karl, 3167
HAYDN, JOSEPH, 3167
Hayes, Carlton J. Generation of Materialism, 5055
———. History of Western Civilization Since 1500, 4989
Hayes, Paul M. Fascism, 1148
HAYES, RUTHERFORD BIRCHARD, 6088-6089
Haykal, Muhammad H. The Cairo Documents, 5716
Haymes, Robert C. Introduction to Space Science, 1896
Haynes, Milton. see Badillo, Herman
Hays, H. R., ed. Twelve Spanish-American Poets, 4302
Hays, Samuel P. Response to Industrialism, 1421
Hayter, Earl W. The Troubled Farmer, 2772
Hayward, Elizabeth. Grand Prix, 3406
Hayward, Max and Crowley, E. L., eds. Soviet Literature in the Sixties, 4585
Hayward, Max and Fletcher, William C., eds. Religion and the Soviet State, 799
Hayward, R. see Pauling, Linus

402

Hazards of Holiness. Antonius, Bro.   3622
Hazelton, Roger. Blaise Pascal, 672
Headley, Joel Tyler. The Great Riots of New York, 1712-1873, 1248
Headstrom, Richard. A Complete Field Guide to Nests in the United States. 2429
Health and Modern Man. Read, Donald A., et al.   2529
Health Foods. Margolius, Sidney, 2832
Heaps, Willard A. Psychic Phenomena, 541
———. Riots, U. S. A. 1765-1965, 903
Hearder, H. and Waley, Daniel P. Short History of Italy, 5427
HEARST, WILLIAM RANDOLPH, 494
HEART
  DISEASES, 2592
  SURGERY, 2620
Heart of the Hunter. Van Der Post, Laurens, 4796
A Heartbeat Away. Cohen, Richard M, 6173
Heat and Thermodynamics. Zemansky, M. W, 2045
Heath, Douglas. Growing Up in College, 1743
Heath, Harry E.   see Gelfand, Louis
Heaton, Eric W. Everyday Life in Old Testament Times, 726
Heaven's Command. Morris, James, 5261
Heavens, O. S. Lasers, 2640
Heavens on Earth. Holloway, Mark, 1504
Hebert, Tom.   see Coyne, John
HEBREW DRAMA, 4594
HEBREW LANGUAGE
  DICTIONARIES, 190
HEBREW LITERATURE — HISTORY AND CRITISISM, 4587-4588, 4590-4592
HEBREW POETRY, 4589
Hecht, Marie B. John Quincy Adams, 5991
Hedblom, Peter.   see Grinspoon, Lester
Hedgepeth, William and Stock, Dennis. The Alternative, 1503
Hedges, David and Meyer, Fred. Horses and Courses, 3448
Hedley, Arthur. Chopin, 3171
Hegel, George W. Philosophy, 665
Heiber, Helmut. Goebbels, 5314
HEIDEGGER, MARTIN, 550
Heiden, Konrad. Der Fuehrer, 5315
Heilbroner, Robert. Worldly Philosophers, 1405
Heilbroner, Robert L. An Inquiry into the Human Prospect, 4657
———. The Limits of American Capitalism, 1422
Heine, Heinrich. Lyric Poems and Ballads, 3996
———. Werke, 3975

HEINE, HEINRICH, 4009
Heinlein in Dimension, a Critical Analysis. Panshin, Alexi, 3744
HEINLEIN, ROBERT ANSON, 3744
Heinrich Heine. Brod, Max, 4006
Heinrich Heine. Hofrichter, Laura, 4009
Heinrich Himmler. Smith, Bradley F, 5325
Heintze, Carl. Genetic Engineering, 2201
Held, R. Burnell and Clawson, Marion. Soil Conservation in Perspective, 2774
HELICOPTERS — HISTORY, 2726
Helicopters and Other Rotorcraft Since 1 37. Munson, Kenneth, 2726
Hellenistic Age. Bury, John B., et al. 4976
Heller, Erich. Disinherited Mind, 3987
Heller, Walter W. New Dimensions of Political Economy, 1539
Hellman, Harold. Energy in the World of the Future, 1474
Hellman, Lillian. The Collected Plays, 3678
———. An Unfinished Woman, 3679
HELLMAN, LILLIAN, 3679
Helm, Peter J. Alfred the Great, 5185
Helm, Thomas. Hurricanes, 2159
Helmer, John. Bringing the War Home. 1000
Helmreich, E. C.   see Black, Cyril E.
Helper, Hinton R. Impending Crisis of the South, 1285
Hemingway and His Critics. Baker, Carlos, ed, 3726
Hemingway, Ernest. Death in the Afternoon, 3290
HEMINGWAY, ERNEST, 3725-3726, 3761
Hemingway, the Writer As Artist. Baker, Carlos, 3761
Hemming, James and Maxwell, Zena. Sex and Love, 972
Hemming, John. The Conquest of the Incas, 6267
———. The Conquest of the Incas, 6277
Hems, Jack.   see Hervey, George F.
Hendel, Samuel. The Soviet Crucible, 1145
Henderson, Bernard W. The Great War Between Athens and Sparta, 4972
Henderson, Gregory. Korea, the Politics of the Vortex, 1174
Henderson, Isabella F. and Henderson, W. D. Dictionary of Biological Terms, 230
Henderson, W. D.   see Henderson, Isabella F.
Hendricks, Gordon. The Life and Works of Thomas Eakins, 3043
Henig, Ruth B. The League of Nations, 1552
Henri, Adrian. Total Art, 2910
Henri, Robert. The Art Spirit, 2886

INDEX

Henry II. Warren, Wilfred L, 5207
HENRY III, 5203
HENRY VII, 5216, 5218
Henry VII. Chrimes, Stanley B, 5216
HENRY VIII, 5218, 5230
Henry VIII. Scarisbrick, J. J, 5230
Henry Clay and the Art of American Politics. Eaton, Clement, 6021
Henry Moore. Sylvester, David, 2982
HENRY, PATRICK, 5940
Henscratches and Flyspecks. Seegar, Pete, 3186
Henson, Matthew A. A Black Explorer at the North Pole, 4850
Herald, Earl. Fishes of North America, 2407
———. Living Fishes of the World, 2405
Heraldic Alphabet. Brook-Little, J. P, 4873
HERALDRY, 433, 4873-4874
Herber, Lewis. Crisis in Our Cities, 2565
Herberg, Will. Protestant - Catholic - Jew, 800
Herbert, George. Poems of George Herbert. , 3793
Herbert, Hiram J. see Rubin, Louis D.
Herbert Hoover and the Great Depression. Warren, Harris A, 6129
HERBS, 2320
Herdeck, Donald E. African Authors, 352
Here I Stand. Bainton, Roland H, 782
HEREDITY, 2249, 2252
Heredity and Development. Moore, John A, 2297
Heren, Louis, et al. China's Three Thousand Years, 5579
Heritage of America. Commager, Henry S. and Nevins, A., eds. 5880
Heritage of Hellenism. Furguson, John, 4731
Heritage of Music. Shippen, Katherine B. and Seidlova, Anca. 3140
Heritage of Wales. Habgood, Noel, 5278
Herman Melville. Arvin, Newton, 3719
Herman Melville. Freeman, John, 3720
Hermannsson, Halldor. The Vinland Sagas, 5888
Hernandez, Jose. Gaucho Martin Fierro, 4325
Hernandez, Miguel. El Rayo Que No Cesa, 4336
Hernani, Librairie. Hugo, Victor, 4164
Hero in America. Wecter, Dixon, 4865
HEROD, HOUSE OF, 4903
Herodotus. Histories, 4877
———. The Persian Wars, 4968
Herods of Judaea. Jones, Arnold H, 4903
Heroic Fiction. Lutwack, Leonard, 3712
Heroic Poetry. Bowra, Cecil M, 3471

Heroic Triad. Horgan, Paul, 6221
Heroin Trail. Newsday, Staff & Editors of, 1726
Heroin Was My Best Friend. Berry, James, 2597
Heroines of Dixie. Jones, Katharine M, 6058
Herold, Christopher J. and Horizon Editors. The Horizon Book of the Age of Napoleon, 5403
Herrick, N. Q. see Sheppard, Harold L.
Herrick, Robert. Poems, 3799
Herring, Hubert. History of Latin America, 6257
Herriot, James. All Creatures Great and Small, 2804
———. All Things Bright and Beautiful, 2805
Herrnstein, Richard J. and Boring, Edwin G., eds. Source Book in the History of Psychology, 566
Hersey, John R. Hiroshima, 5140
Hersh, Seymour M. Chemical and Biological Warfare, 1685
———. My Lai 4, 5683
Herskovits, Melville J. The Human Factor in Changing Africa, 5699
———. The Myth of the Negro Past, 5700
Herskowitz, Irwin H. Principles of Genetics, 2294
Hervey, George F. The Complete Illustrated Book of Card Games, 3345
Hervey, George F. and Hems, Jack. Illustrated Encyclopedia of Freshwater Fish, 262
Herzen, Alexander I. My Past and Thoughts, 5501
HERZEN, ALEKSANDR I., 5501
Herzog, Maurice. Annapurna, 3391
Hess. Hutton, J. Bernard, 5318
Hess, Karl. see Reeves, Thomas
Hess, Robert L. Ethiopia, 5719
HESS, RUDOLF, 5318
Hess, Stephen and Broder, David. The Republican Establishment, 1392
Hesse, Hermann. Beneath the Wheel, 4056
———. Gertrude, 4057
———. Glass Bead Game, 4058
———. Der Steppenwolf, 4055
Hesseltine, William B. and Smiley, D. The South in American History, 6209
Hetzler, Stanley A. Technological Growth and Social Change, 879
Heuvelmans, Bernard. In the Wake of the Sea Serpents, 2372
Hewish, John. Emily Bronte, 3927
Hewitt, James, compiled by. Eye-Witness to Wagon Trains West, 6234
Hey, Nigel S. The Mysterious Sun, 2005
Heyerdahl, Thor. Aku-Aku, 4845

———. Kon-Tiki, 4697
———. The RA Expeditions, 4687
Heywood, Rosalind. Beyond the Reach of Sense, 529
Hi-Fi Stereo Handbook. Boyce, William F, 2654
Hibbard, Howard. Poussin, 3052
Hibbert, Christopher. The Dragon Wakes, 1317
———. Edward the Uncrowned King, 5275
———. Garibaldi and His Enemies, 5438
Hick, John. Philosophy of Religion, 684
Hickling, Charles F. and Brown, Peter L. The Seas and Oceans in Color, 2138
Hickman, Mae and Guy, Maxine. Care of the Wild Feathered and Furred, 2826
Hicks, John D. The Populist Revolt, 1394
Hicks, Wilson. Words and Pictures, 489
Hidden Forest. Olson, Sigurd F. and Blacklock, Les. 2319
Hidden History of the Korean War. Stone, Isidor F, 5613
Hidden Order of Art. Ehrenzweig, Aaron, 2883
Hidden Persuaders. Packard, Vance O, 2858
High Employment Without Inflation. Committee for Economic Development, 1543
High Priests of Waste. Fitzgerald, Arthur E, 1679
High School, 1980. Eurich, Alvin C. and Academy for Educational Development Staff, eds. 1779
Higham, Charles. The Art of the American Film, 1900-1971, 3274
Highet, Gilbert. Juvenal the Satirist, 4422
Highland Clans. Pine, Leslie G, 5153
Highlights of the Olympics from Ancient Times to the Present. Durant, John, 3383
Highways and Our Environment. Robinson, John, 1807
HIJACKING OF AIRPLANES, 1719
HIKING, 3386-3387
Hill, Brian H., compiled by. Canada, 1875-1973, 5779
Hill, Gladwin. Madman in a Lifeboat, 1635
Hill, John E. The World Turned Upside Down, 5239
Hill, Raymond. see Peter, Laurence J.
Hillas, A. M. Cosmic Rays, 2064
Hillbilly Women. Kahn, Kathy, 980
Hillegas, Mark R. The Future As Nightmare; H. G. Wells and the Anti-Utopians, 3920
Hillerbrand, Hans J. The World of the Reformation, 786
Hilsman, Roger. To Move a Nation, 1341

HIMMLER, HEINRICH, 5325
Hinckley, Ted C. The Americanization of Alaska, 1867-1897, 6248
Hindenburg. Mooney, Michael M, 2735
Hindley, Geoffrey. Medieval Warfare, 1670
Hindu Tradition. Embree, Ainslie T., ed, 846
HINDUISM, 846, 848
Hindus, Maurice G. Cossacks, 5485
Hinkelbein, Albert. Origins of the Universe, 1990
Hinschfield, Robert S., ed. The Power of the Presidency, 1640
Hinshaw, David. Rufus Jones, Master Quaker, 815
Hippie Ghetto. Partridge, William L, 915
HIPPIES — U.S., 915, 1503
Hippler, Arthur E. Hunter's Point, 966
Hirmer, Max. see Lange, Kurt
Hiro, Dilip. Black British, White British, 1024
HIROHITO, EMPEROR OF JAPAN, 5117
Hiroshima. Hersey, John R, 5140
Hiroshima. Yass, Marion, 5142
HIROSHIMA — BOMBARDMENT (1945), 5140-5142
Hirsch, Richard. The National Aeronautics and Space Administration, 1636
Hirschfeld, Albert. see Atkinson, J. Brooks
His Toy, His Dream, His Rest. Berryman, John, 3624
Hiscocks, Richard. Poland, 5361
Hiss, Alger. In the Court of Public Opinion, 1714
HISS, ALGER, 1622
Histoire de la Littérature Française. Des Granges, C. M, 4107
Histoire de las Littératures Française Contemporaine. Lalou, Rene, 4110
Histoire Illustrée de la Litterature Française. Abry, Emile, et al. 4103
Historia de la Literatura Española. Del Río, Angel, 4312
Historia de una Escalera. Buero Vallejo, Antonio, 4349
Historian As Detective. Winks, Robin W., ed, 4666
Historian's Craft. Bloch, Marc, 4662
Historian's Fallacies. Fischer, David H, 4650
Historians of Greece and Rome. Usher, Stephen, 4969
Historic Costume for the Stage. Barton, Lucy, 3303
Historic Costuming. Truman, Nevil, 1814
Historical Anthology of Music. Davison, Archibald T. and Apel, Willi. 3146
Historical Atlas of Latin America. Wilgus, A. Curtis, 394

INDEX

Historical Atlas of the Religions of the World. Al Faruqi, Isma'il R, 400
Historical Atlas of the United States. Lord, Clifford L. and Lord, Elizabeth S. 393
Historical Catastrophes. Brown, Billye and Brown, Walter R. 2153
Historical Documents of Canada, 1914-1945. Stacy, C. P., ed, 5799
An Historical Geography of Western Europe Before 1800. Smith, C. T, 4706
Historical Introduction to Modern Psychology. Murphy, Gardner, 560
Historical Sites of Israel. Pearlman, Moshe, 4786
Histories. Herodotus, 4877
HISTORY, 379
    ANCIENT, 434-435, 474, 4876-4881
    BIBLIOGRAPHY, 73
    DICTIONARIES, 380
    METHODOLOGY, 4650, 4662, 4664-4666
    MODERN, 60, 437, 4667, 4672, 4677-4678, 5057, 6099
    PHILOSOPHY, 4645, 4648-4649
History and Description of Roman Political Institutions. Abbott, Frank F, 4919
History and Geography of the Most Important Diseases. Ackerknecht, Erwin H, 2560
History of Africa. Gailey, Harry A, 5709
History of Africa. Gailey, Harry A, 5710
History of African Civilization. Murphy, E. Jefferson, 5706
A History of American Education. Good, Harry G. and Teller, James D. 1761
A History of American Law. Friedman, Lawrence M, 1545
A History of American Life Series. 6185
A History of American Pewter. Montgomery, Charles F, 3003
History of American Philosophy. Schneider, Herbert W, 649
A History of American Political Theories. Merriam, Charles E, 1198
History of American Presidential Elections. Schlesinger, Arthur M., Jr. and Israel, F. L. 137
History of Architecture. 2979
History of Architecture. Fletcher, Banister, 2962
History of Art. Janson, Horst W, 269
History of Art and Music. Janson, Horst W. and Kerman, Joseph. 2873
History of Assyria. Olmstead, Albert T, 4916
History of Astrology. Zolar, 540
History of Australia. Clark, Charles M, 6287

A History of Bolshevism, from Marx to the First Five Years' Plan. Rosenberg, Arthur, 5524
A History of Brazil. Burns, E. Bradford, 6270
History of China. Fitzgerald, Charles P. and Horizon Editors. 5577
A History of Christianity in the World. Manschreck, Clyde L, 779
History of East Asian Civilization. Reischauer, Edwin O., et al. 5571
History of Egypt. Breasted, James H, 4883
A History of Electricity and Magnetism. Meyer, Herbert W, 2049
History of England. Trevelyan, George M, 5176
A History of English. Strang, Barbara, 1870
A History of English Literature. Quennell, Peter, 3772
History of Florence and of the Affairs of Italy. Machiavelli, Niccolo, 5433
History of French Literature. Cazamian, Louis, 4106
History of French Literature. Nitze, William and D'Argan, E. 4113
History of German Literature. Robertson, J. G, 3990
History of German Literature. Rose, Ernst, 3991
History of Greece. Bury, John B, 4953
A History of Greek Literature. Hadas, Moses, 4438
A History of Hungary. Kosary, Domokos G, 5364
History of Impressionism. Rewald, John, 3030
History of Instructional Technology. Saettler, Paul, 1772
A History of Islamic Philosophy. Fakhry, Majid, 613
A History of Israel. Bright, John, 4899
A History of Italian Fascism. Chabod, Federico, 5448
History of Italian Literature. Wilkins, Ernest H, 4287
History of Italian Renaissance Art. Hartt, Frederick, 2925
History of Italy. Guicciardini, Francesco, 5432
A History of Jazz in America. Ulanov, Barry, 3192
A History of Judaism. Silver, Daniel J, 860
A History of Korea. Hatada, Takashi, 5606
History of Latin America. Herring, Hubert, 6257

INDEX

A History of Latin American Art and Architecture from Pre-Columbian Times to the Present. Castedo, Leopoldo, 2949

A History of Latin Literature. Hadas, Moses, 4398

History of Medieval Europe. Thorndike, Lynn, 5010

History of Mexico. Parkes, Henry B, 5807

A History of Modern France. Cobban, Alfred, 5369

A History of Modern Germany. Holborn, Hajo, 5286

A History of Modern Hebrew Literature. Klausner, Joseph, 4592

A History of Modern Southeast Asia. Bastin, John and Benda, Harry J. 5670

History of Music. 3256

History of Music and Musical Style. Ulrich, Homer and Pisk, Paul A. 3141

History of Music in Sound. 3255

History of Music Series. 3257

History of Musical Instruments. Sachs, Curt, 3201

History of New England. Adams, James T, 6188

History of Philosophy. Hartnack, Justus, 515

History of Photography. Newhall, Beaumont, 3109

A History of Polar Exploration. Mountfield, David, 4852

History of Political Theory. Sabine, George H, 1131

History of Portugal. Marques, Antonio H. R. de, 5478

A History of Presidential Elections. Roseboom, Eugene H, 1382

A History of Preventive Medicine. Wain, Harry, 2559

History of Religion. 878

History of Rocketry and Space Travel. Ordway, Frederick I., Jr. and Braun, Wernher Von. 2760

A History of Russia. Pares, Bernard, 5490

A History of Russia. Riasanovsky, Nicholas V, 5491

History of Russia. Vernadsky, George, 5494

A History of Russian Literature. Mirsky, D. S, 4497

History of Russian Philosophy. Zenkovsky, Vasilii V, 676

History of Scepticism from Erasmus to Descartes. Popkin, Richard H, 524

A History of Science and Its Relation with Philosophy and Religion. Dampier, William C, 1922

A History of Scotland. Mitchison, Rosalind, 5152

A History of South Africa. Were, Gideon S, 5738

History of Spanish Civilization. Altamira y Crevea, Rafael, 5455

History of Tammany Hall. Myers, Gustavus, 1137

History of the American Frontier, 1763-1893. Paxson, Frederic L, 5868

History of the American People. Carman, Harry J., et al. 5856

History of the American Revolution. Alden, John R, 5912

History of the American Working Class. Bimba, Anthony, 1436

A History of the Ancient World. Starr, Chester G, 4881

History of the Arabs. Hitti, Philip K, 5625

History of the Belgians. De Meeus, Adrien, 5545

History of the Book. Dahl, Svend, 2847

History of the Byzantine Empire. Franzius, Enno, 5550

A History of the Byzantine Empire, 324-1453. Vasiliev, Alexander A, 5551

History of the Christian Church. Walker, Williston, 781

A History of the Crusades. Runciman, Steven, 5018

A History of the Czechoslovak Republic, 1918-1948. Mamatey, Victor S. and Luza, Radomir. 5349

A History of the Czechs and Slovaks. Seton-Watson, Robert W, 5350

History of the Dance. Kraus, Richard, 3326

History of the Ecumenical Movement, 1517-1948. Rouse, Ruth and Neill, Stephen C., eds. 780

A History of the English Language. Baugh, Albert C, 1866

A History of the English-Speaking Peoples. Churchill, Winston L, 5171

A History of the Great War, 1914-1918. Cruttwell, Charles R, 5068

History of the Greek and Roman Theater. Bieber, Margarete, 4450

History of the House of Representatives. Galloway, George B, 1361

History of the Incas. Metraux, Alfred, 6269

History of the Indians of the United States. Debo, Angie, 5745

A History of the Jews. Sachar, Abram, 4906

A History of the Jews Since the First Century A.D. Schweitzer, Frederick M, 4907

INDEX

History of the Kingdom of Naples. Croce, Benedetto, 5454
History of the Kings of Rome. Dyer, Thomas H, 4928
A History of the Modern World. Palmer, Robert R. and Colton, Joel. 4672
History of the Monroe Doctrine. Perkins, Dexter, 1352
History of the Peloponnesian War. Thucydides, 4973
History of the Persian Empire. Olmstead, Arthur T, 4918
History of the Racing Car. Lurani, Giovanni, 2751
History of the Roman World, 146 to 30 B.C. Marsh, Frank B, 4930
History of the Roman World, 753 to 146 B.C. Scullard, Howard H, 4924
History of the Second World War. Liddell Hart, Basil H, 5101
History of the Sikh Gurus. Gupta, Hari R, 850
A History of the South. 6219
History of the Spanish Stage from Medieval Times Until the End of the Seventeenth Century. Shergold, N. D, 4364
History of the Theatre. Brockett, Oscar G, 3308
History of the Theatre. Freedley, George and Reeves, John A. 3313
History of the United States Army. Weigley, Russell F, 1663
History of the United States Naval Operations in World War II. Morison, Samuel E, 5143
A History of the Vikings. Jones, Gwyn, 5536
History of the Western World Series. 5566
A History of Ukraine. Hrushevy, Michael, 5532
History of U. S. Political Parties. Schlesinger, Arthur M., Jr, 1377
History of Violence in America. Graham, Hugh D. and Gurr, Ted R. 882
History of West Africa. Webster, J. B, 5724
A History of West Africa to the 19th Century. Davidson, Basil, 5722
History of Western Civilization Since 1500. Hayes, Carlton J., et al. 4989
History of Western Education. Boyd, William, 1756
A History of Western Music. Grout, Donald J, 3136
A History of Western Philosophy. Russell, Bertrand, 518
A History of Western Technology. Klemm, Friedrich, 2491
A History of Zen Buddhism. Dumoulin, Heinrich, 837

History Will Absolve Me. Castro, Fidel, 5828
Hitler. Fest, Joachim C, 5311
Hitler, a Study in Tyranny. Bullock, Alan, 5308
Hitler, Adolf. Mein Kampf, 5316
HITLER, ADOLF, 1304, 5121, 5304, 5308, 5310-5311, 5315, 5324, 5449
Hitler Moves East, 1941-1943. Schmidt, Paul K, 5135
Hitler's Generals. Humble, Richard, 5121
Hitsman, J. Mackay. Incredible War of 1812, 5986
Hitti, Philip K. History of the Arabs, 5625
———. Makers of Arab History, 4858
HITTITES, 4984
Ho. Halberstam, David, 5682
HO-CHI-MINH, 5682, 5684
Hobshawm, Eric J. The Age of Revolution, Europe, 5056
Hochhuth, Rolf. The Deputy, 4019
———. Soldiers, 4020
HOCKEY, 3412-3414
Hockey! The Story of the World's Fastest Sport. Beddoes, Richard, 3412
Hocking, Richard, see Hocking, William E.
Hocking, William E. and Hocking, Richard, eds. Types of Philosophy, 509
Hodge, Alan. see Graves, Robert
Hodge, Jane A. Only a Novel, 3922
Hodges, Henry. Technology in the Ancient World, 2490
Hodgson, Robert D. and Stoneman, Elryn. A Changing Map of Africa, 5701
Hodous, Lewis. Folklore in China, 1832
Hoedeman, J. J. Naturalists' Guide to Freshwater Aquarium Fish, 263
Hoeltje, Hubert H. Inward Sky, 3718
HOFFA, JAMES RIDDLE, 1446
Hoffer, Eric. The True Believer, 896
Hoffman, Banesh. The Strange Story of the Quantum, 2032
Hoffman, Banesh and Dukas, Helen. Albert Einstein, 2025
Hoffman, Frederick J. The Twenties, 3540
Hoffman, Martin. The Gay World, 984
Hoffman, Michael J. The Subversive Vision, 3541
Hofmannstal, Hugo Von. Deutsche Erzahler, Ausgewahlt und Eingeleitet von Hugo von Hofmannsthal, 4071
———. Selected Writings, 3976
Hofrichter, Laura. Heinrich Heine, 4009
Hofstadter, Albert. Agony and Epitaph, 507
Hofstadter, Dan. Mexico, 1946-1973, 5819
Hofstadter, Richard. Age of Reform, 6110
———. America at 1750, 1114
———. American Political Tradition, 5861

INDEX

———. Progressive Movement, 1900-1915, 5881

———. Social Darwinism in American Thought, 884

Hofstadter, Richard and Wallace, Michael, eds. American Violence, 5862

Hogan, Robert G. After the Irish Renaissance, 3854

———. Seven Irish Plays, 1946-1964, 3855

Hogarth. Paulson, Ronald, 3092

HOGARTH, WILLIAM, 3092

Hogg, Ian. *see* Batchelor, John

Hogg, Syd. The Art of Cartooning, 3008

Hohauser, Sanford. Architectural and Interior Models, 2960

HOHENZOLLERN, HOUSE OF, 5338

Hohne, Heinz. The Order of the Death's Head, 5317

Holborn, Hajo. A History of Modern Germany, 5286

Holden, Alan. Shapes, Space, and Symmetry, 1949

Holden, Anna. The Bus Stops Here, 1750

Holden, David. Greece Without Columns, 5554

A Hole in the Bottom of the Sea. Bascom, Willard, 2105

Holiday, F. W. Great Orm of Loch Ness, 2373

HOLIDAYS, 151-152

Hollander, Hans. Early Medieval Art, 2901

Hollander, Paul. Soviet and American Society, 1090

Hollander, Zander, ed. Modern Encyclopedia of Basketball, 3354

Hollander, Zander and Bock, Hal, eds. The Complete Encyclopedia of Ice Hockey, 3414

Holloway, Mark. Heavens on Earth, 1504

Holm, Nora S. Runner's Bible, 3380

Holmes, Richard T., *see* Campbell, Bruce

Holocaust. Levin, Nora, 5105

HOLOCAUST, JEWISH (1939-1945), 3494, 5107

Holography. Klein, H. Arthur, 2042

Holt, Alfred H. Phrase and Word Origins, 157

Holt, John. How Children Fail, 1775

———. How Children Learn, 1749

———. The Underachieving School. , 1762

Holt, Peter M. Egypt and the Fertile Crescent, 5642

Holt, Peter M., et al, eds. Cambridge History of Islam, 382

Holtman, Robert B. The Napoleonic Revolution, 5047

Holweck, Frederick G. A Biographical Dictionary of the Saints, 110

Holy Bible. Confraternity Edition. Bible, 703

Holy Bible. Four Prophets. Bible, 731

Holy Bible. King James Version. Bible, 704

Holy Bible. Bible, 705

Holy Scriptures. According to the Masoretic Text. Bible, 716

Holzman, William and Lewin, Leonard. Holzman's Basketball, 3355

Holzman's Basketball. Holzman, William and Lewin, Leonard. 3355

Home Book of Bible Quotations. Stevenson, Burton E, 101

Home Book of Modern Verse. Stevenson, Burton E., ed, 3784

Home Book of Quotations. Stevenson, Burton E., ed, 340

Home Book of Verse, American and English. Stevenson, Burton E., ed, 366

Homecoming. Pinter, Harold, 3912

Homer. Iliad, 4466

———. The Iliad, 4463

———. The Odyssey, 4464

———. Odyssey, 4465

HOMER, 4461-4462, 4468-4469

Homer. Steiner, George and Fagles, Robert, eds. 4468

Homer and the Heroic Tradition. Whitman, Cedric H, 4469

HOMER, WINSLOW, 3041

L' Homme Revolté. Camus, Albert, 4201

Homo Faber. Frisch, Max, 4049

Homosexual Liberation. Murphy, John, 985

HOMOSEXUALITY, 984-985, 2595

Honest to God. Robinson, John A, 747

Honest to God Debate. Edwards, David L., ed, 745

Hongkong. Rand, Christopher, 4776

Hood, Graham. American Silver, 3002

Hood, Sinclair. The Minoans. , 4734

Hooded Americanism. Chalmers, David M, 1705

Hoofed Mammals of the World. Mochi, Ugo and Carter, T. Donald. 2462

Hoopes, Donelson F. The American Impressionists, 3044

HOOVER, HERBERT CLARK, 6129

Hope, C. E. and Jackson, G. N. The Encyclopedia of the Horse, 261

Hopf, Alice L. Wild Cousins of the Dog, 2470

Hopis. Okane, Walter C, 5763

Hopkins, Edward W. The Religions of India, 847

Hopkins, Gerard M. Poems, 3826

HOPKINS, GERARD MANLEY, 3830

Hopkins, Jeannette. *see* Clark, Kenneth B.

Hopkins, Jerry. Elvis, 3231

Hora Actual Dela Novela Espanola. Alborg, Juan Luis, 4308

409

INDEX

Horace Greeley. Van Deusen, Glyndon G, 6042
Horace Tabor. Smith, Duane A, 1369
Horatius Flaccus, Quintus. Odes and Epodes, 4417
―――. Satires, Epistles, and Ars Poetica, 4418
Horgan, Paul. The Heroic Triad, 6221
Horizon Book of Great Cathedrals. Horizon Editors, 2976
Horizon Book of Great Historic Places of Europe. Davidson, Marshall B, 4740
Horizon Book of Makers of Modern Thought. Horizon Editors, 4859
Horizon Book of the Age of Napoleon. Herold, Christopher J. and Horizon Editors. 5403
Horizon Book of the Arts of China. Horizon Editors, 2930
Horizon Book of the Arts of Russia. Horizon Editors, 2928
Horizon Book of the Middle Ages. Bishop, Morris, 4995
Horizon Book of the Renaissance. Plumb, J. H., ed, 5029
Horizon Concise History of Scandinavia. Butler, Ewan, 5533
Horizon Concise History of the Low Countries. Bailey, Anthony, 5543
Horizon Cookbook and Illustrated History of Eating and Drinking Through the Ages. Horizon Cookbook Editors, 2829
Horizon Cookbook Editors. The Horizon Cookbook and Illustrated History of Eating and Drinking Through the Ages, 2829
Horizon Editors. The Horizon Book of Great Cathedrals, 2976
―――. The Horizon Book of Makers of Modern Thought, 4859
―――. The Horizon Book of the Arts of China, 2930
―――. Horizon Book of the Arts of Russia, 2928
Horizon Editors. see Fitzgerald, Charles P.
Horizon Editors. see Herold, Christopher J.
Horizon History of Africa. Josephy, Alvin M., et al, eds. 5702
Horizon History of Russia. Grey, Ian, 5483
Horn, Stanley F. Invisible Empire, 1373
Hornung, Clarence P. Treasury of American Design, 290
Horowitz, I. A. The World Chess Championship, 3336

HORSE-RACING, 3448-3449
HORSE-TRAINING, 3446
HORSEMANSHIP, 3447
HORSES
  DICTIONARIES, 261, 2808
  U.S., 2463, 2806-2807
Horses and Courses. Hedges, David and Meyer, Fred. 3448
Horses, Hitches and Rocky Trails. Back, Joe, 3447
Horses in America. Haines, Francis, 2806
Horspiele. 4021
Horton, Edward. The Illustrated History of the Submarine, 2684
Horwitz, Elinor L. Communes in America, 1505
Horwitz, Sylvia L. Francisco Goya, 3063
Hoskins, Eric and Gooders, John. Wildlife Photography, 3120
Hotham, David. The Turks, 5653
Houck, Louis. Boundaries of the Louisiana Purchase, 5973
Hough, John T., Jr. Peck of Salt, 1126
Hough, Lindy. see Grossinger, Richard
House of Intellect. Barzun, Jacques, 457
House of Life. Brooks, Paul, 2222
HOUSE PLANTS, 2794-2798
House Plants. Compton, Joan, 2794
HOUSEHOLD APPLIANCES, 2629
Housman, Alfred E. Collected Poems of A. E. Housman, 3837
Houston, Beverle. see Kinder, Marsha
Houston, Mary G. Ancient Egyptian, Mesopotamian and Persian Costume and Decoration, 1811
―――. Ancient Greek, Roman and Byzantine Costume and Decoration, 1812
HOUSTON, SAMUEL, 6225
How Children Fail. Holt, John, 1775
How Children Learn. Holt, John, 1749
How Communist China Negotiates. Lall, Arthur, 1318
How Did Sports Begin? A Look at the Origins of Man at Play. Brasch, Rudolph, 3350
How Did You Think of That? An Introduction to the Scientific Method. Killeffer, David H, 1911
How It Works. Graf, Rudolf F. and Whalen, George J. 2629
How the Great Religions Began. Gaer, Joseph, 820
How the Other Half Lives. Riis, Jacob A, 969
How the Racers Ski. Witherell, Warren, 3420
How Things Work. Byrd, E, 1889
How to Be a Survivor. Ehrlich, Paul R. and Harriman, Richard L. 942

How to Be a Winner at Chess. Reinfeld, Fred, 3338
How to Break Ninety-Eight-Par. McAdams, Cliff, ed, 3369
How to Drive Better and Avoid Accidents. Kearney, Paul W, 2571
How to Kick the Habit. Alexander, Clifton and Alexander, Sandy. 1696
How to Know American Antique Furniture. Bishop, Robert, 3024
How to Make Money with Your Crafts. Clark, Leta W, 2854
How to Play Championship Tennis. Laver, Rod and Pollard, Jack. 3363
How to Play the Guitar. Silverman, Jerry, 3251
How to Write and Deliver a Speech. Ott, John, 3491
How Your Car Works. Jutty, Sam, 2744
Howard, Frank and Gunston, Bill. The Conquest of the Air, 2715
Howard, John T. Our American Music, 3182
Howard, Michael. The Franco-Prussian War, 5293
Howard, Neale E. The Telescope Handbook and Star Atlas, 1975
Howarth, David. Waterloo, 5546
Howat, John K. The Hudson River and Its Painters, 3026
Howe, Irving. Sherwood Anderson, 3729
Howell, Bill. *see* Jones, Barbara
Howell, Margaret. *see* Price, Mary R.
Howes, Barbara, ed. The Eye of the Heart, 4379
Howl, and Other Poems. Ginsberg, Allen, 3640
Hoy Es Fiesta. Buero Vallejo, Antonio, 4347
Hoyle, Fred. Frontiers of Astronomy, 1963
———. Galaxies, Nuclei and Quasars, 1982
———. Man in the Universe, 508
———. Nicolaus Copernicus, 1973
Hrushevy, Michael. A History of Ukraine, 5532
Hsieh, Chiao-Min and Salter, Christopher L. Atlas of China, 404
Hsü, Immanuel C. Y. The Rise of Modern China, 5583
Hsueh-Chin, Tsao. Dream of the Red Chamber, 4603
Huart, Clément I. Ancient Persia and Iranian Civilization, 4909
Hubben, William. Dostoevsky, Kierkegaard, Nietzsche and Kafka, 551
HUDSON RIVER, 4831
Hudson River. Boyle, Robert H, 4831
Hudson River and Its Painters. Howat, John K, 3026

HUDSON VALLEY — DESCRIPTION AND TRAVEL — VIEWS, 3026
Hudson, Winthrop S. American Protestantism, 801
———. Religion in America, 690
HUDSON'S BAY COMPANY, 5801
Huebener, Theodore. The Literature of East Germany, 3988
Huey Long. Williams, T. Harry, 6222
Hughes, Emmet J. The Living Presidency, 1641
Hughes, Gervase. Dvorak, 3172
Hughes, H. Stuart. Contemporary Europe, 5092
———. United States and Italy, 1342
Hughes, Langston. I Wonder As I Wander, 3643
———. Langston Hughes Reader, 3644
Hughes, Langston and Bontemps, Arna W., eds. Book of Negro Folklore, 1833
HUGHES, LANGSTON, 3643
Hughes, Quentin. Military Architecture, 2975
Hughes, Serge. The Fall and Rise of Modern Italy, 1168
Hugo, Victor. Hernani, Librairie, 4164
———. La Légende des Siecles, 4123
———. Les Miserables, 4219
———. Notre Dame de Paris, 4220
———. Quatre-Vingt Treize, 4221
———. Ruy Blas, 4165
HUGO, VICTOR MARIE, 4279
Huisman, Philippe and Dortu, M. G. Lautrec by Lautrec, 3053
Huizinga, Johan. Erasmus and the Age of Reformation, 787
———. The Waning of the Middle Ages, 5000
Hulley, Clarence C. Alaska, 6249
Hulsizer, Robert and Lazarus, David. The World of Physics, 2019
Human Be-Ing. Pietsch, William V, 591
HUMAN BEHAVIOR, 588, 2193, 2457, 2483
Human Body. Best, Charles H. and Taylor, N. B. 2507
Human Brain. Asimov, Isaac, 2524
HUMAN ECOLOGY, 935, 940, 947, 952, 955, 1119, 1635
HUMAN EVOLUTION, 525, 2191, 2193, 2196-2197, 2200
Human Evolution. Campbell, Bernard, 2194
Human Factor in Changing Africa. Herskovits, Melville J, 5699
HUMAN GENETICS, 2202-2204, 2257
Human Genetics. McKusick, Victor, 2202
Human Nervous System. Noback, Charles R, 2523

INDEX

Human Organism. DeCoursey, Russell M, 2509
HUMAN PHYSIOLOGY, 251, 2507-2510
Human Poisoning from Native and Cultivated Plants. Hardin, James W. and Arena, James W. 2335
HUMAN REPRODUCTION, 2551
Human Sexuality. McCary, James L, 2520
Human Teaching for Human Learning. Brown, George I, 1769
Human Values in the Classroom. Hawley, Robert C, 1748
Human Zoo. Morris, Desmond, 588
HUMANISM, 5028
Humanist As Hero. Maynard, Theodore, 5226
HUMANITIES INDEXES, 94
Humanities Index. 88
Humble, Richard. Hitler's Generals, 5121
Humboldt and the Cosmos. Botting, Douglas, 1900
HUMBOLT, ALEXANDER FREIHEUR, 1900
Hume, David. Moral and Political Philosophy, 652
Hume, John. The Abolitionists, Together with Personal Memories of the Struggle for Human Rights, 1830-1964, 1289
Humphrey, Philip S., see Bates, Marston
Humphries, Rolfe. Coat on a Stick, 3573
———. Collected Poems of Rolfe Humphries, 3574
A Hundred Years of Philosophy. Passmore, John, 517
Hundred Years of War. Falls, Cyril, 4675
HUNDRED YEARS' WAR (1339-1453), 5016, 5199
Hundred Years' War. Perroy, Edouard, 5016
HUNGARY
    HISTORY, 5364, 5366-5368
    POLITICS AND GOVERNMENT, 5343, 5365, 5368
Hungry Future. Dumont, Rene and Rosier, Bernard. 1517
HUNS, 4685
Hunsaker, David M. see Smith, Craig R.
Hunt, Edward E., Jr. see Coon, Carleton S.
Hunt, Gaillard. Life of James Madison, 5983
Hunt, John. The Conquest of Everest, 3392
Hunter, Beatrice T. Consumer Beware!, 2862
———. Gardening Without Poisons, 2784
———. The Natural Foods Primer, 2831
Hunter, C. Bruce. A Guide to Ancient Maya Ruins, 4803
Hunter, Sam and Jacobus, John. American Art of the 20th Century, 2945

Hunter's Handbook. Knap, Jerome J, 3457
Hunter's Point. Hippler, Arthur E, 966
HUNTING, 3450, 3457-3461
Hurlbut, Cornelius, Jr. Minerals and Man, 2089
Hurlimann, Martin. France, 4755
Hurlimann, Martin and King, Francis. Japan, 4778
L' Hurluberlu, ou Le Réactionnaire Amoureu. Anouilh, Jean, 4145
HURRICANES, 2153, 2159
Hurricanes. Helm, Thomas, 2159
Hurst, Michael, ed. Key Treaties for the Great Powers, 1814-1914, 141
Husain, S. Abid. Destiny of Indian Muslims, 1060
Hutchinson, John. Imperfect Union, 1441
Hutchinson, Peter. Evolution Explained, 2280
Hutson, Arthur E. and McCoy, Patricia, trs. Epics of the Western World, 3505
Hutton, J. Bernard. Hess, 5318
HUXLEY, ALDOUS, 3951
Huxley, Aldous L. Brave New World Revisited, 897
———. The Perennial Philosophy, 692
Huxley, Anthony. see Edlin, Herbert L.
Huxley, Elspeth. Florence Nightingale, 2497
Huxley, Julian. Evolution in Action, 2281
Huxley, Thomas H. On a Piece of Chalk, 2282
HUXLEY, THOMAS HENRY, 2221
Huyen, N. Kha. Vision Accomplished, 5684
Huygens, Christiaan. Treatise on Light, 2039
Hyams, Edward. A Dictionary of Modern Revolution, 134
Hyams, Joseph. see King, Billie J.
Hyde, Douglas A. Communism Today, 1497
Hyde, George E. Indians of the High Plains, 5751
———. Indians of the Woodlands, from Prehistoric Times to 1725, 5752
Hyde, Margaret O. Mind Drugs, 2543
———. The New Genetics, 2295
———. V.D. The Silent Epidemic, 2611
HYDROFOIL BOATS, 2754
Hydrofoils and Hovercraft. Gunston, William T, 2754

INDEX

HYDROGEN BOMB, 1668
HYDROLOGIC CYCLE, 2261
HYDROLOGY — TABLES, CALCULATIONS, ETC., 2261
HYDROPONICS, 2797
HYENAS, 2474
HYGIENE, 251, 2530
Hyman, Arthur and Walsh, James J., eds. Philosophy in the Middle Ages, 629
Hyman, Harold M. see Thomas, Benjamin P.
Hynds, Ernest C. American Newspapers in the 1970's, 498
HYSTERIA (SOCIAL PSYCHOLOGY), 1196, 6120

I Am a Camera. Van Druten, John, 3893
I and Thou. Buber, Martin, 664
I Can Sell You Anything. Stevens, Paul, 2859
I Can Teach You to Figure Skate. Noyes, Tina and Alexander, Freda. 3416
I CHING, 870
I Ching; or, Book of Changes. Baynes, Cary F., tr, 870
I Have Spoken. Armstrong, Virginia I., ed, 5743
I Wonder As I Wander. Hughes, Langston, 3643
Ianni, E. R. see Ianni, Francis A.
Ianni, Francis A. and Ianni, E. R. A Family Business, 1712
Ianniello, Lynne, ed. Milestones Along the March, 1259
Iberia. Michener, James A, 5459
Iberians. Arribas, Antonio, 5456
Iberoamérica. Castro, Americo, 4301
Ibsen, Henrik. Eleven Plays, 4094
IBSEN, HENRIK, 4085
Icarus. Shroder, Maurice Z, 4116
Ice Age. Kurten, Bjorn, 2165
Ice Age Lost. Schultz, Given, 2166
Ickis, Marguerite. Book of Festivals and Holidays the World Over, 151
Icon and the Axe. Billington, James H, 5481
ICONS, 2891
Icons and Their History. Rice, David T. and Rice, Tamara T. 2891
Idea of the Jewish State. Halpern, Ben, 5664
Idea of the South. Vandiver, Frank E., ed, 6217
Ideas and Institutions in European History, 800-1715. Mendenhall, Thomas C., et al. 4990
Identity. Erikson, Erik H, 580
Ideological Origins of the American Revolution. Bailyn, Bernard, 5913

IDEOLOGY, 634
Ideology and Organization in Communist China. Schurmann, Franz, 1500
Ideology, Politics and Government in the Soviet Union. Armstrong, John A, 1169
Idols Behind Altars. Brenner, Anita, 2941
Idyll, C. P., ed. Exploring the Ocean World, 2139
IEEE Standard Dictionary of Electrical and Electronics Terms. Institute of Electrical & Electronics Engineers, 255
Ignition. Clark, John D, 2861
IK (AFRICAN PEOPLE), 932
Ikram, Sheikh M. Muslim Civilization in India, 5628
Iliad. Homer, 4466
Iliad. Homer, 4463
Ilios. Schliemann, Heinrich, 4982
Illich, Ivan D. Deschooling Society, 1751
Illustrated Encyclopedia of Freshwater Fish. Hervey, George F. and Hems, Jack. 262
Illustrated English Social History. Trevelyan, George M, 5177
Illustrated Hassle-Free Make Your Own Clothes Book. Rosenberg, Sharon and Wiener, Joan. 2839
Illustrated History of Baseball. Smith, Robert M, 3376
Illustrated History of Magic. Christopher, Milbourne, 3334
Illustrated History of Ships and Boats. Casson, Lionel, 2680
Illustrated History of the Submarine. Horton, Edward, 2684
ILLUSTRATIONS — BIBLIOGRAPHY, 61
I'm Not Stiller. Frisch, Max, 4048
I'm OK, You're OK. Harris, Thomas Anthony, 2604
I'm Somebody Important. Mitchell, George, 1033
Im Westen Nichts Neues. Remarque, Erich M, 4068
Imaginary Poets. Sprague, Rosemary, 3544
IMAGINATION, 4654
Immensee. Storm, Theodor, 4069
Immigration As a Factor in American History. Handlin, Oscar, 1278
L' Immoraliste. Gide, André, 4214
IMMUNOLOGY, 2257
Impeachment. Berger, Raoul, 1569
Impeachment. Black, Charles Lund, 1571
Impeachment. Brant, Irving, 1606
Impeachment and Trial of Andrew Johnson. Benedict, Michael, 6081
Impeachment and Trial of Andrew Johnson. DeWitt, David, 6083

INDEX

Impeachment Congress. Grayson, Cary R. and Lukowski, Susan, eds. 1363
IMPEACHMENTS
  GREAT BRITAIN, 1569
  U.S., 1569, 1571, 1606, 1644-1645
Impending Crisis of the South. Helper, Hinton R, 1285
Imperfect Union. Hutchinson, John, 1441
Imperial Germany. Rosenberg, Arthur, 5297
Imperial Japan, 1800-1945. Livingston, Jon, 5621
Imperial Presidency. Schlesinger, Arthur, Jr, 5869
Imperial Republic. Aron, Raymond, 1327
Imperial Rome. Hadas, Moses, 4943
Imperial Spain. Salmon, Edward D, 5460
IMPERIALISM, 1211, 1216, 5057
Imperialism. Koebner, Richard and Schmidt, H. D. 1211
Imperialism and Nationalism in the Fertile Crescent. Allen, Richard, 1182
IMPRESSIONISM (ART), 3030, 3044
Improvization for the Theatre. Spolin, Viola, 3295
In His Own Image. Simon, James F, 1610
In Hitler's Shadow. Bell, Leland V, 1146
In Praise of Folly. Erasmus, Desiderius, 4432
In Praise of Hands. Paz, Octavio, 3012
In Search of a Responsible World Society. Bock, Paul, 767
In Search of Ancient Gods. Von Daniken, Erich, 474
In Search of Dracula. McNally, Raymond T. and Florescu, Radu. 3531
In Search of Lake Monsters. Costello, Peter, 2371
In Search of Roosevelt. Tugwell, Rexford G, 6146
In Someone's Shadow. McKuen, Rod, 3652
In the Coral Reefs of the Caribbean, Bahamas, Florida, Bermuda. Hannan, Hans, et al. 2265
In the Court of Public Opinion. Hiss, Alger, 1714
In the Interlude. Pasternak, Boris L, 4512
In the Paradise of Krishna. Klostermaier, Klaus, 848
In the Service of Their Country. Gaylin, Willard, 1673
In the Shadow of Man. Van Lawick-Goodall, Jane, 2481
In the Trail of the Wind. Bierhorst, John, ed, 4638
In the Wake of the Sea Serpents. Heuvelmans, Bernard, 2372
In Whitest Africa. Frye, William R, 1049

Inadmissible Evidence. Osborne, John, 3905
INCAS, 6266-6267, 6269, 6277
Inclusive Flame. Cambon, Glauco, 3554
INCOME — U. S., 1540
Incompleat Folksinger. Seegar, Pete, 3238
Incredible War of 1812. Hitsman, J. Mackay, 5986
An Index to Criticism of British and American Poetry. Cline, Gloria S. and Baker, Jeffrey A. 365
Index to Fairy Tales, 1949-1972. Ireland, Norma, 153
Index to Illustrations. Ellis, Jesse C, 61
Index to Literary Biography. Havlice, Patricia P, 68
Index to the Dictionary of the History of Ideas. Wiener, Philip P., ed, 378
INDEXES, 67, 333, 335
INDIA, 1124, 3391, 5929, 6132
  HISTORY, 440, 5626-5627, 5630, 5635
  POLITICS AND GOVERNMENT, 1180, 1562, 5631, 5634
  RELIGION, 835, 847
India. Kublin, Hyman, 5629
India, a Modern History. Spear, Percival, 5630
INDIA-PAKISTAN CONFLICT, 5637
Indian. Commission on the Rights and Liberties and Responsibilities of the American Indians, 5766
Indian Art in America. Dockstader, Frederick J, 2938
INDIAN DRAMA, 4481, 4599
Indian Heritage of America. Josephy, Alvin M, 5753
INDIAN LITERATURE, 4636-4637, 4478, 4486
INDIAN POETRY, 4601
Indian Removal. Foreman, Grant, 5770
Indian Treaties, 1778-1883. Kappler, Charles J., ed, 446
Indianapolis 500. Engel, Lyle K, 3405
INDIANS, 1978, 2230, 5756, 6265
Indians. Kopit, Arthur, 3699
INDIANS OF MEXICO, 2941, 4737, 5747, 5757, 5808
INDIANS OF NORTH AMERICA, 75, 445-446, 876, 1835, 2464, 2938, 2898, 4736, 5743-5756, 5760-5776, 5793, 5886, 5995, 6073, 6078, 6191,6221, 6230, 6250
Indians of North America. Driver, Harold E, 5747
INDIANS OF SOUTH AMERICA, 4737, 5748, 5753
Indians of the Americas. Embree, Edwin R, 5748
Indians of the High Plains. Hyde, George E, 5751

INDEX

Indians of the Woodlands, from Prehistoric Times to 1725. Hyde, George E, 5752
INDIANS, TREATMENT OF — U.S., 5759, 5766-5767, 5769-5770, 5775
India's Freedom Movement. Shiva Rao, B, 5634
Indigo Bunting. Sheean, Vincent, 3618
Indira. Bhatia, Krishan, 5631
Indira Gandhi Speaks on Democracy, Socialism, and Third World Nonalignment. Gandhi, Indira, 5635
INDONESIA, 6283
  HISTORY, 1562, 5689-5690, 6282
Indoor Water Gardener's How-to Handbook. Loewer, H. Peter, 2797
INDUSTRIAL ARTS — HISTORY, 4749
Industrial England, 1776-1851. Marshall, Dorothy, 1411
Industrial Revolution. Beard, Charles A, 1410
INDUSTRIAL WORKERS OF THE WORLD, 1438, 1445
INDUSTRY — HISTORY, 5056
Inequality and Poverty. Budd, Edward C., ed, 1540
Infinite River. Amos, William H, 2261
Inflation. Friedman, Irving S, 1455
INFLATION (FINANCE), 1455
Influence of Sea Power Upon History, 1660-1783. Mahan, Alfred T, 1688
INFORMATION STORAGE AND RETRIEVAL SYSTEMS, 47, 1264
INFORMATION THEORY, 464
Ing, Catherine and Pond, Grace. Champion Cats of the World, 2812
Inge, William. Four Plays, 3696
Inger, Robert F. and Schmidt, Karl P. Living Reptiles of the World, 2412
Ingmanson, Dale E. and Wallace, William J. Oceanology, 2140
Inkeles, Alex. Social Change in Soviet Russia, 1091
Innes, William T. Exotic Aquarium Fishes, 2819
Innocent Killers. Van Lawick-Goodall, Jane and Van Lawick-Goodall, Hugo. 2474
Inorganic Chemistry. Sanderson, Robert T, 2079
An Inquiry into the Human Prospect. Heilbroner, Robert L, 4657
INQUISITION, 794
Inquisition. O'Brien, John A, 794
INSECT CONTROL — BIOLOGICAL CONTROL, 2784
Insect Societies. Wilson, Edward O, 2392
Insect Zoo. Ewbank, Connie, 2813
INSECTS, 243-244, 2389-2394, 2777-2778, 2813
Insects and How They Function. Callahan, Philip S, 2390

Insects of North America. Klots, Alexander B. and Klots, Elsie B. 2393
Insects of the World. Linsenmaier, Walter, 243
Inside Pitching. Jenkins, Ferguson, 3373
Inside Swimming. Schollander, Don and Cohne, Joel H. 3433
Inside the Confederate Government. Kean, Robert G, 6059
Inside the Third Reich. Speer, Albert, 5326
Insiders' Guide to the Colleges. Yale Daily News, ed, 1789
INSTINCT, 2360
Instinct and Intelligence. Barnett, Samuel A, 2351
Institute of Electrical & Electronics Engineers. IEEE Standard Dictionary of Electrical and Electronics Terms, 255
INSTRUCTIONAL MATERIALS CENTERS, 23, 35
INSTRUCTIONAL MEDIA CENTERS, 1
Instrumental and Chamber Music. Ewen, David, 3155
Instruments of Flight. Siberry, K. M, 2737
Instruments of Music. Donington, Robert, 3200
INTELLECT, 577-578
Intelligence - What Is It? Cohen, Daniel, 577
Intelligence Establishment. Ransom, Harry H, 1296
Intermezzo. Giraudoux, Jean, 4161
Internal Politics of China, 1949-1972. Domes, Juergen, 1176
INTERNAL SECURITY — U. S., 1336
International Book of Trees. Johnson, Hugh, 236
INTERNATIONAL ECONOMIC RELATIONS, 1083, 1795
International Encyclopedia of the Social Sciences. 128
International Encyclopedia of Winter Sports. Bass, Howard, 3411
INTERNATIONAL LAW, 1555
International Medical Encyclopedia. Bennett, Hastin, 2586
INTERNATIONAL RELATIONS, 1154, 1293-1294, 1548
INTERPLANETARY VOYAGES, 473-474
Interpreter's Bible. 104
Interpreter's Dictionary of the Bible. 105
Interpreter's One Volume Commentary on the Bible. 106
Into the Hidden Environment. Critchlow, Keith, 2136
Into the Ocean World. Ward, Ritchie, 2268
Introducing Op Art. Lancaster, John, 2911

INDEX

Introducing the Single-Camera VTR System. Mattingly, Grayson and Smith, Welby. 3116

Introduction to African Civilization. Jackson, John G, 4792

Introduction to African Literature. Beier, Ulli, 4624

An Introduction to Anglo-Saxon England. Blair, Peter H, 5179

An Introduction to Argentina. Alexander, Robert J, 6273

Introduction to Automated Data Processing. Langerbach, Robert, 2846

An Introduction to Comparative Government. Blondel, Jean, 1142

Introduction to Computers in Information Science. Artandi, Susan, 47

An Introduction to Ecology and Population Biology. Emmel, Thomas C, 2239

Introduction to Electronics. Branson, Lane, 2644

Introduction to German Poetry. Gray, Ronald D, 4007

Introduction to Human Anatomy. Francis, Carl C, 2503

Introduction to Human Genetics. Sutton, Elton H, 2204

Introduction to Logic. Copi, Irving M, 593

Introduction to Mathematical Linguistics. Wall, Robert, 1859

An Introduction to Modern Economic Theory. Moore, Basil J, 1400

An Introduction to Modern Economics. Robinson, Joan and Eatwell, John. 1401

An Introduction to Music. Boyden, David D, 3135

Introduction to Oceanography. Ross, David A, 2141

Introduction to Organic Chemistry. Depuy, Charles H. and Rinehart, Kenneth L. 2083

Introduction to Scandinavian Literature. Bredsdorff, Elias, et al. 4082

Introduction to Space Science. Haymes, Robert C, 1896

An Introduction to Spanish-American Literature. Franco, Jean, 4314

An Introduction to Spanish Literature. Northup, George T, 4315

Introduction to Teleprocessing. Martin, James, 2642

Introduction to the French Poets. Brereton, Geoffrey, 4136

An Introduction to the History of Central Africa. Wills, Alfred J, 5742

An Introduction to the History of Mathematics. Eves, Howard, 1942

An Introduction to the Study of African Culture. Ayisi, Eric O, 925

Introduction to the Theory of Games. McKinsey, John C, 1954

Introduction to Thermodynamics. Rolle, Kurt C, 2044

Introduction to Tomorrow. Abernethy, Robert G, 6099

An Introduction to Western Philosophy. Flew, Anthony G, 636

Introduction to Yugoslav Literature. Mikasinovich, Branko, et al, eds. 4586

Introductory Concepts in Biology. Becker, George, 2207

Invention of the Aeroplane, 1799-1909. Gibbs-Smith, Charles H, 2712

INVENTIONS, 1924, 2488-2489, 2493-2494

INVENTORS, 2495, 4863

Inventors and Inventions of the Ancient World. Baldwin, Gordon C, 2488

INVERTEBRATES, 2378-2381

Invertebrates of North America. Milne, Lorus and Milne, Margery. 2381

Invisible China. Alexander, Garth, 1314

Invisible Empire. Horn, Stanley F, 1373

Invisible Government. Wise, David and Ross, Thomas B. 1624

Invisible Universe. Verschuur, Gerrit L, 1977

Invitation to Biology. Curtis, Helena, 2212

Invitation to Poetry. Cotter, Janet, 3473

Invitation to the Theatre. Kernodle, George Riley, 3314

Inward Sky. Hoeltje, Hubert H, 3718

Ionesco, Eugene. Rhinoceros and Other Plays, 4166

IRAN
    ANTIQUITIES, 4910
    HISTORY, 4909, 4917-4918, 4961, 4970, 5640-5641

IRAQ — HISTORY, 4912, 5659

IRELAND
    CIVILIZATION, 5161
    DESCRIPTION AND TRAVEL, 4745
    EMIGRATION AND IMMIGRATION, 1513
    HISTORY, 5160, 5162-5164
    POLITICS AND GOVERNMENT, 1161, 5165-5166, 5169

Ireland, Norma. Index to Fairy Tales, 1949-1972, 153

Ireland Since the Rising. Coogan, Timothy P, 5164

Irish. Connery, Donald S, 5161

IRISH DRAMA (ENGLISH), 3854-3855

Irish Journal. Boll, Heinrich, 4745

IRISH LITERATURE — TRANSLATIONS INTO ENGLISH, 4492
IRISH POETRY — COLLECTIONS, 3778
IRISH QUESTION, 5166
IRISH REPUBLICAN ARMY — HISTORY, 5163
Irish Stories and Plays. Carroll, Paul Vincent, 3890
Iriye, Akira. Across the Pacific, 929
Irrational Man. Barrett, William, 549
Irrelevant English Teacher. Morse, Josiah M, 1884
Irrepressible Conflict, 1850-1865. Cole, Arthur C, 6004
Irrungen, Wirrungen. Fontane, Theodor, 4046
Irving Berlin. Freedland, Michael, 3157
Irwin, Graham, see Morris, Richard E.
Irwin, Leonard B. Black Studies, 18
Is God a White Racist? A Preamble to Black Theology. Jones, William R, 746
Isaac Newton, a Biography. More, Louis T, 2026
Isaacs, Neil D. and Zimbardo, Rose A., eds. Tolkien and the Critics, 3942
Isei and Nisei. Kitagawa, Daisuke, 1064
ISLAM, 614, 863-865, 4684
Islam. Guillaume, Alfred, 864
ISLAMIC COUNTRIES — HISTORY, 382
ISLAMIC EMPIRE
 BIOGRAPHY, 4858
 HISTORY — HANDBOOKS, MANUALS, ETC., 441
Islamic Philosophy and Theology. Watt, W. Montgomery, 614
Islamic Tradition. Christopher, John B, 4684
Island Race. Churchill, Winston L, 5172
Islands of the Caribbean. Hannan, Hans W, 4801
Isms. Golob, Eugene O, 894
ISRAEL, 4785-4786, 5667
 ANTIQUITIES, 4786
 FOREIGN OPINION, 895
 FOREIGN RELATIONS, 1323
 HISTORY, 5661, 5663, 5665
Israel. Naamani, Israel T, 5667
Israel and the Arab World. Dodd, Charles H., compiled by. 5662
Israel and World Politics. Draper, Theodore, 5648
Israel-Arab Reader. Laqueur, Walter, ed, 1323
ISRAEL-ARAB WAR (1948-1949), 5643, 5645
ISRAEL-ARAB WAR, (1967), 5647-5650
ISRAEL-ARAB WAR (1973), 5651-5652
Israel at the Crossroads. Schweid, Eliezer, 859
Israel, F. L., see Friedman, Leon

Israel, F. L. see Schlesinger, Arthur M., Jr.
Israel's War of Independence, 1947-1949. Lorch, Netaniel, 5645
Issues in the Future of Asia. Lowenthal, Richard, ed, 1178
It Happened Last Year. Cornell, James, ed, 1897
Italian Art. Chastel, Andre, 2923
ITALIAN DRAMA, 4293-4294
 COLLECTIONS, 4295-4297
ITALIAN FICTION — HISTORY AND CRITICISM, 4298
ITALIAN LANGUAGE — DICTIONARIES, 182
Italian Painters of the Renaissance. Berenson, Bernard, 3055
ITALIAN POETRY, 4291, 4299-4300
Italians. Barzini, Luigi, 5426
ITALO-ETHIOPIAN WAR, (1935-1936), 5720-5721
ITALY
 ANTIQUITIES, 4727
 CIVILIZATION, 4531-5432
 FOREIGN RELATIONS, 1342, 5108, 5449
 HISTORY, 5427, 5429-5430, 5433-5435, 5437-5438, 5441-5443, 5445-5448, 5450-5451
 POLITICS AND GOVERNMENT, 1167-1168
 SOCIAL LIFE AND CUSTOMS, 5426
Italy. Mack-Smith, Denis, 5446
Italy After Fascism. Mammarella, Giuseppe, 5447
Italy from Napoleon to Mussolini. Albrecht-Carrie, Rene, 5443
Italy Under Mussolini. Leeds, Christopher A, 5451
Ivask, Ivar and Von Wilpert, Gero. World Literature Since 1945, 3524
IVES, CHARLES, 3161
Ives, J. M. see Currier, Nathaniel
Iyer, Raghaven. The Moral and Political Thought of Mahatma Gandhi, 620
Izbrannoe. Solzhenitsyn, Aleksandr I, 4561
Izbrannye Proizv. Nekrasov, Nikolai, 4511

J. M. Barrie. Dunbar, Janet, 3966
Jablonski, Edward and Stewart, Lawrence D. The Gershwin Years, 3213
Jack London, Sailor on Horseback. Stone, Irving, 3736
JACKSON, ANDREW, 5995-5998
Jackson, G. N. see Hope, C. E.
Jackson, Gabriel. Spanish Republic and the Civil War, 1931-1939, 5470
Jackson, George. Soledad Brother, 1736
Jackson, John G. Introduction to African Civilization, 4792

INDEX

Jackson, Joseph H. Anybody's Gold, 6244
———. Pictorial Guide to the Planets, 1996
Jackson, Kenneth H., ed. A Celtic Miscellany, 4491
Jackson, Kenneth T. The Ku Klux Klan in the City, 1915-1930, 1374
Jackson, Robert V. South Asian Crisis, 5637
Jackson, Stanley. Caruso, 3205
JACKSON, THOMAS JONATHAN, 6051
Jacksonian Era. Van Deusen, Glyndon G, 5997
Jacob, Francois. The Logic of Life, 2296
JACOBITE REBELLION, 5158
Jacobs, David. Architecture, 2963
———. Bridges, Canals, Tunnels, 2689
Jacobs, G. Walker. Stranger Stop and Cast an Eye, 3088
Jacobs, Harold R. Mathematics, a Human Endeavor, 1933
Jacobs, Jane. Death and Life of Great American Cities, 1253
Jacobs, Lewis, compiled by. The Documentary Tradition, 3275
———. The Emergence of Film Art, 3276
Jacobs, Wilbur R. Dispossessing the American Indian, 5772
Jacobus, John. see Hunter, Sam
Jaffe, Hans. Twenty Thousand Years of World Painting, 3027
Jahn, Mike. Rock, 3222
JAMES I, 5240, 5248
James, Dorris C. Years of MacArthur, 1676
James First. Mathew, David, 5240
James, Glenn and James, Robert C., eds. Mathematics Dictionary, 209
James, Henry. Theory of Fiction, 3488
JAMES, HENRY, 642
James Joyce. Ellmann, Richard, 3939
James Joyce and His World. Anderson, Chester G, 3935
James, Marquis. The Raven, 6225
James Monroe. Ammon, Henry, 5981
James, Muriel. Born to Love, 2605
James, Muriel and Jongward, Dorothy. Born to Win, 2606
James, Robert C., see James, Glenn
James Russell Lowell. Duberman, Martin B, 3556
James, William. Varieties of Religious Experience, 693
———. William James, 645
JAMES, WILLIAM, 642
Jameson, J. Franklin. The American Revolution Considered As a Social Movement, 5917
Jan Smuts. Crafford, F. S, 5740
Jane Addams, Pioneer for Social Justice. Meigs, Cornelia L, 1693

Jane Austen. Jenkins, Elizabeth, 3923
Jane Austen and Her World. Laski, Marghanita, 3924
Jane's Pocket Book of Commercial Transport Aircraft. Taylor, John, ed, 2729
Jane's Pocket Book of Major Combat Aircraft. Taylor, John, ed, 2676
Jane's Pocket Book of Major Warships. Moore, John E., ed, 2682
Janson, Horst W. History of Art, 269
Janson, Horst W. and Kerman, Joseph. History of Art and Music, 2873
Janus, Christopher G. and Brashler, William. The Search for Peking Man, 2205
JAPAN
    CIVILIZATION, 4779, 5614, 5618
    DESCRIPTION AND TRAVEL, 4778
    FOREIGN RELATIONS, 1304, 5608
    HISTORY, 2933, 5615-5620
        SOURCES, 5614, 5621, 5623
    MAPS, 405
    POLITICS AND GOVERNMENT, 1562, 5117
Japan. Hane, Mikiso, 5616
Japan. Hurlimann, Martin and King, Francis. 4778
Japan. Maraini, Fosco, 4779
Japan. Reischauer, Edwin O, 5617
Japan. Sansom, George B, 5618
Japan. Smith, Bradley, 2933
Japan in Postwar Asia. Olson, Lawrence A, 931
Japanese. Seward, Jack, 4780
Japanese Americans. Kitano, Harry L, 1065
JAPANESE DRAMA, 4599
JAPANESE FICTION — HISTORY AND CRITICISM, 4616
JAPANESE POETRY, 4601, 4612-4614
Japan's Decision to Surrender. Butow, Robert J, 5118
Japan's Imperial Conspiracy. Bergamini, David, 5117
Japan's Modern Century. Borton, Hugh, 5620
Jarman, Cathy. Atlas of Animal Migration, 239
Jarrell, Randall. Complete Poems, 3645
Jaspers, Karl. The Great Philosophers, 516
———. Nietzsche, 662
Jastrow, Robert. Red Giants and White Dwarfs, 1985
Jastrow, Robert and Thompson, Malcolm H. Astronomy, 1964
Javits, Jacob K. and Kellerman, Don. Who Makes War, 1580
Jazz Masters of the '20's. Hadlock, Richard, 3190
Jazz Masters of the '40's. Gitler, Ira, 3189

JAZZ MUSIC, 3187, 3189-3192, 3196
JAZZ MUSICIANS, 3243, 3247, 3249
Jazz Story from the '90's to the '60's. Dexter, Dave, 3187
Jeal, Tim. Livingstone, 4795
Jean-Christophe. Rolland, Romain, 4244
Jean Cocteau. Fowlie, Wallace, 4156
Jean Giraudoux. Le Sage, Laurent, 4168
Jean-Paul Sartre. La Farge, René, 673
Jean Piaget. Evans, Richard I, 581
JEANNERET-GRIS, CHARLES EDWARD, 2961
Jeb Stuart. Thomason, John W, 6050
Jeffers, Robinson. Beginning and the End, and Other Poems, 3575
Jefferson and Hamilton. Bowers, Claude G, 5962
Jefferson Davis. Tate, Allen, 6047
Jefferson, Thomas. Life and Selected Writings, 1076
JEFFERSON, THOMAS, 1076, 5915, 5962, 5974
Jeffersonian Republicans. Cunningham, Noble E., Jr, 1389
Jencks, Charles. Modern Movements in Architecture, 2973
Jenkins, Elizabeth. Jane Austen, 3923
Jenkins, Ferguson. Inside Pitching, 3373
Jenkins, Francis A. Fundamentals of Optics, 2040
Jenkins, Marie M. The Curious Mollusks, 2383
Jennings, Ivor. British Constitution, 1560
———. Cabinet Government, 1652
———. Parliament, 1359
Jensen, Merrill. The New Nation, 5965
Jensen, William A. and Salisbury, Frank B. Botany, 2311
Jenson, Oliver. see American Heritage Editors
Jerrold, Walter C. A Book of Famous Wits, 3961
JERUSALEM
    ANTIQUITIES, 4902
    SIEGE, (1948), 5643
Jerusalem. Join-Lambert, Michel, 4902
Jerusalem Bible. Bible, 708
Jespersen, Otto. Growth and Structure of the English Language, 1867
———. Language, 1856
JESUS CHRIST, 748-750
Jesus of Nazareth. Bornkamm, Gunther, 749
JESUS PEOPLE, 775-776
Jesus People. Enroth, Ronald M., et al. 776
Le Jeu de l'Amour et du Hasard. Marivaux, Pierre C. de, 4170
Jevons, Frederick R. The Biochemical Approach to Life, 2227

Jew and His Family. Kaplan, Benjamin, 1050
A Jew in Christian America. Gilbert, Arthur, 1059
JEWISH-ARAB RELATIONS, 389, 895, 924, 1182-1183, 1322-1323, 5644, 5646, 5662
Jewish Art. Roth, Cecil, 2892
JEWS
    CIVILIZATION, 857, 4901
    HISTORICAL GEOGRAPHY — MAPS, 389
    HISTORY, 1054, 4899, 4901, 4904-4907
    LITURGY AND RITUAL HAGGADAH, 861
    PERSECUTIONS, 5328
    POLITICAL AND SOCIAL CONDITIONS, 1052, 5105
Jews Among the Nations. Kahler, Erich, 1054
JEWS IN GERMANY, 5319
JEWS IN LITERATURE, 3536
JEWS IN PALESTINE — HISTORY, 5661
Jews in Their Land. Ben-Gurion, David, ed, 5661
JEWS IN WARSAW — HISTORY — SOURCES, 5362
JFK and LBJ. Wicker, Tom, 1646
Jiménez, Juan Ramón. Platero and I, 4380
———. Three Hundred Poems, 1903-1953, 4343
Jiménez, Juan Ramón. see García Lorca, Federico
JOAN OF ARC, 5377
Joan of Arc. Michelet, Jules, 5377
JOANNES XXIII, POPE, 751
Jocelyn. Lamartine, Alphonse de, 4124
Joe Egg. Nichols, Peter, 3904
Joesting, Edward. Hawaii, 6290
Johann Gutenberg and the Invention of Printing. Harris, Brayton, 2865
Johann Sebastian Bach. Geiringer, Karl and Geiringer, Irene. 3158
Johannsen, Robert W. Stephen A. Douglas, 6023
John Adams and the American Revolution. Bowen, Catherine D, 5932
John Brown's Body. Benet, Stephen Vincent, 3595
John C. Calhoun. Coit, Margaret L, 5976
John Calvin. Walker, Williston, 812
John D. Rockefeller. Nevins, Allan, 1533
John Dewey on Education. Dewey, John, 1745
John Donne. Bald, R. C, 3795
John Foster Dulles. Gould-Adams, Richard J, 6164
John Keats. Ward, Aileen, 3819

INDEX

JOHN, KING OF ENGLAND, 5201
John Locke. Aaron, Richard, 651
John Muir and the Sierra Club. Jones, Holway R, 1462
John Paul Jones. Morison, Samuel E, 5955
John Quincy Adams. Bemis, Samuel F, 5990
John Quincy Adams. Hecht, Marie B, 5991
Johnsen, Russell H. see Grunwald, Ernest
JOHNSON, ANDREW, 6080-6084
Johnson, Bruce D. Marihuana Users and Drug Subculture, 1700
Johnson, Burges, ed. New Rhyming Dictionary and Poets' Handbook, 173
Johnson, Edgar. Charles Dickens, 3928
———. Sir Walter Scott, the Great Unknown, 3964
Johnson, Eric W. Love and Sex in Plain Language, 2518
———. V.D, 2612
Johnson, Haynes. Bay of Pigs, 5833
Johnson, Hugh. The International Book of Trees, 236
Johnson, James W. Gods Trombones, 3603
JOHNSON, JOHN ARTHUR, 3703
Johnson, Lady Bird. A White House Diary, 6171
JOHNSON, LYNDON BAINES, 1646, 6170-6171
Johnson, Paul. Pope John XXIII, 751
Johnson, Samuel. Johnson's Dictionary, 164
JOHNSON, SAMUEL, 3963
Johnson, Thomas H., see Miller, Perry
Johnson, Thomas Herbert. Emily Dickinson, 3568
Johnson, Walter and Evans, Carol, eds. The Papers of Adlai E. Stevenson, 6161
Johnson, William O., Jr. All That Glitters Is Not Gold, 3384
Johnson's Dictionary. Johnson, Samuel, 164
Johnston, Harold W. The Private Life of the Romans, 4922
Johnston, Mary. Roman Life, 4923
Johnston, Verna. Sierra Nevada, 1907
Join-Lambert, Michel. Jerusalem, 4902
Jonathan Sewall. Berkin, Carol, 5944
Jones, Arnold H. Herods of Judaea, 4903
———. The Later Roman Empire, 284 to 602, 4951
Jones, Barbara and Howell, Bill. Popular Arts of the First World War, 3013
Jones, David. The Plays of T. S. Eliot, 3896
Jones, Edmund D., ed. English Critical Essays, 3954
———. English Critical Essays, 3953

Jones, Gwyn. A History of the Vikings, 5536
Jones, Holway R. John Muir and the Sierra Club, 1462
Jones, Howard M. and Ludwig, Richard M. Guide to American Literature and Its Backgrounds Since 1890, 354
Jones, John F. On Aristotle and Greek Tragedy, 4453
JONES, JOHN PAUL, 5955
Jones, Katharine M. Heroines of Dixie, 6058
Jones, Kenneth L., et al. Drugs and Alcohol, 2547
Jones, Leroi. Black Music, 3196
———. Four Black Revolutionary Plays, 3697
———. Two Plays, 3698
Jones, Phyllis M., ed. English Critical Essays, 3955
Jones, Rufus. Spiritual Reformers of the 16th and 17th Centuries, 4869
JONES, RUFUS MATTHEW, 815
Jones, Virgil C. Roosevelt's Rough Riders, 6098
Jones, William R. Is God a White Racist? A Preamble to Black Theology, 746
Jongward, Dorothy. see James, Muriel
Jonson, Ben. Five Plays, 3860
JOPLIN, JANIS, 3229
Joravsky, David. Soviet Marxism and Natural Science, 1917-1932, 1910
Jordan, Emil L. Animal Atlas of the World, 2446
Jordan, Winthrop D. White Over Black, 5883
Jordi, Lisa and David. Rubin, Theodore I, 2627
JOSEPH II, EMPEROR OF GERMANY, 5291
Joseph P. Kennedy. Koskoff, David E, 6168
Joseph, Peter. Good Times, 6172
Joseph, Stephen. Theatre in the Round, 3294
JOSEPHINE, CONSORT OF NAPOLEON I, 5406
Josephson, Matthew. Al Smith, 6126
———. The Politicos, 6070
———. President Makers, 1896-1919, 6103
———. Robber Barons, 6071
———. Stendhal; or the Pursuit of Happiness, 4283
Josephus, Flavius. Complete Works, 4904
Josephy, Alvin M., et al, eds. The Horizon History of Africa, 5702
———. The Indian Heritage of America, 5753
Josiah Quincy, 1772-1864. McCaughey, Robert A, 5977

420

Journal of Urban Law Editors. Riot in the Cities, 908
JOURNALISM, 485, 487-489, 492, 495-496, 498, 504
Joy of Music. Bernstein, Leonard, 3131
Joyce Cary, a Biography. Foster, Malcolm, 3940
JOYCE, JAMES, 3935, 3939
Juan de Mairena. Machado, Antonio, 4327
JUAN, DON, 874-875
JUAREZ, BENITO PABLO, 5814
JUDAISM, 851-852
  DICTIONARIES, 122
  DICTIONARIES AND ENCYCLOPEDIAS, 123
  HISTORY, 857, 860
  ISRAEL, 859
  U. S., 853
JUDGES, 1609, 1612
JUDICIAL REVIEW, 1613
Judson, David M. Ghar Parau, 2129
Julie, ou La Nouvelle Héloise. Rousseau, Jean Jacques, 4246
July, Nineteen Fourteen. Geiss, Immanuel, compiled by. 5074
July, Robert W. The Origins of Modern African Thought, 5723
Jung, Carl G. Basic Writings of C. G. Jung, 528
JUNG, CARL JUSTAV, 563
Junge Frau von 1914. Zweig, Arnold, 4070
JUNIOR COLLEGES — U. S. —
  DIRECTORIES, 148, 1787
Junkie Priest. Harris, John D, 2598
Jupiter. Asimov, Isaac, 2000
Jupiter Effect. Gribbin, John R. and Plagemann, Stephen H. 2115
Jusserand, Jean A. English Wayfaring Life in the Middle Ages. , 5186
Justice. Harris, Richard, 1648
Justice on Trial. Todd, Alden L, 1620
Justices of the U. S. Supreme Court, 1789-1969. Friedman, Leon and Israel, F. L., eds. 1618
Justinian and the Later Roman Empire. Barker, John W, 5547
JUSTINIANUS I, 5547
Jutty, Sam. How Your Car Works, 2744
Juvenal the Satirist. Highet, Gilbert, 4422
Juvenalis, Decimus Junius. Satires, 4423
JUVENALIS, DECIMUS JUNIUS, 4422
JUVENILE DELINQUENCY — U.S., 1593, 1603

Kafka, Franz. Die Romane, 4059
———. Das Urteil und Andere Erzählungen, 4060
KAFKA, FRANZ, 551, 4080
Kafker, Frank A. and Laux, James M., eds. The French Revolution, 5395
Kagan, Jerome. Personality Development, 582
Kahin, George McT. Nationalism and Revolution in Indonesia, 6283
Kahler, Erich. Jews Among the Nations, 1054
Kahler, Heinz. The Art of Rome and Her Empire, 2918
Kahn, Ely J. The Separated People, 1244
Kahn, Kathy. Hillbilly Women, 980
Kailins, Marvin and Andrews, Lewis M. Biofeedback, 2580
Kaiser and His Times. Balfour, Michael, 5300
Kai-Yu, Hsu, ed. Twentieth Century Chinese Poetry Anthology, 4604
Kajubi, Senteza, et al, eds. African Encyclopedia, 443
KALAHARI DESERT — DESCRIPTION AND TRAVEL, 4796-4797
Kalb, Marvin L. Kissinger, 6175
Kalendergeschichten. Brecht, Bertolt, 4041
Kalidasa. Shakuntala and Other Writings, 4481
Kallir, Otto. Grandma Moses, 3045
Kampf, Avram. Contemporary Synagogue Art, 2890
Kannik, Preben. Military Uniforms of the World in Color, 1671
Kant, Immanuel. The Philosophy of Kant, 666
Kapitanskaia Dochka. Pushkin, Aleksandr S, 4558
Kaplan, Abraham. New World of Philosophy, 609
Kaplan, Benjamin. The Jew and His Family, 1050
Kaplan, Carol, *see* Kaplan, Lawrence
Kaplan, Chaim A. Scroll of Agony, 5362
Kaplan, Justin. Lincoln Steffens, 3758
Kaplan, Lawrence and Kaplan, Carol, eds. Revolutions, 1081
Kaplan, Martin, compiled by. The Harvard Lampoon Centennial Celebration, 1876-1973, 3751
Kaplan, Sidney. The Black Presence in the Era of Revolution, 1770-1800, 5935
Kappler, Charles J., ed. Indian Treaties, 1778-1883, 446
Karalus, Karl E. and Eckert, Allan W. The Owls of North America, 2442
Karen. Killilea, Marie, 2594
Karl Barth. Mueller, David, 741
Karl, Frederick R. An Age of Fiction, 3934
———. Reader's Guide to the Contemporary English Novel, 3931

INDEX

KARL I, EMPEROR OF AUSTRIA, 5344
Karl Marx. Berlin, Isaiah, 1491
Karl Marx. Bottomore, Tom, ed, 1492
Kasner, Edward and Newman, James. Mathematics and the Imagination, 1934
Kasper, Raphael. *see* Ebbin, Steven
Kassof, Allen, ed. Prospects for Soviet Society, 1092
Kaster, Joseph, ed. Wings of the Falcon, 4889
Katz, Robert. The Fall of the House of Savoy, 5444
———. A Giant in the Earth, 1518
Katz, William A. and Gargal, Berry. Magazines for Libraries, 10
Katz, William L. The Black West, 6235
———. Eyewitness, 1025
Katzner, Kenneth. The Languages of the World, 1853
Kauffeld, Carl. Snakes, 2822
Kauffman, Stanley. Living Images, 3277
Kaufmann, Walter A., ed. Existentialism from Dostoevsky to Sartre, 552
———. Philosophic Classics, 611
———. Religion from Tolstoy to Camus, 694
Kaufmann, William J. Relativity and Cosmology, 1979
Kaun, Alexander S. Leonid Andreyev, 4553
Kavaler, Lucy. Freezing Point, 2225
———. Noise, 2567
Kavenagh, W. Keith. Foundations of Colonial America, 1276
Kavkazskii Plennik. Tolstoi, Leo N, 4566
Kawabata, Yasunari. Snow Country, 4609
Kayatta, Ken and Schmidt, Steven. Successful Terrariums, 2800
Kazin, Alfred. Bright Book of Life, 3730
Kean, Robert G. Inside the Confederate Government, 6059
KEAN, ROBERT GARLICK HILL, 6059
Kearney, Paul W. How to Drive Better and Avoid Accidents, 2571
Keats, John. Complete Poetical Works, 3812
KEATS, JOHN, 3819
Kecskemeti, Paul. Unexpected Revolution, 5367
Kee, Howard C., et al. Understanding the New Testament, 735
Kee, Robert. The Green Flag, 5166
Keen, Clifford P., et al. Championship Wrestling, 3409
Keene, Donald, ed. Anthology of Japanese Literature, 4610
———. Modern Japanese Literature from 1868 to Present Day, 4611
———. Modern Japanese Novels and the West, 4616

———. Twenty Plays of the No Theater, 4615
Keene, Frances, ed. Neither Liberty nor Bread, 5445
Keer, Bhananjay. Mahatma Gandhi, 5633
Keil, Charles. Urban Blues, 3235
Keith, Arthur B. The Religion and Philosophy of the Veda and Upanishads, 835
Kellas, James C. Modern Scotland, 5159
Keller, Werner. The Bible As History, 713
———. The Bible As History in Pictures, 712
———. The Etruscans, 4729
Kellerman, Don. *see* Javits, Jacob K.
Kelley, Austin P. and Sotheby Parke Bernet Staff. Anatomy of Antiques, 3017
Kellog, A. Remington, et al. Wild Animals of North America, 2450
Kellogg, Charles F. NAACP, 1026
Kellogg, Walter G. The Conscientious Objector, 5075
Kelly, Amy. Eleanor of Aquitane and the Four Kings, 5206
Kelly, Francis M. and Schwabe, Randolph. Short History of Costume and Armour, 1066-1800, 1813
Kelsey, Robert J. Walking in the Wild, 3386
Kemeny, John G. Man and the Computer, 470
Kempton, Murray. The Briar Patch, 1598
Kendall, Paul M. Louis XI, 5376
———. Richard III, 5210
———. The Yorkist Age, 5211
Kendrick, Alexander. The Wound Within, 5685
Kendrick, Benjamin B. *see* Hacker, Louis M.
Keniston, Kenneth. Uncommitted, 909
———. Young Radicals, 993
Kennan, George F. Memoirs, 1925-1963, 1343
———. Realities of American Foreign Policy, 1344
———. Russia and the West Under Lenin and Stalin, 1309
KENNAN, GEORGE F., 1343
Kennedy. Sorensen, Theodore, 6169
Kennedy, John F. Profiles in Courage, 1365
KENNEDY, JOHN FITZGERALD, 1341, 1646, 6169
KENNEDY, JOSEPH PATRICK, 6168
Kennedy, Robert F. Thirteen Days, 6166
Kennedy, Rose F. Times to Remember, 6167
KENNEDY, ROSE FITZGERALD, 6167
Kenner, Hugh. Bucky, 2632

INDEX

———. A Reader's Guide to Samuel Beckett, 4286
Kennett, Audrey and Kennett, Vincent. The Palaces of Leningrad, 4765
Kennett, Vincent. *see* Kennett, Audrey
Kenny, John. Business of Diving, 2694
Kensington Rune Stone. Blegen, Theodore C, 5884
Kent, Frank R. Democratic Party, 1391
Kent State. Michener, James A, 6176
Kenyon, Gerald S., *see* Loy, John W., Jr.
Kenyon, Kathleen M. Archaeology in the Holy Land, 4719
Kerensky, Alexander. The Catastrophe, 5521
Kerensky, Oleg. Anna Pavlova, 3325
Kerman, Joseph. *see* Janson, Horst W.
Kernan, Alvin B., ed. Classics of the Modern Theater, 3506
Kerner, Robert J. The Urge to the Sea, 5486
Kernodle, George Riley. Invitation to the Theatre, 3314
Kershmer, William K. Flight Instructor's Manual, 2722
Kessel, Neil and Walton, Henry. Alcoholism, 2601
Ketcham, Ralph L. From Colony to Country, 5966
Ketchum, Richard M. The Secret Life of the Forest, 2327
———. The Winter Soldiers, 5952
Key Treaties for the Great Powers, 1814-1914. Hurst, Michael, ed, 141
Key, Wilson B. Subliminal Seduction, 2856
Keynes, Geoffrey. Life of William Harvey, 2500
Khadduri, Majid. Arab Contemporaries, 1157
———. Political Trends in the Arab World, 1158
Khruschev Remembers. Khrushchev, Nikita S, 5530
Khrushchev, Nikita S. Khruschev Remembers, 5530
Kice, J. L. and Marvell, E. N. Modern Principles of Organic Chemistry, 2084
Kieffer, William F. The Mole Concept in Chemistry, 2067
Kieran, John and Daley, Arthur. Story of the Olympic Games, 3385
Kierkegaard. Grimsley, Ronald, 677
A Kierkegaard Anthology. Kierkegaard, Soren, 678
Kierkegaard, Soren. A Kierkegaard Anthology, 678
KIERKEGAARD, SOREN AABYE, 551, 677
Kiernan, Thomas. *see* Root, Leon

Killam, G. D. The Novels of Chinua Achebe, 4633
Killeffer, David H. How Did You Think of That? An Introduction to the Scientific Method, 1911
Killilea, Marie. Karen, 2594
Kilroy-Silk, Robert. Socialism Since Marx, 1484
Kimball, Warren F. The Most Unsordid Act, 6135
Kimble, David. A Political History of Ghana, 5726
Kimche, Jon. There Could Have Been Peace, 1322
Kimmell, Stanley. The Mad Booths of Maryland, 3323
Kinchen, Lila A. *see* Erwin, Mabel D.
Kind and Usual Punishment. Mitford, Jessica, 1739
Kinder, Marsha and Houston, Beverle. Close-up, 3278
King and No King. Beaumont, Francis and Fletcher, John. 3857
King, Billie J. and Hyams, Joseph. Billie Jean King's Secrets of Winning Tennis, 3362
King, Coretta Scott. My Life with Martin Luther King, Jr, 1257
King, Francis. *see* Hurlimann, Martin
King, H. G. R. Antarctic, 4851
King, Henry C. Pictorial Guide to the Stars, 2007
King James VI and I. Wilson, David H, 5248
King, Martin Luther, Jr. Stride Toward Freedom, 1027
———. Where Do We Go from Here, 1028
———. Why We Can't Wait, 1029
KING, MARTIN LUTHER, 1257, 1710
King, Noel Q. Religions of Africa, 872
King of Two Worlds. Grierson, Edward, 5464
King Solomon's Ring. Lorenz, Konrad, 2354
King Who Lost America. Lloyd, Alan, 5250
King William the Fourth. Ziegler, Philip, 5255
Kingdom and the Power. Talese, Gay, 503
Kingdom of Oil, The Middle East. Viker, Ray, 1523
Kingdom of the Seashell. Abbott, R. Tucker, 2385
Kingdom of the Sun. Martin, Luis, 6268
Kings and Philosophers, 1689-1789. Krieger, Leonard, 5034
Kings Depart. Brodsky, Alyn, 4900
Kings Depart. Watt, Richard M, 5306

423

INDEX

Kinkead-Weekes, Mark and Gregoe, Ian. William Golding, 3952
Kip, Arthur F. Fundamentals of Electricity and Magnetism, 2047
Kipling, Rudyard. Verse, 3827
KIPLING, RUDYARD, 3965
Kirk, H. L. Pablo Casals, 3246
Kirk, Ruth. Desert, 2248
Kirkendall, Lester A. and Whitehurst, Robert N., eds. The New Sexual Revolution, 973
Kirkpatrick, Frederick A. Spanish Conquistadors, 6260
Kissinger. Kalb, Marvin L, 6175
Kissinger, Henry A. American Foreign Policy, 1345
KISSINGER, HENRY ALFRED, 6175
Kitagawa, Daisuke. Isei and Nisei, 1064
Kitano, Harry L. Japanese Americans, 1065
Kitchener. Magnus, Philip, 5260
KITCHENER, HORATIO HERBERT, 5260
Kite Craft. Newman, Lee S. and Newman, Jay H. 3352
KITES, 3352
Kitson-Clark, George S. The Making of Victorian England, 4748
Kitto, Humphrey D. Form and Meaning in Drama, 4454
———. Greek Tragedy, 4455
———. The Greeks, 4959
Kittrie, Nicholas N. F., see Alexander, Yonah
Kjellstrom, Bjorn. Be Expert with Map and Compass, 3389
Klass, Philip J. Secret Sentries in Space, 1687
———. UFO's Explained, 472
Klausner, Joseph. A History of Modern Hebrew Literature, 4592
Klein, Aaron. see Pearce, W. E.
Klein, Aaron E. The Electron Microscope, 1913
———. Trial by Fury, 2593
Klein, H. Arthur. Holography, 2042
Kleiner Mann - Was Nun? Fallada, Hans, 4044
Kleist, Heinrich Von. Works, 3977
Klemm, Friedrich. A History of Western Technology, 2491
Kline, Morris. Mathematics in Western Culture, 1935
KLONDIKE GOLD FIELDS, 6251
Klostermaier, Klaus. In the Paradise of Krishna, 848
Klots, Alexander B. and Klots, Elsie B. Insects of North America, 2393
———. Living Insects of the World, 2389
Klots, Elsie B. New Field Book of Freshwater Life, 2270
Klots, Elsie B. see Klots, Alexander B.
Klyuchevsky, V. Peter the Great, 5498
Knap, Jerome J. The Hunter's Handbook, 3457
Knapp, J. Merrill. The Magic of Opera, 3206
Knapton, Ernest J. Empress Josephine, 5406
———. France, 5372
Kneale, Martha. see Kneale, William
Kneale, William and Kneale, Martha. Development of Logic, 594
Knight, Melvin M. The American in Santo Domingo, 5842
Knight of the Burning Pestle. Beaumont, Francis and Fletcher, John. 3858
Knigin, Michael and Zimiles, Murray. The Technique of Fine Art Lithography, 3091
Knobler, Nathan. The Visual Dialogue, 2877
Knobloch, Irving W., ed. Readings in Biological Science, 2219
Knock. Romains, Jules, 4180
Knorr, Klaus E. Military Power and Potential, 1656
Knots and Lines Illustrated. Snyder, Paul and Snyder, Arthur. 2687
KNOTS AND SPLICES, 2686-2687
Know Your Woods. Constantine, Albert, 2328
Knowing the Atomic Nucleus. Ellis, R. Hobart, Jr, 2058
Knowing the Outdoors in the Dark. Brown, Vinson, 2210
Knowles, Ruth S. America's Oil Famine, 1527
KNOX, JOHN, 813
Knudsen, Jens W. Biological Techniques, 2310
Kobbé. see Harewood
Kobbé's Complete Opera Book. Harewood and Kobbé. 3204
Kobler, John. Ardent Spirits, 1235
———. Capone, 1713
Koch, Winston E. Seeing Sound, 2038
Koebner, Richard and Schmidt, H. D. Imperialism, 1211
Koedt, Anne, et al. Radical Feminism, 981
Koestler, Arthur. Dialogue with Death, 5471
———. The Sleepwalkers, 701
Kohl, Herbert T. The Open Classroom, 1770
———. Thirty-Six Children, 1777
Kohlmeier, Louis M. God Save This Honorable Court, 1608
———. The Regulators, 1625
Kohn, Bernice. The Organic Living Book, 2775

Kohn, Hans. The Mind of Germany, 5294
———. Mind of Modern Russia, 5487
Kokes, R. J. see Andrews, Donald
Koller, John M. Oriental Philosophies, 612
Kolodin, Irving. The Metropolitan Opera, 1883-1966, 3207
Kon-Tiki. Heyerdahl, Thor, 4697
Konvitz, Milton R., ed. Bill of Rights Reader, 1581
Kopit, Arthur. Indians, 3699
———. Oh Dad Poor Dad, Mama's Hung You in the Closet and I'm Feelin' So Sad, 3700
Koran. Muhammed, 865
Korbonski, Stefan. Fighting Warsaw, 5115
Kordemsky, Boris. The Moscow Puzzles, 3333
KOREA
    CIVILIZATION, 4777
    HISTORY, 5605-5606, 5608
    POLITICS AND GOVERNMENT, 1174, 1413
    SOCIAL LIFE AND CUSTOMS, 5607
Korea. Choy, Bong-Youn, 5605
Korea, the Politics of the Vortex. Henderson, Gregory, 1174
Korean Development. Cole, David C., et al. 1413
KOREAN WAR, 900, 5609-5613
Korean War. Ridgway, Matthew B, 5612
Koreans and Their Culture. Osgood, Cornelius B, 4777
Korea's Heritage. McCune, Shannon, 5607
Korngold, Ralph. Citizen Touissant, 5847
Korschelt, O. The Theory and Practice of Go, 3339
Kortright, Francis H. The Ducks, Geese, and Swans of North America, 2430
Kosary, Domokos G. A History of Hungary, 5364
Koschatzy, Walter. Durer Watercolors, 3051
Koskoff, David E. Joseph P. Kennedy, 6168
Kousoulas, D. George. Modern Greece, 1172
———. Revolution and Defeat, 1397
Kozol, Jonathan. Death at an Early Age, 1752
———. Free Schools, 1766
Kramer, Edna. The Nature and Growth of Modern Mathematics, 1936
Kramer, Jack. The Complete Book of Terrarium Gardening, 2801
Kramer, Jane. Allen Ginsberg in America, 3646
Kramer, Samuel Noah. The Sumerians, 4913
Kranzberg, Melvin and Pursell, Carroll W., Jr., eds. Technology of Western Civilization, 2492
Krappe, Alexander H. The Science of Folklore, 1834
Kraus, Richard. History of the Dance, 3326
Krause, Chester L. and Mishler, Clifford, eds. Standard Catalog of World Coins, 283
Krause, Ernst. Richard Strauss, 3173
Krause, Lawrence B. European Economic Integration and the U. S, 1798
Kraushaar, Otto F. American Nonpublic Schools, 1767
Kreh, Bernard L. Fly Fishing in Salt Water, 3453
Krieger, David, see Borgese, Elisabeth Mann
Krieger, Leonard. Kings and Philosophers, 1689-1789, 5034
Krishna, Gopi. The Secret of Yoga, 621
Krishnamurti, Jiddu. The Only Revolution, 622
Kristol, Irving, see Bell, Daniel
Kritzeck, James, ed. Modern Islamic Literature, 4597
Kropotkin, Petr. Memoirs of a Revolutionist, 5504
Krout, John A. and Fox, Dixon R. The Completion of Independence, 1790-1830, 5863
Krow, Harvey. Stock Market Behavior, 1457
KU KLUX KLAN, 1373, 1705-1706, 6077
Ku Klux Klan. Randel, William P, 1706
Ku Klux Klan in the City, 1915-1930. Jackson, Kenneth T, 1374
Kubler-Ross, Elisabeth. On Death and Dying, 584
Kublin, Hyman. India, 5629
Kuhn, Thomas S. The Copernican Revolution, 1992
Kunen, James S. Strawberry Statement, 1785
Kunitz, Stanley J. and Colby, Vineta, eds. European Authors, 1000-1900, 426
Kunitz, Stanley J. and Haycraft, Howard, eds. American Authors, 427
———. British Authors Before 1800, 428
———. British Authors of the Nineteenth Century, 429
———. Twentieth Century Authors, 430
Kuper, Leo. An African Bourgeoisie, 1099
Kurdish Revolt, 1961-1970. O'Ballance, Edgar, 5659
Kurlansky, Mervin and Naar, Jon. The Faith of Graffiti, 465
Kurten, Bjorn. The Ice Age, 2165
———. Not from the Apes, 2196
Kurtz, Stephen A. Wasteland, 2970

INDEX

Kuspira, John and Walker, G. W. Genetics, 2301
Kuwait. Freeth, Zahra and Winestone, H. V. 4781
KUWAIT (STATE) — HISTORY, 4781
Kwame Nkrumah. Omari, T. Peter, 5727
Kwami, T. S., see Djoleto, S. A.

Labichne, Eugene and Martin, E. Voyage de Monsieur Perrichon, 4167
LABOR AND LABORING CLASSES, 1432-1433
   U. S., 1428-1429, 1434, 1436, 1442-1443
Labor in America. Dulles, Foster R, 1439
Labor Wars. Lens, Sidney, 1443
La Bruyère, Jean de. Les Caracteres, 4275
Lacey, Robert. Robert, Earl of Essex, 5220
———. Sir Walter Raleigh, 5221
LACROSSE, 3366
Lacrosse Fundamentals. Evans, G. Heberton and Anderson, R. E. 3366
Ladies of Seneca Falls. Gurko, Miriam, 979
Lady Gregory. Adams, Hazard, 3894
Lady Jane Grey. Mathew, David, 5223
Lady Luck. Weaver, Warren, 1952
Lady Mary. Waldman, Milton, 5232
Lady of the Two Lands. Cottrell, Leonard, 4884
Lady's Not for Burning. Fry, Christopher, 3902
La Farge, Rene. Jean-Paul Sartre, 673
Lafayette and the Close of the American Revolution. Gottschalk, Louis, 5934
LAFAYETTE, MARIE JOSEPH PAUL, 5934
LaFayette, Marie M. de. La Princesse de Cleves, 4222
LaFeber, Walter. America, Russia, and the Cold War, 1945-1971, 1310
Laffin, John. Fedayeen, 5644
La Fontaine, Jean de. Fables, 4223
———. Selected Fables, 4224
Lafore, Laurence. The Long Fuse, 5076
Lagarde, André and Michard, Laurent. Les Grands Auteurs Français Du Programme, 4109
LAGERLOF, SELMA, 4091
Lagowski, J. J. Modern Inorganic Chemistry, 2077
La Guardia. Mann, Arthur, 6197
La Guardia Comes to Power, 1933. Mann, Arthur, 6198
LA GUARDIA, FIORELLO HENRY, 6197-6198
Laing, R. D. Self and Others, 590
Laird, Charlton G. The Miracle of Language, 1854
———. You and Your Language, 1864

Laird, Donald A. Techniques for Efficient Remembering, 579
Lall, Arthur. How Communist China Negotiates, 1318
Lalou, René. Histoire de las Littérature Française Contemporaine, 4110
Lamartine, Alphonse de. Graziella and Raphael, 4225
———. Jocelyn, 4124
———. Meditations, Poétiques, 4125
Lamb, Brian. see Lamb, Edgar
Lamb, Edgar and Lamb, Brian. Colorful Cacti of the American Deserts, 2793
Lamb, Lawrence E. What You Need to Know About Food and Cooking for Health, 2830
Lambert, Jacques. Latin America, 1205
Lamont, Lansing. Day of Trinity, 2669
Lancaster, Bruce. The American Heritage Book of the Revolution, 5918
Lancaster, John. Introducing Op Art, 2911
Lanctot, Gustave. Canada and the American Revolution, 1774-1783, 5790
Land Above the Trees. Zwinger, Ann H. and Willard, Beatrice E. 2246
A Land of Our Own. Meir, Golda, 5666
Land of the Giants. Lavendar, David, 6242
Landeck, Beatrice. Echoes of Africa in Folk Songs of the Americas, 3236
Landes, Kenneth K. Petroleum Geology of the United States, 2170
LANDFORMS — U. S., 4816
Lands Between. Palmer, Alan W, 5287
Lands of St. Peter. Partner, Peter, 5453
LANDSCAPE ARCHITECTURE HISTORY, 2957
   U. S., 2958
LANDSCAPE GARDENING, 2791
Landscape of Nightmare. Baumbach, Jonathan, 3715
LANDSCAPE PAINTING, AMERICAN
LANDSLIDES, 2122
Landslides and Their Treatment. Zaruba, G. and Mencl, U. 2122
Lane, J. see Miller, Madeline
Lane-Fox, Robin. Alexander the Great, 4975
Lang, D. M., see Dudley, D. R.
Lang, Paul H. George Frederic Handel, 3174
———. Symphony, 1800-1900, 3240
Lang, Serge. Basic Mathematics, 1937
Langacker, Ronald W. Language and Its Structure, 1857
Langdon, George D., Jr. Pilgrim Colony, 6194
Lange, Kurt and Hirmer, Max. Egypt, 2915
Langer, Richard W. Grow It Indoors, 2796

Langer, William L. The Diplomacy of Imperialism, 1890-1902, 5057
———. Encyclopedia of World History, 379
———. Political and Social Upheaval, 1832-1852, 5058
Langer, William L. and Gleason, S. E. Challenge to Isolation, 1346
Langerbach, Robert. Introduction to Automated Data Processing, 2846
Lange's Handbook of Chemistry. Dean, John A, 215
Langgasser, Elisabeth. Mithras. Lyrik und Prosa, 3997
Langgasser, Elizabeth. Das Unauslöschliche Siegel, 4061
Langley, Lester D. The Cuban Policy of the United States, 1347
Langone, John. Goodbye to Bedlam, 2602
———. Vital Signs, 2588
Langsam, Walter C. The World Since 1919, 4677
Langston Hughes Reader. Hughes, Langston, 3644
Language. Jespersen, Otto, 1856
Language. Sapir, Edward, 1855
Language and Its Structure. Langacker, Ronald W, 1857
LANGUAGE AND LANGUAGES, 1853-1857, 1887
Language and Silence. Steiner, George, 3464
Language in Thought and Action. Hayakawa, Samuel I, 1882
Language of Space. Turnill, Reginald, 259
Languages of the World. Katzner, Kenneth, 1853
Lanham, Urless N. The Bone Hunters, 2177
Lanier, Sidney. Poems of Sidney Lanier, 3569
Lansberger, Henry A., ed. Latin American Peasant Movements, 1001
Lansing, Marion F. Liberators and Heroes of Mexico and Central America, 5806
Lanson, Gustave. Essais de Methode de Critique et d'Histoire Litteraire. Peyre, Henri, ed, 4114
———. Voltaire, 4276
Lanson, Gustave and Tuffrau, Paul. Manuel Illustré d'Histoire de la Littérature Française, 4111
LaPierre, Dominique. see Collins, Larry
Lapp, Ralph E. The Logarithmic Century, 1423
———. The Weapons Culture, 2670
Laqueur, Walter. Confrontation, 5651
———. The Israel-Arab Reader, 1323
———. The Road to Jerusalem, 5649
———. Weimar, 5303

Larg, David G. Giuseppe Garibaldi, 5439
Larkin, J. A., see Benda, Harry J.
Larkin, Maurice. Gathering Pace, 5021
La Rochefoucald, François Duc De. Maximes, 4277
Larousse. Encyclopedia of the Earth, 223
———. Nouveau Dictionnaire Etymologique, 180
———. Nouveau Petit Larousse, 179
Larousse Editors. Grand Larousse Encyclopedique, 83
Larousse Encyclopedia of Archaeology. 407
Larousse Encyclopedia of Byzantine and Medieval Art. 273
Larousse Encyclopedia of Modern Art. 276
Larousse Encyclopedia of Prehistoric and Ancient Art. 272
Larrowe, Charles P. Harry Bridges, 1442
Larsen, Otto N., ed. Violence and the Mass Media, 902
Larus, Joel. Nuclear Weapons Safety and the Common Defense, 2671
Lasagna, Louis. The VD Epidemic, 2613
Lasch, Christopher. The Agony of the American Left, 1249
LASERS, 2639-2640
Lasers. Brown, Ronald, 2639
Lasers. Heavens, O. S, 2640
Lash, Joseph P. Eleanor, 6137
———. Eleanor and Franklin, 6136
Laski, Marghanita. Jane Austen and Her World, 3924
La Sor, William S. Dead Sea Scrolls and the New Testament, 720
Lassaigne, Jacques. Van Gogh, 3070
Lasswell, Harold D. Propaganda Technique in World War I, 5084
Last Americans. Brandon, William, 5744
Last Battle. Ryan, Cornelius, 5132
Last Exodus. Schroeter, Leonard, 1242
Last Hundred Days. Toland, John, 5137
Last of the Ruling Reptiles. Neill, Wilfred T, 2423
Last Pharaoh. McLeave, Hugh, 5717
Last Plantagenets. Costain, Thomas B, 5202
Last Play. Ridgeway, James, 1476
Last Stuart. Daiches, David, 5158
Last Trek of the Indians. Foreman, Grant, 5771
Last Tudor King. Chapman, Hester W, 5215
Later Roman Empire, 284 to 602. Jones, Arnold H, 4951
LATIN AMERICA, 6252
   ANTIQUITIES, 6265
   BIBLIOGRAPHY, 72
   BIOGRAPHY, 4866, 6258

INDEX

CIVILIZATION, 6253
CONSTITUTIONS, 1590
DESCRIPTION AND TRAVEL, 4841
DICTIONARIES AND
  ENCYCLOPEDIAS, 455
HISTORICAL GEOGRAPHY —
  MAPS, 394,
HISTORY, 6253-6258, 6260-6263
POLITICS, 1204-1206
SOCIAL CONDITIONS, 1001, 1204-1205
Latin America. Arciniegas, German, 6253
Latin America. Bailey, Helen M., et al. 6254
Latin America. Lambert, Jacques, 1205
Latin American Peasant Movements. Lansberger, Henry A., ed, 1001
Latin American Politics. Tomasek, Robert D., ed, 1206
Latin American Thought. Davis, Harold E, 680
Latin Americans. Alba, Victor, 6252
Latin Dictionary. Lewis, Charlton T. and Short, Charles. 186
LATIN DRAMA
  COLLECTIONS, 4409
  COMEDY, 4411, 4445
  HISTORY AND CRITICISM, 4410
LATIN HISTORIANS, 4969
LATIN LANGUAGE — DICTIONARIES, 185-186
LATIN LITERATURE, 4422-4428
  COLLECTIONS, 4394-4395
  DICTIONARIES, 410
  HISTORY, 4396-4399, 4429-4431, 4434, 4452
Latin Literature in Translation. Guinagh, Kevin and Dorjahn, Alfred P., eds. 4395
LATIN ORATIONS, 4421
LATIN POETRY, 4403, 4406, 4408, 4413-4419
  COLLECTIONS, 4401-4402
  HISTORY AND CRITICISM, 4404-4405, 4407, 4412
Latin Poetry. Mendell, Clarence, 4404
Latourette, Kenneth S. The Chinese, 5580
———. A Short History of the Far East, 5570
Lattimore, Richmond. Themes in Greek and Latin Epitaphs, 4433
Lattimore, Richmond. see Grene, David
Laufe, Abe. Broadway's Greatest Musicals, 3209
Laurel, Alicia B. Living on the Earth, 2828
Lautrec by Lautrec. Huisman, Philippe and Dortu, M. G. 3053
Laux, James M., see Kafker, Frank A.
Lavendar, David. American Heritage History of the Great West, 6236

———. Land of the Giants, 6242
Laver, Rod and Pollard, Jack. How to Play Championship Tennis, 3363
LAW — U. S. — HISTORY AND CRITICISM, 1545
LAW ENFORCEMENT, 908, 1704, 1707
Law of War. Friedman, Leon, ed, 1556
Lawrence and Oppenheimer. Davis, Nuel P, 2057
Lawrence, David H. Selected Poems, 3838
LAWRENCE, DAVID HERBERT, 3943-3944
LAWRENCE, ERNEST ORLANDO, 2056-2057
Lawrence, Nathaniel M. Alfred North Whitehead, 653
Lawson, Joan. European Folk Dance, 3331
Layman's Guide to Individual Rights Under the U. S. Constitution. U. S. Congress. Senate. Committee on the Judiciary. Subcommittee on Constitutional Rights, 1588
Layman's Guide to Negro History. Salk, Erwin A. 17
Lazarus, David. see Hulsizer, Robert
Leach, Douglas E. Arms for Empire, 5902
———. The Northern Colonial Frontier, 1607-1763, 6189
Leach, Maria, ed. Standard Dictionary of Folklore, Mythology and Legend, 154
Leaders of the American Revolution Series. 5961
Leaders of the French Revolution. Thompson, James M, 5401
Leading Constitutional Decisions. Cushman, Robert E, 1575
Leaf, Russel C., see De Bold, Richard C.
LEAGUE OF NATIONS, 1551-1552, 5721, 6122
League of Nations. Henig, Ruth B, 1552
Leakey, Louis S. Animals of East Africa, 2448
———. By the Evidence, 2184
LEAKEY, LOUIS SEYMOUR BAZETT, 2184
Leamer, Laurence. The Paper Revolutionaries, 499
Lear, Edward. Complete Nonsense Book, 3828
Learmonth, Andrew T. and Learmonth, Nancy. Encyclopedia of Australia, 456
Learmonth, Nancy. see Learmonth, Andrew T.
Learning for Tomorrow. Toffler, Alvin, ed, 1755
Learning Parliamentary Procedure. Sturgis, Alice F, 1357
Leaves of Grass. Whitman, Walt, 3564
Leckie, Robert. Warfare, 1660

428

Lectures Classiques et Modernes. Hall, Marie-Louise Michaud and Michaud, C. Regis. 4097
Lectures on Greek Poetry. MacKail, John W, 4444
Ledesert, D. M. see Ledesert, Rene
Ledesert, Rene and Ledesert, D. M. Harrap's New Standard French and English Dictionary, 181
Ledesma, Francisco N. Cervantes, 4392
Lee, Alfred M. The Daily Newspaper in America, 495
Lee, Don L. Directionscore, 3647
LEE, ROBERT EDWARD, 6049
Leeds, Christopher A. Italy Under Mussolini, 5451
Leek, Sybil. ESP, 530
Lee's Lieutenants. Freeman, Douglas, 6048
Lefebvre, Georges. The Coming of the French Revolution, 5396
———. French Revolution from 1793-1799, 5397
Left Hand of the Electron. Asimov, Isaac, 1917
Legacy of Egypt. Harris, John R., ed, 4888
Legacy of Greece. Livingstone, Richard W., ed, 4960
La Légende des Siecles. Hugo, Victor, 4123
LEGENDS
  FRENCH, 4119
  JEWISH, 854
Legends of Our Time. Wiesel, Elie, 5328
Legends of the Jews. Ginzberg, Louis, 854
Legends of the Patriarch and Prophets and Other Old Testament Characters. Baring-Gould, Sabine, 723
Lehmann-Haupt, Hellmut. The Book in America, 2848
Leighton, Isabel, ed. Aspirin Age, 1919-41, 6104
Lemke, Antje and Fleiss, Ruth. Museum Companion, 265
Lenin and Philosophy, and Other Essays. Althusser, Louis, 1494
Lenin and the Russian Revolution. Shukman, Harold, 5525
LENIN, VLADIMIR ILYICH, 1494, 5509, 5525
LENINGRAD
  PALACES, 4765
  SIEGE, (1941-1944), 5134
Lens, Sidney. The Labor Wars, 1443
Lenz, Siegfried. The German Lesson, 4062
———. The Lightship, 4063
Leonard, George B. Education and Ecstasy, 1763

Leonard, Jonathan N. Ancient America, 4737
Leonardo. Calder, Ritchie, 3057
Leonardo and the Age of the Eye. Calder, Ritchie, 3058
LEONARDO DA VINCI, 3057-3058
Leone, Mark P., see Zaretsky, Irving
Leonid Andreyev. Kaun, Alexander S, 4553
Leonov, Leonid. Vor, 4554
Leopardi, Giacomo. Poems and Prose, 4299
Leopold, Aldo. A Sand County Almanac and Sketches Here and There, 1903
Leopold, Luna B. Water, 2151
Lermontov, Mikhail Y. Demon, 4508
———. Geroi Nashego Vremeni, 4555
———. Lermontov Reader, 4578
Lermontov Reader. Lermontov, Mikhail Y, 4578
Lerner, Max. America As a Civilization, 5864
Le Sage, Alain-René. Gil Blas, 4226
———. Turcaret, 4227
Le Sage, Laurent. Jean Giraudoux, 4168
Lessing, Gotthold E. Dramen, 4022
Lessing, L. and Fortune Editors. DNA, 2252
Lesznai, Lajos. Bartok, 3159
Let 'er Buck! Hall, Douglas K, 3289
Let Them Live. Curry-Lindahl, Kai, 2338
Letters. Plinius Caecilius Secundus, Gaius, 4428
Letters and Papers from Prison. Bonhoeffer, Dietrich, 811
Letters from Attica. Melville, Samuel, 1737
Letters on the Short Story, the Drama and Other Literary Topics. Chekhov, Anton P, 4573
Lettres de Mon Moulin. Daudet, Alphonse, 4205
Leuchtenburg, William E. Franklin D. Roosevelt and the New Deal, 6138
———. The Periods of Prosperity, 1914-1932., 6111
———. A Troubled Feast, 6152
Levertov, Denise. The Sorrow Dance, 3648
———. With Eyes in the Back of Our Heads, 3649
Leveson, David. A Sense of the Earth, 2095
LEVI-STRAUSS, CLAUDE, 887
Levin, Harry. Gates of Horn, 4264
Levin, Murray B. Political Hysteria in America, 1196
Levin, Nora. The Holocaust, 5105
Leviton, Alan. Reptiles and Amphibians of North America, 2415

INDEX

Levitt, I. M. Beyond the Known Universe, 1986
Lewin, Leonard. see Holzman, William
Lewin, Roger. Nervous System, 2343
Lewine, Richard and Alfred, Simon. Songs of the American Theater, 1900-1971, 3214
Lewis, Alfred. Clean the Air, 2708
LEWIS AND CLARK EXPEDITIONS, 6233
Lewis, Charlton T. and Short, Charles. Latin Dictionary, 186
Lewis, Clive S. The Four Loves, 755
———. Mere Christianity, 738
———. The Problem of Pain, 702
———. The Screwtape Letters, and Screwtape Proposes a Toast, 761
Lewis, Geoffrey L. Modern Turkey, 5654
Lewis, Howard. With Every Breath You Take, 2566
Lewis, John W., ed. Party Leadership and Revolutionary Power in China, 1398
Lewis, Oscar. Five Families, 1100
———. La Vida, 1042
———. Life in a Mexican Village, 1101
Lewis, Paul. The Grand Incendiary, 5936
Lewis, Richard S. The Voyages of Apollo, 2767
Lewis, Richard W. Edith Wharton, 3723
LEWIS, SINCLAIR, 3731
Lewis, Warren H. The Splendid Century, 5382
Leyburn, James G. The Haitian People, 5848
Liberal Arts Physics. Bailey, John M, 2014
Liberal Tradition in American Thought. Volkomer, Walter E., ed, 1149
LIBERALISM — U. S., 1149, 6151
Liberators. Nicholson, Irene, 6258
Liberators and Heroes of Mexico and Central America. Lansing, Marion F, 5806
Liberties and Responsibilities of the American Indians. see Commission on the Rights
LIBERTY, 897, 1112
LIBRARIES
  AUTOMATION, 47
  CENSORSHIP, 475
  HANDBOOKS, MANUALS, ETC., 82
  UNIVERSITY AND COLLEGE, 22
LIBRARY ARCHITECTURE, 20-21
Library of Congress. Goodrum, Charles A, 476
Library of Great Museums. 3081
Library of Great Painters. 3082

LIBRARY RESOURCES — U. S. — DIRECTORIES, 81
LICE, 2609
Lichtenstein, Grace. A Long Way, Baby, 3364
Lichtheim, George. Europe in the Twentieth Century, 5059
Licit and Illicit Drugs. Brecker, Edward M. and Consumer Report Editors. 2541
Liddell, Henry G. and Scott, Robert, eds. Greek-English Lexicon, 187
Liddell Hart, Basil H. A Greater Than Napoleon, 4931
———. History of the Second World War, 5101
———. The Real War, 1914-1918, 5085
Lieber, Hugh G. and Lieber, Lillian R. Mits, Wits and Logic, 596
Lieber, Lillian R. The Einstein Theory of Relativity, 2031
Lieber, Lillian R. see Lieber, Hugh G.
Lieberman, E. James and Peck, Ellen. Sex and Birth Control, 2519
Lieberman, Mark. The Dope Book, 2548
Life. Brandwein, Paul F., et al. 2209
Life. Luria, S. E, 2307
LIFE — ORIGIN, 1985
Life Along the San Andreas Fault. Fried, John J, 2120
Life and Death in a Coral Sea. Cousteau, Jacques-Yves and Diole, Philippe. 2135
Life and Death of Carthage. Picard, Gilbert C. and Picard, Colette. 4986
Life and Death of the Salt Marsh. Teal, John and Teal, Mildred. 2244
Life and Death of Yukio Mishima. Scott-Stokes, Henry, 4618
Life and Labor in the Old South. Phillips, Ulrich B, 6213
Life and Language in the Old Testament. Chase, Mary Ellen, 725
Life and Literature in the Roman Republic. Frank, Tenney, 4397
Life and Selected Writings. Jefferson, Thomas, 1076
Life and Times of Akhnaton, Pharaoh of Egypt. Weigall, Arthur E, 4898
Life and Times of Cavour. Thayer, William R, 5441
Life and Times of Eamon de Valera. Fitzgibbon, Constantine and Morrison, George. 5165
Life and Times of Muhammad. Glubb, John, 863
Life and Works of Thomas Eakins. Hendricks, Gordon, 3043
Life Between Tidemarks on Rocky Shores. Stephenson, T. A. and Stephenson, Anne. 2260

INDEX

LIFE (BIOLOGY), 1892, 2215, 2296, 2306-2307
Life Game. Calder, Nigel, 2306
Life in a Medieval Castle. Gies, Joseph and Gies, Francis. 4999
Life in a Mexican Village. Lewis, Oscar, 1101
Life in Photography. Steichen, Edward, 3125
Life in Shakespeare's England. Wilson, John D, 4750
Life Library of Photography. 3129
Life Magazine Editors. World's Great Religions, 822
Life Nature Library. 2484
Life of Birds. Dorst, Jean, 2427
Life of Captain John Cook. Beaglehole, John C, 4701
Life of Dylan Thomas. Fitzgibbon, Constantine, 3849
Life of Ezra Pound. Stock, Noel, 3588
Life of James Madison. Hunt, Gaillard, 5983
Life of James Monroe. Morgan, George, 5989
Life of Mozart. Fischer, Hans S. and Besch, Lutz. 3166
Life of Nelson. Southey, Robert, 5254
Life of Samuel Johnson. Boswell, James, 3963
Life of Stephen F. Austin, Founder of Texas, 1793-1836. Barker, Eugene C, 6224
Life of the Mind in America. Miller, Perry, 4828
Life of Vertebrates. Young, John Z, 2402
Life of William Harvey. Keynes, Geoffrey, 2500
Life on a Medieval Barony. Davis, William, 4997
LIFE ON OTHER PLANETS, 473, 2277, 2308, 2377
Life on the English Manor. Bennett, Henry S, 5200
Life on the Planet Earth. Morowitz, Harold J. and Morowitz, Lucille S. 2216
Life Process. Butler, J. A, 2226
Life Science Library. 2485
Life Studies. Lowell, Robert, 3650
Life World Library. 4856
Lifesaving. American National Red Cross Editors, 2570
Lifton, Robert J. Death in Life, 5141
Lifton, Robert J. and Olson, Eric. Living and Dying, 585
Lighting for Photography. Nurnberg, Walter, 3099
Lightship. Lenz, Siegfried, 4063
Limbacher, James L., ed. Feature Films on 8mm and 16mm, 52
Limits of American Capitalism. Heilbroner, Robert L, 1422

Lincoln, Abraham. Political Thought, 1077
LINCOLN, ABRAHAM, 1589, 6013, 6035-6036, 6053
Lincoln and the Negro. Quarles, Benjamin, 6013
Lincoln and the Tools of War. Bruce, Robert V, 6053
Lincoln, C. Eric. The Black Muslims in America, 1061
Lincoln, James H. The Anatomy of a Riot, 1593
LINCOLN, MARY (TODD), 6038
Lincoln Steffens. Kaplan, Justin, 3758
Lindbergh, Charles A. Spirit of St. Louis, 2716
Lindley, Ernest K. Roosevelt Revolution, 6139
Lindsay, Jack. Cézanne, 3054
Lindsay, Robert B. The Nature of Physics, 2053
Lindsay, Vachel. Selected Poems, 3604
LINDSAY, VACHEL, 3607
Lingelbach, William E. Austria-Hungary, 5340
Lingeman, Richard R. Drugs from A to Z, 253
LINGUISTICS, 1857
Linguistics and Reading. Fries, Charles C, 1887
Link, Arthur S., et al. American Epoch, 6112
———. Woodrow Wilson, 6118
———. Woodrow Wilson and the Progressive Era, 6119
Link, Arthur S. and Catton, William B. The Era of the Cold War, 1946-1973, 6157
Linklater, Eric. The Voyage of the Challenger, 1919
Linklater, Eric and Smith, Edwin. Scotland, 4744
Linn, Charles F. The Golden Mean, 2872
Linsenmaier, Walter. Insects of the World, 243
Linton, Ron. Terracide, 2707
Lion and the Throne. Bowen, Catherine D, 5236
Lion in the North. Prebble, John, 5154
LIONS — BEHAVIOR, 2467, 2469
Lipking, Lawrence I. and Litz, Walton A., eds. Modern Literary Criticism, 1900-1970, 3463
Lipman, Jean and Winchester, Alice. The Flowering of American Folk Art 1776-1876, 3016
Lippmann, Walter. Early Writings, 6113
———. Men of Destiny, 4868
Lipscomb, David M. Noise, 2568
LIQUID PROPELLANTS, 2861
Liss, Sheldon B. Canal, 1348
Listen to the Blues. Cook, Bruce, 3194

INDEX

Listen to the Warm. McKuen, Rod, 3653
Listening to Music Creatively. Stringham, Edwin John, 3132
Lister, Margot. Costumes of Everyday Life, 1816
Liston, Robert A. The Right to Know, 1596
Liszt. Perenyi, Eleanor, 3160
LISZT, FRANZ, 3160
Literary History of Rome. Duff, John W, 4396
Literary History of the American Revolution. Tyler, Moses C, 5929
A Literary History of the Arabs. Nicholson, Reynold A, 4598
Literary History of the United States. Spiller, Robert E., et al. 357
Literary Market Place. Neal, Jack A., ed, 264
Literatura Hispanoamericana, Antologia e Introducción Historica. Anderson-Imbert, Enrique and Florit, E. 4303
LITERATURE, 3521, 3523
    BIBLIOGRAPHY, 14, 68, 94
    COLLECTIONS, 3493, 5020
    COMPARATIVE, 4391, 4572
    DICTIONARIES, 322-324, 325, 327-328
    HISTORY AND CRITICISM, 3464, 3466, 3482, 3484
    MEDIEVAL, 5007, 5030
    MODERN, 343-344, 3524, 5466
    PRIMITIVE, 2897
    TERMINOLOGY, 326, 331
Literature and the Sixth Sense. Rahv, Philip, 3523
Literature and Theatre of the States and Regions of the U. S. A. Gohdes, Clarence L, 69
Literature by and about the American Indian. Stensland, Anna L, 75
Literature of East Germany. Huebener, Theodore, 3988
Literature of Eighteenth Century Russia. Segel, Harold B., tr, 4498
Literature of the American Jews. Gross, Theodore L, 3536
Literature of the New Testament. Scott, Ernest F, 732
Literature of the Old Testament. Bewer, Julius A, 724
Literature of the Spanish People. Brenan, Gerald, 4309
Literaturlesebuch. Fleissner, Otto S. and Deutsches, E. M. 3982
LITHOGRAPHS, 3098
LITHOGRAPHY — TECHNIQUE, 3091
Little Book of Bells. Hatch, Eric, 3253

Little Commonwealth. Demos, John, 987
LITTLE, MALCOLM, 1014, 1016, 1031, 1152
Little Treasury of American Poetry. Williams, Oscar, 3552
Little Treasury of British Poetry. Williams, Oscar, 3787
Little Treasury of Great Poetry. Williams, Oscar, 3502
Little Treasury of Modern Poetry. Williams, Oscar, 3503
Little Treasury of Modern Poetry. Williams, Oscar. 3788
LITTLEFIELD, MILTON SMITH, 6064
Litto, Frederic M. Plays from Black Africa, 4634
Litwack, Leon F., *see* Stampp, Kenneth M.
Litwhiler, Daniel. Baseball, 3374
Litz, Walton A., *see* Lipking, Lawrence I.
Liu, Wu-Chi. Confucius, His Life and Time, 869
Live or Die. Sexton, Anne, 3662
Lively Years, 1920-1973. Atkinson, J. Brooks and Hirschfeld, Albert. 3320
Livermore, Harold B. New History of Portugal, 5477
Lives. Plutarch, 4473
Lives of a Cell. Thomas, Lewis, 2218
Lives of the Painters. Canaday, John, 3035
Lives of the Poets. Untermeyer, Louis, 4871
Living Amphibians of the World. Cochran, Doris M, 2410
Living and Dying. Lifton, Robert J. and Olson, Eric. 585
Living Bible. Bible, 707
Living Birds of the World. Gilliard, Thomas E, 2425
Living Black American Authors. Shockley, Ann A. and Chandler, Sue, eds. 356
Living Cell. Scientific American Editors, 2254
Living Fishes of the World. Herald, Earl, 2405
Living Ideas in America. Commager, Henry S., ed, 5879
Living Images. Kauffman, Stanley, 3277
Living Insects of the World. Klots, Alexander B. and Klots, Elsie B. 2389
Living Mammals of the World. Sanderson, Ivan T, 2447
Living off the Country. Angier, Bradford, 2531
Living on the Earth. Laurel, Alicia B, 2828
Living Plants of the World. Milne, Lorus and Milne, Margery. 2312
Living Presidency. Hughes, Emmet J, 1641
Living Races of Man. Coon, Carleton S. and Hunt, Edward E., Jr. 2187

Living Reef. Faulkner, Douglas, 2263
Living Reef. Greenberg, Jerry, 2264
Living Reptiles of the World. Inger, Robert F. and Schmidt, Karl P. 2412
Living Trees of the World. Everett, Thomas H, 2326
Livingston, Jon. Imperial Japan, 1800-1945, 5621
———. Postwar Japan, 1945 to the Present, 5623
Livingstone. Jeal, Tim, 4795
LIVINGSTONE, DAVID, 4795
Livingstone, Elizabeth A. see Cross, F. L.
Livingstone, Richard W., ed. Legacy of Greece, 4960
Livius, Titus. Roman History with an English Translation, 4426
Lizaso, Felix. Marti, Martyr of Cuban Independence, 5834
Lloyd, Alan. The King Who Lost America, 5250
———. The Making of the King, 1066, 5187
———. Marathon, 4961
Lloyd, Peter C. Africa in Social Change, 1096
Lloyd, T. O. Empire to Welfare State, 1085
Lloyd, Tom C. Electric Motors and Their Applications, 2637
Loades, David M. The Oxford Martyrs, 795
Local Anesthetic. Grass, Gunther, 4052
Locke, Alain, ed. The Negro in Art, 2914
Locke, David M. Enzymes, 2512
———. Viruses, 2587
Locke, John. An Essay Concerning Human Understanding, 654
LOCKE, JOHN, 651
Lockley, R. M. The Private Life of the Rabbit, 2453
Lockspeiser, Edward. Debussy, 3175
———. Music and Painting, 3130
Lockwood, George B. The New Harmony Movement, 1509
Lockwood, Lee. Castro's Cuba, 5835
———. Conversations with Eldridge Cleaver, 1250
Lodewijk, T., et al. The Way Things Work, 2487
Loeb Classical Library. 4475
Loebl, Suzanne. Conception, Contraception, 958
Loewer, H. Peter. The Indoor Water Gardener's How-to Handbook, 2797
Loftis, Anne. see Girdner, Audrie
Loftus, Tony, ed. The Earth and Man, 398
Logan, Rayford W. The Betrayal of the Negro, 1258
———. Haiti and the Dominican Republic, 5850

Logarithmic Century. Lapp, Ralph E, 1423
LOGIC, 592-596
Logic. Salmon, Wesley C, 595
Logic of Life. Jacob, Francois, 2296
Loken, Newton C. Tumbling and Trampolining, 3382
Lomax, Alan and Abdul, Raoul, eds. Three Thousand Years of Black Poetry, 3498
Lomax, Alan. see Lomax, John A.
Lomax, John A. and Lomax, Alan. American Ballads and Folk Songs, 3237
Lomax, Louis. The Negro Revolt, 1030
LONDON — DESCRIPTION, 4747
London, Grelun. see Stambler, Irwin
LONDON, JACK, 3736
London, Joan and Anderson, Henry. So Shall Ye Reap, 1444
Lonely Crowd. Riesman, David, et al. 544
Lonely Hunter. Carr, Virginia S, 3727
Lonesome Road. Redding, J. Saunders, 1273
Long African Day. Myers, Norman, 2449
Long Fuse. Lafore, Laurence, 5076
Long Generation. Meyer, Henry C, 5295
LONG, HUEY PIERCE, 6222
LONG MARCH, (1934-1935), 5597
Long March, 1935. Wilson, Richard G, 5597
Long March to Power. Harrison, James P, 1177
Long Way, Baby. Lichtenstein, Grace, 3364
Long Week-End. Graves, Robert and Hodge, Alan. 5272
Longest Day. Ryan, Cornelius, 5133
Longfellow and His Poetry. Smeaton, Oliphant, 3560
Longfellow, Henry Wadsworth. Poems, 3557
LONGFELLOW, HENRY WADSWORTH, 3560
Longford, Elizabeth. Queen Victoria, 5258
———. Wellington, 5251
———. Wellington, 5252
Longworth, Philip. Cossacks, 5488
Look Back in Anger. Osborne, John, 3906
Looking for Dilmun. Bibby, Geoffrey, 4733
Lootens, J. Ghislain. Lootens on Photographic Enlarging and Print Quality, 3111
Lootens on Photographic Enlarging and Print Quality. Lootens, J. Ghislain, 3111
Lope de Vega, Felix de. Five Plays, 4356
Lopez, Alfredo. The Puerto Rican Papers, 1043
Lorca, the Poet and His People. Barea, Arturo, 4341
Lorch, Netaniel. Israel's War of Independence, 1947-1949, 5645

INDEX

Lord, Clifford L. and Lord, Elizabeth S. Historical Atlas of the United States, 393
Lord, Elizabeth S. see Lord, Clifford L.
Lord Palmerston. Ridley, Jasper G, 5263
Lord, Walter. Day of Infamy, 5128
Lord Weary's Castle. Lowell, Robert, 3651
Lords of Creation. Allen, Frederick L, 1449
Lorenz, Konrad. King Solomon's Ring, 2354
———. On Aggression, 2355
LOS ANGELES — RIOTS (1965), 1123, 6245
Los de Abajo. Azuela, Mariano, 4367
Lost Cities of Africa. Davidson, Basil, 4791
LOST CONTINENTS, 1847
Lost Continents. DeCamp, L. Sprague, 1847
Lost Discoveries. Ronan, Colin A, 1924
Lost Leviathan. Ommanney, F. D, 2455
Lost World of Quintana Roo. Peissel, Michel, 4802
Lost World of the Kalahari. Van Der Post, Laurens, 4797
Lot, Ferdinand. The End of the Ancient World and the Beginnings of the Middle Ages, 5001
Loth, David. see Freuchen, Peter
Loti, Pierre. Pecheur d'islande, 4228
Louis Napoleon and the Second Empire. Thompson, James M, 5412
Louis XI. Kendall, Paul M, 5376
Louis XIV and the Craft of Kingship. Rule, John C, 5385
Louis XIV at Versailles. Saint-Simon, Louis, 5386
LOUISIANA PURCHASE, 5973
Louria, Donald B. Overcoming Drugs, 2544
LOVE, 570, 605, 755, 972
Love and Death in the American Novel. Fiedler, Leslie A, 3714
Love and Sex in Plain Language. Johnson, Eric W, 2518
Love and Will. May, Rollo, 570
Love Bugs. Stiller, Richard, 2616
Love, Kenneth. Suez, 5646
Love, Sex and Being Human. Bohannan, Paul, 2517
Lovejoy, Clarence E. Lovejoy's College Guide, 1788
Lovejoy's College Guide. Lovejoy, Clarence E, 1788
Lovell, Colin R. English Constitutional and Legal History, 1561

Lowell, Amy. Complete Poetical Works, 3605
Lowell, James Russell. Complete Poetical Works, 3558
LOWELL, JAMES RUSSELL, 3556
Lowell, Robert. Life Studies, 3650
———. Lord Weary's Castle, 3651
Lowenfels, Walter. From the Belly of the Shark, 3576
———. The Writing on the Wall, 3550
Lowenthal, Richard, ed. Issues in the Future of Asia, 1178
Lower Animals. Buchsbaum, Ralph and Milne, Lorus. 2379
Lower Depths and Other Plays. Gorky, Maxim, 4532
Lowie, Robert H. Primitive Religion, 829
Lowry, Bates. Renaissance Architecture, 2972
Lowry, Peter and Griffith, Field. Model Rocketry, 2769
Loy, John W., Jr. and Kenyon, Gerald S., eds. Sport, Culture and Society, 920
Loyalists in Revolutionary America, 1760-1781. Calhoon, Robert M, 5945
LSD, Man and Society. De Bold, Richard C. and Leaf, Russel C., eds. 2578
LSD Story. Cashman, John A, 2577
Lubbock, Percy. The Craft of Fiction, 3489
Lucas, A. T. Treasures of Ireland, 2921
Lucas, Frank L. Tragedy, 3482
Lucas, Noah. The Modern History of Israel, 5665
Lucas, Robert. Frieda Lawrence, 3943
Luce and His Empire. Swanberg, W. A, 491
Luce, Gay. Body Time, 2514
LUCE, HENRY ROBINSON, 491
Luce, John V. see Stanford, William B.
Lucie-Smith, Edward. Primer of Experimental Poetry, 3504
Lucretius Carus, Titus. De Rerum Natura, 4406
Ludwig, Richard M. see Jones, Howard M.
Lueders, Edward, see Dunning, Stephen
Lukas, J. Anthony. Don't Shoot - We Are Your Children!, 990
Lukowski, Susan, see Grayson, Cary R.
Lulu Plays. Wedekind, Frank, 4023
Lumley, Frederick. New Trends in 20th Century Drama, 3527
LUNAR GEOLOGY, 2163
LUNAR ROCKS, 2168
Lunar Rocks. Mason, Brian and Melson, William G. 2168
Lunatic Express. Miller, Charles, 5733
Lunatics, Lovers and Poets. Croyden, Margaret, 3311
Lundquist, James. Sinclair Lewis, 3731

Lurani, Giovanni. History of the Racing Car, 2751
Luray, Martin. *see* Tokle, Art
Luria, S. E. Life, 2307
Lusitania. Simpson, Colin, 5090
LUSITANIA (STEAMSHIP), 5090
Luther. Osborne, John, 3907
Luther, Martin. Martin Luther, 788
LUTHER, MARTIN, 782
LUTHERAN CHURCH, 788
Lutwack, Leonard. Heroic Fiction, 3712
Lutwaffe War Diaries. Bekker, Cajus, 5139
Luza, Radomir. *see* Mamatey, Victor S.
Lycan, Gilbert L. Alexander Hamilton and American Foreign Policy, 1349
Lynch, John. The Spanish American Revolutions, 1808-1826, 6261
Lynd, Staughton, ed. Nonviolence in America, 1252
Lyon, Peter. Eisenhower, 6162
Lyons, Eugene. Workers' Paradise Lost, 1093
Lyons, Marvin. Nicholas II, 5505
Lyric Poems and Ballads. Heine, Heinrich, 3996
Le Lys dans la Vallée. Balzac, Honoré de, 4196
Lytle, C. *see* Cortner, R.
Lyttle, Richard B. Paints, Inks, and Dyes, 2863

Maas, Peter. Serpico, 1631
———. Valachi Papers, 1720
Mabee, Carleton. Black Freedom, 1224
McAdams, Cliff, ed. How to Break Ninety-Eight-Par, 3369
McAlester, Archie L. and Hay, E. A. Physical Geology, 2110
McAlister, John T. Vietnam, 5679
McAlister, John T., Jr. and Mus, Paul. The Vietnamese and Their Revolution, 1187
MACARTHUR, DOUGLAS, 1676, 5611
Macaulay, David. Cathedral, 2977
———. City, 2953
McCaffrey, Donald W. The Golden Age of Sound Comedy, 3279
McCall, G. J. Meteorites and Their Origins, 2002
McCall, Robert. Our World in Space, 2756
McCarry, Charles. Citizen Nader, 1544
MCCARTY, JOSEPH RAYMOND, 6160
McCary, James L. Human Sexuality, 2520
McCaughey, Robert A. Josiah Quincy, 1772-1864, 5977
MCCLELLAN, GEORGE BRINTON, 6054
McCloskey, Paul N. Truth and Untruth, 1197
McClurg, David R. The Amateur's Guide to Caves and Caving, 3396

McColley, Robert. Federalists, Republicans, and Foreign Entanglements, 1789-1815, 1350
McConahy, John B. *see* Sears, David O.
McCormack, Arthur. The Population Problem, 953
McCoy, Donald. Calvin Coolidge, 6127
McCoy, Patricia, trs. *see* Hutson, Arthur E.
McCrory, G. Jacobs. Softball Rules in Pictures, 3375
McCullers, Carson. Member of the Wedding, 3680
MCCULLERS CARSON SMITH, 3727
MacCulloch, John A., et al, eds. Mythology of All Races, 119
McCullough, David. The Great Bridge, 2693
McCune, Shannon. Korea's Heritage, 5607
McDonagh, Don. Martha Graham, 3329
MacDonald, Donald F. The Age of Transition, 5259
MacDonald, Dwight, ed. Parodies, 3962
McDonald, Elvin. The World Book of House Plants, 2798
MacDonald, Gordon A. Volcanoes, 2118
MacDonald, Gordon A. and Abbott, Agatin T. Volcanoes in the Sea, 2173
MacDonald, H. Malcolm, et al. Readings in American National Government, 1633
MacDonald, J. W. and Saxton, J. C., eds. Four Stages, 3507
MACDONALD, SIR JOHN ALEXANDER, 5797
MacDougall, Curtis D. Principles of Editorial Writing, 486
McEwan, P. J., ed. Africa from Early Times to 1800, 5703
———. Nineteenth-Century Africa, 5704
———. Twentieth-Century Africa, 5705
MacFarquhar, Roderick. The Origins of the Cultural Revolution, 5599
McGill, Ralph. The South and the Southerner, 6210
McGinley, Phyllis. Times Three, 3577
McGovern, George S., ed. Agricultural Thought in the 20th Century, 1511
MCGOVERN, GEORGE STANLEY, 1380
McGovern, James. To the Yalu, 5611
McGovney, D. O. and McGovney, Howard. Cases on Constitutional Law, 142
McGovney, Howard. *see* McGovney, D. O.
McGraw Encyclopedia of World Art, 270
McGraw-Hill Dictionary of Art, 274
McGraw-Hill Dictionary of Modern Economics. Greenwald, Douglas, 138
McGraw-Hill Editors. Dictionary of Scientific and Technical Terms, 201
———. McGraw-Hill Encyclopedia of Science and Technology, 202

INDEX

———. The McGraw-Hill Encyclopedia of World Biography, 416
McGraw-Hill Encyclopedia of Environmental Science. 125
McGraw-Hill Encyclopedia of Science & Technology Editors. Basic Bibliography of Science and Technology, 59
McGraw-Hill Encyclopedia of Science and Technology. McGraw-Hill Editors, 202
McGraw-Hill Encyclopedia of World Biography. McGraw-Hill Editors, 416
McGraw-Hill Encyclopedia of World Drama. 346
McGraw-Hill Yearbook of Science and Technology, 1975. 204
Machado, Antonio. Juan de Mairena, 4327
———. Poesías Completas, 4326
McHale, John. The Ecological Context, 935
Machiavelli. Prezzolini, Giuseppe, 1141
Machiavelli and Renaissance Italy. Hale, John R, 5436
Machiavelli, Niccolo. History of Florence and of the Affairs of Italy, 5433
———. The Prince, 1140
MACHIAVELLI, NICCOLO, 1141, 5436
La Machine Infernale. Cocteau, Jean, 4153
MACHINERY — HISTORY, 2635
Machines and Liberty. Roberts, Martin, 5025
McHugh, Tom. The Time of the Buffalo, 2464
MacIntyre, Alasdair C. A Short History of Ethics, 600
McIntyre, Joan. Mind in the Waters, 2458
MacKail, John W. Lectures on Greek Poetry, 4444
Mackay, James A. The Dictionary of Stamps in Color, 292
McKelvey, Blake. The Emergence of Metropolitan America, 1915-1966, 967
———. Urbanization of America, 1860-1915, 968
MacKendrick, Paul. The Greek Stones Speak, 4732
———. The Mute Stones Speak, 4727
———. Roman France, 4726
McKenna, Marian C. Borah, 6123
McKenzie, John L. The Roman Catholic Church, 809
MacKenzie, John P. The Appearance of Justice, 1609
Mackett-Beeson, E. J. Chessmen, 2992
McKinley, Bryan and the People. Glad, Paul W, 6093
MCKINLEY, WILLIAM, 6093
McKinney, H. Lewis. Wallace and Natural Selection, 2290

McKinsey, John C. Introduction to the Theory of Games, 1954
McKitrick, Eric L. Andrew Johnson and Reconstruction, 6084
———. Slavery Defended, 1286
Macksey, Kenneth and Batchelor, John H. Tank, 2679
Mack-Smith, Denis. Italy, 5446
McKuen, Rod. In Someone's Shadow, 3652
———. Listen to the Warm, 3653
McKusick, Victor. Human Genetics, 2202
McLachlan, James. American Boarding Schools, 1768
McLanathan, Richard B. Art in America, 2946
McLaughlin, Mary M., see Ross, James B.
McLeave, Hugh. The Last Pharaoh, 5717
MacLeish, Archibald. Poetry and Experience, 3477
———. The Wild Old Wicked Man and Other Poems, 3606
McLennan, Barbara N., ed. Crime in Urban Society, 1731
McManama, Jerry. see Shondell, Donald S.
McManus, Edgar J. Black Bondage in the North, 1004
Macmillan, William M. Bantu, Boer and Briton, 5736
MacMullen, Ramsay. Constantine, 4950
McNally, Raymond T. and Florescu, Radu. In Search of Dracula, 3531
McNeal, E. H. see Thatcher, Oliver J.
MacNeice, Louis. Collected Poems, 1925-1963, 3850
McNeil, Elton B. Being Human, the Psychological Experience, 891
McNeil, William H. The Shape of European History, 4992
McNickle, D'Arcy. Native American Tribalism, 5773
MacQuarrie, John, ed. Dictionary of Christian Ethics, 111
———. Existentialism, 553
———. Studies in Christian Existentialism, 739
Macridis, Roy C. and Ward, Robert E., eds. Modern Political Systems, 1143
———. Modern Political Systems, 1144
MacVey, John. Whispers from Space, 1976
McWhirter, Norris and McWhirter, Ross, eds. Guinness Book of World Records, 477
McWhirter, Ross, see McWhirter, Norris
Mad Anthony Wayne and the New Nation. Tucker, Glenn, 5953
Mad Booths of Maryland. Kimmell, Stanley, 3323
Madame Bovary. Flaubert, Gustave, 4209

INDEX

Madame de Pompadour. Mitford, Nancy, 5383
Madame Sarah. Skinner, Cornelia O, 3306
Madison, Charles A. Book Publishing in America, 2850
———. Critics and Crusaders, 4870
———. Yiddish Literature, 4593
MADISON, DOLLEY (PAYNE) TODD, 5982
MADISON, JAMES, 5983
Madman in a Lifeboat. Hill, Gladwin, 1635
Madmen and Geniuses. Barzman, Sol, 5853
Madow, Leo. Anger, 569
Maenchen-Helfen, Otto J. The World of the Huns, 4685
MAFIA, 1709, 1711-1712, 1720
Mafia Is Not an Equal Opportunity Employer. Gage, Nicholas, 1711
MAGALHAES, FERNAO DE, 4702
Magazines for Libraries. Katz, William A. and Gargal, Berry. 10
Magazines in the Twentieth Century. Peterson, Theodore, 478
Magazines in the United States. Wood, James P, 479
Magellan of the Pacific. Roditi, Edouard, 4702
MAGIC, 537, 3334
Magic Mountain. Mann, Thomas, 4066
Magic of Opera. Knapp, J. Merrill, 3206
Magic, Supernaturalism and Religion. Seligmann, Kurt, 537
Magie, William F. A Source Book in Physics, 2035
Magill, Frank N., ed. Cyclopedia of Literary Characters, 342
MAGNA CARTA, 1262, 5203
Magna Carta. Pallister, Anne, 1262
MAGNETISM, 2047, 2049
Magnificent Birds of Prey. Callahan, Philip S, 2438
Magnificent Century. Costain, Thomas B, 5203
Magnus, Philip. Kitchener, 5260
Mahabharata. Narasimhan, C. U., tr, 4486
MAHABHARATA BHAGAVADGITA, 844-845
Mahan, Alfred T. Influence of Sea Power Upon History, 1660-1783, 1688
———. Story of the War in South Africa, 5741
Mahatma Gandhi. Keer, Bhananjay, 5633
Mahler, Alma. Gustav Mahler, 3176
MAHLER, GUSTOV, 3176
Mahoney, M. The Mathematical Career of Pierre de Fermat, 1601-1665, 1947

Mahood, H. R. and Angus, Edward L., eds. Urban Politics and Problems, 1629
Maiden Voyage. Marcus, Geoffrey, 4698
Maids; Deathwatch. Genet, Jean, 4157
Maid's Tragedy. Beaumont, Francis and Fletcher, John. 3859
Mailer, Norman. The Armies of the Night, 3759
Mailer, Peter R., et al. The Marvels of Animal Behavior, 2356
Main, Jackson T. The Sovereign States 1775-1783, 5919
Mainstreams of Modern Art. Canaday, John, 2908
Major Documents in American Economic History. Hacker, Louis M., ed, 1419
Major Governments of Asia. Callard, Keith, et al. 1562
Major Legal Systems in the World Today. Brierley, John E. and David, Rene. 1546
Major Poets. Coffin, Charles M. and Roelofs, Gerrit, eds. 3775
Major Religions of the World. Bach, Marcus, 817
Majority Party Leadership in Congress. Ripley, Randall, 1368
Makers of America. Encyclopedia Britannica, 126
Makers of Arab History. Hitti, Philip K, 4858
Makers of Modern England. Costigan, Giovanni, 5277
Makers of Modern Strategy. Earle, Edward M., ed, 1669
Makers of the Modern World. Untermeyer, Louis, 4863
Makers of the Russian Revolution. Haupt, Georges and Marie, Jean-J. 5520
MAKEUP, THEATRICAL, 3305
Making Movies from Script to Screen. Bobker, Lee R, 3112
Making of a Counter Culture. Roszak, Theodore, 912
Making of a Library. Taylor, Robert S, 22
Making of a Quagmire. Halberstam, David, 5678
Making of a State. Masaryk, Thomas G, 5352
Making of a Surgeon. Nolen, William A, 2621
Making of an American. Riis, Jacob August, 1280
Making of China. Chang, Chun-shu, 5574
Making of Modern English Society from 1850. Roebuck, Janet, 1086
Making of Modern Ireland, 1603-1923. Beckett, James G, 5160
Making of Modern Mexico. Brandenburg, Frank R, 5823

INDEX

Making of the King, 1066. Lloyd, Alan, 5187
Making of the President, 1972. White, Theodore H, 1385
Making of Victorian England. Kitson-Clark, George S, 4748
Mal-Nourished Mind. Shneour, Elie, 578
MALAWI — HISTORY, 5742
MALAYSIA — HISTORY — SOURCES, 5676
Malaysia and Its Neighbors. Gullick, J. M, 5676
Malcolm, George A. The Commonwealth of the Philippines, 6284
Malcolm X. Clarke, John H., et al. 1016
Malcolm X Speaks. Breitman, George, ed, 1014
Malcolm X and Haley, Alex. The Autobiography of Malcolm X, 1031
Maldonado, Manuel. Puerto Rico, 5851
Male and Female Homosexuality. Saghir, Marcel T. and Robins, Eli. 2595
Malkevitch, Joseph and Meyer, Walter. Graphs, Models, and Finite Mathematics, 1938
Malkoff, Karl. Crowell's Handbook of Contemporary American Poetry, 358
Mallarme, Stephanie. Selected Poems, 4126
Mallett, Michael. The Borgias, 5428
Mallory, James R. The Structure of Canadian Government, 1190
Mallowan, Max E. Early Mesopotamia and Iran, 4910
MALNUTRITION, 578
Malo, John W. Malo's Complete Guide to Canoeing and Canoe-Camping, 3426
Malone, Bill C. Country Music U.S.A. A Fifty-Year History, 3227
Malo's Complete Guide to Canoeing and Canoe-Camping. Malo, John W, 3426
Malquerida. Benevente, Jacinto, 4345
Malraux, André. Anti-Memoirs, 4278
———. La Condition Humaine, 4229
MALRAUX, ANDRÉ, 4278
Mamatey, Victor S. and Luza, Radomir. A History of the Czechoslovak Republic, 1918-1948, 5349
MAMMALS, 247, 2446-2448, 2450-2452, 2462
   DICTIONARIES, 2444
Mammals of North America. Orr, Robert T, 2451
Mammals of the World. Walker, Ernest P., et al. 247
Mammarella, Giuseppe. Italy After Fascism, 5447
Mammoths, Mastodons and Man. Silverberg, Robert, 2183
MAN, 507, 525, 1921, 2483

INFLUENCE OF ENVIRONMENT, 398, 2955
INFLUENCE ON NATURE, 125, 1466, 2235, 2239, 2707
ORIGIN AND ANTIQUITY, 2192, 2194, 2196
Man Against Cancer. Glemser, Bernard, 2617
Man and Aggression. Ashley Montagu, compiled by. 571
Man and God in Art and Ritual. Brandon, Samuel G, 762
Man and the Atom. Barnaby, Frank, 2663
Man and the Computer. Kemeny, John G, 470
Man and the Natural World. Goin, Coleman J. and Goin, Olive B. 2213
Man Changes the Weather. Bova, Ben, 2160
A Man for All Seasons. Bolt, Robert, 3899
Man in the Universe. Hoyle, Fred, 508
Man, Nature and Ecology. Reid, Keith, et al. 2235
Man of Principle. Barker, Dudley, 3937
Man on Fire. Abels, Jules, 5975
MAN, PREHISTORIC, 401, 474, 2197-2199, 2205-2206, 2488, 4709, 4712, 4715, 4724-4725, 4735, 4738
MAN, PRIMITIVE, 4709
Man the Designer. Evans, Helen M, 3018
Manchester, William. Arms of Krupp, 1587-1968, 1531
———. The Glory and the Dream, 6140
Manchild in the Promised Land. Brown, Claude, 1120
Mandate of Heaven. Melby, John F, 5595
Mandell, Maurice. Advertising, 2857
Mandl, Matthew. Fundamentals of Electronics, 2645
Manhattan Project. Groueff, Stephen, 2668
Mann, Arthur. La Guardia, 6197
———. La Guardia Comes to Power, 1933, 6198
Mann, Felix. Acupuncture, 2582
Mann, Thomas. Bekenntnisse des Hochstaplers, Felix Krull, 4064
———. Buddenbrooks, 4065
———. Magic Mountain, 4066
———. Der Tod in Venedig und Andere Erzahlungen, 4067
MANN, THOMAS, 4078
Manned Kiting. Poynter, Dan, 3443
MANNED SPACE FLIGHT, 2768
Manned Spacecraft. Gatland, K, 2768
Mannes, M. see Sheresky, Norman
Manning, Harvey. Cry Crisis, 1475
Manon Lescaut. Prévost, Abbé, 4239
Man's Best Friend. National Geographic Society, ed, 2811

Man's Religions. Noss, John B, 823
Man's Rise to Civilization As Shown by the Indians of North America, from Primeval Times to the Coming of the Industrial State. Farb, Peter, 5749
Mansbach, Richard W. Dominican Crisis, 1965, 5843
———. Northern Ireland, 5168
Manschreck, Clyde L. A History of Christianity in the World, 779
Manual for School Evaluation. New England Association of Schools & Colleges, 49
Manual for Writers of Term Papers, Theses, and Dissertations. Turabian, Kate L, 329
Manual of Botany. Gray, Asa, 234
Manual of Cultivated Plants. Bailey, Liberty H, 232
A Manual of Style. University of Chicago Press Editors, 2849
Manuel des Études Littéraires Françaises. Castex, Pierre-Georges and Surer, Paul. 4105
Manuel, Frank Edward, ed. Utopias and Utopian Thought, 1134
Manuel, George and Posluns, Michael. The Fourth World, 5754
Manuel Illustré d'Histoire de la Littérature Française. Lanson, Gustave and Tuffrau, Paul. 4111
Manuel Tamayo y Baus. Flynn, Gerard C, 4362
MANUSCRIPTS — CONSERVATION AND RESTORATION, 33
Many Winters. Wood, Nancy, 3667
Mao. Papers. Mao, Tŝe-tung, 5600
Mao, Tŝe-tung. Mao. Papers, 5600
MAO, TŜE-TUNG, 1175, 4278, 5596
Mao Tŝe-Tung's Cultural Revolution. An, Tai-Sung, 1153
Mao's Way. Rice, Edward, 5596
Mao Tŝe-Tung. The Political Thought of Mao Tŝe-Tung, 1214
———. Selected Readings, 1179
Mapping. Greenwood, David, 2013
MAPS, 2013, 3389
Maraini, Fosco. Japan, 4779
Maran, S. P. see Brandt, John C.
Marathon. Lloyd, Alan, 4961
MARATHON, BATTLE OF, 4961
March of Archaeology. Ceram, C. W, 4707
March to Tunis. Moorehead, Alan, 5129
Marchand, Leslie A. Byron, 3813
Marchetti, Victor and Marks, John D. The CIA and the Cult of Intelligence, 1295
Marckwardt, Albert H. American English, 1879

Marcus, Abraham. Basic Electricity, 2048
Marcus, Abraham and Marcus, W. Elements of Radio, 2649
Marcus Aurelius. Sedgwick, Henry D, 4946
Marcus, Geoffrey. Maiden Voyage, 4698
Marcus, Steven. Dickens, 3932
Marcus, W. see Marcus, Abraham
La Mare au Diable. Sand, George, 4250
Marek, George R. Beethoven, 3177
Mares, Colin. Rapid and Efficient Reading, 1888
Margaret Mitchell of Atlanta. Farr, Finis, 3728
Margolius, Sidney. Health Foods, 2832
Maria Theresa. Bright, James F. 5342
MARIA THERESA, EMPRESS OF AUSTRIA, 5342
Marianne Moore. Hall, Donald, 3572
MARIE ANTOINETTE, 5380
Marie Curie. Reid, Robert, 2027
Marie, Jean-J. see Haupt, Georges
MARIHUANA, 1597, 1697
Marihuana. U. S. Commission on Marihuana & Drug Abuse, 1699
Marihuana Reconsidered. Grinspoon, Lester, 2542
Marihuana The Deceptive Weed. Nahas, Gabriel G, 1697
Marihuana Users and Drug Subculture. Johnson, Bruce D, 1700
Marine Aquarium Keeping. Spotte, Stephen, 2821
MARINE BIOLOGY, 2135, 2265-2266, 2268, 2346
MARINE ECOLOGY, 2267, 2374
Marine, Gene. America the Raped, 1463
Marine, Gene and Van Allan, Judith. Food Pollution, 2557
MARINE GEOPHYSICS, 2148
MARINE MAMMALS, 2456
Marine Mammals and Man. Wood, Forrest G, 2461
MARINE POLLUTION, 2703
MARINE RESOURCES, 1478-1479, 1557, 2131, 2143
Mariner, James L. Understanding Ecology, 2232
Mariner 6 and 7 Pictures of Mars. Collins, Stewart A, 1999
MARITIME LAW, 1557
Marius. Pagnol, Marcel, 4175
Marivaux, Pierre C. de. Les Fausses Confidences, 4169
———. Jeu de l'Amour et du Hasard, 4170
———. Le Paysan Parvenu, 4171
Mark Twain. Wagenknecht, Edward C, 3753
Mark Twain's Notebook. Clemens, Samuel L, 3756

INDEX

Markandaya, Kamala. A Handful of Rice, 4482
———. Nectar in a Sieve, 4483
Markings. Hammarskjold, Dag, 4092
Markov, Vladimir. Russian Futurism, 4525
Markov, Vladimir and Sparks, Merrill, eds. Modern Russian Poetry, 4522
Markowitz, Norman D. The Rise and Fall of the People's Century, 6141
Marks, Geoffrey. The Medieval Plague, 2610
Marks, Geoffrey and Beatty, William K. The Story of Medicine in America, 2502
Marks, John D. *see* Marchetti, Victor
Marks, Lionel. *see* Baumeister, T.
Markus, John. Electronics and Nucleonics Dictionary, 257
MARLBOROUGH, JOHN CHURCHILL, 5235
Marlowe, Christopher. Works, 3861
Marnell, William H. The Right to Know, 1582
Marques, Antonio H. R. de. History of Portugal, 5478
Marrin, Albert, ed. War and the Christian Conscience, 769
Marriott, Alice and Rachlin, Carol K. American Indian Mythology, 1835
Mars. Moore, Patrick and Cross, Charles A. 1998
Mars and the Mind of Man. Bradbury, Ray, et al. 1920
Marsden, Walter. The Rhineland, 4752
MARSH ECOLOGY, 2244
Marsh, Frank B. History of the Roman World, 146 to 30 B.C, 4930
Marsh, Henry. The Caesars, 4944
MARSH, OTHNIEL CHARLES, 2177
Marshall, Dorothy. Industrial England, 1776-1851, 1411
Marshall, George and Poling, David. Schweitzer, 773
Marshall, Samuel L. Crimsoned Prairie, 5774
MARSHALL, THURGOOD, 1601
MARSHALS, FRANCE, 5405
Martha Graham. McDonagh, Don, 3329
MARTHA'S VINEYARD, MASSACHUSETTS — DESCRIPTION AND TRAVEL, 4830
Martí, José. Páginas Escogidas, 4328
MARTÍ, JOSÉ, 5834
Marti, Martyr of Cuban Independence. Lizaso, Felix, 5834
Martialis, Marcus Valerius. The Epigrams, 4419
Martienssen, Anthony K. Queen Catherine Parr, 5222
Martin, Alexander C. Weeds, 2325

Martin, Bernard. Strange Vigor, 5590
Martin Buber. Diamond, Malcolm L, 619
Martin, E. *see* Labichne, Eugene
Martin Gardner's Sixth Book of Mathematical Games from Scientific American. Gardner, Martin, 3332
Martin, Graham. Eliot in Perspective, 3897
Martin, James. Introduction to Teleprocessing, 2642
Martin, James K. Men in Rebellion, 5942
Martin, Jay. Nathaniel West, 3732
Martin, Laurence W. Arms and Strategy, 1667
Martin, Luis. The Kingdom of the Sun, 6268
Martin Luther. Luther, Martin, 788
Martini, Fritz. Deutsche Literaturgeschichte von den Anfangen bis zur Gegenwart, 3989
MARTYRS, 792, 795
Marvell, Andrew. Complete Poems, 3800
Marvell, E. N. *see* Kice, J. L.
Marvels of Animal Behavior. Mailer, Peter R., et al. 2356
Marvin, Ursula B. Continental Drift, 2126
Marx, Karl. Capital and Other Writings, 1677
MARX, KARL, 556, 1491-1492, 1494
Marx, Karl and Engels, Friedrich. Communist Manifesto, 1493
Marx, Wesley. The Frail Ocean, 1479
———. Oilspill, 2701
MARY, CONSORT OF LOUIS XII, 5228
MARY I, QUEEN OF ENGLAND, 5232
MARY II, QUEEN OF ENGLAND, 5247
Mary, Queen of Scots. Fraser, Antonia, 5157
MARY STUART, QUEEN OF THE SCOTS, 5157
Mary Todd Lincoln. Turner, Justin G. and Turner, Linda L., eds. 6038
Mary Tudor, the White Queen. Richardson, Walter C, 5228
Masaryk, Thomas G. Making of a State, 5352
———. The Spirit of Russia, 5489
Masefield, John. Poems, 3839
Mason, Alpheus Thomas. The States Rights Debate, 1583
Mason, Brian and Melson, William G. Lunar Rocks, 2168
Mason, Germaine. A Survey of French Literature, 4112
Mason, Jerry, ed. The American Sportsman Treasury, 3450
Maspero, Gaston C. The Dawn of Civilization, 4878
MASS MEDIA, 463, 901-902
Massa, Ann. Vachel Lindsay, 3607

MASSACHUSETTS
  HISTORY — COLONIAL PERIOD
    (NEW PLYMOUTH), 6194
  POLITICS AND GOVERNMENT,
    1375
Massacre. Payne, Robert, 5638
Massie, Robert. Nicholas and Alexandra, 5506
Master Builders. Blake, Peter, 2961
Master Builders of the Animal World. Hancocks, David, 2363
Masterpieces of Modern French Theater. Corrigan, Robert W, 4190
Masterpieces of Russian Literature. Turkevich, Ludmilla B., ed, 4500
Masterpieces of the Modern German Theatre. Corrigan, Robert W., ed, 4027
Masterpieces of the Modern Italian Theatre. Corrigan, Robert W., ed, 4297
Masterpieces of the Modern Russian Theatre. Corrigan, Robert W., ed, 4538
Masterpieces of the Modern Spanish Theatre. Corrigan, Robert W., ed, 4361
Masterpieces of the Russian Drama. Noyes, George R., ed, 4539
Masters, Donald C., ed. Canada, 5782
Masters, Edgar L. New Spoon River Anthology, 3608
Masters of Ancient Comedy. Casson, Lionel, ed, 4445
Masters of the Occult. Cohen, Daniel, 531
Masters, Robert V., compiled by. Complete Book of Karate and Self-Defense, 3410
Masur, Gerhard. Simon Bolivar, 6262
Mathematical Career of Pierre de Fermat, 1601-1665. Mahoney, M, 1947
Mathematical Discovery on Understanding, Learning and Teaching Problem Solving. Polya, Gyorgy, 1941
MATHEMATICAL LINGUISTICS, 1858-1859
Mathematical Models. Cundy, Henry M. and Rollett, A. P. 1930
Mathematical Models in Linguistics. Gross, Maurice, 1858
MATHEMATICAL RECREATIONS, 1943, 3332-3333
MATHEMATICIANS, 1943, 1945
MATHEMATICS, 210, 1927-1939, 1941
  DICTIONARIES, 209
  HISTORY, 1942-1944
  PHILOSOPHY, 644
  TABLES, ETC., 208, 215
Mathematics, a Human Endeavor. Jacobs, Harold R, 1933

Mathematics and the Imagination. Kasner, Edward and Newman, James. 1934
Mathematics Dictionary. James, Glenn and James, Robert C., eds. 209
Mathematics for the Modern Mind. Fuchs, Walter R, 1932
Mathematics in the Modern World. Scientific American Editors, 1939
Mathematics in Western Culture. Kline, Morris, 1935
MATHEMATICS, PRIMITIVE, 1940
Mather, Kirtley F. The Earth Beneath Us, 2111
Matheson, Maureen. see Cooper, Barbara
Mathew, David. James First, 5240
———. Lady Jane Grey, 5223
Matisse, Henri. Matisse on Art, 2878
Matisse on Art. Matisse, Henri, 2878
Matrix of Man. Moholy-Nagy, Sibyl, 2954
Matthews, Constance M. Place Names of the English Speaking World, 4688
Matthews, Donald R., ed. Perspectives on Presidential Selection, 1379
Matthews, William H. A Guide to the National Parks, 1472
Matthiessen, Francis O. The Achievement of T. S. Eliot, 3578
Matthiessen, Peter. The Cloud Forest, 4841
———. Sal Si Puedes, 1448
———. The Wind Birds, 2428
Matthiessen, Peter and Porter, Eliot. The Tree Where Man Was Born, 4793
Mattingly, Garrett. The Armada, 5224
———. Catherine of Aragon, 5225
Mattingly, Grayson and Smith, Welby. Introducing the Single-Camera VTR System, 3116
Matusow, A. J., see Bernstein, Barton J.
Maupassant, Guy de. Contes Choisis, 4230
———. Pierre et Jean, 4231
Maurer, Armand A. Medieval Philosophy, 631
Mauriac, François. Désert de l'Amour, 4232
———. Le Noeud de Vipéres, 4233
———. Thérèse Desqueyroux, 4234
Maurois, André. Ariel, 3814
———. Prometheus, 4235
———. Victor Hugo, 4279
Maxim Gorky, Romantic Realist and Conservative Revolutionary. Hare, Richard, 4534
Maximes. La Rochefoucald, François Duc De, 4277
Maximilian and Carlota. Smith, Gene, 5816
MAXIMILIAN, EMPEROR OF MEXICO, 5816
Maxwell, Zena. see Hemming, James

INDEX

May, Arthur J. Age of Metternich, 1814-1848, 5341
May, Ernest. The World War and American Isolation, 1914-1917, 5079
May, George S. A Most Unique Machine, 2738
May, Herbert G. Oxford Bible Atlas. , 108
May, Judy G. Scuba Diver's Guide to Underwater Ventures, 3438
May, Rollo. Love and Will, 570
Maya. Coe, Michael D, 5758
Mayakovski, Vladimir. Stikhovoreniia Poemy, 4509
Mayakovsky. Brown, Edward J, 4507
MAYAS, 4802-4803, 5758, 5809
Mayer, Milton S. They Thought They Were Free, 5319
Mayer, Peter, ed. Pacifist Conscience, 1549
Mayer, Ralph. Dictionary of Art, 266
Mayer, Tom. Climb for the Evening Star, 2717
MAYER, TOM, 2717
Maynard, John. Russia in Flux, 5507
Maynard, Theodore. The Humanist As Hero, 5226
Mayr, Ernst. Populations, Species and Evolution, 2347
Mazlish, B. *see* Bronowski, Jacob
Mazo, Joseph H. Dance Is a Contact Sport, 3327
Mazzaro, Jerome, ed. Modern American Poetry, 3570
————. William Carlos Williams, the Later Poems, 3609
Mazzini. Salvemini, Gaetano, 5440
MAZZINI, GUISEPPE, 5440
Mbiti, John. African Religions and Philosophy, 873
Mead, Douglas S., ed. Great English and American Essays, 3516
Mead, Frank S. Handbook of Denominations in the United States, 802
Mead, Margaret. Changing Culture of an Indian Tribe, 5776
————. Continuities in Cultural Evolution, 916
————. Culture and Commitment, 910
Meaning of Czech History by Thomas Masaryk. Wellek, Rene, ed, 5351
Meaning of Modern Sculpture. Wilenski, Reginald H, 2996
Meaning of Relativity. Einstein, Albert, 2030
Meaning of the Qumran Scrolls for the Bible. Brownlee, William H, 718
Meaning of the Twentieth Century. Boulding, Kenneth E, 917

MECHANICAL ENGINEERING — HANDBOOKS, MANUALS, ETC., 254
MECHANICAL MOVEMENTS, 2629
Mechanisms of Inorganic Reactions. Basolo, Fred and Pearson, R. G. 2078
Medeiros, Robert W. Chemistry, 2068
Medes and Persians. Culican, William, 4917
Media and Methods. 40
Media Programs. NEA, Division of Audiovisual Instruction, 23
Medically Based No-Nonsense Beauty Book. Chase, Deborah, 2841
Medicated Society. Proger, Samuel, 2576
Medici. Schevill, Ferdinand, 5434
MEDICI, HOUSE OF, 5433-5434
MEDICINE
  CASES, CLINICAL REPORTS, STATISTICS, 2591
  DICTIONARIES, 248-249, 252, 2586
  HISTORY, 2502, 2560-2561
  PRACTICE, 2590
MEDICINE AS A PROFESSION, 2496
Medicine for Mountaineering. Wilkerson, James A., ed, 2622
Medicine Power. Steiger, Brad, 876
MEDICINE, PREVENTIVE — HISTORY, 2559
MEDICINES, PATENT, PROPRIETARY, ETC, 2556
Medieval Cities. Saalman, Howard, 2952
Medieval Germany, 911-1250. Barraclough, Geoffrey, tr, 5289
Medieval Mind. Taylor, Henry O, 5008
Medieval Panorama. Coulton, George G, 5196
Medieval People. Power, Eileen E, 5004
Medieval Philosophy. Maurer, Armand A, 631
Medieval Plague. Marks, Geoffrey, 2610
Medieval Russia's Epics, Chronicles and Tales. Zenkovsky, Serge A, 4584
Medieval Village. Coulton, George G, 4996
Medieval Warfare. Hindley, Geoffrey, 1670
MEDITATION, 740, 759
Meditations, Poétiques. Lamartine, Alphonse de, 4125
Mediterranean. Bradford, Ernle D, 4683
Mediterranean and the Mediterranean World in the Age of Philip II. Braudel, Fernand, 4689
MEDITERRANEAN REGION, 4683, 4689
Medlicott, William N. Contemporary England, 5271

Meggers, Betty J., et al. Tropical Forest Ecosystems in Africa and South America, 2245
Meier, August. From Plantation to Ghetto, 5865
———. Negro Thought in America, 1880-1915, 1032
Meier, August and Rudwick, Elliott. CORE, 1236
Meier, Matthew S. and Rivera, Feliciano. The Chicanos, 1044
Meigs, Cornelia L. Jane Addams, Pioneer for Social Justice, 1693
Meilach, Dona Z. Contemporary Art with Wood, 2990
Mein Kampf. Hitler, Adolf, 5316
Meir, Golda. A Land of Our Own, 5666
MEIR, GOLDA MABOVITZ, 5666
Meister Dramen. Zuckmayer, Carl, 4024
Melbourne. Cecil, David, 5256
MELBOURNE, WILLIAM LAMB, 5256
Melby, John F. Mandate of Heaven, 5595
Melchinger, Siegfried. The Concise Encyclopedia of Modern Drama, 316
Mellaart, James. Earliest Civilizations of the Near East, 4722
Mellers, Wilfred. Twilight of the Gods, 3232
Mellow, James R. Charmed Circle, 3765
Melson, William G. see Mason, Brian
Meltsner, Michael. Cruel and Unusual, 1599
Meltzer, Milton and Cole, Bernard. The Eye of Conscience, 3121
MELVILLE, HERMAN, 3719-3720
Melville, Keith. Communes in the Counter Culture, 1506
Melville, Samuel. Letters from Attica, 1737
Member of the Wedding. McCullers, Carson, 3680
Memoir of a Revolutionary. Djilas, Milovan, 1222
Memoirs. Truman, Harry S, 6154
Memoirs of a Revolutionist. Kropotkin, Petr, 5504
Memoirs of Chief Red Fox. Red Fox, William, 5764
Memoirs of the Right Honorable Alexander Macdonald. Pope, Joseph, 5797
Memoirs, 1925-1963. Kennan, George F, 1343
Men and Dinosaurs. Colbert, Edwin H, 2180
Men and Masks. Gossman, Lionel, 4163
Men and Molecules. Metzger, Norman, 2228
Men and Music in Western Culture. Walter, Don C, 3142
Men and the Matterhorn. Rebuffat, Gaston, 4768

Men, Beasts, and Gods. Carson, Gerald, 2803
Men in Rebellion. Martin, James K, 5942
Men, Messages and Media. Schramm, Wilbur, 463
Men of Destiny. Lippmann, Walter, 4868
Men of Mathematics. Bell, Eric T, 1945
Men to Match My Mountains. Stone, Irving, 6239
Men Who Play God. Moss, Norman, 1668
Menard, H. W. Geology, Resources, and Society, 2096
Mencken, Henry L. American Language, 1880
Mencl, U. see Zaruba, G.
Mendel, Arthur P., ed. Essential Works of Marxism, 1489
MENDEL, GREGOR, 2300
Mendell, Clarence. Latin Poetry, 4404
MENDELSOHN-BARTHOLDY, FELIX, 3153
Mendelssohn, Kurt. The Riddle of the Pyramids, 4890
Mendenhall, Thomas C., et al. Ideas and Institutions in European History, 800-1715, 4990
———. Quest for a Principle of Authority in Europe, 1715 to the Present, 5022
Menen, Aubrey. The Mystics, 849
Las Meninas. Buero Vallejo, Antonio, 4348
Menke, Frank G. The Encyclopedia of Sports, 321
Mensching, Gustav. Tolerance and Truth in Religion, 758
Merchants and Masterpieces. Tomkins, Calvin, 2893
Merck Manual of Diagnosis and Therapy. 249
Mercury. Montague, Katherine and Montague, Peter. 2583
MERCURY — TOXICOLOGY, 2583
Mere Christianity. Lewis, Clive S, 738
Merimée, Prosper. Colomba, 4236
Merriam, Charles E. A History of American Political Theories, 1198
Merrill, James. Braving the Elements, 3654
Merrill, James M. William Tecumseh Sherman, 6055
Merrill, John C. The Elite Press, 493
Merrill, W. K. The Survival Handbook, 2535
Mersand, Joseph, ed. Great Narrative Essays, 3746
Merton, Robert K. and Nisbet, Robert. Contemporary Social Problems, 885
Merton, Thomas. The Asian Journal of Thomas Merton, 740
———. Faith and Violence, 770
Mertvye Dushi. Gogol, Nikolai V, 4549

INDEX

Merz, Charles. Dry Decade, 6114
Meschkowski, Herbert. Ways of Thought of Great Mathematicians, 1943
Meserve, Ruth, see Meserve, Walter J.
Meserve, Walter J. and Meserve, Ruth, eds. Modern Drama from Communist China, 4605
MESOPOTAMIA
   ANTIQUITIES, 4720, 4910
   CIVILIZATION, 4911-4912
Messages and Voices. Cosgrove, Margaret, 2367
METALS, 2584
Metamorphoses. Ovidius Naso, Publius, 4408
METAPHYSICS, 519
Metcalf, Keyes. Planning Academic and Research Library Buildings, 21
METEORITES, 196, 1897-1898, 2002-2003
Meteorites and Their Origins. McCall, G. J, 2002
Methvin, Eugene H. The Riot Makers, 1721
Metraux, Alfred. History of the Incas, 6269
Metric Power. Deming, Richard, 1809
METRIC SYSTEM, 1808-1809
METROPOLITAN AREAS, 970
Metropolitan Opera, 1883-1966. Kolodin, Irving, 3207
Metternich's Europe. Walker, Mack, ed, 5065
Metzger, H. Peter. The Atomic Establishment, 1524
Metzger, Norman. Men and Molecules, 2228
MEXICAN AMERICANS, 1040-1041, 1044-1046, 1237, 4825-4826, 5875
Mexican People. Gutierrez de Lara, Lazaro, 5813
Mexican Revolution. Cumberland, Charles C, 5818
Mexican War. Singletary, Otis A, 6020
MEXICO, 5805
   ANTIQUITIES, 2941, 4800, 4803
   BIOGRAPHY, 5806
   DESCRIPTION AND TRAVEL, 4802
   HISTORY, 5802-5804, 5807, 5810-5815, 5817-5820, 5822-5823, 6259
   SOCIAL CONDITIONS, 1100-1101, 5821
Mexico. Cheetham, Nicolas, 5802
Mexico. Cumberland, Charles C, 5803
Mexico. Tannenbaum, Frank, 5821
Mexico, Three Thousand Years of Art and Life. Bernal, Ignacio, 4800
Mexico, 1946-1973. Hofstadter, Dan, 5819
Meyer, Fred. see Hedges, David
Meyer, Henry C. The Long Generation, 5295
Meyer, Herbert W. A History of Electricity and Magnetism, 2049
Meyer, Robert, Jr. Festivals U.S.A. and Canada, 1820
Meyer, Walter. see Malkevitch, Joseph
Mezey, Robert, compiled by. Poems from the Hebrew, 4589
Michael, Paul and Parish, James R., eds. American Movies Reference Book, 314
Michard, Laurent. see Lagarde, André
Michaud, C. Regis. see Hall, Marie-Louise Michaud
Michelangelo. Complete Poems and Selected Letters, 4300
Michelangelo. Brandes, Georg, 2922
MICHELANGELO BUONAROTTI, 2302-2305
Michelet, Jules. Joan of Arc, 5377
Michell, Humphrey. Sparta, 4978
Michelsohn, David R. Atomic Energy for Human Needs, 2060
Michener, Charles D. The Social Behavior of the Bees, 2399
Michener, James A. Iberia, 5459
———. Kent State, 6176
———. Modern Japanese Print, 3090
Micro-Organisms and Man. Wyss, Orville and Eklund, C. E. 2305
Microbes and Morals. Rosebury, Theodor, 2614
Microbial World. Stanier, Roger Y., et al. 2304
MICROBIOLOGY, 2302-2305
Microbiology. Pelczar, Michael J. and Reid, Roger D. 2303
MICROFILMS, 27
Microscope and How to Use It. Carona, Philip B, 2309
MICROSCOPE AND MICROSCOPY, 200, 1913, 2309
Midcentury America. Bode, Carl, compiled by. 6002
MIDDLE AGES, 4993, 4999
   HISTORY, 436, 4996, 4998, 5002-5003, 5005, 5007, 5010-5010 5015, 5018
      CHRONOLOGY, 381
      SOURCES, 5009
      INTELLECTUAL LIFE, 4994, 5000, 5008
Middle Americans. Coles, Robert and Erikson, Jon. 998
MIDDLE CLASSES
   AFRICA, SOUTH, 1099
   POLITICAL ACTIVITY, 1070
   U. S., 995, 998
Middle East. Adams, Michael, ed, 442
Middle-English Dictionary. Stratmann, Francis H, 174

Middleton, Christopher and Hamburger, Michael, eds. Modern German Poetry, 4005
Migel, Parmenia. Titania, 4093
Mighty Stonewall. Vandiver, Frank E, 6051
MIGRANT LABOR —U. S., 996
Mikasinovich, Branko, et al, eds. Introduction to Yugoslav Literature, 4586
Milagros de Nuestra Señora. Berceo, Gonzalo de, 4318
Milestones Along the March. Ianniello, Lynne, ed, 1259
Milestones of the Air. Taylor, John, 2730
Milford, Nancy. Zelda, 3733
Militant Dissenters. Coblentz, Stanton A, 4668
Militant South, 1800-1861. Franklin, John H, 6206
MILITARISM, 1164, 1659, 1662, 6202
Militarism, U. S. A. Donovan, James A, 1659
Military and American Society. Ambrose, Stephen E. and Barber, James A., Jr., eds. 1067
Military Architecture. Hughes, Quentin, 2975
MILITARY ARCHITECTURE — HISTORY, 2975
MILITARY ARTS AND SCIENCE, 1654-1655, 1657-1658, 1660, 1669-1670, 4937
Military Establishment. Yarmolinsky, Adam, 1664
MILITARY HISTORY, 144, 1658, 1665, 1669-1670, 4671, 4678
ATLASES, 385
A Military History of the Western World. Fuller, John F, 4671
MILITARY POLICY, 1661
Military Power and Potential. Knorr, Klaus E, 1656
MILITARY SERVICE, COMPULSORY — U. S., 1674
Military Transport of the First World War. Ellis, Christopher, 1681
Military Transport of World War Two. Ellis, Christopher, 1682
Military Uniforms of the World in Color. Kannik, Preben, 1671
MILKY WAY, 1988-1989
Milky Way. Bok, Bart J. and Bok, Priscilla F. 1988
Milky Way. Branley, Franklyn M, 1989
Mill, John Stuart. Utilitarianism, Liberty and Representative Government, 1129
Millard Fillmore. Rayback, Robert J, 6022
Millay, Edna S. Collected Poems, 3610

MILLAY, EDNA ST. VINCENT, 3618
Miller, Albert J. Confrontation, Conflict and Dissent, 57
Miller, Arthur. Collected Plays, 3681
MILLER, ARTHUR, 3682
Miller, Arthur R. The Assault on Privacy, 1264
Miller, Bessemay. see Doris, Lillian
Miller, Charles. The Lunatic Express, 5733
Miller, John C. The Federalist Era, 1789-1801, 5967
———. Origins of the American Revolution, 5920
———. The Triumph of Freedom, 1775-1783, 5921
Miller, Jonathan, ed. Freud, 561
Miller, Madeline and Lane, J. Harper Bible Dictionary, 103
Miller, Merle. Plain Speaking, 6153
Miller, Nathan. Sea of Glory, 5954
Miller, Orson K., Jr. Mushrooms of North America, 2333
Miller, Perry. Life of the Mind in America, 4828
———. The New England Mind, 4829
———. New England Mind, 6190
———. The Transcendentalists, 547
Miller, Perry and Johnson, Thomas H., eds. The Puritans, 3538
Miller, Shirley. The Vertical File and Its Satellites, 24
Miller, William. The Ottoman Empire and Its Successors, 1801-1927, 5655
Miller, William R. Nonviolence, 911
Millgate, Michael. The Achievement of William Faulkner, 3734
Millis, Walter. Road to War, 5082
Mills, John F. Treasure Keepers, 481
Milne, Alan A. Vinni - Pukh I Vse-Vse-Vse, 4556
Milne, Lorus and Milne, Margery. The Animal in Man, 587
———. The Arena of Life, 2233
———. The Cougar Doesn't Live Here Anymore, 2339
———. Invertebrates of North America, 2381
———. Living Plants of the World, 2312
Milne, Lorus. see Buchsbaum, Ralph
Milne, Margery. see Milne, Lorus
Milner-Gulland, Robin, ed. Soviet Russian Verse, 4523
Milton. Tillyard, Eustace M, 3802
Milton Cross' New Encyclopedia of the Great Composers and Their Music. Cross, Milton J. and Ewen, David. 298
Milton, David, et al, eds. The China Reader, 5591
A Milton Handbook. Handford, James H, 3798

INDEX

Milton, John. Complete Poetry and Selected English Prose, 3801
MILTON, JOHN, 3798, 3802
Mind Drugs. Hyde, Margaret O, 2543
Mind in the Waters. McIntyre, Joan, 2458
Mind of Germany. Kohn, Hans, 5294
Mind of Modern Russia. Kohn, Hans, ed, 5487
Mind of the Founder. Myers, Marvin, ed, 5984
Mind of the Middle Ages, A.D. 200-1500. Artz, Frederick B, 4994
Mind of the Old South. Eaton, Clement, 6203
Mind of the South. Cash, Wilbur J, 6201
MINERALOGY, 2087, 2089, 2167, 2169
   DICTIONARIES, 219, 227
   PICTORIAL WORKS, 2088
Minerals. Campbell, Jan, 2087
Minerals and Man. Hurlbut, Cornelius, Jr, 2089
MINES AND MINERAL RESOURCES, 223, 2103, 2666, 4844
Minetree, Harry. Cooley, 2620
Minoans. Hood, Sinclair, 4734
Minoans, Philistines, and Greeks. Burn, Andrew R, 4963
MINORITIES — U. S., 126, 1005-1007, 1022-1023
Minow, Newton N., et al. Presidential Television, 1130
Minton, Madge R. see Minton, Sherman A., Jr.
Minton, Sherman A., Jr. and Minton, Madge R. Giant Reptiles, 2413
———. Venomous Reptiles, 2417
Mintz, Morton. The Pill, 2555
Mintz, Morton and Cohen, Jerry S. America, Inc. Who Owns and Operates the United States, 1199
Miracle at Philadelphia. Bowen, Catherine D, 1572
Miracle of Haitian Art. Rodman, Selden, 2942
Miracle of Language. Laird, Charlton G, 1854
Mirror and the Lamp. Abrams, Meyer H, 3462
Mirsky, D. S. A History of Russian Literature, 4497
Les Miserables. Hugo, Victor, 4219
Misericordia. Pérez Galdós, Benito, 4382
Mishima, Yukio. Confessions of a Mask, 4621
———. Sound of Waves, 4619
———. Temple of the Golden Pavillion, 4620
Mishler, Clifford, see Krause, Chester L.
Missile Crisis. Abel, Elie, 6163

Missiles of the World. Taylor, John W. and Taylor, Michael J. 1684
MISSISSIPPI VALLEY — HISTORY, 5868, 5978
Mr. Justice Holmes and the Supreme Court. Frankfurter, Felix, 1617
Mistral, Gabriela. Selected Poems, 4329
Mrs. James Madison. Arnett, Ethel S, 5982
Mitchell, Broadus. The Price of Independence, 5922
Mitchell, Charity. see Sutton, Roberta B.
Mitchell, Dick. Mountaineering First Aid, 2572
Mitchell, George. I'm Somebody Important, 1033
Mitchell, J. P. see Creasy, Edward S.
Mitchell, John G. and Stallings, Constance L., eds. Ectotatics, 936
MITCHELL, MARGARET, 3728
Mitchison, Rosalind. A History of Scotland, 5152
Mitford, Jessica. Kind and Usual Punishment, 1739
Mitford, Nancy. Madame de Pompadour, 5383
———. The Sun King, 5384
Mithras. Lyrik und Prosa. Langgasser, Elisabeth, 3997
Mits, Wits and Logic. Lieber, Hugh G. and Lieber, Lillian R. 596
Miyakawa, T. S., see Conroy, Hilary
Miyoshi, Masao. Accomplices of Silence, 4617
Mizener, Arthur. The Far Side of Paradise, 3735
MNEMONICS, 579
MOBS, 1225
Mochi, Ugo and Carter, T. Donald. Hoofed Mammals of the World, 2462
Model Rocketry. Lowry, Peter and Griffith, Field. 2769
MODELING, 2988
Modern American Literature. Curley, Dorothy Nyren, et al, eds. 3539
Modern American Novel. Westbrook, Max, ed, 3724
Modern American Poetry. Mazzaro, Jerome, ed, 3570
Modern American Poetry. Untermeyer, Louis, ed, 3551
Modern American Sculpture. Ashton, Dore, 2983
Modern and Contemporary European History. Schapiro, Jacob S, 5026
Modern Architecture. Scully, Vincent J, 2974
Modern Archives. Schellenberg, T. R, 25
Modern Book of Whittling and Woodcarving. Tangerman, Elmer J, 2991

Modern British Poetry. Untermeyer, Louis, ed, 3786
Modern Business Letter-Writer's Manual. Cloke, Marjane and Wallace, Robert. 2844
Modern Capitalism and Other Essays. Sweezy, Paul, 1408
Modern Carpentry. Wagner, Willis H, 2870
Modern Constitutional Law. Cortner, R. and Lytle, C. 1573
MODERN DANCE, 3330
Modern Dance Fundamentals. Schurman, Nona and Clark, Sharon. 3330
Modern Drama and Social Change. Raines, Robert A., ed, 3511
Modern Drama from Communist China. Meserve, Walter J. and Meserve, Ruth, eds. 4605
Modern Encyclopedia of Basketball. Hollander, Zander, ed, 3354
Modern Genetics. Papazian, Haig P, 2298
Modern German Drama. Garten, H. F, 4028
Modern German Literature. Hatfield, Henry C, 3986
Modern German Poetry. Middleton, Christopher and Hamburger, Michael, eds. 4005
Modern Germanic Literature. Domandi, Agnes K., ed, 373
Modern Germany. Pinson, Koppel S, 5296
Modern Greece. Campbell, John and Sherrard, Philip. 5549
Modern Greece. Kousoulas, D. George, 1172
Modern Greek Stories. Brown, Demetra V. and Phoutrides, Aristides, trs. 4474
Modern History of Egypt. Vatikiotis, Panagiotis J, 4896
Modern History of Israel. Lucas, Noah, 5665
Modern History of Japan. Beasley, William G, 5619
Modern Humanists Reconsidered. Robertson, John, 890
Modern Ibsen. Weigand, Hermann J, 4085
Modern Inorganic Chemistry. Lagowski, J. J, 2077
Modern Iran. Avery, Peter, 5640
Modern Islamic Literature. Kritzeck, James, ed, 4597
Modern Italian Novel from Manzoni to Svevo. Pacifici, Sergio J, 4298
Modern Japanese Literature from 1868 to Present Day. Keene, Donald, ed, 4611
Modern Japanese Novels and the West. Keene, Donald, 4616
Modern Japanese Print. Michener, James A, 3090
Modern Japanese Stories. Morris, Ivan I., ed, 4622
Modern Literary Criticism, 1900-1970. Lipking, Lawrence I. and Litz, Walton A., eds. 3463
Modern Masters. 4642
Modern Military in American Society. Ackley, Charles Walton, 1066
Modern Movements in Architecture. Jencks, Charles, 2973
Modern Norwegian Literature, 1860-1918. Downs, Brian, 4095
Modern Novel. West, Paul, 3933
Modern Political Systems. Macridis, Roy C. and Ward, Robert E., eds. 1143
Modern Political Systems. Macridis, Roy C. and Ward, Robert E., eds. 1144
Modern Principles of Organic Chemistry. Kice, J. L. and Marvell, E. N. 2084
Modern Prints and Drawings. Sachs, Paul J, 3093
Modern Romance Literatures. Curley, Dorothy N. and Curley, Arthur, eds. 341
Modern Rowing. Wilson, Paul C, 3424
Modern Russian Poetry. Deutsch, Babette and Yarmolinsky, Avrahm. 4521
Modern Russian Poetry. Markov, Vladimir and Sparks, Merrill, eds. 4522
Modern Russian Short Stories. Gibian, George and Samilov, M., eds. 4548
Modern Scotland. Kellas, James C, 5159
Modern Spanish Novel. Eoff, Sherman, 4391
Modern Spanish Theatre. Benedikt, Michael and Wellwarth, George. 4359
Modern Sportswriting. Gelfand, Louis and Heath, Harry E. 485
Modern Tradition. Ellmann, Richard and Fiedelson, Charles, Jr., eds. 3493
Modern Turkey. Lewis, Geoffrey L, 5654
MODERNISM (ART), 2905, 2908
Modernization of Iran, 1921-1941. Banani, Amin, 5641
Modigliani. Werner, Alfred, 3060
MODIGLIANI, AMADEO, 3060
MOHOLE PROJECT, 2105
Moholy-Nagy, Sibyl. Matrix of Man, 2954
Moi Universitety. Gorky, Maxim, 4577
Molding of American Banking. Redlich, Fritz, 1453
Molds and Man. Christensen, Clyde M, 2330
MOLDS (BOTANY), 2330
Mole Concept in Chemistry. Kieffer, William F, 2067
MOLECULAR BIOLOGY, 2258, 2307
Molecular Biology. Smith, C. U, 2229

INDEX

MOLECULES, 2066, 2075-2076
Molecules in the Service of Man.
　　Drummond, A. H., Jr, 2066
Molière, Jean B. Complete Works, 4172
MOLIÈRE, JEAN BAPTISTE, 4163
MOLLUSKS, 2383-2385
MOLLY MAGUIRES, 1437
Molly Maguires. Bimba, Anthony, 1437
Moment in the Sun. Rienow, Robert, 955
Monarchs of England. Morris, Jean, 5174
MONASTICISM AND RELIGIOUS
　　ORDERS, 790
Monkey. Wu Ch'Eng-En, 4607
MONKEYS, 2477
Monkeys and Apes. Napier, Prue, 2477
MONROE DOCTRINE, 1352, 5988
Monroe, Earl and Unseld, Wes. The
　　Basketball Skill Book, 3356
MONROE, JAMES, 5981, 5989
Montague, Katherine and Montague, Peter.
　　Mercury, 2583
Montague, Peter. see Montague, Katherine
Montaigne. Frame, Donald, 4270
Montaigne, Michel E. de. Essais, 4271
———. Selected Essays, 4272
MONTAIGNE, MICHEL EYGUEM DE,
　　4270
Montesquieu, Charles de. Oeuvres
　　Complètes, 4273
Montet, Pierre. Eternal Egypt, 4891
———. Everyday Life in Egypt in the Days
　　of Ramesses the Great, 4892
Montezuma. Burland, Cottie A, 5810
MONTEZUMA II, 5810
Montgomery, Charles F. A History of
　　American Pewter, 3003
Montherlant, Henri de. Célibataires, 4237
Montross, Lynn. War Through the Ages,
　　1657
Moody, Christopher. Solzhenitsyn, 4579
Mooers, Robert L., Jr. Finding Your Way in
　　the Outdoors, 2710
MOON, 1993
　　EXPLORATION, 2763-2764, 2767
　　PHOTOGRAPHS, 1994
Moon. Branley, Franklyn M, 1993
Mooney, Michael M. The Hindenburg,
　　2735
Moons and Planets. Hartmann, William K,
　　1991
Moorcraft, Colin. Must the Seas Die?, 2703
Moore, A. D. Electrostatics, 2050
Moore, Basil J. An Introduction to Modern
　　Economic Theory, 1400
Moore, Harry T. and Roberts, Warren. D.
　　H. Lawrence and His World, 3944
MOORE, HENRY, 2982
Moore, John A. Heredity and Development,
　　2297

Moore, John E., ed. Jane's Pocket Book of
　　Major Warships, 2682
Moore, John R. Daniel Defoe, 3921
Moore, Marianne. Complete Poems of
　　Marianne Moore, 3579
MOORE, MARIANNE CRAIG, 3572
Moore, Patrick. Atlas of the Universe, 211
———. Watchers of the Stars, 1969
———. Yearbook of Astronomy, 1975, 212
Moore, Patrick and Cross, Charles A. Mars,
　　1998
Moore, Patrick and Hardy, David A.
　　Challenge of the Stars, 2757
Moore, Ruth. Charles Darwin, 2284
———. The Coil of Life, 2215
———. The Earth We Live On, 2104
———. Niels Bohr, 2061
Moorehead, Alan. The Blue Nile, 5713
———. Darwin and the Beagle, 2288
———. The March to Tunis, 5129
———. The White Nile, 5714
Moquin, Wayne and Van Doren, Charles,
　　eds. A Documentary History of the
　　Italian-Americans, 4824
———. Documentary History of the
　　Mexican Americans, 5875
Moral and Political Philosophy. Hume,
　　David, 652
Moral and Political Thought of Mahatma
　　Gandhi. Iyer, Raghaven, 620
Moral Responsibility. Fletcher, Joseph, 753
Morality and the Mass Media. Haselden,
　　Kyle, 901
Moravia, Alberto. Red Book and the Great
　　Wall, 5601
More Light on the Dead Sea Scrolls.
　　Burrows, Millar, 719
More, Louis T. Isaac Newton, a Biography,
　　2026
More Nineteenth Century Studies. Willey,
　　Basil, 658
MORE, SIR THOMAS, 5226
More Words of Science. Asimov, Isaac, 198
Morgan, Edmund S. The Birth of the
　　Republic, 1763-1789, 5923
———. The Puritan Dilemma, 5903
Morgan, George. Life of James Monroe,
　　5989
Morgan, H. Wayne. American Writers in
　　Rebellion, from Mark Twain to Dreiser,
　　3542
———. From Hayes to McKinley, 1388
———. Gilded Age, 6072
Morgan, Lael. And the Land Provides,
　　6250
Morgan, Richard E. The Supreme Court
　　and Religion, 1584
Morgan, Robert J. A Whig Embattled,
　　6001

448

Morgan, Robin, ed. Sisterhood Is Powerful, 982
Morgenstern, Sam, *see* Barlow, Harold
Morison, Samuel E. Admiral of the Ocean Sea, 5889
———. The European Discovery of America, 5890
———. The European Discovery of America, 5891
———. The Growth of the American Republic, 5867
———. History of the United States Naval Operations in World War II, 5143
———. John Paul Jones, 5955
———. The Oxford History of the American People, 5866
———. Samuel De Champlain, 5793
———. Sources and Documents Illustrating the American Revolution, 1764-1788, and the Formation of the Federal Constitution, 5924
———. The Two-Ocean War, 5144
Morison, Stanley and Day, Kenneth. The Typographic Book, 1450-1935, 2867
Morowitz, Harold J. and Morowitz, Lucille S. Life on the Planet Earth, 2216
Morowitz, Lucille S. *see* Morowitz, Harold J.
MORPHOLOGY, 1894
Morris, Desmond. The Human Zoo, 588
———. The Naked Ape, 2483
Morris, Donald. The Washing of the Spears, 5737
Morris, Eric. Blockade, 5337
Morris, Ivan I., ed. Modern Japanese Stories, 4622
Morris, James. Heaven's Command, 5261
Morris, Jean. The Monarchs of England, 5174
Morris, John. The Age of Arthur, 5188
Morris, John J., ed. Alaska, 4839
Morris, Richard B. The Peacemakers, 5925
———. Seven Who Shaped Our Destiny, 5937
Morris, Richard B., *see* Commager, Henry S.
Morris, Richard B. and Commager, Henry S., eds. Encyclopedia of American History, 451
Morris, Richard E. and Irwin, Graham, eds. Harper Encyclopedia of the Modern World, 380
Morrison, Donald G. Black Africa, 1097
Morrison, George. *see* Fitzgibbon, Constantine
Morrison, Kathleen. Robert Frost, 3611
Morriss, James E. *see* Freedman, Russell
Morrow, William L. Congressional Committees, 1366

Morse, Josiah M. The Irrelevant English Teacher, 1884
MORTALITY, 130
Moscow Puzzles. Kordemsky, Boris, 3333
Mosén Millán. Sender, Ramón J, 4386
MOSES, ANNA MARY (ROBERTSON), 3045
Moshe Dayan. Teveth, Shabati, 5669
Moss, Norman. Men Who Play God, 1668
Mosse, Claude. The Ancient World at Work, 1432
Mosse, George L. The Crisis of German Ideology, 5320
———. The Reformation, 789
Mossman, Archie. Conservation, 1467
Most Dangerous Man in America. Bowen, Catherine D, 5949
A Most Unique Machine. May, George S, 2738
Most Unsordid Act. Kimball, Warren F, 6135
Mostert, Noel. Supership, 1805
Moth and the Star. Pippett, Aileen, 3945
Motion Pictures. Fulton, Albert R, 3273
Motion Will Be Denied. Schultz, John, 1600
Motorcycle Racing in America. Spence, James and Brown, Gar. 3408
Motorcycle World. Schilling, Phil, 2749
MOTORCYCLES, 2747-2749, 3408
Motz, Lloyd, *see* Boorse, Henry A.
Moulton, Charles W. Moulton's Library of Literary Criticism of English and American Authors, 362
Moulton's Library of Literary Criticism of English and American Authors. Moulton, Charles W, 362
Mountain People. Turnbull, Colin M, 932
MOUNTAINEERING, 3388, 3391-3392, 3394-3395, 4767-4768, 4783
 ACCIDENTS, 2572, 2622
Mountaineering First Aid. Mitchell, Dick, 2572
Mountaineering Handbook. Casewit, Curtis W. and Pownall, Richard. 3388
Mountfield, David. A History of Polar Exploration, 4852
Movement for the Acquisition of All Mexico, 1846-1848. Fuller, John D, 6019
Movers and Shakers. Sochen, June, 983
Movie Magic. Brosnan, John, 3268
Movies. Schickel, Richard, 3282
Moving Continents. Golden, Frederic, 2125

INDEX

MOVING-PICTURE ACTORS AND ACTRESSES, 314
MOVING-PICTURE CARTOONS, 51, 3114
MOVING-PICTURE FILM COLLECTIONS, 26
MOVING-PICTURE PLAYS, 3263, 3485, 4088
MOVING-PICTURES, 3269, 3276
    BIOGRAPHY, 313, 3281
    CATALOGS, 50, 52-53
    CRITICISM, 3266, 3278
    DICTIONARIES, 313
    HISTORY, 3264, 3267, 3271, 3273-3274, 3280, 3282
    PICTORIAL WORKS, 3265
    PRODUCTION AND DIRECTION, 3112-3113, 3115, 3281
    REVIEWS, 312, 3277
    SETTING AND SCENERY, 3268
MOVING-PICTURES, DOCUMENTARY, 3272, 3275
MOVING-PICTURES, SILENT, 65, 3261-3262
Mowat, Charles L. Britain Between the Wars; 1918-1940, 5273
Mowat, Farley. Never Cry Wolf, 2471
Mowbray, A. Q. The Transplant, 2624
Mowry, George E. Era of Theodore Roosevelt, 6115
Moynihan, Daniel P. see Glazer, Nathan
MOZART, WOLFGANG AMADEUS, 3166
Ms.-M.D. Fenten, D. X, 2496
Muckrake Years. Chalmers, David M, 496
Mueller, David. Karl Barth, 741
Mueller, John E. War, Presidents, and Public Opinion, 900
MUHAMMAD, 863
Muhammed. Koran, 865
MUIR, JOHN, 1462
Muirden, James. The Amateur Astronomer's Handbook, 1965
Muller, Herbert J. The Uses of the Future, 4658
———. The Uses of the Past, 4646
Müller, Vladimir K. English-Russian Dictionary, 188
Mumford, Lewis. The City in History, 2951
———. The Pentagon of Power, 4652
———. Sticks and Stones, 2968
———. Technics and Human Development, 4653

MUNAZZAMAT AYLUL AL-ASWAD, 1183
MUNICIPAL GOVERNMENT, 1372, 1626-1628, 1630
MUNITIONS, 1796
Munn, Glenn G. Encyclopedia of Banking and Finance, 139
Munson, Kenneth. Airliners Between the Wars, 1919 to 1939, 2724
———. Airliners Since 1946, 2725
———. Bombers in Service Since 1960, 2677
———. Fighters in Service, 2675
———. Helicopters and Other Rotocraft Since 1907, 2726
———. Pioneer Aircraft 1903-1914, 2727
———. Pocket Encyclopedia of Seaplanes and Flying Boats, 2728
Munson, Thomas N. The Essential Wisdom of George Santayana, 646
Muraoka, Kageo and Okamura, Kichiemon. Folk Arts and Crafts of Japan, 3014
Murdoch, Iris. Sartre, 669
Murphy, C. T., see Oates, Whitney J.
Murphy, E. Jefferson. History of African Civilization, 5706
Murphy, Gardner. Historical Introduction to Modern Psychology, 560
Murphy, John. Homosexual Liberation, 985
Murray, Bruce C. see Davies, Merton
Murray, Harold J. Short History of Chess, 3337
Murray, J. A., et al, eds. Oxford English Dictionary, 165
Murray, Linda. see Murray, Peter
Murray, Margaret A. The Splendour That Was Egypt, 4893
Murray, Peter and Murray, Linda. Dictionary of Art and Artists, 275
Murray, Robert K. The Harding Era, 6124
———. The Politics of Normalcy, 6125
———. Red Scare, 6120
Mus, Paul. see McAlister, John T., Jr.
Muschenheim, William. Elements of the Art of Architecture, 2959
Museum Companion. Lemke, Antje and Fleiss, Ruth. 265
MUSEUM TECHNIQUES, 481
MUSEUMS — DIRECTORIES, 480
Mushkat, Jerome. Tammany, 1378
Mushroom Hunter's Field Guide. Smith, Alexander H, 2331
Mushroom Pocket Field Guide. Bigelow, Howard E, 2332
MUSHROOMS, 2331-2333
Mushrooms of North America. Miller, Orson K., Jr, 2333
MUSIC, 303, 3131-3133, 3135, 3247
    BIBLIOGRAPHY, 62, 302
    COLLECTIONS, 3146

DICTIONARIES, 296-298, 301
HISTORY AND CRITICISM, 304-305, 2873, 3134, 3136-3138, 3140-3143, 3145-3146, 3148, 3150-3151, 3154, 3156, 3187-3188, 3193, 3197-3198
LOUISIANA — NEW ORLEANS, 3247
Music. Grunfeld, Frederic V, 3137
Music. Walton, Ortiz, 3198
MUSIC, AMERICAN — HISTORY AND CRITICISM, 3182-3185, 3227
Music and Musical Life in Soviet Russia .1917-1970. Schwarz, Boris, 3181
Music and Painting. Lockspeiser, Edward, 3130
MUSIC, BAROQUE, 3144, 3147
Music from the Middle Ages to the Renaissance. Sternfeld, Frederick W, 3143
Music in the Baroque Era. Bukofzer, Manfred F, 3144
Music in the Classic Period. Pauly, Reinhard G, 3148
Music in the Modern Age. Sternfeld, Frederick W, 3151
Music in the 20th Century. Austin, William, 3149
Music Is My Mistress. Ellington, Duke, 3248
MUSIC, POPULAR (SONGS, ETC.), 3202, 3221-3224, 3226
DICTIONARIES, 307, 310-311
DISCOGRAPHY, 63
HISTORY AND CRITICISM, 3194
MUSIC, RUSSIAN, 3181
Music Through the Ages. Bauer, Marion and Peyser, Ethel. 3134
MUSICAL INSTRUMENTS, 3199-3201
Musical Instruments. Buchner, Alexander, 3199
MUSICAL NOTATION, 3186
MUSICAL REVUE, COMEDY, ETC., 3209, 3211-3212, 3259
MUSICAL REVUES, COMEDIES, ETC., 3214, 3216-3217
MUSICIANS, 3165, 3196, 3242, 3259, 4867
Muslim Civilization in India. Ikram, Sheikh M, 5628
Muslim Spain. Chejne, Anwar G, 4760
MUSLIMS IN INDIA, 1060
Musset, Alfred de. La Confession d'un Enfant du Siècle, 4238
———. Oeuvres Complètes, 4173
Mussolini, Benito. Fascism, 1218
MUSSOLINI, BENITO, 5449-5451
Mussolini's Italy. Gallo, Max, 5450
Must the Seas Die? Moorcraft, Colin, 2703

Mustangs. Ryden, Hope, 2463
Mutch, Thomas A. Geology of the Moon, 2163
Mute Stones Speak. MacKendrick, Paul, 4727
Muted Revolution. Hangen, Welles, 1163
Die Mutter. Brecht, Bertolt, 4011
My Country. Eban, Abba A, 5663
My Friends the Wild Chimpanzees. Van Lawick-Goodall, Jane, 2482
My Greatest Race, by Twenty of the Finest Motor Racing Drivers of All Time. Ball, Adrian, ed, 3403
My House. Giovanni, Nikki, 3642
My Lai 4. Hersh, Seymour M, 5683
My Life with Martin Luther King, Jr. King, Coretta Scott, 1257
My Orphans of the Wild. Collett, Rosemary K, 2823
My Past and Thoughts. Herzen, Alexander I, 5501
Mycenae and the Mycenaean Age. Mylonas, George E, 4980
Mycenaeans. Taylour, William, 4981
Mydans, Carl and Mydans, Shelley. Violent Peace, 4678
Mydans, Shelley. see Mydans, Carl
Myers, Clayton R. The Official YMCA Physical Fitness Handbook, 2537
Myers, Gustavus. The History of Tammany Hall, 1137
Myers, Marvin, ed. The Mind of the Founder, 5984
Myers, Norman. The Long African Day, 2449
Myers, Robert J. and Hallmark Cards Editors. Celebrations, 152
Myers, Rolls H., ed. Twentieth Century Music, 3150
Mylonas, George E. Mycenae and the Mycenaean Age, 4980
Myrdal, Gunnar. An American Dilemma, 1272
———. Asian Drama, 1414
———. Challenge of World Poverty, 1536
Myrdal, Jean. Report from a Chinese Village, 1094
Mysterious Britain. Bord, Janet and Bord, Colin. 4725
Mysterious Sun. Hey, Nigel S, 2005
Mystery of Heredity. Fried, John J, 2292
MYSTICISM, 557-558, 763, 849, 862
Mysticism. Harkness, Georgia, 763
Mysticism. Underhill, Evelyn, 558
Mysticism East and West. Otto, Rudolf, 557
Mystics. Menen, Aubrey, 849
Myth of Sisyphus, and Other Essays. Camus, Albert, 4268

INDEX

Myth of the Negro Past. Herskovits, Melville J, 5700
MYTHOLOGY, 119, 543, 824, 826-828, 877, 3525
    DICTIONARIES, 118, 120-121, 154
    INDEXES, 153
Mythology. Bulfinch, Thomas, 824
Mythology. Hamilton, Edith, 828
Mythology of All Races. MacCulloch, John A., et al, eds. 119
Myths, Models, and Paradigms. Barbour, Ian G, 682

N E A, Division of Audiovisual Instruction. see NEA, Division of Audiovisual Instruction
NAACP. Kellogg, Charles F, 1026
Naamani, Israel T. Israel, 5667
Naar, Jon. see Kurlansky, Mervin
Nabokov, Vladimir, tr. Song of Igor's Campaign, 4510
———. Speak, Memory, 3763
NABOKOV, VLADIMIR, 3763
Nadel, Norman. A Pictorial History of the Theatre Guild, 3315
Nader, Ralph. Unsafe at Any Speed, 2739
———. Working on the System, 143
NADER, RALPH, 1544
NAGASAKI — BOMBARDMENT,(1945), 5142
Nagler, A. M. Source Book in Theatrical History, 3316
Nagy-Talavera, Nicholas M. The Green Shirts and the Others, 5365
Nahas, Gabriel G. Marihuana - The Deceptive Weed, 1697
Naked Ape. Morris, Desmond, 2483
Naked Masks. Pirandello, Luigi, 4294
Naked Poetry. Berg, Stephen, ed, 3547
Naked to Mine Enemies, the Life of Cardinal Wolsey. Ferguson, Charles Wright, 5218
NAMES
    DICTIONARIES, 417
    GEOGRAPHICAL — ENGLISH, 4688
    U. S., 432, 1880
Names and Structures of Organic Compounds. Benfey, Otto F, 2081
Namier, Lewis. England in the Age of the American Revolution, 5253
Nana. Zola, Émile, 4261
Nanry, Charles, ed. American Music, 3183
Napier, Prue. Monkeys and Apes, 2477
NAPLES (KINGDOM) — HISTORY, 5454
NAPOLEON I, 5045-5046, 5394, 5403-5404

NAPOLEON III, 5411-5412
Napoleon III. Smith, William H, 5411
Napoleon Bonaparte. Thompson, James M, 5404
Napoleon Third and Mexico. Hanna, Alfred J. and Hanna, Kathryn A. 5815
Napoleoni, Claudio. Economic Thought of the Twentieth Century, 1406
Napoleonic Revolution. Holtman, Robert B, 5047
Napoleon's Marshals. Young, Peter, 5405
Narasimhan, C. U., tr. The Mahabharata, 4486
Narayan, R. K. The Financial Expert, 4484
———. Swami and Friends and The Bachelor of Arts, 4485
NARCOTIC HABIT, 2547, 2577-2578, 2596, 2598
NARCOTIC LAWS — U. S., 1597
NARCOTICS, CONTROL OF, 1726
Narrative of the Life of Frederick Douglass, an American Slave, Written by Himself. Douglass, Frederick, 1290
Narratives of the Witchcraft Cases, 1648 to 1706. Burr, George L., ed, 5898
Nash, Gary B. Red, White and Black, 5904
Nash, Gerald D. The American West in the 20th Century, 6237
Nash, J. M. The Age of Rembrandt and Vermeer, 3071
Nash, Jay R. Bloodletters and Badmen, 145
Nash, Ogden. Verses from Nineteen Twenty-Nine on, 3580
Nash, Roderick, compiled by. American Environment, 1464
———. Wilderness and the American Mind. , 4812
Nason, Alvin and Dehaan, Robert L. The Biological World, 2217
NASSER, GAMAL ABDEL, 5715-5716
Nassour, Ellis and Broderick, Richard. Rock Opera, 3215
Nat Turner's Slave Rebellion. Aptheker, Herbert, 5992
Nathaniel West. Martin, Jay, 3732
A Nation in Torment. Ellis, Edward R, 1106
Nation Takes Shape, 1789-1837. Cunliffe, Marcus, 5963
National Aeronautics & Space Administration. Earth Photographs from Gemini III, IV, and V, 2010
———. Earth Photographs from Gemini VI Through XII, 2011
National Aeronautics and Space Administration. Hirsch, Richard, 1636

NATIONAL ASSOCIATION FOR THE ADVANCEMENT OF COLORED PEOPLE, 1026
National Football League. Official Encyclopedia History of Professional Football, 3359
National Geographic Society, ed. Alaska, 4840
———. Everyday Life in Bible Times, 714
———. Man's Best Friend, 2811
———. Those Inventive Americans, 2495
———. Vanishing Wildlife of North America, 2340
———. Wilderness U. S. A, 4813
National Geographic Society Editors. Vanishing Peoples of the Earth, 2189
NATIONAL PARKS AND RESERVES
AFRICA, 2467-2469
U. S., 1462, 1472, 1904-1906, 2274, 4810
NATIONAL SOCIALISM, 1151, 1395, 5283, 5312, 5316, 5319-5321, 5323
NATIONAL SOCIALIST PARTY, 5317, 5322
National Study of Secondary School Evaluation. Evaluative Criteria, 48
Nationalism and Revolution in Indonesia. Kahin, George McT, 6283
Native American Tribalism. McNickle, D'Arcy, 5773
Natural Foods Primer. Hunter, Beatrice T, 2831
NATURAL HISTORY, 196-197, 1897-1899, 1901-1908, 2210, 2248, 2259, 2271-2275, 2288, 2353, 2369, 2375-2376, 2464, 2467, 2469, 4798, 5689
DICTIONARIES, 222
Natural History of Infectious Disease. Burnet, MacFarlane F. and White, D. O. 2607
Natural History of Man. Swanson, Carl P, 2191
Natural Light Photography. Adams, Ansel, 3101
Natural Mind. Weil, Andres, 2549
NATURAL RESOURCES, 955, 1465, 1469-1470
DICTIONARIES, 222
NATURALISTS, 2823
Naturalists' Guide to Freshwater Aquarium Fish. Hoedeman, J. J, 263
Nature and Growth of Modern Mathematics. Kramer, Edna, 1936
Nature Atlas of America. Clement, Roland, 197

NATURE CONSERVATION, 1471, 2240, 2824, 4812
Nature in the Urban Landscape. Gill, Don and Bonnett, Penelope. 2240
Nature of Earth Materials. Tennissen, A, 2169
Nature of Physics. Lindsay, Robert B, 2053
Nature of Revolution. Beals, Carleton, 4667
Nature of Roman Comedy. Duckworth, George E, 4411
Nature's Guide to Successful Gardening and Landscaping. Flemer, William, 2791
NAVAL ARCHITECTURE — HISTORY, 2680
Nayman, Jacqueline. Atlas of Wildlife, 241
Nazi Years. Remak, Joachim, ed, 5323
NEA, Division of Audiovisual Instruction and N E A, Division of Audiovisual Instruction. Media Programs, 23
Neal, Jack A., ed. Literary Market Place, 264
Neale, John. Queen Elizabeth I, 5227
NEAR EAST
ANTIQUITIES, 4722
CIVILIZATION, 4784
HISTORY, 389, 441-442, 727, 1322, 5642
POLITICS, 1147, 1181-1182, 1184
SOCIAL CONDTIONS, 1523
A Near East Studies Handbook, 570-1974. Bacharach, Jere L, 441
Nectar in a Sieve. Markandaya, Kamala, 4483
Nedorosl' Fonvizin, Denis I, 4530
Negative. Adams, Ansel, 3106
Negotiating with the Chinese Communists. Young, Kenneth T, 1355
NEGRO CHILDREN, 1019
Negro Genius. Brawley, Benjamin G, 4867
Negro Ghetto. Weaver, Robert C, 1274
Negro in American Culture. Butcher, Margaret J, 2874
Negro in American History. 127
Negro in Art. Locke, Alain, ed, 2914
Negro in the Civil War. Quarles, Benjamin, 6033
Negro in the Making of America. Quarles, Benjamin, 1035
Negro Revolt. Lomax, Louis, 1030
Negro Thought in America, 1880-1915. Meier, August, 1032
NEGROES, 962, 966, 1009-1012, 1017-1018, 1020, 1031, 1121, 1243,1272-1274, 1420, 1752, 1777, 1877, 3196, 3267, 4827, 5700, 6013, 6235
BIBLIOGRAPHY, 17-18
BIOGRAPHY, 1273, 1292, 4860, 5935, 6223

INDEX

HISTORY, 17, 127, 1008, 1028, 1032, 1034-1035, 1037, 1258, 1270-1271, 1287, 1291, 1723, 4860, 5796, 5865, 5883
   SOURCES, 1025, 5882
  MORAL AND SOCIAL CONDITIONS, 1008, 1036, 1038, 1123, 1283
  POLITICS AND SUFFRAGE, 1240-1241, 1261, 1399
  RELIGION, 681, 746, 871
  SEGREGATION, 1019, 1030, 1036, 1099, 1274-1275
NEGROES IN ART, 2914
Negroes in the American Revolution. Quarles, Benjamin, 5938
NEHRU, JAWAHARLAL, 4278, 5636
Neill, Alexander S. Neill! Neill! Orange Peel! An Autobiography, 1778
———. Summerhill, 1771
NEILL, ALEXANDER SUTHERLAND, 1778
Neill! Neill! Orange Peel! An Autobiography. Neill, Alexander S, 1778
Neill, Stephen C., see Rouse, Ruth
Neill, Wilfred. Twentieth Century Indonesia, 5689
Neill, Wilfred T. The Last of the Ruling Reptiles, 2423
Neither Liberty nor Bread. Keene, Frances, ed, 5445
Nekrasov, Nikolai. Izbrannye Proizv, 4511
Nelson, Benjamin. Arthur Miller, 3682
Nelson, Clemens A. see Zumberg, James H.
NELSON, HORATIO, 5254
Nelson, J. Population and Survival, 954
Nelson, Jack L. and Carlson, K., eds. Radical Ideas and the Schools, 4659
Nelson, Lowry, Jr., ed. Cervantes, 4390
Nelson, Walter H. The Soldier Kings, 5338
Nelson, William D. Surfing, 3431
Nemerov, Howard. Blue Swallows, 3655
———. New and Selected Poems, 3656
———. Reflections on Poetry and Poets, 3478
Nemesis of Power. Wheeler-Bennett, John W, 5307
Nemiroff, Robert, ed. To Be Young, Gifted and Black, 3701
Nepal. Bernstein, Jeremy, 4782
NERO, 4948
Nero. Warrington, Brian H, 4948
Neruda, Pablo. Selected Poems, 4330
NERVOUS SYSTEM, 2343, 2506, 2523
Nervous System. Lewin, Roger, 2343
Nestyev, Israel V. Prokofiev, 3178
Netboy, Anthony. The Salmon, 1481

Netherby, Steve, ed. The Experts' Book of Freshwater Fishing, 3455
NETHERLANDS
  HISTORY-GERMAN OCCUPATION, 5114, 5116
  SOCIAL LIFE AND CUSTOMS, 5000
Nettels, Curtis P. Roots of American Civilization, 5905
Netzer, Dick. Economics and Urban Problems, 937
Die Neuen Wirklichkeiten. Bloecker, J, 3983
Neumann, Franz. Behemoth, 5321
Neushul, M. Botany, 2313
Neusner, Jacob. American Judaism, 853
Never Cry Wolf. Mowat, Farley, 2471
Never in Anger. Briggs, Jean L, 926
Never Tire of Protesting. Seldes, George, 482
Nevins, Allan, et al, eds. Civil War Books, 79
———. Grover Cleveland, 6092
———. John D. Rockefeller, 1533
———. Ordeal of the Union, 6009
Nevins, Allan, see Commager, Henry S.
New Age of Franklin Roosevelt. Perkins, Dexter, 6142
New American Nation Series. 6186
New American Philosophers. Reck, Andrew J, 647
New American Society. Bensman, Joseph and Vidich, Arthur J. 995
New America's Wonderlands. Bennett, Ross, ed, 4810
New Anatomy of Britain. Sampson, Anthony, 1087
New and Selected Poems. Nemerov, Howard, 3656
New Anthology of Spanish Literature. Chandler, Richard E. and Schwartz, Kessel, eds. 4304
New Astronomies. Bova, Ben, 1960
New Australia. Simpson, Colin, 4844
New Biology. Chedd, Graham, 2258
New Birth Control. Wylie, Evan McLeod, 2554
New Black Playwrights, an Anthology. Couch, William, Jr., ed, 3670
New Black Voices. Chapman, Abraham, ed, 3533
New Century Cyclopedia of Names. 417
New Century Handbook of Classical Geography. Avery, Catherine B., ed, 406
New Century Handbook of English Literature. 359
New Century Handbook of Leaders of the Classical World. Avery, Catherine B, 411
New Chemistry. Sherwood, Martin, 2071

454

New Class. Djilas, Milovan, 1496
New Columbia Encyclopedia. 86
New Complete Book of Bicycling. Sloane, Eugene A, 3401
New Complete Book of the American Musical Theater. Ewen, David, 3211
New Complete Walker. Fletcher, Colin, 3387
New Dictionary of American Family Names. Smith, Elsdon C, 432
New Dimensions of Political Economy. Heller, Walter W, 1539
New Emily Post's Etiquette. Post, Elizabeth, 1822
New Encyclopedia Britannica. 87
New Encyclopedia of Furniture. Aronson, Joseph, 282
New Encyclopedia of the Opera. Ewen, David, 309
NEW ENGLAND — HISTORY, 6188, 6190-6191, 6193
  SOURCES, 6192
New England Association of Schools & Colleges. Manual for School Evaluation, 49
New England Frontier. Vaughan, Alden T, 6191
New England in the English Nation, 1689-1713. Haffenden, Philip S, 6193
New England Mind. Miller, Perry, 4829
New England Mind. Miller, Perry, 6190
New English. Chisholm, William, 1863
New English Bible, with the Apocrypha. Bible, 706
New Field Book of Freshwater Life. Klots, Elsie B, 2270
New Field Book of Reptiles and Amphibians. Cochran, Doris M. and Goin, Coleman J. 2411
NEW FRANCE — DISCOVERY AND EXPLORATION, 5786, 5793
New French Revolution. Ardagh, John, 1089
New Functional Hebrew-English, English-Hebrew Dictionary. Goldberg, Nathan, 190
New Genetics. Hyde, Margaret O, 2295
NEW HARMONY, INDIANA — HISTORY, 1509
New Harmony Movement. Lockwood, George B, 1509
New History of Portugal. Livermore, Harold B, 5477
New History of Spanish Literature. Chandler, Richard E. and Schwartz, Kessel. 4310
New Horizons in Astronomy. Brandt, John C. and Maran, S. P. 1961
New Industrial State. Galbraith, John Kenneth, 1409

New Irish Poets, Anthology. Garrity, Durin, ed, 3778
New Jewish Encyclopedia. Bridger, David and Wolk, Samuel J., eds. 122
New Journalism. Wolfe, Tom, 504
New Larousse Encyclopedia of Mythology. 120
New Mathematical Library. 1957
New Mind, New Body Biofeedback. Brown, Barbara B, 2513
New Music Lover's Handbook. Siegmeister, Elie, ed, 303
New Nation. Jensen, Merrill, 5965
New Outline of Science. Dietz, David, 1892
New Oxford Annotated Bible. Bible, 709
New Oxford History of Music. 305
New Physics. Taylor, John G, 2055
A New Pictorial History of the Talkies. Blum, Daniel, 3265
New Pocket Anthology of American Verse. Williams, Oscar, 3553
New Prometheans. DeRopp, Robert S, 1890
New Pronouncing Dictionary of the Spanish and English Languages. Velazquez-de-la-Cadena, Mariano, et al, eds. 184
New Rhyming Dictionary and Poets' Handbook. Johnson, Burges, ed, 173
New Rumania. Fischer-Galati, Stephen, 5564
New Science of Skin and Scuba Diving. Council for National Co-Operation in Aquatics, 3436
New Sexual Revolution. Kirkendall, Lester A. and Whitehurst, Robert N., eds. 973
New South Creed. Gaston, Paul M, 6207
New Spoon River Anthology. Masters, Edgar L, 3608
New Sweden. Fleisher, Frederic K, 5535
New Trends in 20th Century Drama. Lumley, Frederick, 3527
New Voices. Harper, Kenneth, et al, eds. 4552
New World of Dreams. Woods, Ralph L. and Greenhouse, Herbert B. 576
New World of Philosophy. Kaplan, Abraham, 609
New World of the Oceans. Behrman, Daniel, 2132
New Writing in Russia. Whitney, Thomas P., ed. & tr, 4569
NEW YORK (CITY), 969, 1022, 1042-1043, 1137, 1248, 1378, 1631, 6197-6198
NEW YORK STATE PRISON, ATTICA, 1735, 1737, 1742
New York Times. The End of a Presidency, 6177
———. The White House Transcripts, 6178

INDEX

New York Times Book of House Plants. Faust, Joan L, 2795
New York Times Book of Vegetable Gardening. Faust, Joan L, 2788
New York Times Encyclopedic Dictionary of the Environment. Sarnoff, Paul, 258
New York Times Film Reviews. Amberg, George, 312
New York Times Garden Book. Faust, Joan L., ed, 2792
New York Times Great Songs of Broadway. 3216
New York Times Index. 93
New Yorker Book of Poems. New Yorker (Periodical) 3779
New Yorker (Periodical) The New Yorker Book of Poems, 3779
NEW ZEALAND
  DESCRIPTION AND TRAVEL, 4843
  HISTORY, 6285
New Zealand. Cameron, William J, 6285
Newfield, Jack and Greenfield, J. A Populist Manifesto, 1115
Newhall, Beaumont. History of Photography, 3109
Newhouse, John. Cold Dawn, 1300
Newman, Edwin. Strictly Speaking, 914
Newman, James R. World of Mathematics, 210
Newman, James R. see Kasner, Edward
Newman, Jay H. see Newman, Lee S.
Newman, John Henry. Apologia pro Vita Sua, 728
Newman, Lee S. and Newman, Jay H. Kite Craft, 3352
Newman, Oscar. Defensible Space, 1728
Newmark, Maxim. Dictionary of Spanish Literature, 375
News from Nowhere. Epstein, Edward J, 483
Newsday, Staff & Editors of. The Heroin Trail, 1726
Newsmongers. Rutland, Robert A, 501
NEWSPAPERS, 493-494
  INDEXES, 93
Newton, Huey P. To Die for the People, 1230
Newton, Huey P. and Blake, Herman. Revolutionary Suicide, 1231
Newton, Isaac. Opticks, 2041
NEWTON, ISAAC, 2026
Newton, Norman T. Design on the Land, 2957
Next Ten Thousand Years. Berry, Adrian, 4660
Nguyen, Du and Nguyen, Huynh-Sang. The Tale of Kieu, 4623
Nguyen, Huynh-Sang. see Nguyen, Du

Nicholas II. Lyons, Marvin, 5505
NICHOLAS II, EMPEROR OF RUSSIA, 5505-5506
Nicholas and Alexandra. Massie, Robert, 5506
Nicholls, A. J. Weimar and the Rise of Hitler, 5304
Nichols, David and Cooke, John. Oxford Book of Invertebrates, 2380
Nichols, Peter. Joe Egg, 3904
Nichols, Roy F., ed. Battles and Leaders of the Civil War, 6031
———. Stakes of Power, 6010
Nicholson, Irene. The Liberators, 6258
Nicholson, Ranald. Scotland, 5156
Nicholson, Reynold A. A Literary History of the Arabs, 4598
Nicht Nur Zur Weignschtzeit. Boll, Heinrich, 4038
Nicks, Oran W., ed. This Island Earth, 2012
Nicolaus Copernicus. Hoyle, Fred, 1973
Nicolaus Copernicus and His Epoch. Adamczewski, Jan, 1972
Nicoll, Allardyce. The World of Harlequin, 3319
Nicolson, Harold G. The Congress of Vienna, 5048
Niebla. Unamuno, Miguel de, 4389
Niebuhr, H. Richard. Christ and Culture, 764
Nieburg, Harold L. Political Violence, 1132
Niels Bohr. Moore, Ruth, 2061
Niemeier, Jean. The Panama Story, 6278
Nietzsche. Jaspers, Karl, 662
Nietzsche, Friedrich W. Thus Spoke Zarathustra, 667
NIETZSCHE, FRIEDRICH WILHELM, 551, 662
Nigeria. Schwarz, Walter, 5729
NIGERIA — HISTORY, 5728-5729
Nigg, Walter. Warriors of God, 790
Night Comes to the Cumberlands. Caudill, Harry M, 1122
Night of the Iguana. Williams, Tennessee, 3710
NIGHTINGALE, FLORENCE, 2497
Nightwatchers. Cameron, Angus, 2441
Nikolaieff, George A. Computers and Society, 921
NILE RIVER, 5713-5714
Nilsson, Lennart. Behold Man, 2505
Nine Classic French Plays. Peyre, Henri and Seronde, Joseph, eds. 4185
Nine Hundred Days. Salisbury, Harrison E, 5134
Nine Modern Classics. Barnet, Sylvan, et al. 3514
Nine Planets. Nourse, Alan E, 1997
Nine Plays. O'Neill, Eugene, 3684

Nineteen Eighty-Four Revisited. Wolff, Robert P., ed, 1203
Nineteen Seventy-Six. Udall, Stewart L, 1119
Nineteenth-Century Africa. McEwan, P. J., ed, 5704
Nineteenth-Century Readers' Guide to Periodical Literature. 89
Nineteenth Century Russian Plays. Reeve, Franklin D., ed, 4541
Nineteenth Century Studies. Willey, Basil, 659
Nisbet, Robert. see Merton, Robert K.
Nitze, William and D'Argan, E. History of French Literature, 4113
Niven, John. Gideon Welles, 6034
Nixon, Marion. Oxford Book of Vertebrates, 2403
Nixon, Richard M. Six Crises, 6158
NIXON, RICHARD MILHOUS, 1718, 6177-6179
NKRUMAH, KWAME, 5725, 5727
No Easy Victories. Gardner, John W, 1109
No Exit, and Flies. Sartre, Jean-Paul, 4182
No Man Knows My History. Brodie, Fawn M, 814
No Name in the Street. Baldwin, James, 1010
No One Will Lissen. Forer, Lois G, 1603
No Victory Parades. Polner, Murray, 5686
Noah's Ark. Fourcade, Marie M, 5100
Noback, Charles R. The Human Nervous System, 2523
Nobile, Philip, see Deedy, John
Noble Gases. Asimov, Isaac, 2080
Nobody Knows My Name. Baldwin, James, 1011
Noel Hume, Ivor. A Guide to Artifacts of Colonial America, 4814
Le Noeud de Vipères. Mauriac, François, 4233
Noise. Kavaler, Lucy, 2567
Noise. Lipscomb, David M, 2568
NOISE POLLUTION, 2567-2568
Nolen, William A. The Making of a Surgeon, 2621
Nolte, Ernest. Three Faces of Fascism, 1151
Non-Book Materials. Riddle, Jean, et al. 46
Nontraditional College Routes to Careers. Splaver, Sarah, 1781
NONVIOLENCE, 620
Nonviolence. Miller, William R, 911
Nonviolence in America. Lynd, Staughton, ed, 1252
Norman Achievement. Douglas, David C, 5197

Norman Rockwell. Buechner, Thomas S., ed, 3038
Norman Thomas. Seidler, Murray B, 1486
NORMANDY — HISTORY, 5195
NORMANS, 5191, 5197-5198
Normans. Baker, Timothy, 5191
Normans and the Norman Conquest. Brown, Reginald A, 5195
Norris, Kenneth S. The Porpoise Watcher, 2460
NORTH AMERICA — HISTORY, 5892, 5902
Northen, Henry T. and Northen, Rebecca T. Greenhouse Gardening, 2802
Northen, Rebecca T. see Northen, Henry T.
Northern Colonial Frontier, 1607-1763. Leach, Douglas E, 6189
Northern Editorials on Secession. Perkins, H. C, 6045
NORTHERN IRELAND, 5163, 5167-5168
Northern Ireland. Mansbach, Richard W., ed, 5168
NORTHMAN, 5536, 5538
Northup, George T. An Introduction to Spanish Literature, 4315
Norton, Boyd. The Grand Tetons, 1905
NORWAY — HISTORY, 5130, 5539
NORWEGIAN LITERATURE — HISTORY AND CRITICISM, 4095
Norwick, Kenneth P., ed. Your Legal Rights, 1604
Norwood, Frederick A. Strangers and Exiles, 793
Noss, John B. Man's Religions, 823
Not from the Apes. Kurten, Bjorn, 2196
Not So Rich As You Think. Stewart, George R, 2697
Notes from Africa. Aynor, H. S, 5694
Notestein, Wallace. English People on the Eve of Colonization, 5241
Notre Dame de Paris. Hugo, Victor, 4220
Nourse, Alan E. Nine Planets, 1997
———. The Outdoorsman's Medical Guide, 2573
Nouveau Dictionnaire Etymologique. Larousse, 180
Nouveau Petit Larousse. Larousse, 179
Novak, Michael. Choosing Our King, 1642
———. The Rise of the Unmeltable Ethics, 1006
Novelas Ejemplares. Cervantes, Miguel de, 4373
Novelists on the Novel. Allott, Miriam, ed, 3486
Novels of Chinua Achebe. Killam, G. D, 4633
Novick, Sheldon. The Careless Atom, 2665
Nowell, Charles. Portugal, 5479

INDEX

Noyes, George R., ed. Masterpieces of the Russian Drama, 4539
Noyes, Tina and Alexander, Freda. I Can Teach You to Figure Skate, 3416
NUCLEAR PHYSICS, 2057-2059
NUCLEAR REACTORS — ACCIDENTS, 2665
Nuclear Weapons Safety and the Common Defense. Larus, Joel, 2671
NULLIFICATION, 5994
Nullification Era. Freehling, William H., ed, 5994
Number, the Language of Science. Dantzig, T, 1931
Nuremberg Falacy. Davidson, Eugene, 1555
NUREMBERG TRIAL OF MAJOR GERMAN WAR CRIMINALS, (1945-1946), 5309
Nurnberg, Walter. Lighting for Photography, 3099
NURSES AND NURSING, 2497
Nussbaum, Frederick L. Triumph of Science and Reason, 1660-1685, 5042
NUTRITION, 997, 2830-2832
Nye, Russel B. The Cultural Life of the New Nation, 5926
———. Society and Culture in America, 1830-1860, 6011
Nystrom, John W. and Haverstock, Nathan A. The Alliance for Progress, Key to Latin America's Development, 930

O Jerusalem! Collins, Larry and LaPierre, Dominique. 5643
O the Chimneys. Sachs, Nelly, 4000
Oakes, George. Turn Left at the Pub, 4751
Oakes, George and Chapman, Alexandria. Turn Right at the Fountain, 4742
Oakley, Stewart. A Short History of Denmark, 5542
———. A Short History of Sweden, 5540
Oates, Stephen B. To Purge This Land with Blood, 6012
Oates, Whitney J. Stoic and Epicurean Philosophers, 626
Oates, Whitney J. and Murphy, C. T., eds. Greek Literature in Translation, 4436
Oates, Whitney J. and O'Neill, Eugene, Jr., eds. Complete Greek Dramas, 4449
Oatley, K. Brain Mechanisms and Mind, 2526
O'Ballance, Edgar. The Kurdish Revolt, 1961-1970, 5659
———. The Third Arab-Israeli War, 5650
Ober, J. Hambleton. Writing, 1860
Oblomov. Goncharov, Ivan, 4551
Obolensky, Dimitri, ed. The Penguin Book of Russian Verse, 4524
Obras Completas. Gongora, Luis de, 4323
O'Brien, Connor C. and O'Brien, Maire. The Story of Ireland, 5162

O'Brien, John A. The Inquisition, 794
O'Brien, Maire. see O'Brien, Connor C.
OBSCENITY (LAW) — U. S., 1596, 1727
O'Casey, Sean. Selected Plays of Sean O'Casey, 3891
Occasional Writings. Dostoevsky, Feodor M, 4575
Occult Explosion. Freedland, Nat, 532
OCCULT SCIENCES, 96, 53-532, 534, 537
OCEAN, 2105, 4694
Ocean. Scientific American Editors, 2143
OCEAN BOTTOM (MARITIME LAW), 1557
OCEANICA — HISTORY, 6281
OCEANOGRAPHY, 1478, 2131-2145, 2150, 2268
    DICTIONARIES, 225
Oceanography. Scientific American Editors, 2144
Oceanology. Ingmanson, Dale E. and Wallace, William J. 2140
O'Connor, Jack, et al. Complete Book of Shooting, 3458
O'Connor, Raymond. Chemical Principles and Their Biological Implications, 2069
O'Connor, Richard. Ambrose Bierce, 3721
———. The German-Americans, 4836
———. The Spirit Soldiers, 5584
O'Connor, Thomas H. The Disunited States, 6032
OCTOPUS, 2388
Octopus and Squid, the Soft Intelligence. Cousteau, Jacques-Yves and Diole, Philippe. 2388
Odes and Epodes. Horatius Flaccus, Quintus, 4417
Odes, and Fragments. Pindarus, 4470
Odets, Clifford. Six Plays, 3683
Odishaw, H. see Condon, Edward W.
Odum, Eugene P. Fundamentals of Ecology, 2234
Odyssey. Homer, 4464
Odyssey. Homer, 4465
Oehser, Paul H. The Smithsonian Institute, 1915
Oeuvres Complètes. Montesquieu, Charles de, 4273
Oeuvres Complètes. Musset, Alfred de, 4173
Oeuvres Poétiques. Villon, François, 4133
Of Men and Morals. Feldberg, Katherine, ed, 3957
Of the Imitation of Christ. Thomas a Kempis, 760
Of Time, Tides, and Inner Clocks. Still, Henry, 2224
Offensive and Defensive Football. Smith, Burt, 3360

INDEX

Official Encyclopedia History of Professional Football. National Football League, 3359

Official Encyclopedia of Baseball. Turkin, Hy, 3378

Official Major League Baseball Playbook. Tanner, Chuck and Enright, Jim, eds. 3377

Official YMCA Physical Fitness Handbook. Myers, Clayton R, 2537

Ogburn, Charlton, Jr. The Winter Beach, 1899

OGDEN, PETER SKENE, 5801

Ogg, David. Europe in the Seventeenth Century, 5023

———. Europe of the Ancient Régime, 5043

Ogilvie, Robert S. Basic Ice Skating Skills, 3415

Ogilvy, C. Stanley. Thoughts on Small Boat Racing, 3429

Oh Dad Poor Dad, Mama's Hung You in the Closet and I'm Feelin' So Sad. Kopit, Arthur, 3700

OHIO STATE UNIVERSITY, KENT — RIOT, (MAY 4, 1970), 1791, 6176

Ohlin, Peter. Agee, 3764

OIL POLLUTION OF RIVERS, HARBORS, ETC, 196, 1897-1898, 2701-2702

Oilspill. Marx, Wesley, 2701

Ojha, Ishwer C. Chinese Foreign Policy in an Age of Transition, 1319

Okamura, Kichiemon. see Muraoka, Kageo

Okane, Walter C. Hopis, 5763

O'KEEFE, GEORGIA, 3042

Old American Prints for the Collector. Ebert, John and Ebert, Katherine. 3089

Old English Customs. Christian, Roy, 1818

Old Regime and the French Revolution. De Tocqueville, Alexis, 5392

Old Testament. Eissfeldt, Otto, 717

Oldenberg, Hermann. Buddha, 838

Oldenbourg, Zoe. Catherine the Great, 5500

O'Leary, Cornelius. see Budge, Ian

O'Leary, Daniel F. Bolivar and the War of Independence, 6263

Olga. Beecham, Justin, 3379

Oliver, Roland A. and Atmore, Anthony. Africa Since 1800, 5707

Olmstead, Albert T. History of Assyria, 4916

Olmstead, Arthur T. History of the Persian Empire, 4918

Olmstead, Frederick L. Cotton Kingdom, 6211

OLMSTED, FREDERICK LAW, 2958

Olney, James. Tell Me Africa, 4627

Olsen, Jack. Slaughter the Animals, Poison the Earth, 2827

Olson, Elder. Theory of Comedy, 3483

Olson, Eric. see Lifton, Robert J.

Olson, Lawrence A. Japan in Postwar Asia, 931

Olson, Sigurd F. and Blacklock, Les. The Hidden Forest, 2319

OLYMPIC GAMES, 3383-3385

O'Malley, C. D. Andreas Vesalius of Brussels, 1514-1564, 2589

Oman, Charles. Art of War in the Middle Ages, 5002

Omari, T. Peter. Kwame Nkrumah, 5727

Omar Khayyám. Rubáiyát, 4490

Ommanney, F. D. Lost Leviathan, 2455

Omnibus of French Literature. Steinhauer, Harry and Walter, Felix, eds. 4117

On a Piece of Chalk. Huxley, Thomas H, 2282

On Aggression. Lorenz, Konrad, 2355

On Aristotle and Greek Tragedy. Jones, John F, 4453

On Creative Writing. Engle, Paul, ed, 3468

On Death and Dying. Kubler-Ross, Elisabeth, 584

On Ice and Snow and Rock. Rebuffat, Gaston, 3393

On Judaism. Buber, Martin, 851

On Poetry and Poets. Eliot, Thomas S, 3476

On Revolution. Arendt, Hannah, 1212

On the Loose. Russell, Terry and Russell, Renny. 3128

On the Side of the Apes. Hahn, Emily, 2476

On the Various Forces of Nature. Faraday, Michael, 2017

On These I Stand. Cullen, Countee, 3599

On Violence. Arendt, Hannah, 880

On Wings of Song. Blunt, Wilfred, 3153

Once Upon a Pedestal. Greer, Germaine, 978

One Heartbeat Away. Bayh, Birch, 1567

One Hundred Famous Haiku. Buchanan, Daniel C., tr, 4613

One Man, One Vote. Graham, Gene S, 1578

One Sunset a Week. Vecsey, George, 1435

One Way. Ellwood, Robert S., Jr, 775

ONEIDA COMMUNITY, 1508

Oneida Community. Robertson, Constance N, 1508

O'Neill. Gelb, Barbara and Gelb, Arthur. 3677

O'Neill, Eugene. Nine Plays, 3684

———. Plays, 3685

INDEX

O'NEILL, EUGENE, 3677
O'Neill, Eugene, Jr., *see* Oates, Whitney J.
O'Neill, Robert J. The German Army and the Nazi Party, 1933-1939, 5322
Onís, Harriet de, ed. Golden Land, 4306
Only a Novel. Hodge, Jane A, 3922
Only Revolution. Krishnamurti, Jiddu, 622
Only Yesterday. Allen, Frederick L, 6107
Onyx Group, Inc. Environment U. S. A. A Guide to Agencies, People and Resources, 1468
Open Classroom. Kohl, Herbert T, 1770
Open Classroom Reader. Silberman, Charles E., ed, 1776
Open Frontiers. Bravmann, Rene A, 2937
Opening up the Suburbs. Downs, Anthony, 961
Openings. Berry, Wendell, 3623
OPERA, 3203, 3207
    DICTIONARIES, 308-309
    HISTORY AND CRITICISM, 3206, 3208
OPERAS — STORIES, PLOTS, ETC., 3204
Oppenheim, A. Leo. Ancient Mesopotamia, 4911
Oppenheimer Case. Stern, Philip M. and Green, Harold P. 1715
OPPENHEIMER, JULIUS ROBERT, 1715, 2057, 2062
Optical Illusions. Thurston, Jacqueline and Carraher, Ronald G. 2885
Opticks. Newton, Isaac, 2041
OPTICS, 2039-2042
Or I'll Dress You in Mourning. Collins, Larry and LaPierre, Dominique. 3288
Orange Man. Roueché, Berton, 2591
ORATIONS, 3518-3519
Orbit of China. Salisbury, Harrison E, 5602
Orchestra Music. Ewen, David, 3244
Ordeal of the Union. Nevins, Allan, 6009
Ordeal of Total War, 1939-1945. Wright, Gordon, 5103
Order of the Death's Head. Hohne, Heinz, 5317
Ordish, George. The Year of the Butterfly. , 2396
Ordway, Frederick I., Jr. and Braun, Wernher Von. History of Rocketry and Space Travel, 2760
Ordway, Frederick I., 3rd, et al. Dividends from Space, 2758
Oregon Trail. Parkman, Francis, 6238
Orel, Harold, ed. World of Victorian Humor, 3958
Orfield, Gary. Reconstruction of Southern Education, 1753
Organic Living Book. Kohn, Bernice, 2775

ORGANICULTURE, 2530, 2775
ORIENTAL LITERATURE, 376, 4476-4477
    DICTIONARIES, 351
Oriental Philosophies. Koller, John M, 612
Origin of Races. Coon, Carleton S, 2195
Origin of Russian Communism. Berdyaev, Nicolas, 1495
Origin of Species and The Descent of Man. Darwin, Charles, 2286
Origins of English Feudalism. Brown, Reginald A, 5181
Origins of Modern African Thought. July, Robert W, 5723
Origins of Modern Germany. Barraclough, Geoffrey, 5282
Origins of Prussia. Carsten, Franz L, 5284
Origins of the American Revolution. Miller, John C, 5920
Origins of the Cultural Revolution. MacFarquhar, Roderick, 5599
Origins of the Second World War. Taylor, Alan J. P, 5106
Origins of the Universe. Hinkelbein, Albert, 1990
Origins of Totalitarianism. Arendt, Hannah, 1216
Origins of Western Art. Powell, Ann, 2899
Origins of Western Art. Wolf, Walther, 2900
Orlinsky, Harry M. Ancient Israel, 4905
Ormond, Clyde. Complete Book of Hunting, 3459
ORNITHOLOGISTS, AMERICAN, 2223
Ornstein, Robert E. The Psychology of Consciousness, 574
Orr, Robert T. Animals in Migration, 2361
———. Mammals of North America, 2451
Orrey, Leslie. A Concise History of Opera, 3208
Ortega Y Gasset, José. Revolt of the Masses, 4647
———. Velasquez, Goya and the Dehumanization of Art, 3064
ORWELL, GEORGE, 3936, 3950
Orzel, Nick, ed. Eight Plays from off-off Broadway, 3671
Osborne, John. Inadmissible Evidence, 3905
———. Look Back in Anger, 3906
———. Luther, 3907
Osburn, William A. *see* Gardner, Weston D.
Oscar Wilde and the Theatre. Agate, James, 3877
Osen, Lynn M. Women in Mathematics, 1946
Osgood, Cornelius B. The Koreans and Their Culture, 4777

INDEX

Osofsky, Gilbert. Harlem, 962
Oswalt, Wendell H. This Land Was Theirs, 5755
Other America. Harrington, Michael, 999
Other Criteria. Steinberg, Leo, 2913
Other Worlds, Other Beings. Anguist, Stanley W, 2308
Otis, Brooks. Ovid As an Epic Poet, 4407
——. Virgil, 4412
Ott, John. How to Write and Deliver a Speech, 3491
Ott, Thomas. The Haitian Revolution, 1789-1804, 5849
Ottemiller's Index to Plays in Collections. Connor, John M. and Connor, Billie M., eds. 333
Otto, Rudolf. Mysticism East and West, 557
Ottoman Empire and Its Successors, 1801-1927. Miller, William, 5655
Ottsy i Deti. Turgenev, Ivan S, 4567
Our American Music. Howard, John T, 3182
Our Crowd. Birmingham, Stephen, 1058
Our Ecological Crisis. Smith, Grahame J., et al. 947
Our Hidden Heritage. Tufts, Eleanor, 2948
Our Living Traditions. Coffin, Tristram P., ed, 1829
Our Mysterious Panics, 1830-1930. Collman, Charles A, 1529
Our Soviet Sister. St. George, George, 974
Our Struggle for the 14th Colony. Smith, Justin H, 5791
Our Vanishing Wilderness. Grossman, Mary L. and Hamlet, John N. 2273
Our World in Space. McCall, Robert, 2756
Out of My Life and Thought. Schweitzer, Albert, 774
Out of Our Past. Degler, Carl N, 5859
Out of the Whirlwind. Friedlander, Albert H., ed, 3494
OUTDOOR LIFE, 2210, 2531, 2828
Outdoorsman's Medical Guide. Nourse, Alan E, 2573
OUTER SPACE, 2054, 2633, 2756-2757
Outline of European Architecture. Pevsner, Nikolaus, 2966
Overcoming Drugs. Louria, Donald B, 2544
Overman, Michael. Water, 2699
Ovid As an Epic Poet. Otis, Brooks, 4407
OVIDIUS NASO, PUBLIUS, 4407
Ovidius Naso, Publius. Metamorphoses, 4408
Ovington, Roy. Basic Fly Fishing and Fly Tying, 3456

OWLS, 2441-2443
Owls of North America. Karalus, Karl E. and Eckert, Allan W. 2442
Oxford Anthology of English Poetry. 3780
Oxford Bible Atlas. May, Herbert G, 108
Oxford Book of Ballads. 3781
Oxford Book of Canadian Verse in English and French. 3499
Oxford Book of Carols. 3220
Oxford Book of Food Plants. Harrison, S. G., et al. 2789
Oxford Book of French Verse, Thirteenth to Twentieth Century. 4139
Oxford Book of Greek Verse. 4442
Oxford Book of Invertebrates. Nichols, David and Cooke, John. 2380
Oxford Book of Latin Verse from the Earliest Fragments to the End of the 5th Century. 4402
Oxford Book of Light Verse. 3782
Oxford Book of Spanish Verse. 4337
Oxford Book of Vertebrates. Nixon, Marion, 2403
Oxford Book of Wild Flowers. Ary, Sheila and Gregory, Mary. 2324
Oxford Classical Dictionary. 409
Oxford Companion to American History. 452
Oxford Companion to American Literature. 353
Oxford Companion to Art. 267
Oxford Companion to Canadian History and Literature. 447
Oxford Companion to Classical Literature. 410
Oxford Companion to English Literature. 360
Oxford Companion to French Literature. 374
Oxford Companion to Music. 302
Oxford Companion to the Theatre. 317
Oxford Companion to World Sports and Games. 319
Oxford Dictionary of English Etymology. 158
Oxford Dictionary of English Proverbs. Smith, William G. and Wilson, F. B., eds. 155
Oxford Dictionary of the Christian Church. Cross, F. L. and Livingstone, Elizabeth A. 99
Oxford English Dictionary. Murray, J. A., et al, eds. 165
Oxford History of England. 5281
Oxford History of the American People. Morison, Samuel E, 5866
Oxford Martyrs. Loades, David M, 795
Oxford World Atlas. Cohen, Saul B., ed, 396

Pablo Casals. Kirk, H. L, 3246

INDEX

PACIFIC OCEAN, 4697
Pacifici, Sergio J. The Modern Italian Novel from Manzoni to Svevo, 4298
PACIFISM, 1299, 1547, 1549
Pacifist Conscience. Mayer, Peter, ed, 1549
Packard, Vance O. The Hidden Persuaders, 2858
Paddock, Paul. *see* Paddock, William
Paddock, William and Paddock, Paul. Famine 1975, 1512
Padfield, Peter. The Battleship Era, 1689
Padover, Saul K. Revolutionary Emperor, 5291
PAGEANTS, 3287
Páginas Escogidas. Martí, José, 4328
Pagnol, Marcel. Fanny, 4174
———. Marius, 4175
———. Topaze, 4176
Paine, R. *see* Soper, A.
PAINTERS, 3035
Painters in a New Land. Bell, Michael, compiled by. 2939
Painters of the Bauhaus. Roters, Eberhard, 3029
PAINTING, 3025, 3033, 3044, 3049
  HISTORY, 3027-3028
Painting. Pignatti, Terisio, 3028
PAINTING, AMERICAN, 3036, 3040, 3046
PAINTING, FRENCH, 3052
PAINTING, ITALIAN, 3055
PAINTING, SPANISH, 3064
Paints, Inks, and Dyes. Lyttle, Richard B, 2863
PAKISTAN — POLITICS AND GOVERNMENT, 1562
Palace Guard. Rather, Dan and Gates, Gary. 1200
Palaces of Leningrad. Kennett, Audrey and Kennett, Vincent. 4765
Palaver. Cartey, Wilfred, ed, 4625
PALEONTOLOGY, 2162, 2175, 2177
PALESTINE
  ANTIQUITIES, 4719, 4786
  HISTORY, 4903, 5660, 5664-5665, 5668
  SOCIAL LIFE AND CUSTOMS, 733
Palisca, Claude U. Baroque Music, 3147
Pallister, Anne. Magna Carta, 1262
Palmer, Alan W. The Lands Between, 5287
Palmer, John. Political and Comic Characters of Shakespeare, 3867
Palmer, Robert R. The Age of the Democratic Revolution. A Political History of Europe and America, 1760-1800, 5044
———. Twelve Who Ruled, 5398
———. The World of the French Revolution, 5049

Palmer, Robert R. and Colton, Joel. A History of the Modern World, 4672
PALMERSTON, HENRY JOHN TEMPLE, 5263
Pamphlets on the American Revolution, 1750-1776. Bailyn, Bernard and Garrett, J. N., eds. 5914
PANAMA — HISTORY, 1348, 6278
Panama Story. Niemeier, Jean, 6278
Panditji. Seton, Marie, 5636
Panorama de la Literatura Espanola. Torrente, Ballesteros, 4316
Panshin, Alexi. Heinlein in Dimension, a Critical Analysis, 3744
Pantagruel. Rabelais, François, 4242
Pantheon Story of Art for Young People. Butterberry, Ariane R, 2894
Panting, John. Sculpture in Fiberglass, 2986
PANTOMIME, 3322
Pantomime. Alberts, David, 3322
PAPACY, 113
PAPAL STATES — HISTORY, 5453
Papazian, Haig P. Modern Genetics, 2298
PAPER MONEY — U. S., 291
Paper Money of the United States. Friedberg, Robert, 291
Paper Revolutionaries. Leamer, Laurence, 499
Paperbound Books in Print. 4
Papers of Adlai E. Stevenson. Johnson, Walter and Evans, Carol, eds. 6161
Papp, Charles S. *see* Swan, Lester A.
Parachutes and Parachuting. Sellick, Bud, 3445
PARACHUTING, 3445
Paradise Below Zero. Rutstrum, Calvin, 3399
Paradox. Westell, Anthony, 5800
Pares, Bernard. A History of Russia, 5490
PARIS PEACE CONFERENCE, (1919), 5078
PARIS, TREATY OF, (1783), 5925
Parish, James R., *see* Michael, Paul
Park, Brad. *see* Gilbert, Rod
Park, Julian, ed. Culture of Contemporary Canada, 5783
Parker, Dorothy. Collected Poetry, 3612
———. The Portable Dorothy Parker, 3766
PARKER, DOROTHY, 3766
Parker, J. A. Angela Davis, 1232
Parker, Tony. The Frying-Pan, 1740
Parkes, Henry B. History of Mexico, 5807
Parkes, James W. Whose Land? A History of the Peoples of Palestine, 5668
Parkinson, C. Northcote. Parkinson's Law, 3959
Parkinson, Roger. A Day's March Nearer Home, 5102
Parkinson, Tom. *see* Fox, Charles P.

INDEX

Parkinson's Law. Parkinson, C. Northcote, 3959
Parkman, Francis. Half-Century of Conflict, 5906
———. The Oregon Trail, 6238
Parlato, Salvatore J., Jr., ed. Films Too Good for Words, 53
Parliament. Jennings, Ivor, 1359
PARLIAMENTARY PRACTICE, 1356-1358
Parodies. MacDonald, Dwight, ed, 3962
Paroles. Prévert, Jacques, 4127
Parone, Edward, ed. Collision Course, 3672
Parrinder, Geoffrey. A Dictionary of Non-Christian Religions, 116
Parry, Albert. The Russian Scientist, 1923
Parry, John H. The Age of Reconnaissance, 4703
———. The Discovery of the Sea, 4699
———. The European Reconnaissance, 4704
Parsegian, V. L. This Cybernetic World of Men, Machines and Earth Systems, 461
Parsons, William B. Engineers and Engineering in the Renaissance, 2630
Partner, Peter. The Lands of St. Peter, 5453
Partridge, Eric. Adventuring Among Words, 1871
———. Dictionary of Slang and Unconventional English, 175
———. Shakespeare's Bawdy, 3868
———. Usage and Abusage, 1883
Partridge, William L. The Hippie Ghetto, 915
Party Leadership and Revolutionary Power in China. Lewis, John W., ed, 1398
Party Politics in the Age of Caesar. Taylor, Lily R, 4940
Pascal, Blaise. Pensées, 4280
PASCAL, BLAISE, 672
Paskar, Joanne, see Wasserman, Paul
Pasmantier, Jeanne, see Resnick, Seymour
Le Passe-Muraille. Aymé, Marcel, 4191
Passing of the Black Kings. Hale, Hugh M, 5735
PASSIVE RESISTANCE, 898, 911, 1220, 1245, 1252
Passmore, John. A Hundred Years of Philosophy, 517
Pasternak, Boris L. In the Interlude, 4512
———. Sochinenia, 4580
PASTERNAK, BORIS LEONIDIVOCH, 4557
Patchen, Kenneth. Collected Poems, 3581
Pather Panchali. Banerji, Bibhutibhushan, 4480
Paths of American Thought. Schlesinger, Arthur M., Jr. and White, Morton M. 648

Paths to the Present. Schlesinger, Arthur M., Jr, 5870
Paths to the Present. Weber, Eugen, ed, 512
Patrick Henry. Tyler, Moses C, 5940
Patrick, Ludmilla A. Six Soviet One-Act Plays, 4540
Patterns in Nature. Stevens, Peter S, 1894
Patterns of American Prejudice. 1053
Patterns of Medieval Society. Adams, Jeremy DuQuesnay, 4993
Patterson, Jerry E. Autographs, 4875
Patterson, Lindsay, ed. Black Theater, 3676
Patton. Farago, Ladislas, 5127
PATTON, GEORGE SMITH, 5127
Paul Lawrence Dunbar and His Song. Cunningham, Virginia, 3566
Pauling, Linus and Hayward, R. The Architecture of Molecules, 2076
Pauling, Linus and Pauling, Peter. College Chemistry, 2070
Pauling, Peter. see Pauling, Linus
Paulson, Ronald. Hogarth, 3092
Pauly, Reinhard G. Music in the Classic Period, 3148
PAVLOVA, ANNA, 3325
Paxson, Frederic L. History of the American Frontier, 1763-1893, 5868
Payne, Donald G. Antarctica, 6291
Payne, Robert. Massacre, 5638
———. Splendor of Israel, 4785
———. The Three Worlds of Boris Pasternak, 4557
———. The White Pony, 4600
Payne, Robert. see Gary, Dorothy H.
Payne, Stanley G. Falange, 5472
———. Politics and the Military in Modern Spain, 5468
Le Paysan Parvenu. Marivaux, Pierre C. de, 4171
Paz, Octavio. In Praise of Hands, 3012
Peace Corps. Carey, Robert G, 1125
Peace of Mind in Earthquake Country. Yanev, Peter, 2869
Peacemakers. Morris, Richard B, 5925
Pearce, W. E. and Klein, Aaron. Transistors and Circuits, 2646
PEARL HARBOR, ATTACK ON, (1941), 5128
Pearlman, Moshe. Historical Sites of Israel, 4786
Pearson, Hesketh. George Bernard Shaw, 3884
Pearson, John. Arena, 4728
Pearson, Lester N. Words and Occasions, 5798
Pearson, Norman H., see Auden, W. H.
Pearson, R. G. see Basolo, Fred
PEARY, ROBERT EDWIN, 4850
PEASANTRY, 1001, 5200, 5507
Pêcheur d'islande. Loti, Pierre, 4228

INDEX

Peck, Ellen. *see* Lieberman, E. James
Peck of Salt. Hough, John T., Jr, 1126
Peckham, Howard H. Colonial Wars, 1689-1762, 5907
Peculiar Institution. Stampp, Kenneth M, 1056
Pei, Mario. Double-Speak in America, 1872
———. Story of the English Language. 1868
———. Talking Your Way Around the World, 1862
———. Words in Sheep's Clothing, 1873
Peirce, Neal R. The Deep South States of America, 4835
———. The People's President, 1265
Peissel, Michel. The Lost World of Quintana Roo, 4802
Peking Man. Shapiro, Harry L, 2206
Pelczar, Michael J. and Reid, Roger D. Microbiology, 2303
Pells, Richard H. Radical Visions and American Dreams, 459
Peltier, Leslie C. Guideposts to the Stars, 1981
Penguin Book of French Verse. 4140
Penguin Book of German Verse. Forster, Leonard Wilson, ed, 4004
Penguin Book of Latin Verse. Britain, Frederick, ed, 4401
Penguin Book of Russian Verse. Obolensky, Dimitri, ed, 4524
Penguin Companion to American Literature. 355
Penguin Companion to English Literature. 363
Penguin Companion to European Literature. 349
Penguin Companion to Literature. 3771
Penguin Companion to Literature, Vol. 4. Dudley, D. R. and Lang, D. M., eds. 351
Penguin Dictionary of Architecture. Fleming, J., et al. 280
Penguin Dictionary of the Theatre. Taylor, John R, 347
PENN, WILLIAM, 1139, 6199
PENNSYLVANIA — POLITICS AND GOVERNMENT, 1139
Pensées. Pascal, Blaise, 4280
Pentagon of Power. Mumford, Lewis, 4652
Pentagon Papers. Sheehan, Neil, et al. 5687
People. Eisenstaedt, Alfred, 3127
Peopled World of Harold Pinter. Esslin, Martin, 3901
Peoples of Old Testament Times. Wiseman, D. J., ed, 727
People's President. Peirce, Neal R, 1265
People's War. Calder, Angus, 5274

People's War. Girling, J. L, 1186
Pepys, Samuel. Diary, 5242
PEPYS, SAMUEL, 5244
Perception of Color. Evans, Ralph M, 568
Le Père Goriot. Balzac, Honoré de, 4197
Pereira, Anthony. Rome, 4759
Perennial Philosophy. Huxley, Aldous L, 692
Perenyi, Eleanor. Liszt, 3160
Pérez Galdós, Benito. Doña Perfecta, 4383
———. Gloria, 4381
———. Misericordia, 4382
PERICLES, 4971
Pericles and Athens. Burn, Andrew R, 4971
PERIODICALS
  BIBLIOGRAPHY, 10-12
  INDEXES, 88-91
Periodicals for School Libraries. Scott, Marian H, 12
Periods of Prosperity, 1914-1932. Leuchtenburg, William E, 6111
Perkins, Bradford. Prologue to War, 5987
Perkins, Dexter. American Approach to Foreign Policy, 1351
———. History of the Monroe Doctrine, 1352
———. The New Age of Franklin Roosevelt, 6142
Perkins, H. C. Northern Editorials on Secession, 6045
Perlis, Vivian. Charles Ives Remembered, 3161
Perman, Michael. Reunion Without Compromise, 6085
Perrett, Geoffrey. Days of Sadness, Years of Triumph, 1116
Perrin, Porter G. and Ebbitt, Wilma R. Writer's Guide and Index to English, 3469
Perroy, Edouard. The Hundred Years' War, 5016
Perry, Richard. The Polar Worlds, 2369
———. The Unknown Ocean, 2374
PERSECUTION
  HISTORY, 793
  RUSSIA, 807
Persecution and Assassination of Jean-Paul Marat As Performed by the Inmates of the Asylum of Charenton Under the Direction of the Marquis de Sade. Weiss, Peter, 4034
PERSIAN LITERATURE, 4489-4490, 4597
Persian Wars. Herodotus, 4968
Personal Memoirs. Grant, Ulysses S, 6069
Personal Memoirs of Julia Dent Grant. Simon, John Y., ed, 6087

PERSONALITY, 562, 580, 582, 590
Personality Development. Kagan, Jerome, 582
Perspective. White, Gwen, 3010
Perspectives on Presidential Selection. Matthews, Donald R., ed, 1379
PERU — HISTORY, 6259, 6266, 6268, 6276-6277
PERVIGILIUM VENERIS, 4415
PEST CONTROL, 2783
Pest War. Fletcher, W. W, 2779
PESTICIDES, 2516, 2564, 2583, 2778-2782, 2827
Pests and People. Pringle, Laurence, 2780
P'esy. Chekhov, Anton P, 4528
Peter, Laurence J. and Hill, Raymond. The Peter Principle, 2852
Peter Principle. Peter, Laurence J. and Hill, Raymond. 2852
Peter Skene Ogden and the Hudson's Bay Company. Cline, Gloria G, 5801
Peter the Great. Klyuchevsky, V, 5498
Peterdi, Gabor. Printmaking, 3087
Peters, H. Frederick. Rainer Maria Rilke, 3998
Petersen, Merrill D. Thomas Jefferson and the New Nation, 5974
Peterson, Harold L. Encyclopedia of Firearms, 2672
Peterson, Houston, ed. Treasury of the World's Greatest Speeches, 3519
Peterson, James A. Finding and Preparing Precious and Semiprecious Stones, 2171
Peterson, Theodore. Magazines in the Twentieth Century, 478
Le Petit Chose. Daudet, Alphonse, 4206
Petit Prince. Saint Exupéry, Antoine de, 4248
PETROLEUM
  ALASKA — PIPELINES, 1521-1522
  GEOLOGY, 2170
  TRANSPORATION, 1805
Petroleum Geology of the United States. Landes, Kenneth K, 2170
PETROLEUM INDUSTRY AND TRADE, 1475, 1520 1522-1523, 1527, 1533, 4781
PETROLOGY, 2169
  DICTIONARIES, 227
Petrow, Richard. The Bitter Years, 5130
Pettingill, O. E. Born to Run, 3449
Petzold, Paul. All-in-One Movie Book, 3113
Petzoldt, Paul. The Wilderness Handbook, 3390
Pevsner, Nikolaus. Outline of European Architecture, 2966
PEWTER, 3003
Peyre, Henri. Contemporary French Literature, 4102
———. French Novelists of Today, 4265

———. Lanson, Gustave. Essais de Méthode de Critique et d'Histoire Littéraire, 4114
Peyre, Henri and Seronde, Joseph, eds. Nine Classic French Plays, 4185
Peyser, Ethel. see Bauer, Marion
Pfeiffer, John E. The Emergence of Man, 2197
Phaidon Dictionary of Twentieth-Century Art. 268
Phenomenon of Man. Teilhard de Chardin, Pierre, 521
PHILIPPINE ISLANDS, 5691, 6284
Phillips, Cabell. From the Crash to the Blitz, 1929-1939, 6143
Phillips, Ulrich B. American Negro Slavery, 1287
———. The Course of the South to Secession, 6212
———. Life and Labor in the Old South, 6213
———. Plantation and Frontier Documents, 1649-1863, 6214
———. Slave Economy of the Old South, 1424
Phillips, Walter A. The War of Greek Independence, 5553
PHILLIPS, WENDELL, 6039
PHILOSOPHERS, 514, 516, 635, 643, 647, 4859, 4863
Philosophic Classics. Kaufmann, Walter A, 611
Philosophical Writings. Descartes, René, 671
Philosophies of India. Zimmer, Heinrich, 623
PHILOSOPHY, 508-515, 517-518, 525, 546, 608-609, 611-618, 622-632, 634-637, 639-641, 643, 645, 647-650, 655-656, 658-660, 663-668, 671, 675-676, 678-680, 685, 832, 835, 884, 1914, 2588, 4471-4472, 5008, 5034, 5489, 5860
  DICTIONARIES, 95
Philosophy. Hegel, George W, 665
Philosophy. Schopenhauer, Arthur, 668
Philosophy in the Middle Ages. Hyman, Arthur and Walsh, James J., eds. 629
Philosophy of Kant. Kant, Immanuel, 666
Philosophy of Marxism. Somerville, John, 556
Philosophy of Religion. Charlesworth, Maxwell J, 683
Philosophy of Religion. Hick, John, 684
Phoenicia. Rawlinson, George, 4983
PHOENICIANS, 4983
PHOTOGRAPHERS, 3121, 3125
PHOTOGRAPHY, 295, 489, 3099-3111, 3122-3124, 3126-3128
PHOTOSYNTHESIS, 2316-2317
Photosynthesis. Asimov, Isaac, 2316

INDEX

Photosynthesis. Devlin, Robert M, 2317
Phoutrides, Aristides, trs. see Brown, Demetra V.
Phrase and Word Origins. Holt, Alfred H, 157
PHYLOGENY, 2178
PHYSICAL FITNESS, 2536-2538
PHYSICAL GEOGRAPHY, 223, 2272. 4689
PHYSICAL GEOLOGY, 2097, 2109-2110
Physical Geology. Flint, Richard F. and Skinner, Brian J. 2109
Physical Geology. McAlester, Archie L. and Hay, E. A. 2110
Physical Science Today. CRM Staff & Contributing Consultants, 1895
Physical Science with Environmental Applications. Wiggins, Arthur W, 2022
PHYSICS, 217, 1895, 2014-2022, 2024, 2035, 2053-2055
 DICTIONARIES, 213-214
Physics for the Modern Mind. Fuchs, Walter R, 2018
Physics, the Pioneer Science. Taylor, Lloyd W, 2020
Die Physiker. Durrenmatt, Friedrich, 4015
PIAGET, JEAN, 581, 887
Picard, Colette. see Picard, Gilbert C.
Picard, Gilbert C. and Picard, Colette. The Life and Death of Carthage, 4986
PICASSO, PABLO, 3061, 3065,
Piccard, Jacques. The Sun Beneath the Sea, 2149
Pickles, Dorothy M. Democracy, 1215
Pictorial Astronomy. Alter, Dinsmore, et al. 1959
Pictorial Guide to the Mammals of North America. Rue, Leonard L, 2452
Pictorial Guide to the Moon. Alter, Dinsmore, 1994
Pictorial Guide to the Planets. Jackson, Joseph H., 3rd, 1996
Pictorial Guide to the Stars. King, Henry C, 2007
A Pictorial History of American Labor. Cahn, William, 1428
A Pictorial History of American Mining. Sloane, Howard N. and Sloane, Lucille L. 2666
Pictorial History of the American Theatre. Blum, Daniel, 3307
A Pictorial History of the Silent Screen. Blum, Daniel, 3261
A Pictorial History of the Theatre Guild. Nadel, Norman, 3315
Pierce, John R. Almost All About Waves, 2037

Piercy, Esther J. Commonsense Cataloging, 29
Pierre et Jean. Maupassant, Guy de, 4231
Pierson, Elaine C. Sex Is Never an Emergency, 986
Piesy. Tolstoy, Aleksei, 4537
Pietsch, William V. Human Be-Ing, 591
Piggott, Stuart. Ancient Europe, 4723
———. The Dawn of Civilization, 4714
———. The Druids, 866
Pignatti, Terisio. Painting, 3028
Pike, D. Australia, 6288
Pikovaya Dara. Pushkin, Aleksandr S, 4559
Pilgrim at Tinker Creek. Dillard, Annie, 1902
Pilgrim Colony. Langdon, George D., Jr, 6194
Pill. Mintz, Morton, 2555
Piloting, Seamanship and Small Boat Handling. Chapman, Charles F, 2681
PINCHBACK, PINCKNEY BENTON STEWART, 6223
Pincherle, Marc. Vivaldi, 3179
Pinchon, Edgums. Viva Villa!, 5820
Pinckney Benton Stewart Pinchback. Haskins, James, 6223
Pindarus. Odes, and Fragments, 4470
Pine, Leslie G. The Highland Clans, 5153
Pinney, Roy. Vanishing Tribes, 2190
Pinson, Koppel S. Modern Germany, 5296
Pinter, Harold. The Birthday Party, 3908
———. The Caretaker and the Dumb Waiter, 3909
———. Early Plays, 3910
———. Five Screenplays, 3911
———. Homecoming, 3912
PINTER, HAROLD, 3901
Pioneer Aircraft 1903-1914. Munson, Kenneth, 2727
Pipe, Ted. Principles of the Wankel Engine, 2660
Pipes, Richard. Formation of the Soviet Union, 5508
Pipes, Richard, ed. Revolutionary Russia. 5522
Pippett, Aileen. Moth and the Star, 3945
Pirandello, Luigi. Naked Masks, 4294
PIRATES, 4693
Pirenne, Henri. Economic and Social History of Medieval Europe, 5003
Pirie, James W., ed. Books for Junior College Libraries, 9
Pirsig, Robert. Zen and the Art of Motorcycle Maintenance, 4815
Pisk, Paul A. see Ulrich, Homer

INDEX

PIUS XII, POPE, 5310
PIZARRO, FRANCISCO, 6259
PL 1 (COMPUTER PROGRAM LANGUAGE), 467
Place Names of the English Speaking World. Matthews, Constance M, 4688
Places for Learning, Places for Joy. Sizer, Theodore R, 1765
Plagemann, Stephen H. see Gribbin, John R.
Plain Speaking. Miller, Merle, 6153
Planet Earth. Press, Frank and Siever, Raymond, eds. 2102
Planet-Girded Suns. Engdahl, Sylvia L, 2277
Planetfall. Cardin, Martin, 1995
PLANETS, 1920, 1995-2001
Planning Academic and Research Library Buildings. Metcalf, Keyes, 21
Plano, J. C. and Greenberg, M. American Political Dictionary, 133
PLANT LORE, 2320
Plantation and Frontier Documents, 1649-1863. Phillips, Ulrich B, 6214
PLANTS, 232-233, 260, 2312, 2315, 2321-2323, 2789-2790, 2802
PLASMA DYNAMICS, 2034
PLASMA (IONIZED GASES), 2034
Platanov, Sergei. Boris Godunov, 5497
PLATE TECTONICS, 2114, 2116, 2164
Plate Tectonics and Geomagnetic Reversals. Cox, Allan, ed, 2114
Platero and I. Jimenez, Juan Ramon, 4380
Plath, Sylvia. Winter Trees, 3657
Plato. The Collected Dialogues of Plato, 4472
———. The Portable Plato, 4471
PLATO, 608
Platt, Anthony, ed. The Politics of Riot Commissions, 1917-1970, 1722
Platt, Rutherford. Great American Forest, 4798
———. Water, 2266
Play Index. 335
Playing Hockey the Professional Way. Gilbert, Rod and Park, Brad. 3413
Playing Soccer the Professional Way. Bradley, Gordon and Toye, Clive. 3358
Plays. Aeschylus, 4456
Plays. Barrie, James M, 3881
Plays. Euripides, 4458
Plays. Galsworthy, John, 3895
Plays. O'Neill, Eugene, 3685
Plays. Shaw, George B, 3887
Plays. Strindberg, August, 4090
Plays for a New Theater. 3508
Plays from Black Africa. Litto, Frederic M, 4634
Plays of T. S. Eliot. Jones, David, 3896

Playwright's Art. Busfield, Roger M, 3480
Pleasants, Henry. The Great American Popular Singers, 3223
Pletcher, David M. The Diplomacy of Annexation, 6016
Pliner, Roberta. see Evans, Charles
Plinius Caecilius Secundus, Gaius. Letters, 4428
Plowden, David. Bridges, 2691
Plumb, J. H., ed. The Horizon Book of the Renaissance, 5029
Plutarch. Lives, 4473
Pocket Encyclopedia of Seaplanes and Flying Boats. Munson, Kenneth, 2728
Poe, Edgar Allan. Poems of Edgar Allan Poe, 3559
POE, EDGAR ALLAN, 3722
Poem of the Cid. Simpson, Lesley B., tr, 4332
Poema de Mio Cid. Smith, Colin, ed, 4333
Poems. Coleridge, Samuel T, 3811
Poems. Cowper, William, 3806
Poems. Goethe, Johann Wolfgang Von, 3995
Poems. Herrick, Robert, 3799
Poems. Hopkins, Gerard M, 3826
Poems. Longfellow, Henry Wadsworth, 3557
Poems. Masefield, John, 3839
Poems. Shelley, Percy B, 3817
Poems. Tate, Allen, 3589
Poems. Thompson, Francis, 3833
Poems and Prose. Leopardi, Giacomo, 4299
Poems and Translations. Rossetti, Dante G, 3829
Poems from Africa. Allen, Samuel W, 3495
Poems from the Hebrew. Mezey, Robert, compiled by. 4589
Poems Nineteen Fifty Seven-Nineteen Sixty Seven. Dickey, James, 3635
Poems of Edgar Allan Poe. Poe, Edgar Allan, 3559
Poems of George Herbert. Herbert, George, 3793
Poems of Pushkin. Pushkin, Aleksandr, 4513
Poems of Sidney Lanier. Lanier, Sidney, 3569
Poems of Stephen Crane. Crane, Stephen, 3565
Poems, Prose, and Plays. Pushkin, Aleksandr S, 4581
Poesias Completas. Machado, Antonio, 4326
Poesies. Ronsard, Pierre de, 4129
Poet in America, 1650 to Present. Gelpi, Albert J., compiled by. 3549

467

INDEX

Poetical and Dramatic Works. Byron, George G, 3810
Poetical Works. Browning, Elizabeth B, 3822
Poetical Works. Browning, Robert, 3823
Poetical Works. Bryant, William Cullen, 3555
Poetical Works. Pope, Alexander, 3804
Poetical Works. Scott, Walter, 3816
Poetical Works. Tennyson, Alfred, 3832
POETICS, 173, 1861, 3474
POETRY, 3473, 3475-3478, 3497, 3504, 3578
    COLLECTIONS, 3496, 3500-3503, 3776
    DICTIONARIES, 350
    HISTORY AND CRITICISM, 350, 3472, 3477, 3479, 3525
    INDEXES, 332-339
Poetry. Drew, Elizabeth, 3475
Poetry. Durrell, Lawrence, 3847
Poetry. Frost, Robert, 3602
Poetry and Criticism of Matthew Arnold. Arnold, Matthew, 3821
Poetry and Experience. MacLeish, Archibald, 3477
Poetry Handbook. Deutsch, Babette, 3474
Poetry in Modern Ireland. Clarke, Austin, 3845
Poetry of Black America. Adoff, Arnold, ed, 3668
Poetry of France. Boase, Alan M, 4135
POETS, AMERICAN, 3544, 4871
Poets of the English Language. Auden, W. H. and Pearson, Norman H., eds. 3774
Poets on Street Corners. Carlisle, Olga, 4520
Poil de Carotte. Renard, Jules, 4243
Pointing the Way. Buber, Martin, 618
Points de Vue. Haac, Oscar A., et al. 4101
POISONOUS ANIMALS, 2368
POISONOUS PLANTS — U. S., 2335
POISONOUS SNAKES, 2417
POISONS, 2584-2585
Poisons Around Us. Schroeder, Henry A, 2584
Polakoff, Keith I. The Politics of Inertia, 1381
POLAND
    HISTORY, 5115, 5361, 5363
    POLITICS AND GOVERNMENT, 1162, 5360
Poland. Hiscocks, Richard, 5361
Poland's Politics. Bromke, Adam, 1162
POLAR REGIONS — DISCOVERY AND EXPLORATIONS, 4852
Polar Worlds. Perry, Richard, 2369

POLICE — U. S., 1704
Police in Trouble. Ahern, James F, 1704
Poling, David. see Marshall, George
Political and Comic Characters of Shakespeare. Palmer, John, 3867
Political and Social Upheaval, 1832-1852. Langer, William L, 5058
POLITICAL CONVENTIONS, 136
POLITICAL ETHICS, 620, 1197
Political Geography. Pounds, Norman J, 4705
A Political History of Ghana. Kimble, David, 5726
Political History of Latin America. Glassman, Ronald, 1204
Political Hysteria in America. Levin, Murray B, 1196
POLITICAL PARTIES, 1387-1388
    ROME, 4940
    U. S., 1195, 1377, 1389, 1393
Political Power and the Press. Small, William J, 1263
POLITICAL PRISONERS — RUSSIA, 1733
POLITICAL SCIENCE, 1075-1078, 1127, 1129, 1131, 1133, 1140
    HISTORY, 1128, 1149-1150, 1158, 1198
Political Systems of the Middle East in the 20th Century. Abboushi, W. F, 1181
Political Thought. Lincoln, Abraham, 1077
Political Thought of Mao Tse-Tung. Mao Tse-Tung, 1214
Political Trends in the Arab World. Khadduri, Majid, 1158
Political Violence. Nieburg, Harold L, 1132
Political Writings. Rousseau, Jean-Jacques, 1078
Politicos. Josephson, Matthew, 6070
Politics and Policies of the Truman Administration. Bernstein, Barton J., ed, 6147
Politics and Society in De Gaulle's Republic. Williams, Philip M. and Harrison, Martin. 5422
Politics and the Military in Modern Spain. Payne, Stanley G, 5468
Politics for Better or Worse. De Grazia, Alfred, 1127
Politics in America. Brogan, Denis W, 1371
Politics in the Gilded Age. Dobson, John M, 1195
Politics in the USSR. Barghoorn, Frederick C, 1170
Politics of Conservation. Smith, Frank E, 1469
A Politics of Fear. Griffith, Robert, 6160

Politics of Grand Strategy. Williamson, Samuel R, 1303
Politics of History. Zinn, Howard, 4649
Politics of Inertia. Polakoff, Keith I, 1381
Politics of Normalcy. Murray, Robert K, 6125
Politics of Palestinian Nationalism. Quandt, William B, 1184
Politics of Polution. Davies, J. Clarence, 1634
Politics of Poverty. Donovan, John C, 1541
Politics of Rescue. Feingold, Henry L, 5104
Politics of Riot Commissions, 1917-1970. Platt, Anthony, ed, 1722
Politics of the Powerless. Binstock, Robert H. and Ely, Katherine. 1069
Politics of Violence. Sears, David O. and McConahy, John B. 6245
POLITICS, PRACTICAL, 959, 1371-1372
Politics, Principle and Prejudice, 1865-1866. Cox, Lawanda and Cox, John H. 6063
Politics, Reform and Expansion. Faulkner, Harold U, 6065
Pollard, Jack. see Laver, Rod
Pollitt, Jerry J. Art and Experience in Classical Greece, 2919
Pollman, Leo. Sartre and Camus; Literature in Existence, 4115
POLLUTION, 938-939, 947, 1526, 2102, 2321, 2584, 2697-2698, 2706-2707
DICTIONARIES, 258
Polner, Murray. No Victory Parades, 5686
────. When Can I Come Home? A Debate on Amnesty for Exiles, Antiwar Prisoners and Others, 1227
Polo, Marco. Travels, 4774
Polsby, Nelson W., ed. Congressional Behavior, 1367
Polya, Gyorgy. Mathematical Discovery on Understanding, Learning and Teaching Problem Solving, 1941
POLYGLOT GLOSSARIES, PHRASE BOOKS, ETC., 156, 1862
POLYHEDRA, 1949-1950
Polyhedron Models. Wenninger, M. J, 1950
Pomeroy, Wardell B. Girls and Sex, 2521
Pomeroy, Wardell B. and Tebbel, John. Boys and Sex, 2522
POMPADOUR, JEAN ANTIONETTE, 5383
POMPEII, 4730
POND ECOLOGY, 2269
Pond, Grace. see Ing, Catherine
POOR — U. S., 999, 1104
Poor Richard's Almanac. Franklin, Benjamin, 3755

POP ART — U. S, 2943
Pop Art and After. Amaya, Mario, 2905
Popcorn Venus. Rosen, Marjorie, 3280
Pope, Alexander. Poetical Works, 3804
Pope, Clifford H. The Reptile World, 2414
Pope John XXIII. Johnson, Paul, 751
Pope, Joseph. Memoirs of the Right Honorable Alexander Macdonald, 5797
Pope-Hennessey, John. Fra Angelico, 3059
POPES — BIOGRAPHY, 113
Popes Through the Ages. Brusher, Joseph S, 113
Popkin, Richard H. The History of Scepticism from Erasmus to Descartes, 524
Poppins, Rollie E. Brazil, 6271
Popular Arts of the First World War. Jones, Barbara and Howell, Bill. 3013
POPULATION, 934, 948, 950-954, 956, 1514-1517
Population Activist's Handbook. Population Institute, 959
Population and Survival. Nelson, J, 954
Population and the American Future. U. S. Commission on Population Growth & the American Future, 957
Population Bomb. Ehrlich, Paul R, 951
Population Dilemma. Hauser, Philip M, 934
Population Institute. The Population Activist's Handbook, 959
Population Problem. McCormack, Arthur, 953
Population, Resources, Environment. Ehrlich, Paul R. and Ehrlich, Anne H. 952
Populations, Species and Evolution. Mayr, Ernst, 2347
A Populist Manifesto. Newfield, Jack and Greenfield, J. 1115
POPULIST PARTY, 1394
Populist Revolt. Hicks, John D, 1394
Porpoise Watcher. Norris, Kenneth S, 2460
PORPOISES, 2460-2461
Portable Age of Reason Reader. Brinton, Crane, ed, 5020
Portable Chekhov. Chekhov, Anton P, 4574
Portable Dorothy Parker. Parker, Dorothy, 3766
Portable Emerson. Van Doren, Mark, ed, 3561
Portable Greek Reader. Auden, Wystan H., ed, 4435
Portable Hakluyt's Voyages. Hakluyt, Richard, 4695
Portable Medieval Reader. Ross, James B. and McLaughlin, Mary M., eds. 5030
Portable Oscar Wilde. Wilde, Oscar, 3880

INDEX

Portable Plato. Plato, 4471
Portable Rabelais. Rabelais, François, 4281
Portable Roman Reader. Davenport, Basil, ed, 4394
Portable Russian Reader. Guerney, Bernard G., ed, 4495
Portable Voltaire. Voltaire, François M. de, 4282
La Porte Étroite. Gide, Andre, 4215
Porter, Cedric L. Taxonomy of Flowering Plants, 235
Porter, Eliot. see Matthiessen, Peter
Porter, H., see Wortabet, J.
PORTUGAL, 4735, 4762, 5476-5479
Portugal. Bradford, Sarah, 5476
Portugal. Nowell, Charles, 5479
Portugal. Reich, Hanns, ed, 4762
Positively Black. Abrahams, Roger D, 1824
Posluns, Michael. see Manuel, George
Posner, Arlene, ed. China, 74
Post, Elizabeth. The New Emily Post's Etiquette, 1822
POST-IMPRESSIONISM (ART), 3031
Post Prison Writings and Speeches. Cleaver, Eldridge, 1018
POSTAGE — STAMPS, 292-294, 1799
POSTAL SERVICE — U. S. — HISTORY, 1800
Poster in History. Gallo, Max, 3097
POSTERS — HISTORY, 3097
Postgate, Raymond W. Revolution from 1789 to 1906, 1213
Postwar German Literature. Demetz, Peter, 3984
Postwar Japan, 1945 to the Present. Livingston, Jon, 5623
Pot Shots. Stepanian, Michael, 1597
Potter, David M. The South and the Sectional Conflict, 6215
Potter, Jeffrey. Disaster by Oil, 2702
POTTERY, 287, 3001
Pound, Ezra. Cantos of Ezra Pound, 3582
———. Selected Poems, 3583
Pound, Ezra and Spann, Marcella, eds. Confucius to Cummings, 3500
POUND, EZRA LOOMIS, 3588
Pounds, Norman J. Political Geography, 4705
Poussin. Hibbard, Howard, 3052
POVERTY, 997, 1540-1542, 1701-1702
Poverty in America. Ferman, Louis A., et al, eds. 1542
Powell, Ann. Origins of Western Art, 2899
Power, Eileen E. Medieval People, 5004
Power, Frank G., Jr. see Cousy, Robert
Power in the Kremlin. Tatu, Michel, 1171
Power of Calculus. Whipkey, Kenneth L. and Whipkey, Mary N. 1948

Power of the Presidency. Hinschfield, Robert S., ed, 1640
Power Over People. Young, Louise B, 2638
POWER RESOURCES, 1460, 1473-1475, 1477, 2634
Pownall, Richard. see Casewit, Curtis W.
Poynter, Dan. Hang Gliding, the Basic Handbook of Skysurfing, 3442
———. Manned Kiting, 3443
Practice of History. Elton, Geoffrey R, 4664
Praeger Encyclopedia of Art. 271
Praeger Library of U. S. Government Departments and Agencies. 1370
PRAGMATISM — HISTORY, 555
Prague's 200 Days. Schwartz, Harry, 5355
PRAIRIE ECOLOGY — GREAT PLAINS, 2464
Prall, Stuart E., compiled by. The Puritan Revolution, 5243
Pratt, George C. Spellbound in Darkness, 3262
Pratt, Julius W. Expansionists of 1898, 6094
Prayers from the Ark. Gasztold, Carmen B., ed, 4121
Pre-Columbian Cities. Hardoy, Jorge E, 6265
Pre-Historic Times As Illustrated by Ancient Remains and the Manners and Customs of Modern Savages. Avebury, John L, 4709
Prebble, John. The Lion in the North, 5154
Precocious Autobiography. Yevtushenko, Yevgeny, 4518
PREDATION, 2467-2469
Prehistoric Man. Simak, Clifford D, 2198
Prehistory. Roe, Derek, 4715
Prehistory of China. Treistman, Judith M, 4718
PREJUDICE AND ANTIPATHIES, 1005, 1007, 1052, 1074
Prejudice, U. S. Glock, Charles I. and Siegelman, Ellen. 1005
Prelude to Modern Europe, 1815-1914. Woodward, Llewellyn, 5066
Preminger, Alex, et al, eds. Princeton Encyclopedia of Poetry and Poetics, 350
Prescott, G. W. The Algae, 2334
Prescott, William H. The Conquest of Mexico, and The Conquest of Peru, 6259
Present at the Creation. Acheson, Dean, 1324
Presidency in Flux. Reedy, George E, 1376
Presidency of Rutherford B. Hayes. Davison, Kenneth B, 6089

President Ford. Congressional Quarterly Service, 6174
President Makers, 1896-1919. Josephson, Matthew, 6103
Presidential Government. Burns, James M, 1639
Presidential Impeachment. Schnapper, M. B., ed, 1644
Presidential Television. Minow, Newton N., et al. 1130
PRESIDENTS, 1130, 1376, 1637, 1639-1641
    ELECTION, 1193, 1265-1266, 1379-1385, 1642, 6093
    HISTORY, 5869
    PUBLIC OPINION, 900
    STAFF, 1200
    SUCCESSION, 1567
PRESLEY, ELVIS ARON, 3231
PRESS — U. S., 482, 494-495, 497, 500, 1263
Press and America. Emery, Edwin, 497
Press, Charles. *see* Adrian, Charles R.
Press, Frank and Siever, Raymond. Earth, 2097
———. Planet Earth, 2102
Preston, Samuel H., et al. Causes of Death, 130
Prestuplenie. Dostoevsky, Feodor M, 4545
Prévert, Jacques. Paroles, 4127
———. Spectacle, 4177
Previews. 41
Previte-Orton, Charles. The Shorter Cambridge Medieval History, 5005
Prévost, Abbé. Manon Lescaut, 4239
Prezzolini, Giuseppe. Machiavelli, 1141
Price, Mary R. and Howell, Margaret. From Barbarism to Chivalry, 5006
Price of Independence. Mitchell, Broadus, 5922
Price of Loyalty. Crary, Catherine S, 5946
Price, Steven D. Take Me Home, 3224
Priestley, Herbert I. The Coming of the White Man, 1492-1848, 5892
Primate Odyssey. Bourne, Geoffrey H, 2478
PRIMATES, 2476-2478, 2483
A Primer of English Verse. Corson, Hiram, 3777
Primer of Experimental Poetry. Lucie-Smith, Edward, 3504
Primitive Art. Boas, Franz, 2897
Primitive Religion. Lowie, Robert H, 829
Prince. Machiavelli, Niccolo, 1140
Prince, J. H. Weather and the Animal World, 2362
Prince of Carpetbaggers. Daniels, Jonathan, 6064
La Princesse de Clèves. LaFayette, Marie M. de, 4222

Princeton Encyclopedia of Poetry and Poetics. Preminger, Alex, et al, eds. 350
Principles of Astrology. Carter, Charles E, 538
Principles of Astronomy. Wyatt, Stanley P, 1967
Principles of Diving. Terrell, Mark, 2695
Principles of Editorial Writing. MacDougall, Curtis D, 486
Principles of Genetics. Gardner, Eldon J, 2293
Principles of Genetics. Herskowitz, Irwin H, 2294
Principles of Geology. Gilluly, James, et al. 2094
Principles of Human Genetics. Stern, Curt, 2203
Principles of the Wankel Engine. Pipe, Ted, 2660
Principles of War. Clausewitz, Karl von, 1655
Pringle, Henry F. Theodore Roosevelt, 6116
Pringle, Laurence. Pests and People, 2780
———. Wild River, 2241
PRINTING
    HISTORY, 2847-2848, 2865
    SPECIMENS, 2866-2868
Printing Types. Updike, Daniel B, 2868
Printmaking. Daniels, Harvey, 3086
Printmaking. Peterdi, Gabor, 3087
Prints and Their Creators. Zigrosser, Carl, 3095
PRISON RIOTS — U. S., 1741-1742
PRISONERS — PERSONAL NARRATIVES, 1735-1738
PRISONS
    GREAT BRITAIN, 1740
    U. S., 1739
Prisons, Protest, and Politics. Atkins, Burton M. and Glick, H. R., eds. 1741
Prittie, Terence C. Willy Brandt, 5335
PRIVACY, RIGHT OF — U. S., 1264
Private Life of the Rabbit. Lockley, R. M, 2453
Private Life of the Romans. Johnston, Harold W, 4922
Private Pressure on Public Law. Bland, Randall W, 1601
Private Realities. Ackley, Clifford, ed, 3122
PRIVATE SCHOOLS — U. S.
    HISTORY, 1767-1768
PROBABILITIES, 1951-1954
Problem of Pain. Lewis, Clive S, 702
Problem of Slavery in an Age of Revolution, 1770-1823. Davis, David B, 1003

INDEX

PROBLEM SOLVING, 1941
Problems in Aesthetics. Weitz, Morris, 2880
Problems in American Civilization. 6187
Problems in Asian Civilization. 5693
Problems in Latin American Civilization. 6280
Problems of European Civilization. 5567
Problems of Political Philosophy. Raphael, David D, 1133
Processes of Organic Evolution. Stebbins, G. Ledyard, 2283
Procession of Life. Romer, Alfred S, 2348
Prochnow, Herbert V. Federal Reserve System, 1454
Proctor, Dennis. Hannibal's March in History, 4932
Proctor, Samuel. Young Negro in America, 1960-1980, 1034
Profiles in Courage. Kennedy, John F, 1365
Proger, Samuel. The Medicated Society, 2576
Progressive Movement, 1900-1915. Hofstadter, Richard, ed, 5881
PROHIBITION — U. S., 606, 1235, 6114
Prohibition and the Progressive Movement, 1900-1920. Timberlake, James H, 606
PROHIBITION PARTY, 1235
PROKOFIER, SERGEI SERGEEVICH, 3178
Prokofiev. Nestyev, Israel V, 3178
Prologue to Sumter. Stern, Philip V, 6041
Prologue to War. Perkins, Bradford, 5987
Promenades Littéraires et Historiques. Cattanes, Helene and Robert, Osmond T. 4099
Prometheus. Maurois, André, 4235
Promise of American Life. Croly, Herbert, 1574
Promise of Bonhoeffer. Reist, Benjamin A, 742
Promises to Keep. Bowles, Chester, 6132
Pronko, Leonard C. Avant-Garde, 4188
PROPAGANDA, 897, 1297, 5941
Propaganda and the American Revolution. Davidson, Philip G, 5941
Propaganda Technique in World War I. Lasswell, Harold D, 5084
Prophet. Gibran, Kahlil, 4595
Prophet Armed. Deutscher, Isaac, 5514
Prophet Outcast. Deutscher, Isaac, 5515
Prophet Unarmed. Deutscher, Isaac, 5516
Prophets for the Common Reader. Chase, Mary Ellen, 730
A Prosody Handbook. Shapiro, Karl J. and Beum, R. 1861
Prospects for Revolution. Conant, Ralph W, 1072

Prospects for Soviet Society. Kassof, Allen, ed, 1092
Protestant - Catholic - Jew. Herberg, Will, 800
PROTESTANTISM — U. S., 801
PROTOZOA, 2382
Protozoa. Vickerman, Keith and Cox, F. E. 2382
Proust, Marcel. Combray, 4240
PROVERBS, ENGLISH, 155
Prusek, ed. Dictionary of Oriental Literatures, 376
PRUSSIA — HISTORY, 5284, 5338
Pruyser, Paul W. Between Belief and Unbelief, 523
Pryce-Jones, David. Evelyn Waugh and His World, 3946
PSYCHIATRY, 2602
Psychic Phenomena. Heaps, Willard A, 541
PSYCHICAL RESEARCH, 529-530, 532, 541
PSYCHOANALYSIS, 527-528, 563
PSYCHOBIOLOGY, 578, 589
Psychobiology. Scientific American Editors, 589
PSYCHOLOGICAL WARFARE, 1310
PSYCHOLOGY, 559-560, 564-567, 570, 577, 581, 587-588, 2351, 2526, 2605
    DICTIONARIES, 97-98
Psychology, Ancient and Modern. Brett, George, 564
Psychology of Consciousness. Ornstein, Robert E, 574
PSYCHOSURGERY, 2625
PSYCHOTHERAPY, 2603-2604
PUBLIC HEALTH, 2529, 2565-2566
PUBLIC OPINION — U. S., 124, 900, 1269
Public Papers of the Presidents. 1079
Public Purse. Ward, Norman, 5785
PUBLIC WELFARE, 1542, 1691
PUBLISHERS AND PUBLISHING, 264, 490, 2850
Pucciani, Oreste F., ed. The French Theatre Since 1930, 4186
Puerto Rican Papers. Lopez, Alfredo, 1043
Puerto Ricans. Wagenheim, Kal, compiled by. 5852
PUERTO RICO, 1043, 4807, 5851-5852
Puerto Rico. Maldonado, Manuel, 5851
Puerto Rico. Wagenheim, Kal, 4807
Pugh, G. Douglas, see Haddad, William F.
Pulse of the Planet. Suroweicki, John, 196
Punch Magazine. Century of Punch Cartoons, 3960
PUNIC WARS, 4986
PUPPETS AND PUPPET-PLAYS, 3286
Purcell, H. D. Cyprus, 5657

Purcell, Victor. The Chinese in Southeast Asia, 1051
Puritan Dilemma. Morgan, Edmund S, 5903
Puritan Revolution. Prall, Stuart E., compiled by. 5243
Puritan Tradition in America, 1620-1730. Vaughan, Alden T., ed, 6192
PURITANS, 555, 3538, 4829, 6190, 6192
Puritans. Miller, Perry and Johnson, Thomas H., eds. 3538
Puritans and Pragmatists. Conkin, Paul K, 555
Pursell, Carroll W., Jr., see Kranzberg, Melvin
Pursuit of Loneliness. Slater, Philip E, 5871
Pursuit of Poetry. Untermeyer, Louis, 3479
Pusey, Merlo J. Way We Go to War, 1643
Pushkin. Simmons, Ernest J, 4582
Pushkin. Troyat, Henri, 4514
Pushkin, Aleksandr. Poems of Pushkin, 4513
Pushkin, Aleksandr S. Boris Godunov, 4535
———. Eugene Onegin, 4560
———. Kapitanskaia Dochka, 4558
———. Pikovaya Dara, 4559
———. Poems, Prose, and Plays, 4581
PUSHKIN, ALEKSANDR S., 4514, 4582
Pygmalion. Shaw, George B, 3886
PYLE, HOWARD, 3037
PYRAMIDS, 4885, 4890, 4895
Pyramids. Fakhry, Ahmed, 4885

Quandt, William B. The Politics of Palestinian Nationalism, 1184
QUANTUM THEORY, 2029, 2032
Quare Fellow; The Hostage. Behan, Brendan, 3898
Quarles, Benjamin. Black Abolitionists, 1291
———. Blacks on John Brown, 6024
———. Lincoln and the Negro, 6013
———. Negro in the Civil War, 6033
———. The Negro in the Making of America, 1035
———. Negroes in the American Revolution, 5938
Quarles, Benjamin. see Fishel, Leslie H.
Quarrels That Have Shaped the Constitution. Garraty, John A., ed, 1577
Quasimodo, Salvatore. Selected Writings of Salvatore Quasimodo, 4290
Quatre-Vingt Treize. Hugo, Victor, 4221
Queen Alexandra, 1844-1925. Battiscombe, Georgina, 5269

Queen Catherine Parr. Martienssen, Anthony K, 5222
Queen Elizabeth I. Neale, John, 5227
Queen of France. Castelot, Andre, 5380
Queen Victoria. Longford, Elizabeth, 5258
Quennell, Peter. A History of English Literature, 3772
———. Who's Who in Shakespeare, 369
Quest for a Principle of Authority in Europe, 1715 to the Present. Mendenhall, Thomas C., et al. 5022
Quest for a United Germany. Vali, Ferenc, 1165
Quest for Arthur's Britain. Ashe, Geoffrey, 5178
Quest for Mind. Gardner, Howard, 887
Quest for Security; 1715-1740. Roberts, Penfield, 5035
Quest for Sumer. Cottrell, Leonard, 4721
Quest for Ulysses. Stanford, William B. and Luce, John V. 2888
Quest of the Historical Jesus. Schweitzer, Albert, 750
Quest of the Holy Grail. Weston, Jessie, 1846
Quezon, Manuel L. The Good Fight, 5691
QUEZON, MANUEL LUIS, 5691
Quiet Crisis. Udall, Stewart L, 1470
QUINCY, JOSIAH, 5977
Quinn, Arthur H. Edgar Allan Poe, 3722
Quinn, Edward, see Gassner, John
Quinn, Edward G., see Campbell, Oscar J.
QUINTANA ROO, 4802
Quisqueya. Rodman, Selden, 5844
QUOTATIONS, 101, 340

RA Expeditions. Heyerdahl, Thor, 4687
Rabelais, François. Gargantua, 4241
———. Pantagruel, 4242
———. Portable Rabelais, 4281
RACE, 1015, 1024, 2185, 2187-2188
Race. Baker, John R, 2185
Race and Nationality in American Life. Handlin, Oscar, 1023
Race and Races. Goldsby, R. A, 2188
RACE PROBLEMS, 1074
RACE (THEOLOGY), 746
Rachlin, Carol K. see Marriott, Alice
Racial Violence in the United States. Grinshaw, Allen D, 1723
Racine, Jean B. Best Plays, 4179
———. Complete Works, 4178
Racism. Froman, Robert, 1074
RACKETEERING — U. S., 1441, 1709, 1712
RADAR, 5652
Radar Fundamentals. Wheeler, Gershon, 2652
RADIATION — PHYSIOLOGICAL EFFECT, 2511
Radiation Injury. Upton, Arthur C, 2511

INDEX

Radical Feminism. Koedt, Anne, et al. 981
Radical Ideas and the Schools. Nelson, Jack L. and Carlson, K., eds. 4659
Radical Right. Bell, Daniel, ed, 1192
Radical Theatre Notebook. Sainer, Arthur, 3317
Radical Visions and American Dreams. Pells, Richard H, 459
RADICALISM, 993, 1203, 1223, 1233, 1506, 4695
Radin, Paul and Sweeney, James J., eds. African Folktales and Sculpture, 1836
RADIO, 1564, 2641, 2648-2651, 2685
Radio Amateur's Handbook. American Radio Relay League, 2648
Radio and Television. Hawker, J. P, 2641
RADIO ASTRONOMY, 1976-1977
Radio Exploration of the Sun. Smith, Alexander G, 2006
RADIOACTIVE SUBSTANCES, 2665
RADIOACTIVITY, 2063
RADIOCARBON DATING, 4724
RAFFAELE, SANZIO, 3056
Rahv, Philip. Literature and the Sixth Sense, 3523
RAILROADS — AFRICA, EAST, 5733
Rainer Maria Rilke. Peters, H. Frederick, 3998
Raines, Robert A., ed. Modern Drama and Social Change, 3511
A Raisin in the Sun. Hansberry, Lorraine, 3694
Rakowska-Harmstone, Teresa, see Bromke, Adam
RALEIGH, WALTER, 5221
Ralph Nader Study Groups Reports. 1650
Ralph Waldo Emerson. Bode, Carl, 3749
Rampage. Briggs, Peter, 2696
Rand, Austin L. Birds of North America, 2431
Rand, Christopher. Hongkong, 4776
Rand, Edward K. Founders of the Middle Ages, 5007
Rand McNally Atlas of the American Revolution. 399
Randall, James G. The Constitutional Problems Under Lincoln, 1589
Randall, John H., Jr. The Career of Philosophy, 641
Randel, William P. The Ku Klux Klan, 1706
Random House Dictionary of the English Language. Random House Editors, 166
Random House Editors. Random House Dictionary of the English Language, 166
Ranger, Terence O., ed. Aspects of Central African History, 5731
———. Emerging Themes of African History, 5708
Rankin, Hugh F. Francis Marion, 5939
Ransom, Harry H. The Intelligence Establishment, 1296
Ransom, John C. Selected Poems, 3613
Ranum, Orest A. The Century of Louis XIV, 5024
Rapahael, Chaim. A Feast of History, 861
Raphael. Berti, Luciano, 3056
Raphael, David D. Problems of Political Philosophy, 1133
Rapid and Efficient Reading. Mares, Colin, 1888
Rapoport, Anatol. The Big Two, 1311
Rapoport, Solomon. The Dybbuk, 4594
El Rapto. Ayala, Francisco, 4365
RARE ANIMALS, 2338-2341
Rather, Dan and Gates, Gary. The Palace Guard, 1200
RATIONALISM, 624
Rationalism in Greek Philosophy. Boas, George, 624
RATS AS CARRIERS OF DISEASE, 2609
Rats, Lice and History. Zinsser, Hans, 2609
Rattigan, Terance. Collected Plays, 3892
Raven. James, Marquis, 6225
Rawlinson, George. Phoenicia, 4983
RAY, JAMES EARL, 1710
Rayback, Robert J. Millard Fillmore, 6022
Raynor, Henry. A Social History of Music from the Middle Ages to Beethoven, 3139
El Rayo Que No Cesa. Hernandez, Miguel, 4336
La Raza. Samora, Julian, ed, 4825
La Raza. Steiner, Stanley, 1046
Reaction and Revolution. Artz, Frederick B, 5052
Read, Donald A., et al. Health and Modern Man, 2529
Read, Herbert E. Wordsworth, 3815
Read, Piers P. Alive, 6274
Reader, W. J. Victorian England, 5262
Reader's Adviser. 14
Reader's Encyclopedia. Benet, William Rose, 322
Reader's Encyclopedia of Shakespeare. Campbell, Oscar J. and Quinn, Edward G., eds. 368
Reader's Encyclopedia of World Drama. Gassner, John and Quinn, Edward, eds. 334
Reader's Guide to African Literature. Zell, Hans and Silver, Helene. 345
Readers' Guide to Periodical Literature. 90

A Reader's Guide to Samuel Beckett. Kenner, Hugh, 4286
Reader's Guide to the Contemporary English Novel. Karl, Frederick R, 3931
Reader's Handbook of Famous Names in Fiction, Allusions. Brewer, Ebenezer C, 324
A Reading of Modern Art. Ashton, Dore, 2907
Reading the Woods. Brown, Vinson, 2318
Readings in American Art Since 1900. Rose, Barbara, ed, 2947
Readings in American National Government. MacDonald, H. Malcolm, et al. 1633
Readings in Biological Science. Knobloch, Irving W., ed, 2219
Readings in Economics. Samuelson, Paul A., ed, 1402
Readings in Russian Civilization. Riha, Thomas, ed, 5492
Ready, William. The Tolkien Relation, 3947
Real Lace. Birmingham, Stephen, 4821
Real Majority. Scammon, Richard M. and Wattenburg, Ben J. 1269
Real War, 1914-1918. Liddell Hart, Basil H, 5085
Real World of 1984. Farmer, Richard N, 4661
Realism and Nationalism. Binkley, Robert C, 5053
Realities of American Foreign Policy. Kennan, George F, 1344
Reality Sandwiches, 1953-1960. Ginsberg, Allen, 3641
Realm of the Submarine. Cohen, Paul, 2683
Reaske, Christopher. Seven Essayists, 3517
Reason Why. Woodham-Smith, Cecil B, 5265
Rebel. Camus, Albert, 597
Rebel Leadership. Downton, James V, 893
Rebels Against War. Wittner, Lawrence S, 1550
Rebuffat, Gaston. Men and the Matterhorn, 4768
———. On Ice and Snow and Rock, 3393
Reck, Andrew J. The New American Philosophers, 647
RECONSTRUCTION, 1381, 6032, 6062-6063, 6067, 6075-6077, 6079-6080, 6080, 6084-6085
    SOURCES, 6066
Reconstruction. Stampp, Kenneth M. and Litwack, Leon F., eds. 6076
Reconstruction After the Civil War. Franklin, John H, 6067
Reconstruction of Southern Education. Orfield, Gary, 1753

Record of American Diplomacy. Bartlett, Ruhl J., ed, 1329
Recovery of Confidence. Gardner, John W, 1108
Red Book and the Great Wall. Moravia, Alberto, 5601
Red China Today. Snow, Edgar, 5603
Red Giants and White Dwarfs. Jastrow, Robert, 1985
Red Men Calling on the Great White Father. Turner, Katharine C, 5775
Red Rock Country. Baars, Donald L, 2161
Red Scare. Murray, Robert K, 6120
Red Star Over China. Snow, Edgar, 5592
Red, White and Black. Nash, Gary B, 5904
Reddaway, William W., et al, eds. Cambridge History of Poland, 5363
Redding, J. Saunders. The Lonesome Road, 1273
Red Fox, William. The Memoirs of Chief Red Fox, 5764
Redinger, Ruby V. George Eliot, 3929
Rediscovery of Black Nationalism. Draper, Theodore, 1241
Redlich, Fritz. Molding of American Banking, 1453
Reed, John. Ten Days That Shook the World. , 5523
Reed, Mort. Encyclopedia of U. S. Coins, 286
Reedy, George E. The Presidency in Flux, 1376
Reese, Terence and Dormer, Albert. The Complete Book of Bridge, 3346
Reeve, Franklin D., ed. Nineteenth Century Russian Plays, 4541
———. Twentieth Century Russian Plays, 4542
Reeves, John A. see Freedley, George
Reeves, Thomas and Hess, Karl. The End of the Draft, 1674
Reeves, Thomas C. Gentleman Boss, 6091
REFERENCE BOOKS, 1, 7-8, 82
Reference Books. Galin, Saul and Spielberg, Peter, eds. 8
Reference Shelf. 1852
Reflections on Poetry and Poets. Nemerov, Howard, 3478
REFORMATION, 782-784, 786-787, 789, 5038
Reformation. Mosse, George L, 789
Reformation Europe. Elton, Geoffrey R, 5038
REFORMERS, 1703, 4869-4870, 6005, 6011, 6068, 6110
Reforming American Education. Eurich, Alvin C, 1760
REGIONAL PLANNING, 970
Regulators. Kohlmeier, Louis M, 1625

INDEX

Rehearsal for Conflict. Bill, Alfred H, 6017
Reich, Hanns, ed. Portugal, 4762
Reichard, Robert. The Figure Finaglers, 1794
Reichswehr and Politics. Carsten, Franz L, 5301
Reid, Keith, et al. Man, Nature and Ecology, 2235
Reid, Robert. Marie Curie, 2027
Reid, Roger D. see Pelczar, Michael J.
Reid, W. Stanford. Trumpeter of God, 813
Reimer, Everett W. School Is Dead, 1747
Reinfeld, Fred. How to Be a Winner at Chess, 3338
Reinhardt, Kurt F. Germany, 5288
Reischauer, Edwin O., et al. History of East Asian Civilization, 5571
———. Japan, 5617
———. Toward the Twenty-First Century, 1294
———. The United States and Japan, 1353
Reiss, H. S. Franz Kafka, 4076
Reist, Benjamin A. The Promise of Bonhoeffer, 742
Relativity and Cosmology. Kaufmann, William J, 1979
RELATIVITY (PHYSICS), 2028-2031
A Relevant War Against Poverty. Clark, Kenneth B. and Hopkins, Jeannette. 1701
RELIGION, 664, 683-686, 692-696, 829, 1495
    DICTIONARIES, 100
Religion and Man. Comstock, W. Richard, 686
Religion and Philosophy of the Veda and Upanishads. Keith, Arthur B, 835
Religion and the Rise of Capitalism. Tawney, Richard H, 765
Religion and the Soviet State. Hayward, Max and Fletcher, William C., eds. 799
Religion and Violence. Brown, Robert M, 768
Religion from Tolstoy to Camus. Kaufmann, Walter A., ed, 694
Religion in America. Hudson, Winthrop S, 690
Religion in Greece and Rome. Rose, Herbert J, 833
Religion in the USSR. Conquest, Robert, ed, 797
Religion in 20th Century America. Schneider, Herbert W, 804
RELIGIONS, 400, 687-688, 817-823, 825, 830, 834
    DICTIONARIES, 116
    ENCYCLOPEDIAS AND DICTIONARIES, 117

SOURCES, 831
Religions in America. Rosten, Leo, ed, 803
Religions of Africa. King, Noel Q, 872
Religions of India. Hopkins, Edward W, 847
Religions of the East. Bancroft, Anne, 834
Religious and Spiritual Groups in Modern America. Ellwood, Robert S., Jr, 688
A Religious History of the American People. Ahlstrom, Sydney E, 715
Religious Movements in Contemporary America. Zaretsky, Irving and Leone, Mark P., eds. 691
RELIGIOUS THOUGHT, 629, 658, 660, 689, 765, 832
Remak, Joachim, ed. The Nazi Years, 5323
Remarque, Erich M. Im Westen Nichts Neues, 4068
Rembrandt and His World. White, Christopher, 3073
Rembrandt and the Italian Renaissance. Clark, Kenneth, 3069
REMBRANDT, HERMENSZOON VAN RIJN, 3069, 3073
Remington, Robin A., ed. Winter in Prague, 5354
Reminiscences of the Cuban Revolutionary War. Guevara, Ché, 5832
Remond, Rene. The Right Wing in France, 1166
RENAISSANCE, 5028-5031, 5431-5432
Renaissance. Setton, Kenneth M, 5031
Renaissance Architecture. Lowry, Bates, 2972
Renaissance in Italy. Decker, Heinrich, 2924
Renaissance of the Twelfth Century. Haskins, Charles, 4431
Renaissance Philosophy of Man. Cassirer, Ernst, ed, 630
Renard, Jules. Poil de Carotte, 4243
Rendezvous with Destiny. Goldman, Eric F, 6068
Rendon, Armando B. Chicano Manifesto, 1237
René. Chateaubriand, François René de, 4203
René Descartes. Vrooman, Jack R, 674
Renfrew, Colin. Before Civilization, 4724
Renner, John W. see Saterstrom, Mary H.
Renshaw, Patrick. The Wobblies, 1445
Report. U. S. Commission on Obscenity & Pornography, 1727
Report from a Chinese Village. Myrdal, Jean, 1094
Report of the President's Commission on Campus Unrest. U. S. President's Commission on Campus Unrest, 1226
Reptile World. Pope, Clifford H, 2414

REPTILES, 2411-2415, 2417-2419, 2421
Reptiles and Amphibians of North America.
  Leviton, Alan, 2415
Republican Establishment. Hess, Stephen
  and Broder, David. 1392
REPUBLICAN PARTY, 1392
De Rerum Natura. Lucretius Carus, Titus,
  4406
RESEARCH, 4663
    RESEARCH GRANTS — U. S., 460
Researcher's Guide to American Genealogy.
  Greenwood, Val D, 4872
Resistance, Rebellion and Death. Camus,
  Albert, 4269
Resnick, Seymour. Selections from Spanish
  Poetry, 4338
———. Spanish-American Poetry, 4339
Resnick, Seymour and Pasmantier, Jeanne,
  eds. Anthology of Spanish Literature in
  English Translation, 4307
Response to Industrialism. Hays, Samuel P,
  1421
Responsibility in Mass Communication.
  Schramm, Wilbur and Rivers, William.
  899
Restless Century. Gaunt, William, 3049
Restless Earth. Calder, Nigel, 2123
Restless Universe. Born, Max, 2016
Restlessness of Shanti Andía and Other
  Writings. Baroja, Pío, 4489
Reston, James B. The Artillery of the Press,
  500
Reunion and Reaction. Woodward, C. Vann,
  6079
Reunion Without Compromise. Perman,
  Michael, 6085
Revizor. Gogol, Nikolai V, 4531
Revolt of the Black Athlete. Edwards,
  Harry, 3351
Revolt of the Masses. Ortega Y Gasset,
  José, 4647
Revolution and Defeat. Kousoulas, D.
  George, 1397
Revolution and Mass Democracy. Amann,
  Peter, 5407
Revolution and the Civil War in Spain.
  Broué, Pierre and Témime, Emile.
  5467
Revolution from 1789 to 1906. Postgate,
  Raymond W, 1213
A Revolution in the Earth Sciences. Hallam,
  A, 2116
Revolutionaries, Traditionalists, and
  Dictators in Latin America. Davis,
  Harold E, 4866
Revolutionary Education in China. Seybolt,
  Peter J., compiled by. 1759
Revolutionary Emperor. Padover, Saul K,
  5291

Revolutionary Generation, 1763-1790.
  Greene, Evarts B, 5900
Revolutionary Russia. Pipes, Richard E., ed,
  5522
Revolutionary Soviet Film Posters.
  Constantine, Mildred and Fern, Alan.
  3096
Revolutionary Struggle, 1947-1958. Castro,
  Fidel, 5829
Revolutionary Suicide. Newton, Huey P.
  and Blake, Herman. 1231
REVOLUTIONISTS, 134, 893, 1488, 5525
REVOLUTIONS, 906, 1081, 1138, 1212-
  1213, 4667-4668, 5060, 5480, 5518, 5582
Revolutions. Kaplan, Lawrence and Kaplan,
  Carol, eds. 1081
Revolutions of 1848, a Social History.
  Robertson, Priscilla, 5060
Rewald, John. The History of
  Impressionism, 3030
Rexroth, Kenneth. Collected Shorter Poems,
  3584
Reynolds, Vernon. Apes, 2479
Rezzuto, Tom. see Selden, Samuel, Jr.
Rh. Zimmerman, David R, 2626
RH FACTOR, 2626
RHINE VALLEY — DESCRIPTION AND
  TRAVEL, 4752
Rhineland. Marsden, Walter, 4752
Rhinoceros and Other Plays. Ionesco,
  Eugene, 4166
RHODE ISLAND — HISTORY
  COLONIAL PERIOD, 6195
RHODES, CECIL JOHN, 5739
Rhodes, Frank H., et al. Fossils, 2176
RHODESIA — HISTORY, 5742
Riabchikov, Eugeny. Russians in Space, 2759
Riasanovsky, Nicholas V. A History of
  Russia, 5491
Ricciuti, Edward R. The American
  Alligator, 2424
Rice, David T. The Appreciation of
  Byzantine Art, 2902
Rice, David T. and Rice, Tamara T. Icons
  and Their History, 2891
Rice, Edward. Mao's Way, 5596
Rice, Elmer. Three Plays, 3686
Rice, Tamara T. see Rice, David T.
RICHARD II, 5202
RICHARD III, 5210
Richard III. Kendall, Paul M, 5210
Richard Strauss. Krause, Ernst, 3173
Richard Wagner. Gutman, Robert W,
  3170
Richard Wright. Webb, Constance, 3741
Richards, Laura E. Abigail Adams and Her
  Time, 5971
Richards, Leonard L. Gentlemen of
  Property and Standing, 1225

INDEX

Richards, Stanley, ed. Best Mystery and Suspense Plays of the Modern Theatre, 3509
——. Best Plays of the Sixties, 3510
Richards, Victor. Cancer, 2619
Richardson, Albert E. Georgian England, 4749
Richardson, E. P. A Short History of Painting in America, 3046
Richardson, Elmo. Dams, Parks and Politics, 1465
Richardson, Emeline. The Etruscans, 4929
Richardson, John A. Art, 2879
Richardson, Tony and Stangos, Nikos, eds. Concepts of Modern Art, 2912
Richardson, Walter C. Mary Tudor, the White Queen, 5228
Richelieu. Auchincloss, Louis, 5379
RICHELIEU, ARMAND JEAN DU PLESSIS, 5379
Richmond, Ian A. Roman Britain, 5189
Richter, Gisela. Handbook of Greek Art, 2920
——. Sculpture and Sculptors of the Greeks, 2995
Richter und Sein Henken. Durrenmatt, Friedrich, 4042
Riddle, Jean, et al. Non-Book Materials, 46
Riddle of Gravitation. Bergmann, Peter G, 2028
Riddle of the Pyramids. Mendelssohn, Kurt, 4890
Riders of the Winds. Dwiggins, Don, 2733
Ridgeway, James. The Last Play, 1476
Ridgway, Matthew B. The Korean War, 5612
Ridley, Jasper. Lord Palmerston, 5263
——. Thomas Cranmer, 796
Rienow, Robert. Moment in the Sun, 955
Riesman, David, et al. The Lonely Crowd, 544
Right to Know. Liston, Robert A, 1596
Right to Know. Marnell, William H, 1582
Right Wing in France. Remond, Rene, 1166
Rights in Conflict. Walker, Daniel, 6226
Riha, Thomas, ed. Readings in Russian Civilization, 5492
Riis, Jacob A. How the Other Half Lives, 969
Riis, Jacob August. The Making of an American, 1280
RIIS, JACOB AUGUST, 1280
Rilke, Rainer Maria. Selected Poems, 3999
RILKE, RAINER MARIA, 3998
Rimbaud, Arthur. Selected Verse, 4128
Rinehart, Kenneth L. see Depuy, Charles H.
Riot in the Cities. Journal of Urban Law Editors, 908
Riot Makers. Methvin, Eugene H, 1721
RIOTS, 903, 905, 908, 1072-1073, 1104, 1248, 1721-1723
Riots, U. S. A. 1765-1965. Heaps, Willard A, 903
Ripley, Randall. Majority Party Leadership in Congress, 1368
Rise and Fall of the Confederate Government. Davis, Jefferson, 6057
Rise and Fall of the Habsburg Monarchy. Tapie, Victor L, 5343
Rise and Fall of the Maya Civilization. Thompson, John E, 5809
Rise and Fall of the People's Century. Markowitz, Norman D, 6141
Rise and Fall of the Third Reich. Shirer, William L, 5324
Rise of Modern China. Hsü, Immanuel C. Y, 5583
Rise of Modern Europe. 5568
Rise of the City, 1878-1898. Schlesinger, Arthur M, 6074
Rise of the Common Man, 1830-1850. Fish, Carl R, 6008
Rise of the New West 1819-1829. Turner, Frederick J, 5978
Rise of the Unmeltable Ethics. Novak, Michael, 1006
Rising Sun. Toland, John, 5119
Rister, Carl C. Border Command, 6073
Ritter, Gerhard. Frederick the Great, 5290
——. The Sword and the Scepter, 1164
RITUAL, 762
RIVERA, DIEGO, 3076
Rivera, Feliciano. see Meier, Matthew S.
Rivers, William. see Schramm, Wilbur
Riviere, William A. Backcountry Camping, 3398
——. The Gunner's Bible, 3460
Roach, Hildred. Black American Music, 3197
Road to Disappearance. Debo, Angie, 5759
Road to Jerusalem. Laqueur, Walter, 5649
Road to Pearl Harbor. Feis, Herbert, 5112
Road to Revolution. Yarmolinsky, Avrahm, 5496
Road to War. Millis, Walter, 5082
Robber Barons. Josephson, Matthew, 6071
Robbins, Herbert. see Courant, Richard
Robbins, Royal. Basic Rockcraft, 3394
Robert Bridges. Sparrow, John, 3841
Robert E. Lee. Freeman, Douglas, 6049
Robert, Earl of Essex. Lacey, Robert, 5220
Robert Frost. Morrison, Kathleen, 3611
Robert Frost. Thompson, Lawrence, 3619
Robert, Henry M. Robert's Rules of Order, 1356
Robert, Osmond T. see Cattanes, Helene

Roberts, Adam. *see* Windsor, Philip
Roberts, Martin. Machines and Liberty, 5025
Roberts, Nancy. The Yoga Thing, 2540
Roberts, Penfield. Quest for Security; 1715-1740, 5035
Robert's Rules of Order. Robert, Henry M, 1356
Roberts, Warren. *see* Moore, Harry T.
Roberts, Willard Lincoln, et al. Encyclopedia of Minerals, 219
Robertson, Constance N. Oneida Community, 1508
Robertson, J. G. History of German Literature, 3990
Robertson, John. Modern Humanists Reconsidered, 890
Robertson, Priscilla. Revolutions of 1848, a Social History, 5060
Robertson, Stuart and Cassidy, Frederic G. The Development of Modern English, 1869
Robespierre and the French Revolution. Thompson, James M, 5402
ROBESPIERRE, MAXIMILIEN MARIE ISIDORE DE, 5402
Robins, Eli. *see* Saghir, Marcel T.
Robinson, Charles A. Ancient History, 4879
Robinson, Douglas H. Giants in the Sky, 2736
Robinson, Edwin A. Collected Poems, 3614
———. Selected Poems, 3615
ROBINSON, EDWIN ARLINGTON, 3586
Robinson, Jay L. *see* Bailey, Richard W.
Robinson, Jerry. The Comics, 3006
Robinson, Joan and Eatwell, John. An Introduction to Modern Economics, 1401
Robinson, John. Highways and Our Environment, 1807
Robinson, John A. Honest to God, 747
Robinson, K. W. Australia, New Zealand and the Southwest Pacific, 4843
Robinson, Norman H. The Groundwork of Christian Ethics, 756
Robinson, Sol. Guidelines for News Reporters, 484
Robot Explorers. Gatland, K, 2755
Robotics. Young, J. F, 2771
ROBOTS, 2755
Robson, Eric. The American Revolution in Its Political and Military Aspects, 1763-1783, 5927
Rock. Jahn, Mike, 3222
Rock Book. Fenton, Carroll L. and Fenton, Mildred A. 2167
ROCK CLIMBING, 3393-3394
Rock Encyclopedia. Roxon, Lillian, 310

Rock Opera. Nassour, Ellis and Broderick, Richard. 3215
Rockefeller, John D. The Second American Revolution, 1117
ROCKEFELLER, JOHN DAVIDSON, 1533
ROCKETRY — HISTORY, 2760
ROCKETS (ASTRONAUTICS) — MODELS, 2769
ROCKS, 227, 2088, 2167
Rocks and Minerals. Desautels, Paul E, 2088
Rocks, Lawrence and Runyon, Richard P. The Energy Crisis, 1477
ROCKWELL, NORMAN, 3038
Rodale, Robert. Sane Living in a Mad World, 2530
RODEOS, 3289
Roderick, Arthur J., ed. Wales Through the Ages, 5279
Rodgers and Hammerstein Song Book. Rodgers, Richard and Hammerstein, Oscar, 3rd. 3217
Rodgers, Richard and Hammerstein, Oscar, 3rd. Rodgers and Hammerstein Song Book, 3217
———. Six Plays, 3675
Roditi, Edouard. Magellan of the Pacific, 4702
Rodman, Hyman. *see* Sarvis, Betty
Rodman, S., *see* Eberhart, Richard
Rodman, Selden. The Miracle of Haitian Art, 2942
———. Quisqueya, 5844
Rodrigues, José H. Brazilians, 6272
Roe, Derek. Prehistory, 4715
Roebuck, Carl. The World of Ancient Times, 4880
Roebuck, Janet. Making of Modern English Society from 1850, 1086
Roelofs, Gerrit, *see* Coffin, Charles M.
Roethke, Theodore. Collected Poems, 3585
Roger Williams. Garrett, John, 6195
Rogers, Carl R. Carl Rogers on Encounter Groups, 2603
Rogers, J. A. World's Great Men of Color, 4860
Roget, Peter M. Roget's Thesaurus in Dictionary Form, 172
Roget's Thesaurus in Dictionary Form. Roget, Peter M, 172
Rogin, Michael P. Fathers and Children, 5995
Roll, Jordan, Roll. Genovese, Eugene D, 6208
Rolland, Romain. Jean-Christophe, 4244
Rolle, Kurt C. Introduction to Thermodynamics, 2044
Rollett, A. P. *see* Cundy, Henry M.
Romains, Jules. Knock, 4180

INDEX

Roman Africa. Graham, Alexander, 4985
Roman Art, from the Republic to Constantine. Brilliant, Richard, 2917
Roman Britain. Richmond, Ian A, 5189
Roman Britain and Early England, 55 B.C. to A.D. 871. Blair, Peter H, 5180
Roman Catholic Church. McKenzie, John L, 809
Roman Drama. Dorey, T. A. and Dudley, D. R., eds. 4410
ROMAN EMPERORS, 4944, 4946, 4950
Roman France. MacKendrick, Paul, 4726
Roman History from Coins. Grant, Michael, 2999
Roman History with an English Translation. Livius, Titus, 4426
Roman Life. Johnston, Mary, 4923
ROMAN LITERATURE — EPITAPHS, 4433
Roman Nobility. Gelzer, Mathias, 4920
Roman Poets of the Republic. Sellar, William Y, 4405
Roman Revolution. Syme, Ronald, 4939
Roman Way. Hamilton, Edith, 4399
ROMANCE LITERATURE — HISTORY AND CRITICISM, 341
Romance of Tristan and Iseult. Tristan, 4130
Die Romane. Kafka, Franz, 4059
Romantic Quest and Modern Query. Driver, Tom F, 3312
Romantic Rebellion. Clark, Kenneth, 2904
ROMANTICISM, 3462, 3541, 4116
ROME
    ANTIQUITIES, 2887, 2953, 4727
    ARMY, 4937
    BIOGRAPHY, 4473
    CIVILIZATION, 4397, 4399, 4942, 4947
    HISTORY, 2999, 4921, 4924, 4928, 4930, 4933-4934, 4938-4939, 4941, 4943-4944, 4946, 4950-4951, 4986
    POLITICS AND GOVERNMENT, 4919, 4939-4940
    RELIGION, 833
    SOCIAL CONDITIONS, 4920, 4935, 4945
    SOCIAL LIFE AND CUSTOMS, 4922-4923, 4925
Rome. Pereira, Anthony, 4759
Rome and the Romans. Showerman, Grant, 4925
ROME (CITY)
    COLOSSEUM — HISTORY, 4728
    DESCRIPTION, 4759
Rome of the Caesars. Africa, Thomas W, 4941
Romer, Alfred S. The Procession of Life, 2348
———. The Vertebrate Body, 2400

———. Vertebrate Story, 2401
ROMMEL, ERWIN, 5138
Rommel, the Desert Fox. Young, Desmond, 5138
Ronan, Colin A. Discovering the Universe, 1970
———. Galileo, 1974
———. Lost Discoveries, 1924
Ronsard, Pierre de. Poésies, 4129
Roosevelt. Burns, James M, 6133
Roosevelt. Burns, James M, 6134
Roosevelt and Batista. Gellman, Irwin F, 1340
ROOSEVELT, ELEANOR (ROOSEVELT), 6136-6137
ROOSEVELT, FRANKLIN DELANO, 1340, 1383, 6133-6134, 6136, 6138-6139, 6142-6144, 6146
Roosevelt Revolution. Lindley, Ernest K, 6139
ROOSEVELT, THEODORE, 6115-6116
Roosevelt's Rough Riders. Jones, Virgil C, 6098
Root, Leon and Kiernan, Thomas. The Doctor's Guide to Tennis Elbow, Trick Knee, and Other Miseries of the Weekend Athlete, 2623
Roots, Clive. Animals of the Dark, 2357
Roots of American Civilization. Nettels, Curtis P, 5905
Roots of National Socialism, 1783-1933. Butler, Rohan D, 5283
Roots of the Republic. Dargo, George, 1194
Roper, Laura W. Flo, 2958
Roscoe, Theodore. United States Submarine Operations in World War II, 5145
Rose, Barbara, ed. Readings in American Art Since 1900, 2947
Rose, Ernst. History of German Literature, 3991
Rose, Herbert J. Handbook of Greek Literature, 4441
———. Handbook of Latin Literature, 4400
———. Religion in Greece and Rome, 833
Rose, M. The Cybernetics Revolution, 462
Rose, Peter I. Seeing Ourselves, 888
———. Study of Society, 889
Roseboom, Eugene H. A History of Presidential Elections, 1382
Rosebury, Theodor. Microbes and Morals, 2614
Rosen, Marjorie. Popcorn Venus, 3280
Rosenberg, Arthur. A History of Bolshevism, from Marx to the First Five Years' Plan, 5524
———. Imperial Germany, 5297
Rosenberg, Bruce A. Custer and the Epic of Defeat, 6086

Rosenberg, Sharon and Wiener, Joan. The Illustrated Hassle-Free Make Your Own Clothes Book, 2839
Rosencrantz and Guildenstern Are Dead. Stoppard, Tom, 3915
Rosenstone, Robert A. Crusade of the Left, 5473
Rosenthal, Eric, ed. Encyclopedia of Southern Africa, 444
Rosier, Bernard. see Dumont, Rene
Ross, David A. Introduction to Oceanography, 2141
Ross, Frank, Jr. Storms and Man, 2152
Ross, Ishbel. First Lady of the South, 6046
Ross, James B. and McLaughlin, Mary M., eds. The Portable Medieval Reader, 5030
Ross, Thomas B. see Wise, David
Rossetti, Dante G. Poems and Translations, 3829
Rossiter, Clinton. The American Quest, 1790-1860, 5968
———. Conservatism in America, 1210
———. Seventeen Eighty Seven, 1585
Rostand, Edmond. Cyrano de Bergerac, 4181
Rosten, Leo, ed. Religions in America, 803
Rostovtzeff, Mikhail. Social and Economic History of the Hellenistic World, 4977
———. Social and Economic History of the Roman Empire, 4945
Roszak, Theodore. The Making of a Counter Culture, 912
Roters, Eberhard. Painters of the Bauhaus, 3029
Roth, Bernhard A. The Complete Beginner's Guide to Motorcycling, 2748
Roth, Cecil. Jewish Art, 2892
Roth, Charles E. Walking Catfish and Other Aliens, 2358
Rothenberg, Jerome, ed. Shaking the Pumpkin, 4639
Rothenberg, Polly. The Complete Book of Ceramic Art, 3001
ROTHSCHILD FAMILY, 1450
Rothschild, Joseph. East Central Europe Between the Two World Wars, 5093
Rothschilds. Cowles, Virginia, 1450
Roucek, Joseph S., ed. Central-Eastern Europe, 4991
Roueché, Berton. The Orange Man, 2591
Le Rouge et le Noir. Stendhal, 4253
Rounds, David. see Edmondson, Madeleine
Rouse, Ruth and Neill, Stephen C., eds. History of the Ecumenical Movement, 1517-1948, 780
Rousseau and Revolution. Durant, Will, 5040

Rousseau, Jean-Jacques. Emile, 4245
———. Julie, ou La Nouvelle Héloïse, 4246
———. Political Writings, 1078
ROUSSEAU, JEAN JACQUES, 5040
Routley, Erik. Words, Music and the Church, 3218
Roux, Georges. Ancient Iraq, 4912
ROWING, 3424
Rowland, Benjamin M. see Calleo, David P.
Rowland, Beryl, ed. Companion to Chaucer Studies, 3792
Rowland, K. T. Eighteenth Century Inventions, 2493
Rowse, Alfred L. The Elizabethan Renaissance, 5229
———. Shakespeare the Man, 3869
Roxon, Lillian. Rock Encyclopedia, 310
Royal Canadian Air Force. The Royal Canadian Air Force Exercise Plan for Physical Fitness, 2538
Royal Canadian Air Force Exercise Plan for Physical Fitness. Royal Canadian Air Force, 2538
Royal, D. The Story of J. Robert Oppenheimer, 2062
Royal Navy in America, 1760-1775. Stout, Neil R, 5943
Rubáiyát. Omar Khayyám, 4490
RUBBINGS, 3088
Rubens and His World. White, Christopher, 3075
RUBENS, SIR PETER PAUL, 3075
Rubin, Louis D. and Herbert, Hiram J. Forecasting the Weather, 2158
Rubin, Theodore I. Jordi, Lisa and David, 2627
Rubin, William S. Dada, Surrealism, and Their Heritage, 3034
Ruchelman, Leonard I., ed. Big City Mayors, 1630
Rudel, Harry W. Birth Control, 2552
Rudhyar, Dane. The Astrological Houses, 539
Rudin, Harry R. Armistice, 1918, 5089
Rudloe, Jack. The Erotic Ocean, 2346
Rudwick, Elliott. see Meier, August
Rudyard Kipling. Stewart, J. I, 3965
Rue, Leonard L. Pictorial Guide to the Mammals of North America, 2452
RUFFIN, EDMUND, 6007
Rufus Jones, Master Quaker. Hinshaw, David, 815
Ruge, Friedrich. Der Seekrieg, 5146
Ruggles, Eleanor. Gerard Manley Hopkins, 3830
Rugoff, Milton A., ed. A Harvest of World Folk Tales, 1837
Ruhe, Robert V. Geomorphology, 2124

Ruiz, Roman E. Cuba, 5836
Rukeyser, Muriel. Breaking Open, 3658
———. Speed of Darkness, 3659
Rule, John C. Louis XIV and the Craft of Kingship, 5385
Rules of the Game. 320
RUMANIA
   HISTORY — (1944-), 5564
   POLITICS AND GOVERNMENT, 5365
Runciman, Steven. A History of the Crusades, 5018
Runner's Bible. Holm, Nora S, 3380
RUNNING, 3380
Runyon, Richard P. see Rocks, Lawrence
Rural Santo Domingo. Clausner, Marlin D, 5840
Russel, Alexander. see Andrews, Howard
Russel, Robert R. Economic Aspects of Southern Sectionalism, 1840-1861, 1425
Russell, Bertrand. The Autobiography of Bertrand Russell, 3967
———. Basic Writings, 1903-1959, 655
———. A History of Western Philosophy, 518
RUSSELL, BERTRAND, 3967
Russell, Douglas A. Stage Costume Design, 3304
Russell, Franklin. Watchers at the Pond, 2269
Russell, Renny. see Russell, Terry
Russell, Terry and Russell, Renny. On the Loose, 3128
RUSSIA
   CIVILIZATION, 2927
   DESCRIPTION AND TRAVEL, 4763
   FOREIGN RELATIONS, 1306-1303, 1316, 1320, 1326, 1333, 5109, 6163, 6166
   HISTORICAL GEOGRAPHY — MAPS, 388
   HISTORY, 1498, 5482-5484, 5486, 5489-5492, 5494, 5497, 5499-5500, 5502-5503, 5507-5510, 5513-5514, 5517, 5519, 5512-5523, 5525, 5528, 5531
      DICTIONARIES, 438
      SOURCES, 5495
   POLITICS AND GOVERNMENT, 1092, 1145, 1169-1171, 5496, 5504-5506, 5511-5512, 5530
   RELIGION, 797-799, 1495
   SOCIAL CONDITIONS, 1090-1093, 5518
Russia. Florinsky, Michael T, 5482
Russia. Harcave, Sidney, 5484
Russia. Werth, Alexander, 5528
Russia and the West Under Lenin and Stalin. Kennan, George F, 1309

Russia in Flux. Maynard, John, 5507
Russia Since 1801. Thaden, Edward C, 5502
Russian America. Chevigny, Hector, 6247
Russian Artist. Frankel, Tobia, 2927
RUSSIAN DRAMA — COLLECTIONS, 4538-4539, 4541-4542
Russian-English Dictionary. Smirnitsky, A. I, 189
Russian Folklore. Sokolov, Yury M, 1838
Russian Futurism. Markov, Vladimir, 4525
RUSSIAN LANGUAGE —
   DICTIONARIES, 188-189, 438
RUSSIAN LITERATURE, 4572-4573
   COLLECTIONS, 4494-4496, 4498, 4500-4503
   HISTORY AND CRITICISM, 4493, 4497, 4499, 4504, 4585, 5489
Russian Literature and Modern English Fiction. Davie, Donald, ed, 4572
Russian Literature Since the Revolution. Brown, Edward J, 4493
Russian Literature Under Lenin and Stalin, 1917-1953. Struve, Gleb, 4499
Russian Marxists and the Origins of Bolshevism. Haimson, Leopold, 1488
Russian Orthodox Church Underground, 1917-1971. Fletcher, William C, 807
RUSSIAN POETRY, 4517
   COLLECTIONS, 4520-4522
   HISTORY AND CRITICISM, 4525
Russian Rebels, 1600-1800. Avrich, Paul, 5480
Russian Revolution of February, 1917. Ferro, Marc, 5519
Russian Revolutions of 1917. Curtiss, John S, 5513
Russian Scientist. Parry, Albert, 1923
Russian Short Stories. Friedberg, Maurice, ed, 4547
RUSSIAN SHORT STORIES —
   COLLECTIONS, 4547-4548, 4552, 4570
Russian Tradition in Education. Hans, Nicholas, 1758
Russians. Yarmolinsky, Avrahm, ed, 4503
Russians in Space. Riabchikov, Eugeny, 2759
Russia's Road from Peace to War. Fischer, Louis, 1308
Russier, Gabrielle. The Affair of Gabrielle Russier, 1738
RUSSO-JAPANESE WAR, 5622
Rutenberg, Michael E. Edward Albee, 3702
Rutherfoord, Peggy, ed. African Voices, 4629
Rutherford B. Hayes and His America. Barnard, Harry, 6088
Rutland, Robert A. The Newsmongers, 501
Rutstrum, Calvin. Paradise Below Zero, 3399

Ruy Blas. Hugo, Victor, 4165
Ryan, Charles W. Sport Parachuting, 3444
Ryan, Cornelius. A Bridge Too Far, 5131
———. The Last Battle, 5132
———. The Longest Day, 5133
Ryden, Hope. America's Last Wild Horses, 2807
———. God's Dog, 2472
———. Mustangs, 2463
Ryder, A. J. Twentieth Century Germany, 5298
Ryuziro, Isido, ed. Atlas of Japan, 405

Saalman, Howard. Medieval Cities. , 2952
Saarinen, Eero. Eero Saarinen on His Work, 2969
SAARINEN, EERO, 2969
Sabato, Ernest R. Tunel, 4384
Sabine, George H. History of Political Theory, 1131
Sablosky, Irving L. American Music, 3184
SACCO-VANZETTI CASE, 1724
Sachar, Abram. History of the Jews, 4906
Sachs, Curt. The History of Musical Instruments, 3201
Sachs, Nelly. O the Chimneys, 4000
Sachs, Paul J. Modern Prints and Drawings, 3093
Sackheim, Eric, compiled by. The Blues Line, 3195
Sackler, Howard. The Great White Hope, 3703
SACRED BOOKS, 818, 821
Saettler, Paul. History of Instructional Technology, 1772
Saffell, David C., ed. Watergate, 1201
Sagan, Carl. The Cosmic Connection, 2377
Sagan, François. Bonjour Tristesse, 4247
Sage, Bryan L. Alaska and Its Wildlife, 2275
Saggs, H. W. The Greatness That Was Babylon, 4915
Saghir, Marcel T. and Robins, Eli. Male and Female Homosexuality, 2595
Saher, P. J. Eastern Wisdom and Western Thought, 685
SAILING SHIPS, 2815
Sailing to Win. Bavier, Robert N, 3427
Sainer, Arthur. The Radical Theatre Notebook, 3317
Saint Exupéry, Antoine de. Petit Prince, 4248
———. Terre des Hommes, 4249
St. Francis of Assisi. Bishop, Morris, 791
St. George, George. Our Soviet Sister, 974
SAINTS — DICTIONARIES, 110
Saint-Simon, Louis. Louis XIV at Versailles, 5386
Sal Si Puedes. Matthiessen, Peter, 1448
Salammbô. Flaubert, Gustave, 4210

Sale, Kirkpatrick. SDS, 1233
Salinas, Pedro. Sea of San Juan, 4331
Salisbury, Frank B. see Jensen, William A.
Salisbury, Harrison E. The Nine Hundred Days, 5134
———. Orbit of China, 5602
———. The Soviet Union, 5531
Salk, Erwin A. Layman's Guide to Negro History, 17
Salk, Jonas E. The Survival of the Wisest, 525
Salkever, Louis K., see Uppal, J. S.
Sallustius Crispus, Gaius. War with Catiline, War with Jugurtha, etc, 4425
Salmon. Netboy, Anthony, 1481
Salmon, Edward D. Imperial Spain, 5460
SALMON FISHERIES, 1481
Salmon, Wesley C. Logic, 595
Salmond, John A. The Civilian Conservation Corps, 1933-1942, 1647
Salter, Christopher L. see Hsieh, Chiao-Min
Saltonstall, Richard. Your Environment and What You Can Do About It, 938
Salvemini, Gaetano. Mazzini, 5440
Samilov, M., see Gibian, George
Samora, Julian, ed. La Raza, 4825
Sampson, Anthony. The New Anatomy of Britain, 1087
———. The Sovereign State of ITT, 1801
Sampson, George. The Concise Cambridge History of English Literature, 364
Samuel De Champlain. Morison, Samuel E, 5793
Samuel Pepys and His World. Trease, Geoffrey, 5244
Samuelson, Paul A., ed. Readings in Economics, 1402
San Francisco Earthquake. Thomas, Gordon and Witts, Max M. 2121
SAN JUAN, PUERTO RICO — POOR, 1042
A Sand County Almanac and Sketches Here and There. Leopold, Aldo, 1903
Sand, George. La Mare au Diable, 4250
Sandbox; Sad Death of Bessie Smith. Albee, Edward, 3688
Sandburg, Carl. Abraham Lincoln, 6035
———. The Complete Poems of Carl Sandburg, 3616
SANDBURG, CARL, 3596
Sanders, Ronald, see Fried, Albert
Sanderson, Ivan T. Living Mammals of the World, 2447
Sanderson, Robert T. Inorganic Chemistry, 2079
Sane Living in a Mad World. Rodale, Robert, 2530
Sanger, Marjory B. Billy Bartram and His Green World, 2223

INDEX

Sanity and Survival. Frank, Jerome D, 604
Sansom, George B. Japan, 5618
SANTAYANA, GEORGE, 646
Sapir, Edward. Language, 1855
Sarmiento, Domingo F. Facundo, 4385
Sarnoff, Paul. The New York Times Encyclopedic Dictionary of the Environment, 258
Sarris, Andrew. The American Cinema, 3281
Sarton, May. Collected Poems, 3617
Sartre. Murdoch, Iris, 669
Sartre and Camus; Literature in Existence. Pollman, Leo, 4115
Sartre, Jean-Paul. Being and Nothingness, 554
———. The Ghost of Stalin, 5368
———. No Exit, and Flies, 4182
———. Théâtre, 4183
SARTRE, JEAN PAUL, 669, 673, 4115
Sarvis, Betty and Rodman, Hyman. The Abortion Controversy, 886
Sastre, Alfonso. Teatro Selecto, 4363
Saterstrom, Mary H. and Renner, John W. Educators Guide to Free Science Materials, 205
SATIRE, 761, 4422-4423
Satires. Juvenalis, Decimus Junius, 4423
Satires, Epistles, and Ars Poetica. Horatius Flaccus, Quintus, 4418
Sauvage, Leo. Ché Guevera, 6264
Savage, George. Dictionary of Antiques, 289
Savory, Hubert N. Spain and Portugal, 4735
SAVOY, HOUSE OF, 5014, 5444
Savoy Operas. Gilbert, William S, 3878
Sawa, Yuki, trs. see Shiffert, Edith
Sawyer, P. H. The Age of the Vikings, 5537
Sax, Joseph L. Defending the Environment, 945
Saxton, J. C., see MacDonald, J. W.
Scagel, Robert F., et al. An Evolutionary Survey of the Plant Kingdom, 2314
Scammon, Richard M. and Wattenburg, Ben J. The Real Majority, 1269
SCANDINAVIA, 5534
    DESCRIPTION AND TRAVEL, 4766
    HISTORY, 5533
Scandinavia. Fullerton, Brian and Williams, Alan. 4766
SCANDINAVIAN FICTION — HISTORY AND CRITICISM, 4086
SCANDINAVIAN LITERATURE, 4087
    HISTORY AND CRITICISM, 4082, 4084
Scandinavian Literature from Brandes to Our Day. Topsoe-Jensen, H. G, 4084
Scandinavians. Connery, Donald, 5534

Scarisbrick, J. J. Henry VIII, 5230
Scarne, John. Scarne's Encyclopedia of Games, 3342
Scarne's Encyclopedia of Games. Scarne, John, 3342
Schachner, Nathan. Alexander Hamilton, 5969
Schafer, William J., et al. The Art of Ragtime, 3193
Schaller, George B. Golden Shadows, Flying Hooves, 2467
———. Serengeti, 2468
———. Serengeti Lion, 2469
Schapiro, Jacob S. Modern and Contemporary European History, 5026
Schapiro, Leonard. The Communist Party of the Soviet Union, 1396
Scharff, Robert. Standard Handbook of Saltwater Fishing, 3454
Scheer, Richard. see Carney, James D.
Scheffer, Victor B. A Voice for Wildlife, 2814
———. The Year of the Seal, 2475
Schell, Orville, see Schurmann, Franz
Schellenberg, T. R. Modern Archives, 25
Schenk, Hans G. The Aftermath of the Napoleonic Wars, 5061
Scheob, Harold, ed. African Images, 4628
Schevill, Ferdinand. The Medici, 5434
Schickel, Richard. Movies, 3282
Schiller, Friedrich Von. Werke, 3978
Schilling, Phil. Motorcycle World, 2749
Schilling, Sylvester P. God Incognito, 700
Schiotz, Arne. A Guide to Aquarium Fishes and Plants, 2820
Schiotz, Askel. Singer and His Art, 3225
SCHIZOPHRENIA, 590
Schlee, Susan. The Edge of an Unfamiliar World, 2142
Schlesinger, Arthur M. The Rise of the City, 1878-1898, 6074
Schlesinger, Arthur M., Jr. The Age of Jackson, 5996
———. The Age of Roosevelt, 6144
———. The Birth of the Nation, 5908
———. The Bitter Heritage, 1354
———. History of U. S. Political Parties, 1377
———. The Imperial Presidency, 5869
———. Paths to the Present, 5870
Schlesinger, Arthur M., Jr. and Israel, F. L. History of American Presidential Elections, 137
Schlesinger, Arthur M., Jr. and White, Morton M. Paths of American Thought, 648
Schliemann, Heinrich. Ilios, 4982
Schlissel, Lillian, ed. Conscience in America, 1675
Schmidt, H. D. see Koebner, Richard

Schmidt, Karl P. *see* Inger, Robert F.
Schmidt, Paul K. Hitler Moves East, 1941-1943, 5135
———. Scorched Earth, 5136
Schmidt, Steven. *see* Kayatta, Ken
Schmidt-Nielsen, Knut. Animal Physiology, 2342
Schmitt, Marshall L. *see* Buban, Peter
Schnapper, M. B., ed. Presidential Impeachment, 1644
Schneider, Herbert W. History of American Philosophy, 649
———. Religion in 20th Century America, 804
Schollander, Don and Cohne, Joel H. Inside Swimming, 3433
Schonberg, Harold C. The Great Conductors, 306
School Is Dead. Reimer, Everett W, 1747
SCHOOL LIBRARIES, 23, 34
School Library Journal. 42
School Library Media Center. Davies, Ruth A, 34
Schooling of the Western Horse. Young, John R, 3446
Schopenhauer, Arthur. Philosophy, 668
Schramm, Wilbur. Men, Messages and Media, 463
Schramm, Wilbur and Rivers, William. Responsibility in Mass Communication, 899
Schreiber, Georg. *see* Schreiber, Hermann
Schreiber, Hermann and Schreiber, Georg. Vanished Cities, 4708
Schreider, Frank. *see* Schreider, Helen
Schreider, Helen and Schreider, Frank. Exploring the Amazon, 4842
Schroeder, Henry A. The Poisons Around Us, 2584
Schroeder, Peter B. Contact at Sea, 2685
Schroeter, Leonard. The Last Exodus, 1242
Schug-Wille, Christa. Art of the Byzantine World, 2903
Schuller, Gunther. Early Jazz, 3191
Schultz, Given. Ice Age Lost, 2166
Schultz, John. Motion Will Be Denied, 1600
Schultz, Leonard, et al. Wondrous World of Fishes, 2406
Schulz, David A. Coming up Black, 1036
Schurman, Nona and Clark, Sharon. Modern Dance Fundamentals, 3330
Schurmann, Franz. Ideology and Organization in Communist China, 1500
Schurmann, Franz and Schell, Orville, eds. China Reader, 5581
Schwab, John C. The Confederate States of America, 1426
Schwabe, Randolph. *see* Kelly, Francis M.

Schwartz, Alvin. Central City-Spread City, 970
Schwartz, Bernard. Commentary on the Constitution of the United States, 1586
Schwartz, Delmore. Selected Poems, 3660
Schwartz, Elliott S. Electronic Music, 3254
Schwartz, Harry. Prague's 200 Days, 5355
Schwartz, Kessel. *see* Chandler, Richard E.
Schwarz, Boris. Music and Musical Life in Soviet Russia 1917-1970, 3181
Schwarz, Urs. Confrontation and Intervention in the Modern World, 1661
Schwarz, Walter. Nigeria, 5729
Schweid, Eliezer. Israel at the Crossroads, 859
Schweitzer. Marshall, George and Poling, David. 773
Schweitzer, Albert. Albert Schweitzer, 663
———. Out of My Life and Thought, 774
———. Quest of the Historical Jesus, 750
SCHWEITZER, ALBERT, 773-774
Schweitzer, Frederick M. A History of the Jews Since the First Century A.D, 4907
SCIENCE, 195, 204, 1890, 1892, 1914, 1917-1918, 1924, 2029
  BIBLIOGRAPHY, 43, 59
  DICTIONARIES, 201-203
  HISTORY, 1891, 1921-1922, 1925-1926
  METHODOLOGY, 205, 1889, 1909, 1911, 2487
  PHILOSOPHY, 596, 1910, 2101
  TERMINOLOGY, 198-199
Science and Anti-Science. Goran, Morris, 1893
Science and Human Destiny. Dessel, N. and Dessel, Nehrich. 1891
Science and Sentiment in America. White, Morton, 650
Science Books and Films. 43
SCIENCE FICTION
  HISTORY AND CRITICISM, 3920
  STUDY AND TEACHING, 3919
Science in Russian Culture. Vucinich, Alexander S, 1925
Science in Russian Culture, 1861-1917. Vucinich, Alexander S, 1926
Science in Utopia. Eurich, Nell, 1208
Science of Folklore. Krappe, Alexander H, 1834
Science of the Earth. Eardley, Armand I, 2107
Science of Zoology. Weisz, Paul B, 2337
Science Study Series. 2486
Scientific American Editors. The Biosphere, 2112
———. Continents Adrift, 2127
———. Ecology, Evolution, and Population Biology, 2238

INDEX

———. Facets of Genetics, 2299
———. From Cell to Organism, 2253
———. Frontiers of Astronomy, 1966
———. The Living Cell, 2254
———. Mathematics in the Modern World, 1939
———. The Ocean, 2143
———. Oceanography, 2144
———. Psychobiology, 589
———. Thirty-Nine Steps to Biology, 2220
SCIENTIFIC APPARATUS AND INSTRUMENTS, 1912-1913
Scientific Breakthrough. Clark, Ronald W, 2494
Scientist Extraordinary. Bibby, Cyril, 2221
SCIENTISTS, 206-207, 1893, 1923, 2026, 4863
SCIPIO THE ELDER, 4931
Scobbie, Irene. Sweden, 5541
Scobie, W. I. see Foley, Charles
SCOPES EVOLUTION CASE, 1591
SCOPES, JOHN THOMAS, 1591
Scorched Earth. Schmidt, Paul K, 5136
Scorer, Richard. Clouds of the World, 2155
SCOTLAND
  DESCRIPTION AND TRAVEL, 4743-4744
  HISTORY, 5151-5156, 5159
Scotland. Cowie, Donald, 4743
Scotland. Donaldson, Gordon, 5151
Scotland. Linklater, Eric and Smith, Edwin. 4744
Scotland. Nicholson, Ranald, 5156
Scott, Ernest F. The Literature of the New Testament, 732
Scott, Ian. Tumbled House, 5732
Scott, Marian H. Periodicals for School Libraries, 12
Scott, Peter and Wildfowl Trust. The Swans, 2436
Scott Publications, Inc. Scott's Standard Postage Stamp Catalogue, 1799
Scott, Robert, see Liddell, Henry G.
SCOTT, ROBERT FALCON, 4853
Scott, Sheila. Barefoot in the Sky, 2718
SCOTT, SHEILA, 2718
Scott, Tom and Cousins, Geoffrey. The Golf Immortals, 3370
Scott, Walter. Poetical Works, 3816
Scott's Specialized Catalog of United States Stamps, 1923- 293
Scott's Standard Postage Stamp Catalogue. Scott Publications, Inc, 1799
Scott's Standard Postage Stamps of the World. 294
Scottsboro. Carter, Dan T, 1594
SCOTTSBORO CASE, 1594
Scott-Stokes, Henry. The Life and Death of Yukio Mishima, 4618

Screwtape Letters, and Screwtape Proposes a Toast. Lewis, Clive S, 761
Scrimshaw and Scrimshanders, Whales and Whalemen. Flayderman, E. Norman, 2997
SCRIMSHAWS, 2997
Scroll of Agony. Kaplan, Chaim A, 5362
Scuba Diver's Guide to Underwater Ventures. May, Judy G, 3438
Scuba, Spear and Snorkel. Borstein, Larry and Berkowitz, Henry. 3435
Scullard, Howard H. From the Gracchi to Nero, 4938
———. History of the Roman World, 753 to 146 B.C, 4924
Scully, Vincent J. Modern Architecture, 2974
SCULPTORS, 2981
SCULPTURE, 2923, 2980, 2983-2984, 2987, 2989, 2993-2996
Sculpture and Sculptors of the Greeks. Richter, Gisela, 2995
Sculpture in America. Craven, Wayne, 2984
Sculpture in Fiberglass. Panting, John, 2986
Sculpture of Life. Borek, Ernest, 2256
Sculpture of the World. Cheney, Sheldon, 2980
SDS. Adelson, Alan, 1783
SDS. Sale, Kirkpatrick, 1233
Sea and the Ice. Halle, Louise J, 2353
Sea Around Us. Carson, Rachel, 2134
SEA LIONS, 2461
Sea of Glory. Miller, Nathan, 5954
Sea of San Juan. Salinas, Pedro, 4331
SEA POWER, 1688
SEA SERPENTS, 2370-2373
SEAFARING LIFE, 2815
Seager, Robin. Tiberius, 4949
SEALS, 2456
SEALS (ANIMALS), 2475
Search for Morag. Campbell, Elizabeth M. and Solomon, David. 2370
Search for Peking Man. Janus, Christopher G. and Brashler, William. 2205
Sears, David O. and McConahy, John B. The Politics of Violence, 6245
Seas and Oceans in Color. Hickling, Charles F. and Brown, Peter L. 2138
Seas in Motion. Smith, F. Walton, 2150
SEASHORE BIOLOGY, 2262
SEASHORE ECOLOGY, 2260
SEASHORES, 1899
A Season in Utopia. Curtis, Edith R, 1507
SECESSION, 6007, 6043-6045
Second American Revolution. Rockefeller, John D, 1117
Second Wave. Taylor, John R, 3888
Secret Army. Bell, J. Bowyer, 5163

Secret History of the American Revolution. Van Doren, Carl C, 5957
Secret Life of Plants. Tompkins, Peter and Bird, Christopher. 2315
Secret Life of the Forest. Ketchum, Richard M, 2327
Secret of the Hittites. Ceram, C. W, 4984
Secret of Yoga. Krishna, Gopi, 621
Secret Sentries in Space. Klass, Philip J, 1687
SECRET SERVICE, 1624, 5123, 5947, 5957
Secrets of the Great Pyramid. Tompkins, Peter, 4895
SECTS — U. S., 803
Secular City. Cox, Harvey, 744
SECURITY CLASSIFICATION (GOVERNMENT DOCUMENTS) — U. S., 1582
Sedgwick, Alexander. Third French Republic, 1870-1924, 5418
Sedgwick, Henry D. Marcus Aurelius, 4946
Seduction of the Innocent. Wertham, Frederic, 586
Seduction of the Spirit. Cox, Harvey, 696
Seegar, Pete. Henscratches and Flyspecks, 3186
———. The Incompleat Folksinger, 3238
Seeing Ourselves. Rose, Peter I, 888
Seeing Sound. Koch, Winston E, 2038
Der Seekrieg. Ruge, Friedrich, 5146
Seele, Keith C. *see* Steindorff, George
Segel, Harold B., tr. The Literature of Eighteenth Century Russia, 4498
Segerberg, Osborn. Where Have All the Flowers, Fishes, Birds, Trees, Water, and Air Gone? What Ecology Is All About, 946
Segmented Society. Wiebe, Robert H, 4820
Segré, Emilio. Enrico Fermi, Physicist, 2033
Segy, L. African Sculpture, 2993
———. African Sculpture Speaks, 2994
Seidler, Murray B. Norman Thomas, 1486
Seidlova, Anca. *see* Shippen, Katherine B.
Selden, Samuel, Jr. and Rezzuto, Tom. Essentials of Stage Scenery, 3301
Seldes, George. Never Tire of Protesting, 482
Select Bibliography. American Universities Field Service, 72
Select List of Books on European History, 1815-1914. Bullock, Alan and Taylor, A. J., eds. 60
Selected Essays. Montaigne, Michel E. de, 4272
Selected Fables. La Fontaine, Jean de, 4224

Selected Latin American One-Act Plays. Colecchia, Francesca Maria, 4358
Selected Plays of Sean O'Casey. O'Casey, Sean, 3891
Selected Poems. Aiken, Conrad, 3594
Selected Poems. Brodsky, Joseph, 4506
Selected Poems. Brooks, Gwendolyn, 3628
Selected Poems. García Lorca, Federico and Jiménez, Juan Ramón. 4321
Selected Poems. Lawrence, David H, 3838
Selected Poems. Lindsay, Vachel, 3604
Selected Poems. Mallarme, Stephanie, 4126
Selected Poems. Mistral, Gabriela, 4329
Selected Poems. Neruda, Pablo, 4330
Selected Poems. Pound, Ezra, 3583
Selected Poems. Ransom, John C, 3613
Selected Poems. Rilke, Rainer Maria, 3999
Selected Poems. Robinson, Edwin A, 3615
Selected Poems. Schwartz, Delmore, 3660
Selected Poems. Shapiro, Karl, 3663
Selected Poems. Simpson, Louis, 3664
Selected Poems. Verlaine, Paul-Marie, 4131
Selected Poems. Warren, Robert Penn, 3591
Selected Poems. Williams, William C, 3593
Selected Poems, 1956-1968. Cohen, Leonard, 3631
Selected Poems of Gabriela Mistral. Godoy Alcayaga, Lucilla, 4322
Selected Poems of Ruben Darío. Darío, Ruben, 4320
Selected Poetry. Yevtushenko, Yevgeny, 4519
Selected Poetry and Prose. Swinburne, Algernon C, 3831
Selected Readings. Mao Tse-Tung, 1179
Selected U. S. Government Publications. U. S. Superintendent of Documents, 6
Selected Verse. Rimbaud, Arthur, 4128
Selected Writings. Capote, Truman, 3767
Selected Writings. Carlyle, Thomas, 3956
Selected Writings. Hofmannsthal, Hugo Von, 3976
Selected Writings and Speeches on America. Burke, Edmund, 1075
Selected Writings of Salvatore Quasimodo. Quasimodo, Salvatore, 4290
Selections. Tolstoi, Leo N, 4565
Selections from Italian Poetry. De Luca, A. Michael and Giulianos, William. 4291
Selections from Spanish Poetry. Resnick, Seymour, 4338
Self and Others. Laing, R. D, 590
SELF-DEFENSE, 3410
Self-Renewal. Gardner, John W, 922
Seligmann, Kurt. Magic, Supernaturalism and Religion, 537

INDEX

Sellar, William Y. Roman Poets of the Republic, 4405
Sellick, Bud. Parachutes and Parachuting, 3445
Sellman, Hunton D. Essentials of Stage Lighting, 3302
Selma Lagerlof, Her Life and Work. Berendsohn, Walter A, 4091
Selma 1965. Fager, Charles E, 1255
Seltzer, L. E., ed. Columbia Lippincott Gazetteer of the World, 383
Selznick, Gertrude J. and Steinberg, Stephen. The Tenacity of Prejudice, 1052
SEMANTICS, 1874
Semantics. Ullmann, Stephen, 1874
Sender, Ramón J. Crónica del Alba, 4387
———. Mosén Millán, 4386
A Sense of the Earth. Leveson, David, 2095
SENSES AND SENSATION, 2344
Separated People. Kahn, Ely J, 1244
SEPHARDISM — U. S. — BIOGRAPHY, 4864
Serengeti. Schaller, George B, 2468
Serengeti Lion. Schaller, George B, 2469
Seronde, Joseph, see Peyre, Henri
Serpent. Van Itallie, Jean-Claude, 3706
SERPENTS (IN RELIGION, FOLK-LORE, ETC.), 2413
Serpico. Maas, Peter, 1631
SERPICO, FRANK, 1631
Serres, Jean. see Wood, John R.
Servin, Manuel P., compiled by. An Awakened Minority, 1045
Seton, Marie. Panditji, 5636
Seton-Watson, Hugh. Eastern Europe Between the Wars, 1918-1941, 5493
Seton-Watson, Robert W. A History of the Czechs and Slovaks, 5350
Setton, Kenneth M. The Renaissance, 5031
Seven Days of Freedom. Barber, Noel, 5366
Seven Essayists. Reaske, Christopher, 3517
Seven Irish Plays, 1946-1964. Hogan, Robert G., ed, 3855
Seven Plays. Brecht, Bertolt, 4012
Seven Short Plays. Gregory, Isabella A, 3883
Seven Who Shaped Our Destiny. Morris, Richard B, 5937
Seventeen Eighty Seven. Rossiter, Clinton L, 1585
Seventeenth Century Background. Willey, Basil, 660
Seventeenth Century France. Treasure, Geoffrey, 5387
Seventeenth Century Literature. Wedgwood, Cicely V, 3773

Seventy-Seven Dream Songs. Berryman, John, 3625
Severn, William. A Carnival of Sports, 3349
SEWAGE IRRIGATION, 2704
SEWALL, JONATHAN, 5944
Sewall, Richard B. The Vision of Tragedy, 3484
Seward, Jack. The Japanese, 4780
SEWARD, WILLIAM HENRY, 6014
SEWING, 2838-2840
SEX, 972
Sex and Birth Control. Lieberman, E. James and Peck, Ellen. 2519
Sex and Love. Hemming, James and Maxwell, Zena. 972
SEX CUSTOMS — U. S., 973
SEX INSTRUCTION, 986, 2517-2522
Sex Is Never an Emergency. Pierson, Elaine C, 986
SEX (PSYCHOLOGY), 570
Sexton, Anne. The Book of Folly, 3661
———. Live or Die, 3662
SEXUAL ETHICS, 2517
Seybolt, Peter J., compiled by. Revolutionary Education in China, 1759
Seyfert, Carl K. and Sirkin, Leslie K. Earth History and Plate Tectonics, 2164
Seymour, Charles. American Diplomacy During the World War, 5080
Seymour-Smith, Martin. The Funk and Wagnalls Guide to Modern World Literature, 343
Sgroi, Suzanne M. VD, 2615
Shaffer, Peter. Black Comedy and White Lies, 3913
———. Equus and Shrivings, 3914
Shaker Music. Cook, Harold E, 3219
SHAKERS — MUSIC — HISTORY AND CRITICISM, 3219
Shakespeare of London. Chute, Marchette, 3865
Shakespeare the Man. Rowse, Alfred L, 3869
SHAKESPEARE, WILLIAM, 3863-3865, 3869, 4750
    CHARACTERS, 369, 3866-3867
    CONCORDANCES, 367, 370
    DICTIONARIES, 368, 371, 3868
    STAGE HISTORY, 3870
Shakespearean Comedy. Charlton, Henry B, 3864
Shakespearean Tragedy. Bradley, Andrew C, 3863
Shakespeare's Bawdy. Partridge, Eric, 3868
Shakespeare's Globe Playhouse. Smith, Irwin, 3870

INDEX

Shakespeare's Predecessors in the English Drama. Symonds, John A, 3856
Shakespeare's Villains. Coe, Charles N, 3866
Shaking the Pumpkin. Rothenberg, Jerome, ed, 4639
Shakuntala and Other Writings. Kalidasa, 4481
Shame of the Cities. Steffens, Joseph L, 1626
Shannon, David A. Between the Wars, 6145
———. The Great Depression, 1458
———. Socialist Party of America, 1393
———. Twentieth Century America, 6105
Shape of European History. McNeil, William H, 4992
Shapes, Space, and Symmetry. Holden, Alan, 1949
Shapiro, Barry. see Boericke, Art
Shapiro, Harry L. Peking Man, 2206
Shapiro, Karl. Selected Poems, 3663
Shapiro, Karl. and Beum, R. A Prosody Handbook, 1861
Shaplen, Robert. Time Out of Hand, 5673
Shapley, Harlow. Galaxies, 1987
Shark. Cousteau, Jacques-Yves and Cousteau, Philippe. 2409
SHARKS, 2408-2409
Sharks. Brown, Theo W, 2408
Sharp, Harold S. Handbook of Pseudonyms and Personal Nicknames, 431
Shaw, Charles B., ed. American Essays, 3748
Shaw, Charles E. and Campbell, Sheldon. Snakes of the American West, 2418
Shaw, George B. Four Plays, 3885
———. Plays, 3887
———. Pygmalion, 3886
SHAW, GEORGE BERNARD, 3882, 3884
Shaw, Harry. Dictionary of Literary Terms, 326
Shaw, Leroy, ed. German Theater Today, 4029
Shaw the Dramatist. Crompton, Louis, 3882
Shawcross, William. Dubcek, 5356
She Stoops to Conquer. Goldsmith, Oliver, 3875
Shea, John G. Woodworking for Everybody, 2864
Sheaves. Tagore, Rabindranath, 4487
Sheean, Vincent. The Indigo Bunting, 3618
Sheehan, Neil, et al. The Pentagon Papers, 5687
SHELDON, DONALD EDWARD, 2713
Shell. Stix, Hugh and Stix, Marguerite. 2387
Shell Makers. Solem, Alan, 2384

Shelley, Percy B. Complete Poetical Works, 3818
———. Poems, 3817
SHELLEY, PERCY BYSSHE, 3814
SHELLS, 242, 2385-2387
Shelton, John S. Geology Illustrated, 2098
Shepard, Daniel and Shepard, Jean. Earth Watch, 1898
Shepard, Francis P. The Earth Beneath the Sea. , 2147
Shepard, Jean. see Shepard, Daniel
Shepard, Thomas R. see Grayson, Melvin J.
Shepherd, Elizabeth. Arms of the Sea, 2242
Shepherd, William R. Shepherd's Historical Atlas, 386
Shepherd's Historical Atlas. Shepherd, William R, 386
Sheppard, Harold L. and Herrick, N. Q. Where Have All the Robots Gone? Worker Dissatisfaction in the Seventies, 1433
Sheresky, Norman and Mannes, M. Uncoupling, 992
Shergold, N. D. History of the Spanish Stage from Medieval Times Until the End of the Seventeenth Century, 4364
Sherican, Walter. The Fall and Rise of Jimmy Hoffa, 1446
SHERIDAN, PHILIP HENRY, 6073
Sheridan, Richard B. Six Plays, 3876
Sherlock, Philip M. West Indian Nations, 5825
SHERMAN, WILLIAM TECUMSEH, 6055
Sherpa, Himalaya, Nepal. Fantin, Mario, 4783
Sherrard, Philip. see Campbell, John
Sherwood Anderson. Howe, Irving, 3729
Sherwood, Martin. The New Chemistry, 2071
Shest' Rasskazov. Chekhov, Anton P, 4543
Shestack, Melvin. Country Music Encyclopedia, 311
Shield and Crest. Franklyn, Julian, 4874
Shiffert, Edith and Sawa, Yuki, trs. Anthology of Modern Japanese Poetry, 4612
Shimer, John A. Field Guide to Landforms in the U. S, 4816
Shinel' Gogol, Nikolai V, 4550
Shipley, Joseph T. Dictionary of Early English, 177
———. Dictionary of World Literary Terms, 327
Shippen, Katherine B. and Seidlova, Anca. The Heritage of Music, 3140

INDEX

SHIPWRECKS, 4986, 4690, 4717
Shipwrecks and Archaeology.
Throckmorton, Peter, 4717
Shirer, William L. The Collapse of the Third Republic, 5419
———. The Rise and Fall of the Third Reich, 5324
Shirley-Smith, H. World's Great Bridges, 2692
Shiva Rao, B. India's Freedom Movement, 5634
Shneidman, Edwin S. Death and the College Student, 1725
Shneour, Elie. The Mal-Nourished Mind, 578
Shoal of Time. Daws, Gavan, 6289
Shockley, Ann A. and Chandler, Sue, eds. Living Black American Authors, 356
Shondell, Donald S. and McManama, Jerry. Volleyball, 3357
Short, Charles. see Lewis, Charlton T.
Short History of Chess. Murray, Harold J, 3337
Short History of Costume and Armour, 1066-1800. Kelly, Francis M. and Schwabe, Randolph. 1813
A Short History of Denmark. Oakley, Stewart, 5542
A Short History of Ethics. MacIntyre, Alasdair C, 600
Short History of Italy. Hearder, H. and Waley, Daniel P. 5427
A Short History of Literary Criticism. Hall, Vernon, Jr, 3465
A Short History of Medieval Philosophy. Weinberg, Julius R, 632
A Short History of Norway. Derry, Thomas K, 5539
A Short History of Opera. Grout, Donald J, 3203
A Short History of Painting in America. Richardson, E. P, 3046
A Short History of Sweden. Oakley, Stewart, 5540
A Short History of the Chinese People. Goodrich, L. Carrington, 5578
A Short History of the Far East. Latourette, Kenneth S, 5570
A Short History of the Italian People. Trevelyan, Janet P, 5429
A Short History of Yugoslavia from Early Times to 1966. Clissold, Stephen, et al. 5559
SHORT STORIES, 3514-3515, 4262-4263
INDEXES, 336
Short Story Index, Plus 4 Supplements. Cook, Dorothy E., et al, eds. 336
Short Victorious War. Walder, David, 5622

Shorter Cambridge Medieval History. Previte-Orton, Charles, 5005
Showdown at Newport. Hammond, Geoffrey F, 3428
Showerman, Grant. Rome and the Romans, 4925
Showman, Richard K., see Freidel, Frank
Shroder, Maurice Z. Icarus, 4116
Shukman, Harold. Lenin and the Russian Revolution, 5525
Shuler, Nettie R. see Catt, Carrie C.
Si le Grain Ne Meurt. Gide, André, 4216
Siberry, K. M. Instruments of Flight, 2737
Sieber, Roy. African Textiles and Decorative Arts, 3015
Siegelman, Ellen. see Glock, Charles I.
Siegmeister, Elie, ed. The New Music Lover's Handbook, 303
Siegner, Otto. Egypt, 4788
Sierra Club. 4857
Sierra Nevada. Johnston, Verna, 1907
Siers, James. Hawaii, 4847
Siever, Raymond. see Press, Frank
Sigler, Jay A., ed. The Conservative Tradition in American Thought, 1150
Sign in Sidney Brustein's Window. Hansberry, Lorraine, 3695
SIGNS AND SYMBOLS, 169
SIKHISM — HISTORY, 850
Silberman, Charles E. Crises in the Classroom, 1764
———. Open Classroom Reader, 1776
Le Silence de la Mer. Vercors, 4254
Silenced Majority. Amundsen, Kirsten, 975
Silent Language. Hall, Edward T, 919
Silent Spring. Carson, Rachel, 2778
Silver, Daniel J. A History of Judaism, 860
Silver, Helene. see Zell, Hans
Silverberg, Robert. Mammoths, Mastodons and Man, 2183
———. The World Within the Ocean Wave, 2267
———. The World Within the Tide Pool, 2243
Silverman, Eliot N. and Brody, Linda A. Statistics, 1955
Silverman, Jerry. How to Play the Guitar, 3251
SILVERSMITHING — U. S. — HISTORY, 3002
Silverstein, Alvin and Silverstein, Virginia. Animal Invaders, 2359
———. Sleep and Dreams, 2528
Silverstein, Virginia. see Silverstein, Alvin
Simak, Clifford D. Prehistoric Man, 2198
El Simbolismo Religioso en las Novelas de Perez Galdos. Corre, Gustavo, 4311

Simkins, Francis B. The Women of the Confederacy, 6060
Simmons, Ernest J. Chekhov, 4536
──. Pushkin, 4582
Simon Bolivar. Masur, Gerhard, 6262
Simon, George T. The Big Bands, 3243
Simon, James F. In His Own Image, 1610
Simon, John Y., ed. The Personal Memoirs of Julia Dent Grant, 6087
Simon, Neil. Comedy of Neil Simon, 3704
──. The Sunshine Boys, 3705
Simon, Sidney B., et al. Values Clarification, 602
Simpson, Colin. Greece, 4769
──. The Lusitania, 5090
──. The New Australia, 4844
Simpson, Lesley B., tr. The Poem of the Cid, 4332
Simpson, Louis. Selected Poems, 3664
Since Nineteen Hundred. Barck, Oscar T, 6108
Since Silent Spring. Graham, Frank, Jr, 2781
Sinclair Lewis. Lundquist, James, 3731
Singer and His Art. Schiotz, Askel, 3225
Singer, Samuel L. The Student Journalist and Reviewing the Performing Arts, 487
Singh, Khushwant. Train to Pakostan, 4479
SINGING, 3225
Singletary, Otis A., ed. American Universities and Colleges, 149
──. The Mexican War, 6020
Sioux. Hassrick, Royal B., et al. 5762
Sir Christopher Wren. Gould, Heywood, 2965
Sir Francis Drake. Thomson, George M, 1690
Sir George Etienne Cartier. Boyd, James, 5795
Sir Walter Raleigh. Lacey, Robert, 5221
Sir Walter Scott, the Great Unknown. Johnson, Edgar, 3964
Sirkin, Leslie K. see Seyfert, Carl K.
Sisterhood Is Powerful. Morgan, Robin, ed, 982
SITTING BULL, 6015
Sitting Bull, Champion of the Sioux. Vestal, Stanley, 6015
Situation Ethics. Fletcher, Joseph, 754
Sitwell, Edith, ed. The Atlantic Book of British and American Poetry, 3783
──. Collected Poems of Edith Sitwell, 3840
SITWELL, EDITH, 3836
Six Crises. Nixon, Richard M, 6158
Six Non Lectures. Cummings, E. E, 3757
Six Plays. Odets, Clifford, 3683
Six Plays. Rodgers, Richard and Hammerstein, Oscar, 2nd. 3675

Six Plays. Sheridan, Richard B, 3876
Six Scandinavian Novelists. Gustafson, Alrik, 4086
Six Soviet One-Act Plays. Patrick, Ludmilla A, 4540
Sixth Sense of Animals. Burton, Maurice, 2344
Sizer, Theodore R. Places for Learning, Places for Joy, 1765
Sjolander, Sverre. see Fichtelius, Karl-Erik
SKATING, 3415-3416
Skeat, Walter W., ed. Etymological Dictionary of the English Language, 159
SKIIS AND SKIING, 3418-3420
Skilling, H. Gordon. The Governments of Communist East Europe, 1159
SKIN DIVING, 3434-3438
Skinner, Brian J. see Flint, Richard F.
Skinner, Burrhus F. Beyond Freedom and Dignity, 562
Skinner, Cornelia O. Madame Sarah, 3306
Sky Pirates. Arey, James A, 1719
SKYDIVING, 3444
Slack, A. V. Defense Against Famine, 2776
Slater, Mary. The Caribbean Islands, 4805
Slater, Philip E. The Pursuit of Loneliness, 5871
Slaughter the Animals, Poison the Earth. Olsen, Jack, 2827
Slave Community. Blassingame, John W, 6200
Slave Economy of the Old South. Phillips, Ulrich B, 1424
SLAVE NARRATIVES, 1002
SLAVE TRADE, 1239, 1792, 5730
Slavery. Elkins, Stanley M, 1283
Slavery Defended. McKitrick, Eric L., ed, 1286
SLAVERY IN THE U. S., 1002-1004, 1039, 1055-1057, 1224-1225, 1234, 1238, 1271, 1281-1290, 1424, 1431, 6013, 6200, 6208, 6211, 6213
SLAVS — HISTORY, 5285
SLEEP, 2528
Sleep and Dreams. Silverstein, Alvin and Silverstein, Virginia. 2528
Sleepwalkers. Koestler, Arthur, 701
Slive, Seymour. Frans Hals, 3072
Sloane, Eugene A. The New Complete Book of Bicycling, 3401
Sloane, Howard N. and Sloane, Lucille L. A Pictorial History of American Mining, 2666
Sloane, Lucille L. see Sloane, Howard N.
Small Arms of the World. Smith, Joseph E, 2673
Small, William J. Political Power and the Press, 1263
Smart, Charles A. Viva Juarez, 5814

INDEX

Smarter Than Man? Intelligence in Whales, Dolphins and Humans. Fichtelius, Karl-Erik and Sjolander, Sverre. 2457
Smeaton, Oliphant. Longfellow and His Poetry, 3560
Smellie, K. B. Great Britain Since 1688, 5175
Smiley, D. see Hesseltine, William B.
Smirnitsky, A. I. Russian-English Dictionary, 189
Smith, Adam. Wealth of Nations, 1403
Smith, Alexander G. Radio Exploration of the Sun, 2006
Smith, Alexander H. The Mushroom Hunter's Field Guide, 2331
SMITH, ALFRED EMANUEL, 6126
SMITH, BESSIE, 3228
Smith, Bradley. Japan, 2933
———. Spain, 3066
Smith, Bradley and Weng, Wan-Go. China, 2931
Smith, Bradley F. Heinrich Himmler, 5325
Smith, Burt. Offensive and Defensive Football, 3360
Smith, C. T. An Historical Geography of Western Europe Before 1800, 4706
Smith, C. U. Molecular Biology, 2229
Smith, Chard. Where the Light Falls, 3586
Smith, Colin, ed. Poema de Mio Cid, 4333
Smith, Craig R. and Hunsaker, David M. The Bases of Argument, 3492
Smith, Duane A. Horace Tabor, 1369
Smith, Edwin. see Linklater, Eric
Smith, Elsdon C. New Dictionary of American Family Names, 432
Smith, F. Walton. The Seas in Motion, 2150
Smith, Frank E. The Politics of Conservation, 1469
Smith, Gene. Maximilian and Carlota, 5816
———. When the Cheering Stopped, 6121
Smith, Grahame J., et al. Our Ecological Crisis, 947
Smith, Horatio, ed. Columbia Dictionary of Modern European Literature, 328
Smith, Howard D. Chinese Religions from 1000 B. C. to the Present Day, 839
Smith, Huston, et al, eds. Great Religions of the World, 830
Smith, Irwin. Shakespeare's Globe Playhouse, 3870
SMITH, JOHN, 5909
SMITH, JOSEPH, 814
Smith, Joseph E. Small Arms of the World, 2673
Smith, Justin H. Our Struggle for the 14th Colony, 5791
Smith, Lacey B., ed. The Elizabethan World, 5231

Smith, Ralph B. Vietnam and the West, 5680
Smith, Rhea M. Spain, 5461
Smith, Richard F. Chemistry for the Million, 2072
Smith, Robert L. Ecology and Field Biology, 2237
Smith, Robert M. Illustrated History of Baseball, 3376
Smith, Welby. see Mattingly, Grayson
Smith, William G. and Wilson, F. B., eds. The Oxford Dictionary of English Proverbs, 155
Smith, William H. Napoleon III, 5411
Smithsonian Institute. Oehser, Paul H, 1915
SMOKING, 2550
Smolders, Peter L. Soviets in Space, 2761
SMUTS, JAN CHRISITAN, 5740
SNAKES, 2416, 2418-2419, 2822
Snakes. Kauffeld, Carl, 2822
Snakes of the American West. Shaw, Charles E. and Campbell, Sheldon. 2418
Snakes of the World. Stidworthy, John, 2419
Sniderman, Florence M. see Breed, Paul F.
Snodgrass, Anthony M. Arms and Armour of the Greeks, 1851
Snow, Charles P. Two Cultures and a Second Look, 458
Snow Country. Kawabata, Yasunari, 4609
Snow, Edgar. Red China Today, 5603
———. Red Star Over China, 5592
Snyder, Arthur. see Snyder, Paul
Snyder, Louis L. Dreyfus Case, 5414
———. Great Turning Points in History, 4673
Snyder, Paul and Snyder, Arthur. Knots and Lines Illustrated, 2687
So Shall Ye Reap. London, Joan and Anderson, Henry. 1444
Soaps. Edmondson, Madeleine and Rounds, David. 3284
Soaring. Carter, William T, 2723
SOCCER, 3358
Sochen, June. Movers and Shakers, 983
Sochinenia. Pasternak, Boris L, 4580
Social and Economic History of the Hellenistic World. Rostovtzeff, Mikhail, 4977
Social and Economic History of the Roman Empire. Rostovtzeff, Mikhail, 4945
SOCIAL BEHAVIOR IN ANIMALS, 2399
Social Behavior of the Bees. Michener, Charles D, 2399
Social Change in America. Cochran, Thomas, 927

INDEX

Social Change in Soviet Russia. Inkeles, Alex, 1091
SOCIAL CONFLICT, 1237
Social Contract. Ardrey, Robert, 2193
Social Darwinism in American Thought. Hofstadter, Richard, 884
SOCIAL EVOLUTION, 884
Social History of Art. Hauser, Arnold, 2881
A Social History of Music from the Middle Ages to Beethoven. Raynor, Henry, 3139
Social Life at Rome in the Age of Cicero. Fowler, William W, 4935
Social Man. Halacy, D. S., Jr, 892
SOCIAL SCIENCES — DICTIONARIES, 128
Social Sciences Index. 91
SOCIAL WORK, 1691, 1694
SOCIALISM, 894, 1207, 1482-1486, 1488-1489, 1491, 1677
Socialism and Revolution. Gorz, Andre, 1483
Socialism in America. Fried, Albert, ed, 1485
Socialism Since Marx. Kilroy-Silk, Robert, 1484
SOCIALIST PARTY, 1393, 1486
Socialist Party of America. Shannon, David A, 1393
Socialist Thought. Fried, Albert and Sanders, Ronald, eds. 1482
SOCIALIZATION, 2842
Society and Culture in America, 1830-1860. Nye, Russel B, 6011
Society and Democracy in Germany. Dahrendorf, Ralf, 1088
Society and Thought in America. Wish, Harvey, 5873
SOCIETY, PRIMITIVE, 2189, 2197
SOCIOLOGY, 888-890, 892, 937, 965, 1000, 1066-1067, 1253
SOCRATES, 608
SOFTBALL, 3375
Softball Rules in Pictures. McCrory, G. Jacobs, 3375
SOIL CONSERVATION, 2774
Soil Conservation in Perspective. Held, R. Burnell and Clawson, Marion. 2774
Sokel, Walter H. The Writer in Extremis, 3992
Sokolov, Yury M. Russian Folklore, 1838
SOLAR ENERGY, 2661-2662
Solar Energy for Man. Brinkworth, B. D, 2661
SOLAR SYSTEM, 1991, 1997
Soldier Kings. Nelson, Walter H, 5338
Soldiers. Hochhuth, Rolf, 4020
Soledad Brother. Jackson, George, 1736
Solem, Alan. The Shell Makers, 2384

Solo. Van Lawick, Hugo, 2473
Solomon, David. see Campbell, Elizabeth M.
Solzhenitsyn. Moody, Christopher, 4579
Solzhenitsyn, Aleksandr I. The Gulag Archipelago, 1918-1956, 1733
———. Izbrannoe, 4561
———. Stories and Prose Poems, 4562
SOLZHENITSYN, ALEKSANDR ISAEVICH, 4579
Solzman, Jack, ed. Years of Protest, 3534
Some Haystacks Don't Even Have Any Needle, and Other Complete Modern Poems. Dunning, Stephen and Lueders, Edward, eds. 3548
Some Ship Disasters and Their Causes. Barnaby, Kenneth C, 4690
Somerville, John. The Philosophy of Marxism, 556
Somewhere Else. Center for Curriculum Research, 92
Sonata de Primavera. Valle-Inclán, Ramón Del, 4334
Song and Dance Man. Gray, Michael, 3230
Song and Garden Birds of North America. Wetmore, Alexander, et al. 2432
Song of Igor's Campaign. Nabokov, Vladimir, tr, 4510
SONGS, 3195, 3216, 3220, 3233-3234
Songs of the American Theater, 1900-1971. Lewine, Richard and Alfred, Simon. 3214
Sonnenfeld, Albert, ed. Thirty-Six French Poems, 4141
Sootin, Harry. Gregor Mendel, 2300
Soper, A. and Paine, R. Art and Architecture of Japan, 2934
Sophoclean Tragedy. Bowra, Cecil M, 4451
SOPHOCLES, 4457
Sophocles. Whitman, Cedric H, 4457
Sorensen, Theodore. Kennedy, 6169
Sorenson, Thomas C. The World War, 1297
Sorin, Gerald. Abolitionism, 1238
Sorrell, Walter. Facets of Comedy, 3530
Sorrow Dance. Levertov, Denise, 3648
Sotheby Parke Bernet Staff. see Kelley, Austin P.
Soul-Force. Barrett, Leonard E, 871
Soul on Ice. Cleaver, Eldridge, 1017
Soule, Gardner. The Greatest Depths, 2145
Sound of Waves. Mishima, Yukio, 4619
SOUND-WAVES, 2038, 2408
Source Book for Medieval History. Thatcher, Oliver J. and McNeal, E. H. 5009

INDEX

A Source Book for Russian History from Early Times to 1917. Vernadsky, George, et al, eds. 5495
A Source Book in Chinese Philosophy. Chan, Wing-Tsit, 615
A Source Book in Physics. Magie, William F, 2035
Source Book in the History of Psychology. Herrnstein, Richard J. and Boring, Edwin G., eds. 566
Source Book in Theatrical History. Nagler, A. M, 3316
Source of Chinese Tradition. De Bary, William T., et al, eds. 5575
Sourcebook on Atomic Energy. Glasstone, Samuel, 2059
Sources and Documents Illustrating the American Revolution, 1764-1788, and the Formation of the Federal Constitution. Morison, Samuel E., ed, 5924
Sources of Indian Tradition. De Bary, William T., et al, eds. 5627
Sources of Japanese Tradition. De Bary, William T., et al, eds. 5614
Soustelle, Jacques. Daily Life Among the Aztecs, 5808
South Africa. Cope, John, 5734
SOUTH AFRICAN WAR, (1899-1902), 5741
South and the Sectional Conflict. Potter, David M, 6215
South and the Southerner. McGill, Ralph, 6210
South Asian Crisis. Jackson, Robert V, 5637
SOUTH CAROLINA — HISTORY
　CIVIL WAR, 6043
　SOURCES, 5994
South in American History. Hesseltine, William B. and Smiley, D. 6209
Southeast Asia. Dobby, Ernest H. G, 4789
Southeast Asia, 1930-1970. Von Der Mebhen, Fred R, 5674
Southeast Asian World. Buchanan, Keith, 5672
Southern Africa Since Eighteen Hundred. Denoon, Donald, 1098
Southern Editorials on Secession. Dumond, Dwight L., ed, 6044
SOUTHERN STATES, 6213
　CIVILIZATION, 4835, 6201-6204, 6207, 6217-6218
　ECONOMIC CONDITIONS, 1121, 1424-1425, 6211
　HISTORY, 607, 6205-6206
　　SOURCES, 6214
　INDUSTRIES, 1426
　POLITICS AND GOVERNMENT, 4835, 6085, 6212

Southey, Robert. Life of Nelson, 5254
SOUTHWEST, NEW — HISTORY, 6220-6221, 6243
Southwest Pacific. Grattan, C. Hartley, 6281
Sovereign State of ITT. Sampson, Anthony, 1801
Sovereign States 1775-1783. Main, Jackson T, 5919
Soviet and American Society. Hollander, Paul, 1090
Soviet and Chinese Communism. Treadgold, Donald W, 1490
Soviet Bloc. Brzezinski, Zbigniew, 4676
Soviet Crucible. Hendel, Samuel, 1145
Soviet Education. Bowen, James, 1757
Soviet Literature in the Sixties. Hayward, Max and Crowley, E. L., eds. 4585
Soviet Marxism and Natural Science, 1917-1932. Joravsky, David, 1910
Soviet Philosophy. Blakeley, Thomas J, 675
Soviet Russian Verse. Milner-Gulland, Robin, ed, 4523
Soviet Union. Salisbury, Harrison E., ed, 5531
Soviets in Space. Smolders, Peter L, 2761
Sowing the Wind. Wellford, Harrison, 2516
Sox and Martin Book of Drag Racing. Sox, Ronnie, et al. 3407
Sox, Ronnie, et al. Sox and Martin Book of Drag Racing, 3407
Space-Age Photographic Atlas. Fitzgerald, Ken, compiled by. 397
SPACE FLIGHT — U. S., 2633
SPACE FLIGHT TO MARS, 1920, 1999
SPACE FLIGHT TO THE MOON, 2762-2763, 2765-2767
Spacetime Physics. Taylor, Edwin F. and Wheeler, John A. 2054
Spaghetti City Video Manual. Videofreex (Organization) 3117
SPAIN, 4735, 4760, 5455-5456, 5458-5459, 5892, 6246
　HISTORY, 5219, 5224, 5457-5458, 5461-5463, 5466-5467, 5469-5471, 5473, 5475
　POLITICS AND GOVERNMENT, 5465, 5468, 5472, 5474
Spain. De Madariaga, Salvador, 5458
Spain. Smith, Bradley, 3066
Spain. Smith, Rhea M, 5461
Spain and Portugal. Savory, Hubert N, 4735
Spain Under France. Gallo, Max, 5474
Spain 1808-1939. Carr, Raymond, 5465
Spalding, C. Sumner, ed. Anglo-American Cataloging Rules, 30

SPANISH AMERICA — CIVILIZATION, 4301
SPANISH-AMERICAN DRAMA, 4358
SPANISH-AMERICAN LITERATURE
  DICTIONARIES, 375
  HISTORY AND CRITICISM, 4314, 4317
SPANISH-AMERICAN POETRY, 4302, 4339
Spanish-American Poetry. Resnick, Seymour, 4339
Spanish American Revolutions, 1808-1826. Lynch, John, 6261
Spanish Armadas. Graham, Winston, 5219
Spanish Book Corp. of America. Spanish Books, 16
Spanish Books. Spanish Book Corp. of America, 16
Spanish Bourbons. Bergamini, John D, 5462
Spanish Civil War. Thomas, Hugh, 5469
Spanish Conquistadors. Kirkpatrick, Frederick A, 6260
Spanish-Cuban-American War and the Birth of American Imperialism, 1895-1902. Foner, Philip S, 6096
SPANISH DRAMA, 4359-4361
  HISTORY AND CRITICISM, 4363-4364
Spanish Empire in America. Haring, Clarence H, 6256
SPANISH FICTION, 4379
  HISTORY AND CRITICISM, 4390-4391
Spanish Labyrinth. Brenan, Gerald, 5457
SPANISH LANGUAGE
  DICTIONARIES, 183-184
  ENCYCLOPEDIAS AND DICTIONARIES, 84
SPANISH LITERATURE, 4304-4305, 4307, 4393
  DICTIONARIES, 375
  HISTORY AND CRITICISM, 341, 4308-4313, 4315-4316
SPANISH MAIN, 4693
SPANISH POETRY, 4322, 4335-4336, 4338, 4340
  HISTORY AND CRITICISM, 4342
Spanish Republic and the Civil War, 1931-1939. Jackson, Gabriel, 5470
Spann, Marcella, see Pound, Ezra
Sparks, Merrill, see Markov, Vladimir
Sparrow, John. Robert Bridges, 3841
Sparta. Michell, Humphrey, 4978
Speak for Yourself, Daniel. Webster, Daniel, 5980
Speak, Memory. Nabokov, Vladimir, 3763
Spear, Allan H. Black Chicago, 1037
Spear, Percival. India, a Modern History, 5630

Spearheads for Reform. Davis, Allen F, 1703
Spectacle. Prévert, Jacques, 4177
Specter, David K. Urban Spaces, 2956
SPEECH, 3491
Speech Index. Sutton, Roberta B, 337
Speech Index. Sutton, Roberta B. and Mitchell, Charity. 338
Speeches. Cicero, Marcus Tullius, 4420
SPEECHES — INDEXES, 337-338
Speed Culture. Grinspoon, Lester and Hedblom, Peter. 2579
Speed of Darkness. Rukeyser, Muriel, 3659
Speer, Albert. Inside the Third Reich, 5326
Spellbound in Darkness. Pratt, George C, 3262
Spence, James and Brown, Gar. Motorcycle Racing in America, 3408
Spence, Jonathan D. Emperor of China, 5585
Spencer, Donald. Computers in Action, 471
Spender, Stephen. Collected Poems, 3851
Spengler, Oswald. The Decline of the West, 4674
Spenser, Edmund. Complete Poetical Works, 3794
Spevack, Marvin. The Harvard Concordance to Shakespeare, 370
Spielberg, Peter, see Galin, Saul
Spiller, Robert E., ed. The American Literary Revolution, 1783-1837, 3543
———. Literary History of the United States, 357
Spinoza, Benedict. Chief Works, 679
Spirit of Russia. Masaryk, Thomas G, 5489
Spirit of St. Louis. Lindbergh, Charles A, 2716
Spirit of Survival. Hay, John, 2435
Spirit of '76. Commager, Henry S. and Morris, Richard B., eds. 5931
Spirit Soldiers. O'Connor, Richard, 5584
Spiritual Reformers of the 16th and 17th Centuries. Jones, Rufus, 4869
Spirituals and the Blues. Cone, James H, 3239
Spirt, Diana L. see Gillespie, John T.
Splaver, Sarah. Nontraditional College Routes to Careers, 1781
Splendid Century. Lewis, Warren H, 5382
Splendid Little War. Freidel, Frank, 6097
Splendor at Court. Strong, Roy, 3287
Splendor of Israel. Payne, Robert, 4785
Splendors of Asia. Gary, Dorothy H. and Payne, Robert. 4773
Splendour That Was Egypt. Murray, Margaret A, 4893

INDEX

Spock, Benjamin M. Decent and Indecent, 1082
Spolin, Viola. Improvization for the Theatre, 3295
Sport, Culture and Society. Loy, John W., Jr. and Kenyon, Gerald S., eds. 920
Sport Parachuting. Ryan, Charles W, 3444
SPORTS, 920, 2623, 3348-3350, 4957
  DICTIONARIES, 318, 320
  ENCYCLOPEDIAS, 319, 321
Sports Car. Campbell, Colin, 2750
Sports Illustrated Editors. Sports Illustrated Swimming and Diving, 3432
Sports Illustrated Skin Diving and Snorkeling. Allen, Barry, 3434
Sports Illustrated Swimming and Diving. Sports Illustrated Editors, 3432
SPORTS MEDICINE, 2622
Spotte, Stephen. Marine Aquarium Keeping, 2821
Spraggett, Allen. The Case for Immortality, 542
Sprague, Rosemary. Imaginary Poets, 3544
SQUASH RACKETS, 3365
SQUIDS, 2388
Staar, Richard F., ed. Yearbook on International Communist Affairs, 140
Stacks, John F. Stripping, 2667
Stacy, C. P., ed. Historical Documents of Canada, 1914-1945, 5799
Stadler, Karl R. Austria, 5347
Stage Costume Design. Russell, Douglas A, 3304
Stage Left. Williams, Jay, 3321
STAGE LIGHTING, 3302
Stage Makeup. Corson, Richard, 3305
Stages of Human Evolution. Brace, C. Loring, 2278
Stakes of Power. Nichols, Roy F, 6010
Stalin. Deutscher, Isaac, 5517
Stalin. Ulam, Adam B, 5527
Stalin and His Generals. Bialer, Seweryn, ed, 5113
Stalin As Revolutionary, 1879-1929. Tucker, Robert C, 5526
STALIN, JOSEPH VISSARIONVICH, 5113, 5509, 5517, 5526-5527
Stalking the Far Away Places. Gibbons, Euell, 1901
Stalking the Good Life. Gibbons, Euell, 2321
Stalking the Healthful Herbs. Gibbons, Euell, 2320
Stallings, Constance L., see Mitchell, John G.
Stallman, Robert W. see West, Ray Benedict
Stallybrass, Oliver, ed. Aspects of E. M. Forster, 3930

Stambler, Irwin and London, Grelun. Encyclopedia of Folk, Country and Western Music, 307
Stampp, Kenneth M., ed. The Causes of the Civil War, 6040
———. Era of Reconstruction, 6075
———. The Peculiar Institution, 1056
Stampp, Kenneth M. and Litwack, Leon F., eds. Reconstruction, 6076
Standard Catalog of World Coins. Krause, Chester L. and Mishler, Clifford, eds. 283
Standard Dictionary of Folklore, Mythology and Legend. Leach, Maria, ed, 154
Standard Handbook for Mechanical Engineers. Baumeister, T. and Marks, Lionel. 254
Standard Handbook of Saltwater Fishing. Scharff, Robert, 3454
Stanford, William B. Ulysses Theme, 4467
Stanford, William B. and Luce, John V. The Quest for Ulysses, 2888
Stangos, Nikos, see Richardson, Tony
Stanier, Roger Y., et al. Microbial World, 2304
Stanislavski, Constantin. An Actor Prepares, 3296
Stanley. Hall, Richard S, 4794
STANLEY, HENRY MORTON, 4794
Stanton. Thomas, Benjamin P. and Hyman, Harold M. 6037
STANTON, EDWIN MCMASTERS, 6037
Stanton, Frank M. Anglo-Saxon England, 5190
Stanyon, Ellis. Card Tricks for Everyone, 3347
Stapler, Harry. The Student Journalist and Sportswriting, 488
Star Names. Allen, Richard H, 2008
Starkie, Enid. Flaubert, 4251
Starr, Chester G. Ancient Greeks, 4962
———. Civilization and the Caesars, 4947
———. A History of the Ancient World, 4881
Starr, Paul. The Discarded Army, 1672
Starr, Richard F. The Communist Regimes in Eastern Europe, 1160
STARS, 2008
Starting from San Francisco. Ferlinghetti, Lawrence, 3639
STARVATION, 2773
STATE GOVERNMENTS, 1649
STATES RIGHTS, 1583
States Rights Debate. Mason, Alpheus Thomas, 1583
Statesman's Yearbook. 129
STATESMEN, 1330, 4863, 6103
Statistical Abstract of the United States. U. S. Bureau of the Census, 132

INDEX

STATISTICS, 58, 129, 131, 477, 1794, 1955-1956
Statistics. Silverman, Eliot N. and Brody, Linda A. 1955
Statistics. Tanur, Judith, et al, eds. 1956
Statistics Sources. Wasserman, Paul and Paskar, Joanne, eds. 58
Staying on Alone. Toklas, Alice B, 3760
Stearns, Peter N. Eighteen Forty-Eight, 5062
Stebbins, G. Ledyard. Processes of Organic Evolution, 2283
Steck, Allen and Tejada-Flores, Lito. Wilderness Skiing, 3417
Steffens, Joseph L. The Shame of the Cities, 1626
STEFFENS, JOSEPH LINCOLN, 502, 3758
Steffens, Lincoln. Autobiography, 502
Stegner, Wallace, ed. The American Novel, 3713
Stegner, Wallace. The Writer's Art, 3515
Steichen, Edward. The Family of Man, 3124
———. A Life in Photography, 3125
Steiger, Brad. Medicine Power, 876
Stein, George H. The Waffen S.S. Hitler's Elite Guard at War, 1939-1945, 5327
STEIN, GERTRUDE, 3760, 3762, 3765
Steinbeck and His Critics. Tedlock, Ernest and Wicker, Cecil. 3738
Steinbeck Country. Crouch, Steve, 4838
Steinbeck, John. America and Americans, 4817
———. Travels with Charley, 4818
STEINBECK, JOHN, 3738
Steinberg, Alfred. The Bosses, 1202
Steinberg, Leo. Other Criteria, 2913
Steinberg, Stephen. see Selznick, Gertrude J.
Steindorff, George and Seele, Keith C. When Egypt Ruled the East, 4894
Steiner, George. Language and Silence, 3464
Steiner, George and Fagles, Robert, eds. Homer, 4468
Steiner, Stan and Witt, Shirley. The Way, 4640
Steiner, Stanley. La Raza, 1046
Steinhauer, Harry and Walter, Felix, eds. Omnibus of French Literature, 4117
Steinilber-Oberlin, Emile. The Buddhist Sects of Japan, 840
Stendhal. La Chartreuse de Parme, 4252
———. Le Rouge et le Noir, 4253
Stendhal; or the Pursuit of Happiness. Josephson, Matthew, 4283
Stensland, Anna L. Literature by and about the American Indian, 75
Stepanchev, Stephen. American Poetry Since 1945, 3545

Stepanian, Michael. Pot Shots, 1597
Stephen A. Douglas. Johannsen, Robert W, 6023
Stephen, David. Dolphins, Seals, and Other Sea Mammals, 2456
Stephenson, Anne. see Stephenson, T. A.
Stephenson, T. A. and Stephenson, Anne. Life Between Tidemarks on Rocky Shores, 2260
Der Steppenwolf. Hesse, Hermann, 4055
STEREOPHONIC SOUND SYSTEMS, 2654-2657
Stern, Curt. Principles of Human Genetics, 2203
Stern, Philip M. and Green, Harold P. The Oppenheimer Case, 1715
Stern, Philip V. Prologue to Sumter, 6041
Sternfeld, Frederick W. Music from the Middle Ages to the Renaissance, 3143
———. Music in the Modern Age, 3151
Stevens, Leonard A. Clean Water, 2704
Stevens, Paul. I Can Sell You Anything, 2859
Stevens, Peter S. Patterns in Nature, 1894
Stevens, Wallace. Collected Poems of Wallace Stevens, 3587
STEVENSON, ADLAI EWING, 6161
Stevenson, Burton E. Home Book of Bible Quotations, 101
———. The Home Book of Modern Verse, 3784
———. Home Book of Quotations, 340
———. The Home Book of Verse, American and English, 366
Stewart, George R. Not So Rich As You Think, 2697
Stewart, J. I. Rudyard Kipling, 3965
Stewart, John H. A Documentary Survey of the French Revolution, 5399
Stewart, Lawrence D. see Jablonski, Edward
Sticks and Stones. Mumford, Lewis, 2968
Stidworthy, John. Snakes of the World, 2419
Stikhovoreniia Poemy. Mayakovski, Vladimir, 4509
Still, Henry. The Dirty Animal, 2698
———. Of Time, Tides, and Inner Clocks, 2224
Still Hungry in America. Coles, Robert and Clayton, Al. 997
Still, William. The Underground Railroad, 1057
Stiller, Richard. The Love Bugs, 2616
Die Stimme Hinter dem Vorhang. Benn, Gottfried, 4010
Stinsons. Underwood, John W, 2719
Stix, Hugh and Stix, Marguerite. The Shell, 2387
Stix, Marguerite. see Stix, Hugh

INDEX

Stock, Dennis. *see* Hedgepeth, William
STOCK EXCHANGE, 1457
Stock Market Behavior. Krow, Harvey, 1457
Stock, Noel. Life of Ezra Pound, 3588
Stoic and Epicurean Philosophers. Oates, Whitney J, 626
Stokes, F. G. Dictionary of the Characters and Proper Names in the Works of Shakespeare, 371
Stolen Apples. Yevtushenko, Yevgeny, 4517
STONE AGE, 4712, 4722
Stone Age Hunters. Clark, Grahame, 4712
Stone, Irving. Clarence Darrow for the Defense, 1611
──── . Jack London, Sailor on Horseback, 3736
──── . Men to Match My Mountains, 6239
Stone, Isidor F. Hidden History of the Korean War, 5613
Stone, Wilfred. The Cave and the Mountain, 3948
Stonehenge Decoded. Hawkins, Gerald S, 5184
Stonehouse, Bernard. Animals of the Antarctic, 2375
──── . Animals of the Arctic, 2376
──── . Young Animals, 2349
Stoneman, Elryn. *see* Hodgson, Robert D.
Stoppard, Tom. Rosencrantz and Guildenstern Are Dead, 3915
Storer, Tracy I. and Usinger, Robert L. General Zoology, 2336
Storey, Eric. *see* Dickens, Michael
Storey, Robin L. Chronology of the Medieval World, 381
Stories and Prose Poems. Solzhenitsyn, Aleksandr I, 4562
Storm, Theodor. Immensee, 4069
──── . Werke in Zwei Banden, 3979
Storms and Man. Ross, Frank, Jr, 2152
Storr, Anthony. C. G. Jung, 563
──── . The Dynamics of Creation, 575
Story of Art. Gombrich, Ernst H, 2896
Story of Indonesia. Fischer, Louis, 6282
Story of Ireland. O'Brien, Connor C. and O'Brien, Maire. 5162
Story of J. Robert Oppenheimer. Royal, D, 2062
Story of Man. Coon, Carleton S, 2186
Story of Medicine in America. Marks, Geoffrey and Beatty, William K. 2502
Story of Philosophy. Durant, Will, 514
Story of the English Language. Pei, Mario, 1868
Story of the Gypsies. Bercovici, Konrad, 4682

Story of the Olympic Games. Kieran, John and Daley, Arthur. 3385
Story of the War in South Africa. Mahan, Alfred T, 5741
Storyteller without Words. Ward, Lynd K, 3094
Stout, Neil R. The Royal Navy in America, 1760-1775, 5943
Strahler, Alan H. *see* Strahler, Arthur N.
Strahler, Arthur N. and Strahler, Alan H. Environmental Geoscience, 2099
Strang, Barbara. A History of English, 1870
Strange Alliance. Deane, John R, 5109
Strange Career of Jim Crow. Woodward, C. Vann, 1275
Strange Story of the Quantum. Hoffman, Banesh, 2032
Strange Vigor. Martin, Bernard, 5590
Stranger Stop and Cast an Eye. Jacobs, G. Walker, 3088
Strangers and Exiles. Norwood, Frederick A, 793
STRATEGIC ARMS LIMITATION TALKS, 1300
Stratmann, Francis H. Middle-English Dictionary, 174
STRAUSS, RICHARD, 3173
STRAVINSKII, IGOR FEDOROVICH, 3180
Stravinsky, Igor. Autobiography, 3180
Strawberry Statement. Kunen, James S, 1785
STREAM ECOLOGY — U. S., 2241
Streetcar Named Desire. Williams, Tennessee, 3711
Strenuous Decade. Aaron, Daniel and Bendiner, Robert, eds. 6130
Strictly Speaking. Newman, Edwin, 914
Stride Toward Freedom. King, Martin Luther, Jr, 1027
STRIKES AND LOCKOUTS, 1448
Strindberg, August. Eight Famous Plays, 4089
──── . Plays, 4090
Stringham, Edwin John. Listening to Music Creatively, 3132
STRIP MINING, 2667
Stripping. Stacks, John F, 2667
Strong Man of China. Berkov, Robert, 5594
Strong, Roy. Splendor at Court, 3287
Stroup, Herbert H. Founders of Living Religions, 687
Structure of American English. Francis, W. N, 1878
Structure of Canadian Government. Mallory, James R, 1190

Structure of the Human Body. Gardner, Weston D. and Osburn, William A. 2504
Struggle Against Fascism in Germany. Trotsky, Leon, 1501
Struggle for Cyprus. Foley, Charles and Scobie, W. I. 5656
Struggle for Mastery in Europe. Taylor, Alan J. P, 5063
Struik, Dirk J. A Concise History of Mathematics, 1944
Strunk, William S., Jr. and White, E. B. The Elements of Style, 3470
Struve, Gleb. Russian Literature Under Lenin and Stalin, 1917-1953, 4499
Stuart, Duane Reed. Epochs of Greek and Roman Biography, 4434
STUART, GILBERT, 3048
STUART, JAMES EWELL BROWN, 6050
Student Journalist and Reviewing the Performing Arts. Singer, Samuel L, 487
Student Journalist and Sportswriting. Stapler, Harry, 488
STUDENT MOVEMENTS — U. S., 1226, 1233, 1783-1784
Students Without Teachers. Taylor, Harold, 1782
Studies in Christian Existentialism. MacQuarrie, John, 739
Studies in Economics. 1427
Studies in History and Politics. 1653
Studies in Medieval and Renaissance Music. Bukofzer, Manfred F, 3145
Studies in Opposition. Barker, Rodney, ed, 1220
Studies in the Institutional History of Early Modern Japan. Hall, John W., et al, eds. 5615
A Study of History. Toynbee, Arnold J, 4648
Study of Society. Rose, Peter I, 889
Study of Urban Geography. Carter, Harold, 960
Sturgis, Alice F. Learning Parliamentary Procedure, 1357
———. Sturgis' Standard Code of Parliamentary Procedure, 1358
Sturgis' Standard Code of Parliamentary Procedure. Sturgis, Alice F, 1358
STYRON, WILLIAM, 3742
Suares, Jean-Claude, ed. Art of the Times, 3009
Suarez, Andres. Cuba, 5837
Subject Collections. Ash, Lee, compiled by. 81
Subject Guide to Books in Print. 5
Subject Guide to Government Reference Books. Wynkoop, Sally, 2

Subject Was Roses, and About Those Roses. Gilroy, Frank, 3693
Subliminal Seduction. Key, Wilson B, 2856
SUBMARINE BOATS, 2683-2684, 2688, 5145
SUBMARINE GEOLOGY, 2146-2147
Subordinate Sex. Bullough, Vernl and Bullough, Bonnie. 976
SUBVERSIVE ACTIVITIES
 BOLIVIA, 1246-1247
 U. S., 1071, 1228, 6120
Subversive Vision. Hoffman, Michael J, 3541
Successful Terrariums. Kayatta, Ken and Schmidt, Steven. 2800
Suchlicki, Jaime. Cuba, 5838
Suez. Love, Kenneth, 5646
Suez. Thomas, Hugh, 5718
SUEZ CANAL, 1804, 5718
Sullivan, Michael. The Arts of China, 2932
SULLIVAN, (SIR) ARTHUR SEYMOUR, 3210, 3878
Sullivan, Walter. Continents in Motion, 2117
Sultans. Barber, Noel, 5555
Sulzberger, C. L. The American Heritage Picture History of World War II, 5122
———. The Coldest War, 1320
SUMERIANS, 4721, 4910, 4913-4914
Sumerians. Kramer, Samuel Noah, 4913
Sumerians. Woolley, Charles, 4914
Summerhill. Neill, Alexander S, 1771
SUMNER, CHARLES, 6029
SUN, 2004-2006
Sun and Its Influence. Ellison, M. A, 2004
Sun Beneath the Sea. Piccard, Jacques, 2149
Sun King. Mitford, Nancy, 5384
SUN YAT-SEN, 5590
Sunday Times, London. The Yom Kippur War, 5652
Sunshine Boys. Simon, Neil, 3705
Supership. Mostert, Noel, 1805
Supplement to the Oxford English Dictionary. Burchfield, R. W., ed, 163
Suppression of the African Slave Trade, 1638-1870. DuBois, William E, 1792
Supreme Court and Its Great Justices. Asch, Sidney H, 1605
Supreme Court and Religion. Morgan, Richard E, 1584
Supreme Court and the Idea of Progress. Bickel, Alexander M, 1614
Supreme Court in U. S. History. Warren, Charles, 1621
Surer, Paul. see Castex, Pierre-Georges
SURF RIDING, 3431
Surfing. Nelson, William D, 3431

INDEX

SURGERY, 2621
SURINAM — DESCRIPTION AND TRAVEL, 2825
Suroweicki, John. Pulse of the Planet, 196
SURREALISM, 3033-3034
Surrealists. Gaunt, William, 3033
SURTSEY, 2231
Surtsey. Fridriksson, S, 2231
Surtsey. Thorarinsson, Sigurdur, 2119
A Survey of European Civilization. Ferguson, Wallace K. and Bruun, Geoffrey. 4988
A Survey of French Literature. Mason, Germaine, 4112
Survey of the Sino-Soviet Dispute. Gittings, John, ed, 1316
SURVIVAL (AFTER AIRPLANE ACCIDENTS, SHIPWRECKS ETC.), 2531, 2534, 6274
Survival Handbook. Merrill, W. K, 2535
Survival of the Wisest. Salk, Jonas E, 525
Sussman, Aaron. The Amateur Photographer's Handbook, 3105
Sutcliffe, Bob. *see* Glyn, Andrew
Sutton, Ann. Yellowstone Park, 1904
Sutton, Ann and Sutton, Myron. The Wilderness World of the Grand Canyon, 1906
Sutton, Elton H. Introduction to Human Genetics, 2204
Sutton, Myron. *see* Sutton, Ann
Sutton, Roberta B. Speech Index, 337
Sutton, Roberta B. and Mitchell, Charity. Speech Index, 338
Swami and Friends and The Bachelor of Arts. Narayan, R. K, 4485
Swan, Lester. Beneficial Insects, 2777
Swan, Lester' and Papp, Charles S. The Common Insects of North America, 2394
Swanberg, W. A. Citizen Hearst, 494
―――. Dreiser, 3737
―――. Luce and His Empire, 491
Swans. Scott, Peter and Wildfowl Trust. 2436
Swans of the World. Wilmore, Sylvia B, 2437
Swanson, Carl P. The Natural History of Man, 2191
Swastika and the Eagle. Compton, James V, 1304
Swazy, Judith P. *see* Fox, Renee C.
SWEDEN, 5535, 5540-5541
Sweden. Scobbie, Irene, 5541
SWEDISH DRAMA, 4089
Sweeney, James J., *see* Radin, Paul
Sweezy, Paul. Modern Capitalism and Other Essays, 1408
Swenson, May. To Mix with Time, 3665

Swieker, Carl B. The Growth of Constitutional Power in the United States, 1587
SWIMMING, 2570, 3421, 3432-3433
Swinburne, Algernon C. Selected Poetry and Prose, 3831
Swindler, William F. Court and Constitution in the Twentieth Century, 1619
Swing Out. Fernett, Gene, 3242
Swinger of Birches. Cox, Sidney, 3597
Swinton, William E. Dinosaurs. , 2182
SWITZERLAND — INTELLECTUAL LIFE — HISTORY, 4753
Sword and the Scepter. Ritter, Gerhard, 1164
Sydenham, M. J. The First French Republic, 1792-1804, 5400
Sylvester, David. Henry Moore, 2982
SYMBOLISM, 54, 1845-1846, 3088
Syme, Ronald. Roman Revolution, 4939
Symonds, John A. Shakespeare's Predecessors in the English Drama, 3856
Symphonic Music. Ulrich, Homer, 3241
La Symphonie Pastorale. Gide, André, 4217
SYMPHONY, 3240-3241
Symphony, 1800-1900. Lang, Paul H., ed, 3240
Synergetics. Fuller, R. Buckminster, 644
Synge, John M. Complete Works. , 3879
Synge, Patrick M. *see* Hay, Roy
SYSTEM THEORY, 644
Szulc, Tad. Czechoslovakia Since World War II, 5357
―――. The United States and the Carribean, 1102

TABOR, HORACE AUSTIN WARNER, 1369
Taborsky, Edward. Communism in Czechoslovakia, 1948-1960, 5358
Tacitus, Cornelius. Dialogus, Agricula, Germania, 4427
Taft, Philip. The A. F. of L. in the Time of Gompers, 1447
TAFT, WILLIAM HOWARD, 1638
Tagore, Rabindranath. The Broken Nest, 4488
―――. Sheaves, 4487
TAIPING REBELLION, 5588
Taiping Revolutionary Movement. Yu Wen, Jen, 5588
TAIWAN — HISTORY — SOURCES, 5604
Take Me Home. Price, Steven D, 3224
Takeuchi, H., et al. Debate About the Earth, 2113
Tale of Kieu. Nguyen, Du and Nguyen, Huynh-Sang. 4623

500

INDEX

Tale of the Reed Pipes. Farzan, Massaud, compiled by. 862
Tales of Ancient India. Van Buitenen, Johannes A. B, 1840
Tales of Power. Castaneda, Carlos, 874
Talese, Gay. The Kingdom and the Power, 503
Talking Your Way Around the World. Pei, Mario, 1862
Talleyrand. Bernard, Jack F, 5390
TALLEYRAND-PERIGORD, CHARLES MAURICE DE, 5390
Talman, James J. Basic Documents in Canadian History, 5794
TALMUD, 855
Tamiment Institute. The Future Metropolis, 971
Tammany. Mushkat, Jerome, 1378
TAMMANY HALL, 1137, 1378
Tan, Chester G. Boxer Catastrophe, 5586
Tan, Lek. see Caldwell, Malcolm
Tangerman, Elmer J. The Modern Book of Whittling and Woodcarving, 2991
Tank. Macksey, Kenneth and Batchelor, John H. 2679
TANK — VESSELS, 1805
Tank, Kurt L. Günter Grass, 4081
Tank, Ronald W., ed. Focus on Environmental Geology, 2103
TANKS (MILITARY SCIENCE), 2678-2679
Tannahill, Reay. Food in History, 2833
Tannenbaum, Frank. Mexico, 5821
Tanner, Chuck and Enright, Jim, eds. The Official Major League Baseball Playbook, 3377
Tansill, Charles Callan. America Goes to War, 5083
Tanur, Judith, et al, eds. Statistics, 1956
TAPE RECORDERS AND RECORDING, 2658
Tape Recording for the Hobbyist. Zuckerman, Art, 2658
TAPESTRY, 3022
Tapié, Victor L. The Rise and Fall of the Habsburg Monarchy, 5343
TARIFF — U. S. — HISTORY, 1797
Tariff History of the United States. Taussig, Frank W, 1797
Tarling, Don and Tarling, Maureen. Continental Drift, 2128
Tarling, Maureen. see Tarling, Don
TAROT, 533
Tarot. Douglas, Alfred, 533
Tartarin de Tarascon. Daudet, Alphonse, 4207
A Taste of Honey. Delaney, Shelagh, 3900
Tate, Allen. Jefferson Davis, 6047
———. Poems, 3589
Tatu, Michel. Power in the Kremlin, 1171

Taussig, Frank W. Tariff History of the United States, 1797
Tawney, Richard H. Religion and the Rise of Capitalism, 765
Taxonomy of Flowering Plants. Porter, Cedric L, 235
Taylor, Alan J. P. Bismarck, 5299
———. English History, 1914-1945, 5276
———. The Origins of the Second World War, 5106
———. Struggle for Mastery in Europe, 5063
Taylor, Alan J. P., see Bullock, Alan
Taylor, Alice, ed. Focus on Southeast Asia, 1095
Taylor, Basil. Constable, 3050
Taylor, Clif. GLM, 3418
Taylor, Edwin F. and Wheeler, John A. Spacetime Physics, 2054
Taylor, Harold. Students Without Teachers, 1782
———. The World As Teacher, 1754
Taylor, Henry O. Medieval Mind, 5008
Taylor, John, ed. Jane's Pocket Book of Commercial Transport Aircraft, 2729
———. Jane's Pocket Book of Major Combat Aircraft, 2676
———. Milestones of the Air, 2730
Taylor, John G. Black Holes, 1980
———. The New Physics, 2055
Taylor, John R. Penguin Dictionary of the Theatre, 347
———. Second Wave, 3888
Taylor, John W. Civil Aircraft of the World, 2731
Taylor, John W. and Taylor, Michael J. Missiles of the World, 1684
Taylor, L. B., Jr. For All Mankind, 2633
Taylor, Lily R. Party Politics in the Age of Caesar, 4940
Taylor, Lloyd W. Physics, the Pioneer Science, 2020
Taylor, Louis. Harper's Encyclopedia for Horsemen, 2808
Taylor, Michael J. see Taylor, John W.
Taylor, N. B. see Best, Charles H.
Taylor, Robert S. The Making of a Library, 22
Taylor, William R. Cavalier and Yankee, 6216
Taylour, William. The Mycenaeans, 4981
Tchaikovsky. Warrack, John H, 3162
TCHAIKOVSKY, PETER ILYICH, 3162
TEACHING, 1769-1770, 1772
Teaching Film Animation to Children. Andersen, Yvonne, 51
Teaching Tomorrow. Calkins, Elizabeth, 3919
Teachings of Don Juan. Castaneda, Carlos, 875

INDEX

Teal, John and Teal, Mildred. Life and Death of the Salt Marsh, 2244
Teal, Mildred. *see* Teal, John
Teatro Selecto. Sastre, Alfonso, 4363
Tebbel, John. *see* Pomeroy, Wardell B.
TECHNICAL EDUCATION — U. S. — DIRECTORIES, 1787
Technics and Human Development. Mumford, Lewis, 4653
Technique of Fine Art Lithography. Knigin, Michael and Zimiles, Murray. 3091
Technique of Screenplay Writing. Vale, Eugene, 3485
Techniques for Efficient Remembering. Laird, Donald A, 579
Techniques of Small Boat Racing. Walker, Stuart H., ed, 3430
Technological Growth and Social Change. Hetzler, Stanley A, 879
Technological Man. Ferkiss, Victor C, 918
TECHNOLOGY, 204, 879, 918, 921, 941, 1423, 1889, 1891, 2487, 2490-2492, 2494, 4652-4653
    DICTIONARIES, 201-202
Technology in the Ancient World. Hodges, Henry, 2490
Technology of Western Civilization. Kranzberg, Melvin and Pursell, Carroll W., Jr., eds. 2492
Tedlock, Ernest and Wicker, Cecil. Steinbeck and His Critics, 3738
Teilhard de Chardin. Braybrooke, Neville, 520
Teilhard de Chardin, Pierre. Christianity and Evolution, 697
———. The Phenomenon of Man, 521
TEILHARD DE CHARDIN, PIERRE, 520
Tejada-Flores, Lito. *see* Steck, Allen
TELESCOPE, 1975
Telescope Handbook and Star Atlas. Howard, Neale E, 1975
TELEVISION, 483, 1130, 1564, 1773, 2641, 2653, 3285
Tell Me Africa. Olney, James, 4627
Teller, James D. *see* Good, Harry G.
Teller, Walter M. Cape Cod and the Offshore Islands, 4830
Temime, Emile. *see* Broué, Pierre
Temple of the Golden Pavillion. Mishima, Yukio, 4620
Temple, Ruth Z. and Tucker, Martin A. Twentieth Century British Literature, 71
Ten Centuries of Spanish Poetry. Turnbull, Eleanor L., ed, 4340
Ten Days That Shook the World. Reed, John, 5523
Tenacity of Prejudice. Selznick, Gertrude J. and Steinberg, Stephen. 1052

TENEMENT HOUSES — NEW YORK (CITY), 969
Teng, Ssu-Yu. China's Response to the West, 1321
TENNIS, 3362-3364
Tennissen, A. Nature of Earth Materials, 2169
Tennyson. Buckley, Jerome, 3824
Tennyson, Alfred. Poetical Works, 3832
TENNYSON, ALFRED TENNYSON, 3824
Ter Horst, Jerald F. Gerald Ford, 6181
———. Gerald Ford and the Future of the Presidency, 6180
Terkel, Studs. Hard Times, 1118
———. Working, 1434
Terracide. Linton, Ron, 2707
Terrarium Book. Evans, Charles and Pliner, Roberta. 2799
TERRARIUMS, 2799-2801
Terre des Hommes. Saint Exupéry, Antoine de, 4249
Terrell, Mark. The Principles of Diving, 2695
Territorial Imperative. Ardrey, Robert, 2360
Teveth, Shabati. Moshe Dayan, 5669
TEXAS — HISTORY — TO 1846, 6224
Thaden, Edward C. Russia Since 1801, 5502
Thales to Dewey. Clark, Gordon H, 513
That Disgraceful Affair. Eby, Cecil D, 5993
Thatcher, Oliver J. and McNeal, E. H. The Source Book for Medieval History, 5009
Thayer, George. The War Business, 1796
———. Who Shakes the Money Tree? American Campaign Financing Practices from 1789 to the Present, 1386
Thayer, William R. The Life and Times of Cavour, 5441
THEATER, 3291-3294, 3319, 3677
    BIBLIOGRAPHY, 64
    DICTIONARIES, 315-317
    HISTORY, 3307-3310, 3312-3314, 3318, 3320-3321, 3287, 4450
        SOURCES, 3316
    PRODUCTION AND DIRECTION, 3298-3299
THEATER AS A PROFESSION, 3300
THEATER GUILD, 3315
THEATERS — STAGE-SETTING AND SCENERY, 3301
Theatre. Cheney, Sheldon, 3310
Théâtre. Cocteau, Jean, 4154

Théâtre. Sartre, Jean-Paul, 4183
Theatre and Allied Arts. Baker, Blanche M, 64
Theatre in the Round. Joseph, Stephen, 3294
Theatre Language, a Dictionary. Bowman, Walter P. and Ball, Robert H. 315
Theatre of Albert Camus. Freeman, E, 4189
Theatre of Bertolt Brecht. Willett, John, 4031
Theatre of Commitment and Other Essays on Drama in Our Society. Bentley, Eric, 3291
Theatre of Protest and Paradox. Wellrath, George E, 3513
Theatre of the Absurd. Esslin, Martin, 3526
Theft of the Nation. Cressey, Donald R, 1709
Themes in Greek and Latin Epitaphs. Lattimore, Richmond, 4433
Theodore Roosevelt. Pringle, Henry F, 6116
THEOLOGY, 681, 697-699, 737, 739, 743, 745, 747, 752, 788, 806
    DICTIONARIES, 99-100
Theory and Practice of Go. Korschelt, O, 3339
Theory of Comedy. Olson, Elder, 3483
Theory of Fiction. James, Henry, 3488
Theory of the Leisure Class. Veblen, Thorstein, 1404
There Could Have Been Peace. Kimche, Jon, 1322
Thérèse Desqueyroux. Mauriac, Francois, 4234
THERMODYNAMICS, 2043-2045
Thermodynamics. Faires, Virgil M, 2043
They Live by the Wind. Bradley, Wendell P, 2815
They Thought They Were Free. Mayer, Milton S, 5319
They Wrote on Clay. Chiera, Edward, 4720
Thiemer, Otto H. A Gentleman's Guide to Modern Physics, 2021
Thinking Metric. Gilbert, Thomas F. and Gilbert, Marilyn B. 1808
Third Arab-Israeli War. O'Ballance, Edgar, 5650
Third French Republic, 1870-1924. Sedgwick, Alexander, 5418
Third Rose. Brinnin, John M, 3762
Thirteen. Cooper, Henry S., Jr, 2766
Thirteen Days. Kennedy, Robert F, 6166
Thirty-Nine Poems. Ciardi, John, 3630
Thirty-Nine Steps to Biology. Scientific American Editors, 2220

Thirty-Six Children. Kohl, Herbert T, 1777
Thirty-Six French Poems. Sonnenfeld, Albert, ed, 4141
Thirty Years of Treason. Bentley, Eric, ed, 1228
THIRTY YEARS' WAR — 1618-1648, 5039
Thirty Years' War. Wedgwood, Cicely V, 5039
This Africa. Gleason, Judith I, 4632
This Country Was Ours. Vogel, Virgil J, 5756
This Cybernetic World of Men, Machines and Earth Systems. Parsegian, V. L, 461
This Fabulous Century. Time-Life Books Editors, 4819
This Hallowed Ground. Catton, Bruce, 6026
This Island Earth. Nicks, Oran W., ed, 2012
This Land Was Theirs. Oswalt, Wendell H, 5755
This Sun of York. Clive, Mary, 5209
This Was Toscanini. Antek, Samuel, 3245
This Way Out. Coyne, John and Hebert, Tom. 1780
THOMAS À BECKET, 5208
Thomas a Kempis. Of the Imitation of Christ, 760
THOMAS A KEMPIS, 760
Thomas Aquinas, St. Basic Writings, 699
THOMAS AQUINAS, 633
Thomas Becket. Winston, Richard, 5208
Thomas, Benjamin P. Abraham Lincoln, 6036
Thomas, Benjamin P. and Hyman, Harold M. Stanton, 6037
Thomas Cranmer. Ridley, Jasper, 796
Thomas, Dylan. Collected Poems, 3852
———. Under Milk Wood, 3916
THOMAS, DYLAN, 3849
Thomas Edison, Chemist. Vanderbilt, B. M, 2860
Thomas, Gordon and Witts, Max M. San Francisco Earthquake, 2121
Thomas, Hugh. Cuba, 5839
———. The Spanish Civil War, 5469
———. Suez, 5718
Thomas Jefferson and the New Nation. Petersen, Merrill D, 5974
Thomas, Lewis. The Lives of a Cell, 2218
Thomas Mann. Berendsohn, Walter A, 4078
Thomas Mann. Hatfield, Henry C, 4075
Thomas, Norman M. Great Dissenters, 4862
THOMAS, NORMAN MATTOON, 1486
Thomas Wolfe. Field, Leslie A., compiled by. 3716

INDEX

Thomas Wolfe. Turnbull, Andrew, 3739
Thomas Wolfe's Characters. Watkins, Floyd C, 3740
Thomas Wolsey, Late Cardinal. Cavendish, George, 5214
Thomason, John W. Jeb Stuart, 6050
Thompson, Francis. Poems, 3833
Thompson, James M. Leaders of the French Revolution, 5401
———. Louis Napoleon and the Second Empire, 5412
———. Napoleon Bonaparte, 5404
———. Robespierre and the French Revolution, 5402
Thompson, John E. Rise and Fall of the Maya Civilization, 5809
Thompson, Kenneth. Dictionary of Twentieth Century Composers, 62
Thompson, Lawrence R. Fire and Ice, 3620
———. Robert Frost, 3619
Thompson, Malcolm H. see Jastrow, Robert
Thomson, David. Democracy in France Since 1870, 5415
———. Europe Since Napoleon, 5064
———. France, 5416
Thomson, George M. Sir Francis Drake, 1690
Thomson, Virgil. American Music Since 1910, 3185
Thorarinsson, Sigurdur. Surtsey, 2119
Thoreau, Henry David. The Variorum Civil Disobedience, 1251
Thoreau's Vision. Anderson, Charles R., ed, 3750
Thorndike, Lynn. History of Medieval Europe, 5010
Thorne, J. O., ed. Chambers Biographical Dictionary, 418
Thornton, Ian. Darwin's Islands, 1908
Those Inventive Americans. National Geographic Society, ed, 2495
Thoughts on Small Boat Racing. Ogilvy, C. Stanley, 3429
Three Comedies. Goldoni, Carlo, 4293
Three Edwards. Costain, Thomas B, 5204
Three Faces of Fascism. Nolte, Ernest, 1151
Three Hundred Poems, 1903-1953. Jimenez, Juan Ramón, 4343
Three Nigerian Plays. Beier, Ulli, ed, 4631
Three Plays. Fry, Christopher, 3903
Three Plays. Rice, Elmer, 3686
Three Thousand Years of Black Poetry. Lomax, Alan and Abdul, Raoul, eds. 3498
Three Tragedies. García Lorca, Federico, 4355
Three Who Made a Revolution. Wolfe, Bertram D, 5509

Three Worlds of Boris Pasternak. Payne, Robert, 4557
Thresher Disaster. Bentley, John, 2688
Throckmorton, Peter. Shipwrecks and Archaeology, 4717
Through the Crust of the Earth. Everglyn, L, 2108
Through the Valley of the Kwai. Gordon, Ernest, 5148
Thucydides. History of the Peloponnesian War, 4973
Thurber. Bernstein, Burton, 3007
THURBER, JAMES, 3007
Thurston, Jacqueline and Carraher, Ronald G. Optical Illusions, 2885
Thus Spoke Zarathustra. Nietzsche, Friedrich W, 667
Thwaites, Reuben G. France in America, 1497-1763, 5787
Tiberius. Seager, Robin, 4949
TIBERIUS, EMPEROR OF ROME, 4949
TIDE POOL ECOLOGY, 2243
TIDES, 2150
Tides of Change. Borgese, Elisabeth Mann and Krieger, David, eds. 1557
Tierney, Brian. Western Europe in the Middle Ages, 300-1475, 5011
Tillich, Paul. The Courage to Be, 607
———. Dynamics of Faith, 695
Tillyard, Eustace M. Milton, 3802
Timberlake, James H. Prohibition and the Progressive Movement, 1900-1920, 606
TIME, 522
Time Atlas of the World. Bartholomew, John, ed, 395
Time Is Short and the Water Rises. Walsh, John and Gannon, Robert. 2825
Time-Life Book of the Family Car. Time-Life Books Editors, 2745
Time-Life Books Editors. This Fabulous Century, 4819
———. The Time-Life Book of the Family Car, 2745
———. Vanishing Species, 2341
Time-Life Library of Art. 3083
Time of Need. Barrett, William, 4655
Time of the Buffalo. McHugh, Tom, 2464
Time on the Cross. Fogel, Robert W. and Engerman, Stanley L. 1431
Time Out of Hand. Shaplen, Robert, 5673
A Time to Speak, a Time to Act. Bond, Julian, 1240
Times Three. McGinley, Phyllis, 3577
Times to Remember. Kennedy, Rose F, 6167
Tin Drum. Grass, Gunther, 4053
Tingsten, Herbert L. Victoria and the Victorians, 5264
Tiny Alice. Albee, Edward, 3689
Titania. Migel, Parmenia, 4093

TITANIC (STEAMSHIP), 4698
Tito. Auty, Phyllis, 5562
TITO, JOSIP BROZ, 5562
Tito's Separate Road. Campbell, John C, 5563
To Be Young, Gifted and Black. Nemiroff, Robert, ed, 3701
To Die for the People. Newton, Huey P, 1230
To Live on Earth. Brubaker, Sterling, 940
To Mix with Time. Swenson, May, 3665
To Move a Nation. Hilsman, Roger, 1341
To Purge This Land with Blood. Oates, Stephen B, 6012
To See a World. Harrington, John W, 2101
To the Finland Station. Wilson, Edmund, 1498
To the Hartford Convention. Banner, James M., Jr, 1375
To the Yalu. McGovern, James, 5611
To Walk in Seasons. Cohen, William H, 4614
Tobacco and Your Health. Diehl, Harold S, 2550
Der Tod in Venedig und Andere Erzahlungen. Mann, Thomas, 4067
Today and Tomorrow and ... Asimov, Isaac, 1918
Today's Isms. Ebenstein, William, 1207
Todd, Alden. Finding Facts Fast, 82
———. Justice on Trial, 1620
Todd, David K., ed. The Water Encyclopedia, 226
Toffler, Alvin. Future Shock, 913
———. Learning for Tomorrow, 1755
Toklas, Alice B. Staying on Alone, 3760
TOKLAS, ALICE B., 3760
Tokle, Art and Luray, Martin. Complete Guide to Cross-Country Skiing and Touring, 3419
Toland, John. The Great Dirigibles, 1806
———. The Last Hundred Days, 5137
———. The Rising Sun, 5119
Tolerance and Truth in Religion. Mensching, Gustav, 758
Tolkien and the Critics. Isaacs, Neil D. and Zimbardo, Rose A., eds. 3942
TOLKIEN, JOHN RONALD REUEL, 3942, 3947
Tolkien Relation. Ready, William, 3947
Toll, Robert C. Blacking up, 3259
Tolstoi, Leo N. Anna Karenina, 4563
———. Kavkazskii Plennik, 4566
———. Selections, 4565
———. Voina I Mir, 4564
Tolstoy, Aleksei. Piesy, 4537
Tomasek, Robert D., ed. Latin American Politics, 1206
Tomasevic, N. Yugoslavia, 5560

Tomkins, Calvin. Merchants and Masterpieces, 2893
Tomkowitz, Gerhard. see Wagner, Dieter
Tomorrow's Child. Alves, Rubem A, 4654
Tompkins, Peter. Secrets of the Great Pyramid, 4895
Tompkins, Peter and Bird, Christopher. Secret Life of Plants, 2315
Toms, Coons, Mulattoes, Mammies, and Bucks. Bogle, Donald, 3267
Tongue, Ruth L. see Briggs, Katharine M.
Toor, Frances. A Treasury of Mexican Folkways, 1839
Top Pop Records, 1955-1970. Whitburn, Joel, 63
Topaze. Pagnol, Marcel, 4176
Topics in Mathematics. 1958
Topics in Modern Chemistry. 2086
Toppings, Earl, ed. Canada, 4799
Topsoe-Jensen, H. G. Scandinavian Literature from Brandes to Our Day, 4084
Torah. 729
TORNADOES, 2153-2154
Tornadoes of the United States. Flora, Snowden D, 2154
Torrente, Ballesteros. Panorama de la Literatura Espanola, 4316
Torres-Rioseco, Arturo. Epic of Latin American Literature, 4317
Torrey, N. L. see Fellows, Otis E.
TOSCANINI, ARTURO, 3245
Total Art. Henri, Adrian, 2910
Totalitarian Rule. Buchheim, Hans, 1217
TOTALITARIANISM, 897, 1216-1217
TOUISSANT LOUVERTURE, FRANCOIS DOMINQUE, 5847
TOULOUSE-LAUTREC MONFA, HENRI MARIE RAYMOND DE, 3053
Le Tour de Monde en 80 Jours. Verne, Jules, 4255
Tourneur, Cyril. see Webster, John
Toward a Democratic Left. Harrington, Michael, 1113
Toward a New Christianity. Altizer, Thomas, ed, 743
Toward a Theory of Instruction. Bruner, Jerome S, 1744
Toward the Twenty-First Century. Reischauer, Edwin O, 1294
Towards a Poor Theatre. Grotowski, Jerzy, ed, 3293
Towards a Visual Culture. Gattegno, Caleb, 1773
Townsend, Robert C. Up the Organization, 2853
Toye, Clive. see Bradley, Gordon
Toynbee, Arnold J. A Study of History, 4648
Toynbee, Jocelyn M. C. Animals in Roman Life and Art, 2887

INDEX

TRADE UNIONS — U. S., 1429, 1439, 1441-1442, 1444, 1446-1447
Tradition and Design in the Iliad. Bowra, Cecil M, 4461
Traditional Asian Plays. Brandon, James R., ed, 4599
TRAGEDY, 3482, 3484, 3529
Tragedy. Corrigan, Robert W, 3529
Tragedy. Lucas, Frank L, 3482
Tragedy of Lyndon Johnson. Goldman, Eric F, 6170
Tragic Era. Bowers, Claude G, 6082
Train to Pakostan. Singh, Khushwant, 4479
Traitor and the Spy. Flexner, John T, 5916
Trans-Vision Book of Health. 251
TRANSACTIONAL ANALYSIS, 2604-2606
TRANSCENDENTAL MEDITATION, 548
Transcendental Meditation. Forem, Jack, 548
TRANSCENDENTALISM (NEW ENGLAND), 546-547
Transcendentalists. Miller, Perry, ed, 547
Transformation of American Foreign Policy. Bohlen, Charles E, 1331
Transistors and Circuits. Pearce, W. E. and Klein, Aaron. 2646
Transplant. Mowbray, A. Q, 2624
TRANSPLANTATION OF ORGANS, TISSUES, ETC., 2590, 2624
TRANSPORTATION — HISTORY, 1793
Transportation Through the Ages. Georgano, George N, 1793
Trattner, Walter I. From Poor Law to Welfare State, 1691
Travels. Polo, Marco, 4774
Travels in Arabia Deserts. Doughty, Charles M, 5624
Travels with Charley. Steinbeck, John, 4818
Treadgold, Donald W. Soviet and Chinese Communism, 1490
Trease, Geoffrey. Samuel Pepys and His World, 5244
TREASON — U. S., 5957
Treasure, Geoffrey. Seventeenth Century France, 5387
Treasure Keepers. Mills, John F, 481
Treasure of Our Tongue. Barnett, Lincoln, 1865
Treasure of Sutton Hoo. Grohskopf, Bernice, ed, 5183
Treasures of Ireland. Lucas, A. T, 2921
Treasury of American Design. Hornung, Clarence P, 290
Treasury of American Folklore. Botkin, Benjamin A, 1826

A Treasury of Asian Literature. Yohannan, John D, 4477
A Treasury of Chinese Literature. Chai, Chu and Chai, Winberg, eds. 4602
Treasury of Great Humor. Untermeyer, Louis, ed, 3520
Treasury of Great Russian Short Stories. Yarmolinsky, Avrahm, ed, 4570
A Treasury of Irish Folklore. Colum, Padriac, ed, 1831
A Treasury of Kahlil Gibran. Gibran, Kahlil, 4596
A Treasury of Mexican Folkways. Toor, Frances, 1839
Treasury of Russian Literature. Guerney, Bernard G., ed, 4496
Treasury of the World's Greatest Speeches. Peterson, Houston, ed, 3519
TREATIES — COLLECTIONS, 141
Treatise on Light. Huygens, Christiaan, 2039
Tree Where Man Was Born. Matthiessen, Peter and Porter, Eliot. 4793
Treece, Henry. The Crusades, 5019
TREES, 236, 2326-2328
Tregear, Thomas R. An Economic Geography of China, 1510
Treistman, Judith M. The Prehistory of China, 4718
Trelease, Allen W. White Terror, 6077
Trevelyan, George M. England Under the Stuarts, 5245
———. The English Revolution, 1688-1689, 5246
———. Garibaldi and the Making of Italy, 5442
———. History of England, 5176
———. Illustrated English Social History, 5177
Trevelyan, George O. The American Revolution, 5928
Trevelyan, Janet P. A Short History of the Italian People, 5429
Trewartha, G. T., et al. Elements of Geography, 4680
Trial by Fury. Klein, Aaron E, 2593
Trial of the Germans. Davidson, Eugene, 5309
TRIALS, 1615, 1715
Tripp, Edward. Crowell's Handbook of Classical Mythology, 121
Tristan. The Romance of Tristan and Iseult, 4130
Triumph of Freedom, 1775-1783. Miller, John C, 5921
Triumph of Science and Reason, 1660-1685. Nussbaum, Frederick L, 5042
Trois Contes. Flaubert, Gustave, 4211
Les Trois Mousquetaires. Dumas, Alexandre, 4208

Tropical Forest Ecosystems in Africa and South America. Meggers, Betty J., et al. 2245
Trotsky, Leon. The Struggle Against Fascism in Germany, 1501
TROTSKY, LEON, 5509, 5514-5516
Trotter, Reginald G. Canadian Federation, 5792
Troubled Farmer. Hayter, Earl W, 2772
A Troubled Feast. Leuchtenburg, William E, 6152
Troyat, Henri. Pushkin, 4514
TRUDEAU, PIERRE ELLIOT, 5800
True Believer. Hoffer, Eric, 896
True Sound of Music. Fantel, Hans, 2656
TRUJILLO, MOLINA RAFAEL LEONIDAS, 5841
Truman Administration. Bernstein, Barton J. and Matusow, A. J., eds. 6148
Truman Doctrine and the Origins of McCarthyism. Freeland, Richard M, 1336
Truman, Harry S. Memoirs, 6154
TRUMAN, HARRY S., 6147-6149, 6151, 6153, 6155
Truman, Margaret. Harry S. Truman, 6155
Truman, Nevil. Historic Costuming, 1814
Trumpeter of God. Reid, W. Stanford, 813
Truth About Kent State. Davies, Peter, 1791
Truth and Untruth. McCloskey, Paul N, 1197
Trythall, J. W. El Caudillo, 5475
Tuchman, Barbara W. The Guns of August, 5088
———. The Zimmerman Telegram, 5077
Tucholsky, Kurt. Eine Auswahl, 3981
———. Deutschland, Deutschland, Uber Alles, 3980
Tucker, Glenn. Mad Anthony Wayne and the New Nation, 5953
Tucker, Martin A. see Temple, Ruth Z.
Tucker, Robert C. Stalin As Revolutionary, 1879-1929, 5526
Tuffrau, Paul. see Lanson, Gustave
Tufts, Eleanor. Our Hidden Heritage, 2948
Tufty, Barbara. Cells, 2255
Tugwell, Rexford G. Brains Trust, 1383
———. In Search of Roosevelt, 6146
Tumbled House. Scott, Ian, 5732
Tumbling and Trampolining. Loken, Newton C, 3382
Tunamuno. Vida de Don Quixote y Sancho, 4393
Tunel. Sabato, Ernest R, 4384
Turabian, Kate L. Manual for Writers of Term Papers, Theses, and Dissertations, 329
Turcaret. Le Sage, Alain-René, 4227
Turgenev. Yarmolinsky, Avrahm, 4571

Turgenev, Ivan S. Ottsy i Deti, 4567
———. Vintage Turgenev, 4583
———. Zapiski Okhotnika, 4568
TURGENEV, IVAN SERGEYEVICH, 4571
Turkevich, Ludmilla B., ed. Masterpieces of Russian Literature, 4500
TURKEY — HISTORY, 5555, 5558, 5642, 5653-5655
Turkin, Hy. The Official Encyclopedia of Baseball, 3378
Turks. Hotham, David, 5653
Turn Left at the Pub. Oakes, George, 4751
Turn of the Century. Bergonzi, Bernard, 3770
Turn Right at the Fountain. Oakes, George and Chapman, Alexandria. 4742
Turnbull, Andrew. Thomas Wolfe, 3739
Turnbull, Colin M. The Mountain People, 932
Turnbull, Eleanor L., ed. Ten Centuries of Spanish Poetry, 4340
Turnell, Martin. The Art of French Fiction, 4266
Turner, Frederick J. The Frontier in American History, 5872
———. Rise of the New West 1819-1829, 5978
Turner, Justin G. and Turner, Linda L., eds. Mary Todd Lincoln, 6038
Turner, Katharine C. Red Men Calling on the Great White Father, 5775
Turner, Linda L., see Turner, Justin G.
TURNER, NAT, 3742, 5992
Turnill, Reginald. The Language of Space, 259
TURTLES, 2420
Turtles of the United States. Ernst, Carl and Barbour, Roger W. 2420
Tusculan Disputations. Cicero, Marcus Tullius, 4421
Tussing, Arlon R. Alaska Pipeline Report, 1522
Twain, Mark. Autobiography of Mark Twain, 3752
Twayne's English Authors Series. 3970
Twayne's United States Authors Series. 3769
Twayne's World Authors Series. 4643
TWEED RING, 6196
Tweed Ring. Callow, Alexander B., Jr, 6196
Tweedie, Michael. Atlas of Insects, 244
Twelve Apostles. Brownrigg, Ronald, 734
Twelve Portraits of the French Revolution. Beraud, Henri, 5389
Twelve Spanish-American Poets. Hays, H. R., ed, 4302

INDEX

Twelve Who Ruled. Palmer, Robert R, 5398
Twelve Year Reich. Grunberger, Richard, 5313
Twenties. Hoffman, Frederick J, 3540
Twentieth-Century Africa. McEwan, P. J., ed, 5705
Twentieth Century America. Shannon, David A, 6105
Twentieth Century Authors. Kunitz, Stanley J. and Haycraft, Howard, eds. 430
Twentieth Century British Literature. Temple, Ruth Z. and Tucker, Martin A. 71
Twentieth Century Capitalist Revolution. Berle, Adolf A., Jr, 1532
Twentieth Century China. Clubb, Oliver E, 5589
Twentieth Century Chinese Poetry Anthology. Kai-Yu, Hsu, ed, 4604
Twentieth Century Ethics. Hancock, Roger N, 603
Twentieth Century Europe. Black, Cyril E. and Helmreich, E. C. 5091
Twentieth Century French Drama. Grossvogel, D. E, 4187
Twentieth Century French Literature. Brée, Germaine, 4098
Twentieth Century Germany. Ryder, A. J, 5298
Twentieth Century Indonesia. Neill, Wilfred, 5689
Twentieth Century Interpretation Series. 3971
Twentieth Century Music. Myers, Rolls H., ed, 3150
Twentieth Century Pacificism. Brock, Peter, 1547
Twentieth Century Russian Plays. Reeve, Franklin D., ed, 4542
Twentieth Century Views Series. 3972
Twenty Decisive Battles of the World. Creasy, Edward S. and Mitchell, J. P. 4669
TWENTY-FIRST CENTURY — FORECASTS, 935, 4658
Twenty Plays of the No Theater. Keene, Donald, tr. from Jap. 4615
Twenty Thousand Years of World Painting. Jaffe, Hans, 3027
Twenty Years' Crisis, 1919-1939. Carr, Edward H, 1548
Twenty Years of Silents, 1908-1928. Weaver, John T, 65
Twiley, W. B. *see* Barker, Lucius
Twilight of France, 1933-1940. Werth, Alexander, 5420
Twilight of Imperial Russia. Charques, Richard, 5503

Twilight of the Gods. Mellers, Wilfred, 3232
Two Cultures and a Second Look. Snow, Charles P, 458
Two Hundred Million Guinea Pigs. Fuller, John, 2556
Two Hundred Million Years Beneath the Sea. Briggs, Peter, 2146
Two Lives of Joseph Conrad. Gurko, Leo, 3941
Two-Ocean War. Morison, Samuel E, 5144
Two Plays. Jones, LeRoi, 3698
Two Tales. Agnon, Shmuel Y, 4588
Two Vietnams. Fall, Bernard B, 5677
Two Worlds of Childhood. Bronfenbrenner, Urie, 2842
Two Years Before the Mast. Dana, Richard H, 4692
Twombly, Robert C. Frank Lloyd Wright, 2964
Tydings, Joseph D. Born to Starve, 956
Tyler, Alice F. Freedom's Ferment, 5979
TYLER, JOHN, 6001
Tyler, Moses C. Literary History of the American Revolution, 5929
———. Patrick Henry, 5940
Type. Gates, David, 2866
TYPE AND TYPE-FOUNDING, 2866-2868
Types of Philosophy. Hocking, William E. and Hocking, Richard, eds. 509
TYPHUS FEVER, 2609
Typographic Book, 1450-1935. Morison, Stanley and Day, Kenneth. 2867
Tyranny on Trial. Harris, Whitney R, 5334
Udall, Stewart L. Nineteen Seventy-Six, 1119
———. Quiet Crisis, 1470
UFO's Explained. Klass, Philip J, 472
UKRAINE — HISTORY, 5532
Ulam, Adam B. Expansion and Coexistence, 1312
———. Stalin, 5527
Ulanov, Barry. A History of Jazz in America, 3192
Ullman, James R. Age of Mountaineering, 3395
Ullmann, Stephen. Semantics, 1874
Ulrich, Homer. Chamber Music, 3250
———. Symphonic Music, 3241
Ulrich, Homer and Pisk, Paul A. History of Music and Musical Style, 3141
Ulrich's International Periodicals Directory. 11
Ultra Secret. Winterbotham, Frederick, 5150
Ulysses Found. Bradford, Ernle D, 4462

Ulysses Theme. Stanford, William B, 4467
Unamuno, Miguel de. Galdós' Novelista Moderno, 4388
———. Niebla, 4389
Das Unauslöschliche Siegel. Langgasser, Elizabeth, 4061
Unbought and Unbossed. Chisholm, Shirley, 1360
Uncertain Giant. Adler, Selig, 1325
Uncommitted. Keniston, Kenneth, 909
Uncoupling. Sheresky, Norman and Mannes, M. 992
Under Milk Wood. Thomas, Dylan, 3916
Under the Mask. Weiss, Karel, 1007
Under Twenty-One. Dorman, Michael, 1602
Underachieving School. Holt, John, 1762
UNDERDEVELOPED AREAS, 1518, 1535-1536
Underdevelopment and Economic Nationalism in Southeast Asia. Golway, Frank H., et al. 1534
UNDERGROUND LITERATURE — RUSSIA, 4764
UNDERGROUND PRESS — U. S., 499
Underground Railroad. Still, William, 1057
Underhill, Evelyn. Mysticism, 558
Understanding Ecology. Mariner, James L, 2232
Understanding Electricity and Electronics. Buban, Peter and Schmitt, Marshall L. 2636
Understanding Historical Research. Block, Jack, 4663
Understanding History. Gottschalk, Louis, 4665
Understanding Magazines. Wolseley, Roland E, 2851
Understanding Poetry. Brooks, Cleanth and Warren, Robert P. 3472
Understanding the New Testament. Kee, Howard C., et al. 735
Understanding the Old Testament. Anderson, Bernhard W, 722
UNDERWATER ARCHAEOLOGY, 4716-4717
UNDERWATER EXPLORATION, 2137, 2149
Underwood, John W. Stinsons, 2719
Unesco World Art Series. 3084
Unexpected Revolution. Kecskemeti, Paul, 5367
Unfinished Revolution. Deutscher, Isaac, 5518
An Unfinished Woman. Hellman, Lillian, 3679
Unfit for Human Consumption. Harmer, Ruth, 2564

Unification of Italy, 1859-1861. Delzell, Charles F., ed, 5437
UNIFORMS, MILITARY, 1671
United Empire Loyalists. Bradley, Arthur G, 5789
UNITED FARM WORKERS ORGANIZATION COMMITTEE, 1448
UNITED MINE WORKERS OF AMERICA — HISTORY, 1440
UNITED NATIONS, 1553-1554
United Nations. Barros, James, ed, 1553
UN. Eichelberger, Clark M, 1554
U. S
   ANTIQUITIES, 4814
   ARMED FORCES, 1066-1067
   BIBLIOGRAPHY, 3, 5, 66, 80
   BIOGRAPHY, 422-423, 4865, 5861
   DICTIONARIES, 135, 421
   CENSUS, 132
   CIVILIZATION, 928, 3522, 4658-4659, 4809, 4811-4812, 4817, 4820, 4828, 5854, 5857-5858, 5864, 5871, 5873, 5905, 5910, 5926, 6002, 6011, 6072, 6131, 6152
     HISTORY, 5870, 5894, 6074
     SOURCES, 5879, 6172
   CONSTITUTIONAL HISTORY, 1563, 1570, 1575, 1579, 1583, 1587, 5924
   CONSTITUTIONAL LAW, 142, 1573, 1577, 1581, 1586-1587
   DECLARATION OF INDEPENDENCE, 5915
   DEFENSES, 1664, 2670
   DESCRIPTION AND TRAVEL, 2272, 2950, 4810, 4818
   ECONOMIC CONDITIONS, 496, 968, 1106, 1113, 1118, 1416, 1418-1419, 1421-1423, 1538, 1541-1542, 1702, 6008, 6065, 6107, 6111, 6131, 6143
   ECONOMIC POLICY, 1539, 1543, 1795
   EMIGRATION AND IMMIGRATION, 1278, 1280
   FOREIGN POPULATION, 126, 1277, 1279
   FOREIGN RELATIONS, 500, 1298, 1304, 1310-1311, 1313, 1315, 1326, 1328-1335, 1340, 1342, 1344-1345, 1347-1349, 1351, 1353-1355, 5109, 5112, 5149, 5576, 5678, 5687, 5925, 5987, 6003, 6096, 6163, 6165
     BIBLIOGRAPHY, 76
     SOURCES, 1343, 6148
     (1815-), 6016
     (1861-), 5815
     20TH CENTURY, 1325
     (1901-), 5079-5080, 5082-5083
     (1933-), 1324, 1339, 1346, 5104
     (1945-), 1327, 1337-1339, 5613,

INDEX

6099
(1953-), 6164
(1961-), 1341
(1969-), 6175
GENEALOGY, 4872
GOVERNMENT PUBLICATIONS —
  BIBLIOGRAPHY, 2, 6
HISTORICAL GEOGRAPHY —
  MAPS, 391-393
HISTORY, 903, 5855-5856, 5859,
  5862, 5866-5858, 5870, 5872, 6100
  BIBLIOGRAPHY, 77-78
  CHRONOLOGY, 449, 451
  DICTIONARIES, 133, 450-452
  SOURCES, 5876-5880, 5984,
    6002, 6101, 6214
  COLONIAL PERIOD, 5892-5893,
    5895, 5898-5901, 5903-5907, 5911,
    5920, 6189
  REVOLUTION, 5253, 5789-5790,
    5893, 5900-5901, 5912, 5914, 5917-
    5923, 5927-5929, 5931-5935, 5938-
    5939, 5947-5948, 5951, 5954-5957
    CAUSES, 5913, 5930, 5936-
      5937, 5941, 5943, 5945
    CAMPAIGNS AND
      BATTLES, 399, 5952
    DICTIONARIES, 453
    SOURCES, 5924, 5931, 5946
  (1783-), 5863, 5923-5924, 5962-
    5965, 5967-5968
  (1812-), 5789, 5985-5987
  (1815-), 5979, 5988, 5996-5997,
    6006, 6009, 6016-6020, 6225, 6231
  (1849-), 6004, 6010, 6067
  CIVIL WAR, 6004, 6025-6030,
    6032-6033, 6035, 6037, 6048, 6052-
    6053, 6056-6060, 6069, 6215
    BIBLIOGRAPHY, 79
    CAUSES, 6006, 6040-6041
    CAMPAIGNS AND
      BATTLES, 6031, 6049-6050
    DICTIONARIES, 454
  (1865-), 6062-6063, 6070, 6076,
    6082, 6088, 6092, 6102
  (1898-), 6096-6098, 6119
  20TH CENTURY, 3540, 6105-
    6106, 6108, 6112, 6114, 6120,
    6122, 6124, 6128, 6145
  (1919-), 6107, 6111, 6124, 6127,
    6144
  (1933-), 1116, 6138, 6140, 6142-
    6143
  (1945-), 5685, 6150, 6157-6159
INDUSTRIES, 1409, 6071
INTELLECTUAL LIFE, 457, 459,
  1249, 5860, 5910, 5966
MILITARY HISTORY, 1662-1663,
  5902, 6003

MILITARY POLICY, 1293, 1296,
  1666, 1668, 1678, 1686
NATIONAL SECURITY, 1666
NAVAL HISTORY, 5985
POLITICS AND GOVERNMENT,
  137, 1189, 1198, 1249, 1382, 1384,
  1387, 1399, 1574, 1576, 1632, 1648,
  1703, 5861, 5870, 6068
  SOURCES, 1633, 5881, 6148,
    6154, 6156
  COLONIAL PERIOD, 1194,
    1276, 5942
  (1783-), 1350, 1389, 1585
  (1815-), 5978, 5981, 5990, 5999,
    6001, 6010, 6041, 6044-6045
  (1861-), 1589
  (1865-), 1195, 1388, 6075, 6079,
    6082, 6093, 6103
  (1898-), 6110, 6113
  20TH CENTURY, 1111, 1196,
    1371, 4868, 6104
  (1901-), 1202, 1638, 6115, 6117
  (1919-), 6125, 6127, 6129, 6222
  (1933-), 1146, 6130, 6132, 6135,
    6139, 6141
  (1945-), 482, 1156, 1203, 1336,
    6147, 6149, 6151, 6153, 6155
  (1961-), 1192, 1390, 6166, 6170
  (1969-), 1115, 1191, 1193, 1197,
    1201, 1360, 1390
POPULATION, 948-949, 957, 959
RACE QUESTION, 1007, 1010-1011,
  1023, 1074, 1104, 1241, 1273, 1723
RACE RELATIONS. 1009
RELIGION, 689-691, 715, 738, 800,
  802-804
SOCIAL CONDITIONS, 927, 995,
  997, 1069-1071, 1105, 1112, 1114,
  1542, 1574, 1576, 6005, 6131
  BIBLIOGRAPHY, 57
  SOURCES, 5881
  (1945-), 955, 1103, 1107, 1109,
    1203
  (1960-), 905, 915, 928, 1082,
    1090, 1110, 1117, 1505-1506
SOCIAL LIFE AND CUSTOMS, 448,
  544, 914, 1841, 4808, 4819, 5896-
  5897, 5908
TERRITORIAL EXPANSION, 5886,
  6016, 6019, 6094, 6229
United States and Canada. Craig, Gerald M,
  1332
United States and China. Fairbank, John K,
  1315
United States and Italy. Hughes, H. Stuart,
  1342
United States and Japan. Reischauer, Edwin
  O, 1353

United States and the Carribean. Szulc, Tad, ed, 1102
United States and the Origins of the Cold War, 1941-1947. Gaddis, John L, 1339
U. S. and World War II. Buchanan, A. Russell, 5120
U. S. Arms Control and Disarmament Agency. Arms Control and Disarmament Agreements, 1959-1972, 1298
U. S. ARMY — HISTORY, 1663, 5086, 6078, 6095, 6098
U. S. Bureau of the Census. Statistical Abstract of the United States, 132
U. S. CENTRAL INTELLIGENCE AGENCY, 1295-1296, 1624
U. S. CIVILIAN CONSERVATION CORPS — HISTORY, 1647
U. S. Commission on Marihuana & Drug Abuse. Drug Use in America, 1698
———. Marihuana, 1699
U. S. Commission on Obscenity & Pornography. The Report, 1727
U. S. Commission on Population Growth & the American Future. Population and the American Future, 957
U. S. Congress. Biographical Directory of the American Congress, 1774-1961, 135
U. S. CONGRESS, 135, 1156, 1361-1368, 1580, 1613, 1643
U. S. Congress. House. Committee on the Judiciary. Constitutional Grounds for Presidential Impeachment, 1645
U. S. Congress. Senate. Committee on the Judiciary. Subcommittee on Constitutional Rights. Layman's Guide to Individual Rights Under the U. S. Constitution, 1588
U. S. CONSTITUTION, 1568
U. S. CONSTITUTIONAL CONVENTION, (1787), 1572, 1585
U. S. CONTINENTAL CONGRESS — BIOGRAPHY, 135
U. S. Dept. of Commerce. Earthquake History of the United States, 224
U. S. Library of Congress. A Guide to the Study of the United States of America, 80
United States Postal Service. Cullinan, Gerald, 1800
U. S. President's Commission on Law Enforcement & Administration of Justice. The Challenge of Crime in a Free Society, 1732
———. The Report of the President's Commission on Campus Unrest, 1226

U. S. PRESIDENT'S COMMISSION ON CAMPUS UNREST, 1722
United States Since 1865. Hacker, Louis M. and Kendrick, Benjamin B. 6102
United States Submarine Operations in World War II. Roscoe, Theodore, 5145
U. S. Superintendent of Documents. Selected U. S. Government Publications, 6
U. S. SUPREME COURT, 1260, 1584, 1599, 1605, 1607-1608, 1610, 1613-1614, 1616-1621
Unity in Diversity. Blackmer, Donald L, 1487
UNIVERSE, 508, 1892, 1980, 1983-1985, 1987, 1990, 2016
UNIVERSITIES AND COLLEGES, 146-147, 149, 1789
University Dictionary of Mammals of the World. Burton, Maurice, 2444
University of Chicago Press Editors. A Manual of Style, 2849
University of Minnesota Pamphlets on American Writers. 3768
Unknown Ocean. Perry, Richard, 2374
Unknown Soldiers. Barbeau, Arthur E, 5086
Unsafe at Any Speed. Nader, Ralph, 2739
Unseld, Wes. see Monroe, Earl
An Unsettled People. Berthoff, Rowland T, 1105
Untapped Resource. Cahill, Kevin M, 1695
Unterecker, John. Voyager, 3621
Untermeyer, Louis, ed. The Book of Living Verse, 3785
———. Lives of the Poets, 4871
———. Makers of the Modern World, 4863
———. Modern American Poetry, 3551
———. Modern British Poetry, 3786
———. The Pursuit of Poetry, 3479
———. Treasury of Great Humor, 3520
Untried Case. Ehrmann, Herbert B, 1724
Up from Slavery. Washington, Booker T, 1292
Up the Organization. Townsend, Robert C, 2853
UPANISHADS, 835
Updike, Daniel B. Printing Types, 2868
Uppal, J. S. and Salkever, Louis K., eds. Africa, 1415
Uprooted. Handlin, Oscar, 1279
Uprooted Children. Coles, Robert, 996
Upton, Arthur C. Radiation Injury, 2511
Urban Blues. Keil, Charles, 3235
Urban Government. Banfield, Edward C., ed, 1628

INDEX

Urban, John T., ed. White Water Handbook for Canoe and Kayak, 3423
Urban Politics and Problems. Mahood, H. R. and Angus, Edward L., eds. 1629
Urban Reader. Cahill, Susan and Cooper, Michele. 965
Urban Spaces. Specter, David K, 2956
URBANIZATION, 967-968, 1731
Urbanization of America, 1860-1915. McKelvey, Blake, 968
Urbanization of the Earth. Arango, Jorge, 964
Urge to the Sea. Kerner, Robert J, 5486
Das Urteil und Andere Erzählungen. Kafka, Franz, 4060
URUGUAY, 6279
Uruguay, a Contemporary Survey. Alisky, Marvin, 6279
Usage and Abusage. Partridge, Eric, 1883
Uses of the Future. Muller, Herbert J, 4658
Uses of the Past. Muller, Herbert J, 4646
Usher, Stephen. The Historians of Greece and Rome, 4969
Usigli, Rodolfo. El Gesticulador, 4357
Usinger, Robert L. see Storer, Tracy I.
Utilitarianism, Liberty and Representative Government. Mill, John Stuart, 1129
Utley, Robert M. Frontier Regulars, 6078
UTOPIAS, 1208-1209
Utopias and Utopian Thought. Manuel, Frank Edward, ed, 1134

Vachel Lindsay. Massa, Ann, 3607
Vaczek, Louis C. The Enjoyment of Chemistry, 2073
VALACHI, JOSEPH, 1720
Valachi Papers. Maas, Peter, 1720
Vale, Eugene. Technique of Screenplay Writing, 3485
Vale, M. G. A. Charles VII, 5378
Valenstein, Elliot S. Brain Control, 2625
Valentine, J. Manson. see Berlitz, Charles F.
Vali, Ferenc. The Quest for a United Germany, 1165
Valle-Inclán, Ramón Del. Sonata de Primavera, 4334
Valliana, Leo. The End of Austria-Hungary, 5344
Values Clarification. Simon, Sidney B., et al. 602
VAMPIRES, 3531
Van Allan, Judith. see Marine, Gene
Van Amerogen, C. The Way Things Work Book of Computers, 464
Van Buitenen, Johannes A. B. Tales of Ancient India, 1840
VAN BUREN, MARTIN, 5999
VANCOUVER, GEORGE, 4846

Van Den Heuvel, Cor, ed. The Haiku Anthology, 3669
Vanderbilt, Amy. Amy Vanderbilt's Etiquette, 1823
Vanderbilt, B. M. Thomas Edison, Chemist, 2860
Van Der Post, Laurens. The Heart of the Hunter, 4796
———. Lost World of the Kalahari, 4797
VAN DER ROHE, MIES, 2961
Van der Zee, Barbara. see Van Der Zee, Henri
Van Der Zee, Henri and Van der Zee, Barbara. William and Mary, 5247
Van Deusen, Glyndon G. Horace Greeley, 6042
———. Jacksonian Era, 5997
———. William Henry Seward, 6014
Van De Wetering, Janwillem. The Empty Mirror, 841
Vandiver, Clarence H. Fur-Trade and Early Western Exploration, 6240
Vandiver, Frank E., ed. The Idea of the South, 6217
———. Mighty Stonewall, 6051
Van Doren, Carl C. Secret History of the American Revolution, 5957
Van Doren, Charles, see Moquin, Wayne
Van Doren, Mark. Anthology of World Poetry, 3501
———. Portable Emerson, 3561
Van Druten, John. I Am a Camera, 3893
Van Gogh. Auden, Wystan H., ed, 3068
Van Gogh. Lassaigne, Jacques, 3070
VAN GOGH, VINCENT, 3068, 3070
Vanished Cities. Schreiber, Hermann and Schreiber, Georg. 4708
Vanishing Peoples of the Earth. National Geographic Society Editors, 2189
Vanishing Species. Time-Life Books Editors, 2341
Vanishing Tribes. Pinney, Roy, 2190
Vanishing Wildlife of North America. National Geographic Society, ed, 2340
Van Itallie, Jean-Claude. The Serpent, 3706
Van Lawick, Hugo. Solo, 2473
Van Lawick-Goodall, Jane. In the Shadow of Man, 2481
———. My Friends the Wild Chimpanzees, 2482
Van Lawick-Goodall, Jane and Van Lawick-Goodall, Hugo. Innocent Killers, 2474
Van Nostrand's Scientific Encyclopedia. Van Nostrand, 203
Van Tyne, Claude H. Causes of the War of Independence, 5930

INDEX

Varieties of Present-Day English. Bailey, Richard W. and Robinson, Jay L. 1875
Varieties of Religious Experience. James, William, 693
Varieties of Visual Experience. Feldman, Edmund B, 2875
Variorum Civil Disobedience. Thoreau, Henry David, 1251
Vasari, Giorgio. Vasari's Lives of the Painters, Sculptors and Architects, 2926
Vasari's Lives of the Painters, Sculptors and Architects. Vasari, Giorgio, 2926
Vasectomy. Fried, John J, 2553
Vasiliev, Alexander A. A History of the Byzantine Empire, 324-1453, 5551
Vatikiotis, Panagiotis J. The Modern History of Egypt, 4896
Vaughan, Alden T. American Genesis, 5909
——. New England Frontier, 6191
——. Puritan Tradition in America, 1620-1730, 6192
V.D. Johnson, Eric W, 2612
VD. Sgroi, Suzanne M, 2615
VD Epidemic. Lasagna, Louis, 2613
V.D. The Silent Epidemic. Hyde, Margaret O, 2611
Veblen, Thorstein. Theory of the Leisure Class, 1404
Vecsey, George. One Sunset a Week, 1435
——. The Way It Was, 3348
Velasquez, Goya and the Dehumanization of Art. Ortega Y Gasset, Jose, 3064
Velazquez-de-la-Cadena, Mariano, et al, eds. New Pronouncing Dictionary of the Spanish and English Languages, 184
VENEREAL DISEASES, 2613, 2615-2612
VENEZUELA, 6263
Venomous Animals of the World. Caras, Roger, 2368
Venomous Reptiles. Minton, Sherman A., Jr. and Minton, Madge R. 2417
Vercors. Le Silence de la Mer, 4254
Der Verdacht. Durrenmatt, Friedrich, 4043
Verdi. Wechsberg, Joseph, 3163
VERDI, GIUSEPPE, 3163
Vergilius Maro, Publius. The Aeneid, 4414
——. Ecologues, Georgics, Aeneid, Minor Poems, 4413
VERGILIUS MARO, PUBLIUS, 4412
Verlaine, Paul-Marie. Selected Poems, 4131
VERMEER, JAN, 3071
Vernadsky, George. History of Russia, 5494
——. A Source Book for Russian History from Early Times to 1917, 5495

Vernadsky, George and Fisher, Ralph T., eds. Dictionary of Russian Historical Terms from the Eleventh Century to 1917, 438
Verne, Jules. Le Tour de Monde en 80 Jours, 4255
——. Vingt Mille Lieues Sous les Mers, 4256
——. Voyage au Centre de la Terre, 4257
Versailles. Dunlop, Ian, 4757
VERSAILLES — HISTORY, 4757
Versailles, Nineteen Nineteen. Czernin, Ferdinand, 5072
VERSAILLES, TREATY OF, 5072, 5078, 5306
Verschuur, Gerrit L. Invisible Universe, 1977
Verse. Kipling, Rudyard, 3827
Verses from Nineteen Twenty-Nine on. Nash, Ogden, 3580
Vertebrate Body. Romer, Alfred S, 2400
Vertebrate Story. Romer, Alfred S, 2401
VERTEBRATES, 2178, 2400-2404
Vertebrates of the United States. Blair, W. F., et al. 2404
Vertical File and Its Satellites. Miller, Shirley, 24
VERTICAL FILES (LIBRARIES), 24
VESALIUS, ANDREAS, 2589
Vestal, Stanley. Sitting Bull, Champion of the Sioux, 6015
VETERANS — U. S., 1000, 1672, 5686
VETERINARIANS, 2804-2805
Vexed and Troubled Englishmen, 1590-1642. Bridenbaugh, Carl, 5237
VICE-PRESIDENTS — U. S., 5853, 5874
Vichy Regime. Aron, Robert, 5417
Vickerman, Keith and Cox, F. E. The Protozoa, 2382
Victor Hugo. Maurois, André, 4279
Victoria and the Victorians. Tingsten, Herbert L, 5264
VICTORIA, QUEEN OF GREAT BRITAIN, 564, 5173, 5256, 5258
Victorian Age, 1815-1914. Evans, R. J, 5257
Victorian England. Reader, W. J, 5262
Victorian England. Young, George M, 5266
Victorian People. Briggs, Asa, 5267
Victorious Expression. Young, Howard T, 4342
La Vida. Lewis, Oscar, 1042
Vida de Don Quixote y Sancho. Tunamuno, 4393
Vida y Obra de Galdos. Casalduero, Joaquin, 4370
VIDEO TAPE RECORDERS AND RECORDING, 3116-3117
Videofreex (Organization) The Spaghetti City Video Manual, 3117
Vidich, Arthur J. see Bensman, Joseph

INDEX

VIENNA CONGRESS, 5048
VIETNAM, 6165
   HISTORY, 1354, 5677, 5680
   POLITICS AND GOVERNMENT, 1185, 1187, 1337, 5678-5679
Vietnam. McAlister, John T, 5679
Vietnam and the West. Smith, Ralph B, 5680
Vietnam Triangle. Zagoria, Donald S, 5688
Vietnamese and Their Revolution. McAlister, John T., Jr. and Mus, Paul. 1187
VIETNAMESE CONFLICT, 900, 1000, 1138, 1185, 1672, 3759, 5681, 5683, 5685-5688
View from Space. Davies, Merton and Murray, Bruce C. 2001
Vigny, Alfred de. Destinées, 4132
Viker, Ray. The Kingdom of Oil, The Middle East, 1523
Viking America. Enterline, James R, 5887
VIKINGS, 5537
Vikings and Their Origins. Wilson, David M, 5538
VILLA, FRANCISCO, 5820
Villon, François. Complete Works of François Villon, 4134
   ———. Oeuvres Poétiques, 4133
Vincent, William. Gymnastic Routines for Men, 3381
Vingt Mille Lieues Sous les Mers. Verne, Jules, 4256
Vinland Sagas. Hermannsson, Halldor, 5888
Vinni - Pukh I Vse-Vse-Vse. Milne, Alan A, 4556
Vinson, James. Contemporary Dramatists, 372
Vintage Turgenev. Turgenev, Ivan S, 4583
VIOLENCE, 572, 768, 770, 880, 906, 1107, 1132, 1138
   U.S., 881-883, 905, 1072-1073, 5862
Violence. Graham, Hugh D., et al, eds. 881
Violence. Hartogs, Renatus and Artzt, Eric. 883
Violence and the Mass Media. Larsen, Otto N., ed, 902
Violence As Protest. Fogelson, Robert M, 905
Violence in the Streets. Endleman, Shalom, ed, 1107
Violent Peace. Mydans, Carl and Mydans, Shelley. 4678
Violent Universe. Calder, Nigel, 1968
Virgil. Otis, Brooks, 4412

VIRGINIA — HISTORY — COLONIAL PERIOD, 5909
VIRUS DISEASES, 2587, 2608
Viruses. Locke, David M, 2587
Vision Accomplished. Huyen, N. Kha, 5684
Vision and the Way. Agus, Jacob B, 858
Vision of Tragedy. Sewall, Richard B, 3484
Visit. Durrenmatt, Friedrich, 4014
Visual Arts - As Human Experience. Weismann, Donald L, 2884
Visual Dialogue. Knobler, Nathan, 2877
VISUAL PERCEPTION, 2882
Vital Signs. Langone, John, 2588
Viva Juarez. Smart, Charles A, 5814
Viva Mexico. Flandrau, Charles M, 5805
Viva Villa! Pinchon, Edgums, 5820
Vivaldi. Pincherle, Marc, 3179
VIVALDI, ANTONIO, 3179
Vogel, Amos. Film As a Subversive Art, 3283
Vogel, Virgil J. American Indian Medicine, 5777
   ———. This Country Was Ours, 5756
Vogelweide, Walther Von Der. Gedichte. Mittelhochdeutscher Text und Ubertragung, 4001
Vogt, Hannah. Burden of Guilt, 5305
A Voice for Wildlife. Scheffer, Victor B, 2814
Voice of the Lord. Wildes, Harry E, 816
Voices from Slavery. Yetman, Norman R., ed, 1002
Voices of the Silent. Gerstenmaier, Cornelia, 4764
Voices of Time. Fraser, Julius T., ed, 522
Voina I Mir. Tolstoi, Leo N, 4564
VOLCANOES, 2118-2119, 2173, 2231
Volcanoes. MacDonald, Gordon A, 2118
Volcanoes in the Sea. MacDonald, Gordon A. and Abbott, Agatin T. 2173
Volkomer, Walter E., ed. The Liberal Tradition in American Thought, 1149
VOLLEYBALL, 3357
Volleyball. Shondell, Donald S. and McManama, Jerry. 3357
Voltaire. Lanson, Gustave, 4276
Voltaire, François M. de. Age of Louis XIV, 5388
   ———. Candide, 4258
   ———. Portable Voltaire, 4282
VOLTAIRE, FRANCOIS, 4276
Von Frisch, Otto. see Von Frisch, Karl
Von Wilpert, Gero. see Ivask, Ivar
Von Daniken, Erich. Gods from Outer Space, 473
   ———. In Search of Ancient Gods, 474
Von Der Mebhen, Fred R. Southeast Asia, 1930-1970, 5674

Von Frisch, Karl and Von Frisch, Otto. Animal Architecture, 2364
Von Frisch, Otto. Animal Camouflage, 2366
Vonnegut, Kurt, Jr. Happy Birthday, Wanda June, 3707
Vor. Leonov, Leonid, 4554
Voyage au Centre de la Terre. Verne, Jules, 4257
Voyage de Monsieur Perrichon. Labichne, Eugene and Martin, E. 4167
Voyage of the Challenger. Linklater, Eric, 1919
Voyager. Unterecker, John, 3621
VOYAGES AND TRAVELS, 4687, 4691-4692, 4695, 4697, 4774, 5890-5891
Voyages of Apollo. Lewis, Richard S, 2767
Le Voyageur sans Bagages, and Le Bal des Voleurs. Anouilh, Jean, 4146
Voznesenskii, Andrei. Antimiry, 4515
―――. Antiworlds, 4516
Vrooman, Jack R. René Descartes, 674
Vryonis, Speros. Byzantium and Europe, 5552
Vucinich, Alexander S. Science in Russian Culture, 1925
―――. Science in Russian Culture, 1861-1917, 1926
Vucinich, Wayne S., ed. Contemporary Yugoslavia, 5561

W. E. B. DuBois. DuBois, William E, 1020
Waage, Karl M. see Dunbar, Carl O.
Waddell, Helen. Wandering Scholars, 4403
Wade, Mason. French Canadians, 5784
Waffen S.S. Hitler's Elite Guard at War, 1939-1945. Stein, George H, 5327
Wagar, W. Warren. Books in World History, 73
Wagenheim, Kal, compiled by. The Puerto Ricans, 5852
―――. Puerto Rico, 4807
Wagenknecht, Edward C. Mark Twain, 3753
Wager with the Wind. Greiner, James D, 2713
Waggoner, Hyatt H. American Poets, 3546
Wagner, Dieter and Tomkowitz, Gerhard. Anschluss, 5348
WAGNER, RICHARD, 3170
Wagner, Rudolph F. Dyslexia and Your Child, 1774
Wagner, Willis H. Modern Carpentry, 2870
Wain, Harry. A History of Preventive Medicine, 2559
Waiting for Godot. Beckett, Samuel, 4149
Wakelin, Martyn F. English Dialects, 1876

Walder, David. The Short Victorious War, 5622
Waldman, Milton. The Lady Mary, 5232
WALES ― HISTORY, 5278-5279
Wales Through the Ages. Roderick, Arthur J., ed, 5279
Waley, Daniel P. see Hearder, H.
Walker, Daniel. Rights in Conflict, 6226
Walker, Ernest P., et al. Mammals of the World, 247
Walker, G. W. see Kuspira, John
Walker, Lewis W. The Book of Owls, 2443
Walker, Mack, ed. Metternich's Europe, 5065
Walker, Stuart H., ed. Techniques of Small Boat Racing, 3430
Walker, Williston. History of the Christian Church, 781
―――. John Calvin, 812
Walking Catfish and Other Aliens. Roth, Charles E, 2358
Walking in the Wild. Kelsey, Robert J, 3386
Walking the Boundaries. Davison, Peter, 3633
Wall, Joseph F. Andrew Carnegie, 1525
Wall, Robert. Introduction to Mathematical Linguistics, 1859
WALLACE, ALFRED RUSSEL, 2289-2290
Wallace and Bates in the Tropics. Beddall, Barbara G., ed, 2289
Wallace and Natural Selection. McKinney, H. Lewis, 2290
WALLACE, HENRY AGARD, 6141
Wallace, Michael, see Hofstadter, Richard
Wallace, Robert. see Cloke, Marjane
Wallace, William J. see Ingmanson, Dale E.
Walsh, James J., see Hyman, Arthur
Walsh, John and Gannon, Robert. Time Is Short and the Water Rises, 2825
Walter, Don C. Men and Music in Western Culture, 3142
Walter, Felix, see Steinhauer, Harry
Waltham, A. C. Caves, 2130
Walton, Hanes, Jr. Black Political Parties, 1399
Walton, Henry. Germany, 5336
Walton, Henry. see Kessel, Neil
Walton, Ortiz. Music, 3198
Wandering Scholars. Waddell, Helen, 4403
Waning of the Middle Ages. Huizinga, Johan, 5000
Waning of the Old South Civilization, 1860-1880. Eaton, Clement, 6204
Wankel. Faith, Nicholas, 2659

INDEX

WANKEL ENGINE, 2659-2660
WAR, 604, 1293, 1580, 1660, 1665, 1667, 1669, 4675, 5002
War Against the Jews, 1933-1945. Dawidowicz, Lucy S, 5107
WAR AND EMERGENCY POWERS — U. S., 1643
War and Politics. Brodie, Bernard, 1293
War and the Christian Conscience. Marrin, Albert, ed, 769
War and the Poet, 1800 B.C.-1945 A.D. Anthology. Eberhart, Richard and Rodman, S., eds. 3497
War Business. Thayer, George, 1796
WAR CRIMES — TRIALS — NUREMBERG, (1945), 5334
War Hitler Won. Bethell, Nicholas, 5097
War in Medieval English Society. Barnie, John, 5199
War in Peacetime. Collins, Joseph L, 5610
War of Greek Independence. Phillips, Walter A, 5553
War, Presidents, and Public Opinion. Mueller, John E, 900
War That Never Ended. Cruden, Robert, 6028
War Through the Ages. Montross, Lynn, 1657
War to End All Wars. Coffman, Edward M, 5087
War with Catiline, War with Jugurtha, etc. Sallustius Crispus, Gaius, 4425
Ward, Aileen. John Keats, 3819
Ward, John. Andrew Jackson, 5998
Ward, Lynd K. Storyteller without Words, 3094
Ward, Norman. Public Purse, 5785
Ward, Ritchie. Into the Ocean World, 2268
Ward, Robert E., see Macridis, Roy C.
Ward-Perkins, J. B. see Boethius, Axel
Warfare. Leckie, Robert, 1660
Warfare in England, 1066-1189. Beeler, John, 5194
Warfare in Feudal Europe, 730-1200. Beeler, John, 1658
Warmbrunn, Werner. The Dutch Under German Occupation, 1940-1945, 5116
Warner, Ezra. Generals in Gray, 6052
Warner, James A. The Darker Brother, 3119
Warrack, John H. Tchaikovsky, 3162
Warren, Charles. Supreme Court in U. S. History, 1621
Warren Court. Cox, Archibald. 1616
Warren, Harris A. Herbert Hoover and the Great Depression, 6129
Warren, Robert P. see Brooks, Cleanth
Warren, Robert Penn. Brother to Dragons, 3590
———. Selected Poems, 3591

Warren, Sidney. Battle for the Presidency, 1384
Warren, Wilfred L. Henry II, 5207
Warrington, Brian H. Nero, 4948
Warriors of God. Nigg, Walter, 790
Washburn, Wilcomb E., compiled by. The American Indian and the United States, 445
Washing of the Spears. Morris, Donald, 5737
Washington, Booker T. Up from Slavery, 1292
WASHINGTON, BOOKER TALIAFERRO, 1032, 1292
WASHINGTON, GEORGE, 5970
Washington Post. The Fall of a President, 6179
Waskow, Howard J. Whitman, 3562
Wasps. Evans, Howard E. and Eberhard, Mary J. 2398
Wasserman, Paul and Paskar, Joanne, eds. Statistics Sources, 58
Wasteland. Kurtz, Stephen A, 2970
Watch Your Language. Bernstein, Theodore M, 1886
Watchers at the Pond. Russell, Franklin, 2269
Watchers of the Stars. Moore, Patrick, 1969
WATER, 2151, 2266, 2699-2701
Water. Leopold, Luna B, 2151
Water. Overman, Michael, 2699
Water. Platt, Rutherford, 2266
WATER — POLLUTION, 2563, 2565, 2702
Water Encyclopedia. Todd, David K., ed, 226
Water Is Everybody's Business. Behrman, A. S, 2700
Water, Prey, and Game Birds of North America. Wetmore, Alexander, 2433
Watergate. Dickinson, William B., ed, 1717
Watergate. Saffell, David C, ed, 1201
WATERGATE AFFAIR, 1201, 1716-1718, 6177-6179
Watergate Hearings. Apple, R. W., Jr, 1191
Waterloo. Howarth, David, 5546
WATERLOO, BATTLE OF, 5546
Watkins, Floyd C. Thomas Wolfe's Characters, 3740
Watson, James D. The Double Helix, 2249
Watson, Robert I. The Great Psychologists, 567
Watt, Richard M. Kings Depart, 5306
Watt, W. Montgomery. Islamic Philosophy and Theology, 614
Wattenburg, Ben J. see Scammon, Richard M.

INDEX

Watts. Bullock, Paul, ed, 1123
Watts, Alan W. The Way of Zen, 842
WATTS, CALIFORNIA — SOCIAL CONDITIONS, 1123
WAUGH, EVELYN, 3946
WAVES, 2037
Way. Steiner, Stan and Witt, Shirley. 4640
Way It Was. Vecsey, George, ed, 3348
Way of Zen. Watts, Alan W, 842
Way Things Work. Lodewijk, T., et al. 2487
Way Things Work Book of Computers. Van Amerogen, C, 464
Way We Go to War. Pusey, Merlo J, 1643
WAYNE, ANTHONY, 5953
Ways of Thought of Great Mathematicians. Meschkowski, Herbert, 1943
We Shall Be All. Dubofsky, Melvyn, 1438
Wealth of Nations. Smith, Adam, 1403
Weapons Culture. Lapp, Ralph E, 2670
Weapons of War. Cleator, Philip E, 1680
WEATHER, 2154, 2157-2160, 2362
Weather. Battan, Louis D, 2157
Weather and the Animal World. Prince, J. H, 2362
Weathering the Storm. Evans, Elizabeth, 5948
Weaver, John T. Twenty Years of Silents, 1908-1928, 65
Weaver, Robert C. Negro Ghetto, 1274
Weaver, Warren. Lady Luck, 1952
Webb, Constance. Richard Wright, 3741
Webb, Walter P. Great Plains, 6241
Weber, Carl J. Fore-Edge Painting, 505
———. Hardy of Wessex, 3949
Weber, David J., compiled by. Foreigners in Their Native Land, 4826
Weber, Eugen, ed. Paths to the Present, 512
Webster, Daniel. Speak for Yourself, Daniel, 5980
WEBSTER, DANIEL, 5980
Webster, J. B. History of West Africa, 5724
Webster, John and Tourneur, Cyril. Four Plays, 3862
Webster's Biographical Dictionary. 419
Webster's New Dictionary of Synonyms. 170
Webster's New Geographical Dictionary. 384
Webster's New World Dictionary of the English Language. 167
Webster's Third New International Dictionary. 168
Wechsberg, Joseph. Verdi, 3163
Wecter, Dixon. The Age of the Great Depression, 1929-1941, 6131
———. The Hero in America, 4865
Wedekind, Frank. The Lulu Plays, 4023

Wedgwood, Cicely V. Seventeenth Century Literature, 3773
———. The Thirty Years' War, 5039
———. William the Silent, 5544
Weeds. Martin, Alexander C, 2325
Wehl, David. The Birth of Indonesia, 5690
Wehr, Hans. Dictionary of Modern Written Arabic, 191
Weigall, Arthur E. The Glory of the Pharaohs, 4897
———. The Life and Times of Akhnaton, Pharaoh of Egypt, 4898
Weigand, Hermann J. Modern Ibsen, 4085
WEIGHTS AND MEASURES — U. S., 1808-1809
Weigley, Russell F. American Military, 1662
———. The American Way of War, 1678
———. History of the United States Army, 1663
Weil, Andres. The Natural Mind, 2549
Weil, Gordon L. The Benelux Nations, 1173
Weimar. Laqueur, Walter, 5303
Weimar and the Rise of Hitler. Nicholls, A. J, 5304
Weimar Culture. Gay, Peter, 5302
Weinberg, Gerhard L. The Foreign Policy of Hitler's Germany, 1305
Weinberg, Julius R. A Short History of Medieval Philosophy, 632
Weiner, Michael. Earth Medicine - Earth Foods, 2501
Weinstein, Allen and Gatell, Otto, eds. American Negro Slavery, 1288
Weintraub, Stanley. Whistler, a Biography, 3047
Weiser, Francis X. Handbook of Feasts and Customs, 114
Weisheipl, James A. Friar Thomas D'Aquino, 633
Weiskopf, Donald. see Alston, Walter
Weisman, John. Guerilla Theatre, 3297
Weismann, Donald L. The Visual Arts - As Human Experience, 2884
Weiss, Karel. Under the Mask, 1007
Weiss, Malcolm E. The World Within the Brain, 2527
Weiss, Peter. The Persecution and Assassination of Jean-Paul Marat As Performed by the Inmates of the Asylum of Charenton Under the Direction of the Marquis de Sade, 4034
Weisz, Paul B. The Science of Zoology, 2337
Weitz, Morris. Problems in Aesthetics, 2880
Welch, William. American Images of Soviet Foreign Policy, 1313

INDEX

WELCH, WILLIAM HENRY, 2499
Wellek, Rene. Concepts of Criticism, 3466
———. The Meaning of Czech History by Thomas Masaryk, 5351
WELLES, GIDEON, 6034
Wellford, Harrison. Sowing the Wind, 2516
Wellington. Longford, Elizabeth, 5251
Wellington. Longford, Elizabeth, 5252
WELLINGTON, ARTHUR WELLESLEY, 1ST DUKE OF, 5251-5252
Wellman, Paul I. Glory, God and Gold, 6243
Wellrath, George E. Theatre of Protest and Paradox, 3513
Wells, Henry W., tr. Ancient Poetry from China, Japan and India, 4601
WELLS, HERBERT GEORGE, 3920, 3938
Wellwarth, George. see Benedikt, Michael
Welty, Paul T. The Asians, 4772
Wendell Phillips. Bartlett, Irving H, 6039
Wendt, Herbert. From Ape to Adam, 2199
Weng, Wan-Go. see Smith, Bradley
Wenninger, M. J. Polyhedron Models, 1950
Were, Gideon S. A History of South Africa, 5738
We're in the Money. Bergman, Andrew, 3264
Werke. Droste-Huelshoff, Annette Von, 3973
Werke. Grillparzer, Franz, 4017
Werke. Heine, Heinrich, 3975
Werke. Schiller, Friedrich Von, 3978
Werke in Sechs Banden. Geothe, Johann Wolfgang Von, 3974
Werke in Zwei Banden. Storm, Theodor, 3979
Werner, Alfred. Modigliani, 3060
Werner, William E. see Benton, Allen H.
Wernham, R. B. Before the Armada, 5233
Wertenbaker, William. The Floor of the Sea, 2148
Werth, Alexander. De Gaulle, 5424
———. Russia, 5528
———. The Twilight of France, 1933-1940, 5420
Wertham, Frederic. Seduction of the Innocent, 586
Wesker, Arnold. The Wesker Trilogy, 3917
Wesker Trilogy. Wesker, Arnold, 3917
WEST
    DESCRIPTION AND TRAVEL, 6233
    DISCOVERY AND EXPLORATION, 6240
    HISTORY, 1480, 5765, 5868, 5872, 5978, 6078, 6228-6232, 6236-6239, 6241
        SOURCES, 6234
West African Prose. Djoleto, S. A. and Kwami, T. S., eds. 4626

West Germany. Balfour, Michael, 5331
West Indian Nations. Sherlock, Philip M, 5825
WEST INDIES
    DESCRIPTION AND TRAVEL, 4805
    HISTORY, 4693, 5825
    POLITICS, 1102
WEST, NATHANIEL, 3732
West, Paul. Modern Novel, 3933
West, Ray Benedict and Stallman, Robert W. The Art of Modern Fiction, 3490
Westbrook, Max, ed. The Modern American Novel, 3724
Westell, Anthony. Paradox, 5800
Western. Fenin, George N. and Everson, William K. 3271
Western Attitudes Toward Death. Aries, Philippe, 526
Western Europe in the Middle Ages, 300-1475. Tierney, Brian, 5011
Western Intellectual Tradition. Bronowski, Jacob and Mazlish, B. 640
Westminster Historical Atlas to the Bible. Wright, George E. and Filson, Floyd V. 109
Weston, Jessie. From Ritual to Romance, 1845
———. The Quest of the Holy Grail, 1846
Westward Expansion. Billington, Ray A, 6229
Wetmore, Alexander, et al. Song and Garden Birds of North America, 2432
———. Water, Prey, and Game Birds of North America, 2433
Whale. Cousteau, Jacques-Yves and Diole, Philippe. 2454
Whale Hunt. Haley, Nelson C, 2816
Whalen, George J. see Graf, Rudolf F.
WHALES, 2454-2455, 2457-2458
Whaley, Barton. Codeword Barbarossa, 5123
WHALING, 2455, 2816
Wharton, David B. The Alaska Gold Rush, 6251
WHARTON, EDITH NEWBOLD JONES, 3723
What Is Existentialism? Heidegger. Barrett, William, 550
What Is History? Carr, Edward H, 4645
What Is Mathematics? Courant, Richard and Robbins, Herbert. 1929
What the Great Religions Believe. Gaer, Joseph, 821
What to Do About Bites and Stings of Venomous Animals. Arnold, Robert E, 2585
What You Need to Know About Food and Cooking for Health. Lamb, Lawrence E, 2830

518

Wheeler, Gershon. Radar Fundamentals, 2652
Wheeler, John A. *see* Taylor, Edwin F.
Wheeler-Bennett, John W. Nemesis of Power, 5307
Wheels and Pistons. Butterworth, W. E, 2741
Wheelwright, Philip, ed. Critical Introduction to Ethics, 601
When Can I Come Home? A Debate on Amnesty for Exiles, Antiwar Prisoners and Others. Polner, Murray, ed, 1227
When Egypt Ruled the East. Steindorff, George and Seele, Keith C. 4894
When the Cheering Stopped. Smith, Gene, 6121
Where Do We Go from Here. King, Martin Luther, Jr, 1028
Where Have All the Flowers, Fishes, Birds, Trees, Water, and Air Gone? What Ecology Is All About. Segerberg, Osborn, 946
Where Have All the Robots Gone? Worker Dissatisfaction in the Seventies. Sheppard, Harold L. and Herrick, N. Q. 1433
Where the Light Falls. Smith, Chard, 3586
A Whig Embattled. Morgan, Robert J, 6001
Whipkey, Kenneth L. and Whipkey, Mary N. The Power of Calculus, 1948
Whipkey, Mary N. *see* Whipkey, Kenneth L.
Whispers from Space. MacVey, John, 1976
Whistler, a Biography. Weintraub, Stanley, 3047
WHISTLER, JAMES, 3047
Whitburn, Joel. Top Pop Records, 1955-1970, 63
White, Christopher. Rembrandt and His World, 3073
———. Rubens and His World, 3075
White, D. O. *see* Burnet, MacFarlane F.
White, E. B. *see* Strunk, William S., Jr.
White Goddess, a Historical Grammar of Poetic Myth. Graves, Robert, 3525
White, Gwen. Perspective, 3010
A White House Diary. Johnson, Lady Bird, 6171
White House Transcripts. New York Times, 6178
White, Morton, ed. The Age of Analysis, 639
———. Science and Sentiment in America, 650
White, Morton. *see* Schlesinger, Arthur M., Jr.
White Nile. Moorehead, Alan, 5714
White Over Black. Jordan, Winthrop D, 5883
White Pony. Payne, Robert, ed, 4600
White Terror. Trelease, Allen W, 6077
White, Theodore H. Breach of Faith, 1718
———. The Making of the President, 1972, 1385
White, Virginia P. Grants, 460
White Water Handbook for Canoe and Kayak. Urban, John T., ed, 3423
Whitehead, Alfred N. Alfred North Whitehead, 656
———. Essays in Science and Philosophy, 1914
WHITEHEAD, ALFRED NORTH, 653
Whitehead, Donald F. F.B.I. Story, 1623
Whitehurst, Robert N., *see* Kirkendall, Lester A.
Whitford, Harold C. and Dixson, Robert J. Handbook of American Idioms and Idiomatic Usage, 171
Whitley, William T. Gilbert Stuart, 3048
Whitman. Waskow, Howard J, 3562
Whitman, Cedric H. Homer and the Heroic Tradition, 4469
———. Sophocles, 4457
Whitman, Walt. Complete Poetry, Selected Prose and Letters, 3563
———. Leaves of Grass, 3564
WHITMAN, WALT, 3562
Whitney, Charles A. The Discovery of Our Galaxy, 1971
Whitney, Thomas P., ed. & tr. The New Writing in Russia, 4569
Who Makes War. Javits, Jacob K. and Kellerman, Don. 1580
Who Shakes the Money Tree? American Campaign Financing Practices from 1789 to the Present. Thayer, George, 1386
Who Was Who. 412
Who Was Who in America. 422
Whole World Is Watching. Gerzon, Mark, 1110
Whorton, James. Before Silent Spring, 2782
Who's Afraid of Virginia Woolf. Albee, Edward, 3690
Who's Who. 413
Who's Who in America. 423
Who's Who in American Art. 279
Who's Who in Shakespeare. Quennell, Peter, 369
Who's Who of American Women. 424
Whose Land? A History of the Peoples of Palestine. Parkes, James W, 5668
Why Men Rebel. Gurr, Ted R, 906
Why We Can't Wait. King, Martin Luther, Jr, 1029
Wiarda, Howard J. The Dominican Republic, 5845

INDEX

Wicker, Cecil. *see* Tedlock, Ernest
Wicker, Tom. JFK and LBJ, 1646
Wiebe, Robert H. The Segmented Society, 4820
Wiener, Joan. *see* Rosenberg, Sharon
Wiener, Leo, ed. Anthology of Russian Literature, 4501
Wiener, Philip P., ed. Dictionary of the History of Ideas, 377
——. Index to the Dictionary of the History of Ideas, 378
Wiese, Benno Von. Die Deutsche Lyrik, 4008
——. Die Deutsche Novelle von Goethe bis Kafka, 4077
——. Die Deutsche Tragodie von Lessing bis Hebbel, 4030
——. Deutschland Erzählt, Von Buchner bis Hauptmann, 4072
——. Deutschland Erzählt, Von Goethe bis Tieck, 4073
——. Deutschland Erzählt, Von Schnitzler bis Johnson, 4074
Wiesel, Elie. Legends of Our Time, 5328
Wiggins, Arthur W. Physical Science with Environmental Applications, 2022
Wigginton, Brooks E., ed. The Foxfire Book, 4832
——. Foxfire 2, 4833
——. Foxfire 3, 4834
Wilcox, R. Turner. Five Centuries of American Costume, 1817
——. Folk and Festival Costume of the World, 1815
Wilcox, Ruth T. The Dictionary of Costume, 150
WILD AND SCENIC RIVERS — U.S., 2241
Wild Animals of North America. Kellog, A. Remington, et al. 2450
Wild Cats. Boorer, Michael, 2465
Wild Cats of the World. Guggisberg, C. A, 2466
Wild Cousins of the Dog. Hopf, Alice L, 2470
WILD FLOWERS, 2324-2325
Wild Food Trailguide. Hall, Alan, 2322
Wild Old Wicked Man and Other Poems. MacLeish, Archibald, 3606
Wild, Peter. Cochise, 3666
Wild River. Pringle, Laurence, 2241
Wilde, Oscar. Portable Oscar Wilde, 3880
Wilder, W. F., *see* Giese, Frank S.
WILDERNESS, 3390, 3397
Wilderness and the American Mind. Nash, Roderick, 4812
WILDERNESS AREAS — U.S., 1471, 4813
Wilderness Cooking. Berglund, Berndt and Bolsby, Clare. 2837

Wilderness Handbook. Petzoldt, Paul, 3390
Wilderness Skiing. Steck, Allen and Tejada-Flores, Lito. 3417
WILDERNESS SURVIVAL, 2321, 2532-2533, 2535
Wilderness Survival. Berglund, Berndt, 2532
Wilderness U. S. A. National Geographic Society, ed, 4813
Wilderness World of the Grand Canyon. Sutton, Ann and Sutton, Myron. 1906
Wildes, Harry E. Voice of the Lord, 816
——. William Penn, 6199
Wildfowl Trust. *see* Scott, Peter
WILDLIFE CONSERVATION, 1459, 2338-2340, 2352, 2449, 2778, 2814, 2825, 2827
Wildlife in Danger. Fisher, James, et al. 1459
Wildlife Photography. Hoskins, Eric and Gooders, John. 3120
WILDLIFE PROTECTION, 1903
WILDLIFE RESCUE, 2823, 2826
Wilenski, Reginald H. The Meaning of Modern Sculpture, 2996
Wilgus, A. Curtis. Historical Atlas of Latin America, 394
WILHELM II, GERMAN EMPEROR, 5300
Wilkerson, James A., ed. Medicine for Mountaineering, 2622
Wilkins, Ernest H. History of Italian Literature, 4287
Wilkinson, Elizabeth M. and Willoughby, Leonard. Goethe, 4079
Willard, Beatrice E. *see* Zwinger, Ann H.
Willeford, William. The Fool and His Scepter, 3258
Willett, John. The Theatre of Bertolt Brecht, 4031
Willetts, Ronald F. Ancient Crete, 5565
Willey, Basil. The Eighteenth Century Background, 657
——. More Nineteenth Century Studies, 658
——. Nineteenth Century Studies, 659
——. The Seventeenth Century Background, 660
WILLIAM I, PRINCE OF ORANGE, 5544
WILLiAM I, THE CONQUERER, KING OF ENGLAND, 5187, 5198
WILLIAM III, KING OF GREAT BRITAIN, 5247
WILLIAM IV, KING OF GREAT BRITAIN, 5173, 5255
William and Mary. Van Der Zee, Henri and Van der Zee, Barbara. 5247
William Blake and the Age of Revolution. Bronowski, Jacob, 3809

520

William Carlos Williams, the Later Poems. Mazzaro, Jerome, 3609
William Golding. Baker, James, 3968
William Golding. Kinkead-Weekes, Mark and Gregoe, Ian. 3952
William Henry Harrison. Goebel, Dorothy B, 6000
William Henry Seward. Van Deusen, Glyndon G, 6014
William Henry Welch and the Heroic Age of American Medicine. Flexner, Simon and Flexner, James T. 2499
William Howard Taft. Anderson, Donald F, 1638
William James. Allen, Gay W, 642
William James. James, William, 645
William Penn. Dunn, Mary M, 1139
William Penn. Wildes, Harry E, 6199
William Styron's Nat Turner. Clarke, John H., ed, 3742
William Tecumseh Sherman. Merrill, James M, 6055
William the Conqueror. Douglas, David C, 5198
William the Silent. Wedgwood, Cicely V, 5544
Williams, Alan. see Fullerton, Brian
Williams, E. Neville. The Ancien Regime in Europe, 5036
Williams, James G. Classified Library of Congress Subject Headings, 31
Williams, Jay. Stage Left, 3321
Williams, Oscar. Little Treasury of American Poetry, 3552
———. Little Treasury of British Poetry, 3787
———. Little Treasury of Great Poetry, 3502
———. Little Treasury of Modern Poetry, 3503
———. Little Treasury of Modern Poetry, 3788
———. New Pocket Anthology of American Verse, 3553
Williams, Philip M. and Harrison, Martin. Politics and Society in De Gaulle's Republic, 5422
Williams, Raymond. Drama from Ibsen to Brecht, 3528
WILLIAMS, ROGER, 6195
Williams, T. Harry. Huey Long, 6222
Williams, Tennessee. Cat on a Hot Tin Roof, 3708
———. Glass Menagerie, 3709
———. Night of the Iguana, 3710
———. Streetcar Named Desire, 3711
Williams, Trevor I. Biographical Dictionary of Scientists, 206

Williams, William C. Collected Later Poems, 3592
———. Selected Poems, 3593
WILLIAMS, WILLIAM CARLOS, 3609
Williamson, Samuel R. The Politics of Grand Strategy, 1303
Willianis, Philip M. French Politicians and Elections, 1951-1969, 5423
Willoughby, Leonard. see Wilkinson, Elizabeth M.
Wills, Alfred J. An Introduction to the History of Central Africa, 5742
Willy Brandt. Prittie, Terence C, 5335
Wilmerding, Lucius, Jr. Electoral College, 1266
Wilmore, Sylvia B. Swans of the World, 2437
Wilpert, Gero Von. Deutsche Literatur in Bildern, 3993
Wilson, Charles M. Green Treasures, 2323
Wilson, David H. King James VI and I, 5248
Wilson, David M. The Vikings and Their Origins, 5538
Wilson, Edmund. The Dead Sea Scrolls, 1947-1969, 721
———. To the Finland Station, 1498
Wilson, Edward O. The Insect Societies, 2392
Wilson Era. Daniels, Josephus, 6117
Wilson, F. B., see Smith, William G.
Wilson, John D. Life in Shakespeare's England, 4750
Wilson Library Bulletin. 44
Wilson, Paul C. Modern Rowing, 3424
Wilson, Richard G. The Long March, 1935, 5597
Wilson, Theodore B. Black Codes of the South, 1243
Wilson, Woodrow. Case for the League of Nations, 6122
WILSON, WOODROW, 5078, 5080, 6117-6119, 6121
Winchester, Alice. see Lipman, Jean
Wind Birds. Matthiessen, Peter, 2428
Wind That Swept Mexico. Brenner, Anita, 5817
Windsor, Philip and Roberts, Adam. Czechoslovakia 1968, 5359
Winestone, H. V. see Freeth, Zahra
Wings of the Falcon. Kaster, Joseph, ed, 4889
Winks, Robin W. The Blacks in Canada, 5796
———. The Historian As Detective, 4666
Winold, Allen. Elements of Musical Understanding, 3133
Winslow Homer. Goodrich, Lloyd, 3041
Winston, Richard. Thomas Becket, 5208
Winter Beach. Ogburn, Charlton, Jr, 1899

INDEX

Winter in Prague. Remington, Robin A., ed, 5354
Winter, Ruth. Beware of the Food You Eat, 2558
Winter Soldiers. Ketchum, Richard M, 5952
WINTER SPORTS, 3411
Winter Trees. Plath, Sylvia, 3657
Winterbotham, Frederick. The Ultra Secret, 5150
WINTHROP, JOHN, 5903
WISDOM, 525
Wisdom of Confucius. Confucius, 616
Wise, David and Ross, Thomas B. The Invisible Government, 1624
Wiseman, D. J., ed. Peoples of Old Testament Times, 727
Wiser, Charlotte. see Wiser, William
Wiser, William and Wiser, Charlotte. Behind Mud Walls, 1930-1962, 1124
Wish, Harvey. Contemporary America, 6106
———. Society and Thought in America, 5873
Wiskemann, Elizabeth. Europe of the Dictators, 1919-1945, 5094
———. Fascism in Italy, 5452
WIT AND HUMOR, 3520
WITCHCRAFT, 536, 5898
Witchcraft. Hart, Roger, 536
With Every Breath You Take. Lewis, Howard, 2566
With Eyes in the Back of Our Heads. Levertov, Denise, 3649
Witherell, Warren. How the Racers Ski, 3420
Within the Sound of These Waves. Chickering, William H, 4846
Witness. Chambers, Whittaker, 1622
Witt, Shirley. see Steiner, Stan
Wittner, Lawrence S. Cold-War America, 6159
———. Rebels Against War, 1550
Witts, Max M. see Thomas, Gordon
Wobblies. Renshaw, Patrick, 1445
Wolf, John B. The Emergence of the Great Powers, 5027
Wolf, Walther. The Origins of Western Art, 2900
Wolfe, Bertram D. Three Who Made a Revolution, 5509
Wolfe, Louis. Aquaculture, 2818
WOLFE, THOMAS, 3716, 3739-3740
Wolfe, Tom. The New Journalism, 504
Wolff, Robert. The Balkans in Our Time, 5557
Wolff, Robert P., ed. Nineteen Eighty-Four Revisited, 1203
Wolk, Samuel J., see Bridger, David
Wolman, Baron, et al. Festival, 3226

Wolman, Benjamin B. Dictionary of Behavioral Science, 98
Wolseley, Roland E. Understanding Magazines, 2851
WOLSEY, THOMAS, CARDINAL, 5214, 5218
WOLVES, 2471
Womack, John. Zapata and the Mexican Revolution, 5822
WOMAN, 977
  HISTORY AND CONDITION OF WOMEN, 974, 976, 981, 983
  LEGAL STATUS, LAWS, ETC. — U. S., 978
  SUFFRAGE, 978-979, 1267-1268
Woman Suffrage and Politics. Catt, Carrie C. and Shuler, Nettie R. 1267
WOMEN — BIOGRAPHY, 424, 783-784, 975, 981-983, 979, 1946, 2718, 3379, 3918
Women in Mathematics. Osen, Lynn M, 1946
WOMEN IN MEDICINE, 2496, 2498
Women in Print. Adburgham, Alison, 3918
WOMEN IN THE ARTS, 2948
WOMEN IN THE CONFEDERATE STATES OF AMERICA, 6058, 6060
Women of the Confederacy. Simkins, Francis B, 6060
Women of the Reformation in France and England. Bainton, Roland H, 783
Women of the Reformation in Germany and Italy. Bainton, Roland H, 784
Women Writers in France. Bree, Germaine, 4096
WOMEN'S LIBERATION MOVEMENT, 982-983
WOMEN'S RIGHTS, 975, 979, 982
Wonder That Was India. Basham, Arthur L, 5626
Wonders of the Earth. Bauer, Ernst W, 2090
Wondrous World of Fishes. Schultz, Leonard, et al. 2406
WOOD-CARVING, 2990-2991
WOOD-ENGRAVERS, AMERICAN, 3094
Wood, Forrest G. Marine Mammals and Man, 2461
Wood, James P. Magazines in the United States, 479
Wood, John R. and Serres, Jean. Diplomatic Ceremonial and Protocol, 1558
Wood, Nancy. Clear-Cut, 2787
———. Many Winters, 3667
Woodcock, George. The Crystal Spirit, 3950
———. Dawn and the Darkest Hour, 3951
Woodham-Smith, Cecil B. The Great Hunger, 1513
———. The Reason Why. , 5265

Woodrow Wilson. Link, Arthur S, 6118
Woodrow Wilson and the Lost Peace. Bailey, Thomas A, 5078
Woodrow Wilson and the Progressive Era. Link, Arthur S, 6119
Woods, Gerald, et al, eds. Art without Boundaries, 2906
Woods, Ralph L. and Greenhouse, Herbert B. The New World of Dreams, 576
Woodward, Bob. see Bernstein, Carl
Woodward, C. Vann. The Burden of Southern History, 6218
———. Reunion and Reaction, 6079
———. The Strange Career of Jim Crow, 1275
Woodward, Llewellyn. Prelude to Modern Europe, 1815-1914, 5066
WOODWORK, 2864
Woodworking for Everybody. Shea, John G, 2864
Woolf, Virginia. Flush, 3834
WOOLF, VIRGINIA, 3945
Woolley, Charles. The Sumerians, 4914
Words and Occasions. Pearson, Lester N, 5798
Words and Pictures. Hicks, Wilson, 489
Words in Sheep's Clothing. Pei, Mario, 1873
Words, Music and the Church. Routley, Erik, 3218
Words of Science and the History Behind Them. Asimov, Isaac, 199
Wordsworth. Read, Herbert E, 3815
Wordsworth, William. Complete Poetical Works, 3820
WORDSWORTH, WILLIAM, 3815
Work and Nonwork in the Year 2001. Dunnette, Marvin D, 1430
Workers' Paradise Lost. Lyons, Eugene, 1093
Working. Terkel, Studs, 1434
Working on the System. Nader, Ralph, 143
Working with Clay and Plaster. Cowley, David, 2988
Works. Akhmatova, Anna, 4505
Works. Catallus, Gaius Valerius, 4415
Works. Kleist, Heinrich Von, 3977
Works. Marlowe, Christopher, 3861
World Almanac and Book of Facts. 131
World As Teacher. Taylor, Harold, 1754
A World Atlas of Military History. Banks, Arthur, 385
World Book of House Plants. McDonald, Elvin, 2798
World Chess Championship. Horowitz, I. A, 3336
WORLD COUNCIL OF CHURCHES, 767
World Food Problem. Cochrane, Willard W, 1516

WORLD HISTORY, 2561, 4673
   DICTIONARIES, 380
World Literature Since 1945. Ivask, Ivar and Von Wilpert, Gero. 3524
World Museum Guide. Cooper, Barbara and Matheson, Maureen. 480
World of Ancient Times. Roebuck, Carl, 4880
World of Ants. Chauvin, Remy, 2397
World of Art. 3085
World of Butterflies. Dickens, Michael and Storey, Eric. 2395
World of Currier and Ives. Currier, Nathaniel and Ives, J. M. 3098
World of Elementary Particles. Ford, Kenneth W, 2036
World of Gwendolyn Brooks. Brooks, Gwendolyn, 3629
World of Harlequin. Nicoll, Allardyce, 3319
World of Herodotus. De Selincourt, Aubrey, 4967
World of Hesiod. Burn, Andrew R, 4964
World of Humanism. Gilmore, Myron P, 5028
World of Mathematics. Newman, James R, 210
World of Musical Comedy. Green, Stanley, 3212
World of Odysseus. Finley, Moses I., ed, 4460
World of Physics. Hulsizer, Robert and Lazarus, David. 2019
World of Rome. Grant, Michael, 4942
World of Southeast Asia. Benda, Harry J. and Larkin, J. A., eds. 5671
World of the Atom. Boorse, Henry A. and Motz, Lloyd, eds. 2052
World of the French Revolution. Palmer, Robert R, 5049
World of the Gull. Costello, David F, 2434
World of the Huns. Maenchen-Helfen, Otto J, 4685
World of the Reformation. Hillerbrand, Hans J, 786
World of the Snake. Harrison, Hal H, 2416
World of Twentieth-Century Music. Ewen, David, 3156
World of Victorian Humor. Orel, Harold, ed, 3958
World Petroleum Market. Adelman, Morris A, 1520
WORLD POLITICS, 482, 1084, 1154, 1337, 1548, 1555, 1661, 4675, 4677, 5057
WORLD RECORDS, 477
World Since 1919. Langsam, Walter C, 4677

INDEX

World Turned Upside Down. Hill, John E, 5239
WORLD WAR,(1939-1945), 4677, 5098, 5101, 5103, 5449
    AERIAL OPERATIONS, 5139
    AFRICA, NORTH, 5129
    ATROCITIES, 5362
    CAMPAIGNS, 5124-5125, 5130, 5133, 5136, 5138
    CAMPAIGNS AND BATTLES, 5127, 5134
    CAUSES, 1304, 5106
    CRY·PTOGRAPHY, 5150
    DIPLOMATIC HISTORY, 1346, 5102, 5110-5112
    ECONOMIC ASPECTS, 6135
    EUROPE, 5137
    EVACUATION OF CIVILIANS, 1062-1064
    FRANCE, 5420
    GERMANY, 5121, 5123, 5126, 5132, 5146, 5307, 5317, 5327
    GREAT BRITAIN, 5098, 5102, 5274
    ITALY, 5108
    JAPAN, 5112, 5117-5119, 5140-5141
    JEWS, 5104-5105, 5114
    MAPS, 403
    NAVAL OPERATIONS, 5143-5144
    PEACE, 5118
    PHILIPPINE ISLANDS, 5691
    PICTORIAL WORKS, 5122
    POLAND, 5907
    PRISONERS AND PRISONS, 5147-5148
    RUSSIA, 5109, 5113, 5123, 5126
    TRANSPORTATION, 1682
    UNDERGROUND MOVEMENTS, 5099, 5100, 5115-5116
    U.S., 1116, 1346, 1682, 5112, 5120, 5149, 6134
World War. Sorenson, Thomas C, 1297
World War and American Isolation, 1914-1917. May, Ernest, 5079
World Within the Brain. Weiss, Malcolm E, 2527
World Within the Ocean Wave. Silverberg, Robert, 2267
World Within the Tide Pool. Silverberg, Robert, 2243
Worldly Philosophers. Heilbroner, Robert, 1405
Worlds-Antiworlds. Alfven, Hannes, 1983
World's Great Bridges. Shirley-Smith, H, 2692
World's Great Men of Color. Rogers, J. A, 4860
World's Great Religions. Life Magazine Editors, 822

World's Number One, Flat-Out, All-Time, Great, Stock Car Racing Book. Bledsoe, Jerry, 3402
Wortabet, J. and Porter, H., eds. English-Arabic, Arabic-English Dictionary, 192
Wound Within. Kendrick, Alexander, 5685
WREN, SIR CHRISTOPHER, 2965
WRESTLING, 3409
Wretched of the Earth. Fanon, Frantz, 923
Wright, Arthur F. Buddhism in Chinese History, 843
WRIGHT, FRANK LLOYD, 2961, 2964
Wright, George E. and Filson, Floyd V. Westminster Historical Atlas to the Bible, 109
Wright, Gordon. The Ordeal of Total War, 1939-1945, 5103
Wright, Louis B. Cultural Life of the American Colonies, 5910
Wright, Mary C., ed. China in Revolution, 5587
WRIGHT, RICHARD, 3741
Writer in Extremis. Sokel, Walter H, 3992
Writer's Art. Stegner, Wallace E, 3515
Writer's Guide and Index to English. Perrin, Porter G. and Ebbitt, Wilma R. 3469
Writer's Handbook. Burack, A. A., ed, 3467
Writers in Arms. Benson, Frederick R, 5466
Writing. Ober, J. Hambleton, 1860
WRITING — HISTORY, 1860
Writing on the Wall. Lowenfels, Walter, ed, 3550
Writings and Drawings. Dylan, Bob, 3202
Wu, Yuan-Li, ed. China, 439
Wu Ch'Eng-En. Monkey. , 4607
Wyatt, Stanley P. Principles of Astronomy, 1967
Wycherley, William. Complete Plays, 3873
WYETH, ANDREW, 3039
WYETH FAMILY, 3037
Wylie, Evan McLeod. The New Birth Control, 2554
Wyman, Donald. Wyman's Gardening Encyclopedia, 2790
Wyman's Gardening Encyclopedia. Wyman, Donald, 2790
Wynar, Christine L. Guide to Reference Books for School Media Centers, 1
Wynkoop, Sally. Subject Guide to Government Reference Books, 2
Wyss, Orville and Eklund, C. E. Micro-Organisms and Man, 2305

Xenophon. Anabasis, 4970

Yale Daily News, ed. The Insiders' Guide to the Colleges, 1789

INDEX

Yale Institute of Far Eastern Languages. Dictionary of Spoken Chinese, 194
Yale University, Dept. of French. Contes et Nouvelles D'aujourd 'hui, 4263
Yanev, Peter. Peace of Mind in Earthquake Country, 2869
Yarmolinsky, Adam. The Military Establishment, 1664
Yarmolinsky, Avrahm. Aspects of Russian Imagination, 4502
———. Road to Revolution, 5496
———. Russians, 4503
———. Treasury of Great Russian Short Stories, 4570
———. Turgenev, 4571
Yarmolinsky, Avrahm. see Deutsch, Babette
Yass, Marion. Hiroshima, 5142
Year of Decision, 1846. DeVoto, Bernard A, 6231
Year of the Butterfly. Ordish, George, 2396
Year of the Seal. Scheffer, Victor B, 2475
Yearbook of Astronomy, 1975. Moore, Patrick, ed, 212
Yearbook on International Communist Affairs. Staar, Richard F., ed, 140
Yearnings. Chevez, Albert C., ed, 3535
Years of MacArthur. James, Dorris C, 1676
Years of Opportunity. Dexter, Byron, 1551
Years of Protest. Solzman, Jack, ed, 3534
Yeats. Ellmann, Richard, 3848
Yeats, William B. Collected Plays, 3889
———. Collected Poems, 3853
YEATS, WILLIAM BUTLER, 3848
Yellowstone Park. Sutton, Ann, 1904
Yetman, Norman R., ed. Voices from Slavery, 1002
Yette, Samuel F. The Choice, 1038
Yevtushenko, Yevgeny. Precocious Autobiography, 4518
———. Selected Poetry, 4519
———. Stolen Apples, 4517
YEVTUSHENKO, YEVGENY, 4517-4518
Yiddish Literature. Madison, Charles A, 4593
YIDDISH LITERATURE — HISTORY AND CRITICISM, 4593
YOGA, 621, 2539-2540
Yoga Thing. Roberts, Nancy, 2540
Yoga Way to Release Tension. Carr, Rachel, 2539
Yohannan, John D. A Treasury of Asian Literature, 4477
Yom Kippur War. Sunday Times, London, 5652
Yorburg, Betty. The Changing Family, 988
Yorkist Age. Kendall, Paul M, 5211

You and Your Language. Laird, Charlton G, 1864
You Know I Can't Hear You When the Water's Running. Anderson, Robert, 3691
Young Animals. Stonehouse, Bernard, 2349
Young Animators and Their Discoveries. Young Filmakers Foundation, 3114
Young, Desmond. American Roulette, 5874
———. Rommel, the Desert Fox, 5138
Young Filmakers Foundation. Young Animators and Their Discoveries, 3114
Young, George M. Victorian England, 5266
Young, Howard T. The Victorious Expression, 4342
Young, J. F. Robotics, 2771
Young, John R. The Schooling of the Western Horse, 3446
Young, John Z. Life of Vertebrates, 2402
Young, Kenneth T. Negotiating with the Chinese Communists, 1355
Young, Louise B., ed. Evolution of Man, 2200
———. Power Over People, 2638
Young Negro in America, 1960-1980. Proctor, Samuel, 1034
Young, Peter, ed. Atlas of the Second World War, 403
———. Napoleon's Marshals, 5405
Young Radicals. Keniston, Kenneth, 993
Young, Robert. Young's Analytical Concordance to the Bible, 102
Young's Analytical Concordance to the Bible. Young, Robert, 102
Your Environment and What You Can Do About It. Saltonstall, Richard, 938
Your Legal Rights. Norwick, Kenneth P., ed, 1604
YOUTH, 580, 602, 990, 993, 1104, 1110, 1223, 1602, 1604, 1784-1785
Youth. Gesell, Arnold, et al. 545
YUGOSLAVIA
  DESCRIPTION AND TRAVEL, 4770
  FOREIGN RELATIONS, 5563
  HISTORY, 5559-5561
Yugoslavia. Edwards, Lovett F, 4770
Yugoslavia. Tomasevic, N, 5560
Yulsman, Jerry. The Complete Book of 8mm Movie Making, 3115
Yu Wen, Jen. The Taiping Revolutionary Movement, 5588

Zadig, Ernest A. The Complete Book of Boating, 3425
Zagoria, Donald S. Vietnam Triangle, 5688
Zaidenberg, Arthur. Anyone Can Sculpt, 2989
Zalacain, e Aventurero. Baroja, Pio, 4369

INDEX

Zapata and the Mexican Revolution. Womack, John, 5822
ZAPATA, EMILIANO, 5822
Zapiski. Dostoevsky, Feodor M, 4546
Zapiski Okhotnika. Turgenev, Ivan S, 4568
Zaretsky, Irving and Leone, Mark P., eds. Religious Movements in Contemporary America, 691
Zaruba, G. and Mencl, U. Landslides and Their Treatment, 2122
Zaslovsky, Claudia. Africa Counts, 1940
Zavalishin, Viacheslav. Early Soviet Writers, 4504
Zelda. Milford, Nancy, 3733
Zeldin, Theodore. France, 1848-1945, 4756
Zell, Hans and Silver, Helene. Reader's Guide to African Literature, 345
Zemansky, M. W. Heat and Thermodynamics, 2045
Zen and the Art of Motorcycle Maintenance. Pirsig, Robert, 4815
ZEN BUDDHISM, 841-842
ZEN (SECT) — HISTORY, 837
Zenkovsky, Serge A. Medieval Russia's Epics, Chronicles and Tales, 4584
Zenkovsky, Vasilii V. History of Russian Philosophy, 676
Zeylanicus. Ceylon, 5639
Ziegler, Philip. King William the Fourth, 5255
Zigrosser, Carl. Prints and Their Creators, 3095
Zilversmit, Arthur. First Emancipation, 1039
Zimbardo, Rose A., see Isaacs, Neil D.
Zimiles, Murray see Knigin, Michael
Zimmer, Heinrich. Philosophies of India, 623
ZIMMERMAN, ARTHUR, 5077
Zimmerman, David R. Rh, 2626
Zimmerman Telegram. Tuchman, Barbara W, 5077
Zink, Harold. City Bosses in the United States, 1372
Zinn, Howard. The Politics of History, 4649
Zinsser, Hans. Rats, Lice and History, 2609
ZIONISM — HISTORY, 5664
Zoitvany, Yves F., ed. French Tradition in America, 5788
Żola, Emile. L' Assommoir, 4259
———. Germinal, 4260
———. Nana, 4261
Zolar. The History of Astrology, 540
ZOOLOGY, 1459, 2336-2337, 2342, 2347, 2353, 2362, 2369, 2375-2376, 2449, 2474, 2825
   ENCYCLOPEDIAS, 238
Zuckerman, Art. Tape Recording for the Hobbyist, 2658
Zuckmayer, Carl. Meister Dramen, 4024
Zumberg, James H. and Nelson, Clemens A. Elements of Geology, 2100
Zweig, Arnold. Junge Frau von 1914, 4070
Zwinger, Ann H. and Willard, Beatrice E. Land Above the Trees, 2246

Z
1035
N2
1976

AUG 24 1976

RAYMOND H. FOGLER LIBRARY
DATE DUE